IMAGING
AMERICAN WOMEN

IDEA AND IDEALS
IN CULTURAL HISTORY

Martha Banta

COLUMBIA UNIVERSITY PRESS
NEW YORK

The Andrew W. Mellon Foundation, through a special grant, has assisted the Press in publishing this volume.

Lyrics for "Cigarettes, Cigars," p. 682, by Harry Revel and Mack Gordon, copyright 1931; renewed © 1959 Miller Music Corporation. Rights assigned to CBS Catalog Partnership. All rights controlled and administered by CBS Miller Catalog Inc. All rights reserved. International copyright secured. Used by permission.

Library of Congress Cataloging-in-Publication Data
Banta, Martha.
Imaging American women.

Bibliography: p.
Includes index.
1. Women in art.   2. Women in literature.
3. Feminine beauty (Aesthetics)—United States
4. Women—United States—Social conditions.   5. United
States—Popular culture—History—19th century.
6. United States—Popular culture—History—20th
century.   7. Women—United States—Psychology.
I. Title.
NX652.W6B36   1987   700'.973   86-14692
ISBN 0-231-06126-9
ISBN 0-231-06127-7 (pbk.)

Columbia University Press
New York   Guildford, Surrey
Copyright © 1987 Columbia University Press
All rights reserved

Printed in the United States of America

To My Friends—My Family

Contents

Illustrations   ix
Preface   xxvii
Acknowledgments   xli
Introduction: Object, Image, Type, and the Conduct of Life   1

PART I: CONTEXTS

Images of Identity
1. American Girls and the New Woman   45
2. Looking for the "Best" Type   92

Images of Desire
3. Artists, Models, and Real Things   143
4. The Aesthetics of Desire   179

Counterimages
5. Masking, Camouflage, Inversions, and Play   221

PART II: DEMONSTRATIONS

Portraits in Private
6. Literary Portraits and Types: Crises   287
7. Literary Portraits and Types: Possibilities   315
8. Studio Studies and Still Lifes   339

Contents

Between the Private and the Public
9. Images of the Ideal   377
10. Angels at the Threshold   428

Public Statements
11. Making the Right Occasions   465
12. Scaling Up to War (1876–1898)   499
13. Poster Lives (1898–1918)   553

Images for Sale
14. Poses on Display   593
15. The Purchase of Grace   632

Epilogue: Looking Back   672

Notes   703
Bibliography   785
Picture Credits   819
Name Index   825
Subject Index   837

Illustrations

Preface 1. Charles Allen Winter, "Political Action Versus Direct Action," *The Masses*, February 1912. xxxvi
2. Maurice Becker [woman hurling brick], *The Masses*, December 1916. xxxvi
3. "Oiling," Colt Patent Firearms Co., Hartford Conn. (1918). xxxviii
4. "The Wick Fancy Hat Bands" (1916). xxxviii
5. "Apollo Bicycles" (1895). xxxviii
6. J. J. Gould, Jr., poster for "Lippincott's Series of Select Novels" (1896). xxxix
7. Cecilia Beaux, "The Dreamer' (c.1894). xl

Introduction 1. *Frank Leslie's Illustrated Historical Register of the Centennial Exposition*, 1878. 2
2. Edwin Howland Blashfield, "A New Factor that Transcends All Others—Speed" (c.1918). 3
3. Harry W. McVickar, frontispiece for *Daisy Miller* (1892). 3
4. Raphael Kirchner, "Chu-Chin-Chow: *Ziegfeld Follies of 1917*." 3
5. Consuelo Vanderbilt (c.1887). 4
6. Consuelo Vanderbilt (1914). 4
7. James Abbott McNeil Whistler, "Two Sisters" (n.d.). 4
8. "The Woman Service of the Nation to the Man Service" (1918). 6
9. Howard Chandler Christy, "The American Girl," from *Liberty Belles* (1912). 8
10. Howard Chandler Christy, "The Western Girl," from *Liberty Belles* (1912). 9
11. Harry W. McVickar, from *The Evolution of Woman* (1896). 9
12. Irma Purman (1904). 10

13. Irma Purman (1914).   10
14. Irma Purman (1909).   11
15. Irma Purman and friends (c.1912).   11
16. Clarence H. White with Alfred Stieglitz [Miss Thompson] (c.1907).   12
17. "Nature, Love, and Billiousness," *Daily Graphic*, February 16, 1880.   16
18. Rodney Thomson, "Militants," *Life*, March 27, 1913.   17
19. Charles Dana Gibson, "His First Love," *Life*, June 3, 1897.   19
20. Daniel Chester French, "Alma Mater," (1903).   20
21. Hamden School for Boys, New Haven (1918).   27
22. Adolph Treidler, "Remember Your First Thrill of American Liberty" (1918).   28
23. Frances Benjamin Johnston [students at Tuskegee Institute] (1902).   29
24. Frances Benjamin Johnston [studio] (1895).   29
25. Telephone Operator's Room, Camp Kearney, Calif. (1918).   31
26. "Models of Natural Expression," from J. R. Palmenberg's Sons, (1893).   33
27. H. Wright, "Special Atlanta Exposition Number," poster for the *New York Sunday Herald*, October 20, 1895.   33
28. Irma Purman (1905).   33
29. From *A Collection of 152 Original Monumental Designs, Compiled by Messrs. Cardoni and Morton* (1883).   34
30. Charles Dana Gibson, "In Silence," from Chambers, *The Common Law* (1911).   34
31. Irma Purman and friends (c.1910).   35
32. Harry W. McVickar, from *The Evolution of Woman* (1896).   35
33. Mme. Bernard Trouser Dress (1914).   36
34. Irma Purman and friends (c. 1912).   36
35. "Have a Cup of Yale Coffee with Me" (1904).   37
36. "Helpmeet," Superior Drill Machinery (1906).   38
37. Irma Purman and friends (c.1913).   38
38. Gertrude Käsebier, "Rose O'Neill Smoking" (c.1900).   39
39. William Schevill, "Lillian Wald" (1919).   39
40. Irma Purman and friends (c.1913).   39

1.1. Hugo Froelich and Bonnie Snow, *Text Books of Art Education. Book 2* (1904).   46
1.2. Hugo Froelich and Bonnie Snow, *Text Books of Art Education. Book 4* (1904).   46
1.3. Irma Purman (1902).   47
1.4. Charles Dana Gibson, "The Seed of Ambition," *Collier's Weekly*, January 31, 1903.   47
1.5. Harrison Fisher, frontispiece for McCutcheon, *Beverly of Graustark* (1904).   48
1.6. J. Alden Weir, "A Gentlewoman" (1906).   49
1.7. Robert J. Wildhack, *Collier's Weekly*, December 17, 1910.   49
1.8. Harry W. McVickar, poster for *The Evolution of Woman* (1896).   50

1.9. Abbott Handerson Thayer, "Head of a Woman with Fur-Lined Hood" (1915).   56

1.10. Thomas Eakins, "Miss Van Buren" (c.1886–1890).   56

1.11. C. Allan Gilbert, poster for *Scribner's Monthly Magazine*, May 1898.   59

1.12. Orson Lowell, "Election Day," *Life*, September 23, 1909.   61

1.13. Cecilia Beaux, "New England Woman" (1895).   63

1.14. Howard Chandler Christy, from "The Cleansing of a Lie," *Harper's Monthly Magazine*, August 1901.   64

1.15. Mrs. Clarence MacKay, from Kincaid, "The Feminine Charms of the Woman Militant," *Good Housekeeping*, February 1912.   66

1.16. Inez Millholland, from Kincaid, "The Feminine Charms of the Woman Militant," *Good Housekeeping*, February 1912.   68

1.17. Inez Millholland (March 1913).   68

1.18. Standiford Studios, Cleveland, "Judge Florence Ellenwood Allen" (1925).   69

1.19. Robert Bolling Brandegee, "Sarah Porter" (1896).   69

1.20. Edward Hughes, "Juliette Gordon Low" (1887).   70

1.21. Sarah J. Eddy, "Susan B. Anthony, on the Occasion of her 80th Birthday" (1900).   72

1.22. Standiford Studios, Cleveland, "Harriet [Mrs. James Lees] Laidlow" (1925).   73

1.23. Mrs. Thomas Jefferson Smith (c.1920s).   74

1.24. Frederick A. Bridgman, "Woman and Rose" (1885), from Sheldon, *Recent Ideals of American Art* (1888, 1889, 1890).   74

1.25. James Breese, "Mrs. Walter Pease," from "The Basis of New York Society," *Cosmopolitan*, August 1899.   75

1.26. Tonnesen Sisters, Chicago (1900), for *Washington Times Supplement*, October 13, 1901.   75

1.27. Harrison Fisher, "Armour's Harrison Fisher Girl" (1906).   75

1.28. Howard Chandler Christy, "On the Beach" (1903), reprinted in Christy, *The American Girl* (1906).   76

1.29. Marion Hollins (c.1908).   76

1.30. Elaine Golding (1915).   76

1.31. Katharine Harley (c.1908).   77

1.32. Elaine Golding (1915)   77

1.33. Annette Kellermann (n.d.).   79

1.34. Tonnesen Sisters, Chicago (1900), for the *Washington Times*, March 24, 1901.   79

1.35. Edith Roberts (1918).   79

1.36. Harriet Hosmer, "Beatrice Cenci" (1857). engraved by W. Roffe for Clark, *Great American Sculptures* (1878).   79

1.37. Dr. Mary Walker (1912).   80

1.38. Romaine Brooks, "Self-Portrait" (1923).   80

1.39. Mrs. A. Van Winkle (1915).   80

1.40. Irene Langhorne Gibson (c.1915).   81

1.41. Charles A. Winter, "The Militant," *The Masses*, August 1913.   81

1.42. Charles Dana Gibson, "Dull for the Girls After Dinner—The Judge and the Governor Discuss Politics," from *Other People* (1911). 82

1.43. "Emancipated Woman" (1900). 83

1.44. "Here Is the New Woman," *New York World*, August 18, 1895. 84

1.45. Charles Dana Gibson, "One of the Disadvantages of Being in Love with a Athletic Girl," *Life*, May 22, 1902. 86

1.46. Burr McIntosh Studio, "Miss [Marie] Doro, No. 13" (1902). 86

1.47. Charles Cox, poster for "Bearings" (1896). 87

1.48. Irma Purman and friends (c.1913). 87

1.49. Van, "New York Against Boston for the Championship," *Life*, September 22, 1887. 87

1.50. Irma Purman (c.1914). 87

1.51. Charles Dana Gibson, "Scribner's for June" (1896). 89

1.52. Binner, "Hall's Hair Renewer 'Grows Bountiful Beautiful Hair,' " (1898). 89

1.53. "Basket Ball—The New Craze for Athletic Young Women," *New York Journal*, May 17, 1896. 90

1.54. Charles Dana Gibson, "Design for Wall Paper. Suitable for a Bachelor Apartment," *Life*, September 18, 1902. 90

1.55. Irma Purman and friends (c.1913). 91

2.1. Stuart Davis, "Gee, Mag, Think of Us Bein' on a Magazine Cover!" *The Masses*, June 1913. 95

2.2. Rudolf Eickemeyer, Jr., "Mrs. John Jacob Astor" (1903). 98

2.3. James Abbott McNeil Whistler, "Arrangement in Black and White, No. 1: The Young American" (1873–1878). 98

2.4. Charles Dana Gibson, "Studies in Expression. When Women Are Jurors," *Life*, October 23, 1902. 99

2.5. Charles Dana Gibson, "In a London Theatre," *Life*, April 9, 1896. 99

2.6. Charles Dana Gibson, untitled, from *The Social Ladder* (c.1901–1902). 105

2.7. From Lavater, *Essays on Physiognomy* (1804). 106

2.8. "Typical Man," from Guyot, *Physical Geography* (1866). 107

2.9. "The Races of Men," from Von Steinwehr and Brinton, *An Intermediate Geography* (1878). 107

2.10. "Which Is the American Princess?" *New York Journal*, January 12, 1896. 108

2.11. Lewis Hine, "Russian Jewess" (1905). 110

2.12. Cusacks, "Columbia," *The Daily Graphic*, January 13, 1880. 113

2.13. "The Great 'Scrub' Race" (1870). 114

2.14. From Simms, *Physiognomy Illustrated* (1891). 114

2.15. Abbott Handerson Thayer, "Portrait of Bessie Price" (1897). 115

2.16. Charles Dana Gibson, "The Wearing of the Green," from *Other People* (1911). 116

2.17. From Simms, *Physiognomy Illustrated* (1891). 119

2.18. From Simms, *Physiognomy Illustrated* (1891). 120

2.19. From Rocine, *Heads, Faces, Types, Races* (1910). 121

2.20. Albert Beck Wenzell, "The Christian Sabbath on Fifth Avenue," from *In Vanity Fair* (1896). 122

2.21. Albert Beck Wenzell, "Long Branch Puzzle—Find the Christian," from *In Vanity Fair* (1896). 122

2.22. J. E. Purdy, "Lottie Adams as 'A Daughter of the Temple' " (1899). 124

2.23. "Gertrude Stein" (c.1895). 125

2.24. Bonney, "Gertrude Stein" (c.1925). 127

2.25. Howard Chandler Christy, "Americans All!" (1917). 128

2.26. "Perfectly Balanced Section," from *Human Nature Study* (1924). 129

2.27. "Isaac Merrit Singer," attributed to Edward Harrison May (1869). 131

2.28. John Singer Sargent, "Miss Elsie Palmer" (1890). 132

2.29. George de Forest Brush, "Miss Polly Cabot" (1896). 133

2.30. Samuel Murray, "Full-Length Figure of Mrs. Thomas Eakins" (1894). 133

2.31. "The Philosophical Type," from Rocine, *Heads, Faces, Types, Races* (1910). 136

2.32. From Lombroso and Ferrero, *The Female Offender* (1895). 137

2.33. Charles Dana Gibson, "A Suffragette's Husband," from *Other People* (1911). 139

3.1. Elihu Vedder, "The Cumaean Sibyl" (1876). 150

3.2. Elihu Vedder, "Jane Jackson," (1863). 150

3.3. William Merritt Chase, "Lady with the White Shawl" ("Portrait of Mrs. C.") (1893). 153

3.4. Davida Johnson Clark (c.1886). 155

3.5. Augustus Saint-Gaudens, first study for head of "Diana" (1886). 156

3.6. Augustus Saint-Gaudens, detail of reduction of "Diana" (c.1895). 156

3.7. Augustus Saint-Gaudens, "Anne Page," model for the head of the Angel in the Shaw Memorial (1895). 157

3.8. Dennis Miller Bunker, "Portrait of Anne Page" (1887). 157

3.9. Augustus Saint-Gaudens, figure from the Shaw Memorial (1884–1897). 158

3.10. Daniel Chester French, studio model (c.1906). 159

3.11. George Du Maurier, "The Soft Eyes," from *Trilby* (1884). 163

3.12. George Du Maurier, "Au Clair de la Lune," from *Trilby* (1894). 163

3.13. John Ferguson Weir, "His Favorite Model" (188–). 166

3.14. Albert Beck Wenzell, frontispiece for Partridge, *The Angel of Clay* (1900). 167

3.15. Charles Dana Gibson, "In the Studio," from Chambers, *The Common Law* (1911). 169

3.16. Alice Barber Stevens, "Female Life Class" (1879). 169

3.17. Anders Zorn, "Augustus Saint-Gaudens with Model" (1897). 175

3.18. Alfred Maurer, "The Model" (c.1902). 176

3.19. Thomas Eakins, "Mrs. Thomas Eakins" (c.1899). 177

4.1. Louis Loeb, illustration for Twain, *Pudd'nhead Wilson*, *The Century*, January 1894.   183

4.2. E. W. Kemble, frontispiece for Twain, *Pudd'nhead Wilson and Those Extraordinary Twins* (1899).   184

4.3. Dennis Miller Bunker, "Jessica" (1890).   194

4.4. Thomas Eakins, "Addie (Miss Mary Adeline Williams)" (c.1900).   195

4.5. Kenyon Cox, from *The Blessed Damozel* (1886).   196

4.6. John Singer Sargent, "Astarte and Neith" (1895–1916).   199

4.7. J. C. Leyendecker, poster for *The Chap-Book* (1897).   202

4.8. Thomas Wilmer Dewing, "Lady with a Mask" (c.1907).   205

4.9. "Artist, Creator of the Famous 'Christy' American Girl Pictures," from Rocine, *Heads, Faces, Types, Races* (1910).   207

4.10. Howard Chandler Christy, "Gold Is Not All," (1904).   209

4.11. Howard Chandler Christy, "Which?" (1902).   209

4.12. Howard Chandler Christy, "The Summer Girl," from *Our Girls* (1906).   211

4.13. Charles Dana Gibson, "The Heiress," *Life*, April 17, 1902.   215

4.14. Charles Dana Gibson, "One of Our Leisure Class," from *Other People* (1911).   215

4.15. Charles Dana Gibson, untitled, *Life*, November 16, 1893.   216

4.16. Charles Dana Gibson, "In the Swim, Dedicated to Extravagant Women," *Life*, September 27, 1900.   216

4.17. Charles Dana Gibson, "Love Will Die," *Life*, March 1, 1894.   217

4.18. Charles Dana Gibson, "His Everlasting Experiments with Ill-Matched Pairs," *Life*, March 16, 1893.   217

5.1. Thomas Eakins, "Nude Woman Seated Wearing a Mask" (1866–1867).   222

5.2. Koloman Moser, from *Ver Sacrum* (1901).   224

5.3. Coles Phillips, advertisement for Oneida Community Silver (1911).   224

5.4. John Singer Sargent, "The Hermit" (1908).   225

5.5. Elihu Vedder, "Memory" (1870).   226

5.6 John Sloan, "The Football Puzzle," for *Philadelphia Press*, October 13, 1901.   227

5.7. Fernand Léger, "Nudes in a Landscape" (1909–1910).   228

5.8. and 5.9. Abbott Handerson Thayer, with Gerald Thayer, Emma Thayer, and Rockwell Kent, "Concealing Coloration in the Animal Kingdom: Copperhead Snake on Dead Leaves" (c. 1900–1909).   229

5.10. Coles Phillips, *Life*, November 25, 1909.   231

5.11. Seymour Joseph Guy, "Making a Train" (1867).   234

5.12. Abbott Handerson Thayer and Richard Merryman, "Peacock in the Woods" (1907).   238

5.13. Alfred H. Maurer, "The Peacock" (c.1903).   239

5.14. James Montgomery Flagg, "The Mask," from *Yankee Girls Abroad* (1900).   241

5.15. Joseph Mozier, "Undine" (c.1867).   242

5.16. Jean Webster, "Any Orphan," from *Daddy-Long-Legs* (1912). 243

5.17. Jean Webster, "News of the Month," from *Daddy-Long-Legs* (1912). 244

5.18. Jean Webster, "Daddy-Long-Legs," from *Daddy-Long-Legs* (1912). 245

5.19. Jean Webster, [Fat Trustee], from *Daddy-Long-Legs* (1912). 245

5.20. Jean Webster, "Are You Bald?" from *Daddy-Long-Legs* (1912). 245

5.21. James Montgomery Flagg, ". . . a fear of being trapped by domesticity and baby carriages," from Hooper, *Virgins in Cellophane* (1932). 246

5.22. James Montgomery Flagg, ". . . every man likes to think his Prize Package is a Virgin in cellophane," from Hooper, *Virgins in Cellophane* (1932). 247

5.23. James Montgomery Flagg, ". . . the prayer of a hot-water bottle," from Hooper, *Virgins in Cellophane* (1932). 248

5.24. James Montgomery Flagg, ". . . I have an insane desire to wrap him up in a pink flannel blanket," from Hooper, *Virgins in Cellophane* (1932). 248

5.25. James Montgomery Flagg, "After a few cocktails all men look alike," from Hooper, *Virgins in Cellophane* (1932). 249

5.26. James Montgomery Flagg, "Stags only see the backs of girls' legs and break in on the prettiest pairs," from Hooper, *Virgins in Cellophane*. (1932). 249

5.27. Harrison Fisher, from McCutcheon, *Beverly of Graustark* (1904). 251

5.28. Harrison Fisher, from McCutcheon, *Beverly of Graustark* (1904). 251

5.29. Edward Penfield, frontispiece for Williamson, *The Princess Passes* (1905). 252

5.30. "Feminine, Womanly," from Balkin, *Human Dictionary* (1923). 253

5.31. From Rocine, *Heads, Faces, Types, Races.* (1910). 254

5.32. From Rocine, *Heads, Faces, Types, Races* (1910). 255

5.33. "The Perfect Man," Hammerslough, Saks & Co. (c.1890). 256

5.34. "Diagram C.—Standard Adult Proportions," from Buttrick, *Principles of Clothing Selection* (1923). 256

5.35. "I'm Glad I'm a Boy," *Ziegfeld Follies of 1909.* 257

5.36. Bristow Adams, "Indiana Normal" (1902). 257

5.37. Irma Purman and friends (c.1913). 258

5.38. Irma Purman and friends (c.1913). 258

5.39. Penrhyn Stanlaws, poster for *Scribner's Monthly Magazine* (1898). 259

5.40. William Sergeant Kendall, poster for *Scribner's Monthly Magazine* (189–). 259

5.41. J. C. Leyendecker, "House of Kuppenheimer" (1921). 260

5.42. J. C. Leyendecker, "Vacation," *Collier's Weekly*, August 17, 1907. 260

5.43. Irma Purman and friends (c.1912). 261

5.44. Irma Purman and friends (c.1913). 261

5.45. Head of the Statue of Liberty, Paris park (1883). 262

5.46. George Brehm, "Tenby, an Arrow Collar for Women" (1910). 263

5.47. Charles Dana Gibson, "One More Victim," *Life*, May 23, 1895. 264

5.48. Charles Dana Gibson, "The Ambitious Mother and the Obliging Clergyman," *Life*, June 5, 1902. 264

5.49. Charles Dana Gibson, "Her Nightmare. How She Saw Herself," *Life*, May 21, 1896. 264

5.50. Irma Purman and friends (c.1912).   265
5.51. Irma Purman and friends (c.1912).   265
5.52. Irma Purman (1908).   265
5.53. Irma Purman and friends (c.1913).   266
5.54. Irma Purman and friends (c.1913).   266
5.55. Irma Purman and friends (c.1912).   267
5.56. Irma Purman and friends (c.1912).   267
5.57. Irma Purman and friends (c.1913).   267
5.58. Irma Purman and friends (c.1911).   268
5.59. Irma Purman and friends (c.1911).   268
5.60. Irma Purman and friends (c.1912).   268
5.61. From "Tabasco Land" (1905–1906).   269
5.62. John Sloan as "Twillbee" (1894).   270
5.63. Frederick W. Taylor as "Lilian Gray" (late 1870s).   271
5.64. F. Scott Fitzgerald, promotion photograph for "The Evil Eye," *New York Times* (1915).   271
5.65. Julian Eltinge, "Friends" (1919).   272
5.66. "Julian Eltinge in Eleven Poses," from *Julian Eltinge Magazine and Beauty Hints* (1904).   272
5.67. "Julian Eltinge With and Without the Julian Eltinge Cold Cream on His Face," from *Julian Eltinge Magazine and Beauty Hints* (1904).   273
5.68. Maude Adams in "L'Aiglon" (1900), from *The Illustrated American Stage* (1901).   274
5.69. Julia Marlowe in "Chatterton" (1897), from *The Illustrated American Stage* (1901).   274
5.70. Hetty King, "I'm Going Away" (1907).   275
5.71. Della Fox, "Good-Bye Maggie May" (1905).   275
5.72. "Vesta Tilley's New Songs" (1894).   276
5.73. Florenze Tempest, "I Love the Ladies" (1914).   277
5.74. Tempest and Sunshine, "Oh You Tease" (1910).   278
5.75. Howard Chandler Christy, from McCutcheon, "When Girl Meets Girl," *Good Housekeeping*, June 1912.   279
5.76. Howard Chandler Christy, from McCutcheon, "When Girl Meets Girl," *Good Housekeeping*, June 1912.   279
5.77. Irma Purman and friends (1914).   281
5.78. Irma Purman and friends (1914).   281

6.1. Francis Picabia, "Gertrude Stein" (1930s).   298
6.2. Benjamin West, "Self-Portrait" (1806).   300
6.3. Floral postal (1906).   303
6.4. John Singer Sargent, "Isabella Stewart Gardner" (1888).   309

7.1. Roy Lichtenstein, "Drowning Girl" (1963).   316

7.2. William Merritt Chase, "Lady in Black" (1888). 320

7.3. John Singer Sargent, "Mrs. Charles E. Inches" (1888). 321

7.4. Gertrude Stein and friends, Radcliffe College (c.1895–1897). 337

7.5. Alvin Langdon Coburn, "Gertrude Stein" (1913). 338

8.1. F. Holland Day, "Black Girl with White Collar" (1905). 340

8.2. Gertrude Käsebier, "Zit-Kala-Za" (c.1898). 341

8.3. Thomas Wilmer Dewing, "The Garland" (n.d.). 346

8.4. Helen Keller, *McClure's Magazine*, June 1905. 347

8.5. Thomas Wilmer Dewing, sketch of woman's head (n.d.). 350

8.6. George Bellows, "Florence Davey" (1914). 351

8.7. Frank Weston Benson, "Girl in a Red Shawl" (1890). 353

8.8. Daniel Chester French, "Memory" (1919). 356

8.9. William McGregor Paxton, "The House Maid" (1910). 359

8.10. Coles Phillips, "The Lure of Books," *Life*, June 8, 1911. 360

8.11. Bessie Potter Vonnoh, "Day Dreams" (1903). 361

8.12. Charles Sprague Pearce, "A Reverie" (188–), from *Recent Ideals of American Art* (1888, 1889, 1890). 362

8.13. Charles Sprague Pearce, "Resting" (188–), from *Recent Ideals of American Art* (1888, 1889, 1890). 362

8.14. John Joseph Boyle, "Tired Out" (1887). 363

8.15. John Singer Sargent, "Repose" (1911). 363

8.16. Edmund Tarbell, "Across the Room" (c.1899). 364

8.17. Frederick Frieseke, "La Chaise Longue" (1919). 365

8.18. C. H. Anderson, San Francisco, "Admiration" (1903). 365

8.19. M. B. Parkinson, New York, "Idle Moments" (1896). 368

8.20. William H. Rau, "Chicken Salad and Oysters After the Matinee" (1900). 368

8.21. William H. Rau, "The Platonic Kiss" (1902). 369

8.22. "Little Daubs of Powder . . ." (1909). 370

8.23. James Montgomery Flagg, "You," *Life*, October 25, 1906. 370

8.24. Mary Cassatt, "Mother and Child" (c.1905). 371

8.25. J. Alden Weir, "The Green Bodice" (1898). 372

8.26. Thomas Wilmer Dewing, "The Mirror" (n.d.). 373

9.1. Samuel L. Waldo, "Mrs. Samuel L. Waldo (Deliverance Mapes)" (c.1826). 378

9.2. George P. A. Healy, "Mrs. John Church Cruger (Euphemia Van Rensselaer)" (1842). 379

9.3. Samuel F. B. Morse, "The Muse—Susan Walker Morse" (1835–1837). 379

9.4. Cephas Giovanni Thompson, "Spring" (1838). 381

9.5. Edwin Howland Blashfield, "Portrait of Evangeline Wilbour Blashfield" (n.d.). 383

9.6. Edwin Howland Blashfield, detail of "The Angel With the Flaming Sword" (1920). 384

9.7. Thomas Wilmer Dewing, "The Angel of Sleep" (n.d.), from Koehler, *American Art* (1886).   385

9.8. Thomas Wilmer Dewing, "Summer" (1890).   385

9.9. Frances Benjamin Johnston, "Spring," from masque of "Friendship" (1906).   386

9.10. Elie Nadelman, "Classical Figure" (c.1901–1910).   387

9.11. Elie Nadelman, "Figure Study" (1913).   388

9.12. Elie Nadelman, "Hostess" (c.1918–1919).   389

9.13. Abbott Handerson Thayer, "Portrait of a Lady: Miss Bessie Stillman" (1883).   390

9.14. Abbott Handerson Thayer, "Girl Arranging Her Hair" (1918–1919).   391

9.15. Abbott Handerson Thayer, "A Winged Figure" (1911).   392

9.16. Abbott Handerson Thayer, "Sketch for an Angel" (c.1889).   393

9.17. M. B. Parkinson, "Daydreams" (1896).   397

9.18. Gerturde Käsebeir, from Tracy, "Shadows of the Artist's Ideal," *Discussions on American Art and Artists* (1893).   397

9.19. J. E. Purdy, "Lillian Lawrence as 'Temperance' " (1899).   398

9.20. John La Farge, "Dawn Comes on the Edge of Night" (n.d.).   398

9.21. Abbott Handerson Thayer, "Diana" (n.d.).   399

9.22. Frances Benjamin Johnston, "Diana," from masque of "Friendship" (1906).   400

9.23. Fritz W. Guerin, [Bacchante] (1902).   401

9.24. Mary Cassatt, "Bacchante" (1872).   402

9.25. George G. Bain, "Mrs. James B. Eustis as a Bacchante" (1909).   402

9.26. William Wetmore Story, "Libyan Sibyl" (1868).   403

9.27. "Frou Frou's Dream of Home" (1870).   403

9.28. Howard Chandler Christy, "Reverie," from *Our Girls* (1907).   404

9.29. Benjamin Falk, "Marguerite" (1894).   405

9.30. Tonnesen Sisters (1900), for *The Washington Times*, March 17, 1901.   405

9.31. Irma Purman (1897).   406

9.32. Johannes Oertel, "Saved" or "The Rock of Ages" (1867).   408

9.33. Von Glahn Memorial (c.1906), Greenwood Cemetery, Brooklyn.   409

9.34. C. H. Anderson, "Clinging to the Cross" (c.1903).   410

9.35. From *Palliser's Memorials and Headstones* (1891).   419

9.36. Daniel Chester French, "Spirit of the Waters," for Spencer Trask Memorial (c.1913–1915).   421

9.37. "Protecting Angels" (1867).   422

9.38. J. H. Adams, "Room in My Heart" (1900).   423

9.39. Albert Beck Wenzell, "Vanitas Vanitatum," from *The Passing Show* (1900).   424

9.40. Edwin Howland Blashfield, "The Christmas Bells" (c.1891), from *Gems of Sacred Song* (1911).   425

10.1. Abbott Handerson Thayer, "Angel" (c.1888). 430

10.2 From Lavater, *Essays in Physiognomy* (1804). 434

10.3. James Montgomery Flagg, "Then and Now" (1907). 434

10.4. Charles Dana Gibson, "An Afternoon Reception in Heraculaneum," *Life*, February 5, 1891. 436

10.5. Charles Dana Gibson, from Davis, *The Princess Aline* (1895). 441

10.6. Charles Dana Gibson, from Davis, *The Princess Aline* (1895). 442

10.7. Charles Dana Gibson, from Davis, *The Princess Aline* (1895). 443

10.8. Charles Dana Gibson, from Davis, *The Princess Aline* (1895). 445

10.9. Augustus Saint-Gaudens, bronze cast of original marble relief, "Bessie Smith White" (1884). 450

10.10. Rudolf Eickemeyer, Jr., "Evelyn Nesbit" (c.1901). 450

10.11. Maude Adams as "Rosemary" (1896). 451

10.12. Burr McIntosh Studio, "Miss Bentley" (1902). 451

10.13. Rudolf Eickemeyer, Jr., "Evelyn Nesbit" (c.1901). 453

10.14. Rudolf Eickemeyer, Jr., "Evelyn Nesbit" (c.1901). 453

10.15. Rudolf Eickemeyer, Jr., "Evelyn Nesbit" (c.1901). 454

10.16. Kenyon Cox, "Femme Inconnue—Louvre," *The Century*, November 1884. 455

10.17. Kenyon Cox, from Rossetti, *The Blessed Damozel* (1886). 458

10.18. Kenyon Cox, from Rossetti, *The Blessed Damozel* (1886). 459

10.19. Kenyon Cox, from Rossetti, *The Blessed Damozel* (1886). 459

10.20. Pilule, "The Chain Complete—No. 7," Prang American Chromo (1875). 460

10.21. Charles Dana Gibson, "When He Once Goes Out It Is Hard To Get Him Back," *Life*, April 19, 1894. 460

10.22. Otho Cushing, *"The Newly Arrived:* 'Say Boss, Give Us A Light From Your Flamin' Sword, Will Yer?' " *Life*, December 8, 1898. 461

10.23. Daniel Chester French, "The Sons of God Saw the Daughters of Men That They Were Fair." 461

11.1 Charles Demuth, "In Vaudeville: Columbia" (1919). 466

11.2. Leon Klayman, "U.S. Grain Arsenal—Food Is Not A Weapon, It Is A Human Right" (c.1975). 467

11.3. John Singer Sargent, "Mrs. George Swinton" (1896–1897). 470

11.4. Thomas Wilmer Dewing, "Lady in Yellow" (1888). 471

11.5. Mrs. H. Bramhall Gilbert, from Van Rensselaer, "The Basis of New York Society," *The Cosmopolitan*, August 1899. 472

11.6. John Singer Sargent, "The Marlborough Family" (1905). 473

11.7. Russell Purman (c.1902). 474

11.8. Augustus Saint-Gaudens, Sherman Monument (1903). 482

11.9. "The Political Sodom and Gomorrah Are Doomed To Destruction," *Puck*, May 10, 1882. 485

11.10. "Through Night to Light," *Puck*, October 25, 1882.   486

11.11. "The Graphic and Its Gifted Pupils," *The Daily Graphic*, March 9, 1880.   487

11.12. "The National Metropolis in the 107th Year of American Independence. Puck's idea of a statue more appropriate for New York than Bartholdi's 'Liberty' " *Puck*, December 12, 1882.   488

11.13. H. S. Phillips, "The Woman That Saved The Union," poster for *Godey's Magazine* (1896).   489

11.14. Philipp Galle, "America" (1581–1600).   490

11.15. J. Scott Williams, "For Victory, Buy More Bonds" (1918).   491

11.16. "The Heroine's March" (1867).   492

11.17. F. L. Mott Iron Co., "The Amazon" (1876), from Weinberg, ed., *Masterpieces of the Centennial International Exhibition.*   492

11.18. Emanuel Leutze, "The Amazon and Her Children" (1851).   493

11.19. "America" (1876), design by John Bell for Prince Albert Memorial, London.   494

11.20. Archie Gunn, "Columbian Amazons" (1894).   494

11.21. Howard Chandler Christy, "Pocahontas," from *Liberty Belles* (1912).   495

11.22. Sibyl Brainerd as "Pocahontas" (1911).   495

11.23. Domenico Tojetti, "The Progress of America" (1875).   497

12.1. Thomas Wilmer Dewing, "The Blue Dress" (1892).   501

12.2. Daniel Chester French, "The Republic" (1918).   502

12.3. Augustus Saint-Gaudens, "Diana," (1886–1891).   503

12.4. "Columbia," from suffrage tableaux, Washington, D.C., March 3, 1913.   504

12.5. Augustus Saint-Gaudens, detail from the Adams Memorial, Rock Creek Cemetery, Washington, D.C. (1891).   505

12.6. John Singer Sargent, "Mrs. and Mrs. I.N. Phelps Stokes" (1897).   506

12.7. Albert Beck Wenzell, from Wharton, *The House of Mirth* (1905).   507

12.8. Charles Dana Gibson, "The Weaker Sex—II," *Collier's Weekly*, July 4, 1903.   509

12.9. "Every Woman Admires a Tall Man" (1904).   509

12.10. George Du Maurier, "It Was Trilby," from *Trilby* (1894).   510

12.11. Charles Dana Gibson, untitled, from *The Social Ladder* (1902).

12.12. Mora, "Mrs. Cornelius Vanderbilt as Electric Light," Vanderbilt ball, March 26, 1883.   511

12.13. Contemporary woodcut, "Liberty," delivered to the American ambassador, Paris, July 4, 1884.   512

12.14. "Margaret Wycherly as 'Woman,' " July 1915.   512

12.15. Mole and Thomas, "Human Statue of Liberty," Camp Dodge, Des Moines, Iowa (1918).   514

12.16. Frances Benjamin Johnston, "The Grand Basin, Columbian Exposition" (1893).   516

12.17. Daniel Chester French, "America," U.S. Custom House, New York (1903–1907).   517

12.18. "Appropriate Group of Statuary for the New York Custom House," *Life*, October 22, 1903.   518

12.19. Kenyon Cox, "Lodgers in a Crowded Bayard Street Tenement—'Five Cents a Spot,' " after a photograph by Jacob Riis, from "How The Other Half Lives," *Scribner's Monthly Magazine*, December 1899.   520

12.20. Charles Dana Gibson, "Waiting for Bread," from *Americans* (1898).   520

12.21. Hendrik Christian Andersen, frontispiece for *Creation of a World Centre of Communication* (1903).   521

12.22. Hendrik Christian Andersen, from *Creation of a World Centre of Communication* (1903).   522

12.23. Will H. Low, from "The Art of the White City," *Scribner's Monthly Magazine*, October 1893.   524

12.24. "The Corliss Engine," from Burr, *Memorial of the International Exposition* (1877).   526

12.25. J. Carroll Beckwith, "The Telephone," from "The Decoration of the Exposition," *Scribner's Monthly Magazine*, December 1892.   531

12.26. Elihu Vedder, "The Pleiades," (1885), from *American Art* (1886).   531

12.27. Coles Phillips, "The Spirit of Transportation" (1920).   533

12.28. Franklin W. Smith, "The Aggrandisement of Washington" (1891).   540

12.29. Augustus Saint-Gaudens, models for coinage (1907).   541

12.30. Edwin Howland Blashfield, "The Law," courthouse, Wilkes-Barre, Pa. (1909).   544

12.31. Edwin Howland Blashfield, "Westward," Iowa State Capitol (1905).   546

12.32. Edwin Austin Abbey, "The Spirit of Light," Pennsylvania State Capitol, Harrisburg (c.1904–1908).   547

12.33. Keinz and Allison, "Coronation of Womanhood" (1885).   548

12.34. G. Y. Coffin, "National American Woman Suffrage Association—28th Annual Convention" (1896).   548

12.35. Edwin Howland Blashfield, "Minnesota, The Granary of the World," senate chamber, Minnesota State Capitol, St. Paul (1904).   549

12.36. Edwin Howland Blashfield, "Carry On!" (1918).   550

12.37. Thomas Cole, "The Course of Empire—Consummation of Empire" (1835–36).   551

13.1. Imre Kiralfy, "Columbia's Triumph," from "America" (1893).   554

13.2. Jules Guerin, drawing for McKim, Mead, White, "Arch of the Rising Sun from The Court of the Universe," Panama-Pacific International Exposition, San Francisco (1915).   554

13.3. "Good-Bye, Dolly Gray" (c.1898).   555

13.4. "Dewey's Victory" (c.1898).   555

13.5. "The American Girl Battleship March" (1898).   556

13.6. Charles Dana Gibson, "Come, Let Us Forgive and Forget," *Life*, August 11, 1898.   557

13.7. Charles Dana Gibson, "These Foreign Relations: 'Do I want to go in with that crowd?' " *Life*, August 25, 1898.   557

13.8. Hedrick, "The Newest Woman," *St. Louis Globe-Democrat* (1898).   558

13.9. Charles Dana Gibson, " 'On the Sidewalks of New York,' " from *Americans* (1898).   561

13.10. Denman Fink, "On the Threshhold of the New Country," from "Among the Immigrants," *Scribner's Monthly Magazine*, March 1901.   563

13.11. Poster for "The Boston Sunday Herald," April 19, 1896.   564

13.12. "Six Young Ladies Wrapped in a Flag" (1918).   566

13.13. Benjamin Falk, "Evangeline Booth—The White Angel of the Slums" (1907).   566

13.14. "The Uncle Sam Range" (1876).   567

13.15. A. E. Foringer, "The Greatest Mother in the World" (1918).   568

13.16. "Pears' Soap," *The Cosmopolitan*, advertising section, May–October 1899).   569

13.17. Fritz W. Guerin, St. Louis, "Cuba Reconciling the North and the South" (1898).   570

13.18. Russell, *St. Louis Globe-Democrat* (1898), from *Cartoons of the War of 1898 with Spain* (1898).   570

13.19. Kenyon Cox, nude study for magazine cover, "Columbia and Cuba" (c. 1898).   571

13.20. George Prince, "Dawn of Day in the Antilles" (1898).   572

13.21. Maud Humphrey, "A Red Cross Nurse" (1898).   572

13.22. Tapestry by Mme. de Rudder, "Civilization" (1897).   573

13.23. Edwin Howland Blashfield, "Belgium," from Wharton, *The Book of the Homeless* (1916).   573

13.24. Cigar label, "Americas Unidas" (c.1885).   574

13.25. Hazel Frazee, "Every Ship Saved a Long Journey Means a Shipload of Soldiers and Munitions to France" (1918).   574

13.26. Daniel MacMorris, "Women in War" (1955).   575

13.27. Howard Chandler Christy, "Gee! I Wish I Were A Man. I'd Join The Navy" (1917).   576

13.28. Cigar label, "Cockade" (c.1885).   576

13.29. "My Baby's Arms," *Ziegfeld Follies 1919,*   577

13.30. Howard Chandler Christy, "The Army Girl," from *The American Girl* (1906).   577

13.31. Starmer, "Why Can't a Girl Be a Soldier?" (1905).   578

13.32. Capranesi, "Sotto Scrivere al Prestito" (1918).   579

13.33. "Motherless, Fatherless, Starving. How Much To Save These Little Lives?" (1918).   580

13.34. Edward Penfield, "The Girl on the Land Serves the Nation's Need" (1918).   580

13.35. Douglas Volk, "They Shall Not Perish" (1918). 580

13.36. Henry J. Glintenkamp, "The Girl He Left Behind Him," *The Masses*, October 1914. 581

13.37. U.S. Food Administration Drawing (c.1918). 582

13.38. Edward Penfield, "Will You Help the Women of France? Save Wheat" (1918). 582

13.39. Howard Chandler Christy, "Observers," *The American Weekly*, *Washington Times*, July 21, 1918. 583

13.40. Charles Dana Gibson, "A Word to the Wives. 'Save' " (c.1918). 583

14.1. Kerr, "The Choir Celestial" (1900). 594

14.2. Louis Rhead, *Cleveland World*, Easter number (1896). 594

14.3. Albert Beck Wenzell, "Until After Easter," from *The Passing Show* (1900). 596

14.4. Frank A. Nankivell, poster for the *New York Journal*, Easter number (1896). 596

14.5. Charles Dana Gibson, "Lenten Confessions," *Life*, February 8, 1894. 598

14.6. Hy Mayer, *Truth*, Easter number (1897). 599

14.7. Irma Purman and friends (Easter 1913). 599

14.8. Charles Schenk, from *Draperies in Action* (1902). 600

14.9. Coles Phillips, "Luxite Hosiery" (1919). 600

14.10. "Madame Dean's Spinal Supporting Corsets" (1885). 601

14.11. "A Blessing to Life's Sunrise, Nestle's Food," *Scribner's Magazine Advertiser* (1900). 601

14.12. "The New Fashion Department," *The Ladies' Home Journal*, January 1908. 602

14.13. "The Bartholdi Statue of Liberty, The Largest in the World: The Brainerd & Armstrong Co's Spool Silk, The Best in the World" (c. 1883). 603

14.14. F. Opper, "Let the Advertising Agents Take Charge of the Bartholdi Business. . . . ," *Puck*, April 1, 1885. 604

14.15. "Liberty Triumphant, 1849–1899," Louis Bergdoll Brew'g Co. (1899). 605

14.16. "Morning Nap, Tarrant's Seltzer Aperient," (1884). 607

14.17. "Edison's Greatest Marvel, The Vitascope" (1896). 615

14.18. "The High-Kicker," J. R. Palmenberg's Sons catalogue. (1893). 615

14.19. Charles Dana Gibson, "Fooled Again," *Life*, September 12, 1895. 616

14.20. Sigismond de Ivanowski, "Lead Us Not Into Temptation," from "The Lord's Prayer: A Series of Paintings," *The Delineator*, December 1908. 616

14.21 a and b. Archie Gunn, "The Curtain Descends On the Season of 95–96," *New York Journal*, May 24, 1896. 619

14.22. Charles Dana Gibson, "The Villain Dies," *Collier's Weekly*, November 12, 1904. 619

14.23. Charles Dana Gibson, "An Argument with the Leading Lady," *Life*, October 10, 1895. 620

14.24. "Margaret Anglin and Her Husband," from "Domesticity and the Theater," *Good Housekeeping*, January 1912.   621

14.25. Archie Gunn, [Edna May in "The Girl From Up There"], from *The Illustrated American Stage* (1901).   622

14.26. Forrest Halsey, [Olga Nethersole as "Fanny Le Grand" in "Sappho"], from *The Illustrated American Stage* (1901).   622

14.27. "The Pony Ballet," from "Tabasco Land" (1905–1906).   623

14.28. Sigismond de Ivanowski, "Lead Us Not Into Evil," from "The Lord's Prayer, A Series of Paintings," from *The Delineator*, December 1908.   623

14.29. Archie Gunn [Bessie Clayton with Weber and Fields], from *The Illustrated American Stage* (1901).   624

14.30. Burr McIntosh Studio, "Miss Doro" (1901).   625

14.31. Evan, Los Angeles, [women on the beach] (1918).   626

14.32. "Phyllis and Aristotle" (c.1400).   626

14.33. Charles Dana Gibson, "The Nursery," from *Americans* (1900).   627

14.34. Irma Purman and friends (1914).   627

14.35. Coles Phillips, "Net Results," *Life*, August 24, 1911.   628

14.36. Raoul Larche, gilded metal electric lamp designed in the shape of Loïe Fuller (c.1900).   629

14.37. M. Morrison, "Lillian Russell" (1898).   630

14.38. Benjamin Falk, "Loïe Fuller" (1901).   630

15.1. Arthur B. Davies, "Dramatical" (n.d.).   633

15.2. George Du Maurier, "Repentance," from *Trilby* (1894).   635

15.3. Howard Chandler Christy, "Her husband and I turned on her together," from "The Lion's Mouth," *Scribner's Monthly Magazine*, December 1900.   635

15.4. Albert Beck Wenzell, from "The Weaker Vessel," *Good Housekeeping*, June 1912.   636

15.5. J. Henry, " 'You nervy little devil, you!' " from Ferber, *Fanny Herself*. (1917).   637

15.6. From "Photographs by Cory," *The Cosmopolitan*, January 1898.   638

15.7. M. B. Parkinson, New York (1897).   639

15.8. Baby Lottie Morse reciting "Faith in the Red, White, and Blue," from Hoyle, *The Complete Speaker and Reciter for Home, School, Church, and Platform* (1902).   640

15.9. Charles Dana Gibson, "Stage-Struck," *Collier's Weekly*, March 25, 1905.   640

15.10. Charles Dana Gibson, "Studies in Expression, An Imitation of the Lady of the House," *Life*, January 23, 1902.   641

15.11. Rosa Mueller Sprague, "Now you stop!" from Morgan, *An Hour With Delsarte* (1889).   644

15.12. Rosa Mueller Sprague, "Alas poor soul! What grief is thine?" from Morgan, *An Hour With Delsarte* (1889).   644

15.13. Rosa Mueller Sprague, "Mine woes afflict this spirit sore," from Morgan, *An Hour With Delsarte* (1889). 645

15.14. Fanny Brice as "Rose of Washington Square," *Ziegfeld Follies* (1920). 646

15.15. Archie Gunn, "Mr. Faversham as the Villain . . . ," *The Illustrated American*, December 22, 1894. 647

15.16. "The Dregs in the Cup," Hasty Pudding Club (1906). 648

15.17. Charles Dana Gibson, "That Evening Her Engagement Was Announced," *Life*, May 25, 1893. 649

15.18. From Ecob, *The Well-Dressed Woman* (1892). 649

15.19. Helen Dryden, *Vogue*, October 1914. 649

15.20. "Watching At The Window," from Hoyle, *The Complete Speaker and Reciter for Home, School, Church, and Platform* (1902). 650

15.21. Howard Chandler Christy, "Awaiting His Coming," from *The American Girl* (1906). 650

15.22. Irma Purman (June 1914). 651

15.23. Charles Dana Gibson, "Advertising à la Mode," *Life*, May 4, 1905. 653

15.24. "Miss Stevens as Egypt," from "Some Society Tableaux," *The Cosmopolitan*, January 1898. 654

15.25. Mrs. Caroline C. Burien as Antigone (1890). 657

15.26. Mrs. Caroline C. Burien as Antigone (1890). 658

15.27. Charles Schenk, from *Draperies in Motion* (1902). 663

15.28. Daniel Chester French, "Andromeda" (1929–1931). 663

15.29. Joshua Reynolds, "Joanna Leigh, Mrs. R. B. Lloyd" (c.1776). 665

15.30. James Abbott McNeill Whistler, "Alma Stanley in 'The Street Walker'[?]" (1983–1896). 667

15.31. Carte de visite of Alma Stanley as "Niobe" (1898). 668

Epilogue 1. John White Alexander, from "The Crowning of Labor" (1906–1907). 675

2. John White Alexander, "The Apotheosis of Pittsburgh," from "The Crowning of Labor" (1906–1907). 676

3. John White Alexander, "The Apotheosis of Pittsburgh," from "The Crowning of Labor" (1906–1907). 677

4. "The Picture the World Loves Best" (1916). 679

5. "I'm in Heaven When I'm in My Mother's Arms" (1920). 680

6. "Angels, We Call Them Mothers Down Here" (1921). 681

7. Alberto Vargas, "Cigarettes, Cigars!" *Ziegfeld Follies* (1931). 683

8. John Sloan, "Three A.M." (1909). 684

9. "Magdalen," from a painting by Murillo and photographs of Miss Teresa Vaughan and Miss Estella Clayton, from Low, "Contrasts of Life and Art" (1893). 685

10. Irma Purman and friends (c.1912). 688

11. Charles Dana Gibson, "She is disturbed by a vision which appears to be herself," *Life*, June 27, 1901. 690

12. Coles Phillips, "The Light Housekeeper," *Life*, October 12, 1911. 690

13. McDougall, "Our Sweet Girl Graduates of 1895," *New York World*, June 23, 1895.   691

14. J. Henry, "Fanny's hands became fists, gripping the power she craved. 'Then I shall have arrived!' " from Ferber, *Fanny Herself* (1917).   693

15. Ruth Eastman, *Motor*, May 1919.   693

16. "The woman 'cop' (a dream)" (1909).   694

17. "How woman policeman would look making an arrest" (1909).   695

18. Charles Dana Gibson, "Keep Still, Please," *Collier's Weekly*, April 29, 1905.   696

19. Coles Phillips, "From the Mirror," *Life*, August 19, 1909.   697

20. John Sloan, "The Bachelor Girl" (1915).   698

21. Thomas Eakins, "Portrait of Margaret Eakins" (c.1880).   698

22. Alfred Stieglitz, "Georgia O'Keeffe" (1918).   699

23. Irma Purman Banta (c.1916).   701

Preface

Imaging. The making of visual and verbal representations (by sculptors, painters, illustrators, writers, advertisers, theater people, journalists) and responses to these artifacts at every level of society.

American. The somewhat arrogant mental appropriation of the entire Western Hemisphere by one of its component parts, the United States of America, whose citizens named certain virtues and values as characteristically "American."

Women. The casting of women into symbolic forms that wore the female mien of contemporary social types (the Charmer, the Outdoors Girl, the New Woman) or of universal abstractions (Virtue, Civilization, Progress).

Idea. The application of the age-old philosophic/scientific concept of "type" by which individuals were made to conform to a series of platonizing classifications.

Ideals. The assignment of select values to womankind and to the nation, as well as the envisioning of a perfected nation as female and the categorization of true women as exemplary Americans.

Cultural History. The analysis of the diverse attitudes held toward women of the United States between 1876 and 1918 and toward the country's achievements defined according to certain so-called female attributes.

This parsing of the title of my book sets down the basic terms which structure its matter, its method, and its spread of time. *Imaging American Women: Idea and Ideals in Cultural History* is a book about the images of women—both visual and verbal—which came into being in the United States between the Philadelphia Centennial Exposition in 1876 and the close of World War I. It is about the making of those images and why they were made in such abundance. By asking sharp questions about the purposes to which these female representations were put, we come closer to understanding that *the woman as image* was one of the era's dominant cultural tics. To be even more precise: *the woman as image of a type.*

Commanding one end of the Grand Basin at the 1893 Columbian Exposition was the gigantic statue of the Republic by Daniel Chester French (see figure 12.16). The 65-foot female figure stood upon a 35-foot base, making it the largest statue ever erected in the United States to that date. (Bartholdi's Liberty statue, dedicated seven years earlier, was a foreign import after all.) Thousands came to Chicago that summer (during one of the worst financial panics of the century) to admire the splendor of the nation placed on display; they acknowledged the figure of the Republic as the central icon of the occasion. One of the fair's strongest admirers, James B. Campbell, who concocted a two-volume *Illustrated History* of the event, referred his readers to a contemporary scientist who was busily trying to prove that Eve had been 200 feet tall, then observed that French's magnificent female gave viewers the sense of the physical immensity of the Original Woman. Even more important to Campbell as an American was the expression he found upon the countenance of the Republic and what it signified: "the features of the statue had a look of proud contentment and happiness, as if there was nothing left to be desired in her existence."

The statue of the Republic represented the type of the nation. The form was that of the female, the type of American womanhood writ large. The sex and the race came together as a visual emblem of the greatness (physical size and moral force) of a nation which had "nothing left to be desired."

In 1912 Ida M. Tarbell (journalist, muckraker, lecturer) wrote *The Business of Being a Woman.* In summing up the current situation under which women in the United States labored, Tarbell employed the typifying phrase "The Uneasy Woman." James Campbell in 1893 interprets an allegorical female statue allegorically and reads what he finds as complete satisfaction. Ida Tarbell in 1912 interprets the actual conditions of actual women and concludes that dissatisfaction is the rule; but Tarbell like Campbell relies on the language of the type. One of these two interpreters of the American scene discovers the truth encapsulated in the form of the contented Republic; the other locates the Uneasy Woman. Both make use of the rhetoric of symbolic classification. So did many (I dare to say most) who commented upon the way this corner of the world looked to them in the years between 1876 and 1918—four decades spanning one of the more volatile periods in United States social history. The 1876 Centennial, the 1893 Columbian Exposition, the Spanish-American War, and the war of 1917–1918 were occasions for the making of pictorial public statements which were then assigned symbolic value on the spot. These events also furnished historians with happenings which have acquired symbolic significance after the fact. Throughout those years, at an accelerating pace, the use of the primary classifications of "woman" and "American" was habitual. Image-making and image-reading had become a major cultural activity, as well as the means for interpreting the nation's achievements and gauging its weaknesses. Even more. "Woman" and "American" coalesced around the types of desire and fear that underlay the very formation of that culture.

There is a little sketch made famous by Ernst Gombrich. A squiggle of lines, it invites the viewer to see now a duck, now a rabbit. Gombrich used this profoundly childlike sign to launch his explication of the complex relations between art and illusion and the importance of making images that match culturally shaped habits of seeing. Social conventions which direct the artist's hand are central to Gombrich's thesis; this and the notion that there is no such thing as an innocent eye, since we see what we expect to find in the world of objects surrrounding us. My book is greatly responsive to all that Gombrich has taught us about acts of perception and cognition. Although I resist coming to the same Gombrichian conclusions, I ask many of the same questions about the nature of the interpretation of images, the forceful part taken by convention, the odd affinities that exist beneath the seemingly contentious surfaces of illusion and reality, and the intriguing fact that we continually "see" and "read" the world in pictorial ways—ways made familiar to us because of the "mémoire involontaire" of which Walter Benjamin spoke when commenting upon the aura artworks cast upon their period. I apply Gombrich's duck/rabbit conundrum to the people of a country (the United States of America), of an era (1876–1918), who were tutored to see objects and persons in the form of generalized types—especially the types of women equated with American principles.

These days, I am happy to note, there is a major reexamination going on over the nature of convention. *New Literary History* put out an issue (Winter 1983) on the matter; it included essays by E. D. Hirsch, Margaret Gilbert, and Menachem Brinker that add new vigor to the realization that conventionality is one of the enduring facts of our social existence. Interest in related issues is also evident at the main watering holes of the critics and theorists. There are clusters of essays in *NLH* and *Critical Inquiry* by Brinker ("On Realism's Relativism"), James Ackerman ("On Judging Art Without Absolutes"), Nelson Goodman ("Realism, Relativism, and Reality"), and Kurt Forster ("Critical History of Art, or Transfiguration of Values?") which test—yet one more time since Socrates and Aristotle—the pugnacious relations between the concrete and the abstract in ways that American art critics and philosophers at the turn of the century would have caught to their bosoms; just as they would have the import of Guilio Argan's queries about "Ideology and Iconology" and Michel Rio's "Images and Words." When Carolyn Porter writes in *Seeing and Being* about Henry Adams and Henry James in the role of "the Participant Observer," and when Evelyn Keller and Christine R. Grontkowski ask in "The Mind's Eye" whether seeing as the primary method for knowing the world is a universal human trait or a culturally induced "masculine" habit, they too raise the theoretical issues this book takes on as a matter of course (clothed with lots of bone and gristle) because, in turn, the book honors the fact that many of the best of the American minds at the turn of the century considered the modes by which we perceive, think, and thereby exist as interpreters of society.

Interpreting the act of interpretation as a necessary but often thankless task forms another important area of current theoretical concern. Clifford Geertz, a major figure in American Studies, writes *The Interpretation of Cultures* (where he states his belief that the natives know their own culture better than the visiting anthropologists do). Jonathan Lieberson retorts in "Interpreting the Interpreter" that all kinds of misreadings creep in when you rely on the locals, and Gerald L. Bruns, in "Loose Talk About Religion from William James," warns of the interpretive conflicts that beset anyone who prefers tidy conclusions. Most of these current appraisals are cautionary in nature, but so were the assessments of the devilishly difficult job of assigning significance to the world of signs set down from the 1880s on. But for each person today who admonishes that we cannot come to terms with pictorial evidence or even thread our way with impunity between different *kinds* of pictures (paintings, photographs, literary portraits), there is someone like Kendall Walton in "Transparent Pictures: On the Nature of Photographic Realism" who assures us that there *is* something to make contact with when we look at a thing; objects don't just dissolve into unsignified signs and fury. And what are the feminist critics and the scholars in the history of women about but trying to show that valid readings of cultural tracings are possible? As long as we do not fall under the sway of canonized conventions that evaluate *a priori* what we see, we have the right—nay, the obligation—to check the nature of conventions, perceptions, and conceptions for the historical and cultural data they assuredly provide.

Because of today's hypersensitivity over the tricky quality of cultural readings, there are those who remind us—constantly, correctly—that the particular conditions governing the United States during the final decades of the nineteenth century and the first two decades of the twentieth are resistant to ready analysis. "Divisions," "dual sensibilities," "schisms," are the terms favored by scholars of the period such as Peter Conn *(The Divided Mind)* and Neil Harris *(The Land of Contrasts)*. Alan Trachtenberg, Gene Wise, and John Higham also read us sermons on the pluralisms that forbid us to find unity in a nation and at a period where there was none.

Yes, no unity, no access to interpretive certainties, no absolutes, no guaranteed rapport between seeing and knowing in a society struggling with conventions that were in the process of creating still newer conventions. There were those at the turn of the century who may have thought they possessed unity, certainty, conclusive knowledge, and self-control; but even they mainly recognized that what they had was the desire for those comforts, not their actuality. Such people are thereby among the most interesting Americans of the period: the ones who were self-critical enough to realize they wanted something that they did not have; those who lived in the midst of a confusion of cultural signs, yet kept on sponsoring the new images they hoped might bring them the clarity they craved and the force that comes through dealing with strong signs—signs such as those provided by *the types*.

Through the years from the 1870s to the 1910s a canon of types remained prominently in view. The categories they pictorialized acted to contain change; at the same time, these elected types revealed the fact that mutations and alterations of meaning were taking place. Merging and diverging, the subforms wrenched from the older traditions were commentaries on the prior state of the original image and also on the new forms in the throes of being born. Unity within multiplicity was the cultural aim, but the cultural fact was multiplicity without unity. A history such as mine of the images apportioned to American women is guaranteed to underscore the stress between the aim and the fact.

To make a distinction familiar to art historians and philosophers, images of American women were *created* as ideas, not *found* as facts. At most, Americans took certain social facts and created ideas from them to suit their needs, not necessarily to report on their historical condition. Too, many images were "found" in the sense that artists borrowed freely from a pictorial and literary iconography already established by tradition; also in the sense that some late-nineteenth-century artists were a near thing to Platonists in their notion that ideal forms exist independently of the imagination. And true, there was much talk at the time about there actually being young women on the social scene who inspired the type of the American Girl. But by and large the image makers acted to impose their ideas upon the culture. What I want to emphasize is the astonishing frequency with which those images were female in form. However masculine the political and commercial activities that controlled "the main world," the images dominating the turn-of-the-century imagination were variations on the figure of the young American woman and permutations of the type of the American Girl.

We hardly need to be reminded that one figure does not a whole carpet make and that it is silly to generalize about the preference of the American Public about anything. (If individuals have had the historical habit of reification, there is no need for us to reify their activities.) Yet it is not necessary to go down in defeat before masses of confusing data. A lively range of examples must be brought to the accounting. That done, it is legitimate business to reach conclusions about the attitudes held by specified people concerning the conventions which held to the significance of particular visual and verbal types of the American female.

Imaging American Women progresses from part 1, "Contexts" to part 2, "Demonstrations." The Introduction and the first five chapters lay down the essential theories, conditions, and opinions which will receive demonstration as individual cases in the remaining chapters. The Introduction provides the views on perception and cognition advanced by contemporary theorists as disparate as Charles Sanders Peirce, Josiah Royce, and the newspapermen of the *Daily Graphic* and the *New York World*. They suggest some of the reasons people saw and understood what they did and why many were taking women as their point of definitional reference. Chapter 1 traces the evolution of the imaged idea of the American Girl into several of its subcategories; these in turn metamorphose into diverse images (pleasing and unpleasant) of the New Woman made use of by various political and social causes. Chapter 2 takes up the uncomfortable fact that the Girl was expected to be young, pretty, unmarried, white, Protestant, and "American" if she were to aid observers (both native-based and visitors from abroad) in the understanding of the nation's unique destiny; this chapter also examines the influence of the pseudoscience of physiognomy upon the racists' need to keep the pure bloodstock of the American Girl inviolate. Chapters 3 and 4 turn to the artists (painters, sculptors, writers, popular illustrators) of the period and their responses to the power of the type as an aesthetic convention capable of prompting the creation of "the real thing." Chapter 5 looks at the gender distinctions exacted of males and females in the United States and also at the playful experiments with those sexual boundaries carried out through the period's fascination with costumes, maskings, and camouflage.

Once we have gone over the fertile terrain of the philosophical, psychological, sociological, aesthetic, and pseudoscientific theories vis-à-vis the type and the historical contexts which led to the application of type classifications to young American women, it is time to turn to demonstrations. Chapters 6 and 7 look at the creation of literary portraits and studies and the problems they inherit, and solve, by using type in the making and matching of private records of a woman's innermost being. Chapter 8 applies these questions of losses and gains to the paintings of women posed within the stillness of interior rooms and ruminations. Chapter 9 introduces the female form into the public arena as an allegorical force; no longer one or another of the types, the forms now represent the Type of abstract eternal verities which are somehow supposed to indicate the press and change of American life. Chapter 10 continues to ask what results when female images are given wings and placed as guardians of the American home, cemetery plots, or courthouse corridors.

Chapters 11, 12, and 13 heighten the stakes still further; they trace the chronology of the changing functions of the female form in American national life wherein images of women represent the patriotic values that moved after 1893 toward aggressively imperialistic statements of moral mission and military might. Chapter 14 deals with the direct selling of female images and the merchandising of consumer products by means of those images; the American marketplace is the locus for the intensified examples of desire shown there. Chapter 15 goes onstage and examines the amateur and professional enthusiasm for the tableau, the spectacle, the "dramatical" pose—methods by which audiences sought the satisfaction of their desires through yet another series of female images. The Epilogue, titled "Looking Back," is about doing just that in more ways than one: what readers do in thinking back over the examples provided by this book about women constantly being looked at; what those women might do for themselves to remedy the impact of all those glances.

A few clarifications concerning my intentions, my methods, my scope.

    1. At times, when discussing the prevalence and significance of type, my argu-

ment may not seem to hew entirely to either women or American culture. This is inevitable, since the idea of type is too old and too broad to be held down entirely to a specific period, place, or subject. But this fact in no way lessens the importance of the connections I shall make between "type," "America," and "women." Yes, I argue the idea of type by using female forms for illustrative purposes. I just as actively discuss the condition of women in the United States that resulted from the ways in which they were perceived and conceptualized. In the end it is the types that are used illustratively so I may meet the charge I take as my primary concern: the clarification of what it must have been like to be a woman looked at *just like that*—viewed as one type or another because of the conventions in image-making then in command.

2. Some of the pictorializations introduced over the course of this book could have been encountered in other climes. England and the Continent had their own cultures that incorporated conventions for imaging women. Indeed, I continually remark about the cosmopolitan nature of American borrowings from abroad: Art Nouveau sinuosities, Belle Epoque posters (which themselves featured Columbia, flag, and eagle mounted on American bicycles for the decoration of Paris kiosks), *The Yellow Book* style picked up by Will Bradley of Chicago, and the French salon traditions that influenced many Americans, including Thomas Eakins, who did their art training in Parisian ateliers. But it is the *Americanization* of these art forms and the shaping from them of a native "art idea" by means of the female figure that centers my discussion.

3. Expressive forms for nation and the female sex were hardly peculiar to the turn of the century. Earlier nineteenth-century American paintings and novels made use of a number of the conventions I present here, but the 1876–1918 span is its own slice of cultural history with its own givens. Certain phenomena do not belong solely to any period or society: the neoplatonizing classifying instinct, uneasiness over the loss of cultural homogeneity and unity, the dispersal of women from home and family, to name but three. But a clean knife-cut indicates what was different from the presentation of these continuing concerns after 1876, as well as after 1893 or 1900 or 1918. Not only did old ideas change, but new facts altered the circumstances that provided their idiosyncratic texture: the improved technology of the print media; the expansion of popular publications; new methods of marketing new products; the influx of new kinds of immigrants; the New Woman as a potential social dislocation; new forms of theater entertainment and public amusements; increased imperialistic zeal; industrialization and commercial enterprises which reached peaks unattainable prior to 1900; the standardization of business and product and the use of mass communication that made possible the spread of an "American" look. Not only does the Girl who figures in the pages of *Collier's Weekly* look different from the Maiden in *Godey's*, but how she was drawn, reproduced, and marketed is significantly other.

4. The matter of class differences and audiences in late-nineteenth-century America remains a problematic tangle for the would-be interpreter. Were there

two cultures? it was asked rhetorically at the time, since it was all too evident there was one for the rich and one for the poor. I go that question several better by asking what about all the other "classes" separated by region, by sex, by race, by ideology. Joanne Reitano has looked at the touchy rapport between working women and middle-class reformers in "Working Girls Unite," and Stuart and Elizabeth Ewen in *Channels of Desire* note the rapidity by which newly arrived immigrants became consumers of "the American look" in clothes and other goods for sale. Neil Harris wishes we could know what the audiences for whom the cultural signs were produced *really* thought, and Lois Banner remarks on the difficulty of gauging middle-class values because there were so many middle classes and so many values. But one wonderful fact appears, offering hope that we can carry on a profitable traffic in ideas and images. If doors were closed between segments of the population, there still were leaks in the floorboards between the cellar and the upper rooms. And if there was a trickle-down process by which fashionable trends descended the social scale, there was also a trickle-up movement by which popular looks were appropriated by the makers of "high art." We may not be able with full precision to say who influenced whom and to what extent, but there *were* mutual responses to many of the images that permeated the whole society. This, I believe, is one of the cultural facts this book's illustrations prove with some conclusiveness.

5. Finally, there is the issue of a representative image maker and image reader. Actually, there is no one exemplary figure around which this book revolves, but Henry James (and to a lesser extent Charles Dana Gibson) comes close to providing the bearings that make its wheels spin. Precisely for some of the reasons that caused Peter Conn in *The Divided Mind* to single out James in his chapter "The Triumph of Reaction" I also make much of what James had to say about types, Americans, and women. George Santayana was right on the mark when he wrote in "The Genteel Tradition in American Philosophy" about the surprising dart away from genteel inertia achieved by William James and his brother Henry. Santayana speaks of them both as having been "as tightly swaddled in the genteel tradition as any infant geniuses could be. . . . Yet they burst those bonds almost entirely. . . . Mr. Henry James has done it . . . by turning the genteel American tradition, as he turns everything else, into a subject-matter for analysis. . . . Thus he has overcome the genteel tradition in the classic way, by understanding it."

I am more sanguine than Peter Conn about the usefulness of James' inbred conventionality, for I find (as did Santayana) that there is merit in being an individual embedded deeply in a set of cultural responses once one is released to express the complexities and ambivalences of those very conventions. Almost everywhere I go throughout the course of this book, Henry James has been there before me and has *seen what has happened*. The conclusions he draws from his interpretations of those events may not please us, but they are usually breathtakingly to the point of what it means for us all to exist "conventionally." Charles Dana Gibson was almost tongue-tied when he had to deal with words, nor did he bring to his own biases the conscious awareness James did; but Gibson's articulate pen had much more to say about his era than his drawings are usually given credit for. But in the end it is Henry James who lets us see what it was like for someone—even though a male, even though from the upper middle class, even though an expatriate—to determine what women had been made to *look like* to his fellow Americans. It is this acknowledgment of James' importance *because of his conventionality* that has given him the central place in two recent studies, Virginia Fowler's *Henry James's American Girl* and Elizabeth Allen's *A Woman's Place in the Novels of Henry James*. Their books—like mine—care about the typing (sometimes dire, sometimes cruel) of women as a cultural act. What I add is my belief that there were occasions when the types, used by clever women, were conducive to self-creation rather than self-annihilation; which was something that James also made note of. There is, in addition, as you will see, a representative American female who, by being—simply, always, marvelously—herself, blesses this book with a visual point of reference from start to last.

David Potter has noted in *History and American Society* that Americans have different cultural experiences depending upon their sex; men and women may share the same countryscape but not what it signifies. Alexis de Tocqueville recognized this fact long ago when he observed the mismatch between the concepts informing democracy in the 1840s and the position held by women in the United States which locked them into notions of "superiority" together with the inequalities of their social condition. Warner Berthoff attests in *The Ferment of Realism* that the testimony of women to the essential lie of their condition became severe by the 1890s; there was no way for their fellow citizens not to hear them declare their objections. Nor to keep them out of sight. In *Women and the Alphabet* Thomas Wentworth Higginson commented that once the woman had been held in "sacred obscurity" as "The Invisible Lady" but now she was fully visible; visible and, in Ida Tarbell's view, uneasy because of her self-exposure. How the Visible Lady as the Uneasy Woman chose to show herself, and how others wished for her to look, and what were the conventions of pose and appearance that either aided or hurt her in her endeavors is the subject of this book. It is of necessity the source of the many contradictions and ambiguities it illustrates.

The allegorical drawing by Charles Winter (figure 1) was placed on the cover of *The Masses* in 1912 in order to suggest two sides of an important contemporary debate: political action (working within the system) or direct action (violent overthrow of the system). In light of its formalistic properties, Winter's figure could just as well have appeared on the covers of politically conservative journals such as *The Century* or *Harper's Monthly*. There is nothing about that hooded head that declares its social sentiments or its sex. Four years later Maurice Becker furnished an untitled illustration (figure 2) for the same journal that is clearly not genteel in its attitudes toward society. It dramatizes the theory of "direct action" which Winter's drawing chose to conceptualize. But Becker's Daumier-like cartoon has one thing in common with Winter's image (very like those of Elihu Vedder): both

1. Charles Allen Winter, "Political Action Versus Direct Action," *The Masses*, February 1912.

2. Maurice Becker [woman hurling brick], *The Masses*, December 1916.

provide a symbolic figure which effaces individuality for the sake of the force of the type which represents an idea and/or emotion for the viewer's consideration. We have one journal that holds a particular political commitment to radical action; we see two images which seem not to share the same social views; we recognize a shared aesthetic based on the functionality of the visual type. The old adage "You can't tell a book by its cover" applies here, for both images need to be "explained" through our understanding of the fuller context. Winter's drawing requires its association with *The Masses* to point up that it is not of the venue of *The Century*. Becker's drawing demands that its locale be identified lest we mistakenly conjecture that it is an instrument of attack by the foes of radicalism who use this frighteningly uncouth, lower-class, unfeminine form to expose the terrors of anarchy. But once an awareness of the "book" is brought to bear upon its "covers," much is revealed to us.

Figure 3 is a government photograph taken during World War I to show how women support the war effort by wearing appropriate work dress in the factory, but the demure pose and the discreet appearance of the young woman might well be that of a lady watering her flower boxes in peacetime. Figure 4 causes one to wonder which are the men, which the women, since all are subsumed under a panoply of Wick's Hat Bands, and John Sloan, in the years prior to the expression of political and artistic radicalism for which he is best known today, participates in "the poster craze" of the 1890s, which conflates pretty young women, the marketing of the newest brake-safe bicycle technology, and art techniques just arrived from Paris (figure 5).

Albert Habegger has argued in *Gender, Fantasy, and Realism in American Literature* that adolescent girls benefited from their reading of the popular romances that crammed the best-seller lists at the end of the nineteenth century; these formula fictions allowed them to dream possibilities for their future. Samuel Jay Keyser has suggested the impact of formulas in advertising and the need to study the strength of those formulas as answers to intense desire. J. J. Gould, Jr.'s book-poster of 1896 (figure 6) and Cecilia Beaux's "The Dreamer" of 1894 (figure 7) are but two of the quite different images by which young women of the period might test who they could become and what formulas for desire they could pursue, following through the "fantastic socialization" processes Charles Horton Cooley was soon to write about. As Alexander Black wrote in *Miss America* in 1898, popular illustrators with their many images of young American women did not reflect the nation's social life as much as they created the forms by which women shaped their own notions of themselves. Under such circumstances, in a country papered from coast to coast by pictorial images, there were constant occasions to assess the available images and to evaluate the quality of the cultural contexts by which they demonstrated their multiple meanings.

In 1915 Scribner's published another novel by Robert Grant, one of its most popular writers. In *The High Priestess* Mary Arnold—architect and designer of monumental sculptured figures—appraises the insidious meaning of the older images on view to the young women of her generation. She passes through a museum stock-

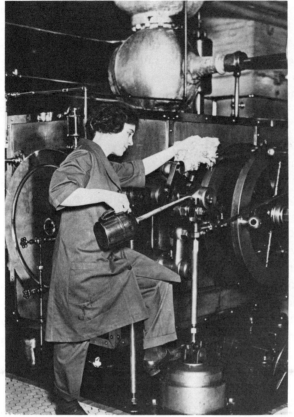

3. "Oiling," Colt Patent Firearms Co., Hartford, Conn.
(1918).

4(*left*). "The Wick Fancy Hat
Bands" (1916).

5(*above*). John Sloan, "Apollo
Bicycles" (1898).

piled with copies of figures such as Canova's "Theseus and the Centaur" (Mino-
taur?) and Cellini's "Perseus and Medusa."

Mary smiled sadly. There under her very eyes was the eloquent object-lesson she was looking for. The entire display she was facing symbolized first of all the glorification of force.
. . . Beginning with mythology and continuing to modern times, exemplars of masculine
might immortalized by plastic genius frowned down proudly on her from their pedestals

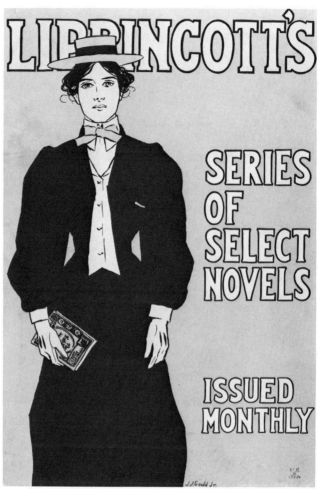

6. J. J. Gould, Jr., poster for
"Lippincott's Series of Select
Novels" (1896).

LIBRARY OF CONGRESS

from every angle of the spacious gallery—Hercules or satyr, Samson or gladiator, Viking or knight of the mailed fist—they were all essentially alike. And what was woman's role among them?—for she freely figured there. That of the suppliant, the rescued, the insipidly modest, the tantalizing, the amorously seductive. Weak, beautiful, and frail—there was man's measure of her in undying marble and bronze for the art student of her own sex to contemplate and copy. Oh, the indignity and humiliation of the libel when spell-bound no longer by the marvels of technique one read its true import!

As one of the New Women, Mary Arnold attempts to do something about this outrageous image-situation. Responsible for the design of one of the many new state capitol buildings rising across the nation, Mary oversees the installation of "a colossal allegorical feminine figure."

She had sought to impart to the features of the allegorical figure, half goddess, half human, a blending of loveliness, initiative, and spirited dignity which should symbolize the woman

7. Cecilia Beaux, "The Dreamer"
(c. 1894).

BUTLER INSTITUTE OF ART

of the future—man's partner on equal terms and also his imaginative, fearless rival. She had aimed to portray her as infinitely tender and deep in her affections, yet consistently self-respecting; no longer a mere slave or echo, yet profoundly sensible to the intensity of sex. . . . The ideal must be human of course in order to be convincing. . . . The truth of such a conception was essential to the betterment of the world. If women were to remain as they had been, civilization could never hope to advance.

Imaging American Women contains the stories, as it were, of many Mary Arnolds (written about by women or by men like Robert Grant who still hope that the new images will "discredit by efficient reasonableness the demon force"); of those who seek new icons to replace false old idols. It also contains images of the kind Mary Arnold never dreamed about. It provides a history of the idea of the type and the ideals represented by the types by whose means women and men tried to think their way into the newness of the cultural conditions provided by a nation en route from one century to the next.

Acknowledgments

After my last book I received a deal of joshing from friends about the statement I made on the (very brief) Acknowledgments page that I had none of the traditional thank-yous to make, since I had done the work almost entirely on my own. This book is quite another story. Deeply grounded in on-location research, it is a different kind of book written under markedly different circumstances. This fact allows me the pleasure of thanking the many who helped me along the way.

First the institutions, since they are the ones with the money that make it possible for private individuals to transform ideas into publishable form. It all began in 1979 with the National Endowment for the Humanities grant for directing a Summer Seminar for College Teachers, conducted at the University of Washington. It was at that time, encouraged by the alert responses of the excellent people who participated in the seminar, that I first tested the thesis which soon resulted in the project-proposal that won me an NEH Senior Fellowship for 1981–1982. That year spent mid the research riches of the museums, archives, and libraries of Washington, D.C., moved me well along with my work. Immediately after came the Senior Fellowship awarded by the Guggenheim Memorial Foundation; its largesse enabled me to start at once to write up my ideas while my notecards and I were still at white-heat. The academic year 1982–83 was spent in Bloomington, Indiana, where I became the unofficial protegée of the Department of English of Indiana University and an official Senior Fellow of the Institute for Advanced Studies. My reentry into the regular life of teaching took place in 1983 at the University of California, Los Angeles; various campus agencies at once took my project to their bosom. Thanks to the UCLA Academic Senate Research Grant I continued to receive financial support of the sort needed to bring my manuscript to its completion. If it costs money to do research and to get a book written, it also costs to produce it. I am grateful to the UCLA College Institute, College of Letters and Science for aid in subsidizing the many illustrations included in my book.

Next there were the individuals who assisted me in various ways. Some of these contributions were obviously major in scope; others might be considered inconsequential by those who are not fully aware of what projects such as this one involve, but *I* know the importance of every gesture made on my behalf, whether it was a question raised at lunch along Chapel Street in New Haven by Richard Brodhead, the stream of pertinent photocopied material supplied by Werner Sollors, the meticulous attention paid to the preparation of the illustrations in the photo duplication laboratories of the Library of Congress, Indiana University, Ohio State University, and UCLA (with the names of Anne Wallmark, Teresa Webb and her crew, and Dorothy Johnson warranting particular thanks), or the dogs-body work done in preparing the book's apparatus that was loyally, efficiently provided by Linda Lohn, one of my UCLA graduate students. The staffs of the Prints and Photographs Division of the Library of Congress and of the research libraries of the National Museum of American Art, the National Gallery of Art, and the Freer Art Gallery were especially helpful. David Warrington of the Lilly Library and Anthony Shipps of the Main Library, both of Indiana University, and Susan Frisch Lehrer of Chesterwood, seat of the Daniel Chester French Archives of the National Trust for Historic Preservation also merit special mention.

I wish to single out those who arranged to bring me onto their campus in order that I might present papers taken from various corners of my research; they gave me the invaluable chance to test my ideas in the early stages of their development. Thanks then to Emory Elliott, Lee Mitchell, Frank Bergon, Sacvan Bercovitch, Robert Scholnick, James Kilroy, George Majeska, Marjorie Perloff, Asher Milbauer, Liz Ciner, and Jerome McGann. I also benefited from being asked to participate in the 1984 WWHA conference held at the Huntington Library, the 1985 American Studies Association Convention, and at several of the functions sponsored by the lively intellectual communities of UCLA. Portions of chapters 3 and 5 of the book appeared in an essay titled "Artists, Models, Real Things, and Recognizable Types," published in *Studies in the Literary Imagination* for Fall 1983.

There were those who were good enough to read early sections from separate chapters, handing along comments I took and pondered in my heart: Daniel Aaron, John Eakin, Terence Martin, and Lee Mitchell. I also wish to thank Thomas Tanselle and R. W. B. Lewis for their continued interest in my project which prompted them to ask after it whenever we met as though it were a growing child about whose well-being they were genuinely solicitous.

Books do not emerge solely out of intellectual give and take. The brutal mechanics of such an elaborate project required the kind of unstinting support I received from Jeanette Gilkison and Nora Elias of the UCLA Department of English. I handed in reams of written matter; they fed them into the word-processor and extracted them in final form, thereby enabling me to meet an unholy deadline under the most unpromising conditions. Waiting at the other end was William P. Germano, then of Columbia University Press, whose faith in my book has been astonishing and whose firm editorial backing has persuaded me that there *are* still candles alight in the naughty, overly commercialized world of publishing. Joan McQuary and Ken Venezio of the CUP staff also helped see the project through its final stages with efficiency and good cheer.

Finally, as at any fine restaurant, there are those who strike the grateful patron as deserving of the biggest tips of all: the friends who read my manuscript in its entirety and *were* my friends precisely because they never once let up applying critical pressure to every turn and twist of my argument. There is Nina Baym, whose reader's conscience refused to let me relax for a moment, Elizabeth Dipple, connoisseur of the philosophers and of Henry James, who continually shook me back into confidence over the worth of my undertaking, and Steven Fink, who often seemed to know the shape of my thesis better than I did, was exceptionally good on the interpretation of pictorial material, great on picking out male fantasies, and top-drawer in everything else he brought to bear as a reader.

Someday it would be fun if someone would extend the scope of the literary genre of the Acknowledgments section to include the names of everyone who proved an obstacle to one's project. I have a private short-list of such human roadblocks sealed away in my memory, but what is heartening is the fact that there were so many more people who helped than those who hindered. If I have left out specific mention of any of those who aided me in any way, I am sorry. For I am grateful to you all.

"If I cannot have you in my thought at all, but only a picture produced by you, I am in respect to you like A confined to the pictures produced from B's room."

Josiah Royce, "The Possibility of Error"

". . . . *a man has as many social selves as there are individuals who recognize him* and carry an image of him in their minds."

William James, *The Principles of Psychology*

   "I am I not any longer when I see.
   "This sentence is at the bottom of all creative activity. It is just the exact opposite of I am I because my little dog knows me."

Gertrude Stein, "Henry James"

IMAGING AMERICAN WOMEN

Introduction: Object, Image, Type, and the Conduct of Life

The following four sets of pictorial renderings of the American female bracket 1876 and 1918. They suggest the kinds of intricate continuities and changes which inform this study of cultural attitudes. They indicate a few of the types which stimulated American imagination during the decades lying on either side of the new century.

Columbia, imaged for the Centennial Exposition of 1876, then reworked by Edwin Howland Blashfield for the 1918 war effort (figures 1 and 2). *The American Girl*, pictured by Harry McVickar for the 1892 edition of Henry James' story "Daisy Miller," and placed center stage in the *Ziegfeld Follies of 1917* (figures 3 and 4). *The Heiress of All the Ages* as Consuelo Vanderbilt the child and as the suffragist in 1914, her constricted life as the duchess of Marlborough now behind her (figures 5 and 6).[1] *The New Woman*, represented by a sketch of two sisters by Whistler in 1884 and by a photograph as a member of "The Woman Service" in 1918 (figures 7 and 8).

Columbia as stabilizing power and aggressive action; the American Girl with charm that is innocent and knowing; the Heiress of All the Ages whose wealth restricts her choice of destiny and whose will empowers her to assume new roles; the New Woman who sits to think or dream and who stands to serve: these diverse pictorial forms represent ideas on the move—ideas that originated in the way American women were looked at between 1876 and 1918.

And *looked-at women* they were, by observers from abroad and by about every-

1. *Frank Leslie's Illustrated Historical Register* of the *Centennial Exposition* (1878)

one at home, many of whom pointed out the extraordinarily pictorial nature of American girls. Technological advances in the printing industry, the surge of new magazines and newspapers, and the growth of promotion techniques used in advertisements, posters, and department store displays, in conjunction with events in the political and art scene, led to a concentration on images that were quick and easy to read. As it worked out, it was inevitable that the American Girl was singled out as the visual and literary form to represent the values of the nation and codify the fears and desires of its citizens.

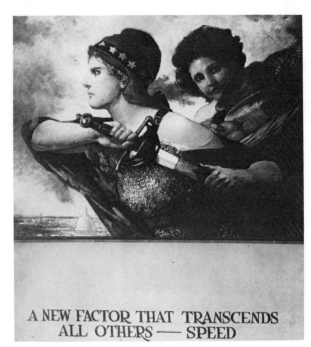

2. Edwin Howland Blashfield, "A New Factor that Transcends All Others—Speed" (c.1918).

NATIONAL ARCHIVES

3. Harry W. McVickar, frontispiece for James' *Daisy Miller* (1892).

LILLY LIBRARY

4. Raphael Kirchner, "Chu-Chin-Chow," *Ziegfeld Follies of 1917*.

ISABELLA STEWART GARDNER MUSEUM

LIBRARY OF CONGRESS

5. Consuelo Vanderbilt (c.1887).

6*(below)*. Consuelo Vanderbilt
  (1914).

7*(above, right)*. James Abbott Mc-
  Neill Whistler, "Two Sisters"
  (n.d.).

LIBRARY OF CONGRESS

"Racial and Ideal Types of Beauty" appeared in the December 1904 issue of *The Cosmopolitan*.[2] Gertrude Lynch, the author of this piece, assumes as a matter of course that these types are female, while going out of her way to make clear that such images do not convey historical truths about the appearance of different races. Quite the reverse; they demonstrate the reality of artists' dreams about racial and national types. The result is "the insertion of art into history."

The art of ideal types has two notable characteristics. It is inspired by "the best," not by "the lowest or mediocre specimens," and it insists upon clear demarcations between racial and national categories.

Some nations are easily classified. The English with their "insular prejudices" are good examples of a people who provide clear, sharp visual signs; so are the Jews because of their "law of exclusion." As the consequence of its inclusiveness and cosmopolitan nature, the United States is one nation that lacks a readily recognizable type. "But if America has no racial type, it certainly has an idea," Lynch observes. By means of that idea, the American artist "is evolving a type which it is hoped will in time resolve itself into a more fixed standard than we have to-day, so that we may know what it really means when the American type is particularized."

Gertrude Lynch's little essay of 1904 is a compact résumé of the way the image as type acted to interpret national values. Developing cultures possess the capacity to inspire ideals—the designation of "the best." National ideals are conveyed to the public by artists and writers who create types for contemplation through "the insertion of art into history." History busily alters the conditions by which the ideals of progressive societies like the United States form and re-form into a series of accepted national types. It is up to the image makers to keep their ideas abreast of the changes, lest the images their imaginations create find no audiences to share in the recognition of their meaning.

The Cosmopolitan piece is written with confidence. The task of evolving images that satisfy artist and public is difficult, but the artist will succeed. Well after the fact of 1904, we may not feel such assurance. Where Gertrude Lynch made statements, we ask questions. How well did the image makers at the turn of the century succeed in making and matching art to history? And if they succeeded as artists by imposing ideas of the type, did they fail humanity? Official images have a way of entrapping individuals, although there is always the outside chance they can be used to express free and unauthorized moments. Which proved to be the case in the American culture of the time?

General questions elicit particular ones. What did the term "type" mean circa 1900? Was it possible at the tail end of the nineteenth century for type to assume the status of the Neoplatonic universals which, in earlier centuries, had commanded great philosophical and emotional force? How could type be used with a straight face and a clear conscience in a secular culture—by writers of literary realism like Henry James, Edith Wharton, and Theodore Dreiser; by experimentalists of the modern persuasion like Stephen Crane and Gertrude Stein; by a diversity of artists (painters, commercial illustrators, photographers) who normally would not give one another the time of day; and by thinkers like Charles Sanders Peirce, Josiah Royce, William James, and John Dewey, who were in the process of defining new modes of philosophy and psychology appropriate for an America that was rushing into the twentieth century?

Questions of this sort push us toward the ontological nature of "real things" and

8. "The Woman Service of the
Nation to the Man Service"
(1918).

the epistemological processes by which one arrives at knowledge. In turn, a study of late-nineteenth-century ontology and epistemology plunges us into the center of the anxiety that underlay the culture. It was anxiety over how to determine the identity of things in a society where there were no commonly accepted patterns to guarantee confident recognition. For could knowing what was real be accomplished in a country where many were announcing their belief that cultural homogeneity had been lost? Once, they told themselves, Americans possessed clear-cut categories for everything under the sun, including sex, race, class, religion, and ethnic derivation. We know better than this. Such matters had been a muddle in America from the start, but people who spoke for late-nineteenth-century values insisted that there had until recently been a clarity to the national scene which was now blurred.

By 1900 questions of identity had become a social obsession, a fact which helps us appreciate the emphasis placed on appearances during the 1890s and the early 1900s. Attention to external physical traits led to a renewed interest in the age-old pseudoscience of physiognomy. Classification of physiognomical signs encouraged yet another ancient mental habit—the use of types to represent the public values and private virtues to which society as a whole was supposed to give its allegiance. But there was something new: the favored type was one variation or other of the American female.

This is the American woman as she was imaged by one of America's most loyal boosters, Howard Chandler Christy, in her guise as the Charmer, an apt image for the nation which envisioned the type as "a veritable queen of the kingliest of races" (figure 9).[3] But here is the American woman as the Western Girl, and here she is as the suffragist putting the hapless male in his place (figures 10 and 11). How are we to make sense of such a mix of seemingly contradictory types? What sort of evolutionary destiny did Americans believe in that accommodated both Christy's sophisticated Debutante and his elemental Western Girl?

The same mix is apparent when we look at photographs—examples of that medium of visual representation with a reputation for social documentation that supposedly hits closer to the mark than paintings and illustrations tainted by make-believe.

This is my mother at the awkward age of twelve (figure 12). The year is 1904. That twelve-year-old is the raw material of the American girl-child born and raised in the terms of small town, middle-class Indiana, but by what cultural fiat does she grow up to possess the silhouette (figure 13) which—when fleshed out by the camera—yields both the type of the Princess (figure 14) and the Pal (figure 15), two images on their way toward incorporation within the primary type of the American Girl?

We are already caught up in a paradox of sorts. The images provided by illustrators and a down-home photographer indicated the varied images whereby a young American woman might express the complexity of her individuality. But these images also underscore the conventionality of their nature. They are images that fall into classifiable categories and clearly assigned types. Where do individuality and actuality take their stand, once convention, category, and type take over? Indeed, what happens to history, change, and reality once they slide over into the realm of timelessness, stasis, and ideality where types are said to exist?

There is little composure these days over the publicity given the American Girl, and slight pleasure taken in the fact of the prevalence of her image. The negative response expressed by both scholars and laity who scan the arts and literature of 1900 is usually prompted by the word "type" or its even more sinister form "stereotype." They would not like, for example, the story appearing in the *New York*

9. Howard Chandler
Christy, "The American
Girl," from *Liberty Belles*
(1912).

Journal of June 7, 1896. The headline coyly states, "Who shall say whether a woman is beautiful or not?" then coyly concludes, "Each person may set up a standard, and decide as individual judgment dictates." The modicum of license allowed for private tastes is paid for heavily by the assumption that general rules of "standard"

10. Howard Chandler Christy,
    "The Western Girl," from
    Liberty Belles (1912).

11 *(above)*. Harry W. Mc-
    Vickar, from *The Evolution
    of Woman* (1896).

and "judgment" prevail and that a woman's value is determined by whether she fits one type of beauty or another.

When faced by novels or paintings of the 1890s students, critics, and women with updated awareness react angrily. "Why must the females always be shown as young, pretty, and marriageable?" they ask, then answer by rejecting most turn-of-the-century female images out of hand. Objections of this kind deserve to be taken seriously. They oblige us to inquire not only which conventions were dominant but also why those particular conventions possessed the force they did. Once we establish the extraordinary pervasiveness of the general type, we will be ready to treat the fact that, more often than not, the types that stood for national values were female in form. We shall also be in the position to determine some of the causes of this turn-of-the-century phenomenon and to gauge the effects the American Girl had upon the private and public imagination. But only when the right

12. Irma Purman (1904).

13. Irma Purman (1914).

questions are asked, and when righteous anger is kept to the minimum, can we approach sound answers concerning the prevalence of cultural "typing" that systematically transformed the American female into a set of powerful iconographic signs.

The Ur-text for an examination of "real things," "knowing," "identity," and "type" is the scene from chapter 19 of Henry James' novel *The Portrait of a Lady*.[4] Isabel Archer and Madame Merle confront one another over the nature of the individual self. "Am I what I wear?" is the gist of what Isabel asks in scorn. "Am I what I appear to society? Am I to be made society's 'type,' or am I my own unique self?" Madame Merle retorts, as it were, "Are you, my dear child, intending to go forth naked into the world?"

Consider the photograph taken about 1907 by Clarence White in collaboration

14. Irma Purman (1909).

15. Irma Purman and friends
(c.1912).

16. Clarence H. White with
Alfred Stieglitz [Miss
Thompson] (c.1907)

METROPOLITAN MUSEUM OF ART, NEW YORK

with Alfred Stieglitz as the Ur-image that accompanies the Ur-text by James (figure 16). Guided by the terms of the argument between Isabel Archer and Madame
Merle, ask what kind of readings we ought to give this image of a young American
at her most essential. Is this soft-porn material by chauvinistic male photographers
who exploit the naked female even though they mask their act as genteel "art

photography"? Is this a mood piece that takes all too seriously its art historical antecedents, incorporating elements ranging from Hiram Power's famous neoclassical statue of 1845 "The Greek Slave" to the peacock-feather-and-vase props currently all the rage in studios devoted to the Pre-Raphaelite and the Japonaise? Is Miss Thompson sister-in-the-skin to the woman depicted in a strikingly similar pose painted that same year by Thomas Eakins for his "William Rush and His Model"? Or is this photograph no accurate visual record of any particular young woman, but rather a Platonic abstraction, an allegory of the pagan Queen of Heaven, what with the sign of the peacock, Juno's special emblem?

Isabel Archer confronts Madame Merle with her theory of self-definition (one soon to be tested on the field of a world given over to "things"): "Nothing that belongs to me is any measure of me; everything's on the contrary a limit, a barrier, and a perfectly arbitrary one." Even as we applaud Isabel for her fine courage in detaching herself from the steel-corseted world of convention represented by Serena Merle, we need to pause to consider whether persons of independent mind ever escape convention altogether. Certainly the world of the studio is no such sanctuary. Even without clothes, Miss Thompson's every look and gesture is set by the combined efforts of Clarence White, Alfred Stieglitz, and, yes, the model herself. But once alone in their own rooms, are Miss Thompson or Isabel Archer free from what serves "out there" as "a limit, a barrier, and a perfectly arbitrary one"? Are women in particular ever entirely "without clothes"? Can they by a mere act of will strip down to deeply personal meanings known only to themselves—down to the bottom-natures studied alike by Henry James, William James, and Gertrude Stein?

Imaging American Women pays attention to bottom-nature, no question about that; but even so, that precious essential self Isabel Archer zealously guards has to take the demands of convention as its context. In the examples that follow, sometimes bottom-nature will seem swamped by limits and barriers; sometimes it will find in convention the best occasions for experiments and self-expression. But whatever the examples, the women imaged in this book (whether they are shown dressed or not) will most likely be "clothed" in the conventional signs of the times.

In order to edge nearer to answers appropriate to the questions raised by today's inquiring minds, and also by many Americans during the decades surrounding 1900, we need to shift our attention from the pristine but particularized image of Miss Thompson toward the pristine and abstract thought of Charles Sanders Peirce and Josiah Royce, two influential American philosophers of the late nineteenth century. We consult them as they expound, often with brilliance, upon the nature of "signs," "identification," and "types."

Charles Sanders Peirce is credited for having fathered semiotics and pragmatism.[5] As early as 1868 Peirce began to develop his position on the triadic process which dictates the relation between *object* (the thing, the signifier, that arouses interest), *representation* (the sign that stands for the object's signified meaning), and *interpretant* (the person who appraises the arousing sign). According to Peirce, this relation not only leads to the assignment of meaning to the object, it influences the way we behave toward that object. Even more precisely, assigned meaning *is* conduct.

The stakes are high. If we respond to faulty objects in inept ways, our social behavior is marred, and behavior constitutes the only reality we have. If we could ever pay the right kind of attention to objects that are worthy because "clear," we would arrive at responsible conduct and a respectable command of the Reality that Peirce held out as the goal we all have the obligation to pursue. How we behave, therefore, in society and as individuals is crucially affected by the objects that first capture our notice and pull us into action.

Peirce was more than willing to admit that we daily encounter a seeming lack of meaning and a plethora of unreliable guides to conduct. Indeed, it is through the world's confusion that we experience "the present moment." Still, Peirce insisted that there is no call for us to ascribe unreasonableness to the universe. It is based on the Real and Reasonableness which wait to be verified "in the long run." Eventually the cosmic "cognizability" will become clear at that happy time when human thought discovers the laws that wait to be discovered and acted upon by all humankind.

Now add the anomalous presence of Josiah Royce, one of the few practicing idealists left in late-nineteenth-century America. Notwithstanding the conflict one might expect between their positions, Peirce and Royce meet at that gathering point where the Real exists as a normative field of truth. This is possible since both men share a belief in the force of "the leading ideas" (hypotheses) by which the collective body of sensitive interpretants may one day identify the world's diverse signs of identity.

How does a procedure that points toward identification and action at the philosophical level work in everyday instances? Let us take as our object *the woman* and as our concept *women*. It is appropriate to do this since "the woman" and "women" were precisely the objects and the leading ideas that aroused thought and shaped conduct in America during the decades when Peirce, Royce, and others of like mind constructed their theories.

As Peirce would have it, philosophers of the nominalist persuasion use a word such as "women" while not believing it stands for anything real. To the nominalists, the idea floats, susceptible on every hand to trivialization and dismissal. In contrast, realists such as Peirce believe that "women" is a sign that represents a particular reality. The tangible object "the woman" lurks nearby, waiting to be joined to its concept.

Peirce's support of the realist position concedes the importance of the verification of material actuality. Still, the object "the woman" does not gain status in the drive toward Reality until it is *thought about* by means of the concept "women." "The woman" *exists* as an actuality, but it is only *recognizable*, now, as an abstract concept. "The woman" and "women" (object and concept together) are potentially *knowable*, in the future, as a fact capable of the fulfillment of its Reality. Viewed alone, the concept "women" does not exist as a universal in the literal sense. Joined with its object and converted into a general "type," it is very real because of its immediate effect upon our daily conduct. The type is the means by which we pierce through to the Reality of all women. If we are female, the type shows us how we function according to the reality of "women." If we are male, it indicates how we are shaped by our behavior toward "the woman."

Premises such as these, which so handily throw around terms like "concept," "type," and "Reality," admittedly grate upon the nerves of common everyday realists whose utilitarian tastes are foreign to philosophical realists with their liking for ideas. Such notions also antagonize feminists who angrily reject the hypotheses beloved of philosophers and scientists (males, every last one) that appear to eradicate the clutter of the personal experience of being female. Misunderstandings also arise within the community of philosophers whenever they think they have caught Peirce in the act of holding either of two unacceptable intellectual positions: belief in an unreal system of absolute truths, or belief in the equally surreal scheme of radical skepticism. It is difficult for lay realists, for feminists, and for Peirce's philosophical adversaries to make out the value of Peirce's argument that signs, images, and types speak to truths that lie fully *within* the scope of human experience. But they do. Rightly used, the type presses us closer to the world of everyday action; it need not act negatively to place us at a remove.

An example is a three-part illustration that appeared in the New York *Daily Graphic* of February 16, 1880 (figure 17). The first panel depicts a wife as she "actually" looks to the world (an ordinary face). The second sketch represents her as she normally appears to her loving husband (a pretty face). The third shows how she looks to him when he has drunk too much at his club (a grotesque hag). In each of these three states of iconic representation, the woman's sign is being actively interpreted. Meaning is assigned according to the impact of the particular *image* by which she is perceived and to the *idea* conceived about her. It is easy enough to say that the face *conceived of* by means of the emotions of love, or the face *perceived* through the mists of whisky, cannot guarantee what this woman is really like. Does the first sketch, thereby, come the closest to being correct? After all, it is the image that is generally accepted as true by the consensus of the woman's neighbors and the shopkeepers with whom she does daily trade.

Peirce would agree that the first of the three drawings might well refer to the actual woman. But this would be the case only if two essential elements are at work: that those who interpret this sign respond to an external reality existing independently of their minds, and that their conduct toward the woman reflects her core-truth as far as outsiders can experience it on the spot. True viewers of this woman must not merely *see* (that is, *perceive*) her physical image. They must *inquire* (that is, *think*) to know who she is. Most important of all, they must *interpret* (that is, *act upon*) that thought.

Consider the extraordinary difficulties thrown daily into the path of the processes that take anyone, whatever the period and the place, through mazes of

THE DAILY GRAPHIC: NEW YORK, MONDAY, FEBRUARY 16, 1880—TWELVE PAGES.

NATURE, LOVE AND BILIOUSNESS.

MRS. FRANK JOLIBOIS, AS SHE APPEARS, MORE OR LESS, IN HER PHOTOGRAPHS AND TO THE WORLD IN GENERAL; AND A VERY CHARMING PERSON SHE IS WHEN ONCE YOU KNOW HER!

MRS. FRANK JOLIBOIS, AS SHE STILL APPEARS TO THAT BEST OF FELLOWS, HER HUSBAND, WHEN IN HIS NORMAL CONDITION; AND LONG MAY SHE CONTINUE TO DO SO!

MRS. FRANK JOLIBOIS, AS SHE APPEARS TO THE SAME, WHEN HE HAS BEEN SUPPING OVER-NIGHT AT THE CLUB, WITH A LOT OF OTHER JOLLY BOYS, AS HE SOMETIMES WILL!

Moral.—DON'T SUP AT THE CLUB. IN POINT OF FACT, DON'T SUP AT ALL.

17. "Nature, Love, and Biliousness," *Daily Graphic*, February 16, 1880.

perception and cognition—blundering past object, idea, and sign. How can casual observers of the world's many images ever know what the signs they encounter mean? How to know?—especially in those societies and at those times when the need for detecting "real things" becomes crucial if one is to survive with any grace. That our own period of history is such a time goes without saying. As for the years at the turn of the century, Neil Harris has written, "Never before had Americans confronted differences so directly, not temporary, peripheral differences, but permanent, pervasive distinctions."[6]

Harris lists the many kinds of guides Americans clung to in their effort to interpret the baffling flurry of signs that confronted them on every street corner. But most of those guides were unreliable. They were governed by what Charles Sanders Peirce called "meaning by intensity" (values that begin and end with subjective responses), or they were based on "meaning by authority" (beliefs imposed by outside agents). They were, all too often, the guides that prompted the likes of the *Life* cartoon of 1913—an arresting variation on the *Daily Graphic* sketches of 1880 (figure 18).

Notwithstanding the inadequacy of the interpretive aids available in the late nineteenth century, the need to "read" correctly was shared by everyone. As a result, some strange bedfellows climbed under the same cultural covers. Reactionaries, who longed to arrange the heterogeneous American population into tidy, dogmatic batches, leagued with liberals, who willingly risked living in the midst of social pluralism. Reactionaries classified out of desperation as they tried to box off enemies from friends. Liberals classified in the hope of detecting a fundamen-

Militants

AS THEY ARE

AS THEY THINK THEY ARE

Rodney Thomson
with apologies to
Orson Lowell

AS THEY APPEAR TO THE POLICE AND SHOPKEEPERS

18. Rodney Thomson, "Militants," *Life*, March 27, 1913.

tally democratic unity in multiplicity. Divergent in their motives, both groups relied on the viewing and interpretation of objects, peoples, and events held to the lowest common denominator, *the type*. When this procedure went wrong, type was used reductively as a method for fixing masses permanently into "the desirables" and "the undesirables." Working through type went well when it followed the enlightened intentions of the theorists with flexible methods that encompassed the rich and fluid texture of the world's primal Reasonableness—based as *that* is upon change, development, and pluralism.

It may seem a dangerous move to place Josiah Royce at the center of a discussion of types that attempts an evenhanded view of those ideas which elicit major social consequences. As we know, Royce was the man of the period who adhered most closely to absolutism and monism—the philosophical position that serves to give "type" a bad name. But if we move past the essays in which Royce set out to prove that only God can know what "the Woman" is (or even "any woman") and come to the gist of the twelve Harvard lectures he delivered in 1893, titled "Topics in Psychology of Interest to Teachers," we are faced squarely with the question of the relation of type to conduct.[7] For this is the Josiah Royce who describes how we think about what we see from the earliest moments of our conscious lives, suggests why we respond as we do to the world of objects, and defines the consequences of the interpretations we heap upon those images we most desire.

Royce's intention was to explain to his audience of teachers the everyday kinds of knowing we all experience. He chose to use tigers as his main illustration. We can keep to his lead in using "tiger" as a concept, but for our purposes it helps to think "woman" as well. While doing this, contemplate the drawing by Charles Dana Gibson titled "His First Love" (figure 19). The reasons for juxtaposing Royce's theory with Gibson's depiction of a small boy in awed rapture over his mother's presence will shortly become apparent.

Royce reminds us that we are introduced to the idea of tigers through having seen the beast at a zoo or in a picture book or by calling upon memories of a poem such as William Blake's "Tiger! Tiger! burning bright." But, Royce declares, "my understanding of the word *tiger* is something more than these mere images of tiger." This "something more" is a matter of "what I should do if I met a tiger at large, say strolling about in Harvard Square."

Royce next gives a nice example of what happens if, out of our ignorance of signs, we fail to feel the terror which accompanies the sight of wild beasts (or women) whose power we recognize. Royce tells the anecdote of a war carried out by Marcus Aurelius. Lions were set loose upon the barbarian hordes in the expectation that the enemy would be frightened into submission. But the ignoramuses did not know enough about lions to fear them. They called the beasts "dogs" and sallied forth to club them to death and to win the battle against the Roman legions.[8]

In an era in which the question "Is it the lady and/or the tiger?" was constantly asked,[9] those with a taste for survival were advised to form social habits that enabled them to move efficiently from external facts to ideas and on to appropriate behavior. But everyone, unwittingly or not, supposedly follows the stages of the learning process Royce outlined in his 1893 lectures.

On the threshold of a child's early years, Royce informs us, there is some object or other the child chooses to contemplate, an object selected from the clutter that surrounds him. His choice is crucial since everything he does thereafter flows from the thing to which he gives "his first love." The original response intitiates the desire to imitate that beloved object. By such simple means, the processes commence by which the infant mind comes to grasp whatever reality the world will hold for him as an adult.

19. Charles Dana Gibson,
"His First Love,"
Life, June 3, 1897.

Perception of the object and the choice to emulate it happen first; cognitive reflection follows; last comes interpretation. As the result of these unfolding stages of consciousness and instinct, each person acquires a unique personality—one which is created by the complex interchange between the pared-down core-self and the engulfing environment. This interchange, mediated by thought, is predicated upon the almost accidental selection of the perceived image which receives its confirming sign as a conceptual type.[10]

It is precisely this initial stage of the development of the social self which Charles Dana Gibson's drawing of "His First Love" represents. Through Gibson's powerful pen-and-ink technique, the Universal Woman looms out of the primal darkness. In precisely this manner, Royce would argue, all vital objects impress themselves permanently upon the wondering mind and the developing self.

That the object shown in Gibson's drawing is a woman in the figure of the mother is of great significance when pursuing Royce's theories down the corridors of late-nineteenth-century American cultural behavior. There is ample evidence that the concept of the value of the American home most favored at the turn of the century rested on the notion that impressionable children turn to the female object as the basis for the moral conduct that will shape their future lives.[11] Homely wisdom, Gibson's drawing, and Royce's theory coalesce—the force of their meaning intensified by the female form placed at their center. And when that form is cast into bronze as the monumental "Alma Mater" by Daniel Chester French and placed dead-center at the heart of Columbia University, meaning is reinforced by further institutionalization (figure 20).

Moral issues seldom absented themselves from the theorizing of Josiah Royce and

20. Daniel Chester French,
"Alma Mater," full-size
model, plaster (1903).

Charles Sanders Peirce, or from the writings of their colleagues and disciples, William James and John Dewey. All four philosophers believed that perception and cognition are connected by causality and choice and that choices are always matters for moral validation. Upon this basic premise they based the following principles. 1) The forces that create the self are not innate; they are a consequence of our existence in society. 2) We do not, however, have a self imposed upon us; we think it into being. 3) What we think is based on the desire to be "more." In Royce's words, the child "learns to conceive himself not as he merely and literally is, but as he more ideally might be." 4) Since so much depends on the choices by which the self develops, a grievous wrong is committed if ever we fall into what Royce called "a viciously acquired naïveté." 5) Ideas about things, to cite Royce once again, "always involve consciousness of how you propose to act towards the thing of which you have an idea"; therefore, ideas are purposes that seek fulfillment.[12]

Recall that to the late-nineteenth-century mind the word "fulfillment" most likely implied evolution (defined as progress), change (defined as the betterment of life), and growth (defined as the attainment of "the highest ideas" which the private heart or public soul could aim for). Josiah Royce meant what he said when he stated, "Our ideas embody our will. And the real world is just our whole will embodied."

During the final years of the nineteenth century and the opening decades of the twentieth, Americans were often fated to receive exactly what they willed. They were formed into the social beings that resulted from their actions as interpreters of signs. It is the central argument of this book that "women" was one of the major ideas out of which Americans created, for better and for worse, the embodiment of their collective will. Particularly the idea of "women" in its various forms (visual and verbal) as the America Girl.

Late-nineteenth-century philosophers sat in their studies meditating over the importance of the mind's movement from object to assigned meaning. Across the way, in studios and classrooms, the makers of artistic forms considered what exactly it involves *to look at* objects. The views held about the nature of the artist's eye, and the applicability of those views to everyday acts of seeing experienced by just about everyone, constitute another significant element in the cultural processes by which the American woman was transformed into the image of a type that is *looked into being*.

The story of the formal training offered by American art schools and the experiences of young Americans abroad in the ateliers of Paris, Munich, Dusseldorf, and London is a familiar one. The details can be found in any number of sources.[13] Among the areas of change were the shift to life classes away from the copying of plaster casts, the increased number of women entering the academies, the use of nude models before mixed classes, the attention given to studies of anatomy, the rise of the sketch and the drawing pad taken outdoors, and the economic conditions resulting in large classes and impersonal instruction. Less well known is the concentration placed during the 1880s, 1890s, and early 1900s upon the training of the eye and the hand, exacted alike of children in the American public schools and vocational schools, of students in the academies, and of professional and commercial artists.

In 1877–78 the U.S. Centennial Commission scolded the administrative heads of elementary schools for failing to train children in the rudiments of industrial drawing. In 1886 the art critic Sylvester Rosa Koehler reminded American art students that they must first learn their trade as draughtsmen if they hoped to succeed in the representation of readily recognizable forms. Although the government reports attended solely to the position of the United States relative to international progress in industrial design and although Koehler's comments applied only to the status of serious studio art, these statements underscored the importance of early training in drawing. More to our purposes are the implications of these admonitions. Both suggest that, according to the way the individual eye is trained to perceive the shapes that fill the world, people become participants in a community of viewers sharing the "American" idea of how things look.

Sylvester Rosa Koehler's stand on the nature of American seeing will be examined in detail in chapter 4. Here, however, I will deal with the position taken by the 1878 U.S. government commission concerning the teaching of the conventions of material forms in the public schools.

In ways analogous to the flurry in the United States over the Soviet launching of the first Sputnik that prompted official mandates in the 1950s on the need to pull a laggard student population up to the mark in mathematics and the sciences, the Philadelphia Centennial Exposition of 1876 stirred alarm over the failure of the American schools to prepare students for careers in the areas of industrial design and technology. The government issued a series of chiding reports, one in 1877 devoted to the training necessary for futures in architecture and engineering, another in 1878 to the sciences and education.[14] In both reports, the emphasis was upon drawing skills taught in the primary grades. Not drawing of the kind practiced by young ladies who paint teacups or young gentlemen who wish to emulate Ruskin in the sketching of mountain streams; but *useful* skills.[15] According to the commissioners, the best early training avoids aesthetic stabs at the imitation of nature. The greatest attention is placed upon geometrical shapes.

The drawing of natural forms should follow, not precede *the drawing of conventional forms*. Such is the order of difficulty, and such, for other reasons, is the true pedagogical order. He who has first drawn geometrical and conventional forms takes larger views of nature, gives less heed to irregular surface details, and more heed to *the general form* and to *the great features* of organic growth. (My italics)

The commission's report was firmly on the side of conventional forms, those shapes the eye has responded to since the time of the ancient Greek geometricians. Through systematic training in the accurate rendering of geometrical forms, Americans would be able to compete with the students emerging from the English, French, and German schools where (especially under the German system) drawing classes adhered to rigorous exercises in the elemental forms. But more than technical skill would be acquired. As a consequence, American schoolchildren would learn a method for creating designs whose meaning would be understandable to all the people.[16] By the maintenance of "academy" standards and the suppression of the "whims" of capricious teachers, "conformity to a single rational standard" would replace "atrocious things" and "indecision and vagary." Meaning would be made accessible to everyone through visual statements founded upon "general principles, having the approval of the safest authorities and widest experience."[17]

Although philosophy and art were not the concern of the government commissions, the uniformity they promoted for the furtherance of the nation's technological progress also answered the needs of anxious American believers in ideal types. Geometry in the factory would join forces with geometry in the philosopher's study and the artist's studio, giving comfort to those who felt lost in a welter of unreadable shapes. Soul and intellect were solaced when the eye could credit universalized representations justified by the ancient truths of geometry. Outside the realm of points, lines, planes, and solids all was erratic unpredictability, whether caused by subjectivist artists who reported on the turmoil of inner feelings or naturalists who copied the accidental facts of the world.

Conformity at the national level has always had hard going in the United States, even in the area of public education. Nothing transpired after 1878 to match the government commission's admiration for the German school system. Installing rigorous training in drawing and design in the elementary grades had to be left to local efforts. Under these conditions, the availability of helpful instruction manuals became a necessity, since the average schoolmistress had none of the advantages of preparatory training that fit the U.S. commission's dream of Prussian efficiency. Into the breach stepped the Prang Educational Company.[18]

Prang had art materials to sell. What better way to persuade schools to stock up on its brand of crayons and pencils than to provide classroom guides even the most thumb-handed teacher could use when the wall clock told her to switch from spelling, arithmetic, and geography to an hour of drawing lessons? During the next quarter-century the Prang manuals supplied what were doubtless the best teachers' aids around. From the start they taught art as a matter of the mastery of geometrical forms. But even more; they inculcated habits of seeing and knowing which run as an undercurrent beneath the theories that artists and philosophers were just then espousing about the relation between object and image.

The Prang manual of 1887 introduces the remarkable notion that children ought to be taught in ways that expand the meaning of "mental" to include touch and sight. The kits of geometrical objects supplied to the teachers for use in classroom demonstration would have pleased the men who wrote the government reports of 1877 and 1878. But the Prang Company also argued that children could be stimulated to grasp abstract concepts through sensual responses to elemental forms. What is more, students were guided through stages of instruction commensurate with their dawning abilities. Through lessons carefully laid out in graded instruction books, children were encouraged to express ideas of form through the experience of making shapes. Conventions and universal standards were central to the exercises, but they were also meant to be personal in their effects.

First, the children as a group learned the mysteries of the sphere, the cube, and the cylinder. Later they drew faces—simple schematic types that expressed pleasure (upturned mouth), displeasure (mouth downturned), or emotional neutrality (mouth a horizontal stroke). But however simplistic or restrictive in its instructions,[19] and however likely that it might lead one to admire only a Poussin or a Puvis de Chavannes, the Prang method could also prepare a child to become an innovator like Frank Lloyd Wright.[20] By the late 1880s the American eye was being instructed in the particular aspects of neoclassicism that later informed modernist modes of seeing. In the next generation that eye might appreciate the experiments of the Cubists in Paris and the verbal symmetries of Gertrude Stein.

The 1904 updated Prang manuals reflect the times and the changes taking place in the way the world was looked at and evaluated. Classroom exercises continue to emphasize designs laid along flat surfaces; the grasp (both perceptual and cognitive) of the principles of geometry is hardly overlooked. But by 1904 the main burden of the printed text is upon the ways young eyes make sense of the surrounding environment by moving through the successive stages of perception, representation, and interpretation.[21]

When you have found something beautiful out of doors, you will wish to tell others about it. You could do this in several ways. You could write a description of it, you could talk about it, or you could make a picture of it. But in one picture you could not put everything you had seen from the window. That would take too long, and you would lose patience. What you could easily do, would be to choose from the whole view some part that would best tell the story, and make a picture of that.

Whereas the 1887 Prang manuals led children to believe that they lived within one great universal geometrical shape, by 1904 the assumption is that they live in diversity—in a modern world complete with trolleys, railroads, and the Kodak Brownie.

When you are riding on the cars, you never tire of looking from the window. Every minute brings a fresh picture. There are far-away hills, wide-spreading meadows, peaceful farmhouses and big red barns, rivers, bridges and towns in quick succession. The window is a frame for hundreds of new and interesting pictures as the train hurries along.

The big wide world of "far-away hills, wide-spreading meadows, peaceful farmhouses and big red barns, rivers, bridges and towns" calls for the use of instant snapshots to assure the "frames" that suggest life on the move.

You have all seen dummies in the show-windows. They have fine figures, and they stand very still. But an artist would rather have for a model, one wide awake boy or girl than all the wax or wooden figures ever made.[22]

Today, you are to make some pictures of real life children. You may call your drawings snapshots because they are to be done very quickly.

It is also a world where the attentive teacher presented the epistemological puzzler "Which is better—the 'real' or the 'apparent' "?

Appearances Deceive Us.

As you grow older you learn that many things beside the sunbeams are not what they seem. This old earth of ours seems flat, and yet we know that it is really like a huge ball. The stars seem like tiny specks of silver, but they are great worlds as large as ours. Distant hills look blue, although they may be covered with grass as green as that at our feet.

Things That You Draw.

It is the same way with things that you try to draw. They seldom appear as they really are.

At this point, teachers were supposed to guide their students in the very special relation between accepted perceptions of shape and form and the "truths" those images convey.

An artist tries to draw things as they appear to be. The lessons in this chapter will help you, not only to see, but to tell truthfully with your pencil or brush just what you see.

Prang-taught children did not draw objects as they "knew them to be," but according to *the conventions of how they appeared.*

In 1907 the American painter, art instructor, and critic Kenyon Cox lamented that art students in the academies knew a great deal about the "science" of "aspects" but lacked practical training in their craft. In Cox's opinion, each student tried "to substitute the charm of his personal sentiment and his individual view of nature for that assured rightness which comes of an accepted body of traditions and the possession of tried methods."[23]

Up to a point Cox would have been correct if he had believed that the current tendency to single out objects for individual attention was one of the results of the instruction schoolchildren received from the Prang manuals, what with all their talk about "snapshots," "selection," and closing one's eyes before cutting out what one sees. But Cox would have been wrong if he had chastised the Prang method in the same way he rebuked the Impressionists for their rampant subjectivity or the Naturalists for placing the eye in bondage to material fact. Notwithstanding Cox's apprehensions and the ring of some of the Prang instructions, the American classroom was still a bastion of universal solids and silhouette outlines. Truth lay in appearances, and appearances paralleled the child's capacity to recognize the elemental shapes that form the sensible world of experience. It was drawing what you "knew" that allowed subjectivity to run amok. Conversely, the world of appearances modeled upon cylinder, pyramid, and square was a world that offered a shared vista. It was a place clearly marked by signs the classroom community could point to and say, *I have drawn what I have seen, therefore I know it,* with the assurance that that same world was there for all to perceive, to know, and to interpret rightly.

The principles set out in the texts of the Prang Company in 1904 and the concerns raised by Kenyon Cox in 1907 are further reflected in remarks made by the art critic D. S. MacColl in his book of 1902 *Nineteenth-Century Art.*[24] MacColl was intrigued by the nature of "modern" vision. We ought to be just as interested as he was, since what he says (conflated with the implications of the Prang method and Cox's assessment of the way artists "see" their worlds into being) has a great deal to do with why women were being transformed into images and types—visible signs to which all manner of "American" values and meanings were attributed.

MacColl argues that what is considered "modern" in 1902 is an age-old mode of vision brought forward into the present by the pitch and heave of the developments affecting our perception of the world. Moderns use the term "camera vision," but it is simply an up-to-date phrase descriptive of the shortcuts to meaning once used by primitive races and, later, by simple mariners and landsmen.

With "camera vision" the eye moves around restlessly. It is not fixed in place by the rules of Renaissance perspective or by the economics of the patronage system which imposed the wishes of the consumer upon the artist. Today's pictures express an artist's "uncommissioned mood." They *let in more* because art is now free, private, "so little a thing of command, or even wide consent." But it is still Everyman's art. The world the artist looks at is very like the world perceived by the ordinary citizen who simply wants to be able to cross crowded thoroughfares without getting run down by the objects hurtling across his path. For the modern, there emerges out of "a vague of space . . . a few signs of distance, of turning places . . . a minimum of signals and recognitions." He now "sees . . . what his mind requires" for survival's sake. His eye looks at objects as farmers, hunters, and fishermen have always looked at them in making their careful way through territory that becomes familiar once it is shaped by recognizable patterns.

The modern eye moves and dances. Nothing is focused. Nothing dominates the center. Nothing is more important than the rest until the eye chooses to make it so. The world is filled with signs and potential meanings, so many the eye cannot bear to track the visual gabble or transform it into usefulness. In self-defense, the eye moves away from extremes of impressionism or naturalism. (Those are arts for the rare persons with the leisure or emotional security that frees them to deal insouciantly with worlds of multiplicity.) The average person and the modern artist try to generalize—to "see broadly" through mental abstractions—in order to focus in on what matters. The result is a workable world made up of discernible patterns that are simultaneously very personal and highly conventionalized. It is the world transformed into public knowledge by an idiosyncratic eye. It is the world Gertrude Stein found when she went up in an airplane over the flatlands of the American Midwest and discovered to her pleasure that the ground below was as familiar to her as the Cubist paintings hanging in her Paris apartment because both the land and the paintings shared the same readable, universal shapes.

The modern eye is, therefore, not an opponent of conventionalized forms. Quite the contrary. But what with the way it darts hither and yon—responding to whatever calls upon its attention before selecting its "first love" and discarding the rest—it would be folly to make unqualified claims about what exactly held the attention of the collective American eye at the turn of the century.

Audience response must be approached with the greatest tact. As long as we pay attention to the problems accruing to the Intentional Fallacy, we shall probably reach a working agreement about what the artist and writers of the late nineteenth and early twentieth centuries said they wished to effect through their use of female iconography. But it would not be very bright of us to make fast conclusions concerning the relation of the viewing public to the representations offered up for its interpretation.

21. Hamden School for Boys,
New Haven (1918).

NATIONAL ARCHIVES

It is 1918 and the young students of the Hamden School for Boys in New Haven are at their desks (figure 21). Since we cannot even swear that the boys are giving their full attention to the books they hold in their hands, how can we say for certain that their minds are ignited by patriotism at the sight of the World War I posters banking the front of the classroom? Poster buffs would give their eyeteeth for a display containing mint examples by such illustrators as Howard Chandler Christy, James Montgomery Flagg, Charles Dana Gibson, and Edward Penfield. Any flag-waving patriot at the time would react with pride to the stirring appeals made by the figures of Columbia, Liberty, and America, in the company of Uncle Sam and the brave boys of the navy, army, and marines. But those bent heads tell us nothing one way or another about what the students felt.

The intentions behind Adolph Treidler's poster for the Second Liberty Loan of 1917 and the particular audience toward which it is directed are clearly indicated (figure 22). But it is sobering to realize that not one of the immigrants pictured at the moment of entrance into New York's harbor turns a "thrilled" look upon the figure of the Liberty statue. A woman pares a piece of fruit. A couple talk. A child sits meditating upon bundles of the family's belongings. A few glance out past the ship's railing, but not up at the Statue of Liberty. It is the harbor patrol boat that catches their attention, not the national icon of worship. And since Treidler "made" this scene, we have to wonder why he let the evidence of his images belie the words of the text. The result here is ambiguity, not clarity of response.

Frances Benjamin Johnston, a highly regarded professional, took a series of pho-

22. Adolph Treidler, "Remember Your First Thrill of American Liberty" (1918).

tographs at the Tuskegee Institute in 1902. Among them is this shot of a history classroom (figure 23). Neatly dressed young blacks, male and female, sit erectly on wooden benches. Framed portraits of Washington, Lincoln, and Webster (each with small American flags stuck at the side) hang along the upper wall, small photo-reproductions of the Apollo Belvedere and the Laocoön rim the wall-moldings, and a crude sign for Captain John Smith is chalked on the blackboard. We have every right to speculate what those particular images of national patriotism and classical culture might have meant to the Tuskegee students. Then there is the lesson written across one of the blackboards.

The Indians of Virginia. Capt. Smith goes in search of the Pacific; he is captured by Indians. Smith's life is saved by Pocahontas; her marriage to *Jno* Rolfe.

What the students of Tuskegee Institute were thinking as they sat for Johnston's photograph is not something a social historian would wish to claim out of hand.

23. Frances Benjamin Johnston
[students in a history class
at Tuskegee Institute]
(1902).

24. Frances Benjamin Johnston
[studio] (1895).

Fruitful speculation is limited to the essential fact that young blacks in 1902 at this institution were being taught history as a mix of myth and fact while seated in a room decorated by images of white American statesmen and classical Greek marbles.

The next photograph offers the kind of visual evidence we have the right to make certain conclusions about (figure 24). Although we may never know exactly what people think when they are set down by authorities in the midst of an environment of images (the classrooms of New Haven or Tuskegee, the ship sailing into New York harbor), it is different when the images that help define the place are of the person's own choosing. Here is Frances Benjamin Johnston in her Washington, D.C., studio. The walls are papered by some of the finest examples of what is now known as the Golden Age of the Poster—the American 1890s. Will Bradley, Charles Dana Gibson, Louis Rhead, Ethel Reed, Will Carqueville—most of the poster greats are on view, promoting the newest magazines and newspaper supplements and touting Packer's Tar Soap. Biographical data tells us that Johnston had an eye for the sophisticated design elements of the poster, and this photograph of her private collection confirms this.[25] It also provides us the sight of one woman's private art gallery which reproduces the same array of female images that filled the shop windows of the 1890s.

Figure 25 takes us inside another woman's private sanctuary. It is 1918 and these are the quarters of a telephone operator stationed at Camp Kearney. We know little about this nameless young woman—her motives for helping the war effort, her past or future. We cannot know whether the navy pennant and the U.S. flag at the window express general feelings of patriotism or whether they are associated in her mind with certain young men in the service. We only have the physical evidence of what she brought into this room to go by. Even there, the exact reasons for what she chose are not altogether clear. Still, the jar of cleansing cream and the bottle of scent on the bureau lined up on the linen runner, together with the two framed photographs, the narrow white bed, the fresh curtains at the window, and the clown-doll propped upon the molding, suggest that she tried to convert the small barrack-room into something to her own liking.

Among the most interesting items in the room are the magazine cutouts rimming the ceiling (one image of a handsome young man in profile, others of pretty, well-coiffed, chic young women) and the "owner" of this environment. The young woman holds a hand mirror; she is also reflected by the mirror above the bureau—doubling the images the photographer includes. Whoever she is, and for whatever reasons she is at Camp Kearney, and to what purpose the government ordered this photograph taken, we come away from the photograph remarking that this young woman of 1918 is a connoisseur of female images and that she has taken care to present an attractive composite image when she knows herself to be looked at. (All this without even taking into account the implied presence of the person who holds the camera.) How she acts to interpret herself by means of the objects with

25. Telephone operator's room, Camp Kearney, Calif. (1918).

which she adorns this space—half impersonal army barracks, half private bou-
doir—serves as a paradigm for our own tasks of interpretation that lie ahead.

Many "histories" affected the images undergoing formation in the United States at
the turn of the century. Many "histories" were created in turn by the nature of
those images. One could pursue to real advantage any of the following historical
accounts between the years 1876 and 1918. The history of the *careers* of individual
writers and artists—such as Henry James, Gertrude Stein, Charles Dana Gibson, or
Abbott Handerson Thayer—whose lives were given over to image-making. The history of the *genres* by which the images of women were presented to the public:
statues of marble succeeded by statues of bronze; the mural arts and the billboard
poster; figure-painting and portraits; the studio photograph and the amateur's
snapshot; the decorative arts handed over to women artists; and the dead-ends and
open doors women professionals experienced through being associated with the
design of household products. The history of *new inventions and public fads* that
had noticeable effects upon the making of images: the technology of mass printing;
the Delsarte method of "attitudes" and tableaux; the reemergence of interest in
physiognomy; the stage spectacle; the increasing interest in the androgyny of cross-
dressing. The history of *ideas*: Charles Sanders Peirce and William James on "the
Self"; the nature of female consciousness; theories of determinism that influenced
the choice of roles the individual assumed in society. The history of *historical
events* and the history of *social developments* of the kind that students of economics, feminism, politics, demography, sociology, urbanization, labor history, and
race relations care most about. But this book takes as its special concern the history of iconographic forms.

One of the main conclusions gained from such a study is this: the images by
which ideas about the American female were being offered to the public between
1876 and 1918 were not only varied to the point of potential self-contradiction,
they were all-pervasive. In recognition of this fact, the Introduction closes with
five sets of "parallel cases." Each set consists of drawings, photographs, paintings,
or posters which suggest that each type of American female form had a number of
rich histories to draw upon—a history of conventions that dictate the nature of
the pose, while not entirely controlling it; a history of the manifold interpretations
prompted by any one pose; a history which contains five times over the figure of a
particular young woman from Indiana who functions as the "constant" this cultural experiment requires.

IDEAL HEADS (figures 26–28): "Models of Natural Expression" (1893); "The Atlanta Exposition" (1895); Irma Purman (1905).

KNEELING ANGELS (figures 29–31): monument design by Cardoni and Morton
(1883); illustration by Charles Dana Gibson for Chambers, *The Common Law* (1911);
Irma Purman and friends (c.1910).

WOMEN IN TROUSERS (figures 32–34): from *The Evolution of Woman* by Harry

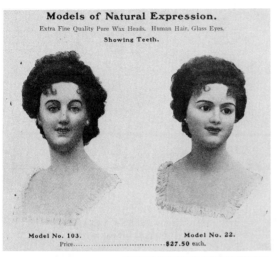

26. "Models of Natural Expression," from J. R. Palmenberg's Sons (1893).

27. H. Wright, "Special Atlanta Exposition Number," poster for the *New York Sunday Herald*, October 20, 1895.

28 *(above, right)*. Irma Purman (1905).

29. From *A Collection of 152 Original Monumental Designs, Compiled by Messrs. Cardoni and Morton* (1883).

30. Charles Dana Gibson, "In Silence," from Chambers, *The Common Law* (1911).

31. Irma Purman and friends
    (c.1910).

32. Harry W. McVickar, from *The Evolution
    of Woman* (1896).

McVickar (1896); "Mme. Bernard Trouser-Dress" (1914); Irma Purman and friends (c.1912).

CONSUMERS ON DISPLAY (figures 35–37): 'Yale Coffee" (1904); "Superior Drill Machinery" (1906); Irma Purman and friends (c.1913).

THE NEW WOMEN (figures 38–40): "Rose O'Neill Smoking" by Gertrude Käsebier (1900); "Lillian Wald" of the Public Health Service by William Schevill (1919); Irma Purman and friends (c.1913).

What agile, imaginative persons young American women had to be to keep up

33. Mme. Bernard Trouser
    Dress (1914).

34. Irma Purman and friends
    (c.1912).

35. "Have a Cup of Yale Coffee
with Me" (1904).

with the images that lay waiting in the various public imaginations, ready to be impressed into service. It was to be hoped they would not be overwhelmed by the meanings attached to the types as a result of the needs emerging from many corners of the culture. It would take luck and stamina, surely, for women to choose to be objects representative of the desires of others that were also commensurate with the significance they tried to create for themselves.

36. "Helpmeet," Superior Drill
Machinery (1906).

37. Irma Purman and friends
(c.1913).

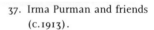

38. Gertrude Käsebier, "Rose O'Neill Smoking" (c.1900).

39. William Schevill, "Lillian Wald" (1919).

40. Irma Purman and friends (c.1913).

Part One

CONTEXTS

IMAGES OF IDENTITY

I

American Girls and the New Woman

The Prang Educational Company, manufacturers of crayons, drawing pencils, papers, and teaching manuals, probably had as much influence in the art training of American children as the McGuffey Readers had in other areas of their education. A study of the manuals Prang brought out over the years is a case in point; it reveals a clearly thought-out pattern of instruction to eye, hand, and mind.[1] Children were introduced to geometric shapes. (This would have gladdened the hearts of Peirce and Royce, since they knew that the cosmos itself is definable as "logic" and as "reasonableness" because predicated on just such pure shapes.) Next, they were assigned the drawing of stick figures that emphasized the Human Form Divine stripped down to the Platonic essentials of movement (figure 1.1). By now the little students were ready to be instructed on how to represent themselves and to identify others.

Fourth graders were presented with significant ontological and epistemological issues. Boys and girls are ostensibly quite different in kind; but perhaps they are not (figure 1.2). This depends on how one thinks of them, as the comments in the Prang manual point out.[2] What matters in drawing class, however, is the way gender identities rely on visible "attributes"—those manifest tokens by which, for instance, one saint is distinguished from another: Saint Catherine with her wheel, Saint Lawrence with his grille. Schematically, the physical shapes of boys and girls are the same, but the boy is "known" by the schoolbag he carries and the trousers he wears, and the girl by her jump rope and her dress.

The child depicted in the 1904 Prang fourth-grade manual as "Type Girl" would grow up to look like one adult female type or another, just as my mother (figure 1.3), herself a fourth grader in 1902, soon came to the time when (as Madame

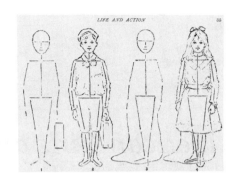

1.1. Hugo Froehlich and Bonnie Snow, *Text Books of Art Education, Book 2* (1904).

1.2. Hugo Froehlich and Bonnie Snow, *Text Books of Art Education, Book 4* (1904).

Merle informed Isabel Archer) she would be known by what she wore and the gestures she made—that array of signs by which she would be perceived and conceived of by the world at large. That there were social types waiting for her to assume went without saying. The question was *which objects* such a little American girl might emulate (figure 1.4) as she moved through the Peircean/Roycean process of imitation, reflection, and interpretation, perhaps even to find along the way the particular "sign" she would claim as her distinctive self.

Three variations, or subclassifications, of the American Girl writ large concern us in this chapter. They are variations marked by a surprisingly complex set of interchanges between the elements possessed by each type. First, the American Girl as Beautiful Charmer, represented by Harrison Fisher's portrait of one of the favorite heroines of the 1890s, Beverly of Graustark (figure 1.5). Second, the American Girl as the New England Woman, with an example by J. Alden Weir (figure 1.6). Third, the American Girl as Outdoors Pal, depicted by Robert Wildhack (figure 1.7). In each instance, the basic physical traits expected of true American Girls (classical regularity of features, lithesomeness of figure) are modified and redefined by the clothes, poses, and settings which contribute to the identification of these subtypes.

These three were the types most frequently pressed into service by the interpreters of the period between the 1890s and the 1910s.[3] They set no easy task. If each type stands opposed at times to the other two (the Charmer charms, the New England Woman thinks, the Outdoors Girl cavorts), there are points at which the three begin to overlap and even to merge. The particular mark of the times becomes apparent when the images of the Beautiful Charmer, the New England

1.3. Irma Purman (1902).

1.4. Charles Dana Gibson, "The Seed of Ambition," *Collier's Weekly*, January 31, 1903.

Beverly

1.5. Harrison Fisher, frontispiece for
McCutcheon, *Beverly of Graustark* (1904).

Woman, and the Outdoors Girl evolve into yet another type—the New Woman. At
this point of convergence, these seemingly disparate variations could be used by
ideologues for explicit political purposes (no matter on what side of the line of
argument they stood), once it came to the contentious subject of woman suffrage
(figure 1.8).

It is relatively easy to sum up the nature of the Beautiful Charmer. This is the
American Girl who, in her many representations, is wonderfully pretty, independent, candid, spontaneous, willful, spoiled, and "nice." Physically alluring, the
Charmer possesses no strong sexual appetites.[4] It is easy for this practical, egoistic
young woman to satisfy social convention on the score of her chasteness; but there
are times when her strength of will intimidates, since society prefers "will" to be
a male's prerogative, not a woman's.

She does what she does without the attribution of questionable motives. Not
that ambiguities are lacking with this seemingly safe variant on the main type.
James' Milly Theale and Euphemia de Mauves and Edith Wharton's May Welland
indicate the problematic qualities of "niceness," "innocence," and "charm." No

1.6. J. Alden Weir, "A Gentlewoman" (1906).

1.7. Robert J. Wildhack, *Collier's Weekly*, December 17, 1910.

NATIONAL MUSEUM OF AMERICAN ART

wonder that the Charmer became the center of the controversy posed in terms of the question, Which is "the fast girl" and which is "the free American"?

This is, of course, "the Daisy Miller question." Almost all who made their way to James' story of 1878 had comments to make about Daisy and the puzzlement she set for a society that preferred to rely on clear identifications of type.[5] As William Dean Howells phrased it, Daisy was rejected by many American women because they were "too jealous of her own perfection to allow that innocence might be reckless, and angels in their ignorance of evil might not behave as discreetly as worse people."[6] *The American Code of Manners*, published in 1880, worried that Daisy was the American type who is sure to be misunderstood, although possessed of "a great moral purity."[7] Daisy was a problem for makers of the rules of etiquette and a catastrophe to herself because types are supposed to be clear in their assigned meaning, and she was not. Too pliant, too difficult to pin down, too uncertain of which position she was taking, Daily Miller as the Beautiful Charmer introduced questions of identity and of its concomitant—correct conduct.

1.8. Harry W. McVickar, poster for *The Evolution of Woman* (1896).

    The Beautiful Charmer stands for will that seeks to fulfill its desires independently of the concerns of others. As Beauty, her meaning resides in the dazzling effect of her appearance. As Nice Girl, ambiguities rush into the cracks between her appearance and her reality. She may look innocent but be a wanton; or she may appear fast while being virtuous. She may seem as though she wishes love and yet be a calculating manipulator of men's hearts; or, in her wistful desire for admiration and esteem, she may be beset by observers who, baffled, take her as being more conscious than she is.

There is a variation on the type of the strong-willed female it is useful to cite at this point. Although neither pretty, young, nor charming, this figure by contrast throws both the type of the willful Beautiful Charmer and the next type we come to, the resolute New England Woman, into clearer relief. This is the intermediate type which Thomas Beer named the Titaness.[8]

In 1926 Beer looked back in real anger to the 1890s and found there "the Middle Western woman . . . a shadowy Titaness, a terror to editors, the hope of missionary societies and the prey of lecturers." The Titaness is not, however, the American Girl grown merely older and shriller. It is her mother, "an emblem, a grotesque shape in hot black silk . . . with her companionable ministers and reformers at heel." Hers is "the voice of the porch shaded by dusty maples along Grand Avenue in a hundred towns, a resolute violence of the cheapest kind, without breeding, without taste." (As one wag commented, at the command of such women, respectable American journals were made to menstruate genteely every month in order to protect the Nice Girls.)

The type of the American female as postmenopausal censor naturally concerned those who wanted to express what the spirit of censorship wished to quell. She usually turned up, imaged with varying degrees of animus, in the editorial remarks of Henry James, William Dean Howells, and others who commented critically on the trying times when the arts had ideas to express that ran contrary to those of the Titaness. On occasion, the type of Censor elbowed her way into the world of legislation (Carrie Nation with her temperance ax as satirized by the cartoonists) or took over the running of the Kingdom of the Spirit (the Mary Baker Eddy figure attacked by Mark Twain as the personification of the hated Moral Sense). But the Titaness had to step aside when Americans wished to compliment themselves for having the greatest number of the nicest girls in the Western world.

The Girl as New England Woman had critics, to be sure: those who perceived that she might become the Titaness because of her frighteningly moral sense of determination. But there were distinct differences between the ways the New England Woman, the Titaness, and the Beautiful Charmer were depicted. If the Beautiful Charmer is the ego, and the Titaness is the superego, the New England Woman is conscience and will that lie so deep and act with such intensity they have the force of the instinctual id. The New England Woman either represents the great tragedy of the American scene, eliciting compassion for what has been done to all such young women of inherent value, or she is seen as the source of the restrictions imposed upon other young American women possessed of greater public appeal.

The New England Woman as an imaginative type was not limited to the geographical area of "Down East," but by the 1870s and 1880s it was the expected thing to open or close a discussion of her type by commenting that she was most likely seen in terms of the New England setting, whether rural or urban. We find her embodied everywhere in Howells' fiction and in James' Boston as Olive Chancellor or "in the country" as Gertrude Wentworth.[9] But Albany, New York, also locates Isabel Archer on a threshold between two worlds that are not merely simple contrasts between America and Europe. Isabel Archer's "America" is based upon the traditions of New England spirituality in distinction to Daisy Miller for whom the society of Schenectady and New York City was nothing like as "pokey" as Boston or the hill villages lying beyond.

It became a commonplace to link the type of the ardent young woman of conscience to the New England past and the pet term "puritanism." For instance, when William Dean Howells compares Thomas Hardy's heroines with their American literary counterparts, he finds that though the British and American national types are of the same racial stock, the American heroine is "a graft upon the parent stem."[10] This is a heroine distinguished from her transatlantic sister by "the ugliness and error and soul-sickness which Puritanism produced in building up our intensely personalized American conscience."

Whether the contemporary explanations accorded this or other of the variations on the American female type are historically accurate is not of concern here. It is unnecessary to marshal the recent scholarship of Sacvan Bercovitch, Michael Colacurcio, Robert Daly, or Emory Elliott to test and correct Howells' 1901 thesis. It more than suffices to notice the prevalence of the idea that a vestigial puritanism lingered on and to observe how this notion influenced the imagery attributed to the type of the New England Woman in the late nineteenth century. Howells' remarks of 1901 were familiar to the American reading public, what with James' *The Europeans* of 1878 and *The Bostonians* of 1886, Howells' own spate of fictive young women, and the essay-portraits that were standard fare in the popular journals. But even if the basic lineaments of the type had long since been sketched out, her merits were continually undergoing reevaluation. Two *Atlantic Monthly* essays of 1878 and 1901 indicate the evolution going on within the conceptualization of the type. It was an evolution which prepared the way for the New England type to come into conjunction, and conflict, with other forms of the American Girl.

The first of the two *Atlantic Monthly* articles was written by Mrs. M. E. W. Sherwood for the issue of August 1878.[11] Sherwood's piece is a lighthearted fictional rendition of the table talk that goes on at a dinner party—a literary mode much favored by the middle-class journals. In this example of the genre, the subject "What is the New England Woman like?" comes up during the first course. Everyone jumps into the discussion with enthusiasm, inspired by the convenient presence of the obligatory visitor from abroad. Mr. Majoribanks, "the most literal and hemmy and hawey Englishman I have lately met," furnishes the Americans with the chance to set him straight in regard to the nation's female sex.

A query by Majoribanks concerning the nature of American "exports" prompts another guest, Harrison, to respond, "Women! Unique women, with a peculiar flavor, local, like that of California wine." Harrison, the man who becomes the evening's champion for the type he most admires, characterizes the New England variant as, above all the others, "the rarest, purest, most peculiar grape in all the world!" Majoribanks observes that the flavor of the New England women he has met is a "little cold, a trifle forbidding, perhaps too intellectual." Harrison rebuts this charge with the terms by which the 1870s gave approval to the nation's "best product": the New England Woman has "a sort of passion for chastity, a clearness of intent . . . a determination not to please any man but her husband."

The outward calm which marks New England Women does not mean they are "cold, bloodless beauties." Physical appearance discloses inner nature, but only if the signs are correctly read. "Why, I have in my mind now a valley in New England where the dark-haired, red-lipped, high-instepped, full figured women seemed to me to have come from Andalusia, instead of from Vermont, they were so graceful, so well complexioned, so well developed. They were of the passionate type, too. . . . And yet," Harrison adds (for he is adamant that the New England variant on the true American Girl cannot be merely passionate), "they were the most thoroughly regulated, studious, industrious, calculating set of Puritans imaginable. . . . Not calculating in the sense of taking advantage of others, but calculating rigidly how much they could take out of themselves."

Harrison's rhapsody continues as he anatomizes the aesthetics of conscience that far overshadows petty matters of pretty exteriors. "They were neat as pins. 'It was their nature to'; not neat because it looked well, but clear because they liked it; sweet as clover-beds, fresh as June roses; but badly shod, badly corseted, badly *coiffée*. Their thoughts, meantime, were keeping noble company; their hands were doing useful work."

There is still more for Harrison to praise about the mind of the New England Woman: her usefulness and her spirituality, as well as her inability to be tempted into unfaithfulness, since she "knows nothing of this side of life." Contrast her with "the European woman in her velvet and pearls [who] at forty [is] busily engaged in being fascinating." The lady from the Continent may possess tact, *esprit*, and *espièglerie*, but her God is herself. Turn away from this fascinating egoist and inquire, "Where is the typical New England woman at forty?" Receive the morally consoling reply, "She is where she had always been, doing her duty." (Harrison's remarks appeared in the same issue of the *Atlantic* as Henry James' serialization of *The Europeans*—the novel which contrasts the Baroness Eugenia with her New England cousins.)

With Harrison still in command, the dinner guests examine the causes for the remarkable nature of this special American type. Climate is not the source of the New England Woman's peculiar force, "for Russia is much colder, and we know what is morality in Russia, Sweden, and Denmark." Not religion, for "I do not think the descendents of the Puritans are religious." Not education, "for what is education but an outcropping of ourselves?" Perhaps tradition is the cause: "the old Puritan atmosphere still circling around Plymouth Rock"—announced by "Diana's crescent, pure and pale," which rises as "the 'field mark and device' of a large and influential type" over the land.

Harrison's conclusion (a view held by many of the lay theorists of the period) is that the present type of the New England female has been fixed by "the iron determination" of history. She is the inheritor of "a warfare . . . within sometimes, certainly without." Nor has this "puritan" stress diminished one whit. Another of the guests concurs: "This abnegation of self, this devotion to principle [is] an integral part of that Anglo-Saxon race from which we spring." For this reason, "the type of the New England woman has not departed; it flourishes still."

The paramount question remains: what *kind* of will does the New England Woman represent? How selfish or self-centered is it? Does she take us (we might ask) toward Mrs. Abel Newsome and Sarah Pocock, or toward Maria Gostrey and Mamie Pocock, in James' *The Ambassadors?* Faced by similar inquiries, Harrison lets tumble a flow of phrases in her defense, some of which twist away toward unpleasantness under the weight of the ambiguity of their implications: "enormous self-respect"; "natural reserve [that] becomes something which appears like a purse-proud disdain"; "made to 'suffer and be strong' "; "wants the best"; "capable of great hardness toward the man she loved if he did not come up to her standards of virtue"; "most unmerciful"; "cut off, by the limitations of her being, from some very admirable vices."

The host of the dinner party observes, "Harrison, you grow incoherent." Indeed he does because of his need to include a wide array of character traits within a single classification of type. Harrison even concedes the varied nature of the type's physical appearance (she can be "the Gainsborough type," follow "the willow pattern," or have the look of "my Andalusians") or geographical location ("We cannot mark off the virtues, the faults, or the manners, by latitude or longitude"). But, Harrison concludes, "Wherever I have seen her on a silver lake, on the secluded shaded wave of a lonely river, my pure New England flower; or on the marshy, disturbed surface of some suburban inlet, or the malarious, broad plane of Western waters, it was the same white flower, it was always the lily."

Twenty-three years after Mrs. Sherwood addressed the readers of *The Atlantic Monthly* through the loquacious, ardent words of Harrison and his friends, Kate Stephens presented her views to the next generation of *Atlantic* readers. The light-hearted celebration of the New England Woman found in the essay of 1878 is replaced by the caustic revisionism of 1901. Stephens skips the genial tone of Sherwood's essay and puts aside the fictional setting of genteel dinner partners in amiable conversation. She chooses to make a straightforward indictment of "a corporate woman known as 'The New England Woman.' "[12] Stephens intends to trace the decline of the type from the original "hearty, even-minded, rosy-cheeked, full-fleshed English lass" to the current type which is "weakly human, intensely feminine, and . . . passing the fabled heroism of saints in self-devotion."

In Stephen's eyes the New England Woman is "an exotic" when viewed in terms of the modern city. There is no *place* for her. Towns have replaced "that community of villages which was formerly . . . her habitat" and "the quiet seclusion of the white homes of these villages" where she gained "her ideals of life." Amid the rush of the decades after the Civil War, she narrowed her life "with a self-limitation almost Greek." Obsessed with service to husband, children, and neighbors, her only true territory became "a secluded ground, shaded by hemlocks or willows, where should stand the headstone marking her dust."

Stephens deplores the life limited to house and to headstone, but she grants the New England Woman her membership in "a great sisterhood . . . indefatigable in what Plato calls women's work." The sad waste that became her destiny resulted from the divisions between what she did and what she thought. The duties to which she gave herself "were of the external world, mainly mechanical and routine." Her thoughts, held to "but one mental path," led her along "the road to introspection." She became "an idealist in all things having to do with the spirit."

What had baffled Mrs. Sherwood's Harrison (that a selfless type might also be self-absorbed) poses no interpretive problem for Kate Stephens. "New England subjectivity"—"like almost every dwarfed or distorted thing in the active practical world"—is her special affliction. "Cut off from the larger world, she was forced into the smaller." Most commonly viewed as a spinster, she has suffered the life of "the undirected impulse."[13] She is seen by others "from a Garden of Eden point of view" which limits "dignified, constructive human expression" to married women. According to "the pronunciamento of the average citizen," the spinster never attains "the end for which women were made": the bearing of children. Because of this communal perception of her failure to join the productive ranks of wives and mothers, "a dynamo force for good was wasted through centuries, and many thousands of lives were blighted."

Kate Stephens' views on the value of the New England Woman are clearly at odds with those held by Mrs. Sherwood via her spokesman, Harrison. But Stephens, like Harrison, assumes that the spirit of the type she analyzes with such rigor must be approached from a study of the visible signs of outward appearance. Stephens wants to make clear the differences between the common view, the crude equation it makes between body and soul, and her own perceptions. These differences reveal the tragic gap caused by years of faulty looking and the errors in social conduct stemming from those misperceptions.

In this great spinster class . . . we may physiologically expect to find an excess of the neurotic, altruistic type, women sickened and extremists, because their nature was unbalanced and astray. . . . In the common conception, when among masculine comrades she should bear herself as a sexless sort of half-being, an hermaphroditic comrade, a weaker, unsexed creature, not markedly masculine, like her brother or the present golfing woman, and far from positively feminine.

If cultural uncertainties about the New England Woman's physical appearance prevent her from holding a steady place as male or female, her inner life is of a piece. It is this soul which Stephens laments, not the ambiguities of her body.

1.9. Abbott Handerson Thayer, "Head of a Woman with Fur-Lined Hood" (1915).

1.10. Thomas Eakins, "Miss Van Buren" (c.1886–1890).

All her ideals were masculine. . . . Her religion was wholly masculine, and God was always "He." . . . In this non-recognition of a woman's sex, its needs and expression in home and family life, and the domination of masculine ideals, has been a loss of grace . . . in short, a want of clarity, delicacy, and feminine strength. It emphasized spinster life—and increased it. It is this that has led the world to say that the New England woman is masculine, when the truth is she is most femininely feminine in everything but sex, where she is most femininely and self-effacingly *it*.

This inward-turning—caused by "the Garden of Eden point of view" about the body of the New England Woman—causes yet a further wasting of that body. After generations of being badly seen and badly acted toward, her exterior has "spent its physical force and wants vitality. She is slight. . . . Her lungs are apt to be weak, waist normal, and hips undersized." True, she has "a marvelously delicate, brilliant, fine-grained skin," eyes that are "pure and preternaturally bright," and features that "would in passport wording be called 'regular.' " But she is no Beautiful Charmer. Although the Charmer is said to be uninterested in sex, that type is ravishingly alluring to men because she possesses the attractive force of her own self-interested will. The New England Woman's sexless refinement of features has no such power to exert. Her will is not her own; it is a masculine will imposed upon from without. Judged body and soul as an Eve who has fallen short of the prescribed type of the true American Girl and future Mother of Americans, she has gained nothing from the cultural transaction that created her. All that introspection combined with selflessness, all that subjectivity leagued with obedience to abstract principle, have only resulted in the subtype of "the spinster"—a woman who is an atavism in her chastity and remoteness from modern life.

In the conclusion of her essay, Stephens takes hope. The New England Woman is past saving. Indeed, she must be sacrificed in order to make American society better for the New Woman. Physically outmoded, the old type will be replaced by a new racial mix as well as a new cultural spirit. "She is already outnumbered in her own home by women of foreign blood, an ampler physique, a totally different religious conception, a far different conduct, and a less exalted ideal of life. Intermixtures will follow and racial lines will gradually fade, and in the end she will not persist. Her unproductivity . . . has been her death."

Let us not here praise great souls and noble women, says Stephens. Let us rather rejoice that the New England Woman and her kind are fast disappearing into the graveyards of the little villages in which they have lived out their pathetic lives. Stephens' source of solace comes through her faith that the passing from the American scene of the New England type will assure the total eradication of a botched species.

As we read Stephens' essay of 1901 it is clear that the stakes are higher than they were for Mrs. Sherwood in 1878. When we look at the paintings of the New England Woman that fill the twenty-three years that separate the two essays, we find a steady supply of images that Sherwood could recognize and praise and that Stephens could single out for disapproval. Abbott Thayer's "Head of a Woman with Fur-Lined Hood" would doubtless please Harrison as an example of one of his "Andalusians," though not so obviously as one of his "lilies." (figure 1.9). On the other hand, Thomas Eakins' "Miss Van Buren" would seem to support Stephens' thesis (figure 1.10). It is the Eakins/Stephens view that is the "newer" one, with Thayer's on the edge of becoming a cultural anachronism.

By 1901 the notion of the failure of the type of the New England Woman achieves true Darwinian proportions. What constituted delightful dining-table conversation in 1878, and what permeates Thayer's painting of 1915 with its haunting quality, is now a matter of grave rebuke. Stephens feels bound to give a stern account of the processes of natural selection by means of which the American woman who is fully responsive to her *Zeitgeist* will move outward from the numbing sphere of village house and graveyard. In Sherwood's essay, talk about the type provides an evening's entertainment and the education of a visiting Englishman. Stephens' grimmer attention to matters of political and social reform requires that she make the type function in her essay as a powerfully negative example of what American life has done to waste "the dynamo force" of its New England virgins.

Kate Stephens did not have the final word. There were many in her generation who disagreed with her. They did this not by reverting to M. E. W. Sherwood's position of the 1870s, or by calling up either of the painter's images produced by Thayer or by Eakins. Stephens had stated that the New England Woman contradicted everything for which the New Woman of 1901 stood, but there were two other political arguments that directly identified the New Woman with the New England Woman, albeit in markedly different ways. The one argument maintained that the New Woman, unfortunately, was as excessively self-sacrificing and as distressingly charmless as was the fading image of her New England cousin. The second position stated that the two types, fortunately, shared the same splendid proclivity to lead lives of principled, energetic, intelligent action for the social good. In this view, rather than heading for the graveyard, the two sisterly types were marching together toward the voting booth.

At this point the classification of the American Girl—that general type which lies by necessity behind whatever subclassifications spin into view—becomes wondrously complex. Both the verbal portraits and the visual images supplied by the early 1900s require careful sorting. We have seen the distinctions made between the American Girl manifested as Beautiful Charmer and the New England Woman, and between the various perceptions of the Girl which superimpose the latter-day New England Woman upon the emerging image of the New Woman. Now we need to see how the American Girl as the New Woman is placed in association with the Beautiful Charmer, though not always to her advantage. Here, as in the case of the variants granted to the type of the New England Woman, *will* is the strand that links Charmer and New Woman. The different purposes to which the female will is put, and the ways this inner quality reflects itself upon the face and body, are what differentiate one form of the central type of the Girl from the others that cluster around it.

To her admirers in 1900 the New Woman was like that earlier manifestation of the Charmer, Daisy Miller (see Introduction, figure 3), only brought up-to-date as the Wellesley Woman (figure 1.11). Both types were granted the traits of physical attractiveness, independence, strong-mindedness, and zest for the experiences of the world. To her detractors, however, the New Woman was all too like the legendary Charmer in her egotism, willful selfishness, and the calculation of her attempts to take command of men and society. By no means was this latter view held only by males who feared for their collective lives because of the forward thrust of the feminists' will. In yet another *Atlantic Monthly* article, this one from

1.11. C. Allan Gilbert, poster for
   Scribner's Monthly Magazine,
   May 1898.

1910, Margaret Deland, a well-known novelist of the period, made clear the deep-seated reservations she held about the New Woman.[14]

By positioning Deland's essay on the opening pages of its March issue, *The Atlantic Monthly* acknowledged the reputation Margaret Deland enjoyed among middle-class readers. (The following year Deland's *The Iron Woman* placed sixth on the best-seller lists.) Women familiar with her novels would take notice of what she had to say. Perhaps they already shared Deland's anxieties over the fact "that this amusing person, who is called the New Woman, is to be reckoned with as a reality which is not entirely amusing." Indeed, the New Woman is not a joke.

. . . there is something more than a joke in all this curious turning upside-down of traditions and theories in regard to women; something more than a joke in the girl with a latch-key; in the matron who gives her time to civic affairs or to berating officers of the law; in myself here on this platform instead of being at home, as a good and contemptuous man said to me once, "making soup."

Deland is most troubled by two cultural trends:

. . . the first is *a prevailing discontent among women*; and the second, *a change in what we might call the "feminine ideal."* Once grant these two things, the discontent and the change, and we find ourselves face to face, not only with the lady herself, but with certain sobering possibilities which accompany her. For that discontent and change are in themselves sobering, as certain as that they are in themselves hopeful. There is always a threat where there is a promise.

This is the point Deland wishes to emphasize: "A hope always implies a menace." Allied to this is the fact that the *ideas* about what constitutes hope in 1910 have changed radically from previous generations. Hope causes the restlessness of women who will go to college, will not live with their parents, will do settlement work, will not go to church, will be active in women's clubs, will not consider marriage and childbirth. Contrast them with their mothers, Deland urges, then ask, "Can we remember that selflessness, and see no difference between it and the present feminine individualism?" Deland takes care to point to the unhappy effects which the sense of self-sacrifice had had upon the lives of an earlier generation of women. She also notes the unfortunate consequences: because daughters are ashamed of their mothers' self-effacement they now turn toward self-centeredness. It is for Deland to set matters straight again and to expose the harm done by "the sense of individualism" that contends against "the sense of social responsibility."

If earlier generations of American women depleted themselves by the strain of caring for others, the current situation is worse. In 1910 young women are "approaching Walt Whitman's ideal woman" whose "vigorous egotism of the healthy animal" replaces "a certain old-fashioned word, *duty*, by two other words, 'to myself'. . . . Now there is a certain regal word, the only word that can finally compel the soul, the word *ought*. Our girls know how to say, 'I want,' and 'I will,' or sometimes 'I must;' but they are not learning to say, 'I ought.' "

The method by which Margaret Deland pursues her argument differs markedly from those of Sherwood or Stephens, both of whom relied upon the pictorial imagination to call up mental images that opposed their likes to their dislikes. In contrast, Deland works almost solely with words, constantly returning to her key terms "selfishness," "individualism," "duty," "myself," "ought," "I want." Words repeated in sequence ("Restlessness, restlessness!") insist upon being noticed. Words made visible through the differentiation of typeface upon the printed page ("You— *you*—YOU") assault the mind.

Deland emphasizes the power of the voice, not the eye. By her voice she combats the Devil who whispers into the ear of the susceptible New Eve, "I will get a divorce, and marry A, B, or C, whom I love (for the time being), and who will make *me* happy." She gets us to eavesdrop upon the Devil in order to expose his lies: "It is base for a man and a woman who hate each other to live together. . . . So we will part!" Thus, Deland instructs her readers, "the frantic voice goes on." But these are words divided against themselves. "While this strident voice is crying in the wilderness for self-culture, self-advancement, self-satisfaction,—the lust of the flesh, the lust of the eye, and the pride of life,—it is crying, on the other side, for power to act for the public good; and that we call the sense of social responsibility."

Instead of staying at home "making soup," Deland elects to launch her jeremiad

1.12. Orson Lowell, "Election Day," *Life*, September 23, 1909.

from the public platform of *The Atlantic Monthly*. She speaks out to quell the voice of the tempter who argues for women's suffrage.

"Am not I," [the New Woman] cries, reproachfully, "I, an intelligent and educated woman, better qualified to vote than my ashman?" "True," replies public opinion, "but shall the suffrage therefore be given to your cook?" But to gratify that desire for power, the New Woman is willing to include her cook; she is willing to multiply by two the present ignorant and unconscientious vote, a vote which many thoughtful persons, anxiously doubting democracy, believe is already threatening our national existence.

The New Woman's voice cries, "All of us—or none of us!" Deland's reply, spoken from the depths of her political conservatism and racial biases (a view reflected the year prior to her article in this cartoon from *Life*—figure 1.12), is this: "We have suffered many things at the hands of Patrick; the New Woman would add Bridget also. And—graver danger—to the voice of that fierce, silly, amiable creature, the uneducated Negro, she would add (if logical) the vote of his sillier, baser female."

In an aside, Margaret Deland changes her tone to her audience which sits, as it were, before her in the public auditorium afforded by the *Atlantic*. "I hope I am not understood as being opposed to woman suffrage. I am only protesting against suffrage for all women; just as I would protest (if there was any use in doing so) against suffrage for all men. In other words, I protest against any extension of the suffrage."

Deland incorporates a string of echoing voices into her attack against the New Woman and the debased form of democracy this type would initiate. From the Bible there is the voice of the "One, who, being the supreme Aristocrat of the world, yet said, 'I am among you as one who serveth'" and the voice of Saint Paul who cautions that "all things are lawful . . . but all things are not expedient." There is also the voice of Bishop Whately who proclaims that "women never reason; or if they do, they either draw correct inferences from wrong premises, or wrong inference from correct premises—*and they always poke the fire from the top.*" Finally, there are the voices that sound through "the beautiful, dark, true words" of Omar Khayyám; through the phrases of the Apostles' Creed; and through Kant's categorical imperative, *"No one may do that which, if done by all, would destroy society."*

Deland has turned her address from the platform into a sermon from a pulpit. We may not have *seen* the New Women, but we have heard them. Deland permits us to hear their voices, but checks their self-congratulatory speech, first, with the admonitions of the preachers from the past, then with her own voice in the final words we hear. "Do not haste. Do not hold back." We at last understand the exact political position held by Margaret Deland in 1910: *wedged in between* two generations, perhaps *at impasse.*

It is not that images are altogether absent in Margaret Deland's presentation. Her opening statement directly alludes to the part popular visual representations of the New Woman have had in transforming the type into a harmless joke, rather than clarifying the grave menace Deland takes it to be. "When I planned to write this paper, I thought I would call it 'The New Woman'; but the last page of *Puck*, and the first of *Punch*, rose before me; ladies in bloomers, with latch-keys, mothers-in-law and club-women and Suffragettes, made the title impossible."

Funny pictures make serious words difficult to attend to. "Indeed, one can hardly say 'The New Woman' with any hope of being taken seriously." The new cultural phenomenon, the New Woman, not only looks like a joke, she sounds like one. Confronted by two sensory assaults, Deland must choose *which* fire she must fight with a like fire. She decides to pit honest words against verbal blandishments, not painterly images placed in opposition to cartoon caricatures. Deland's absorption with words and voices rests in her belief that the threat posed by the New Woman is that creature's siren call inviting other women to sing a celebratory "Song of Myself." The New Woman has listened to the deceitful whisperings of the Devil of selfishness; she must be drowned out by reasoned speech and rational discourse.

Nonetheless, an array of readily recognizable visual types lies behind Deland's words. Her essay depicts a contest between the eternal qualities of the New England Woman with her selfless duty toward "you" (here imaged by Cecilia Beaux—figure 1.13) and the restless variables of the Beautiful Charmer with her selfish will to please "me" (represented by one of the Christy Girls—figure 1.14). How useful these pictorial types were proving to be. Different speakers with different social ends in mind (a Kate Stephens or a Margaret Deland) could freely move the types (constantly undergoing definition and redefinition) across the chessboard of their power plays. And how useful these variables are for our own purposes, when as literary critics we wish, for example, to trace the bloodlines that extend between James' Daisy Miller and Fitzgerald's Daisy Buchanan, or when as cultural historians we need to understand, say, the disjunctions between Evelyn Nesbit and Jane Addams.

1.13. Cecilia Beaux, "New England Woman" (1895).

PENNSYLVANIA ACADEMY OF THE FINE ARTS

Good Housekeeping was one of the newly created women's magazines playing a double game.[15] It reassured its readers that the home and family would remain at the center of American society, no matter what unsettling new changes came into being. It also flattered them with the sense of their modernity, parading before them the changes it described as pleasing, practical, and fun. In contrast to *The Atlantic Monthly*, which did not use illustrations to support its written texts (one of the reasons Henry James preferred it for publishing stories with his own kind of images), *Good Housekeeping* went in heavily for photography and drawings; its

1.14. Howard Chandler Christy, from "The Cleansing of a Lie," *Harper's Monthly Magazine*, August 1901.

visual format was part of the appeal it held for readers of a less literary turn than those who preferred verbal forms of persuasion and information.[16] For the February issue of the 1912 *Good Housekeeping* Mary Holland Kinkaid wrote a sunny article, "The Feminine Charms of the Woman Militant: The Personal Attractiveness and Housewifely Attainments of the Leaders of the Equal Suffrage Movement, Illustrated with Portraits."[17] Kinkaid immediately declares her sympathies with the suffragists, women who "have patiently endured ridicule and misunderstanding [because they] could afford to smile at the unchangeableness of the jests about deserted homes and neglected babies, unused cook stoves and undarned socks, since life was teaching the value of the vote to millions of women whom economic conditions have forced into wage-earning employments."

Pleased as Punch with the message she has to bear, Kinkaid reports, "Gradually women of every type have been united by this common bond of sisterhood, and in their union they have come to know that the woman suffrage movement is not altogether political. They have realized its spiritual significance, since they can make their citizenship mean impetus to all that is best in national life."

Kinkaid's wording is conventional enough, but her purpose is to allay the fears of persons such as Margaret Deland. She proclaims, "The women who have the highest ideals of life are the women who make their homes the centers of beauty and harmony." Because of "the doubts cast upon the housekeeping attainments of advocates of equal suffrage," women with "the responsibility of leading the battle for the ballot" have taken upon themselves "a special preparation in the domestic arts." Thus the domesticity of "the woman militant" is both a natural affinity and a clever political strategy.

Kinkaid presents an honor roll of the original stalwarts of the feminist movement. She declares that the most famous suffragists were all accomplished in the women's sphere. Elizabeth Cady Stanton was the "head of a beautifully ordered home." Amelia J. Bloomer was attentive to "every detail in the keeping of her pretty cottage." Susan B. Anthony was "an adept with her needle" and "did the most exquisite darning when she was thinking of her speeches." Carrie Chapman Catt still "goes into the kitchen to make pumpkin pies . . . [from] real pumpkins, not base tinned imitations . . . [for her] famous Thanksgiving dinners."

In assessing the possible political impact of the Kinkaid article, we must take into account that her words of praise are just words. They are the same ones that had been flowing forth for decades from suffragist camps. At the late date of 1912 there was no guarantee that a few more verbal assurances like Kinkaid's would make the unconvinced suddenly *hear* the truths they had been resisting up to that point. But unlike Margaret Deland, Kinkaid does not rely on words alone. She realizes her audience needs visual evidence concerning the look of the "safe" suffragist. She reinforces her printed argument with ten photographic portraits. Each reinforces her assertion that feminist leaders are every bit as attractive to look at as they are exemplary to read about.

Margaret Deland talked on and on about the importance of the female unselfishness that declares itself only when women attend solely to the needs of the home. Mary Holland Kinkaid "shows" the converse to be true. It is *because* these women work vigorously for the right to vote that they are the unselfish mainstays of society. Furthermore, *because* they are unselfish mainstays of society, their appearance appeals.

The photograph of Mrs. Clarence MacKay (figure 1.15) is accompanied by the names and pictures of Miss Vida Sutton, Mrs. Jean Nelson Penfield, Mrs. Ernest

1.15. Mrs. Clarence MacKay, from
Kincaid, "The Feminine Charms
of the Woman Militant," *Good
Housekeeping*, February 1912.

Thompson Seton, Mrs. James Lees Laidlaw, Mrs. Martha Nelson McCan, Miss Harriet May Mills, Mrs. Charles Farwell Edson, and Miss Inez Milholland. Most of these feminists are society women and college graduates. (The University of Chicago, Cornell, and Vassar are cited as part of their credentials.) All possess impeccable upper-class status and a staff of servants to do the exacting work in their kitchens, but Kinkaid does not consider this fact to be cheating. She insists that each one of these New Women knows very well how to run a home. Each is capable of utilizing, in both home and public arena, "the executive ability" for which she is famous. The admission that Inez Milholland has no time "to solve housekeeping problems" and "may not be familiar with formulas for desserts or salad dressings" is of little consequence. There is "no doubt that in any domestic crisis she would master all cooking difficulties by mixing brains with reliable recipes." Figure 1.16 shows Milholland posed as Cornelia, mother of the Gracchi, taking part in a charity tableau. Although Kinkaid's article appeared a year too early to be able to mention the fact, Milholland—an exceptional woman in many ways[18]— was to demonstrate her talents for representing types of exemplary womanhood in March of 1913. Figure 1.17 depicts her on horseback, acting as herald in the march to the U.S. Treasury Building where a highly publicized suffragist pageant was presented before a large crowd of often obstreperous spectators.

Kinkaid's article carries its own *Good Housekeeping* Seal of Approval by way of an "Editor's Note" printed at the start of the piece. It reads, "The popular misconception [that the suffragist is a] strident creature, mannish in attire and of unattractive personality," is untrue, "as the facts and pictures in this article will prove." The editor and Kinkaid take for granted (as would most of her readers) that an attractive exterior signifies inner moral beauty: therefore this type of the New Woman can never signify the asocial behavior of Deland's New Woman who says, "I want, I will, I must." Kinkaid's suffragist is blessed by both "feminine charms" and the vigor of "the woman militant." She promises Americans a society with both pumpkin pies and selfless lives dedicated to that motto, "I serve."

By 1912 photojournalism had found its métier. Muckrakers and the progressivist press used photography to expose hidden scandals that menaced the stability of society and the home. First Jacob Riis, then Lewis Hine, among others, provided graphic images of the ugliness and disordering effects of slum housing and child labor. They stripped away the concealments created by the indifference of silence or by verbal prettification. Notice how Mary Holland Kinkaid takes the same reform tactics and inverts them. She employs the techniques used by the reformer's photo essay to right falsehoods. But in her case photos are not employed to reveal new kinds of ugliness; rather, they disclose the *attractiveness* of the New Woman. Instead of exposing the unpleasant forces disrupting American society, her photos promise the steadying support the ever-evolving New Woman brings the age-old values of home and family.

Even more is at work in Kinkaid's piece of journalism. The New Woman presented through visual images combines the best of all the types at which we have looked. Kinkaid's "Woman Militant" is the Beautiful Charmer with heart and the New England Woman without neurasthenia. She is the political activist, but she is also—in fact or theory—spiritual mentor, intelligent wife, mother, and homemaker.

By 1910 the lines were blurring between the many types into which young Amer-

1.16. Inez Milholland, from
      Kincaid, "The Feminine
      Charms of the Woman
      Militant," *Good House-
      keeping*, February 1912.

1.17. Inez Milholland, March 1913.

1.18. Standiford Studios, Cleveland, "Judge Florence Ellenwood Allen" (1925).

1.19. Robert Bolling Brandegee, "Sarah Porter" (1896).

ican women were classified. It was often hard to know when one type dissolved into its opposite or began to turn into an obvious variant. Nowhere is this sleight of hand more apparent than in two further areas where the apolitical Charmer and the politicized New Woman met and converged. "Roses at the Breast" is one subtype and "Bicycles" is the other. Respectively, they give us the look of the suffragist as Charmer and of the Charmer as the active sportswoman. It seemed as though American women might execute a major coup only if a composite image could be formed from these three distinct types—the female activist, the girl of superb bodily health, and the woman with the pretty face. Somehow all three had to enfold into the single image of that newest and finest form of the American Girl—the New Woman. Only then might the public's fears be placated. It was common knowledge that ugly faces and unattractive manners meant the collapse of the basic American institutions of marriage, family, and home. But if the New Woman could be *perceived* through her attractive exterior as being good for society, then an affirmative *idea* about her inner nature would be backed by public *conduct* that acted in her favor.

A studio photograph was taken of Judge Florence Ellenwood Allen in 1925 (figure 1.18). It is a no-nonsense likeness of a professional woman who wears her robes of office as though she clearly has the right to them. The portrait oil executed in 1896 of Sarah Porter, founder of Miss Porter's School for Women, conveys the same statement (figure 1.19). Allen and Porter make no allowances for the public's taste for attractive feminine types. One accepted them or not (after the manner of Er-

1.20. Edward Hughes, "Juliette
Gordon Low" (1887).

NATIONAL PORTRAIT GALLERY

nest Hemingway's comment about Gertrude Stein) according to whether one is
willing to have a woman look like, thus behave like, a Roman emperor.

A painting of Juliette Gordon Low who went on to found the Girl Scouts in 1915
is in marked contrast to the visual statements made by Sarah Porter and Florence
Allen (figure 1.20). A word of caution, however. Even if we had not seen the
evidence of Kinkaid's 1912 *Good Housekeeping* article, we should know better than
to assume from the 1887 date of the portrait of Low that the image of the Beautiful
Charmer had lost its appeal by the time Sarah Porter sat for her portrait in 1896,

fifty-three years after opening her day school in Farmington, Connecticut. Whatever the decade—the 1880s, 1890s, or 1920s—young women sitting for a social portrait received a visual treatment different from the treatment considered appropriate for professional women, particularly those who were no longer bright young
things and whose full lives of service elicited respect from their portrayers. But we
must also be careful about concluding that the visual typing accorded to Juliette
Low at age twenty-seven was somehow prophetic of a woman who later devoted
her energies to instructing girls in the domestic skills to which the scouting movement was a party, activities thrown into disrepute by feminists who distrust with
equal fervor social butterflies dressed for a ball or little mothers gathered around a
campfire. If there is no reason to think that Sarah Porter and Florence Allen as
young women might not have been pictured according to the conventions of the
Charmer, there is no reason to believe that Juliette Low as founder of the Girl
Scouts would be shut out of the authentic look, whatever *that* is, of the New
Woman.

The political life of Susan B. Anthony was far more feisty than that of the tra-
dition-bound Mrs. Low. But examine this adulatory painting of 1900 (figure 1.21).
Anthony at eighty is too old to pose as a Southern belle with fan and ball gown.
But her image is not that of Sarah Porter or Florence Ellenwood Allen. Painted at
the moment of receiving floral tributes from adoring children, Anthony is given
attributes more common to female saints than to secular charmers. Indeed, this
New Woman possesses the iconic references associated with the Holy Mother Mary.
But the 1887 painting of Low as Charmer and the 1900 painting of Anthony as
Saint and Virgin share the same rosy glow of saving femininity. (In each, pink is
the dominant color.) The softness of tone and sweetness of demeanor emphasized
in both portraits would go a long way toward assuaging the suspicions the public
might hold toward the social causes such women supported. Furthermore, the inclusion of similar signs in their typing as New Women helped bridge whatever
ideological distance separates the cautious feminism of Juliette Low and the more
radical femininity of Susan B. Anthony.

Two photographic studies confirm and extend the force of the new iconographic
convention by which the Female Militant could be perceived by the general public
as attractively feminine. Harriet Burton Laidlaw (figure 1.22), like Mrs. Thomas
Jefferson Smith (figure 1.23), was active in the upper ranks of the National American Woman Suffrage Association.[19] Both women assume poses for the camera that
follow the visual formula I call "roses at the breast." Mrs. Laidlaw faces frontally.
The cast of her jaw and the direct gaze of her eyes are as forthright as those of
Judge Allen or Sarah Porter, but her arm (crooked to press a blossom to her bosom)
fits an ageless convention that associates pleasing femininity with the delicacy of
flowers. The pose taken by Mrs. Smith, the recording secretary of NAWSA, has one
obvious precedent in Francesco Parmigianino's "Madonna of the Long Neck," painted
in 1535, or closer to hand, Frederick A. Bridgman's "Woman and Rose" of 1885
(figure 1.24). Mrs. Smith looks pensively off to the side, her shoulders discreetly

1.21. Sarah J. Eddy, "Susan B.
Anthony, on the Occasion
of her 80th Birthday"
(1900).

NATIONAL MUSEUM OF AMERICAN HISTORY

but charmingly bared, the roses caught just above her breast cleavage, as though
she were a tremulous debutante hoping to be asked for the next dance. (Pansy
Osmond's role model perhaps?) [20]

The basic pose of demure damsel, ivory shoulders, and just-opening blossoms was
a well-used visual convention picked up for a variety of random purposes well into
the 1900s. In 1899 *The Cosmopolitan* magazine ran a piece on New York high
society, and as standard procedure included this study by James Breese, well known
as a photographer of the upper classes (figure 1.25). In 1901 hired models fell into

1.22. Standiford Studios, Cleveland, "Harriet [Mrs.
James Lees] Laidlaw"
(1925).

LIBRARY OF CONGRESS

the same pose on instructions from the Tonnesen Sisters Studio of Chicago which
provided this photograph for the Sunday supplements (figure 1.26) as a form of
viewer titillation. In 1906 the Armour Meat Products Company mounted an advertising campaign (figure 1.27). A set of "Armour's Girls" drawings was free for the
asking, including one by the popular artist Harrison Fisher. In 1907 Howard Chandler Christy's "She Held a Deep Red Rose" was drawn for a gift-book whose title
brings together all these poses into a single social context. That title is *Our Girls*.[21]

It was important to supporters of the suffrage movement to be perceived by the
public as being one of "our girls." These women were willing to abide by a visual
convention that stressed their normalcy, even though the pose linked them to com-

1.23. Mrs. Thomas Jefferson Smith (c.1920s).

1.24. Frederick A. Bridgman, "Woman and Rose" (1885), photogravure, from Sheldon, *Recent Ideals of American Art* (1888, 1889, 1890).

mercial and social enterprises that had nothing to do with the goals of the New Woman and, indeed, expressed ideas antithetical to feminist principles.

The motives of such women to be portrayed by camera or oils were varied. They might pose as they did to convince themselves that they *were* examples of what their contemporaries considered attractive womanhood; or they might make use of the roses-at-the-breast convention as a calculated political strategy. But although we can only speculate about the motives that lay behind individual cases, there are some things we *can* state with certainty. First, the image of the Beautiful Charmer was potentially a *useful* convention since it quickly identified a woman as the type of the attractive female. Second, it was also an ambiguous sign since the actual political beliefs held by the woman might be overshadowed by the statement the pose made about her appearance. In this sense, roses at the breast was a *useless* convention unless other statements could simultaneously be made that connected her with the right-to-vote movement.

The demure debutante was a pose that could be assumed by both the charmer and the suffragist during the 1890s and early 1900s. But what about the growing num-

1.26. Tonnesen Sisters, Chicago (1900), for *Washington Times Supplement*, October 13, 1901.

1.25. James Breese, "Mrs. Walter Pease," from Van Rensselaer, "The Basis of New York Society," *Cosmopolitan*, August 1899.

1.27. Harrison Fisher, "Armour's Harrison Fisher Girl" (1906).

ON THE BEACH

LIBRARY OF CONGRESS

LIBRARY OF CONGRESS

1.28. Howard Chandler Christy, "On
    the Beach" (1903), reprinted in
    Christy, *The American Girl*
    (1906).

1.29. Marion Hollins (c.1908).

1.30 *(above, right)*. Elaine Golding
    (1915).

ber of female athletes who were moving into public visibility by 1900? One might
think they would aggressively shun any pictorial formula that threatened to nudge
their particular expression of female emancipation closer to the conventional image of the American Girl. What had their vigorous athleticism to do with the
scores of vanity images calculated to show off lithe figures and buoyant spirits
(figure 1.28)? The frivolity of such poses certainly had nothing to do with the
discipline of mind and body that serious sportswomen exacted of themselves.

A snapshot of Marion Hollins shows an accomplished golfer whose eyes resolutely follow the arc of the ball she has just hit with the force of her well-trained
body (figure 1.29). This photograph of the champion swimmer Elaine Golding catches

1.31. Katharine Harley (c.1908).

1.32. Elaine Golding (1915).

her climbing out of a cold February ocean in 1915 upon completing a successful swimming race. (figure 1.30).

But what of this photograph of Katharine Harley, National Woman's Golf Champion of 1908 (figure 1.31)? Harley stands in the pose of the-lady-golfer-is-beautiful. Eyes directed at the camera, her feet and hand grip function for photogenic effect, not for walloping a nonexistent ball. Here is Elaine Golding again, now removed to a "studio" setting (probably along the boardwalk) where she stands in a rather painful attempt at looking seductive (figure 1.32). It would be kind of us to say that Golding was a better athlete than a bathing beauty. *That* role was taken with far more assurance by Annette Kellermann, the Esther Williams of her day, whose good looks took her curvaceous body out of the water and into the locker room and the photographer's studio and finally onto the stage as a professional entertainer (figure 1.33).[22]

Kellermann's basic pose turns up again and again, with variations. This nymph-by-the-brook produced in 1901 for the Sunday supplements by the indefatigable Tonnesen Sisters seems innocently unaware of the provocative nature of her veilings and supine position (figure 1.34). This beach shot taken in 1918 (figure 1.35) matches Kellermann's in its forthright self-consciousness, though its calculated coyness is already pointing to the cute seductiveness soon made familiar by the Mack Sennett comedies and by the Miss America contests that commenced in 1921. Conventionality of pose lets these diverse examples share together the formalistic tradition of the Reclining Female. But if the intrinsic *look* is immediately recognizable, how the particulars are to be interpreted is not that evident. Harriet Hosmer's marble "Beatrice Cenci," sculpted in 1857, portrays a woman victimized by incestuous assault, her reputation tarnished, her death untimely (figure 1.36). The pose of her woe approximates *in form* the poses assumed by Kellermann, the Tonnesen model, and the Los Angeles beach girl, but hardly their *moods*. The question whether any of these poses serves to penetrate the deepest nature of the women on view is yet another reason for hesitating to assign generalized meaning to these female forms. But it is time to put a halt to this round of deconstructive acts. There is a point at which we have the right to stop and consider the possible social declarations that poses might make concerning a woman's innate talents and commitments.

Consider what it meant to be a feminist at the turn of the century in light of the problems of identification created by her ideological position. A woman who elected to advance a body of social and political principles was compelled to resolve the question of how to embody those abstract values pictorially.

Women who advocated dress reform might go into public wearing trousered suits as part of their political stance, tucking a rose into the bosom of their shirts, as did Dr. Mary Walker at eighty (figure 1.37).[23] Women who were apolitical but sexually radical in their advocacy of lesbianism could assert their divergence from the social norm after the manner of Romaine Brooks (who, as an artist, controlled the image she gave to the world by painting it herself [figure 1.38]).[24] Their task was simplified if they wore judge's robes, the academic regalia of a college president, or—as in the case of the painting of Lillian Wald (see Introduction, figure 39)—the uniform of the Public Health Service. The clothes of professional women helped to indicate that they had obtained some release from social limitations.

Suffragists could also declare their beliefs by their gestures. When they went into the streets to participate in rallies for the vote wearing standard feminine dress, symbolic poses and props served as visual "demonstration" of the twofold fact that they held radical political beliefs, even while possessing the look of the True American Woman (figure 1.39). *Pace,* Isabel Archer! The way a woman dresses and

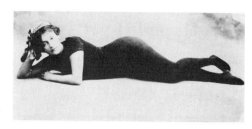

1.33. Annette Kellermann
(n.d.).

LIBRARY OF CONGRESS

1.34. Tonnesen Sisters (1900),
for the *Washington
Times*, March 24, 1901.

LIBRARY OF CONGRESS

LIBRARY OF CONGRESS

1.35. Edith Roberts (1918).

1.36. Harriet Hosmer, "Beatrice Cenci"
(1857), engraved by W. Roffe for
Clark, *Great American Sculptures* (1878). (Original at the
Mercantile Library, St. Louis.)

1.37. Dr. Mary Walker (1912).

1.38. Romaine Brooks, "Self-Portrait" (1923).

1.39. Mrs. A. Van Winkle (1915).

The Militant

1.40. Irene Langhorne Gibson (c.1915), from Downey, *Portrait of an Era as Drawn by C. D. Gibson.*

1.41. Charles A. Winter, "The Militant," *The Masses*, August 1913.

looks may be the means by which she displays her ideas to the world, as well as revealing her complex affiliation with the very society she wishes to alter.

What about the New Woman taken just as she is? Stripped down to her essential self, she looks very much like any other woman. If she chooses, she disappears into a blur of domestic poses and roses. She becomes one of "our girls" with pensive look, bared shoulders, flowers at the breast, protected by the coloration she needs to stay within the system she hopes to reform. From their photographs alone, how can one tell the difference between Mrs. MacKay, Mrs. Laidlaw, and Mrs. Smith (all active feminists) and Mrs. Charles Dana Gibson, popularly thought to be the original model for the Beautiful Charmer (figure 1.40)? Based on visual evidence alone, the ardent young woman on the vaguely medieval cover of *The Masses* of August 1913 (figure 1.41) seems no more "The Militant" than Inez Milholland caparisoned as a medieval herald (see figure 1.17). Milholland and *The Masses* both *stand for* social change; Mrs. Gibson does not. Obviously image alone does

1.42. Charles Dana Gibson, "Dull for the Girls After Dinner—The Judge and the Governor Discuss
Politics," from *Other People* (1911).

not make clear one's political intentions; but image is often the immediate means
taken toward the desired-for end.

Few feminists wished to go as far as the painter Romaine Brooks did in her public
effort to transform her lesbianism into a "man-made" artifact. Even so, most resented the simplistic choices illustrated by Gibson's drawing "Dull for the Girls
After Dinner—the Judge and the Governor Discuss Politics" (figure 1.42). They
preferred to believe that American women did not have to choose, on the one
hand, between pretty girls bored by reform issues and, on the other hand, grossly
unattractive females. Somehow the feminist had to *dress* her ideas and her inner
convictions in order to let them be expressed, however inadequately, by the surface she presented. Rather than appear as a female who alienated by her public
behavior the very society she wished to better (figure 1.43), the feminist had to
find ways to inspire her viewer to follow the Peircean mode of interpretation. Only
then might society's perception of her image translate into collective conduct that
would advance her principles and protect her from hostility and ridicule.

1.43. "Emancipated Woman" (1900).

NATIONAL ARCHIVES

The *New York World* of August 18, 1895, featured a piece on the New Woman. The sketch accompanying the article (figure 1.44) is glossed by the following statements:

A great deal has been said about the new woman, but nobody, until to-day, has had the opportunity of looking her in the face. The above picture is a composite of the new woman.

1.44. "Here Is the New Woman," *New York World*, August 18, 1895.

It is faithfully made up of twelve excellent likenesses of the twelve most prominent new women in the world. . . .

It will be seen at once that the composite new woman has a strong face. It is an intellectual face, and—it is said with some regret—possibly, a stern, unyielding face.

The newspaper piece praises the face of the type of the New Woman since it "indicates character and progress," but the main issue is the response the male reader (the Old Man) has to this composite image. The question is asked "whether he would like to marry the woman he sees pictured here." By implication, a related question is asked of the female reader. Does she want to be like that "intellectual-looking person" whom men would probably rather not wed?

Prominent writers of the period had to deal with the marriageability of the women they portrayed in their stories. Henry James insists that Isabel Archer is not the kind of beautiful heroine required by the romantic novels he saw as his main competition in the marketplace. His Verena Tarrant and Milly Theale are also a little odd and have quantities of eccentric red hair. James continually comments upon Maggie Verver's plainness and casts her into the shade caused by the glowing magnificence of Charlotte Stant. But even though James intentionally presents his female centers as unconventional in looks and actions, he wraps them in a language of such style its elegance rubs off on them. The New Womanish quirks of his heroines are modified by the sheen of the beauty of James' words. William Dean Howells also falters in the face of the question of his heroines' looks. He does his best to make his fictional women of will and spirit unattractive, so better to emphasize his point that physical beauty is not necessary for the true American heroine. In *The Rise of Silas Lapham* of 1885 he moves Penelope Lapham well away from the conventions dictating female appearance, but even he cannot go so far as to make her unmarriageable.

Many compromises were involved when the roses-at-the-breast image was donned like a costume. It came distastefully near the old convention of the sweetly feminine, romantically fragile women whose meaning was "limitation." Other poses had to be found—up-to-date poses that portrayed vigor of body and mind—if the American Girl were to declare herself truly new by 1900.

Among the various solutions coming into view in the 1890s, one stands out. The young American woman who plunged (without roses, but with enthusiasm) into a merry round of sports seemed just the type to demonstrate how winning an example of the New Woman might be. Such a girl might be difficult for a man to keep up with, but she was considered a charmer all the same (figure 1.45). The feminist per se had only an independent mind to display, but the young woman who was physically active appeared to state her bodily and mental freedom through the clothes she wore and the poses she struck.

As we have seen clarity of image did not mean absence of ambiguity in the reading of the meaning of athletic poses. Is a woman "authentic" only when she is like Marion Hollins knocking off a solid shot (see figure 1.29). In contrast, is a woman the betrayer of her sex's aspirations for independence when, like Katharine Harley, she takes up a pretty pose for the camera (see figure 1.31)? What about Marie Doro, one of the pets of Charles Frohman's musical comedy company (figure 1.46)? Is Doro any less a version of the New Woman because she uses a prop golf

1.45. Charles Dana Gibson, "One of the Disadvantages of Being in Love with a Athletic Girl," *Life*, May 22, 1902.

1.46. Burr McIntosh Studio, "Miss [Marie] Doro, No. 13" (1902).

1.47. Charles Cox, poster for "Bearings" (1896).

1.48. Irma Purman and friends (c.1913).

1.49. Van, "New York Against Boston for the Championship," *Life*, September 22, 1887.

1.50. Irma Purman (c.1914).

stick in a photographer's studio as one means by which she (as a kind of Sister Carrie) makes her way up in the theater world of stagy make-believe?

There is an even bigger issue at stake. When we ask, "Where does the fantasy end and the reality begin?" (figures 1.47 and 1.48), we want to know whether either image lacks accuracy as a report of the changes taking place in American life because it seems reflective only of conventions and popular expectations. That is, in the instance in which my mother figures (figure 1.48), can I "read" her pose as an Outdoors Pal to any purpose?

My own answer to the question is this. Although such images carry different meanings which are sometimes set in opposition, I believe that such images *are* useful as evidence. They can signal the vigor of determined young women making real changes in American society, or they can stand for fun-loving girls who offer no direct threat to the status quo. This is exactly the point I want to make. It is the ability of types *to flow past their containers* into the realms of ambiguity and paradox that is the source of their importance to us as cultural artifacts.

The history of the Beautiful Charmer in her particular manifestation as the Outdoors Girl is a good example of one way by which women found the means to appropriate the "strong" look of the New Woman, while gaining the approval of the general public. During the 1870s and 1880s female athleticism was often viewed negatively (figure 1.49). Since the women who participated in sports might be directly linked with the suffrage movement, athletics and suffrage joined as a single idea in the public's imagination. The New Woman who wanted to vote and to play ball was discredited. But by the early 1900s a young woman who was a swimmer (figure 1.50) had won at least partial approval for the overt display she made of her bodily and mental freedoms.[25]

The girl who went cycling (figure 1.51) might not raise a finger to urge the vote for women, but her *image* as the type of the American Girl became part of the process that altered social perceptions and formed new conceptions of what it was possible for females to do and to be. As a near-contemporary of Charles Dana Gibson remarked, "The Goddess of the Wheel, as Gibson and many another artist now drew her, was . . . a pretty American girl speeding joyously along on a bicycle. On that simple machine she rode like a winged victory, women's rights perched on the handlebars and cramping modes and manners strewn on her track."[26]

By 1900 many women expressed genuine interest in athletics. Others were enticed by the attention given to female sports by newspapers and magazines. Publicity persuaded many women that such activities were the surest way to acquire the free-spirited look now expected of lively American Girls. The type of the Outdoors Girl could image a revolutionary process that promised the self and society would never be the same again. The type also supported the views of conservatives who reasoned that their daughters should cultivate an excellent physique as insurance for a stable society founded on sound motherhood. Or the type could be used to promote beauty products in an avidly consumer society (figure 1.52).

There are few limits to what types, placed in different hands, might mean. Rather than quelling questions, they continue to arouse them. Images of the kind that activate the complex processes by which Charles Sanders Peirce, William James, and Josiah Royce say we come to knowledge are no guarantee that meaning can easily be won. This is why they are stunning examples of what *meaning* is.

1.51. Charles Dana Gibson, "Scribner's for June" (1896).

1.52. Binner, "Hall's Hair Renewer 'Grows Bountiful Beautiful Hair,' " (1898).

COLUMBIA UNIVERSITY LIBRARIES

In the early years of the twentieth century the phrase "the American Girl" was neither mere fiction, abstract theory, nor fraudulent fact. Solidly backed by images that flowed quickly across the visual horizon of the American public, this complex composite of types was available for use by anyone who wished to use it for whatever reasons—commercial, personal, aesthetic, political. When the type of the American Girl was at the height of her glory between 1895 and 1915, Royce, Peirce, Dewey, and William James would have recognized, as clearly as did Henry James, Edith Wharton, and William Dean Howells, that she was a type that could be "looked at." As one observer at the time commented, the Girl had "a face and figure [that lent] themselves to [the] sort of reproduction" the new forms of media

1.53. "Basket Ball—The New Craze for Athletic Young Women," *New York Journal*, May 17, 1896.

1.54. Charles Dana Gibson, "Design for Wall Paper. Suitable for a Bachelor Apartment," *Life*, September 18, 1902.

were just then rushing into existence.[27] Because of this fact, the Girl gave Americans the expressive forms by which they could realize their fears (Vassar girls possessed by a craze for basketball) and their desires (a bachelor's apartment literally wallpapered with dreams) (figures 1.53 and 1.54).

1.55. Irma Purman and friends
(1912).

Once the 1893 Columbian Exposition had come and gone from the flatlands of Chicago, an official American image began to compose itself from the fluid elements of the times. "America" was female, young, pretty, Protestant, and northern European. She was the heiress of America's history as edited by the American Whigs. Her features were "regular" and Caucasian. Her bloodline was pure and vigorous. That she might have "nerves," and that her will was at times inconveniently strong, was, after all, to be expected of any physical or psychical type that represented the nation's own restlessness and independence of spirit. Whether too selfless or too selfish, whatever else the Girl was, her various images had power over the public imagination. She was problematic, just as the country was.

Questions of whether the surge of energy the Girl embodied would prove a future force for ill or for betterment spurred the outpourings of the popular press *and* the writings of the best authors. They stimulated the commercial artists who promoted laundry soap and bicycles *and* the painters who executed memorably acute portraits and emblematic allegorical figures. But above all there was the question, Would that energy ever be directly enjoyed by the actual American women which the Girl was supposed to represent (figure 1.55)? For after all, the young woman you see to the right of this photograph is what that child whom I showed you at the beginning of the chapter (see figure 1.3) had become just ten eventful years later. By 1912 she had, almost by the accident of history, become one of the New Women. But to what end?

2

Looking for the "Best" Type

From one end of the nineteenth century to the other, two literary devices were put into play by observers who wished to call attention to peculiarities prevailing in the United States. One (given particular emphasis in the early decades of the 1800s) sounds the note of absence and lists the historical and cultural scenery, costumes, and props that America does not possess. The other reiterates the splits running from top to bottom through the country's social strata, economic structures, political allegiances, geography, gender relations, tastes, and aims. Emphasis upon absences and fragments led to an American scene imaged as both a blank and a welter: *what was not there* and *what there was too much of.*

The need for signs to help guide the way in either case is apparent. In an empty landscape and a culture lacking in the details which indicate appropriate conduct, something (formula or code) is wanted to stand in for the missing things. If the sojourner (whether native citizen or visitor from abroad) feels overwhelmed by detail, this messiness stirs a craving for clear signs to identify, make known, bring control.

All those strangers crossing the ocean into the States (especially after 1883 with the burst of czarist energies against the Jews) heaped problems of identification upon those already dug in. The resident northern European stock perceived the faces, skulls, and torsos of the immigrants from central Europe or the Orient as blanks (people who were not really *there* since unknown and unusable as information) and as contradictory data (people whose latent meaning was confusing and indecipherable).

Setting aside the famous listings of what these United States do not provide the analytic eye schooled by European expectations (lists furnished by Crèvecoeur, de Tocqueville, Cooper, Hawthorne, and Henry James, to name some of the masters of the American genre of "no this" and "no that"), let us concentrate instead upon late-nineteenth-century references to American culture described in terms of splits, contrasts, and divisions among incompatible peoples living at cross-purposes with one another. Then we can determine what part was assigned to the American Girl in this affair, whether as the queen of cultural misrule or as the lady who reconciles and heals.

The two Americas of wealth and poverty are not the focus here. Rather, the primary concern is with the refusal of one group to allow other groups the privileges and profits of "being American"—a debacle of faulty perception and bad conduct in the Peircean sense which resulted because the first group viewed the latter as "wrong" in the racial and ethnic types they represented. The clues we seek are who is and who is not perceived as being "American" amid the welter undergoing simplifications of the kind that denied immigrant and minority groups visual identification as "the best type."

In 1907 William Graham Sumner published *Folkways: A Study of the Sociological Importance of Usages, Manners, Customs, Mores, and Morals*, his conscious effort to propose scientific norms for the analysis of the behavior of social entities. Sumner's book argues the differences between "the we-group or in-group, and everybody else, or the other-group, out-groups."[1] In making an issue of the brute fact that there are *us* and *them*, Sumner shook up one of the public's favorite fantasies about itself. The shock did not come from the fact that the United States was experiencing major cultural rifts. The shock derived from the realization that it is in the nature of human communities to be divided and that life in the New World is no different on that score from life in the flawed societies of the Old World.

It had been years since anyone had put any trust in the notion that the peoples of the United States held a culture in common. Still, it had been one of the nicer daydreams to argue that this was a nation with a special talent for homogeneity of race, culture, and social interests. Hadn't Hector St. John de Crèvecoeur said this back in the 1780s in *Letters from an American Farmer*, and hadn't the Schoolroom Poets assumed that we were all New Englanders at heart, and hadn't the Civil War been won and the Union Pacific Railway been laid to prove that North, South, East, and West were essentially one?

True, observers from afar who came on visits to the United States and stayed long enough to write up their reactions—friendly or hostile in nature—noticed fairly quickly that American culture was not as much of a piece as it was made out to be, since even the prevailing Anglo-Saxon type was known to wear coats of differing colors. It is just such foreign analysts to whom we turn: the Frenchman Paul Bourget, the Scot James Fullarton Muirhead, and the Norwegian Hjalmar Hjorth Boyesen. Not only did they have the outsiders' sharp eye for American contradictions in general, they were convinced by the constant, attention-drawing presence of young American women that it was necessary to read American culture in their light.

It is Paul Bourget with whom we start, and his book of 1895 *Outre-Mer: Impressions of America*.[2] Bourget does not necessarily provide the best interpretations for his own impressions. Point to point, Muirhead may be the soundest note taker of the three (Baedeker Guidebook specialist as he is). But Bourget is right on the mark when he makes two observations about how to go about reading American life. First, look for representational types—the forms by which the visitor can regularize the foibles of individual specimens. Second, trust the types which are most in the public eye. Once these two elements are in place, Bourget adds the third that makes the whole process work. Choose as one's preeminent representational type the most visible form on the American social scene. It will be the American Girl in all her guises.

As a writer who wants to understand the national culture, Bourget approaches the problem as would a painter. He has a great deal to say about American artists, illustrators, and cartoonists. He is astute in regard to the pictorial mode that makes constant reference to easily recognizable images of the Girl. He recognizes how this repetition guarantees the Girl's appeal. Bourget takes the example of the Beauty, "the most artless of these young girl types." The Beauty literally exists because she has a face and a figure that "lend themselves to that sort of reproduction of which newspapers are so fond"—fond because the Beauty *prints* so well. The iconic quality of the Beauty even affects the procedures in the composing rooms where metal typeface is set in "columns devoted to 'Social Gossip.' " The "types spontaneously form her name, so often have the compositors set it up." Sanctioned by the printers' habitual use of typeface, the face of the type of the Beauty "enters upon a sort of official, almost civic existence. . . . In all countries where universal suffrage is the rule, it becomes necessary to speak to the people by means of pictures. They see everything as a whole, and naturally like coarse and striking things."

Not "coarse," however, in the manner of Mag and her friend seen on the cover of *The Masses*, where Stuart Davis made a deliberate political statement through his parody of the popular, yet reactionary, taste for banal pictorializations of American girls (figure 2.1). The "right" girls hold their place as the national type because their look prints up as being "American." However individualized the nuances of their actual appearance, their images must lend themselves to pictorial homogeneity and easy translation upon the page; they must also be "pretty."

Three years after Bourget's remarks about the symbiosis between social type and pictorial method demanded by the American public, James Fullarton Muirhead published *The Land of Contrast: A Briton's View of His American Kin*.[3] A professional compiler of handbooks on unfamiliar places, Muirhead wished to emphasize similarities between the transatlantic members of the Anglo-Saxon race. He was generally pleased with the likenesses he found, but he was most attentive about the wondrous new sights he encountered. What impressed Muirhead most was the "*relative* strikingness" of the American Girl. Like Bourget, he realized it was im-

2.1. Stuart Davis,
"Gee, Mag,
Think of Us Bein'
on a Magazine
Cover!" *The
Masses,* June
1913.

perative to try to understand her significance through the visible signs she presented her viewer.

"Compared to the appearances of the American girl in books written about the United States, that of Charles I's head in Mr. Dick's memorial [cited in Dickens' *David Copperfield*] might perhaps be almost called casual. . . . It need not be asserted," Muirhead continues, "that all the references to her are equally agreeable. . . . But the fact remains that almost every book on the United States contains a chapter devoted explicitly to the female citizen; and the inevitableness of the record must have some solid ground of reason behind or below it."

The Marquis de Chastellux, Moreau de St. Méry, Hector St. John de Crèvecoeur, and Alexis de Tocqueville are but four of the early travelers in the America of the colonial period and the days of the early republic who attested to what Muirhead would later declare was the "inevitableness of the record." Why observers from abroad were compelled to write about the female presence, and why he himself believes he must continue the tradition, Muirhead sets out to discover.

Observers have usually found it possible to write books on the social and economical traits of other countries without a parade of petticoats in the headlines. This is not to say that one can ignore one-half of society in the writing of it; but if you search the table of contents of such books as Mr. Philip Hamerton's charming "French and English," or Mr. T. H. S. Escott's "England: Its People, Polity, and Pursuits," you will not find the words "woman" or "girl," or any equivalent for them. But the writer on the United States seems irresistibly compelled to give woman all the coordinate importance which is implied by the prominence of capital letters and separate chapters.

Muirhead insists that the visibility given women within the accounts of foreigners is not "a phase of the 'woman question,' technically so called. It has no direct reference to the woman as voter, as doctor, as lawyer, as the competitor of man; the subject of interest is woman as woman, the *Ding an sich* of German philosophical slang."

The focus, then, is upon the woman as type, with the type given full acknowledgment as that means by which one comes to "know America."

The European visitor to the United States *has* to write about American women because they bulk so largely in his view, because they seem essentially so prominent a feature of American life, because their *relative* importance and interest impress him as greater than those of women in the lands of the Old World, *because they seem to him to embody in so eminent a measure that intangible quality of Americanism*, the existence, or indeed the possibility, of which is so hotly denied by some Americans. (My italics)

The "strikingness" of the young American woman, and her capacity for the embodiment of "intangible quality," are, to Muirhead's mind, precisely what serious students of American mores need to consult as a kind of combination Baedeker and Oxford English Dictionary. The iconography of the Girl spurs observers to use their own talents for visualization. Analogies proliferate; pedantry disappears in the excitement of interpreting images and projecting interpretations by means of the creation of still more images.

Here is an example. Muirhead concludes that "America" viewed through the transparent figure of the Girl means "opportunity"—the nation's refusal "to play second fiddle" because of "consciousness of efficiency." To confirm his belief in American self-confidence, he provides his own set of figures. He refers to the look of two caryatids which are on view at the Vatican. One of them, Muirhead says, represents America; the other is Great Britain. The American type follows the caryatid taken from the Erechtheum which "seems to bear the superincumbent architecture easily and securely, with her feet planted squarely and the main lines running vertically." In contrast, the English type is like a caryatid of a much later period. Feet "placed close together" and drapery folded in a "prevalence of curved lines," this is England summed up by its "air of insecurity."

Muirhead is no anthropologist. He is open to criticism for the sweep of his cultural assertions. But he knows enough to remark that observers like himself ought not to equate the atypical American woman with typical American habits of conduct. For this reason he is careful to avoid settling on the American heiress as the figure for primary examination. He recognizes that the heiress is the type favored by the popular press of the 1890s, by the writers of romances, and by popular illustrators, but he argues that rich young American women simply do not "look out on the world through genuinely American spectacles." They are "biased by a point of view which may be somewhat paradoxically termed the 'cosmopolitan-exclusive.' " To tap home his warning, Muirhead turns for confirmation to his generation's main iconographer of American literary types. "As Mr. Henry James puts it: 'After all, what one sees on a Newport piazza is not America; it is the back of Europe.' "

Indeed, this photograph (taken in 1903 by Rudolph Eickemeyer, Jr.) of Mrs. John Jacob Astor presents us with a splendid caryatid, pillar of a thoroughly Europeanized society, but not by a long shot the Girl of "opportunity" and "efficiency" (figure 2.2). Nor is this image of Mrs. Astor like the one painted by James McNeill Whistler in the 1870s and titled "Arrangement in Black and White, No. 1" (figure 2.3). Charles Freer, who purchased the painting in 1904, gave it the title "The Young American" and a description which likens her to Muirhead's notion of the American caryatid.[4] About "to step out of ivory darkness into an unknown world," the Girl shows "no sign of fear." She not only *fronts* her own nation, she is eager to *confront* Europe. She is Isabel Archer, not Mrs. Astor as Madame Merle.

Visitors from abroad made a genuine effort to study the young American woman so that they might imbibe "that intangible quality of Americanism." But could they do this without uncritically worshiping the caryatids they met or without hating what they found? Surely they had to protect themselves from oversimplifying the equation between the culture and the Girl through recognizing there were as many types as there were strands to the social weave. As a native, Charles Dana Gibson believed he knew exactly what to do with American females. "Studies in Expression" sets out a gallery of female types responding to a courtroom drama (figure 2.4). But watch Gibson take the English type and place it within a London theater (figure 2.5). The same bony, pinch-mouthed, elongated countenances fill the picture, no matter the difference in emotions or class status each figure represents. What if visitors to the United States falsified this country's culture as, perhaps, Gibson simplified England's?

Muirhead's repertoire of American types was somewhat meager. The writer of the 1890s who offered the most extensive list was Paul Bourget, analyst of the Beauty, the Girl of Ideas, the Tomboy, and the Collector.[5] Bourget was also more alert than Muirhead to the problems which accompany the advantages of employing cultural categories. He insisted that each classification he listed is an "individ-

NATIONAL MUSEUM OF AMERICAN HISTORY

2.2. Rudolf Eickemeyer, Jr., "Mrs.
John Jacob Astor" (1903).

2.3. James Abbott McNeill Whistler,
"Arrangement in Black and
White, No. 1: The Young Ameri-
can" (1873–1878).

FREER GALLERY OF ART

uality . . . amply developed" only when watched over the course of time. Inevitably, types "work themselves out" into meaning, but any "traveller of a few months'
experience" was beset by the lack of time needed for detecting individuality "in
even the most general way."

As we follow Bourget's attempt to isolate his data, we are led to a valuable
definition and working principle for analysis of the type: the American Girl is the
individual young American woman snatched out of time. The type is momentarily

2.4. Charles Dana Gibson, "Studies in Expression. When Women Are Jurors," *Life*, October 23, 1902.

2.5. Charles Dana Gibson, "In a London Theatre," *Life*, April 9, 1896.

fixed in place by the observer's stare. Such fixity keeps her this side of full development (and thereby without the complete Reality that Charles Sanders Peirce believed came only "in the long run"). But her time-free quality is also what guarantees that the Girl's signs as such can be seen and read with a certain accuracy and some gain in the understanding of her iconic reference.

Hjalmar Hjorth Boyesen, the Norwegian novelist and essayist who came to the United States in 1869 and stayed on to teach at Columbia University, was confident that he could extract authoritative meaning through his study of types of the American female.[6] Like Bourget, he tried to be careful about rendering the *variety*—therefore, the particularity—of those types. The foreign observer's need to differentiate was itself an indication of the special quality of the American female. When Boyesen set Americans over against the peoples of England and Germany, he found the women to "have more vivacity, more character, more freedom of speech and manners. . . . They have a more distinct, and as a rule a more piquant, flavor of personality. They are not merely specimens of the feminine gender more or less attractive, and labelled for the sake of convenience Minnie, Jennie, or Fannie, but they are primarily Minnie and Jennie and Fannie . . . endowed with and modified by their feminine gender.''

The Englishman James Muirhead could agree with Bourget and Boyesen on the matter of individuality—that paradoxical basis by which generalizations could be made about the Girl.

The American girl . . . strikes me as individual, as varied. In England when we meet a girl in a ball-room we can generally—not always—"place" her after a few minutes' talk, she belongs to a set of which you remember to have already met a volume or two. . . . In the United States every new girl is a new sensation. Society consists of a series of surprises. Expectation is continually piqued. A and B and C do not help you to induce D; when you reach Z you *may* imagine you find a slight trace of reincarnation.[7]

But of the three foreign visitors—Muirhead, Boyesen, and Bourget—it is Bourget who emphasizes the need to recognize the range of individualism that continually folds and unfolds within the boundaries of the type. He is also able to identify two further reasons why misreadings are often made of the Girl. First, most foreign visitors do not bother to look at her assiduously enough. Second, the girls out of whom the Girl is formulated make sustained looking difficult because of their freedom of action.

At first glance this absolute freedom makes all the young girls look alike. They are the model after whom many authors—some of them very distinguished, but none of whom has taken the trouble to come here—have composed the type which has become classical with us,—the American woman of the romance and the theatre. Our visitors manufacture her of the simplest possible materials,—very bad manners upon a background of simplicity; there you have the walking doll.[8]

It is the Walking Doll, the Daisy Miller type, Bourget notes, that has been accepted as the dominant American female type. Her supremely self-confident independence offers the only "America" taken up by most observers; she is the one who has become the reigning sign for the nation's culture. Yet this is the type who immediately causes confusion in the minds of the very people who wish to simplify the process of "knowing Americans."

Most males, for instance, faced the danger of misconstruing the Girl's goodness for impropriety. There was another danger they did not acknowledge as readily— that they would pass over what was *not* goodness in their eagerness to reinterpret "free American ways" as a kind of raw innocence. Observers of the Girl seemed willing to sink back upon the comforting conclusion "She was good-natured, generous to a fault, and brimming with energy."[9] And when they added, "She recognized no law except her own sovereign will," they stopped short of asking what the social consequences might be of the release of such energy and will upon the world by the Girl or the nation she stood for. If many men viewed individual American women as a possible source for social upheavals because of their willfulness, think of the epistemological problems the Girl provoked when viewed as a national symbol. How can a bright young thing help society if she flaunts its conventions? And can a literary or pictorial type be useful to its interpreters if it does not know its place by remaining obedient to accepted formal expectations? The presence of headstrong, independent will undermines the very foundation of the literary or visual genre of type, as much as it does the social principles upon which "true womanhood" is founded. After all, the type as an aesthetic and philosophical category was joined with the idea of the woman's sphere to represent the virtues of fixity, timelessness, and subservience to the normative mold. Yet here was the type of the American Girl—volatile, unpredictable, a blur of will-strong emotion and motion, upsetting the applecarts alike of writers, artists, and cultural reporters.

Paul Bourget reported on a nation which was extraordinarily confident that what it desired it could get, which is exactly what the Girl—its image—believed in for herself. The pictorial America observed by H. H. Boyesen was a different place with different women—those who aspired without hope of receiving satisfaction. The images emphasized by the Frenchman and the Norwegian are in striking contrast, but actually the two men were looking at the top and flip side of the same coin of the realm. *Will* that expects gratification comes in the image of the enchanting young American Girl as the Beautiful Charmer. *Will* that resigns itself to loss is imaged by the wan American female typified by the New England Woman at her most feeble.

In 1890 Boyesen took Kate Stephens' New England Woman and called her more generally "the Aspiring Woman."[10] "She is frequently anaemic, and in New England inclines to be flat-chested. The vigor of her physical life usually leaves much to be desired; the poverty of diet in ascetic ancestors has often reduced her vitality, making her undervalue the concerns of the flesh, and overvalue the relative importance of the things of the spirit."

The Aspiring Woman does not pay attention to her external appearance, but Boyesen as an earnest interpreter of visible types does because he wishes to define her soul. Whatever appearance this type takes (and there are several since it "is so extensive and numerous a species"), there is "one trait, however, which [these women] all have in common: they are all bent upon improving themselves." In fact, if there is "any single trait which radically distinguished American society, as a whole, from European society, it is a universal hopefulness and aspiration." Bourget, agreeing, would then have gone on to declare it was the American women who got what they aspired to. In contrast, Boyesen believed it was the males in America who aspire and attain, but not the women. To Boyesen, the latter group are "animated by an ambition which in many cases was pathetic. I met, during my sojourn in Ohio and Illinois, daughters of farmers and mechanics who were cultivating themselves in secret, groping their way most pitifully, without help or guidance."

Boyesen does not focus, as Bourget does, upon the Beauty, the woman who gives herself over to resignation once she has willed and won the supreme social prize of marriage. Boyesen studies the Souls—aging, anemic women of toil who are stirred by an ambition of the soul which never concedes defeat. Once the Beauty in her visibility goes down in defeat to the married state, her image is lost to the tabloids and the public which dotes upon the *possibilities* only open to unwed girls. In contrast, the invisible Souls of Boyesen's concern are overlooked, first and last. But Boyesen sees them, and sees them as contributing "something valuable" to American life. "When the failure is, at last, tacitly acknowledged and the hope of success abandoned, something yet remains, which is beyond the reach of hostile critics and an indifferent public. This may be a mere heightened self-respect, with a touch of defiance, or it may be the lifting of the character to a higher plane than it would have reached without the futile aspiration."

Kate Stephens and the feminists argued that the will of frustrated "New Englandish" women, knotting in upon itself, would reassert itself fruitfully if given expression through the suffrage movement. Boyesen cannot agree. He looks at the group of political activists contained within his larger category of aspiring women. What he finds there only stirs more pity. "Some few have vigorous, well-trained intellects and naturally feel their superiority to the majority of men with whom they associate. They then rashly conclude that women, as a rule, are the intellectual superiors to men, or would be if the same opportunities of education were afforded them; and presently we find them in woman-suffrage conventions, petitioning legislatures and agitating for social reform."

Boyesen pauses. He genuinely wants to be fair about this new type—the American type—but he cannot keep from pressing the point that the very quality of aspiration he most appreciates is exactly what these women will forgo if they insist upon their political ambitions. His admiration forms the basis of what he most fears. "Though I do not sympathize with some of their aims, I cannot but admire their intrepidity, their fortitude, their noble enthusiasm. . . . The influence of their work is good, and we could ill afford to dispense with it. It is not to be denied, however, that they forfeit much of *that charm which, in the present condition of the world, constitutes to the benighted male the chief attraction of the sex.*" (my italics).

Boyesen indicates a conflict he considers to be inevitable—one whose nature is of great importance to any discussion of the cultural images attributed to American women. He is talking about *desire*. He believes that women who place the energy of their aspirations upon getting the vote fail to win what they crave even more: marriage and home. Assertion of the will to gain social equality with men is made at the tragic cost of the means—charm—by which women achieve the private gain of love. The female will that denies the need to be charming comes into conflict with the desire of males to be charmed. Getting the vote entails losing love and marriage. "I believe there is inherent in all women what may be called, without invidious inference, *a yearning for the commonplace—for the normal lot.* Those who protest most strenuously against the injustice of society to their sex, are as a rule willing to exchange their uncomfortable prominence for the contented obscurity of a domestic hearth" (my italics).

Boyesen's imagination cannot *perceive* a radically different type of American woman, one who would satisfy her twin desires for public equality and personal satisfaction. He cannot *know* the New Woman as a charmer (with or without roses at her breast), or as the vigorous outdoors girl who constructs a happy life by cycling from the polls to her place of employment, then home to her hearthside. He can only *see* what the artist for the *New York World* saw in 1895: a stern, forbidding unmarriageable type (see figure 1.44). As the result of what he is limited to seeing, what Boyesen understands about the New Woman is also limited. He believes that she does not wish to be different from the way women have "always been." She wants to confirm an ageless norm—the type of the Eternal Woman. Boyesen's New Woman holds to the term "type" in its original, Platonistic sense and thereby contradicts herself profoundly. To him she is, deep down, an unyielding form that possesses its identity so fully it has nowhere else to go.

Boyesen was not of the party of Charles Sanders Peirce. Peirce investigated Reality by reference to forms which evolved and altered with the course of cosmic development. Boyesen's American female was predicated on Platonic types which rejected the onward roll of the national scene that inflicted change upon all cultural forms. As far as Boyesen was concerned, the essential desire of the American woman was for invisibility, for self-absorption back into the common fact. She did not desire a life of conspicuous spectacle and the visible fulfillment of social aspirations.

When Boyesen wrote his reports in 1890 the New Woman in America was one of the things that was especially new about being American, but he was incapable of comprehending this kind of newness. The types he picked out to analyze were not types in the authentic American sense. Boyesen's version of the so-called American New Woman is actually a model displaced from Europe—the Bluestocking; although he named her as the best sign for understanding contemporary American society, she limited him to terms appropriate to the Continent. Boyesen missed the point that the New World society requires modes of pictorialization that emphasize what is new and visible. By failing to perceive correctly, Boyesen failed to conceive of a volatile culture in which seemingly unchanging universals are constantly overwhelmed by the particulars of history. What is worse, he was dead off the mark when it came to responding to one of the peculiarities of American desire—its craving for what *flows onward*.

Margaret Deland concluded her essay of 1910 on the New Woman with the words "Do not haste. Do not hold back." In 1890 Boyesen wound down his own essay with a similar admonition. Honor stasis, he says. Stay with a life that keeps within the normal development of "the national flavor." Develop in ways that do not attach one to change. Obviously, Boyesen is starting to contradict himself by making two mutually exclusive demands. He states that the type of the American Girl must remain what the female has always been. At the same time, he calls up the type as representative of a country caught up in events which jerk it away from

its previous forms. The American female type must satisfy its desires through remaining unexceptional and inconspicuous. At the same time the type must somehow image an American culture fated to be different and visible.

Contradictions of the kind Boyesen made became an inevitable part of the process of analysis late-nineteenth-century observers brought to bear upon the contradictory nature of the American scene. But over "the long run" (as Peirce would
say), patterns were working themselves toward a sort of clarity. Once the dust had
settled, those who came along later usually detected which side of the cultural
contradiction had taken command. (Not as a matter of which side was truer, but
rather which had the strength to survive.) Boyesen's belief in the type of the American female as the eternal form of stasis fell away before the forces of change.
Carried forward by the flow was the type of the Girl who really means what she
represents: to be different, to be visible, to be "American."

To speak of the American Girl and the culture she represents is of necessity to
speak of time, change, and evolutionary theory in terms of visible signs. In turn,
this entails talk of race, gender, and the eugenics of type.

Discussion about the look of the American Girl began to turn nervous during the
1890s and the early years of the twentieth century. It became imperative to classify
what it was right for the Girl to be and to keep lists of the biological factors threatening her role as the nation's primary means for identifying its values to the world.
Fear grew that the Girl might falter under the forces of change and come to image
irregular sexual traits and faulty racial stock. If this happened, the figure of hope
for America's future would be transformed into an image foreshadowing the end
of all that was good in the culture (biological and social). The American Girl
could only be as fine as she looked, and looking fine meant looking like the WASP
Princess (figure 2.6).

As it was sweepingly referred to by the rank and file, evolutionary theory was a
mental mix of the very new and the very old. Among the oldest elements claiming
current attention was an updated version of the pseudoscience of physiognomy
that had made its somewhat smarmy way from classical times through the Middle
Ages and into the nineteenth century. By 1900, hand-me-down notions concerning
the classification of "the best types" were still relying on the eighteenth-century
principles authorized by Johann Casper Lavater, the Swiss pastor whose *Essays on
Physiognomy* repopularized the ancient belief that external appearance is governed by inner moral qualities.[11]

Condescending as Lavater's essays now appear, their main purpose had been the
promotion of love. In Lavater's mind, the act of classifying racial types leads to
knowing the world's peoples in all their diversity; and to know is tantamount to
loving.[12] It also promised a future of hope through Lavater's conviction that all
members of the human race would eventually share the glad fate of "becoming
Apollo." (Figure 2.7 details twelve of the stages in the ascent from frog to god.)

One hundred years later the text and pictures in the mid-ninteenth-century geo-

2.6. Charles Dana Gibson, untitled, from *The Social Ladder* (c.1901–1902).

graphies used in the instruction of American schoolchildren took for granted that only one world race—the Caucasian—would ever attain the look of the Apollo Belvedere (figure 2.8). This illustration from Arnold Guyot's text of 1866 shows all other races forever set apart from the central and superior stem.[13] The route through biological history taken by the female physiognomy was just as clear. A textbook illustration of 1878 places the ideal woman at the center of the wheel, morally and genetically (figure 2.9). Around her rotate masculine deviations from the racial norm she sets. No classical statue is needed as her prototype. This perfect maiden could have stepped out of any popular American novel of the decade. The particulars of her physical appearance reflect the notions of feminine beauty held in the 1870s—particulars different in detail from those praised by the end of the century (see figure 2.6).[14] However, the inward moral qualities which the female image represented to its own generation remained resolutely Aryan.

Certain pressures were exerted in the 1890s to extend the accreditation granted to the ideal female type. Enlightened moral and intellectual reasons for inclusivity were slow in coming, as we shall see; but if nothing else, there were strong commercial arguments for tolerance in the matter of who might qualify as the American Girl. The circulation of the popular press depended on its ability to attract the favor of the immigrant groups, especially in the face of the fact that the latter were setting up their own native-language papers. The Pulitzer and Hearst publications could hardly go too far in making derogatory comments or printing offensive pictures that excluded the new people from what those same papers proposed American life had to offer to everyone. If the chance to become the American Girl was part of the bright promise, then that promise had to be open to all pretty young women who might "pass" socially, economically, or racially for the true type.

Figure 2.10 is taken from William Randolph Hearst's *New York Journal* of January 12, 1896. Gertrude Vanderbilt (descendant of a poor, uneducated immigrant from the Netherlands) is visually paired with Bertha Krieg of the Bowery (most likely German in origin, perhaps Jewish as well, although no details of her lineage are given). The picture and the accompanying article joins them (and separates

2.7. From Lavater, *Essays on Physiognomy* (1804).

them subtly) by posing the catchy headline question "Which Is the American Princess?" This is no trivial question, as the lead-in indicates. "A Type Worthy of Earnest Study and Respectful Admiration" is placed before the readers as an appellation equally applicable to the young woman "whose father is as powerful as king"

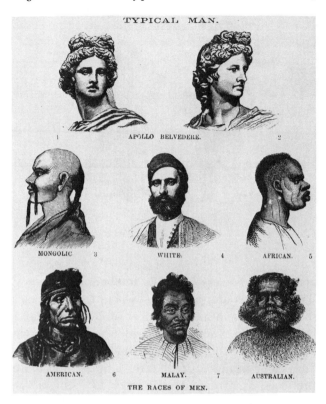

2.8. "Typical Man," from Guyot, *Physical Geography* (1866).

2.9. "The Races of Men," from Von Steinwehr and Brinton, *An Intermediate Geography* (1878).

2.10. "Which Is the American Princess?" *New York Journal*, January 12, 1896.

and to "the Bowery Girl." By implication, those who are not of the socioeconomic Vanderbilt set are invited to associate their lives, somewhat circuitously, with the social power and aesthetic chic of Fifth Avenue. In turn, through the force of the headlines and the pictorial evidence, Bertha Krieg (the type of most of those who bought the *Journal*) is likened by implication to the young woman who has been "in place" in the United States long enough to qualify, according to the biases of the 1890s, as a true native; likened to "being a Vanderbilt"—one who, through the hard work expected of all who became Americanized, now enjoys the accumulation of fortune and social prestige initiated by her ancestors, the lowly Van der Bilts.

The 1896 *Journal* story points up the moral imperatives required of American Princesses. They differ of course from Vanderbilt to Krieg. Gertrude is "No Pampered Darling of Fashion." This "millionaire's child" is innately charitable, accomplished, and "above all, thoroughly American." Bertha, on the other hand, is still in the early stages of contending for the title of American Princess; still engaged in "brave struggle" as the oldest of seven children of a widowed mother. Not a dangerous radical of the kind feared by the nativists, Bertha is "a self-respecting maiden, who is contented with her lot and does not envy Miss Vanderbilt a bit." As a reward for her commitment to "pluck" (as her boss at the dry-goods shop calls it) and apolitical sentiments, this daughter of relatively recent immigrant stock wins the right to pose prettily next to the millionaire's child, notwithstanding the distance that separates her in the evolutionary spectrum from the Vanderbilt ideal.

Berthas are accepted when the mental arrows of their aspirations fly in the correct direction. They want *to be like* Gertrude precisely because they are now what the Vanderbilts once were and because they may yet attain what the Vanderbilt heiress now possesses. Nor do they merely covet the economic status held by the plutocracy. Fortunately not, since doing so might involve political upheavals and the revolutionary overthrow of the status quo. Bowery Girls take the proper tone by aspiring to the aesthetic of the American Girl which can be copied by way of cheap versions of expensive clothes and by imitating, gratis, Fifth Avenue poses and gestures.

What luck that it is Gertrude Vanderbilt who provides the visible sign for an immigrant girl to emulate in her evolutionary climb. Both the lead caption and the printed text of the *Journal* article bear this out. Gertrude is an *American* (thus, democratic) Princess. Had she been a monarchist of the imagination, someone who slavishly followed the European manner (standing with her back to the United States like Mrs. John Jacob Astor, or like her cousin Consuelo, married a year earlier to the Marlborough title), the model she set for the American lower classes would be of questionable social value. For in Europe the only way for the lower-class girls to become princesses is to throw bombs and to overrun palaces.

Do not be misled, however, by the presence, side by side, of Gertrude and Bertha. Do not think that just anyone was invited by the Hearsts and the Pulitzers into the classification "the American Girl." Bertha Krieg would not fit the appointed type if there were something wrong in her appearance; not in a society that placed increased emphasis upon physiognomy as the direct reflection of the health of one's mind, one's soul, and one's biological stamina. The Girl had, at the very least, to *look like* the best breeding stock. Only then could she hope to sustain her position as a representative of a nation dedicated to the highest ideals.

Still more was exacted of the Girl's appearance. She had to be visibly feminine, thus eminently marriageable, lest the truth, goodness, and beauty she emblematized go to waste and the "Americanness" of her bloodline be subsumed by the unassimilable alien hordes proliferating like rabbits in slum neighborhoods and prairie towns.[15]

The American Girl is not the type of the Mother. She stands before us in her crystalline, virginal state, not in that later, more shadowy state of fecundity. But her physical suitability, the guarantee that the future of the United States will be populated by the right kind of Americans, is always implied. One day, the immigrant girls currently pictorialized as participants in the aesthetics of assimilation might be admitted into the imagined realm of American motherhood; just now, they are safely imaged as long as they remain unmarried. In contrast, take this Russian Jewess, newly arrived at Ellis Island, photographed by Lewis Hine in 1905 (figure 2.11). However, lovely of face and form, this young woman is *visually* too close to her un-American origins to be acceptable. She has no imagined present as the American Girl and no imagined future as the Mother of Americans. Until she can evolve into the likes of Bertha Krieg, she is deprived, imaginatively, of a future in which she figures through marriage and motherhood as "being American."

It is necessary to review certain of the particulars which influenced the selection of the physical norms by which "Americanness" was designated at the turn of the century and by which racial and ethnic deviance was determined. This story—painful and embarrassing to all concerned—is a familiar one, for who has escaped

2.11. Lewis Hine, "Russian Jewess" (1905).

its hurts or its guilts? But some of the texts and illustrations spread abroad in the land during the 1890s require our attention at this point. Only with an immediate understanding of the potent force granted to those signs by which "the best types" were supposedly read with ease by the native-born is it possible to conceive the national significance credited to the various sanctioned images of the American Girl.

Images of males rule most of the material (verbal and pictorial) introduced in the following section because this is how the physiognomical treatises of the time chose to present their arguments. But deeply implied in the words and pictures dedicated to the definition of the correct American masculine type is the sexual role accorded to the American female as mother, wife, and daughter. The nation run by American men would continue to be strong and worthy through the perpetuation of the right bloodlines. It was imperative that women, who were the only guarantee of racial continuity, fit the same racially attractive categories exacted of the men. The desired end was a nation that rested solidly on fine American male stock; the means were women who passed the test of the type exemplified by the American Girl.

The urge to classify all the world's many things is an impulse which has received encouragement from science ever since Aristotle. It grew stronger under the hands of Linnaeus and Buffon. By the mid-nineteenth century, botany, zoology, anthropology, and medicine were among the disciplines devoted to marking the formal boundaries that separate one organism from another. (The social sciences with their avidity for categorizing behavioral patterns were already elbowing their way forward with statistics, charts, and lists of norms and averages.) By the final decades of the nineteenth century whatever "republican" resistance there might previously have been to ranking classes in comparative terms of "better" and "worse" was fast breaking down in America.

The relatively benign attitude held by Johann Casper Lavater in the 1770s had changed radically by the 1890s. The Swiss pastor and amateur dabbler in the science of interpreting external bodily forms equated the act of classification with knowing, appreciating, and (perhaps) loving. Latter-day adherents of physiognomy stopped short after completing the first two steps: classifying and knowing. Investigative science, not romantic aesthetics or social ethics, became the standard to emulate, although investigative science was hardly as objective in its evaluations as its advocates insisted it was.[16] Once the polemicists of physiognomy (highly questionable in its own status as a scientific discipline) took over in America, the formula went like this: one classifies in terms of what one already knows the truth to be. In the description of sexual and racial differences, this meant an emphasis upon physical traits that appeared to distinguish superior from inferior types; it meant favorable response to external signs which seemed familiar and unfavorable reactions to those which did not.[17]

By the end of the century many nativists were convinced that true Americans could only be produced by the races which had always been considered "the best"—those members of the northern European club very loosely termed "Anglo-Saxon." Others were not rabid on the subject, though they indicated their aesthetic preferences for the "classical" or "English" look which the Gibson Girl was said to convey with brilliance, even while patently a daughter of the Declaration of Independence which had freed the colonies from British rule. As advocates of the melting-pot theory, the moderates envisioned a future in which a diversity of settlers—legatees of age-old Teutonic, Nordic, Norman, and English values, and practitioners of a mix of Christian beliefs—would live together in mutual confidence. They agreed with the gist of the argument set down a century earlier by Hector St. John de Crèvecoeur. *Letters from an American Farmer* had rejoiced in the idea of the assimilation of ethnic groups as diverse as Germans, Swedes, or Scots; it saw only good resulting from Protestant denominations placed next to the more outré Roman Catholic or Quaker persuasions. The happy result would be a serene society based on a citizenry indifferent to difference. It was assumed that the melting pot would simmer away without mishap because these were people unalike in degree, not in kind. All were Christian. All came from one part or another of northern Europe. All hastened to take up English as their language and Great Britain as the source of their mores.

The easygoing methods for "making an American" proposed by Hector St. John de Crèvecoeur had a certain staying power through the end of the nineteenth century, although they did not solve "the Irish problem." Ironically, that problem had been partially the result of the active encouragement by Columbia, the ultimate American Girl, who pressed the lowly bog trotter to emigrate with his family to a New World of hope (figure 2.12). Once the Irish arrived in mid-century, however, they quickly became part of the larger "servant problem"—the disruption caused by monkeylike creatures who joined with apelike Negroes to make the lives of middle-class homemakers unbearable. The only solution to *that* problem was for the American Girl with her wit and know-how to forgo servants entirely; to take up the newest Eureka Mop and beat out the inferior races in the race toward efficiency and cleanliness which only she was racially fit to win (figure 2.13). In 1891 the Irish are still pictured as mired in the historic bog. Figure 2.14 fixes the Irish physiognomy in that limbo inhabited by those of "Imaginativeness Small." Contrast that face with Lamartine's, a member of one of the European races favored by "largeness of Brain form" and "a highly sensational organization."[18]

But (some agreed) the Irish—Catholics and Celts though they were—were at least *imaginatively* assimilable. Abbott Thayer's 1897 portrait of Bessie Price, the young servant girl recently arrived from Ireland to take service in the Thayer household, endows Bessie's face with the moral seriousness and physical attractiveness generally reserved for native-born Americans (figure 2.15). And Charles Dana Gibson's drawings give a piquancy of charm to his young Irish women often absent in his renditions of the more aloof "English" type (figure 2.16). But these young Irish women were northern European, Caucasian, and Christian, after all.

2.12. Cusachs, "Columbia," *The Daily Graphic*, January 13, 1880.

The notion of their evolution into the true American type could be countenanced. It was all the others—the Indians, Negroes, Mediterraneans, Asians, Slavs, and Jews—who could not be conceived of as being Americans.

Physiognomy received the flush of renewed interest in the United States at the moment when the northern European balance of the population was altered by the push of the "wrong" types after the 1880s; by types that trundled ashore, loaded down by the baggage of unfamiliar languages, customs, religions, and genes, under the watchful eye of the colossal American Girl set on her pedestal since 1886 in New York's harbor. An immediate consequence of the new waves of immigration was an increase in the anxious theorizing needed to support the American Girl as the WASP icon. Not a little nastiness was involved in the creation of the Girl. In order to love her for the normalcy she represented (aesthetic, moral, and genetic),

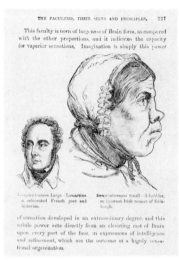

2.13. "The Great 'Scrub' Race" (1870).

2.14. From Simms, *Physiognomy Illustrated* (1891).

other attributes—linked to deviant races and aberrant sexual natures—had to be held in contempt and trepidation.

In the United States of the 1890s only the Indians had not come from somewhere else. Since there had never been a time when Indians had not lived within the American landscape, they were the only true "native Americans." But they were unrecognized as American by the nativists because their ahistorical, acultural barbarism placed them beyond the pale of civilized peoples. By limiting the "right" blood to the settlers of the New England colonies and the Virginia plantations who had *entered into* American history at just the right moment (and by ignoring the presence of ethnic groups other than those enclosed within the vague but popular term "Anglo-Saxon"), the origin of the preferred American type was firmly located in history.[19] Furthermore, it was assumed that this historical happenstance of correct timing continued to mark the faces of succeeding generations. The nature of that readable sign was constantly designated as "regularity."

2.15. Abbott Handerson
Thayer, "Portrait of Bessie
Price" (1897).

COURTESY OF HENRY C. WHITE

Anyone who has attended a meeting of the Daughters of the American Revolution or examined the physiognomical portraits painted by Norman Rockwell knows
full well that regularity sits uneasily, if at all, upon "American" faces. According
to the wisdom of the times, however, authentic citizens were registered in the
nativists' American Kennel Club for all to see because their features approximated
the contours sanctioned by neoclassical art. Physiognomical "regularity" meant

2.16. Charles Dana Gibson, "The Wearing of the Green," from *Other People* (1911).

the straight, slender nose, the full yet controlled line of the lips, and the high "pure" brow made familiar from endless plaster casts of Greek statuary. Features which followed these standards indicated, by a leap of faith in the accepted racial theory, a "regularity" that very few Carters, Lowells, Rhinelanders, Smiths, or Joneses actually possessed. This fact did not, however, diminish belief in the visual ideal that supposedly lay, like a shadowy Platonic form, behind the ordinary diversity of such faces.

Remarks taken from *The Bazar Book of Decorum* of 1870 reflect an early preference for the sharp-edged symmetry that was assumed to be the privilege of the native-born physiognomy; they make clear a dislike of the irregularities thought typical of imported peasant dough. The "decorum" of features depicted here would become an obsession with many by 1900.[20]

It is common for foreigners to praise our people for their good looks, and the American face is certainly remarkable for its regularity. It seldom presents those extraordinary deviations from the classical ideal so frequently observed in foreigners. Those monstrous developments of the features, which are not seldom found in the German or Irish countenance, and approximate it to the various types of the lower animals, are rare among native-born Americans. As people of all nations come hither, we have, of course, every kind of face. There are, accordingly, all varieties of disproportion and degrees of ugliness to be occasionally seen. These, such as the low heads and crumpled faces which look as if they had been squashed in the making; the nasal appendages fleshly and pendent, like abortive elephants' trunks; the ears tumid and misshapen as gigantic oysters; the thick lips, eviscerated mouths, and projecting under jaws, are generally of foreign importation.

The author of this gem of grotesquerie, Robert Tomes, then sums up the advantages gained when a nation has a clear pictorial criterion as its guide to racial "decorum." "Compare the peasant face of Europe with that of working people of this country. The former appears like a mass of dough rolled into a uniform surface; the latter is full of lines, distinct and expressive as those of a steel engraving."

When the crudities of bake-oven gingerbread men were set over against the refinements of the steel engraving (the best art that people with good taste might place in their parlors), the aesthetic contest was easily won by the American face.

While Daniel Boorstin is discussing the processes of assimilation by which many of the new immigrants tried to fit into the American warp, he remarks that "they took on the protective coloration" of native speech, clothing, and customs. Millions disappeared from view as "foreigners." They became "featureless figures" instead.[21] But some did not escape all the way into invisibility. Those were the people whom the nativists set to *featuring* in strongly pictorial terms.

In 1891 and 1910 three books were published (among many of their kind) which analyzed "the others" and found them wanting in the looks attributed to representatives of the "best"—the "American"—type. The first of the three was the doing of the Reverend Josiah Strong, general secretary of the Evangelical Alliance for the United States, New York. *Our Country: Its Possible Future and Its Present Crisis* was originally published in 1885 under the auspices of the American Home Missionary Society. Strong revised his argument in 1891; the new edition incorporated statistics for the physical stature of recent arrivals to the United States which he borrowed from the 1890 government census. Strong argued that these figures upheld his case that native stock would be adversely affected if the genetic and moral effects of the foreign horde were not stopped in time.

True to his name, Strong favored "strong races."[22] Unlike those who believed that Americans were attaining "civilization" at the cost of the strength of their nerves, Strong associated "the finest nervous organization" with "the highest civilization" and increased physical "scale of sizes"—then referred all three to the kinds of racial stock of which he approved. He wrote at length about the amalgam of "Celt and Gaul, Welshman and Irishman, Frisian and Flamand, French Huguenot and German Palatine" that would take the United States toward greatness. To back his cautious ecumenism, Strong quotes Herbert Spencer. "From biological truths it is to be inferred that the eventual mixture of the allied varieties of the Aryan race, forming the population, will be to produce a more powerful type of man than has hitherto existed, and a type of man more plastic, more adaptable, more capable of undergoing the modifications needful for complete social life."

The crucial distinction Strong wants to make is this: "the Aryan race" bears up under the arduous voyage across the ocean; its men survive and prevail. As for the non-Aryan, once his "old associations are broken," he will "sink to a lower moral level." When transplanted "from a forest to an open prairie . . . he is smitten with the blast of temptation." Rather than being transformed, as is the Aryan, into that better, "more powerful type" common to America, the non-Aryan who survives the ocean voyage pays back his host country with crime, disease, drunkenness, socialism, Mormonism, Roman Catholicism, and tobacco.

The Reverend Josiah Strong's position was hardly new or news by 1891. Relying solely on the evidence of his theories, it would be difficult to locate him exactly in time. What marks him as one of the pseudo social scientists of the tag end of the nineteenth century is Strong's constant referral to statistics of bodily strength or weakness and the way his racist rhetoric combines mathematical abstractions with the pulpit language of militant mission.[23]

Physiognomy Illustrated was published in its sixth edition by Joseph Simms the same year as the 1891 edition of Josiah Strong's *Our Country*. Its message, first launched in 1874, continues to speak to the 1890s, but Simms' particular use of verbal and visual pictorializations gives away the fact of its slightly earlier origins. By underscoring the way strangers and friends appear to the mind's eye, Simms—like Strong—separates the strong from the weak. But Strong reads bodies as a mathematician. Simms, who likens faces to landscapes and portraits, reads appearances after the manner of a finicky art critic.[24]

Through Joseph Simms' *Physiognomy Illustrated; or, Nature's Revelations of Character: A Description of the Mental, Moral, and Volitive Dispositions of Mankind, as Manifested in the Human Form and Countenance*, readers learn that Indians are stupid; the mere juxtaposition of their faces next to Samuel Clemens reveals this as a fact (figure 2.17).[25] One could *see* that the white child is already on his way to success in the American vein, while the Negro boy is fixed in his inborn ignorance (figure 2.18). Simms' written text is somewhat difficult to comprehend because of his penchant for the jargon of a primitive brand of the social sciences and the labels of classification he continually coins. In contrast, the biases behind the crudely drawn pictures are read all too easily.

V. G. Rocine's *Heads, Faces, Types, Races* was published in 1910. Rocine takes Simms' and Strong's notions of the "folkways" of ethnocentrism nineteen years farther along the route toward the nativists' uncurbed vilification of racial types.[26] Strong wanted to save America's maleness by protecting its physical and political stature. Simms wanted to insure the nation's moral tone. Rocine wants to be certain that the right people are in charge of making the country's money.

In personal appearance (balding and unbearded)[27] and in prose style (short, snappy sentences; pithy title), Rocine is the "new" physiognomist. Gone are the elaborate paragraphs and mid-nineteenth-century metaphors for moral uplift that forestall the speed-reading of Simms' earnest book. Simms' ropy sentences, like Strong's evangelical exhortations, are replaced by the punch of Rocine's on-your-toes approach to success.[28] Rocine's book intends to spread the word that "brain philosophy" can profit artists, doctors, ministers, parents, politicians, teachers, and—especially—salesmen. The book's definition of success is simple. Be one of the right kind, and be smart at knowing which of the competition is of the wrong kind.

The lessons start from the first page, but in case the readers of Rocine's book are not as bright as they might be, lesson 29 makes it all come clear. Being the type of "the true American" means *not* being the Semite or the Turanian, those types who are "disinclined for culture, refinement, manners and the polite arts" and capable of neither "society life nor progress." Indeed, the worst accusation which Rocine can make against the non-Aryan (his favorite term for those of inferior status) is

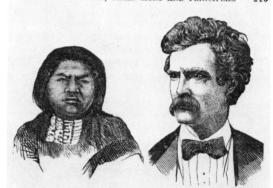

THE FACULTIES, THEIR SIGNS AND PRINCIPLES.　215

Salitiveness Small—Ute Indian, of Salt Lake, as witless as a dry stump.

Salitiveness Large — Mark Twain, author of "Innocents Abroad," and several other amusing works.

SUBLIMITASITY.—ADMIRATION OF THE SUBLIME.

THE EXPANSIVE SWELLING OF THE SOUL THAT APPRECIATES THE ELEVATED GRANDEUR OF NATURE AS WELL AS THE ELEVATING, LOFTY EXPRESSION OF THOUGHT AND FEELING. "ALL THAT EXPANDS THE SPIRIT YET APPALS."

This quality or faculty of the mind largely abounds in a fine organization in which the upper portion of the face is larger and wider than the lower. Also the towering form, if well cultivated mentally, indicates nobleness of character.

Alone of all the animal kingdom man maintains a posture erect and towering to heaven; and he alone is capable of lofty aspirations and of ennobling contemplation. Arguing *a priori*, we naturally conclude that the form

2.17. From Simms, *Physiognomy Illustrated* (1891).

that he is "stationary." Whereas the American is "the man for the future," the non-Aryan is "the man of the past."

We have previously run across a similar distinction between stasis and progress and the generic types to which each condition is apportioned. Hjalmar Hjorth Boyesen genuinely desired to help the American woman when he advised her not to "aspire." He believed her happiness depended upon her rejecting any unnatural craving for progress as a New Woman; better for her to return to the stasis promised by containment within the sphere of the Eternal Woman. By the fact of her biological gender status, she is precluded from being "the woman for the future"— that better time which it is the destiny of American men to bring to pass. Rocine's position is both like and unlike Boyesen's. Rocine is talking about Jews, Negroes, Indians, and Asians; his motives are hardly those of compassion and concern; nor

white boy was brought to me for an examination, and in no instance have I seen a better example of a high sensational nature, intensity of organization, and a true type of "Young America." Such children need rural life, plain food, and complete abstrusion from books and school. This

White Boy.   Orison J. Stone, of Boston, who   Negro Boy.
  learned his letters at three years of age,
 and could repeat a large book from memory
   when three years and six months old.

negro boy, with his feeble intellect, which meagreness he inherited from his forefathers, who cultivated only their animal passions and motary powers, can accomplish very little; while the white boy's ancestors were among the best educated families in the world, and he inherited a large brain and intense sensations from those who had used and enlarged their powers of sensation before him. He is cognoscitive, and known to be capable of much mental labour. The negro boy, after many years' schooling, can hardly write his own name, or solve the plainest problem in arithmetic. The white boy is an adept in memorizing and retention.

2.18. From Simms, *Physiognomy Illustrated* (1891).

does he think that Semites and Turanians have any choice in the matter. But he shares Boyesen's view in this sense: he is convinced that the best people to run America are Aryan males, and he bases his conviction on the belief that all other types are incapable of successful action. The inertia Boyesen attributes to the ideal American woman is like the backwardness ingrained in Rocine's flawed races. Together with Jews, Negroes, Indians, and Asians, women stand forever outside the world of progress promised, in Rocine's words, to the true American male (figure 2.19).

The Aryan is tall, warlike, industrious, strong and enterprising. He is proud, dignified, highly intelligent, trustful and patriotic. . . . He has given us our sciences, systems of education, government and law. He has soft hair, blue or gray eyes, fine soul quality, strong feelings, active sympathies, a lively imagination, artistic taste, musical sentiments and an inventive

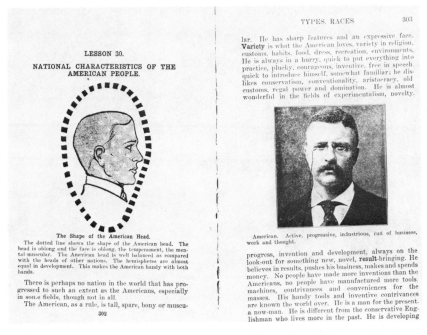

LESSON 30.

NATIONAL CHARACTERISTICS OF THE
AMERICAN PEOPLE.

lar. He has sharp features and an expressive face. **Variety** is what the American loves, variety in religion, customs, habits, food, dress, recreation, environments. He is always in a hurry, quick to put everything into practice, plucky, courageous, inventive, free in speech, quick to introduce himself, somewhat familiar; he dislikes conservatism, conventionality, aristocracy, old customs, regal power and domination. He is almost wonderful in the fields of experimentalism, novelty.

The Shape of the American Head.
The dotted line shows the shape of the American head. The head is oblong and the face is oblong, the temperament, the mental-muscular. The American head is well balanced as compared with the heads of other nations. The hemispheres are almost equal in development. This makes the American handy with both hands.

There is perhaps no nation in the world that has progressed to such an extent as the Americans, especially in some fields, though not in all.

The American, as a rule, is tall, spare, bony or muscu-
302

American. Active, progressive, industrious, full of business, work and thought.

progress, invention and development, always on the look-out for something new, novel, **result**-bringing. He believes in results, pushes his business, makes and spends money. No people have made more inventions than the Americans, no people have manufactured more tools, machines, contrivances and conveniences for the masses. His handy tools and inventive contrivances are known the world over. He is a man for the present, a now-man. He is different from the conservative Englishman who lives more in the past. He is developing

2.19. From Rocine, *Heads, Faces, Types, Races* (1910).

mind. . . . He has large temples, a high tophead, a large forehead, indicating a high degree of reason, culture, thought and development. He is progressive, interested in education and development: new things arouse his attention. The Aryan is the race of evolution.

Rocine does not need to identify the world's most famous American (above to the right of figure 2.19). Nor would Rocine want to single him out as a named individual. Theodore Roosevelt's physiognomy represents the *type* of American "zip and pep." The face alone is the visual tag for "free schools, liberal politics, versatility, restlessness, tools, machinery, progress, travels, speculative spirit and tendency to acquire and spend." The physical attributes of Rocine's Roosevelt are less than those of Lavater's Apollo. But his achievements are clearly those of "the best type" and so Rocine gives him his unstinting approval—working back from the fact of success to the assigned physiognomical qualities which guarantee success.

Joseph Simms' book of 1891 does not even mention the presence of Jews. It was a little too soon for them to be taken as a visible menace to the ingrained principles of American culture and progress. What V. G. Rocine leaves out and what he adds in 1910 to his roster of undesirables is just as revealing. Rocine ignores the Irish, though he continues to cite the Indian and the Negro as racial types doomed to failure. In the crude, cruel parallels Rocine charts between snake, Indian, and Negro, there is no promise of an evolutionary leap from frog to Apollo, as there had been in Lavater's treatise. What strikes one most when going through Rocine's book is the new threat he elaborates upon. It is the Jew—the male counterpart of the alien force photographed with such tenderness by Lewis Hine (see figure 2.11).

2.20. Albert Beck Wenzell, "The Christian Sabbath on Fifth Avenue," from *In Vanity Fair* (1896).

2.21. Albert Beck Wenzell, "Long Branch Puzzle—Find the Christian," from *In Vanity Fair* (1896).

Anti-Semitism did not have to wait until 1910 to receive coarse visual jokes at the expense of the Jewish profile.[29] The well-known illustrator Albert Beck Wenzell included two vignettes of Hebrew infiltration into the American scene in his picture book *In Vanity Fair* of 1896 (figures 2.20–2.21). Wenzell's Jews are ludicrous creatures. They exist behind noses whose enormity signals their difference from "Americans"—those who are graced with the perfect nose granted them by the license of the artist's pen. Of course, one of two acts would demolish Wenzell's little joke: either make the noses given to the Jews match the norm assigned by cultural fiat to the native-born, or render American noses honestly. That is, either extend the fantasies about physiognomical "rightness" to both groups, or insist upon a rigorously accurate account of noses in general. Either way, facial differences would melt away and with them the so-called racial distinctions. The other clues to type that Wenzell offers—the dress and poses of this zestful, affluent group—would thereby offer only food for thought concerning their socioeconomic status and their varied temperaments; not their race.[30]

The *idea* of the Jew sometimes figured in the late nineteenth century as an acceptable addition to the entrenched heritage of American culture. This came about during that Sunday School mood when it was thought proper to remind the churchgoing public that Jews and Christians share a common spiritual heritage.[31] Not that this studio pose staged by a Boston photographer in 1899 makes much of the Hebrew physiognomy (figure 2.22). There is no sure way that one can state whether Lottie Adams is really "one of them," since what does an actual Christian or Jew look like anyway? Only through the use of costume and props and the attachment of a title—not through her appearance—does Lottie Adams provide her viewers with a safely romanticized, vaguely uplifting reference to the ancient days of the Temple before Jews made the unfortunate historical mistake of killing the Christ.

To be a woman and a Jew in the 1890s was not as easily remedied by a photographic trip back into time. One had to be willing to assimilate the decade's prevailing Gibson Girl look that set the norms for what it meant to look like a true woman and a real American. Figure 2.23 shows Gertrude Stein trapped in a photographer's studio during her Radcliffe years in the mid-1890s. Like thousands of American girls of whatever racial antecedents, Stein lacked the height, the elongated torso, and the heft of hair to fit the ideal regularized by Gibson's drawings during that same decade. Many American women continued to fret (just as they would after the Gibson Girl was replaced by John Held's Flapper) that they did not fit the images raised up for their emulation. But Stein at last found the look that was right for her (figure 2.24). This splendid profile shot (taken about 1925) brings out the full beauty of her head. It also suggests that Stein had had another choice to make. Not only did she reject the prevailing styles in feminine appearance required of the American Girl, whether it was 1897 or 1925, she also decided not to identify herself primarily as a female.

As the preceding résumés of the books by Strong, Simms, and Rocine indicate,

Lottie Adams as
" A DAUGHTER OF THE TEMPLE "

LIBRARY OF CONGRESS

2.22. J. E. Purdy, "Lottie Adams as 'A Daughter of the Temple' " (1899).

as well as the reference to Boyesen's belief in the static quality of true woman-hood, not much time of day was given by the professional physiognomists to the place of the American Girl on the evolutionary ladder; not when their immediate concern was with stabilizing the nation's political and economic strengths. As we have seen before, and shall see again, the American Girl was not placed within a pictorial context where Theodore Roosevelt was apt to appear. Observers of the social scene from home and abroad constantly placed women at the center of their

2.23. "Gertrude Stein" (c.1895).

BEINECKE RARE BOOK AND MANUSCRIPT LIBRARY, YALE

evolutionary interpretations of American culture, but the men who wrote the manuals about public success in the United States concentrated almost entirely upon the face and figure of the male.

The note of maleness is sounded with clarity in two final examples taken from the literature of American fitness. George Barr McCutcheon had war on his mind when he asked in 1918, "What is it to be an American?" in tones that sound more like the famous rhetorical question Crèvecoeur asked in 1782 than it does like the evangelical militancy of Josiah Strong's *Our Country* in 1891.[32] The circumstances of World War I brought ethnic competitiveness under some disrepute. McCutcheon was convinced that racial types had to be brought together into a cohesive fighting unit. (Figure 2.25 is Howard Chandler Christy's poster version of McCutcheon's views.) Which type would lead this group effort against the Hun was clear. "Our backbone is Anglo-Saxon; the sinews of our vast body may come from a hundred hardy races, but our backbone comes from but one."

Like Strong, Simms, and Rocine, McCutcheon has no difficulty in imagining Anglo-Saxons cooperating with others of the general type of the Caucasians, since "we are cast in as many moulds as there are white races under the sun." He makes no mention of Rocine's Turanians (the American Indian, Negro, or Asian) and no reference to the Semite. Locating whatever anxieties he feels solely to the ill effects of divided loyalties among European ethnic groups, McCutcheon is still able to speak with pleasure of the contributions of the Americanized Irishman and Pole. He exacts only one requirement. Using the first person plural which associates him directly with the Anglo-Saxon "backbone," McCutcheon states that "we insist" that Irishman or Pole "shall be one of us. There is no going behind that."

In this early version of "America: Love Her or Leave Her," McCutcheon concludes, "The United States offered everything to the [immigrant], and in return she merely asks that the man who comes shall be one of us." Homogeneity of purpose is at stake. The imaginations of Americans must overcome the habit of their divided nature. "In these days of war a man cannot be a German and an American at the same time and still be one of us. He must be an American."[33] McCutcheon wants it both ways. The Anglo-Saxon type is the one which supplies the norm; other racial and national types are worthy only insofar as they follow the lead of the American male ready to succeed at peace or at war. Yet the terms of his argument has made this allegiance an impossibility. The "Anglo-Saxon" is in actuality a vaguely mongrelized amalgam of just about any ethnic group from north of the Pyrenees and west of Vienna. All the same, for McCutcheon and thousands like him, the term stands for the idea of a unified, unchanging, "pure" culture against which all other national types are placed in contrast as miscreants. McCutcheon calls for newly arrived Poles and Germans to be loyal Americans, but he proceeds to assign them the fate of being forever hyphenated. Only the "Anglo-Saxon" is one man, notwithstanding the hyphen that ties together the two segments of his mythic antecedents. In contrast, Irish-, Italian-, Polish-, or German-Americans straddle the New World and the Old, relegated in McCutcheon's mind for all time to being only *half* the true American.

The war concluded, Americans got back to the business of business. Simms' focus on the moral nature of the commercial man was generally forgotten. The new business success was less like Jesus than Jesus was like the man of Madison Avenue.[34] Even McCutcheon's demand for warm fellowship of American soldiers in the trenches was no longer needed for survival. What mattered to the people running the Human Nature Study Bureau in Grand Rapids, Michigan, in 1924 were techniques of self-classification by which a man could learn to "drive" his "personality type" straight toward success.

The little manual of text and drawings put together by Lila Gillian Farrell for the Human Nature Bureau is, however vulgar in its phrasing, sunny and good-natured, as well as being full of Rocine's vaunted "zip and pep." It is a book for nice Kiwanians, not for followers of the Grand Dragon of the Ku Klux Klan. Gone are exemplary illustrations of Aryan and Semite, Teuton and Negro, Anglo-Saxon and Indian. Since racial types do not explicitly enter into Farrell's discussion, it is

2.24. Bonney, "Gertrude Stein"
(c. 1925).

impossible to say whether the "Cadillacs" that win out are northern European in make and whether the "Flivvers" that break down along the highway to fame and fortune represent an inferior ethnic group.[35] A person's racial type seemed to make no difference to the Human Nature Bureau, or the cast of his nose, as long as he was one of the swift. It was taken for granted that the best "cars" were "made in America"—masculine mechanisms headed into a bright future of materialistic success. "Every normal person can achieve success, providing he takes as much care of his human car as he takes of his automobile. So the first problem in ones [*sic*] happiness is to learn the make of car he drives and to plan his life's route by it."

Fortunate the man who discovered he was the happy composite of "the thoracic

HONOR ROLL

Du Bois
Smith
O'Brien
Cejka
Haucke
Pappandrikopolous
Andrassi
Villotto
Levy
Turovich
Kowalski
Chriczanevicz
Knutson
Gonzales

2.25. Howard Chandler Christy,
"Americans All!" (1917).

type," "the vital type," and "the mental type," blended into "the ideal type" be-cause helped along in self-knowledge and self-help by the friendly advice of the Human Nature Bureau (figure 2.26). The American "science" of physiognomical studies had come a long way from Johann Casper Lavater's *Essays*. American males no longer needed to strive to transform themselves from Frog Prince into Apollo. The type of the Cadillac was good enough.

But what if one's "car" began to break down? What if one's physical and emo-tional stamina reached that level where it was beyond repair? What if the true American started to revert to one of the races retarded by brain and biology into the status of the unfit? Once fears like these were voiced, as they were in the 1890s, the importance of the physical type of the American Girl received concerned at-tention, and her image sharpened in focus.

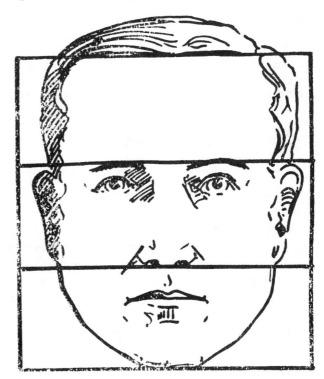

2.26. "Perfectly Balanced Section," from *Human Nature Study* (1924).

Chart 56
Perfectly Balanced Section

Images of the American Girl fed the hope that, through the continuity of her bloodlines, national degeneracy might be allayed. Other images, also identified as the American Girl, were used to signify the decay which had come with fatal inevitability to "the best type" itself.

In 1908 Henry Dwight Sedgwick published *The New American Type and Other Essays*. Its opening chapter (the one that gives the volume its title) announces that something has happened in American life. Its effects cannot be overlooked, not when one compares portraits painted in colonial times with those painted during Sedgwick's generation; particularly not when one looks hard at the images of American women placed in the public eye by the turn of the century.

The accepted racial type of the American Girl continues to be northern European, but in these modern times that type is nervous and disordered, deeply bruised, in Sedgwick's words, by "the exigencies of our epoch."[36] The shift from sturdiness of character to edginess of female nerves is clearly on view when one compares the looks of portraits painted before and after the alteration of American stock that took place during the nineteenth century.

Throughout the eighteenth century, portraits gave evidence of a pure national breed, wherein like bred with like in happy homogeneity, traits paired with consanguineous traits, racial habits and national predispositions mated after their kind; the physiological and psychological niceties, which spring from the differentiation of races and nations, were protected from the disquiet and distress of cross-breeding, deep affinities herded together, and the offspring were saved from the racking strain and distortion that beset a hybrid generation. This physical stability begot mental calm; peace of body insured peace of mind.

Speaking like a knowledgeable stockbreeder, Sedgwick reflects upon the "hardy animal foundation" that gave the preindustrial society its look of "self-satisfied *benedicte*." Figure 2.27 shows that look in the person of Isaac Merrit Singer, one of the men who helped propel American life into its new phase through the extraordinary success of the Singer sewing machine.[37]

Sedgwick is in a good mood throughout his essay. He reveals none of the agitation or acid contempt marking the arguments of Josiah Strong, Joseph Simms, and V. G. Rocine, nor any of the anxieties expressed by Henry James and Henry Adams over the recent decline in American physical and mental tone. Sedgwick merely wishes "to present evidence concerning our American bodies and souls." For that evidence, Sedgwick singles out John Singer Sargent, since Sargent was an artist "born to depict a hybrid people, vagabonds of the mind, to portray a strain of physiological and psychological transformation in the evolution of a new species." Sargent's portrait of "Miss Elsie Palmer" of 1890 might well be one of the kind Sedgwick has in mind (figure 2.28).

Given our general notion of Sargent's sitters as women with high social pedigrees and resoundingly WASP names, Sedgwick's view concerning their hybrid, vagabond nature may strike us as odd. But Sedgwick, like Howard Chandler Christy and others of his generation, quite literally means it when insisting that the true American type formerly consisted solely of settlers from England, Scotland, and Wales. Families of Dutch and German Protestant stock were accepted (though not by Robert Tomes of *The Bazar Book of Decorum*) if their forebears had arrived in America prior to 1800, and if they had put in the requisite number of years plowing their fields as honest yeomen or had overseen others in their agrarian toils. In contrast, the hybrid Americans of Sargent's portraits evidence "disquiet, lack of equilibrium, absence of principle [and the] general sense of [being] migrant tenants." Such was the consequence to the basic American blood strain of the influx of exotica like the Scandinavians, the French, and the Swiss during the mid-nineteenth century.

What stands out in Sedgwick's mind is that American women are the main victims of this altered state. Women are "the first to reveal the strain of physical and psychical maladjustment. The thin spirit of life shivers pathetically in its 'fleshly dress'; and yet in the intensity of its eagerness it is all unconscious of its spiritual fidgeting on finding itself astray."[38] Primed by Sedgwick's suggestions, we can see what he saw in a number of the portraits painted between 1800 and 1910. The young woman imaged by George deForest Brush (figure 2.29) is a "gentle-

2.27. "Isaac Merrit Singer," attributed
to Edward Harrison May (1869).

NATIONAL PORTRAIT GALLERY

woman"—a term which is both a social compliment and a potential biological
curse. Samuel Murray's 1894 statuette of Mrs. Thomas Eakins (figure 2.30) [39] mirrors the thin, bony body and puffed area under the eyes we also find in the painting of his wife that Eakins began shortly after his marriage to Susan Macdowell in
1884. The wall card placed beside that portrait where it now hangs in the Metropolitan Museum of Art somewhat apologetically explains that the new Mrs. Eakins "was thirty-two and no doubt looked younger and less careworn." But familiarity with Eakins' portraiture indicates he had a penchant for the careworn look.
He seemed either to seek it out or to add its marks to the faces of the females in
his portraits. Whatever Eakins' private feelings on the subject, his paintings stand
as further evidence of the "spiritual fidgeting" of American women noted in Sedgwick's essay of 1908.

Little wonder that others—more uncompromising in their notions of racial and
ethnic purity than the relatively sanguine Sedgwick—wished to put a halt to genetic developments that were simultaneously making the Girl more refined in spirit
and more frail of mind and body. Think of the irony of the situation into which
her defenders were placed. They had chosen the Girl to be the ruling model for the

2.28. John Singer Sargent,
"Miss Elsie Palmer"
(1890).

COLORADO SPRINGS FINE ARTS CENTER

nation's ideals at exactly the time when the arts were reflecting the physical changes which that racial type had undergone over the preceding decades. They feared that the symmetrical beauty of feature and the moral and physical vigor of body they prized most as an image would be lost in actuality through the random workings

2.29. George de Forest Brush, "Miss Polly Cabot" (1896).

2.30. Samuel Murray, "Full-Length Figure of Mrs. Thomas Eakins" (1894).

HIRSHHORN MUSEUM AND SCULPTURE GARDEN

PHILADELPHIA MUSEUM OF ART

of events. It was natural for conservative minds to try to fix the Girl in place as a universal type. But since they also believed in one form of evolutionary progress or another, they had to assure a place for the Girl's symbolic worth within a hybrid society whose genetic alterations made the purity of type a historic impossibility and confidence in the steadiness of her nerves a sometime thing.

The moment we hear about the edginess attributed to highly sensitive American women, we are likely to think of the influential book on the subject written in 1881 by Dr. George Miller Beard. It is right that we remind ourselves of *American Nervousness, Its Causes and Consequences: A Supplement to Nervous Exhaustion (Neurasthenia)*. But we not only need to learn what this late-nineteenth-century medical practitioneer thought about mental agitation and fatigue, we need to picture the appearance by which Beard identified female sufferers of the malady he specifically defined as American and modern. As much a student of the physiognomy of the nervous type as Simms and Rocine were physiognomists of racial and gender types, Beard delineates "fine organization" in the chapter he titles "Signs of American Nervousness." The signs are clear in a woman: "fine, soft hair, delicate skin, nicely chiselled features, small bones, tapering extremeties."[40]

High-strung femininity continued to be imaged in the terms set by Beard throughout the next two decades, usually with the accompaniment of a note of pity or anxiety over the state of affairs that made women susceptible to every quiver of modern times. Frank Norris, for one, found no pleasure in fine-boned women of fragile nerves; nor did he think them of any use to the literary scene. In 1901 he wrote a short piece for the *Boston Evening Transcript* called "Why Women Should Write the Best Novels; and Why They Don't." Norris picked out the physical and psychological traits frequently associated with New England types at that time. He did not explicitly state it was the New England woman of whom he wrote, but the Boston setting of his newspaper piece and the description he provided points to the frail body and tense nerves by which we recognize the latter-day Olive Chancellors of turn-of-the-century literature and portraiture.

In Norris' view women writers fail because they lack the bodily and mental stamina required for success in "the midst of that great, grim complication of men's doings we call life."[41] Norris seems genuinely sorry that women sufficiently sensitive to write imaginative literature have insufficient strength to accomplish anything of literary merit, but his reasoning is of a piece with the physiognomical principles of Simms, Rocine, and Beard. Woman's susceptibility to mental fatigue is due to the fact that she biologically possesses "the more specialized organ."

Dr. George Beard did not have the fate of American literature to consider, only the physiognomical aesthetics of the nation's females. The "queens in social life" who spent half their days sitting in Beard's waiting room awaiting treatment for neurasthenia gave him a kind of genuine pleasure from the appearance they presented. "The same climatic peculiarities that make us nervous also make us handsome; for fineness of organization is the first element in all human beauty, in either sex. . . . [Fineness] is supplemented by expressiveness of features—which is its second element; by the union of these two, human beauty reaches its highest."

Beard admits that handsome women are occasionally found in Great Britain, and—at times—on the Continent, "but in America, it is the extent—the common-ness of this beauty, which is so remarkably, unprecedentedly, and scientifically interesting." Beard's national pride is touched by "the fact that the American type is to-day more adored in Europe than in America; that American girls are more in demand for foreign marriages than any other nationality; and that the professional beauties of London that stand highest are those who, in appearance and in char-acter have come nearest the American type."

Aware that he must compare the American beauty with her British rival if he is to make his case hold, Beard advances an intriguing thesis.

. . . yet American beauty has this sovereign advantage—that it best bears close observa-tion. . . . The American face bears the microscope, mainly by reason of its delicacy, fine-ness, and mobility of expression—qualities that are only appreciated on inspection. . . . It is no hard task for one travelling in Great Britain or on the Continent to distinguish Amer-ican ladies from those of any other nationality, by the finely cut features and mobility of expression.

How odd to realize that Americans of Beard's bent of imagination who wander in strange lands are meant to take pleasure in "a typical American when they recognize in her face, expression, gait, and bearing . . . *the functional nervous disease which she had long endured"* (my italics).

Chapter 1 of *Imaging American Women* makes much of the burst of vigor pro-moted by the type of the Outdoors Girl and by the increased attention given to physical fitness during the mid-nineties and after. We also know that there was growing concern over healthful diet, sensible clothing, and enlightened medical care. The young woman of statuesque bearing and strong limbs is as much a mark of the period as the examples cited by Beard and Sedgwick or visualized by Sar-gent, Dewing, Eakins, and Brush. Neither set of opinions on the nature of the American Girl cancels the other. Images both strong and delicate were part of the diverse ways in which the Girl was presented to the public's mind's eye.[42]

The bloodlines of the American Girl were of obvious importance to her support-ers. Her fertility was of equal concern since the future of the nation led by the likes of Theodore Roosevelt depended on the healthy reproductive capacity of the best sort of female. The paradox of the situation addressed by Henry Sedgwick in "The New American Type" emerges here in full force: the more winningly femi-nine and sensitive the American Girl appears—the more she signifies the refine-ments of an advanced society—the less able the Girl is to bear the vigorous sons needed to further America's commercial and political ambitions. What might the country expect if Theodore Roosevelt or Isaac Singer were replaced by "The Phil-osophical Type" (figure 2.31)? The American Girl was intended to be socially static, protected from the ways of the male world by remaining within her private sphere.

The Philosophical Type.

2.31. "The Philosophical Type," from Rocine, *Heads, Faces, Types, Races* (1910).

Still, she not only had *to stand for* the spirit of progress, she had *to reproduce* men of progress as well.

As long as the image of the Girl conveyed the spirit of civilization, the physicality of that image had to be restrained. When her image was intended as a guarantee that she was a good breeder, then the lineaments of good breeding were curtailed, even to the point of allowing her the look of pert vulgarity and frank sensuality. Unless, that is, someone like Charles Dana Gibson or Howard Chandler Christy was able to draw a composite figure possessed of the signs of both physical energy and regal good manners.

Material progress and spiritual evolution are not what female atavisms contribute to society. The threat of regression lay behind women who looked like those catalogued in Cesare Lombroso's *The Female Offender*, published in English in 1895 (figure 2.32). Though the attention it drew was transnational, Lombroso's book had an especially strong impact upon the imagination of Americans.[43] Lombroso's theories of criminology and genetic determinism give us yet another indication of

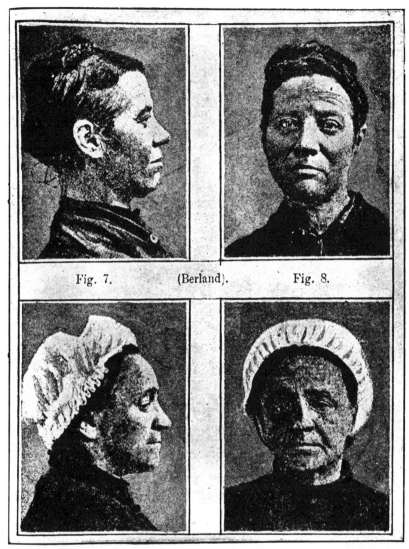

Fig. 7.   (Berland).   Fig. 8.

2.32. From Lombroso and
Ferrero, *The Female*   Fig. 9.
Offender (1895).   (Thomas.)   Fig. 10.

the widespread interest during the 1890s in the power of external signs, of the heightened wish to break the human mass down into discrete categories, and of the notion that society was viewed as involved in a continuing drama played out between unfamiliar, inferior types and "the best people."[44] The anxieties expressed by Lombroso's books on female and male criminal types were shared by numerous segments of Western society, but to many Americans these types seemed to represent peculiarly American problems once the cities began to fill up with what they deemed the dregs of all nations.

The core of Lombroso's thesis concerning the basic type of the social deviant must not be overlooked. One is not stamped as a murderer, felon, or streetwalker, Lombroso argued, because he or she is born in Sicily, the Irish slums of Boston, or the back alleys of Warsaw. Rather, a criminal is a person, of whatever origin, who has been born out of joint with the times. Lombroso does not platonize the "normal" person, but he does the deviant. "Good" people are individuals affected by the particulars of historical events and the flow of evolutionary processes. "Bad" people are universal types who exist beyond the reach of circumstance, trapped within the envelope of timelessness back where human life began.

Females who offend the laws of society are "strong" examples of the consequences of biological atavism. Whatever their ethnic or racial derivation, they can be recognized as criminals and deviants because they cannot be "seen" as *women*. Although they are not males by sex, they *look like* men and act like men. True men and true women (biologically restricted by nature's evolutionary laws to one of two markedly different physical types) keep up with history. In contrast, female offenders remain unnaturally fixed in the caves and swamps of prehistoric times. Placed out of time and the compulsion of history toward ascent, these creatures share a single, brutish subhuman form with the lowest males of the species.

Lombroso's theories set paradoxes running like hares before the fox, particularly when their implications are laid next to the teachings of the physiognomists of the period. Indian, Jews, blacks, and Asians are "the lost races"—irrevocably marred by cultural inertia and genetic regression. In contrast, northern European males are members of that race and that gender which will progress as long as the health of their genetic inheritance is sustained. American females of the same stock are the finest specimens of their sex in the world. They are very pretty and very good, although an alarming number are excessively delicate of frame and emotions. Their moral and pictorial "rightness" is guaranteed as long as they "stay back" out of the bustling world of commerce and politics, continue to bear sturdy male babies for America's future, and do not attempt to be "pushy" and "forward" about their social and political advancement. The true American woman must, therefore, *stay in history but out of the world*. In menacing contrast to this type there is another "lost race"—that of the female offender identifiable to society by great strength of limb, aggressive behavior, and masculine appearance. This, the worst sort, must never be allowed to mother America's children, just as the best type must be encouraged to overcome the biological frailties that would keep her from fulfilling her duty to family and to nation. "Spirit" must prevail, lest the masculinized female, the primitivistic seed of crime and immorality, take command by the fact of her frightening vigor as a reproductive organ.

American males need strong mates, but what man would wish to be tied to one of Lombroso's criminal types? None, no more than a man would wish to marry the New Woman pictured in the *New York World* in 1895 (see figure 1.44). Such a man, yoked to a genetic throwback, figures as the shriveled partner in Charles Dana Gibson's "A Suffragette's Husband" (figure 2.33). Lombroso's females offend

2.33. Charles Dana Gibson, "A Suffragette's Husband," from *Other People* (1911).

against society with crimes of theft and prostitution. The crime portrayed by the female in the Gibson drawing is a political one. She is no mere Gibson Girl grown naturally old and fat; she is the unnatural New Woman at her most frightening. From the look of the man in the Gibson drawing, any respectable male bound to a suffragette is emasculated, unfit to sire children. Sexual give-and-take between such unlike creatures is unthinkable. Only criminals can breed with one another, but their spawn will prove more deviant still, endangering the necessary evolution of "the best types."

At the end of the century there were more than a few anxious observers of the American scene. They felt—and thought they could *see* from visual evidence—that time had been yanked out of its warp. The True Woman was prized for the fineness of her femininity and purity of her racial type, but her constitution was chancy when it came to mothering strong citizens. The New Woman was either suspect for the deviant virility of her mind and body or for the impurities of her genetic composition. How could "correct" Americans be born under such aberrant conditions? How was the American Girl to remain the female Americans could identify as the right type and possess as the image of their desires?

IMAGES OF DESIRE

3

Artists, Models, and Real Things

One day in 1900 Mrs. Joseph W. Drexel did not feel like returning to Thomas Eakins' studio for yet another sitting for the portrait he was in the process of painting. She sent her maid instead. Eakins was upset by the notion that an original could be replaced by a substitute, and he called off the project. He explained in a letter that he could not proceed under conditions that would result in "a portrait of you that did not resemble you, would be false, have no historic value, and would not enhance my reputation."[1]

Since the 1870s (upon Eakins' return to Philadelphia from his studies under Gérôme and Bonnat at the École des Beaux-Arts), he had been "enhancing" his reputation as a resolute realist. He had remained true to the belief expressed in his letter to Mrs. Drexel that pictorial representations of the human form should be based on keen observation and the avoidance of falsification. Fidelity to the person under scrutiny also had added value as a historic record of identification; it "recognized" that person as having existed during a particular time and in a particular place. Nonetheless, the principles to which Eakins dedicated his stubborn energies did not preclude his manipulation of the literal facts of his "givens." Nor did his adherence to accurate imitation keep him from imbuing his subjects with emotional readings based on his own notions concerning their essential nature.

In 1876 Eakins recreated his idea of what William Rush's studio had looked like in 1809 when the sculptor carved a wooden allegory of the Schuylkill River from a female nude model. To execute this "manifesto" that declared the right of artists to use live models without fear of censure,[2] Eakins used photographs he had taken in Paris of paintings by his teacher Gérôme. These images-on-file suggested to Eakins how he could compose a "realistic" rendering of Rush's studio almost seventy years after the event. Eakins took his horse Billy as the model for the sculptured mounts ridden by Lincoln and Grant when he worked on the Brooklyn Civil War Memorial Arch in 1894. And according to stories of the day, he strapped J. Laurie Wallace naked to the roof of his Mt. Vernon Street studio in 1880 in order to visualize the effects he needed for his painting of the Crucifixion.[3]

Celebrated as the finest realist in painting that nineteenth-century America produced, Eakins in fact employed an array of substitutes for objects he purported to represent directly: models for absent personages or things; photographic studies of nude males with panpipes or young women draped in Grecian gowns for scenes of classical Arcady; references, via sketch or photograph, to oft-repeated images handed down by painters from previous generations. To report these practices is not to charge Eakins with betraying the cause of realism. Rather, it serves to introduce a complex of issues that concerned many late-nineteenth-century American artists who were attempting to create images (visual or verbal) that met their exacting standards for realistic representation.

The artistic forms assigned to the American Girl are an integral part of the views that evolved during the 1880s and 1890s over the nature of realism, for the Girl was "real" in some crucial sense or she was nothing at all. The figure of the Girl was projected as a variety of types. Types, in turn, were made to bear the weight of significant cultural meaning. That figure and those types and their projected meanings drew directly upon the crush of arguments over *what is real* about both actual objects and ideal representations.

The way certain painters used female models in their studios and the manner in which certain fictional works depicted artists and models raises an important issue. It is the question of "real things" and what that term implied—in theory and practice, in fact and in fiction—during the period when advocates of realism and idealism, imitation and imagination, were at odds with one another. This question, of necessity, touches upon concerns expressed by Americans who felt that objects of all kinds were no longer easily recognizable. Possessing a sense of a thing's "reality" might give one a fighting chance when encountering the baffling, pluralistic, unruly American scene. Inevitably modes traditionally used to signify reality were brought into play. But labels such as realism or romanticism (whether defined as specific formalistic practices or as general responses to experience) were frequently supplemented by another, still-older term that came to dominate contemporary practice and theory: *the type.*

The year 1892 is a good place to start. As we shall see, it is the year for which the events of the Philadelphia Centennial of 1876, and the principles expressed there, had served as a kind of messianic preparation. In 1892 the public occasion that best images the problematic nature of the period's search for the recognizable got underway. In a former swampland in the southern part of Chicago thousands of workmen, artisans, and artists were busily erecting and decorating what the delighted visitors to the next year's event would know as the White City. Poised at the edge of Lake Michigan, the fairgrounds of the Columbian Exposition (filled with colossal images of ideal female figures placed around vast architectural structures and reflected like a mirage in the central lagoon) opened during the summer of 1893 at a time of severe economic depression. The pure white buildings were ringed by a gaudy Midway loud with hawkers and slums that stretched toward Dreiser's city of high dreams and bitter frustrations.[4] But the official imagery embodied by the White City informed the crowds of visitors to the fair that they were witnesses to the glorious culmination of events which the coming of Columbus to the New World had set in motion four hundred years before. The designers in charge made the City a visual statement of American peace, progress, and prosperity. It was also (what with its mix of some truths and much wishful thinking) a tangible form of the question disturbing the minds of a number of the nation's citizens: *What exactly is it we have here in America?*

The same year the building of the Columbian Exposition got under way Henry James published "The Real Thing." The original notion for this short story as projected in James' notebooks indicates that he viewed the artist's life as one more example of the struggle of the fittest to beat out the inadequate—"the way superficial, untrained, unprofessional effort goes to the wall when confronted with trained, competitive, intelligent, *qualified* art."[5] The theme of precisely which artists capture public attention is an apt topic for any writer. In James' generation, the acute pressure for painters and authors to pull ahead of the pack made it necessary to explore the particular demands which the 1890s placed on the representational arts. In order to size up the public's hunger for the real, artists had to ask what "being real" involved.

The matter of "real things" also engaged the interest of late-nineteenth-century philosophers of aesthetic theory, of psychologists tinkering with the relation between random perception and focused cognition, of painters who paused long enough in their work to consider the nature of imitation, and of academics excited by discussions of contending epistemologies and ontologies. It would hardly seem to be a theme that was meat for a best-seller. However, the motif James chose for his story of 1892 would resurface, combined with a love story (that necessary ingredient for general popular consumption), in several romances of the next two decades: *Trilby*, *The Angel of Clay*, and *The Common Law*. In James' handling of "The Real Thing" it is the infusion of an asexual "IDEA" (as he described his inspiration for the tale) that brought passion to his narrative—not boys and girls in love. That idea was the drama of how an artist, through the medium of art, locates those types by which he *recognizes*, and perhaps even *knows*, real human forms.

The narrator of "The Real Thing" is particularized as a man who has gained a certain commercial reputation as the illustrator of popular romances. His present assignment is the chance he needs to break through to fame and money. It will place his work before the public in prestigious relation with the writings of "the rarest of the novelists . . . one of the most independent representatives of English letters."[6] The high praise accorded the author of *Rutland Ramsey* is filtered through the narrator's point of view, a view which requires some skepticism on our part. It is possible that the anxious efforts of the narrator to create images that live up to the greatness of the novel are ironically misplaced; *Rutland Ramsey* may actually be a rum effort. However this may be, the artist-narrator *is* clear about two matters: his professional career is assured if his illustrations provide "satisfaction" to his publishers; his publishers define "reality" in light of what the current market wants in the way of likeness to high-society figures.[7]

As James presents the case, the answer to the ontological matter of "real things" lies in the choices the artist-narrator makes in his studio. He must decide whether to hire amateurs possessed of a social identity that literally coincides with the characters in the *Ramsey* volume or to hire professional models adept in devices for suggesting, not what they happen to be, but what the illustrations call for. With these choices as the story's donnée, James makes it our task as readers to assess, along with the narrator, *the kinds of identity* Mrs. Monarch (the amateur) and Miss Churm (the professional) provide. Unlimited by narrow notions of what is authentic and what is not, and undistracted by petty oppositions between art and life, we, like the narrator, must respond with immediacy to the nature of "real things."

Mrs. Monarch has "singleness." She is "complete"—too much so. "She was the real thing, but always the same thing." She has no visible character, only "obsessional form"; it is a form that, as it "couldn't be everybody's," might "end in being nobody's." Her bodily perfection had led to her being called "the Beautiful Statue," but she lacks the imperfections by which we sense humanness behind the art. For ready identification, she carries a name card. She quickly produces a collection of photographs that show off the settings and the clothes—*the things*—that go along with being a "lady." Significantly, she prefers being paid to model her silhouette, not her face. Faces are the locus of a person's particular identity, whereas figure outlines provide generalizations that, even if "sold," preserve the privacy of the inner life. Her inner life relies on *being Mrs. Monarch* in concentrated form. She is unable to *act out* "Mrs. Monarch" as an approximation.

The Monarchs, husband and wife, appear on the narrator's doorstep with the plea to be taken on as paid models, but prior to this date the couple has been up for sale for some time. Throughout years of financial instability, the Monarchs had presented themselves in a semiprofessional capacity as guests in great houses where their function was to decorate the scene. Serving as furniture and art objects, they were comparable in kind to the accessories of the refined life shown in the photographs they carry about. By the time James' story commences the Monarchs' finances have come to such a pass they are forced into the next stage of their social decline: that of selling themselves directly as images on the open market. The narrator gets credit for realizing that the Monarchs indeed have value—the kind that accrues to the intangible quality of their "ladyness" and "gentlemanlyness."

But this native value does not transmit itself into cash terms. They are unable to provide the pictorial look of a social reality that Miss Churm can serve up with the quick turn of the head or the cock of an elbow.

Miss Churm is not "single." She is infinite variety, working outward from fluidity of character toward the rounding off of whatever figure the day's assignment at the studio requires. She is "like" whatever pays; she does not have to bother with "being" the represented object. Her genius is her ability to convey the sense of "the real thing" which art demands. In contrast, "the authentic thing" of Mrs. Monarch's existence is beside the point in the world of the studio. As a cockney woman of uncertain age and in wobbly command of her haitches, there is some slippage between what Miss Churm is and the poses she takes as a highborn lady. Discrepancies like these make her fall short of the requirements exacted of scientific models. But artists (whether realists or romanticists) do not exact the total accuracy of the laboratory. Suggestive approximations work best. They supplement the other aids to representation that guide the artist through his working day—the formal training that moves his hand just so across the surface of canvas, paper, or marble; the replicas of traditional art forms he carries in his memory or that decorate the walls of his work area; the freshly conceived images that float in his brain, prompted either by private imaginings or by direct observations of the natural scene.

Mrs. Monarch is herself "the lady," now and always. She cannot lend herself to the *suggestions* it is Miss Churm's cockney genius to convey. Unassuming by temperament, she is too intensely what she is, with no chance of ever becoming anything else of interest. By contrast, Miss Churm is a consummate actress who has at her beck whatever type is needed for the moment. As a studio model, she does not have to move about a theater stage or (fortunately, because of her lower-class accent) to open her mouth. Mute and motionless, she acts up a storm, composing her body into the shapes and gestures that represent the glimpse of recognizable identity upon which the artist builds. She is hired specifically to supplement the other data by which the artist stimulates his perceiving eye and prompts his mind's activity.

It would be nice if Mrs. Monarch, failure as a professional model, could succeed as a professional "personality." But in a period when the market value of being a celebrity was increasing with great rapidity, she cannot even sell herself as herself. Not only is she unable to hire herself out as one who projects imagined identities, she has no personal trademark by which she can be recognized as a conveyor of desire.[8] This is the irony that keeps her from winning her daily bread: she is too distinguished to be striking. She is also "less" than Miss Churm who has "more" to offer. Self-effacing and modest, Mrs. Monarch is a raving egoist when it comes to identity. Limited to herself and conscious only of her own nature, she possesses the Wordsworthian ego that disqualifies her in the artist's studio. In contrast, Miss Churm is a fine example of Shakespearean negative capability. She can take suggestions from the artist and give suggestions to his imagination in return. She realizes intuitively that a living is to be made by an exaggeration, a coarsening, of what she is actually. At the same moment, she can draw back toward subtle sublimations of the self in order to approximate the type. The type as art, not the fact of nature, is Miss Churm's commodity. Such an altered self is not less real for all that. It is *more real* when taken as the occasion for the disclosure of the value of type in the processes of *making* reality. Using art, Miss Churm prompts others to make artistic products. Denying her self as such, she projects herself outward. The artist seizes that projection and fashions from it a product that possesses the reality lying within even the most meretricious of pictorial and verbal representations.

Who Miss Churm is, back in her little London flat, as her own real thing, does not enter into the story. Her ability to work up, chameleon-like, a variety of expansive gestures precludes James' need to turn her into the center of a narrative about "The Problem of Identifying Miss Churm." *That* story James would tell in *The Ambassadors* through Madame de Vionnet—an actress of such infinities of meaning that she baffles Lambert Strether in his literal-mined search after the reality of her inner nature: as good or bad, as lady or as servant girl weeping over her lover. "Identifying" the woman is also the story that lies at the base of *Trilby, The Angel of Clay*, and *The Common Law*. But in his tale of 1892 Henry James concentrates upon a theme that makes him a literary version of Talcott Parsons, since both the novelist and the sociologist place emphasis upon the value people derive from the social functions they perform.[9] Today, career-placement advisers administer tests to clients like the Monarchs in order to determine what is marketable about them. But neither Parsons nor job counselors (and certainly not agents who sign up celebrities for public-appearance tours) would have succeeded in persuading James' artist-narrator to hire the candidates they sent around to his studio. That is, not unless they had a profound sense of the true nature of modeling or an acute awareness of the ontology of the type.

The 1890s and early 1900s tossed forth several romantic novels that twist their plots around the question of the true identity of the studio models who bring both professional inspiration and love interest to the artist-heroes. Before turning to three of these fictions it helps to be aware of the work habits of actual artists of the period who had to mediate between the presence of live models and images of "real things."

Take Elihu Vedder, for example. He is commonly described as a mystic, a visionary, a concocter of ideal forms and allegorical themes. But as Vedder himself expressed it in his memoirs, his attention split from the start between realism and the ideal. Set against his love for color, solidity, landscapes, emotion, sketches that catch on-the-spot details, and the imitation of carefully perceived objects (traits that point his art toward both naturalistic portrayals and modern formalism) is Vedder's delight with drawing, atmosphere, figures, thought, finished pictures, and the creation of cognized images.[10]

Vedder is usually represented in museums and art books by allegorical studies such as "The Cumaean Sibyl" (figure 3.1), but Vedder's recollection of how he came to execute this particular mythic image undercuts the notion that he relied heavily upon fanciful fabrications as the source of his representational forms. Years before rendering the "Sibyl," Vedder had sketched the head of Jane Jackson, an ex-slave whom he found selling peanuts on a New York street corner (figure 3.2). He also had a photograph taken of her as she sat crouched over her wares. Later, when he was "in a mood," he went back to his studio file. Plucking out these two closely observed versions of Jane Jackson's face, he produced an image of brooding emotions, embodied in the onward rushing figure of the sibyl. Vedder's conviction that the mind must work upon what it sees does not deny his empiricism. The "aim of Art," he wrote is, "first [to] have an idea, and then from your experience and the nature about you get the material to clothe it." That is, have an idea about the sibyl. Then cast around to retrieve useful data. The result will be "the reality" the artist recognizes about sibyls which emerges from "the thing" seen in Jane Jackson's face. In either instance, Vedder drew a realistic representation of a female, but like many romantics he chose to shift from an image of the reality of a street vendor to an image that conveyed the nature of sibylline powers.

If *the idea* was the mannequin for Vedder and *nature* the clothing (with *the type* the consequence of the happy combination), the method could be reversed as well. This was the case in the work produced by Edwin Austin Abbey, an immensely successful artist slightly younger than Vedder. Abbey is best known for his recreations of the historical past (especially of his beloved Italian Renaissance) and for his illustrations of Shakespeare's comedies and the poetry of Robert Herrick. Still and all, two critics of the contemporary art scene noted Abbey's exceptional talent for using studio models and lay mannequins to create things that were approximations of the "real" more than they were results of the fancy that falsifies. One of these critics was Royal Cortissoz; the other was Henry James.

Cortissoz furnishes an anecdote that compares the manners by which Abbey and John Singer Sargent responded to studio props.[11] One day the two painter friends set themselves to rendering a wooden lay figure dressed in a troubadour's hat and coat and with a lute in its "hands." "Sargent's was an unmistakable 'actuality,' the picture of a mannikin provided with studio properties. Abbey's was the portrait of a living troubadour. . . . Sargent had made a record of exactly what he saw. Abbey had given free play to his imagination and endowed a senseless thing with life."

Abbey's studio was known by friends and colleagues as a warehouse of props and costumes—as an archives where he carried out his painstaking research into the look of the past. Even as an art student he had disliked sketching from antique casts. Like a Socrates in disgust over copies placed at several removes from original forms, he preferred direct observation. But for all the objects he accumulated, for all his use of grids and squarings to assure correct proportionings, and for all his

3.1. Elihu Vedder, "The Cumaen Sibyl" (oil on canvas) (1876).

3.2. Elihu Vedder, "Jane Jackson" (1863).

reliance upon detailed preliminary sketches and cartoons, photographs, lantern slides, and mannequins—all the tricks of his trade—Abbey consistently turned back to his mind's eye for verification. It was a very special eye, however.

Henry James, a close friend, recognized that Abbey worked within an exceptional mental world. Extreme attention to concrete objects existed alongside a vivid memory. It was as though Abbey *saw through* those objects, windowlike, into the past where—in highly particularized scenes—living personages acted out their reality before his eyes. Always one to speculate upon what it takes to be a good storyteller, James asked himself what it would mean to write the way Abbey drew—that is, to be able "directly [to observe] figures, scenes, places that exist only in the fairyland of . . . fancy." Abbey's discovery about the advantages of working with type answered James' question. James, like Abbey, came to realize that the figure placed at the center of the carpet of the imagination was a model or mannequin. Its inclusion guaranteed that whoever stepped on that carpet was on solid footing.

If we go by the *subjects* painted by Vedder or Abbey, we call them romantics, even idealists, just as we do when assessing the writings of the American Romantics. If we take under consideration the *look* of the strong, clearly defined forms they placed upon the sheets of paper, the canvases, or the walls that provided the tactile medium for their images, we need to admit that they cannot be classified as romantics without further thought, just as we must qualify any initial simplifications when applying such labels to Melville, Hawthorne, or Thoreau. If we also include an account of the *methods* Vedder and Abbey used to reproduce the human form (manual techniques and mental processes), we are hard put not to see them as disciples of realism. Even so, why press down on one or another of these terms? It is closer to the point to say of them that they tried to render reality by means of the type. Types wander with the arrogance of authority back and forth across the genre boundaries separating romanticism from realism. They act to deflate and to conflate the artificial classifications by which we attempt to protect reality from its adversary, unreality.

To appreciate the freedom to roam which artists of the type take as their due, turn from so-called painters of the ideal like Vedder and Abbey to the self-named realist William Merritt Chase, to see how he confiscated models of "real things."[12]

Next to Eakins, Chase is the painter of the period who is most commonly singled out for the commitment he made to pictorial realism. Trained in such diverse places as Indianapolis, New York, Munich, and Venice, Chase's single-minded drive toward success was under way by the 1880s. At the time of his death in 1916 Chase was acclaimed as "sane, unsentimental, truthful and unpretentious." He was credited with being the best exponent of "the natural style" ("a composite, blending indistinguishably the influence of old and new schools of painting") and a painter who succinctly captured "the nervousness, crispness, intensity of American life."

To a large extent Chase eschewed the anecdotal; certainly, the didactic. He prided himself on being a painter who looked closely at things and recorded them for their own sake in terms of "the brush treatment, the color, the form." The models he used ranged from codfish (he could paint a masterly still life of one in an hour's time) to Alice Gerson, the young woman who became his wife, to his eight children, and to a parade of other sitters—professional and amateur. The attitude he took toward the use of models was as commonsensical as it was toward the other tools of his trade. Models were the occasion for a demonstration of the adroit brush techniques by which he represented physical forms. They helped him produce canvases filled with strokes of color that satisfied the artistic eye; they prompted likenesses that mediated confidently between an academic tradition dedicated to the correct illusion of perspective and the contemporary interest in paint as light and shadow. Yet when Chase came to write a little piece in 1908 for *The Delineator* (then under the editorship of Theodore Dreiser), he revealed that he (like Dreiser) may be termed a "realist" only if that classification includes the reverberations of "type."

Chase recalls the day in 1893 when a model was ushered into his Tenth Street studio in New York.[13] Good models were hard to come by, and he often sent his servant Daniel into the streets to find someone suitable for posing. That day Daniel returned with a woman who turned out to be the Mrs. Clark who supposedly served as the original model for the Gibson Girl. Charles Dana Gibson had translated the particulars of Mrs. Clark's character into the general type that was well on the way in 1893 to becoming the accepted, romanticized image for the American Girl. The "sane, unsentimental" Chase also found in the "clear-cut, classic face with splendid profile" the "perfect type of American womanhood," Irish though she was. He painted her just as he found her in her plain black dress, adding only one touch. Around her shoulders he threw a white shawl that hung nearby. "That was sufficient, the picture was complete" (figure 3.3). The model; the studio; the shawl; the artist's recognition of a type that he insisted "could have been done only by an American artist": the result is simultaneously "the real thing" supplied by artist and model in easy collaboration, the universalized type of American national values, and the particularized portrait of a woman with an identity that is hers alone.

Sculptors make use of models in a somewhat different way than painters do. In preparation for meeting the sculptor who serves as the hero of the novel *The Angel of Clay*, note how certain late-nineteenth-century practitioners in bronze and marble set about representing reality. The result is a clearer understanding of the fact that artists of the ideal made use of mechanical props, while artists of the naturalist persuasion practiced the art of the type.

The author of *The Angel of Clay* was William Ordway Partridge, a professional sculptor. Partridge was a fanatic about "real things" taken in the restricted sense of Neoplatonic forms. Even so, he shared the current view that sculpture is by the nature of its medium the only naturalistic art. A sculpted piece is a rounded form; it approximates actual figures more directly than can the flatness of the painted canvas. However, statues representing ideal forms escape the ignominy of strict

3.3. William Merritt Chase,
"Lady with the White
Shawl" ("Portrait of
Mrs. C.") (1893).

PENNSYLVANIA ACADEMY OF THE FINE ARTS

naturalism by the fact that the sculptor works with the white purity of marble, not the tawdry colors by which the painter's palette falsifies the soul's truth in the name of fidelity to external appearance. Notwithstanding Partridge's allegiance to the ideal, his book *Technique of Sculpture* (published five years before his novel *The Angel of Clay*), is filled with sketches of mannequins, armatures, and the other mechanical apparatuses by which molders and carvers coerce solid materials into shape.[14] Partridge's working practices, therefore, as a matter of course belie the extreme position taken by his idealism.

Six years after Partridge's *Technique*, the London-based Edouard Lanteri brought out the first of three volumes that demonstrate the opposite side of the sculptor's coin; they reverse the priority given to the ideal placed in antagonism to physical form. Lanteri's work was immediately judged by practitioners of the art on both sides of the Atlantic as "*the* classic treatise on the techniques of figurative sculpture" backed by "at least three thousand years of accumulated studio lore."[15] Lanteri rejected the academy's advocacy of mental forms as the basis for representational art; he championed exact copying from nature. He was outspokenly against "narcissism," the term he applied to the intrusion of the maker's subjective moods. He also objected to the rendition of ideal images and insisted that knowledge of anatomical principles must be supplemented by the study of living models whose individualistic traits qualified overly generalized laws of bodily structure. Yet even Lanteri believed in "the mirror" by which an artist's personal feelings infiltrate the sculpturing process, and even he argued that the artist should pursue "characteristic" and "typical" traits when developing sculptured forms. Artists, like scientists, must understand the ordering principles that lie behind their copies. If artists ignored the type, they would be left with the trivia of the empirical report, and the balance between expressive feelings and regressive subjectivity would be lost.

The practices of Daniel Chester French and Augustus Saint-Gaudens, sculptors in marble and bronze, provide further examples of the constant movement to and fro between the open cities of realism and romanticism, with "the type" serving as the artist's password. Like Elihu Vedder and Edwin Austin Abbey, French and Saint-Gaudens are usually associated with the idealized subjects they created between the 1870s and the close of World War I. But they, like Vedder, Abbey, Chase, Lanteri, and even Partridge, were objectivists and empiricists in training and method. Through their continued reference to type, French and Saint-Gaudens went beyond the limitations imposed by too strict an obedience to the conventions of realism or romanticism.

During the 1880s the favorite studio model of Augustus Saint-Gaudens was Davida Johnson Clark.[16] Figure 3.4 shows Davida's image captured naturalistically by the camera. Figure 3.5 is a marble bust of 1886 that treats that same high-held head as it proceeded en route from the actual (the particulars of Davida seen in the photograph) to the ideal (the head of the "Diana" which later graced the pinnacle of Stanford White's Madison Square Garden, the Ann Maria Smith tomb, and the

3.4. Davida Johnson Clark
(c. 1886), archival pho-
tograph.

DARTMOUTH COLLEGE LIBRARY

decorative figure piece known as "Amor Caritas.") Figure 3.5 is the second stage; it is "the real thing." It has the universalized qualities that possess the sign that is both Davida Johnson Clark and *more than Davida*. It is not yet the allegorical abstraction of Diana, the figure guarding the tomb of the dead, or the look of Love (figure 3.6). It is not yet, that is, the type of the Ideal.

Figure 3.7 is Saint-Gaudens' bronze study made in 1895 of Anne Page in prepa-ration for his work on the Shaw Memorial. Compare it with the portrait painted in 1887 of the same woman by Dennis Bunker (figure 3.8). The Bunker painting expresses, as it were, Anne Page as Miss Churm resting upon the studio platform between stints as a model. The details of dress, the use of colors, the three-quarter-length view, the sitter's direct gaze, the inclusion of roses: all act as reminders of this young woman's individual nature, however much Bunker works with conven-

3.5. Augustus Saint-Gau-
dens, marble bust—first
study for head of
"Diana" (1886).

3.6. Augustus Saint-Gau-
dens, detail of reduc-
tion of "Diana"
(c.1895).

tions that qualify the naturalistic tendencies of his portrait. In contrast, the Saint-Gaudens bronze is Anne Page as Miss Churm at work; as "the real thing" used to guide the artist's eye and mind toward his discovery of the way the Angel of Death might look. The detachment of head from body, the nonnatural tone and texture of bronze, the stare into the middle distance: all encourage a sense of remoteness from Anne Page's public personality. Only after he had done "the real thing" of this bronze study was Saint-Gaudens prepared to execute the model for the angel which would float in its ideality upon the Shaw Memorial dedicated upon Boston Commons in 1897 (figure 3.9).

Do not, then, be too hasty to label any of these six figures (3.4 through 3.9) as being strictly "romantic" or "realistic." Analysis of the allegorical forms that appear at the end of a long artistic journey is best served when we note the representations of *the actual* and *the real*, the imaginative stages that precede the creation of *the ideal*.

The working habits of Daniel Chester French inform us how French achieved allegorical forms by means of techniques that demanded the naturalist's eye and hand. During 1981–82 Susan Frisch Lehrer, curator of the collection at Chesterwood, French's home and studio in the Berkshires, mounted an exhibit titled "Setting the Stage for Sculpture: Models and Props."[17] Lavishly documented by photo-

3.7. Augustus Saint-Gaudens, "Anne Page," model for the head of the Angel in the Robert Gould Shaw Memorial (1895).

3.8. Dennis Miller Bunker, "Portrait of Anne Page" (1887).

SAINT-GAUDENS NATIONAL HISTORIC SITE

LOS ANGELES COUNTY MUSEUM OF ART

3.9. Augustus Saint-Gaudens, figure from the Robert Gould Shaw Memorial, Boston (1884–1897).

BROOKLYN MUSEUM

graphs taken between 1903 and 1915 of French's studio, of his many female models, and of the props he used, the exhibit detailed the procedures by which French evolved such groupings as the Trask Memorial, the "Four Continents" for the New York Custom House, the "Alma Mater" for Columbia University, the "Mourning Victory" for the Melvin Memorial, and the "Memory" that hovers over the Marshall Field Memorial. Figure 3.10 gives one example of the fact that behind French's idealized forms stood a particular woman who served as his "real thing."

French seems to have been unable to do without models and tangible prompters for his imagination. On file at Chesterwood are boxes of photographs of family, friends, and models in various poses, *cartes de visite* gathered from studio photographers in Europe, costumes, wooden lay figures (cheaper to use, French said, than live models who received five dollars for three hours of posing), reproductions of Old Masters, and plaster casts from the Caproni works in Brooklyn. Recent interviews with Mitchell Shapiro, once hired by French to make photographic studies of his models, and with Ethel Cummings, one of his favorite sitters, add to the evidence that French used every conceivable means to assure accuracy in his observations.[18]

French (who owned a copy of Partridge's *Technique of Sculpture*) followed the practice outlined by both Partridge and Édouard Lanteri for conflating the features of many models into a single type. Like them, he believed in the form that arises from composites of the best available features. One of French's "angels," for instance, had a beautiful mouth and false teeth. He sensibly concentrated upon her mouth alone. Another model—a male immigrant from the Middle East—did quite nicely as George Washington when rigged up in an old revolutionary war uniform. French could take what he needed from actual models and props, while ignoring what did not further the broader references assured by the use of the type.

French believed that the studio model must (like a Miss Churm) be able to "drop into the pose of the 'Spirit of Light' or the 'Angel of Death' and *not* to look like a prizefighter."[19] Yet if he had been commissioned to prepare a monument to honor

3.10. Daniel Chester French,
studio model (c.1906).

CHESTERWOOD MUSEUM ARCHIVES

prizefighters, he might have relied on the same model who had shown him "light" and "death" to reveal the type of "the fighter."

The novels toward which we shall turn in a moment lock their artists and models into fervid emotional entanglements. In contrast, French and his female models took a practical, unself-conscious approach to their work together. The recollections of Ethel Cummings, the young domestic from nearby Stockbridge who began to pose for French at seventeen, make this clear. After she appeared from behind the screen where she disrobed and he had set her pose for the day, French went silently to work. He went so far as to comment once to Cummings that she had "perfect ears," but it was only the workmen on the grounds of Chesterwood who became excited over the presence of naked sitters to the extent of peering through holes in the wall. But Mrs. French reported that the models viewed the business of posing nude quite simply. They believed that if one's figure is beautiful, there need be no embarrassment. The models' perfection was their armor; that and their professionalism. The images the sculptor took away from the sight of their bodies had nothing to do with them personally. He wanted from them the real things of the type; they retained the actual thing of their individuality. It was completely otherwise, as one model expressed it to Mrs. French with a tone of disgust, when fashionable ladies appeared at balls in deep décolletage. "I don't see how they *can* show off their figures that way—just for the sake of showing them off." Amateurs *offered* breasts that were literal *products* for sale. Professional models *revealed* breasts that were *ideas* an artist had every right to respond to, while leaving the models in full possession of their own bodies.

Two years after the appearance of James' "The Real Thing," *Trilby* burst upon the reading public in Great Britain and the United States. George Du Maurier (who had planted the "germ" for James' "The Real Thing" in his friend's mind) also offered this story line to James, but James turned it back to Du Maurier to write. The result was *Trilby*, a publishing success of the kind James never managed to bring off, and a story to which Americans reacted as part of a transoceanic contract by which they extracted whatever images they wished in order to satisfy their own cultural needs.[20]

What does *Trilby* have as a narrative that "The Real Thing" does not? In many ways they share similar elements for public interest—their setting (artist's studio and professional model) and the question prompted by the situation (Which is the real thing?). But the differences between the two works are crucial. For one, James' tale is a passion of ideas; it deeply wants to know how the images are created by which we come to recognize certain types. Feelings for persons are underplayed. In contrast, Du Maurier's novel does without almost everything but the emotions stirred by the powerful icons of Trilby and Svengali. James' story is harshly realistic in its pursuit of functional authenticity, so much so that the artist-narrator's responses form the only "furniture" the story contains. Consider Du Maurier's romance, from the paragraph that opens the narrative through to the final page. The narrative is crammed with realistic props: plaster casts of arms and legs, Dante's mask, a Michelangelesque Leda and the Swan, reproductions of an Elgin marble, Old Master drawings, animal figures by Barye, and Clytie's bust—all the trappings of an art student's digs. By means of its inventory alone, Du Maurier's readers are assured they are being given an inside look at *la vie de bohème*.

This doting upon *things* is not a guarantee of the narrative's realism. Rather, it is the giveaway that verisimilitude in *Trilby* is included for the sake of fantasy. But to things Du Maurier adds feelings. James' story has no romantic plot and no reference to love except the gently expressed affections the middle-aged Monarchs share with one another and the pathos the narrator starts to feel toward the people whose grasp around his neck he must loosen. Such low-keyed feelings hardly turn "The Real Thing" into a parade of popular emotions. Du Maurier's novel meets the rules for a love story, if we can put up with no lovemaking and an excess of brain fevers and broken hearts caused by unrequited sentiments. Sexuality, of course, is implied by the hold Svengali exerts over the hypnotized woman in his power. The fact that he is also repulsive to look upon, Semitic, and villainous in character—a creature of vile and unmentionable forces—made the story's white slavery motif even more appealing to contemporary readers.[21] James' artists and models are magicians of the imagination, but it is Du Maurier who knows how to throw an aura of black magic around Svengali and his "creation."

Trilby may appear to be without an idea in its head of what it is about (the primary element James exacted of worthy fictions), but Du Maurier's narrative provides the obsessions that spill over the edges of the story. It is *out there* that those who desire more than a "good read" have a chance to consider what the tale of Trilby and the artist's studio conveys about the relation of human identity to artistic type.

The males in Du Maurier's romance are men only through the convention of their chronological age. Actually, they are boys who have yet to grow out of the diminutives and nicknames by which a familial society gives them a kind of probationary identity. Taken together, Taffy, the Laird, and Little Billee do not add up to one adult masculine figure. Rather, the boyish worship Billee gives to Trilby is matched by Taffy and the Laird, who treat their little friend as the perfect child and woman.

By contrast, Trilby O'Ferrall is a complete self, as rounded a personage as a young woman who lives by intuition and soul can be. True, at the outset she is a woman more in stature than in emotional maturity. The blithesomeness that makes Trilby such fun to be with, as the story makes clear in wholesale lots, is what one has when one has not yet "suffered." For her to count as a thoroughgoing Du Maurier heroine, she must undergo the pain of loving Billee, experience shame, and have a brain fever. But what matters to my present argument is that Du Maurier's Trilby is both James' Miss Churm *and* Mrs. Monarch. Trilby is an Irish/Parisian/Bohemian version of the cockney model in light of her scruffy antecedents, her knock-about upbringing, and her social classification as an artist's model. She is also (and naturally—without having to act her way into the type) as much a lady as Mrs. Monarch. These considerations, which Du Maurier let seep into his story, give the novel *Trilby* whatever ties it has with literary realism; they are also what link *Trilby* to the concerns held alike by American and Continental artists.

Du Maurier works hard in the narrative to point up the need for recognizing Trilby's true type. He borrows freely from Dumas' *Camille*, since the figure of the misunderstood Marguerite Gautier furnishes shortcut references to what happens when one is not known for what one *typically* is. Early in the story, Trilby weeps

over the plight of a stage Camille in unconscious prophecy of the shame and sorrow that lie ahead for her. When Little Billee's mother comes to plead with Trilby
to give up her son for the sake of his sister's happiness within respectable society,
Taffy tries to convince Mrs. Bagot (bigot?) that Trilby has a soul as beautiful as
her face; but the mother depends entirely upon ingrained methods for recognizing
identity. She looks only at Trilby's apparent social function and class. When it is
patently too late to do Trilby or Little Billee any good, a handsome reconciliation
scene takes place. Billee's mother acknowledges that Trilby's public activities as a
model (which had automatically categorized her as immoral) are countered by
the moral authenticity of her real self. Trilby is revealed to proper society as a
lady; she is honored in her dying hours (à la Camille) as the type of the angel and
the lily—as the accepted icon of sacrificial love.

During the days when Trilby practices her profession as a model (figure 3.11),
she inspires an entire *arrondissement* of artists, including Leon Gérôme. She is named
Galatea to one sculptor's Pygmalion; she prompts Billee to create what is acclaimed as one of the masterpieces of the Western world—the soul-stirring outline
of her left foot chalked upon a wall. But then fate strikes. She becomes the muse
of Svengali, who thrusts his dark sexual longings upon her diaphragm, throat, and
mouth. It is noticeable that Trilby's identity is continually being anatomized. Synecdoche takes over whenever male fantasies attach themselves to one part or
other of her body. Not breasts, buttocks, or thighs, however. Rather, discreet portions (foot, throat) act as erotic substitutes for those other "real things" which Du
Maurier's descriptions of his beautiful model choose to omit.

A major disclosure is made at the end of the novel. Trilby, who was so wonderfully one person at the start of the story (present model and lady, future angel and
martyr), has undergone the purgatory of having another self imposed upon her (or
discovered within herself) by means of Svengali's hypnotic powers. That second
self is "the Beautiful Statue" (to allude to one of Mrs. Monarch's attributes). This
is the public figure which appears onstage, its perfect foot posed upon a pedestal-
like stool (figure 3.12).[22] The original young woman who simply *is* and the subsequent marble form that *performs* give us a switch on Miss Churm. Miss Churm has
the admirably intuitive gift of acting which makes her the real type, in contrast
to Mrs. Monarch's real form which keeps the latter limited to the marbleness of
her ego. The figure of Trilby offers Du Maurier an intriguing doubleness of means
and ends, of external image and inner type; but he failed to resolve the narrative
splits her doubleness causes. Further, he did not fully convert these dualities into
the aboutness of his story. We are left with Trilby returned to her original wholeness, but dying. She has been overwhelmed (as was Du Maurier's imagination) by
that other entity—the Beautiful Statue—which is swept into the narrative by way
of Svengali's creative force. The type is done in by the dark arts of the Type maker.

The Angel of Clay was written by William Ordway Partridge, practicing sculptor
and frustrated participant in modern times. Published in 1900, Partridge's novel did
not make the best-seller lists which *The Bookman* instituted in 1895, but this is

3.11. George Du Maurier, "The Soft Eyes," from *Trilby* (1884).

3.12. George Du Maurier, "Au Clair de la Lune," from *Trilby* (1894).

not the main evidence for the kind of failure it demonstrates. What Partridge's narrative lacks that both *Trilby* and *The Common Law* possess is nicely summed up in a contemporary appraisal of the power possessed by good popular novels.

The Bookman of April 1906 states that Richard Harding Davis' heroines are "the kind of women about whom a man wants to muse wistfully in his bachelor den, to idealise, to invest with a thousand attributes of heart and mind and soul—and then go out to dinner."[23] That is, successful popular fiction allows readers a royal good time of dreaming their way through a world of romantic imagery, while releasing them, without too much strain, back into the world of dinners; back to reality. Partridge, as it were, never goes out to dinner. He stays imprisoned within "his bachelor den"—in his case, the sculptor's studio.

Partridge's narrative is given over to obsessive struggles between angels of marble (the elevated ideal of feminine purity) and angels of clay (the debasing actuality of female sexual appetites). The result is a story that falls apart at the level of imaginative coherence. What prevents him from providing the pleasures possible from Davis, Du Maurier, and (as we shall see) Chambers is that Partridge does not seize the chance to make something forceful of types. He feels (deeply and with embarrassing earnestness) but fails to locate those feelings in coherent images. He writes about types but cannot present them as strong images. He only manages stereotypes, not the type as "the real thing." It is for these reasons that Partridge's *The Angel of Clay* acts as the contrast which makes distinct the other side of the theoretical coin.

Ellerton Lawrence, the hero of Partridge's novel, refuses to mix real life with ideal life (the sort of thing, he scornfully says, the French do). He wants to live purely and to banish mixtures altogether, but into his life comes Julia Hartmann, a beautiful young woman whom he takes first to be his studio model, later his wife. Julia is a model who is also a woman; she is a combination of the diverse types which all human beings assume in the actual flesh. Alas, what Ellerton wants is a "model"—an absolute Type which will inspire the Platonic ideas he desires to turn into marble for an eternity of worship.

From page one we learn that Ellerton will not be having any fun in his studio life. Partridge signals at the start that the sculptor's studio is dedicated to life as real and as earnest, in contrast to the frivolous existence of the dandies of the easel. He leads into chapter 1 with a poem by Michelangelo that elevates Platonic truths of eternity above counterfeit images bound to the mundane. We are also subjected to a lecture concerning the reality pure marble possesses in opposition to the infantile appeal of the palette of colors. We are told that Ellerton's studio—a workshop where muscle and determination create great art—is the arena where his soul struggles against the uncontrollable feelings which actual female beauty arouses when that force is not contained and freed from taint by marble.

As a practicing artist (one who has undoubtedly studied the Partridge *Technique of Sculpture*), Ellerton is painfully aware that the sculptor's work involves the shaping of a clay prototype. His immaculate conceptions of heaven's virtue have to pass through the world's muck. But Ellerton, self-blinded both by his infatuation and his idealism, refuses to let the full implications of the conflict between Julia's qualities (wonderful clay!) check his vision of her as a cold, perfectly pure image in marble. It would have been wiser had he contented himself, as did John Ferguson Weir, with a wooden lay figure as "His Favorite Model" (figure 3.13).

Two actual angels rule Ellerton's life. One is his mother, the stereotype of New England purity to whom he turns in time of need. She is his "sweetheart" who lets him lie in her arms as if he were the marble Christ in the marble lap of the Virgin of Michelangelo's "Pietà." The other angel is Mabel Frothingham, an allegorical personification of Patience and Hope. Her brow of marble informs us hundreds of pages before Ellerton realizes (since he is uncommonly dense about such matters) that *she* is the angel to whom he ought to be offering his personal adoration; the one he ought to be imaging through his art. Unfortunately, Ellerton only thinks of Mabel as a sweet child. A child is what Julia, his new model, is not.

Julia has the look of perfect beauty and she possesses all the working techniques of a practiced model, but she lacks a soul. Her father was of the "northern" races (representing spirit), but her mother was Italian, a "southern" type (representing sensuality). Her body is as flawless as a classical statue, while her face is that dangerous kind that weakens the moral fiber of anyone who looks upon it. Once while she lies sleeping in his studio, Ellerton notices that her complexion is a dream of color. This fact ought to have warned a man who is convinced that "truth" comes only with the repudiation of earthly hues and the acceptance of marmoreal whiteness. But Ellerton is misled by his belief (the same as Lavater's) that it is impossible for external physical beauty to disguise inner moral ugliness. Thus thrown off the track of the proper identification of Julia's type, he plans to carve her as a marble Aurora. Visitors to the studio see that she would do better as a model for a painting of Zenobia, Eastern queen robed in scarlet and jewels. Practiced readers might also pick up on the suggestion that Ellerton Lawrence is caught between Mabel Frothingham as Priscilla and Julia Hartmann as Zenobia in a latter-day version of Miles Coverdale's dilemma in Hawthorne's *The Blithedale Romance*.

Through a sequence of unbelievable events, Julia becomes Ellerton's wife. At once he sees his mistake. Even his original fevered interest in her body vanishes once he possesses it. "Realization" is less exciting than the "anticipation" enjoyed while his imagination mounted through endless spires of form. He immediately trades his earlier obsession for another. He will try to correct Julia's complex reality of type. He will attempt to elevate her to the level of the Platonic Idea he seeks to impose upon the variety of her human types.

The story line of *The Angel of Clay* proceeds to detail the wretchedness that results when an idealist finds himself yoked to a woman whose beauty now makes him think of Sappho, not Aurora. He adds wings to Julia's sculptured form, but they do little to alter the blunt fact that his wife possesses a bottom-being formed by heredity, environment, and a mess of unholy experiences. Poor Julia wants very

3.13. John Ferguson Weir, "His
Favorite Model" (188–).

much to improve her "mould." Only then, she believes, might her "cast" cease
being that of the type of the Bohemian model. But Julia is unable to remove the
taints inherited from her Italian mother and her past life. She confirms everything
the Mrs. Bagots of the world conceive artists' models to be like. She is fated to
repeat her parents' folly through her marriage to Ellerton; once again "New England" rectitude is linked with "Italian" sensuality.

Julia ponders a photograph of Mabel Frothingham that Ellerton keeps close by.
Perhaps, Julia thinks, if she associates her own longings for perfection with this
image of pure womanhood, her flawed nature may change for the better. Perhaps
she can trade the "real thingness" of her human character for the inhuman truth
of Mabel's Platonic form. But the possibility that Mabel's image might act as Julia's talisman of hope is dashed when Ellerton cruelly compares Julia to an image
of darkness and Mabel to an angel of light. In desperation, Julia kneels in prayer
before a Murillo Madonna. No wonder she fears that the massive marble angel
that looms above her in her husband's studio will one day topple, crushing the life
from her all-too-human body (figure 3.14).

3.14. Albert Beck Wenzell,
frontispiece for Partridge,
The Angel of Clay (1900).

In the meantime Partridge informs his readers that his hero, through the pain he has suffered and the asceticism he practices, has learned how to love. When one wintry night he finds Julia dead outside in a snowdrift, frozen into purity at last, he is able to forgive her. He rejoices that she has been transformed into the angel of his ideal, even though it requires death to bring her the cold stability of spirit and the defeat of the warm variations of her flesh.

The Angel of Clay describes what happens when a zealous artist of the ideal misreads the images he sees in the course of his Neoplatonic repudiation of corporeal images. Ellerton Lawrence prefers that spirit replace the body. That such gestures of Savonarolan iconoclasm appear in a late-nineteenth-century narrative is remarkable, especially when it comes from a man like Partridge who was both a practicing sculptor and novelist—those two professions dedicated to the way of physical images and the creation of human types. But renunciation of materiality is what Ellerton Lawrence, the novel's hero, and William Ordway Partridge, its author, insist upon. They take up the cause of the supra-earthly Type—the ultimate Platonic form that denies the types, the real things, which find their vigorous existence in the midst of the world.

The last of this group of four fictional narratives that treat artists and models is Robert Chambers' best-seller of 1911, *The Common Law*, illustrated by the man to whom Chambers dedicated his novel, Charles Dana Gibson.

Chambers' hero, Louis Neville, matches the fantasies often held by art students. Still in his handsome twenties, Neville has already achieved popular fame, critical honors, and wealth. "Thousands" stand in awe before his paintings that hang in major museums. His current commissions include the decorations for a palatial new theater and murals for the state capitol. He is a Harvard man, with an impeccable old-Eastern family whose country house graces the area near the city. He runs an unending salon in a studio whose immense spaces can be filled with guests.[24] While he—perched high on a ladder—paints winged creatures on a vast canvas, someone plays a baby grand piano in one corner, and friends gather around tea things in another (figure 3.15). He also serves intimate little breakfasts to lovely models—catered repasts that consist of "chilled grapefruit, African melon, fragrant coffee, toast, and pigeon's eggs poached on astrakan caviar." Neville's studio, enhanced by a few extravagant details of *luxe*, is uncommonly like those that excited the readers of the Sunday supplements of the period: the famous Tenth Street establishments run by William Merritt Chase or the equally well-known studio of Howard Chandler Christy on West 67th Street. All this, and (as the illustrations make clear) the looks of the Gibson Man. As Neville admits, fortune is his mistress, one who has perhaps been too generous.

True to the conventions of this grouping of artist-and-model narratives, Neville is too dedicated to his art, too fond of his male companions, and too preadolescent to have much interest in women. Women are dimly in the background, adding aesthetic fillip to studio life. All this leaves the story wide open for Valerie West to walk through the door and ask if she may be his model.

In the parlance of Hollywood, Neville and Valerie "meet cute." He mistakenly thinks she is a seasoned professional and brusquely tells her to disrobe because he wishes to use her as the type of a nymph-on-a-cloud he is in the midst of painting. In fact, she is a blushing virgin and this is her first time out as a model; the agonies she suffers over removing her clothes go quite past Neville when she emerges from behind the dressing screen to stand before him in naked splendor. (Gibson and Chambers chose not to have this scene illustrated, but figure 3.16 is a 1879 painting

3.15. Charles Dana Gibson, "In the Studio," from Chambers, *The Common Law* (1911).

3.16. Alice Barber Stevens, "Female Life Class" (1879).

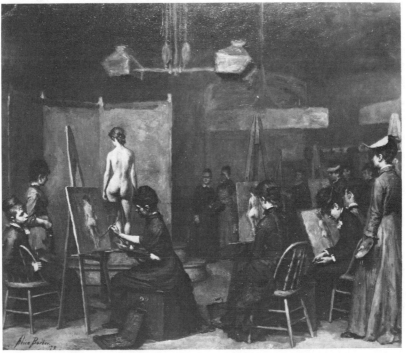

PENNSYLVANIA ACADEMY OF THE FINE ARTS

by Alice Barber which depicts a nude model protectively sheltered by a circle of female artists.) Neville is properly businesslike. He writes down Valerie's name and physical description in his notebook (not the bachelor's proverbial little black book): "Height, medium; eyes, a dark brown; hair, thick, lustrous, and brown; head, unusually beautiful; throat and neck, perfect."

Unlike the glum hero of *The Angel of Clay*, Neville has no interest in hiring beautiful souls. He simply wants a highly professional model whose figure and face will guide his trained hand and instructed imagination. He certainly does not want a model he might have to give thought to. Still, Neville finds himself listening intently as Valerie reports shyly that prostitution is perhaps the only other way open for a lonely, attractive young woman in the city.

Neville is obtuse when it comes to the human heart. He admits, however, that he has been told he needs to experience suffering and its consequence—love. Otherwise, he will never acquire the warm sympathy for humanity that could correct his fatal facility as a painter. It is Valerie who will be the making of Neville as an artist and a man and the undoing of the smug male conventionality of his heart and mind. For Valerie is Chambers' version of the type of the New Woman and of the subtype, the Professional Model; redemptive, both. But, as the novel's title indicates, Valerie must first solve certain conundrums concerning the nature of "common law." Only then will she be prepared to tutor Neville in the bracing truths about the relationships between art, life, and love she has herself discovered.

In terms of plot, the question raised by *The Common Law* is whether a nice orphan girl (who passed the entrance examination to Barnard College but was too poor to matriculate) can find happiness with a handsome Harvard man bound to society's conventional views about marriage (deemed a stay against social chaos) and illicit liaisons (declared the destruction of civilization). As for the narrative's intellectual commitment, conventional terms such as "art" and "common law" must undergo rigorous redefinition.[25] "Art" is more than technique that results in skillfully executed generalizations. In *The Common Law* art requires the heart's overflow that particularizes individual motives, desires, and principles. "Common law" is more than a socially questionable relationship of the kind that fits the public notion of what goes on in the demimonde of artists and models. In Chambers' novel people in love have to reexamine their dependence upon desiccated social conventions and look for guidance to the natural laws of emotional response. Art and love are the two areas of education through which Louis Neville, type of the Handsome Artist, must progress toward knowledge, guided by Valerie West, type of the Beautiful American Girl imaged even more specifically as New Woman and Model.

The course of education does not run smoothly in 1911 (as Henry Adams was just then in the process of noting down in his big book on the subject). Not when Neville has everything yet to learn about what loving and art actually consist of. His experience of "the real thing" Valerie represents is different from the stereotypes held by him and his class as preconceived judgments against professional models.

Neville labors under the fact that he comes from a particularly stuffy family. His sister faces Valerie and tells her—as Mrs. Bagot does Trilby and as Armand Duval's father does Marguerite Gautier—that she must give up her hold on Neville in order to save him from social ruin. His parents are depicted as tottering relics from a bygone age of innocence. In 1911 his mother still wears a lace cap and a long black antebellum gown; his father is bearded, eats bread and milk from a bowl with a large spoon, reads outmoded literary journals such as the *Atlantic*, appreciates Bierstadt, Hiram Powers, and Herbert Spencer, and angrily sends his son from the room for saying the word "seraglio" in the mother's presence.

Neville has a further difficulty to overcome before he himself can become more than an imperfect type, a man flawed by the lack of complete identity. Neville's character is an uneasy patching together of two subtypes. Neville is "Louis" (worried, conventional, vulnerable, very human) and he is also "Kelly" (the nickname by which friends refer to his godlike, supremely self-assured nature). Although Valerie tells him she loves both the personalities he possesses, he will have to merge the two before he can recognize what his own "real thingness" consists of. He must do this for his own sake, but also so that he may not impose destructive splits upon others of the kind that brought poor Trilby and poor Julia to their deaths.

Since Valerie is the figure of saving grace in Chambers' novel, she (like the Trilby who existed before Svengali took her into his power) represents wholeness and completed self-identity. Within her type she contains pluralities—all that is pure, intelligent, amusing, serious, frolicsome, tender, questioning, knowing, beautiful: the qualities exacted in 1911 of the American Girl when approached by authors, illustrators, and the public at large. Neville and his friends keep coming across new aspects of Valerie's unity-in-multiplicity. Variety is what makes her such a successful artist's model. Like Trilby, Valerie is both Miss Churm (actress) and Mrs. Monarch (lady). Like Trilby, she has the beautiful soul to match her beautiful body. And like Trilby, she must be "discovered." When this revelation takes place it causes the shock Aristotelian poetics define, whether exemplified by the disclosure of Oedipus' true nature or by Camille's reversion from courtesan to saint.

Neville paints Valerie in a variety of forms ranging from a radiant allegorical nude for a theater mural to "just a girl in street clothes." He now wants to show her *entire*. Not in the "altogether" (to use Du Maurier's quaint phrase), but (to use Neville's comment) as a representation that is "very much 'all of you.' " But Neville is puzzled over which form best portrays Valerie in her rich indeterminacy and her complex simplicity.

Neville's fellow artists like to escort Valerie after hours because she can "impersonate" anyone. Both casteless and placeless, she is fun to be with. She is also safe. When these men encounter relatives while in her company, they know Valerie can pass as a lady even though she is a model. But readers who have caught on to the drift of Chambers' theme realize that Neville and his friends have not yet *recognized* Valerie; the studio coterie continues to look at the superficial stereotype that disguises the real thing and the true type.

Present fun with Valerie precludes future bliss. According to these young blades of good blood, the very adaptability of this young woman (one who has no proper place in proper society) means that she is *out of* the world they and Neville possess by right of birth. If she ever gave herself to Neville in common-law marriage, he would *come down* to her level of debasement. Neville suggests ways for Valerie to raise herself socially, but she rejects them. She is not interested in the respectable jobs open to women of the period: type-writer, milliner, store clerk. She wants to prove she can be free and pure—*as a model.*

Valerie quickly becomes a "personality" in the same way the fresh appeal of Evelyn Nesbit at sixteen took New York by storm during the previous decade. Valerie's image appears everywhere: on the back-advertising covers of leading magazines and in Sunday supplement photographs. But she insists upon her private life; she lives virginally in a small white room—spotless and tidy as a nun's cell—in this, providing no neat parallel to the life of Nesbit.

Valerie must have it both ways. She demands that society allow her an identity so right she can go anywhere and do anything because committed to an antinomian belief in her authority to choose what kind of "real thing" she is. As novelist, Chambers also wishes to have it both ways; to a point. His readers are given the enjoyment of seeing this lovely young woman of twenty take down social convention and Neville's ingrown snobbery several pegs, but they are still protected by Chambers' narrative from witnessing a radical revolt against the properties. Valerie shapes her identify as she wills, but since she never sins, all her little freedoms are kept this side of what is considered unacceptable. The threat of her modernity and her realism as the type of the New Woman are carefully contained by the fact that Chambers guides the plot and keeps her pure.

Neville, immersed *within* the narrative, cannot realize how safe it is for him to love Valerie. Chambers provides a rousing confrontation scene (very like the one in which Camille is publicly insulted by Armand). It is New Year's Eve. Neville is morosely in the company of friends and a woman named Maizie, the type of the wanton. (Chambers' readers could classify her easily by means of his description and Gibson's illustration.) Suddenly Neville looks up and sees Valerie. She is with a rival artist, standing on top of a table pelting the revelers with rosebuds, her gown torn free from her beautiful shoulders. Neville is outraged, but he does not understand that what he feels is jealousy and desire. All he knows is that he *doubts.* Her appearance, which had previously brought him delight over the innocence it represented to his imagination, is now that of a loose woman: *a model.* Throughout Chambers' novel, Neville has been written up very much in the manner of Edith Wharton's male protagonists Newland Archer and Lawrence Selden. As nervous as they in his doubts, Neville instantly casts Valerie (as Archer and Selden do Ellen Olenska and Lily Bart) into the shadows.

Disconsolate, Neville returns to his studio. There he broods before his painting of Valerie in the pose of a bride, the one everyone tells him is the most brilliant thing he has ever done, the proof he has at last learned about suffering. He suffers because he does not recognize that the type of the bride in his painting matches "the real thing" of Valerie's nature.

This very long novel winds to its close when Valerie offers herself to Neville, with or without a wedding ring, as a "bride" who is—she insists—"all new". But before she presents herself, she prepares for her sacrificial act of love by kneeling beside her little white bed to ask instruction in interpreting "the law" (see Introduction, figure 30). Her prayer is answered by the only "god" she has—her heart's intuitions.

Chambers' readers may have feared (and been titillated by) the thought that the story would conclude with "common law" redefined as the situational morality that flies in the face of social law. But their fears were laid to rest (and their expectations dashed). In her own way, Valerie comes around to the position earlier argued by Neville's sister: that marriage is the only safety a woman has and that women need the personal limitations of marriage in order to enjoy the social freedoms allowed them once they are married. But to give credit to Valerie-as-written-by-Chambers, she goes beyond this somewhat self-serving stance. At the basis of her decision is the discovery she makes about the biological fact that, if she and Neville joined their lives, there might be children, and that it is *they* she must protect. (Babies getting born is something that had never occurred to her until that moment.) Having come into the possession of this startling piece of knowledge, Valerie concludes that marriage is indeed right. It alone blends nature's laws (biology and birth) with man's laws (society and order).

All ends happily for the artist and his model. Aided by the impact upon Neville's family of his painting of her as a bride, Valerie's true identity as a marriageable "soul" is made clear. The sacred quality of the painted image, inspired by "the real thing" that lies harbored within the physical form of Valerie the model, is now recognized by society at large. Not only is Valerie lifted into Neville's social world, he rises into the realm of her free and natural spirit where the real things dwell. Through the penance he suffers and the reward he gains by learning how to love, he finds his own realness as a painter and the breach between "Louis" and "Kelly" is healed. By the conclusion of Chambers' novel, art, love, and self—those potentially dangerous qualities—are made safe. Appearances are saved because they are matched to what is actually there.

In face of the obvious fudging and compromises exposed by the conclusion of Chambers' novel, it is imperative to realize that the narrative use of the type of the New Woman as Professional Model is not what defaults on the possibilities set loose by Valerie's story. It is Chambers' final timidities as an author that do this. Instead of throwing caution to the winds, what he throws away is an opportunity to push the type of the young American woman to the edges of realism and romance, and beyond.

The problematic relation of pretense to actuality is relentlessly at the center of narratives about artists and models. In these stories, the sharp lesson the skeptics must learn is that beauty is not necessarily a disguise for immorality, and that the concealments required by professionalism need not belie inner integrity.

There are those among us like Mrs. Bagot and Neville's sister who conclude that posing, self-representation, and the marketing of personal value are marks of the bad woman, corrupt society, and worse art.

The accepted position is to speak of "realism" as though it were the only way by which "reality" can be laid hold of. Often the critical hands that do the laying on are heavy ones. If the platonist can be oppressively literal minded at times, so can the empiricist. If the idealist can be preachy about the morality of the true, the good, and the beautiful (flinging them into the face of what is deceptive, evil, and morally ugly), so can literary critics who wish to save the collective American soul from the deceits of a corrupted society given over to commercialized "shows" and "sells." Such arguments are as old as those found in *The Republic* and as new as those presented by the Frankfurt School or Fredric Jameson. But it does not help for cultural historians and literary critics to start sounding like Ellerton Lawrence in their craving for social-political angels of marble; or to denounce the immoral fraudulence of actresses and models in the tones of Mrs. Bagot or Louis Neville's parents. Professional models often live in the shadow of the artists who employ them. This is suggested by Anders Zorn's 1897 drawing in which Augustus Saint-Gaudens dominates the foreground, while one of his models, "clothed" only in Zorn's thick pen strokes, crouches behind him (figure 3.17), and by the still, tall, isolated figure of Alfred Maurer's painting "The Model" (figure 3.18). Models ought to be brought back into the light of common day where acting and posing can be recognized for what they are: a reputable means for the identification of one's essential nature and the possible placation of one's desires.

In Philip Fisher's essay on Dreiser's *Sister Carrie* he notes, "Acting . . . is not sham, but rather a form of practice. . . . Acting draws its moral meaning not from a world of true and false but from a dynamic society where all are rising or falling."[26] True, Fisher trots out Jean-Jacques Rousseau's diatribe against acting through a paraphrase that makes it a bit difficult to know where Rousseau ends and where Fisher picks up in agreement. "The essence of acting is, of course, representing what one is not. . . . To value and foster the skills of the actor is to reward those able to not be themselves, not feel what they really feel and, therefore, to strike at the heart of a social order based on full individual being and public self-representation."

We are on sounder ground when Fisher follows this quotation about Rousseau's peeves with a comment about Carrie Meeber's artful ways. Where Theodore Dreiser goes beyond Rousseau, Fisher observes, is in "his refusal to contrast acting with sincerity, his refusal to oppose the representation of what one is not to authentic self-representation."

3.17. Anders Zorn, "Augustus Saint-Gaudens with Model" (1897).

Exactly! Dreiser's position was also Henry James'. Even though James continually pointed up the slippage between inner lives and social exteriors (especially amid the bruising pressures exerted by corrupt cultures), he maintained to the end the value of representation. Pitfalls abound in a society filled with "artists and models." Fraud and self-deception lurk behind every flick of the painter's brush or twist of the model's body. But authenticity of expression is still possible in the exchanges that take place in "studio lives." Even when representation incorporates the special strengths of the type.

At the turn of the century the theory of types could be and was roundly abused and misused by racists and sexists. Facile labels and distorting classifications were applied with appalling ease when people began to generalize about individuals with the purpose of tidily identifying them as friends or enemies. But the irresponsible use of categories of type should not lead to our ignoring the other occasions when the type was put responsibly to work. One such occasion arises from our need to break free from the notions that realism and romanticism are the only two ways we have for dealing with the world's diversity and that the validity of the art of the type collapsed with the fall of the Bastille.

In the same year that Robert Chambers gave his readers a story about the meaning of "the common law," Gertrude Stein was writing *Three Lives* and pondering

3.18. Alfred Maurer, "The Model" (c.1902).

"The Making of Americans"—two narratives by means of which she redefined the universals of personality. In the thirties Stein regaled the public with her tales of artists and models in Paris in *The Autobiography of Alice B. Toklas,* but by then Stein had become an expert at experimenting with one of the oldest known forms of identification—the type. And on that day in Philadelphia in 1900 Thomas Eakins could have used the surrogate model sent to sit in for Mrs. Drexel—that is, if she had had the facility of Miss Churm. (And who is to say out of hand that she did not?) Or Eakins could have turned to his wife and asked her to pose for "the real thing" of the absent portrait subject.

Susan Macdowell Eakins had once been an art student and a painter.[27] In her youth she had worked alongside Eakins at the Pennsylvania Academy. Before their marriage she posed nude for him in a charming photograph he tucked away in his file of studies of the human form. As his wife, she sat for him many times. The results of these sittings are some of the finest portraits contained within the American collections of the nation's galleries. But when we look at the painting Eakins

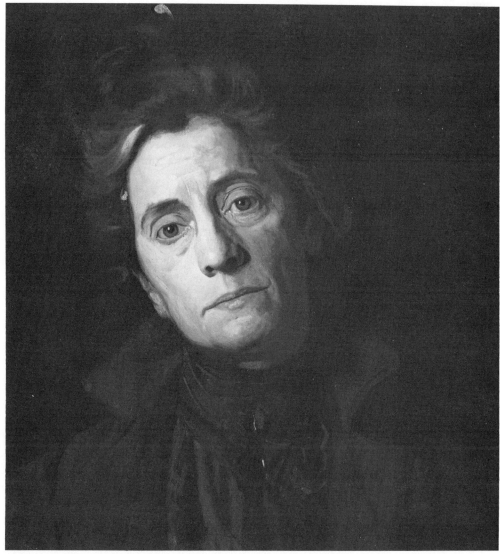

3.19. Thomas Eakins, "Mrs. Thomas Eakins" (c.1899).

did of his wife around 1899 (the year before he threw down his brush in disgust before his unfinished canvas of Mrs. Drexel), can we state flatly that this "Mrs. Thomas Eakins" is a literal, "realistic" imitation of Susan Macdowell Eakins as she really was (figure 3.19)? As the story goes, she had asked her husband to let her wear a brightly colored dress for the portrait he planned to do of her. He said no, he saw her as wearing a somber gown.[28] As the result, we have Eakins' version of his wife as it hangs in the Hirshhorn Museum, a painting lauded as a perfect example of the realistic mode. But who is to say which is the "real" Susan Macdowell Eakins: the woman represented by her husband's painting or the woman whose mood was dismissed at the moment she felt the need to flare forth in living hues?

We cannot know whether Eakins captured the particulars of his wife in the Hirshhorn Museum portrait, even though we conclude that the painting is realistic (based on observation), not romantic (constructed solely according to a mental image). In one sense it does not make much difference. What we have to go by is a painted surface that may strike us as being one of the great real things which American artists at the end of the nineteenth century were capable of producing. If this is indeed the effect Eakins' painting has upon its viewers, it comes about as the consequence of his brilliant creation of an essential type through the transaction that transpired then, and still does, between artist and model.

4

The Aesthetics of Desire

Desire was the origin of the art of representational forms. So the old story has it, a story retold by many during the late nineteenth century.[1] One day in 600 B.C. a young woman named Corinthea was parted from her beloved. Realizing the sense of loss his absence would cause her, she traced the shadow of his form cast by a candle upon the wall of her room. Thereafter her yearning had a form; she now possessed the likeness of the love she had once had and now had not. And so, the story concludes, representational art was born of the occasion of Corinthea's pain and the means she used to assuage it.

Corinthea's act led to the arts of portraiture, and also to philosophies of type and physiognomical theories of identity. To Socrates the Cave of Shadows stood for the deceptions under which mortals lie when imprisoned far from True Forms, but to others—Johann Casper Lavater among them—the power of the silhouette was great and good. Such men accepted the ancient notion that the absent reality is held in memory through "shadows," "shades," and "profiles"—terms used interchangeably with "silhouette."[2]

Silhouette or outline-drawing supplies a substitute image that simultaneously placates the emotion of loss and continues to press upon the nerve of that emotion. But what of the desire one feels for what one has never experienced directly but has only dreamed about? Does the dream object require other plastic forms and other modes of visual identification than the outline? Yes, and the chapters ahead will be filled with examples of the alternate forms given to desire and identification. But this chapter focuses upon the outline—"the pure form" that expresses

types and real things—favored by many late-nineteenth-century American art theorists and artists.

Granted, the range of art forms gathered under the rubric "representational" has
long since strayed from the original simplicity of the outline shadowed upon Corinthea's wall; but the subcategory "arts of pure form" still adheres to that primary
image. This chapter sketches the history of pure forms during the last two decades
of the nineteenth century and the early years of the twentieth century as they
provided the artistic means to the ends of registering deep wants. This chapter
advances what the earlier chapters introduced—the complex and evolving relation
between desire and identification invoked by practitioners and theorists of representational art forms for the pleasure and instruction of the American public.

All the things there were for people to want, and the many ways high or low
art had for representing those things, were validated by a variety of formulations
and practice we can call an aesthetics of desire. And everywhere Americans looked,
on almost every level of the nation's pictorial life, the image used with the greatest
frequency to suggest the nature of desire was the image of the female.

There is a clear history of the issues raised by American critics and artists over the
nature of representation in the years between 1876 and 1918. But another matter
takes precedence: what desire is like, what its source is, and the means by which
one tells the difference between desires spurious and authentic. Art historical over-
views are fine; they are what we need and will receive by the conclusion of this
chapter. But first we ought to look at the trees that made up the forest of turn-of-
the-century concerns (compulsion, actually) over the nature of desire, real things,
and true art.

We can name three species of the trees in that forest. They are "Rhoda," "Humphrey," and "Walter"—the persons caught up in an imaginary epistolary debate
set down in 1896 by Henry Bennet Brewster in a little book titled *The Statuette
and the Background*.[3]

Rhoda is a dreamer of "the inner life" who asks that each painting convey a
special message just for her. She writes to Humphrey that art is like a carrier pigeon. "I search at once for the letter at its neck." Expert rendering of objects does
not interest her, only the feelings they stir. A latter-day Luther, she demands not
works but faith. She thinks of the artist as one who prays to be judged by the
intensity of the longings his paintings express, not by their accuracy.

Humphrey writes back to Rhoda in a huff. He accuses her of "having moods"
and of liking art that dissolves under the force of her "invisible self." As for his
position on the matter, "it is the hard, insensible, exterior part of us that counts."
But even a sensible fellow like Humphrey the positivist turns to allegory to make
his point. The story Humphrey tells Rhoda is aesthetic theory in the form of "The
Heart of Darkness," written, as it were, in collaboration with Josiah Strong, Joseph
Simms, and whoever was just then classifying cultural acts in terms of race and
gender.

There is an island, Humphrey says, where white men are busy colonizing the coastal areas, but the natives pass along rumors of a mysterious kingdom in the interior ruled by a veiled queen. Enticed by these tales, foolhardy colonists plunge into the jungle to seek "the dark Eldorado." The moral of this tale, Humphrey informs Rhoda, is that the useful part of our nature stays along the shoreline, absorbed in the white man's business. The other part "wanders inward towards the mysterious self that reigns in the land of dreams." Rationality and adult "Aryan" activities dominate the coast; feelings and "childhood play" lie buried in the "aboriginal" interior. Eager to warn Rhoda away from the jungle of desire, Humphrey encapsulates the history of the white male as the progress away from "theology, philosophy, and magic; pentagrams and meditations on the essence of things" toward the present where "the best" give their time to "building dams and clearing wastes."

In this epistolary exchange, Humphrey emerges as the male and the Aryan, while Rhoda is the female, the child, the aboriginal who plays with dolls and idols. Humphrey closes with these words of rebuke: "To you, intensity of life means inward pageants and rites . . . and you watch with beautiful, pained eyes, the hard men who are doing the work of the world. In them are no whispering avenues down which theories, clad in white, bear incense to the palace of memory."

Fine letter to receive from someone you thought your friend! Devastated by Humphrey's attack, Rhoda turns next to Walter, whose position on the relation of art, the self, desire, and reality is more moderately phrased, in keeping with his location on the sexless, casteless middle ground between objective coastline and subjective jungle interior.

Walter agrees with Rhoda that some moods are "works themselves, the products of a great and silent industry, revealed to us in . . . monuments of the most delicate architecture." He also agrees that moods of desire have value; not because of the feelings that clothe them but for "the constructive force, the power of organization from which they result." (Force and power are Walter's forte, but he makes them neither masculine nor feminine in nature.) Thoughts or feelings placed upon the painter's canvas must be used as "agents in a scheme of visual organization," lest they ebb into efforts that are no more than the literary, the sentimental, or the moralistic.

Overly refined persons (Rhoda) wish to please the soul with works of art. Coarser individuals (and even Humphrey is superior to this) expect anecdotes that satisfy their common sense. Both types miss the purpose of true art. Art should ravish the eye, not merely provide pictures for "the Illustrated Psychical News." If Humphrey errs in being a materialist, Rhoda errs in placing her spirituality on high like an idol. Walter knows he acts correctly by insisting on the presence of pure forms. He follows "the supreme reality . . . an all-prevailing, constructive force"—even though it is "only revealed in forms that are not its essence," which is what causes the sorrow that is the distinguishing mark of desire.

Having let Rhoda, Humphrey, and Walter sound their positions on the nature of art and desire,[4] Henry Brewster steps forward in the second half of his book to speak directly to the reader. Brewster's stance is Walter's stance but amplified. No art-for-art's-sake man, Brewster's argument shows an uncanny likeness to the philosophies of Charles Sanders Peirce and Josiah Royce that advocate an ultimate Reality founded upon consensus agreements about what we crave most.

People who harp on "truths" never move beyond "a particular relation of images to the things they mirror," Brewster states. He denies the validity of outer forms achieved through mimetic means and inner forms conjured up through symbolism. "I ask for the Real Presence without the wafer. What you offer me is the wafer in commemoration of my own presence!"

Brewster's wants are based neither on subjectivity nor objectivity; neither knowledge nor imitation. Art is his religion, the nature of art is desire, and the aim of desire is to possess "consubstantiality." Myths, not truths, express the presence of "real things." Since myths act collectively, they are not lodged in subjective, random feelings or in "outlaying models or stimuli." They exist in, and act to express, "the reality of things themselves."

Brewster is aware of the dangers that trail in the wake of collective desires. But whereas Frank Kermode warns that once we believe our fictions are true, fictions become falsified as myths,[5] Brewster urges us to put our faith in the reality of myths, not in the deception of truths. He finds it distressing that social groups are frequently drawn together through their allegiance to "orthodox opinions," misled into believing that their opinions are scientific, commonsense rejections of what is untrue. Led by error, such groups make judgments. Replacing aspirations toward reality with formulas for truth, they start to sing the same song—then enforce its singing by institutionalizing it as the national anthem. They do what we see that Edward Kemble did when assigned by Harper to draw illustrations for Mark Twain's *Pudd'nhead Wilson*.

In 1894 Louis Loeb illustrated the serial version of Mark Twain's novel for *The Century*. He supplied a picture of Roxy the slave woman that follows the description in Twain's written text (figure 4.1). Loeb's drawing clearly bears out the irony of the situation which condemns Roxy to be "seen" as black and a slave by the society in which she lives, notwithstanding the fact that her appearance is that of a white woman. In 1899 Harper and Brothers brought out the second American book edition.[6] Edward Kemble, a longtime associate of Mark Twain and the illustrator considered the best "coon" artist in the business,[7] turned his hand to a representation of Roxy (figure 4.2). Kemble did not draw the Roxy Mark Twain portrays. He set down the accepted fictions, "the orthodox opinions," governing turn-of-the-century identification of inferior racial types. A stroke of Kemble's pen wipes out the verbal irony by which Mark Twain set up cross-currents among what Roxy looks like, her bottom-nature, and the racial tag placed upon her by society.

According to Brewster's theories of the nature of reality, Kemble does the sort of thing Humphrey would be capable of perpetrating, and Rhoda too during one of her off moments; but not Walter/Henry, who pushes away "the wafer" of social

4.1. Louis Loeb, illustration for Twain, *Pudd'nhead Wilson*, *The Century*, January 1894.

fictions about truth while demanding real Presence. It is unfortunate but evident that social groups made up of sensible folk like Humphrey believe their collective desires are truths. Personal symbols are just as useless—the interior mannerisms followed in futility by people like Rhoda. Individuals are tied—would they but know it—not merely to society but to the universe and its core of unity, the one authentic source of true desire.

Take for example the desire for God—the ultimate confirmation of unity and

4.2. E. W. Kemble, frontispiece
for Twain, *Pudd'nhead
Wilson and Those Extraor-
dinary Twins* (1899).

reality. (Identifying God is Brewster's example, just as mine was knowing Roxy.)
To Rhoda God is a subjective feeling, and hers alone. God to Humphrey is a law
everyone conforms to as objective reality; this means God has no more value than
any "book of statutes and regulations" copied out by social groups for study and
obedience. In contrast, Brewster's God is something *that he is meant to be*. This
does not mean Brewster becomes part of a pantheistic merger; he is not *that* kind
of romantic. It means, rather, *this* kind of paradox: we cannot merely be absorbed
into a common ideal; we must struggle to assault the reality of what we desire
through the act of defining it. If we ever did arrive at an authentic "representation" of God, we would lose "consubstantiality" and "communion." Therefore, we
must resist synthesis and remain somewhere between desires (the signs we get in
"the short run" about the reality we covet) and Reality (what exists only in "the
long run," never to be obtained).

Brewster concludes his odd, touching little book with a description that eerily echoes the passage found in chapter 7 of Henry James' *The Portrait of a Lady*, that Poesque passage where James images Ralph Touchett's nature as a house with outer rooms masking the chambers that lie within. Brewster tells us that in every house and every person there are two areas. One is the back room where each of us lives out his grave, self-martyred love for the absent Being; the other spot, the public rooms where music and revelry conceal the inner sadness.

There is a sound of lutes and viols in the anterooms, a sparkle of carelessness on the whole scene; the pages playing at dice in the court, the guests banqueting in the hall. You push aside some curtain, and find yourself suddenly in presence of the Pensieroso, whose eternal dream stretches out beyond the horizon.

Neither area of the human house ought to be shut off. Neither taken alone is the truth. Both taken together constitute the experienced myth which is our reality.

The little forest seeded by Henry Brewster's book of 1896 yields the following disagreements over the nature of desire: there is Humphrey who wants clear, objective, male, aryan, coastline, social truths; Rhoda who dreams of vague private, female, aboriginal, jungle feelings; and Walter/Henry who yearns for the universal fact of the Real Presence but is resigned to existence in the halfway house of desire, verification of his life's authenticity. Through this brief flurry of letters and the gloss supplied by Brewster, the key concerns which bear further examination in this chapter are in place. But this is only one corner of the forest.

A latter-day Henry Brewster, Richard Bernheimer proposes distinctions for mastering the problems of evaluation that arise whenever we are faced, on the one hand, by images ("the real things") that exude "constructive force" and, on the other, by images that falter in their force even though they mimic the first group in theme or pose.

Bernheimer's book *The Nature of Representation: A Phenomenological Inquiry*, reflects upon the way the meaning of images move over time. Like many students of the conventions of universal types (of which Ernst Gombrich is an obvious exemplar), Bernheimer is convinced that long ago there were objects which directly absorbed the reality of the demoniac, sacred powers they represented and which elicited overwhelming emotions from those who looked upon them.[8] Such absolute objects Bernheimer refers to as "primary" or "denoted."

Time passes. Objects which now exist on this side of "the great traditions" find their significance, if any, in the realm of the relative and the everyday. These Bernheimer names as "designated subjects." Whereas denoted subjects apply to self-contained images held with "an established system of interest," designated subjects demand "no more from the interpretant than a memory of common visual elements" out of which the viewer casually extracts "an established iconographic type" for momentary referral. The sharp "specialness" of the denoted is replaced by the wandering associationalism of "the familiar and the obvious." The experience of "one incandescent unity" is lost and the mood shifts to acceptance of the "motifs of daily life." Such are the occasions in modern life that leave Rhoda bereft and inward-turning, Humphrey satisfied with dams and cleared wastelands, and Walter girding the loins of his imagination in the search for "the constructive forms" of Real Presence.

To demonstrate the distinctions between denoted and designated, Bernheimer describes the dual nature of the image of the Virgin Mary as it appears in our times. "[The] painting will not only represent the Madonna, referred to in the Gospels and the Apocrypha and venerated by members of the Orthodox and Catholic church, but it will also belong to an iconographic type called 'the Madonna,' which we put in quotes to indicate that we are now concerned with a conventional type rather than with realities."

Humphrey has little interest in original paintings of Madonnas. He makes do with a photogravure copy picked up at the nearest religious art shop. For her part, Rhoda looks deep within her heart to find an image of holiness linked with some vague sense of the transcendent. Walter takes great pains to seek out as finely wrought an expressive form of the Virgin as a mid-1890s art gallery allows. He at least understands why Bernheimer insists that an artistic type cannot be more "than an empty exercise in iconographic distinctions and subtleties if it did not draw its life—its authorization, if you will—from a higher quarter; for all potential value resides in and spreads from the denoted subject."

Bernheimer (and Henry Brewster) assert the primacy and "consubstantiality" of the denoted subject. The designated subject (the mere wafer handed out before the tacky altar of a tastelessly ornamented church) is only a poor imitation. But exchange between the two forms is necessary. Take "works of art whose arrangement reflects established usage" and in which "the designated subject is paramount." The signs by which these works are recognized *"must first be applied to the type before we can inform ourselves about the reality beyond"* (my italics).

That is, we perceive an object as the type of a designated subject that quotes prior conventions which establish ways of responding to that object. However unwittingly, we reflect upon the sacred past of that object before we return it to the present and ground it in the social and historical context it shares with us. Some images are more affected than others by the circuit they make through our memories. Many objects come back from their forays into the past almost totally denuded of the primary powers of the denoted; but other objects, even in the day and age of Rhoda, Humphrey, and Walter, emerge out of the memory bearing the faint but steady radiance of the Real.

As the theoretician who has been carefully distinguishing between "good" and "bad" times and "strong" and "weak" images, Richard Bernheimer lifts a finger of caution. The human craving to possess desired presences by means of effective representational forms is largely a history of frustration because the mind's capacity to want is the source of its own unhappiness. "Drives have a tendency to vest their objects with impossible, synthetic perfections, endowing them with a glittering ideality that no substitute can ever hope to match. When such ideals are not embodied in existing objects, as they are in the early phases of human love, the result may be a permanent and fretful dissatisfaction with life which no real experience can cure."

If an individual has no private beloved, he turns to the world at large. There he will again be frustrated because of an absence of a "treasure of common experiences and certainties" and the lack of a "common stock of images, religious or patriotic." Failed by his civilization, he is assaulted by "his own drives" and besieged by images welling up "from an undirected and unreconstructed inner life."

Sounding a bit like Humphrey chastising Rhoda and Walter, Bernheimer moves in with his advice. "The makeshift world of the confirmed idealist becomes bearable only if he learns either to appreciate the greater perfection shining even through the humblest phenomena or to turn his gaze from the things which cannot suffice him toward a reality beyond. Only then will the object of his drive cease to be an idealized member of a species and reveal itself as a truly irreplaceable individual."

Imaging American Women is about the members of a particular society who were not very good at taking sound advice. It is about a time in the nation's history when those flare-ups by which we identify cultural interests, achievements, and failures were frequently caused by the fact that Americans, male and female, were encouraged to want, yet were often offered faulty images which augmented those wants at the cost of much common sense and some human decency.

When exactly did the world of frustrated desire open up in history and the sacred actuality absent itself from the earth? It all depends upon how one calculates such matters. Denoted figures might be said to have existed in full force only *prior to* Andrew Jackson's presidency, or the French Revolution, or the Council of Trent, or the taking of Constantinople by the Saracens, or the toppling of the Temple of Solomon, or the loss of the Phidian Zeus, or the disappearance from memory of the magic signs brushed upon the walls of the Altamira caves. The line that separates *before* and *after* is relative to what is held most sacred to the individual heart and what is judged as determining a supreme cultural moment. What moment does this book single out in its examination of the craving for the denoted that figures with exceptional force? It is the period of the American Renaissance.

As used here, "American Renaissance" does not refer to the years just before the Civil War portrayed well after the fact in F. O. Matthiessen's famous study of 1941. It refers to the United States during the 1880s and 1890s when people on the spot were likening contemporary American culture to the flourish of arts, business, and politics that had characterized the Italian quattrocento and cinquecento. Just as the original Renaissance meant different things to want for those who lived during those years, the American Renaissance is marked by many kinds of desire and just as many ways for getting or losing them. J. P. Morgan and Henry C. Frick were probably as satisfied as Lorenzo de Medici or Pope Julius II in getting what they went after. The painters of the Boston School (Edmund Tarbell, Frank Benson, and J. Alden Weir) were most likely as content with their lot as Raphael in Rome.

Manual laborers in the crowded quarters of Florence no doubt felt the same itch for what they could never have as the people herded into the darker corners of Chicago or New York. But of all the people of desire fostered by the American Renaissance, it is the Rhodas and the Walters upon which I wish to concentrate just now, not the Humphreys who perfected the marvels of the Brooklyn Bridge, the Corliss engine, the electric light, or Madison Square Garden. And of the two, it is the Walter type which receives the most attention—the man with a heart and mind like a latter-day Michelangelo who first reached out toward the richly designated figure of Vittoria Colonna, then beyond toward the shadowy perfection of denoted power for which even Vittoria offered too ordinary an image of desire.

Late-nineteenth-century Americans who desired "the idealized member of the species" instead of "the truly irreplaceable individual" had not learned the hard truths with which poets of the sixteenth-century Renaissance came to terms. The latter fended off frustration through aesthetic means that are a variant on Bernheimer's admonition to stay with what is on hand in the world. With tact and verbal agility, they tried to do without "the unlike us," "the better," and the sacred "other" whose presence is constantly denied by the material world.[9] Certain artists of the American Renaissance (Saint-Gaudens, Henry James, Thomas Dewing among them) created fine fictions which directly treated the pathos of the gap between what is grand and what is ordinary; they consciously developed a demystified language of art that bridged the space between the designated and the denoted.[10] But the late-nineteenth-century art world generally held back from attempting a full reconciliation with shabby markdowns of the everyday.

The degree of desire felt by each individual and the possibilities for satisfying that need varied widely. The Rhodas of the time were downright wretched, ruled as they were by the anxieties Angus Fletcher says plague people devoted to the allegorical in an antiallegorical world.[11] The Walters cautioned their contemporaries not to insist on "truths" when they would be better served by reality, but not many listened in their rush to "figure forth" what was absolutely "better." Some had nerves strong enough to break loose from bondage to moralistic axioms and irrevocable universals, but they did this at the cost of becoming like Rhoda, cast back upon the minutiae of private feelings, or like Humphrey, congratulating themselves on the concrete particulars of dams and drains.

It is Walter's middle way of longing which figures most prominently in this chapter. He reminds us of the artists and audiences of the period who set out as calmly and reasonably as they could to attain that third Hegelian stage of reality—that "Absolute Reality"—which Marshall Brown identifies as an important, though unlikely, segment of nineteenth-century realism.[12] To hardheaded individuals of this persuasion, the world of "Absolute Necessity" was desirable for its "realism of types" and its "meaningful forms and significant relationships." It is, Brown notes quite accurately, the world of universals "revived by C. S. Peirce and William James, whose ideas and phrases are echoed by Henry James in the preface to *The American*: 'The real represents to my perception the things that we cannot possibly *not* know, sooner or later, in one way or another.' "

The world these artists and their fellows-in-desire wanted was hardly the American society they possessed. In *that* society everything seemed to conspire to prevent them from knowing, "sooner or later, in one way or another," the real things. All the more reason that they turned to "the realism of types" in order to have the means to represent the values that engrossed their minds. The formulations of their theories were usually general in nature; the specific images which resulted from those theories were often female in form.

In 1879 a call was made for some supreme event, the coming of an era of "greatness" that could be praised for "its intellectual power, its sanity, its adequacy to average human needs," as well as for arts characterized by "growth, experiment, preparation, and acquisition." In voicing the nation's need, Sylvester Rosa Koehler put an exact name and motive to this event: a "Renaissance" that gives "tangible, material form to the ideal."[13] But Koehler knew that the Renaissance was unavailable in 1879. He turned to the vocabulary used by earlier Americans to express cultural omissions. His statements are very close to those made in 1864 by James Jackson Jarves, who also thought he knew exactly what was missing (a bona fide American art idea) and where the gaps were located (between science and art, materialism and idealism, perceived facts and cognized significance, wealth and poverty, knowledge and love).[14]

As Koehler's decade tilted toward the 1880s, social conditions demonstrated the same diminished quality of American life Jarves had experienced in the 1860s. The American art world had not moved much since Jarves defined the elements that contributed most to the public's satisfaction: the "art-trickery" of the German decorative school that served up trumpery to the sensuous eye; the aftertaste of the Pre-Raphaelites whose scientific rigor of observation led to excesses of "the photographic," "the microscopic," and "the mechanical";[15] and a feminized art that soared "above the level of the worldly and vulgar" (this the single "good" art idea for Americans, imported though it was from the French salons).

Fretful observers of the American cultural scene in the late 1870s had plenty of reasons for aspiring to a better idea for a national art, but they were held back by their inability to suggest a method for expressing that idea. European positivism opened still wider the old lesions between art's ideals and science's facts, exacerbating the frustration of Americans who wanted a way to create effective representations of the denoted. The current theories relied on an uneasy mix of German aesthetics and British empiricism; they placed confidence in "psychology without psyche" and "science of beauty without sense of beauty."[16] Bereft of a clearly developed theory for the expression of types and values that answered specific American needs, artists felt threatened from outside (no public tutored to under-

stand what they wished to achieve) and from within (no unclouded personal vision or trained artist's hand to show them the way to execute a soundly conceived
art idea for America).[17]

Before Sylvester Rosa Koehler's essay appeared in 1879 there had, of course, been
the 1876 Centennial Exposition held in Philadelphia's Fairmount Park. Some of the
thousands who streamed past the displays of sewing machines and embroidered
cushions believed this was the great event American culture had been waiting for,
but most agreed that materialism, science, and "male" reasoning reduced to insig-
nificance the scattered, second-rate examples of idealism, art, and "feminine" feelings.[18] It would take seventeen years before the United States gained international
recognition as the land of "the American Renaissance" and before the nation's
desire for a unified culture received concrete form and official fulfillment in Chicago's Jackson Park.[19]

Midway between "The Promise" made visible by the displays at the 1876 Centennial Exposition and "The Outcome" (for better or worse) symbolized by the
1893 Columbian Exposition, yet another essay by Koehler appeared that spoke of
promises and outcomes. Koehler had named his desire and voiced his doubts about
"The Future of Art" in 1879; now it was 1886 and he asked his questions once
again. This time around, he made it even clearer what he wanted the American
art of aspiration to be like; he also formulated the means by which artists might
both create and satisfy their needs.[20]

Koehler edited two volumes published in 1886, *American Etchings* and *American Art*.[21] In his preface to the second of the two volumes he stated his dual aims:
he wished "to restore [art] to that intellectual position to which it is entitled, but
which it has all but lost" in the United States, and he wished to examine the cause
of "a deplorable estrangement between" the public and the artist. Koehler quickly
tempered the pessimism of his preface with the opening sentences of his first chapter, titled "From 1876–1886: The Promise." The preceding decade had been important in the development of a true American culture. Whatever later critics might
decide, "the fact must remain that it was a period of awakening, of high hopes,
and of honest endeavor." Emerging from the often tarnished time known as the
Gilded Age, American artists were coming to the realization that they must act as
"the interpreters of [their] own thoughts and aspirations." Koehler spoke for them,
since he believed it was a common need to find art forms that express "ideas growing out of the circumstances that surround us, out of our attachment to the free
institutions which the fathers have left to us . . . which it is our duty to purify
and develop as the civilization of the world advances."[22]

Once Koehler makes clear what "The Promise" is (American art that provides
forms expressive of the nation's noblest desires), he turns to "The Outcome." He
first runs down the list of the obstacles standing between the ideals and their fulfillment, such as the lack of technique that keeps young American artists from
being good painters. That done, Koehler moves to the center of his argument. Poor
technique hurts, but there is another failure which harms artists even more. This

is the lack of a distinctive style, a visual sign of unity by which the world might identify what they do as "American."

The solution Koehler proposes for rectifying the absence of a national art signature may seem vague to us in the extreme, but it is the solution others of Koehler's persuasion decided was the only certain way to achieve an effective culture. It is, after all, an art critic's version of what Hector St. John de Crèvecoeur's Farmer James assumed as an accomplished fact when he wrote "What Is an American?" one hundred years before. It is also a variation of Walt Whitman's manifesto of 1871, *Democratic Vistas.*

Artists, Koehler states, must consciously think and feel like "Americans," giving themselves wholeheartedly to a "brotherhood" of "new men." This done, they will be empowered to express "a greater, broader humanity than is possible among the better defined nationalities of the old world." Through the encouragement of diversity and "cosmopolitan thought," they will lay claim to the unifying force of "the essence, the subject, the thing, *or rather the idea,* represented" (my italics).

Koehler's first chapter, "The Promise," proposes the ideal of a unified culture. "The Outcome" proclaims his hope that this ideal will be achieved once artists share *the idea of being Americans,* thereby gaining the ends promised by the original democratic impulse. Ever since the Declaration of Independence cast its Corinthean shadow upon the wall of the American republic in 1776, the desire for human fulfillment had its denoted image and the circumstances which served to frustrate that desire. But now it was 1886 and perhaps, Koehler argued, a society formerly held down to the diminished level of designated objects could return to the "constructive force" of the true American idea out of which the republic was formed.

It is easy for us to see the many disappointments lying in wait for the generation of American artists who grew into their craft immediately after the Civil War. It was good that they had an art critic such as Sylvester Koehler to needle them into the realization they could no longer afford to be well-intentioned young ignoramuses and that they must learn the use of palette and canvas, prop and model— all the necessary tricks of their trade. But we wonder to what purpose Koehler instructed them to aspire to "being Americans" and to nourish ideas of the great Idea. Whitmanesque aesthetics of a unified culture always sound fine, but it was devilishly hard in 1886 to know what to do with such a theory when the prevailing social conditions were constantly cutting the ground away from both art idea and American Idea.[23]

Before one assumes too quickly that Koehler was no better than a reactionary or a naïf, observe that Koehler's comments indicate he was aware of the circumstances with which his young artists had to come to terms. Wherever they look, he wrote, there is "a 'society' whose reliance is stock-jobbing and stock-watering," and whose main goal is "the senseless piling of money upon money." But even though the nation is "oppressed by an ever-growing idle class without any other aim but self-indulgence," Koehler continues to urge Americans to substitute for the designated objects of a demeaned society the denoted art idea dedicated to "love, truth, and the sense of justice, and the desire to make pleasant without rude disregard of the rights and the comforts of others."

Although we may quarrel with the occasional limpness of Koehler's written word and the limitations of the conditions he sets for a reformed society, we ought not fault the good intentions he had for that society and the art by which he hoped it would gain its clearest expression. And how can we escape the poignancy of Koehler's conclusion? "We are not wholly bad, therefore, and hence our art also cannot be wholly bad."

But what, artists and art critics had to ask, is the point of aspiring to a good art produced by good artists in the name of a good society if there is no audience for their achievements?

The wants of the middle-class public diverged sharply from what many writers and artists sought to give them. The fears that marred the lives of the genteel poets,[24] the frustrations that sent literary folk the likes of Henry James, Edith Wharton, and Henry Brewster abroad into self-exile, and the pathos that marked the careers of painters as diverse as Thomas Eakins and Abbott Thayer were inevitable. A great deal of the friction between artist and audience came down to what people wanted to see and how they expected to see it.[25] Painters who were learning new techniques or polishing old ones questioned the notion that "reality" sticks to conventions of surface appearance, but members of the public often took their pleasure in just such surfaces—liking the art of anecdote that tells a story anyone can see with the sense he is born with, or the art of *trompe d'oeil* that places ordinary objects right there ready to be touched. Painters were discovering that art forms have their own value and impose their own autonomies; but the viewers and purchasers usually dug in their heels on this matter—preferring art that announces its moral purpose and its relation to everybody's world. Painters were reaching out toward an international style;[26] but the public usually appreciated local scenes and native references recognizable at a glance. Painters were defining art as a mode of knowing that goes beyond formal knowledge; but the public enjoyed receiving reinforcement in home truths and an education in new facts from the pictures it looked at. Painters were blending European notions of art for art's sake with American ideals of art for the sake of spirit; but the public (however open to uplifting themes) thought there was more use to be had from pictures about things.

The impasse of imagination which blocked the commerce of response between artist and audience was a variation of the same old problem: how to get Americans to respond in common to a world of signs at a time when the diversity within society increases with a rapidity beyond the capacity of established concepts and vocabularies of perception to express them with "constructive force."[27]

It was 1879 when Sylvester Koehler first called for an American Renaissance. The next year William Brownell announced that the nation had achieved this high aim. In 1886 Koehler bannered the news of "The Promise" and Mariana Van Rensselaer quoted Emerson on dawns and new beginnings. There seemed to be little question that major shifts were taking place which made the art of the 1880s appear to be quite different in kind from that of the 1870s.[28] There were clashes of opinion, however, concerning the nature of those changes.

One consideration repeatedly introduced into the critical fray was whether the new art was primarily feeling or thought. William Brownell's essay of 1880 "The Younger Painters" stated flatly that feelings were sovereign. "Almost without exception, nature is to them a material rather than a model; they lean toward feeling rather than toward logic; toward beauty, or at least artistic impressiveness, rather than toward literalness; toward illusion rather than toward representation."[29]

But if Brownell places American art within Rhoda's private fiefdom of feelings, others defined the developing expressive style as Walter/Henry would: emotions disciplined by an art idea that committed them to an arduous journey toward "the Absolute Necessity" of Hegel, the Reality of Peirce and Royce, or (to use Brewster's term) the Real Presence.

The more extreme forms of self-reflexive art on display in the 1890s were already in evidence by the mid-1880s. Later, twentieth-century abstractionism and the formalism characteristic of postimpressionism and symbolism underscored the return to universals that had played a significant role in the formulation of the art of the 1880s and 1890s.[30] The studio realists and the *plein air* crowd may have thought they were overturning predilections toward "idea" through their direct observation of nature and life, but their approach to painting (through what they said they saw) was constantly supplemented by the devices of those who painted what they said they thought (and in some cases dreamed).

The example of James Abbott McNeill Whistler, with his disavowal of Courbet's realism in the late 1860s and the slant he gave the Aesthetic Movement of the 1870s,[31] represents only one of the more celebrated slides away from nature's details toward art's abstractions. A classicizing style, an aesthetics of idealism with the sting of moralism removed, formalized arrangements, timeless gestures, and the elimination of illusion-making notations: these elements marked Whistler's art and those of his comrades in the art of design and desire, just as surely as the butterfly with which Whistler signed his paintings. Several kinds of art give the 1890s its authenticity of achievement, but among them the art of idea held its own against the competition.

The full impact of what Koehler called "The Outcome" of "The Promise" of the 1880s did not make itself known until the 1890s, but by the time Koehler wrote the preface to *American Art* in 1886, artists as unlike one another as Abbott Thayer, Edwin Austin Abbey, Kenyon Cox, William Merritt Chase, Thomas Eakins, and John La Farge were establishing the art vocabularies required to represent their thoughts, not simply their emotions. Thayer, Abbey, and La Farge were romantics; Chase and Eakins are best known today as realists; Cox was the self-proclaimed

4.3. Dennis Miller Bunker,
"Jessica" (1890).

MUSEUM OF FINE ARTS, BOSTON

champion of classicism. As watery as these terms can be,[32] they apply with a fair amount of accuracy to the surfaces these men painted. The look of a heroine out of Shakespeare by Abbey, the look of La Farge's "Spirit of the Water Lily," or the look of Dennis Bunker's dreaming "Jessica" (figure 4.3) make it common sense for us to label their style romantic when their works are compared with the assessments of individual character made by Eakins' realist brush (figure 4.4). One would have to labor to find a better tag than "neoclassicism" for Kenyon Cox's *fin-de-siècle* version of Botticelli's "Three Graces (figure 4.5). But these artists were, to a greater or lesser extent, painters of types which were born of an American art idea, not of representations fostered entirely from the world's clay.

John La Farge suggests the peculiar dilemma of his and the next generation of artists; or, as a recent art critic has phrased it, the unending dilemma of any independent artist who tries "to enlarge the limits of traditional painting without actually breaking away from them."[33] La Farge delivered a group of lectures at the Metropolitan Museum of Art in 1893. He took the occasion to make it clear that although he opposed the mimetic arts, he refused to force a wedge between "realism" and "idealism."[34] Speaking as though his friend William James were at his shoulder, La Farge cautioned that "there can be no absolute view of nature." Take an artist to ten different places and he turns out *"ten copies of his manner of looking at* the thing he copies."[35] In the same way, ten artists render ten different versions of a single object. Given such innate divergences, rigid theories about

4.4. Thomas Eakins, "Addie (Miss Mary Adeline Williams)" (c.1900).

PHILADELPHIA MUSEUM OF ART

genres are a waste of the practicing artist's time. Only the individual eye, relying on its own perceptions, conceives a painting and makes it happen.

Having advanced his case for the art of realism based upon private acts of response, La Farge speaks to the shared perceptions which the art of convention makes possible. Since the immediate occasion for his lectures was the analysis of outline, La Farge takes an example from Rembrandt to demonstrate how a few scratched lines suggest a grove of trees. Through the most meager of signs, viewers enter "the dreamland" into which the artist invites them. Those lines appear to be "the thing itself," though they are merely the "bridge" that joins what the

4.5. Kenyon Cox, from *The Blessed Damozel* (1886).

painter has seen and what viewers desire to see. The illusion "suggested by the artist's work is directed by him, but mostly made by us." Art is a cooperative act. It synthesizes object, interpretant artist, and viewer, with the latter having the final say when looking at the supposedly "finished" piece. Artists happily draw upon perceptual conventions so that the public may just as happily alter (not destroy) the nature of their authority. "What we can feel sure of is that nothing has been done once for all . . . and that no matter how completely all has been done, all the more chance for you to do it again: to make once for all, another time, the Runner, the Sower, the Thrower of the Disc."

In his own fine way La Farge is describing the community of interpretants who reside at the center of the philosophies of Charles Sanders Peirce and Josiah Royce.[36] We all move through signs that are personally interesting and collectively significant. One day this process of shared perceptions will provide the full experience of a correctly conceived world, whose patterned whole is constituted of laws which are the true conventions.

John La Farge stresses perception over conceptualization, but his remarks side with the position held by theorists who care about the manner by which universal types are revealed as the real thing. The generalizing outline with its symbolic suggestiveness characterizes what La Farge historicizes as "late forms of art," but this sophisticated, intensely concentrated, very modern mode is also "the mode of art of the savage" and "the mode of art that children understand and first care for." What Humphrey's male elitist colonizing mind cannot abide when rebuking Rhoda for her emotional submission to the inferior arts of the jungle and nursery, La Farge praises as the elemental "hieroglyph" capable of evoking "certain images of memory" available to all. An American culture, unified by a "sign" and an "idea" recognizable by everyone, for which Sylvester Rosa Koehler pleaded in 1886, appeared to have found the art form it needed by the 1890s—oddly enough, from among the practitioners of the art of the outline and the type.

There is a worm, however, lodged at the core of the great democratic dreamland into which all are supposed to enter. The art idea of the universal and the art form of the type *exclude*. How else could it be with La Farge and other artists and critics continually insisting upon purity as the way to direct the flow of perceptions toward the consubstantiality of real things? How else when both artists and viewers were expected to use objects selectively for the stimulation of the memory of "higher things"?

Countless statements coming out of the 1890s argued the need for art to represent individual human experiences, but these admonitions were often held in check by the proviso that artistic expression be "ennobled" and free of ugliness. The eye was to pick and choose its way with great honesty through the world; at the same time that eye was asked to discard whatever was unpleasant. The contradictory nature of these demands was felt both in the studios and in society at large. The purity exacted by spokesmen for the art of the represented type was related to the purity required of the human type viewed sociologically. Purity lay behind the incantatory phrases that repeated the belief that everyone in America ought to be free *(with the exception of . . .)*; that various ethnic groups entering the United States would all become authentic Americans *(with the exception of . . .)*; that American women were guaranteed the rights to do anything they liked *(with the exception of . . .)*. Once purity was used to justify acts of exclusion, it was inevitable that someone would be singled out as not pure enough. By the cultivation of such habits, exclusivity took hold in the midst of democracy.

Strange things went on in the 1890s when the art of ideal forms was discussed. From the subjectivism of the individual artistic act came "realism"—a realism filled with "ideality" that defined itself as "purity of spirit." An expansive reality because it rejected narrow notions of mimetic illusion-making, it was also restrictive because it tended to repeat a select repertoire of signs. Viewers had a strong hand in the traffic between the artwork and the impressions taken away from that work; but the selective eye of the artist still preset the terms of what would be seen. This aesthetics preached the democratic equality of human desires but gave its approval only if certain aristocratic forms kept their privileged place within the range of the desiring eye: "the only ideal that is ultimately worth the serving, the only leader who goes on unfaltering to the end, the only goddess whose feet are not of clay, is she to whom you can say . . . 'I never knew a whiter soul than thine.' "[37]

In the words just quoted, the art critic Royal Cortissoz attempts to reconcile unique woman with universal type and to merge realism with idealism, but he still proposes that the public save its soul by serving the American goddess who offers the "right" things to yearn for. What, then, about the Julia Hartmanns of the nation? Are such women to die like William Ordway Partridge's victimized female, outside in the snow, once the artist-lover discovers her body is made of clay, not of marble?

This chilly fate was not, however, the only one that awaited the followers of the art of type and the aesthetics of desire in the 1890s. It was possible, with care, to escape the consequences of equating the ideal entirely with exclusivity and purity. After all, in 1896 Henry Brewster went on record that we each contain complexly cloaked emotions hidden within the various partitions of our imagination. It is not feasible for us to say, "This is good, bright, and cheerful and *what we say we are*," while rejecting all that is troubled, dark, sad, and *what we fear to admit we may be*. And when Henry James wrote his 1898 story of the house at Bly with its many rooms and varied secrets, he had the governess awaken for an instant to the question put to us all at those moments we undergo a truly profound confrontation with type: "[F]or if he *were* innocent, what then on earth was I?"

Vernon Lee stands before John Singer Sargent's murals at the Boston Public Library in 1899.[38] From what she sees and says she suggests how one might find a way out of the purity trap; that is, if one were not snatched back at the moment of breaking free. For like Henry Brewster and Henry James, Lee knows that for all our faith in wholes we are, of necessity, thrust into the middle of contradictions.

Lee's thesis is tested to its limits when she looks up—past Sargent's image of the goddess Astarte hovering in moon mist—at a vision that contains extremes within a single emotional field. Looming from the center of the vault is "a terrible black colossal woman's face" coiled around with pythons (figure 4.6). It is the inverted head of the Egyptian goddess Neith, a presence much like the veiled goddess that Humphrey believes lies at the heart of darkness; it is very unlike the goddess without feet of clay whom Royal Cortissoz described as "the only ideal that is ultimately worth the serving." Yet Vernon Lee suggests that *this* is the female image for the modern imagination.

But just when we think we have finally found in Neith that goddess whose dark soul makes the exclusion of the unseemly impossible, and in Sargent's rendition of ambiguities an art for the times that exists beyond the "higher" laws, Vernon Lee informs us otherwise. Even Sargent's mural guarantees a safe, jungle-free future that a Humphrey would like. The male figure of Apollo, wrapped about by the

4.6. John Singer Sargent, "Astarte and Neith" (1895–1916).

pythons that coil Neith's nightmare face, is represented in the act of striking at the heart of the terror with his spear.[39] Goodness, rationality, and the beauties of light will prevail. Humphrey's dams will be built in the darkness colonized by sane and energetic Aryans. When Vernon Lee asks, "Will the visions of terrible or ambiguous divinities of nature then be dispelled?" her reply unfortunately is "We may imagine so." But at least she does not say, "We may know so."

Vernon Lee has offered one more example of the obsessive need for certain late-nineteenth-century imaginations to *save* everything in sight, even though that imagination is "fed . . . only by what the artist thinks he sees, not by what, were such a thing psychologically possible, he actually verifies as existing."

Lee does not go as far as Peirce and Royce in their demands that Reality serve as the end of desire. She does not believe that the Absolute Necessity is necessary. Simply to see what one feels and to create what one thinks is business enough for a world pervaded by "terrible or ambiguous divinities." Vernon Lee goes far, indeed, to validate clay images that are not "pure" or "uplifting." She releases the mind from bondage to trivializing truths. She encourages "the lazy activity of daydreaming, of mingled fancy and belief" typified by powerful female forms that bear a vision containing extremes within a single emotional field. But even with Lee, there is satisfaction that, somewhere within that field of vision, the figure of Apollo with his spear stands ready to strike, lest desire transform itself into the nightmares neither Humphrey nor Vernon Lee can bear to share the world with. The seventeen years spanning the Centennial Exposition of 1876 and the Columbian Exposition of 1893 replaced the "Hebraism" of American puritanism with the secular freedoms of "Hellenism,"[40] but John Singer Sargent's pagan pantheon still assured Bostonians that the god of light would triumph over the goddess of night as long as one viewer was left to interpret their twin images as didactic signs for the struggle between good and evil.

In the art world of the late nineteenth century another way around the exclusionary clause—one more authentic than Vernon Lee's—was being written into the documents of the art of the ideal. It is ironic that this way is also reached through purity. Pure forms, pure tones, pure intelligence, pure design and pattern: these were modes of art that shook the canvas free of representations of pure spirit; they were the source of images that commanded the field of commercial art and were the means by which female forms were placed before avid audiences bent on the gratification of sensory desire, not necessarily the saving of their souls.

Female form *as design* is entrapped, if you choose to see it this way, within a formalism which effaces the individuality of the women it images. Yet pure form could be used at the turn of the century to release the meaning of "woman" from the controls of a society that preferred to read female images moralistically as truth, goodness, and beauty. For a contrast to forms of purity that serve allegories of Virtue or Victory, consider the pure form exampled by J. C. Leyendecker's 1897 design for *The Chap-Book*. The formal pattern allows equal interest and merit to all it contains—from cat to lettering, costume to books, stern Dante to lazing Woman (figure 4.7).

It was not that the turn-of-the-century decision to supplement exclusory forms dedicated to spiritual purity with pure forms marked by generosity of inclusion was considered a frivolous one. Advocates of the design aesthetic often stated their wish to attain the pure essence of real things—what others of a more traditional bent called "God." But the method of these practical mystics was to use design, not denoted objects.

Around 1903 the Cambridge, Massachusetts, art teacher and lecturer, Jay Hambridge declared he had found the way through his use of the almost magical properties of geometry. Calling his method "dynamic symmetry," Hambridge enthusiastically traced its genealogy back to the Egyptians and Greeks. Dynamic symmetry was inspired by the patterns that shape growth in man, shells, or plant life (as distinct from the static symmetry of snow crystals) and that make the human skeleton its chief icon. "We must now regard this framework of bone," Hambridge wrote, "as the chief source of the most vital principles of design."[41] Through Hambridge's advocacy, D'Arcy Thompson and the science of morphology were brought into the artist's studio to be used—for example—by George Bellows and Robert Henri.

Hambridge rejected the notion of copying "blindly what nature provides"; the artist has to "select" and "direct his creations so as to express some ideal." But not a merely mental ideal, isolated in the artist's head; rather, that ideal that springs into mind when the artist perceives nature as divine geometry. For Hambridge's brave new theory was simply an updated approach to "the old Greek point of view that there is an eternal something in character more real than surface appearance."[42]

In the same years Jay Hambridge plunged into the white silences of pure geometry, James McNeill Whistler's life came to its end. Whistler's drive to achieve pure art took him in another direction from that of Hambridge and his pupils. While the neo-geometricians attempted to represent the core of nature in terms of the absolutes of the rectangle, Whistler strove to record arrangements of color phrased as tonalities of absolute music. Hambridge sought pure bone; Whistler hovered near pure tone. Whereas Hambridge's dynamic symmetry did not tempt him to forgo the look of nature, Whistler's efforts affected many sympathetic viewers as a "love for pure art [that] pushed painting as far from imitation as it can go without ceasing to be painting."[43] But both Hambridge and Whistler had similar goals—a way past what Hambridge named the cause of "the weakness of modern art"— "too much sex, too much sentiment, and too little design."

A third man was also working away from petty notions of realism and restrictive idealisms toward the more inclusive wholeness promised by the arts of design. This was Thomas Dewing, an artist who aspired to the representation of pure intelligence by placing sensuous forms in patterns that propose perhaps the only signification possible to art.

4.7. J. C. Leyendecker, poster for *The Chap-Book* (1897).

In April 1908 Charles Caffin wrote in *Harper's Monthly* of the remarkable changes Thomas Dewing had made in the visual language normally used to define "meaning." Caffin's essay is filled with phrases such as "intellectually sensuous," "pure abstract enjoyment," and "not passion, but its essence" by which he characterizes Dewing's paintings and points to the fact that the mind's plunge is now the subject of art.[44] But Caffin's Dewing is an artist who neither images universals as chaste females or clayless goddesses nor traps his viewers inside a personal world that excludes everything but the artist's psyche.

Caffin realizes he is making distinctions that are hard to follow. In order to clarify what viewers experience when they look at a Dewing painting, he provides an analogy—one which describes an authentic "modern" vision which takes in everything by the act of focusing upon one part of the great design.[45]

From some high vantage point in the upper Alps I have looked down on a tiny village. . . . But it is a mere spot in the vast panorama that enfolds it; and one presently loses consciousness of the village, to become absorbed in the miracle of vastness that widens out in successive ranges of snowy peaks, soaring into sky that has no limits. Then, if again one's gaze drops to the little village, *it is to see it in a new way*, to feel in it a new significance. It is no longer an isolated human unit; *it has become to one's imagination the focal point on which converge the impressions of its vast environment*. . . . To Dewing *the concrete significance of the model becomes less and less as he gradually invests it with some of that suggestion which he has drawn from the vast outside*. (My italics)

It is 1908 and American art has come a long way from traditional obeisance to natural objects. Although *things* are in no way banished from modern painting, they have been taught their place in the new scale of values that came into force once the mimetic mode began to slide from favor in the 1880s. Nature remains the occasion for the artistic process, but it is no longer its end.

Caffin wants his readers to recognize that yet another kind of repudiation is under way. The subjective mode that translates natural phenomena into tense bursts of emotion is being replaced by the intellectual, abstracting workings of the mind. The old *pictures* impressed upon the heart by piety are nothing like the new *designs* imprinted upon the artist's mind by "the abstract truth and beauty of the universe." In Dewing's case, as we shall soon see, they are designs which begin and end with the imaged type of the woman.

Exclusion remains in force wherever desire for "the better thing" (defined according to social conventions of virtue) controls the content of art. In contrast, there is no room for disgust per se with objects included within patterns laid across art surfaces. But finally design exacts correctness; it excludes forms that do not meet its stern criteria for aesthetic beauty. We can see this other snobbery at work in the way the word "pure" shifts about during the final decades of the century.

In the 1870s and 1880s purity in art generally referred to moralistic representations of physical chasteness, spiritual innocence, and elevated feelings. The "higher" qualities of the denoted object took preference over the "lower" qualities of the designated, since it was argued that certain things had "more" and "better" meanings to offer the soul than other objects. By the late 1890s and early 1900s artists were more likely to talk about pure geometry, pure color, and pure form.[46] But even when traditional matters of virtue are left out, aesthetic moralism acts to honor essences that cohere and to reject elements that disturb "the abstract truth and beauty of the universe." As chapter 2 demonstrated, the nativists of the 1890s and 1900s were upset over the mongrelization of the northern European races by the "new" immigrants. In an analogous situation, American artists of ideal types hoped to protect the pure forms that they believed were the sole source of good art. In either instance, limits were placed upon one's freedom *to include*.

For example, the female forms in a Dewing painting are not set apart in their specialness through the imposition of social conventions that place "ladies" here and "the others" over there. But Dewing does segregate his figures through the painterly techniques by which he renders their forms and the pictorial space that surrounds them. Oddly, the result is somewhat the same as if he had restricted his vision to "good women" (figure 4.8). As Caffin phrases it, Dewing's women exist "detached from ordinary usage and suggestion. They lived apart, in a medium of their own; they are no longer personal, individual; they are not figures and objects; *they are Presences.*"

Dewing's female types are kept holy (which is not the same as "virtuous") through what looks like their removal from the realm of the particular, the historical, and the life of the everyday. This protective enclosure is possible because he transforms them into the "focal point" of the painting, assigning them the arduous task of being the design-sign for the "abstract truth and beauty of the universe."

I return to Thomas Dewing and the question of the exclusionary quality of his female forms in chapter 8. There I shall argue that Dewing's paintings—even when approached as sociopsychological records—are not the elegant prison cells or restricted psychic spaces they are often taken to be. But just now I acknowledge that—as designs—Dewing's females are powerfully held in place within the cloisters of a formal purity.

But surely there were artists within the turn-of-the-century world of serious art who broke down the barricades and freed the eye from strictures that image the heart's desire at the cost of exclusion? In 1907 the young mavericks of the Eight made it clear that the reigning art critics had no right to act as the only spokesmen for American art. Just as the Ten had pulled away in 1877 from the National Academy, the Eight now brushed away the dust motes of the established art world. Just as Jarves and Koehler had (as true American artists always seem to), the Eight wished to seal the cracks between art and life. For them this meant including the squalor and the fun of everyday life. But even the Eight had their own little rites of exclusion. Patricia Hills gives their game away when, in praising their brave and lusty attempts to act as artists of real life, freed from the genteel encasements of official art, she comments that the Eight were thoroughgoing believers in the myth of the happy poor.[47] All right then, what about the unhappy ones? Not "pure" enough to be granted entry into the pictured space of the true American art idea?

The Eight were involved in further acts of exclusion than those which arise from sociopsychological choices of content and mood. Their paintings of ashcans were aesthetically limited to the anecdotal, sociological, and mimetic, in contrast to a Jay Hambridge who attended to the expansive universals of the rectangles of trash containers or to a James McNeill Whistler who could absorb such cans into infinite arrangements of blacks, grays, and whites. In the end, just like the Ten, the Eight were held down to the minutiae of realism, rather than released toward suggestions of the unlimited real.

Geometry, color, idea, meant "significance" to certain kinds of turn-of-the-century artists, but not to most members of the public or to painters who aspired to

4.8. Thomas Wilmer Dewing,
"Lady with a Mask"
(c.1907).

CORCORAN GALLERY OF ART

join art and society together into a unified culture that responds in kind to the same sets of images. In the past, the academy had placed too much reliance on imitation. In the present, official mavericks like La Farge, Cortissoz, Caffin, Sturgis, and Cox erred in the direction of abstraction. Concurrently, realists dedicated to particulars believed that realists of type excluded life, whereas realists committed to rendering types accused realists of the particular of shutting out everything that really matters. Then, as now, the oscillations of this perennial debate between nature and art, eye and mind, make the Perpetual Motion Machine seem sluggish by comparison. It is time to step in, once again, to point out the odd double life of the art of real things that held its own ground, even when confronted by the ever-growing forces of the art of realism.

The art of real things was sired by turn-of-the-century aristocrats of privileged vision, yet its own by-blows included many of the popular art forms of the period. The designs, patterns, and formalistic pictorial values used in magazine illustrations and advertising art appealed to audiences that probably had little eye for either the paintings of Thomas Dewing or Robert Henri. In the marketplace abstract forms and design offered the immediate identification of desirable objects. Over the course of time the silhouette which Corinthea put upon her wall in 600 B.C. became the billboard poster, the theater marquee, the newspaper advertisement, and the art of the calendar—"signs" in the form of commercial and promotional images that stimulated an insatiable wish for the denoted in the midst of a society posited on the production of the designated.

The American Girl as drawn (and constantly explicated) by Howard Chandler Christy suggests how an image can successfully stir up emotions it does not itself possess. Christy was chosen by V. G. Rocine to represent the physiognomical type of the Artist (figure 4.9). We can choose the Christy Girl to analyze the way a type wins popular acclaim; more important, how a designated image borrows the appeal of the denoted subject although lacking the power "to penetrate to realities beyond."[48]

Christy's illustrations are designated objects in every sense of Richard Bernheimer's definition. As pictorial signs, their range of human reference is restricted to minimal signs for sex, age, and class. Paucity of information is not simply the result of Christy's incompetence as a technician (particularly feeble in the rendering of hands and feet and in the arrangement of figures across the plane of his drawing sheet) or of his limited repertoire of feminine poses and facial expressions (ample only when compared with the even more limited formulas he applied to his male figures). What most impoverishes Christy's illustrations are his notions of what it signifies to be a female and an American.

Patriotic apotheosis, together with racism and sexism, is the extent of Christy's contribution to the call made by Jarves and Koehler for a true American art idea. In the texts Christy wrote to accompany his drawings he parades his theories of evolution which single out the American Girl as the sign that the nation has reached its apex of youth, vigor, and beauty. Christy is such a chauvinist, such a jingoist, when it comes to boasting of the preeminence of American virtues—so blatant in his conflation of brave nationhood with pure-blooded and chaste maidenhood—that the cultural historian in us falls upon his neck with cries of glee, however repugnant or silly his opinions. The pleasure we can take in Christy comes from the realization that we would have to go a long way before finding better samples than his of the evasions, the contradictions, and the irresponsible nastiness which are always ready to engulf images of the American Girl.

Up to now, I have avoided words such as "cliché" and "stereotype" because they are too frequently applied with haste to discussions of the theory of types. But those words are clearly appropriate when judging Christy's perceptual/cognitive responses to race, nation, class, and sex. Yet there is something more. Between 1898 and 1920 the Christy Girl claimed a life of her own that had no relation to the existences of actual women, strictly speaking. But the fuzzy outlines, the crude coloration, the hackneyed tricks of come-hither smiles and haughty tosses of the head, together with the highly questionable blend of romance, evolutionism, and chauvinism borne by Christy's images, have a force that cannot be denied. This force is most evident when the discrepancy is exposed between what Christy drew and what he (and his contemporaries) said. Take roses, pipe dreams, and flags, for

4.9. "Artist, Creator of the Famous 'Christy' American Girl Pictures," from Rocine, *Heads, Faces, Types, Races* (1910).

example—the tokens by which the Christy Girl sublimates sexuality into patriotism and exteriorizes inner desires that are not quite as wholesome as they appear.

The sociopolitical complexity introduced into the dog-eared convention of the maiden holding a rose has already been noted. In chapter 1 we saw examples of how women of quite different stamp posed as "our girls," at whatever cost. In *Our Girls: Poems in Praise of the American Girl, with Illustrations by Howard Chandler Christy*, the illustrator matches the dedicatory poem "To the American Girl" with the drawing titled "She Held a Deep Red Rose."[49] The verses by one H. K. read as follows:

> When God was in His rarest skill
> He tore from out the rose its heart
> And of it wrought you, wonder one!
>   To be the triumph of His art!
>
> He lit the stars to be your eyes;
>   Black glooming night your tresses wove,

> And Venus' self your graces planned
> Then envied you your treasure-trove.
>
> He raped the Seas of Ind for pearls
> To jewel in your coral-bands.
> He made your mouth an altar vale
> Then sent you flawless, from his hand.

God appears as a violent maker who rapes and tears the world of nature apart in order to create the perfect female, representation of the American nation. If the American Girl is the ripped-out heart of the rose, over what kind of garden does she hold sway? The marvelous thing about Christy is that a question like that never strikes his mind. It struck, however, the more supple and cynical imagination of Paul Bourget ten years earlier.

Wishing to comment upon the excesses of the American scene in the mid-1890s, Bourget refers to the hothouse rose, "so justly called 'the American beauty.' "[50] In former times, this rose was controlled by the classicism of its natural form, but today it has been transformed by man into a flower "so intensely red, so wide open, and so strongly perfumed, that it does not seem like a natural flower." The level of energy reached by American "vigor of blood and nerves" shows nature outdoing itself. "It requires the greenhouse, the exposition, a public display." Bourget's America is the Columbian Exposition as Rappaccini's Garden. The American Girl is a beauteous, amoral Beatrice who breathes her poison upon "the senseless prodigalities of high life" accumulated by "the fathers" who are dedicated to "conquest" and "splendor."

How perceptive Paul Bourget was to read the signs of late-nineteenth-century American society and to turn rose, Girl, and country into a stunning triumvirate of misused social and political power. This thought and pictorialization are exactly the sort of thing Howard Chandler Christy is incapable of. Having illustrated an ambiguous text with the most problematic of images, he walks away with his imagination unscathed and his public settled in for a sound night's sleep—certainly part of the appeal Christy's images exerted over the popular imagination. But he was able to do more than skim over the dangerous deeps of social fears. His images also express the pleasures located in private desires. We realize this other talent when we hear about the sketch which first brought him fame.

Scribner's Magazine, Harper's Monthly and *The Century* assigned Christy to Cuba during the Spanish-American War. His big moment came with a drawing for a story by Richard Harding Davis called "The Soldier's Dream" that pictured a lovesick soldier weaving the phantom form of his ideal woman from the smoke drifting from his pipe. The success of this single, banal image was immediate. Reproductions of "The Soldier's Dream" went up on the walls of countless American homes. Marriage proposals arrived addressed to the girl in the drawing, and hats, shoes, and gowns were marketed in her name. The Christy Girl was born in 1898 as a pipe dream, and Christy's career as one of the country's most successful illustrators was under way.[51]

4.10. Howard Chandler Christy,
"Gold Is Not All," (1904).

4.11. Howard Chandler Christy,
"Which?" (1902).

LIBRARY OF CONGRESS

LIBRARY OF CONGRESS

"The Soldier's Dream" joins two palpable national values: the brave American serviceman bone weary from serving his country's cause in alien jungles and the dream-image of the girl who represents what he fights to protect. Christy found a formula he could work for all it was worth in the years ahead, as figures 4.10 and 4.11 make clear.[52] But what matters is what the formula does to incite the will to win on fields of battle or in Alaskan goldfields. Manly American males who long to possess the charm of intensely feminine women are translated into images of patriotic zeal, and patriotism is turned back "nicely" into sexuality through the provocative form of his Girls.[53] From the early images of the Christy Girl there is a straight line, never wavering, that leads to the WASP queens seated on imperial thrones (see Introduction, figure 9) and the World War I posters of healthy, young, pretty, "good" girls enthusiastically urging men to join (see figure 13.27). It is a pattern of desire that appeals to men and women alike; the Girl is what men want to have and what women want to be. But as is the case with most images of desire, the possibility of guilt is present for both sexes. The man who does not do his duty and the girl who chooses the slacker in dinner dress over the worthy wounded soldier are as much "the wrong types" as the examples of "our inferiors" described in the pages of Josiah Strong, Joseph Simms, V. G. Rocine, and Cesare Lombroso.

Howard Chandler Christy succeeded because he never asked the "primary" questions his designated images evoke or rummaged beneath the simplistic surfaces of feelings expressed as the child-like "I want this" or "I ought not to want that." This is the wondrous fact: beyond the banality of Christy's illustrations lie real problems, but because he repeatedly ignored them he was able to serve up a poisoned drink which his public swallowed with the impunity of a latter-day Mithradates.

Give or take the rise and fall of various financial booms and panics, the United States had become a successful business nation by 1900. It was an open secret, however, that the means by which men achieved corporate power were often corrupt. There was an increase of success for individuals of privilege, but also of the failures which sensitive critics laid against the nation. Meanwhile the qualities of fineness and fairness traditionally associated with the American system were, with a noticeable lift in emphasis, being imaged in the form of American females. But how could this be, when actual young women were kept at a remove from the political and commercial centers of male authority? The logic of this act of exclusion and segregation was questioned by those who wondered aloud why females (whether actual woman or symbolic Girl) were absolved from a history in which males get power and make money; they also asked how an impure society dare flaunt images of pure womanhood for patriotic purposes.

Writers asking the tough, essential questions created fictional heroines who stray near the centers of energy which threaten their personal decency with social violation. Like-minded artists imaged women in confrontation with the disturbances of an unsettled society. But writers and artists who used images of the American woman to test with fierce rigor what "America" signifies were not the ones who most appealed to the general public. Christy kept his Girls well away from the places of practical action. Charm and a knack for inspiring manly acts are the extent of their personal power. But that is precisely the source of their public influence as images. The truth factor of signs is here smoothly replaced by the capacity of signs to block knowledge. Christy's images free his viewers from *having to know what it is they see.*

An interpretant who never questions and only affirms does not have the kind of

4.12. Howard Chandler Christy,
"The Summer Girl," from
Our Girls (1906).

mind Charles Sanders Peirce was after when he asked that we do all we can to "make our ideas clear," but Henry James did. In contrast to Christy's obscuration, James led readers toward "the sacred terror." Looking at Christy's "The Summer Girl" (figure 4.12), it is impossible to guess that James was just then expressing his concern over "The Summer Problem"—imaged by the idle willfulness of pretty girls whose sole aim is to have a good time and make a good catch.[54] But it is precisely this ability of Christy's—to present the image of the Girl in a void, absolved from the problematic—that assured him his far-reaching success as a spokesman for that segment of the nation's public which preferred not to know.

Between 1894 and 1914 Charles Dana Gibson portrayed desire to near perfection. He did not do this as Christy did by ignoring all questions or placing his Girls in a cultural time warp. Nor did Gibson go in for national apotheosis through the placement of the American Girl at the static apex of her evolutionary ascent. Chapter 13 indicates the occasions during 1898 when Gibson set the type of his tall beauties over against the symbolic "shortness" of lesser nations, but overt nationalism was not his pictorial passion; the same chapter also cites his artistic failure as a waver of flags during World War I because of his inability to make the visual equation between sexuality and patriotism that came with such ease to Christy. The secret of Gibson's artistry and the source of his interest to us as limner of American cultural values comes from his exceptional ability to image longing in and of itself.

Aside from the merit derived from Gibson's forceful use of the motifs of desire, there is the obvious fact of his skill as a draughtsman and design maker. The lines of his pen and ink move and are seldom still. They writhe into the far corners of the illustration, then circle back into the energetic centers of action. His compositions make adroit use of the white areas of the page. Spaces suddenly open out in the midst of the blackness; his vigorous cross-hatching threatens to swallow the objects. Gibson's sense of perspective, the control he holds over outline, the inspired use he makes of silhouette, the sweep of the diagonals that tilt his verticals and horizontals into motion: all testify to his remarkable artistry as a master of the pure forms carved out of space by the strong lines of his pen.

Gibson was lucky, of course. The era in which his black and white technique came to its peak exactly matched the perfecting of mechanical modes of reproduction for the magazine and book trade. With the invention of zinc cuts and photo-engraving, the time was right for the display of superior draughtsmanship. The earliest of Gibson's biographers has stated, "For him art and science were in fortunate conjunction. Pen—camera—printing press. Not until the coming of motion picture and radio would there exist comparable media for reaching masses."[55] The availability of the right technology for making contact with a large public hardly suffices, however, for explaining Gibson's impact. This came about, I believe, because he was one of the period's great delineators of desire, and its best pictorial analyst of frustration.

From childhood Gibson had had the ability to turn stories into picture-signs. Even before he began to draw, he perfected a significant talent. At the age of five he was cutting out silhouettes—indicating the minimal structures of animals and human forms that succinctly reveal identity through type.[56] When Gibson was sixteen he was apprenticed to Augustus Saint-Gaudens' studio, but he quickly realized that the three-dimensional bulk of sculptural forms was not what he was after. His interests lay in the direction of outlines and the single profile by which he could swiftly sum up "essence" in ways appreciated by such as Corinthea, Jay Hambridge, and the editors of the Prang manuals. Gibson sold his first drawings to *Life* in 1886 when he was nineteen. Within seven years he was the most sought-after commercial artist in the United States, with a contract of $100,000 for the production of 100 drawings.

Just as the origins of Howard Chandler Christy's popular success lay in the first sketch he did in 1898 for *Scribner's Magazine* of a soldier's dream-vision, Gibson's initial drawing for *Life* in 1886, however rudimentary, carries the same prophetic import. Gibson's sketch—drawn to accompany the little lyric "The Moon and I," sung by Yum-Yum in Gilbert and Sullivan's hit *The Mikado*—shows a dog chained to his house. The dog gazes with longing at the heavens, its black head silhouetted against the huge whiteness of the moon. Unlike Christy's drawing, Gibson's vignette suggests nothing about nation and patriotism; nor is the figure of a woman included. As simple in its meaning as the silhouettes he cut out as a child, Gibson's drawing for *Life* is desire at its most basic. His dog represents the inborn instinct of all creatures (whether Keats' Endymion, Stephen Crane's Jimmy Johnson, or Frank Norris' Vandover the lycanthropist) for lunar longings. All yearn after that object of desire—remote, beautiful, unattainable—traditionally associated with the female; an object which men crave to possess and women wish to become.

The actual presence of attractive young American women made Gibson's personal aesthetics concrete and shareable. He took bits and pieces of the pretty girls he saw and printed them like snapshots in his memory, then formed them into a series of images marked by the bodily health and the elegance of stature which he, then his public, appropriated as the sign of the times—interpreting the Girl's appearance as the outward show of the nation's vaunted independence of spirit and proud self-confidence. Gibson's artistic techniques developed noticeably over the two decades of his greatest popularity, but their evolution had nothing to do with the racist notions of the perfecting of superior types favored by the physiognomists and by Christy. Gibson's drawings reflect both artistic and social changes according to the principles that underlie the morphology of forms. Up to a point at least, they pictured the natural growth of a culture undergoing constant alterations, with matters of "inferior" and "superior" set to the side. The Gibson Girl retained remnants of a stable core of reference to the ideal (as do all denoted objects), but she was also a designated type, flexible enough to mutate absolutes, alter essences, and catch change within continuity.[57] The specific type represented by Gibson's Girls is the type of the dream *at the point of coming true*. It never will, but it offers that hope because it is committed to process.

Gibson's fame was enhanced when he—already known as the Gibson Man—met and wed an actual Gibson Girl. As the press told its readers, Gibson and Irene Langhorne (one of three beautiful sisters from Virginia) first met at Delmonico's; she posed for him; they married. Like Keats' Adam, Gibson had dreamed Irene into existence on paper even before she materialized to epitomize the composite of the beauty of all the young women he had ever delighted in.[58] Shortly before he died, Gibson was asked why he had made a career of drawing lovely women. As awkward with words as he was skillful with his pen, he could only answer, "If I had been an oyster, I'd have drawn girl oysters. Wherever I looked I saw those beautiful girls, and who was I to resist."[59] However feebly put, Gibson's remark underscores an important fact: *wherever I looked I saw* . . . It matches the realization expressed in 1905 by one of his admirers: "the fact remains that we saw her first in the pictures of Gibson, and then we began to see her—or did we only fancy this?—in the circles of wealth and fashion."[60] If we translate these two observations into terms proposed by Charles Sanders Peirce and Josiah Royce, we can say that Gibson had *seen*, thus *known*. (Or as the Prang manuals would have it, he *drew,* thereby *knew.*) As a consequence, he expressed in pen and ink what his generation came *to know,* thus *to see.* The *New York World* acknowledged this interchange in the statement "Before Gibson synthesized this ideal woman, the American girl was vague, nondescript, inchoate."[61] The girls lying behind the Girl had been seen, but not as readable meaning. Once Gibson created the sign of the Girl, young American women were associated with the grace and glamour he gave to his drawings.[62]

Gibson was off to a good start when he chose as the focus of his art the "right" person (the female with features and figure that followed, and influenced, current American social norms of beauty) and the place (the reaches of mid- and high society). He was also fortunate in his ability to select the best narrative forms for this person and this setting—simple stories of courtship and melodramas of corrupt alliances made for money or foreign titles. Also working in Gibson's favor was the fact that he had the necessary artistic technique for rendering types in black and white—that "rare taste for picking out the characteristics which could be transferred to paper."[63]

Gibson had the object, the setting, the basic plots, and the artistic skill it took to be noticed. But other artists of the period met those same qualifications for popular success, if that was all that was needed; they were traits his imitators quickly picked up.[64] Gibson's special genius lay in his ability to express with intensity what many of his generation wanted to be or to have; he shared with them his awareness of what it is like always to dream and generally to experience the frustration of those longings. Charles Belmont Davis saw this at the time. "And so I believe that every woman and every man who look on the fair, fine women of Gibson imagine that they see a possibility for themselves."[65]

But the point (the one which pours power into those images) is that *there are no such possibilities.* "They are only made so by the infinite art of the artist. The Gibson girl does not exist in real life; she is a finer thing than mere clay; she is at best an example, a forlorn hope for the dressmaker to hang her dresses on, and the hat-maker and the hair-dresser to strive after as best they may."

The very special force of Gibson's drawings, one which is absent in the derivative figures that aped their look, came from the realization that the Girl means more than commerce and objects that can be sold and bought. Although she was marketed for all she was worth,[66] the Gibson Girl went beyond the business of business and into the nonnegotiable area where sacred objects and primary types lie beyond the constrained level occupied by the designated type.

The Gibson Girl also *made a difference* in the world. Social behavior was shaped as men tried to be worthy of the young women who, in turn, attempted to live up to the images Gibson presented for their contemplation.[67] Safe behavior, of course. One could desire innocently to be or to possess the Girl, since her image had been created in innocence. Dreams that activated her image were no danger to society. They prompted no radical ideas, for the Girl served as a useful substitute for longings not yet sanctioned for young American women. "Little girls everywhere, who

4.13. Charles Dana Gibson, "The Heiress. She Cannot Talk, She Cannot Sing, She Looks a Fright; But Folks Aver Ten Millions Have Been Set Apart To Talk and Sing and Look For Her," *Life*, April 17, 1902.

4.14. Charles Dana Gibson, "One of Our Leisure Class," from *Other People* (1911).

relinquished the ambition to be President to little boys and who did not then even hope to be Madame Secretaries in the Cabinet, did determine to be Gibson Girls when they grew up."[68]

But there were, as Henry James might say, *consequences*. However much the Gibson Girls were contained within the cautious limits of the collective imagination, the images strained after darker visions. The wonder is that Gibson not only allowed these visions, he pressed them home in a series of drawings that are among the most affecting to be found among the popular art of the period.

Gibson perfected pen strokes of satire. He delineated society's susceptibility for imbalances of gold: too much for some, poverty for others (figures 4.13 and 4.14).

4.15. Charles Dana Gibson, untitled, *Life*,
      November 16, 1893.

4.16. Charles Dana Gibson, "In the Swim,
      Dedicated to Extravagant Women,"
      Life, September 27, 1900.

But these are public matters. Gibson excelled at translating into visible forms the
more private emotions. Christy toyed with romantic longings and sublimated sexuality with easy patriotism or dreams of America's past, but he never came near
an expression of the physical passion of which Gibson's art was sometimes capable.
In Gibson's drawing of 1893 (figure 4.15) bodies are locked together, heads obliterated by black cross-hatching. This could be a visualization of the final paragraph

4.17. Charles Dana Gibson, "Love Will Die," *Life*, March 1, 1894.

4.18. Charles Dana Gibson, "His Everlasting Experiments with Ill-Matched Pairs," *Life*, March 16, 1893.

of Henry James' novel *The Golden Bowl* when Prince Amerigo embraces Maggie, his "primary type." "I see only you," he says, expressing joy but also fear; fulfillment but also frustration.

Gibson did not leave it at this. The lover's embrace is the conventional sign-off that trivializes a story only if we are forbidden to consider the possible consequences of longing. A man drowns in a woman's willfulness, the face of the goddess of night smiles at his suffering, and no god of light comes to his rescue (figure 4.16). Where sacred trust is betrayed and Cupid lies dead on the bier, the attitudes struck by the two figures powerfully appropriate the conventions of melodramatic despair and shock the stark images into emotional reality (figure 4.17). Ill-matched pairs are bound together in a Dantesque vision of struggle and loathing from which no escape seems possible (figure 4.18).

Contrast the darkness of Gibson's pages (literally and figuratively) with the pale pages where the Christy Girl exists sealed off from harm. No Christy Girl ever loses the right man. No real man is ever denied his Christy Girl. No wedding night ever disturbs the wedding day. No questions ever have to be asked. No fears have to be faced.

Given the two kinds of Girl drawn by Howard Chandler Christy and Charles Dana Gibson, which set of images have had the most pernicious effect on the lives of actual American women? Your answer to this question depends upon whether you think it is more dangerous for women to be likened to Isabel Archer (in the manner of Gibson) or to John Smith's Pocahontas (after Christy's fashion in figure 11.21), and whether you think a woman's reality is damaged more by the strong Gibsonian types that express the complexity of private desires or by the weak Christy types that further the pretty lies of a society in love with itself.

COUNTERIMAGES

5

Masking, Camouflage, Inversions, and Play

Masks are an odd aspect of the larger issues of identity and the interpretation of signs. As a student in Paris in the late 1860s, Thomas Eakins attended life classes in which the nude female models wore black masks (figure 5.1). The time came in 1877 when, as an instructor at the Pennsylvania Academy of the Fine Arts, he wrote up an advertisement inviting models to apply for work in the life classes. He included the promise that if the models chose they might cover their faces during working hours with a mask.[1] What purpose did this concealment serve? Perhaps it freed the artist to discover what the poses of the unfaced models suggested about real things, since he did not have to take their everyday "Miss Churmness" into account. And perhaps masks assured models the privacy of thoughts whereby their identities were kept safe from possession by male eyes.

In apparent contrast to the protective masks worn out of modesty by models, ceremonial masks call attention to the face; but even they focus the eye upon a superimposed image that conceals the identity behind the mask.[2] When masks are used in religious rituals, viewers forget who wears the mask and turn toward the rare presence signaled by the outward image.

By the close of the nineteenth century new forms of protective, ceremonial disguise had come into play—methods for altering appearance that concealed identities and revealed presences, and that acted to repress particulars of individuality in order to emphasize associations with the type. Some of these forms became

5.1. Thomas Eakins, "Nude Woman Seated Wearing a Mask" (1866–1867).

PHILADELPHIA MUSEUM OF ART

means for self-protection. One such was the technique of camouflage that found favor in the art world prior to its adoption by the military during World War I.

Camouflage conceals by *the obliteration* of visual signs. It invites observers to forget that there is anything to look at. In contrast, masks cover up by means of *the declaration* of an alternative presence. Masks bewilder by complicating easy acts of identification, while blazoning forth the idea of identity. But both camouflage and maskings depend upon effective design and the dominance of type.

Design became one of the major trends in the development of the fine and applied arts during the second half of the nineteenth century. We find its strong traces among the Pre-Raphaelites in the 1850s, the European dévotées of Asian arts in the 1860s, and the French Impressionists in the 1870s and after. The heavily patterned look of Art Nouveau in the 1880s continued the preference for the negation of narrative content and naturalistic forms. An object's potential "story" was subsumed by the marks hatched upon a sheet of drawing paper or the easel canvas. Individualizing traits were swallowed by the brute assertion of flat colors or the ingratiating play of lights and shadows.

By the mid-1890s poster art and book design turned pictorial surfaces into a maze. Figure 5.2 gives an example of the kind of book format that was pervasive by 1901, both in Europe and among American sophisticates. Design blurred the outlines that commonly give recognizable shapes to unique objects or, as in figure 5.2, that distinguish between multiple planes. Everything within the grip of the design became part of the same boldly flattened-out field: wonderful to look at, somewhat a puzzle to read.

This state of affairs was unusual, actually, given the need of commercial art to identify objects for show and for sale. But the trade artists who pushed their experiments in design well into the 1920s seemed more interested in a design's ability to seize attention, however obliquely it presented the literal object. Figure 5.3 is such a design, executed by Coles Phillips, a highly successful commercial artist who perfected the technique he called "fade outs."[3] The advertisement Phillips prepared in 1911 for Oneida Silverware is a handsome exercise in concealments and omissions. The women, their clothes, and the room's decor, blending into one flat pattern, are clearly present. The product, made doubly provocative because left invisible, is "there" in the sense that the design dwells upon the *idea* of silverware as the object every stylish home requires.

Design also affected the art of the painter. In John Singer Sargent's "The Hermit," design returns the naked body of the man to the painted splotches of the picture's all-encompassing field (figure 5.4). This technique is thematically appropriate. The hermit has, for his religious beliefs, given up his worldly identity in order to merge with God. Flesh assimilated into spirit is the equivalent of disappearing into Sargent's colors. As painted by Sargent (known as the worldliest of portraitists, in the employ of some of society's vainest people), the form of the hermit evaporates into the shimmer of the forest glade, and his psychic self vanishes from view.

We might expect the annihilation of earthly forms to come from the hand of a visionary painter, as in Elihu Vedder's "Memory" (figure 5.5). Here the sea and sky only faintly reveal the glimmer of a face, suggesting by symbolic means that the uniqueness of personality is held as an image solely through the powers of remembrance—not by the mortal eye. But the mentalist tradition Vedder in part represents was only one of the elements that prompted the arts of concealment that resulted, forty years later, in Sargent's "The Hermit." Just as much an inspiration was delight in design for its own sake (which, of course, is evidenced by Vedder's work as well).

Behind Sargent's experiment with painterly camouflage lie the patterned canvases of William Dyce and John Brett, minor members of the Pre-Raphaelite entou-

5.2. Koloman Moser, from *Ver Sacrum* (1901).

5.3. Coles Phillips, advertisement for Oneida Community Silver (1911).

rage, and the Impressionists' sun glare that strikes the surfaces of wheat fields, rivers, and meadows. Farther back are Joseph Mallord Turner's forms veiled in glazes of light. Just ahead are the Pointillists' stipples of paint that disclose a world formed of an infinitesimal series of colored dots. Such works anticipated or confirmed Sargent's 1908 tour de force. So did the popular puzzle-pictures of the kind that urge children, "Find the face hidden in the leaves of the tree," or (as in this

5.4. John Singer Sargent, "The Hermit" (1908).

design executed by John Sloan in 1901) that invite newspaper subscribers to hunt for the figures enfolded within a woman's skirt (figure 5.6). And as we all know, at the very time Sargent completed "The Hermit," Cubists busily split forms and used collage to reveal forms by seeming to disguise them. Randomly chosen objects were dismantled, then reassembled into shapes too foreign to their native contours to allow for quick recognition, at the same moment they challenged viewers to rediscover their deeper significance (figure 5.7).

During the opening days of World War I Pablo Picasso and Gertrude Stein put their heads together. They decided that the way lay clear for the military to exploit the artists' tricks of optical illusion for the purpose of concealing tanks, planes, and buildings from the enemy. But almost a decade before Picasso and Stein, the American painter Abbot Handerson Thayer had striven to introduce his theory of "protective coloration."

Although Thayer is known today (where known at all) as the painter of idealized female types, his first training was in the drawing of animals, birds, insects, and reptiles found in their natural settings. After a period of painting allegorical

5.5. Elihu Vedder,
"Memory" (1870).

LOS ANGELES COUNTY MUSEUM OF ART

figures and the portrait heads of sternly beautiful women and children, in the 1890s he returned to his first passion.[4] Thayer became obsessed (the correct term to use for the missionary intensity he brought to his activities) with the way animate forms assume disguises through color-patterning. He prepared careful notes about the designs embodied by nature's creatures that obliterate signs of their presence. Thus hidden from sight, they either steal upon their prey to take them by surprise, or—if they are among the meek of the earth—they lie low upon the mutually patterned earth, escaping the notice of their own predators.

The certitude with which Thayer argued his theory antagonized a number of his contemporaries. When his book appeared in 1909—*Concealing-Coloration in the Animal Kingdom, an Exposition of the Laws of Disguise Through Color and Pattern*—professional scientists, and amateur naturalists such as Theodore Roosevelt, blasted his ideas. Thayer's personal manner (anything but ingratiating or persua-

5.6. John Sloan, "The Football Puzzle," for *Philadelphia Press*, October 13, 1901.

sive) did not help his cause; not did his blunt assertion that only artists comprehend the techniques of natural camouflage. But whatever objections are laid against
Thayer's theory along strictly scientific lines, it fits exceptionally well into our
considerations about modes of identification and disguise.[5]

This is the law according to Abbott Thayer: nature paints an exact picture when
it places a snake in relation to its leaf bed; nature as an artist does not merely
approximate the general form of something else (figures 5.8 and 5.9). The stabs at
representation made by human artists also rely on the biological principles of optical illusion, but in nature's case the artifice is real and the deceptiveness is founded
upon truth. Yet if nature is more true in its processes of illusion-making than the

RIJKSMUSEUM KRÖLLER-MÜLLER, OTTERLO

5.7. Fernand Léger, "Nudes in a Landscape" (1909–1910).

imitations to which artists fumblingly aspire, at least artists (unlike scientists) understand the pictorial devices by which the world presents itself. Artist work with the same methods as and have similar aims to those of nature; they are head and shoulders above scientists who approach the visible world with totally inappropriate questions on their lips. (There are, by the way, many conscious echoes in Thayer's life of the theories of the New England Transcendentalists he called his heroes.)

The erroneous view of types taken by men of science is, Thayer maintained, the main obstacle to the full appreciation of protective coloration. Nature's laws cannot be described by the mathematics of averages. Man-made rules used by life insurance companies and laboratory naturalists falsify. Such rules eradicate differences; they are content with generalized abstractions set midway within a numerical range. In contrast, the artist realizes that natural types involve the notation of distinctions in the midst of universals. Every bird is simultaneously a representative member of its species and unique; each creature is marked by differences from its fellows, however minute. But late-nineteenth-century scientists were reluctant to assign value to the individual case placed within the wider spectrum of the species. In Thayer's assessment, the result of this asinine blindness was that 99 percent of the creatures seething through the world went undetected. For Thayer—the artist who *saw*—the world is filled with the secret lives of a plentitude of types so beautifully adjusted to the environment, notwithstanding the specialness of their own nature, that the authenticity of their existence is borne out by their very invisibility.

5.8. and 5.9. Abbott Handerson Thayer, with Gerald Thayer, Emma Thayer, and Rockwell Kent, "Concealing-Coloration in the Animal Kingdom: Copperhead Snake on Dead Leaves" (c. 1900–1909).

NATIONAL MUSEUM OF AMERICAN ART

At the start of the First World War Thayer tried unsuccessfully to interest the military heads of the Allied forces in his proposals for the protection of ships at sea from marauding Germans. Techniques of camouflage eventually came into common use over the next years, but Thayer's own efforts were dismissed. His son believed that this fact contributed to the sadness of the final years of a man who had studied, with the greatest seriousness, the relationship of type to matters of identification and survival.

World War I and its military needs are well behind us, but the cultural concerns of that period linger on. I want to transfer the gist of Thayer's law of protective coloration into the making of a workable metaphor for one of the methods for "making do" that the "natural creatures" of late-nineteenth-century American society acted upon with the instinctiveness of Thayer's copperhead.

The Theory of the Leisure Class was published in 1899. In this book Thorstein Veblen described the obverse of Thayer's law in specifically social terms. According to Veblen, certain human types become obsolete once they cease having a function in a world where usefulness is their sole guarantee for survival. Wasteful and parasitic, holdovers from earlier stages of human existence, these atavisms are instantly recognized because of their conspicuousness. Having become too visible, they are thereby marked out for extinction.

The narratives of artists and models at which we looked in chapter 3 demonstrate the implications of the theories of Thayer and Veblen. In Henry James' "The Real Thing" the Monarchs are types who possessed value as long as society had a specific function for the lady and the gentleman. Their current economic plight is not caused by the fact that they are unreal. Quite the contrary. They are being pushed toward obsolescence ("selected out" from human species of survival) precisely because their presence has become too visible, too conspicuous. They exist without function in a world of functionaries. They are left to stand there, exposed, vulnerable to dismissal after a cursory, contemptuous glance by a society that judges them to be of no earthly use. The Monarchs are so far out of it they cannot employ the protective deceptions which flourishing species (such as the Monarch butterfly) use in their pretense that they do not exist. No predators, the Monarchs are easy prey to the world's indifference, and indifference is as certain a means toward the destruction of the obsolete as any direct form of attack.

Valerie West in Robert Chambers' novel *The Common Law* almost goes the way of the Monarchs, but for reasons that involve a different time scheme from that which endangers the characters in "The Real Thing." The Monarchs are types of a species that once thrived in the past; they are of no use in the present. Valerie is the New Woman of the future who challenges entrenched laws of social behavior. As long as she lives by definitions for the terms "common" and "natural" that differ markedly from what is accepted as "the law" by the social environment that surrounds her, Valerie remains nakedly visible. She exists too far in advance of the present time; she lacks the protective veiling that enwraps activities that fit the here and now. But Valerie draws back from destruction in time. *In time* she adjusts to the rules appropriate to her milieu, once she detects what seem to her to be reasonable relations between marriage, biology, and social ordering.

People are accounted failures when they do not perform useful functions in society and when they do not learn how to disguise unique differences. They have not the knack for blending creatively with their environment. There are various causes for the inability to survive according to the law of protective coloration. Neutral tints (read as self-effacement) are not automatic guarantees of safety. Nor is flamboyance the quickest way toward self-destruction. It all depends on the environment and the nature of the adjustments involved.

Charles Darwin's careful observations concerning the vivid plumage of males and the drab look of females characteristic of many species indicate that both kinds of coloration work to the creatures' advantage. It is simplistic to state, as did Eugene Benson (painter and critic of American culture during, and immediately after, the period of the American Civil War), that women and society are best served if feminine dress is quietly unobtrusive and the social outrage of scarlet

5.10. Coles Phillips, *Life*,
November 25, 1909.

and purple is avoided. Benson's argument in *The Round Table* of January 1864 does
not hold up—not when the taste of the period went in for purple, as a follow-up
piece in the same periodical admits.[6] Later on, red-haired women wearing yellow-
green Pre-Raphaelite gowns fit the scene perfectly in certain social and aesthetic
corners of late-nineteenth-century Britain and America, just as Coles Phillips'
Christmas cover for *Life* in 1909 presses red against red for a fine reciprocity between women, dress, and holiday season (figure 5.10).

Those in need of protective coloration who possess a dual nature are in double
jeopardy. They have to find a fit for several selves within the prevailing social
expectations—an especially tricky task when that "personality" we call society is
itself marred by splits and dualities. Being a woman who contains qualities pulling
her in differing directions makes it all the worse.

In *The Common Law* the hero is split between conventional "Louis" and free-wheeling "Kelly," but he survives the tensions of dualism aided by the fact that he is a male. The reigning social view accepts each of Neville's contending natures because that is "the way men are." In contrast, females like Valerie West (or Trilby or Julia Hartmann) are at a disadvantage. What studio models do in the course of their professional activities—assume a series of poses—is acceptable enough. But the model cannot be countenanced who wants to live out the role of society belle, bride, or mother in the "nice" world. What models experience as the wholeness of their complex identities is limited to the studio; that fullness is not supposed to be unleashed upon proper society after hours.

It is the same with Edith Wharton's heroines of *The Age of Innocence* and *The House of Mirth*. Once Ellen Olenska returns from Europe, the completeness of her character begins to fall into fragments when placed against the alien background of New York society, while Lily Bart suffers from a personality consisting of shards of mirror images inflicted upon her from childhood on. Splitting open is also the fate suffered by Edna Pontellier of Kate Chopin's *The Awakening*. In this novel of 1899, the Edna who is indolently on holiday on the Grand Isle of the Gulf Coast and the Edna who is the proper wife and hostess in the big house in New Orleans are an acceptable duo, but add to them the new self that takes up residence in the little house around the corner and tremors are felt at once by staid society. Only death by drowning allows *that* Edna to disappear protectively into the blank coloration of the universe; *that* Edna cannot survive intact within the Louisiana society of Chopin's narrative.

There are many other female victims of nonassimilation in the fiction of the period, women who stand exposed to the looks turned upon them by potential predators. Stephen Crane's Maggie is a Darwinian "sport," the flower that emerges by accident from the mud of the gutter. Once Pete gets an eyeful of her "shape" and once her silhouette stands out sharply against the squalor of the tenements, Maggie is doomed. She lacks the strength that comes from possessing "the real thing." The flashy entertainers in "the hilarious halls" where Pete takes Maggie have the trick of survival down pat. So does Nell, who is the prostitute-as-successful-actress. These women know how to function in a society full of contentious splits and contradictory passions; how to disappear out of harm's way even while standing fully in view. Maggie is a "looker" (defined both as a helpless spectator and as a pretty girl whom men single out to take advantage of). Maggie ends her brief existence as a prostitute who is not good at her job, dead by drowning. Like Edna Pontellier, Maggie Johnson does not have the will to grow "wings" from her shoulder blades. Wearing wings, as Mademoiselle Reisz tells Edna, is the best way to survive as an "artist"—the one who masters protective diversity by soaring over the restrictions of the social world below. As for those who are not artists and cannot soar: they do best by learning to blend with the scene.

Not all heroines fail when they stay down where society sets the rules. One succeeds wonderfully well, and in just the terms that Abbott Thayer's theory expressed, although she is hardly the kind of "ideal woman" Thayer spent a lifetime adoring through his paintings. This is Undine Spragg of Edith Wharton's *The Custom of the Country*, published in 1913, yet another novel about a young woman's self-absorbed quest after the nature of "the common law." Once Undine assimilates the meaning of that law, she matches her type to the "coloration" of the social milieu she enters as a fully functioning member.

As a child Undine Spragg liked "to 'dress up' in her mother's Sunday skirt and play lady before the wardrobe mirror."[7] "Lady" for Undine does not mean what the Monarchs assume it means. Being a lady places Mrs. Monarch out of control in her environment; to play at being a lady puts Undine in charge of events. Undine is also different from Miss Churm. Whereas Miss Churm makes a living by inspiring others' creativity through the effacement of her private "thingness," Undine earns her keep by flaunting before her audience the public self it is her function in life to provide. Miss Churm's talents diverge from Undine's because she perfects the conventional arts of self-concealment, while Undine excels at modern modes of conspicuous disguise.

At the opening of Wharton's novel Undine is eighteen years old. We catch sight of her in her bedroom mimicking an imagined scene in anticipation of its actual enactment, just as she has been doing since childhood (figure 5.11). She is pleased "to see in advance just what impression she would produce on Mrs. Fairford's guests. For a while she carried on her chat with an imaginary circle of admirers, twisting this way and that, fanning, fidgeting, twitching at her draperies, as she did in real life when people were noticing her."

Shortly after, Undine goes to an art gallery with the intention of testing her home skills at "secret pantomime" and "the joy of dramatizing her beauty" before a live audience. Undine places herself on display in a public place lined with pictures on exhibition for seeing and for sale (though she cannot later recall what they were). She also comes to seek out "the originals" of New York's "golden aristocracy." Undine can identify her idols at once because of her "passionate poring over the daily press." People such as "the wife of a Steel Magnet" are clearly discernible types, with the look she recognizes from the printed page.

The identification Undine makes of Peter Van Degen, "the hero of 'Sunday supplements,' " excites her most. Taken just as he is, he has "bulging eyes and [a] queer retreating face" and a "grotesque saurian head, with eye-lids as thick as lips and lips as thick as ear-lobes." He is a Beast from whom any Beauty would feel compelled to flee. But Van Degen is viewed by Undine in relation to the rest of the social scene. Once Undine places him within that particular "design," he causes no repugnance. Quite the contrary, the sight of "his odd physiognomy called up some agreeable association of ideas." What Undine "sees" is the type of the wealthy and eligible young man of the newspaper write-ups, someone she appropriates to her own needs.

Undine's experience at the art gallery is paradigmatic for many of the scenes in Wharton's novel. The paintings on the walls are ignored; she concentrates on the images of the guests identified with the "functions" assigned them by the press.

5.11. Seymour Joseph Guy,
"Making a Train" (1867).

PHILADELPHIA MUSEUM OF ART

Undine tracks them down, not to destroy them, but in order to merge with the pack. She fixes their categories according to how they might help her attain the social functionality she plans for herself. In fact, *The Custom of the Country* is structured by a series of scenes that record Undine's eagerness to identify the wealthy and the glamorous. But something more is gained through Wharton's use of the narrative theme of the interpretation of external signs. As these episodes flow in sequence, Undine converts her talent for *looking at types* into the means by which *she* gains full recognition for herself as a type fit for a place within the inner circle.

In chapter 5, for instance, Undine is at the opera. We can trace how far she has come from chapter 2 in her campaign for acceptance. Earlier, she was a spectator gazing with longing at newspaper images made flesh. Here Undine moves in closer upon the "sacred" stalls of the opera house. No longer a mere onlooker at an art gallery, she is now "hung" in exhibition at the opera framed in proximity to that array of "Sunday supplement sketches" which constitute the society on show. Even after Undine marries Ralph Marvell and moves inside the magic circle, she continues to use the gestures she once practiced before the bedroom mirror. Then she imitated the poses drawn from her study of press photographs; now she herself originates the poses.

Undine's presence is never conspicuous in the sense that she is placed in radical dissociation from the ruling powers at society's center. Quite the contrary. She learns to adjust her look and gestures to each new illusion. Although she falters at times (she is not good at being a French count's *country wife*), she quickly pulls herself toward the custom of the country that suits her best (leaving the count behind, without wife or heirloom tapestries). Some of the people around Undine are not real things, of course. Only shallow shapes, lacking in authentic force, who have no talent for staying the course. But Undine *is* what she poses as. Because her imagination directly participates in everything she sees and does, her success is tremendous.

Even as early as the events described in chapter 5, we see how well Undine's assimilative powers work for her. She notices that Van Degen's opera box is empty. Mentally, she quickly fills it with information taken from that day's newspaper notice of a lavish club dinner he is hosting that night. Ever alert to such tips, she is able to interpret the empirical evidence, while taking into account what is going on outside the range of her bodily eye. What better way for a predator to be prepared to act, or for a potential victim to know which protective actions to take. But a far more important truth comes to Undine that evening while seated next to Mabel Lipscomb, the girl who had previously acted as her guide to New York society.

It had become clear to Undine that Mabel Lipscomb was ridiculous. . . . No one would care to be seen talking with her while Mabel was at her side: Mabel, monumental and moulded while the fashionable were flexible and diaphanous; Mabel strident and explicit while they were subdued and allusive. . . . It was precisely at this point that there dawned on Undine what was to be one of the guiding principles of her career: *"It's better to watch than to ask questions."*

By adjusting her self-image to the suggestive images that surround her, and by looking rather than by talking, Undine is ready to move upward and onward.

Undine's single-minded ascent through life as image maker and the interpreter of types has a dire effect upon the men in her life who are idealists enough to yearn after Platonic forms. She is a realist, a woman who thrives by constantly adjusting to the world's ever-shifting reality. Idealists remain fixed to fantasies of desire for unreal things; they are anomalies who remain exposed and apart, at a loss for the protective coloration by which developing organisms stay *within* their changing context.

Undine's "first" husband, Ralph Marvell (first in point of public disclosure, if not in point of fact), is inept in the custom of the country in the same way Ellerton Lawrence is in *The Angel of Clay*; in the same way demonstrated by the "Louis" side of Neville in *The Common Law*. Marvell shapes Undine into the form of an allegorical Andromeda he believes it is his allegorical duty to save from the dangers of a false society. Like Lawrence and Neville, Marvell cannot recognize the true type of the woman who stands before him. For his failure to adjust his vision to the signs by which the new society signals its customs and celebrates its successful types, his ideals are shaken and his life is shattered. It is significant that the successive stages of Marvell's disillusionment are marked by the newspaper accounts Wharton cleverly plants within the narrative. The press is accurate in its record of Undine's accomplishments. Marvell's dream-vision of a marble creature is entirely different from the gloriously malleable clay of which Undine's nature consists.

By the end of the novel, Undine has mounted close to the apex of her earthly desires (a parody of Peter Bembo's ascent toward divine truth). Left far behind her is her little son Paul. Like his father Ralph Marvell, Paul only "knows" his mother by looking through the scrapbook of newspaper clippings and publicity photographs that give visual proof that Undine has got almost everything she wanted. She has created herself after the images of a cultural ideal that offer her access to her desires. She has dismissed as unreal the ideal images Paul and Marvell dream up for her. The discrepancy between what she wants and gets and what they want and are denied is fatal to the two males and a triumph for her.

Undine's success is, of course, not flawless, even on her own terms. Nor could it be in the presence of the ironies with which Wharton characteristically tells her stories. The last sentence in the novel images Undine dressed and bejeweled for the evening as the wife of Elmer Moffat (the man identified by the papers as the type of the Collector—the successor to Undine's penultimate husband, the Count). But Undine is upset. She has just been informed that she, as a woman twice divorced, may never be the wife of an ambassador. The Ambassador's Wife is exactly the picture she has been holding up to inspire her facile imagination. By having, however, become the other real things she set out to be, she has by necessity become the Divorcée. She has blocked the way toward adding another—the crowning—type to her life's repertoire. In almost every other way, she has adjusted with astonishing precision to the protective requirements dictated by the social background she has chosen as her own. In this one instance she stands apart—too conspicuous ever to receive society's sanction as the Ambassador's Wife. How like Undine that *that* is the self she declares is "the one part she was really made for."

Undine is intellectually incapable of realizing that it is her constant dissatisfaction with the present moment and her need to change which keeps her in line with the world around her. Her capacity *to desire more* enables her to *move with* a society whose members believe in change as long as change brings them nearer their hearts' desire. But the same fluidity that lets Undine flourish in a world of flux prevents her from saying, "There, at last, I have *it*—the one real thing I want to be, now and always."

Still, if the image of the Ambassador's Wife eludes Undine's grasp, this image is only one of the sequence of images that has assured her survival. By living up to all the types her mind imagines, Undine has the kind of protective coloration that works. In contrast, all poor Ralph Marvell possesses is the image of the Andromeda (divorced as it is from any of the tints and tones of the current social scene); it casts him, conspicuous and vulnerable, beyond the safety of a milieu into which he and his ideals can never blend.

Many of the remarks I have made concerning Undine Spragg's successful use of protective coloration are hugely ironic. Ironic, because of the gaps they disclose; not necessarily ironic when viewed in terms of the social field out of which these

fictional characters emerge and into which they blend. Irony means gaps that separate the false from the real; irony indicates what is *conspicuously different*. Thayer's peacock is not ironic in its gaudy blending with its bed of leaves (figure 5.12);
nor is Undine's perfect assimilation as "the Peacock" (here imaged by Alfred Maurer,
figure 5.13). Only those of us who, in our function as the type of the Critic, stand
outside the scene, make use of irony.

Critics uncover the protective duplicities by which nature and society's laws
give safekeeping to the world's organisms. Critics call upon ironies that could prove
their own destruction if they were forced to exist within the environment they
comment upon as spectators. Theodore Dreiser is an example of a writer who comes
very close at times to disappearing into the setting when the images singled out by
his pictorial eye start to reflect his own desires. He always escapes at the last
instant, just when irony seems to disappear from his narrative; he saves himself
for the critic's life by a sudden thought that places him to one side of the camou-
flaged object.

Early in chapter 5 of *Sister Carrie* the narrative voice tells us of the pleasure
Charlie Drouet takes in Fitzgerald and Moy's saloon, which represents all Drouet
desires.[8] We are shown what Charlie sees "from a Chicago standpoint": the saloon
as "gorgeous," "handsome," "graceful," "sumptuous," "fancy," and "rich." Equated
by Drouet with the power of greenbacks, the place has the sound "reputation"
that promises future success and offers present satisfaction. The passage suppresses
the suggestion that the saloon's appearance is a cheat once a man learns its interior secrets. If the physiognomical manuals of the period had specialized in analyses of places as well as persons, this glittering place would receive top marks for
its perfect consistency of type. It, indeed, seems to be "a truly swell saloon."

When George Hurstwood appears in the next paragraph, the fit between the figure he cuts and his setting is perfect. Both look the part of substantiality. True,
Hurstwood's position as manager is a special one. He has no executive or financial
powers. His plain little office behind the scenes is like a dressing room where an
actor retreats when not onstage playing the star role. We who read the novel to
its end come to know much more; we learn what happens when Hurstwood leaves
the saloon where he had been completely in focus. But just here we are given no
hints about the circumstances that will dislodge him from his position as the Manager; not until the passage placed farther along in the chapter where the critic's
eye takes over from Drouet. The setting is now interpreted from the perspective of
"one not inclined to drink, and gifted with a more serious turn of mind." Only at
that carefully delayed moment of revelation does irony enter. It is irony that discloses that the saloon and its denizens, hitherto disguised in the form of confident
and successful men, are actually "the light of the flame" and "the moths" which
come in "endless procession, to bask" in the glow. Viewed from within the spell
of the images cast by the saloon, "One might take it after all as an augur of the
better social order." Viewed, however, by one "outside, under the serene light of
the eternal stars," the saloon and its dreams "must seem a strange and shiny thing."

Compare Stephen Crane's treatment of the Bowery tavern in *Maggie: A Girl of*

5.12. Abbott Handerson Thayer
and Richard Merryman,
"Peacock in the Woods"
(1907).

NATIONAL MUSEUM OF AMERICAN ART

the Streets to that of Dreiser's Chicago saloon. Crane immediately reveals to us that what glitters before the ignorant eyes of Pete and Jimmy is sham. The narrator's knowing eye constantly badgers us with the corrected vision of which the Bowery folk are incapable. Crane in *Maggie* is the ironist as reporter covering a costume party who knows exactly what lies behind each disguise. Dreiser in *Sister Carrie* joins with his characters as a fellow guest at a masked ball, delaying the moment when he separates himself from the mindless frivolity and unleashes the burden of his ironic knowledge of true identities. But what about individuals—particularly women—who have something to gain by staying in costume? Perhaps critics with irony to burn are not always the best judges of what it means to be a woman with an identity she wishes to conceal, to reveal, or to discover for herself by means of the social disguises she assumes and the costumes she wears.

Costume parties were a popular form of entertainment in the years between the 1880s and the 1910s. (The Butterick Pattern Company issued a little booklet with instructions on how to dress like various figures from history or legend—down to

5.13. Alfred H. Maurer, "The Peacock" (c.1903).

the right buttons to use and what kinds of flounces to add to the cuff.) [9] There was also a vogue for masked balls. Compare a party where a woman goes masked with a party where she limits herself to dressing up as Cinderella or Mary, Queen of Scots. At the latter affair, she wears a costume that sets up a pattern of make-believe; she adds a wig and fancy headgear; but her *face* (that everyday signature of her social self) is fully in view. No real transformation takes place in her identity; no disclosures are made about what lies hidden within.

In contrast, the woman at a masked ball covers her face in addition to altering the everyday look of her body. Certain new powers come into her grasp. At the least, she neutralizes her public identity for the evening; she is a free-floating receptacle for whatever may turn up, especially a bit of romantic playfulness. At the most, she seizes the occasion to express some quirk of the self kept under cover and out of bounds until that night. She needn't be as lawless as a second-story man, a Klansman, or an assassin, but she can be a princess in disguise on a "Roman holiday" among the plebs, or a commoner who moves freely in the midst of the lordly circles she secretly claims as her birthright. By means of costume and mask, she blends with impunity into a setting (the masked ball) where "revealing" disguises are in order. Dressing as Joan of Arc on Main Street at high noon might not be wise; doing it at a masked ball lets her be woman, warrior, martyr, and saint to general acclaim and with no harm done.

There is yet a greater moment to come at the ball. It is that "midnight" moment when the mask is removed. A drawing of 1900 by James Montgomery Flagg shows a young woman, her body enveloped in a disguising domino, who has just taken off her mask (figure 5.14). That she was disguised and that she is now revealed is what titillates Flagg. But what I want to ask is, Could this girl *go back into* disguise as easily as she came out of it? Could she (like Thayer's copperhead shown in figures 5.8 and 5.9) master the laws of protective coloration to the extent that she may continue either to prey upon others or to shield herself from predators?

Undine Spragg can. She learns how to match the patterns of "consumption" of her social world with such exactitude she is no longer "conspicuous" in the Veblenian sense of standing out in exposed vulnerability. Like Abbott Thayer's peacock (figure 5.12), Undine becomes *just as glittering as* the gilded foliage of the New York and Continental society into which she plunges. The red costume worn by the young woman imaged by Coles Phillips blends into the red that forms the entire design (see figure 5.10). Wharton's Undine (four times married, thrice divorced) is a "scarlet woman" who fits neatly into that level of society which condones divorce (except for ambassadors' wives). Hawthorne's Hester Prynne, by contrast, is seen as a figure of scandal because she and her sin (given visible identification by the embroidered letter A and her elf-child Pearl) stand out against the grays and browns of old Salem's moral laws.

Traditionally, self-value resides in the face, most specifically in the area of the eyes. According to this line of argument, the eyes are windows to the soul; if those windows are shuttered to prevent Peeping Toms from staring voyeuristically in upon one's private nature, then the happenstance that one's private parts are exposed is of relatively small importance. So Eakins' advertisement of 1877 implied. What, though, about the marble statue of "Undine" by Joseph Mozier in 1867, a neoclassical personification of the mythic water creature sculpted fifty years before the heroine of Wharton's novel came into being (figure 5.15)? The face and body of Mozier's Undine are veiled, but does the statue suggest a woman who is concealed or one who is revealed—at the least, called attention to? The face, which might give viewers a sign of who she is, is obliterated; but the body, just as heavily draped, is accentuated by the sinuous marble veilings. What is more, it is the figure's sex that cries out to us; it raises the same questions about the nature of concealment and identification as does the sketch Thomas Eakins made of the masked nude model (see figure 5.1).

It is time to stand the matter of disguises and concealments on its head. We shall look at examples of inverted identities by which women consciously switch gender categories, making themselves unconventional through the creative use of conventions that distinguish male from female. The codified distinctions between the sexes in late-nineteenth- and early-twentieth-century society acted as an incitement to the testing of the types. A woman could push the gender categories toward their limits and remain within the accepted social game, as long as the nature of those limits remained clear. The unconventional act required a sharp

5.14. James Montgomery Flagg,
"The Mask," from *Yankee
Girls Abroad* (1900).

sense of the conventions, even though that sharpness constantly felt the dulling edge of change.

Two popular novels, one of 1912 and the other of 1931, serve as a useful set of time brackets. Each narrative indicates the social climate surrounding heroines in the process of asking "Just who am I?" This is a very old question, but each generation has to ask it for different reasons, even generations separated by only nineteen years. In answering, these heroines were aided or abetted by the degree of confidence they had in imaging what it means to be a woman. Obviously, the evidence extracted from two novels asked to stand for two complexly patterned periods cannot sustain the burden of any general truth. But however selective these

5.15. Joseph Mozier, "Undine" (c. 1867).

references, the novels suggest the kind of gender identifications two women au-thors, at least, believed were possible in the 1910s and 1930s.

In 1912 Jean Webster wrote and illustrated *Daddy-Long-Legs*, a light romantic comedy that satisfied the expectations we bring to the fairy-tale motif of the or-phan girl who marries the prince. Add to this familiar theme Webster's use of the epistolary tradition, known to us through narratives such as Samuel Richardson's *Pamela*, in which spunky young women from the provinces go out into the big, frightening world and win.

Jerusha Abbott has been raised as "Any Orphan" (figure 5.16) in a dreary chil-dren's home. Her name was given her by the matron who took "Jerusha" from a tombstone and "Abbott" from a telephone directory, but the heroine knows very well that those names are just "not me." The story recounts what happens when an unknown benefactor from among the trustees of the orphanage selects Jerusha as the lucky girl sent off to Vassar for an education.

DADDY-LONG-LEGS

(as you doubtless know and heartily approve of) is to turn the ninety-seven orphans into ninety-seven twins.

    The unusual artistic ability which I ex-
hibit, was developed at an early age through

A NY O R PH A N

Rear Elevation   Front Elevation

5.16. Jean Webster, "Any Orphan,"
from *Daddy-Long-Legs* (1912).

35

Two powerful desires are set into motion from this point on. The first, and simplest, is for Jerusha to find out who she "really" is and to match that inner self
with the social image that correctly expresses her true worth. This is rapidly determined. Lo! "Jerusha" is transformed like magic into "Judy." "Any orphan" attains her rightful inheritance as a "Vassar Girl" (figure 5.17). Since this pleasant
discovery and the merger of private and public selves take place almost at once,
what sustains the rest of the story is Judy's long quest (one that takes her through
four years at college and some months beyond) to find out the identity of her
benefactor. He is known to her as "Mr. John Smith," but she dismisses this name
as obviously not being the right one for him, just as she has repudiated the name
"Jerusha" for herself.

    Judy has had one brief glance of "John Smith." It was a shadow cast upon a
wall, an outline she likens to that of a daddy-long-legs (figure 5.18). She also knows
what he is *not* like. He is not one of the other trustees, imaged as a fat bug (figure
5.19). Judy informs her benefactor of her stabs at definition through the drawings
she includes in letters she sends, through an intermediary, to "Mr. Smith," or, as
she chooses to call him, "Daddy." Judy badgers Daddy to give her hints to his real
identity. She proposes a schematic figure that suggests his probable height but may
fault on the amount of hair he actually has (figure 5.20). Judy experiments in a
vacuum of information, trying through the process of elimination to determine the
true nature of the man who gave her the chance to discover her own identity.

    In the meantime, Judy begins to feel affection for Jervis Pendleton, the uncle of

DADDY-LONG-LEGS

Will you forgive me this once if I promise
never to flunk again?

> Yours in sackcloth,

> J UDY.

5.17. Jean Webster, "News of the
Month," from *Daddy-Long-Legs*
(1912).

one of her classmates. By the novel's end, the separate identities of "John Smith,"
"Daddy-Long-Legs," and "Jervis Pendleton" merge into a composite type. Dreamed-
up abstractions are replaced by the confirmed identity of the man Judy has come
to love. Long since, *she* has moved beyond being the anonymous orphan; she has
enjoyed being college woman and budding author. Now she adds another piece of
solid social identification to her repertoire: wife of the wealthy Pendleton, the
"Daddy" who is simultaneously "father," "husband," and potential "lover."

The happy ending of this romantic little tale stands at a far remove from what
happens to the heroine-narrator of *Virgins in Cellophane: From Maker to Con-*

DADDY-LONG-LEGS

Sunday.

Dear Daddy-Long-Legs,

Is n't it funny? I started to write to you yesterday afternoon, but as far as I got was the heading, "Dear Daddy-Long-Legs," and then I remembered I'd promised to pick some blackberries for supper, so I went off and left the sheet lying on the table, and when I came back to-day, what do you think I found sitting in the middle of the page? A real true Daddy-Long-Legs!

I picked him up very gently by one leg. and dropped him out of the window. I

DADDY-LONG-LEGS

benevolent. He pats one on the head and wears a gold watch chain.

That looks like a June bug, but is meant to be a portrait of any Trustee except you. However — to resume:

I have been walking and talking and having tea with a man. And with a very superior man — with Mr. Jervis Pendleton of the House of Julia; her uncle, in short (in

December 19th.

Dear Daddy-Long-Legs,

You never answered my question and it was very important.

ARE YOU BALD?

I have it planned exactly what you look like — very satisfactorily — until I reach the top of your head, and then I *am* stuck. I can't decide whether you have white hair or black hair or sort of sprinkly gray hair or maybe none at all.

Here is your portrait: But the problem is, shall I add some hair? Would you like to

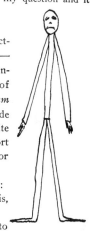

5.18. Jean Webster, "Daddy-Long-Legs," from *Daddy-Long-Legs* (1912).

5.19. Jean Webster, [Fat Trustee], from *Daddy-Long-Legs* (1912).

5.20. Jean Webster, "Are You Bald?" from *Daddy-Long-Legs* (1912).

5.21. James Montgomery Flagg,
". . . a fear of being
trapped by domesticity
and baby carriages," from
Hooper, *Virgins in Cellophane* (1932).

sumer Untouched by Human Hand, written by Bett Hooper and illustrated by James
Montgomery Flagg in 1932.

The protagonist of Hooper's narrative (significantly unnamed) tells her own unhappy story. She sees herself caught up in the dilemma of her times. A latter-day
Carrie Meeber, this young woman has come to the city to find herself. The city is
Washington, D.C., and she is a government secretary caught between fat and lust-
ful congressmen by day, while after hours she finds herself in cynical combat with
any number of young men on the make. What she wants is romantic love. What
she doesn't want is "old-fashioned" bondage as housewife and mother (figure 5.21).
But what the males in her life want of her complicates matters no end. This is
because they ask her to be two self-contradictory objects: one of the "virgins in
cellophane" (figure 5.22), and also the "hot-water bottle" men take to bed whenever it pleases them (figure 5.23).

The heroine of Hooper's story knows she will receive no useful counsel from her
mother's generation on what to do to resolve her dilemma. By 1931 female lives
have altered too much for that. Only Bertrand Russell is on hand, and he says,
"Do exactly what you feel like doing, since that is nature's way." This is no help,

5.22. James Montgomery Flagg, ". . . every man likes to think his Prize Package is a Virgin in cellophane— direct from makers to consumer, untouched by human hand," from Hooper, *Virgins in Cellophane* (1932).

she decides, since she feels so many different things. Among these conflicting desires are the need to be free and the need to mother (figure 5.24).

If only our heroine could find out *what being a woman means!* Exactitude about the nature of women, and men as well, would make the difference. But "all men look alike when you're drunk," she discovers (figure 5.25), just as men only see women as a pair of legs, blotting the rest from view (figure 5.26).

What sharpens the contrasts between Hooper's narrative and Webster's? It is this:

5.23. James Montgomery Flagg, ". . . the prayer of a hot-water bottle," from Hooper, *Virgins in Cellophane* (1932).

5.24. James Montgomery Flagg, ". . . I have an insane desire to wrap him up in a pink flannel blanket with white rabbits on it," from Hooper, *Virgins in Cellophane* (1932).

although Judy Abbott has to decide which social signature matches her untried self and to discover the true identity of the wonderful "bug" she has grown to love, it is what she does *not* have to worry about, and what the Hooper heroine does, that matters.

First, Judy's responses to the man who turns out to be Jervis Pendleton cover quite a range. She is a *daughter* to his "Daddy" (a child who is at times dutiful, at times rebellious). She wants to *mother* him when she learns he has become seriously ill. She desires to be his *wife*. But these various emotional conditions are

5.25. James Montgomery Flagg, "After a few cocktails all men look alike," from Hooper, *Virgins in Cellophane* (1932).

5.26. James Montgomery Flagg, "Stags only see the backs of girls' legs and break in on the prettiest pairs," from Hooper, *Virgins in Cellophane* (1932).

never, in her mind at least, confusing or tormenting, as they very much are to the young woman of 1931.

Second, it is taken for granted that Judy will arrive in Jervis' arms as a virgin in cellophane *and* that the love they will share, in marriage, will not transform her into a hot-water bottle, a sex object.

Third, and most important, the identification of who and what is male and who and what is female is never in doubt in Jean Webster's world, even though we realize that this is a foolish assumption on her part, given the ambiguities that riddled the issue of gender in 1912. By 1931 and Hooper's novel, however, we appear to have come around to what William Wasserstrom in his book *The Heiress of All the Ages: Sex and Sentiment in the Genteel Tradition* foretold might happen. Once the sexual revolution comes, the dream of romantic love between a man and a woman will be shaken, if not lost.[10] But not merely romantic love is lost. Also absent from *Virgins in Cellophane* is the clear sense of what it means to be free to be female or male—freedoms possible under the conditions created by the social conventions the heroine associates with her grandmother's generation.

Three popular novels of the 1890s and early 1900s portray just what that grandmother counted on, at least if she believed as the authors of these romances did that women and men fit prescribed categories of class and gender. But note that none of the three novels takes place in the United States; they are located in the never-never lands of Ruritania, Graustark, and a romantic's vision of Europe where disguises abound, just as they once did in Shakespeare's Forest of Arden.

The hero of Anthony Hope Hawkins' *The Prisoner of Zenda* of 1894 (the best-selling novel for which Charles Dana Gibson furnished the illustrations) takes over the identity of his physical double, the Prince of Ruritania. The switch enables the followers of the menaced prince (the legitimate heir to the throne) to defeat the forces of evil. As an inevitable consequence of the disguise, romantic complications develop. The commoner hero falls in love with the Princess Flavia. She loves him in return, both before and after it is disclosed that, although he is a well-born Englishman, he is not of royal blood. By the close of the story the lovers have to part, with only one last embrace to carry in their memories.

George Barr McCutcheon's *Beverly of Graustark* of 1902, illustrated by Harrison Fisher, replaces Ruritania with Graustark. But in McCutcheon's version of the established formula romance, it is the charming, plucky American girl who passes as a princess in order to help good defeat evil. There is an additional twist. It is she who falls in love with an uncouthly dressed huntsman. In figure 5.27 we are shown Beverly asking in apprehension, "Who are you?" By the end, each discovers who the other one is. Beverly no longer has to pretend she is a princess, and he reveals that he is the prince. In figure 5.28 Beverly takes the face of the mysterious stranger in her hands (a face she has loved and hated because of the deceptions involved). But in this story the lovers can marry. The American Girl becomes a real princess, beloved by the true Graustarkian prince.

In both *The Prisoner of Zenda* and *Beverly of Graustark*, what is at issue are disguises used in regard to class identity; gender concealments are not at their core.[11] Compare, however, two other popular novels in which the nature of the heroine's sex is held in some confusion. In the case of *Trilby*, George Du Maurier's romance of 1894, this confusion is only momentary. At one point Trilby escapes from a situation of unrequited love by disguising herself as a boy. When she reappears, it is unquestionably as a woman, although one who is now "masked" (even to herself) as the "mouthpiece" of the enchanter Svengali.

Much more thoroughgoing in its rendition of gender disguise (since it is a theme which extends over the course of the entire novel) is *The Princess Passes*. This novel of 1905 was written by C. N. and A. M. Williamson, a husband and wife team, and illustrated by the famous magazine-cover and poster artist Edward Penfield. *The Princess Passes* is a complicated variant on the Shakespearean romantic

"Who—who in heaven's name are you?" she
faltered.

5.27. Harrison Fisher, from
McCutcheon, *Beverly of
Graustark* (1904).

5.28. Harrison Fisher, from
McCutcheon, *Beverly of
Graustark* (1904).

"I hated you to-night, I thought," she cried,
taking his face in her hands.

comedy motif of the young woman (unhappy in love) who dons a boy's costume
(figure 5.29), then trails after the hero in his travels, deeply in love with him, but
unable to reveal her identity or sex. The story's emphasis is placed upon the shifts
taking place in the emotional attitudes felt by the hero toward the seeming boy.
He first thinks of his pert companion as the Brat, then as the Boy, next as My
Little Pal, even as the Beloved—at which time he becomes worried over the feelings he has toward this handsome lad. At last it is disclosed that his boyish companion is a fabulously wealthy American heiress, a true "princess" who is "passing" as one of his own sex. All ends very well, with the hero, an impoverished
British lord, gaining marriage, money, and romantic love with the Beloved whom
he can now fully, conventionally adore.[12]

None of these popular romances undermines social norms concerning what women
and men are supposed to be, although the threat of possible upheaval continues to
the final scenes. The "boy" disguises allow the romantic couples to meet charmingly, the woman's figure is enhanced by her boyish attire, and the final revelation

5.29. Edward Penfield, frontispiece for Williamson, *The Princess Passes*
(1905).

scenes are knockouts. Emotionally, these narratives of the inversion of identity are both satisfying and soothing: satisfying since they allow the imagination to toy with the pleasures of change; soothing because whatever has been upended is returned to its proper place by the story's conclusion. In the actual world nothing was that certain or contained, but as long as there were romances to read the right and proper differences between "princesses" and "heroes" were confirmed; as long

123

FEMININE, WOMANLY

(Masculine)

Concave upper and convex lower type of profile.

Brunet or dark color of hair, skin and eyes.

Small size.

Fine texture of hair and skin.

Mental or brainy and nervous type of structure.

Small delicately carved features.

5.30. "Feminine, Womanly," from Balkin, *Human Dictionary* (1923).

Round and wide-open eyes, with arched eyebrows.

too as there were physiognomical manuals to state the absolutes of gender identification.

Signs for the sexes had become standardized to the level of pictographs in *Human Dictionary*, the handbook patched together by Harry Balkin in 1923 (figure 5.30). *Heads, Faces, Types, Races*, written by V. G. Rocine in 1910, defined the genders at more length than did Balkin's brisk dictionary entries, but Rocine was hardly less simplistic (figure 5.31). Female: "Quality fine but delicate; susceptibility to culture, love of society life, high aspiration, health delicate." Male: "Large body, heavy neck, vital, motive temperament. Adapted for cattle industries."[13]

Quality fine, but delicate. Temperament here is the mental. Good development of the chin. The color faculty strong, the temples well developed, the face pyriform. This means refinement, susceptibility to culture, love of society life, high aspirations, beauty of person, refinement, culture, agreeableness of manner. Health delicate.

Large body; heavy neck; large lower face; small tophead; weakly developed temples; fleshy, heavy, muscular, base of brain predominating and acting with a large development of the will faculties. Here the quality is rather low. This is a vital, motive temperament. Adapted for cattle industries.

life. A very small chin, jaw and neck go with a delicate constitution. A wide chin means strong amative feelings and a desire for society. A very small, sharp, retreating chin, with thin lips, a wide head and a sharp nose, go with an unsociable, hermit-like nature.

This chin is long and triangular, the nose is artistic, the eyes open and the face indicates that the temperament is mental-osseous. The heart and circulation are good, but the lungs are weaker. This man has a literary, poetic and highly intelligent development.

5.31. From Rocine, *Heads, Faces, Types, Races* (1910).

Men with feminine traits caused Rocine great concern, even when their refinement brought them close to "the highest type" to which any man could aspire—Jesus Christ (figure 5.32). Rocine was unable to see what the feminized male in the figure of a Reverend Mr. Caine (shown to the right of the page spread) had to contribute to "the zip and pep" required by an American capitalistic system founded upon aggressive maleness. Refinement in a man could only lead to the type of the American Genteel, just as George Santayana said it would in his Berkeley address the year after Rocine's book came out.[14] American society was burdened by men like Reverend Mr. Caine, described by Rocine as "a genuine benefactor and minister of the gospel, but a poor business man. Here vitality is weak. Subject to neurasthenia and indigestion." The type of the cattle baron shown in figure 5.31 was what America needed to direct its business life. As for the nation's political activities, Theodore Roosevelt was the exemplary type Rocine picked to represent true American maleness—squeaky voice, poor digestion, and all (see figure 2.19).

Feminized American males were bad enough. If American society did not watch out (what with all the current talk about the New Woman), American females might become squat, mannish figures. This warning was clearly stated in the sixth

It is the inventive, experimental, imaginative, idealistic, mystical and altruistic shape of forehead. The Hindoo has this shape to his upper forehead. He has the same approximate characteristics. He is active in abstract and speculative religion, but lazy, when it is a question of industry. He believes in caste and rank magi, mysticism and speculative philosophy.

The most prominent characteristics of those people are experimentation, speculation, theorization. They always take an interest in that which is new, in that which is not known, in new doctrines, new art, new

High Forehead.
A high-square tophead, medium sidehead, long, narrow face, harmonious features. From a phrenological standpoint, this is the tophead of a highly spiritual minded, religious and peaceful man. It is supposed to be the picture of Jesus Christ, the Savior of the world. His head and face certainly are of the highest type.

People who have a high forehead are believers; they believe that the mind is all and that "thoughts are things." They believe that something will "turn up," while people who have a low forehead turn things up themselves. The Hindoo turns gold into ashes, but the heavy-set Italian turns ashes into gold.

High Forehead, Rev. Caine.
A high tophead; a long narrow face; a strongly developed face in the center; an honest mouth; a sincere eye; large, active ears; an energetic nature. A genuine benefactor and minister of the gospel, but a poor business man. Here vitality is weak. Subject to neurasthenia and indigestion.

philosophy. They have an experimental mind, delve into inventions, experimental speech and languages, speculative religion, experimental breeding of animals, the improvement of fruit varieties, experimental eugen-

5.32. From Rocine, *Heads, Faces, Types, Races* (1910).

edition of *Physiognomy Illustrated*, brought out in 1891 by Joseph Simms. Simms felt some compassion for the frustrated lives of deviants from the feminine norm, but he was unable to fathom how a sound society could accommodate their freakishness. Where would marriage and family enter in if the masculinized New Woman took over?[15]

Not only the future of the general human race lay in jeopardy if males and females failed to keep to their proper categories. Since the accepted national types that were in place by the 1890s demanded that American men be very male and that American women be recognizably feminine, the specific *American* quality of the country's population was threatened by any drastic shuffle of gender types. The family. The nation. Even more was at stake. The vigor of the growing ready-to-wear garment industry and the dress-pattern market depended upon the careful classification and mathematical standardization of body types. As early as the 1870s and 1880s, dressmakers, manufacturers, and merchandisers laid down specifications along practical, apolitical lines.[16] The Perfect Male was defined by one ready-made suit maker in 1890 just prior to the publication of Simms' book (figure 5.33), while the Standard Woman helped consumers select printed dress patterns in 1923

5.33. "The Perfect Man," Hammerslough, Saks & Co. (c. 1890).

Table of
Standard
Adult
Proportions

Unit of
Measurement
One Head

(from top
of head
to under
chin)

·GS·

top of
breast bone
shoulders

fullest
part of
bust

waist

hips

neck

1st
head

2nd
head

3rd
head

4th
head

5th
head

6th
head

7th
head

8th
head

5.34. "Diagram C.—Standard Adult
Proportions," from Buttrick,
Principles of Clothing Selection
(1923).

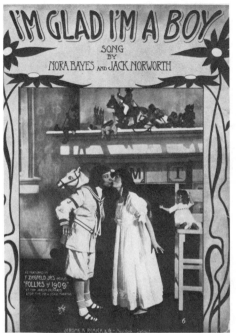

5.35. "I'm Glad I'm a Boy," *Ziegfeld Follies of 1909.*

5.36. Bristow Adams, "Indiana Normal" (1902).

at the same moment Harry Balkin's "dictionary" regularized definitions for the feminine type (figure 5.34).

In an atmosphere in which the male and female forms could be diagramed with precision, audiences for the *Ziegfeld Follies* found amusement when well-known performers, dressed up as little boys and girls, sang songs in celebration of *la dif- férence* (figure 5.35). The second verse of this piece from the 1909 *Follies*, "I'm Glad I'm a Boy," leads off with "I'm Glad I'm a Girl," a declaration by Nora Bayes that being female also has its pleasures. The visual joke, exploited by the *Follies'* pairing of "children," came from the fact that grown-up men and women could enjoy biological differences through the sexual activities permitted to adults. In contrast, actual little girls were limited to child's play, no real fun for them in a culture that permitted a wide range of activities only to little boys.[17] But once boys and girls grew past the supposedly asexual, schematized forms depicted in the Prang drawing manuals (see figure 1.2), the fun of relationships based on being female and male could commence. Even when overt sexuality was kept carefully in check by adherence to social mores concerning proper premarital conduct for

5.37. Irma Purman and friends
(c.1913).

5.38. Irma Purman and friends
(c.1913).

nice young women, heterosexual attractions were given space for experiment and play.

Fun between the sexes was predicated on an instant recognition of everyone's gender. In the state of "Indiana Normal" (figure 5.36), men and women are recognized as such—even when seen on the run in the distance (figure 5.37), or when only their faces show and two of the women sport men's hats (figure 5.38). All the figures are alike in the physical zest they display and in their readiness to mug, and no pronounced cultural distinctions separate feminine from masculine conduct, but which are women and which are men is easy enough to determine, even if one goes by hairstyles alone. (These two snapshots, taken in 1913, are of my mother and her friends, who were passing their energetic young adulthood in a small Indiana community. More photographs of the group will appear later.) [18]

For every Gibson Girl it was hoped a Gibson Man would materialize. This ideal male type was figured by the popular novelist and gentleman-adventurer Richard Harding Davis (figure 5.39) and by the square-cut jaw of Charles Dana Gibson himself (figure 5.40). There was also the androgynous look which J. C. Leyendecker introduced to the advertising world in the service of promoting masculine tailoring (figure 5.41). [19] As this Kuppenheimer advertisement suggests, American male *racial* types were more distinct from one another than was the Leyendecker male from the female, but when Leyendecker women took up the tailored look they remained well inside the physical category considered appropriate to their

5.39. Penrhyn Stanlaws, poster
for *Scribner's Monthly
Magazine* (1898).

5.40. William Sergeant Kendall,
poster for *Scribner's
Monthly Magazine* (189–).

sex (figure 5.42). Leyendecker males might look somewhat feminized at times, but his women appeared feminine even when wearing versions of male clothing or when falling under the signs allocated to the New Woman or the Outdoors Girl.

When Leyendecker men and women gathered together, they were imaged as "pals" (to use a favorite term of the times) intended to represent distinct gender types. Any confusion caused by Leyendecker's sometimes sexually ambiguous figures is clarified when the motifs he presented through drawing are repeated through the medium of the snapshot. My mother and her friends stand next to a Leyendecker billboard poster for Kuppenheimer Suits, showing off their own highly tailored costumes with impunity (figure 5.43). They pose wearing sailor blouses and sports cardigans in the company of a male companion, together with that essential prop of the Arrow Shirt advertisements Leyendecker made famous—the low-slung roadster—never doubting that everyone along Montpelier's main street would recognize them as female (figure 5.44).

5.41. J. C. Leyendecker, "House of Kuppenheimer" (1921).

5.42. J. C. Leyendecker, "Vacation," *Collier's Weekly*, August 17, 1907.

    Ambiguities of form and feature abounded, of course, alongside the conventions set in place for the identification of the male and the female type. Ambiguities appear with frequency in the allegorical statues placed on public display (figure 5.45). But when this stern Liberty head is viewed at the distance required by its gigantic proportions, it signals its sex by the drapery of its classical dress, albeit on a disturbingly heroic scale. After all, turn-of-the-century representations of "America" were intended to be *female*, not feminine. "America" as a public form had to possess *virtus*, in the original Roman sense of power. The American theater, as you will shortly see, also provided occasions for calculated confusions of sex distinctions. But by and large, in the commercial world of hard-cash products with wide consumer appeal, items were explicitly classified. The words "for women," together with the wine-glass waist, accentuated bust, abundant hair, and ripe mouth, attest which of two Arrow audiences is being asked to buy the mannish collars shown in figure 5.46.

5.43. Irma Purman and friends
(c.1912).

5.44. Irma Purman and friends
(c.1913).

Young American women were daily surrounded by gender distinctions of the kind that threatened to limit them to prescribed social categories. What did it mean, for instance, when they tried to achieve a fair imitation of the Gibson Girl image? Did their appropriation of the physical and psychological set of "attitudes" clustering around this well-known sign consign them to the sole fate of getting married, since getting married is what Gibson had in mind when he portrayed his romantically feminine, albeit vigorous and statuesque, young women?

Charles Dana Gibson knew what might happen to the woman limited to love and marriage. She might become "One More Victim," or she might be the prey of a scheming mother abetted by a blinded clergyman (figures 5.47 and 5.48). Gibson believed that young American women could protect society's virtues only if these women were protected from society's vices. He did not know the way out of this impasse. Many of his illustrations give direct evidence that he was aware of the conditions that undercut his hope that the social system would save its own best saviors. Still and all, as Gibson imaged the American Girl, the Girl's dream was to be included—to stay inside that magic circle where men are men and women are women waiting to be wanted. For the Gibson Girl's nightmare is being ignored, thereby *left out* (figure 5.49).

Here follows a series of eight family photographs featuring my mother and her friends in the years between 1908 and 1913. These photographs explicitly attempt to record what "being left out" *looks like* in terms of the conventional poses by which rejection is recognized without the need for captions or explanations. They also suggest alternative "attitudes" by which the socially humiliating condition of

5.45. Head of the Statue of Liberty, Paris park (1883).

exclusion can be resolved. They are poses playfully enacted before the camera of a young professional photographer in Montpelier, the husband of the one member of the group who was already married. The young women moved with enthusiasm into those moments of play because they knew their exact status within their hometown. They were, after all, charter members of the LOPH Club, the group they formed after leaving high school in order to commemorate the fact that they (all but the one) had been "Left on Papa's Hands."

Figure 5.50 is the first of three poses dramatizing the sorry plight of the failure to fit into the expected romantic pairing of one woman to one man. Figure 5.51 is another variation, whereas figure 5.52 portrays my mother "jilted" at sixteen years of age, left alone to moon over old love letters (actually laundry bills supplied by the photographer, who had an eye for props beyond those of fur rug and silk kimono). Next come five poses in which the LOPH Club experiments with how *not* to appear superfluous. Figure 5.53 shows one man with two women inserted in the middle of the standard pairings. By taking up the slack, this threesome is supposedly as happy as any set of two can be. Figure 5.54 places two men and one woman

5.46. George Brehm,
"Tenby, an Arrow
Collar for Women"
(1910).

and two women and one man in alternating holding patterns. Figure 5.55 provides
a further twist: all the players are female, but everyone is given a romantic partner
when half dress as women and half as men. The following photograph pushes the
idea of cross-dressing all the way (figure 5.56). The young women are attired as
male chums; there are no "women" present to feel excluded. The final arrangement also solves the exclusion problem, but not by the mathematical means of
two-by-two or all-as-one used in the preceding poses (figure 5.57). Here the extra
woman obliterates the question of rejection altogether with a shrug that says, "Who
gives a damn!"

What do these photographs suggest in regard to a theory of self-assessment and
self-determination? In 1890 William James' *The Principles of Psychology* pointed
out the tendency of people to "see" others into being according to the way they
applied their own standards of identification. James wrote that *"a man has as
many social selves as there are individuals who recognize him* and carry an image

5.47. Charles Dana Gibson, "One More Victim," *Life*, May 23, 1895.

5.48. Charles Dana Gibson, "The Ambitious Mother and the Obliging Clergyman," *Life*, June 5, 1902.

5.49. Charles Dana Gibson, "Her Nightmare. How She Saw Herself," *Life*, May 21, 1896.

5.50. Irma Purman and friends
(c.1912).

5.51. Irma Purman and friends
(c.1912).

5.52. Irma Purman (1908).

of him in their minds."[20] But if James' *Principles* instructed his generation that each individual has several "social selves" furnished with images provided by the outside world, the book made clear that another element is also at work. There is some choice in the matter. Those "selves" and those "images" are not solely imposed from without. The inner core claimed as one's own has its own source of energy and the will to create its own array of signs.

5.53. Irma Purman and friends
(c.1913).

5.54. Irma Purman and friends
(c.1913).

In 1902 Charles Horton Cooley wrote *Human Nature and the Social Order.*[21] It was a provocative "new" study of the ways by which children use private play as a means of progressing toward a future sense of self-identification. They do this, Cooley argued, by the process he called "fantastic socialization." Throughout his book Cooley emphasized the crucial difference between that self as an *object* which is given its identity by others and the self that is drawn from the *sentiment* one has about oneself. Cooley argued the use of costumes for make-believe. No matter how infrequently one wears such all-enveloping "masks," fantasy costumes enable the curious child and the young adult to experiment with a variety of possibilities for self-created identities. It is during such times of play that individuals discover and enact their private desires at the same time they are coming to terms with their more public "social selves."

Look now at a series of tableaux recorded by the camera held by the same omnipresent young photographer of Montpelier, Indiana. His photographs give further evidence of the tricks of identity conversions the members of the LOPH Club were ready to try out, albeit in the privacy of their own homes.

5.55. Irma Purman and friends
(c.1912).

5.56. Irma Purman and friends
(c.1912).

5.57. Irma Purman and friends (c.1913).

Figure 5.58 shows the young women as free spirits of a Felliniesque circus world. See Introduction, figure 31, which shows them kneeling in the conventional attitude of angels and virgins. (One of the group *was* married, while the others were still virgins; but all could "act" and "look" immaculate in such a pictorial display of chaste innocence.) The next (figure 5.59) lines them up as variations on "Poor

5.58. Irma Purman and friends
(c.1911).

5.59. Irma Purman and friends
(c.1911).

5.60. Irma Purman and friends
(c.1912).

Butterfly"—documentary evidence of the current interest taken in the David Belasco play and the Puccini opera.²² It also reflects one consequence of America's
recent imperialistic moves into the Pacific by which males (such as U.S. naval
officers) annexed new territories of female innocence to betray. But in figure 5.60
these twenty-year-olds avoid the possible threats of sexual exploitation by regressing visually into the "safe" prepuberty period of dolls and teddy bears.

Let us leave Indiana and its young women at play behind for now in order to
see what certain young men of the same period were doing "for fun" with their
gender identities. Princeton University seems to have been an especially propitious
place for acting out gender switches, what with the Triangle Club's annual pro-
ductions-in-drag (figure 5.61). Then there is the youthful John Sloan, shortly before he became a well-known artist (figure 5.62). Here he poses in the costume he
wore during an 1894 amateur performance that parodied George Du Maurier's best-
seller *Trilby*. Figure 5.63 presents Frederick Winslow Taylor. Taylor is known to us
as the austere Father of Scientific Management—the system he originated for analyzing the time spent by workers on the production line—but this is Taylor as
"Miss Lilian Gray."²³ Figure 5.64 identifies F. Scott Fitzgerald dressed as a chorus
beauty for the 1915–16 Princeton Triangle Club's production. This publicity photograph, which ran in the *New York Times*, caught the attention of a Broadway
theatrical manager who tried to sign Fitzgerald on as a female impersonator.²⁴
Fitzgerald had other things in mind than going on the professional stage, but not
Julian Eltinge.

5.61. From "Tabasco Land"
(1905–1906).

TRIANGLE CLUB ARCHIVES, PRINCETON

Julian Eltinge was the top female impersonator in the American theater between 1905 and 1928.[25] The sheet-music covers of the lyrics featured in his acts usually image Eltinge's dual social selves (figure 5.65). The large photograph shows him in the person of a woman; the small inset records what he is "naturally." Even more striking are the photos Eltinge ran in the magazine *Beauty Hints* he published to promote his own brand of cold cream.[26] Figures 5.66 and 5.67 present Eltinge's several "social selves" for the edification of his women readers.

Female impersonators had held a place in the American theater since the days of the minstrel show, as Robert C. Toll's *On with the Show* makes clear. By 1900 fifty-five such acts were booked into the theaters as "respectable" family entertainment. The men displayed themselves as feminine beauties, not as grotesques or comic types. Toll argues that the responses of the members of the audience, mutually approving, varied according to their gender: males were excited by the performances of the female impersonators, yet could feel sexually superior to the men wearing the costumes; women in the audience were fascinated by the high-fashion look of the "women" onstage, but did not need to view them as potential rivals since their feminine attractiveness was not "real."[27]

But what of male impersonators during this period?

There was a long tradition of serious stage actresses who played male roles taken from the classical and Shakespearean repertoire.[28] In 1900 two of America's favorite stage stars were Maude Adams and Julia Marlowe. They were women praised for their winsome femininity, but they also achieved renown on Broadway in the roles of doomed young men (figure 5.68 and 5.69). Maude Adams, who portrayed Edmond Rostand's hero L'Aiglon, was, of course, the same actress who originated

5.62. John Sloan
as "Twillbee"
(1894).

the role of Peter Pan, the boy who never grows up into sexual or emotional maturity. Julia Marlowe's major triumph was as Juliet, but she could switch over to play the role of the poet Thomas Chatterton.

Even more interesting than these dramatic enactments of male roles are the stage turns of women who impersonated men on the musical-comedy and vaudeville circuit. In the early 1900s Hetty King was featured as a saucy sailor boy with such songs as "I'm Going Away," whose lyrics recount the trials of the handsome sailor with too many girls in every port (figure 5.70). Della Fox was chunkier of build than the boyishly slender Hetty King, but she mounted a successful act with such

TRIANGLE CLUB ARCHIVES, PRINCETON

5.64. F. Scott Fitzgerald, promotion photograph for "The Evil Eye," *New York
Times* (1915).

5.63. Frederick W. Taylor as "Lilian Gray"
(late 1870s).

songs as "Good-Bye Maggie May," "The Little Trooper March," and "One Little
Soldier Man" (figure 5.71).

Two of the most intriguing examples of male impersonation are provided by
Vesta Tilley and Florenze Tempest. Tilley was the biggest name in the business. An
Englishwoman who had her first success in America in 1894, she continued to be
top-of-the-bill until the First World War. The wife of a producer of British variety
shows, Tilley became Lady de Frece after his knighting. She always took pains
during newspaper interviews to emphasize her femininity and the distaste she felt
toward coarsely masculine women. An enthusiastic public picked up on both these
"social selves": her personal status as a True Woman and her theatrical renown as
a dapper male.[29]

Vesta Tilley's New York stage hit was "Algy" (figure 5.72). What stands out in

5.65. Julian Eltinge, "Friends"
     (1919).

5.66. "Julian Eltinge in Eleven
      Poses," *Julian Eltinge
      Magazine and Beauty
      Hints* (1904).

this 1894 production is the cynicism of some of the lyrics Tilley sang, and the fact
that their bitterness is mostly directed at women. The title song tells us of a drunken young man of wealth who is taken for his money, then jeered at by the calculating women into whose hands he has fallen. Another song exposes the fraudulent disguises assumed by a man and a woman who mutually trick one another
into marriage, each in the belief that the other has money. The song's conclusion
focuses upon the plight of the duped male. Deserted by his conniving wife, he
paces back and forth in a cold tenement room with their abandoned child in his

5.67. "Julian Eltinge With and Without the Julian Eltinge Cold Cream on His Face," from *Julian Eltinge Magazine and Beauty Hints* (1904).

PRINCETON UNIVERSITY THEATER COLLECTION

arms. Outside in the streets, a drunk sings the mocking refrain "Ah, Dear Heart!" Another song is titled "Following in Father's Footsteps." It reveals that a lecher and lush named Percy had a father who was Percy's model for the betrayal of his own marriage vows. In this song alone of those Tilley presented in "Algy," sympathy swerves toward the woman. One wonders about Vesta Tilley's complex heart when she appeared upon the stage dressed as a man, backed by widespread publicity that featured her as the perfect wife and charming woman.

Florenze Tempest also introduces certain puzzling twists and turns as to the gender identity she intended to present to her audiences. Tempest was featured in the *Ziegfeld Follies* between 1910 and 1914 as "Our American Boy" (figure 5.73). Conventional minds could easily accept her as the girl next door having a bit of fun in her brother's clothes. But the sheet-music cover for "Oh, You Tease!" cuts closer to the bone in regard to the frustration of desire common to either heterosexual or

5.68(*left*). Maude Adams in
"L'Aiglon" (1900), from
*The Illustrated American
Stage* (1901).

5.69(*above*). Julia Marlowe in
"Chatterton" (1897), from
*The Illustrated American
Stage* (1901).

homosexual relationships (figure 5.74). Tempest's partner Sunshine portrays the
girl who coyly withholds her favors from the suitor costumed as a man, but even
were Sunshine to give in to "his" opportunings, the sexual satisfaction this pair
would enjoy would not be the kind expected by heterosexual couples.

Still other emotional convolutions are involved. Tempest and Sunshine are look-
alikes, just as their stage names suggest they are "L'Allegro" and "Il Penseroso"
sides to a relationship. As "twins" they embrace, staring out at the audience, daring anyone to state conclusively which is the "girl." Here we see the distinction
Charles Cooley made between "the sentiment of identity" and "the objective identity." In Tempest's performances the "sentiment" comes from her clothes, while
the "objective" quality arises from the pronouns of gender reference in the lyrics
she sings. Sometimes the clothes and the pronouns begin to contradict one another. In "Cute and Cunning Wonderful Baby-Doll" or "I Love the Ladies," the

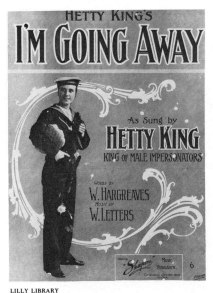

5.70. Hetty King, "I'm Going Away" (1907).

5.71. Della Fox, "Good-Bye Maggie May" (1905).

masculine clothing Tempest wears matches the lyrics "he" sings, since the verses are addressed to females. But when Tempest sings "I Want a Boy to Love Me" and "Supposing I Make You Wait till We Get Married," she reverts to her biological status as a woman. Tempest is a kind of sexual Mobius strip—a female, dressed as a man, who sings of "her" desire to have a boyfriend.

Late-nineteenth- and early-twentieth-century impersonators put the traditions of male and female dress to the test, but not the mandates of physiognomy; the prized look and gestures for either male or female impersonators remained essentially feminine. Impersonators also bent the theories of Charles Sanders Peirce, Josiah Royce, and William James that detailed the processes that move individuals through stages of perception to the conceptualizations out of which they form private and public identities. Acts of impersonation that loop the loop between genders tend to obscure the relation between exterior appearance and the "performance" of the innermost self; but whatever the ontological and epistemological difficulties raised by cross-dressing, the artifice of gender-posing, and the occasional ambiguity of lyrics that failed to match the singer's persona, pretense as such pleased the audiences of the period. Aware of the illusion in progress, spectators perceived the "play" presented for their entertainment. The fact that the performers' actual sex was different from the costumes, gestures, and lyrics meant that detours were taken along the route from perception to conceptualization. But all was safe for society as long as the impertinence of these theatrical acts stayed within the conventions that structure "fantastic socialization."

5.72. "Vesta Tilley's New Songs" (1894).

I conclude with a piece of prose fiction whose effectiveness depended back in 1915 upon its readers' being able to detect at once what was "wrong" in regard to the gender identities at work in the story. "When Girl Meets Girl" by George Barr McCutcheon is one of the kind I call "inversion narratives." They are either presented, as is McCutcheon's story, as parodies on the New Woman and her belief that she can do anything males had traditionally done; or the narratives are presented with a straight face as romances in which charming young women assume male disguises until they can reveal their true selves at the moment of the final romantic embrace—as in *The Princess Passes*.

McCutcheon's story was part of an announced "leap year series" proposed by

5.73. Florenze Tempest, "I Love
the Ladies" (1914).

LILLY LIBRARY

Good Housekeeping.[30] The opening illustration by Howard Chandler Christy depicts the story's hero, Cuthbert Reynolds (wealthy, excessively eligible bachelor), cowering under the power of Elinor Crouch (figure 5.75). Elinor is a strong-willed young woman who has had Cuthbert kidnapped by a gang of coarse amazons who bark out the order "Don't spoil his face!" as they overwhelm him with brute force. Cuthbert is locked away in a dark cell where he is kept on meager rations. His protests are jeered at, and his determination to protect his "virginity" is mocked. Elinor intends to marry Cuthbert, although he wants none of her. Like Samuel Richardson's Clarissa threatened by the rake Lovelace, Cuthbert repeatedly replies "Never!" to Elinor's demands that he capitulate. But his resistance seems all for naught. Elinor "clasped him in her strong, young arms" and rained "passionate kisses upon his lips, his brow, his cheek." Elinor plans to bring a female justice of the peace to Cuthbert's cell where a forced marriage will be performed; but just in the nick of time a young woman, heavily veiled in motoring dress, appears at his side. "Thank God, you are alive," the mystery woman whispers. "I am not too late."

Cuthbert faints from terror. He awakens from his swoon to find himself cradled

5.74. Tempest and Sunshine, "Oh You Tease" (1910).

in the arms of his savior. Elinor Crouch reenters the cell. Cuthbert takes refuge under his cot (figure 5.76). The unknown woman wrestles on the floor with Elinor for possession of a revolver. She triumphs, since, "lithe and sinewy and as cool as a veteran in the line of battle," she resorts "to a new trick in wrestling that had just come into practice among athletic women." Cuthbert is returned to freedom, "leaning feebly on the arm of his deliverer." She turns out to be Linda Blake, the woman for whom he now feels the love and gratitude any weak thing has for its

5.75. Howard Chandler Christy, from McCutcheon, "When Girl Meets Girl," *Good Housekeeping*, June 1912.

5.76. Howard Chandler Christy, from McCutcheon, "When Girl Meets Girl," *Good Housekeeping*, June 1912.

protector. The story ends with true love assured, even though the final words mock the premise of the whole parodic plot. "It's too good to be true."

Stories like McCutcheon's apparently had a ready market in the women's magazines of the period. Their success was possible, in part, *because* athletic, energetic young women actually existed in America. The types of Elinor Crouch and Linda

Blake were receiving ample attention in books, magazine articles, and the popular press, aided by the visual assist provided by the illustrations of Gibson, Christy, and Leyendecker. Those who did not really mind the advent of the New Woman and those who only mildly disliked the type were free to enjoy inversion narratives; in either case, not much was at stake when switches in gender roles were shown as essentially silly. Others of the period with much more to lose—fervent feminists and entrenched believers in the True Woman and the Real Man—most likely found McCutcheon's tale distasteful in the extreme; neither group could afford to take the possible revolution in types lightly.

For those who were at ease with the changes taking place on every side, stories that inverted gender signs simply confirmed that men were males and women (old or new) were females after all. All Howard Chandler Christy had to do was to parade his familiar pictorial forms (spunky but feminine young women, worshipful but manly males), then invert expected behavior patterns to create a parody of the conventional tale of beleaguered womanhood. His partner George Barr Mc-Cutcheon took up the well-tested romance formula that had already proven so successful in his *Beverly of Graustark* (brave but victimized heroine; menacing male villain; stalwart rescuing hero), then stood these formula figures on their heads. Christy and McCutcheon clung to the faith that radical overturnings of gender would never be allowed in American society. Their own deepest fears were tied to the threat of social inversion imaged by the New Woman as Elinor Crouch, not by Linda Blake, the type of the adorable Outdoors Girl. They could use the fact of their fears to try to contain the wilder meanings of leap year.

But look at the photograph in figure 5.77. Here is a man entrapped, his head swathed in a blinding wrap of cloth. He looks much like Cuthbert did at the moment of his abduction. Actually this is my father in 1914, and that is my mother to his left, holding firmly to his elbow. The story he always told his friends was that, upon first seeing her at a dance—even before being introduced to her—he announced to his friends, That's the woman I'm going to marry. But this piece of documentary evidence makes one wonder who captured whom, even in play.

The visual examples filling this chapter prompt the following speculations concerning the way things were during the 1890s and the early years of the twentieth century in regard to the formation of "social selves," and private ones too. There was an active repertoire of conventions and norms on tap to identify masculine and feminine. "Proper" standards were applied to physiognomical appearances, costuming, poses, and general behavior, just as they always had been. At the same time, a new sportiveness had entered into the relationships between the sexes, as well as greater leeway for experiments within the boundaries of gender identities.

The playfulness on view in this chapter was not part of a subversive movement that had to be kept out of sight in a cultural underworld. Gender switches took place out in the open, sanctioned by popular romances, amateur theatricals, and the *Ziegfeld Follies*. They certainly caused no social uproar in small-town Indiana, for they were not in the vein of the overt political statements made by feminists

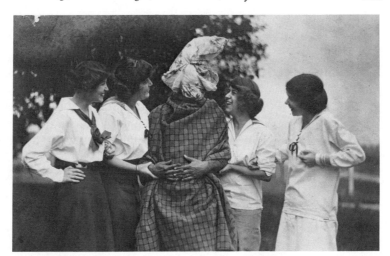

5.77. Irma Purman
and friends (1914).

5.78. Irma Purman
and friends (1914).

such as Dr. Mary Walker or by lesbians like Romaine Brooks who repudiated their heterosexuality altogether (see figures 1.43 and 1.44). The costumes worn in Montpelier, Indiana, by the members of the LOPH Club were just that: play-dressing and poses put on for brief and special occasions. They were not uniforms that expressed a permanent, radical commitment to a New Heaven and a New Earth for the sexes. However this may have been the case, this does not state the entire matter. Fictional inversions of the kind found in "When Girl Meets Girl" confirmed the sexual status quo that their author and illustrator wished to maintain. But other acts of crossing over, even when limited in duration and extent, were also used to try out genuinely new attitudes toward established social definitions. Throughout this chapter the emphasis has been upon the creative occasions when individuals played out and experimented with *as many possible ways of being a man and a woman* as the going conventions would bear (figure 5.78).

What is remarkable is the variety and subtlety of experimentation that conventions not only permitted but invited. Some of these experiments clearly imply the radical social and political changes of the future whereby many of these conventions would eventually be toppled. But other forms of play sidestepped large political gestures to focus upon the emotional relationships between the sexes. Practicing what Charles Cooley called "fantastic socialization," young women won the right to be pals with men and the confidence to express, through the zest of an enhanced life of the imagination, their evolving sense of themselves as females.

Part Two

DEMONSTRATIONS

PORTRAITS IN PRIVATE

6

Literary Portraits and Types: Crises

There seems to be something wrong with James' *The Portrait of a Lady* from the start; or rather, at the start and throughout the first half. The sense of things being amiss lies in the acclaim accorded to the novel's heroine. Everyone within the narrative (with the exception of Mrs. Touchett, who is dry in her responses to anyone anyway)—from old Mr. Touchett and the younger men, down through Warburton's sisters and Bunchie the dog—immediately and automatically finds Isabel Archer charming, witty, special, superior. There is just too much unquestioned adulation heaped upon the figure of Isabel. All this young woman has to do is stand there and be viewed across vistas and through doorways, and her companions fall over themselves to make a great "ado."

In the preface to the 1908 volume of the New York edition, James reflects upon how he got going on the story for *The Portrait of a Lady*. From the onset (early jottings, next a running précis recorded in a notebook entry of 1879), James realized he had a difficult technical problem to resolve, what with the focus of his story being "too exclusively psychological."[1] His preface, written almost thirty years after the inception of the narrative, is even more explicit about the nature of the task he faced. He had to take the "image of the young feminine nature" that had slipped into his mind—"a constituted, animated figure or form," "my vivid individual"—and *do* something of value by showing "this single small corner-stone" in the act of "affronting her destiny."[2] The difficulty did not lie in persuading his readers of the existence of the type of "the mere slim shade of an intelligent but presumptuous girl." "Millions of presumptuous girls, intelligent or not intelligent, daily affront their destiny." The authorial strain came from his having to endow "this slight 'personality' . . . with the high attributes of a Subject." Otherwise, as James knew, an impertinent question "that we should make an ado about it?" arises over the merits of a type.

Such "female fry" are "typical, none the less, of a class difficult, in the individual case, to make a centre of interest." They are incorrigible enough to cause such skilled authors as Dickens, Scott, and Stevenson "to leave the task unattempted" and others (both writers and painters) "to assume it to be not worth their attempting." But the "pusillanimity" involved in an artist's avoiding the issue altogether does not come from the lack of value contained by a young female character; it stems from the artistic problems of "positively organizing an ado" about that "shade," that "apparition," that "thinness." Artists may sincerely believe they had found "truth" and "value" in the type and class of the eager young girl, but "it is never a tribute to any truth at all, that we shall represent that value badly."

Upon encountering the figure of Isabel Archer in the first half of *The Portrait of a Lady*—pages given over to trumpeting her value—many readers conclude that James has indeed flubbed his obligation. The claims about Isabel's worth do not artistically hold firm. James is in and out of the narration propping up Isabel's image, insisting that she has an almost arrogant right to our attention. At the same time, he carries out a Kantian "Critique of Pure Intuition" of his own. But even as he singles out Isabel's flaws in reasoning which deflate any unduly high opinion of her as the American idealist, he fondly remains "our heroine's biographer." We are read little lectures in forbearance that are somewhat obvious in their manipulation of our feelings on Isabel's behalf, however engagingly expressed.

. . . she would be an easy victim of scientific criticism if she were not intended to awaken on the reader's part an impulse more tender and more purely expectant.

. . . Smile not, however, I venture to repeat, at this simple young woman from Albany . . . She was a person of great good faith, and if there was a great deal of folly in her wisdom those who judge her severely may have the satisfaction of finding that, later, she became consistently wise only at the cost of an amount of folly which will constitute almost a direct appeal to charity.

It is one thing as readers to be told to put up with Isabel's frailities of character, and even to love them; it is quite another to have to deal with James' frailties as a portraitist. The critics' frequent demurrers against Isabel's enthusiasm, or their pleas for sympathy on her behalf, are moral in nature, but this focus deflects attention from considerations of James' methods for presenting Isabel to our mind's eye. I wish to place the causes of the unease felt by readers who sense an inadequacy in the portrait-images that fill the first half of a novel audaciously titled *The Portrait of a Lady*. I shall do this by referring to the considerations opened up in the beginning chapters of *Imaging American Women* and its examination of the

American Girl, the type that (as James observes of his Isabel version) is "a class difficult, in the individual case, to make a centre of interest."

Is the story of Isabel simply (and too simplistically) the story of Daisy Miller writ larger? Did "Daisy Miller," that artificial (though effective, because relatively slight) "study" of 1879 concerning the prototype of the American Girl Abroad, betray James aesthetically in 1881? Did he make a fatal mistake in judgment by turning a novel-length narrative over to a mere *type*? Had Daisy Miller merited success as a heroine because the meagerness of outline and thinness of substance provided by the type of Beautiful Charmers Misunderstood were held down in scale? Was Isabel's chance of carrying off the first half of a long narrative scotched because James sent a type (the Girl) to accomplish what only the highly individualized portrayal of a lady could convey in response to what James put as "my primary question, 'Well, what will she *do?*' "?

This is what I propose as an answer to the issue of the possible deficiencies of form affecting the content of *The Portrait of a Lady*: Henry James—the writer largely responsible for creating the literary type of the American Girl as Beautiful Charmer in the years just prior to his writing of Isabel Archer's story—introduces that same slight slip of a type into the vasty reaches of the traditional novel-length narrative form; and he does it for a purpose.

Like an ingenue sent onstage to enact the role of Phaedre when a famed tragedienne is taken ill just before the curtain rises, Isabel arrives upon the lawn of Gardencourt, still a type and not yet a portrait. James then sets to work to demonstrate how the "heroine's satellites, especially the male," go on and on about how wonderful, charming, and superior she is. They do this in exactly the way the English-language public was just then going on and on about the American Girl.

James *exposes* how ready his contemporaries are to fall under the spell of the image of a young girl who has not yet earned the power that her admirers assume to be radiating from her own person. The attributes of charm and glamour (viewed in their original meanings of sacred force) are *given* to Isabel at this stage. She does not yet merit the right (moral or aesthetic) to be thought of as more than an ordinary girl, one who is rather ludicrously misperceived as someone special. Misperceived, since the men are busy falling in love with the private image they hold of feminine values in the abstract. Lord Warburton tells Ralph, "You wished a while ago to see my idea of an interesting woman. There it is!" It is devilishly easy for these males of whatever national background to *see* such an *idea* manifested in the form of the American Girl which Isabel provides them once she wanders into their sight lines. They are ready to hang this notion of "being interesting" upon any recognizable form that fits the conceptual formulas they have become enamored of.

It is risky for James to go on for so many pages, centering a big-time novel on a type upon whom the satellite characters place more value than it can competently bear. Of course, *The Portrait of a Lady* is greatly concerned with all its characters' inability to curb their tendency to misperceive and misconceive. Isabel has hard lessons ahead to learn concerning the Perfect Friend she initially takes Madame Merle to be, and about the Ideal Husband she believes Gilbert Osmond to represent to the extent of marrying this, her fondest "idea." But it is dangerous for James to place the untested and perhaps inadequate idea of "an interesting woman" at the heart of a novel committed by its very title to the portrait technique, therewith committing it to the forceful depiction of a unique individual. Dangerous, because we commonly assume that it is better to own a good portrait than a blurred image set within an ornately carved frame that consists of the gloss of varnish and little substance.

Once James elects to begin with a type (or intimates this is the way he will proceed), his task is twofold: he must give (a) an immediate indication that the American Girl is (in Richard Bernheimer's terms) a designated type—one which has a denoted type ready to burst past the bounds of the formula's limits; (b) a follow-through which develops this expanded type and richly informed formula into the portrait of a woman who embodies the particular values of the lady—yet another type, perhaps, but one which at its best contains worlds of experience. The story proves to be about a woman known truly as a "lady"—that type which may not be reduced to a category of mere class status (thereupon vulnerable to repudiation on ideological grounds); it becomes that type by which important qualities of human character define themselves. James' novel progresses, therefore, *away from* the threat of turning out to be a much-to-do about nothing and *toward* an ado about something that merits interest.[3]

That the aesthetic and conceptual shift between inadequacy and adequacy comes after Isabel gets married is a matter of great significance. To tout Isabel Archer as the American Girl who is never to be seen again in public once she has said yes to one of her adoring suitors would be the wreck of the narrative values built up during the earlier scenes of courtship. This reluctance to let Isabel's fate end with a rousing wedding-day scene does not arise from James' notion that young unmarried American women have no intrinsic interest. What concerns him is that a reader's ideas about such women may be limited to the ideas they are portrayed as thinking about.

James allowed that no story can be any better than the quality of the intelligence the story's author happens to possess.[4] He certainly hoped, although he often despaired, of having readers equipped with intelligence. He also realized that whatever ideas he or his readers have about portrait-images are affected by the ideas the fictitious person is shown as being capable of. The ideal merger that combines writer, reader, and the imaged subject into a forceful dynamic of thought takes place in the scene from the *Portrait* which James singled out as the best his novel provides. It comes in chapter 42 when Isabel sits and deliberates through the night. Although this scene is a "representation" in James' words "simply of her motionlessly *seeing*," it is at this point that we as readers can say, "*There* is an interesting woman!"

Isabel as the type of the unmarried girl just arrived in Europe does not give James that scene. Isabel as the portrait of a married woman can. When James came to write the story of Milly Theale in 1902, the American Girl who most stunningly does *not* get married, James accepted the need to endow Milly's ideas and images with interest. Some readers are not persuaded that he succeeded. The reservations they have about the figure of Milly which they encounter throughout the narrative devoted to her "ado" are like those they have about Isabel before marriage, in contrast to the strengths they find in Isabel after marriage. In fact, the differences between Milly and Isabel testified to by many readers are analogous to the differences in impact many viewers locate in paintings by Thomas Dewing and Thomas Eakins of women gazing into the middle distance.

Powerful, affecting, realistic portrayals of women who are powerful, affecting, and real: this is what is usually said of Eakins' work. Vapid, inconsequential, slick paintings of women who are vapid, inconsequential, and slick: this is Dewing's reputation overall. Such distinctions are odd on the face of it when one deals with subject matter alone, leaving matters of technique out of the issue. These judgments appear to rest upon the notion that Dewing's women do nothing more than sit gracefully around, in contrast to the interesting life of the mind they attribute to the women of Eakins' paintings.

Granted, it is difficult to credit the full social value of silent female forms, whoever paints them. Still, viewers are driven to ask what these imaged women are thinking, or whether they are thinking at all, or whether they ought to be out somewhere overturning society rather than musing while seated in almost empty rooms. Such questions are compounded when the images veer toward the type of the American Girl—by definition young, unmarried, and untried.

The American Girl who adorns the calendars for Swift Meat Products, greeting cards, billboard posters, and gift books is not expected to think. She exists only as an icon for others, thoughtlessly, to adore. She hangs suspended in the blank time-space between the end of her schooling and the commencement of marriage, on holiday from thought. The only temporality that concerns her is the fairy-tale interlude which begins with the summer months that follow upon her graduation, proceeds to her coming-out in the autumn or early winter, plays out in the social triumphs of Her Year, and concludes with a big June wedding.

The twelve-month agenda just outlined forms the only plot available to *The American Girl as Seen and Portrayed by Howard Chandler Christy*. Unbeknown to her in her innocence, the type of the Christy Girl is threatened by "Old Father Time" and the "Old World" whose "guile and guilt" will be exposed after her marriage,[5] but since Christy never presents her as a portrait, Time and the World are blocked from the pictured scene.

Female portraits have identities assigned by their titles: "Portrait of Miss So-and-So." They are intended as records of individuals who have histories formed by what they have thought or felt about the Old World and Father Time. They are visual biographies which invite us to consider the consequences of the marriage ceremony. Such portraits in their specificity are different in formalistic, conceptual, and psychological terms from the essential anonymity of "studies" of the type of the Lady. When, however, James set out to represent *the portrait of a lady*, he did it by crafting a narrative in two parts. The first is a "study" of the American Girl; the second is the "portrait" of a married woman as lady. The effect of a narrative divided into before (type) and after (portrait) is further enhanced by the fact that marriage brings an end to each party's self-delusions about the other's type. Isabel weds Gilbert Osmond not as he is but rather as *the type of possibility* she believes he possesses. In turn, Osmond marries what he thinks Isabel to be, based on his notion (encouraged by Isabel during the courtship) that she is *the type of fixed behavior* who will confirm his ideas of her by fully conforming to them.

Henry James, William Dean Howells, and Edith Wharton offer some of the best portraits of women at the turn of the century. All three pull their female characters beyond the nuptial moment in order to give their erstwhile American Girls *something to deliberate about*. Still, it is off the mark if we conclude from this fact that the execution of good portraits means denial of the type. Those who make this denial fall into the trap of that variation on the biographical fallacy which equates "knowing" with factual data of the kind that generalized studies of unnamed figures do without. Those who think they can do without type also lose sight of the advantages gained when an actual person is endowed with the unnameable forces of the denoted.

Artists and art critics are not the only ones given to the notion that paintings become silly and shallow whenever they contain types. Writers and literary critics are just as susceptible to the idea that they rid themselves of impending aesthetic disaster by rejecting universalized forms. Their distaste is understandable when the examples they offer hold to the kind of botched work Mark Twain had on his hands with *Those Extraordinary Twins*. One naturally wants to give a "light-weight heroine" "the grand bounce" the way Twain did Rowena when he realized that "making such a to-do over her affairs" was leading him nowhere.[6] At the head of chapter 17 of his story-draft the chastened author writes, "Rowena went out in the back yard after supper to see the fireworks and fell down the well and got drowned." This is admittedly an abrupt way to get rid of a troublesome heroine, but Twain argued that "it loosened up Rowena from where she was stuck and got her out of the way."

Mark Twain regularly had difficulties with his female characters, types or not. He finally took Roxana the slave woman, the potent portrait introduced into the story of the twins that had evolved into *Pudd'nhead Wilson*, and "killed" her off by turning her into the type of the Mother, heartbroken and broken-spirited. But writers with steadier nerves than Twain learn that the narrative depiction of a portrait life may come *by way of* the development of the powers latent in the types. Start with a type; just don't conclude with one.

Writers and painters can work directly with the special powers of denoted types, or with designated forms that contain the seed of the denoted. Either way, good portraiture adroitly exploits the processes by which type is transformed, not annihilated; studies of types yield the streaks of the tulip by which portrait particulars enhance the categories and subcategories of genus and species. By the close of the 1910s Gertrude Stein did away with portraits limited to traditional notions of biographical factuality. She specialized in portraits created by expressing the type in its most extended form. But there is a way to go before we come to Stein's experimentations at the opening of the new century. It is that way we shall trace just now.

One of the seemingly safe things about portraiture is the useful information it is supposed to give us. We look at portraits with the comforting sense that we could recognize those individuals if ever we should pass them on the street. But the turn of the century was a time (besides its other muddles) of changing attitudes toward the "self." Disorderliness in the area of the psychology of personality formation contributed to a crisis in portrait-making.

As chapters 1 through 4 have indicated, the emphasis placed by the new psychology upon the complex relation between seeing and thinking was of great importance. In order for there to be significance, the eye had *to be concerned;* otherwise it merely expounded.[7] If thinking relied solely on itself without the instigation of sight, the process of paying attention broke down. Halfhearted, uncompleted thought fell short of attaining the status of belief. As William James might have phrased it, "The Will to See Is Believing."

In *The Principles of Psychology* of 1890, chapter 10, William James presented the various components of "the consciousness of self" out of which will and belief take their form. Self arises from the sense of an empirical Me (what a person *owns* that no one else has). This ownership depends on, first, the *display* of that Me on a material and social level (what is *recognized* by others); and next, an innermost center which actively attempts to know through *taking interest.* Persons with a fully developed self possess a satisfying amount of what James calls warmness, sameness, and continuity. They are "at home" in what James describes alternately as "the nest," "the nucleus," "the kernel," and "the sanctuary."

The nature of the self formulated by William James had important implications for the meaning of "type." It continually broached the question concerning *which* of the several "persons" rising up within the container of the composite being was the "true self," the "sanctuary self," the "real thing."

By the 1890s the position held by the French psychologists Theodore Ribot and Pierre Janet gained credence in American circles. This position maintained the importance of traumatic emotional experiences and the life of the subconscious; it replaced the somatic school, which had held sway through the 1880s.[8] The self that lies at the bottom—the one which reveals itself in sleep and reverie and is created by memory—is the essential type and the one by which we are identified to ourselves. This type is not the *average* of our nature—that public creature which walks abroad by daylight and attends to the demands placed upon it by respectable society. Averages and means are arrived at by adding up every jot and tittle, then dividing them to gain "a value intermediate between the value of two or more other qualities" (as *Webster's New Universal Unabridged Dictionary* defines these numerical results). In contrast, the self uncovered by the new psychology cannot be likened to the sum and division of the parts of a whole formed from everyday behavior; rather, it is approximated by that whole which transcends and transforms daily averages. Turn-of-the-century psychologists recognized the presence and social functionality of *the self as the mean;* they also acknowledged the presence of *the self as the original*—an energy unbounded by social rules even when its representations conformed to the cultural conventions of look and pose. The self as the type of the original follows that definition advanced by Melville's *The Confidence Man*, which speaks of figures which are unique yet universal (unique *because* universal); forms that can be duplicated many times without loss of the power to astound; centers that exist apart from the distracting clutter of surface facts. Under these terms, Frank Norris' *Vandover the Brute* is the real thing; Vandover the Harvard man is at most a sometime-thing.

Artists came to some of the same conclusions about the dual nature of the self, whether they were familiar or not with the new psychology. However inadvertently, many elected to represent those selves in art by means of one of two distinctly different modes. Artists with a classical bent preferred regularized representations of the public individual; for them "personality" was the type of the average of a person's several selves, the collective being that displays itself before others, the "designated" at its most diffuse. In contrast, other artists represented "originality"—the type as the hidden but ever-present sanctuary self, the authentic bottom-nature, the "denoted" in its most concentrated form.

Reading types is one way of gaining control in a society whose diversity is almost too much to bear. The type of the average serves an effective way to acquire mastery over others. When Harry Balkin as "the success doctor" published the *Human Dictionary*, a set of pictographs imaging traits of personality, he assumed that the public look is all there is (see figure 5.30). Whatever lies unseen below the represented surface is directly revealed in "the psychic hand" or "the feminine curve." The preface to Balkin's manual declares its intention is the instruction of men who wish to control employer or employees, customers, and business associates. Balkin does not hesitate to offer advice on how to read the average types of one's children or social companions; but the emphasis is upon the successful male in the marketplace who needs to gain authority over those who come within range of his interpreting eye.

Others did not limit themselves to Balkin's mastery game as "the success doctor" or to the superficiality of public pictographs. They sought signs of their own authenticity and control of their private originality. In 1892 (the same year Henry James' "The Real Thing" appeared) Helen Gilbert Ecob brought out *The Well-Dressed Woman: A Study in the Practical Application to Dress of the Laws of Health, Art, and Morals.*[9] The book counsels women in the pursuit of self-possession and the completely "natural" look. Clearly an absolutist because of her assertion that "the beautiful is eternal," Ecob promotes self-presentation that reflects "the highest and best." The look Ecob urges lies beyond rules and means. "Conventional" women, Ecob argues, are self-conscious and unsure of themselves. They passively accept images from outside sources for the shape of their body. They submit to corseted bodies that are *ab*normal, unhealthy, graceless containers for that falsest of types— the average "social" woman. In happy contrast, the "artistic" woman wears Pre-Raphaelite gowns which represent the type of the "true," because self-possessed, woman. According to Ecob's theories, Isabel Archer can succeed in being herself only if she takes Madame Merle's advice on social dressing seriously. If Isabel applies that advice to the nature of her originality, she will gain mastery over herself, while avoiding the vicious averages imposed by Merle and Osmond, whose own selves are "corseted" by their enslavement to conventionality.

Interpreters of the American scene were looking for large answers to questions of self-definition. Chapter 2 indicated that many foreign visitors to the United States spoke of the need to study the American Girl as the master type by which they might understand the intangibles of the American character. William Butler Yeats never made the transoceanic voyage to America or gave himself over to the contemplation of the American Girl, but he was clearly concerned with determining the nature of "the real self," the paradoxes contained within the female image, and the special aura attached to the type. In 1922 Yeats made certain comments that point up the discoveries possible when one asks questions that are more interesting than those put by vocational counselors like Balkin or even by perceptive America watchers such as Paul Bourget and James Muirhead.

"Man is nothing till he is united to an image." That is the Yeatsian statement of purpose as articulated in *The Player Queen*. Not any image; only the image of the woman can show the man the way out of the incompleteness of his native nothingness by offering him the services of her "antithetical being." In the words of Robert Langbaum, "[T]he 'real' self the man wants to fathom is the woman— an unreconstructed individual, before she has been united to an image."[10] "But it is the woman as archetype, the woman united to an image, who awakens passion and whose true individuality shines forth."

The image the Yeatsian male desires, however much to his chagrin, is the type of the original: the unique and private self that exists in antithesis to cultural averages. The "saving image" that "reconstructs" the man's old self forgoes the Arnoldian notion of culture as the sincere self that walks in the light of day. The Yeatsian new self is acquired when a man imitates the heart's passion that "shines forth" from the image, masked as a female, whose nature is comprised of his passion. Yeats' poor duffer must painfully learn the comic lesson the narrator of James' "The Real Thing" and Louis Neville of Chambers' *The Common Law* also have to learn. And like the suitors in the path of Isabel Archer's sweep through the pages of *The Portrait of a Lady*, the Yeatsian self must experience the difference between an Isabel Archer as the lesser type favored by the Realists (the average American Girl who dominates the first half of James' novel) and an Isabel as the type of the original disclosed by the new breed of psychologists (the portrait of the lady which empowers the passionate nature of the novel's later stages). Like Isabel herself, the Yeatsian self combats the images enforced by "the present culture." Lest "the reconstructed self," like Isabel's, be ground in the mills of the conventional, this self (the core-of-being joined to the image it imitates) "must be perpetually renewed through perpetual conflict with the object of imitation and with the temptation to rest in the unreconstructed self."

Notions of "bottom-nature" look back toward the classifications of type formulated by Johann Casper Lavater and ahead toward the experimentations in portraiture initiated by Gertrude Stein. Lavater's *Essays on Physiognomy* emphasizes both "the powers of the understanding" and "the moral part, or the expression of the feeling and sensitive powers" as they work their way outward to affect material forms.[11] For this reason, Lavater argues, the traditional practices used by painters for representing external forms of beauty are inadequate for the portrayal of the fullness that lies beneath surfaces waiting to rise up and be noted.

Lavater devoted a chapter to the painting of portraits. He stated that the true painter has to be a philosopher, one who is stimulated by the fact that "the countenance is the theatre on which the soul exhibits itself." The Lavaterian view, couched in terms recognizably Jamesian, singles out the face as the location where life's "scenes" go onstage; the face is where the drama of the "thinking and feeling soul" displays the images that occasion its revelation and recognition. But Lavater's true painter spurns vulgar "realism" as much as he does a formalism limited to thoughtless pictographs. In Lavater's view, realists believe that features have to be in motion in order to display what Yeats' misguided man believes to be his "unreconstructed individualism." According to Lavater's moral aesthetics, the soul shows itself best when "in a state of tranquility, or rest." Certain traditions of the theater (for Lavater the *tableau vivant*; for Yeats the Noh drama) serve the artist better than nature does. In nature "nothing is fixed, all is swift, all transition," but in the tableau and Noh traditions it is stillness which expresses the self's core.

The taste for portraits primed by the tableau and the principles of physiognomy continued well into the 1890s. The portraiture developed by Gertrude Stein during the opening decades of the twentieth century called upon other, more recent painterly and psycho-physiognomical traditions; but Stein, like Lavater, sought a theater of repose for the display of what Stein called not soul but bottom-nature.

When Paul Alkon questions the purpose of the sixteen photographic portraits Gertrude Stein included in the first edition of *The Autobiography of Alice B. Toklas*, he asks good questions.[12] Do these photographic representations overlap, supplement, or falsify the written text? Do they give information or do they act only to suggest vague symbolic meanings? Do they give us Stein from the outside, from where the camera is placed, or do they yield inside/outside views from that spot where Gertrude Stein stands pretending to be Alice? Alkon concludes that Stein stresses surfaces, not inner qualities, because of her fear-ridden wish to conceal what Alkon terms "the moral emptiness of a soul that is not so much displayed as denied." These conclusions are set askew by Alkon's failure (among others) to distinguish between the typology of the average and of the original; between the self in motion and the self at rest. That is, Alkon has not noticed that there are types and there are types and there are types. If a rose is a rose is a rose, it is also true that there are roses of varying kinds once we start to count the streaks on their individual petals.

Artists can use types that ride along detailed surfaces; the ones that occasion the vulgar realism Lavater objected to and Stein found of scant interest. Or types can represent the inner/outer areas of a subject through unimaginative schematizations; the ones executed by artists of the average of whom neither Lavater nor Stein could approve. There are also types that hover between daylight and dusk, that rest and muse, dream and meditate; the ones done best by portraitists who report on an essential self that is simultaneously universal and unique. When Picasso painted a likeness of Gertrude Stein as she was not just yet but was soon to be, he achieved a portraiture of "soul" (Lavater's term) and of "bottom-nature" (Stein's phrase). Lavater and Stein, analysts of the type, were separated by 150 years and uncounted shifts in cultural values, yet they shared a similar intention: to examine the particular type which both accommodates and lies beyond—in Lavater's words—"all [that] is swift, all [that is] transient."

The commonplaces of physiognomy as practiced by Lavater and the pseudoscientists who tagged after him rely too easily upon the "arithmetical averages" of faces and clothes. All too frequently, they stop dead with the viciously absurd labels which V. G. Rocine and Joseph Simms dropped irresponsibly upon the calipered foreheads of various races and sexes. But the "physiognomical awareness" stimulated by Lavater's theories, by which we are encouraged to analyze how fictional characters are looked into being by the people around them, serves equally well to increase our understanding of Jamesian narratives and Steinian portraiture.

When put to service as inspiration for literary portraiture, turn-of-the-century practices of physiognomical awareness had two results.[13] They either upheld the confidence expressed by viewers within the narratives that they could assess appearances correctly, or they confirmed the doubt that such assessments are possible. Whichever, a significant point is made. Portraiture based on the principle of inner-matching-outer de-emphasizes the designation of the self by external signs alone; it underscores the need for literary portraits devoted to the correlation between private core and public image—between what I call the type of the original and the type of the mean.

Another major point remains to be made. Gertrude Stein was not satisfied by the *identity* supplied by what others see, by "I am I because my little dog knows me" (figure 6.1).[14] Still, she realized that the *entity* of bottom-nature which portraiture projects remains a creation by outsiders, although not by the casual, social "other" which one's little dog is. Right and proper portraits cannot really be self-portraits;

6.1. Francis Picabia,
    "Gertrude Stein"
    (1930s).

they have to be fashioned by "artists," whether lovers prompted by the heart's affections or by painters who feel compelled to test the boundaries of the representational arts. Part of Melanctha Herbert's woe in *Three Lives* is that she does not see herself; but Gertrude Stein can. Stein experiences *rigolo* by letting herself be seen through the eyes of Alice B. Toklas, who muses about what it is like to live elbow-to-elbow with genius; or by letting Pablo Picasso place on canvas the form that her future being is certain to take.

The relationships between inside and outside that we find in Stein's *Three Lives* of 1909 or *The Autobiography of Alice B. Toklas* of 1933 are analogous, in reverse, to the strain caused James' Mrs. Monarch by the fact that she is generally incapable of seeing anyone but herself. It takes an artist to see her, and to discover why her particular kind of Wordsworthian ego identity does not lend itself to the portraiture of real things, just as it takes an artist to detect the many entities possessed by Miss Churm that extend far beyond the rumpled cockney woman of the type that little dogs deal with day after day.

Arthur C. Danto has some highly interesting (if controversial) comments to make about the nature of real things in relation to their having to be viewed from outside. Aptly titled *The Transfiguration of the Commonplace*, Danto's book is essentially concerned with the differences between the average and the original, and with the type of the public and evident image and the type of the private and unique.

In his chapter "Metaphor, Expression, and Style" Danto assigns himself the task of defining style as a historical code of identification.[15] The historian who wants to differentiate one period from another does this by attending to "its outward surface." A period *is* that "solely from the perspective of the historian." After all, "for those who lived in the period it would just be the way life was lived." In contrast, the "life" which the historian examines from without is not "simply the way things were." Style is the evidence he uses; it is also the consequence of his being the one looking on.

After the manner of Bourget, Boyesen, and Muirhead who look at the American Girl, the historian looks at period. Both periods and people possess styles that are little more than an "external physiognomy of an inner system of representation." Cultural time zones have "shared representational modes which define what it is to belong to a period," whereas individuals possess their own representational mode. In either instance, "those qualities . . . which are the man"—or the period—are "seen from the outside, physiognomically." "The qualities of [the] representation are for others" to see—not the man immersed in the period or the period that encloses him. Danto argues that the artist is the sole agent who creates periods and individuals; he accomplishes this act by the style his "portraits" provide, since works of art are the factor for "externalizing a way of viewing the world, express-ing the interior of a cultural period, offering itself as a mirror."

Mirror theories of art exist to be questioned. No one-to-one equation between products of the studio and society at large is likely. But Danto is not really being that simplistic. The problem with Danto's thesis lies elsewhere, at the cost of the full coherence of his argument. Danto maintains that historians are able to read what has happened in the past *because* they stand outside that past; *because* they meditate upon works of art whose style indicates the nature of a particular period in time. According to this notion, artworks must act on two levels and be of two minds. They are things (analogous to the period and to the persons living in that period) which *do not know themselves* because they exist *inside* and can only express themselves "immediately and spontaneously." They are also things which are made by artists who self-consciously stand *outside*, reflecting the physiognomy of the objects they represent through their artistic methods.

Are not the artists themselves part of the period? Are they not representative individuals who stand inside and are thereby lacking in "physiognomical aware-ness"? Are not artists susceptible to the "style" of their times and the pressures of historicism which keep them forever self-blinded?

James Abbott McNeill Whistler may be a possible exception. This man who "chose" not to be born in Lowell, Massachusetts,[16] freed himself to live outside his American generation; he thereby seized the occasion to create one of the major styles by which we recognize his epoch. But the effect of expatriation upon artists

6.2. Benjamin West, "Self-Portrait" (1806).

PENNSYLVANIA ACADEMY OF THE FINE ARTS

like Whistler is not the real issue. Residence in Europe is not needed for an Archimedean interpretation of history. Gertrude Stein managed it in *The Autobiography of Alice B. Toklas*, but not because she was an American in Paris. Benjamin West also suggests how to be inside while being outside, as we shall see from one of the paintings he executed a century before.

One of the primary modes by which art breaks down the walls between inside and outside is positioning. The printed text of *Alice B. Toklas* is an "autobiography" of Gertrude Stein, an artifact that cannot see itself fully or act as witness to its own style. In contrast, the maker of the book is the "biographer," skilled at expressing the nature of the self at which the writer looks. Since we are in on Stein's little joke, we know that *Alice B. Toklas* contains two "places": first, the stylish stylelessness of the insider who (to repeat Danto's words) experiences the early years of the 1900s as "simply the way things were"; second, the style of the onlooker who attends to the "outward surface" of the era. The effect Stein's literary manipulations have on us is suggested visually by the odd little work by Benjamin West titled "Self-Portrait" (figure 6.2). The artist stands in front of what is supposed to be an easel-portrait of his wife. But no frame is evident to divide creator from created, actuality from image. The usual signs are missing by which we distinguish between the painted likeness of an artist and the portrait-image that same artist places on a fictive canvas. Surfaces, proportions, perspectives: all co-mingle willy-nilly to resist our ability to separate the two planes within the canvas space. We cannot say that *this* image is of Benjamin West and is his autobiograph-ical self-portrait, and that *that* image is of a portrait (a "biography") of his wife. The consequence of this ambiguity upon the sensitive observer is similar to what happens when reading Stein's text. One is beckoned toward the inside, then left lingering on the threshold of the multifold spaces which form historical identity and personal entity.

Another possible answer to the nature and origin of style is suggested by the loving emphasis given to the portrait head by many artists of the late nineteenth century, as it had been given since the days of ancient Rome. That the head is the synecdoche for individual personality was assumed by the period's manuals of physiognomy, by the popular press, and by many studio artists.[17] The *face* was the evidence by which the artist-observer defined the sitter's style; *the body* repre-sented the sitter's sense of self. To apply Danto's distinctions, we could say that the head is where "history" and "biography" locate themselves, whereas the body carries on the more problematic function of the autobiography.

Masks, Heads, and Faces, with Some Considerations Respecting the Rise and Development of Art was published in 1892 (the same years as James' "The Real Thing" and Helen Gilbert Ecob's *The Well-Dressed Woman*). Ellen Russell Emerson introduces her anthropological, iconographic study by stating that faces evolve throughout historical time and are transfigured by the increased complexity of civilization.[18] Emerson admits that the plastic arts are inadequate to capture the "high-wrought palpitating fabric of accumulated growths" which distinguish the "modern face" from the "smooth lineaments of the primitive," but she maintains that it is only through the study of the face and the head that one approaches "identity, individuality, nay . . . specialized and human existence." It is the head, therefore, at which we now look before turning later to a consideration of the whole figure posed in the manner of Isabel Archer Osmond framed in a doorway, exacting from viewers an act of interpretation which must include all the ele-ments of artful costume, setting, gesture, and expression.

How are we to proceed when we have writers, not painters, acting as the stylists and historians of the portrait head? More specifically, what distinguishes pictorial representations found in popular romances by Richard Harding Davis and George Barr McCutcheon from the heads and faces taken from works by Edith Wharton and Henry James? We still have James' *The Portrait of a Lady* to return to and a discovery to make concerning how the novel manages to move from the inade-quate images of Isabel as type of the mean to Isabel as a portrait-type of the orig-inal. A look at the conventions of popular literary portraiture of James' day affect-ing the two planes of style and narrative content points to what he did differently.

In 1906 Arthur Bartlett Maurice of *The Bookman* wrote the first of a series of articles on "Representative American Story Tellers."[19] Maurice's essay briskly sizes up the appeal of the ever-popular Richard Harding Davis. The Davis hero is "the office-boy's idea of a gentleman." Davis' heroines match lower-class fantasies about high society by radiating "the charm of elusiveness and unattainability" of a woman glimpsed riding by in a carriage. The manufacture of such dreams and fantasies does not entail originality; it relies on using the comfortable formulas Davis had ever ready to hand. "Paint in at hazard a face and figure from Mr. Charles Dana Gibson's sketch-book, and you have a portrait that will do for" all female charmers in Davis' works.

Maurice seems to be likening the images of desire that populate formula fiction to the cutouts casually borrowed from an illustrator's sketchbook. There is another useful analogue we can use. It refers to practices common to the commercial trade of the day: the studio-prop photo and the holiday postal, both methods that set the face within a symbolic framing device and superimposed its fleshly reality against a painted backdrop.

Vacation time for the working girl often meant stopping by a photographer's studio or a boardwalk stall.[20] She thrust her head through a hole in the painted canvas. At once she was part of a fantasy scene: dressed in a curvaceous bathing suit, seated on a bicycle for two, or trucked out in a wedding dress and veil. Or she bought sentimental postal cards with an array of photographed heads set within the outline of her own name—spelling out, for instance, "Daisy" or "Lily" (figure 6.3). Such portrait-postals were similes satisfying her simplest need for explicit self-identification by providing a series of surrogate "Daisy" types to send off over her signature. The head-through-the-hole gambit furnished the indirect comparisons offered by metaphors. She was herself, but placed in the middle of the make-believe of how she wanted most to look, whether the pretty bather, cyclist, or bride. Either way, her name or head embellished by art became the sign for the fulfillment of a personal dream-image.

Young women who thrust their heads through painted studio canvases or purchased cards celebrating their names enhanced their identities. Something like what happens with such holiday postals and photographs occurs when people read formula fictions. The nature of their desires are regulated by the gender divisions ruling those images. Women readers who stick their heads through the holes of the painted backdrop of the narratives usually satisfy their fantasies; they become the objects looked at adoringly by others in the novel. In contrast, male readers have to do the looking at the faces fronting them across the fictive canvas; their desires to have what they look at may well remain unsatisfied.

Henry Dwight Sedgwick directly took up the issue of what makes popular fiction work in the chapter titled "The Mob Spirit in Literature" from his book of 1908 *The New American Type and Other Essays*.[21] Concern about "art" is limited to "the educated body" of readers, that small group whose disciplined, intellectual authority is resented by the mass of readers that prefers to respond to "the gusty impulses of instinct" and "the waves of contagion." The "mob spirit" is itself hardly

6.3. Floral postal (1906).

uniform. The "mobbish" in general break down into three categories: "the upper bourgeoise type," "the proletarian reading mob," and "the lower bourgeoise reading mob." Sedgwick is himself most interested (as am I just now) in the tastes in fiction commonly read by "the upper bourgeoise type." In order to mark the exact level of this type's "intellectual development," Sedgwick prints extracts from several popular novels of the day.[22] Each is dominated by images of young women meant to be looked at and desired.

Her skin was like velvet; a rich, clear, rosy snow, with the hot young blood glowing through it like the faint red tinge we sometimes see on the inner side of a white rose leaf. Her hair was a very light brown, almost golden, and fluffy, soft, and fine as a skein of Arras silk. She was of medium height, with a figure Venus might have envied. Her feet and hands were small, and apparently made for the sole purpose of driving mankind distracted. . . . Her greatest beauty was her glowing dark, brown eyes, which shone with an ever changing lustre from beneath the shade of the longest, blackest, upcurving lashes ever seen. (From *When Knighthood Was in Flower*)

. . . a tall, beautiful girl, with an exquisite ivory-like complexion, and a wonderful crown of fluffy red hair which encircled her head like a halo of sunlit glory. I could compare its wonderous lustre to no color save that of molten gold deeply alloyed with copper. It was red, but it also was golden, as if the enamored sun had gilded every hair with its radiance. . . . [It] fringed her low, broad forehead, and upon the heavy black eyebrows, the penciled points of whose curves almost touched across the nose . . . the rosy-tinted ivory of her skin . . . the long eyes which changed chameleon-like with the shifting light, and varied with her moods from fathomless green to violet, and from violet to soft voluptuous brown. (From *Dorothy Vernon of Haddon Hall*)

A slender girl . . . of that age, when nature paints with her richest brush. Her hair was a wave of russet lights, with shadows of warmer brown. Her face, rose-stained, was the texture of a rose. Her mouth, below serious eyes of blended blue, gave a touch of willfullness. If there was intentness on the brow, so was there languor in the lips, red, half-ripe, the upper short and curved to smile. She was all raptures—all sapphire and rose-gold, against the dark cushion. (From *Hearts Courageous*)

The checklist of desire included in these three passages concentrates wholeheart-edly upon the feminine face: hair, skin, eyes, lips. The size and shape of the body are passed upon in general terms. Tactility is important: velvet, snow, soft and fine as a skein of Arras silk, inner side of a white rose leaf, ivorylike, fluffy, molten gold, texture of a rose. These are young women that men yearn to caress and that women yearn to become. What each image offers to the hand is warmth. Even the skin of snow is "rosy" because of "the hot young blood glowing through it"; fur-thermore, skin like snow is also skin likened to a rose leaf. Eyes glow and shine; hair radiates in a sun's halo or falls in "a wave of russet lights."

Together with tactility, warmth, radiance, there is also variety. Eyes shine "with an ever changing lustre" or ripple "chameleon-like with the shifting light." If there is "intentness on the brow, so was there languor in the lips." Such variety promises delight but it is also evidence of "a touch of willfulness." These imaged faces frus-trate the male desire for easy satisfaction, while bringing pleasure to the female desire for mastery, for these are heroines formed "for the sole purpose of driving mankind distracted."

Johann Casper Lavater, the father of "physiognomical awareness," would not be happy in a society governed by the desires of the "mobbish" as found in the "upper bourgeoise novel." Absence of intellect in these fictional females would not sur-prise Lavater, since it did not occur to him that intelligence could be part of the portrait of a lady. But he would wonder where the soul was. Unlike Lavater, Sedg-wick's turn-of-the-century "mob reader" was pleased with verbal images of lushly physical young women. Lush but virginal; or to use Paul Bourget's term, marked by "chaste depravity."[23]

There are further succulent examples of the popular romance type to be taken from Jeanne Howell's novel of 1892 *A Common Mistake*.[24] Here is Sylvia Gilchrist at eighteen on the night of her coming-out ball.

The expression of her face was bright and intelligent, her eyes were deep blue, large, wide open, questioning, like the doll's. Her mouth betrayed a disposition to mockery, her nose was small and sharp, her jaw had a tendency toward squareness, and a phrenologist would have judged from it that the little lady had her share of obstinancy. . . . She was *piquante*, original, fascinating, but she was not beautiful. . . . She had remarkably small hands and feet, and no end of fascinating little ways which one failed to observe at the first glance, but which added infinitely to her charm. She took short steps in walking, and had a child-ish, almost babyish demeanor. She was graceful, without being dignified, and undeniably stylish.

Howell is serious about the ways her heroine is being looked at, sized up, and judged. The narrative is concerned (albeit at a more facile level) with what con-cerns Edith Wharton's *The House of Mirth* in 1905: from the "common mistake" that stems from faulty "physiognomical awareness" and the tragedy to which it leads, down to a strikingly similar ending.[25] From the start, Howell is careful to point up that Sylvia's inner nature is constantly likened to, then thought to be contradicted by, her outward appearance.

At eighteen, casual viewers judge Sylvia's face and soul to be one and the same. "As Sylvia appeared at this moment, she looked the incarnation of innocent girl-hood, the French ideal of a *jeune fille innocente et pure*. Dressed in white tulle, which fell in diaphanous folds about her slender figure, her fair hair, caught up in a mass of little curls on the top of her head, and falling in a soft, wavy fringe over her forehead, she had a positively angelic look."

But Sylvia's fate is Lily Bart's fate, and the time quickly comes when she is looked at with growing suspicion. Howell's narrative tries to answer the ruling question "Who is Sylvia?" by means by means of a patchwork of portrait-images. The following shows Sylvia at twenty-five at the opera.

> She wore a costume of black tulle, which set off her white satiny skin to the greatest advantage; her corsage was *décolleté* in the extreme, and held in place over the shoulders by diamond clasps in lieu of sleeves. Her fair hair was dressed high, so as to reveal the perfect contour of her head and throat, her sole ornament being a diamond aigrette supporting a little black pompon. She attracted the attention of everyone in the house, but remained impassive under the scrutiny of many eyes, secure in the knowledge of her own charms and in the classical lines of her figure.

At eighteen Sylvia is glimpsed at the moment of "coming out"—placed on public display for the first time. Her body is a mixture of the exposed and the sheltered, as this description indicates. "A tight fitting satin bodice showed to advantage, and even served to exaggerate the contour of her figure, leaving exposed to view her shoulders and arms, save where a wreath of roses which served as garniture and sleeves dropped their snowy petals against her soft flesh, as though, in their modesty, they would screen her."

But if Sylvia's figure sends out mixed signals as to her innocence, the fresh "naturalness" of her face still tips the interpretation of her moral type toward the angelic. Once Sylvia is in her mid-twenties—garbed in black tulle, not white; ornamented with diamonds, not roses—the gazing public "began to wonder whether the beauties so freely offered to admiration were real or artificial." By this point it is her body's sexuality that dictates the reading of her character, not the soul portrait provided by the female head.

The female images cited in Sedgwick's anthology and in the passages extracted from Jeanne Howell's *A Common Mistake* are possessed as "pictures" by the men who look upon the young women. The heroines are viewed across spaces, physical and psychological. That they are placed in large, public reaches such as a ballroom or an opera house is somewhat beside the point. Heart's desire is what creates the condition of distancing.

George Barr McCutcheon's 1904 best-seller *Beverly of Graustark* gives a clue to the workings of the "mobbish" technique of the spatial.[26] Initially Beverly Calhoun is looked at from a distance by everyone (the characters within the novel, the narrator, and the reader). But these generalized views are replaced by accounts of how Beverly appears to those to whom her portrait matters most: the novel's hero and the reader who takes up the hero's cause because of his or her own needs.

The author first tries to stir responses to the *availability* of Beverly Calhoun's face. Promising satisfaction to all who see it, her face is "one that painters coveted deep down in their artistic souls. It never knew a dull instant; there was expression in every lineament, in every look; life, genuine life, dwelt in the mobile countenance that turned the head of every man and woman who looked upon it."

Beverly's public identity as the type of the mean is contained within the liveliness of her waking, daylight hours. Compare this with the intensity of desire created by looking at Beverly across the distance caused by her falling into the state of sleep. In this scene the hero gazes upon the still life of the sleeping woman as they ride together within the confines of a coach. He is completely alone with the image of a face that gives him a glimpse of her bottom-nature, her portrait as the type of the original. "One little gloved hand rested carelessly in her lap, the other upon her breast near the delicate throat. The heart of Baldo was troubled. The picture he looked upon was entrancing, uplifting; he rose from the lowly state in which she had found him to the position of admirer in secret to a princess, real or assumed."

Time is suspended. Youth and beauty cannot be threatened; the "violence" of bodily contact is delayed. Images prompting masculine desire are potent only as long as touch is withheld. When handling comes—as it will during the mandatory embrace with which such romances close and with the implied aftermath of the heroine's wedding day—the image of the sleeping princess disappears. Desire lasts as long as the heroine exists as the sacred one who lies asleep. Once she is kissed back into the "reality" of the everyday, the other reality she possesses as a "still life" is dispersed and desire is disrupted.

"Looking at" is the gist of what portrait artists and their audiences do. Being "looked at" is the condition the portrait sitter must undergo. Under such circumstances the psychological relationships are understandably intense, but on whom is the act the hardest?

We often tend to assume that the sitter is the one placed most firmly within another's power. We know of the fear of spirit violation reported by roving anthropologists of the *National Geographic* variety; natives resist having the evil eye of the camera thrust upon their private entities. We are also familiar with gothic tales of psychic rape, such as Poe's "The Oval Portrait," which cause the portrait sitter to fade into nothingness under the terrible scrutiny of the artist-voyeur. But when one comes to specific narratives written during the 1890s and 1900s in which a young woman sits to her portrait, a reversal of roles controls the matter of who has the power.

The Common Law, The Angel of Clay, and *Trilby* trace the authority of the artist's eye that threatens to block accurate identification of the models' authentic nature. But these novels also record the slow and painful (and in the case of Partridge's narrative, unsuccessful) process by which the artists' eyes are opened to the real thing at which they have been looking all along. By the conclusions of their stories the corrected images of Trilby and Valerie West take command.

The possible power held by the woman who sits for her portrait is stated with even more force in Edith Wharton's *The Custom of the Country* and Henry James' *The Tragic Muse*. Undine Spragg Marvell sits to Claude Popple; Miriam Rooth comes to Nick Dormer's studio. In both instances, the women dominate the situation. Their presence "paints" the force of their image upon the imaginations of the viewers. In James' novel, the imaginations aroused are those of a man (Nick) and a woman (Julia Dallow); in Wharton's, the sitter's image enthralls the males in attendance. Both audiences are reduced to becoming recorders of the authority the sitters exude.

Miriam Rooth's social status is as questionable to the upper class through which she picks her lordly way as is the position held by Valerie West, Julie Hartmann, or Trilby O'Ferrall. It is further complicated by her racial type (fathered by a Jew) and by her profession as an actress. When the very proper Julia Dallow arrives at Nick Dormer's studio, she comes by chance during the interval when the artist and his sitter are seated at ease before the canvas Nick has been painting of Miriam. Julia instantly registers the shock of the irregularity of the situation as she sees it. "She had taken a step forward, but she had done no more, stopping short at the sight of the strange woman, so divested of visiting-gear that she looked half undressed, who lounged familiarly in the middle of the room and over whom Nick had been still more familiarly hanging."[27]

Julia goes pale, and "Nick, observing it, instinctively looked back to see what Miriam had done to produce such an effect. She had done nothing at all, which was precisely what was embarrassing; only staring at the intruder, motionless and superb. She seemed, somehow, in indolent possession of the place."

What Julia sees does *not* disclose to her how fine a "lady" Miriam is, as similar recognition scenes do in the novels by Chambers and Du Maurier. Rather, Nick believes that Julia recognizes how "low" his life as an artist seems in comparison with the assured status he would hold as her husband and as the representative to Parliament from Harsh. This reading of Miriam (based upon Nick's interpretation of Julia's response) is unkind, but it is also accurate. Nick realizes that Julia has identified a threatening source of energy. Nick sees Julia seeing him as Miriam's lover; Nick sees himself reacting to Miriam's image as an artist who thinks, "How I should like to paint her *that* way!" In either instance, Miriam's presence which animates the studio has nothing to do with the decency of English upper-class life backed by generations of self-restraining service in the public realm. Her image releases the wildness of art and the assertation of a self by which Miriam (as actress and as model) overturns the safe worlds of "identity" Julia and Nick once thought they controlled.

Undine Spragg Marvell's sitting to her portrait has a similar effect upon Old New York's version of Julia Dallow's aristocratic English society. As in the case of Miriam Rooth, Undine is herself more effective than the portrait propped on the artist's easel. Claude Popple assures Undine that he has had no need to idealize her image (i.e., to make "pleasing"), since "nature herself has outdone the artist's dream." Energized as always by flattery, however shallow, "Undine, radiantly challenging comparison with her portrait, glanced up at it with a smile of conscious merit."[28]

The forward thrust of the vivid faces of Undine and Miriam shocks the social fabric. They are winners; their faces are in control. There is no Poesque fading away for them. The power of their presence includes but goes beyond sexuality. It comes to them through the males who respond to the beauty of their faces and forms, or (as in the case of Julia) the women who identify them as threats to their own control. But Miriam and Undine also appropriate the images they find imprinted upon the faces of their observers; they mold them into self-portraits which they claim by the authority of the arts of portraiture they themselves employ. They do not exist merely at the behest of the portraitists in the studio (the artist and the onlookers). They win because they avoid becoming designated subjects—objects to be possessed by the social gaze. They become denoted subjects—icons with the sacred power others must obey.

Yes, women portrayed as icons are threatened by another danger. They chance losing their unique human identity by having it replaced by a superimposed figure set on high for public adoration or fear. And yes, they are still *what is being looked at*. But control over the situation is at stake, and idols have it hands down over whores in a society bound to conventions of identity. If Miriam Rooth and Undine Spragg ever fail to retain authority, their fate is to be identified with women of diminished reputation and little power.

Paul Bourget describes a portrait by John Singer Sargent he saw at an exhibition (figure 6.4).[29] Bourget does not know the name of the original sitter, but this is of no significance to him. He gives the picture his own meaning. He calls the woman in the painting "The American Idol" and praises it as a portrait by an artist "who, back of the individual found the real, and back of the model a whole order."

The woman is standing, her feet side by side, her knees close together, in an almost hieratic pose. Her body, rendered supple by exercise, is sheathed—you might say moulded—in a tight-fitting black dress. Rubies, like drops of blood, sparkle on her shoes. Her slender waist is encircled by a girdle of enormous pearls, and from this dress, which makes an intensely dark background for the strong brilliance of the jewels, the arms and shoulder shine out with another brilliance, that of a flower-like flesh,—fine, white flesh, through which flow blood perpetually invigorated by the air of the country and the ocean.

Thus far Bourget has focused his gaze upon the figure of the American Idol, but it is the head that contains the power.

The head, intellectual and daring, with a countenance as of one who has understood everything, has, for a sort of aureole, the vaguely gilded design of one of the Renaissance stuffs which the Venetians call *sopra-risso*. . . . It is a picture of an energy at once delicate and invincible, momentarily in repose, and all the Byzantine Madonna is in that face, with its wide-open eyes.

Yes, this woman is an idol, for whose source man labors, which he has decked with the jewels of a queen, behind each one of whose whims lie days and days spent in the ardent battle of Wall Street.[30]

6.4. John Singer Sargent, "Isabella
Stewart Gardner" (1888).

ISABELLA STEWART GARDNER MUSEUM

There is obviously a darker side to women who present themselves for their portraits. Private as such occasions are meant to be, the inevitable publicity of the moment entails a potentially dangerous voyeurism. Novels of the period which treat of sexuality rather than the essentially tamed sensuality of the "upper bourgeoise" romance indicate the hurt that comes to women who are constantly looked at. Stephen Crane's *Maggie: A Girl of the Streets* is a strong example of the case in which a woman is damaged irremediably because she lacks the ability to dictate the "reading" or the social behavior that results from the stares turned upon her.

Stephen Crane's Maggie Johnson loses the protective coloration she needs to survive under the squalid conditions of the New York slums of the 1890s. "When a child, playing and fighting with gamins in the street, dirt disguised her. Attired in tatters and grim, she went unseen. There came a time, however, when the young men of the vicinity said, 'Dat Johnson goil is a puty good looker.' "[31]

Maggie is a "miracle," a rose blooming in the gutter, but that miracle dooms her since it robs her of the concealments of "tatters and grime."[32] In happier circumstances the unexpected appearance of a rose in unlikely places is taken as the sign of the presence of a female saint or the Virgin. But Maggie's sudden flowering in the Bowery does not raise her to the heights of power granted to peasant girls at Fatima or Lourdes; for her there is no elevation to the heights of the Rose Window of Notre Dame or Chartres. As a Darwinian "sport"—an anomaly in a naturalistic world which does not take kindly to divine miracles or to biological mistakes—Maggie's "portrait" is drawn by crass young men like Peter who are attracted to "lookers." To be told, "Say, Mag, I'm stuck on yer shape. It's outa sight"—to be told, "Mag, yer a bloomin' good looker"—is to be made conspicuous in ways Undine Spragg manages to avoid. Maggie's failure to mask or hide herself propels her *outside*. In naive imitation of "high," "uptown" society, her people cast her out of whatever "place" she once held in the "low" society of the tenements.

Crane presents Maggie's slide down into the dark river of her death through a series of portrait-types. Readers never see Maggie directly even though she is constantly referred to as being seen. We have to see her through the perceptions of Pete, who is pulled toward whatever he looks at (i.e., lusts after); through the people who spill into the hallways of the tenement house to witness Maggie's public humiliation when her mother repudiates her; through the men of the street whom Maggie encounters during the final dark night of her soul. They all see Maggie in terms of her sexuality, shame, and sin. "Maggie considered she was not what they thought her," but their authoritarian stares overwhelm her. In turn, Crane controls the way we as readers look at and judge the others who look at, and misjudge, Maggie's signs.[33]

Crane's narrative furnishes none of the traditional details of hair, eyes, lips, or skin savored by the "mobbish spirit." Maggie would not last a minute in an "upper bourgeois" text of the kind cited by Henry Sedgwick. Before she becomes a looker, Maggie does not even have a name; she is identified only as the "small ragged girl," "the little girl." Nor is she granted the vivid colors her massive mother appropriates to her own image. Purples, reds, yellows, and blues that shock the mind's eye are the primary colors possessed by persons, places, things, or events packed with instinctual drives and cravings; they paint a poster world in which primal types exist furiously and die in futility, but Maggie has no place in its garish design because she provides no "colors" (no force) of her own.

Nor does Maggie as the looker possess detail. She exists—"blushing" and "glistening" in response to Pete's splendor—as the blank in the narrative upon which the portrait makers in the Bowery world impose their feelings. " 'Dere's yer sister. Lookut her! Lookut her! . . . Through the open doors curious eyes stared in at Maggie. Children ventured into the room and ogled her as if they formed the front row at a theatre."

We know that Maggie has left home by the notation that her jacket and hat are missing from the room, not through any direct description of her departure. She becomes "a girl of the painted cohorts"—as vulnerable to annihilation as a poster figure that peels away from the wall and blows into the gutter. Faceless, Maggie is interchangeable with "the forlorn woman" her brother Jimmy once seduced and abandoned; she is interchangeable with all the forlorn women with no way to survive. Nell, a "woman of brilliance and audacity," commands what others see in her. Poor Maggie becomes what others have seen her to be. She does not even know for herself what that self is. "She wandered aimlessly for several blocks. She stopped once and asked a question of herself: 'Who?' "

It is appropriate that we last see Maggie Johnson as a void set against the glare of the theater streets. Yes, "some men looked at her with calculating eyes," but that stare does not hold her in place. She rapidly fades away until she arrives at the eternal blankness of the river's darkness and silence.

Popular fiction at the turn of the century usually avoided the direct treatment of sexuality. It preferred the sensuality of desire which accompanies the act of looking. There is sensuality in Kate Chopin's 1899 *The Awakening*—so much that it has little patience for sexuality. Sexuality requires at least two people, and Edna Pontellier is so wrapped in desire for her emerging body and self that we are given a portrait of a woman staring herself into life in a mirror. The intensity of the narrative's self-reflection, by which the heroine, the author, and the admiring readers are absorbed by the contemplation of unending mirror images of the awakened senses, turns Chopin away from the "novel" toward the "mob" romance of the "upper bourgeois" persuasion.[34]

Edna Pontellier is yet another "drowned woman" from that undeniable tradition of American letters that also gives us Hawthorne's Zenobia and Crane's Maggie. Upon first looking upon Kate Chopin's heroine it seems unlikely to conceive of her as doomed. Not only are her social and economic circumstances far and away superior to those of Maggie Johnson of the Bowery slums, she is vividly *there* in the narrative as poor vacant Maggie fails to be. But it is Adèle Ratignolle whose face and figure fit the hole in the painted scenery which, as Henry Sedgwick indicates, is the sign of the popular portrait and the True Woman.

There are no words to describe her save the old ones that had served so often to picture the bygone heroine of romance and the fair lady of our dreams. There was nothing subtle or hidden about her charms; her beauty was all there, flaming and apparent: the spun-gold hair that comb nor confining pin could restrain; the blue eyes that were like nothing but sapphires; two lips that pouted, that were so red one could only think of cherries or some other delicious crimson fruit in looking at them. She was growing a little stout, but it did not seem to detract an iota from the grace of every step, pose, gesture. One would not have wanted her white neck a mite less full or her beautiful arms more slender.

Physiognomical awareness is also given to Edna. But hers is the look of the New Woman—one which shivers through the narrative from first to last, providing intensity and modernity.

Mrs. Pontellier's eyes were quick and bright; they were a yellowish brown, about the color of her hair. She had a way of turning them swiftly upon an object and holding them there as if lost in some inward maze of contemplation or thought.

Her eyebrows were a shade darker than her hair. They were thick and almost horizontal, emphasizing the depth of her eyes. She was more handsome than beautiful. Her face was captivating by reason of a certain frankness of expression and a contradictory subtle play of features.

Edna Pontellier is there to be looked at, but Edna's appearance is more difficult to read than Adèle's, more hidden, subtle, and in motion; less open and immediate in its effects. Even the "charm of Edna Pontellier's physique stole insensibly upon you. . . . A casual and indiscriminating observer, in passing, might not cast a second glance upon the figure. But with more feeling and discernment he would have recognized the noble beauty of its modeling, and the graceful severity of poise and movement, which made Edna Pontellier different from the crowd."

The best interpreter of this newly awakened woman is the one with the artist's eye. It is he or she who sees the "modeling" and "poise" of the real thing. But these notes on Edna's appearance come early in the narrative. Hers is still essentially a public image. It is not a developed portrait.

The portrait comes once Edna emerges from the cocoon of the type of the average and begins to look candidly at herself. The following description is of a woman privately examining the secret parts of a bottom-nature she is in the act of discovering.

Edna, left alone in the little side room, loosened her clothes, removing the greater part of them. She bathed her face, her neck and arms in the basin that stood between the windows. She took off her shoes and stockings and stretched herself in the very center of the high, white bed. How luxurious it felt to rest thus in a strange, quaint bed, with its sweet country odor of laurel lingering about the sheets and mattress! She stretched her strong limbs that ached a little. She ran her fingers through her loosened hair for a while. She looked at her round arms as she held them straight up and rubbed them one after the other, observing closely, as if it were something she saw for the first time, the fine, firm quality and texture of her flesh. She clasped her hands easily above her head, and it was thus she fell asleep.

After this important interlude, the public Edna again shines forth, but with more obviousness to her beauty. We are shown Edna as she appears on the street, in her new house, and at a splendid dinner party. Here the images Chopin introduces approach the fantasies encouraged in readers by the mobbish romance. One wonders just whose desire her look best nourishes—that of the male or the female.

She looked handsome and distinguished in her street gown. The tan of the seashore had left her face, and her forehead was smooth, white, and polished beneath her heavy, yellow-brown hair. There were a few freckles on her face, and a small, dark mole near the under lip and one on the temple, half-hidden in her hair. . . .

Arobin found her with rolled sleeves, working in company with the house-maid when he looked in during the afternoon. She was splendid and robust, and had never appeared hand-somer than in the old blue gown, with a red silk handkerchief knotted at random around her head to protect her hair from the dust. . . .

The golden shimmer of Edna's satin gown spread in rich folds on either side of her. There was a soft fall of lace encircling her shoulers. It was the color of her skin, without the glow, the myriad living tints that one may sometimes discover in vibrant flesh. There was some-thing in her attitude, in her whole appearance when she leaned her head against the high-backed chair and spread her arms, which suggested the regal woman, the one who rules, who looks on, who stand alone.

Where does this sequence of portraits take Edna? It takes her to the seashore where she disrobes and moves *outside* the clothes which, as Madame Merle advised Isabel Archer, furnish the marks of a woman's social identity. Edna "finds" what lies beneath her clothes and discards them altogether, as Isabel does not. Edna "knows" herself more than Maggie Johnson ever does, as she stands "for the first time in her life . . . naked in the open air, at the mercy of the sun, the breeze that beat upon her, and the waves that invited her." It is ecstasy that Edna feels at this moment, something foreign to both Isabel and to Maggie. "How strange and awful it seemed to stand naked under the sky! how delicious! She felt like some new-born creature, opening its eyes in a familiar world that it had never known."

But this world of self-discovery is an ocean world. This is not the shore life where the type of the mean works out its existence. Edna moves into the waves where, rumor tells us, the universal, essential, eternal "original" takes its source. And Edna drowns. The haunting question left by Kate Chopin's novel is whether Edna dies because she has awakened to the real thing she is, or because she, like so many of her sisters, has made "a common mistake" and misread what she thought she had looked upon and knew about herself.

Edna Pontellier's watery death in the Gulf Stream is prettier in its language than the drowning of Maggie Johnson. It has been likened by some enthusiasts to a soaring apotheosis into the Oversoul or to a transcendent absorption of entity into an element certainly less soiled by the oil slicks, drifting debris, and water rats native to New York's East River.[35] But Chopin's heroine is just as dead at the conclusion of *The Awakening* as is Maggie, triumphs of the will aside. Edna, like Maggie, gives us the portrait of a type which has *no more to do*; no more for an author to make an "ado" about. Drowning is the annihilation of the images of the social selves by which human life defines itself. Drowning may let a woman enter upon the reality of her bottom-nature and enjoy an absolute of privacy, but living requires that the woman possess the type of the mean that can be looked at, as well as the type of the original that exists only "under water."

7

Literary Portraits and Types: Possibilities

The final pages of the New York edition of *The Portrait of a Lady* contain the image of a woman on the point of drowning. Isabel Archer is, of course, not in danger of annihilation in any literal waters. What she experiences "was but a subjective fact, as the metaphysicians say; the confusion, the noise of waters, all the rest of it, were in her own swimming head."[1] But Isabel has to struggle none-theless against "this act of possession." If she submits, as do Maggie Johnson and Edna Pontellier, to that engulfing force, she will be saved from what Caspar Good-wood calls in disdain "the bottomless idiocy of the world." She will be flung into that other world he claims they alone would inhabit. It "seemed to open out, all round her, to take the form of a mighty sea, where she floated in fathomless waters."

Isabel pleads with Goodwood, "Don't kill me." The future he plans for her seems like a series of upheavals in the natural world consisting of a "rushing torrent," "the hot wind of the desert . . . potent, acrid, strange," "white lightning, a flash that spread, and spread again, and stayed." She sinks beneath these onslaughts, her head filled with the "train of images" experienced by "those wrecked and un-der water." She senses that Goodwood's "help" is "the next best thing to her dying. This belief, for a moment, was a kind of rapture, in which she felt herself sink and sink." Then she breaks free of Goodwood's embrace, running now upon the "very straight path" that leads her back to Rome, Gilbert Osmond, and a lifetime as "the portrait of a lady."

7.1. Roy Lichtenstein, "Drowning Girl" (oil and synthetic polymer paint on canvas) (1963).

MUSEUM OF MODERN ART, NEW YORK

But is Isabel imaged at the novel's conclusion as a lesser type, or as a fully realized individual?

The ending of *The Portrait of a Lady* stirs controversy over the nature of Isabel's future: whether she is now capable of facing life's complexity or whether she has perversely resigned herself to a dead marriage; whether she wins the right to be the subject of a portrait which denotes her as a Lady or whether she remains a probationary character, limited to the designated type of the American Girl. Perhaps, even after all the *good writing* James provides, we are left with a cartoon figure, Roy Lichtenstein's "Drowning Girl," whose only stab at self-determinism is to whimper, "I don't care! I'd rather sink than call Brad for help!" (figure 7.1).

The judgments we make as readers about Isabel's worth are largely governed by the sequence of pictorial images the novel offers. There is no "decisive moment" through which Isabel comes into complete and instant focus. This is true even in chapter 42 where she is shown (rendered after the manner of an Eakins or a Dewing) sitting and thinking her way into the next stage of her pictorial status. James' "Isabel" is created from a string of postures caught, momentarily, out of time. These altering postures are then linked and informed by their progression through narrative time. All the Isabels combine to reveal the grid of relationships out of which her portrait emerges.[2]

Isabel's grid consists of everything she detects in herself; it also gathers together what others see in her. Isabel initially believes she has come to Europe to "look around" in order to know and to be ready to choose the life she will enjoy. But in large part her knowing and her choosing are regulated by the intensity with which others look at her.

The Portrait of a Lady consists of a six-year record in the form of a photographic album. Readers turn the pages, following the development of an identity in stages dictated (in terms Gertrude Stein would recognize) by what all "the little dogs" know: from Madame Merle and Bunchie the Touchett terrier on through suitor after suitor. In terms familiar to Josiah Royce and Charles Sanders Peirce, Isabel is the image held up by Ralph and by Warburton, respectively, as "His First Love"— the model after which each man thereafter shapes the conduct of his life.

Ralph Touchett defines his life as "watching" Isabel; what happens to her equates with what happens to him. Lord Warburton is rejected by Isabel because his identity has been fixed by his class status and his national characteristics. (As fierce a chauvinist as the physiognomist V. G. Rocine when it comes to separating desirables from undesirables, Isabel fears that the qualities of her "American type" might be contaminated by Warburton as the type of the British lord.) Warburton's future is thereby dictated by the fact that he is seen, "read," and rejected by the one woman he finds "interesting."

Goodwood and Osmond seem to be types in opposition (the man of iron will and the failed dilettante), but they are alike in how they try to stare Isabel out of countenance and to mold the social behavior of the young woman they look upon. Isabel's acceptance of Osmond turns out to be an ironic acceptance by proxy of Goodwood's desire to make her his "thing." Isabel *is* her ideas; she is also the ideas men have about her. It is a pity that her ideas lead her toward men like Goodwood and Osmond who want to destroy them, and thereby her bottom-nature.

Isabel is also an "idea" to Warburton and to Ralph—kinder men with finer ideas. Neither of them, however, can save Isabel. In James' world, "saving" is not something one person can do for another. But if Warburton is unable to help Isabel because incapable of giving her anything beyond his dutiful mournfulness, Ralph at least gives her a deathbed gift (a far more useful one than the money he transmits to her through his father's deathbed will). He gives Isabel an idea of herself that counters the killing idea Osmond has thrust upon her. Isabel and Ralph "look at" life together and see it as somehow good.

The scene between Ralph and Isabel (the giving of esteem that enables Isabel to keep from drowning in Goodwood's idea about her) comes almost at the end of the novel. We must go back to the very start in order to see Isabel presented through a sequence of scenes as the type which has as yet to find the way to become a portrait.

The following "pictures" show Isabel *before* her marriage.

On first viewing across the lawn at Gardencourt, Isabel—"a tall girl in a black dress, who at first sight looked pretty"—is represented as the one who is doing the looking. "She was looking at everything, with an eye that denoted clear perception—at her companion, at the two dogs, at the two gentlemen under the trees, at the beautiful scene that surrounded her."

She is unquestionably an observer, but one who draws the glances of others. Once the significant nature of this personality-picture is established, there is time for James to paint a Whistlerian portrait of Isabel in tones of black and white. We are shown that "her white hands, in her lap, were folded upon her black dress; her head was erect, her eye lighted, her flexible figure turned itself easily this way and that, in sympathy with the alertness with which she evidently caught impressions."

Soon after, Ralph guides Isabel through the portrait gallery at Gardencourt. As they stroll slowly about, he notes her height and the litheness of figure, the color of her eyes and hair. He finds himself "bending his eyes much less upon the pictures than on her presence. He lost nothing, in truth, by these wandering glances, for she was better worth looking at than most works of art."

By the next chapter the narrator finds it incumbent to provide the marks of an inner physiognomy. It is part of the task he shoulders as Isabel's "biographer," lest those who observe her from the outside overlook the signs that really matter. He concentrates, of course, on her mind. It is a mix of "errors and delusions," "a tangle of vague outlines," together with "a certain nobleness of imagination" that deludes her into thinking a great deal about "beauty and bravery and magnanimity."

Chapters 11 and 12 follow the sequence set up by chapters 5 and 6. First Isabel is seen "seated on a garden-bench, within sight of the house, beneath a spreading beech, where, in a white dress ornamented with black ribbons, she formed among the flickering shadows a graceful and harmonious image"—as neat and effective a portrait as one painted by Frank Benson or Edmund Tarbell, members of the Boston School who specialized in the portraiture of well-bred young women given to sitting on garden benches.[3] Then the image of Isabel's mind immediately comes after. We are shown what Isabel sees herself to be ("a character," someone with a "sublime soul"). But we are also told what the narrator realizes we may make her out to be (rather a smug fool), and what the narrator asks us to see clairvoyantly ("a person of great good faith" who will suffer from her own follies in ways "which will constitute almost a direct appeal to charity").

The novel continues to inch forward by means of pictures of Isabel inside and out; of Isabel as she sees herself and as others in the story see her; of Isabel as the Jamesian narrator realizes the readers are probably looking at her; and of Isabel viewed through the corrective vision offered first-hand by the narrator. In chapter 14, for example, Warburton visits Gardencourt and it is Isabel's turn to take him on a tour of the portrait gallery. This device gives Warburton and us another fine chance to watch Isabel placed against the array of painted portraits. Once again the narrator notes what an excellent painting she herself makes. "Isabel walked to the other side of the gallery and stood there showing him her charming back, her light slim figure, the length of her white neck as she bent her head, and the density of her dark braids. She stopped in front of a small picture as if for the

purpose of examining it; and there was something so young and free in her movement that her very pliancy seemed to mock at him."

But something is different in this scene from that which took place earlier in
Gardencourt's gallery. Isabel is not absorbed in looking at paintings or persons. She
is looking far within herself, her eyes blurred with tears over the fact of what she
has just discovered about herself: that she cannot escape her fate.

By chapter 28 Isabel is in Rome, deeply involved in the courtship put into play
by Osmond and Madame Merle. We see her as the disconsolate Warburton and the
others in attendance at the opera performance see her. She is on display, under
"operatic conditions." She is seated in her box, "the clear profile of this young
lady defined against the dim illumination of the house," marked by "radiance"
and "exaltation." In chapter 29 Osmond comes to Isabel at her Rome hotel. The
room is a private one, but the setting is still operatic. "The chairs and sofas were
orange; the walls and windows were draped in purple and gilt. The mirrors, the
pictures had great flamboyant frames; the ceiling was deeply vaulted and painted
over with naked muses and cherubs. For Osmond the place was ugly to distress;
the false colors, the sham splendor were like vulgar, bragging, lying talk."

Osmond cannot recognize ·the similarities between his own character and this
awful room. Since he considers himself aesthetically flawless, he is unaware that
sham expresses itself in ways other than cupids and gilt. He does not realize how
"vulgar" the "decor" of his mind is. Nor is Osmond fully cognizant of why Isabel
looks so beautiful amid such tawdry surroundings. To him she has the power of
physical beauty that overcomes flawed settings because of her aesthetic quality.
He does not recognize that it is her mind that carves the space for her image to
occupy as she sits "alone in a wilderness of yellow upholstery," a book in her lap,
"her finger vaguely kept in the place," as she muses upon her future.

By now we have been prepared to see a young American girl make, once more,
"the common mistake." Since we have been taken inside and out, up and down,
and across Isabel's character and her "look," we understand (though we wince at
the moment when it comes) how easily she falls into the woman trap formed by
Osmond's idea of her. Gone is the resistance she brought to bear to Goodwood and
Warburton's earlier overtures. When Osmond announces himself as "I'm convention itself" and tells her she will always be "the most important woman in the
world," she does not shy away from the telltale juxtaposition of these two statements. What could "the most important woman" be to a man who is "convention
itself" but a woman fated to be "ground in the very mill of the conventional"?
Isabel disregards the warning signs. She pleases herself by contemplating the portrait of the lady she believes she has become. "Isabel looked at herself in this
character—looked intently, thinking she filled it with a certain grace."

The narrative has reached its midpoint. James now has to show us Isabel Archer
as Isabel Archer Osmond. He must provide through verbal means a shift in image
comparable to the shift one makes in glancing from William Merritt Chase's "Lady

7.2. William Merritt Chase, "Lady in Black" (1888).

in Black" (figure 7.2) to John Singer Sargent's "Mrs. Charles E. Inches" (figure 7.3). Chase's young woman dressed in a daytime frock, standing easily with hand on arched hip, her frank eyes taking in what lies directly ahead, is Isabel before her marriage. Sargent's young woman gowned and coiffed for evening display, shown three-quarters-length—perhaps seated, perhaps with hands folded in her lap—her expression controlled, her guarded eyes averted from the viewer, is Isabel after she

7.3. John Singer Sargent, "Mrs. Charles E. Inches" (oil on canvas) (1888).

weds. What Chase in a "study" of a type and Sargent in a "portrait" of a particular lady accomplished in painted moments of time, Henry James had to evolve over the final half of his narrative.

We first see the married Isabel through the connoisseur's eye of Edward Rosier. He adds the particular quality of appreciation based "on his eye for decorative character, his instinct for authenticity; but also on a sense of catalogued values, for that secret of a 'lustre' beyond any recorded losing or rediscovering." Rosier's look is that of an incipient Bernard Berenson making use of the methods of "attribution" developed by Giovanni Morelli.[4]

She was dressed in black velvet; she looked high and splendid . . . and yet oh so radiantly gentle! . . . The years had touched her only to enrich her; the flower of her youth had not faded, it only hung more quietly on its stem. She had lost something of that quick eagerness to which her husband had privately taken exception—she had more the air of being able to wait. Now, at all events, framed in the gilded doorway, she struck our young man as the picture of a gracious lady.

James does not leave us with Edward Rosier as our interpreter-guide. Rosier is a thoroughly nice young man, and his taste for art objects does not incapacitate him for recognizing nuances of human thoughts and feelings; but his "looks" are for Pansy Osmond mostly, since gazing with desire at that version of the expatriated American Girl is the only satisfaction he can expect. Ralph Touchett's eye is the one James uses to supplement his own, for Ralph's physical existence is predicated on his intention to watch Isabel make her way through the world. The nearer to dying he comes, the higher the stakes he places in coming to "know" what her life is like.

Ralph's sharp eye reads as much as is possible from external evidence. He notes that she appears "to be leading the life of the world." He records that she does this "with a certain magnificence" and that "the hand of the master [Osmond]" is involved in producing the "studied impressions" for which Isabel has "no faculty." Ralph notes Isabel's new love of movement, gaiety, and fatigue, and "a kind of violence in some of her impulses, of crudity in some of her experiments." There is more "amplitude and a brilliancy" to her image than in her unmarried days, and "a touch of insolence to her beauty." Now her "light step drew a mass of drapery behind it; her intelligent head sustained a majesty of ornament." The physical transformation Ralph finds in Isabel is remarkable. "The free, keen girl had become quite another person; what he saw was the fine lady who was supposed to represent something. What did Isabel represent?" Ralph has no answer to this, the final question. All he is clear about is that Isabel's function is to represent Gilbert Osmond, not herself.

A few chapters after James outlines the impasse of interpretation to which Ralph has been brought, he takes us into Isabel's room where she sits meditating before the fire. The sequence of thoughts that take her through that fateful evening begins by her looking at Osmond. There is nothing really different in his appearance. He is the same man except that he "had grown slightly stouter since his marriage"; he still "might strike one as very distinguished." The alteration in Osmond comes down to the fact that Isabel now *looks at* him differently. "It was the same face she had looked into with eyes equally earnest perhaps, but less penetrating, on the terrace of a Florentine villa." But by that particular night in Rome, she turns a gaze—both earnest and penetrating—upon her husband and herself. She has many more things yet to learn before the novel's end (Madame Merle's complicity in her marriage; the truth of Pansy's birth; the part Osmond demands she take in his plans for Pansy's marriage), but the start she makes that night in correcting her vision is momentous.

Isabel finds herself crossing over "a dusky, uncertain tract which looked ambiguous and even slightly treacherous, like a moorland seen in the winter twilight." Once across the terrain which represents what her married life with Osmond has become, she realizes how he has blighted her soul with a force she likens to an "evil eye." It was as if her husband had left her in darkness by "deliberately, almost malignantly," putting "the lights out one by one." Notwithstanding the lengths to which he has gone to blind her and the fact that she had previously complied by shutting her eyes to his character, Isabel now stares at the mind of the man with whom she lives: "then, *then* she had seen where she really was," and it was indeed "the house of darkness, the house of dumbness, the house of suffocation."

The preface to *The Portrait of a Lady* that James wrote years after the novel's publication in 1881 expresses his pleasure over the challenge he faced and met by creating the great central portrait of chapter 42. "It is a representation simply of her motionless *seeing*, and an attempt withal to make the mere still lucidity of her act as 'interesting' as the surprise of a caravan or the identification of a pirate."

James brought off a remarkable achievement in this scene, one similar to those attempted by many portrait painters during the same period. He established the value of a woman imaged as "motionlessly *seeing*" through his insistence that renditions of the still life of the female mind have great beauty and extensive significance.

In the pages that follow the night in Isabel's room, further pictorial "studies" open up the bottom-nature that lies beneath the protective social mask Isabel wears in Osmond's "house of darkness." At first, Ralph Touchett only catches brief glimpses of that nature. He finally sees everything about her, and she about him. On Ralph's deathbed, the two examine together the life she had once wanted to look at freely but was not allowed to because bound to the ways others looked at her. With Ralph dead, Caspar Goodwood suddenly appears at her side in that abrupt way of his; but not to *see* her, especially not when he seizes her in his arms and almost effaces her with the idea he has of her. Moments later Isabel escapes the threat of drowning in the waters of his will and disappears from our view. All we are left with at the conclusion is the sense that she has seen where it is she must go.[5]

Perhaps we can test the extent to which James succeeds in *The Portrait of a Lady*. We can compare his novel with a work of popular fiction that draws its basic story line from the ways people look at others according to the pictorial ideas they import into the relationship. The mistakes in identification that occur when the heroine drastically misreads the signs of her two suitors place Eugenia Brooks Frothingham's novel of 1906, *The Evasion*, within the same tradition followed by James' narrative (and those of Edith Wharton).[6]

Gladys marries Arthur, who looks like a Greek hero. She has turned against Dick, who looks like a brute. She believes the accusations laid upon Dick's character for cheating at cards. Since he looks like "a proven scoundrel," she is unable to realize that it is her Greek god who is the dishonorable cheat. Dick returns from exile a few years after Gladys' marriage, a time during which she, like Isabel, has lived feverishly in an attempt to present another "face" to the world and to disguise the fact of her failure to interpret the signs of character. Dick looks as rough as ever, but Gladys is now drawn to the look of his hands—"knotted and scarred," "honest hands." She falls in love with everything those hands tell her about his true nature.

The final chapter of *The Evasion* is titled "Realization." In it Dick (who is the type of a "good" Caspar Goodwood) urges Gladys to leave Arthur, who has betrayed her with her friend Diana, but Gladys repels his argument. She delivers a brief for the sanctity of the marriage vow as society's one stay against chaos. She repeats almost verbatum Osmond's own statement on the subject to Isabel. Gladys excuses Arthur's flaws (as Isabel does to some extent for Osmond) by admitting she had not given her husband the kind of love he had expected to receive from her; but unlike Isabel, Gladys maintains that Arthur is now purified by despair, remorse, and moral and physical suffering. When Dick insists that she is his and uses the strong hands she adores to pull her into his arms, Gladys resists with "an untamed, unconquered spirit shining in her eyes." She kneels on the ground and tells Dick he is killing her with his love, but that she must return to Arthur's side.

It is Eugenia Brooks Frothingham who does the final cheating in a book full of evasions (a charge which some readers also lay at the feet of James as well). Gladys knows that Arthur, now gravely ill, is going to die within a short time (though Isabel cannot count on getting rid of Osmond so easily). Gladys only has to wait a while longer and she can have her American Girl conscience and Dick's hands after all.

In 1881 Henry James developed the narrative process by which he made full-length literary portraits—as opposed to a linked series of type images or abbreviated portrait-busts. He learned how to present the drama which arises from "physiognomical awareness." He engaged novelistic characters and the readers of novels in a mutual act of perceiving and knowing; he furnished them both with a sequence of gallery portraits to study. In 1908 Eugenia Frothingham had all these techniques at her disposal, as did any writer of the time; she also knew the proven popular appeal of stories about people who misread and are misread by others. The one thing missing in *The Evasion* that really counts in the long run is the quality of the author's mind.

Gladys, Arthur, Dick, and Diana are "mobbish" types. They create no sense of "ado." As figures in *The Evasion*, they evade doing what is required of portraits: *registering thought* about what it is they look at and what it feels like to be stared into being. That they do not is no fault of the popular romance as such, just as success at portraiture does not automatically follow the incorporation of that device within so-called serious novels. The fault or credit lies not in the genre or the formula, dear Brutus; it lies in the nature of the writers' minds.

Set over and against *The Portrait of a Lady*, *The Evasion* makes us aware that Henry James wins hands down. Part of his strength comes from the fact that James is a better writer than Eugenia Brooks Frothingham, a fact that has to carry some weight. Part is the fact that he takes some chances as a writer. Part is the canny way James uses conventions in order to analyze them. But what makes the difference between his products and those of any other writer of the period is the addition of *the thought* by which he registers his awareness of what he has to do with the literary portrait and with the depiction of life as a series of interpretive acts.

Theories alone do not insure a writer supremacy at his trade. In the case of raw geniuses, the absence of theoretical thought is not only to their advantage, it is to our benefit as readers. We wince to think what ideas placed in consecutive order might do to the exuberance of Mark Twain and what it does at times to Theodore Dreiser's prose. Still, writers often like to natter on about character, plot, and such. Some are quite good at this. But James' case is more special. He is so good a theorist that some readers pay too much attention to his observations concerning the profession of writing while slighting the specifics of his actual performance.

Granted the dangers of robbing Peter the practitioner to pay Paul the theorist, we must allow that James writing on the care and nurture of theory in "The Art of Fiction" of the 1880s avails us, to our advantage, of his early attitudes toward the novelistic portrait. James analyzing Balzac's theories of narrative in "The Lesson of Balzac" in 1905 takes us even further into the subject. The essays prepare us to link James' art of identification and desire with the experiments upon which Gertrude Stein had entered by the time James delivered his meditation on Balzac. The emphasis James as theorist applies to the differences between portraits crafted from words and those created with paint also helps us when we come to consider the achievements of portraitists such as Thomas Dewing, Thomas Eakins, John Singer Sargent, and others who worked directly with the visual qualities James and Balzac had, perforce, to talk about.

In 1884 Henry James published "The Art of Fiction" in response to the lawless principles—the poetics without rules—he detected in the public vagaries of Walter Besant. In 1888 he included a revised version of his essay in the volume *Partial Portraits*. Early and late he insisted that writers should have a theory, *a chosen position*, which protects them from naïveté.[7] Conscious, convinced, chosen art forces writers to "take notes" and to think their way toward skillful execution. For James, a theory about the representation of life is the same as possessing "a latent core of conviction."[8] This interest endows the writer's work with "a consciousness of it-self." The work becomes "the expression of an artistic faith, the result of choice and comparison."

In evolving his notions about the practice of writing novels, James sharpened his views about the separate functions performed by painters and authors. Like a latter-day Lessing, James reiterated the commonly held distinctions between paint-ings (immediate effects) and writings (gradual unfoldings over time), but he was even quicker to notice the differences which marked the status of literature in the 1880s in relation to painting's special authority. James claimed as a historical and cultural fact that contemporary paintings followed rules, whereas literary works did not. Our own legacy from James, as a result of his pronouncements on "the art of fiction," is the heightened awareness of just such writers' rules, but all James could sense in the 1880s was that literature lacked the critical point of view he was persuaded great art requires. To his mind, works of literature need to be "looked at" hard. Only then will thoughtful critics be able to give them the finish of exact perception and conceptualization to be found in fine easel portraits.

"The Art of Fiction" of 1884 develops a program for literature that matches the techniques employed by the masters of painterly illusion: character analysis, treat-ment of surfaces, insinuation of unseen motives by means of the glimpsed sugges-tion, approximation which uses selection, design, and arrangement to further the "illusion of life," and—above all—"a selection whose main care is to be *typical*, to be *inclusive*" (my italics).

Between 1884 and 1888 the revisions James made in his essay, slight and subtle as they appear, act to deemphasize the mimetic rage felt by artists who desire to *compete* with life. By 1888 James' tilt is toward an art that *represents* life and does not attempt to duplicate it. The novel continues to be "history," while the picture is "reality," but in either case writers and painters traffic in images of the world. The writer continues to joust "with his brother the painter in *his* attempt to render the look of things, the look that conveys their meaning."

"Guy de Maupassant," an essay James wrote in 1888, states, "Every good story is of course both a picture and an idea, and the more they are interfused the better the problem is solved."[9] Eleven years later, in "The Future of the Novel" of 1899, James was still insisting that novelists satisfy the reader's "general appetite for a *picture*."[10] But he had still not fully investigated the relation of ideas to the looked-at image. It is this issue which centers the address James gave before the Contem-porary Club of Philadelphia on January 12, 1905.

James was on a visit to the United States after a twenty-year absence. He paused in his travels to present the Philadelphia audience with his views of Honoré de Balzac, the genius at work. In "The Lesson of Balzac," a biography-by-portrait, James details the attributes governing modern portraiture which affect the inter-connections existing between picture and idea.[11] In former times the artist ren-dered "a world of ideas, animated by figures representing these ideas." Now he must point to "the packed and constituted, the palpable, provable world before him" before obtaining that picture "by the study of which ideas . . . inevitably find themselves thrown up."

The writer's picture is not an image of life itself. Life cannot be directly represented by words; not when it is "the unconscious, the agitated, the struggling, floundering cause." But life "in its sources" can be caught upon the page by imaging instead the "intimate, essential states and feelings" of one's consciousness.[12]

Between 1884 and 1905, therefore, James had shifted the literary act (a) from idea as picture, (b) to idea and picture interfused, (c) to a greater emphasis upon the picture itself, (d) to the picture as representative not of the writer's *ideas*, but of the *mind* of the writer.

In 1905 James also wished to ponder the particular "lesson of Balzac" and why his writings affect us as they do. James sketches a portrait of the mind which constitutes Balzac's art, calling upon various analogues to define that mind. Some are directly pictorial. ("The individual strong temperament" of Balzac's fiction is "the color of air," one which "unconsciously suffuses his picture.") Sometimes James slips in one of his favorite metaphors—the mirrored reflection. (Balzac's fiction is "something that proceeds from the contemplative mind itself, the very complexion of the mirror in which the material is reflected.") Sometimes James' references are architectural. (Using his favorite image of the House of Fiction, he likens our experience of the thoughts of a genius to living intensely within the corridors and galleries of his soul and consciousness.) James even combines a number of these images. (Balzac's thoughts are portraits that line a gallery in a villa overlooking a garden centered by a monument to "our towering idol.") Painting. Mirror. Gallery. Palace. Monument. All are approximations which possess "closeness," "weight," "mass;" all attempt to image that entity that has no image since it is quite simply the great I AM—the "very presence, [the] spiritual presence, in his work."

James has his little joke. He concedes that novelists, whose sole form is the mind, cannot really write novels. Painters *can* paint pictures; they have tangible material with which to work. Novelists only *pretend* to write novels—to give representations of life as "portraits of the mind."

In certain ways, the "pretense" of which James speaks is the age-old attempt at illusion-making which began with Apelles' painting of the grapes that fooled the greedy crow. Precisely because art is not the world's kind of reality, crows are beguiled into pecking at painted fruit and readers are lulled into believing in the actual presence of Balzac's Cousine Bette and Père Goriot. Because illusory things often seem more real than reality, fretting over the Reality Principle is a thankless task. Not only thankless but unnecessary. Why quibble whether portraits are closer to life than types are, or whether any portraiture (verbal or visual) is more than cunning sleight of hand? As long as we accept the notion that "Art *makes* life, makes interest, makes importance,"[13] faith, not facts, is what counts in the matter of whether these imaged selves exist. The self consists of a grid of doubts, relations, occasions. Totality, not particulars, mount the "field" out of which the portrait arises. In this, the self (the mind) which the novelist (Balzac *cum* James) tries to represent is equivalent to the novelist's work. The self and the writer's art is a single great book; it is total presence; it is the "weight" of "the mass." It is Presence.

Types as presences blend the remarkable with the usual. They take command over our attention quite as firmly as the individual does who is naturalistically rendered and placed within history. In a paraphrase of the opinions of Georg Lukács, types are useful to the dedicated interpreter of social life. "A type is the fusion of the extraordinary and the typical, it is a character that 'stands out' not because he is different from his contexts . . . but because he embodies them. The characteristic occasions of his historical period are immanent in his life."[14]

The sophisticated employment of the literary type is one of the strengths James brought to the novel once he began to view the genre as essentially the art of making and matching pictures.[15] James' conclusions about the nature of the pictorial and the type are similar to those toward which Gertrude Stein was working at the time James wrote "The Lesson of Balzac." In 1905 Stein was in Paris writing *Three Lives*. She was consorting with Matisse and Picasso, learning how to do verbal portraits of them as portrait makers in oils. When Stein finally set down her theories of portraiture in the 1930s, her discoveries about "being new" were close to what William Dean Howells in 1882 said James knew then.

Art consists of what the writer has to say; it is based on the portrait of the writer's mind, not upon a story being unraveled. It fixes impressions and helps us see objects; it does not twaddle through time in the nature of old-fashioned plot narratives. It sponsors the value, for example, of murder mysteries, since that genre features a corpse—a fixed object whose own story is over and done with. Force of impression is what matters in the end, not clarity of statement from the start. Statements belong to a past era when facts and knowledge were thought to have some importance. Alexander Pope and Josiah Reynolds made statements. Henry James and Thomas Eakins look as though they have statements in mind, but they are only pretending. Gertrude Stein and Pablo Picasso do not even bother to dissimilate.

In Mary Doyle Springer's study of James' updated manipulation of the ancient narrative technique of "the apologue character," Springer points out that these archetypal figures are fixed, intense, and—above all—functional.[16] They surround the main figures with their fixed force; they forgo an autonomous identity or stories of their own to tell. Living on the rim of the narrative, their duty is to throw the meaning of the Isabel Archers, the Milly Theales, and the Lambert Strethers into prominence. Such type figures are very much engaged in the narrative action, but only if the traditional obligations of realistic portraiture are not exacted of them. James' Lord Deepmere at the Bellegarde ball, Miss Barrace at Chad Newsome's little soirées, the monkey-countess to whom Beale Farrange introduces

Maisie—all are baroque embellishments, figures in the carpet that exist to lift the patterns of the main character into focus and to give heft to the whole.

Gertrude Stein had her own use for the apologue character in her "autobiographies" and "biographies"; for instance, to help define the type Genius by showing what not being a genius is like. *The Autobiography of Alice B. Toklas* is redolent with the sense of geniuses because we see their "wives" who also come to the party. Fernande, *le douanier Rousseau*, and Alice Derain with her "brutal thumbs" are apologue characters, just as much as is Hélène,the Steins' cook, or the friendly garage mechanics who fix up the auto Gertrude Stein drives away in en route to a glorious rendezvous at the war front. Even Matisse, Picasso, and Apollonaire function to make it clear through the force of their presence who the book's true genius is, which is Gertrude Stein. Of course, even *petits fonctionnaires* sometimes upset the pecking order. Picasso always threatens to take over any scene he shares with Gertrude. Alice B. Toklas (with her flowered hats and needlepoint) sometimes plays the same trick; on occasion Alice reverses the clever reversals which have named her the titular type of the book in order to lead us toward its true subject—Gertrude as Genius. In just such games of hide-and-seek and king of the mountain, we watch Gertrude Stein—like James and like Balzac—make everything (person and type) part of the portrait of the artist's mind that encloses them within the picture's frame.

Verbal portraiture did not stand still during the early years of the 1900s. That ancient literary mode tried to find even better ways to express the intensity of the original sanctuary self and to devise methods by which the averages of the social self stand out against the general scrim of historical events. Portraiture moved forward into modernism by going back, as it were, toward the habitual usages of type. This done, it sprang its surprising force by employing type to new ends.

Literary realism was a bit tame by 1900. It had restricted itself too often to commonsensical views of how things are—defined in terms of recognizable objects and shared signs. Naturalistic fiction whose characterizations were slashed through by expressionist colors and chiaroscuro textures was at least alive to the intensities of inner drives; it knew how to reduce the depiction of human desires to the universals that lurk beneath the particulars. But naturalists were under the double burden of being dispassionately objective and passionately committed to some political, social, or philosophical cause.

In contrast, the Steinian portraiture of the early years of the twentieth century was free of commitment to clarity, depths, particulars, and meaning per se. In the cheerful attention it paid to bright surfaces, universals, and forcefulness, it is perhaps the most truly modern in its approach to image-making of any mode in evidence before 1920. Take "Melanctha," for example.

Making note of the central panel of Stein's 1909 triptych *Three Lives* causes more than a little embarrassment these days. In *The Autobiography of Alice B. Toklas* Alice-Gertrude describes this portrait of a young black woman living and dying in

Baltimore as "the first definite step away from the nineteenth century and into the twentieth century,"[17] yet we have the right to describe the story as racist. "Melanctha" contains passages scarcely less tasteless than those printed on the smarmiest pages of V. G. Rocine's *Heads, Faces, Types, Races.*

Rocine: The jaws are heavy, the quality is coarse, hair is bushy, coarse and dark, skin is brownish or copper-colored, the body is hairy. . . . It is a coarse, primitive type. . . . He is, as a rule, cunning, cautious, cruel, treacherous and savage in instinct.[18]

Stein: Rose Johnson was a real black, tall, well built, sullen, stupid, childlike, good looking negress. She laughed when she was happy and grumbled and was sullen with everything that troubled.

Melanctha Herbert was a graceful, pale yellow, intelligent attractive negress. She had not been raised like Rose by white folks but then she had been half made with real white blood.[19]

Of course, it is possible to stand back, take a second closer look, and come around to an aesthetic appreciation of the portrait of types contained in "Melanctha." We can, for instance, trace the influence of the interest in non-European cultures currently exerting their appeal over artists, psychologists, and anthropologists in the early 1900s. The sour taste that lingers as the result of Stein's staying so close to racist classifications of blacks as "bad," "mindless," or "happy-go-lucky" might further be sweetened by literary considerations that reject sociopolitical questions in favor of the analysis of formalistic effects. Even so, Stein's portraiture-via-type is vulnerable to attack for that reason as well. Damned if her portraits of cultural types are directly offensive to our social sensibilities; damned if she commits the sin of asocial formalism. In her twofold culpability, Stein provides the perfect example of the fraught situation that confronts any writer who dares to work with the art of the types—that unceasingly abuseful mode of literary expression.

There is more here, however, than meets the mind's eye at first or second glance; more than is taken in by the mind of the socially sensitive critic who sees "Melanctha" solely in terms of its implicit sexism (females live only by emotion) and its explicit racism (blacks exist as sensual animals, while a modicum of white blood transforms the animal into a person, intelligent and worthy of attention). More than is accepted by the mind of the formalist critic who narrows his interest to the story's linguistic and aesthetic impact. Let us rather follow Stein's own mind's eye. Seen from where she stands, literary portraits of types force the writer to deal with "real things" that are ultimately, profoundly, humanistic.

Stein's methods are primarily those of the artist of forms, not of ideologies. On this score alone, she can be taken to task for her social lapses. Feminists see her edging away from a politically courageous stance in regard to her own lesbianism. Others recognize how dangerously obtuse Stein was about the anti-Semitism let loose upon the European scene in the 1930s. As long as lesbianism and anti-Semitism are the main issues under consideration, Stein deserves to be called to account. Many insist that just such issues must always, and solely, be what matters. Others suggest that there is also art and that art has a way of existing beyond politics without denying its human responsibilities.

Even when judged on the terms of pure aestheticism, Stein can be criticized. Often her theories get in the way of her practices, and her ideas can obscure her performance. In such instances her eye is either too clever by half or too astigmatic to perform its assigned task. But let us take Stein on her own terms and see what is there to say about her use of types. I shall argue that when Stein is working well she gives us images that are the *essence* of the object represented, although not its public *meaning*. Identity arrived at by traditional means is beside the point since representation as such is what our little dog understands; it is what we are said to be by others; it is not what we really are as an entity.

> I am I not any longer when I see.
> This sentence is at the bottom of all creative activity.
> It is just the exact opposite of I am I because my little
> dog knows me.[20]

"Melanctha" was published in 1909, though it had been in the works since 1905. The story gives us the portrait of a young woman who wanders the byways of Baltimore in an attempt to discover a life of peace and adventure.[21] Melanctha does not realize that the life she leads is the result of the bottom-nature she already possesses and that it controls her to the exclusion of any chance to change her fate. The fact that she wanders, is "bad," is tormented, is sensual, emotional, and self-destructive, is not the consequence of her classification as a member of the black race; nor is it the condition of her white blood that she is burdened by intelligence and complexity. The components in her nature that are "primal" and those that are "civilized" are no more determined by the biology of her racial mix than are the type traits which rule other Stein portraits. Such components are, however, simultaneously universal and culturally induced.

Stein believed that the black race is part of a very ancient, narrow culture; as a result its people suffer, she said, from "nothingness."[22] Blacks are static and fixed; they are complete as Madame Merle is complete. For such people "there it remains. Consequently nothing does or can happen." When working in the same vein with her type portrait of Pablo Picasso or the typology by which she notes "the making of Americans," Stein reveals she is similarly "racist" in her views of Spaniards and Americans: both are breeds determined by like cultures and temperaments that assure they will be "abstract and cruel."

In the 1934 essay "The Gradual Making of *The Making of Americans*," Stein gives the history of her discovery of the type and (through that discovery) her realization that it would relieve her from the superficiality of identity. She explains how classification as a conceptual practice provides a set of handy verbal signs that point toward the universals and particulars from which each person's bottom-nature derives its characteristic mix.[23]

While in college studying psychology:
. . . one of the things I did was testing reactions of the average college student in a state of normal activity. . . . I was supposed to be interested in their reactions but soon I found I was not but instead that I was enormously interested in the types of their characters that is what I even then thought of as the bottom nature of them.

After medical school:
I then began again to think about the bottom nature in people . . . how everybody said the same thing over and over again with infinite variations. Then I became very interested in resemblances, in resemblances and slight differences between people. I began to make charts of all the people I had ever known or seen, or met and remembered. . . . I was sure that in a kind of way the enigma of the universe could in this way be solved. That after all description is explanation.

By 1912 (upon her first trip to Spain) and 1914 (when *Tender Buttons* was published) Stein gave herself over to resolving the fact that "She always was, she always is, tormented by the problem of the external and the internal."[24] Stein began to write the verbal studies she called still lifes. Through them "she began to describe the inside as seen from the outside." She used a trick as old as physiognomical readings and as up-to-date as writing that consists of "exact reproduction of either an outer or an inner reality."

"Melanctha" of 1905 is a progress report on Stein's career as an experimentalist in types. It marks the point Stein had reached midway between the years at Radcliffe and Johns Hopkins and the time of her visit to Spain and the publication of *Tender Buttons*. It is, first, a portrait of the two types defined by the statistical mean which Melanctha represents to those who only see her "socially." To Rose, to Jeff, and to her father, her identity is that of a hybrid racial and cultural type that mixes the primitive and sexual (black) with the civilized and thinking (white). But "Melanctha" is, second, an "entity" portrait of a woman who experiences an inward conflict between primalism (impulse) and civilization (control). Melanctha's defeat comes when others refuse to see her at the deeper psychological level of the type of the original, and continue to see her at the social level of the type of the average.[25]

"Portraits and Repetitions"—written in 1930—is one of Stein's most useful discussions about what she wanted to achieve through experimentations in literary forms.[26] A lover of questions despite the fact that she sensed there are no answers, she decided that simply to pose the question "How do you like what you have" takes you straight to the making of a portrait. What you "have" is entity. Writing down how you feel about this unshakable possession is how portraits are made. Portraits consist of shared, eternal elements: *the type that I am* which is also what a Melanctha has, or a Picasso possesses. Still, portraits move and flow since the essence contained within the type is by no means frozen: " . . . my ultimate business as an artist is not with where the car goes as it goes but with the movement inside that is the essence of its going." At the same time, what moves is self-contained. "The composition we live in changes but essentially what happens does not change. We inside us do not change but our emphasis and the moment in which we live changes."

We live in terms of, and in indifference to, the flowing waters of the stream to which Heraclitus and William James (Stein's former professor) liken our consciousness: "existing as a human being, that is being listening and hearing is never repetition . . . because naturally each time the emphasis is different. . . . nothing changes from generation to generation except the composition in which we live."[27]

In 1932 and 1933 Gertrude Stein amplified theory and practice with *Four in America*. "Henry James" is the subject she takes as her demonstration of what the modern portrait has come to. It is appropriate as a choice, since her act of portraiture suggests what Henry James attempted in *The Portrait of a Lady* in 1881.

"Entity" is "I see"—the self in the act of viewing an object.[28] In James' novel Isabel Archer's "identity" fills the novel. The narrator is the "entity" commenting on what Isabel looks like. Isabel is initially presented through a series of types, then as a portrait; but she attains her status as portrait by means of descriptive devices common to other novels of the 1880s. In contrast, it is the Jamesian narrator who furnishes the new kind of portrait-image that Stein defined as modern fifty years later. *The Portrait of a Lady* is literary portraiture in the accepted work-aday sense of the term insofar as Isabel-as-lady is looked at. In Stein's view, the central and significant portrait is that of Henry James doing the looking.

Of course, James lets Isabel usurp his role as portrait whenever she sits still long enough *to see for herself*—as during the scene of the long night of her soul (or, to use Stein's term, the long night of her entity). At that moment Isabel does what the writers of novels have traditionally done: she renders a "portrait" of Gilbert Osmond. Significantly, she does this by imaging Osmond's mind. Even more significantly, Isabel images his mind by defining it as the process that has turned her into a looked-at object—a portrait for his collection. Once she is able to look at him looking at her, she snatches back her mind from his grasp for her own uses and becomes herself.

An entire spectrum of literary history unfolds over the course of *The Portrait of a Lady*. As readers, we experience the stages of the evolution by which modern novelistic portraiture came into being: first Isabel enters the narrative as a type who is an idea—an identity—in the minds of those who look at her; next she becomes a portrait when, prompted by the narrator, she is seen by us as a real thing—an entity; finally she herself becomes the creator of portraits—her own narrator—once she begins to think about others' thoughts.

Whenever Isabel Archer does the looking and thinking, she too has to resist falling into the habit of classifying others in terms of the ideas she holds about them. Otherwise she will once again repeat the process which ruled the first half of *The Portrait of a Lady*, where the chapters are filled with types being scanned by a type. Even in the second half those moments are rare when the characters are capable of viewing one another as a portrait. Usually that function is filled by James, the Steinian portrait who observes accurately by the fact of his mind's capacity to enfold all he sees. It is at these choice moments that we receive the great recognition scenes: Isabel vis-à-vis Osmond's mind as the home of darkness; Madame Merle gazing at Osmond and back to the cracked cup he and she have made of her soul/entity; Ralph and Isabel examining together what love is. When these scenes come, in the stillness that marks profound acts of looking, we are in the presence of the presences which constitute "the new novel." "I wonder now if it is necessary to stand still to live if it is not necessary to stand still to live, and if it is if that is not perhaps to be a new way to write a novel."[29]

The difficulty most readers have with the final pages of *The Portrait of a Lady* lies with the question whether Isabel reverts from the power of self-creation to being the merest kind of object. Upon entering the straight and narrow path back to Rome, does she regress from the point of portraiture she has struggled to attain? Certainly Isabel is a type to Caspar Goodwood when he clasps her to his breast, and she will surely slide back to the type of the mean if she returns to Osmond and once more becomes his identification of her, or if she capitulates to being society's stupid notion of what a "lady" represents. But I am one of those who believe that Isabel not only wins her way through to becoming a portrait by chapter 42, but that she is a portrait, triumphantly, to the end of the novel. I may be your victim, she has said to Osmond before departing for England and Ralph's deathbed, but I am not your dupe. Entities do not necessarily have power over their destinies, but once a woman knows how she looks to herself—all the way down past classifiable surfaces to the entity of her bottom-nature—a woman will no longer be duped into becoming another's idea.

The conclusion of James' *The Portrait of a Lady* has force, not clarity. In the 1880s James accomplished through the traditional narrative what Gertrude Stein attempted in the 1930s, sans the novel form. Stein freed herself from the narrative form when she recognized that the plot's events distract readers from the strong presences of authors, even authors like James who pretend they are not the portrait that is the point of the whole affair. Hardly as self-deprecatory as James, Stein makes it known that it is her portrait that counts, even when she is ostensibly writing a portrait of someone else.

"Henry James" is about Gertrude Stein.[30] It is a representation of her entity on the lookout to detect the true entity of the object *Henry James*. That object is what catches her attention at the moment, and her attention is the writing's subject. It is her success as a looker—as an alert mind—which brings success to this portrayal of James as a successful personage. Successful things are seen, she says, because seen rightly. Unsuccessful things are ineptly seen as types-as-identity by observers who are themselves restricted to being types-as-identity.

Now, everyone has entity. There is no reason why the basic meaning of this person or that cannot be caught out by relentlessly programming their classifications in the manner of such adroit physiognomists as Linnaeus and Buffon. But entity discovered accidentally lends "lively" writing and the sense of having "begun." This in contrast to the smooth fatality of identity that is forever relegated to the category of "going to be written."

Of course, even "lively writing" requires intention and preparation. It is not the same as being overly prepared or as being too complete. Lively writing is essence played out "little by little"; what has been from the beginning is finally *come to*. James did this sort of writing well. It is why he is the kind of general Stein's portrait discovers him to be: the writer who does not need to win battles or wars because instead he wins the army. "If Henry James was a general who perhaps would win an army to win a battle he might not know the difference but if he could he would and if he would he might win an army to win not a war but a battle not a battle but an army."

Unsuccessful generals "do not." They master no battles or wars. Generals who are successful in the traditional sense "do." They emerge from the fray with the battle and the war in hand. In contrast, great generals like James (and Stein, since the genius she describes here, as elsewhere, is a portrait of herself looking at herself) "do do do."

Given Stein's terms, I propose that at the conclusion of her campaign in Europe Isabel Archer is a great general. She is undefeated by the loss of her war with Osmond because her bottom-nature is always in preparation, always "just written." Isabel's return to Rome at the narrative's close guarantees her a life of "to have begun." In contrast, Madame Merle and Gilbert Osmond (and Goodwood and Warburton; and Ralph too, because he dies) are "complete" and "prepared." Thus they remain types and identities, excellent in the functional force they contribute to the story. But Isabel is a portrait at last, and one that will last. She (like her portraitist Henry James) has *more to do*. She is thereby the "ado" James recognized was the challenge his novel had to meet or be defeated by.

Stein underscores the essential condition of life which James' art presented as a major theme and a primary technique as early as the 1880s: the condition of human instability. Stein realizes how Henri Matisse approaches the problem. He uses color symmetries as though they were the harmonies of music, but understands that harmony added to what is irretrievably unharmonious results in certain distortions. No wonder the figures of women presented in Matisse's paintings or in Stein's writings gain stability at the cost of being cast askew.

Theoretically, the abstraction and harmonies available to the high period of Greek culture or to eighteenth-century neoclassicism matched exterior to interior truths. The conscious strain required to make this fit work was disguised as grace and serenity. Belief in stability led to a conspiracy of acceptance by the makers and viewers of classical art. Coordinations between aesthetic forms and cultural norms assured the look of consistency, tranquillity, and beauty. In contrast, the symmetries and categories available either to archaic art or to Stein and her friends forgo the pretense that any entity lives at peace within the world. The result is the candid note of cruelty Stein attributes to processes that introduce abstraction and harmony to the figure.

The look of ugliness, distortion, unease—held within the formalistic harmonies of written or painted text—is what makes the work a masterpiece, an object executed by a genius.[31] Yet notice that the objects Stein, Matisse, and Picasso represented are often domestic ones. Stein frequently declared she preferred comfort, the middle way, and the making of pleasant arrangements in a difficult world. Changes brought restlessness, confusion, and unhappiness, especially once peace was declared after the end of a long and disharmonious war.[32] Stein liked things that last and are not lost. Friendships are easily lost, as *The Autobiography of Alice B. Toklas* endlessly recounts. But words last. So do the lives of saints and Negroes, sharing as they do qualities of elemental abstraction, creativity, and force. Words, saints, and Negroes figure among the static, ordinary, wonderful things. They are fragments of eternal nothingness, set apart from the rush of modern life that is filled with novelty and everythingness.

In many ways, then, the ordinariness of "everybody" interested Stein more than the specialness of a "somebody." The everyday life of inside/outside often seemed more important to her than exceptional events and the quirks of the subconscious. But when Stein gave herself as a genius to making portraits of types, she was not content for long with the type of the mean. It is the genius in us all, our type of the original, that constitutes our uniqueness; it also constitutes our one true community. Stein's portraits are at their sharpest and most successful ("and anything seen is successful," she writes in "Henry James") when they represent the values of the steadying primary life of bottom-being shared in common by the diverse members of humankind.

I have synthesized mightily concerning the processes by which Steinian types mount the spires of form to arrive at the kind of portrait Gertrude Stein believed matched the truths of both the universals of human nature and the vagaries of human culture. The minute particulars of the development of Stein's writing from her Radcliffe College themes to the 1930s when her theory and practice of portraiture were laid before the public are intricate ones. They cannot be done full justice in such a cursory summing up. However, the following résumé of her early career places her within a progression that is able to move forward because it swerves back to the origins of portraiture—back to Corinthea's room and the silhouette of frustrated desire that young woman traced upon the wall.

The tradition of the literary portrait Stein, along with everyone else, inherited was the late-nineteenth-century version of the Aristotelian type of the mean. According to this tradition the soul is made apparent through the body's appearance. Individuals are merged with generalized, evaluative modes of behavior. The image *equals* the person, and the person is equated with the usual, the mimetic, and the informational.

Stein had an even older tradition of portraiture to work with, but one which

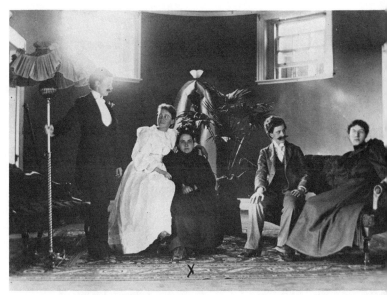

7.4. Gertrude Stein and friends, Radcliffe College (c.1895–1897).

BEINECKE RARE BOOK AND MANUSCRIPT LIBRARY, YALE

could just as easily have been handed her by Charles Sanders Peirce. This is the portrait as indexical, a reality statement that points to a specific object, an image that *replaces* the person. It is an iconic sign that refers to *the idea* of character, not to appearance alone; it provides *evidence*, not conclusions; it *resembles* and does not imitate.

As Wendy Steiner lavishly argues throughout her book-length study of Steinian portraiture, Stein played with both the indexical-symbolic (which is what literature usually does) and the indexical-iconic (the mode picked up by most painters).[33] Always Stein stayed with the representation of surfaces. Whether she tried her hand at "still lifes" or "portraits," the thing and the person are present to be looked at, thought about, interpreted, and enjoyed.

Throughout the period 1905–1911, Stein experimented with scientific classification, the manipulation of the ordering of events, the repetition and rearrangement of sentences, and the presentation of the ruling passions through synecdoche and other devices of literary generalization. Those were the years when her goal was "collective being." Thereafter, Stein tended toward visual orientation; she merged verbal and painterly methods in order to arrive at "pure individuals." In either instance—and this is my main point—Gertrude Stein put her money on *the type of the original*.

Figure 7.4 is a snapshot of Gertrude Stein at Radcliffe with her fellow students. While four are busily being types of the average (grouped as pairs into little dramas by the looks they pass or—as in the case of the woman to the right—stave off), Gertrude neither looks at nor is looked at by the others. She defends her bottom-nature by staring out at the only viewer who matters—the rest of the world.

7.5. Alvin Langdon Coburn,
"Gertrude Stein" (1913).

Figure 7.5 is Alvin Langdon Coburn's portrait-photograph of 1913, as evocative of the type of the universal/unique as the photographs he prepared for the New York edition of Henry James' novels and tales.[34] Stein sits in the same pose as in the Radcliffe photo: hands clasped, face an oval. But the group photograph is a set of four Aristotelian portraits intruded upon by a single iconic sign. Coburn's portrait is indexical-iconic all the way. In my interpretation of this pose (subjective in that it is I who look at the one who looks at me), Stein leans forward, the "general" who wins armies, the mind that furnishes the subject of our attention, the force that takes command, the type that indicates the innate genius that is the subject of "everybody's autobiography."

8

Studio Studies and Still Lifes

Gertrude Stein lived between pictures and words. Consideration of her writing inevitably glances toward the paintings which hung upon the walls of 27 rue de Fleurus. There remains, however, the lingering unease we feel as the result of having been chided by generations of critics about our right to move freely between the sister arts. Is "portrait" a term that coexists on an interchangeable basis between literature and the visual arts? Can "biographies" come out of the studio as well as the study? Gertrude Käsebier, who had become a leading art photographer by 1900, thought so. "From the first days of dawning individuality, I have longed unceasingly to make pictures of people, not maps of faces, but pictures of real men and women as they know themselves, to make likenesses that are biographies, to bring out in each photograph the essential personality that is variously called temperament, soul, humanity."[1]

Others are unable to agree with Käsebier that "biographies" appear as readily upon photographic paper or easel canvas as upon a writing pad.[2] At least they do not want to think that these two acts of making (visual and verbal) exist along the same plane.

The bothersome matter of the sister arts is just one of the problems surrounding any consideration of late-nineteenth-century portraiture. To pursue the subject of portraits all the way would oblige us to discuss at some length the status of photographic portrait studies vis-à-vis the easel portrait or the *au plein* sketch, and then get down to an analysis of how each differs from the various modes of literary physiognomy. Written into the same ideal agenda: the status of racial and ethnic portrait-images and the question whether anyone at the turn of the century ac-

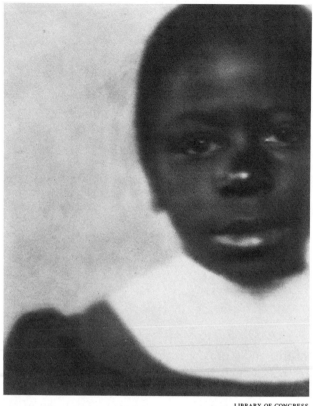

8.1. F. Holland Day, "Black
Girl with White Collar"
(1905).

LIBRARY OF CONGRESS

corded them the interest given to "Portrait of an American Girl." We should wonder what the social aesthetics of that period had to say about F. Holland Day's
photograph of a young black woman (figure 8.1) or Käsebier's study of "Zit-Kala-
Za" (figure 8.2).[3] As for the general label "American," we could ask whether
paintings by Sargent and Whistler are really that in the strict sense or whether
they are not more closely linked to European modes of portraiture.

There are other matters we could take up. Among them, the position of women
painters in the general art scene and whether anything special transpires in paintings of women by women.[4] When concerning ourselves about events that shaped
the ways in which portraits of women were made and viewed, we might deliberate
over those distinctions between genres that have helped to determine the history
of the artist's studio.[5]

None of these issues will be discussed here, although each has received some
treatment in chapters 3 and 4 and will be referred to in chapters 9 and 10 as a
matter of course. To pause at this point out of a blinding sense of duty to say all
there is to say on these and related subjects would mean writing still more volumes
than the several "books" already contained within these covers. It is not practicable to make a commitment to keeping complete records, interesting and appro-

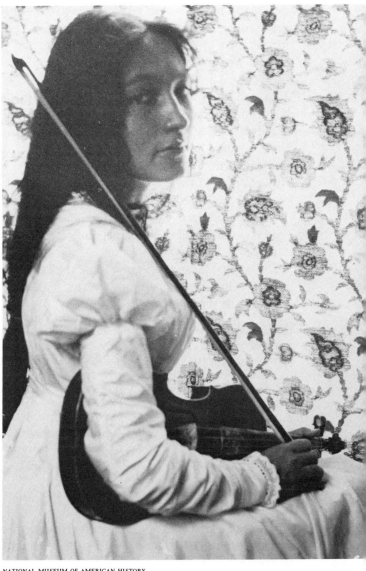

8.2. Gertrude Käsebier, "Zit-Kala-Za" (c.1898).

NATIONAL MUSEUM OF AMERICAN HISTORY

priate as these issues are. Instead my concentration will fall upon two grouped sets of portrait studies. The first represents women sitting in various attitudes of contemplation and/or repose. The second is of women with mirrors. A look at these two groupings invites us to consider several of the matters just mentioned: the sister arts, photography, women painters, "Americanness," and the genres. Mainly, though, this approach points up the kinds of power (social and psychological) imaged by these particular portrait studies. Later chapters present the public means by which female forms were imprinted almost stridently upon the national consciousness, but it would be a mistake to assume that intimate studies of women, surprised as they muse within their own worlds, have no meanings that translate into broader cultural terms. The stillness and privacy inhabited by these women of paint and photography have much to tell us.

We approach paintings of women seated in meditation and relaxation by the route of the still life and the landscape. There is masterful evidence in *The Ambassadors* of 1903 of the ways Henry James negotiated this journey. A brief review of what James accomplishes in this late novel suggests the tack to take for interpreting the paintings which lie just ahead.

By chapter 3 of the sixth book of *The Ambassadors* Lambert Strether has come a long way in his education concerning the nature of types. He has learned that there are more than the two (male and female) acknowledged by Woollett, Massachusetts. But Strether still finds elusive "the idea of the *femme du monde"* as represented by Madame de Vionnet.[6]

The night Marie de Vionnet appears, "dressed for a great occasion," at the dinner given by Chad Newsome, Strether has the occasion he needs to study her "in her habit as she lived."

Her bare shoulders and arms were white and beautiful; the materials of her dress, a mixture, as he supposed, of silk and crape, were of a silvery grey so artfully composed as to give an impression of warm splendour; and round her neck she wore a collar of large old emeralds, the green note of which was more dimly repeated, at other points of her apparel, in embroidery, in enamel, in satin, in substances and textures vaguely rich. Her head, extremely fair and exquisitely festal, was like a happy fancy, a notion of the antique, on an old precious medal, some silver coin of the Renaissance; while her slim lightness and brightness, her gaiety, her expression, her decision, contributed to an effect that might have been felt by a poet as half mythological and half conventional.

This portrait—intensely visual, lavishly verbal, its aspects "half mythological and half convention"—approximates the "various and multifold" nature of the woman herself. Marie de Vionnet has a talent for concealing her entity from sight when it pleases her to do so, then revealing it in tantalizing glimpses, all the while casting doubts as to her final identity. Who she is will be known only when all the types she contains are seen and experienced by the man who looks at her with such speculative ardor. "She had aspects, characters, days, night . . . showed them by a mysterious law of her own. . . . She was an obscure person, a muffled person one day, and a showy person, an uncovered person the next. He thought of Madame de Vionnet to-night as showy and uncovered, though he felt the formula rough, because, thanks to one of the short-cuts of genius, she had taken all his categories by surprise."

Sensitive to a fault concerning the ambiguous, Strether senses that in her present brilliance (little more than one expects from a sleek portrait by Anders Zorn or Giovanni Boldini), this woman might just be all identity and no entity. It is the

Marie de Vionnet whom Strether catches sight of by accident in the following chapter who seems to offer him a clearer revelation of her true being.

Strether is in Notre Dame, seeking refuge from the many things (himself, justice, and injustice) that lie "outside, in the hard light" of the city. At a distance he notices "a fellow visitant." It is a lady sitting in "the shade of one of the chapels." Her posture's "supreme stillness" has a "suggestive effect" upon him. The unknown woman is not prostrate or vulgarly exaggerated in her attitude. "She only sat and gazed before her, as he himself often sat."

As Strether studies the still form in the shadows, he interprets what he sees according to his ingrained method for reading literary texts. "She reminded our friend—since it was the way of nine tenths of his current impressions to act as recalls of things imagined—of some fine firm concentrated heroine of an old story, something he had heard, read, something that, had he had a hand for drama, he might himself have written, renewing her courage, renewing her clearness, in splendidly-protected meditation."

Although Strether sees only the back of the seated woman, "his impression absolutely required that she should be young and interesting"—someone whose tilt of head indicates she possesses "a discernible faith in herself, a kind of implied conviction of consistency, security, impunity."

The Jamesian narrator intrudes at this point to remind us that Lambert Strether is a romantic whose conclusions are frequently off the mark, shaped as they are by what he wants to believe he is seeing. "Strether's reading of such matters was, it must be owned, confused." Admittedly, what he saw was "a good deal to have been denoted by a mere lurking figure."

Once this portrait of a woman seated in meditation stirs into motion, Strether's perceptions are relocated from the general to the particular. His easeful contemplation of the abstract painterly qualities of the scene now have to take account of the woman in the directness of her condition. From one moment to the next, "the person whose attitude before the glimmering altar had so impressed him" is transformed from an abstraction into Marie de Vionnet. Strether has to contend with "the special interest" excited in him by his vision of "his companion's identity." But this shift does not disturb him; rather, it acts to confirm his beliefs. The attitude—the pose of meditation held by the unknown female figure—"fitted admirably" with his conviction that Marie's "connection with Chad" was pure. "It helped him to stick fast at the point he had then reached. . . . Unassailably innocent was a relation that could make one of the parties to it so carry herself."

What Strether does not recognize is that he has simply replaced one idea with another. The first was the patently abstract views about Pure Love he drew from the sight of the unnamed woman in the chapel. The second is a more subtle abstraction, an excited belief about Marie's "innocent" relations with Chad.

Soon after, Strether's interpretation of Marie de Vionnet's bottom-nature undergoes further changes. This time the shock of what he sees is immense. This alteration comes when once again he places her pictorially. As with the scene at Notre Dame, Strether moves through a sequence in which an unknown figure is suddenly recognized for someone he knows; or rather, someone he is in the process of recognizing and knowing.

Strether is in the country. Lounging at the rail of a riverside inn, he gazes out upon the landscape.

> What he saw was exactly the right thing—a boat advancing round the bend and containing a man who held the paddles and a lady, at the stern, with a pink parasol. It was suddenly as if these figures, or something like them, had been wanted in the picture, had been wanted more or less all day, and had now drifted into sight, with the slow current, on purpose to fill up the measure. . . .

> For two very happy persons he found himself straightway taking them—a young man in shirt sleeves, a young woman easy and fair, who had pulled pleasantly up from some other place and, being acquainted with the neighborhood, had known what this particular retreat could offer them. The air quite thickened, at their approach, with further intimations; the intimation that they were expert, familiar, frequent—that this wouldn't at all events be the first time.

These figures are momentarily fixed within a painted landscape. Then they move back into the world, just like the still figure of the silent woman in Notre Dame. Not only does Strether identify these previously abstracted figures, he acts to interpret their meaning. But as long as they exist as pictorial types within a frame, he is able to identify and interpret them in safety as types viewed at an aesthetic, emotional remove. Once the frame is removed, however, and he has names to attach to the figures he sees, the burden of identification and interpretation is harsher, more immediate; greater stakes are involved.

Previously, Strether had accorded Marie de Vionnet the identity of a woman virtuously given to love. Now he recognizes Marie as the focus of Chad Newsome's nonplatonic absorption. The river image of familiar lovers is not overturned; it is confirmed as the reality of the relationship between the man in shirt-sleeves (now known as Chad) and the woman with the pink parasol (now identified as Marie). What is radically altered is that the twofold image and actuality of Marie at Notre Dame (pictorial type of the Innocent and portrait of an innocent lady) has been replaced by the twofold image and actuality of Marie by the riverside (pictorial type of the Mistress and portrait of a compromised woman).

Strether initiates this process of interpretation once he sees an anonymous female form as a still life or as a fixed figure in a landscape. But such figures continually move back *into the world* where Strether stands with his eager interpretive eye.[7] From his first meeting with Marie at Glorianni's party, Strether keeps encountering her as *a figure* posed in generalized attitudes which press abstract ideas upon his imagination. But Marie acts as *a woman* to transform those attitudes into the significance which attaches to special cases. To have seen Marie as she appeared that evening at Chad's dinner in her guise as a showy figure was to take delight in her beauty and her movements. But that kind of image does not aid

Strether in interpreting her hidden nature. Marie as a public *femme du monde* has nowhere the value for the assessment of interiorized entities that the still life or the landscape figure provides upon being pulled back into the motion of the world.

That women in their realness are better "known" through images of meditation and repose flies in the face of the pronouncements made by several authorities in the field of late-nineteenth-century painting. Even more damning is their allegation that what we *can* know of these image-women (since they exist "far removed from the reality of our own experience") may prove of little worth.[8]

Women caught in attitudes of reading, staring into the motes of the middle distance, musing within the silence that encloses their forms, or occupying stilled space are evidence (so the arguments go) of "upper class women hermetically sealed off from the everyday world." Such figures are more to be pitied than to be scorned, perhaps. A male society has placed them in these dreamworlds of "idyllic irresponsibility." History has harmed them and left them "psychically scarred." But pity aside, pictures like these tell us nothing we today need or want to know about the active lives of women in the world.

The primary example cited by the critics of quiet women is the painterly world of Thomas Dewing or the studies done by members of the Boston School. Patricia Jobe Pierce and Patricia Hills are particularly stern about these female images,[9] represented here by Dewing's "The Garland" (figure 8.3).

They are more often than not spiritual, gaunt, austere, cold and removed from reality. They are puritanical, lacking individuality or personality, and one wonders if they are human because they are so dream-like.

The women were transformed into beautiful objects. . . . These women idle away their hours playing cards, playing musical instruments, and reading, or . . . writing letters.

Drained of energy and passion and turned into decorative objects and idols, such women "do nothing." Because of this visible fact, they are women with little of value to offer society or themselves. By implied contrast, only paintings of women in action—placed at the greatest possible remove from the conventions of still lifes and landscape figures—represent *real* women; a woman's only fulfillment comes by doing *real* things through engagement in the world of industry, business, and politics. See a woman posed as reading, thinking, or daydreaming; see a life exposed as indolence, passivity, emptiness, and negation.

I have to disagree with arguments like these. They place *all* the weight of social worth upon the merits of doing—particularly "doing" limited to the kind of sociopolitical and economic bustle presented in the press's coverage of feminist activities. Such views would deny Jane Addams, Frances Willard, and Susan B. Anthony the stillness out of which their thoughts and character took shape. A portrait study of Isabel Archer's passionate meditation beside the dying coals in her room or of Marie de Vionnet's praying in the gloom of the chapel in Notre Dame or of any woman who withdraws to "a room of her own" could thereby be called a study in

8.3. Thomas Wilmer Dewing,
"The Garland" (n.d.).

FREER GALLERY OF ART

nothingness. Under these terms, "the useless life" would have to be the final assessment given to the young woman portrayed in this photograph of 1905 who
lived, literally, within the silence of her senses; for this is Helen Keller (figure
8.4).[10]

Some take formalism in art as a conscienceless denial of social irregularities and
the force of history. Others use it as the evidence they wish to denounce social
flaws. Once images of women are painted to provide wealthy patrons with arrangements in silver and pink, and once these surface-designs are seen as analogues
to the lives of women who have been reduced to the level of decorative possessions
by an elitist society, the way is wide open to read these pictures solely as signs for

8.4. Helen Keller, *McClure's Magazine*, June 1905.

the dehumanizing effects of consumerism and capitalism. In one of her examinations of Thomas Dewing's career, Susan Hobbs quite rightly notes that his "elegant, fine-boned women" suggest "the tensions and ambivalence women experienced in an industrial nation with increasing leisure and rising expectations for their sex."[11] One could launch counter-arguments in favor of the humanistic uses of formal aesthetic surfaces (aware of the fact that humanism itself is susceptible to attack), but even when female images are not wholly swallowed up by compositional demands, we still need to ask whether representations of *doing nothing more than thinking* express only negative truths about these women's lives.

Several factors influence how painters address the subject of pure being. The late nineteenth-century art world furnished various modes for show and tell. Genre painting gave anecdotes of everyday life; didactic murals presented historical events or went all the way toward allegorical emblems. The genre painting, the history-telling mural, or the allegorical format were public art directed at large audiences. Studies of privacy and the interior life were a means for presenting objects some favored as being aristocratically refined and others denounced for being aloofly undemocratic. This was easy enough to do if the stilled object standing at the center of self-isolated circles of form and mood was considered as a thing apart from either the hectic social actuality or the elevated plane of democratic principles.

Works given to privacy and silence do not, however, lie altogether outside the American tradition. They find their place within certain slots in the accepted nineteenth-century canon. For example, there is a steady line to be traced between American paintings of flowers and mountains and portraits of women poised in the midst of meditation and stillness.[12] But traditions of art-content aside, painterly representations of the inner life were influenced by the theories of *how people see* that came into prominence during the final decades of the nineteenth century.

The artificially unified systems of perspective perfected by Italian Renaissance artists resulted in a world that *looked like* the logic of Euclid.[13] Taking command over the flat surfaces all painters are condemned by their medium to manipulate, the men of the Renaissance used their new skills to create an illusional art of three dimensions based on a pretense they were under no obligation to reveal to their viewers. But everyone understood they actually lived in a world where accidental details make mock of Euclid's tidiness or Raphael's designs for "The School of Athens." They too lived in the midst of what William James later called a buzzing, booming chaos. By the 1890s, when James' comments about life's fragmented nature appeared in *The Principles of Psychology*, artists were also beginning to expose the old optical tricks that had been codified to sustain the illusion of man-made unity.

D. S. MacColl's *Nineteenth-Century Art* of 1902 distinguishes between the basic modes of vision in contention at the end of the century.[14] The first MacColl calls "camera vision." This vision is appropriate for a modern age in which the eye denies the public quality of data and prefers the private pleasures of the particular. The camera eye moves on the prowl, in the midst of a world of multiplicity and disunity. By so moving, it constantly alters its relationships to the objects it views. It centers on the middle distance, causing nearer and farther forms to fall out of focus. The result: "an oval with one clear spot, going off into a muzzy penumbra."

Over against "modern" selective camera vision, MacColl sets the traditional eye left over from the Renaissance that places objects into equal focus from its fixed position at the voyeur's keyhole or from the X on the floor where the artist stands before his easel. This eye sees broadly; it likes to account for wholes. But the person—artist or layman—who looks at the new world of the 1900s in old ways is one whom MacColl calls "the misunderstander." Of course, the modern camera eye cannot fend off contradictions entirely, not when the world it perceives has only that "one clear spot," with the rest fading away into "a muzzy penumbra." Still and all, panoramic public vision is no longer feasible. Those who think it is, in their quest for simplicity and unity, possess a picture of the world that is more liable to contradictions than the one perceived by camera vision, which is why Henry Adams was screwing up *his* eye in just the way he did at this time. At least the contemporary eye makes meaning of the moment; at least its seeing is attuned to the *kind* of world there to be seen.

MacColl comes near to defining yet a third kind of vision. The occasion arises when he derides a painting of a chapel interior that contains within the single canvas "all that would be noticed by the architect, by the worshipper, by the dreamer, and by a person looking about the floor for pins." Working under pressure to be completely inclusive, this eye attempts to see broadly *and* narrowly; it crowds in universals *and* particulars; it scoops up the sacred *and* profane; it offers a multiplicity of perceptions through the eye of a solitary viewer. It does this (or tries to) by making use, as it were, of a whole battery of camera lenses: wide-angle, zoom, and microscopic, with motion-picture gear thrown in for good measure.

The public portraiture of Joshua Reynolds typified the old seeing perfected by Brunelleschi and Alberti. Theoretical and mathematical, it relied on a system of logic adopted by rational minds everywhere. There are some resemblances between the Reynolds method and camera vision. Even though the latter was more localized in its range, both indicate how people move around in the world without bumping into one another; both are based on a commonsense view of things shareable with others of common sense. But the world of 1902 is best matched, MacColl suggests, by the eye that dives into realms of deepest privacy. That vision provides brooding glimpses of the outward scene like those gained when one looks out past the veil of one's lashes and the mask of one's thoughts (figure 8.5).

One can depict intensity of contemplation by the use of abstract expressive forms or by representational means that convey "concretion, absorption, concentration, packing into the symbol infinitely more than is present to the eye." [15] Pictures of the inner life are possible in the painterly tradition of scientific naturalism, but they just as freely emerge from that older, idealizing strain, one of whose paths leads toward allegorical heads overdetermined by titles such as "Meditation" and "Dreams." That is, they can appear as naturalistic portraits like George Bellows' "Florence Davey" which contains what Ingvar Bergström calls "disguised symbolism" (figure 8.6), or as conventionalized studies of the kind we have with Frank Benson's "Girl in a Red Shawl" which contains what I shall call "disguised naturalism" (figure 8.7). [16]

Pictures of women seated in a brown study can result from any number of painterly techniques and formalistic traditions. That fact conceded, we still need to ask what rights these quiet images can claim in an American culture which V. G. Rocine defined as the bastion of masculine "zip and pep." It is John Dewey who presents the case for contemplation in a society that aspires to be modern, democratic, activist, and—even when the currents of the times promote little more than public busyness—the source of fine souls.

One is not likely to accuse John Dewey of being a dreamy idealist of the old school. A dutiful son of pragmatism and himself the father of modern educational methods predicated upon the fully experienced life, Dewey bustles through the everyday world setting up practical rules for dealing with contingencies and facts. Dewey is an enthusiast who encounters the world through a series of concrete

8.5. Thomas Wilmer Dewing,
   sketch of woman's head
   (n.d.).

FREER GALLERY OF ART

responses, not through a haze of ideas. He complains about the limits of classicism (it presents an adventure that is completed and stale) and realism (it particularizes the world upon a basis of insufficient perceptions). He likes what is "naturalistic," defining that mode as the life marked by inclusivity of response and by aspiration to the experience of rhythms and wholes.

Now, certain recent observers of the late-nineteenth-century scene argue that the figures we find poised in the stillness of thought and dream are the damaged goods of a paralyzing egotism, the painfully apt representations of a sick society desperate for escape from the unresolvable tensions of modern times.[17] These historians of turn-of-the-century malaise are correct up to a point. But they should be obliged to deal with John Dewey's appraisal of the high worth of thought and dream as he treats them in *Art as Experience*.[18]

Dewey thinks that instability is useful; it provides the conditions "out of which [one] forms purposes." True, loss of stability can lead to a series of personalized, internalized oppositions based on the fear of what life brings. But when he proposes the kind of aesthetic that is possible under conditions of uncertainty, we realize that this practical man is working through a theory of art as experience

8.6. George Bellows, "Florence
Davey" (1914).

which furthers fulfillment, encourages the collective, unified life, and resists maladies of the sick soul.

Dewey favors intense perceptions marked by dramatic interplay; he rejects idle viewings that limit themselves to stereotypes—the figures we get when recognition is arrived at too quickly or when "apathy" and "lassitude" take over. Dewey's emphasis upon intensity precludes giving much credit to "the quality of serenity" or to any diminution of "resistance, tension, and excitement." "Art as experience" cannot put up with "dead spots" of unorganized energy. Experience, not ideals, are what matter because experience contains power—"a power more germinal and more significant than any revealed ideal, since it includes them in its stride, shatters and remakes them."

Dewey wants a vigorous aesthetic that defines artistic energy through its relation to the essential power base of experience. What, then, has he to do with art that centers upon images of contemplation, detachment, reverie, and thought? A great deal, since he reads "seeking and thinking" as part of "the perfecting of the process of perception itself": "Not absence of desire and thought but their thorough incorporation into perceptual experience characterizes esthetic experience, in its distinction from experiences that are especially 'intellectual' and 'practical.' "

Dewey does not consider thought the spoiled brat of idle moments and irresponsible self-indulgence. Thought devoted to desire is of vital importance to the life dedicated to activity. "Since life is activity, there is always desire whenever activity is obstructed. . . . In the kingdom of art as well as of righteousness it is those who hunger and thirst who enter. . . . Nor does the man whose perception is *dominated* by desire or appetite enjoy it for its own sake; his interest in it is because of a particular act to which as a consequence his perception may lead; it is a stimulus, rather than an object in which perception may rest with satisfaction."

Once Dewey assures himself that the juices of desire are part of the stir of interest and activity by which he defines the "good life," he is ready to find value in paintings which stimulate contemplation. By implication, he is able to approve the images of contemplation a painting may take as its representational content.

Our needs are drafts drawn upon the environment, at first blindly, then with conscious interest and attention. To be satisfied, they must intercept energy from surrounding things and absorb what they lay hold of. . . . While instinctive need is impatient and hurries to its discharge . . . impulse that has become conscious of itself tarries to amass, incorporate, and digest congenial objective material.

Contemplation is perception raised to the conscious level. It satisfies a "primitive need" for attachment to objects of desire. It is perception "for its own sake" and leads to "full realization of all the elements of our psychological being." Sensitive as he is to degrees and permutations of the contemplative state, Dewey acknowledges, "It is not practical, *if* by 'practical' is meant an action undertaken for a particular and specialized end outside the perception, or for some external consequence." But Dewey is impatient with the intrusion of questions about mere practicality. He finds "this conception of 'practical' is a limitation of its significance." He is more concerned about the true practicality of those special states in which contemplation can (though not always) encourage interest and energy.

The chief objection to the association usually connected with the term "contemplation" is, of course, its seeming aloofness from passionate emotion. . . . It signifies, in fact, only that different impulses mutually excite and reinforce one another so as to exclude the kind of overt action that leads away from emotionalized perception. Psychologically, deep-seated needs cannot be stirred to find fulfillment in perception without an emotion, and affection that, in the end, constitute the unity of the experience.

In conclusion, the object for our contemplation (a painting) and objects represented in a state of contemplation (the subject matter of a painting or a work of literature) carry great psychological value. To cite the title Dewey gives to the chapter in which he rehearses these matters, such objects are part of "The Human Contribution." The position Dewey takes also clarifies the features of artistic creation which have mistakenly led to the belittlement of Thomas Dewing's art.

The ideas of disinterestedness, detachment and "psychical distance," of which much has been made in recent esthetic theory, are to be understood in the same way as contempla-

8.7. Frank Weston Benson, "Girl in a Red Shawl" (oil on canvas) (1890).

MUSEUM OF FINE ARTS, BOSTON

tion. "Disinterestedness" cannot signify uninterestedness. . . . "Detachment" is a negative name for something extremely positive. There is no severance of self, no holding of it aloof, but fullness of participation.

John Dewey is pungent on the subject of the "unfortunate" usefulness of fantasy and escape. But he believes in the importance of "impractical" desire, even when it seeks its answers in detachment and contemplation. Expressions of desire arise from our experience and lead back toward the fulfillment of purpose; they also (a matter of paramount concern to Dewey) affect good conduct.

Contemplation and repose provide conditions for asserting the reality of our needs. The relaxed mind in contemplation of the universal is momentarily freed from the limiting rigors of will and the unproductive nagging of frustrated desires. Desires spawned by fantasy are continually thwarted in the world of practical attainments which simultaneously encourages fantasies and balks them. Desires born of productive thought, seized by the world of art, embody what is "not elsewhere actualized." To Dewey, "embodiment [is] the best evidence that can be found of the true nature of imagination."

Dewey's "art as experience" mediates between this world (whose sheer actuality inspires the unsatisfied mind to escape into the paralyzing realm of fantasy) and the world of thought (whose very distance from actuality inspires the attempt to achieve one's purpose). Dewey describes the "conflict" that artists and philosophers undergo as they oscillate between the two worlds of vision—the inner and the outer. As a loyal member of the pragmatist camp, Dewey asks that creators of visual and mental images come around to the objective state in order that their "speculations . . . have body, weight, and perspective." But their return to the world of experience does not mean they surrender the vision by which ideas achieve embodiment; not when the embodiment of ideas supplies the means by which one is given the chance to live with vitality in the midst of objective fact.

Chapter 11 of *Art as Experience*, "The Human Contribution," makes a brief for the value of contemplation as a significant form of experience. Chapter 12, "The Challenge to Philosophy," analyzes states of reverie and repose in their relation to the creation of purpose through involvement with acts of art. Purpose, as always, is Dewey's main goal; that and self-control. Purpose and self-control are the means by which the floating properties of reverie are made *to go somewhere*.

Ever the advocate of reality, Dewey prefers an aesthetics which adheres more closely to play theory than to dream theory. He concludes,

Now there is enough conflict between the needs and desires of the self and the conditions of the world to give some point to the escape theory. . . . The issue does not concern this trait, true of all the arts, but has to do with the way in which art performs liberation and release. The matter at stake is whether release comes by way of anodyne or by transfer to a radically different realm of things, or whether it is accomplished by manifesting what actual existence actually becomes when its possibilities are fully expressed.

For Dewey the necessary "manifesting" is accomplished "through an objective material that has to be managed and ordered in accord with its *own* possibilities." Dewey insists that the artist *use* reverie, and use it well, by being certain "his images and emotions are also tied to the object." (In this, Dewey sounds the same note Henry James struck in his famous commentary on the practices of the romancer found in his preface to *The American*.) Reverie fosters ideas that are "floating, not anchored." If allowed to remain aloft of their "own sweet will," they may "be only fanciful and unreal." But "the experience of the 'real '" is possible, even when elements of reverie and dream are included in the creation of art, because reverie and dream "release" a "subconscious fund of meaning" upon the "relaxed" but controlled mind of the artist. Such relaxation *pays* its way toward reality and meaning; it does not hang suspended in the realm of make-believe with nowhere to go.

Dewey takes care to separate the wheat of the human value contained within desires directed toward the purpose of fulfillment from the chaff of the wasteful frustration of desires that obstruct life. The greatest dangers from repose arise when one is trapped within "recurrence, complete uniformity [and] inertia of habit"— that is, within clichés which override "adaptation of the meaning" to the actual world. The greatest benefits of reverie accrue when the imagination controls the manifestations by which the "possibilities" of existence "are fully expressed."

With Dewey's suggestions concerning "art as experience" in hand, we approach the work of a number of American portraitists from a new position. Dewey's business was the delineation of the states of mind by which painters create art, but we can appropriate Dewey's ideas when considering works of art that image women who are themselves in states of contemplation and desire.

We would be as careful as Dewey to make distinctions between wasteful reverie and purposeful repose. Not that this is easy, since the visual evidence is often meager. We can only speculate intelligently concerning whether *this* painting is of a woman productively engaged in thought or whether *that* painting is of a woman idling her futile way toward apathy. But at least we shall not automatically set aside such female images, calling them no more than representations of victims reduced to the level of bought objects or repressed or mindless creatures incapable of passion.

There is yet another element we ought to take into account. It is the remembered past in relation to the immediate moment, and the method for its augmentation comes to us from Gertrude Stein.

Dewey values any kind of contemplation that leads toward experience, purpose, and inner power. He does not dicker over the fine points of which moments of time are best for gaining the benefits of repose. In contrast, Stein separates drifts of thought aimed toward the past from energetic mental activity apparently committed solely to the present. According to the criteria laid down in Stein's essay "Portraits and Repetitions," painters like Frank Benson, William Merritt Chase, Mary Cassatt, Cecilia Beaux, and Thomas Dewing include rather more "suggesting and remembering" in their paintings than Stein had a taste for; which is why her eye went to Matisse and Picasso, painters who were given to "looking and listening."[19]

Stein's aesthetics honor the artistic bent taken by members of her group who placed conscious emphasis upon the creation of "the thing in itself." Stein has her point, just as William Blake did when he chastised art made subservient to the Daughters of Memory. But where we now stand we can turn to portraits imaging women as "suggesting and remembering" that were painted by artists who were "looking and listening."

A book devoted, as this one is, to conventions and types can hardly ignore the essential fact upon which these devices depend: memory and continuity. By shaking ourselves free from Stein's relentless valorization of the present moment we can appreciate paintings whose mental time exists between the now and the then; we can accept figures of the contemplative female that come in forms other than those sanctioned by Steinian aesthetics—as for instance, Daniel Chester French's marble "Memory," which does not contemplate the face reflected in the mirror but whatever lies behind (figure 8.8).[20]

8.8. Daniel Chester French,
"Memory" (1919).

METROPOLITAN MUSEUM OF ART, NEW YORK

M. H. Spielmann's 1898 essay "Coincidences and Resemblances" goes beyond the matter under appraisal: penitent, reflective Magdalenes painted in almost identical poses by several generations of post-Renaissance European artists. Spielmann raises still-vital questions about the place of repetition, quotation, and the plagiarism of forms in the creation of literary and plastic images—semilarcenous acts cheerfully practiced by those criminal types, the modernists, about whom Stein would have much to say.[21]

Originality as opposed to derivativeness; the merits of using conscious resemblances; making it always new or working from a frame of familiar references: these are considerations which art historians, art critics, and artists still confront.

They are clearly matters which apply to the images of women depicted either as thinking their way into a future of new possibilities or as locked into the endless repetitions of reverie. Historians and critics have the means to evaluate the results of artists who bring memories of forms and tropes to their work; they can assess the accomplishments of those who take out on loan the conventions stored in the cultural repertoire. But let us focus upon the women *in* the paintings, limiting ourselves to considerations of what such figures might do with their reveries and their thoughts.

In order to take the fullest, somewhat perverse enjoyment from the interpretive risks that come with speculating about the inner lives of represented images, recall that the aim here is to read possible answers to sharp social questions keyed to a particular time and place (turn-of-the-century America). The irony is that we work with images which resist localization on two counts. These images recreate conventions which have appeared throughout generations and across cultural and national boundaries. These images reflect an interiorized life that exceeds the empirical clues which give us the comfort of hard facts and demonstrable social significance. We are thrown back upon those areas of "appearance" and "being" where physiognomists have plied their often questionable trade and where psychologists and philosophers work their earnest way through the ambiguities of the relationship between the manifest and the latent.

When checking through inventories or *catalogues raisonnés* of turn-of-the-century art or when examining collections of commercial posters, magazine illustrations, sheet-music covers, and the like, one legitimate reaction to the sheer number of examples one finds of women in poses of reading, musing, or simply sitting back in attitudes of relaxation and repose is astonishment. The enormous quantity of these examples (suggesting an industry) inevitably prompts certain questions.

Women who read books can be viewed negatively in at least two ways. First, they shut themselves off from the actual world by entrapping their minds within bookish abstractions and irresponsible fantasies. This was the argument used for generations against the higher education of women. It had a life of its own in America from the time of the seventeenth-century New England settlements through the period when the bluestockings were baited in the early 1800s to the late nineteenth century when renewed anxiety was expressed over the effects of study upon a young woman's reproductive capacities. But the urgency of today's continuing animus against women caught in the act of reading is not based on discredited notions of physiological or neurological damage. Much more directly a social critique, it is similar to the current distaste in some quarters for fictional characters like Isabel Archer, a young woman who is viewed as having ill-prepared herself for "real life" because of the years she spent reading and dreaming in the back room of the Albany house.

In the 1890s and early 1900s there were strong socioeconomic reasons for the ideological position which evaluates the silences characteristic of intellectual ac-

tivities well below the tangible gains of social activism. Women forced by economic necessity to work in factories and sweatshops had no time to read. Parasitic
women of the leisure class did. A woman seen reading became equated with the
belief that she did not have to work. Not having to work was a condition to which
"real women" ought not to aspire. Reading meant having "culture"; it meant not
being a participant in the stark realities of the workplace or the worthy arenas of
political achievement; it meant being disqualified as a functioning member of those
social classes which replaced leisure with the moral merit or the economic necessity of activity.

Equating acts of reading and meditating with questionable social behavior cannot be done with impunity, not before several questions are thought through with
care. Is reading unsupportable because it separates women who "have" from those
who "have not" in terms of what all women ought to possess—the leisure to read?
Or is the point that all women are better off, even under improved economic conditions, when they are not reading but doing?

Take two paintings, "The House Maid," an oil by William McGregor Paxton
painted in 1910, and "The Lure of Books," the cover Coles Phillips prepared in 1911
for the June 8 issue of *Life* (figures 8.9 and 8.10). The subject of the first is identified in the title as a servant; the second may be the woman of the house, but her
hours are as regulated by the routine of dusting and cleaning as those of the paid
housemaid. Both, however, are shown here as pausing in their labors to take up a
book. Have these women momentarily gained the victory all women have the right
to—to stop to read and to contemplate—or do they demonstrate one of the subtle
forms by which females are enslaved to the bourgeois, essentially masculine notion
that women's desires are best kept under control within the walls of the home and
the covers of a book, rather than being released as action in the world of public
affairs?

Take the book out of the woman's hand and beyond her gaze. Show her with it
on her lap while her attention wanders (figure 8.11) and her "social condition"
becomes even more ambiguous. She is no longer in contact with the printed text,
which might possibly have something of value to convey to her mind. It is difficult
to know precisely where the line cuts between the studies of contemplation and
meditation which John Dewey praised and the portraits of reverie which he argued
were dangerous because they cast the mind afloat in fantasies of escape. Visually,
poses of contemplation and reverie share the same set of externals. It is impossible
to trace with complete confidence where the mind has wandered in this little bronze
by Bessie Vonnoh. Has contemplation ("useful" thought) here slid into that mindless state of inertia to which late-nineteenth-century artists gave titles such as
"Repose," "Contentment," "Idle Hours," or—as in Vonnoh's case—"Daydreams"?
Are such interludes of privileged relaxation to be rejected on psychological grounds
because no useful mental activity takes place, or made the object of a socioeconomic mandate against an aristocracy which claims the right to be thought-less?

George Sheldon's *Recent Ideals in American Art* of 1890 includes two paintings

8.9. William McGregor Paxton, "The House Maid" (1910).

CORCORAN GALLERY OF ART

by Charles S. Pearce. One is titled "Reverie" (figure 8.12); the other is "Resting" (figure 8.13). The former is of a young Frenchwoman pictured at three-quarters-length, seated sideways in a chair, lost in thought. By the fact of her "situation" (the pose equated with her class), she could be identified as one of the idle; at least, she is apparently not one of those who toil. The second painting, Pearce's "Resting," is a vignette of peasant life of the kind popularized by the Barbizon School. The simple details of the young woman's pose do not tell us all we need to know about her inner condition. We cannot be certain whether Pearce launches a critique against the utter exhaustion of a peasant's demeaned state or whether he accepts the situation by treating the scene as a romanticized setting in which working girls respond to the pleasures of the natural world, grateful for snatched moments of rest.[22]

But the same female model appears to have been used by Pearce for both paintings. The clothing worn by the young woman in "Reverie" and the chair in which she sits are characteristic of the rural poor rather than of privileged, upper middle-class homes.[23] If this is the case, one could argue that because the two probably share similar social conditions, value is being given to these privileged moments of reverie and rest. Of course, it might be countered that the very use of the conventional pose of young women seated in thought invalidates them both as authentic representations. We are left with another question: which "fact" takes

8.10. Coles Phillips, "The
Lure of Books," *Life*,
June 8, 1911.

precedence—the social class to which the figure in an artwork belongs or the pose
in which that figure is placed? Does allegiance to the "good" economic theory and
the "right" classes necessitate a repudiation of all poses that qualify the values of
the active life or seem to ignore the hardships of those who toil?

According to this thesis Dorothea Lange's famous photograph of the 1930s "The
Migrant Mother" is the only honest social representation of "repose" we can hope
for. At least Lange's photograph invites ironic interpretation, as does "Tired Out"—
a bronze by John J. Boyle of 1887 (figure 8.14). Boyle depicts a mother who sinks
back exhausted into her chair, her sleeping children's bodies pressed against her
sides. This, like Lange's photograph, might be construed as a "true" work of art

8.11. Bessie Potter Vonnoh,
"Day Dreams" (1903).

because the "reality" of its subject makes it so: the state of motherhood, equated with social oppression and male domination, expressed by a woman who lies back in utter weariness. In contrast, John Singer Sargent's "Repose" supposedly exposes the great gulf between what it means for women from different classes *to sink back* (figure 8.15). Sargent represents a handsomely dressed young woman in essentially the same physical position used by Boyle, but without the weight of children flung across her slanting body. Boyle provides a woman with the right props (children) and the correct title ("Tired Out"). Is Boyle's bronze therefore of greater social value, because of a more worthy subject, than Sargent's painting (formal values of artistic mastery aside) because *the type of woman* Sargent makes his subject does not merit our concern?[24]

When social issues take precedence over all other considerations, and when social evaluations are apportioned according to the presence or absence of certain pictorial conventions, we know in advance what will be made of scenes of women who picnic on the lawn or lean back upon a silken couch (figure 8.16). They represent that group of weary neurotics we find it as easy to scorn as did scores of contemporary interpreters of the late-nineteenth-century American scene. When William Dean Howells satirized the city women who fled to New England summer resorts in order to recuperate from their fretful, empty lives and "the servant problem,"[25] or when activists of the time such as Charlotte Perkins Gilman attacked the parasitic, trapped lives of women, the well-aimed words of these critics exposed the world depicted by Edmund Tarbell's "Across the Room" as a shame to womankind in general because such women appear in a "regulated painting of a regulated life."[26]

Discussions leveled entirely along psychosocial lines of necessity turn matters of artistic technique and aesthetic conventions to small account. Differences in painterly value between John Singer Sargent and Frederick Frieseke disappear.

8.12. Charles Sprague Pearce, "A Reverie" (188–), typo-gravure, from Sheldon, *Recent Ideals of American Art* (1888, 1889, 1890).

8.13. Charles Sprague Pearce, "Resting" (188–), typo-gravure, from Sheldon, *Recent Ideals of American Art* (1888, 1889, 1890).

8.14. John Joseph Boyle, "Tired Out" (1887).

PENNSYLVANIA ACADEMY OF THE FINE ARTS

Evaluated by subject matter alone, nothing separates the brilliance of Edouard Manet's famed "Olympia" from Frieseke's more pedestrian "La Chaise Longue," servant woman and all (figure 8.17). That is, unless we claim the right to greater interest in Manet's painting because the indolent, marvelously insolent woman who sprawls in repose across his canvas is a working woman. But if the woman's class status constitutes the whole case for Manet's merit over Frieseke, the social worth of a 1903 studio photograph with its "naturalistic" treatment of a nude at ease must be the finest of the lot (figure 8.18). It is certainly more immediate in its ideological appeal than the paintings by Frieseke, Sargent, and others who used women of the upper classes as their images of repose.

My tone has been somewhat sardonic over these past few pages. It is not because I deny the intrinsic need to pose questions concerning content as well as (probably even more than) matters of technique. I am the last person to consider it of small interest to read paintings and photographs in light of the clues to social and economic structures they offer attentive viewers. Conventions—particularly those which

NATIONAL GALLERY OF ART

8.15. John Singer Sargent, "Repose" (1911).

METROPOLITAN MUSEUM OF ART, NEW YORK

8.16. Edmund Tarbell, "Across the Room" (c.1899).

HIRSHHORN MUSEUM AND SCULPTURE GARDEN

8.17. Frederick Frieseke, "La
     Chaise Longue" (1919).

8.18. C. H. Anderson, San
      Francisco, "Admiration"
      (1903).

LIBRARY OF CONGRESS

give solace to the status quo and imply the retrograde imagination—must continually be put to the test. But I shall not back off from my belief that it was ill-considered at the time and that it still is to assume that the use of conventions which portray women in outward attitudes reflective of inward stillness are gross evidence of the moral turpitude of an entire culture.

Paintings whose subjects break away from the world of everlasting *doing*, and manage it by the adroit use of conventional poses for *just being*, merit our consideration. When men at the turn of the century suggested to their womenfolk that they ought not to bother their pretty little heads and that they should go in and lie down and take a nice nap, we instantly deplore the pernicious mind-set which equates being female with being mindless to the point of a permanent state of stupor. A variation on this point is advanced, however, in *American Imagination and Symbolist Painting* by Charles Eldredge. In the chapter "American Visions and the American Dream" Eldredge argues that paintings of women asleep were the means by which alienated artists expressed their dissatisfaction with American culture. Well and good. We all have dissatisfactions with American culture we want to voice. But the implication, here as in the rest of Eldredge's comments, is that a significant body of American artists at the turn of the century could only be angry in weak and questionable ways. Reading Eldredge's book you feel sorry for the poor bastards whose sensitive souls had to settle for small effects in a raring, tearing masculine society of business and profits. The particular examples of fantasy paintings highlighted by Eldredge probably merit no more respect than John Dewey would have given them. What is unfortunate about this well-documented, richly illustrated, and absorbing book is that it leaves one with the notion that the artists who portrayed female sleepers and dreamers were themselves "womanishly" trying to flee an impossible American life; further, that the poses they painted represent timorous escapes of the kind condoned by all vigorous males who urged naps upon their little women in order to shield them from society and the intellectual life.[27]

As chapter 5 suggested, women who play have a right to exist in the overall sociopolitical scheme. So do women who think and dream and rest. Strong images of women are not necessarily of women engaged in forms of work. Portraits of women who live for the time being within their minds or their unconsciousness may in fact be portraits of women doing useful work. It is private work they do, not public. And payment of some kind has to be paid for the possession of privacy. This is the crucial moment when the type of the original sets itself in stubborn opposition to that type of the average which ultimately exacts its social will and demands the public's attention.

Women with mirrors prompt further questions about solipsism, narcissism, and the attempt to escape the life of the average. There are numerous worst-case versions of this visual motif which shared its popularity at the turn of the century with images of women in moments of reverie. The mirror motif is insistently in evidence in photographs of chorus girls who preen in their dressing rooms under the voyeuristic eye of viewers positioned as stage-door Johnnies, or in those pictures of pretty women whose private charms are projected through clever reflections.

Take a dip into the file boxes housed at the Prints and Photographs Division of the Library of Congress. "Idle Moments" is one of a series produced by M. B. Parkinson in 1896 (figure 8.19). A reclining woman is discreetly covered by classical drapery, but the mirror into which she looks permits a straight journey for the eye into her cleavage. In 1900 William Rau composed a photographic sequence of back-stage scenes of the kind Degas had recently painted with greater asperity and aesthetic detachment. "After the Opera" shows a dancer gazing into her dressing-table mirror. The mirror in "The Bath" coyly reflects the same young woman half-submerged in a tub. "The Mash-Note" poses the dancer and her friend before an-other mirror. "Premier Seconde" shows our girls again; one of them looks into the mirror as she adjusts her stockings. "The New Slippers" is another variation of the pose by means of which shapely legs are repeated by the mirror's reflection. "A Good Story" puts Rau's heroine back in the tub and her friend in a rocker at her side, their charms doubled by the ever-watchful mirror. Many of these scenes con-tain other photographs, other mirrors, and other art forms of the naked body in settings packed with image cannibalism (figure 8.20).

In 1902 William Rau created another series, but the photographs are now more than sentimentally realistic vignettes of backstage life. The chorus-girl models are surrealistically enclosed in worlds of self-admiration. In "Behind the Scenes" the young woman looks into a mirror (which displays her breasts with uncommon clarity); a "friend" adjusts the dancing slippers of the one who turns toward the mirror, but she looks straight ahead, cutting off contact between themselves. "Fin-ishing Touches" repeats the same odd, isolating act. "Reflections" and "Admira-tion" center upon a chorine who gazes raptly into a mirror, with a second mirror that reflects her from the side, while "The Platonic Kiss" takes the narcissistic impulse all the way (figure 8.21).

Rau's 1902 photographs were doubtless taken with commercialized prurience in mind, but the source of their intensity is not that of breasts, legs, backs, faces, and heads cunningly multiplied through a series of visual tricks. Intensity derives from the extreme self-absorption of young women who are relentlessly looked at by the photo's viewers while caught out in obsessive rituals of looking at themselves.

Mirrors are part of the working equipment of dancers and actresses. Appearance is all-important in a profession which requires a woman constantly to appraise her face and body and enhance her surfaces by the cosmetic arts. And always, outside the dressing room door, an audience waits, wanting to see "all." Mirrors with their doubling, revealing properties provide studies in sexual titillation. Even in the sen-timentalized scenes of 1900, privacy is invaded. Peeped-at flesh is the product Wil-liam Rau learned how to peddle with skill.

But the soft pornography of the theater world is by no means the only form taken by the self-mirrored life at the turn of the century. Comic photographs served to mock, not to stimulate, desire. Figure 8.22, a photo vignette of 1909, places the type of the plain woman, no longer young, before her vanity mirror; the futility of the arts she practices is derided in the verses accompanying the images.[28] Adver-tisements promoted the joys of a dainty complexion, as when Pears' Soap used pretty girls in petticoats posed before their mirrors. Howard Chandler Christy, Charles

8.19. M. B. Parkinson, New York,
"Idle Moments" (1896).

8.20. William H. Rau, "Chicken Salad
and Oysters After the Matinee"
(1900).

8.21. William H. Rau, "The Platonic
Kiss" (1902).

Dana Gibson, and James Montgomery Flagg all drew girls given to gazing at "You,"
with Flagg's drawing but one example (figure 8.23).

The stakes held by images converging at points of self-identity and self-desire
increase when we turn to the representations of women with mirrors painted by
well-known artists. Mary Cassatt, James McNeill Whistler, William Merritt Chase,
J. Alden Weir, Thomas Dewing, and Robert Reid are among the many who placed
women in intimate relation to mirror reflections. The conventions they use are
little different from those absorbed by Parkinson or Rau's girlie shots. Women either
look directly into the reflecting surfaces, or they turn to offer their sides or their
backs to the greedy mirrors. The technical skills of these painters are usually of a
high level; the composition of their paintings is often brilliant. But once we pull
past the sensual pleasures of their painted surfaces, unsettling questions arise—and
they are not unlike those elicited by the studies of women who read, meditate, or
relax.

What are these women looking at, and why are we insistently asked to look into
a space whose primary point of reference is the mirror? Have they learned to their

8.22 *(left)*. "Little Daubs of
Powder. . ." (1909).

8.23 *(above)*. James Montgomery Flagg, "You," *Life,*
October 25, 1906.

advantage to see themselves down to the depths of their bottom-nature, or are they
limited by the mirrors to what others see? As always, it is difficult to read beneath
surfaces in the world of paint. We think we are better off when we encounter
narrative mirror scenes. In James' *The Wings of the Dove,* Wharton's *The House
of Mirth,* and Dreiser's *Sister Carrie,* respectively, Kate Croy, Lily Bart, and Carrie
Meeber look intently into mirrors in a desperate attempt to evaluate themselves.[29]
Kate finds she is magnificent and thoroughly salable. Lily is horrified to detect the
lines of age which diminish her value on the marriage market. Carrie sees herself
in light of her own dreams as marvelously pretty, and in terms of the social norms
concerning sexual proprieties as a woman who is "bad." But painted mirror scenes
have no words to provide a guiding context; they push would-be interpreters to
the wall. We ask, but cannot know for certain, how far toward death by drowning
in the seas of narcissism these mirrored images go.

Mary Cassatt's women seem safe enough in their world of mirrors. They do not
implant platonic kisses upon their reflected images, nor do they discover the insta-

8.24. Mary Cassatt, "Mother
and Child" (c.1905).

NATIONAL GALLERY OF ART

bility of their monetary value in a society that prefers its women to be pretty, and salable, and apparently chaste. Cassatt's mirrors are where they are because they are useful to women who bathe their children or themselves or who are having a dress fitted or need to tidy up their hair before going out to the opera. The plot thickens somewhat in Cassatt's "Mother and Child" of 1905 (figure 8.24). The mother assists her little daughter in learning how to look at herself in a hand mirror, while the whole scene is composed by the wall mirror that reflects and insulates them both. It seems very much a culturally instructed "woman's world" they occupy.

The mirrors included within the studies of the upper middle class by J. Alden Weir seem at first to serve two relatively tame purposes: they are part of the over-all decorative pattern the artist has chosen to spread across his canvases, and they are a natural part of the decor of the lives of the women reflected here (figure 8.25). His painting serves, however, to heighten the sense of self-conscious posing which accompanies mirror-viewing.

The mirrors of Thomas Dewing offer yet another occasion for the working out of "the intellectual sensuousness" which Charles Caffin claimed for Dewing's paintings (figure 8.26). Dewing's reflecting surfaces never merely suggest the essentially practical utensils of Cassatt's orderly world, nor are they merely decorative count-

METROPOLITAN MUSEUM OF ART, NEW YORK

8.25. J. Alden Weir, "The Green Bodice" (1898).

8.26. Thomas Wilmer Dewing,
"The Mirror" (n.d.).

ers arranged adroitly across the face of the painted surface. They are much more. Mirrors are minds in Dewing's world. They invite us to consider the possibility that the women who gaze into them are looking at their own thoughts, not at their countenances. Even in those arrangements in which the women are shown positioned to the side or the front of mirrors into which they do not bother to look, their minds seem to be acting in ways analogous to the silver-backed glass on the wall. If this is so, then Dewing's mind pictures nicely match the definition given years before by Johann Casper Lavater when discussing the perfect portrait: "a countenance in a mirror, to which we would speak, that speaks to us, that contemplates more than it is contemplated."[30]

There are well-known paintings from all periods in the history of Western art in which women do not look directly at the mirroring agents that reflect their forms. In such instances it is we as viewers who are given privileged access to the self's multiplicity. Picasso's "Girl Before a Mirror" of 1932 is such a work. As our eyes prowl around the female figure, we are engaged in a visual pun. The physical form *before* the mirror is comprised of *four* sides which we are expected to take in perceptually as a whole. It would be cheating for artists like Picasso to eclipse all but one view; they crave to expose them all. But neither Picasso nor his friend Gertrude Stein was entirely successful at achieving a totality of pictorial revelation. *Gertrude Stein in Pieces* is the title Richard Bridgman gave his critical biography of Stein's career. Bridgman's notion is that Stein was a woman whose consciousness consisted of fragments caused by fears too deep to mend. He argues that she wrote in the attempt to reassemble the shards, but that she was never entirely able to put the pieces back together through the sentences she wrote and the portraits she imaged.

Stein-as-envisioned-by-Bridgman is like the mirror portraits of Dewing and those we find in the novels of James and Wharton. But even though we are not provided with the whole view of the examined object, we are shown artists attempting to represent women who attempt to see more of themselves than is *commonly* on view. The artists labor to produce private, not public, portraits. One of the devices they incorporate into these scenes is the mirror, but the woman's image is not "l'image du miroir"; it is "l'image speculaire." These two kinds of mirror images appear in Merleau-Ponty's *The Primacy of Perception* as part of his general discussion of the "major fact that concerns the development of consciousness of one's own body"—"the acquisition of a representation or a visual image of the body itself, in particular, by means of the mirror."[31] But as the translators of the Merleau-Ponty text point out, the author insists on the difference between "the physical, episodic event of a body reflection in a mirror" ("l'image du miroir") and "the image of himself [or herself] that is gradually acquired by the child from experience of his [or her] own reflection in the mirror" ("l'image speculaire").

It is *the speculative image* which the best of the portraitists (verbal or visual) attempt as they work through the personal toward the universal. Sometimes they use mirrors, sometimes the open book, sometimes the far-off and inward gaze as the means of and sign for their explorations. The images captured by the most audacious of these artists represent the entity which lies beyond both particulars and averages in that special space where the real thing of the exterior life meets and merges with inner being.

BETWEEN THE PRIVATE
AND THE PUBLIC

9

Images of the Ideal

Walk slowly around Gallery 219 of the Metropolitan Museum of Art in New York City and experience a review of pre–Civil War paintings of portraits and types. You will also encounter yet another kind of visual representation: the female form as allegory—that is, the type of the Type, herewith capitalized to mark its function as the conveyer of extraterrestrial signification, in distinction to "type," which denotes categories of the mundane.

Four works in particular indicate the boundaries within which many American painters practiced in the first half of the nineteenth century. The earliest painting is dated around 1826, the latest is an oil of 1842, but there is no forthright evolution of a single convention for image-making in Gallery 219. What is on view are the several choices that artists during a single period in American artistic life had for presenting female forms.

The first of the group is "Mrs. Deliverance Mapes Waldo," an oil on wood painted by Samuel L. Waldo about 1826 to commemorate the occasion of his second marriage (figure 9.1). The portrait is unfinished in the details of background and costume, but the head facing frontally is finely complete. Mrs. Waldo's hair is dark and covered with a wisp of a white cap. Her eyes glance up slightly and to the side. Her features are strong, intelligent, and carefully detailed. The painting appears an exact study of Deliverance Mapes Waldo; it is a type of the original possessed by a particular young woman as interpreted by her new husband.

The last of the four to be painted is titled "Euphemia White Van Rensselaer" (figure 9.2). An oil on canvas, it is the work of George P. A. Healy in 1842 and said to be typical of the many portraits which brought Healy his reputation as the

9.1. Samuel L. Waldo, "Mrs. Samuel L. Waldo (Deliverance Mapes)" (c.1826).

painter of socially prominent, fashionable women. The painting is of the Beautiful Charmer, the American Heiress as the type of the average—here represented by Euphemia White Van Rensselaer, later Mrs. John Church Cruger.

Nearby is a painting by Samuel F. B. Morse, dated 1835–37 (figure 9.3). It is of Morse's daughter, but the title indicates the double function he gave to her image: "The Muse—Susan Walker Morse." The female figure is seated, aureoled by the "attributes" traditionally associated with the spirit of inspiration. The painting is also the likeness of an actual woman dressed and coiffed in the mode of the American 1830s. This is a particular young woman, identified as the portraitist's daughter; but she also serves as an allegorical representation of the abstract qualities that male artists have long associated with female images of the Muse. This painting functions as Type at the same time it represents an individual.

9.2. George P. A. Healy, "Mrs. John Church Cruger (Euphemia Van Rensselaer)" (1842).

METROPOLITAN MUSEUM OF ART, NEW YORK

9.3. Samuel F. B. Morse, "The Muse—Susan Walker Morse" (1835–1837).

METROPOLITAN MUSEUM OF ART, NEW YORK

The fourth painting drops all interest in offering an identification of an individual woman. An oil on canvas of 1838 by Cephas Giovanni Thompson, it is titled "Spring" (figure 9.4). The image is of a pretty young female who wears a large straw hat and a white dress. The figure—placed in a tableau pose—holds a few flowers in the bud and leans lightly upon a fringed shawl embroidered with cherries that is cast over a ledge in the foreground. Behind the figure there is a vaguely defined outdoors scene dominated by a large classical urn. The image is of no person. It offers an evocative appeal to the pleasant emotions prompted by such familiar signs as fruit, flowers, foliage, an urn, and a sweet young female face and form. This is the Type, pure and simple, without the double burden exacted by Samuel F. B. Morse who attempted to give viewers both the portrait of his daughter and an allegory of that force for inspiration which stirs all artists.

Commonly presented in the plastic arts through paintings or sculpture and on occasion attempted through the written word, the primary function of the Type is the making of statements about abstract qualities. Such qualities do not spring directly from the material, historical, and personal realities we call "the actual world." We are more likely to experience joy than Joy or to know what it is to be hungry rather than to encounter Famine. This is not to say that there are hard and fast distinctions to be made between portraits, types, and the Type. The description I just gave of the four paintings placed on view in one gallery of the Metropolitan Museum indicates that variations on the female form can be subtle. The visual differences between the portrait of "Mrs. Deliverance Mapes Waldo" and the allegory by Cephas Giovanni Thompson are clear enough. The conceptual space between "The Muse—Susan Walker Morse" and "Spring" is less so. There is an even tighter fit between the Morse portrait/allegory and Healy's "Euphemia White Van Rensselaer."

The artist's willingness to mix painterly styles and conceptual modes evidenced by the four paintings from the studios of pre–Civil War America continues into the present, as we well know. But what concerns us here is the strength of popular taste for universals tumbled in with delight over particulars that continued throughout the final decades of the nineteenth century and the years of America's involvement in the First World War. Four classifications were in simultaneous use: *portraits*—clearly labeled by title and technique as representations of individual women; *studies*—where the identity of the model was subsumed under a generalized title ("Study in Pink and Silver" or "The Reverie") while retaining the whiff of bottom-nature that signals a woman's thingness; *types*—images such as the New England Woman, the Outdoors Pal, or the Beautiful Charmer; *Type*—pictorial signs for Civilization, Inspiration, or Motherhood.

If one longs to follow chronological trails, it is possible to press toward certain conclusions. The neoclassicism that penetrated mid-century, upper middle-class homes and public places in the form of white marble images of the ideal was furthered by the sculptors Thomas Crawford, Hiram Powers, and Robert Rogers.[1] There is also the arresting fact that energetic female carvers like Harriet Hosmer, Ed-

9.4. Cephas Giovanni Thompson, "Spring" (1838).

METROPOLITAN MUSEUM OF ART, NEW YORK

monia Lewis, Anne Whitney, and Vinnie Ream Hoxie, joined by Louisa Lander, Emma Stebbins, Margaret Foley, and Florence Freeman, formed the group of professionals Henry James called "the white, marmorean flock."[2] But neoclassical sculpture as the generation prior to the Civil War knew it was definitely on the slack by the end of the century. New attention was given to painting, specifically to canvases whose subjects are reflective of the comparable interest growing in literary circles for realistic portraits of women. Even with a rise in experimentation in impressionistic tonal arrangements of female face and form, the dominant taste was for images which represented recognizable human types existing in recognizable cultural and social contexts.

The ideal figure was *not* the characteristic mode of the late nineteenth century, whether in literature or art. To think that it was is to make a common mistake.

Yet figures of the ideal held on with a tenacity that belies the ethereality of their subject matter. They were not displaced from favor that easily just because the tastes of the reading and viewing public had been affected by the attention given to the everyday and to the social particular.

The Type had a life of its own in the years between the Philadelphia Centennial and the close of the first World War, and we shall see how the allegorical image functioned on its own self-contained terms as Type in many places and for several purposes, but most frequently images of abstract qualities existed alongside other female images which—when viewed as part of a spectrum—subtilize the progress from portrait to type to Type. Such nuances make our movement through these decades an excursion analogous to walking around the gallery of the Metropolitan Museum where the four paintings by Waldo, Healy, Morse, and Thompson hang. For convenience's sake, let us then think of the years between 1876 and 1918 as a kind of Gallery 219.

The careers of certain artists contain examples of female forms that range from highly particularized acts of social identification to conceptualized statements that suggest almost totally abstracted qualities, moods, or concepts.

Figure 9.5 is an undated portrait of Evangeline Wilbour Blashfield painted by her husband Edwin Howland Blashfield. Figure 9.6 is a detail from the 1920 Blashfield mural in the Parish House of the Church of the Ascension in New York City that pictures "The Angel with the Flaming Sword." Blashfield's reputation as a muralist was extensive by the turn of the century. He received many commissions to paint allegorical scenes for universities, courthouses, the expensive new churches which were part of the program of physical expansionism furthered by wealthy congregations, and the new state capitol buildings that appeared at the heart of every central city able to raise the funds.[3] Blashfield was a better painter of the Type than of portraits, but in his generation it was not unusual that he tried his hand at both.

Figure 9.7 is an engraving of "The Angel of Sleep" which Thomas Dewing painted in the 1885. As chapter 8 proposes, Dewing's portraits and studies suggest that he generally stayed within the bounds of an identifiable social world in which women exist together with chairs, tables, mirrors, and books, even when the edges of that world blur toward the evocative rather than remain a hard-edged object that invites sociological inventories. Dewing's more ethereal painting mode is exemplified by "Summer" (figure 9.8). This mood scene of four dancing figures and a harpist engaged in a somewhat unlikely pavanne in a forest glade makes use of this world's women as suggestive types, not as the Type of Summer. "The Angel of Sleep" is, therefore, somewhat of an anomaly in Dewing's career. But the allegorical mode existed, as much for him as for other artists, as yet one more possible method ready for use.[4]

Thomas Eakins' "Arcadian" photographs of naked boys playing panpipes and classically draped young girls are a legitimate part of the life of the imagination

9.5. Edwin Howland Blashfield, "Portrait of Evangeline Wilbour Blashfield" (n.d.), from *The Works of Edwin H. Blashfield* (1937).

experienced by this dedicated Realist. John Singer Sargent is correctly placed among the Realists by the nature of many of his portraits of society women, but he also plunged with enthusiasm into the design of murals for the Boston Public Library and the Museum of Fine Arts in Boston on such subjects as "The Unveiling of Truth" and the Goddess of Darkness. We need, therefore, to take account of Dewing's "Angel," Eakins' Arcadian scenes, and Sargent's allegories. These images are as much a part of their careers as Frances Benjamin Johnston's "'Spring" is of hers (figure 9.9). We look with interest at Johnston's naturalistic photographs of women factory workers, young girls practicing on the parallel bars of a Washington, D.C., high school gym, or students of the Tuskegee Institute (see Introduction, figure 23). We should also consider Johnston's involvement as an image maker during a May fete in 1906 when a masque in celebration of "Friendship" called upon her talents as an allegorist.

Elie Nadelman provides another telling sequence of images, and in what quick succession they come. "Classical Figure" of 1909–1910 (figure 9.10) is followed by "Figure Study" in 1913 (figure 9.11) and by "Hostess" of 1918–19 (figure 9.12).

One could pursue in detail the evolutionary process of artistic forms through which Nadelman moved in a ten-year period: from a marble bust of the neoclassical persuasion through a highly stylized figure which draws upon habits of Art Nouveau ornamentation and on to the satiric abstraction of the Type of the Hostess. Watch Nadelman clamber out of one mid-nineteenth-century figurative tradi-

PARISH HOUSE OF THE CHURCH OF THE ASCENSION, NEW YORK

9.6. Edwin Howland Blash-
field, detail of "The An-
gel With the Flaming
Sword" (1920).

tion and into a variation on another turn-of-the-century style before arriving at a personal style marked as "modern" by its irony and wit. The first two pieces are abstract statements about sculptured forms which accept both the forms and the kinds of women they depict. The third is a statement about aesthetic form which adds a jab about women whose social roles consume them so totally they cease

9.7. Thomas Wilmer Dewing,
   "The Angel of Sleep"
   (n.d.), engraving by Robert Hoskin, from Koehler,
   American Art (1886).

9.8. Thomas Wilmer Dewing,
   "Summer" (1890).

9.9. Frances Benjamin Johnston, "Spring," from
masque of "Friendship"
(1906).

LIBRARY OF CONGRESS

being even the average type of the hostess and become merely an allegorical function.

Even when we put to the side an extended analysis of Nadelman's career evidenced by these three works, we come away with the correct observation that
between 1909 and 1919 one active imagination was busy working through the aesthetic permutations of types and the Type.

Abbott Handerson Thayer's career yields a series of images that graphically indicate the complex web of his experimentations with the forms of the portrait, the
type, and the Type. Figure 9.13 is "Portrait of Miss Bessie Stillman," painted in
1883. It uses a number of the prevailing conventions for presenting the likeness of
a young lady who comes for a sitting into the artist's studio: the figure in a chair
set sideways to the front of the canvas; the head turned toward the viewer; the
hands clasped in the lap; the white dress; the obligatory expression of sweet attentiveness. There is even the addition to this contemporary setting of the faint image
of a tall lily to the left of the canvas that stirs echoes of pictures of virgins poised
at the moment of an Italianate Annunciation. Nothwithstanding the borrowings
from past paintings of maidens in white, we have the right to say, Here is an

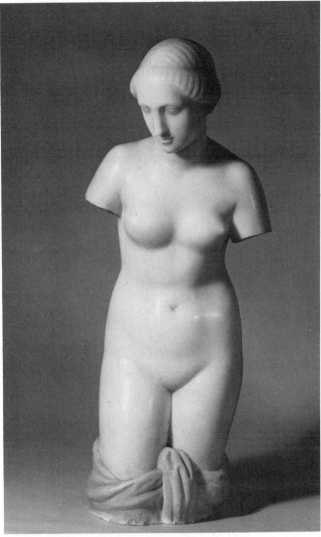

9.10. Elie Nadelman, "Classical
Figure" (c.1901–1910).

HIRSHHORN MUSEUM AND SCULPTURE GARDEN

identifiable likeness of the young woman who is Bessie Stillman—a form we could use to identify the original if we ever encountered her by the light of common day.

Figure 9.14 is Thayer's "Girl Arranging Her Hair," a study painted during 1918–19. This is one of many paintings Thayer did of Alma Wollerman, the woman with the haunting face who married his son Gerald in 1911.[5] The Alma personality which shines through Thayer's renditions of her face cannot be repressed. Here its distinctive qualities are subordinated to an aesthetic evocation of that special, sensual, private moment experienced by women in the act of arranging their hair. It is a psychological portrait of a mood. It is also an exercise in art historical memory:

9.11. Elie Nadelman, "Figure Study" (1913).

HIRSHHORN MUSEUM AND SCULPTURE GARDEN

the classical drapery, the angle of hand and arm that calls upon images taken from Greek sculpture, Italian Renaissance goddesses, Pre-Raphaelite poses, and Degas' women surprised at their toilette. But whatever else this picture is, "Girl Arranging Her Hair" signifies a woman with an identity grounded in a history that is her own.

In contrast to the two previous examples, figure 9.15 is Thayer's conscious effort to paint an ideal Type—"A Winged Figure" of 1911. The beckoning gesture of the hands, the haloing arch of wings and laurel leaves, the folds of drapery, the light pressure of the figure's foot upon a space that is closer to heaven than to earth: all

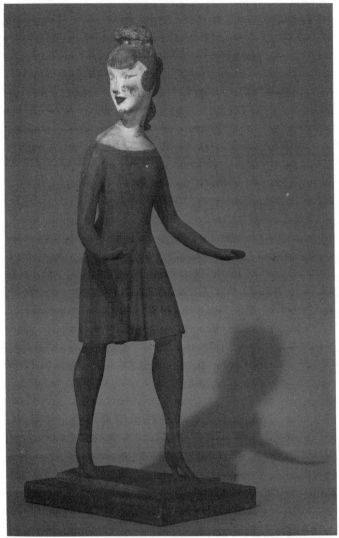

9.12. Elie Nadelman, ''Hostess''
(c.1918–1919).

HIRSHHORN MUSEUM AND SCULPTURE GARDEN

fit the conventions Thayer extracted from Greek sculpture, Fra Angelico wall panels, and Victorian angel images. The face within the halo is modeled directly upon the countenance of Thayer's daughter Gladys, but the paraphernalia used to signify angelic natures tend to overwhelm the somewhat pelutant expression of her face. Gladys' identity is not entirely lost, but in ascendance is the Type of the Angel as Thayer often depicted it—stern, self-absorbed, almost menacing.

Then we come to figure 9.16, an oil on canvas upon which Thayer was working around 1889. This is the image that best suggests the way in which images (verbal and visual) can slide between categories while intimating them all. The pose is of

9.13. Abbott Handerson
Thayer, "Portrait of a
Lady: Miss Bessie Stillman"
(1883).

CHAUNCEY STILLMAN COLLECTION

a young woman in white, seated slightly at an angle, intent of expression, very much a presence, with the face we recognize as that of one of Thayer's favorite models, the Irish servant Bessie Price. The force of the young woman's personality lies strongly across the surface of the canvas. Given these visual terms, what Thayer presents is not a portrait, perhaps, but it is surely a study of a particular young woman as much of this world as is Alma Wollerman musing through the down-drift of her dark hair. But to the right of the canvas (however unfinished in its execution) there is the telltale outline of a great feathered wing. Now we know what we have. It is what the title confirms it is: "Sketch for an Angel." This single painting is like a Gallery 219: it contains portrait, study of a type, and an intended allegorical image, all in one

There is a story by Henry James, written in 1875, "Madame de Mauves." Across its verbal canvas appears the slipping, sliding image of a female form which is sometimes a portrait, sometimes a study of a type, and sometimes (most disturbingly) the Type. If we are able to look at Abbott Thayer's "Sketch of an Angel" with impunity, we are not that safe when gazing at the image of Euphemia de Mauves. Indeed, the havoc done to the men within the story by this woman's presence is

9.14. Abbott Handerson Thayer, "Girl Arranging Her Hair" (1918–1919).

NATIONAL MUSEUM OF AMERICAN ART

great. One is dead from a self-inflicted gunshot; the other is moribund in the region of his heart. The tale's tension comes from the questions it raises about the nature of Madame de Mauves. The men are unable to decide whether she is one kind of abstract personification or another, or is a very human woman. Perhaps they turn to stone precisely because they do decide that she is the Type, yet are incapable of the strain of looking upon her inhuman form; perhaps they are done in by desire for a strong-willed woman they prefer not to identity in her own terms. Whichever, James suggests the dangers of living with and for a person who oscillates between being the type of the American Girl married to a foreigner she no longer respects and the Type of the Ideal; that is, the dangers of living at the behest of a female whose wings now you see and now you do not.

"Daisy Miller" of 1878 is the obvious piece of in-training work which developed into James' masterpiece of 1881, *The Portrait of a Lady;* but "Madame de Mauves" of 1875 is an essential preparation for that novel. Euphemia has married into an artistocratic French family. She is looked at and pondered over by Longmore, the

9.15. Abbott Handerson
Thayer, "A Winged Figure"
(1911).

FREER GALLERY OF ART

young American who tries (like Ralph Touchett, Caspar Goodwood, and Edward
Rosier) to decipher whether the demeanor of this quiet young woman is the result
of her having married badly—of having misjudged the man to whom she gave
herself because of her American innocence and idealism.

Longmore receives information about Madame de Mauves from an old school
friend of hers—a crisper, more detached version of Madame de Vionnet's erstwhile
classmate Maria Gostrey. Longmore listens to what he is told, then takes under
study those details of Euphemia's behavior and appearance that are supposed to
tell him why she looks as she does. But Euphemia is difficult to interpret. Defined
largely by negations and paradoxes,[6] she appears as fixed in her being as the type
of the blank-browed Greek statue.

As Longmore's initial curiosity turns into admiration and admiration grows into
fervid love-longing, Euphemia's image becomes "brighter" to him. Although she
remains a rigid "type" in her husband's eyes, she is transformed into that "ideal"
which Longmore and all poets of female virtue adore. Oddly enough, Longmore
finds he is just as much at a distance from her now as when she seemed merely
the type of the American Girl in Europe. His own role as spectator has not altered.[7]
Nor is Euphemia less the "statue" once he has moved her toward the "idea." What
has changed is the *quality* of the atmosphere which now surrounds her. It is not,

FOGG MUSEUM OF ART, HARVARD

9.16. Abbott Handerson Thayer, "Sketch for an Angel" (c.1889).

however, a secular atmosphere that charms in the way that Whistlerian twilights do. It is the atmosphere of magic that connotes the power of a sacred presence.

A type of this thing or that thing is an object one can afford to be curious about, but according to fairy tale and legend an ideal, a Type, is what the male protagonist desires and but often fears to possess. Fear is exactly what Euphemia's husband learns to feel about her once he begins, like Longmore, to view her as an object of power. Originally Longmore's curiosity had been stirred by the question of whether she was unhappy at the hands of her husband's indifference. What is now at stake is the nature of the sway she holds over them both.

Longmore learns an answer to this question. As the type of the suffering wife and the betrayed American innocent, Euphemia is interesting but essentially weak, in the same way Daisy Miller is weak as long as she is considered a type to be scorned or pitied. But Euphemia as the ideal Type "kills" her husband and causes Longmore to flee once more to the other, safer side of the riverbank. Feeling fear, Longmore decides it is better to worship an ideal statue at the remove of memory; up close, its presence exerts too strong a pull away from the solaces of the commonplace.

As assiduously as he avoids specifying the nature of the evil in *The Turn of the Screw* (such as saying of Miles that "he stole" or "he said things"), James avoids naming a category for what exactly this Type might be. He will not assign the iconographic meaning of Purity or Innocence to Madame de Mauves, or Vengeance or Moral Rectitude. It is unnecessary for James to do such a thing. He only has to let Longmore and Baron de Mauves do themselves in by means of this impossible act of naming.

Nor is James presenting an allegory in his narrative "Madame de Mauves." It is a realistic tale about the psychological consequences which overwhelm men who respond to a woman as though she were some value or other, abstracted to the highest degree on an allegorical plane. We, however, have the right to see Euphemia as a version of the American Idol which Paul Bourget located in the hieratic image painted by John Singer Sargent (even though we are careful not to let that Type efface for us the portraits of Isabella Stewart Gardner or Euphemia de Mauves contained within those frames).

In "Madame de Mauves"—as in "Daisy Miller," *The Portrait of a Lady, The Ambassadors*, and elsewhere—James studies the psychological effects upon characters who make brave and foolhardy attempts at reading signs. He likes telling stories of people who go wrong because they make grievous miscalculations about what they think they are looking at. He believes that bad interpretations are almost inevitable, whether the female image under the observer's eye is that of an individualized portrait study, or is one social type or another, or—as in the case of Euphemia de Mauves—is a human type taken for an abstract Type. The inability to read signs correctly always brings hurt, but James is good at suggesting that the hurt will be the greater the further the act of identification places the person from her central human self. Hurt is *done to* Isabel Archer, Daisy Miller, Marie de Vionnet, and Milly Theale because they are misread as being types other than, or less than, the real things they actually are. In contrast, Euphemia de Mauves appears to escape from harm because she is converted by male longings into an object which exists beyond the bounds of human vulnerability. Like many American Idols, she becomes the figure with the power to hurt. For if any one characterizing name may be applied to the form of the Ideal, it is that of Will. Will is not itself open to being harmed; it is what does the harming. We shall see how this works on the national scale in chapters 11–13 once we are surrounded, almost suffocated, by the often frightening figures of Columbia, Liberty, and America.

Harmful or not, the Ideal Form has to be interpreted by whoever comes across its path. Poor male mortals, in particular, will most likely be done in by their failure to assign correct meaning to the icon they try to read in order to worship it; but for them to evade asking what the Form represents is to step aside from the particular human need James writes almost obsessively into his narratives: the need to ask the questions out of which our consciousness takes its shape.

In 1895 the wife of James' friend, the highly successful artist Edwin Austin Abbey, asked James to help her prepare the written description of the murals Abbey had completed for the Boston Public Library. Abbey's murals—arranged in panels around the walls of the second-level book-delivery area—represent "The Quest and Achievement of the Holy Grail." The fifth panel shows Sir Galahad in the Castle of the Grail. Passing before the hero-knight is the bearer of the Grail, a damsel with a Golden Bowl, two knights with seven-branched candelabras, and one with the Bleeding Spear.

Henry James is hardly the man one thinks of keeping company with richly medieval and allegorical figures, but ever attentive to requests from friends James presumably supplied the following text to describe the scene.[8]

The duty resting upon him [Galahad] is to ask what these things denote, but, with the presumption of one who supposes himself to have imbibed all knowledge, he forebears, considering he is competent to guess. But he pays for his silence, inasmuch as it forefeits for him the glory of redeeming from this paralysis of centuries the old monarch and his hollow eyed Court, dying and never dead, whom he leaves folded in their dreadful doom.

Years later, as depicted in Abbey's eleventh panel, Galahad returns to the Castle of the Grail, "and this time, grown wise by knowledge and suffering, he asks the Question."

The text James provided for the Abbey murals is unique in his long writing career, but the admonition he places within this legendary context—to ask "the Question"—is a familiar one for him. The introductory paragraph to the Abbey brochure refers—appropriately enough, given the Grail story—to the "transcendent vessel" which is "made manifest" to Galahad the perfect knight. However, nothing is more human than that Galahad be required to offer "an interpretation of what it means," lest he suffer and cause suffering because of a silent, prideful avoidance of asking, What is this I see? This is the same obligation James places upon all his major characters, down to Maggie Verver, the damsel with the Golden Bowl.

We take our leave of Henry James at this point in order to turn to others of his generation who worked more frequently with allegories and ideal forms; but it would be wise of us to realize that "the Question" is the act called for whether the female image consists of the usual Jamesian portrait or type, or whether it is the Type in all its potential for magic force and secular abuse.

Writers like James at work on stories such as "Madame de Mauves," and philosophers and psychologists intent on the need to ask the Question, were not the only ones to express an interest in variations on ideal forms. Traffic in conventional poses representing types of the Type was brisk. Studio photographers, purveyors of inexpensive print reproductions, sheet-music illustrators, and salesmen for cemetery markers joined with serious artists in putting the Ideal to profitable uses. One of the consequences of this busy manhandling of female images was the steady secularization that altered the nature of images once thought sacred.

Later chapters are devoted to an examination of the selling of images; they take as one of their best examples the transformation of the religious iconography of the Easter season into up-to-the-minute sales-window displays. As a taste of what lies ahead, we can riffle through a series of illustrations that indicate how fast and loose certain images of the ideal were treated at the same time they were expected to keep to the underlying significance that guaranteed them the broad recognition and acceptance they enjoyed.

Anything vaguely Greek had ready access to the studios of commercial photographers. The Grecian type (which by tradition was the official Type, since Platonism rubbed off upon all creatures in diaphanous draperies) could just as easily turn up in Gretchen-style braids (figure 9.17). It justified images that were morally uplifting, aesthetically ethereal, and emotionally prurient, all at once. Those are real breasts, after all, but a little bit of allegory goes a long way in making idealized females tell "good" stories. Gertrude Käsebier's art photography (figure 9.18) is more high-minded; it comes with the caption that sets the proper mood—"Divinely isolate in mournful thought."

Granted, the incipient naturalism of the camera keeps the impact of such images on the near side of the Ideal. They fall more appropriately into the classification of images discussed in chapter 8—the evocation of reverie and contemplation expressed by women who are demonstrably human. But precisely because the photographs by Parkinson and Käsebier are not the strongest examples of true Types, they indicate how poses and props could state "Type" concurrent with the photographic medium's insistence upon the look of human types.

A mix of the naturalistic and the ideal is apparent in the 1899 studio photograph captioned "Lillian Lawrence as 'Temperance' " (figure 9.19). The pose and the label prod us to read the image directly as allegory. At the same time, the photographic presence of an identifiable woman, an actress consciously caught in the act of posing as an ideal quality—together with the painted backdrop and the "splash" of confiscated wine reminiscent of cartoons of Carrie Nation—weakens the tenuous hold the allegorical image has on our mundane imaginations. We tend to naturalize and to make worldly the material objects at which we look. Everything in this photograph fights against our entering into an allegorical mood. Still, the familiarity of the pose, reinforced by the authoritative label "Temperance," sustains the social act of recognizing ideal signs, which was as common in 1899 as it was in the days of Cesare Riga's and Charles Le Brun's encyclopedias of the iconic.

John La Farge's drawing "Dawn Comes on the Edge of Night" banishes the dis-

9.17(*left*). M. B. Parkinson, "Daydreams" (1896).

9.18(*above*). (Gertrude Käsebier,
from Tracy, "Shadows of the
Artist's Ideal," *Discussions on
American Art and Artists* (1893).

tractions of the commercial photographer's studio which exist between the naturalistic and the fantastic (figure 9.20). Looking at La Farge's drawing prompts aesthetic considerations such as the strokes which enclose ocean, sky, and figure's
drapery within a single swirl. How to help noticing the extreme tilt of the line by
which La Farge slashes a diagonal design across the sheet of paper or his echoes of
Elihu Vedder's treatment of figure and drapery? The belief that this figure is a
palpable sign for the natural phenomenon we speak of as the "coming" of dawn
plays no part in an appreciation of the drawing as a work of art. Our "atheism"
on this score does not exclude a recognition and acceptance of what La Farge did
beautifully with a conventional image and its ascribed meaning.[9]

Turn-of-the-century Americans continued to have a taste for the Grecian look.
The public could select its favorite female poses from a large and generalized pool

9.19*(left)*. J. E. Purdy, "Lillian Lawrence as 'Temperance' " (1899).

9.20. John La Farge, drawing, "Dawn Comes on the Edge of Night" (n.d.).

of classical images. For example, *the idea* of passage of time through the day or the year inspired a plethora of Auroras, Autumns, and Springs. These pictures were decorative, not admonitory. They contain no sense of the urgency to be great in the time allotted one on earth that is found, for example, at the conclusion of Thoreau's *Walden* or in Emerson's "Days." This mood of moral relaxation provides the pleasures of Louis Rhead's cover designs for *The Century* with their female forms, lightly gowned in Pre-Raphaelite robes, who lie languidly in woodland glades, or of Dewing's "Autumn" of 1883 with lute, panpipes, peacocks, a marble exedra, and Grecian-draped female figures. These illustrations and many others like them were quite predictable and rather lovely.

The Diana figure abounded in the urban reaches of late-nineteenth-century America. The merger of chastity and wildness in the images of the virgin goddess of the hunt held a special appeal. Figure 9.21 is a fine example by Abbott Thayer, whose imagination was untiring in its search for the female ideal which for him,

9.21. Abbott Handerson
Thayer, "Diana" (n.d.).

as for many men of his generation, appeared as one form or another of the Virgin Mother. Frances Benjamin Johnston's Diana (figure 9.22) is less the Virgin than it is the type of the New Woman—a conflation of the twin traditions of the huntress and the Amazon brought down into contemporary life. What is notable is that the Diana pose served both poles of an ideological sweep, and satisfied the needs of both Thayer and Johnston.

Bacchantes were another matter altogether. They were obvious subjects for photographs that featured enticing young women adorned with grapes, posed for the sake of their aesthetic pleasingness or in order to promote the sale of champagne (figure 9.23). They could also suggest a more dangerous explosion of forces by recalling the myth of Pentheus, the unfortunate male who is torn to bits by an insanely furious mob of women. Mary Cassatt's bacchante of 1872 (figure 9.24) is hardly that threatening, but neither is it as safely domesticated as the later studies of mothers for which she won her reputation.[10] Oddly enough, it is a series of slick photographs by the Bain Brothers, commissioned to record a New York society tableau in 1909, that offer the greatest edge of incipient violence. Figure 9.25 is of

9.22. Frances Benjamin Johnston, "Diana," from masque of "Friendship" (1906).

LIBRARY OF CONGRESS

Mrs. James B. Eustis, one of many photographs taken prior to the performance in which the painter Albert Herter (shown in the garb of the male victim with an understandably apprehensive look) meets his fate at the hands of maddened society matrons. The participants in the 1909 tableau are amateurs, but even the poorly lighted photographs of the stage scenes suggest that more than a little wildness was let loose. No doubt about it, the bacchante was one type, together with that of the Diana as Amazon, which veered more toward the forceful type of the New Woman than it regressed toward comfortable exercises in the academic.[11] The only thing that saved Albert Herter from certain multilation was the fact that these bacchantes were only types, not the lethal Type.

The sibyl and the sphinx—female forms weighed down by wisdom which men desire to possess—are images whose origins disappear in time. (Figure 9.26 is one example of the ancient image, a product of William Wetmore Story's Roman studio in 1860–1861.) But rather than emphasizing that forceful version of the contemplative Type which holds answers to the great Question of the ages, mid- and

9.23. Fritz W. Guerin, St. Louis [Bacchante] (1902).

late-nineteenth-century tastes tended toward variations on figures lost in thought which do not know or may not even be in search of knowledge. Figures 9.27 and 9.28 are sisters in innocence, notwithstanding the years of historical experience that open between the sheet-music cover of 1870 and the Christy sketch of 1907. The titles attached to each give away the fact that the special power once attached to sibyline knowledge has been lost. Story's "The Libyan Sibyl" is replaced by "Frou Frou's Dream of Home" and by "A Reverie." We can only hope these are "constructive contemplations" of the kind approved by John Dewey rather than negative escape dreams, for it would be a pity if these young women, types of the average in a state of musing, not only had no answers but were unaware there were questions.

The image of Innocence which asks is the obvious inspiration of the prolific Tonnesen Sisters of Chicago and Benjamin Falk of New York. "Marguerite" by Falk and the untitled pose by the Tonnesens (both taken around 1900) offer "uplift" through the canny use of child models (figures 9.29 and 9.30). These are not sibyls upon whom age and knowledge hang heavily. These are the pure of heart who ask out of innocence to have truth revealed.[12] Falk's visual reference to Goethe's Mar-

9.24. Mary Cassatt, "Bacchante"
(1872).

9.25. George G. Bain, "Mrs. James B.
Eustis as a Bacchante" (1909).

guerite and the Vedder-like veiling traditional to holy women used in the Tonnesen photograph elevate the idea behind the poses (ludicrous as they appear to worldlier eyes) to metaphysical heights. Those really are large questions the child models are represented as seeking answers for; questions of the kind the popular literature of the period was couching in terms of "Quo Vadis" and "Wherefore Art Thou—My Savior and My Truth?" They are not simply "the dream of home" little Frou-Frou wonders about.

When we turn to the next photograph (figure 9.31), it appears to be yet another highly conventionalized studio image conceived along the general lines of cute pensiveness, although it is probably a paying client who sits to the camera rather than a professional. This is indeed a bought photograph. It was taken of my mother at the age of five in 1897. The chin on the hand and the far-off gaze are closer in type to the posture of William Wetmore Story's "Sibyl" than to the clasped hands laid along the side of the cheek favored by the sheet-music illustrator of 1870 or by Christy. The child's eyes look out (not upward as in the Falk and Tonnesen poses) and into the distance at some unseeable thought. It would seem a designated type, and an especially weak one at that, with little to be said in its favor other than what it indicates about small-town photographers and fond mothers who turn a pretty child into a sentimentalized version of a Down-Home Quester.

This is not the case, however; not the case at all. Yes, the occasion for the photograph was the familiar one of the mother who takes her child to the local

9.26. William Wetmore Story, "Libyan Sibyl" (1868), engraving by E. W. Stoddart, from *Great American Sculpture* (1878). (Original in National Museum of American Art.)

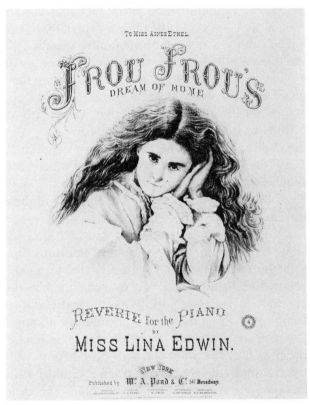

9.27. "Frou Frou's Dream of Home" (1870).

9.28. Howard Chandler Christy,
     "Reverie," from *Our Girls*
     (1907).

studio and of the photographer who arranges the proffered child in one of his meager repertoire of overdetermined poses. What cannot be read by the signs of this pose taken in and of itself is the fact that certain very deep emotions lay behind the mother's visit and the child's expression.

The youngest member of the family, a baby girl, had recently died of diphtheria, the disease which decimated so many families throughout the 1890s. The mother wished to have a lasting record of the daughter who remained (who could tell how long *that* child might be spared), and the child was bereft at the inexplicable loss of her little sister. The mother was greatly concerned over the little girl's reactions to the death of the baby. Too young to understand what had happened, the child internalized her bewilderment and sat for long periods staring into space. The *pose* into which the photographer placed the child that day was the conventional one which covers the spectrum from the One Who Knows to the One Who Asks. By accident, the outlines of the pose of the questioner matched the *emotions* the child was actually feeling.

Axiom: poses need not signify authentic emotions, but this fact does not preclude the possibility that authentic emotions lie behind the poses.

In this rude photograph the designated type—the identity—of one who idly muses about life's little mysteries is overwhelmed by the entity of the child with a great question to ask. Not just, What is death? but also, Why do we suffer it? In its technique and motif, this is an ordinary photograph of a child who has been imposed upon by the period's taste for commercialized sentimentality. But behind the fiction of the photograph lies the history of a particular child's experience of the troubled thoughts about tragic events that take human beings as near to the metaphysics of Type as they ever come. The child, of course, is not the sibyl who

9.29*(right)*. Benjamin Falk,
New York, "Marguerite"
(1894).

9.30. Tonnesen Sisters, Chicago
(1900), for *The Washing-*
ton Times, March 17,
1901).

knows. The chin on the hand and the faraway gaze mark the mortal who *desires to know* the answers only sibyls possess.

The photograph is somewhat silly when one lacks the privileged information about why it was taken; it is somewhat disturbing when one has that information. But the pose does not mock its latent meaning. The choice made by the photographer was conventional rather than inspired; still, that pose—oddly, sadly—has something to do with an authentic moment it can never hope to express. It is this tendency of allegorical poses to have *something to do with* heartfelt human feelings and thoughts which gives them whatever force they possess, even in an age where enfeebled designated types tend to take precedence over the force of real presences.

Images of the ideal are serious by nature. Even images that represent Joy are shaped from an implied pairing with Melancholy, for John Milton was astute when he joined "L'Allegro" with "Il Penseroso." (In the late nineteenth century, especially,

9.31. Irma Purman (1897).

it was easy to cheapen the notion of Joy by projecting it without reference to its opposite in the form of scantily veiled females featured on calendars or magazines of the men's "smoker" variety.) Socrates established the philosophical tradition for images of Truth, Beauty, and Goodness. Greek writers of tragedy, epic, and the odes dealt constantly with Woe, Pride, Fortune, Calumny. The medieval allegorists continued the line with Faith, Sin, Falsehood, and Beatitude. With this kind of pedigree, any image imported from the past that was less than weighty might be construed as pagan, secular, and morally questionable. Covers of irreverent and arty journals like *Mlle. New York* displayed satyrs, Pans, and other mythical rogues in the manner of Aubrey Beardsley's *Yellow Book* drawings (an offensive import from abroad, in the eyes of respectable Americans), but the acceptable Types of the late nineteenth century were resolutely spiritual in resonance and confined themselves to conventions about life and death which allowed no irony.

Unrelenting seriousness was particularly apparent in the monument designs of the period. Families paid for the comfort of the sentiments represented by granite grave markers. Death and the family's need to select an appropriate memorial from samples on view at the local monument maker or taken from design books supplied by traveling salesmen were not the occasion for testing how far the conventions could be stretched. But new conventions for memorial art did appear on the scene. We can even assign a date to one of the most popular. Once "The Rock of Ages" was conceived as an image in 1867 the time came when there would be few cemeteries of any pretension that did not contain its replica.

"The Rock of Ages" entered the pictorial repertory when Johannes Adam Simon Oertel of Westerly, Rhode Island, painted an oil of a young girl in white clinging to a stone cross; below her feet, the figures of other victims of the shipwreck sink beneath the water (figure 9.32). By the 1870s Oertel was writing aggrieved letters concerning the "theft" of his design by commercial poachers of successful images.[13] "The Rock of Ages" gained the reputation of being one of the most popular paintings in America, as famous as "The Spirit of '76"—that other example of an image that captured the public imagination without regard to where, when, or by whose hand it first came into being once it was reproduced a thousandfold through the cheap printing processes currently coming into play.[14] Images like "The Rock of Ages" are not easily protected by legal methods. They go everywhere, without laws or taste to keep them within bounds.

Sheet-music covers for the hymn tune "Rock of Ages" were commonplace. The Von Glahn Memorial (erected sometime shortly after August 1906) in the Greenwood Cemetery of Brooklyn shows what a three-dimensional version of the basic motif looks like (figure 9.33). Meanwhile, in San Francisco a photographer named C. H. Anderson rigged up a variation on the theme in 1900 (figure 9.34). In his preface to *The Turn of the Screw* Henry James notes that two ghosts are better than one. By that reasoning, two young women in white (together with assorted doves, lilies, ferns, and a lyre) give double the value of Oertel's original image, even though the photograph lacks the hand of the drowning man, the ship's spar, and the crashing waves provided by Oertel's painting. In the language of semiotics, "The Rock of Ages" is an overloaded sign, indeed. The same year Anderson posed his picture, L. Frank Baum (better known to us as the originator of Dorothy, the plucky girl from Kansas who takes on tornadoes and the oddities of Oz without the help of any cross to sustain her) suggested a surefire window display for the Easter season in *The Art of Decorating Dry Goods Windows and Interiors*. The photograph accompanying Baum's text shows a child's doll that clings to a cross constructed of snowy white handerkerchiefs.[15]

Neither L. Frank Baum nor C. H. Anderson had a "theory"—semiotic, metaphysical, aesthetic, or otherwise—when they arranged their models and props to image the ideal.[16] Yet the nature of ideal was constantly under discussion by philosophers, instructors in art schools, ministers, politicians, and poets. If idealism in

9.32. Johannes Oertel, "Saved"
or "The Rock of Ages"
(1867).

America was a notion whose time had passed with the waning of the Transcendentalists' fervor at Concord, the closing down of *The Platonist* in 1888, and the final meeting of the American Akademe on June 21, 1892, there were many Americans who were not yet aware of this fact.[17]

This and the following chapter round off the subject of ideal images in late-nineteenth-century America with the consideration of two related pictorial conventions. In each, the use of female forms is paramount and thereby of importance to an understanding of how American women were being perceived. These are the Winged Female and the Blessed Damozel. The former is a Type per se; the latter exists on the threshold between Type and the type. Before examining examples of these ideal forms, we need to touch down upon some of the talk from the turn of the century that debated the status of the ideal. Although the ideal was on a slow slide out of favor, it was still very much an issue in the minds of those concerned with the effect of belief in the absolutes upon aesthetic procedures and social conduct.

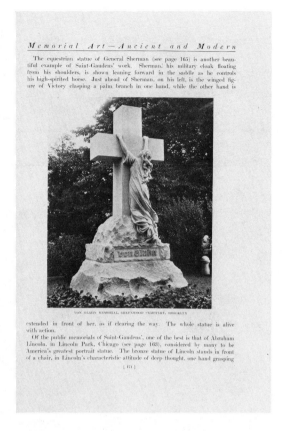

Memorial Art — Ancient and Modern

The equestrian statue of General Sherman (see page 165) is another beautiful example of Saint-Gaudens' work. Sherman, his military cloak floating from his shoulders, is shown leaning forward in the saddle as he controls his high-spirited horse. Just ahead of Sherman, on his left, is the winged figure of Victory clasping a palm branch in one hand, while the other hand is

VON GLAHN MEMORIAL, GREENWOOD CEMETERY, BROOKLYN

extended in front of her, as if clearing the way. The whole statue is alive with action.

Of the public memorials of Saint-Gaudens', one of the best is that of Abraham Lincoln, in Lincoln Park, Chicago (see page 163), considered by many to be America's greatest portrait statue. The bronze statue of Lincoln stands in front of a chair, in Lincoln's characteristic attitude of deep thought, one hand grasping

[171]

9.33. Von Glahn Memorial (c.1906). Greenwood Cemetery, Brooklyn.

Many realized the ideal was a matter of how one sees. The visible nature assumed by the ideal in its tangible forms took center stage whenever theories of the symbolic or the metaphoric came under consideration, or when J. A. Symonds' aesthetic movement of Symbolism was taken into account, or when it was time to discuss the rights and privileges of allegory, or when iconology was set head-to-head against iconography. Mimesis, imitation, and matching were all matters of the eye. And even though image and symbol were matters of the mind, the language used to discuss them (itself a convention) referred to inward "seeing."

Questions were asked. How obliged is one to repeat images from the past, and with what confidence might one create new forms for the ideal? Did the "modern" ideal serve the individual, or did it remain obedient to traditional notions of essence in general? Were such paintings literary in their allusions, or self-contained even though representing objects "out there," or completely abstract? Might the art of the ideal be depicted through a sensuous haze of color, or ought artists to restrict themselves to figures whose outlines were as severely geometrical as the moral concepts they stood for? Were literary renditions of the ideal meant to rely

9.34. C. H. Anderson, San Francisco, "Clinging to the Cross" (c.1903).

LIBRARY OF CONGRESS

on language as such, or might they pass beyond language's logic into areas familiar to the painted image or music?

Questions about methods and means went the rounds of the critics, the theorists, and the practicing artists and writers. Philosophers, theologians, and social critics also entered the debate. There was nothing petty about the nature of the ideal when it came down to the question of ends, and so the questions multiplied. Ought the ideal to reflect truth or beauty? Could the ideal represent both without betraying either? Were images of truth primarily educational, public, and utilitarian, or were they best kept apart for conceptual, inspirational, and private ends? Were beautiful forms mainly aesthetic (meant to induce innocently pleasurable sensations, even if on occasion they threatened to appeal to amoral tastes), or must they be explicitly moral in order to further principles of love and virtue? Was it required that each generation collaboratively create and declare its own social and aesthetic standards, codes, and norms for ideal truth and beauty? Or was the ideal a matter of individual preference, individual since the experience of truth and/or beauty can neither be created nor discovered but can only—simply, amazingly—happen?

In and among the issues under consideration at the century's end, the position of the ideal vis-à-vis permanence is the most important to the main matter of this book. The comfort offered by Eternal Types in a world of uncertain equilibrium was unquestionably the basis for the insistent use of female forms. Change, contingency, and expediency were male. Continuity, stability, and principle were female. Modernism and movement wore a harried masculine face. Classicism and serenity were feminine in feature and arrayed in the white folds of a Grecian garment. Ordinary men might want to go forth to "make" a society founded upon stable rules of thought and conduct, but women (like proper Bostonians and the headgear they inherit) "have" ideals. Men are recognized by the deeds they accomplish. Women are identified by the ideals they represent.

Even the staunchest supporters of stability had to admit that there was precious little about late-nineteenth-century life that satisfied their taste. It was not enough for them to repeat the tiresome fact that permanence was what they desired, although it was not what they had. The visual representations of virtuous order which the American advocates of ideal values commissioned for the walls, corridors, and rotundas of churches, libraries, and courthouses existed in a tarnished world. They had to justify representations of serene forms in the midst of the raucous "rotary system" of modern times.[18] Self-consciousness about the current state of affairs in the United States—the awareness that caused the desire for permanence in the first place—instilled the need to argue for the presence of stone images of Charity and Knowledge or elaborate murals centered by Justice and Bounty.

True, some Americans tried to go home again into the timeless realms where absolute principles supposedly once existed in happy contiguity with great men and women (whether in Greece, Arthur's Britain, or the Italy of Michelangelo, Vittoria de Colonna, and Raphael). But most of those committed to idealism tried to bring its tenets to bear directly upon the particular American scene in which they were fated to live. If they were to escape the psychic damage done to those who merely lament the decline of society, they had to bring idealism into line with provocative new ideas of evolution.

The world was changing. Idealists could not blink that fact. If they could read change as development, perhaps they could uncover the hitherto hidden process by which Reality in America is en route to the Ideal. Then all those statues and paintings of allegorical subjects would be validated by the future; they would prove to be symbolic representations which wake up to find they are true, as in Keats' telling of Adam's dream. Raw change meant the future doom of still greater instability and of knowledge replaced by chaos. Evolution promised a future of the permanence of truth and of things set to rights. In that happy time, the faith placed in the Winged Female as the visual vehicle for all good things would be vindicated. Human conduct and human thought would become what wings had been expressing all along.

The desire to reach into the past to the magic source of visual conventions of the ideal in order to bring order and stability to every level of contemporary society was a philosophical botch. Ideals based on conventions require lost origins, yet we can never go back far enough.[19] Without command over true beginnings, true endings are illusive. One could, as did Emerson and Peirce, concoct aesthetically beautiful theories of history that spiral society toward a future where sign at last merges with signifier, or one could devise notions by which the mind evolves through progressive stages of perception and thinking. But even these carefully articulated theories of history or mind in forward motion could not wholly offset the backward drag exerted by convention—especially the pull of past images. How then to create vital *connections* among past conventions, present beliefs, and future fulfillments?

George Richardson published his *Iconology* in 1779 with the intention of bringing the 1603 emblem book of Cesare Riga up-to-date.[20] Richardson's introduction declares that the source of images for abstract ideas and qualities drawn from classical myths and saints calendars is exhausted. He wants his glossary of ideal images to expand the range of the standard repertoire for the new times. He expects to aid modern artists by incorporating Raphael's and Poussin's innovations, as well as new concepts such as "Democracy," "Liberty," and "America." He aspires to replenish the old stock of ideal forms in readiness for a rich future.[21] But how precisely to determine the life span of a symbol or convention? At what point does it begin and where in time does it wear out its meaning, both in terms of what is considered history and what is imagination?[22]

Arcadia is "the most perfect time," but it *was*. How might photographs taken by Thomas Eakins or F. Holland Day repossess Arcadia's reality through the use of seminude models posed at Avondale, Pennsylvania, or Norwood, Massachusetts? The best that American creators of images and the scholarly compilers of image books could do was to *make meanings* that *looked like* their ideas of ideal values. That is, they themselves had to have a hand at reading the signs by which they recognized past cultures. They had to alter the conventions by which present and future cultures were shaped.[23] But they were powerless to recreate reality to match those conventions they invented, and it was best if they accepted this fact.

This is not iconoclasm. The most drastic act undertaken by believers in the ideal was the proposal of innovations in existing conventions. For them, any radical overthrow of the cultural codes by which ideals are dressed in manifest forms would be a contradictory, counterproductive act. A victory of sorts was possible if they carefully inserted conventions into the stream of time, albeit with the intention to conserve permanent values. It would be a victory on a par with what Gertrude Stein says great generals like Henry James achieve when they lose battles and wars but win the army.

Contemporary American commentators on the uncertain status of the ideal were not all as naïve as we may now think them to be. In her 1892 study of masks, heads, and faces, Ellen Russell Emerson is aware of the severe limits placed upon the conventional in the last decades of the nineteenth century.[24] But even the Greeks had been unable to capture truth directly; their art "removes the absolute expression and substitutes a sign" which exists without "accurate realism." Any society may choose to make virtues out of what it cannot achieve. In that case, the beauty and symmetry of representations achieved through plastic means are themselves elevated into the status of truth.[25]

The calm overview provided by Ellen Russell Emerson is missing in an essay written six years earlier in 1886 by (and this fact is significant) a man. "The Decay of Art" states William Stillman's belief that even the word "idealism" has undergone corruption.[26] He tells us this in distraught tones that lack the steady firmness characterizing the remarks of Ellen Russell Emerson. Yet what Stillman is decrying is *the feminization of American culture*—the widespread emotionality which betrays the very meaning of the ideal.

According to Stillman, idealism refers to absolutes that ride out the tides of history because they exist in a reality that is independent of the mind's turmoil. Ideal forms of true art possess a realism and objectivity that counter the effects of a materialist art that merely imitates the crude facts of a world pretending to be the real thing. In the late nineteenth century, Stillman groans, "naturalistic art" (the art favored by history, physics, geology, botany, and portraiture) has become the so-called objective art, while "idealistic art" has degenerated into the uncurbed expression of the artist's subjective biases. Corrupt ideal art is therefore but another name for modern art in which the once-noble language of symbol is betrayed twice over: by aiding artists to escape the need to combat materialism, and by indulging them in the decoration of buildings with the trivia of illusion. What Stillman wants but thinks American society has lost by 1886 is art's intellectualism. He concedes that the tradition of idealism in which he believes is mental; but it is not mental defined as "fanciful." Stillman distinguishes between naturalistic art (the stuff of mindless brutes) and corrupt idealistic (that is, expressionistic) art dreamed up by self-indulgent children (females). Over against these degenerate forms he sets the true art of the ideal conceived by adult (male) minds.

Stillman's stand and the paradox it represents are both the cause of the problem and the result of the position held by ideal art in late-nineteenth-century America. According to Stillman, ideal art curbs the brutes (the amoral, masculine force found alike in the supersensual world of cosmic forces and in human societies devoted to commerce and industry). Ideal art encourages the citizenry to fight for the public values of intelligence, loveliness, and moral radiance. But the art of the ideal is in the hands of artists whose soft subjectivism Stillman characterizes as intuitive, emotional, and subject to whim and fashion—that is, as infantile and feminine. How then to have an ideal art (which by convention calls upon the image of the female as the sign for the primary moral virtues) that possesses the force of the intelligence?

Ellen Russell Emerson calmly walked away from the shambles left by the failure of human expression to find accurate images for essential cosmic truths. The agitation of William Stillman's diatribe is more common to the times. We may prefer Ellen Emerson's approach to William Stillman's, but his position is the more predictable. However broadly or idiosyncratically the habitual definition given to the word, idealism continued to impress the belief that development and intelligence are male qualities and that tranquillity and intuition are female; it also led to the creation of the paradox whereby the energetic male principle was equated with amorality and the static female principle with virtue. But new habits of thought can be formed, as Charles Sanders Peirce and William James were just then arguing. Visual conventions for ideal forms were soon to be greatly affected by *the masculinization of the feminine ideal.*

In 1913 E. D. Adams of Stanford University published *The Power of Ideals in American History.* The other, better-known Adams had already distributed privately printed copies of *The Education of Henry Adams.* That book told what it was like to grow up according to ideals that had been bludgeoned to their knees by the events of the nineteenth century. Hardness helped one survive; weakness did not. But since only the "female" seemed worth the saving, its visible forms had somehow to be accommodated into the maleness of the American culture.

Immediately after the Civil War wealthy patrons had come to the support of American sculptors. Dedicated to the education of the populace, large figures of American heroes in bronze and granite were set out in public squares and parks, replacing the small-scale "parlor" images of Puck or Psyche commissioned of sculptors earlier in the century. What with all the practice they gained by 1900, the sculptors' studios would be ready when the time came to produce the commemorative statues ordered for the dead of World War I.

The need to use public statuary as the means to encourage public virtue was at its strongest between 1880 and 1910. Growing interest in English Pre-Raphaelitism and the French Impressionists had taken the edge from the previous vogue for neoclassicism in art or philosophy, and genre scenes, landscapes, and portrait figures gained in popular appeal, but the 1876 Centennial revived a taste for the American past. Artists and historians turned to the creation of allegories of perfect beginnings as the inspiration for citizens of a not altogether ideal present. And where there were heroes there were also heroines. Christopher Columbus caught the attention of American schoolchildren, poets, politicians, and commercial illustrators,[27] but he had to share that interest with Pocahontas, Betsy Ross, Evangeline, Priscilla, and Sacagawea. American parks now had their bronze generals and explorers, but they featured idealizations of the stalwart Pioneer Mother as well.

Late-nineteenth-century scholarship brought details to the surface concerning the distinctions between early and later forms of classical art. Critics and artists reappraised the works of the ancients and decided they liked the forms which were expressive and decorative more than they did the ones that were mimetic.[28] And once Socrates, Plotinus, Raphael, and Poussin—the traditional references for idealism in thought and art—were supplemented by interest in Asian philosophies and aesthetics, ideal forms could hardly be what they had been prior to the 1880s.[29]

Through all these shifts and modulations, old-style "American" idealism with its reliance on female images kept a fingerhold upon the present. The plastic arts adapted themselves to the times by quickly adding newly valorized images of Pocahontas and Priscilla to the ranks of traditionally winged females, but the philosophers had more of a struggle to keep up. New thoughts called for new kinds of thinkers who could make the essentially sexless realms of philosophical ideas palpable for a society with a strong taste for the pictorial. The creation of ideal women of marble, stone, and bronze was not in the philosophers' line of action. Nevertheless, they found themselves constantly *talking about images.*

"The Battle of the Absolute" that Josiah Royce fought with William James by the mid-1890s was waged by a man who was an "extensive doubter." Caught in the midst of a mercantile society, Royce had already decided in 1880–81 that "The business of thought is to think out coherent and significant schemes of reality" even when surrounded by limits.[30] By 1896 Royce's post-Kantian idealism was comprised of a bit of Hegel and a bit of Fichte, but it was also touched by Schopenhauer's pessimism about the hard materialty of existence.[31]

Royce realizes that when we first turn from the world of ideas to the actual world ("a World of Doubt"), it is not a happy time.[32] He never pretends that it is we who make the world. Indeed, the very nature of our "finite personality" is a continual expression of "what is just now a dissatisfaction" over facing the world as fact. Nor does Royce want to withdraw into a mental realm of mathematical ideas that swallows up the individual in the bright glow of the absolute. Royce struggles to retain the values of the individual experience in the midst of a sticky coagulation of facts, but all for the purpose of receiving the reward of what he calls the "Real Things." The "type" of the Truth has likenesses that can be imitated, but images of "the Other" are severely restricted by our experiences and the indeterminacy of our ideas. If ever we fulfill our longing and perfect our will, we shall seize the Type, but the accomplishment of this seizure seems well-nigh impossible in the light (or rather, shadow) of the nature of finite experience. The main difference between Royce and William James is in the extent to which each man goes in pursuit of outrageous ends. James curtails his longings and decides that finite experience suffices; he stops short in the presence of actuality. Royce needs to go *through* the experience of the actual, and the surrogate images it casts in our path, to arrive at the Other. He wants to go beyond, where the imageless Real Things are and where desire no longer exists.

Charles Sanders Peirce believed that we are born out of indeterminacy (a generalized potentiality) and die into nothingness.[33] In between these two points we exist with particularized Forms of potentiality. The Peircean universe functions according to Norms, although we have to do daily commerce with the mundane norms which define to us the way things are. Peirce notes that ideal images continually develop within a culture, moving from the state of complete spontaneity toward rules and regularity. Out of their essential helplessness in the midst of un-shaped experience, people cultivate "icons" (which only *describe* "resemblances" but fail to work as "real qualities"), "indexes" (which can only *point*), and "symbols" (which *signify* the laws of the universe that remain indifferent to our individual desires).

Peirce believed that although our attempts are feeble, we can at least *embody* our ideas according to our experience of the laws' brutishness. If we did not have these embodiments we would be left with conjectures—those "lifeless things" without power to fend off the forces of nature Peirce likened to the Margin or "the corpse." Without ideas and the signs by which we set them to work, we appear to drown in a universe that has no final cause. Peirce's great need is for Cause, which means unity, identity, and meaning. He refuses, though, to say that our thoughts and their signs affect truth. Quite the reverse. When an *object* affects the sign and the thought, only then do we realize a Truth. No wonder that of the three philosophers (Peirce, Royce, and William James), Peirce is the one who insists on the primary importance of objects. James does not bother to incorporate a system of objects into his writings about the conflict between experience and desire (perhaps because he somewhat casually took objects for granted). Royce discusses embodiments but tries to get beyond images. It is Peirce who insists that objects (and the cultural signs they constantly stimulate) provide us with those good aims—the ultimates—to which we attach the critical processes of our thought.

George Santayana can be viewed as either more realistic or more cynical than William James, Royce, or Peirce.[34] According to Santayana's nonhumanistic naturalism, matter is the first fact. Ideas get dragged in later. Genteel egotism separates itself from experience and tries to create a world imaged by the ego. The ultimate forms of existence, which have no purpose and are present for no reason that any human imagination can detect, betray human fictions about the realm of Essence. Not an entirely pretty picture from our point of view, but Santayana accepts his status as a cosmic alien. He chooses to live with disillusionment. Images of the ideal and notions of morality are to him fairy tales told by the genteel to keep from being scared by the animal intelligence of American businessmen that was being used to further wars, not decent conduct. Santayana's philosophical position gave him a box seat from which to watch his generation. From that point of elevation above the crowd, he observed the pluralism of American cultures; he viewed the chasm between raw forces responsive to direct action on the one hand, and—on the other—ephemeral ideas in the form of bronze sculpture, stained-glass windows, and the muted verses of those who long for what never was nor ever will be.

Philosophical considerations concerning images that placate minds filled with the desire for Ideal potentiality did not disturb the daily rounds of entrepreneurs like the San Francisco photographer C. H. Anderson. "Clinging to the Cross," "Rock of Ages," or what have you were labels near to hand (see figure 9.34). Countless variations on the free-market prototypes were available for any number of uses. Little wonder that the image of the female (nothing so earthy as "girl" or "woman") that dominated the Ideal industry was confronted at almost every turn in American life.

The female form conveyed (however vaguely) the sense of permanence, unity, and perfection. The female was elected the mainstay of the American home, the protecting angel of the nation, and the muse of the world's civilization. Her form was the signified and the signifier for what the finite mind desired most because she *was* Desire. The American Girl expressed many of the qualities Americans liked best—the type of youth, physical attractiveness, charm, energy, and independence. But it remained for the pure Type, the Ideal unattached to daily life, to represent that final space the mind aspires to when there is no place else on earth to go.

Attempts to assign an image to Desire are clumsy. The failures to create adequate representations of the undefinable bear out Josiah Royce's notion that "meaning" (what we desire in order to feel satisfied) negates the use of images. But it is Peirce's theories we follow in large part throughout this book, and he was one to stick with images—albeit verbal signs rather than visual ones. Peircean signs represent the objects which stimulate our thought and our conduct; they regulate our cultural vocabularies even when they falter in leading us toward the Reality that Peirce's philosophy held as its final aim. It is, therefore, with the images of the ideal—those pawky, fascinating, often self-destructing cultural notations for desire—which we take here as our intellectual commerce.

Recall the haunting sketch by Abbott Thayer (figure 9.16) in which the female image poises midway between earth and heaven en route to desire's attainment. The human form divine in which Thayer placed his faith casts forth the clear suggestion of the painted wing by which we identify the angelic. Because of the unfinished nature of Thayer's image, we "see" what Peirce and Royce meant when they defined human existence as the state that lies between unformed mass and the final shape that will be taken with the universal fulfillment of Reality. Some of us prefer things that are incomplete anyway, even when it means frustration to stay with images whose wings are not yet defined.

The general public liked its angelic forms presented complete, down to the last feather.[35] This requirement poses dangers. Perfection inserted into the middle of imperfection demands a bit of death. Poor Julia Hartmann of Partridge's *The Angel of Clay* experiences this pressure as a personal tragedy; most artists recognize that representations of the ideal may threaten the aesthetic life of the product and limit their professional success.[36]

Mimetic art is based on the belief that direct signification of objects is possible; it trusts the mathematics of the objective correlative. In contrast, allegorical art is founded on the undoing of that faith. The woman who is allegorized is, by that act, summed up as zero.[37] Her original identity is lost in the effort to image the imageless entity of Woman. Students of allegory instruct us not to worry over this loss and to realize it is a waste of time to apply terms like "realism" while in pursuit of perfect types. They say we make better use of our time when we ask why certain cultures choose the allegorical mode to express simplicity of intention, purposeful drive, and the denial of doubts.[38] But many people do worry. They attack the male fascist, chauvinistic mentality that imprisons individuality within frozen forms.[39] Wings in particular enrage those with animosity to burn about everything that went wrong in turn-of-the-century America. But wings are of the greatest importance in societies where traditional religious doctrines have been undercut and where people want the feelings, if not the meaning, of those doctrines.[40]

Paradoxically, the concert of death, perfection, and wings is the reason the monument people did a flourishing business. In *Memorial Art*, Harry A. Bliss comments that perfection resides only with the dead[41]—which is the reverse side of others' recognition that perfection is a form of death. The cool forms of stone or marble achieve what those arts of the living—painting, literature, or music—are wise to avoid. But the aesthetically moribund images of winged females which stand guard over the property of the dead lie well within the decorum of memorial art. Like to like makes a good fit for cemetery still lifes.

What was good business for the monument salesmen who traipsed across the United States in search of clients might be death if applied to perceptions of American women.[42] It is redundant to speak of the damage done to women when the spiritual and aesthetic qualities expected of them by society left no room for human frailties and earthly energies. Late-nineteenth-century women were "idealized," "placed on pedestals," and viewed by males as "paragons of virtue" in order to keep them under control. We all know this often-told story, and each of us can refer to heinous examples of how women were penned within notions of perfection so they might not participate in a human world as human beings.[43] And we realize that the social behavior which resulted from all this talk of perfection was done in the name of saving the collective soul of the "feminized" segment of American society which believed it had been victimized by the "masculine" sector of commerce and industry.

Jackson Lears has had a great deal to say about the lack of intellectual and emotional force that characterized the late-nineteenth-century genteel community, about the oppressive weight of materialism upon the spirit, and about the devaluation of once-potent symbols by modern doubts.[44] Protestant angels were recruited by the enervated to remedy conditions under which they could otherwise count on "no lyrical lift, no aroma of poetry, no wings of spiritual imagination, no vital communion with sublime natures." In compensation for the culture's grossness, angels floated across stained-glass windows, murals, and bas-relief reredos in churches wealthy enough to have been designed by William Morris Hunt, Augustus Saint-Gaudens, and John La Farge.[45] Outside, in the corporate world, granite representations of stout gentlemen in frock coats named Grady stood on top of markers circled by marble lady-angels (figure 9.35). The deceased who car-

9.35. From *Palliser's Memorials
and Headstones* (1891).

ried the concerns of the boardroom into the afterlife were not themselves imaged as angels whose function it is to kneel and pray, but their souls were.

A society divided between the outward Grady (materialism) and the inward man (spirituality) did not remain fixed. Once angelic forms denoted sensitive souls, whether male or female; they acted as signs for the high seriousness of masculine intelligence which hoped it remained uncorrupted by corporate greed. Now winged images came to stand for frivolous feelings associated with the feminine love of hedonistic pleasure. Previously, "blue-nosed Presbyterians" had caused Saint-Gaudens and Stanford White no end of annoyance, as when their tomb designs for angels of resurrection were rejected in 1879 by a client who thought the angels looked like creatures on their way to a party.[46] In contrast, Samuel Isham in 1905 noticed the lack of austerity characterizing the work of younger artists. "They are of their time, with its cheerful optimism, its absorption in material affairs, and its desire to know and to enjoy."[47] The new artists made a new breed of angelic forms to match the changing moods of the people. In the 1870s and 1880s angels supposedly soared toward thoughts of death, immortality, and hope. By the 1900s angels were often the casual afterthoughts of skilled interior decorators, with all gravity lost.

By 1889 Sylvester Koehler was already chiding the "embalmed art" of the ideal. He admitted that much of the fault for the inadequacy of late-nineteenth-century allegorical art lay with the times. "Modern doubt" (one of the period's favorite explanations for all sorts of maladies) was part of it,[48] but the greatest problem lay in the fact that artists were asked not only to supply the arts "but to make the occasion for them." It is unfair, Koehler admitted, to "accuse the artists because they are forced to mirror the kaleidoscope image of our times, with all the senile images which are its heritage." "If 'great efforts' are not made by our artists, it is because we do not provide the occasion." Neither church nor state gives occasions,

hence our so-called religious painting is either coldly reflecting and calculating, or of a sensuousness which records as little with the negation of the flesh as the exclusiveness of rich pewholders does with the doctrine of brotherly love.

If the ideal which it discloses is of the earth earthy, those who dislike it will have to quarrel with the spirit of the times, that is with themselves. . . .

. . . it stands to reason, therefore, that, no matter how many Venuses we may fish up out of the sea, they should be nothing but mortal women, posing to exhibit the beauty of their nakedness. For the divinity has evaporated, and only the very considerable dregs of a lusty humanity with which it was mixed have remained.

A people may be partial to "lusty humanity," but when it has been in divine company, the absence of the ideal makes itself felt.

Koehler apologizes for the fact that his 1889 volume of illustrations and commentary concerning the "new arts" is a mix that ranges from "weary angels to dead robbers, from the Pleiades to copper kettles, from fairy maidens to Chianti wine flasks," yet this combination registers what he finds in the American art scene. After 1890 angels, weary or not, must share space with all the other "things" cluttering the eclectic minds and flighty imaginations of the public.

Koehler believed that the purchase of ideal art by enlightened private collectors was the only remedy for the cultural blanks caused by the failure of the church and the state to serve as patrons, but such collectors were not around in great numbers. There were exceptions—men like Charles Freer with his bounty of angels supplied by Abbott Thayer, or Cornelius Vanderbilt II who requested Augustus Saint-Gaudens to sculpt the "Amor" and "Pax" figures for the mantelpiece designed by John La Farge, or the commission from the trustees of the Boston Public Library that gave Edwin Austin Abbey the chance to paint ranks of the blessed for the Grail murals. But the best "occasions" for the display of winged females were provided by families who ordered stone angels for memorials of the kind which brought Daniel Chester French his main livelihood and national reputation (figure 9.36).

The angels that filled the American cemetery landscape were private tokens given public exposure, but so were the illustrations reproduced in the large-circulation magazines, on sheet-music covers, in the Prang art instruction manuals, and in the pages of the catalog for P.P. Caproni, makers of plaster reproductions of sculptural decorations.[49] Fancy gift books of drawings such as Albert Beck Wenzell's *The Passing Show* of 1900 and the sales catalogs printed by the designers of memorial markers (not all that dissimilar in tone) were two more ready sources for angelic images.[50]

9.36. Daniel Chester French,
    "Spirit of the Waters," for
    Spencer Trask Memorial
    (c.1913–1915).

The essential signs remain largely unchanged, whatever the context for their display. Winged figures soar and hover as they had for decades. Faces reflect changing fashions for feminine beauty and offer a running revew of stylistic changes in the ideal. The cover for the mazurka "Protecting Angels" is easily datable from the 1860s (figure 9.37). The *Jugendstil* illustration for "Room in My Heart" of 1900 is more neo-Bathroom in its use of a mosaic motif than in its resemblance to the saints of Byzantine Ravenna (figure 9.38). Wenzell's angels which swoop across the folio pages of *The Passing Show* are high-society ladies from one of Mrs. Astor's costume balls. Wenzell locates the settings for "The Vision," "Vanitas Vanitatum," "Inspiration," and "Christmas Fantasy" in decadent corners of Saint Patrick's or in private High Church chapels of the more opulent Fifth Avenue mansions (figure 9.39). Into these fashionable Gothic spaces rush Wenzell's belles, with elongated eyelids and bowed lips, the same women who appear elsewhere in the gift book, without wings, in the company of languid suitors.

9.37. "Protecting Angels" (1867).

Perhaps Edwin Howland Blashfield's "The Christmas Bells" of 1891 most succinctly represents the general taste (figure 9.40). First exhibited at the 1893 Columbian Exposition, Blashfield's painting went on display again at the Paris Salon of 1911. There it prompted the observation "It is doubtful if any American painting has had a more popular vogue. . . . It is almost a 'household picture.'"[51] J. A. Symonds, who described the age-old function of angels in *Sketches and Studies in Southern Europe*, was credited as the immediate source for Blashfield's design. Angels, Symonds wrote, are "the vivid thoughts and intense longings of the prophets, who gradually came to give them human forms and titles." By means of their image, "the whole unseen world is made a home to us by their imagined presence." "Vivid thoughts and intense longings" certainly had a place in America after 1900, notwithstanding the crush of new times. The Paris Salon showing of

9.38. J. H. Adams, "Room in
My Heart" (1900).

LIBRARY OF CONGRESS

"The Christmas Bells" prompted another observation. Even when traditional methods for imaging angels goes on the decline, "the poetry of it half redeems it from the improbability of human beings supported by wings."[52] It was true that the art style was breaking down by 1911, but not the poetry of the sentiment incarnated by the angelic forms.

In 1861 Johannes Oertel, the originator of "The Rock of Ages" (that other famous American "household picture"), described the appeal which emblems of faith had then for "the popular mind."[53] "Symbolical and typical expression is the most primitive and the most suggestive. . . . By simple emblems a great number of thoughts are often comprehended and various and manifold relations suggested. . . . In this manner many of the deepest truths and broadest facts are associated in the popular mind with simple signs and phrases." Sixty years after Oertel praised the wisdom of the masses, doubts were being raised about the public's ability to judge the artistic merits of similar memorial figures. The writer of a series of articles for *Granite Marble & Bronze* (later gathered into book form in 1923 as *Memorial Art*) defined the problem as one in which those uneducated in matters of

9.39. Albert Beck Wenzell, "Vanitas Vanitatum," from *The Passing Show* (1900).

9.40. Edwin Howland Blash-
field, "Christmas Bells"
(c.1891), from *Gems of
Sacred Song* (1911).
(Original in the Brooklyn
Museum.)

taste confused the imitation of natural forms with the invention of conventional forms.[54] By skill alone, a stonecutter turns out naturalistic renditions—objects accepted by people who "like that which they can recognize at a glance." But an object treated as a convention bewilders the stone-cutter without "trained artistic conceptions" and those consumers lacking in "standards of recognition or appreciation"; both makers and buyers are "puzzled by it—[are] made to feel ignorant."

The worried writer for *Granite Marble & Bronze* continues his criticism of those cemeteries whose planning is left in the hands of the untutored. Almost echoing James Jarves' 1864 distaste for the ugliness of American burial plots,[55] he writes that "the average burying ground presents a depressing exhibition of flaunting egotism and uncultivated taste." From his view, the convention of winged figures—representative of the faith that the soul of good American citizens will enjoy an eternity of peace—was being put to the test: not the test of faith, but of taste. Taste requires training, education, special knowledge—a *poetic* sensibility.[56]

In sad contrast, the average member of the community does not want poetry. He likes crude naturalism. It takes "the better sort" to prefer conventions; the "meaner kind" want mimesis.

Gone were the days, it seemed, when the Type coexisted with both the "natural" woman and the type of the female; gone the days when American culture provided a Gallery 219 where visual conventions of several kinds comfortably shared the same imaginative space. Not only had the cozy terms of pre–Civil War significations gone by the board, no gain in evolutionary power had resulted. Allegorical types now reflected the random push of change, not the steady movement toward perfection through clearly ascribed sets of meaning which responsive minds could perceive, consider, and benefit from.[57]

There were any number of ways in which Type was still used in America. We have seen a sampling of this variety. But these images did not seem to be saying anything of importance to the individual spirit or pointing to a national future marked by elevated social principles. They were merely the common material that made helter-skelter statements about private griefs or public reputations (in cemetery markers), revealed a religiosity often embarrassingly deficient in doctrinal weight (in stained-glass windows), and compounded the confusion men felt over whether they liked female images to be erotic or sanctified (in popular lyrics and calendar art).

There appeared no way that winged females might resolve the impasse between well-intentioned feelings and bad taste. For some, conventionality itself was the culprit. (Art critics like Samuel Isham and Sylvester Koehler derided the "popular mind" that bound artists in a "weightless" and secular age to aesthetic conventions that had lost whatever force they formerly possessed.) For others like the writer for *Granite Marble & Bronze*, the preference that ordinary people felt for the mimetic arts was the cause of the death of good art. (Unless people of refinement exerted their authority, the rage for "real objects" and simplistic pieties would mean the end of expressive, poetic conventions.) Others argued that simple faith and unthought impulse, imaged through age-old image patterns, could still assure the future of true art.

Images of winged females were caught in the middle of this late-nineteenth-century debate over the value of the Type. These images had held their place for centuries as an important convention by means of the collaboration between the bereaved who sought ways to express their loss and the artisans who supplied the expected forms of *orants* and *imago clipeata*.[58] By tradition, angels and souls bore religious connotations. By 1900 they also had to stand as signs for a variety of social and aesthetic arguments. They were pressed into service as the objects around which the following questions asked: Which of many factors ought to define American culture—genteel or popular taste? refinement or common sense? intuition or professionalism? artistic sensibility or the business mentality? the spirit or the real world?

American women were assigned a place—not as the arguers but as the argued about—in the debate over the nature of the nation's culture; so were images of the female. Both the women and the images symbolized the splits pervading the American scene. The particular role filled by representations of winged females was a touchy case in point. More than the aesthetic quality of American grave markers was at stake. Important matters regarding women's lives had to be resolved that went well beyond lesser questions concerning the tasteful decoration of American schoolrooms, churches, and public libraries. Analogous to the functions required of angels of stone, marble, stained glass, bronze, and plaster was the manner in which American women were perceived as participants in society. Would it not be painful if angels, stopped dead in the midst of their unearthly flight toward Reality, became the sign for impasse, thereby blocking the advance of actual women through the realities of American life?

10

Angels at the Threshold

The impasse was more apparent than real, however. American angels had not been brought to a full stop, marked by frozen forms of cold marble and stone. The conditions set for both actual women and ideal images were those of *rites de passage*. Aesthetic conventions for the Winged Angel at rest were undergoing transformation; they contributed to the sociology of the New Woman in action. If women were going through a period of transition on the social scene, so were crafted images of angels, as we discover when looking at the products of Abbott Thayer's easel and Saint-Gaudens' studio. The wings attached in the past as a matter of course had not all been cast aside, but there were frequent indications that flesh lay beneath the paint and stone. Sentiments of the human voice began to replace the high rhetoric of the visual and verbal arts.[1]

Any image with wings is unsatisfactory when tested against the needs and values of wingless lives. But it is the nature of historical and psychological transitions to be painful. The people caught in the midst of change wonder why it is they sense that something is wrong. Hindsight knows why, and is often nasty in its uses of that knowledge, preferring to describe transitional forms as aesthetically ugly and emotionally imprisoning. In contrast, those on the spot at the time of change are not as confident in their judgments. Much of what they see appears to be bright and good, even if somehow not quite right.

Of course, if one stands at exactly the right spot in history, the meaning of angels is clear and there are no doubts. A Boston newspaper article of 1862 looks at Johannes Oertel's painting "The Final Harvest" and praises what it finds.[2] "We have all seen angels in other pictures. Over beautiful, human forms, more or less exalted, floating . . . drapery . . . is painted, wings of quill and feather are added, and you have your angel complete. But in Mr. Oertel's picture the robes of right-eousness are a part of the angelic essence, and the wings are powers mighty and harmonious."

Angels for the 1890s were a different matter. By the time the decade was half over, Abbott Thayer shrugged over the loss of an audience of the kind sympathetic to Oertel's efforts in the 1860s. He declared, "My art had its moment of fashion and then went out."[3] But Mrs. Arthur Bell, writing in *The International Studio* in 1899, liked what she found in two paintings of the late 1880s in which Thayer's daughter Mary is portrayed with and without wings. Bell describes the wings in Thayer's "Angel" (figure 10.1). "Soft and light though they are, however, they yet convey the idea of sufficient strength to bear the pure visitant back to her heav-enly home, and the white arms balancing the wings are stretched out with a ges-ture expressive of an absolutely frank and childlike character, innocent of all knowledge of evil."[4]

Bell then contrasts Mary as angel with Mary as she appears appears in a painting executed two years later, "Portrait of a Young Girl." There "the angel, her wings laid aside and her features a little older and a little sadder for her two years' fur-ther experience of the earth life, looks out at the spectator with the expression of quiet pathos." Bell realizes that a very real young girl exists in both paintings which image the changing world of the girl's self. Whether she has wings or not, Mary Thayer's entity has not changed, but her pictorial identity reflects the natu-ral alterations that come from insertion into human time.

As acerbic as Samuel Isham could be on occasion, he found no cause in 1905 to criticize the way Abbott Thayer's females swing between heaven and earth.

They do not make Welsh rabbits or go skating, those virgins of Thayer. They are set up frankly for our adoration, and it goes to them at once without reserve, they are so strong and beautiful and pure. It is a noble ideal, a sort of revivifying of the figures of Phidias with modern spirituality, and the execution corresponds with it. . . . It could not have been produced on the Continent, and scarcely in England; but, though Thayer gives to it its highest expression, the conception is widespread in America. At base it is the woman of Winslow Homer, less robust, more graceful, but with her soundness of body and mind.[5]

Although his passion for painting a certain type of young woman had been es-tablished by the early 1880s, Abbott Thayer did not begin his career as an artist with wings as his major leitmotif. Not until the 1890s did the crucial change in manner come into view. Thayer started to place his models within the "frames" of formulas derived from Renaissance art—formulas personalized and pulled into the intimate life of his studio.[6] Sometimes he used photographs to record poses taken by one model which he later superimposed upon another. Sometimes he painted directly from models like Bessie Price, Elise Pumpelly, or his two daughters and his son. In Thayer's private life he had sought an "angel in the house,"[7] but

10.1. Abbott Handerson
Thayer, "Angel" (c.1888).

it was "the angel in the studio" that best suited his desires. Bessie the young Irish servant girl or Mary his eldest daughter were two of the "brood of angels" Thayer "reared up around his own fireside . . . to whose humanity he fitted wings."[8]

In that stretch of countryside which the locals around Dublin, New Hampshire, called "Thayeryland,"[9] this mingling of earth and heaven occasioned inconsistencies. But an art and life marked by contradictions were an inevitable consequence of Thayer's wish to possess images which are fine precisely because they exist with two centers of gravity. The powerfully painted wings he attached to Bessie Price "might well lift an Irish servant girl some feet off the ground," but he did not let those wings deny "the physical weight of the figure [or the] questioning eyes and sensual mouth set so securely in the well-modeled head."[10] Thayer was a "soul-painter" devoted to expressing the presence of "the Other"; at the same time he attempted to keep soul and body in union. In this he and the females he painted are, alike, figures in transition. Artist and models characterize a noteworthy segment of the late-nineteenth-century American cultural ideal.

Augustus Saint-Gaudens often accomplished what Abbott Thayer did without suffering the particular strains of Thayer's obsessions. From first to last, Saint-Gaudens was praised for his representations of "invented personalities." He was appreciated for artistic forms that were simultaneously portraits incised with individuality and types marked by dignity.[11] He also received credit for ending the "dead-alive conventionality" of early-nineteenth-century art through the freshness of the forays he made into the studio conventions of fifteenth-century Italy.[12] Saint-Gaudens' incorporation of "the Spirit of the Renaissance" was precisely the act that assured his art its lively look of the present moment. The Renaissance mode gave to "that spirit its personality—individualism—independent study." Viewers of his work realized a "modern mind [had] been at work." For example, when Saint-Gaudens glanced back to the quattrocento for models for the caryatids he sculpted for the Cornelius Vanderbilt mansion, his mind returned to New York's Fifth Avenue bearing a special kind of female image. Although these "are not women who *have* lived, they are women who might have lived and have loved and, assuredly, have been loved."

There is a difference, however, between Augustus Saint-Gaudens' sculptured caryatids who live between real and imaginary worlds and Thayer's portraits of young women living in transition between the winged and wingless state. Saint-Gaudens cares very much about the beauty he creates in his studio but is free from the burden of having to worship beauty during each heightened moment of his daily life. But when Thayer describes the work of Thomas Dewing (and, by implication, his own art), we glimpse the difference between the artist whose heart is free to concentrate on "performance" and the artist committed to "worship." "Talent shows off while genius throws itself prostrate in worship, and in the deepest sense *only* records worship rather than the look of successful performance."[13]

A great deal more was at stake for Thayer the worshiper than for Saint-Gaudens the performer. Life for this moody, irascible, obsessed man was difficult, and it was difficult for his family. Thayer wished to keep his women out of the world with its grit and stress. He fully endorsed the notion of a sphere set apart from society within which women enacted roles that were both heroic and domestic. His self-portraits have been accurately likened to those of an avenging archangel, but he also gave his female images the charge of standing as sentinels of moral values at the gates blocking the way between the world and "Thayeryland."[14] The psychological exactions of such duties kept the keepers hovering at the threshold—neither fully inside, guarding the cozy center of "the 'woman' sphere," nor outside where the corrupt wander freely and rapaciously through the masculine world.

Protection of property is central to the issue of the function of angelic forms. What else is the task of stone and marble cemetery figures but to watch over burial plots and dead souls? Not literally, of course, just as Thayer was never literal about the functions his angels perform. But there is an analogy between graveside images installed as guardians of both moral and real estate values and what Christy reports in *The American Girl as Seen and Portrayed by Howard Chandler Christy*. When questioned why American lawns and American women risk no danger of physical violation, Christy replies for all his countrymen that in this land no man ever hurts his own property.[15] Henry Adams wrote about similar matters, though in a more ironic and knowing way. In "Primitive Rights of Women" of 1876 Adams points out that male societies consistently protect property and that from earliest times women and family have been man's most prized possession.[16] Thayer's sentinel angels—under orders from Thayer the archangel, the commander of the forces of truth—have a double duty, therefore: first, to protect the sacred centers of home and family from intruders or defectors; second, to protect their own value as the "property" of the Ideal.

The visual symbols, representative of the psychological and social states experienced by Thayer and the women he made his angels, suggest the strain of human lives that oscillate between command over the Ideal and captivity to its demands. As examples of the painting art, however, Thayer's angels reflect an extraordinary freedom of the imagination. They live beyond genre and require no explanation.[17] Superficially, they have the look of the conventional signs by which allegory and didacticism proclaim wisdom, but those same signs austerely counter the possibility, and the need, of giving information about the actual world. Wings became Thayer's means to do away with narrow claims to knowledge.

Visual formulas often limit reference to particular occasions and persons, but they do this by insisting upon classifications. Add this or that attribute to a figure and it is compartmentalized stylistically in the same way that the physiognomists classified "true Americans," "Christians," or "feminine women." In contrast, Thayer gave wings to a woman in order that she could stand "as one neither Greek, heathen, nor Christian."[18] He let her image yield "its own intangible, unthought message." By cutting himself loose from the definable world of classifications and its promises of manifest meaning, Thayer first fated himself, then freed himself from "vainly [having] to strive to explain something that defies meaning." He endowed himself and his women with "a high and precious sense of beauty," notwithstanding the cost of "a nervous incapacity to complete his utterance."

What Abbott Thayer did in his paintings of angels, Gertrude Stein did in her portraits of people.[19] What Thayer and Stein do, aesthetically, is a very modern thing, in contrast to the social terms by which their work can be judged as reactionary, even somewhat unpleasant. But it is true that the implications of their art are psychologically problematic. Any attempt to present persons simultaneously as individuals and as universals—as portraits, types, and Type—takes its toll in a sometimes "nervous incapacity to complete one's utterance." The double-edged efforts of Thayer and Stein are comparable in their achievements, but also in the costs exacted of the vocabularies by which American women were having to create their own "utterances" at home and in the world. The strain all around was of the greatest.

In the midst of the blur of wings framing idealized faces, it is hard for us to realize the extent to which many turn-of-the-century artists insisted that it was this world and this time to which they gave their attention through the adroit use of the conventions of ideal forms.

Back in the 1770s Johann Casper Lavater considered the matter of classical norms, then aligned himself with those who advocated the "natural." Citing Johann Winkelmann's pronouncements concerning "the characteristic of truth" and "the true characters of nature" as being one and the same,[20] Lavater next applied the twin tests of truth and nature to the profiles the ancients gave their goddesses (figure 10.2). "We have here what is called a Grecian profile; the famous descent of the forehead to the toe in one continued right line. But can any person, having a sense of truth and nature, suppose this natural and true? . . . This countenance is, in fact, merely imaginary, and only betokening the vapid and unimpassioned countenance of a maiden."

In 1907 James Montgomery Flagg seemed to make a similar point (figure 10.3). It is up for question, of course, whether the American Girl Flagg portrays in her modernity avoids "the vapid and unimpassioned countenance of a maiden" which Lavater abhorred in the Grecian face. At least Flagg's visual statement suggests two things: regular features in the Grecian mode are a continuing requirement for "American" beauties (in order to distinguish them from the physical and moral lumpishness of "other" races), and facial symmetry complemented by an upswept hairstyle places the Girl in Flagg's own day. That is, the regularity of the classical profile acts to universalize the interior qualities considered necessary for "our people" at all times; but such universalizing traits do not go untouched by the "natural truths" of current fashions in feminine beauty.

Flagg can never be blamed for profundity, but his sketch is an analogue to cultures in which women are asked to live in terms of both "then and now." Unwittingly, he images "the threshold women."

Threshold women, as defined by Victor W. Turner in *The Ritual Process*, contribute an important element of the thesis advanced by Lee R. Edwards in her book *Psyche as Hero: Female Heroism and Fictional Form*.[21] They are women who live on the margin. They slip through classifications. They have no special spaces. They exist in states of transition, although struggling to gain spiritual community with those from whom they are estranged. However marked by feminine passivity, they are still expected to succeed heroically at completing the "masculine" ordeals to which they have been set by a hostile society.

I take up the Turner/Edwards notion in order to extend it. I make it cover the conditions affecting three related areas of concern: the idealized images of females which were everywhere to be seen in the United States at the turn of the century; the position held by young American women of the period which the images were intended to represent; and the views which American artists of the Ideal held about their own status in that society.

Henry Adams said that the once-sacred literary and cultural tradition of "the Woman and the Rose" was dead in France by 1300, replaced by satire.[22] Where is the Virgin now? he asked, and answers, She has been preempted by the Dynamo. But not entirely. We have seen that the convention of women bearing roses at the breast had a pictorial life of its own well into the 1900s. As an image, it may not have been the kind of universal truth Adams was seeking, but it possessed a volatile cultural reality. And of course, there was Elizabeth Cameron, who served as

10.2. From Lavater, *Essays in Physiognomy* (1804).

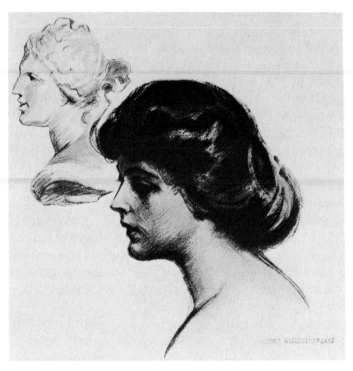

10.3. James Montgomery Flagg, "Then and Now" (1907), reprinted in *City People* (1909).

Adams' Virgin. He kept her in his imagination as the "threshold woman" upon which he imposed the "heroic ordeal" of being the Psyche to his Lord of Love.[23]

Henry James came close to the mark in *The American Scene* about the matter of lives lived by women at the threshold.[24] There he describes in detail the ordeal exacted of all Americans who by nature of their national fate edge out an existence on "the Margin." He also singled out for specific notice the sorry state of women forced to live "uptown" at the edge of American life, isolated from the so-called real world "downtown" where masculine business interests go on every day.

Henry Adams and Henry James believed in the notion of the woman's sphere. They showed no more wisdom than Abbott Thayer did on this subject. But Adams and James at least expressed their exasperation over the "false position" into which American males had placed their women by insisting that that sphere is both of this world and out of it. Precisely because Adams and James were themselves threshold people (one of the reasons they occasionally had a hand at endowing their women with wings), they were acute observers of women who tread the space between old and new ideals and realities. After all, a large part of the credit and blame for the creation of images of angels at the threshold goes to the artists, male and female, who were themselves marginalia. Add to the fact of the peripheral status commonly held by artists in the United States the fact that the society from which the artists felt estranged who also affected by the opposed values of the spiritual and the material. *Living at the threshold* was what 1900 meant to many Americans. They did not need to have wings to feel the tension.

When Gertrude Käsebier drapes young women in classical robes for one of her exercises in art photography, we notice how archaeologically correct the details of costuming are, down to the clasps on the shoulder and the fastenings in the hair (see figure 9.18). We also catch the incorrectness of the expression in the model's face, so "modern" is she.[25] It is the same with many of the artists' careers. The "clasps" on the ideals to which they dedicate their artistic lives match the tenets of the past. The "expressions" of what they feel about those conventions give away the sign of the times. Their artistic intentions and techniques are embedded in ancient Greece or quattrocento Italy; their responses derive from the totally different world of late-nineteenth-century America.

Clever artists find ways to avoid the error of placing figures representative of the universals into modern dress.[26] The deceased Mr. Grady in his stiff business suit atop a pedestal surrounded by Greco-Christian maidens is silly (see figure 9.35). "An Afternoon Reception in Heraculaneum" (drawn with satire on his mind by Charles Dana Gibson) could just as well be teatime at Newport (figure 10.4). But even when the props and costumes have been checked out with fidelity worthy of a classics professor, there is always something a bit off the mark. It's not just the rendered figures who exist on the threshold between then and now; the artists in the anachronisms of their desire live there too.

Arthur C. Danto's argument (advanced in chapter 6) maintains that artists give

10.4. Charles Dana Gibson, "An Afternoon Reception in Heraculaneum," *Life*, February 5, 1891.

each epoch its style. One of the styles by which we recognize the final decades of the nineteenth century is the style of the Margin. We find it expressed in painting and literature; we find it in the artists' statements about their careers. Henry Adams said that if you want to know why American women have failed, you examine the failures of American men.[27] Several American male artists became experts at reporting on their failed lives. Through their analysis of wherein they were "incorrect," we understand how astutely they conceived the "incorrectness" of women who have not yet made the passage from one plane of existence to the next.

Edwin Austin Abbey was enamored of medieval and Renaissance aesthetics; he was also a master of the newest processes of photolithography. Emotionally and professionally, he lived somewhere between quattrocento Florence, the "retrospective spirit" of the mid-nineteenth century, and the ash-can-and-tenement realism common to turn-of-the-century-Brooklyn.[28] Thomas Dewing's paintings have both the modern feel and a traditionalist's sense of canvas space. Abbott Thayer's techniques of strong brush and palpable shadows fit him to be a realist, even though not a member of the Realist school and a companion of Thomas Eakins; his painterly references to the principle of rationality and nobility ally him to the classical tradition, though not to Neoclassicism. It is Thayer's dreams which place him with the Romantics. John La Farge's talk make him one of the most influential conveyors of new ideas about the new art forms; the actual art forms he produced lag behind the forward thrust of his mind.[29]

From his perspective as a historian of the theology of the sacred and profane arts, Gerardus van der Leeuw explains the general nature of the failures of male artists and their winged progeny. Late-nineteenth-century art suffers from its dual allegiance to sacred magic (a frozen moment about to thaw under the agency of its own holy heat) and to profane beauty (aesthetics fixed permanently "into a powerless thing").[30]

The sense of powerlessness and the lack of magic that enveloped painters, writers, and philosophers of the Ideal have received a fair amount of attention from recent analysts.[31] But these appraisals often overlook the testy insistence by the artists who believed that it was *they* who were rejecting the feeble techniques and conceptions of the moderns, not they who were being rejected for being out of date. Like boys who whistle their way through dark cemeteries, they said they had the power to overcome their rivals because they held to the magic of faith in the Ideal, not to fraudulent arts committed to the denial of wings.

Kenyon Cox, Cecilia Beaux, and the young artists in Robert Chambers' novel *The Common Law* make it clear they will have none of what serves for art at the Armory Show or in Matisse's studio, for why put up with imported decadence or everyday egotism? By present standards, these are entrenched and conservative views; but these critics of modern art made a point of moving *above* the times. Better to be briskly dismissive of the aesthetic rot they found in the art world around them than be like Abbott Thayer confessing that his day had come and gone, or like Daniel Chester French confronted by the news that an avant-garde culture preferred Rodin's and Maillol's sculptured women to his own.[32] But those who went on the attack rather than lie down to die amid the forward rush of aesthetic change still knew they were *outside* the sources of energy other Americans were making their own. This was particularly true of those with the least shadow of a wing painted to one side of their life's canvas.

The feeling that one is somewhat out of it is hardly limited to the generation of the 1890s and early 1900s. Check the comments made by artists from 1800 onward, and the perpetual dissatisfaction of one group of artists or another is clear. Artists believe (and like to believe) in their separateness—whether it stems from their being too far ahead or too far behind. But turn-of-the-century artists who held to the classical tradition in techniques, subject matter, and theories recurrently went on record to express their beleaguered status. Heaven knew they were not like a Picasso or a Matisse who cleverly transformed "The Dancing Graces" or Parthenon figures into frolicsome and revolutionary art.

Artists of the Ideal lacked faith in progress. Not only in the progress demonstrated daily by American technology; also in the worth of progress itself. It hurt them to think that the old aesthetic virtues of visual clarity and conceptual significance were losing out to the new amoral force of technique practiced for its own sake. Above all, they suffered from the absence of "occasion" about which Sylvester Koehler and Henry James wrote with such feeling.

James' description of William Wetmore Story growing up in pre–Civil War New England points to the strain experienced by the young man who set his wish to be an artist in contention with the "proper" things expressed by the life of his "Puritan" father. Was Story meant to follow a career in law (Truth), or was he free to serve art (Beauty)?[33] By 1900 the legacies young American males inherited from their fathers generally took the form of business (Money, Power), but the dull drag exerted by either parental counterforce continued to check artistic aspirations. Men with nerve tips like Van Wyck Brooks' found it hard to be happy in such a society. There was not much they could do but testify to the divisions which placed them precariously in between the achievements exacted of males and the restrictions expected of females.[34]

American males who felt out of it, whether as professional artists or as amateurs of artistic sensibility, had to make their own arrangements with their generation. The recorded lives of men like Henry Adams, Henry James, and George Santayana annotate the more or less successful resolutions they made of a bad thing by leaving the United States for extended periods and by becoming the nation's critics. But many stayed on at home to fight and also to encourage the life of the mind and spirit.

Josiah Royce, one of the few philosophers of the time with the intelligence and the tenacity to do so reckless a thing, dedicated his life to a defense of the Absolute. It is telling that Royce based his philsosophy on the assertion that everyone lives as an outsider: that "just now" we all possess only "threshold lives." "Just now" is the source of the general condition of human "dissatisfaction." Our "intentions" are *to come inside*, where the stable values are and where we shall receive answers to the significance of our lives assessed as a whole. Unfortunately, poised as we are in the "just now," we are limited to a particular segment of experience which frequently makes life seem ugly, tragic, or ridiculous. Under the circumstances Royce describes, his attempts at reconciliation with this unhappy state had to take the form of a celebration of the human will. The "will to do something" might just bring us all back inside, away from conditions that guaranteed the perpetual frustration of our desire.

Functioning as pragmatists, William James and John Dewey had not the distance to travel that a philosophical idealist like Royce had. They, too, recognized the need for acts of the will to overcome the sense of exclusion from good things, but James and Dewey proposed that we make our peace with the "just now." They did not ignore the fact of present dissatisfaction; hardly that. Still they suggested that we make a home for ourselves within experience per se. This necessitates limiting ourselves in our desires. Best to declare that it is idle to know everything and that it is folly to require a soul while denying the body. Unattainable desires like knowledge and souls only cause us to feel humiliation and experience oppositions; they place us at the threshold between what we have and what we want and cannot have.

John Dewey admitted to the times when we ache to know what lies beyond the immediate fact, but he thought it more exciting for organisms to live inside their contextual frame. The persuasiveness of Dewey's argument for optimism lies in his giving us a view of both sides of the threshold. Since harmony is "outside" our frame, then disharmony (where we presently and irremediably are) is our real value. Disharmony means we are vividly "inside," although forever moving toward harmony. Held to this side of the passageway, we exist in moments of transition—that state of being which brings us our greatest sense of intensity.[35]

It is unwise to make pat statements about the responses felt by American males who experienced the unpleasantness of living as outsiders to American society. Painters as different as Abbey, Thayer, Whistler, and Eakins saw to it that the studio world of their artistic imaginations was the best place to be. They converted their marginal status into the kind of intensity of experience praised by William James and John Dewey. In their studio they were totally inside; they could view the world of American business concerns lying outside the frame of their activity as a matter of indifference. What Henry James remarked of Edwin Austin Abbey he could have remarked about his own life: the artist "had *had* it," after all; "he hadn't missed it: he had sat at the full feast and had manfully, splendidly lived."[36]

It is gratifying to realize the masterful coups by which American males of rare sensitivity "manfully, splendidly" succeeded at converting possible personal disasters into lives of decent achievement. But little triumphs of the will made in opposition to a masculinized American culture were possible for men like Abbey, Thayer, Adams, Henry and William James, Royce, and Dewey. They were men with just enough "wings" to their imaginations to cause them trouble in "Mr. Grady's" society, but as males they still had access to the privileges of the Grady world. But what about all the *women* set by their generation upon the threshold? Samuel Isham might have nice things to say about the female *images* in the paintings of Abbott Thayer, but what about the *lives* of the Thayer women?

Alice James did the best she could with the methods for success proposed by her brothers William and Henry. She, like them, attempted to will intensity into the days she spent in the invalid's bedroom on Argyll Road. Emily Dickinson did a fair job of incorporating into her own life the private programs of reconciliation proposed by sensitive male souls like Ralph Waldo Emerson or Henry Adams; she created on her own terms an existence expressive of the passionate sense of loss and denial. Edith Wharton came to terms with being Mrs. Jones' daughter, a lady of high society, the divorced wife of Teddy Wharton, and the protégée of Henry James; then she set herself to the task of becoming a writer with a genius for appealing to the tastes of both popular audiences and serious critics. But Alice James, Emily Dickinson, and Edith Wharton were required to start from much farther behind, and had many more psychic traumas to overcome, than the men of their generations.

Many men felt at least partially estranged from the hurly-burly of turn-of-the-century America, but at least—as males—they had an inborn chance at access to that world. All American men were considered biological citizens of the same realm, however far they wandered from home territory as the result of their tastes and training. But American women were often raised in the belief that they had been born outside "real life" as it was commonly defined in the United States.

It is an odd fact that if many women did not have the United States as their true home, they were given "America" as their special sphere of influence. "America" was what they were meant to represent before the world, either as the American Girl (that earthly ideal) or as the various allegorical forms, with wings, by which the primary American virtues took their tangible shape. As females and as images, American women were asked to civilize the culture. At the same time, they were criticized for having feminized that culture. As outsiders, they were expected to bear witness to principled lives on the margin of a society where the insiders continued to run a generally scruffy show. When the women complied by carrying out the social allegories assigned to them and elevated the general tone, they risked gibes for being moral bores or cultural excrescences. And if they tried to reverse this deadly pattern by becoming insiders (by entering the male professions or by agitating for male positions in business and politics), they were criticized for having lost their special power as ideal forms at the cost of gaining nothing much in return.

James McNeill Whistler once said that artists are likened to dreamers and that dreamers are likened to women.[37] Artists, dreamers, and women were the same breed: outsiders. But of this somewhat sorry lot, women had the worst of it. It was expected of them alone that they be both inside and outside, in time and out of it, human and divine.

There is a popular romance by Richard Harding Davis that is wonderfully suggestive about the burdens placed upon women by the male need to identify them as objects of their desire. Davis' *The Princess Aline* contains not one but two female images at the threshold. There is Edith Morris the earthly ideal, the type of the American Girl who stands near to the hero's side, and there is the princess herself, the ideal Type with wings who hovers in the distance of his imagination.

The Princess Aline was published by Harper's in 1895. Thanks to the combined efforts of two of the major image makers of the 1890s (Richard Harding Davis who wrote the story and Charles Dana Gibson who provided the illustrations), the novel was a best-seller and a popular delight. For our purposes, it acts as an anthology of references to the ways a male goes about making up images and for what reasons.[38]

Davis' hero is Morton Carlton, an American painter and bachelor who has studied in Paris at the Académie Julian. At twenty-six, he is a smashing success, singularly accomplished in the two worlds of artistic "female" fame and material "male" fortune. But although "beautiful women of all nationalities and conditions sat before his easel," Carlton wishes he had been born in an age of knight-errantry. In those days he would have been free to serve all women without having to marry any one of the sex. He is "a devotee of hundreds of them as *individuals*"; he also has a "romantic and old-fashioned ideal of women *as a class*" (my italics).

One day at his New York club, Carlton sees a newspaper photograph of the Princess Aline. His painter's eye and his lover's heart are immediately captivated by her pose and appearance. Since he is certain that "the 'not impossible she'

10.5. Charles Dana Gibson, from Davis, *The Princess Aline* (1895).

existed somewhere," Carlton decides to go to Europe in pursuit of the princess. On board the ocean liner, he meets Edith Morris, a young American woman. Edith, together with her aunt as chaperon, joins the party in which Carlton is traveling (figure 10.5). Soon they discover that the royal entourage of the Princess Aline is taking a parallel path across the continent, with Athens as its destination.[39]

Carlton has made a sketch of the Princess Aline (figure 10.6). It is the compound of the recollected newspaper photograph and his own mental image of the ideal she represents. This sketch, together with a drawing made of him by a fellow artist, falls by chance into the hands of Aline (figure 10.7). Through these representations-by-proxy, which image the ideal relationship of which she also dreams, Aline quickly becomes as absorbed in Carlton as he is in her.

Carlton's heart is blind; his imagination is set upon the elusive Aline whom he has not yet met. He is unable to look at Edith Morris with more than "an artist's eye." He admires the aesthetic effect of Edith's "free light step, the erect carriage, the unconscious beauty of her face," but likens her to "a tall, handsome boy." In a description reminiscent of the one given to Brett Ashley upon entering Hemingway's *The Sun Also Rises* (though without the sexual effect it had on Jake Barnes), Edith appears in a blue sweater under a reefer. "The jersey clung to her and showed the lines of her figure, and emphasized the freedom and grace with which she made every movement." Edith's face appears especially "delicate" and "fair" because it rises "from the collar of the rough jersey, and contrasted with the hat and coat of a man's attire." This pairing of feminine face and masculine clothing sets up the erotic shiver felt along the spines of males more alert than Carlton. Carlton is too obtuse to recognize that Edith is the American Girl waiting with an invita-

This is she
do you wonder I travelled
4000 miles to see her ?

10.6. Charles Dana Gibson, from Davis, *The Princess Aline* (1895).

tion to true love, but those who read Davis' novel and look at Gibson's pictures know this.

Now in Greece and on an outing to the Acropolis, Carlton approaches nearer his ideal, the Princess Aline. He stands below and looks up at her where she stands with her companions at the center of a tableau into whose pictorial design he wishes to penetrate. As always, Edith stands nearby, on his level. As before, Carlton turns to study the young American woman appreciatively, as painters do interesting objects. She looks like a winged Victory with wind blowing her skirt and hair, and he tells her, " 'I'd like to paint you just as you are standing now, only I would put you in a Greek dress; and you could stand a Greek dress better than almost any one I know. I would paint you with your hand up and the other hand pressed against your breast. It would be stunning.' He spoke enthusiastically, but in quite an impersonal tone, as though he were discussing the posing of a model."

10.7. Charles Dana Gibson,
from Davis, *The Princess
Aline* (1895).

Carlton is going to have to stop looking at Edith like that, incapable of seeing anything more than conventional forms to translate into easel art. He is caught between viewing the Princess Aline as the ideal image of desire and eyeing Edith Morris as an excellent artist's model for the satisfaction of his aesthetic needs. It is imperative that he finally perceive Edith as the woman he can love. It comes as a bit of a jolt to realize he is able to do this only after he sees her in terms of yet another aesthetic/emotional type—the American Girl as Queen.

Later in that important day at the Acropolis, Carlton passes nearby where the princess is seated alone, a sketch pad on her lap. Rather than approach her, he busies himself fending off an amateur photographer who has aimed his camera at Aline. Such priers into private lives were a new phenomenon on the social scene in the 1890s, as Richard Harding Davis was aware. After all, Carlton's own pursuit of the princess had been initiated by the fact that the popular press prints photographs of celebrities. But Carlton is enraged by that breed of male who takes advantage of "helpless women" through an implied kind of violence—through "shooting" them with a camera. Such voyeurs defile the virginal privacy of princesses whom Carlton, alone, wishes the privilege of watching. Like a proper Davis hero, Carlton bundles the photographer off the scene. Getting rid of men like that is one of the deeds by which modern heroes are now known. Romantic acts of earlier days consisted of shooting down, or knocking over, would-be assailants; hustling intruders beyond camera range is one of the forms taken by the new romanticism.

Once the photographer is out of the way, Carlton just as aggressively captures the princess' image in his own mind's camera eye. He begins to contemplate painting a group portrait of Aline and Edith as contrasting types: the princess (the "image" of desire upon which his imagination consciously directs itself) and Edith (the "model" of art toward which his heart is veering without his full awareness).

This is what he would paint: "the one girl standing upright, looking fearlessly out to sea, on the top of the low wall, with the wind blowing her skirts about her, and her hair tumbled in the breeze, and the other seated, bending intently forward, as though watching for the return of a long-delayed vessel: a beautifully sad face, fine and delicate and noble, the face of a girl on the figure of a woman."

Carlton takes this moment to meditate upon the passing of princesses as a historical type. It grieves him to think that future young men must choose their heroines "from lady lawyers and girl politicians and type-writers. What a stupid world it will be then." But Carlton is lucky. He may never be able to approach the Princess Aline, or she him, but he is about to learn that the true female type (not lawyer or politician or secretary) has been by his side all along. It is simply that he has been unable to recognize her or to identify the nature of his own desire. The Big Recognition Scene is about to begin.

A reception is being held in the royal gardens in Athens. Suddenly Edith Morris appears before Carlton (figure 10.8). She is no longer the pal with whom he has been traveling these past weeks. In an 1890s version of the Hollywood movies in which the mousy girl takes off her glasses and loosens her hair from its bun, Edith stands transformed before Carlton. Edith's hair is dressed high and she is garbed in a gown with décolletage and sweeping train. Carlton feels as though he has never seen her before—this "taller, fairer, and more radiant personage." But what exactly is the difference her change of appearance has had upon his feelings? Previously, Carlton's responses to Edith were limited to those of the brothering American and the impersonal artist. They are replaced by the necessary ingredient of romance fictions of the 1890s—awe.

Carlton tells Edith he is now rather afraid of her because she is "so very resplendent and queenly and different." At this crucial moment he is also given information he had not earlier bothered to inquire about: she is not engaged, as he had formerly thought she was. Her physical appearance, her marriageable status, and her place in his emotions are completely altered. He sees her "for the first time." Now he knows what love is. Now he knows that it is the American Girl he wants, not the Princess Aline.

Edith Morris is Pal and Queen. She is American. Carlton can have her because he wants to have her as he never really wanted to possess Aline. The story ends happily, and predictably, for Carlton and Edith. The mandatory note of romantic sadness is introduced when the princess, standing on the palace balcony (literal and figurative metaphor for her distanced position), looks down to see the lovers kiss. Wistfully, she puts away the treasured sketches of Carlton and of herself. She tells her entourage that she is tired of traveling and wishes to return home. Where else may outmoded images who exist solely in the dreamy minds of young artists go but "home" to mythical kingdoms of the past? Reality is the domain of the

10.8. Charles Dana Gibson, from Davis, *The Princess Aline* (1895).

American Girl who gets what she wants; the present is Edith's time to triumph as an imperial force of the imagination.

What is the import of this tale by Richard Harding Davis about two lovely young women and the artist who quests for the ideal female? What emotions does it express that placed it fifth on the best-seller list of 1895?

Aline as a European princess is an anachronism. Her wings are all too evident. They bar her from the present-day "American" world of Carlton and Edith where wishes can be fulfilled. She exists only to wait; she is forever placed passively in the middle distance; she is vulnerable to seizure by voyeuristic eyes; she is terribly, terribly frustrated in her desires. At the end of the story there is no place for the princess to go but "home" to her Old World kingdom—a goddess surrounded by palace walls and the impersonal homage of her court.

The American Queen is no anachronism. She acts out the winning strategies, while reversing the roles, of the original legend of Psyche and Eros. As the modern Psyche, Edith sees to it that it is Carlton, the Lord of Love, who has to undergo the "heroic ordeal" of sifting out the seeds from the chaff of his perceptions. It is Carlton as Eros (actually, more like a tepid Cupid), not Edith as Psyche, who must come to "see" who his unknown lover is by the light of the lamps hanging in the dark palace garden at Athens. Edith inverts the ordeal traditionally exacted of passive female victims whom society punishes for audaciously wanting what is "different"—for demanding the right to know at firsthand what Love looks like. The trials Edith undergoes are real. She has to put up with Carlton's inability to recognize that she is more than the Pal or the Artist's Model. But her trials do not daunt her because she brings to them her American energy and playfulness.

Readers in 1895 did not have to worry for long whether Edith Morris would win, proving once again the superiority of earthly ideals disseminated by "America" imaged in a female form. Prior to the Columbian Exposition of 1893 many Americans had been anxious about the feebleness of their country's cultural values, but no longer. Young men like Morton Carlton could count on having luck at their side in the sprightly form of the American Girl; at least in the format of a Davis romance and a Gibson drawing.

The imperialistic policies of the United States government were full-blown by 1900. They had been anticipated, however, by the symbols of world power offered by the Girl in popular romance and popular illustration. Davis' Edith Morris, McCutcheon's Beverly Calhoun, and the Williamsons' Mercedes were American princesses in command. To their delight, Americans were discovering that European landscapes and society could be boring and limited. The cultural tokens supplied by Eton, Derby Day, castles, and ruined abbeys (whose lack was noted with a certain pique by Henry James during one of his off-days) [40] were swept away by the energy of brash young things from odd places like Schenectady and Albany. What else did American culture need when it had its Girls?

Henry James' heroines often share their creator's sense of destructive American Margins. Often unsure of his power to satisfy the popular taste, he places his American Girls in relationships to European culture that raise more questions than they settle. But Beverly Calhoun in Ruritania, Mercedes wherever she goes throughout the European travelogue lands provided in *The Princess Passes*, and Edith Morris in ancient Greece have an American "zip and pep" even V. G. Rocine would have to admire.

As in the case of truly effective parables, disturbing elements are present, even if overlooked by the general reader. They are there in Davis' *The Princess Aline*. Why couldn't Carlton have "seen" Edith Morris as she was prior to the recognition scene in the palace gardens? Why couldn't Davis and Gibson recognize Edith's force as a lively, intelligent young woman without having to give her the wings of an imperial queenship? But no, they have to transform Edith in her football jersey into a mysterious presence that strikes awe in the manly bosom of her perceiver. Edith the type of the American Girl with her large claims upon "real" American living has to undergo the age's mandatory metamorphosis into Miss Morris, the Type of the American Idol.

Edith Morris is introduced into the story to represent the vigor of the future which Paul Bourget attributed (in the same year *The Princess Aline* was published) to all American Idols created from and consecrated to Will. I have already observed that it is safer for females to be depicted as powerful idols than to be perceived as artists' models vulnerable to killing by disrespect. It is also safer to be the American Idol who represents the force of a developing society than it is to be the European princess dragged down by the wings of the past. But we may not leave the situation where Davis and Gibson left it. Edith gains power at the cost of having to fulfill Carlton's desire for the ideal female image. The independence and will of the Pal in the football jersey is sunk under the regalia of the Queen.[41] Edith wins, but only by being imaged with wings. "America" wins too, but like Edith's triumph it is a Pyrrhic victory after all.

A good way to locate the nature of the crime being done to angels at the threshold is to inquire about the status of women at the century's turn as lover and as beloved, set in contrast to images of women who desire and are desired.

American females imaged with varying degrees of wings at their shoulders are not figures altogether caught in an impasse. But the Princess Aline is. She is wedged in the past. Her image is static. She remains outside the flow of the American faith in getting what you want—a faith which put the entire culture on wheels. In contrast to figures like Aline, idealized forms of American women are at least figures traversing the distance between the past and the future. After all, Undine Spragg is not named after an undine (a water sprite fated to live eternally between two planes of existence); she is named after the hair-wave lotion her father put on the American market, one of the products that promise women the beauty that wins them their hearts' desire. Undine is not held back by legends; she is not like Ralph Marvell dead for love of his image of her as Andromeda. Undine's ability to move *all the way* past the threshold into a future of her making is admittedly an uncommon talent, but hers is the general direction taken by American women set in motion by desire.

Richard Harding Davis' romance suggests the damage done to American women when the type of the Girl is turned inside out to become the type of the American Idol. Not much room to move within *that* type. But there *is* a means for relief from such a boxed-in state. It involves risks, however, since the precious allowance of psychic space given to Idols depends on whether American women are thought capable of getting love or only of inspiring desire.

First, I propose the following as working definitions to distinguish the two terms "love" and "desire." "Love" is felt for a woman who is *here*—immediately, directly present in her full actuality. "Desire" is expressed for the figure of the female who is *elsewhere*—other, beyond, at an imaginative remove.[42] To borrow the terminology of the semiotic critics: whereas love recognizes no difference between sign and signifier, desire registers an existence in which sign and signifier are forever at odds. Next, I maintain that one of the beliefs ruling perceptions of women in late-nineteenth-century America was that they were youthful figures for male desiring and vulnerable creatures filled by desire. Mature women who love passionately and are loved in kind are rarely seen on this landscape of the imagination.

Considerable attention has been paid to the problematic relationship between love and late-nineteenth-century women. When Henry Adams wrote *Mont-Saint-Michel and Chartres* to explain the difference between the Middle Ages and the late nineteenth century, he hit upon the right distinction. In Adams' view, medieval culture joined love and woman into one force; the Virgin, Eve, and the French queens were, all of them, love expressed directly.[43] In modern times women have lost the power to love or possess force; what is left is the indirection of desire. Richard Le Gallienne's "A Vindication of Eve," written for *The Cosmopolitan* in 1899, explains the fatalism of this situation.[44] The first male was passive, stupid, ordinary, obedient to God's will. The first woman was aspiring, joyful, distinguished, full of love for her mate. Eve's capacity for love was too assertive an act of will for God to permit. In consequence, God punished women and blessed men. God fixed the woman in her place in heaven and home as an object of desiring, not a force for love.

Mark Twain is not the best man to turn to for profound insights into the state of being a woman, but the observations he makes in *The Diaries of Adam and Eve* of 1905 support the slant on "history" expressed by Adams in 1904 and by Le Gallienne in 1899. During the brief time Eve and Adam were together in Paradise, Adam (stupid, passive, ordinary, obedient to God's will) did not recognize that Eve loved him so greatly she felt no need to attend to laws imposed from outside their paradise. Only after Eve dies does Adam realize the power of her feelings and how wondrous they were. Typical of Twainian males (and typical of the male types imaged in literature throughout this period), it is not love Adam now expresses for his lost Eve. It is desire—an intense longing for someone who is now other and elsewhere.

Tragicomedies of errors concerning love and desire appear at the sad core of many American narratives at the turn of the century. In Edith Wharton's *The Age of Innocence* Ellen Olenska is the type of the Woman of Experience. May Welland is the story's Angel (tall white marble statuary designed for the finest family mausoleum that money can buy) and Diana (an allegorical figure for display in Newport ballrooms). But May is displaced from the emotional center of Wharton's novel because she merely has love to offer and Ellen satisfies Newland Archer's taste for the unattainable. True, Archer calls what he feels for Ellen "love," but it is actually desire. Archer marries the woman who loves him and continues to dream of the woman who goes far away from his side. In time, May dies and Archer is free to go to Ellen, but in keeping with the gentle, beautifully expressed malaise of frustrated longing projected throughout Wharton's novel, Archer chooses not to take the final steps to where Ellen sits waiting for him. To go to Ellen now would mean that Archer would have to love her, while putting aside the bittersweet pleasures of his desire.

The intensity of feeling Wharton conveys in her fine novel is high. Wharton wins this intensity by incorporating the sense of enforced distance that separates Ellen from Archer in scene after scene. May Welland Archer is always *right here* and *one of us*, just as Edith Morris is always *with* Carlton up to the moment in the royal gardens when she is elevated by the awe Carlton now feels in her presence. In contrast, Ellen Olenska is always *over there* and *one of the others*, as is the Princess Aline. One mark of the effectiveness of *The Age of Innocence* is that most readers would not have it any other way. The special pleasure Wharton's novel provides as a "read" comes from the frustrations shared alike by the readers, Archer, and Ellen. Set outside the aura of romance cast over the people of desire, May with her love seems a dull drag on Archer's heart. But in turn, what a drag he is on May's life as he shuts himself off in the threshold world of his study, the place where he is safe from the commonplace, insistently present, facts of love.

In *The Rise of Silas Lapham* William Dean Howells dramatizes some of the same problems which arise for the characters in *The Princess Aline* and *The Age of Innocence* because they falter in the face of love. The beauteous Irene Lapham looks like a natural candidate for projection as an ideal image of desire, but actually she is a real woman who wants simply to love. Plain Penelope Lapham looks like the ordinary woman for whom everyday loving is the only fate she can count on, but for a good part of the novel Penelope is wretched with desire. Fortunately for her, Tom Corey shakes some realism into her heart by defusing her wish to take up a lifetime career of longing. Ironically (something one can expect from a Howells novel), Irene is the sister left behind without someone to love and only Tom to desire.

Inevitably reactions set in against the obsessive idealization of women, whether imaged as types or as the Type. Marcel Duchamp's series of satiric studies came at exactly the moment when the image of the pure American virgin seemed inviolable. Duchamp's "Virgin No. 1," "Virgin No. 2," and "Passage from Virgin to Bride" were painted in France in 1912 and 1913,[45] but they do not merely exemplify the decadent wit which disapproving Americans usually expect of the Gallic imagination. They also suggest the cultural "trends" taking place in the American mind of the kind Newland Archer's mother feared would replace old sureties with puzzling new signs.

Augustus Saint-Gaudens came to the conclusion Marcel Duchamp did, but even earlier. Saint-Gaudens was as impatient as Wharton's Julius Beaufort was when he looked May Welland up and down and found her a flawless but chilly, boring type of the Virgin Bride. Saint-Gauden's impatience is suggested by his treatment of the

10.9. Augustus Saint-Gaudens, bronze cast of original marble relief, "Bessie Smith White"
(1884).

10.10. Rudolf Eickemeyer, Jr.,
"Evelyn Nesbit" (c.1901).

thin, restrained mouth of the bas-relief he designed at the time of the marriage of
his friend Stanford White to Bessie Smith in 1884 (figure 10.9). Saint-Gaudens neither took to women who promised a man a lifetime of repressed emotions nor to
those who passed for angels but were not. When White was murdered by Harry
Thaw because the two men had both wanted the perfect body of Evelyn Nesbit,
Saint-Gaudens wrote in anger that Nesbit had "the face of an angel and the heart
of a snake" (figure 10.10).[46] The touch of irony is the fact that Saint-Gaudens was
himself caught between staying in love with the woman he married and making
love to young models—women for whom he felt desire and who also inspired him
to make sculptured representations of longing. Saint-Gaudens was a practical, realistic man, and he did the most practical, realistic thing men of his generation
could do: restrict Love to what one feels for the woman one marries and keeps at

10.11. Maude Adams as "Rosemary" (1896), from *The Illustrated American Stage* (1901).

10.12. Burr McIntosh Studio, "Miss Bentley" (1902).

LIBRARY OF CONGRESS

home and allocate Desire to what one experiences for the women kept "out there" in the world of the studio.

In edgy contrast to Saint-Gaudens, Abbott Thayer was an impractical man. He loved his first wife, but she went mad and then died. Thayer was forced to be like Mark Twain's Adam—endlessly expressing his sense of loss as longing for the ideal female. Since Thayer was a painter, he could at least relocate his inexpressible feelings in the faces of his models where he caught glimpses of what lay beyond his reach.

The Type is of little use as a record of love since love exists in the present without wings or ceremony. Nor can Type register the presence of sexuality in clear conscience. The physical expresses itself either as the realism of love or as the mechanics of pornographic fantasy that has stripped its gears. Neither physical function can take place when pure acts of worship intrude.

Maude Adams was a great success on the stage playing romantic ingènues (figure 10.11) or the perennially boyish Peter Pan whose best "pal" is Tinker Bell and whose "love" is Wendy—a name he cannot remember once she leaves his side.[47] In the theater world Maude Adams' status as the Type of the Ideal extended her appeal beyond that which the type of "Miss Bentley" could command, for all her sexiness (figure 10.12). But the public figure with the greatest power of all was

Evelyn Nesbit. Not Nesbit the coyly sensual vamp (figure 10.13), nor Nesbit as the traditional dark lady (figure 10.14), nor Nesbit posing too obviously as the angel of purity (see figure 10.10). Power is what one encounters in this exquisite head bound with chrysanthemums (figure 10.15). Once one confronts this face, love or sex is not the issue. It is, instead, the special force which "the Unknown" possesses. For what else is the Type in its essence but "La Femme Inconnue"?

Kenyon Cox concludes the 1884 essay he wrote for *The Century* with an examination of a bust from the Louvre known only as "La Femme Inconnue" (figure 10.16). Cox's "Sculptors of the Early Italian Renaissance" appeared in this comfortably respectable family magazine together with a chapter from Howells' *The Rise of Silas Lapham* and H. E. Scudder's essay "Vedder's Accompaniment to the Song of Omar Khayyám." All three writers for *The Century* dealt in literary and visual examples—realistic and visionary—of desire, but the intention Cox declares for his essay (to review the importance of quattrocento Florentine sculpture) at first makes it seem the tamest of the lot.[48]

Cox opens by reference to schools of painting which emphasize color. He rejects the notion, by way of John Ruskin, that color is "absolute fidelity to nature." Quite the contrary, Cox states. The use of color allows artists to restore "her veil to Nature and wrap her in the mystery of atmosphere. . . . therefore nothing is shocking." In contrast, artists of outline are the tough-minded ones, for they dare to "strip nature" down to "the facts."

Cox's argument is complex, even when he does not fully realize the implications of the distinctions he makes between the naturalistic, the classical-romantic, and the ideal. Nature expressed naturalistically has the "rough grandeur and homely beauty" of the everyday world. Nature expressed in the classical-romantic manner by painters who lavish color upon their canvases has the charm of "deep, vague harmonies and . . . impenetrable shadows." In contrast to the "homely beauty" of naturalistic records and the charming "shadows" of classical-romantic paintings, nature expressed as the ideal is brutal and blunt. To have to face the "absolute truth of things as they are, with no softening of angles or hiding of ugliness—Mother Iris without her veil—would be intolerable to us."

Cox lingers over thoughts of the third of the three ways art has to negotiate with nature: the perception of the world offered by "the schools of the line"—a world that is "hard, dry, and defined . . . under the glare of . . . white light." Followers of the ideal offer a vision which might seem the most realistic of the three, but it is not. Theirs is the world imaged as desire. Because "the human mind [has] a natural shrinking from bare, hard fact," artists of outline "cannot bear the least defect, the least commonness, the least *naturalness*—of nature, but refine upon and polish their forms, finding nothing pure or noble enough for them."

What Cox intuits in his essay is something like what Herman Melville gives all of *Moby-Dick* to expressing. Both men have experienced the shock to sensitive minds occasioned by encounters with the natural world. Not by the rude, likable,

10.13. Rudolf Eickemeyer, Jr.,
"Evelyn Nesbit"
(c.1901).

NATIONAL MUSEUM OF AMERICAN HISTORY

10.14. Rudolf Eickemeyer, Jr.,
"Evelyn Nesbit"
(c.1901).

NATIONAL MUSEUM OF AMERICAN HISTORY

10.15. Rudolf Eickemeyer, Jr., "Evelyn Nesbit" (c.1901).

everyday world of naturalism or by the pretty, refined studio world of color. The shock originates in that other, terrible realm of nature as outline. Nor is it nature red in tooth and claw that contains the final terror. *That* is the sort of thing that upsets the tender sensibilities of men like Tennyson and Ruskin, Longfellow and Howells. The terror testified to by Melville and intimated by Cox rises from the

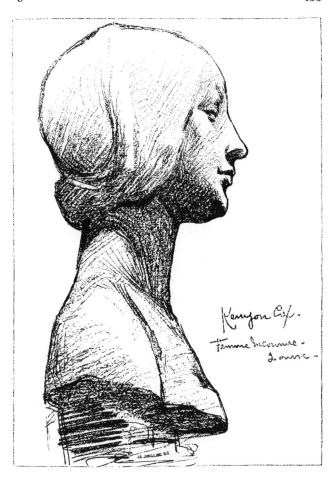

10.16. Kenyon Cox, "Femme Inconnue—Louvre," *The Century*, November 1884.

white world of "bare, hard fact" that Melville's Pip discovers beneath the surface of oceans. The insurmountable paradoxes are these: first, the truth which discloses itself as the Ideal is itself the terror; second, the art of idealization acts to fend off confrontations with the fact of the Ideal.

In Cox's review of the different techniques used by artists to survive the awfulness of truth, he pays particular attention to sculpture. Sculptors deal directly with form—"itself a fact"—while avoiding "the stumbling block of too great reality." Whereas painters duck the shock of the Ideal through the romanticizing technique of color realism, sculptors bypass the Ideal by carving outlines representative of purity and nobility, not of amoral force.[49] Either way, the blunt truths are evaded.

What does Cox's *Century* essay have to do with the state of affairs that results when Americans choose female images of desire over portraits of women in love? A great deal. Direct onslaughts of nature's "bare, hard fact" are analogous to loving a woman with "the absolute truth of things as they are." The main way to bear the unbearable is to evade both nature and love by one means or another.

The means one takes for the evasion of love lie in the same direction as art's evasion of nature: the election of the Type. First, there is the painterly realism of color which restores "her veil to Nature"; it makes everything mysterious, but divulges "nothing [that] is shocking." This is comparable to Evelyn Nesbit whose face disappears into dark furs (see figure 10.14). Second, there is the sculptured idealism of outline—"hard, dry, and defined"—created by artists who search for images without "the least defect, the least commonness, the least *naturalness*." This is the Nesbit of figure 10.15. Both methods produce images of desire. The former yields types with names such as "The Dark Lady"; the latter images the nameless Type. Neither dares to confront the truth which love furnishes to the human signifier.

Kenyon Cox concludes his essay in *The Century* with a description, accompanied by his own sketch, of "the concentration and quintessence of Renaissance art" he finds in "La Femme Inconnue" of the Louvre (see figure 10.16).[50] The pleasure he takes from this image formed "for our delight" is borne out by the verses he pens. They complete his discussion on the need of the beleaguered human spirit to gain relief from "the fact." Cox's poem speculates that the image is of an anonymous lady of Florence living centuries ago who was loved by an unknown artist.

> Full happy was his fate.
> He saw her, heard her speak; he was not born
> Four hundred years too late.

"Being born too late" is the condition Kenyon Cox accepts as the condition of his own life. It grounds his training as an artist, his years as an instructor at the Art Students League, and the essays and books he wrote in support of the traditions of classical and Renaissance art. He is quite literal when he specifies the years that gape between the 1300s and his own era as the reason that he and artists of like mind are "out of it."

Men like Henry Adams go even further than Cox. Adams extended the sense of being lost beyond the use of standard references to calendar time and historical periods. He testifies to the effects of an existential condition shared with other "artists" out of touch with the lines of force that constitute the facticity of society. All such uncentered men live at the Margin and worship the idol that appears in the form of "The Unknown Woman." If they wish, they can elect to call that image "Elizabeth Cameron" or "Evelyn Nesbit," but their acts of naming are beside the point. The Type does not need a name.

Kenyon Cox wrote his little essay of 1884 about the paradoxes involved when artists attempt to evade (in Henry James' phrase) "the hungry, triumphant actual."[51] As essayist, Cox offered the 400-year-old form of an unknown Florentine woman as his particular example of the type of frustrated desire. Two years later, as an artist, Cox expressed the longings he believed brought to modern times their characteristic flavor.

In 1886 Dodd, Mead and Company printed a handsome folio volume of Dante Gabriel Rossetti's "The Blessed Damozel," perhaps the premier English poem of yearning of the mid-century. Kenyon Cox furnished the line drawings which form their own text and both complement and alter the sense of Rossetti's poem.[52] Cox depicts the Damozel as a soul who remembers but cannot requite her life of the body and the passions (figure 10.17). In her longing for the lover who remains on earth, she dreams that she leans down from the clouds to touch him as he sits with his head buried in his arms. She dreams he at last comes to her where she waits holding out her arms in welcome (figure 10.18).[53] The two lovers stand together in the presence of the Lady Mary. Finally—and finest of all—they are joined by the Lord of Love in a ceremony of eternal union (figure 10.19). At the conclusion of the poem, however, the Damozel is wrenched from her dream of love. She is returned to her eternal state of longing, lost forever in that dream of desire which defines her existence for the rest of eternity.

The Blessed Damozel was, notoriously, Rossetti's foremost object of desire whose idea pervaded his autobiography and his canon. As an image, the Damozel is just as central to Cox's own imagination; he was moved to reshape it to match his own very personal and American imagination. She is also Cox's reformulation in 1886 of the feelings he expressed in 1884 about the bust of "The Unknown Woman" in the Louvre.

The most telling of the sheaf of carefully executed drawings Kenyon Cox prepared for the Rossetti poem is figure 10.19. The Blessed Damozel's progress through the sequence of Cox's drawings is not an allegory of Glorianna's Triumph but of the Soul's frustration. But there *is* that brief interlude when the Damozel dreams she has what she longs for. The image Cox provides for this moment of joy is the magnificent figure of a winged creature. But this figure who stands enrobed by the weight of mighty wings is not the Damozel or even the Lady Mary. It is a *male* figure.

Kenyon Cox's drawings are partly classical, partly Christian.[54] The winged male can refer to Eros of the Psyche legend, the Archangel Michael, or the Christ who has, on occasion, been represented as a powerful winged nude figure. Whether Eros, Archangel, or Christ, this is the image of Love and Reality whose pure force is the only one capable of ending frustration. If ever Josiah Royce or Charles Sanders Peirce had given anthropomorphic form to their mathematical signs for Reality (the Reality occasioned by the fulfillment of purpose), this is the form it would take. It could not, one speculates, be a female form; not in the United States of the 1880s.

In the special sphere where late-nineteenth-century American culture placed its women, Love is imaged as a childish Cupid. On his good days he brings lovers together, though hardly in the manner of the mighty male force exemplified by the Cox drawing (figure 10.20). But Love imaged as Cupid is frail. He can be sent away from the setting where Gibson's replica of the Unknown Woman of the Louvre (one of the flawed lares and penates of a loveless household) stares down from

10.17. Kenyon Cox, from Rossetti, *The Blessed Damozel* (1886).

PRINCETON UNIVERSITY LIBRARY

her pedestal (figure 10.21). He can be killed outright in a sad ceremony of dis-reconciliation (see figure 4.17).

In 1869 William Rimmer painted "Evening, the Fall of Day" as a Lucifer figure cast into the pathos of eternal darkness. In 1898 *Life* satirized the archangels who guard the portals to America's paradise (figure 10.22). John Singer Sargent sketched winged males while working out ideas for his projected murals commemorating World War I. But neither the Rimmer oil, the *Life* cartoon, nor the Sargent drawings represent a figure of Love. Indeed, I am aware of but one full-scale rendition of the winged male in the guise of lover (figure 10.23). It is Daniel Chester French's "The Sons of God Saw the Daughters of Man That They Were Fair"—a biblical version of Yeats' "Leda and the Swan" in which the winged forces seized the mortal woman. This is the lust of possession, not the love that passeth understand-

10.18. Kenyon Cox, from Rossetti, *The Blessed Damozel* (1886).

10.19. Kenyon Cox, from Rossetti, *The Blessed Damozel* (1886).

ing.[55] Kenyon Cox's winged god of love and reconciliation perhaps stands alone in the canon of the period. If this is true, this fact helps underscore the peculiar position of powerlessness held by American images of winged women and blessed damozels who are fated to want and never to receive. Passivity is not the same as the power of stillness. The stillness of the portraits of women who sit and think, displayed in chapter 8, are replaced here by the tense nervousness or languid dissatisfaction of women who only stand and wait.

The *absence* of certain images has been at issue throughout this chapter. There

10.20. Pilule, "The Chain Complete—No. 7," Prang American Chromo (1875).

10.21. Charles Dana Gibson, "When He Once Goes Out It Is Hard To Get Him Back," *Life*, April 19, 1894.

have been a number of images of the Type—winged images representing females who are objects of desire or of females who are themselves consumed by longing. There are no images that point to the woman who loves and is loved, esteemed, liked, valued—as we say—for herself.

Some gains are traceable, however, in these images. Some of the figures suggest, albeit fleetingly, a *rite de passage*. This is not to say there are clear lines of progress. As presented by Richard Harding Davis and Charles Dana Gibson through the figure of Edith Morris, the American Girl is not necessarily evolving toward a better world for women. But at least Edith is "modern" and "American." At least

10.22. Otho Cushing, *"The Newly Arrived:* 'Say Boss, Give Us A Light From Your Flamin' Sword, Will Yer?' " *Life*, December 8, 1898.

10.23. Daniel Chester French, "The Sons of God Saw the Daughters of Men That They Were Fair."

CORCORAN GALLERY OF ART

she is saved from being like the Princess Aline, an anachronism of Europe and the past.

Dead meanings and embalmed forms comprise only part of the story disclosed by a study of the various treatments given to the Ideal by turn-of-the-century artists and writers. The "new idealism" furthered new art forms. It put a great deal of employment into the hands of women artists. It helped develop new kinds of production in the marketplace. Cultural historians of the arts like Germaine Greer and Arnold Hauser would be impressed by the social/economic influence which the fabrication of winged women once had upon the American scene, whatever objections they might raise to the consequences. From the point of view of the history of ideas, however, the effects are even more striking.

The greatest impact exerted by renderings of angels and damozels (and the most disturbing one by far) came in the years between 1898 and 1918. Some changes were seen as early as the years spanning the Philadelphia Centennial and the Chicago Exposition, but it was not until the aftermath of the events of 1898 that the American ranks of ideal forms revealed a sharp division. Protective, maidenly icons common to the tradition of the woman's sphere remained, and were now called Love of home and country, not Desire. But such essentially powerless images were forced into the shadows newly cast by female figures with sword, shield, and helmet. The new images were of the Type, not of mere types. They did not signify the domestic truths of woman's world, but the masculine, imperial might of a nation engaged upon its newfound mission to save the world for Truth.

PUBLIC STATEMENTS

Making the Right Occasions

"All great art is Praise," said John Ruskin, but he distinguished between art that is the gesture of "the priest" who offers signs for truth and the gestures by which "the magician" deceives the populace with falsehoods.[1]

Allegories of national pride and self-congratulation proliferated in the United States after 1876. Confronted by the increasing paraphernalia of self-praise, the loyal citizen might conclude that the bronze statues, painted murals, marching songs, celebratory posters, and triumphal arches were, indeed, great art; unless that citizen thought to detect in those gestures the hand of the magician rather than of the priest.

It would have been better if the United States had had more skeptics acting to quell the ardors of the glory years; between 1898 and 1918 especially. It would also have been wise if the activists had seen fit to express their doubts in the same form as the principles they placed under attack. That is, critics of the United States should have used the fire of female allegorical forms to fight fire. Some of the worst excesses in the nation were being advanced by the false magicians in the guise of the noble figures of Columbia, America, or Liberty. A pity that more dissenters did not avail themselves of those same figures for acts of dispraise.

Angus Fletcher maintains that allegory can be used ironically; its makers may set its figures to work to diminish objects and to indicate shifts downward in authoritarian status.[2] But aside from the artists who regularly featured devastating allegories of male capitalist bosses in The Masses between 1913 and the magazine's demise in 1917, there were precious few practitioners like Charles Demuth with his "In Vaudeville: Columbia" who were willing, however slyly, to desanctify fe-

11.1. Charles Demuth, "In Vaudeville: Columbia" (1919).

COLUMBUS MUSEUM OF ART

male icons of national pride (figure 11.1). It appeared as if one had to wait until the mid-1970s for artists like Leon Klayman, representing the anger of "The Wilfred Owen Brigade," to convert the central icon of patriotic piety into an instrument of attack, though Klayman's method is, significantly, to transform the revered female symbol into the sign for evil suggested by Henry Kissinger's pudgy maleness (figure 11.2).

It is not surprising that the soldiers of doubt had small success in infiltrating the legions of praise by 1900.[3] In a nation that had lacked sufficient official "occasions" for self-congratulation, occasions now seemed to abound. There had, of course, been generations of American citizens given to florid Fourth of July celebrations and oratorical testimonials to victories in war, but those had been relatively small and provincial affairs, not of the scale guaranteed to impress the rest of the Western world. But by the late 1890s matters of national morale were looking up; occasions of some magnitude increased in number and size. With them came the

11.2. Leon Klayman, "U.S. Grain Arsenal—Food Is Not a Weapon, It Is a Human Right" (c.1975).

willingness to accept at face value the meanings read in the sculptured and painted objects newly installed in public parks and civic buildings around the country.

Sylvester Koehler, writing in 1879 on "The Future of Art," had astutely pointed out the relations between doubt, faith, and effective art.[4] Koehler wrote his essay at the end of a decade in which the American political system seemed on the verge of self-destructing. The scandals of the Grant administration, the Tweed ring, and the *Crédit Mobilier*, Black Friday, the revolt of Chief Joseph, squalid conditions in the slaughterhouses, railroad and coal strikes, and continuing financial panics prompted Koehler to sum up the period as a time when old faiths were torn apart and new faiths were hidden out of sight. The "old-established political institutions are subverted, and the whole social fabric is threatened with radical change," Koehler declared. As a consequence of "these periods of doubt and inquiry," the public psyche felt yet "more earnest yearnings for and striving after the ideal. . . . It is but natural that this state of things should manifest itself in art. . . . it is but natural that the apparent aimlessness of art should be more conspicuous at the present day than ever before. Nor is it to be wondered at that of all countries of the earth the United States should most markedly show the symptoms of this condition."

Koehler in 1879 was unhappy about the fragmentation he found in American life, the "diffuseness and want of concentration" he detected in American art, and the "doubts and inquiry" that replaced a settled confidence in past ideals. But Koehler urged himself and others not to give themselves to pessimism. Perhaps, he concluded, American artists, together with the American public in general, "shall rally around a common ideal, or shall see the ideal under one common aspect." At that moment, Americans will have great art, and—by inference—the cohesive political and social system made possible by the presence of a faith in achieved ideals unhampered by doubts that America would be true to its citizens.

Less than twenty years after Sylvester Koehler's somewhat anxious assessment of a society caught in the midst of drift, many Americans began to believe that unity, purpose, and achievements were what the nation actually possessed. Not only was the great democratic experiment working within the boundaries of the ocean-girt continent, it seemed that the United States was now in a position to indulge its taste for imperial occasions. The Columbian Exposition appeared on the scene in the summer of 1893 to make this hope manifest through its ranks on ranks of gleaming white buildings and gigantic female statues rimming the Grand Basin.

"Occasions" was the point at issue. Some continued to believe that the United States possessed nothing that passed for the right occasions, not even when the great fair at Chicago was ten years in the past. While on his visit to New York City in the winter of 1904–1905 Henry James observed that so-called occasions, paraded in the form of ostentatiously dressed women guests at an upper Fifth Avenue society event, were "as a purple patch without a possible context. . . . The scene of our feast was a palace, and the perfection of setting and service absolute; the ladies, beautiful, gracious and glittering with gems, were in tiaras and a semblance of court-trains, a sort of prescribed official magnificence; but it was impossible not to ask one's self with what, in the wide American frame, such great matters might be supposed to consort or to rhyme."[5]

Here was money in all its glitter, but where was the context which is what converts mere show into "occasion"? "The material pitch was so high that it carried with it really no social sequence, no application, and that, as a tribute to ideal, to the exquisite, it wanted company, support, some sort of consequence." It wanted, that is, a priest to provide an authentic occasion, not a magician to create the illusion of one.

John Singer Sargent's oil "Mrs. George Swinton" shows us such a fine lady dressed for a public occasion in satin and jewels (figure 11.3) Thomas Dewing places his "Lady in Yellow" within characteristically private spaces in contrast to the splendid "ballroom" space that Sargent's portrait suggests, but the tiara makes a comment on the social void in keeping with James' observations (figure 11.4). The contained social space in which Dewing's lady sits is perhaps more accurate a record of the American scene provided by high society than the apparent fullness of the space surrounding Sargent's Mrs. Swinton. It is arguable, of course, whether James himself wished to rectify the situation by adding the aristocratic accoutrements of the Court of St. James to New York society in order to make the tiaras "right," or whether he was urging the removal of tiaras altogether in order that American women might correctly represent a democratic, nonroyalist social scene. Whichever way James' own tastes took him, he accurately reported that women with tiaras and the principles of an American culture were at odds.

Lack of space and occasion did not stop the dreams of regal glory expressed by Mrs. Swinton, or by Mrs. H. Bramhall Gilbert, whose photograph appeared in *The Cosmopolitan* in 1899 (figure 11.5). Such poses make it painfully clear that if American women aspired to "occasions," they should go to England where empire was already a social fact; only there might they attain the swirling baroque apotheosis by which Sargent surrounds Consuelo Vanderbilt, now the duchess of Marlborough (figure 11.6).

With these visual precedents, no matter how fraudulent in fact, it is not surprising that Howard Chandler Christy placed his American Girl upon a throne as "A Veritable Queen" (see Introduction, figure 9) or that the only child of a Fort Wayne, Indiana, merchant was enthroned by a local photographer as a regal figure in white lace (figure 11.7). These portraits of American Queens date from the late 1880s to 1906. Keep in mind that those which come before 1893 are more obviously creatures of fantasy; those which come after are fantasies on the way toward making themselves true. Not "true" as Henry James defines the truth of authentic occasions, but "true" to an imperialistically minded society which *thinks* its reality into being.

Throughout the period, objections were being voiced to the sleight of hand taking place in the perception of American values and in the conceptions that evolved from what was supposedly "seen." An interpretation of allegorical images is announced by Jacob Riis at the very start of *How the Other Half Lives*, published in 1890. Riis wants to expose what it is like to live in New York City without tiaras and palaces. At the head of his introduction, Riis sets "A Parable"—verses written by James Russell Lowell in 1848 (yet another year whose social upheavals at home and abroad stirred pity and doubts). In Lowell's "Parable" Christ denounces the injustice done by the complacent to the poor and the suffering. The "good citi-

11.3. John Singer Sargent,
"Mrs. George Swinton"
(oil on canvas) (1896–
1897).

ART INSTITUTE OF CHICAGO

zens" try to beg off from guilt with the claim that they follow the faith by honoring the images of God set in place by their ancestors. As the gentry draw back "for
fear of defilement" from the presence of a haggard artisan and a motherless working girl, Christ speaks:

> "Lo, here," said he,
> "The *images* ye have made of me!"

11.4. Thomas Wilmer Dewing,
"Lady in Yellow" (1888).

ISABELLA STEWART GARDNER MUSEUM

In 1879 Sylvester Koehler comments that the failure of American art images (in-effectual at best, false at worst) is the result of a transitory society without faith in itself. In 1890 Jacob Riis would cite Lowell's verses to point up the danger of images created by a society that unquestioningly accepts its own values. Society's "magicians" set up ungodly images which "priests" like Riis must expose through the conscious creation of photographic figures employed as instructive allegories of destitution and neglect.

Jacques Derrida and Paul de Man declare that "being awry" is precisely what is *always* "signified" by all signs, but many Americans have been slow to come to that view. (The many examples offered in the nation's history of persons given to radical skepticism about language, truth, and everything else suggest that the American deconstructionist is made, under the pressures of experience; not born to that condition, as appears to be the case in France.) The exact moment that Americans first began to lose faith in the composite truth of signs and signifiers cannot be fixed in historical time. Most likely signifiers were perceived as some-

11.5. Mrs. H. Bramhall Gilbert, from Van Rensselaer, "The Basis of New York Society," *The Cosmopolitan*, August 1899.

thing of a botch by the time the first Europeans landed on the shores of the North American continent, but that did not stop them from stocking the landscape with imported ideas and images out of which they determined the significance of what they saw. Mumford Jones, Hugh Honour, Samuel Eliot Morison, and others have demonstrated that the centuries of exploration and settlement furnished the silt of myths and ideologies that lie in impenetrable layers of meaning. Spaniards, En-

BLENHEIM PALACE COLLECTION

11.6. John Singer Sargent, "The Marlborough Family" (1905).

glish, Italians, and French each contributed images which manifested confidence in the colonists' ability to identify what they discovered and their willingness to locate desire in the New World.[6] Let us settle on the latter-day making of one particular American icon—the Constitution of the United States. This single example reemphasizes the fact that from the inception of the Republic there were grievous problems in getting allegory to match actuality.

The Constitution declares the value of the abstractions of Law, Property, Cen-

11.7. Russell Purman (c. 1902).

trality, and Union; but as a document shaped from theories of governance over a diverse people, it has little chance against the physical processes of history.[7] In 1789 Law and Union were retrospective ideals, already complete as far as "meaning" goes, but in that year they were appropriated by a society which placed its faith in *the processes of history* as the only kind of meaning it understood. By the end of the nineteenth century, political cartoonists, Henry Adams, and other working skeptics imaged the failures of the American constitutional system in allegorical terms. They pictured the battle in which the absolutes of Law and Social Unity were pitted against the relativism of Finance and Big Business. The irony that besets their allegories of attack is that the very conditions they criticized were inevitable once the allegorical status of the Constitution was dragged into combat with the ways of the world. Law became laws; Union became individuals and communities; Finance became the making of money; Property became possessions. Laws, individuals, communities, money-making, and possessions might possibly shape a good and proper society in the United States, but they could never fit the look of the "occasion" declared by the Constitution's original commitment to abstract ideals. The American system functions best through the avoidance of the Ideal by its citizens; at the same time, the Ideal and its signifiers are exactly what many place at the center of their civic celebrations. The only way to lessen the tensions of such a situation is to let Americans give praise to national values without having to obey them.[8]

The creation of "false historical beliefs" began very early. Thomas Bailey's essay on "The Mythmakers of American History" indicates the social needs that led to the rapid cultivation of the patriotic legends that surround George Washington, Crispus Attucks, Daniel Boone, and Andrew Jackson.[9] An allegorizing popular imagination supplies stories of social unity, adding the Devil Theory wherever cohesion and mono-causation appear to be absent. Neoclassical ideals of order, mimesis, and universal relevance are patched together with romantic ideals of freedom, originality, and the expressive moment. Slapdash but effective, the result is an idea of American nationalism that accommodates history and timelessness, progress and stability, clarity and mystery, logic and soul. Obviously such a pastiche has to be created by magicians, not priests; and by a special breed of magicians—those who are unaware of the sleight of hand with which they treat the facts.

The burgeoning business that produced civic art in the monumental forms of architecture, sculpture, and mural paintings was as effective a force for educating the multitudes in what they needed to believe as were the McGuffey Readers in inculcating Whiggish principles for an expansionist, morally militant nation that joined Hamiltonian politics with Puritan pieties.[10] Two of the best at their job were Cass Gilbert and Augustus Saint-Gaudens.

Cass Gilbert was a highly successful architect. He designed a number of notable public buildings, among them the Minnesota State Capitol in Saint Paul. Gilbert genuinely believed in the statements his architectural structures made about American civic values and national progress. The public building and the decorations that enhanced it existed for the purpose of being "read" by the citizens who passed in awe through the marble corridors and meeting chambers.[11] The meek and lowly viewed material designs and images with particular enthusiasm. "It is an inspiration toward patriotism and good citizenship, it encourages just pride in the state, and it is an education to on-coming generations to see these things, imponderable elements of life and character, set before the people for their enjoyment and betterment."

Unable to afford great works of art in their homes, they ease their "natural craving for such things in the enjoyment of which all may freely share." But whoever enters the new state capitol buildings, all "alike may find the history of the state and the ideals of its government set forth in an orderly way in noble inscriptions, beautiful mural paintings and sculpture and in the fine proportions and good taste of the whole design."

In 1908 the Metropolitan Museum prepared an exhibition of major works by

Augustus Saint-Gaudens. One of the reviewers in attendance was pleased to see the "embodiment of such thoughts as leadership and heroism in war and states-manship" in the sculptured forms Saint-Gaudens handled with skill and confidence.[12] He noted the enthusiasm of viewers who had come in the tens of thousands to stand in the presence of "freedom and slavery; the ancestral memories of pioneers and founders; the acceptance and presentation of contemporary life; the shaming of sordid aims; the sense of dignity and beauty in every vision." In the eyes of these multitudes Saint-Gaudens was the good priest because of his "indefatigable search for higher truths and more perfect forms." By dominating "an era in American sculpture," Saint-Gaudens' art "helped to make for us Americans an ideal actual."

The year before the Saint-Gaudens exhibition Henry Adams finished writing *The Education of Henry Adams* in which he recorded his own lifelong search for "higher truths and more perfect forms." He too had once wished that Americans might discover the means to make "an ideal actual." As early as 1889 he turned over a chapter in the first volume of his *History of the Administration of Thomas Jefferson* to an analysis of "American Ideals" in order to argue that nation's citizens indeed have ideals, not just greed for money and power.[13] But whenever Adams tested the heft of American idealism he found it lacking the "gravity" of those true forms by which more established societies define and express their ideals. As far as Adams could make out, the particular art forms the citizenry received, for all their wishful thinking, were the dynamo and the bronze horse. Saint-Gaudens created bronze horses, and Adams believed them to be very good ones from a formalistic point of view, but they merely symbolized the energy of horsepower, not the primary forces of steam and electricity. Adams craved forms that directly join force with symbol, and this neither Saint-Gaudens nor any other American artist was capable of providing. American art was thereby only "occasional." It did without all the right occasions which both create true forms and are created by them.

Another man was also on the lookout for public forms of art by which to interpret the terms of American nationhood. During the months Henry James spent prowling the American scene in 1904 and 1905, he looked at a great many monuments. Although he has been misunderstood in regard to the meanings he assigned to the faces of "the aliens" he encountered, surely there can be no question of James' success when analyzing the disparities between signifier and signified provided by architectural masses and sculptured forms.

James immediately responded to the adequacy of Philadelphia's Independence Hall as a place for a great occasion.[14]

One sees them immediately as "good," delightfully good, on architectural and scenic lines, these large, high, wainscoted chambers, as good as any could thinkably have been at the time. . . . One fancies, under the high spring of the ceiling and before the great embrasured window-sashes of the principal room, some clever man of the period, after a long look round, taking the hint. *"What* an admirable place for a Declaration of something! What could one here—what *couldn't* one really declare?" And then after a moment: "I say, why not our Independence?—capital thing always to declare, and before any one gets in with anything tactless. You'll see that the fortune of the place will be made."

Once the "declaration" was made in 1776, *everything* (as Henry James was always ready to comment) *remained to be said and done* about what the principles of individual and national independence announced in this admirable place would lead to. By 1904 James was concerned that it had come to little more than empty rhetoric. "What therefore will the multitudinous and elaborate forms of the Washington to come have to 'say,' and what, above all, besides gold and silver, stone and marble and trees and flowers, will they be able to say it *with?*"

Henry James had been training as a "restless analyst" of American patriotic tokens since the mid-1860s. When still in his twenties, he was comparing the image of Andrew Johnson incised on a medallion struck off at the time of Johnson's inauguration to the image of Abraham Lincoln, the assassinated President. Johnson could offer the United States only the crudest of figureheads; his was the type marked by a sameness which had no reference to anything outside itself. In contrast, Lincoln had been a type which was unique. Splendid in style and significance, that rough-hewn head had been exactly right as the visual representation of the ideals of the Union.[15]

Now, forty years later, Henry James went up and down the East Coast visiting monuments raised in praise of the abstract forces of money, progress, and things. Nowhere he looked were there signs that these piles of material commemorated the lives of individual Americans. For example, the recent expansions within Harvard Yard—"more lands and houses and halls and rooms, more swimming-baths and football-fields and gymnasia—were perverting not a little . . . the finer collegiate idea." Harvard University was currently following out the theory that,

with all the wrought stone and oak and painted glass, the immense provision, the multiplied marbles and tiles and cloisters and acres, "people will come," that is, individuals of value will, and in some manner work some miracle. In the early American time, doubtless, individuals of value had to wait too much for things; but that is now made up by the way things are waiting for individuals of value.

A bad situation, and one that persuaded James that the occasion for "things" was at hand; the occasion for "individuals of value" was not. James questioned "the advantage to the spirit" offered by those traditional institutions—the university, the museum, and the hospital. But what of the monuments raised to great Americans that were intended (according to Cass Gilbert and many of his contemporaries) to educate the masses?

Upon James' visit to Grant's Tomb on the bluff overlooking the Hudson River, he found he "distinctly 'liked' it," though he was hard-pressed to say why since its design was in "complete rupture with old consecrating forms." He tried to puzzle out whether the "old sensibilities" traditionally associated with "the Presence" of the hero had been replaced by "new forms," or whether the absence of recognizable forms signified that "the sentiments implied *are* extinct." James could not decide how to decipher Grant's Tomb. Either it was "one of the most effective of commemorations" or it was "one of the most missed."[16]

The equestrian statue raised to Robert E. Lee in Richmond was not the puzzle that Grant's mausoleum had been to James. Its isolated placement at a vague urban crossways suggested "the very heaven of futility" to which Lee gave his life, and the figure of the Confederate hero spoke of the fate which comes to those who have "worshipped false gods." As James looked back "at Lee's stranded, bereft image," he "recognized something more than the melancholy of a lost cause. The whole infelicity speaks of a cause that could never have been gained."

By 1904 forms—architectural and sculptural, inadequate or not—had been erected to commemorate the winners and losers of the Civil War fought to preserve the abstractions "declared" at Independence Hall in 1776 and institutionalized by the Constitution in 1789. But there was still Washington, D.C., for James to read. The totality of its architectural mass must be attended to. There James might discover whether historical occasions, artistic forms, and the nation's citizens had anything of interest to say to one another about the "education" of Americans living on the margin and at the threshold.

The American Scene is notable for the way its literary structure allows Henry James to demonstrate that the United States is a nation where principles are lacking and blanks hold dominion. But actually the book's chapters are crammed with references to the material forms which pack city and landscape wherever James looks. James' main concern is the absence of *fit* which ought to prevail between the forms (architectural and social) and the feelings that forms are meant to express. The new American society upon which James casts his restless eye has created many occasions for itself, together with the paraphernalia that accompanies them, but the question remains in James' mind whether the occasions and the paraphernalia make any sense to the people caught at the historical threshold between what had been declared in 1776 in the fine, well-lighted rooms of Independence Hall and what is taking place in the "terrible" modern American cities of 1904. We can also add our own question (one which is implied at many points of James' argument): what fit is there between the independence granted in the abstract to all Americans and the "independence" directing the diverse spheres of influence that separate males and females in American society?

New York City gave James numerous causes for concluding that American women live under sorry conditions because kept as outsiders to the *real* America of action and power. It was in the nation's capital, however, that the lessons of a separatist society cleaved in twain came home to him with the greatest clarity; a clarity that resulted from the ambiguities he found there.

New York City is divided between uptown, where women function as social and cultural forms, and downtown, where men go to make money and to gain power. James finds the city split geographically and psychologically into "Wall Street" and "Fifth Avenue." The future unification of such separate "occasions" seemed impossible. But New York is only a single example of the nation's cities, albeit the fiercest of the new monster metropolises James discovers upon his return to America. New York has "happened"; it is what history-as-accident is like. (It is analogous to the Constitution shoved out into the world.) In contrast, Washington, D.C., is "planned"; it is the symbol for a nation based on premeditated principles. (It is analogous to the Constitution as ideal document.) Therefore, James counts on Washington to show him the *look* of the system and to predict its failings or success for the future.

Upon his first arrival in the nation's capital, James believes he has found two cities. There is the "public and official, the monumental . . . or, as we nowadays put it, Imperial part" which is "overweighed by a single Dome and overaccentuated by a single Shaft." Symbolically, this is the male world of politics and power, suggestive of the "real" world of New York City represented by Wall Street. But James considers that what he sees may be illusion, not reality. Perhaps the city of the Dome and the Shaft is merely "an immense painted, yet unfinished cloth," he muses once he experiences the impact of the other city he finds contained within Washington. This separate place seems "to represent the force really in possession; though consisting but of a small company of people engaged perpetually in conversation." What marks it as unusual is the way men and women live there on the "common ground" of "*conscious* self-consciousness." With a shock of pleasure, James realizes that *these* people are not "in 'business' "—not absorbed in Wall Street finance or Dome-and-Shaft politics. Nor do they exist in the capital's version of a gilded entrapment—the "Fifth Avenue" sphere—which women alone inhabit. "The other Washington" is a society whose participants—male and female—have consciously crafted the right occasions.

James did not generalize from the happy state of affairs he stumbled upon in Washington. He did not conclude that the "good" society of the nation's capital (which brings men and women together in social and intellectual concert) represents the "real" society of the nation. The City of Conversation was in fact "independent" of the rest of the country; an anomaly and a freak. "Official" Washington (the city of the Dome and Shaft, of politics and power) signaled what America was really like.

In 1904 any segment of American society which included both men and women engaged in good talk on equal terms was simply too "European," too parochial, to have anything positive to say about the state of affairs in the rest of the United States. Unfortunately, the forms created by "the colossal greed" of New York were the authentic ones by which to test the culture. These were the forms which gave shape to the decisions being made within the marble buildings on Capitol Hill. The country as a whole was being run, according to the rules of "Wall Street," by the insiders. Outside were the American woman and those odd males who thought to give her "space" on this side of the threshold.

As James turns his face back to the city of Dome and Shaft he is still bewildered. He acknowledges that the City of Conversation has little to do with the concerns of the rest of the United States; because it does not fit into the Union of the entire society, this vital fragment is stripped of its reality. On the other hand, the "Imperial part" of the nation's capital also seems unreal. It is there that James hears once again the insistent note sounded by an architecture of "expensive effort" which he had accepted as the truth of New York City. There the male is once again in control. But still and all, James insists, this *is* Washington, D.C., the symbolic center of the nation. Surely its forms have something to say about "the *democratic assimilation*" of the parts (the pluralistic population) into the whole (the abstraction of Union).

We promptly take in that, if ever we are to commune in a concentrated way with the sovereign people, and see their exercised power raise a side-wind of irony for forms and arrangements other than theirs, the occasion here will amply serve. Indubitably, moreover, at a hundred points, the irony operates, and all the more markedly under such possible interference; the interference of the monumental spittoons, that of the immense amount of vulgar, of barbaric decoration . . . the unassorted marble mannikins in particular, each a portrayal by one of the commonwealths of her highest worthy, which make the great Rotunda, the intended Valhalla, resemble a stonecutter's collection of priced sorts and sizes.

Amid the "monumental spittoons" and "marble mannikins," the "great Federal future" is suggested through "the general exhibition of a colossal conscience, a conscience proportionate to the size and wealth of the country." Everything here is very male and very large. Under such conditions, where is there room for those *other* images—images of those who stand outside on the margin of a society itself characterized as the Margin; who stand at the threshold of a nation itself in transition?

James caught a few surreal glimpses of persons whom he felt were generally cast to the side. For one, there was "a trio of Indian braves dispossessed of forest and prairies." (He saw them standing by the Capitol, projecting for one moment an image of their historical presence; the next moment they vanished from the "immaculate, the printless pavements of the State.") For another, while wandering the corridors of the Capitol itself, James had fleeting vision of the congressional offices as "the warm domestic hearth of Columbia herself. . . . motherly, chatty, clear-spectacled Columbia, who reads all the newspapers, knows, to the last man, every one of her sons by name . . . and is fenced off, at the worst, but by concentric circles of rocking-chairs."

The circles of power upon which James cast his analyst's eye in 1904–1905 were *not* going to accommodate these presences: no Indian brave, no cozy Columbia. Images of Indians and of Columbia were indeed made much of in late-nineteenth-century America (as the illustrations that follow make clear), but such images were forced to fit the "occasions" the nation was fashioning for itself through forms commensurate with the "Imperial part," not the other way around. If the femaleness of Columbia might be appropriated to represent "colossal conscience," more often than not the male "monumental spittoons" and "marble mannikins" of Washington represented the brute "size and wealth of the country." That is, unless massive female figures could in turn be used to join conscience (virtue) with power *(virtus)*, the task they would be assigned in the decade between the publication of *The American Scene* and the conclusion of World War I.

The Grand Army Plaza of New York City gave Henry James the sharpest sense of the crazy lack of fit between civic forms and authentic meaning. It was there that he responded to the irony of images that cross the wrong thresholds into misconceived areas of action. James stood before the Saint-Gaudens bronze that had been installed in 1903 to do honor to General William Tecumseh Sherman's victories over the forces of the Confederacy (figure 11.8). In this monumental equestrian grouping, James encountered something hitherto missing from the other groupings (social and architectural) he had studied. Neither New York City, nor "official" Washington, D.C., nor the rest of the country seemed to favor male and female images integrated into representations of the nation's progress. Nowhere had he happened upon examples of a patriotic emblem that joined the forms of the two sexes. However, here it was at the center of Central Park: male and female united in one aesthetic whole. But as James mused over Sherman astride his horse and the young woman bearing a palm branch who precedes him, he noted "a certain ambiguity."

It was clear to James what the Sherman figure represented. It was "the Destroyer." But matters were muddled by the incorporation of "a messenger of peace . . . with embodied grace [in] the form of a beautiful American girl, attending his business." James has been wanting to see *inclusions* of the female in the "business" of the male; but in this case, something was askew. "And I confess to a lapse of satisfaction in the presence of this interweaving—the result doubtless of a sharp suspicion of all attempts, however glittering and golden, to confound destroyers with benefactors."

The "confounding" of masculine with feminine spheres was precisely the event that had taken place within the American imagination throughout the decade just past. And it was confusion of a particularly jolting kind, since those two spheres usually declared the presence of an unabridgeable gap between male social power and female moral authority.

Henry James had been away from the United States since the early 1880s. During the twenty years of his absence the image of the American Girl had had thrust upon it the double-edged meanings of bloody force and saving grace, innocence and destructiveness; meanings which had been honed even more sharply since 1898 and the events in the Caribbean and the Philippines. By 1904 this image had been lifted with increasing frequency to that plane of masculine monumentality it had begun to occupy in 1886 and 1893 with the installation of Bartholdi's "Liberty" in New York's harbor and of Daniel Chester French's "Republic" at the Columbian Exposition; installations which were themselves the result of impulses at work since the Philadelphia Centennial of 1876. The Saint-Gaudens grouping was a consequence of those years of mounting nationalism, but James decided that there was something it could not give him. Neither this nor any other of the images of

11.8. Augustus Saint-Gaudens, Sherman Monument, New York (1903).

SAINT-GAUDENS NATIONAL HISTORIC SITE

American virtue and power formulated in the years prior to World War I gave support to his belief that "monuments should always have a clean, clear meaning."

Henry James was nonplussed by Saint-Gaudens' aesthetic decision to link the form of the General with that of the American Girl, but others at the time found nothing contradictory in the fine, tall female presence whose wings swept a path of praise through history for the horse and its rider. In the previous year Kenyon Cox (ever the indefatigable commentator on the relations between art and the public) found everything to like about Saint-Gaudens' inclusion of the "Victory" figure.[17] In Cox's opinion the equestrian figure of Sherman and his horse approached the mastery of the formalistic tradition exemplified by Donatello's "Gattamelata" and Verocchio's "Colleoni." But Cox also thought that the Saint-Gaudens version was thoroughly representative of the most laudable national values precisely because it is an American Victory who leads an American male astride an American horse.

The female figure called up Cox's particular commendation. He told the general public that it was wrong when it assumed that Saint-Gaudens was best at rendering "dainty portrait reliefs of women and children, his exquisite caryatids and angelic figures." The strength and vigor of the "Victory" exposed this error. "She has a certain fierce wildness of aspect, but her rapt gaze and half-open mouth indicate the seer of visions: peace is ahead and an end of war."

What Henry James perceived when he looked at the Saint-Gaudens rendition of the American Girl is not what Cox and others perceived. It is, however, the former of the two evaluations that took precedence. The Saint-Gaudens Girl, described by Kenyon Cox in 1903, is one of the dominant images, translated into poster art, that sped the United States to its victory in the war of propaganda fought during the years 1917–18. It resulted in a victory for an aesthetic of force over the Jamesian principle of clarity.[18]

To be sure, there was disagreement at the time over the best forms to use to educate the people in the democratic virtues; there was also disagreement over what constitutes a clear form in the first place. Henry James finds force but not clarity in the Girl and the General; Kenyon Cox discerns both. Cass Gilbert believes wholeheartedly that allegories of triumphant winged females fill the new state capitols with clarity and effectiveness; John Commons of Wisconsin agrees up to a point as he weighs the value of agricultural realism against classical idealism. "Of course a cow is just a cow, and can never become a Winged Victory, but within her limits she is capable of approaching an ideal. And, more than that, she is an ideal that every farmer and farmer's boy—the despised slaves and helots of Greece—can aspire to."[19]

In the end, the argument was won by just about everyone but Henry James. During the World War I years the Victory figure inspired the Women's Land Army and the U.S. Food Administration. The nation needed female winged figures on its posters as much as it needed women to take to its fields and to care for its cows.

Certain complications resulted when the means (the Victory figure) to the ends (the stirring of patriotic emotions) struck the officials in charge in the wrong ways. In 1919 Daniel Chester French was commissioned to design a Victory figure to commemorate the dead of the First Division of the American Expeditionary Force, but the general in charge of overseeing the monument refused to accept French's model. It was not that Major General Charles P. Summerall shared the earlier compunctions felt by Henry James concerning the thoughtless use of female forms to celebrate masculine values. It was rather that Summerall believed that the lightly draped female figure designed by French was "suggestive."[20] The general was repelled by the thought that the "meaning" assigned to a monument in honor of dead soldiers might be construed as sexual in nature. He was not disturbed, as James had been, by the interpretational difficulties raised when visual tokens of war incorporate female forms. By 1919 the official function of such figures was to make forceful statements about power, death, and the ideal; they were not the nation's signifiers for the clarity of love, peace, and sex.

Girlish forms suggestive of pert physicality were hardly ignored in the making of patriotic images. The Beautiful Charmer and the Outdoors Pal figured prominently in the Spanish-American War and World War I as the types that fighting men reluctantly leave behind. A more morbid sexuality was conveyed by images of feminine vulnerability that suggested the probable fate in war of Everyman's wife or sister. In 1917 men were stirred to go into battle against an enemy whose whole motive, it would seem, for following the Kaiser was to rape and murder good women.

But the dominant emblems marshaled for patriotic inspiration derived from two essentially sexless female types. One was the Protecting Angel (often shown without wings), the type which stood for the gentler virtues of home and conservatism. The other was the Militant Victory (often given bold, weaponlike wings), the image which declared the nation's aggressive determination to fight for the masculine values of progress and expansionism. The former figure adopted aspects of the familiar form of the New England Woman as Mother, Teacher, and—a little later—Red Cross Nurse. The latter figure was an acceptable version of the New Woman, now caparisoned as Warrior and Conqueror. The former advanced civilization by staying in or near the home to tend the national hearth fires; the other protected civilization by extending the American mission into benighted areas beyond the continental limits. The one was the idea of idealism; the other was the ideal of power. The one was the Virgin; the other was the Dynamo. Most forceful of all were the occasions when the two figures joined forces. Notwithstanding what skeptics like Henry James and Henry Adams had to say, Augustus Saint-Gaudens had indeed achieved the most ironically successful work of art produced by American nationalism up to that moment. The Sherman group includes both the Virgin and the Dynamo, both taste and force—and does this through *staying with* the ambiguities.

Saint-Gaudens' bracketing of female Victory with masculine force in 1903 would be taken even further by 1918. First, see how far the female image had had to come before the Sherman grouping was feasible. Two cartoons from the pages of *Puck* in 1882 suggest the strength of the pictorial conventions which identified American political power with figures of the male. On May 10, 1882, the *Puck* editors (who were aligned with the New Party which supported reform of the civil service and the curtailment of monopolies) ran a drawing centered by the familiar figure of a winged angel (figure 11.9). The timid children "Political Honesty" and "Political Wisdom" are led forth by their protectress from the dark plains of the Republican Sodom and the Democrat Gomorrah. These two orphans of the political storm will be mothered by the New Party until they grow up to bring a better future to the nation. On October 25 of the same year, *Puck* was still on the attack against the forces of corruption. This time the editors sent a man, not a woman, to represent their message to the public (figure 11.10). If a winged female takes tender care of Honesty and Wisdom by leading them away from doomed cities, the figure who directly confronts the foes of the New Party is a male warrior armed with sword and shield.

The use of female images was hardly new to the iconography of political reform movements, but in mid-century America such images were largely restricted to functions bound to tradition: *Puck*'s mothering angel; the schoolmarm of the New York *Daily Graphic* logo who instructs her male pupils in the home truths they will take into the world to rectify social ills (figure 11.11); or the enchained victim (imaged in parody of Hiram Power's "Greek Slave") whose plight inspires males to

11.9. "The Political Sodom and Gomorrah Are Doomed To Destruction," *Puck*, May 10, 1882.

champion her civic cause (figure 11.12).[21] Before the 1890s it was possible, but uncommon, for the popular press to assign female figures (allegorical or representational) the political power to alter events directly (figure 11.13).[22]

One image, however, habitually associated the female form with male physical force. It was not the Liberty figure as such. *That* allegorical figure fell more easily into the visual patterns associated with Beautiful Charmers and Protecting Angels.[23] No, the source for the figure of Columbia the Warrior is the Amazon Queen. It is the Amazon Queen who aggressively clears the way for the World War I poster images which featured the Red Cross Nurse projected as the Protecting Mother Angel accoutred as an armed Angel of Wrath.

Hugh Honour relates the fecund history of the nude figure of the dusky female who strides through an exotic landscape with ax, bow, or spear in hand. Almost from the start of the European settlement of the North American continent, this figure was associated with the unknown dangers of the new territories, exciting the imaginations of early explorers and of those safely back home in dull, everyday

THROUGH NIGHT TO LIGHT!

11.10. "Through Night to Light,"
Puck, October 25, 1882.

Europe.[24] The female warrior sketched in 1581 by the Belgian artist Philipp Galle is only one of a continuing run of similar images (figure 11.14). This version of "America" is usually large and muscular of body, clad (if at all) in feathers, and placed upon a desolate plain or within a lush jungle crowded with parrots, armadillos, and alligators. Sometimes she lies indolently in a hammock, but most often she is depicted on the prowl, weapons in hand, clutching—as we see in the Galle drawing—the severed head of an unfortunate male.

11.11. "The Graphic and Its Gifted Pupils," *The Daily Graphic*, March 9, 1880.

The figure of the Amazon Queen represents raw force, individual freedom, and what it would later be fashionable to call Nietzschean will. Nothing as limiting as reason or the discontents elicited by civilization sullies the libido of such creatures. How intriguing it is to learn, through Honour's fascinating survey, that centuries later a similar figure was incorporated into a ceiling decoration (painted around 1870 by Hans Makart) for a Viennese palace. There the American Amazon is a voluptuous woman in a low-cut evening gown drinking champagne, an "America" as *die Dollarprinzessin*.[25] Paul Bourget, William James, and observers of late-nineteenth-century mores would recognize this particular female manifestation of the free enterprise system. She is the Bitch Goddess Success worshiped in the Gilded Age and beyond—the American Heiress let loose upon the modern world. But the sixteenth-century image of the powerful Amazonian "America" also took another route into the future.

PUCK.

LAW-RIDDEN
NEW YORK
THE CITY OF
CONSTRUCTIVE
CONVICTS.

ABSURD LAWS

BLUE LAWS

ANNOYANCES. RESTRICTIONS. ARRESTS.

JAIL.

THE NATIONAL METROPOLIS IN THE 107th YEAR OF AMERICAN INDEPENDENCE.
Puck's Idea of a Statue More Appropriate for New York than Bartholdi's "Liberty"

11.12. "The National Metropolis in the 107th Year of American Independence. Puck's idea of a statue more appropriate for New York than Bartholdi's 'Liberty' " *Puck*, December 12, 1882.

Even the Amazon's more ascetic sister represented the power of the almighty dollar. (Her profile with Liberty cap or Indian feathers was incised by Augustus Saint-Gaudens upon the nation's coins by the direct commission of President Theodore Roosevelt.) But unlike the self-centered greed signified by *die Dollarprinzessin*, this other America stood for the economic and political power of a nation committed to a grand moral mission.[26] Through her image, *virtus* (the Roman term for male military might) joined with *virtue* (the quality generally delegated to the woman's sphere). In the 1890s the male heads swinging as trophies of victory from the hand of the new American Amazon gave warning what would happen to those with the audacity to obstruct the national values of Law, Justice, Truth, and Liberty which the warrior-woman now represented (figure 11.15).

Between 1581 and 1918 Galle's cannibal queen was transformed into a monumental figure of moral righteousness. For this transformation to take place, certain changes had to be made in the depiction of the original type and the ideas it

GODEY'S MAGAZINE

FOR SEPTEMBER

TEN CENTS A COPY
ONE DOLLAR A YEAR

THE WOMAN
THAT SAVED
THE UNION

ANNA ELLA CARROLL, "Secret Member of Lincoln's Cabinet"

11.13. H. S. Phillips, "The Woman That Saved the Union," poster for
Godey's Magazine (1896).

conveyed. Amoral jungle force had to be converted into the modern heroism required for survival in the wilderness of urban wickedness. Figure 11.16 gives the
Indian queen of 1867 a crown, a cross, and a sword. She is Sir Walter Scott's High-
land heroine, complete with Scotch-Irish virtues, transported to the howling forests of the North American continent. The iron Amazon (iron of will as well as of
material) which caused a stir at the Philadelphia Exposition enumerates the merger
of unlikely attributes that had come to characterize the "America" figure by 1876
(figure 11.17). Liberty cap, antique spear, stallion looted from an Italian eques-

11.14. Philipp Galle, "America" (1581–1600).

11.15. J. Scott Williams, "For Victory, Buy More Bonds" (1918).

trian pedestal, and African lion: these diverse elements are compressed into the single romanticized token of the power upon which nineteenth-century Americans liked to express their mastery of the American frontier.

In 1886 John J. Boyle prepared a small bronze grouping titled "Stone Age in America." In it the type of the Amazon warrior is conflated with the established tradition of the brave mother who protects her young. But the fierce stride of the stalwart female figure, the stone ax gripped in one hand, the child at her breast, and the body of the slain bear at her feet make this image far less like the protecting angel of the *Puck* cartoon of May 1882 than like the male warrior of the October *Puck* of the same year. The Amazon has been incorporated into the canon of mothers and protectors; but these mothers and protectors are also fearsome warriors. However domesticated as an image to the needs of late-nineteenth-century civilization, the original wildness of the type of the Amazon is by no means lost in the process of her transformation into a figure with the strength to stand for virile American values.

Emanuel Leutze made a major patriotic icon of George Washington by pitting the general against the Sodom and Gomorrah of British tyranny in his 1850 painting commemorating the crossing of the Delaware River. Leutze also gave his compatriots "The Amazon and Her Children" in 1851 (figure 11.18). This figure does not speak directly to the American national virtues as does the Washington figure. Conversely, it raises questions as to the exact nature of the statement conveyed

11.16. "The Heroine's March" (1867).

11.17. F. L. Mott Iron Co.,
"The Amazon" (1876),
engraving by W. Roffe,
from Weinberg, ed.,
Masterpieces of the Centennial International Exhibition, 1876 (1877).

by the woman's posture, the sword at her side, and the battling children (girls perhaps) whom she observes with (perhaps) approval, although what is most likely *not* being represented is Columbia Viewing with Horror the Forces of the South and the North Which Threaten Her Beloved Union. But other Amazonian figures emerging from the visual and symbolic center of the Philadelphia Exposition in 1876 allowed few such ambiguities, whatever questions *we* have to ask of the mélange of elements defining the American destiny displayed in figure 11.19. Three females with feathers, crown and Liberty cap, scepter, shield, spearlike staff, ax, and torch; Aztec warrior; bison: this is an inventory of symbolic props worthy of a road-company troupe.[27] Here the warrior spirit necessary for wilderness survival is supplemented by the symbolic signs of authority needed for progress in the modern world.

The convention of the Amazonian female is wondrously ample. It contains several subspecies. We have seen the Pioneer Mother. It also accommodated the stock of newly created American heroines—Pocahontas, Evangeline, and Priscilla—which mid-century poets and historians were sketching in for the public imagination. All images chance the danger of rapid trivialization. These figures were no exception. Figure 11.20 is a burlesque show poster. It shows how easily the heroic baring of breasts seen in "The Heroine's March" of 1867 (figure 11.16) or the iron statue

11.18. Emanuel Leutze, "The Amazon and Her Children" (1851).

CORCORAN GALLERY OF ART

piece of 1876 (figure 11.17) could be tarted up as a chorus line where "Columbian" legs, hips, and bosoms are more important than are symbolic representations of courage in the wilderness. Howard Chandler Christy's "Pocahontas" of 1912, part of his historical sequence of *Liberty Belles*, takes the Pocahontas myth on a downward plunge toward banality that even Henry Adams' grave attempt in 1867 at correcting rank historical errors could not predict,[28] nor John Barth's more manic vision in *The Sot-Weed Factor* of 1960 (figure 11.21). At least the costumed Indian pose taken by Sibyl Brainerd in honor of a ground-breaking ceremony in San Diego takes its romanticized sensuality seriously (figure 11.22). And at least the sheaf of Evangeline and Priscilla figures, drawn in 1903 and 1905 by Christy for the Bobbs-Merrill reprints of Longfellow's poems, represents sanctified images of pure young women using weapons of Christian piety against the threats of displacement, loss, and injustice incurred in strange new lands.

But examine the historical vision projected by Christy in *Liberty Belles*. His Pocahontas is the first of the *Eight Epochs in the Making of the American Girl*—published, by the way, at the same time as Gertrude Stein's *The Making of Americans*. Pocahontas represents the original stage of the nation's moral evolution, with the Puritan Priscilla next in line. By the time Christy enthrones the American Girl (see Introduction, figure 9), we realize that Christy is not being frivolous after all; he only seemed that way. The sequence of eight images from Indian Queen to American Queen is simply his way of recording the progress of civilization from Philipp Galle's Amazonian warrior to Hans Makart's *Dollarprinzessin*.[29] Once this imperial figure is placed on her seat of power in 1912 with the publication of *Liberty Belles*, it is a short distance to the apotheosis of the American Girl that lies just beyond: the Warrior Queen of the posters of World War I.

Howard Chandler Christy's images catch the popular mood of the early 1900s with almost dismaying accuracy. There were many in America who sensed, as did Christy, that America's newly acquired international powers somehow lay rooted

11.19. "America" (1876),
Doulton terra-cotta
design by John Bell
for Prince Albert Me-
morial, London; en-
graving by W. Roffe
from Weinberg, ed.,
*Masterpieces of the
Centennial Interna-
tional Exhibition,
1876*, vol. 2 (1877).

11.20. Archie Gunn, "Columbian Amazons" (1894).

COLUMBIAN AMAZONS.

in the image of the Indian heroine whose courage had "protected" the white European hero from death in the wilderness.[30] The forces of civilization would win
over the forces of whatever moral wilderness was let loose in the twentieth century because the Amazon Queen had spawned the dynasty whose finest modern

11.21. Howard Chandler
Christy, "Pocahontas,"
from *Liberty Belles*
(1912).

11.22 *(above)*. Sibyl Brainerd
as "Pocahontas" (1911).

PRINCETON UNIVERSITY LIBRARY

representation was the American Girl, whether her guise was that of Charmer, Protectress, or Warrior.[31]

A great deal depends upon the level of our tolerance for nationalistic emblems. The examples by Christy and the others of the American Girl en route to imperial glory can strike us as silly or as pernicious, or both. Pernicious in the unquestioned values they celebrate; silly in the slapdash mixture of symbolic references with which these images are loaded. Let us talk about the matter of their silliness first. They are not that, entirely; not when tested against the criteria by which "cosmic images" are judged as successful in what they have to say. In describing the ways in which images such as banners and stars function as meaning, Angus Fletcher notes that they are isolated by their status as surreal objects from the logical demands imposed by scientific perspectives and spatial relationships. Discordant elements are yoked together as a matter of course.[32] However great an emphasis they may give to appearances, the revelation of what lies beneath surfaces is the main purpose of allegorical emblems. The Amazon heroine with sword in hand, the Stone

Age Mother with club in hand, Pocahontas allowing homage to be given her by Captain Smith: all are brilliantly *found* objects—"discovered" in the midst of the clutter of American history and transformed into supposedly recognizable "truths." Taken at face value, they have little or no use; that is, if they are taken for fragments bouncing about in a void of meaning. What makes them work in the minds of true believers is the fact that their latent nature consists of a network of feelings they stand ready to arouse. There is yet another factor in the peculiar power they possess: they *look and act* like tamed types of the average and everyday, while they *feel* like those potent values which cluster around types of the original and the extraordinary.

The years spanning the national expositions of 1876 and 1893 mark a train of events which political scientists, historians, economists, and sociologists currently study with care in order to learn what *actually* took place in the United States.[33] During that same period, a second, celebratory history was being created by the imagination of Americans. People, places, and events from the past and the present were assessed for their patriotic force. New heroes and heroines were uncovered, discarded, or tailored out of whole cloth. Paul Bunyan, Johnny Appleseed, Mike Fink, and the Yankee Pedlar existed on the same plane as George Washington, Light Horse Harry Lee, Stonewall Jackson, and the newly resuscitated figure of Christopher Columbus. By 1893 Columbus was admired for his American "pluck" in opening the North American continent to European access, a concept that the unlucky sailor from Genoa might not have comprehended back in 1492. But Americans liked the way Columbus slipped easily in beside other favorite American "adventurers" like Daniel Boone and Davy Crockett.[34] In the same manner, students of American history and religion worked together to reshape icons for Christianity and democracy which would bless the American enterprise, even though they might not promise redemption or probation.[35]

Figures of historic male heroes were being elevated in the Exposition years to the level of near-mythical status, but female forms were pitched even higher. Pocahontas, Priscilla, Virginia Dare, Sacagawea, Evangeline, Molly Pitcher, and Betsy Ross became notable American heroines. They were the type of the spunky American Girl who brought the same pleasure to their admirers as did George McCutcheon's Beverly Calhoun or Richard Harding Davis' Edith Morris. To know the type of the heroines of the new American "history" was to recognize the type who centered the current popular romance.

The New Woman as Charmer and Outdoors Pal refers straight as an arrow to Christy's Pocahontas, but she does not really go back to the Amazon Queen of Philipp Galle. The Amazon's progeny were made of sterner, loftier stuff than was Beverly Calhoun braving the wild things of Graustark. The daughters of the female image by Galle were assigned a mighty mission. It was for them to provide the types of ideal virtue that reigned in marble or bronze or as painted murals along the corridors of the Library of Congress and of the state capitols of Saint Paul and Des Moines. They became the statuary that ornamented the grounds of the Colum-

11.23. Domenico Tojetti, "The
Progress of America"
(1875).

OAKLAND MUSEUM OF ART

bian Exposition and the public parks of the City Beautiful movement in the decades after 1893.

"The Progress of America," painted by Domenico Tojetti in 1875, put into visible form the verses of Bishop Berkeley's "Westward the Path of Empire Takes Its Way" (figure 11.23). The wild Indian and the buffalo flee before the approach of the goddess Columbia in her Roman chariot, presented in the high style of late Italian Renaissance altar paintings. But then Tojetti was still new to the United States. Old World baroque models were still too close to his mind's eye. Other artists more familiar with local habits of symbolic reference soon placed the figure of "America" in imperial poses extracted from that odd mix of aesthetic traditions and iconographic conventions (drawn from both American and European art practices) we recognize as characteristic of late-nineteenth-century art.

Traces of the European aesthetic signature are to be found everywhere in the patriotic art produced in turn-of-the-century American art studios, but that art is stamped "American" through the tension that prevails between the cozily anecdotal and the awe-inspiring grandeur of the sublime. The physical and emotional scale common to Old World goddesses contended with the just-folks flavor that gives the New World picturesque its particular domestic proportions. In the art that proliferated during the 1890s and early 1900s there are figures which aspire to a lofty "feudal" intensity of coherence, honor, and order. There are also the figures which give themselves to the downward slope of kitsch that has no higher goals than to talk about the pleasures of money and home.

Angus Fletcher and Clement Greenberg have written on the social implication of the arts of the feudal and sublime set in opposition to the arts of the kitsch and picturesque. The applicability of their arguments to the patriotic art of late nine-teenth-century America will be touched upon at the conclusion of chapter 13, set within the frame of pertinent remarks by Edward Said. But before we turn to what these critics have to suggest for our consideration, I want to show *the look* of American patriotic art that incorporates female forms. I want to provide demon-strations of three related artistic expressions: the sublime, the picturesque, and examples which crazily contain elements of the first two within a single image. It is necessary (although not always pleasant) to go through an extended experience of forms which mix contraries and proclaim impossibilities, which are not always as intelligent or critical of their own means and ends as we might like. Paramount among the forms that will be placed on view are images of the Warrior and the Angel that declare identifiable civic values, while suggesting the most personal and shrouded of desires.

12

Scaling Up to War (1876–1898)

Scale is an important consideration in neoclassical aesthetics and in the design of the official arts of the ideal,[1] just as it is an essential element in the creation of colossal figures. Mathematics of perspective and the academy's devices for the incitement of sublime emotions join to form a logical basis for the making of immense forms. Since many such figures were erected in public places in the United States at the turn of the century, it is appropriate to ask whether male or female forms claimed the privilege of scale and on what occasions these outsized forms were expected to represent notions of national vastness.

Initially, gender is not what matters in the creation of large-scale works of art. John Flaxman's *Lectures on Sculpture* point out this fact; delivered before the Royal Academy between 1810 and 1826, the English designer's views continued to command an audience in mid-nineteenth-century America of those interested, like earlier neoclassicists, in the relation of form to representations of ideal values.[2] Beautiful bodies are like rational architecture, Flaxman argued; through the perfection of their proportions, they function with the clarity of iconic statements. The significations expressed by male and female forms modeled on the human scale are distinct: the male tells of power and exertion; the female of tenderness and grace. But once colossal scale is assigned to sculptured forms, the sign of sacred might is possessed by gods and goddesses alike.[3]

The implications of Flaxman's lectures for American sculpture of the public, patriotic kind are important in two ways. First, once sculptors arrive at the aesthetic decision to inspire awe through the making of colossi, they can use either a female or a male figure. Second, sculptors working during periods when the idea of the female is tied to ideas of national virtue can extend its cultural meaning to include the imperial might associated with physical forms shaped on the grand scale.

Absentmindedness over strict gender distinctions was common under conditions where eclecticism was the habit of mid-nineteenth-century American sculptors. William Wetmore Story proposed willy-nilly to sculpt a colossal female "Jerusalem," an outsized William Cullen Bryant, and a gigantic female "America" mounted with a like figure of Francis Scott Key.[4] There is a charming photograph of Harriet Hosmer posed like a female Tom Thumb on a high scaffold next to an immense statue of Thomas Hart Benton. But these were random works of large-scale art that just "happened," as it were, because their creators wished them so. In contrast, William Ordway Partridge's *Technique of Sculpture* of 1895 reflects the attempt of one late-nineteenth-century artist to assign good reasons for the proportioning of male and female figures. Not that Partridge is completely clear on the matter, but his remarks suggest a move toward the making of such distinctions in scale.[5]

A traditionalist through and through, Partridge relied heavily on precedent. It is with an almost audible sigh of relief that he turns to the type of the Venus de Medici and the Venus de Milo in order to lay down certain principles in regard to sculptural proportion. Academicians in America and Europe already "knew" that the Medici figure represented softness and grace; they also accepted the Venus de Milo as the *different* Venus—the type of magisterial dignity.[6] Not surprisingly, Partridge abides by the usual gender distinctions which linked softness and grace with the feminine and magisterial dignity with the masculine. He proceeds to make explicit the means by which Greek sculptors achieved the effect of grace through the elongation of the torso, exemplified by the Medici Venus. But if Partridge clearly associates elongation with feminine grace, he fails to pick up the second term of the comparison by explaining how the ancients achieved the visual effect of masculine force in the type of the Venus de Milo. Partridge has allowed that there are two types of female forms (the soft and the powerful), but he does not follow through on the matter of there being two possible kinds of scaling: the elongated and the immense.

Partridge's contemporaries were experimenting with exactly those elements of elongation and immensity. The results were varied, but certain new patterns emerged. There was the type of the "divinely tall, divinely fair" American Girl. Greatly lengthened through the torso in enhancement of her "divine' qualities of feminine softness and grace, her scale remained within the range of the human (figure 12.1). There was also the Type of America, Columbia, Liberty, or the Republic—allegorical figures created on a colossal scale appropriate for public deities expressive of traditional masculine *virtus* (figure 12.2).

These two categories did not remain closed to one another. There was an exchange of notations between the elongated form of the tall American Girl and that of the colossal bulk of the "America" figure. The importance of these separate yet related symbols is great. Joined together they offered an embodiment of national-

12.1. Thomas Wilmer Dewing,
"The Blue Dress" (1892).

FREER GALLERY OF ART

istic statements about the position of the United States in the world scheme. Heroic representations of George Washington, Abraham Lincoln, or Roosevelt the Rough Rider had to compete with the authority newly assigned to off-scale images in female form.

Sculptors and painters of tall female forms turned to an ample inventory of classical references familiar to a broad constituency of viewers. There was the Diana figure, itself a mélange of references to the hunt, chastity, and childbirth. She could be visualized with overlays of the bacchante and the Amazon (see figure 9.22) or appear as the gigantic Saint-Gaudens figure that had its day atop Stanford White's Madison Square Garden (figure 12.3).[7] Minerva also had a rich iconic history. She served as the female prototype for militant force. She personified the love

12.2. Daniel Chester French,
"The Republic," 20-foot
enlargement of the 1892
working model (1918).

CHESTERWOOD MUSEUM ARCHIVES

of wisdom which conservators of civilization set up as their favorite deity. She expressed justice with helmet and sword, an apt figure for use in the feminist pageant of 1913 which advanced the cause of woman's suffrage (figure 12.4). Any one of these Minervas was ready to inspire necessary wars or essential missions on either side of the political divide, conservative or progressive.

There was also the tradition of Venus, a touchy image to incorporate into the life of the official emotions of the United States. A parochialized Venus de Medici of feminine grace nicely served American gentility as the Beautiful Charmer. Discreetly draped versions of the Venus de Milo might see service as the indomitable New Woman. But the Venus Genetrix whose sexual energy creates and sustains the earth's life appeared to have no patriotic work to do for America.

Henry Adams scouted out the Venus Genetrix in medieval France and mourned her absence in the United States. Adams was convinced that the American imagination would never accommodate the special power of female sexuality and creative love.[8] He feared that even the most skillful of American artists would fail to give that ancient figure of primal force an "American" look. We can, however, find strong traces of this Venus in the figures which Augustus Saint-Gaudens mod-

12.3. Augustus Saint-Gaudens, "Diana," 18-foot weather-vane, first version (1886–1891).

SAINT-GAUDENS NATIONAL HISTORICAL SITE

eled upon his mistress Davida Johnson. Davida was the source of Saint-Gaudens' "Diana," the "Amor Caritas," and the Sherman "Victory." With her fine form and classical features, Davida perhaps comes the closest to combining into a significant visual whole the all-encompassing myth of the Venus Genetrix. But even the Davida figure and face required the referential addition of a male component to sustain their meaning. Stanford White stands, as it were, behind the "Diana," General Sherman behind the "Victory," and Saint-Gaudens himself behind the "Amor Caritas." Besides, these three forms (even the "Diana") depend upon elongation. Their final effect is that of soft grace and charming femininity. Scaled up though they are, they lack the self-contained authority borne by messengers of political power or sexual energy.

Only one of the Saint-Gaudens monuments truly stands alone, needing no com-

12.4. "Columbia," from suffrage tableaux, Washing-
ton, D.C., March 3, 1913.

plementing figure or association to express its power, nor even proportions lifted beyond the usual. It is the form Saint-Gaudens sculpted for his friend Henry Adams as the memorial figure for Marian Hooper Adams' tomb (figure 12.5). Unnamed, unspecified in its intentionality of meaning, unappropriated to any particular signification of religion, patriotism, philosophy, or emotion, it is a figure which forbids interpretation. In its silence it simply is, and is therefore Presence, the greatest of all force, one whose imaginative scope is without scale. But it is not, however, the kind of figure most Americans were looking for; not when there was a national rage to identify and be identified with worldly and moral influence.

Adams' view of things was hardly representative of the common impulse to assign meaning and significance to everything in sight. If possible, the public would have given a tag to the Saint-Gaudens memorial figure, even though that meant turning the silent form into something as legible as a label for Macy's pants.[9] And

12.5. Augustus Saint-Gaudens,
detail from the Adams
Memorial, Rock Creek
Cemetery, Washington,
D.C. (1891).

SAINT-GAUDENS NATIONAL HISTORICAL SITE

if Americans liked grave markers to say right out what they meant, they wanted even more to have the way they lived furnished with a sign the whole world could read. Size was one label that was readily understandable, even to those who knew no English. But how to manifest the size of their national aspirations in a single, effective image?

What an easy formula it turned out to be. The formula for America that pleased the largest possible audience—that displayed American pride, American immensity, American morality, American material success—was the often tall, sometimes colossal, form of the American Girl.

The attenuated figure of the American female received attention from a number

METROPOLITAN MUSEUM OF ART, NEW YORK

12.6. John Singer Sargent, "Mr. and Mrs. I. N. Phelps Stokes" (1897).

12.7. Albert Beck Wenzell,
from Wharton, *The House
of Mirth* (1905).

of well-known artists of high and low degree. John Singer Sargent's 1897 painting
of Mr. and Mrs. Isaac Newton Phelps Stokes attests to where the interest lies (figure 12.6). Mr. Stokes hovers in the background, but it is his exuberantly "lengthy"
wife who captures the viewer's attention.[10] Howard Chandler Christy turned out
tall women by the ream, as did Albert Beck Wenzell. Figure 12.7 depicts the monumental Lily Bart supplied by Wenzell for the first edition of Edith Wharton's *The
House of Mirth* in 1905, with little regard for Wharton's description of Lily as someone with more litheness than *embonpoint*.

In a diary entry of 1894, Morton Fullerton (the man who became Wharton's
lover some fourteen years later) provides the erotic dream image that lies behind
the emergence of a form with the capacity to fill the mind's widest spaces.[11] Notice
the architectural setting for the appearance of his ideal woman—"a splendid palace . . . of long corridors and high ceilings and airy rooms." It is this setting and

this woman which would, with variations, dominate American fantasies of feminine force during the 1890s and early 1900s; they would then become, with the greatest ease, fantasies of national power. "She was of perfect classic beauty, divinely tall, and divinely fair, magnificently serene in her movements, big-browed, gentle-eyed, with round arms and fully modulated curves of breasts, and belly. . . . She was very grand, and as big, I swear it, as the ladies of the Erechtheum. I wished to worship at her shrine."

James Montgomery Flagg phrased the pleasure he took in female amplitude in words less elegant than Fullerton's; but he was just as emphatic. "A woman must be tall, well-built and have good breasts—that's important—finely made hands and feet and long legs . . . I don't give a damn what other people think."[12]

What most other people *did* think fell into agreement with the tastes of Fullerton and Flagg. There were some who took exception, however. An editorial appearing in the *New York Sun* during the first years of the Gibson Girl craze of the 1890s accused Gibson of encouraging the desire for extravagant height in the hearts of the population, even though that era was a time of short men and shorter women.[13] Statistics for 1889 indicate that the average height of female college students was 5 feet 2.5 inches. Males at college were 5 feet 7 inches. True, by 1918 improvements in hygiene and nutrition made possible a sampling of young Boston women which raised the average to 5 feet 5 inches, while Boston men stretched up to 5 feet 8.7 inches. These are nice heights, surely, but nothing out of the way in terms of sublime grandeur or cultural apotheosis. What mattered was not the averages of ordinary and actual women but the norms required by the public's desires.[14]

The editorialist in the *Sun* described the Gibson type as a "cathedral-like lady with . . . extraordinary reach and Atlantean shoulders." He also likened her to "the cedars of Lebanon . . . the tower of Babel . . . [and] to M. Bartholdi's Liberty Statue." He chided Gibson for setting up "giantesses" who loom over the hapless American male, as in this example from the series "The Weaker Sex" (figure 12.8). The marketing world agreed with the Gibsonian image, however, not with the stodgy facts of female height, and planned their products and promotions accordingly (figure 12.9).

However much the editorialist for the *New York Sun* disliked what he saw taking place in the American imagination, he provided a useful résumé of age-old aspirations after bigness. But although he called upon the past and the Old World (Babel, Atlantis, Lebanese cedars, Gothic cathedrals), what signifies is the focus he placed upon the Statue of Liberty as exemplum of his contemporaries' growing interest in the monumental. The copper-clad colossus by Frédéric Bartholdi had been welcoming the immigrant ships that steamed into New York's harbor for less than a decade; but its original links with a long French tradition of revolutionary fervor had already been replaced in the mind of the public with sentiments that had undergone a sea change between Europe and the United States.[15] Bartholdi's art gift became (with reluctance at first on the part of its recipients) an *American*

12.8. Charles Dana Gibson, "The Weaker Sex—II," *Collier's Weekly*, July 4, 1903.

12.9. "Every Woman Admires a Tall Man," The Cartilage Co., Rochester, New York (1904).

Every Woman Admires a Tall Man

If you are short, you will appreciate the unpleasant and humiliating position of the little man in the above illustration. But you are probably unaware that it is no longer necessary to be short and uncomfortable.

The Cartilage Company, of Rochester, N. Y., is the owner of a method whereby any one can add from two to three inches to his stature. It is called the "Cartilage System" because it is based upon a scientific and physiological method of expanding the cartilage, all of which is clearly and fully explained in a booklet entitled "**How to Grow Tall,**" which is yours for the asking.

The Cartilage system builds up the entire body harmoniously. It not only increases the height, but its use means better health, more nerve force, increased bodily development and longer life. Its use necessitates no drugs, no internal treating, no operation, no hard work, no big expense. Your height can be increased, no matter what your age or sex may be, and this can be done at home without the knowledge of others. This new and original method of increasing one's height has received the enthusiastic endorsement of physicians and instructors in physical culture. If you would like to add to your height, so as to be able to see in a crowd, walk without embarrassment with those who are tall, and enjoy the other advantages of proper height, you should write at once for a copy of our free booklet "**How to Grow Tall.**" It tells you how to accomplish these results quickly, surely, and permanently. Nothing is left unexplained. After you read it, your only wonder will be "Why did not some one think of it before?" Write today.

THE CARTILAGE COMPANY, 74 P, Unity Building, ROCHESTER, N. Y.

idol; it was disassociated from the inefficient way the French conduct their revolutions, run their republics, and create images of their women.

What was happening to the image of the American Girl during the 1890s was not, according to most Americans, being duplicated in other countries. Take the important example of *Trilby*. The novel was all the rage in the United States after its publication in England in 1894, but contemporary commentators on American mores made it clear that Du Maurier's heroine, however tall and charming, should not be mistaken for the national paragons provided by Gibson and his fellow American artists. Trilby might appear in garb which made her look somewhat like the Columbia figure (figure 12.10). But Trilby was, after all, a common girl from the

12.10. George Du Maurier, "It
Was Trilby," from *Trilby*
(1894).

Parisian bohemian quarter. In contrast, the chastity of the American Girl and the niceness of her social circle were irreproachable. Her force as a national symbol was not that alone of physical bearing. Like Galahad, her force was the force of ten because her heart, mind, and body were pure.[16]

However single-minded Americans were about the chasteness they exacted of this lithe young girl, they managed to make her image complex in other ways. Gibson drew the Girl raising a stirrup cup after riding to the hounds, to signify the spontaneous naturalness of her free and independent spirit (figure 12.11). The American female was also the unapproachable high-society queen. Mrs. Cornelius Vanderbilt (neither tall nor willowy) who appeared at her costume ball as "The Electric Light," arm lifted high (figure 12.12). Both figures share the ambiguous gesture made familiar to us by the Statue of Liberty (figure 12.13). With or without a torch, that arm may extend a gesture of welcome. Or it may be raised in lordly dominion. Or it might signify the command "Halt, go no further! This land is off-limits to all but the great."[17]

The Liberty gesture is also incorporated into an appeal by "Woman"—an allegorical figure who asks for political rights from a government which, although willing to glorify the power of her image, is reluctant to grant power to actual women (figure 12.14). How, then, were middling-sized Americans like Margaret Wycherly to collapse the distance between their own essential ineffectuality on the social scene and the female figures named as emblems of national might?

Most women were considered "picturesque" elements upon the American male

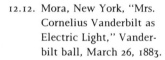

12.11. Charles Dana Gibson, untitled, from *The Social Ladder* (1902).

12.12. Mora, New York, "Mrs. Cornelius Vanderbilt as Electric Light," Vanderbilt ball, March 26, 1883.

scene. In contrast, female icons like the Liberty statue convey the sublime. What is picturesque can be dismissed. What is sublime can hardly be overlooked. Certain contemporary responses to Bartholdi's "Liberty" indicate what that figure possesses which American women lacked as social and political entities. Margaret Wycherly stands in the pose of the Liberty statue, but her personal scale and setting are ordinary. In like manner the Bartholdi statue *as a design* is nothing in particular. But add to the preliminary design its great size and its placement on Bedloe's Island at the throat of New York harbor, and emotional force is guaranteed.

Bartholdi knew what he wanted to express through the scale of his figure. "The immensity of form should be filled with the immensity of thought, and the spectator, at the sight of the great proportions of the work, should be impressed before all things else, with the greatness of the idea of which these ample forms are the envelope, without being obliged to have recourse to comparative measurements in order to feel himself moved."[18]

BIBLIOTÉQUE NATIONALE, PARIS

12.13. Contemporary woodcut, "Liberty," delivered to the American ambassador, Paris, July 4, 1884.

12.14. "Margaret Wycherly as 'Woman,'" July 1915.

LIBRARY OF CONGRESS

Bartholdi's explanation of how the designer of symbols gets from object to response is a bit dry, depending as it does on his attention to "comparative measurements." But terror, then delight, are the effects of the great scale, capable of overwhelming the spectator upon first encounter.[19] "The first sentiment inspired by this enormous head, nearly thirty feet high, is almost terror. Its gigantic dimensions are stupefying; but by degrees the eye becomes accustomed to the colossal forms, and the mind reconciles itself to the extent of those great lines, and we discover in the midst of them the majesty and the light which the author has endeavored to give to the features."

This, a Frenchman's complex response, was set down well before the completion of the Liberty project. But what of the responses typical of the minds of the Americans who were asked to assimilate the gigantic female form into a mythic conception of themselves as citizens of a mighty and generous nation? "Majestic and beautiful . . . serene and grand, a fit emblem to meet the new comer to our shores."[20]

Bartholdi thinks about measurements and site, as a designer must at the onset of his project. A French contemporary moves through successive states of emotional reaction: from a feeling that is "almost terror" and is certainly "stupefying," to the mind's reconciliation with the humanly impossible, on to the stage in which "majesty and light" are the happy result. It is that third and final stage of response which Americans have tended to appropriate. Mathematical considerations and Gallic *frisson* are replaced by an American sublime which is simultaneously majestic and serene, colossal and cozy.

"America the Beautiful" with its spacious skies and prairies where the deer and the antelope roam is a "home" that is grand and inviting at the same time. The potentiality for sublime terror is latent but held down; the emphasis is on the pleasures of a power that is safe for the folks at home. Once again, American imaginations want it both ways. Majestic power perceived about themselves; intimidating force perceived by potential foes. A colossal form that is on "our side" provides stirring emotions; it also helps one to forget that such might can be turned against the nation for which it stands as "a fit emblem."[21]

To return for a moment to Margaret Wycherly in her Liberty pose (see figure 12.14): to a public reluctant to espouse her cause, a woman as a suffragist in 1915 suggests the kind of force that is neither sublime nor safe. Granted that she is only an ordinary woman of average height, vaguely dressed and loosely posed as a national symbol. Still she "demonstrates" for an idea of freedom which would pry women away from their traditional sphere of domestic influence. The signs she presents to unconvinced interpreters are negative. The actuality of her person and the principles of her cause counter acceptable conventions about statuary figures with torches held aloft; they reinforce the notion that Liberty in the form of women like *that* prophesy a future that is neither majestic nor serene. For popular appeal, another version of the Liberty symbol far surpasses that of Margaret Wycherly (figure 12.15). In 1918 18,000 soldiers on duty at Camp Dodge outside Des Moines, Iowa, were ordered to stand in ranks specified by the Chicago photographers Mole and Thomas.[22] The visual result (shot from an American eagle's eye view) is an immense Liberty figure which *contains* thousands. Now, this is one way that the female form can swallow up male members of the population and still find acceptance (except, perhaps, by the soldiers themselves who may have been hot, bored, and irritated by this meaningless little exercise in the allegorical). But a suffragist like Margaret Wycherly, in her own person, could hardly hope to make a patriotic gesture on so effective a scale, particularly one which suggests the military might of the nation, not the political aspirations of its women.

Celebration of the elongated grandeur of the female form was not the general case in the years prior to the Civil War. An apparent exception to this fact is Walt Whitman. From the first issue of *Leaves of Grass* in 1855 Whitman celebrated size—that expansiveness of space and time he equated with the generous soul of America. His verses fondle such words as "enormous masses," "colossal outposts," "vast," and "great." Even though his poem is extravagantly full because it is his own form

12.15. Mole and Thomas, Chicago, "Human Statue of Liberty," Camp Dodge, Des Moines, Iowa (1918).

he celebrates ("Walt you contain enough, why don't you let it out then?"), "Democracy"—imaged as the impressive female form of "Ma femme!"—is one of the vessels into which he poured his and the nation's greatness. But few of the female figures which appeared in the popular literature of Whitman's day were as statuesque as Whitman's vision of democratic greatness implied.[23] For every exception to the generally middling height of the American male (such as Abraham Lincoln), a squat Mary Todd Lincoln stands at his side. Nathaniel Hawthorne's Hester, Zenobia, and Miriam are intimidating as fictional characters precisely because they tower over the fashion-plate dolls sponsored by *Godey's Lady's Book*. Alcott's Jo March and E.D.E.N. Southworth's tall and vigorous heroines have to contend with the taste, later decried by Charlotte Perkins Gilman, for the "small," "dainty," and "delicate."[24]

Take Harriet Beecher Stowe's *Uncle Tom's Cabin* as one particularly instructive example. Stowe's novel gives us several versions of the ideal type of the child-as-mother and the mother-as-childlike in size and manner. Matching Little Eva in stature and maternal impulse is the diminutive figure of Mrs. Bird. She is hardly distinguishable from Eva in either her appearance or her function as Saving Grace in the narrative. As described by Stowe, Mrs. Bird was a familiar type for readers of the the popular fiction of the 1850s: "a timid, blushing little woman, of about four feet in height, and with mild blue eyes, and a peach-blow complexion, and the gentlest, sweetest voice in the world."[25]

Mrs. Bird is like Eva, however: a moral slave driver who commands hulking males to be good, no matter the worldly inconvenience. Eva has the bulk of Tom to twist around her finger; Mrs. Bird has her husband, the senator. A statistical study of 1866 reveals that U.S. senators averaged 5 feet 10.5 inches, well above the national average,[26] but even their fictional counterparts were no match for the imposing piety of the child crusaders.

By the late 1890s citizens of the United States took as their moral mission the obligation to save the dusky children of the Caribbean, the Philippines, and Latin America. The roles and symbolic scale allocated to savior figures were reversed from Stowe's day. Diminutive mothers and physically frail children of great moral strength were replaced as champions of the helpless. Gigantic female forms now expressed the sense of national destiny; they redefined the nature of the protective zeal that went with the new moral and territorial imperialism.

Consider two of Daniel Chester French's designs for monumental figures representative of American nationhood. "The Republic" stood alone and aloof upon her pedestal 100 feet above the waters of the Grand Basin at the 1893 Columbian Exposition. (See figure 12.2, a 20-foot enlargement of the working model, and figure 12.16, the original statue in place at the fair.) In 1906 "America" was one of four massive pieces commemorating the world's continents which French sculpted for the approach to the U.S. Custom House. Notice the difference (figure 12.17). The 1906 grouping is smaller in physical scale than "The Republic," but the "scale" of what the "America" figure now takes as her duty to perform is greatly enhanced. The increase in influence is expressed by French's addition of the two figures over which "America" directs her command. An Indian (remnant of the race removed forever from its place in the processes of Western historiography) crouches behind the seated female. Beside her (protected by her outflung arm) is the kneeling male form of Progress.

A contemporary commentator enthusiastically described the success of the symbolism of French's sculpture.[27] His words suggest how aggressively virtuous the nation had become in the eyes of her admirers. "The woman's figure here is that of the ideal woman of the New World—young, strong, alert, every line instinct with vitality. The face is the clean-cut, markedly intellectual type that has come

12.16. Francis Benjamin Johnston, "The Grand Basin, Columbian Exposition" (1893).

LIBRARY OF CONGRESS

to be accepted as distinctly American, and the pose of the figure suggests a readiness to spring into instant and vigorous action."

In this description there is no questioning of what this massive, muscular sculpture signifies, nor are there doubts that the "America" figure represents a nation that is destined to create, guide, and protect the future of other nations. Not, surely, the doubts expressed by this cover cartoon from *Life* in 1903 captioned "Appropriate group of statuary for the New York Custom House" (figure 12.18). Here a winged America strong-arms those without the power to protest their treatment at the hands of the government officials; here America's "readiness to spring into instant and vigorous action" is no way benign.

In 1906, the same year French completed the Custom House sculpture, Christy made uncomfortably plain what America's relation with the rest of the world was meant to be. In *The American Girl as Seen and Portrayed by Howard Chandler Christy* the author and illustrator is nothing if not explicit about the special power his Girl represents in heralding the near future when she will "become a veritable queen of the kingliest of races."[28] Happy consequence of the evolutionary process, the Girl rapidly progresses toward the fulfillment of the northern European physiognomical and cultural ideal. What else, Christy asks rhetorically, could be the culmination of a democratic society blessed by mellifluous climate, rural virtue, pioneer spirit, and strict habits of hygiene and morality than "the incomparable she!"

The Spanish-American War and the takeover of the Philippines lie just behind the publication of Christy's book. The still-greater glory of the First World War waits on ahead to welcome the Girl who hastens like a female Messiah to enter "upon her wider kingdom." America's daughter of the people symbolizes the pic-

12.17. Daniel Chester French, "America," U.S. Custom House, New York (1903–1907).

DANIEL CHESTER FRENCH PAPERS

turesque virtues of simplicity, but she is also "the heiress of all the ages," so sublimely costly that "to make her all that she is countless millions have lived and died." By the 1930s Scott Fitzgerald concerned himself about the price paid to engender Nicole Warren and Daisy Buchanan, but Christy's Girl confirms her value

12.18. "Appropriate Group of
Statuary for the New
York Custom House,"
Life, October 22, 1903.

in 1906 as "the culmination of mankind's long struggle upward from his barbarism
into civilization." That there may be no question concerning the Girl's national
origins, Christy sets her majestic bearing in sharp contrast to puny immigrant women
who take their "awkward blundering way . . . stupidly [staring] upon the wonders
of the New World." Unlike this alien presence, Christy's "America" is "an acknowledged Queen" at the peak of her perfection, with the physical scale to prove
it.

Once again we have to consider the strange situation which occurred when visual standards based upon so-called white Anglo-Saxon Protestant traits were imposed by a society that was being reshaped daily by an influx of racial and ethnic
groups whose bodies and faces did not confirm to officially sanctioned images. "The
other half" was constantly reminded of what it was not and ought to be but could
never hope to become. *That half* of the American urban population was described
in 1893 by a writer for the *New York Times* as follows: "hatchet-faced, pimply,
sallow-cheeked, rat-eyed young men of the Russian-Jew colony."[29] Even earlier, in
1885, Josiah Strong warned his readers about the "diminishing" effect the European peasant would introduce into American life. The type was one "whose horizon has been narrow, whose moral and religious training has been meager or false,
and whose ideas of life are low." There was nothing "tall" about such people,
judged as they were by their "betters."

The drawings by Kenyon Cox which appeared in Jacob Riis' initial presentation of *How the Other Half Lives* show stunted people in stunted places (figure 12.19). So do Gibson's sympathetic drawings of 1898 in which bodily verticals result from the effects of hunger, not from the "tallness" of power (figure 12.20). During 1909–1910 Franz Boas compiled statistics on newly arrived immigrants.[30] Young women from Bohemia averaged 5 feet 2.4 inches, and the men 5 feet 5.1 inches. The monumental sweep of the Gibson Girl was something else altogether. According to their detractors, immigrants totally lacked the grand moral stature which the American Girl represented to the country's pictorial imagination. Even Christy admitted the good fortune of the fact that generations spent in the New World environment had helped make the Girl what she now was. But mainly at issue was the question whether several lifetimes spent in the United States would eventually strengthen the physical and moral fiber of the new immigrant stock, without doing damage to "Americans" in the process.[31]

There were occasional instances of futuristic visions which did not impose any one nationalistic "scale" upon the world, or attempt to set up specific bodily images that demeaned "the others" by contrast. In 1903 such a vision was proposed that gloried in extremes of scale while imaging equality among nations. It was a city plan proposed by Hendrik Christian Andersen, and remarked upon by his close friend Henry James, in the same year Saint-Gaudens' General and the Girl went on view to disturb James no end.

The frontispiece Andersen prepared for *Creation of a World Centre of Communication* images a world city envisioned on a scale far exceeding that of the White City of Chicago in 1893.[32] It is commanded by two nude figures. The one to the left is the female of the pair which leads the future toward global peace (figure 12.21). This patron saint of the dream space Andersen proposed only a few years before Woodrow Wilson's vision of the League of Nations is a type-for-all-the-world. Her figure has nothing in common with the American Girl who springs from the aspirations of a specific nation; it possesses none of the ambiguities of the Girl who represents a country with a complex sense of itself that contains the paradox of feminine virtue and masculine power.

Another piece of sculpture taken from Andersen's city plan of 1903 also points to some of the differences between images that are simple and those which bear excrutiatingly complicated messages. Figure 12.22 shows one of the hundreds of sculpted figures Andersen designed for the immense central fountain of his world city.[33] A naked woman astride a horse, it stands in marked contrast to the numerous equestrian statues erected in the United States by the close of the century in honor of heavily uniformed male generals expert in the arts of war. It supplies a vivid counterimage to the Saint-Gaudens grouping of the same year. Here the Girl rides the horse. Nearly androgynous in form, "she" is also "he." And the occasion she marks is not the fact of war but the assurance of peace.

On formalistic grounds alone, Andersen's rider cannot be mistaken for the American Girl whose clearly female, fully clothed form stirred American male imagi-

12.20. Charles Dana Gibson,
"Waiting for Bread,"
from *Americans* (1898).

12.19. Kenyon Cox, "Lodgers in a Crowded Bayard Street
Tenement—'Five Cents a Spot,'" after a photograph
by Jacob Riis, from "How the Other Half Lives,"
Scribner's Monthly Magazine, December 1889.

nations; and although there are similarities in form, this figure cannot be placed within the American tradition of Amazon Queens described in chapter 11. Ideological considerations prevent her from joining the iconic tribe beginning with Philipp Galle's "America" which led to the female warriors of World War I poster art. Andersen's equestrian figure is the herald of worldwide community; it denies the intense nationalism and imperial possessiveness that many Americans had assimilated into their sense of scale by 1903. Andersen's icon is intended as a celebration of universal friendship and the union of the male and the female; it refuses to honor the need for enemies and oppositions required by Americans who favor wars fought for the cause of might and right—whether between nations or between the sexes.

On one score alone does Andersen's equestrian figure seem to share with the American Girl and the Amazon Warrior the troublesome and ambiguous imagery of power, as the critique supplied by Henry James makes clear. Andersen was the close companion of James during the latter years of the novelist's life. Whatever the facts concerning the intimacy the two men shared,[34] it is certain that James cared a great deal for the young sculptor's friendship. However, when James read Andersen's massive text-with-illustrations of 1903, he deplored what he found. Writing to Andersen, James told him that the imagined city was based on "megalomania," "la folie des grandeurs," and "the infatuated, and disproportionate love and pursuit of, and attempt at, the Big, the Bigger, the Biggest, the Immensest Immensity, with all sense of proportion, application, elation and possibility madly submerged."

12.21. Hendrik Christian Andersen, frontispiece for *Creation of a World Centre of Communication* (1903).

Andersen's sometimes female, sometimes androgynous figures and the American Girl were, alike, threatened by the loss of "proportion, application, elation and possibility"—that is, by the loss of that private scale of individuality which out-sized icons forgo.

One of the prerogatives which an idol (especially one which stands for a nation's sense of righteousness) takes for granted is not to have its power questioned. Symbolizing as it does the unyielding meaning of absolute virtue, the Ideal Form and the state of ambiguity surely have little to do with one another. But ambiguity is

12.22. Hendrik Christian Andersen, from *Creation of
a World Centre of Com-
munication* (1903).

what we constantly confront when in the presence of the American Girl. Nowhere
was this fact more apparent than in Chicago at the Columbian Exposition of 1893
where the public was exposed to a morally entangled complex of duty, mission,
and power which quickly figured among its main preoccupations. If the incorporation of America found its early material expression at the Columbian fairgrounds,[35] Chicago was also the first major testing ground for imperial fantasies of
progress and influence and the occasion for the authorization of tall female forms
as leading symbols for the nation's aspirations.

The men in charge of designing the Columbian Exposition furnished the architectural spaces for the display of the manly power of technology and marketing,
and also the occasion for the mounting of allegorical versions of the Girl which
represented Americans at their best (that is, their largest). Males still assumed
direct social and political authority, but the iconic statements intended to inspire
their authority and to interpret the consequences of their actions were female in
form. The Exposition's buildings were based on Renaissance models and spoke of
male money power; the statues, classical in nature, became appropriate signs for
the female properties which both monitored and encouraged male power.

The center of the Chicago fairgrounds was dominated by a series of monumental
architectural ensembles in gleaming white.[36] Several were crowned by female colossi with the interchangeable tags of "Victory," "Liberty," or "Freedom." Each
represented, just as interchangeably, Columbia, America, or the Republic. There
was Philip Martiny's "Victory" (14 feet high atop a dome 125 feet high). There
was Daniel Chester French's "Republic" dominating one end of the Grand Basin
(see figure 12.16). Most splendid of all was the fountain executed by Frederick
MacMonnies where "Columbia" sat upon a barge propelled by eight standing fe-

males, guided by "Time" and heralded by "Fame"—none of the figures less than 12 feet in height (figure 12.23).

Will H. Low, one of the artists working at the Exposition, provides a contemporary overview of the sights that most astonished visitors to Chicago. Low was particularly struck by the grandeur of the MacMonnies "Columbia." He singled out the rowers of the imperial barge as superlative expression of "the epitome of youth [which] fills such a large part of our [American] experiment."[37] Low explicitly identified the rowers with the women of Smith and Wellesley who had been given the honor to bear Columbia, the symbol of the nation, on her journey into Time and Fame. Columbia was an abstraction for the nation—the Girl caught up in the present moment. The young women of Smith and Wellesley furnished the historical particulars of future progress. Statistics for 1893 indicate that the average height of the Wellesley woman was only 5 feet 3.2 inches,[38] but when it came to depicting the type in monumental art, the size was doubled in order to complement the Girl in scale and significance. Taken together as an imaginative mass, the MacMonnies ensemble was a visual promise that Americans would continue to enjoy "the youth and hope which we fondly believe to be the characteristic of our nation."

It is not enough to speak of the material fact of the large-scale figures of the Republic or of Columbia which gleamed around the Court of Honor in the summer of 1893. The public significance assigned to these colossal females has to be drawn from the symbolic context offered by the Columbian Exposition and by its predecessor, the 1876 Centennial celebration held in Philadelphia.

The primary and secondary material available on the Centennial Exposition of 1876 fails to match the data provided by the events in Chicago of 1893. But the displays mounted in Philadelphia's Fairmount Park suggest that males won hands down over females in terms of symbolic force— further confirmation of the gender splits which Henry Adams, Henry James, and others were already assigning to the culture of the Gilded Age.

Machinery, money, industry, progress (all those *masculine* things), overwhelmed the exhibition areas featuring the arts, domestic crafts, and educational aspirations of the United States (the *feminine* ideals). The entirety of the Centennial's offerings received the dutiful, cheerful interest of the visitors, but two contemporary accounts indicate that the attention of the thousands who came to the fairgrounds was divided between the *things* that counted and the *ideals* that did not.

In 1877–78 the federal government published reports by the Centennial Commission; they clearly state disapproval of what the commission had found at the Exposition in regard to the current level of education in the United States. The crowds might bear "unconscious testimony to the elevating power of those institutions and agencies, political, educational, and religious, which have given Americans an honorable rank. . . . But of education proper much less can be said."[39] One of the reports concluded that visitors to the fair were "an over-confident, procrastin-

12.23. Will H. Low, from "The Art of the White City," *Scribner's Monthly Magazine*, October 1893.

ating people, less appreciative of education . . . than proof of their material progress and power."

An essay by William Dean Howells for *The Atlantic Monthly* makes clear the nature of the gaps in achievement (actual and symbolic) reported by the government commission; the gaps, that is, between *ideas*, *ideals*, and *things* referred by convention to the opposed spheres of male and female endeavor. Howells lauds the general success of the 1876 Exposition in touching the hearts of the crowd. The display areas could not fail "to grow upon the visitor's liking." As emblems of virtue and vigor, they filled the public with "a thrill of patriotic pride." But in all candor, the intellectual content of the displays was often provincial—lackluster, barren, slovenly.[40] Or as the commission report would have it, the exhibits were inspirational, not educational. There was, however, one stunning exception to the general intellectual and spiritual vagueness. It was, Howells declared, the Corliss engine whose monumental scale dwarfed all who stood before it in the Machinery Building (figure 12.24). Whoever came into its august presence experienced the same truth: "the superior elegance, aptness, and ingenuity of our machinery is observable at a glance. Yes, it is still in these things of iron and steel that the national genius most freely speaks."

The 1876 Philadelphia Centennial gave no foreshadowing of the female icons that later dominated the 1893 Columbian Exposition—no "Republic" by Daniel Chester French, no MacMonnies "Columbia" attended by the young women of Smith and Wellesley, no Woman's Building erected by the force of will of Bessie Potter Palmer and her Board of Lady Managers. The central icon of the Centennial was the "majesty of the great Corliss engine." Enthroned in "its vast and almost silent grandeur," it was "an athlete of steel and iron with not a superfluous ounce of metal on it." It was a "giant" with "a hoarded power that makes all tremble." It was, in fact, the primary statement male America had to make about itself.[41] Other remarks about America's national destiny, projected through other images, would come into evidence only in Chicago in 1893.

Between 1876 and 1893 something happened to image-making in America. It may have come about because of the intellectual mood that led Charles Sanders Peirce to write "How to Make Ideas Clear" in 1879 and William James to begin work on *The Principles of Psychology* that same year.[42] On the one hand, James emphasized the roles of habit and the unconscious—those essentially solitary moves a person makes in the creation of the will. On the other, Peirce stressed the strength which comes to individuals who shift from doubt to belief by means of participation in a community of interpretations. Although James and Peirce were at odds over the issue of whether one should go it alone or as a member of a group, both men pursued a common goal: the understanding of what causes the mind to initiate the processes by which social selves are formed and human will is imposed upon the world.

By 1890 the two volumes of James' *The Principles of Psychology* were in print. The exciting, secret sensations that crawl out of the jungle of our sanctuary self were given appropriate images and explanations. In 1892–93 Peirce delivered his Lowell Lectures in circumspect praise of the mind's power to accelerate the processes of civilization and to enhance the general good. The clean, clear Peircean mind is not the Jamesian jungle self. Rather, it is likened to modern mathematics; in turn, mathematics is associated by Peirce with an ordered, artistic, reposeful, quasi-Hegelian garden. The mind given over to mathematics reveals the relation of the universals to the world of time and change and proves them to be neither

12.24. "The Corliss Engine," from Burr, *Memorial of the International Exposition* (1877).

inhumanly abstracted nor romantically idiosyncratic.[43] But whether the self is as James described it (warm, moist, dark) or as Peirce characterized it (cool, firm, clear), and whether it is imaged as a solitary thing or as a garden community of like minds, both men agreed that the self is founded on human will.

James and Peirce realized we cannot elect the range of choices we have, but from the choices we get we erect the visible structure of our lives.[44] It is a structure that calls for its own icon, one expressive both of the individual American and of the American community. And human will requires a different icon from the Corliss engine.

The choices made at the 1893 Columbian Exposition came in response to real, not just apparent, changes. The 1876 Centennial Exposition had been about what the United States thought it was becoming but was not yet actually.[45] Among the "real things" that had come into being by 1892 when the later Exposition was in its planning stage was the recognition that American culture *ought to be* a balance between business and the arts; between what the masculine endeavor symbolizes and what the female image represents. That recognition was made official by the design of the Exposition's grounds and displays.

Some of the on-the-spot appraisals of the 1893 Columbian Exposition announced that American life—traditionally symbolized by a split between masculine and feminine values—had finally achieved the unification it had never before possessed. They may not have said, Ah, at last men and women are equal in the United States, but they did say, See, American business and arts are on a par at last. Other commentators were not as sanguine; they realized that *the facts* of the displays did not bear out *the perception* of unity of purpose. Still, even they insisted on the visible signs of hope that were father and mother to deeds which would come to realization in the near future.

The city of Chicago itself—symbolic of the aggressive masculine urge to make money and acquire corporate power—offered evidence that the male business elite could join with the women's groups in charge of the arts.[46] The motives of these men and women were complex and the consequences of their activities somewhat questionable. Conflicts that pertain to the inevitable differences between elitism and democratic procedures, and between practical action and idealistic behavior, could not be resolved by the fact that Chicago tycoons offered financial support for the dissemination of music, painting, and architecture. Just because Harriet Monroe was able to persuade influential men to back the big send-off she planned for her "Columbian Ode" at the 1893 Exposition (or, later on, the new magazine *Poetry* she created in 1912) does not prove that the aims of women and men had come fully into harmony. Fifteen years after the Columbian Exposition Henry Adams and Henry James were (correctly) still pointing to the profound failures marring American life caused by the masculine/feminine split. Nonetheless, the 1893 displays served as a major occasion for imaging through tangible symbols a conscious awareness that a balance must be struck between machines and civilization.

As an "occasion," the Columbian Exposition was itself a symbol. Across the grounds and throughout the buildings there were many objects which promised that wished-for-balance, however suspect to astute latter-day students of American culture.[47] Official and semiofficial pronouncements defining for the public what is "American" and "good taste" are always problematic. Just such pronouncements filled the pages of the country's newspapers and magazines with puff and gush. Most of the words produced by the fair's boosters make us doubt whether harmony was all that apparent at the Court of Honor. Even though some *aesthetic* harmony was achieved we may still wonder about the *social* cost of that drive toward unity. But the visual forms by which the Exposition's designers expressed their desires are our concern just now. Images are as capable of the big lie as words, but images 100 feet high are susceptible to analysis. Expositions like the one held in 1893 offer through their official images good examples of *what* is exposed when the public values that are intended are checked over against the values that are revealed.

In 1876 men and women were unequal in political and economic strength. Although gains were made during the next seventeen years, they were unequal still in 1893. The visual nature of the Columbian Exposition's architecture seemed to enforce these differences. The main buildings were massive after the manner of the neo-Renaissance style which is commonly associated with masculine money power. The single building designed by a woman (the twenty-one-year-old Sophia Hayden, a recent graduate of the Massachusetts Institute of Technology) was itself "read" as feminine through and through. A writer for *The American Architect* called Hayden's design "weak and commonplace" and likened the roof garden to "a hen-coop for petticoated hens, old and young."[48] Henry Van Brunt, one of the period's best-known architectural critics, was far more gracious, but he also characterized the Woman's Building in gender terms. He believed that the physiognomy of the design was clearly female.

It is eminently proper that the exposition of woman's work should be housed in a building in which a certain delicacy and elegance of general treatment, a smaller limit of dimension, a finer scale of detail, and a certain quality of treatment, which might be designated in no derogatory sense as graceful timidity or gentleness, combined, however with evident technical knowledge, at once differentiates it from its colossal neighbors, and reveals the sex of its author.

If the design of the Woman's Building was female because of its "smaller limit of dimension" and "finer scale of detail"—a fact that made it stand apart "from its colossal neighbors"—the items on display within that building were also viewed in traditional gender terms. Women run things well, the praise went, and the places they run best are the spaces that signal "home": the model kindergarten, the scientific kitchen, and the lodging house at the edge of the fairgrounds run for the comfort of women visitors to Chicago. Feminine architectural structures are similar to female home functions. Both are "accomplished" when they furnish recognizable signatures for the sex which inscribes them.

This is not to say that the participation of women at the Columbian Exposition was then, or should be now, considered of little consequence. "Successful" is an accurate term to use for what that intelligent, energetic, creative, and sometimes contentious band of women brought into being.[49] But it was success achieved within the expected woman's sphere, even though the boundaries of that sphere had been pushed farther from its constricted center. But I am not directly addressing the state of affairs in 1893 under which women lived out their lives in the United States. I shall not even say much more about the images at the Exposition expressive of the idea of Woman. It is time to concentrate upon another area (intricately related, of course, to any general discussion about the placement of women in society and the images they inspire). It is not images of the Woman or of women of which I now speak, but images of *the idea of America as female*.

The Columbian Exposition taught its visitors lessons they liked about the unique qualities of will Americans were said to possess in abundance. It also began to teach them how will can be represented by female forms scaled up in size and significance beyond anything the country had seen before. To deal with American women directly as citizens or as individuals—or even to speak of them as the Woman (as a distinctive, albeit symbolic, "other" sex)—entailed an embarrassing exposure of the social and political fissures that continued to separate men's deeds from women's needs. On the other hand, to talk about or to image forth through various art forms one's pride in the United States was to transcend the petty details of gender concerns. It was the means for achieving the spirit of unification that, however illusory, was meant to subsume an entire population under the single happy sign "America."

The female figures on display at the Columbian Exposition were not home free as fully effective symbols for American will. There was a way to go before the import of their material size was matched by the importance of the signification accorded them by the general public. That importance fell into place by 1898 in Cuba and the Philippines and was confirmed by the events in France of 1918. But what happened in 1893 in Chicago out at Jackson Park provided the first and necessary step toward the approaching sense of national apotheosis.

The eye-catching colossi of Daniel Chester French's "Republic" and the Mac-Monnies "Columbia" held the attention of the press and dominated the general chitchat about the state of the civic arts in 1893. These statues could not claim, however, to be the true symbolic foci of the fair. Majestic and isolated on their pedestals, they were unable to counter the massive collective power of the architecture of the White City.

Henry Van Brunt suggests the relations that developed between the female and male values through a metaphor of his own. He says that the arts and the machine were mated through the displays. Beauty with fitness; serenity, grace, and harmony with materialistic power—they had come together at last like Aphrodite with Hephaestus.[50] This is a pretty phrase and it serves to indicate the aesthetic effects that enabled the Exposition's supporters to detect the presence of the balance between the male and the female that had been overtly absent in Philadelphia in 1876. But consider what we know about Hephaestus. He creates the form of the first female, and it is Pandora, the ancients' version of Eve—the female force for discord and disobedience. Hephaestus catches his wife Aphrodite in his net and shames her in the sight of the gods. No matter her charms, the Goddess of Love cannot rule the God of the Forge. No matter the gifts Pandora brings to mankind, Hephaestus sees to it that she becomes the symbol for mankind's bad luck.

The exhibition buildings representative of masculine corporate power were to the Columbian Exposition what the Corliss engine had been to the Philadelphia Centennial.[51] The immense female statues by Daniel Chester French and Frederick MacMonnies were the largest that had ever been designed by Americans up to that time. But they had size, not the "scale" which accrues to objects perceived by the general public as possessing the greatest possible symbolic power. The Republic and the Columbia at the Grand Basin clearly imaged the ideals of civilization. They stood for art and education, for truth, beauty, and goodness, for everything that the type of the Wellesley and Smith girl connoted in the early 1890s. But immense as they were as physical objects, the values they imaged were still women's values—the values of "uptown." As such, they could not contest the authority of the buildings surrounding them. The Beaux Arts architecture visualized a male telos—one that symbolized the goals of the Italian Medici and the French Bourse brought into union with the "downtown" vigor of Chicago's stockyards and New York's Wall Street.

The time was close at hand when massive female figures would command the imaginative power possessed by a Richardson warehouse, a Burnham skyscraper, or a McKim, Mead, and White railroad station. By 1898 Columbia directly signified the nation's political and military strength. By 1918 the "America" figure was a potent propagandistic image of power. But until the close of the nineteenth century only the Bartholdi Statue of Liberty was able to hold its own visually against the industrial might of the Corliss engine or the institutional grandeur of banks, museums, mercantile houses, and public libraries. The drawback was the nation's peace-time status. Peace was too feminine in its appeal. The coming of the occasions of war would give the "America" figures the symbolic authority they had been waiting for.

There was, however, a cluster of female forms at the Columbian Exposition of 1893 ready to be exploited as the kind of "real" force the public could respond to: the symbolic force of electricity.

When the buildings were set aglow at the turn of the central switch, visitors to the Exposition experienced their finest moment.[52] Thousands of lights glancing off the white buildings, reflected by the waters of the Grand Basin, were a sight those who saw it never forgot; it gave tangible form to the fact of electricity, the modern American miracle. Experimentations in electricity had been advanced in the 1750s by Benjamin Franklin. Electricity had been put into practical use in 1882 by Thomas Edison, the man who was yet another version of that favorite American type—the inventor with brains and business know-how. Franklin and Edison were that happy mix of the sublime and the picturesque. Together they packaged the Representative Man and the Boy Who Makes Good. They stood, superbly, for the meaning of the republic expressed as a history of male success.

But electrical power causes practical problems for symbol makers. It is the source of visible light and the invisible flow of communication, but of itself electricity is an invisible force. We only see what it touches and what it affects. The great concepts of light, knowledge, energy, and industry are the results of electrical power. But to have to sum them up in an electric light bulb! The *idea* of electricity had to be given an exciting, aesthetically pleasing form if it were to be presented properly at the Columbian Exposition as a forceful statement of American progress; it needed an image that could persuade Americans they were blessed to live in a country where the practical application of electricity had both its birthplace and its future. This time the image makers sent women, not men. A statue of Benjamin Franklin and a tower in honor of Thomas Edison formed part of the Electrical Building at the Columbian Exposition, but public notice went to the lights encircling the noble brow of Daniel Chester French's "Republic" and to the murals with allegorical females who represented the gifts brought by electricity to a progressive society (figure 12.25).

Nymphs holding lamps were already a cliché long before the late 1880s.[53] But

12.25. J. Carroll Beckwith, "The Telephone," from "The Decoration of the Exposition," *Scribner's Monthly Magazine*, December 1892.

12.26. Elihu Vedder, "The Pleiades," (1885), engraved by F. E. Fillebroun, from Koehler, *American Art* (1886). (Original in the Metropolitan Museum of Art, New York.)

traditional notations that linked females with flames became "Americanized" and modernized once Bartholdi gave the United States an emblem with a raised torch, once Archibald Willard (creator of the "The Spirit of '76") painted three large angels representing the Telegraph, the U.S. Mails, and Electricity,[54] and once Elihu Vedder's "Pleiades" exuberantly began to swing their lifted cords (figure 12.26). Americans of the period liked to associate female forms with ideas of electrical power, even though we may think Mrs. Cornelius Vanderbilt a bit silly for dressing up as "The Electric Light" (see figure 12.12). Franklin and Edison were the historical figures who testified to the development of electricity, but the female furnished the favored image for the force itself.[55] By World War I the telephone and telegraph operator was a popular pictorial type. Her image stood for the brave and skillful young women who controlled the vital communication lines that encircled America and linked it with the rest of the world. But even the iconography surrounding this new variant on the modern working girl had had its source with the likes of Bartholdi, Vedder, and Beckwith. Allegories of the type of Electricity came first, followed by the type of the American woman switchboard operator.

In 1893 female figures were being converted into allegories of the spirit of electricity. Potentially at least they were images capable of subverting the public's taste for the Corliss engine, the masculine icon that had commanded the American imagination since the 1876 Centennial. The Corliss was massive in size; it represented incredible power and invisible energy. In contrast, the random allegorical pieces dedicated to electricity at the Columbian Exposition were of no particular size. Clearly, it was the essentially masculine symbolism of the Exposition's architecture, taken as one grand whole, which served to form the public's conception of the nation's achievements. But once the buildings were torn down, one thing that remained was the new habit of imaging light and communication in female terms.

The figures representing the Republic and Columbia received great attention and much praise at the Chicago fair, but they were never more than reminders that time-honored principles can be given national reference on a grand scale through the use of neoclassical forms associated with the traditional female virtues of truth, goodness, and beauty.[56] Not until the United States went to war in 1898 and 1917 did those massive symbols for moral virtue leave the woman's sphere and move into areas previously empowered by male symbols of force and glory. In contrast, the symbols which adhered most closely to attributes of the feminine were forms equated with electricity and communication. They matched, and eventually surpassed, the industrial machine as the peacetime American icon. Beckwith's "Telephone" (see figure 12.25) or Coles Phillips' winged "Transportation" (figure 12.27) became the pretty new muses for a nation that was discarding outmoded symbols. No longer limited to being signs for the eternal moral verities and the gentler arts, the female figure usurped Mercury's role as messenger for the gods. A practical, modern American idol, she was fit for industry and business—ready for use as a mural for a corporate boardroom or as a calendar pinned up in a mechanic's shop.

12.27. Coles Phillips, "The Spirit of Transportation" (1920).

There is admittedly something trivial in the scale of these Electricity Girls, something hand-me-down about the aesthetic traditions that lie behind their unsexy bodies and smooth faces. A profitable future lay ahead of such images in advertising pages for the popular magazines, but they lack the imposing scale necessary for effective civic symbols. But scale, symbolic force, and the fulfillment of grandiose aesthetic and emotional needs are exactly what came into focus in 1893 once night fell over Jackson Park. By day French's Republic and the Columbia of the MacMonnies fountain were fine to look upon, although finally not sublime enough. But when the lights came up and the crown of the Republic shone and the Smith and Wellesley girls floated upon a sea of reflecting luminosity, hearts swelled and sublimity held dominion over the grounds of the Exposition. Here at last the United States had its visual answer to the severance of the two cultures of masculine and feminine—the perfect expression of progress as a merger of power and peace.

She was not present at the Columbian Exposition, but there was yet another American female icon in existence in 1893—one with an increasing part to play in peace and in war over the following two decades. This was the image which hung in an upper room of the Boston palazzo of Isabella Stewart Gardner—a dazzling sight when the electric light over the painting shone upon its dark surface and caught the details of jewels and magnificent stuffs (see figure 6.4). This was the icon Paul Bourget saw in 1889 at an exhibition of paintings by John Singer Sargent before it came to rest in the Gardner household. As we have seen in chapter 6, Bourget used his impressions of the Sargent in defining the awesome power of the American Idol. But Bourget wished to do more than describe the feelings he had in its presence; he wanted to locate the force which had created her.

Frenzy of speculations in land, cities undertaken and built by sheer force of millions, trains launched at full speed over bridges built on a Bael like sweep of arch, the creaking of cable cars, the quivering of electric cars, sliding along their wires with a crackle and a spark, the dizzy ascent of elevators, in buildings twenty stories high, immense wheat-fields of the West, its ranches, mines, colossal slaughter-houses,—all the formidable traffic of this country of effort and struggle, all its labor,—these are what have made possible this woman, this living orchid, unexpected masterpiece of this civilization.[57]

Formed of such forces, representative of such powers, this "deification of woman" could not be expected to stand as a sign for the mid-century values of Louisa May Alcott's Marmee or even of Jo March. This was the new "national spirit" of the early 1890s, imaged by a female figure whose attributes of body and soul revealed a new kind of "supreme glory."

This woman can do without being loved. She has no need of being loved. What she symbolizes is neither sensuality nor tenderness. . . . Everything is illuminated . . . at the gaze of these fathomless eyes, in the expression of which the painter has succeeded in putting all the idealism of this country which has no ideal; all that which, perhaps, will one day be its destruction, but up to the present time is still its greatness,—a faith in the human Will, absolute, unique, systematic, and indomitable.

This is the image of American Will—without the tenderness of love, the intimacy of the sensual, or the Ideal that solicits idealism. It is an amoral energy under no obligation to uphold the national virtues of truth, goodness, and beauty promised by previous female emblems. As Will it is the source of the nation's present success and the possible cause of the nation's future destruction. It is the Virgin as the Dynamo, Civilization as Energy, masculine force subsumed within female form. At long last, Venus Genetrix had come to America in all her fecundity and terror.

The American Idol—Will personified in the figure of a fascinating, soulless female—was Paul Bourget's notion of the idea which motivates late-nineteenth-century American society. It was not the idea commonly accepted at the Columbian Exposition. For one thing, that creature was too ruthless and amoral to sit well with the national desire of Americans to think well of themselves, whether singly or as a corporate political unit. For another thing, the Idol represented what Americans already had; it was their immediate reality, and therefore *not enough*.

Chapters 9 and 10, which worked with winged females and lived at the threshold, argued that turn-of-the-century imaginations were stimulated by the idea of what is *not yet*. There was pleasure in an idea of the ideal as the final form desire might take in the future. As much as anyone else, Americans of the 1890s gave themselves to their own times, but their taste for desiring what lay ahead was very strong. Conversely, the Idol described by Bourget possessed no ideals drawn from the past and no concern for ideals fulfilled by the future. She was the sheer, somewhat terrifying presence of the present moment. As Bourget himself described the Exposition, that occasion acted as the national conscience for the desires of a national culture which were not yet achieved.[58] The MacMonnies Columbia was rowed into the future by twelve-foot-tall college girls. Beckwith's Telephone Girl leaned forward in expectation toward the technological society which electrical power was still in the process of creating. The airy female figures in Mary Cassatt's painting for the Woman's Building pursued the butterfly of possibility right off the edge of the mural. All these images longed for something that had not yet happened. Doing so, they nicely summed up one-half the meaning of the Exposition.

The other half of the Columbian Exposition was devoted to the enjoyment of immediate pleasures, whether the Ferris wheel on the Midway or the exhibition hall displays that compared (favorably) the achievements of the United States with the efforts of other participating nations. The official and semiofficial guidebooks and gift books were solemn in their insistence about the present fact of "the American Paradise of 1893."[59] The context for the pride of attainment experienced by the fair's visitors was the horrors of an irrational past Americans hoped to have put behind themselves.[60] Certainly, many believed, the United States had reached the peak of civilization and was forever fixed in the mastery of the arts.[61] But still and all, the language used by those who wrote most commandingly of the fair was couched in the future tense.

The artists and the architects who designed the Exposition were clear in their own minds that theirs were designs for things to come. What they had done in Jackson Park (and they liked it very well) was not enough. They sensed to greater or lesser degree that the displays exposed splits; they realized that more remained to be done before the ideal of cultural, aesthetic, and political unity to which their designs had been dedicated was achieved. Some visitors to the fair even identified this condition as a matter of the division between the sexes. One wrote that the men dutifully visited the exhibits which featured the arts and domestic activities of their womenfolk, while the women just as dutifully walked through "soulless acres of manufacturing."[62] People at the fair might fool themselves that they were in the presence of the mutual triumph of materialism joined with "sweetness and light," but perceptive viewers recognized this as an illusion that would last only through the summer of 1893.[63]

The fact that the Columbian Exposition was considered a charming dreamland by many of its viewers has received a great deal of recent attention from the scholars. Often their assessments are negative.[64] One argument takes the line that, if a public occasion is perceived and accepted as dreamlike, this response constitutes a conscious denial of the ugliness which actually pervades the culture; an irresponsible *social* crime is thereby committed. Another argument states that the dreamland response exposes the wrongheaded notion that a culture has reached a fixed point of absolute achievement; the guilt committed is one of *philosophical* error. Yet a third variant of the argument against those with a taste for dreamland occasions points to the irony of the fact that, even while the public busily celebrates the nation's progress, fear prevails; disclosed here is the *psychological* flaw in the public's psyche.

Not always so. I disagree that denial, error, and fear are the interpretations that *must* be assigned to the dream quality of the 1893 Exposition. Many who came to the White City, passing through the parklike grounds that separated it from the dark city of Chicago, took the dream world they found there as an affirmation of the future reality Americans might possess if they chose wisely and well.

The names of those fully responsive to the possibilities imaged by the design of the Columbian Exposition were hardly legion. The majority were like Frank Millet, the man in charge of planning the decorations, and Montgomery Schuyler, the noted architectural critic: they saw only so far but no farther. Millet spoke of the buildings of the White City as "sketches."[65] He praised the light touch of the organizing committee which encouraged the informal working out of individual impulses to meet the common goals of uniformity-as-process and order-as-flexibility.[66] Schuyler wrote of the Arcadian, festal quality of the buildings of the White City, which he viewed as a fair city of "the artificial infinite." He decided its aesthetic success came from the completeness of its illusion. One need not consider while there the actuality of American cities. Remote, mythic, classical, spotlessly white, and clothed in electricity, the White City existed as a privileged place, remote from the world of "naked and open daylight."[67]

Henry Van Blunt and William Dean Howells brought more depth to their analyses of the benefits gained from the organized making of illusion. Van Blunt emphasized that the buildings in Jackson Park stood in strong contrast to the look of Chicago and the rest of the United States, but he also suggested that the uniform, ceremonious style of "scenic" display offered precisely the "practicable models" required by professionals and interested citizens for the furtherance of better urban design. Following the lead of the Exposition, city planners would be inspired to join their understanding of technology with the aesthetic ideals of rest and harmony. Only then might the value of the spirit be reinstated within the modern city.[68] Howells' fictitious Altrurian Traveler contrasted the futuristic White City with the present nightmares of Chicago and New York, thereby giving Howells the means to attack the social inequities of the American democratic system and the sordid failure of American cities.[69] The delight expressed by this "tourist" from the perfect republic to the dreamland of the Exposition also gave Howells the chance to animate his plea for what Americans must strive to attain.

To critics like Van Blunt and Howells, the Exposition was not a mode of escape into never-never land; it was a display of choices. It promised its visitors that if egotism, competition, and brutality in the United States are everyday facts, there is also the altruism, cooperation, and beauty that was made manifest during the brief summer beside the Grand Basin of Jackson Park.

Responses prompted by illusory effects are hugely problematic. The heedless could walk cheerfully away from the White City in the belief that its impact upon the public imagination was wholly beneficial. Newspaper accounts reported that the eyes of visiting farm women filled with tears over the memories of the loveliness they experienced at the fair, but did those ephemeral moments compensate the gnarl-handed women for the years of poverty and disappointment?[70] Will H. Low celebrated the summer when Americans were rewarded by the dream of the need to be larger, finer, better. Low extolled the vision taken away by farmers, mechanics, and shopkeepers upon their return to the deadly monotony and toil of the endless "flatlands" (geographical and psychological) which surrounded Chicago, itself "hidden in a pall of smoke." But could one not take as damning evidence the contrasts Low made between life "inside" the "high white wall" and "outside" where the rest of the nation lay inert?[71]

One must also be wary of enthusiastic blueprints for perfect cities of the future based on suspect dreamlands of the present. In 1893 there were all too many official statements of complacent pride. But for those who today do not automatically accept unity, harmony, and grace as primary values, there is something repellent in contemporary assertions that the White City was simultaneously the symbol of the nation's current achievements and the correct design for its future.

One can reject as irresponsible nostalgia Richard Watson Gilder's twin poems about the joys of that glorious summer of 1893 and the sadness he felt over the loss of the White City.[72] One may dismiss as meretricious shtick Imre Kiralfy's flamboyant spectacle staged in honor of the Exposition with grand ballets and tableaux in which Darkness and Bigotry are defeated and America—surrounded by Progress, Liberty, Invention, and the Spirit of Chicago—accepts homage from the nations of the world.[73] One can observe all this, then discard it as nonsense, but one may not lightly reject the possibility that diagrams for the ideal possess their own authenticity and worth.

Many factors at work in late-nineteenth-century culture led to a faith in having designs on the ideal. Today we wonder how nice the ideals upheld by Americans were. Often we are very certain that they could only have been harmful. But even allowing for the abuses caused by the creation of false images, there is always the chance that "the theoretical proposal," "the study sketch," or "the conceptual prototype" have human merit.[74] Problem-solving by means of hypothetical models that project ideas into a hypothetical future is a sound methodology in technology and business.[75] Charles Sanders Peirce and Josiah Royce found the formulation of theoretical models necessary to the psychological process by which we "make our ideas clear." Cultural historians frequently examine models emerging from the past, particularly when they want to know what people once believed was *absent from* their lives.

In 1893 Henry Adams took up a perch in Jackson Park, a position he always assumed in the presence of some new force. He looked out over the shimmering display of the Columbian Exposition and pondered about the nature of the "new power" all around him and what it meant for the nation. He asked, "[D]id it pull or did it push? Was it a screw or thrust? Did it flow or vibrate? Was it a wire or a mathematical line?"[76] Then he asked, "Did he himself quite know what he meant? Certainly not! If he had known enough to state his problem, his education would have been complete at once." This Adams did know: "Chicago asked in 1893 for the first time the question whether the American people knew where they were driving." As for himself, though he was unaware of the direction the United States was taking, Adams "would try to find out." "Chicago asked" and some were trying to answer. One thing many artists, writers, and architects believed that the White City was telling them was that the models and images it provided revealed what the nation's future could *look like* if they would only will it so.

In 1904 the New York City trolley lines reminded Henry James of the strangling entanglements of the Laocoön.[77] In 1924 Lewis Mumford criticized domestic dwellings whose structures were determined by the factory, not by the needs of the people who had to live in them.[78] In the first instance technology had gone wild and out of control; in the second case the problem was caused by overly systematized machine production. James and Mumford give us the look of the early-twentieth-century city beset by the social and economic factors set loose in Chicago. They marshal concrete examples of the lasting effects of *facts* that were first "exposed" at the 1893 Exposition. But occasions also beget "occasions." We realize we need to trace certain consequences of the *ideas* shaped at the fair, and how, in turn, those consequences (the City Beautiful movement, inexpensive reproductions marketed for schoolroom use, national coinage, state capitol buildings, and civic murals) became the material conditions by which the female form took command as the primary container for American values between 1898 and 1918.

In 1895 Cortissoz singled out the yet unbuilt Library of Congress as evidence of the exemplary cultural life that lay ahead in the nation's future.[79] Government buildings, Cortissoz wrote, usually yield ugliness, but when he shut his eyes and contemplated the plans for the Library, he was confident they promised the inspiration needed if the citizenry were to enjoy public beauty. Need, however, is not the same as deed. Something had happened that caused both the sense of need and the energy to bring this excellence to pass. Daniel Burnham's essay of 1902, "White City and the Capital City," declares the reasons why the Library and like projects

were being actively put forth in Washington and elsewhere at this time.[80] Burnham states that the City Beautiful movement is the direct legacy of the Columbian
Exposition, and Burnham should know. During 1892–93 he was in charge of the
men appointed to design Chicago's White City. Ten years later he was heading the
government commission whose assignment was the improvement of the prospect
of Washington, D.C. Burnham felt he knew the fertile connections between historical points A (his activities in Chicago) and B (his new responsibilities in the
nation's capital). Drawing upon the language of portent made familiar by the Book
of Revelations and by the Annunication story, Burnham pointed out that the White
City had "embodied" the vague feelings of the public in the early 1890s and that
it persisted into the new century as the guiding model for the future development
of the Capital City.

We too can trace the line that runs from the ephemeral White City—surrounded
by the jumble of the Midway and the pomp and chaos of late-nineteenth-century
Chicago—to the tourist attractions and government manufactory of that odd mix
of the homey, the squalid, and the splendid which characterizes the present-day
District of Columbia. That line did not, however, result in an unalloyed Acropolis
of America (figure 12.28). Not with the petty interferences of federal bureaucracy
which assured that the "average" would defeat the "superior."[81] Those who felt
less than sanguine about the ability of the nation's capital to take the lead in
perfecting the City Beautiful in tangible forms placed their hopes in the state capitol buildings then under construction around the country.

The high expectations held for architectural projects funded by the states may
have resulted from reversion to lingering myths of Jacksonian individualism and a
new faith in a states' rights program for the imagination. Or perhaps the zest with
which the states erected their capitols was analogous to the current incorporation
of business interests which was drawing power away from the center of federal
government. Whatever causes prompted the urge to construct, the energies released during the first decade of the twentieth century in Saint Paul, Des Moines,
Harrisburg, Madison, and Providence were immense. True, these great domed
buildings extended the beneficent wings of their cultural ideals over only a block
or two in jerry-built cities which might in all other regards be the confused Laocoön tangles of which Henry James spoke; but their architects, sculptors, painters,
and politicians happily planned ceremonial areas filled with works of art intended
to teach harmony and to inculcate the love of beauty in the hearts of the citizenry.

The state capitols, as well as the new buildings in Washington, D.C., were flung
open to the public for its general edification.[82] Yet it was an era when travel was
not within everyone's means; those rare cities possessed of displays of civic beauty
might be thousands of miles from those who sought inspiration. The lifting of civic
and national pride had to depend upon other modes of communication. Increasingly accurate and inexpensive forms of print reproduction disseminated the look
of America's self-assigned significance into middle-class homes through books and

12.28. Franklin W. Smith, "The Aggrandisement of Washington" (1891).

magazines. Just as important for conveying the visible signs of the nation's pride was the use of schoolrooms as "galleries" for "history-study pictures." As the Prang Company people put it, beautiful images from the American past excited the children's souls; beautiful deeds for America's future would stem from the inner beauty instilled by those scenes.[83] The pictures rimming the classroom walls included many often-disconnected images—ancient ruins, the Fireside Poets, John Alden and Priscilla, Flaxman's Trojan heroes, Columbus, Blashfield's angels, Indians, scenes from the lives of the Puritans, Lincoln, and Tennyson's *Idylls*—but the pervasive effect was that of heroic action, high principles, progress, and confidence in the way history in America justifies itself.[84]

Coins offered another "occasion" to display the signs of national self-esteem coming into focus by 1900. Coins held in the hand act as solid reminders that money is value. They are also imprinted with words that proclaim two other favored American mottos: *Trust in Providence* and *Unity in Multiplicity*. Designers of the government coinage gave thought to the visual images by which the nation's history was given a readable face and the force of the ideal.[85] The head of Liberty was chosen as the best signature for a democracy—one that was certainly more appropriate than the use of portraits of powerful individuals.

To trace the physical evolution of the Liberty-head coins is like attending a historical pageant in honor of the American Girl or flipping through *cartes de visite* of reigning beauties who reflect the changing tastes in feminine beauty between 1873 and 1921.[86] A Philadelphia schoolteacher, chaste and beautiful, was the model for the 1878 coin. In 1896 the coin traced the head of Miss Anna W. Williams, praised in the press for her modesty, her nearly perfect profile (because "even" and "regular"), and her milkmaid physique. In 1907 the famous Saint-Gaudens coins featured an Indian bonnet (for "who, other than Indians, are 'pure Americans'?") and showed the attributes of a Greek Nike (figure 12.29). Saint-Gaudens' designs remind us of his "Victory" ready to do battle while welcoming peace; they are

12.29. Augustus Saint-Gaudens, models for coinage (1907): upper, plaster model for U.S. one-cent piece, Pergamene Nike, unused design; lower, plaster model for U.S. ten-dollar gold piece, Indian bonnet.

variations of the American Girl who accompanies the mounted Sherman statue placed on public view in 1903. The MacNeil quarter of 1917 prompted newspaper stories about its model. Once the young woman had been a semi-invalid, but she pulled herself together and did service as a Red Cross nurse during the war, thereby transforming herself into "the perfect type" required by the nation's coinage. A decline then set in. The 1921 "Peace" dollar modeled upon his wife by Anthony De Francisci had the profile of a vapid flapper; it stood in contrast to the Liberty heads designed between 1896 and 1917 which provided effective symbols for a nation that approved of the combined power of money, republican virtue, and military vigor.

Statues, buildings, reproductions of historical scenes and personages, and coins:

all these occasions and symbolic forms advanced the visual impact of signs which identified the nation's values. The artistic vocabulary of statues and coinage were especially amenable to the didactic use of female forms and faces. In contrast, the architectural masses of large public buildings were obviously masculine in design and reference. So were the study pictures used in the country's schoolrooms which featured the famous men who made up the official history of the United States. The only exceptions were images of women like Priscilla and Pocahontas who had achieved mythic status through the influence of the literary arts. Since statues and coins seemed to furnish the best surfaces for the display of abstractions and myths, it was natural for the female form to take command over coinage and commemorative groups in marble or bronze. But by 1900 another display surface had been added upon which the American Girl figured in the telling of stories of the nation's present success and future glory. This was the mural.

Murals lined the inside walls of the vast new civic buildings, just as sculpture was used to decorate their exterior surfaces. By these means those essentially masculine bastions of architectural expression were infiltrated and dominated by images of the female.

Muralists did not automatically achieve the power to express and command public attention. Visitors to the Woman's Building in Chicago in 1893 were not altogether approving of the murals placed on display high (too high) above their heads. Professional and amateur critics alike decided that Mary MacMonnies' painting of "Primitive Woman" was a noteworthy example of ideal art but judged that Mary Cassatt's apple pickers were ugly and "realistic." Yet if mural painting stumbled a bit on its way into the twentieth century, by 1902 a full-scale "history" of the mural tradition in the United States was called for and the mural's importance as a major art form recognized.[87]

Before the Columbian Exposition, murals had been used sporadically.[88] After 1910, critics began to associate murals with the art-for-art's-sake crowd and tended to reject them as designs based upon impersonal notions of beauty.[89] But what murals did best—combine the decorative with the didactic—came into focus during the period of heightened artistic activity between 1892 and 1910.[90]

Compare the way it had been prior to the Exposition. John La Farge and William Morris Hunt had had to teach themselves the art of decorating interior architectural surfaces at the time when easel painting was unquestionably the favored art form. Trinity Church in Boston and the Albany state capitol were the only fully realized instances of mural art the American art scene could offer during the 1870s. The 1880s were the time of apprenticeship for the young men who served as assistants on the few projects that came their way. When their chance came in 1892 to prepare the biggest display of public art ever conceived with the intention to tell a nation what it stood for and where its future lay, these men were ready, and so were the women muralists who mounted the scaffolding at the Woman's Building.[91] All during the summer of 1893 newspapers and magazines across the country carried the word about the murals on view at the White City, and visitors came away accepting them as "evidence of the devotion of the ideal, which is as distinctly American as a turn for mechanics."[92]

In the swell of the interest created in the newly revived art form, murals were incorporated into designs for a number of important buildings under construction in the mid-1890s. The Boston Public Library brought John Singer Sargent and Edwin Austin Abbey back from England, and Puvis de Chavannes from France. In 1894 the Walker Art Building on the campus of Bowdoin College (designed by Charles McKim) was decorated by designs commissioned of La Farge, Abbott Thayer, Kenyon Cox, and Elihu Vedder. In 1896 the Library of Congress became an encyclopedia of mural artists. Its spaces were painted by Charles Sprague Pearce, Edward Simmons, Henry Oliver Walker, John White Alexander, Walter McEwen, Elihu Vedder, Edwin Blashfield, Robert Reid, Walter Shirlaw, Frank Benson, George Maynard, Kenyon Cox, William Dodge, and Gari Melchers. In 1899 the appellate courtroom of the Criminal Courts Building of New York City signed on H. Siddons Mowbray, Willard Metcalf, Simmons, and Reid.

Female images appeared everywhere brushes touched the wide expanses of wall and ceiling. Drawing upon the portfolio of significant gestures and poses already available to the American studio imagination, mural artists included examples of almost every female type from the Warrior Queen as Protector of Truth to the Beautiful Charmer as Inspiration for the Arts. In the words of Pauline King, who acted as historian on the spot of American mural art, Blashfield's "The Law" executed for the Wilkes-Barre Courthouse pictures a female figure which "towers above a woman of the poorer class" with an "awful and determined countenance [which] would strike terror to the guilty, and uphold the faith of the innocent" (figure 12.30). At the other end of the spectrum from the stern Type of Law float Frank Benson's "The Graces" and "The Seasons," appropriate decorative embellishments for the Library of Congress. These are "delicate figures [who] have clearly been inspired by high-bred American girls, whose beauty is as much intellectual as physical"; they are "recognizable portraits of well-known types" as well as "fine and distinguished likenesses of contemporary womanhood" with the "lovely faces and forms that are the admiration of the world."

Ends and means seemed to be clear when ideal types were displayed in the mural form—the most publicly effective mode possible to the painted figure.[93] The American Girl in her several manifestations offered the true face and figure: newly erected architectural spaces provided the necessary areas for display; large wall paintings satisfied the need of the populace for old myths in new guises.

In "The Persistence of Traditional Ideals," one chapter from his *America as Art*, Joshua Taylor comments that people entering foyers and corridors lined by mural paintings felt immersed in a great decorative scheme that bound them to a glorious past and a confident present.[94] As Kenyon Cox stated the case in 1914, mural art (together with commercial illustration) was the one truly popular art. Like the ubiquitous illustration and unlike easel work isolated in the studio or museum, murals let painters and viewers share images intended for civic life.[95]

12.30. Edwin Howland Blashfield, "The Law," court-
house, Wilkes-Barre, Pa.
(1909), from *The Works
of Edwin H. Blashfield*
(1937).

According to the assumptions lying behind the act of mural-painting in late-
nineteenth-century America (though the actuality may have been otherwise), the
relation of the work to its viewers was the relation of teacher to pupil and of
preacher to congregation. It was the contemporary, secularized version of the sacred instruction once presented upon the walls of medieval cathedrals. The lesson
put before the enthralled viewers was patriotism (faith in the nation's virtue), not
religious doctrine (faith in virtue itself). Like murals from the past, the modern
mode incorporated large scale and elevation combined with compelling flatness of
design.[96] The resulting simplicity and grandness of style of the imagery had carrying power. Subjects were immediately recognizable, and lingered in the memory.
Upon entering the spacious civic buildings meant to be their "home," the people
were met by familiar sights, albeit in dimensions that expanded and soared. They
could count on understanding at once the significance of what they saw and on
remembering the greatness of the past by means of beautiful forms. The images
they looked at were both modern and American. They were decorative, not in
spite of their function, but because of it. The core of mural art was the ideal, and
ideal art had the power to generalize the everyday and the individual instance
away from the accidental and ineffectual. It arrived with assurance at *what is
more*—"more beautiful, more robust, more simple, than is the daily habit of humanity."

Those who realized how to achieve this *more* commanded the field of mural painting. The sense of prior accomplishments and portents for the years ahead had to
be contained within one forceful design. As it turned out, the look lent by female
images was what gave an expertness of perceived form to the twin concepts of past
and future.

One of the biggest names during the high times of the mural was Edwin Howland Blashfield. His early fame as the painter of "The Christmas Bells" was replaced by his later achievements as practitioner, lecturer, and teacher of the mural arts.[97] Blashfield's most frequently viewed design is the collar for the rotunda of the main reading room of the Library of Congress—"The Evolution of Civilization."[98] But it is the murals Blashfield executed for the state capitols in Des Moines and Saint Paul which prove how well he knew what he was about in terms of what he had to say about American ideals. His greatest talent lay in his ability to enclose the historical past, the contemporary moment, and the time-free universal within one visual design which made the world of the actual reverberate with allegory and the realm of the allegorical seem realistic.

It remains a touchy matter, this merging of contrary planes of existence and time. The muralist must bring it off if he or she hopes to image the public meaning of American life and to persuade viewers that what they see is *their* America.

In 1906 an unnamed correspondent for Gustav Stickley's *The Craftsman* wrote an essay titled "Mural Painting—an Art for the People and a Record of the Nation's Development" after a visit to the new Iowa State Capitol.[99] The essayist was displeased by the cartoons designed for the future murals in Des Moines. The people of the state pay for the art placed in their public buildings; they have the right to their money's worth by receiving clear records of a history they can personally understand. But several of the lunette designs were not effective, especially not the one by Kenyon Cox centered by "a colossal figure representing Agriculture," or another dedicated to "Herding" comprised of Iowa hogs clustered around a Greek herdsman holding panpipes. "The whole series is undeniably decorative but it has no more relation to the State Capitol of Iowa than it has to ancient Rome. There is not even the feeling of the West, for the atmosphere and landscape are those of New England, the architectural accessories, of classic Italy."

But then the writer for *The Craftsman* was introduced to the panel titled "Westward" executed by Edwin Howland Blashfield (figure 12.31). Success! In Blashfield's mural ox-drawn wagons and winged creatures "typifying progress and prosperity" go forth together with stalwart farmers and their women into the new frontier. The realistic is mingled with the fanciful in ways that yield the most readable of symbols, commemorating "an important local fact." The reason why Blashfield's design worked as the other murals had not was clear to the essayist. Blashfield had given all the figures—whether sturdy Iowans or allegorical female angels—faces that were "distinctively and typically American." Each head was true to the national type. The pioneers who headed west in confidence that Providence would guide them and the Protecting Angels who led the way were, alike, Americans in both their physiognomy and their inner soul.[100]

Lest we think that Protecting Angels and covered wagons refer to events placed too far in the past (however recognizable by Iowans in 1906 as informing the immediate realities of their agrarian present), there are other murals devoted to a direct imaging of early-twentieth-century technology. In them muralists just as

12.31. Edwin Howland Blashfield, "Westward," Iowa State Capitol (1905), from *The Works of Edwin Howland Blashfield* (1937).

busily hurl the public imagination into the future as they instruct it about its past. Figures 1 to 3 in the Epilogue, painted in 1907 by John White Alexander, depict workers from the Pittsburgh steel mills in league with soaring winged females. "The Spirit of Light" (shown here in figure 12.32 is one of the lunette designs surrounding the central mural of "The Apotheosis of Pennsylvania" painted by Edwin Austin Abbey during 1907–1908.[101] Vertical patterns of derricks and angels, translated into the flames they bear aloft, celebrate the power of natural gas and oil.

The murals by Blashfield, Alexander, and Abbey take pictorial risks—the risk of allowing visual splits to occur between the different design elements and the risk of conceptual shifts that dislocate the time factors involved. The muralists had to help the physical eye and the mind's eye synthesize diverse elements into one significant whole, lest the picture plane break down into ludicrously contradictory entities. Their solution was the use of female forms to perform the dual functions of decoration and education that could not be expected of male figures.

A large part of the public assumed that American history was a matter of the lives of famous men. As a matter of course history paintings per se excluded the figures of women. Nonetheless, certain objections to this habit and certain exceptions to the rule are on record. Three marble busts by Adelaide Johnson of "The Founding Mothers" (Frances Willard, Lucretia Mott, and Susan B. Anthony) finally found a place of display (however out of the way) in the crypt of the U.S. Capitol.[102] Caproni Prints sold likenesses of those acceptable American females Julia Ward Howe, Frances Willard (since Temperance sentiments were strong just then), and Harriet Beecher Stowe. But these were meager pickings, and when the plans for the decoration of the Library of Congress were made public, one Sarah Freeman Clarke of Marietta, Georgia, wrote to protest the exclusion of women's images from the "immortals" to be depicted in the main reading room.[103]

Representations of actual women seldom entered the visual record of American

12.32. Edwin Austin Abbey, "The Spirit of Light" (c.1904–1908), oil study for the Pennsylvania State Capitol, Harrisburg, from *Edwin Austin Abbey, Royal Academician* (1921).

history during the nineteenth century. In contrast, the female image was constantly before the public's eye in the form of legendary or semi-allegorical figures. Associated with ideal principles, such figures slid into place as recognizable signs for a dense cluster of cultural and historical values. But more than this, female forms enabled muralists of a historical bent to secularize the sacred without embarrassment, while elevating the mundane without awkwardness.

The representation of male heroes from the annals of the United States has often proved a problem without easy aesthetic resolution. The pretentious arts of the monarchic tradition, with its foolish notions about the divine rights of kings, could not be allowed to corrupt the visual forms of statesmen and Presidents.[104] The suggestion that American heroes might themselves be divine was even more dangerous. Elevate the male figure too high and accusations of the sacrilegious or the ridiculous were certain to follow.[105] In the late nineteenth century, however, female figures could safely represent extraterrestrial powers in a secularized, masculine society. The country's semi-official adherence to Protestantism sanctified such figures without explicitly assigning them the significance of the Virgin Mary. It was assumed that they could be ethereal without being silly, since the ethereal was the true nature of the female, after all.

The following examples may seem pictorially impossible to our minds, but in 1883 and 1896 representations like these still meant what they imaged. Figure 12.33 layered suffragists and their male supporters together with as many patriotic images as the space allows. Figure 12.34 honored the Twenty-eighth Convention of the NAWSA by seating George Washington, Utah, Wyoming, Susan B. Anthony, and Elizabeth Cady Stanton together upon one platform. Not in spite of, but because of, their composite nature, it was confirmed that Americans "really" exist on two planes: the historical and the ideal. It was the female as imaged by American

12.33. Lithograph by Keinz and Allison, "Coronation of Womanhood" (1885).

12.34. G. Y. Coffin, "National American Woman Suffrage Association—28th Annual Convention" (1896).

12.35. Edwin Howland Blashfield, "Minnesota, The Granary of the World," senate chamber, Minnesota State Capitol, St. Paul, (1904), from *The Works of Edwin Howland Blashfield* (1937).

artists which alone possessed the aesthetic power to command both as her true spheres of influence.

The dimensions of history and the ideal altered in degree if not in kind by the year 1898. They led to a major shift in the function and configuration of the female images filling the nation's ample space—physical and imaginative. After 1876 patriotic pride grew less timid before the rest of the world. In 1898 at the White City it "thrilled" over the possibilities promised by the future. Prior to 1893, however, discussions concerned with the nature of the visual evidence by which Americans might express their worth were largely held to debates over the importance of technological achievements (the masculine) relative to the arts (the feminine) and to examples contained within the boundaries of the United States. After 1898 the scope for American self-congratulation took on a new dimension, new terrain, and an extended use for familiar images. Pleasure over regional achievements now incorporated interest in the nation as a whole. In turn, the sense of national pride increasingly found expression in internationalistic terms. Even old animosities between North and South were seemingly laid to rest by the common stand against Spain, as figure 13.17 shows. It is during the twenty years between 1898 and 1918, when the United States asserted its political and economic force before the world, that the figure of the American Girl in various new forms attained the summit of its visual force.

Edwin Howland Blashfield created three images that suggest the nature of the change: "The Christmas Bells," the easel painting dating from 1891 (see figure 9.40); "Minnesota, the Granary of the World," the mural of 1904 which stretches across the wall at the state capitol in St. Paul (figure 12.35); "Carry On!" one of the most famous posters of World War I (figure 12.36).

In the first, angels float charmingly upward through the air of Blashfield's easel painting. In the second, a grave goddess centers the triangular space at the Minnesota capitol, while soldiers, workers, pioneer women, Liberty, and Columbia turn their eyes toward the "mother" who will feed them with the unending supply of grain which makes her mighty.[106] In the third, the figures of Liberty and Columbia (extracted, as it were, from the two edges of the Minnesota mural) are merged,

12.36. Edwin Howland Blashfield, "Carry On!"
(1918).

and their poster composite is placed upon the battlefields of France. The lightsome drift of the winged females which act as agents for the Christmas season, and the majestic weight of the goddess of peace and prosperity, have been replaced in 1918 by the Warrior Queen. Armed with sword, flag, and screaming eagle, this figure lunges forward in attack. This is no Psyche, the desirous victim of desire, a figure trembling on the threshold; nor is she Ceres who, as woman and provider, is kept

12.37. Thomas Cole, "The Course of Empire—Consummation of Empire, Third of the Series, 1835–1836."

on the margin of the world of masculine power. This is the American Idol, leader of America's fighting men, and her new names are Will and War.

Frederick Jackson Turner declared the closure of frontier space in a paper delivered before the American Historical Association convened at the 1893 Columbian Exposition. But other modes of space were prompting Americans to think in terms of vastness. Not the least of these inspirations was the Exposition itself. Americans who banked their hopes upon the promise of the geographical expanse of the North American continent clung to an obsolete sense of agrarian space. Conversely, the design of the White City, with its displays of industrial and commercial power, suggested a new kind of scale that pointed forward into the future.

At first, the visible signs of prosperity and progress occasioned by the exhibition grounds at Chicago were interpreted as possibilities to be played out within the boundaries of the nation. By 1898 scale in the grand manner was relocated to an international context. The Oregon Trail had dwindled into a dead end at the Pacific shore, and lands open to homesteaders and cattlemen were drastically curtailed, but' not the imaginative space appropriated by the accelerating industrial, commercial, and political empire of the mind. Within five years of the Columbian Exposition *the spreading of America* was an idea that was actively proselytized from Cuba to the Philippines. An unsettling mix of ideas about democratic mission and aristocratic imperialism was in place. It was not long before notions of mental grandeur were converted into explicit policies of expansion. The warning imaged by the extravagant White City of Thomas Cole's "Consummation of Empire" (painted in 1835–36 to depict the fate of a nation where mobbish greed replaces republican restraint)[107] was generally not the line taken sixty years later (figure 12.37). For those who *did* dislike either modern democracy or updated imperialism, Cole's city tottering on the brink of excess was a prophecy in the act of fulfilling itself before their eyes.

At every step of the way toward the Caribbean and the Pacific rim we find the figure of the American Girl (divinely tall, divinely fair). She moves through that "splendid palace" of "long corridors and high ceilings" described in Morton Fullerton's prophetic dream—a palace similar to the new civic architecture decorated by murals and sculpture that educated the American people in their rights to power. Whatever innocence the Girl had possessed prior to 1893 was lost somewhere along the main promenade beside Chicago's Grand Basin. By 1898 the Girl was consciously the Mother who feeds the world. By 1918 she was transformed into the Warrior Queen. There was no turning back for *that* icon toward the gentility of culture or the gentle virtues of the home. The cry was now "Carry On!"

13

Poster Lives
(1898–1918)

As Henry May has noted in *The End of American Innocence*, the base of idealism narrowed greatly after 1900.[1] Many variations on the American Girl functioned actively at the turn of the century to represent a variety of ideals, but once the Girl became the symbol for the nation as a political entity, she was assigned as a strong image harboring explicitly imperialistic connotations. Columbia as a patroness of culture, cattle, and local industry paled in comparison with Columbia in triumph receiving homage from "The Earth's Great Nations" (figure 13.1).[2] It was a period of victory arches (figure 13.2).[3] They may have led nowhere or been torn down as rapidly as they went up, but street corners and exhibition grounds turned (however briefly) into duplicates of ancient Rome. The Roman Empire had lacked the stimulus of sheet music, but not the new American imperial imagination. Popular tunes and lyrics promoted patriotism, helped along by appropriate cover images—whether pretty Dolly Gray, the girl whom the brave serviceman leaves behind in order to have someone to return to (figure 13.3), or the quadriga figures J. Q. A. Ward designed for the official Dewey Arch (figure 13.4).[4]

The cover of "The American Girl Battleship March" is a fine example of the merger of wartime sentiment and the feminine touch (figure 13.5). In the background is a sketch of the warship which will become a material reality because of the determination of the young woman in the photograph, demure of pose, heart locket at her throat. To quote from the *New York Herald* of September 4, 1898:

13.1. Imre Kiralfy, "Columbia's Triumph," from "America" (1893).

13.2. Jules Guerin, drawing for McKim, Mead, White, "Arch of the Rising Sun from the Court of the Universe," Panama-Pacific International Exposition, San Francisco (1915).

The idea to build an American Girl battleship as a twin for the proposed American Boy was originated by Miss Maude Mears, of No. 538 Burling Street, Chicago. . . . Miss Mears is patriotic from head to foot and has taken particular interest in the developments of the Spanish-American war because seven of the young men whom she has taught at Sunday school are serving their country in the navy.

. . . The scheme [to raise funds through popular subscription] has been cordially indorsed [*sic*] by leading Chicago citizens, and has taken a strong hold upon many members of the fair sex, young and old, who see in it an opportunity to prove to the world that the girls of the country are fully as patriotic as the boys.[5]

One young American girl is inspired "to give the nation a great floating monument to the memory of the heroes of the Maine." It is only proper that that mon-

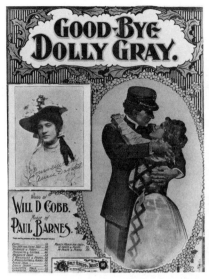

LILLY LIBRARY

13.3. "Good-Bye, Dolly Gray" (c.1898).

13.4. "Dewey's Victory" (c.1898).

LILLY LIBRARY

ument be called "The American Girl."[6] In and of herself, Miss Maude Mears is not strong enough an image to carry the patriotic ideal through to completion. The sketched-in promise of the battleship helps, but the magic comes from linking the two ideas "American Girl" and "Battleship."

Woman plus Nation equates with propaganda about Empire, R. G. Collingwood concluded in his book *The Principles of Art*. Art plus the magic of Empire captures the public emotions.[7] The United States attained the full expression of this magical equation during World War I through poster art of women imaged as the Nation; but as early as the Spanish-American War popular images pointed the direction the country was taking toward poster lives.

The Monroe Doctrine of 1823 had warned the world beyond the rim of the Western Hemisphere to stay out. On August 11, 1898, Charles Dana Gibson pictures Columbia as a gracious, albeit towering, figure who suggests to Spain, the sullen runt, "Come, let us forgive and forget" (figure 13.6). But two weeks later, Columbia in bathing dress—as aloof as a society belle disdainful of associating with her inferiors—asks herself, "Do I want to go in with that crowd?" (figure 13.7). Clearly there is a feeling of ambivalence in this national comedy of manners. Is Columbia to act as hostess for the hemisphere or to remain an isolationist? Whichever way

13.5. "The American Girl Battleship March" (1898).

13.6. Charles Dana Gibson, "Come, Let Us Forgive and Forget," *Life*, August 11, 1898).

13.7. Charles Dana Gibson, "These Foreign Relations: 'Do I want to go in with that crowd?' " *Life*, August 25, 1898.

she chooses to turn, she is a figure of moral superiority, in command of drawing-room politics transferred to the ocean shores.

The *St. Louis Globe-Democrat* of 1898 featured an overtly militant Columbia (figure 13.8). Unlike the situations shown in the Gibson cartoons, there is no chance for gate-crashers to receive an invitation to join the social circle commanded by a reigning belle. This "Newest Woman" is one kind of vigorous American woman-hood the *Globe-Democrat* can sanction; she acts aggressively to challenge Spanish military pretentions, not the masculine system of American politics. Rejecting the classical dress of earlier Columbia figures and the bathing garb of the Outdoors

13.8. Hedrick, "The Newest
Woman," *St. Louis Globe-
Democrat* (1898), from
*Cartoons of the War of
1898 with Spain* (1898).

Girl (the relatively tame costumes Gibson uses in his two cartoons), the *Globe-Democrat*'s Columbia wears the no-nonsense uniform of Theodore Roosevelt's Rough Riders. That she intends to end "the swagger and tyranny" of Spain's greed for "universal dominion" is ironic in ways that were less noticeable at the time than they are to us through hindsight.[8]

What Angus Fletcher calls the "Big Lie" has been a major component of patriotic fervor since Thucydides shaped his record of the Peloponnesian War to suit the emotional needs of his fellow Athenians.[9] But lies are not perceived as such by those who have *seen* the truth. As Charles Sanders Peirce continually reiterated, societies fashion their conduct through interpretation of signs. The nature of national conduct between 1898 and 1918 was governed in large part by the signs Americans were choosing, as well as the ways they chose to read them.

There is an epitaph engraved upon the headstone of the grave of Senator George Frisbie Hoare (1826–1904) in the cemetery of Concord, Massachusetts. (It is not too far down the line from the grave of Henry David Thoreau, who had had harsh things to say in 1848 concerning American excursions into lands across the southern border.) No incised image marks the stone over the senator's grave, only the words of a man's faith in the moral rightness of his country.

I have no faith in fatalism . in destiny . in blind force

I believe in God . the living God . I believe in the American people a free and brave people who do not bow the neck or bend the knee to any other and who desire no other to bow the neck or bend the knee to them

I believe that a republic is greater than an empire

I believe finally . whatever clouds may darken the horizon that the world is growing better . that today is better than yesterday and that tomorrow will be better than today

Senator Hoare died still believing that a republic is greater than an empire,[10] but there were many images (as well as expressions of national will) that were turning that faith into a lie. Images which supported the concepts upheld by Hoare were gentle variations on the American Girl portrayed as Freedom and Truth. The images which falsified those concepts were aggressive representations of the Girl as WASP Savior of a tainted world.

Where did the immigrants fit in? Jews had been arriving in ever-greater numbers since the czarist pogroms picked up in pace if not in elegance during the 1880s. Italians, Slavs, and Asians acted according to their own rhythms of despair and hope by flooding into first Castle Garden, then Ellis Island, during the 1890s. The immigrants had many bewildering new vocabularies to learn. Not just the English language of those who bossed the economic and political systems into whose cracks they tried to scramble. Not just the argot of the slums where diverse races, religions, and ethnic groups had to shift for themselves in often hostile proximity one to another. Not just the physical language of cityscapes and landscapes for which memories of their homelands were inadequate preparation. In addition to this polyglot of New World signs there was the "language" of the sign that was visible wherever they looked: the sign of the American Girl of impeccable northern European Protestant physiognomy and values.

We have already seen evidence of the fact that the children of "the Others" frequently tried to adapt the look and the values of the Girl to their own desires. Chapter 14, in its dealings with the commercial marketing of that icon, gives further instances of the power of the pictorial idea of the American Girl, whatever the place of origin of its consumers. But what did it cost the psyche to make that identification and to cultivate those desires?

Time after time we come upon those painful occasions where the immigrant physiognomy was held up by newspapers and magazines in comparison with the "true" American look—held up as a thing that is physically ugly and morally repellent. In almost the same breath, the press took for granted that the lower classes and inferior peoples wanted to be like that other, finer, truer "American" image. Then (still holding that same breath) the press turned around to repeat the belief that such assimilations were an impossibility. The immigrants' common lot was to be insulted at one moment, encouraged at the next, then condescended to once again. Every time they encountered accepted signs for the American national spirit, they "read" in visual terms the charge that they must (but could not) lift themselves from a state of racial and moral deformity to the evolutionary heights.[11]

There is a tradition of some weight of immigrant contribution to American patriotic art. Constantino Brumidi and his crew of Italian craftsmen worked at the U.S. Capitol throughout the 1860s. Emanuel Leutze's "Washington Crossing the Delaware" of 1850 and Domenico Tojetti's painting "The Progress of America" (see figure 11.23) added notable images to the repertoire that underscored the country's sense of dynastic purpose. By 1910 American art schools enrolled an increasing number of first- and second-generation immigrants drawn from groups arriving after 1876.[12] But no matter what these new Americans did to advance the nationalistic spirit, their *look* posed a problem for those who were already dug in. The Irish did not rate inclusion in V. G. Rocine's ethnic rogue's gallery of 1910, but conversely Howard Chandler Christy denied the Irish—and the Italians, Slavs, and Jews— entry into his picture books of praise for native superiority imaged in the form of the American Girl. (Blacks and Asians were considered such an impossibility as "Americans" they could be depicted outright in pictorially derogatory terms without having to be "seen." They were "invisible" because literally unthinkable.)

Christy had no visual space available for the female immigrant. Charles Dana Gibson gave immigrants, male and female, his sympathy when they were poor (figure 13.9) and his approval when they were pretty (see figure 2.16), but not much of his time. We have already seen what Albert Beck Wenzell could do with the Hebraic nose (see figures 2.20 and 2.21) and how James Montgomery Flagg could slip in an anti-Semitic profile in passing (see figure 5.26). It was left to those who were themselves moving from the outside slowly toward the inside to record with accuracy the looks of the people destined to become the New Americans. It is important to recognize that immigrants shaped this record of transition under essentially the same conditions of suspicion and reluctance that dogged the way of the often-despised new women who sought to create more favorable images of themselves as the New Woman.

We are familiar with the images provided through the photographs of Jacob Riis (rather too much the fastidious Danish immigrant to take real pleasure in the look of the Italians, Jews, and blacks of the Bowery) and of Lewis Hine (who offered dignity without flinching to the new masses). I wish to show another image by an artist who is not well known. I do this because the pictorial method used by Denman Fink is not that of the photo document. Instead, Fink employed the strong flat patterns of the poster, the medium which had already won its place on the American scene during the 1890s as an effective agent for selling products and which was soon to become the single most important visual means for promoting American national values during the war of 1917–18.

In March 1901 *Scribner's Magazine* ran an essay by Arthur Henry, "Among the Immigrants," together with illustrations by Denman Fink.[13] The main points made by Henry pertain to the lack of guile, the worthiness, and the touching vulnerability of "the three hundred or more creatures packed like cattle on the barge"

13.9. Charles Dana Gibson, " 'On the Sidewalks of New York,' " from *Americans* (1898).

that had brought them to Ellis Island one bitter winter's day. Under Henry's sympathetic, attentive eye, these "creatures" sort themselves out into assorted types representing different categories of race, ethnic derivation, age, sex, and physical and mental conditions. He *sees* them as gentle, hopeful, and patient. Each face and figure represents personal stories that are "simple and brief, but so real and the tragedies so apparent" that the listener's eyes fill with tears.

The verbal lesson the essay leaves with the readers of *Scribner's* is clearly put. They need not fear. All will be well for American society in the course of time. "It is a mistake to think that this country is being made a dumping-ground for Europe's rubbish. Year by year we are acquiring, by a process of natural selection, the pick of the nations. Those who possess thrift, courage, and ambition make their way here. The dull, the indolent, and the hidebound stay at home. The third and fourth, if not the second generations from these sturdy emigrants give us good Americans."

These are nice words and sincere sentiments for 1901. They are written by an observer of "aliens" who wishes them well and realizes their future value to their new homeland. But the *strong* images of the presentation come from the illustrations by Denman Fink. True to the lavish art layouts permitted by magazine editors in those halcyon days of photoengraving, Fink provides ten illustrations, spread over ten pages, plus the full-page drawing which stands as the frontispiece to the March issue of *Scribner's Magazine* (figure 13.10). The poster method Fink uses throughout his drawings acts two ways in relation to Henry's words. Visually, these are indeed "creatures" who slowly emerge from the dark background with which the artist surrounds their mass. They do not stand forth as full-fledged individuals in the "American" sense (with the exception of a pencil sketch of a tall Russian mountaineer, pictured in his own space apart from the others). Rather, the immigrants are shown in groups—either as part of the huddled masses filling the waiting rooms of Ellis Island, or as smaller family units of mother and children, or as a crowd of Italians who have come to welcome an old man to his new home.

Figure 13.10 is titled with wonderful accuracy "On the Threshold of the New Country." These are indeed "threshold people" of the kind discussed in chapter 10 in terms of gender identities. The most compelling aspect of Fink's drawing is the pictorial force that lies latent within the flat poster surface. It suggests the social force contained in the expectant, forward thrust of the old man's body and the bundles he carries; it is there in the hooded, wary features of the two figures who peer over the old man's shoulder. This is energy on hold; it is energy at the threshold. But it is energy ready to be released—*to come on inside.*

The half-hidden energy shown in figure 13.10 is analogous to the energy that Henry Adams and others (usually with some fear implied) assigned to women in America. But while the immigrants of Denman Fink's pictures of Ellis Island waited their turn to express their pent-up force within American society, the image of the American Girl had already reached that point in history where it expressed itself directly as energy in motion. The immigrants were given images that put them *in place* within the American scheme of national growth (figure 13.11). The Girl *placed* the values of that society by means of the images which, in turn, Americans had assigned to her.

In World War I, as in World War II, the Girl He Left Behind figures in the popular art forms that served to back the war effort in their own way. In World War II it is likely that the greatest emotional weight was carried by just that on-the-fringe art: the pinup decals stuck to the sides of U.S. bombers, the glossy stills of Betty Grable and Rita Hayworth, the illustrations by Vargas and Petty. These were cute, sexy charmers, visibly *willing* to do their all. In contrast, the official poster art of 1941–45 was bland to the point of negation when it made use (as it did over and over) of images of sturdy WACS, WAVES, and WAFS, or of determined home-front heroines working on the swing shift. James Montgomery Flagg continued to do his bit. His favorite model Georgia MacDonald became the standard image for the soothing hands of mercy extended by the Red Cross or for the nurses attached to the military services. But even when these images escape dull respectability, they are too close to the type of the Beautiful Charmer—too like a parody of Daisy Miller Goes to War, too much the type of the average—to possess the power exerted by the female forms which transformed a significant number of World War I posters into a strange, unsettling, yet unquestionably effective state of mind.

The female type took full command over two categories of posters for World War I. One is the Amazon Warrior (called for official purposes Columbia, Liberty, or America). The other is the Protecting Angel (labeled as the Red Cross nurse, the Rescue Mission lady, the YWCA girl, or the women in the Land Army). It is fascinating to watch images from one category start to infiltrate the emotional shadows of the other group and to notice at what juncture images pull apart for the fulfillment of their distinctive functions. It is also instructive, and eerie, to watch the figures of 1917–18 emerge from the repertoire of images that had come into favor after 1876, by now shaping their significance within entirely new contexts.

13.10. Denman Fink, "On the Threshold of the New Country," from "Among the Immigrants," *Scribner's Monthly Magazine,* March 1901.

13.11. Poster for the *Boston
Sunday Herald*, April 19,
1896.

The emotional point at which the Warrior and the Angel converge is that point at which their (largely invisible) wingspread meets upon the poster sheet. The wings once found in marble cemetery figures, on sheet-music covers, or in Daniel Chester French's versions of "Victory," "Hope," and "Peace" are seldom in evidence in the war posters issued by the various armed services, the Liberty Loan drives, the relief agencies, and the dozens of home-front organizations. But the values remain for which wings were once the token. The strong and the good still unfurl their spirit in order to protect the weak and the worthy, but now these militantly protective figures are in battle dress, and actual wings are neither practicable nor necessary for the mission they carry out.

By 1918 a long visual history (reaching far back into Western art traditions) lay behind the images which the U.S. government used to image its ability and duty to shelter helpless victims from the oppression of wicked foes. But the essential prototype for Columbia as Manifest Destiny came out of the past of Roman Catholic Renaissance Italy, as in the magnificent "Madonna of the Misericordia" by Piero della Francesca, painted for the Church of San Sepolchro in the years between 1445 and 1448. In the della Francesca mural the figure of the Great Mother (itself the légatée of still-earlier renderings by the Italian primitivists) towers over suppliants who huddle and kneel within the shadow of her outstretched cloak. Late-nineteenth-century Americans were more at ease with the spreading wings of Protestant angels than with Mary's cloak of mercy, but inherited props and gestures served to signal the same meaning. From orphans wrapped in an American flag (figure 13.12) to Evangeline Booth of the Salvation Army protecting barefoot waifs (figure 13.13), secular versions of the Mary of Miseries and Mercy took their place in the visual memories of Americans.

The new type of the Columbia figure was more explicitly nationalistic in sentiment than were figures denoting private charities devoted to sheltering the homeless. Like them, Columbia gestures the way into a good future for the backward nations of the earth; at the same time, that hand gesture declares her power to dominate because of the might that lies behind the spirit of mission. We have already seen how Daniel Chester French's Custom House "America" simultaneously holds back and urges forward (see figure 12.17), but let us be reminded of earlier, more homey, less awesome variations on the theme. They help mark the contrasts made apparent by 1900.

In this advertising poster of 1876 (figure 13.14), Uncle Sam, with eagle perched on his shoulder, heads the laden table that provides for the world's children. (The bill of fare that itemizes the foods "typical" of other nations is a gastronomical version of the racist slurs found in the physiognomical manuals of the next decades. The "Saddle of Horse" from France, the "Rats Fricasseed" from China, and Ireland's "Potatoes, Fried, Boiled, Stewed, Roasted, Baked, Mashed, Raw" cannot match the American turkey for good taste.) Columbia is the bustling housewife who lays the board while a happy darky tends the splendid cooking stove which is the product this sunny piece of chauvinism sets out to sell. Forty years later there is no more coziness. In 1918 "The Greatest Mother of the World" is the looming American Mary of Miseries that holds a tiny, off-scale body, reminder of all Christlike men sacrificed in atonement for the world's wickedness (figure 13.15). The essential Roman Catholic image of the Pietà has been appropriated at that precise moment in history when the great secular saint of America pits the nation's benevolence against the world's evil. We are now out of the kitchen and onto the cosmic battlefield.

In 1876 Columbia stood poised at the edge of a precipice. As she looked out over the kingdoms of the world, she appeared unaware of the possibility she might be tempted by satanic history into believing she was the lord of all she surveyed (see Introduction, figure 1). What we read as hubris and the potential for becoming one of the world's less agreeable powers, the editors of *Leslie's Historical Register* proposed as right and proper self-confidence. But even the bold position taken by *Leslie's* Columbia is eased somewhat by the (admittedly deceptive) friendliness of

13.12. "Six Young Ladies
 Wrapped in a Flag"
 (1918).

13.13. Benjamin Falk, New
 York, "Evangeline
 Booth—The White Angel
 of the Slums" (1907).

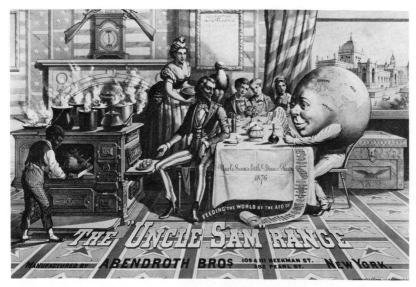

13.14. "The Uncle Sam Range" (1876).

the Columbia who busies herself during the same year at the Uncle Sam Range, offering the abundance of her domestic domain for the world's sustenance and the profit of her farmers. Both images represent twin impulses of the Centennial years. They give signs denoting the new mood of patriotism; they are part of the workable pictorial vocabulary for the aspirations of Americans that would markedly increase over the next forty years.

Occasionally a male figure appears in American magazines at the turn of the century to carry a generalized message of moral mission, as in this Anglophile version of the burdens of empire from *The Cosmopolitan* of 1899 (figure 13.16). But Pears' Soap is the true icon of virtue here; the naval office is only an acolyte in service of a product for sale. Once the focus is placed upon national allegories, females are the figures that count; theirs are the signs that confirm the march to supremacy.

The following images based on the theme of reconciliation and union indicate the shift of attention from Uncle Sam to the "America" figure. In a cartoon of 1875 Joseph Keppler for *Leslie's Monthly Magazine* Uncle Sam joins the hands of the North and the South in the hope that a reunited nation might combat "Conkling, Morton, Poland, and the rest, with their dreadful Ku-Klux emblems . . . the war's bitterness, *Crédit Mobilier* frauds, 'rings' of all kinds, nepotism and Caesarism."[14] In 1898 Captain Fritz W. Guerin, a Union veteran and St. Louis photographer, stages a tableau that celebrates the reconciliation of the North and South that has helped free "poor little Cuba" (figure 13.17). Uncle Sam is no longer present. Cuba herself, a winsome, golded-haired Little Eva whose chains have been broken by the mutual effort of her grandfatherly saviors, is the figure which reconciles and blesses. Little Cuba unites the estranged brothers under one banner and saves their

13.15. A. E. Foringer, "The Greatest Mother in the World" (1918).

souls in reward for her liberation. In figure 13.18 Uncle Sam appears in a cartoon of 1898 for the *St. Louis Globe-Democrat*, but he leans back in his chair, thumbs tucked into his vest, while Columbia flourishes flag and trumpet in order to announce to Cuba, the Philippines, and Puerto Rico that it is she who has freed them. That same, very busy, year Kenyon Cox prepares a drawing intended for a magazine cover (figure 13.19). Cuba is a lovely but frail and naked maiden in distress. To her aid comes Columbia. Proud, tall, splendidly nude, she throws her

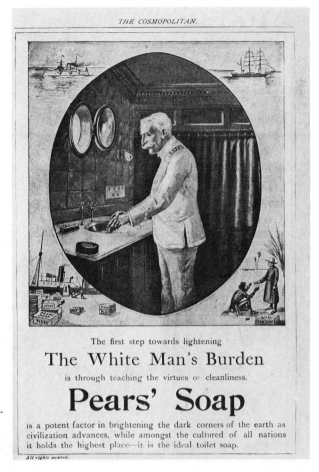

THE COSMOPOLITAN.

The first step towards lightening

The White Man's Burden

is through teaching the virtues of cleanliness.

Pears' Soap

is a potent factor in brightening the dark corners of the earth as civilization advances, while amongst the cultured of all nations it holds the highest place—it is the ideal toilet soap.

13.16. "Pears' Soap," *The Cosmopolitan*, advertising section, May–October 1899.

arm protectively around her weaker sister, needing no further support from male representations of American power. *This* is the image which had been in the process of formation since the Centennial years. Although prone to silliness or cloying cuteness—as in "Dawn of Day in the Antilles" (figure 13.20) or this vignette of the girl-child playing at being the mother of mercy (figure 13.21) [15]—images of protecting might are now ready to advance with frightening earnestness toward 1917–18.

Poor Little Cuba is replaced by Poor Little Belgium when it comes time for a new country to be saved by the military and moral strength of the United States. In 1889 Belgium, itself an empire, was imaged as "Civilization"—the great lady who brings learning and technical skills to the blacks of the Congo colonies (figure 13.22). [16] By 1914 Belgium is now the victim, and Columbia is the one power capable of saving her (figure 13.23). [17]

Occasionally we catch a glimpse of images that suggest that the United States is just one among many nations, an economical and political entity that benefits

Demonstrations

13.17. Fritz W. Guerin, St. Louis, "Cuba Reconciling the North and the South" (1898).

13.18. Russell, *St. Louis Globe-Democrat* (1898), from *Cartoons of the War of 1898 with Spain* (1898).

13.19. Kenyon Cox, nude study for magazine cover, "Columbia and Cuba" (c.1898).

from pursuing a policy of cooperation among equals. Figure 13.24 is one of many cigar labels from the 1880s which present Columbia bound in sisterhood (and by the needs of the tobacco industry) to other countries of the Western Hemisphere. Figure 13.25 is one of the few examples from World War I which shows Columbia sharing her glory and efforts with other nations. But judging from the rarity of this pictorial union of female figures, the formalistic motif of "The Three Graces" did not possess the popular appeal exerted by the single, solitary figure of "The Greatest Mother of the World" (figure 13.26).[18]

The visual attributes common to the Sacred Mother inform the images of both the Amazon Warrior and the Protecting Angel. The look of masculine militancy adapted

13.20 *(left).* George Prince,
   "Dawn of Day in the
   Antilles" (1898).

13.21 *(above).* Maude Humphrey, "A Red Cross
   Nurse" (1898).

to the female form also characterizes each of these two types. The Mother image
had a long history before it arrived at the point where it was ready to do service
for the American cause in World War I. The image of the female soldier also came
onto the scene of battle in 1917 preceded by a diverse history of iconographic
expression.

   The look of the military is introduced to the female form in a number of ways,
each with its own subtradition. The pert and sexy girls of the theater world often
appeared in male uniforms. The "Columbian Amazons" indicated the burlesque
circuit's taste for abbreviated versions of nineteenth-century dress uniforms (see
figure 11.20). Breasts and hips were accentuated by the snug hussar's jacket and
broad belt. Add epaulets, a helmet or shako, a smart little sword, gold trim and
tights, and the Carrie Meebers of an 1890s chorus line were ready to make their
jaunty entrance. Howard Chandler Christy's famous poster for the U.S. Navy (figure 13.27), reputed to have persuaded 15,000 men that the U.S. Navy was their
destiny, is close in its tone to the burlesque poster, to this cigar label of about 1885
(figure 13.28), and to the cover for the 1919 *Ziegfeld Follies,* "My Baby's Arms"

13.22. Tapestry by Mme. de Rudder, "Civilization" (1897),
from Whitby, "The Art
Movement, An Unusual
Form of Decorative Art,"
The Magazine of Art (December 1898).

13.23. Edwin Howland Blashfield, "Belgium,"
from Wharton, *The Book of the
Homeless* (1916).

(figure 13.29). It is surely closer to those sexy images than to the sober female figures in uniform he presented as national emblems in 1906 (figure 13.30). Conversely, Christy's "The Army Girl" (like its companion "The Navy Girl") refers to the tradition of Amazonian warriors illustrated in chapter 12 and to earnest visual statements which asked, "Why Can't a Girl Be a Soldier?" (figure 13.31).

During World War I photographs recorded the look of American women as uniformed participants in the war effort on the home front. The women of these photographs are neither the sexy figures of the theater world nor the bravura images of the poster world. Their uniforms are utilitarian and do little to enhance their appearance, but they *do* indicate that the women are doing their "bit." Limited in physical and imaginative scale, such real women are safe and therefore usable as public symbols. Photographed marching in patriotic rallies, they could not be mistaken for militant suffragists; not be taken as a possible threat to the nation's family life.[19] The realistic scenes prepared by the government photographers place their subjects firmly in that domesticated middle ground that merges the home

13.24. Cigar label, "Americas Unidas" (c.1885).

13.25. Hazel Frazee, "Every Ship Saved a Long Journey Means a Shipload of Soldiers and Munitions to France" (1918).

EVERY SHIP SAVED A LONG JOURNEY MEANS A SHIPLOAD OF SOLDIERS & MUNITIONS TO FRANCE.

front with the war effort abroad.[20] These women were national heroines, but of the kind intended for return to the regulated life once peace was achieved. In contrast, government poster art created a fantasy world where the heroic female image reaches for the timeless and the sublime.

American poster artists borrowed gestures from previous visual vocabularies such as the Mariannes of Eugene Delacroix and François Rudi, but the Gallic edge of profile possessed by the French national icon was altered to accord with that of the American Girl who claimed the "regular" physiognomy of Athenian Nikes and Anglo-Saxon princesses. Italia defying the Hun was a serviceable image for the Italians but entirely too Old World for American needs (figure 13.32).[21] American posters incorporated the by-now-familiar attributes (or what the ad men rushed into the propaganda effort called "trade-marks")[22] of eagle, Liberty cap, flag, and helmet.

Photographs documented the wartime activities of women attired for fund-raising events in flag-draped dresses; but physiognomically those women looked like anyone else from any place in the Western world. They had no particular mark distinguishing them as specific national types or as representatives of particular

13.26. Daniel MacMorris, "Women in War" (1955).

national virtues; certainly not as the type of the Warrior and Mother who leads the women who serve. The activities of actual women working at home or abroad in the various auxiliary units received their most effective publicity through posters that symbolized their efforts: Red Cross nurse (figure 13.33); members of the Land Army (figure 13.34); stalwart defenders of the helpless children of beleaguered nations (figure 13.35). Photographs *recorded* the roles these women played, but posters *dramatized* whomever they touched. Even antiwar sentiments did best when they countered one poster image with another, as when Henry Glintenkamp's 1914 cover for *The Masses* (figure 13.36) tries to plow the ground out from under Edward Penfield's heroic figures (figures 13.34 and 13.38).

Photographs and drawings were often excessively busy in detail. Although they made artistic use of selection and setting, it was sometimes difficult to know just where the viewer's eye was meant to light and what merited special attention. They might take as long to interpret as this drawing prepared for the U.S. Food Administration (figure 13.37). An attack against women slackers, it lacks the impact of the Penfield poster incorporated into the pages of the magazine at which the woman idly gazes (figure 13.38). Posters made the same points photographs and drawings did, but made them more aggressively through the use of silhouettes, flat patterns of color, and bold typeface. Posters simplified and amplified the message expressed by each visual unit, conveying force through clear, instantaneously recognizable signs.

The artists who prepared the most effective wartime posters had had prior experience in the effective making of signifiers. They had served their apprenticeship during the American poster craze of the 1890s or worked with advertising agencies that cultivated the poster format. Edward Penfield, J. C. Leyendecker, Herbert Paus,

13.27. Howard Chandler Christy,
"Gee! I Wish I Were a Man. I'd
Join the Navy" (1917).

13.28. Cigar label, "Cockade"
(c.1885).

Albert Sterner, and Adolph Treidler were experts in the design of flat color planes, hard-edged outlines, and print graphics. Men trained solely as illustrators did not do as well. Christy's posters for the navy and marine recruitment were adequate but only his design for "Gee, I Wish I Were a Man!" comes off with force—as much because of the vertical slash of blue to the left, balanced by the cocky lettering that runs down the right side, as for any emotional appeal it makes to the masculinity of its male viewers. Many of Christy's posters expose his shakiness as a draughtsman and his sloppy eye for design. The illustrations he did for propaganda purposes (as for the *King Albert's Book*) are often artistic and conceptual disasters. Witness the design he prepared for the *Washington Times*' Sunday supplement (figure 13.39). Even James Montgomery Flagg succeeded best when he centered his posters with male figures. His famous image of Uncle Sam, who usurps Lord Kitchener's pose with finger pointed like a rifle to the heart, is a thoroughly male symbol. In comparison, Flagg's use of female figures for idealizing, patriotic purposes was usually uninspired.[23]

Charles Dana Gibson offers even better proof that artists who excelled at illustrations frequently failed at the design of effective propaganda posters (ironic since Gibson was the head of the government's Division of Pictorial Publicity).[24] Gibson's superb draughtsmanship and his eye for compositional arrangement across the design surface could not compensate for the fact that he worked best with small-scale figures and complex contrasts of light and shadow. There is also the fact that his female figures intended as determined Valkyries were too gently fem-

13.29. "My Baby's Arms," *Zieg-feld Follies 1919.*

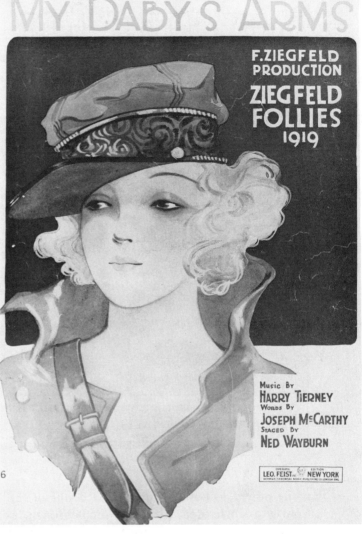

THE ARMY GIRL

13.30. Howard Chandler Christy, "The Army Girl," from *The American Girl* (1906).

LILLY LIBRARY

inine to suggest the force of a nation at war. A Chicago window display feebly tries to compensate with swags of bunting for the visual inadequacy of the delicate Gibson drawing at its center (figure 13.40). From the start of his career and throughout his service in the World War I propaganda effort, Gibson could master every patriotic variation of the American Girl but the Girl as Warrior Queen.

Early in 1918 the poster authority C. Matlack Price, in collaboration with Horace Brown, rushed a pamphlet into print under the sponsorship of the Washington, D.C., National Committee of Patriotic Societies. It outlined why posters are the most successful of all visual forms of propaganda and why certain designs work

13.31. Starmer, "Why Can't a Girl Be a Soldier?" (1905).

LILLY LIBRARY

while others do not.[25] The dos and don'ts of the Price/Brown manual are clear. Convey a single idea through a simple design, using silhouetted figures that are easy to remember. Appeal to the emotions, not the intellect; there is not enough time (or need) to rely on thought. Direct the message to the Common Man in the Street (and the Common Woman in the Home). Avoid complicated allegorical figures; they take too long to decipher. Feel duty-bound to reject techniques previously developed by German poster artists.[26] Above all, as the pamphlet announces in its boldface title, the trick is to know HOW TO PUT IT—PATRIOTIC POSTERS—THE STUFF THAT MAKES PEOPLE STOP—LOOK—ACT!

When 1917 came the United States was ready for a poster war. The government fumbled its way into the tardy training and equipping of troops for overseas combat, but signboards and marketing devices were already at hand. Advertising agencies had created experts at the sale of goods to American consumers by means of emotional appeals that stimulated desire. With the inception of the war effort, the

13.32. Capranesi, "Sotto Scrivere al Prestito" (1918).

NATIONAL ARCHIVES

same men were ready to sell Americans a new set of desires based on the notion of service to the nation. Before the war, posters urged self-indulgence; now, they instructed self-denial. What remained a constant was their calculated incorporation of female figures as vehicles for the simplified representation of a complex of values.

Before the war the wonders of American know-how were presented daily to housewives (products for their homes) and young women (products to enhance their charms). Advertising images also tutored men in the need to protect those homes and wives, to please those young women, and to uphold their nation's pride in industrial progress. Once 1917 came, the basic set of images had not far to go to become images for war. Only a thin boundary to cross and consumers moved away from billboard posters created in the private sector that informed them of the pleasures of prosperity and progress. Now the public had government posters created by the same advertising men for the purpose of winning the war. Advertising techniques and poster art would help to insure the salvation of the Western world and a future dedicated to American principles which included, among others, the Gold Dust Twins and the Mazda Lamp.

Two works of short fiction fit with advantage into this discussion of patriotic emblems. One is "Editha," written as an after-view of the heady events of the summer of 1898 by William Dean Howells.[27] The other is "DeLancey—Himself," written by Frederick Orin Bartlett for *The Marines' Bulletin* in the white-heat of the

13.33. "Motherless, Fatherless,
Starving. How Much To
Save These Little Lives?"
(1918).

13.34. Edward Penfield, "The
Girl on the Land Serves
the Nation's Need"
(1918).

13.35. Douglas Volk, "They
Shall Not Perish" (1918).

13.36. Henry J. Glintenkamp, "The Girl He Left Behind Him," *The Masses*, October 1914.

battle of propaganda during World War I.[28] Each story depicts a man and a woman who live poster lives during poster wars; the one is presented with irony, the other is not.

Howells' story of 1905 is retrospective. It looks back in irony upon the summer

U. S. Food Administration.

13.37. U.S. Food Administration drawing (c.1918).

13.38. Edward Penfield, "Will You Help the Women of France? Save Wheat" (1918).

13.39. Howard Chandler
Christy, "Observers,"
The American Weekly,
Washington Times, July
21, 1918.

13.40. Charles Dana Gibson, "A
Word to the Wives.
'Save.' " Mandel Bros.,
Chicago (c. 1918).

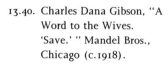

NATIONAL ARCHIVES

of 1898 when the "air was thick with the war feeling, like the electricity of a storm which has not yet burst." Into this palpable atmosphere Howells inserts his young American girl and the young man whom she wishes to woo into the arms of war. At first the attitude of George Gearson toward the question of war is "relaxed" and marked by "want of seriousness." In contrast, Editha's "lips are parted, and panting with the intensity of the questions." She says of the war, "How glorious!" but George laconically replies twice over, "It's war." He wishes a rational career at home in the law. She passionately wills him "to perfect himself" in battle as an act of faith.

With her red hair, blue eyes, and face "with the color painted out by the white moonshine," Editha is a stunning poster image for George to behold.[29] He must contend with her nature "pulling upon his nature, her womanhood upon his manhood." He has to resist the fact that her "whole soul willed him" to be a hero. Passionately, she repeats "the current phrases of the newspapers": *"That ignoble peace! It was no peace at all, with that crime and shame at our very gates."* Passionately, she "seized his hand in her two hands, and poured her soul from her eyes into his." Passionately, her "heart stopped a beat before it pulsed on with leaps that she felt in her neck."

George consecrates himself at last to the service of Editha's "god of battles." She tells him: "You don't belong to yourself now; you don't even belong to *me*. You belong to your country." As her reward for having "recruited" him, she repeats the vow that "satisfied her famine for phrases": "I am yours for time and eternity—time and eternity."

George Gearson is killed during one of the first skirmishes of the war. Editha journeys out west to the home of George's mother. There for the first time she meets the invalid woman whose husband had lost his arm during the Civil War and whose only child is now dead. They confront one another in a darkened room where at first neither can see the other. Some light is let in, and we glimpse Editha, "tall and black in her crapes," and the mother, seated low in a deep armchair. The mother has a "powerful voice" which is startlingly like George's. With that voice as her weapon, she accuses Editha of having killed her son by sending him out on a mission to kill the sons of other mothers. Then by a sheer act of will and the force of her still-powerful arms, the accuser lifts her helpless body partway out of the chair. "What you got that black on for?" she asks Editha. "Take it off, take it off, before I tear it from your back!"

Editha returns home, crushed by this encounter. Soon after, while sketching "Editha's beauty, which lent itself wonderfully to the effects of a colorist," a young woman friend talks with Editha about the matter. As the sketcher looks at "Editha's lips in nature and then at her lips in art," she passes judgment on the shameful behavior of the mother who had so cruelly rebuked Editha's fine sentiments. " 'How perfectly—excuse me—how *vulgar!*' A light broke upon Editha in the darkness which she felt had been without a gleam of brightness for weeks and months. The mystery that had bewildered her was solved by the word; and from that moment she rose from grovelling in shame and self-pity, and began to live again in the ideal."

Editha's red, white, and blue beauty is saved "aesthetically" by the right *word*. The right *look* is restored to her when set in contrast to a pictorial effect that is merely "vulgar." Her innate *taste* for glorious phrases and passionate deeds is vindicated. The realism of killing and being killed is replaced by a life of the ideal; by a poster life.

The fact that George was crushed between the powerful wills of two forceful women is not lost upon Howells. Mrs. Gearson is the Amazon Mother ("wounded" by war, just as her husband and son have been) who rises up out of the darkness before Editha as an Avenging Angel. Editha is the Poster Girl whom George has left behind him for "time and eternity." Howells portrays neither woman as being sublime; both are only picturesque. But Howells makes it clear that the pictorial can destroy the man caught in the middle. However trivial it may be, the picturesque is enough to cause a man's death, although it guarantees that he dies for nothing much.

Frederick Orin Bartlett's "DeLancey—Himself" appeared, with illustrations by Howard Chandler Christy, in the Christmas number of the newly formed *Marines' Bulletin*. It is the start of the year 1918, and the *Bulletin* announces its mission to recruit young men into the corps. By selling the image of the marines, the *Bulletin* hopes to offset the prestige already possessed by the army, navy, and newly formed air corps. "DeLancey—Himself" is a piece of prose fiction which demonstrates the same techniques of public relations discussed in the feature article of the same issue, "Leading Advertising Experts Commend Success of Marines' Publicity Campaign."[30] (The story also uses several of the devices for gaining mass acceptance that Edward Bernays developed into a marketing science after the war's end.)[31] In World War I the marine corps had the perfect occasion to make a name for itself, and Bartlett's tale is made to order to fit that occasion.

As the story opens it is the early months of America's entry into the European war. DeLancey is a successful matinee idol of the New York stage. The plays in which he appears are of no account in any scheme of real things. To use Daniel Boorstin's term, they are pseudo-events. They are merely excuses for the presence on stage of "Himself," that self-fabricated personage DeLancey's agent promotes through large posters displayed outside the theater entrance. Even time has stood still for DeLancey who lives, as it were, outside history. Although his dresser has aged in his service, the actor at thirty-two years is whatever age he wishes to imitate. The world moves deeper into the facts of history with each day of the war, but the only difference the international upheavals make in DeLancey's life is his decision to star in a romantic drama about a war hero. DeLancey is a stickler for verisimilitude, and so he pins a real medal for bravery (one he picked up in a shop) on the military jacket of his stage costume.

One day a note is delivered to DeLancey's dressing room. It is on letter paper marked HRH. (When opening the envelope, he automatically assumes the conventionalized pose of a man of the world "receiving notes from princesses.") The message is from the Princess Eleanore of Boldavia requesting that he come to her. (Another version of Ruritania and Graustark, Boldavia here represents all the beleaguered "little" countries invaded by the bestial Huns which must turn in their need to the United States as their savior.) DeLancey sets forth to meet a real princess. After years of portraying handsome young Americans who meet and love stage princesses, he is excited by the thought, at last, of having an authentic experience.

On the sidewalk in front of the theater DeLancey sees soldiers passing by. He idly thinks that they lack color and interest. They look like practical working men on their way to do jobs for some employer or other. They certainly do not strike him as anything like the brave figure of the bemedaled hero he nightly portrays onstage. But then, the idea of soldiering does not appeal to him. He is an artist; he is not in "business." (He is, thereby, another example of that "feminine" side of American society noted by Henry James, George Santayana, James McNeill Whistler, and Henry Adams.) Just then DeLancey notices a passing soldier who pauses to look at the poster of "Himself" in stage uniform on display before the theater entrance. The man in khaki comments sarcastically, "Some soldier that, eh?" With a start, DeLancey hurries on before he is recognized.

Once he arrives at the hotel where he is to meet the princess, DeLancey's confidence is restored. He mentally compares himself with the photographs of royalty he has seen in the newspapers, and knows he looks even more royal than they. Then the princess appears before him—"tall and slight and dressed in black," "the most beautiful woman" he has ever seen.[32]

DeLancey immediately notices what any actor would. The Princess Eleanore wears no jewels. Lacking the props of royalty, she is thrown back on "herself," in contrast to DeLancey—the "Himself" who must rely on an actor's aesthetic compounding of costume, manner, and self-assurance. The princess has no doubts, however, about DeLancey's authenticity as an actual American patriot. She reads the image he presents to her as the real thing. For her, his looks represent the United States of America—the nation which signifies the Flag of Freedom and the Savior of Mothers and Babies. Automatically, DeLancey's person is brought into firm conjunction with those emblems and those roles.

The Princess Eleanore has summoned DeLancey to congratulate him for bearing her country's highest decoration for bravery—the Cross of the Chevaliers, the medal she has seen him wear at the theater. (For her, signifier and signified are one.) Hitherto poised and self-assured, DeLancey is thrown into confusion by the shame he suddenly feels over not being "real." His feelings are an intensification of what he had momentarily experienced when the passing soldier made mock of his poster. He returns to his dressing room and stands before the omnipresent mirror, looking hard at himself for the first time. He has been stripped of the fraud of his stage uniform by the "honest eyes" of the princess. He is left with the cold fact of a medal he is unworthy of wearing. What *is* he? he asks. What is he as an *American*, not merely as one who acts out the type of the Hero?

Since this is a recruitment story, written in support of the marines' publicity campaign, Walter DeLancey answers his self-questioning by joining the corps. He decides he must match the princess' perception of him with commensurate conduct. Only by committing himself to the war can he close the gap between the heroism she exacts of him and the external appearance he bears. (And only thus could he figure as a wry example of the theories of Peirce and Royce concerning the relations between image and act.)

DeLancey endures the ordeal of boot camp aided by the memory of the princess' reassuring smile. Resplendent in his new dress uniform of marine blue (for he is still in costume, of course, though it is now a costume issued by the U.S. government), he goes to see Eleanore for the last time. She is thrilled by his appearance, every bit as much as she had been by his stage attire. But now, she tells him, he is "so much more." Please, she begs, try not to spill any of the red of your nation's flag or the blood of your veins upon that splendid blue uniform. DeLancey is genuinely inspired by the image-idea of himself provided by both the princess and the corps (an image which stands manfully up to whatever reflection he now finds in his mirror). He declares he is ready to sacrifice his life for all those Boldavian mothers and babies; not because of "heroics," but because of his faith in the authenticated sense of "himself" he possesses at last.

In the final scene of Bartlett's story, the princess pins the Cross of the Chevaliers upon DeLancey's uniform in a private ceremony. (He had earlier handed it over to her when he realized a mere actor was unworthy to wear it.) Fudging a bit on the direct relation between fact and appearance (but true to Peirce's notion that an object's reality lies in its potential for future function), Princess Eleanore informs DeLancey the medal is already his to keep because of the deeds of bravery that lie ahead for him on the battlefield. DeLancey strides off to war, "his head erect, his shoulders back, his eyes far away." With a stab of insight, one whose irony we can safely assume neither Bartlett nor the marine corps was privy to, the final sentence in the story is spoken by DeLancey's former theater agent: "DeLancey—Himself . . . God, man—what a poster you'd make now!"

In the terms by which Bartlett tells his story, a person is identified as an American when replicating the national ideals by a pictorial merger of image and gesture. Furthermore, this identification takes place in a special way. In the princess' words, "In America one meets with such extraordinarily dramatic surprises." Dramatic surprises are possible because "America" is a poster outside a theater. This poster promises action on the stage and action in France; both are spectacles audiences enjoy and applaud. This is why the poster of Himself as stage hero can be transformed overnight into a marine who looks like a recruitment poster. When the princess interprets "the message" of DeLancey Himself, she finds it "means" what it says as a visual statement. "I have found the good God in America. He is coming with his sons. I have seen them striding down the avenue, their shoulders back, their lips set, their eyes leveled across the ocean! I have sent the message ahead. 'They are coming, mothers,' and soon I will go and shout it to them with my own lips. 'They are coming, mothers and little babies!' "[33]

It hardly counts that the pronouns the princess uses here are masculine. De-Lancey is Bartlett's true "heroine"—the one who *becomes* a pictorial composite of flag, medal, uniform and marine marching forward to save mothers and babies on the battlefield. He wins his "manhood" by becoming "Herself"—the Warrior Queen and the Greatest Mother of the World. Certainly, the greatest *poster* of them all!

When writing of the uses to which allegory has been put over the centuries, Angus Fletcher speaks of "walking Ideas"—those literary figures treated formulaically which move through the realms of a structured Providence.[34] Because Editha, DeLancey, and the Princess Eleanore believe in a systematized world of meaning, they are capable of functioning as walking poster messages. The only difference (and it is a big one) is that Frederick Orin Bartlett does not question either the validity or the consequences of the lives that DeLancey and the princess exact of themselves in accordance with poster images. When it comes to William Dean Howells' Editha, questions are asked.

Howells' irony not only alters the ideas his story proposes about the meaning embodied by Editha and George's mother, it alters the genre designation of the story itself. Editha believes herself to be sublime in her effect upon her lover's heart, but as a character she is reduced by the events to the level of the pictur-esque—an aesthetic unit lacking the further dimensions of spirit to which Editha aspires. On the other hand, Bartlett allows DeLancey and the princess to become as sublime and as picturesque as their hearts wish them to be.

Angus Fletcher argues a psychic kinship between the sublime and the pictur-esque since the one does not necessarily cancel the other out of the picture. Am-bivalent as emotions, the sublime and the picturesque may exist in a union of contraries. This odd mix, Fletcher observes, is most readily possible in the areas of surrealism and commercial art. It is a merger one detects in many of the posters of World War I. The techniques of commercial art (salable ideas thrust forward through effective simplicity of design) are placed at the service of palpable desires. (Send the Marines! Save Mothers and Babies!) The techniques and the desires are pow-erful because absolved from having to follow the rules of rational discourse. When-ever logic enters, poster designs fail in the ways Matlack Price and Horace Brown say they will. Don't clutter surfaces with details that a viewer has to stop to dis-cover, measure, and assess as meaning. Keep to outlines that can be read on the run. That's sublime emotion conveyed pictorially. It is picturesque as well, be-cause it is about mother, home, sweetheart.

The sublime as an emotion is somewhat too cold, too rarefied (unless touched by darkness and terror, and this is not the kind of sublime that poster art likes best). Old-style traditions for picturing the Eternal Victim or the Providential Savior lack impact for viewers who have learned to receive ideas and desires through "trademarks" and "slogans" about glory, sacrifice, honor, and service. Trademarks and slogans bring the ideal back into the world they know. (A little Belgian girl in pigtails menaced by the Hun reminds us what victims and brutes are like. The Red Cross nurse who looks like Columbia is surely the way Providence would manifest itself.) "America" figures are trademarks and slogans; they make emotions visible and comprehensible. Commercial artists know that ads that entice you to buy dreams of Beauty and Luxury require the pictured presence of Pears' on the nightstand and the solid bulk of a Pierce-Arrow under the porte cochere. Poster artists know that love of country calls for a Columbia that is both an awesome ideal form and an American Girl with the look of someone you think you know.

It would be interesting to ask Clement Greenberg what he thinks of DeLancey and of the poster lives that lie behind the work of Blashfield, Penfield, and Leyendecker. Greenberg has argued that up to 1870, middle-class art still believed in itself.[35] Art retained intact the feudal intensities that "possessed" a culture based on the values of emotional risk, honor, order, coherence, and self-consciousness. After 1870, Greenberg says, the middle class lost confidence in itself. It gave itself over to concerns of the prosaic and the petered-out. Equality before the image of money replaced aristocratic belief in sublime specialness. Aesthetically, the hauteur of the sublime was replaced by the kitsch of realism. One result of the reaction to the shock of the normal was the modernism that followed quickly after.

I suggest that the posters of World War I and the poster mentality of the two decades between the Spanish-American War and the close of the European conflict furnish a remarkable meeting point for all three of the aesthetic and ideological moves through history pointed out by Greenberg: the aristocratic, the bourgeois, and the modernist. Posters have an arrogant, aristocratic intensity of dedication to infinity, honor, and order; they image those values by means of heroes and heroines that "possess" their own culture. Posters make their reconciliation with the everyday world of leveling down and money comforts; they sustain them through bourgeois memories of girls back home and mothers who raise boys to do their duty. Posters reflect the modernist absorption with visual representations of force and speed; they employ art techniques that confirm the essential poster quality of early-twentieth-century societies.[36] That is, the poster world of war retains aristocratic values imaged by the rhetoric of the sublime, makes use of the design mannerisms of modernism that reflect society's infatuation with technology, and grounds the supposedly contentious qualities of the aristocratic and the modern (their social predilections and their pictorial tricks) in the images and desires of the petty bourgeois taste for nation, home, and sweet womanhood.

Edward Said adds a final element to this brief analysis of the particular, peculiar powers demonstrated by the American poster lives of the war period. Said speaks of the "good" shift that takes place once we move from a life of dreams (conveyed to our minds by the intensity of images) to one dedicated to clarity (gained through the diffuse generalities of words).[37] He cites Freud, Peirce, and Foucault as advocates of the better state of affairs we have when we leave off our insatiable craving for representations and turn ourselves over to discourse.

The departure from images to words would not do at all for the American imagination addressed by the posters of World War I. Talk about talking without images was useless. Editha is in love with the verbal phrases cast up by the wartime press. DeLancey as an actor lives in a theater of words. But both Editha and DeLancey are converted to lives of the image. Such poster lives use few words;[38] they get things done through representations that point out identifications and delineate desires. In contrast, can't you just hear Foucault talking, on and on, about war posters! He would be brilliant about the paper prisons of social oppression they erect around the victims they lead to slaughter. He would be nearly right in what he had to say. But Foucault's mind and method are not about what makes posters work by means of their own kind of perverse brilliance. Foucault, like Freud and Peirce, could understand what posters do and he would be able to analyze why; but none of his dazzling *talk* about social meanings directly suggests the pictorial and emotive techniques which "make" a war.

Neither Freud, Peirce, nor Foucault has the power the American Girl had to be what the many Americans thought they needed most between 1898 and 1918. She was the aesthetic form that lent itself to be "thought about" as an emotion. She was a concept that could be translated from impulse into picture, and from picture into a particular conduct of life.

When the occasion is war, and when the one catalyst required is will, then the American Girl (as Warrior Queen, Protecting Angel, or whatever) is ready to be pressed, vividly, into service, no matter the consequences.

IMAGES FOR SALE

14

Poses on Display

New temples built on soil that covers buried cities risk getting cracks in their foundation. Religious celebrations set upon layers of earlier ritualistic practices also experience slippage. Christmas and Easter are notorious pastiches of pagan elements which are not as decorous as Christian doctrine would like. Especially Easter, what with remnants of fertility rites that prove an embarrassment when Resurrection, not erection, is the event the devout are meant to celebrate with solemn joy. At the turn of the century, when the Easter season approached, good American Christians were met by a jumble of lilies, rabbits, crosses, eggs, agape and eros, in churches, store windows, and the popular press. Under such conditions, what was the American Girl to do in preparation for a properly WASP commemoration of Lent and Easter Sunday?

According to Edith Wharton's novel *The Age of Innocence*, the need to set a date for the springtime wedding of May Welland and Newland Archer caused a furor. It would have been unthinkable to break the established Lenten practice of abstaining from such worldly pleasures as getting married. But the days of which Wharton speaks—when sacred *social* rituals held firm in old New York—were of the 1870s. By the mid-1890s what Newland Archer's mother anxiously describes as "trends" had turned Easter and its imagery into a pictorial free-for-all.

Figure 14.1 shows the cover for sheet music on a sacred theme, distributed in 1900 as a promotional device. The artwork contains the traditional stalk of lilies. The robes are ecclesiastically rich, though hardly what Methodists or Presbyterians were used to seeing their ministers wear during the Easter Sunday processional. The wearer of the robe has no wings to signal that she is the angel standing outside

14.1. Kerr, "The Choir Celestial" (1900).

14.2. Louis Rhead, *Cleveland World*, Easter number (1896).

the empty tomb. She is a young girl, pretty in a vaguely Art Nouveau manner. This is *design*, not sacred doctrine, on display.

The front and back pages of the *Cleveland World* of April 5, 1896, provide another exercise in the beauty and holiness of a design format current both in America and abroad (figure 14.2). A roster of "The Greatest Writers Living" are etched on a plaque commemorating their fame. The Kimball Piano Company, having wrested "the title of supremacy from all others" in the competitive struggle for contented customers, promises a joy more lasting than the Christian doctrine of the Resurrection. Lilies, jonquils, wings, halo, and a Dante Gabriel Rossetti angel are the offerings made to the season by the famous poster artist Louis Rhead.

The substitution of taste and the arts of good design for the theology of sacred writ is discreet enough in these two examples. The basic religious elements are still in place. Although more faith is placed in the techniques of commercial design than in the gospel truths, the notion that Easter had to do with Christ's triumph over death has not been entirely set aside. However, Mr. Hearst's *New York Journal* in 1896 and 1897 takes a different view.

On April 5, 1896 (the same day the *Cleveland World* featured Louis Rhead's design), the *New York Journal* placed an angel on its Easter Sunday cover. The pose, the facial expression, the accompanying props of wings and lilies, dutifully follow the traditional motifs which Louis Tiffany was just then placing in stained-glass windows around the country.[1] The inside spread of the *Journal* is more to the point of the times. A Beauty of the type analyzed by Paul Bourget in his book of 1895 stands at the entrance to a ballroom, helped off with her cloak by Mephistopheles. The cover of the *Journal* signals that Christ is risen; all good Christians are given the promise of the moral life. But the inside spread heralds the cessation of the restraints of Lent and gives the great good news that American Girls may reenter the world of temptation. This sentiment was a familiar one, often expressed, as in Albert Beck Wenzell's drawing "Until After Easter" (figure 14.3).[2] The Beauty stops on the steps of the church while Mephistopheles loiters nearby, twirling his waxed mustaches and murmuring the text from Acts 24:25—"I will call for thee."

Neither the *Journal*'s spread for Easter 1896 nor Wenzell's drawing of 1900 falls within the genre of pulpit sermons which take seriously their duties in the instruction of virtue. Lighthearted titillation is the motive in each case, not innocence tragically hovering on the edge of taint. Images of susceptible beauties and suave male tempters are played off against age-old traditions of social restraint. The Lenten "sanctuary" of forty days of enforced purity is more mocked than supported. Doctrinal assurances of the soul's salvation are put aside. In these representations it is only a matter of time before the Girl gives in—and it makes no real difference that she does.

Easter of 1897 rolls around and once again the *New York Journal* is ready (figure 14.4). Frank Nankivell's promotional poster does not even bother with the sly juxtapositions featured in the *Journal*'s two-part 1896 Easter edition. Angel of Resurrection on the cover and Beauty at the Ball on the inside spread are replaced by a

14.3. Albert Beck Wenzell,
"Until After Easter," from
The Passing Show (1900).

14.4. Frank A. Nankivell,
poster for the *New York
Journal*, Easter number
(1896).

single design, as playfully sacrilegious as any free spirit then living in the United States could hope for. The powerful art memories inherited from Piero della Francesca's noble fresco of Christ rising from the open tomb are overlaid, and overwhelmed, by the figure of Cupid and his worshipers—unrepentant Magdalenes whose joy is uncontained. Della Francesca's example cannot contend in its spirituality against current European ventures into Belle Epoque layerings of pagan and Christian motifs. Nor is any Mephisto in view to suggest that the fun might be spoiled, although the headlines announcing the debate stirred by Marie Corelli's "Modern Marriage Market" intimate where today's pleasures will lead these American Girls who are *so glad* it is Cupid, not Christ, who has come back to them.[3] Charles Dana Gibson's drawing "Lenten Confessions" does, however, raise the possibility that Cupid may soon want to crawl back inside the security of the tomb. Aghast, he shuts his ears upon hearing what the Girls have gotten away with during the Lenten period when they were supposed to forgo the free distribution of the "roses" cast at the foot of the confessional box (figure 14.5).

Easter 1897 as drawn by Hy Mayer for the little magazine *Truth* strips away all remaining religious paraphernalia (figure 14.6). No lilies, halos, or tomb. The jolly friar (not a common sight around America but a part of the Beardsley tropes such designs call up) is the Mephisto figure converted into a lively dancing partner for the Girl. Set within the flat, detail-free white background of the cover, the two have no past or future, no society or social codes, to concern them; all is present revelry. And then in Easter of 1913 three Presbyterians and a Roman Catholic visited the local photographer's studio in a small Indiana town to pose for an Easter egg cutout (figure 14.7).

"Trends" indeed!

American print displays were noticeably enlivened by the playful sacrilege of turn-of-the-century Easter imagery. American store windows did not lag behind. When L. Frank Baum wrote a book in 1900 about effective window displays, he informed his audience of store owners that next to the Christmas season Easter is the most important American holiday, and that the cross is a sales object "suitable for any line of merchandise."[4] Baum urged that the weeks leading up to Easter be treated as a "campaign"—one that had to be "well-managed" if the period were to prove "a boundless harvest to every merchant." "[Easter] comes after a season of comparative dullness, and as it is a time of joy and brightness, of full purses and generous hearts, extraordinary efforts are made to delight the public with gorgeous and pretty displays, and to tempt the good folks to purchase liberally all those knick-knacks and articles of apparel of which orthodox church members have denied themselves during the penitential days of lent."

By 1900 the general economy of the United States was moving toward a period of "resurrection." After several seasons of "comparative dullness' (if not downright fiscal disasters),[5] members of the American public were able to buy the things they had been denied during "the penitential days" of recurring financial panics. Eco-

14.5. Charles Dana Gibson, "Lenten Confessions," *Life*, February 8, 1894.

nomic factors that regulated patterns of production growth or that encouraged the increase of sales through newly created areas of commerce were being supplemented by another set of factors: shifts in the promotion of *the images of what there was to want.*

New items for purchase were continually being introduced into the American marketplace by the 1890s. But more was involved than what took place in the factories and corporate boardrooms. Markets were affected by an expansion of the imagination of "things" held by a widening public of desirers. More products gained more immediate recognition once the visual field for the eye's avarice broadened. That intended field included images formerly limited to the sacred cause of church and state. Shopkeepers and moneylenders once relegated to the courtyard outside the temple were now inside the sanctuary. Or rather, customary locations for worship now had to accommodate the fact that department stores and theaters were the new temples and that sales catalogs were the Bible of the new faith in the power of the heart's desire.[6]

It was not that nothing was sacrosanct in the turn-of-the-century world of promotion and sales. It was simply that images once considered privileged through their association with established bodies of worship were now available for anyone's use. High quality for low prices is the age-old come-on in the marketplace. What would enhance mundane products more than the glow cast by the powerful aura of the denoted? What could scale up products better than the appropriation of images of the American Girl merged with symbols of piety and patriotism?

Pretty girls posed in patriotic attitudes served the commercially minded during the same period that national and state arts commissions sanctioned their use for civic murals and sculptures. Her body lightly skimmed by gauze, a young woman acts as standard bearer for one of Charles Schenk's 1902 *Draperies in Action* (figure

14.6. Hy Mayer, *Truth*, Easter number (1897).

14.7. Irma Purman and friends (Easter 1913).

14.8).[7] In 1919 Coles Phillips sets in motion the equally provocative draperies worn by his upper-class heroine (figure 14.9). The topical occasion is a young officer, crippled in the war, placed under the care of the Phillips Girl, but that occasion is belied by other factors. The body language of the Girl's arm and the officer's gaze seems to point to something of interest out past the right of the frame. But Phillips' design undercuts both the patriotic subject and the narrative red herring. This is not really a celebration of the Greatest Mother of All who tends the brave men wounded in the recent conflict. Legs dipped like gold in Luxite Hosiery is what the entire affair is about.

Angels of pious tradition swoop down to deliver Madame Dean's Spinal Supporting Corset in 1885 (figure 14.10). As a contented user states in the copy beneath the drawing, "It has proven to me a *godsend.*" In 1900 a winged archangel confers "a blessing to life's sunrise" represented by putti gathered at the foot of the shrine

14.8. Charles Schenk, from
Draperies in Action
(1902).

14.9. Coles Phillips, "Luxite
Hosiery" (1919).

Hose as Shapely as the Curves of the Fig.

THE translucent shimmer of Luxite Hosiery half reveals and half conceals. Its texture i
wonderfully soft and silken you can draw a Luxite silk stocking through your finger *
Luxite launders beautifully because these hose contain no adulterations whatever—nothing
super-fine materials and pure dyes. Naturally Luxite Hosiery wears long and always looks beauti

Women's Silk Faced, $1.10. Pure Thread Japanese Silk, $1.30 to $2.25. Other styles 55c upward.
Men's Silk Faced, 65c; Pure Thread Japanese Silk, 85c and $1.10. Other styles 35c up. Children's, 55c up.

LUXITE TEXTILES, Inc., 654 Fowler Street, Milwaukee, Wisconsin
New York   Chicago   San Francisco   *Makers of High Grade Hosiery Since 1875*   Liverpool, England   Sydney, A
LUXITE TEXTILES OF CANADA, Limited, London, Ont.

to Nestle's Food (figure 14.11) and the New Fashion Department of Edward Bok's
Ladies' Home Journal is heralded by another angel of light in 1908 (figure 14.12).

The Statue of Liberty was not even in place in the mid-1880s when its familiar
figure was acknowledged to be the world's tallest, largest, and best pedestal for the
display of consumer products. Figure 14.13 is one example from many, demonstrat-

14.10. "Madame Dean's Spinal Supporting Corsets" (1885).

14.11. "A Blessing to Life's Sunrise, Nestle's Food," *Scribner's Magazine Advertiser* (1900).

ing a practice common enough to attract F. B. Opper's satiric swipe in the pages of *Puck* (figure 14.14).

The 1890s was capable of going all solemn over the Columbia figure, but this did not stop the brewery people. An Anheuser Busch advertising poster for 1893 tied in its products with the glories of the Columbian Exposition. In 1899 the Louis Bergdoll Brewery Company went Anheuser Busch several better. It made references to the company's fifty years as a Philadelphia beer maker, the Spanish-American War, George Washington, William McKinley, tribute money from Old World monarchies, and "Liberty Triumphant" (figure 14.15).

Inherent complications of interpretation were always present in such examples. The eye perceived familiar signs everywhere it looked. The objects were recognizable and identifiable. Memories of what was once considered sacred were overlaid with new sets of responses; a welter of designated types was contained within a

THE LADIES' HOME JOURNAL

THE NEW FASHION DEPARTMENT
WITH OVER 100 FASHION PICTURES

14.12. "The New Fashion Department," *The Ladies' Home Journal*, January 1908.

single visual and emotional field. If one's mind had been trained to expect that lilies, wings, flags, and the Liberty torch made individual statements conforming to established American texts (religious or patriotic), the visual jumble of such promotional pieces was certain to be confusing. But to live during the 1890s and early 1900s when nothing was *surely* sacred in the pictorial life of Americans meant living with contradiction: that juxtaposition of objects or ideas it is impossible to believe in at one and the same time.

We gain a better sense of the years between 1876 and 1918 if we familiarize ourselves with the particular kind of contradictory signs thrown into the marketplace for everyone to look at; it also helps to examine a contemporary evaluation of promotional practices that is itself in the act of becoming contradictory.

In 1912 Herbert Duce, a Chicago ad man, published a book called *Poster Advertising*. His intention was to outline the commercial advantages of billboards. The

14.13. "The Bartholdi Statue of Liberty, The Largest in the World: The Brainerd & Armstrong Co.'s Spool Silk, The Best in the World." Advertising card (c.1883).

NATIONAL MUSEUM OF AMERICAN HISTORY

text is pretty standard stuff until one comes to two separate passages that introduce a series of flaming discrepancies. Duce wants to analyze why, of all current art forms, American society is best defined by the advertising poster. He begins by comparing the representative arts of past and present. Once, the château and the cathedral were the visible forms by which the common people were exorted, "Pray, obey, sacrifice thyself, adore God, fear the master, respect the King."[8] Today the

PUCK.

LET THE ADVERTISING AGENTS TAKE CHARGE OF THE BARTHOLDI BUSINESS,
AND THE MONEY WILL BE RAISED WITHOUT DELAY.

14.14. F. Opper, "Let the Advertising Agents Take Charge of the Bartholdi Business. . . . ," *Puck*, April 1, 1885.

14.15. "Liberty Triumphant, 1849–1899," Louis Bergdoll Brew'g Co. (1899).

paper billboard poster delivers a message quite unlike the solid stones of the past. It "speaks to us only of ourselves, our pleasures, our tastes, our interests, our health, our life."

Duce takes pride in contrasting the self-gratification encouraged by a free and democratic society, for which the American billboard poster stands as the primary symbol, with the self-sacrifice exacted by aristocratic societies. But then he shifts his position, casting his eye elsewhere. Is not the poster, he asks rhetorically, "the natural and logical effect of an age of individualism and of excessive egotism? Is not this indeed the modern monument, the chateau of paper, the cathedral of sensuality, in which all that we have in us of culture and of esthetics finds nothing to occupy itself with except the exaltations of its comfort and the tickling of its instincts?"

By this point Duce's responses to the poster life of his age are already in conflict. Self-gratification is good, because democratic. Self-gratification is bad, because egotistical. In a later chapter he suddenly makes yet another perceptual shift. Three-fourths of all billboard posters feature women, he states. Those female figures do not take their source from the hectic, self-indulgent, time-driven society for which the modern poster is cause and symptom. They descend from on high, from the realm of timeless, universal, absolute values. In the short term posters use women's images to sell products. In the long run these visual manifestations of "The True Woman" act as testimonials to "the sure hope of future advancement" promised to all Americans. (They act in the same way that Cass Gilbert declared murals do when placed in public buildings.) Just as Theodore Roosevelt's image gave assurance to the readers of V. G. Rocine's book on physiognomy, Duce's poster woman attests to "the superior civilization" which protects America from "the inward rot" of degenerate races and promise the nation a future of "world-wide ascendency."

This is a lot to ask of posters selling Uneeda Biscuits, Tip-Top Bread, and Tarrant's Seltzer Aperient, even if the pictorial devices of the latter call up memories of various Madonnas of the Chair (figure 14.16). But Duce proceeds in full cry. "If we read aright the lessons of history, the more expanded the sphere of human knowledge" accorded to the masculine mind, "the greater will be found to be man's need of a regulating influence to guide and sustain him." Modern "knowing" requires the corrective of ageless "perceiving." What the male "knower" must *see* is the female image—one that is not merely the purveyor of cake flour, laundry soaps, and seltzer, but also "that element of the Godhead of which love and the other harmonies of nature are emanations."

At this point in Duce's tottering argument, the female poster image is the icon of the modern democratic world (a world, in turn, both estimable and sleazy); it is also associated with the chatelaine of the château and the Madonna of the cathedral—those representative figures of the bad old days that Duce, in his democratic fervor, has supposedly rejected out of hand. Faced with having to resolve the several *purposes* to which the poster is put (a task made even harder by his impossible mix of past and present, the timeless and the temporal), Duce can only fall back upon the rhetoric of his roving eye to "save the appearances."

We have something more to learn from watching Duce's efforts to resolve the mass of contradictions swimming in his line of vision. Throughout his argument he has been climbing steadily upward on the ladder of metaphor: up from the

14.16. "Morning Nap, Tarrant's Seltzer Aperient," advertising card (1884).

LIBRARY OF CONGRESS

gutter where the paper poster blows in the ill winds of an egotistical consumer society, up toward the ethereal sphere of the True Woman. But now he mounts still higher, up to Omniscience.

In the last sentence of that chapter in which Duce defines the nature of his country's culture, he lifts himself beyond the sharp, time-bound distinctions he had previously made between the ages of stone and of paper. "Seen from a certain height, the eternal and the ephemeral are no longer distinguished from each other, and stone and paper become confounded in the finite." Up there (at a point analogous to where some of us stand poised as scholar-critics), Duce loses his hold on the clarity that comes, paradoxically, through the establishment of the distinctions out of which contradictions arise. Distinctions are replaced by a "confounding" that makes all cultures look alike once human perception drops away before the authority of divine cognition.

However much Duce tries to lessen the difficulties that adhere to acts of cultural interpretation by lifting us out of history altogether, the problem remains. It is an old and familiar one; it occurs whenever unlikely juxtapositions blur the evidence used to identify and evaluate public images. A life-size statue of a Spanish conquistador made of home-grown prunes was placed in prominent view in the California State Building at the 1893 Columbian Exposition. That prunes furnished the structural material for the horse and rider was logical enough since there is a line of association between the state's historical past and the present fact of its agricultural bounties.[9] But there has to be taken into account the troublesome role played by conquerors (Spanish and others) in the California territory. Still, there are fewer contradictions involved in that mounted military figure of prunes than in Saint-Gaudens' bronze general on horseback led by the American Girl, or in the monument described in Wallace Stevens' poem "Dance of the Macabre Mice" where mice run along the length of the marble general's outstretched sword, or in the sight of winos sprawled at the base of a statue placed in a public park to honor some local dignitary.

The possibility of making a clean fit between an object, the material of its composition, its setting, the didactic intention for its placement, and the responses of a varied public is so unlikely that it would be a contradiction of American life itself if we expected no contradictions to appear. Any sustained study of what is placed next to what, and for what purposes, during any specified time frame, must make generous allowances for illogicality and bad matches. Charles Sanders Peirce asked his contemporaries to do their best to make their ideas clear, but they were often too busy trafficking in the sale of images to pay attention to sensible requests of this kind. It is historians after the fact who are supposed to be in the best position to ponder the shaky relations between ideas and images as shapers of cultural values.

Certain broad conclusions have been advanced by students of the image. Daniel Boorstin, for one, argues that between the mid-1870s and the early 1900s *ideas* (conveyed through idealized images) were replaced by *images* existing independently of *ideals*.[10] Formerly, images were used as the means to the decent ends of instructing the public in concepts of permanence and order, beauty and law. Today, images function as their own ends. They exist only to entertain by introducing excitement and novelty or to sell objects exuding glamour and pleasure. Once, images referred to "large" unified ideas. Now, images are "small" and fragmentary.

Boorstin substantiates the shift from *ideas about ideals* to *images as illusion*—from images as the good means to the fine ends of *real things* to images as base *pseudo-events*. The examples he amasses are many and vivid (e.g., the electric sign at a 1913 convention of advertising men that lit up to spell TRUTH). His sprightly yet frightening references encourage us all to recall personal experiences of living in an Andy Warhol world of hype and show. But try to execute a full-scale historical review—pushing back, back through documents of the past in an attempt to say *just when* ungrounded images gained ascendancy over clear ideas and significant ideals. It is then that Boorstin's notion that the precise moment for the big change took place during the last days of the nineteenth century begins to falter.

Richard Altick's and Martin Meisel's visual examinations of the public shows and popular theater of Victorian London, and Walter Benjamin's exposé of "phantasmagoric events" in mid-nineteenth-century Paris, suggest that Americans (admittedly always a bit slow on the cultural uptake) had a dense European past in illusion-making to draw upon.[11] When extolling the glories of the plate-glass window in 1900, L. Frank Baum observes that for centuries pedlars went through the streets crying their wares; later, but still years ago in our past, shopkeepers stood outside their premises calling, "Buy! Buy!" to the passing throng; now, great glass windows filled with enticing objects do the merchants' work. But perhaps it is only the media *forms* and the intensified *rate* of the promotion of desirable products that have changed, not the marketing impulse itself. Surely, the sly, shifting commerce between ideas, ideals, and images has too extensive a history for us to be able to place a date for its origin solidly within the past century.[12]

Rather than going back and forth in a debate over when commerce in images began and who was to blame for its growth, this chapter concerns itself with one particular aspect of the sometimes smarmy, always fascinating business of images for sale: the means by which female figures, displayed in a series of conventional poses, became an important mode for identifying and stimulating the public's taste for wanting. In the examples to follow, there is more than enough evidence to suggest a capitalistic, sexist society founded on entrepreneurial scams, a mass consumerism financed by corporate schemes, and an elitist culture that encouraged the passive acceptance of yearned-for "things." But there are other signs as well—the kind that suggest occasions for the exuberant enjoyment of poses and performance in a "dramatical" world and discoveries that advanced the needs of both the private and the social self.

The relation between show and tell in the years between the 1870s and 1900 underwent certain noticeable changes. The earlier compulsion to expound moral tales to a people who were nervous over not being moral enough was replaced by expanded methods for giving the public the shows that entertain.[13] The newest display techniques were more theatrical (because obvious in their illusory methods) and less static (because making use of ideas set into motion).[14] The sense of movement even infiltrated the spectacle and the tableau, two performance modes usually characterized by the fixed frame of timelessness. Stimulated by the poses placed before them on the stage, spectators' minds could enact private melodramas of desire. These inward plots were not figured by images of Good or Evil in the manner of the traditional melodrama. Instead, they were centered by images of hope ("There is no limit to what you can have") and images of fear ("There are forces—natural and social—that limit the attainment of your wishes").

Another important difference between earlier and later responses to pose and display was what was meant to watch "democratically." American culture was severely marked by nondemocratic differences between class and kind, but the marketplace was open to all images. A common source of images and a shared terrain of desires were available to almost everyone. Lines blurred between fine

arts and the popular arts, amateurs and professionals, rich and poor, precisely because the nature of the images on display transformed everyone who looked at
them into "have nots" yearning to "have."

The purposes to which the favorite poses were put were also blurred. Poses could
be identifying acts by which persons announced the kind of social self they might
like to become. Poses could also be used to deceive others or to frustrate self-inter-
pretation. It is doubtful whether Lily Bart (heroine of Edith Wharton's 1905 novel
The House of Mirth) actually learned who she was the evening she assumed the
"attitude" of Joshua Reynolds' "Mrs. Lloyd" at the Welly Brys' entertainment. It
is questionable whether Lawrence Selden or the other males in the audience were
able to *see* the bottom-nature which lay beneath the smashing figure which Lily
cut while posing in diaphanous garments on the little stage. We ask what it was,
if anything, Sister Carrie discovered about herself in the stage roles assigned to
"Carrie Madenda" that took her to stardom as a public object of desire. We wonder
whether the young women of Boston's Saturday Morning Club who presented an
elaborate production of *Antigone* for a females-only audience in 1890 furthered
the cause of women's rights and the sisterhood of suffering womanhood by participating in their amateur theatrical. The codification of attitudes perfected by François Delsarte, which took women's groups in the United States by storm during the
1880s and 1890s, raises similar questions. Was the Delsarte system one of the best
things to happen to female imagination at that time? Did its "attitudes" provide
the means by which women could pictorialize their true thoughts and feelings? Or
did "the Delsarte craze" have as pernicious a residual effect on the ways women
were imaged in the 1890s as Lavater's principles of physiognomical identification
had upon the racist, sexist texts of the same period?

The examples which lie ahead in this chapter invite interpretations on either
side of the argument, although certain tentative conclusions are possible concerning what the poses reveal about the complex relations that pertain between perception and cognition. What keeps such conclusions tentative is the fact of our
not knowing fully the responses of the people toward whom the poses and performances were directed.

Meanings assigned after the fact to commodities placed on display in theater
and store are sometimes dim. Statements concerning their intention are plain enough;
not simply the intention of ends, which was to promote the desirability of the
images, but the intention for the means, which was to make what the images
signified easily understood by the largest number of viewers, notwithstanding the
often contradictory nature of the materials. This usually involved placing the image in a pose. A female figure standing stiffly on display did not suffice to convey
an identifiable emotion to its viewers. A figure striking an "attitude"—whether of
joy, surprise, woe, curiosity, anger—was potentially an effective agent for the promotion of a product, a personality, or (*pace* Boorstin) a considered ideological
position.

The proclaimed purpose for Delsarte recitations, amateur tableaux, stage spectacles, advertising posters, store window displays, magazine covers, and political pageants was clarity of image and meaning. The perceiving eye was meant to move smoothly from the pose to the object and an appropriate response. This seems simple enough and not a matter for concern, but in *Art as Experience* John Dewey likens the recognition offered a tag or label to that given to a salesman's sample.[15] Samples are not, Dewey points out, the product itself. Here Dewey faces the ontological/epistemological crisis experienced by all philosophers since Socrates. Images *are* at a remove from the original reality. The gap that subverts the fit between "the real thing" and its substitute inevitably causes worry to earnest thinkers, whether they are theologians fretful over idolatry, Lacanian linguists suspended between the world of signified and signifier, or Marxists arguing over the separation between labor expended and payment earned.

The promotion of desire points toward the purchase of an object. It is a social act, one that modifies an earlier decision *not* to want and *not* to buy. An image stirs the desire and sells the object, however, only if that image can be identified. Once, Dante followed the Way of Images to salvation, but in late-nineteenth-century America could the way of material images be taken in all seriousness as the means to the end of identifying one's deepest need?

Charles Dana Gibson's drawing of "His First Love" (see Introduction, figure 19) shows the child's mother in a pose that likens her to a queen on her throne. Her image stimulates awe and desire in the child and affects his subsequent social behavior as he tries throughout the rest of his life to purchase the unattainable reality represented by his mind's first important image. Dante saw Beatrice when she was sixteen. He never possessed her in the literal sense, but the remembered image of that early desire prepared Dante's imagination to receive, first, the vision of Beatrice imaged in Paradise and, finally, the imageless vision of the Virgin and the Wheel of Bliss.[16] Reference to Gibson's drawing and to Dante's verbal representation of divine desire in *The Divine Comedy* serves as an analogue to the processes by which tangible images of mundane things such as the Pierce-Arrow or a stage celebrity lead toward the social acts by which we express our loves. The comparison is not ludicrous. Both sets of images share the same possibility for perversion once desire is turned toward ideals that are as false as the images that point in their direction. The only real difference lies in our notion of which image is worthy for the wanting and which is not.

Neither Gnostics nor post-Kantians nor political radicals have any business applying for positions in a commercial art studio. But if they could ever surmount their distaste for images (since images fail the standard tests they exact for "truth" and "realism"), they might notice certain similarities between their own cherished notions of clarity and those adhered to by display artists. The immensely successful illustrator, J. C. Leyendecker once described the process by which he resolved on his drawing board the "picture puzzle" of identity. The meticulous procedure by which he linked idea with naturalistic sketch and completed image helped him compose forthrightly Platonistic magazine covers.[17] The compiler of a little booklet of 1916 on advertising techniques also asserted the excellence of the pared-down silhouette or outline.[18] Such forms, he wrote, insure the accurate identification of objects by forgoing the complexity of physical and emotional character of which images of the ideal take little note.

Identifiable objects properly do without the clutter and distraction of details. Methods of elimination and concentration for the sake of schematized pictorial or verbal designs have long been the secret of poets, artists, and philosophers who adhere to the Way of Images. But it is not necessarily the case that one person who serves the cause of "real things" will agree to what another person does to advance that same cause.

In 1899 Lorado Taft (a sculptor known in his day for his idealized forms) gave a talk before a convention of the Photographic Association of America.[19] He criticized the photographers for their failure to do away with visual details that negated the forceful recognition of the true subject. Taft named one of the photographs on exhibit at the convention—a woman wearing a large hat—as one such culprit. What he objected to was the way the camera concentrated upon the hat and forgot the woman's face. "The shadow under the hat is fine; that was evidently the object sought in the representation. It is a beautiful piece of modelling; but, after all, it is the hat that cries out for attention. I get a little tired of the punctures around the hat, the embroidery, etc. . . . The impression on me is not that of a portrait of a lady, but of a lady's hat."

As an artist devoted to the representation of types, Lorado Taft was correct in disliking portraits which obscured the reality of pure form; in this instance, the failure to eliminate whatever distracted attention from the woman's face. Ah, but what if the image and the pose were intended to be *about hats*, or even *to sell hats?*

Painters, photographers, and novelists who dedicate their efforts to the clarification of universals will always be at odds with artists of the naturalistic school who try to report on "everything." But the kinds of artists who want "hatlessness" include far more people than Lorado Taft thought he spoke for. They number those who work with carefully controlled designs committed to drawing attention to what matters, which may be the hat after all. The pose singled out for undivided attention from the public could be that of Taft's lady, or her hat, or a Butterick dress pattern, or Ada Rehan as Viola, or Quaker Oats, or Inez Milholland as Herald of the NAWSA march in Washington, D.C., or a recruitment poster. J. C. Leyendecker, Lorado Taft, and Charles Sanders Peirce were arguing on the same side. Whatever one's "hat" may be, attempt to make your signs clear, although the pressures of a culture's ambiguities will do all they can to defeat that effort.

Effective display of images requires judicious choice of settings. The object, personality, or idea up for promotion must be located in space that commands attention for the image, not for itself. There *are* occasions when a display area creates more pleasure than do the images within its enclosure, as when the decoration of a

theater auditorium or the layout of a department store or shopping arcade dominates the eye. But—as we shall see—these are the occasions when *place* is the
"hat" up for sale, not the objects themselves.

A number of components are involved in shaping settings that sell. Whether it
is a theater or a department store, at least three sets of agents are at work. Makers
of the product function backstage as unseen authorities—stage managers, theater
producers, or corporate officers. The marketers of the product appear onstage—
actors or clerks in direct contact with the audience. Promoters stand outside calling attention to the wares within. They are there to stimulate consumer interest
in what the makers and the marketers have to sell through magazine advertisements, billboard posters, window displays, mail-order catalogs, and newspaper promotions.[20]

By the 1890s the mass market magazines and newspapers (aided by the enhanced
quality and lowered costs of new printing techniques) were simultaneously "products" and "displays."[21] The print media entered homes at every economic level,
encouraging readers to go forth into the city to buy. Once the people arrived at
the shopping areas, they often found themselves enveloped within the city's show-
places. The institution of the department store had become as much a part of the
entertainment world as the theater, museum, and exposition hall. Big stores such
as A.T. Stewart, Altman's, Wanamaker's, Marshall Field's, and Macy's were "containers of things," the "inside" into which customers came, pulled by the lure of
"outside" agents. The grandest of the stores displayed their wares in the manner
of museums and exposition halls. Mercantile arcades and national fairs became
interchangeable spaces for the promotion of desire. Home-bred citizens, visitors
from abroad, and newly arrived immigrants, enthralled by the idea of America
"sold" at the national expositions in Chicago, St. Louis, and Buffalo, were drawn
by the same kind of forceful images into the big stores. Could they not buy "America" at Wanamaker's? Was not the American Girl the enthroned queen of the imperial palace—whether she reigned over Marshall Field's or the Court of the Universe at the San Francisco Exposition of 1915?

Newspaper advertisements, reviews, and magazine features promoted the newest
musical comedies, song lyrics, vaudeville comics, or nickelodeon shows. The public spaces that joined home and theater were also dedicated to the display of the
marketable goods of entertainment. Among the most effective points of contact
between consumers and sellers were the store windows and the public thoroughfares. Streets lined by advertising billboards were likened to art galleries for pedes-
trians. Large plate-glass windows fronting the business avenues, complete with lavish
lighting effects and mechanical display pieces, served the same function. The main
goal of the sellers was to bring potential customers in through the doors. Once
inside, the people found "The Great Good Place" where they were given relief from
the mundane and a plunge into the pleasures of the senses.[22]

Although department stores were not the specific haven Henry James had had
in mind when naming his own paradise, James was very good at describing the

longing stirred by public displays. James' 1900 story "The Great Good Place" was followed in 1913 by *A Small Boy and Others;* in the latter he defined desire as that state of being that a child possesses who presses his nose against the window of a pastry shop.[23] But back in 1892 the writer of a piece called "The Art of Shop Windows" went even further with the same analogy.[24] The effect of looking through store windows was likened to peering at pastry shops, but also at the Chicago Exposition, the theatrical offerings of tableaux, pantomimes, and spectacles, and the paintings at the Metropolitan Museum of Art. Frank Baum's *Art of Decorating Dry Goods Windows* of 1900 is not quite as high-flown in its references, but it exuberantly expresses the love of things and the delight over mechanical innovations we expect of the creator of Oz and its material wonders. Baum's is a book written by an Edison, not a Bernard Berenson or a Henry James. Even so, Baum knows what desire is like and how to encourage it. Baum considers the art of framing an indispensable tool of the window dresser; framing is what sets off items for special attention. But so do the "Speech-Makers"—silhouette forms that point to printed banners identifying the object on sale. "Illusion-Makers" also stop passersby in their tracks, as when a live female model pops up out of a display pedestal. But Baum believes that the most effective sales device of all is the physical fact of the plate-glass windows that act as both lure and barrier. On one side of the window is the item to be looked at and longed for; on the other side, the onlookers stand, separated by material that is transparent but nonetheless the means for keeping the desirers and the desired apart, thereby augmenting the need to strive after what lies just beyond their reach.

Leon Alberti's theories stimulated artists during the Italian Renaissance to develop the mimetic arts of illusion-making whose influence lasted throughout four fertile centuries. Alberti's perspective theory was based on the notion that a painting is like a window that gives viewers access to whatever lies beyond the aperture. By the 1890s the immense windows of the handsome new storefronts were conversely being likened to paintings. In turn, the Edison "Vitascope" screen converted theaters into a gallery where spectators focused upon a single framed picture (figure 14.17). To give the pictorial possibilities yet another turn, shop windows were transformed into a music-hall stage when a mechanical high-kicker was sent into action (figure 14.18). Art gallery, store window, theater stage, Vitascope house: all functioned as major framing devices for the display of poses whose primary function was to incite, and sell, desire.

What were the consequences for turn-of-the-century American culture of this all-pervasive business of illusionism? Gibson's "Fooled Again" raises the perennial question of art's deceits (figure 14.19). When the image at which the spectator gazes proves not to be the ideal he longs for, we ask whether this is old-fashioned fantasy at work, or whether this exposure of the ambiguities of appearance is part of the era's "new realism," as the Jamesians maintained. But theoretical issues of aesthetics or ontology are of less concern here than the social implications involved.

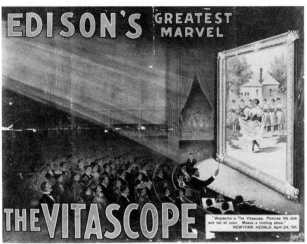

14.17. "Edison's Greatest Marvel, The Vitascope" (1896).

LIBRARY OF CONGRESS

14.18. "The High-Kicker," J. R. Palmenberg's Sons catalog (1893).

NATIONAL MUSEUM OF AMERICAN HISTORY

There were people at the time who worried about the immorality of desire stimulated by the increased display of material goods. "Lead Us Not Into Temptation" (one of the paintings commissioned in 1908 by *The Delineator* to illustrate the Lord's Prayer) took the store window as an apt symbol for the lust of the eye (figure 14.20). But today's economists and social historians often follow in the tradition of Thorstein Veblen, or of Henry James' report on "the rotary system" of planned product obsolescence. Like Veblen in 1899 and James in 1907, they prefer to study the social effects of a consumer class controlled by powerful industrial and commercial interests. They concern themselves with the immorality of illusion-making that leads to the waste of energy, the violation of historical continuity, and the fragmentation of communities.

14.19. Charles Dana Gibson, "Fooled Again," *Life*, September 12, 1895.

14.20. Sigismond de Ivanowski, "Lead Us Not Into Temptation," from "The Lord's Prayer: A Series of Paintings," *The Delineator*, December 1908.

The "conspicuousness" Veblen associated with the lives of the leisure class was, however, exactly what seems to have won the approval of popular audiences. If the theater provided varied pleasures at low rates, the posters on display on sidewalk billboards and in shop windows were free for the looking. Advertising posters were commonly called "the poor man's picture gallery,"[25] and some observers went so far as to praise the social advantages of these devices of mercantile display. Posters and windows served to unite, not to divide, the populace by tutoring the people in what they could buy.[26]

Edna Ferber's 1917 novel *Fanny Herself* sees to it that everyone on both sides of the store window profits from the exchange.[27] Fanny's widowed Jewish mother, struggling to keep the family together through the money she makes in her small shop, has been left with a large supply of Christmas crèche figures. They are not moving off the shelves, and Mrs. Brandeis is in despair. Along comes the friendly neighborhood priest. He shows Fanny's mother how to trim her little show window with Nativity figures. Passersby crowd around the display, come in to buy, and the episode ends with the mother's cash box overflowing and her heart filled with self-confidence over her newly discovered talents as a promoter.

Always, always we want to ask, Yes, but what did *actual* people at the time *really* think about the constant come-ons to which they were exposed? Edna Ferber writing popular fiction about warm, gutsy lower-class characters is as much an advocate of the business ethic of showy display as the contemporary advocates of poster and window pushing the profitable pleasures of enticement. How much did the working class care about the artful shows that surrounded them? Worst thought, did they care too much?

A brochure for an exhibition of posters put on for the Massachusetts Mechanics Association in 1895 lauds the occasion;[28] it maintains that the workers are persuaded that posters prove that nothing is too humble when it comes to artistry and that great art is not a luxury for the few. But the posters the mechanics looked at with pleasure in the exhibition hall could also be used to draw them into the shops to buy. Then posters promoted desires that cost money. They were windows that introduced workers not merely to aesthetic pleasures provided gratis, but to new economic outlays in the name of necessity. At this point (so goes one argument) posters become the enemies, not the friends, of the people.

Name the various forms of art developing in the United States during the 1890s and you identify elements that (if you will) unify the culture, or that (if you will) divide it between the exploiters and the exploited: the stereopticon; the magazines of the middle range such as *McClure's, The Cosmopolitan, Collier's Weekly*; the intellectually subversive yet culturally elitist "little magazines"; chromolithographs; the legitimate theater; the stage spectacle; illustrations by Charles Dana Gibson, Phil May, and William Smedley; best-selling romances; the parody shows put on by the men of Harvard and Princeton; tableaux presented at society functions, settlement houses, and burlesque houses; Japanese woodcuts and advertising posters. Even where it is ideologically useful to offer political interpretations of these phenomena, it is an error to attempt clean divisions between genteel art that sustains the authority of upper- or middle-class culture and an art expressive of the popular mood.

In many instances, lines of class demarcation in the arts of display and performance were nonexistent, or else so loose that the passage of images back and forth between them was made quite casually. The vocabulary of poses on display and in performance was shared by a large and miscellaneous audience, furnishing occasions of much pleasure. Many turn-of-the-century Americans were having fun and liked having fun; they were capable of dismissing those spoilsports who had embarrassing questions to ask about social inequities. Their own nonchalance concerning social issues ought not to cause historians to desist from their critical evaluations; but the genuineness of this talent for pleasure ought not to be overlooked. And if it is important to determine the effects of commercial images upon individual segments of the class structure and the motives that lay behind the promotion of those images, it is just as important to analyze the particular visual forms taken by the images on show.

Archie Gunn, the Al Hirschfeld of the 1890s, commemorated the delights of the 1895–96 New York theater season just past (figure 14.21). Two pretty show girls hold back the swags of a descending curtain long enough for the readers of the *New York Journal* to review the past year's pleasures. Lillian Russell, Loïe Fuller, Eleonora Duse, Sarah Bernhardt, Ellen Terry, and Yvette Gilbert were among the stars on display in the "window" of New York's proscenium stage. The celebrities were supplemented all over the United States by performers of vaudeville, burlesque, the regulars of the Yiddish and ethnic theaters, and companies of the second and third rank which brought spectacles, melodramas, musical comedies, and pantomimes to large cities and small towns alike. And everywhere the lookers-on! (figure 14.22)

In certain significant ways the 1890s was "a day of little things." Brander Matthews made this observation in praise of the posters advertising household articles which he preferred to history paintings, heroic sculpture, and grandiose architectural ventures.[29] In 1893 the novelist and social commentator Robert Grant said that a good motto for life in those days was "Use Pears' Soap."[30] In 1896 Julian Ralph (twenty years a reporter for the *New York Sun*) observed that young women of the slums saved up to buy cheap photographs of actresses or paid neighborhood photographers to take their own pictures in tights so that they too could dream of looking like their stage idols.[31] These were small lives that needed to be scaled up, but in terms of the real things that surrounded them, whether posters for Pears' Soap or photographs of burlesque stars.

Glamour that is purchasable as a comestic aid or a new hat was more in keeping with modern times than glamour defined in its original sense—as magical power sanctioned only for special personages of semidivine authority. The older, elitist form of glamour necessitated having "character." New forms of glamour, reinforced by media presentation, appeared to require "personality" alone. Celebrity came to females with something to display that audiences were willing to make an effort to see.[32] The female celebrity ought not to be too far above the ordinary, lest a Bowery girl dares have no dreams. Still, that star must surely be "other," sexy, in motion, and "dramatical."

Being "other" meant being either prettier than most or, if she could not offer a dimpled smile and rounded thighs, more mysterious. It did not mean being domesticated and forthrightly average. Gibson's petulant leading lady (figure 14.23) is far more arresting than Margaret Anglin posed in connubial harmony at home (figure 14.24). That is why *Good Housekeeping* hastens to point out that a famous actress like Anglin enjoys the best of two worlds—each one providing an arena for the display of her skill at arranging effects. Onstage, Anglin has actors pretending nightly to adore her; at home she has a handsome husband who gives her his true

14.21a and b. Archie Gunn, "The Curtain Descends on the Season of 95–96," *New York Journal*, May 24, 1896.

14.22. Charles Dana Gibson, "The Villain Dies," *Collier's Weekly*, November 12, 1904.

love and a staff of well-trained servants who ease her daily transition between theater and home.

Good Housekeeping did its best to make stage actresses exciting but safe for middle-class consumption, just as it tried to redeem the activists of the suffrage movement. The year the magazine featured Margaret Anglin at home and in the theater it also featured Mary Kinkaid's article on feminists who were physically attractive and excellent home managers. But if it was in the interests of *Good Housekeeping* to demonstrate that feminists and actresses (women whose lives de-

14.23. Charles Dana Gibson,
"An Argument with the
Leading Lady," *Life*, Oc-
tober 10, 1895.

pend upon successful public "demonstrations") were really "like us," other audiences remained entranced by looks that emphasized "otherness." *Difference* was
exactly what the promoters were glad to give them. "The Girl from Up There" and
"Sappho" removed women from the home and placed them within the kind of
fantastical settings and costumes only a Wanamaker's window display might match:
for the otherworldly Edna May, there were icebergs, hovering sun ball, and cas-
cading tresses (figure 14.25); for the very worldly Olga Nethersole, there were a
sumptuous fur-edged cloak, feathery hat, seductive side glance, and lighted ciga-
rette (figure 14.26).

Sexuality was clearly a marketable product by the 1890s, both as an item for
direct sale and as a come-on for the readers of the tabloid press. It was a long time
since Eugene Benson had had to plead for the reinstatement of "the pagan element" in American culture.[33] Princeton and Harvard boys parodied the kick line
that was already a staple of the exposure exploited by vaudeville and burlesque
houses (figure 14.27). Newspaper stories and magazine illustrations fed the public
imagination for orgies associated with the night world of conspicuous consumption, as in this scene by Sigismond de Ivanowski for his "Lord's Prayer" series (figure 14.28). The Harry Thaw murder trial of 1907 was everyone's favorite sex scandal, supplemented by stories about the Girl on the Red Velvet Swing and the 1895
studio party hosted by society photographer James Breese where naked women
wearing Liberty caps were chased by amorous males.[34]

Paul Bourget maintained that young American women lacked sexual passion,
but he limited himself to observations of the Newport and New York social circuit.[35] Bourget's thesis is a fascinating one which ought not to be dismissed too
quickly because of the narrowness of his range of reference. It forms part of his
larger argument about the frightening willpower exerted by everyday versions of
the American Girl. Bourget and others believed that this lack of sensuality was the

14.24. "Margaret Anglin and Her Husband," from "Domesticity and the Theater," *Good Housekeeping*, January 1912.

possible cause for the cool look of self-love they found in the haughty heads and postures of the nineties debutantes, as well as in the poses practiced by young women of less exalted class, whether unmarried or married. But the "chaste depravity" Bourget describe—the "virgin nature which remains pure by calculation," gains its "advantages," and indulges its "whims"—may have been prompted by reasons other than those named by Bourget. He calls it a failure of the national

14.26*(left)*. Forrest Halsey, [Olga Nethersole as "Fanny Le Grand" in "Sappho"], from *The Illustrated American Stage* (1901).

14.25*(right)*. Archie Gunn, [Edna May in "The Girl from Up There"], from *The Illustrated American Stage* (1901).

physiognomy. We can call it willed choice, as Edith Wharton comes near to doing in *The House of Mirth*: a choice prompted by social conventions which encouraged young women of the upper classes to put a higher price on sexual restraint than lower-class women were free to practice.

Whatever the social and economic causes for the distance kept between virginity and promiscuity in turn-of-the-century America, unrestrained sexuality was not the look that displayed itself the best before the general public. *Outline, silhouette, design, shape,* and *pose* are—once more—the terms most applicable; in this case, to the selling of personality and the attainment of celebrity.

The safe poses were cute and cozy, as in the William Rau photographs which peeped in upon female legs and breasts hidden away in backstage dressing rooms (see figures 8.20 and 8.21). Hips and torso were lightly covered, but accentuated. Neck, shoulders, and bosom were exposed to view, but in a friendly way. Pertness was the source of Bessie Clayton's fame as a member of the Weber and Fields troupe (figure 14.29). Provocative winsomeness made Marie Doro one of the favorites of Charles Frohman's musical comedy company (figure 14.30). Flesh more exposed than concealed by black furs set off the charms of anonymous models who had no need for names to be "personalities" (figure 14.31). The truly dangerous poses were those which teased men's eyes while aggressively withholding gratification.[36] These were poses which put women in control and left men helpless.

Aristotle, the wise philosopher, was ridden by lust for Alexander's whore. Medieval cautionary tales and art pictured him reduced in his humiliation to playing horse to Phyllis' jockey (figure 14.32). Charles Dana Gibson was more playful in his rendition of this traditional image of male defeat, although he continued to

14.27. "The Pony Ballet," from "Tabasco Land" (1905–1906).

TRIANGLE CLUB ARCHIVES, PRINCETON

14.28. Sigismond de Ivanowski, "Lead Us Not Into Evil," from "The Lord's Prayer, A Series of Paintings," from *The Delineator*, December 1908.

hold the little man to the nursery (figure 14.33). The frolicsome crowd from Montpelier, Indiana, would try almost anything, even the notion that mastering women could "ride" men (figure 14.34). But what was funny to some was fear for many. It was the fear attached to the image of the fatal woman, whether depicted as a temptress enthroned in a low dive (see figure 14.28), the python-ringed head of the goddess Neith (see figure 4.6), or a spider casting her web (figure 14.35).[37]

Women in control suggested female energy possessed to excess. Energy (or electricity as Henry Adams sometimes called it, being more the physicist and the philosopher than the sexologist) was good, since Adams liked the sexuality that guarantees the reproduction of life from phase to phase in human history. But even Adams feared female energy (and its reverse, inertia) when it expressed itself as political force. Only the literal minded and unimaginative at the turn of the century were easily upset by the threat of unchanneled eroticism. Tabloids focused on

14.29. Archie Gunn, [Bessie Clayton with Weber and Fields], from *The Illustrated Amerian Stage* (1901).

decadence defined in conventional physical terms, but more thoughtful critics knew society would not be overthrown by rampant sexuality. Susan B. Anthony was a greater outrage than the Black Crook Girls. Spicy novels, girlie photographs, and the exotic eroticism expected of oversexed Jewesses, Negresses, and Orientals were less an incitement to the dangerous display of energy than the potentially inflammatory speeches of the feminists.

Female celebrities did not call upon sexuality for effective self-display. Rather, they enhanced their popularity by being *shapes in motion*. Their energy meant fun, not threats, because contained within the frame of the proscenium stage or the windows of stores. Whether run by electrical voltage of the kind J. R. Palmenberg's offered for $100, or run by the inner zest that Loïe Fuller exhibited nightly with her dances before audiences in Paris and New York, figures in motion got attention.

14.30. Burr McIntosh Studio,
    "Miss Doro" (1901).

Let us return to the New York theater season of 1895–96 set out with vigor by Archie Gunn (see figure 14.21). Compare a star in ascent with a star on the wane in order to arrive at the primary meaning of "display." It is motion in contrast to stasis; shape viewed at a tantalizing distance in contrast to the accessibility of the close-up portrait; the impact of intangible energy in contrast to the savored particulars in a beauty's face.

Loïe Fuller was known as "an instrument of light." In Paris artists of Art Nouveau persuasion annexed her shape as the focus of their designs (figure 14.36), and Toulouse-Lautrec, Jules Chéret, Emmanuel-Joseph-Raphael Orzai, Pal, and Georges du Feure turned Fuller's swirling veils into posters for public kiosks. When Fuller arrived in New York the newspapers could not get enough of her act. Hearst's *New York Journal*, for example: on March 1 of 1896 the *Journal* ran two feature stories across from one another, one on Fuller, the other on Lillian Russell. Alan Dale wrote the review of Russell's new theater piece, and the omnipresent Archie Gunn provided the illustration. (Gunn also designed a back cover with the statuesque Russell for the *Illustrated Police News* on April 26 to satisfy another of her consti-

14.31. Evan, Los Angeles,
[women on the beach]
(1918).

14.32. "Phyllis and Aristotle,"
bronze aquamanile
(c.1400).

14.33. Charles Dana Gibson, "The Nursery," from *Americans* (1900).

14.34. Irma Purman and friends (1914).

14.35. Coles Phillips, "Net Results," *Life*, August 24,
1911.

tuencies.) Dale described Russell's role in "The Goddess of Truth" as a masterpiece
of stasis. She appeared onstage in the opening scenes surrounded by plain women
and stupid men, standing forth in physical magnificence without diamonds or motion and wearing only a simple Grecian gown. Later in the show, Russell reap-
peared to stand still once more, but drenched now in the jewels Dale said her
audience had come to expect as part of her self-display. "The Goddess of Truth"
was Russell the star-as-inertia. She was handsome as a window mannequin, but
not one powered by electricity like Mr. Palmenberg's models.

Across the page from Dale's piece on Russell, reviewers celebrated Loïe Fuller as
"the Lily of the Nile"—a blur of motion and light. The next week (March 8) the
dancer was mentioned again when comments about Stephen Crane's newly repub-
lished novel *Maggie: A Girl of the Streets* likened Crane's heroine to a "Bowery
Loïe Fuller."[38] The week after that (March 15) the *Journal* devoted an entire article to the elaborate stage effects which turned Fuller—dressed in 500 yards of
silk—into an ecstasy of movement. By May, as the result of the odious comparisons
upon which fame rises or collapses, the *Journal* and its audiences were ready to
name their choice of favorites.

On May 10 of 1896 the *New York Journal* featured an array of well-known actresses and asked which ones had lost the charm of youth and beauty to aging.
Blunt, cruel, and direct, the article points to the matronly stoutness, the wrinkles,
the boring sedateness, and the coarsening voices of stage personalities on their way
out. Lillian Russell is on that list. On May 31 the *Journal* got down to business. It
singled out Russell to tell a story of lost popularity and dollar decline in marketing

14.36. Raoul Larche, gilded metal electric lamp designed in the shape of Loïe Fuller (c.1900).

COURTESY OF LILLIAN NASSAU

appeal. Once Russell was worshiped. Now the fickle public was indifferent to her charms.

The encroachment of years was, of course, part of the cause of Russell's failure to keep her hold on the public's favor. Formerly she had been a young woman blessed with "girlness," new bloom, and the promise of a crescent Diana, but at thirty-five years, her figure following the divine law of rhythm, Russell was full moon and summer ripeness.[39] Where she had previously flowed, she was now corseted, "dowagered up," and weighted down with too many diamonds and clothes. The *New York Journal*'s critique is borne out by this photograph of 1898 (figure 14.37). Russell is a plump woman with a pretty face and rich textures of skin, hair, jewelry, plumes, and laces. She is planted "there" solidly. She never had moved much, reviewers noted. She was certainly not moving now.

14.37. M. Morrison, Chicago, "Lillian Russell" (1898).

14.38. Benjamin Falk, New York, "Loïe Fuller" (1901).

In contrast, there is Benjamin Falk's photograph of Loïe Fuller (figure 14.38). She is hardly a pretty woman by any standards. One can only guess what her body is like, hidden as it is under masses of material. The halo around her head and the wingspread of her costume make Fuller look less like a love goddess than one of the Blessed of Paradise painted by Fra Angelico. But she is ready for the motion captured by Raoul Larche in the statuette shown above (figure 14.36) and by the scores of posters pasted up around Paris in the nineties. Even in Falk's photograph, where movement is only a potential, Fuller conveys the sense she is about to release herself upon space.[40]

By 1896 the static pleasures of solid, milky flesh are moving out of fashion. *Energy and light* in continual flow are more appropriate to the decade in which the Virgin imaged as the source of electricity becomes a near match for the masculine force of the Dynamo.

15

The Purchase of Grace

Static, self-contented beauty has several faults. It is seldom "dramatical." Dramatical is Loïe Fuller in action. It is a quality present in the nervous twist of the head, the slide of the eye glance, and the arch of the torso, covered or not (figure 15.1). Dramatical means *effect* and *statement* attained through poses expressive of emotion, the more intense the better. The painting by Arthur B. Davies, who was a painter of types if ever anyone was, indicates the particular art medium that works the best to present such effects. In the business of display the general type is better by far than individualistic particulars. Morrison's photograph of Lillian Russell is a naturalistic reading of the feel of skin, curve of lips, film of silk, and sheen of jewels (see figure 14.37). It does this through a peering, up-close shot which only portraits manage. But displace the details of the head to a distance of several hundred feet, to the point where people in a theater auditorium see it. Couple that head with a body that stands still in thickening stasis. Then compare this image with the type whose energy seizes the occasion of distance and converts it into excitement. The Falk photograph of Loïe Fuller is dramatical because it forgoes particulars in order to intimate presence (see figure 14.38). Fuller's shape (not her nondescript features and her frizzy hair) made fine art as a theater poster or a lighting fixture. Hers was a pose that carried across the footlights, *that performed well* once let loose upon the stage.

Several theatrical traditions were in practice at the turn of the century. I single out a particular cluster of related "dramatical" forms which used the art of the pose in ways analogous to print and window promotions. Whether it was the marketplace or the theater that provided the public occasion for acts of display, the

15.1. Arthur B. Davies,
"Dramatical" (n.d.).

HIRSHHORN MUSEUM AND SCULPTURE GARDEN

function of the forms was essentially the same for both: to draw attention to salable goods, to assure their recognition as "celebrities," and to incite desire in the minds of their viewers.

Melodrama is the catchall term that applies to the related theater traditions of which I speak. It subsumes the arts of recitation, the tableau, and the pantomime.[1] All these techniques rely on the type; all have received their share of contempt from the critics, although historians of popular culture are careful to point to their importance in the sociology of the theater.[2] But the issues (epistemological and aesthetic) with which I am most concerned here have been finely addressed in two recent studies of the nineteenth-century French and British theater by Peter Brooks and Martin Meisel. Brooks and Meisel concentrate upon the excitement generated once the dramaturgy of melodrama converted the theater stage into what

Brooks calls "the universe of pure signs."[3] Meisel further, and brilliantly, demonstrates that the universe encompassed the painting, the novel, and the drama. He persuasively argues that these late nineteenth-century Victorian art forms simultaneously strained to express the real and the ideal by means of melodramas of pose and gesture.[4]

"Dramatical" types, displayed in reference to codified meanings, were as much a part of late-nineteenth-century American culture as they were sources for "the universe of signs" that quickened the French and English popular imagination. The pages of popular and serious magazines and novels furnished a ready stage upon which the types played out their emotions.[5] Du Maurier's Trilby lies distraught upon her humble cot in the familiar pose of the repentant Magdalene struck by a newly awakened conscience (figure 15.2).[6] Howard Chandler Christy depicts the stiffening back of the accused woman and the forward crouch of the accusing husband whose hand stays his chair from crashing in anger to the floor (figure 15.3). Albert Beck Wenzell spotlights an actress (figure 15.4) who has just discovered her authority as a performer. "For a few minutes that she was on the stage she utterly held the house. . . . There seemed to lurk in her some sort of primeval and elfin power." (That fateful night at the Elks Club theatricals Dreiser's Sister Carrie will realize that she too possesses the power to enthrall.) In an illustration for Edna Ferber's 1917 novel *Fanny Herself*, J. Henry throws the scene upon the printed page as though upon a movie screen (figure 15.5). "You nervy little devil, you!" the caption reads, but audiences of prose romance or silent film needed no words to appreciate the plight of a young woman at bay.

The poster poses that filled the patriotic imaginations of Americans between 1898 and 1918, and the poster lives of the American consumers described by Herbert Duce, were matched by lives pictorialized by the gestures of theater posters, movie stills, and illustrations for popular fiction. For every mood there was a pose to strike, and for each pose there was an appropriate "dramatical" poster, drawing, or photograph.

Under such conditions, a young thing could not start too early to rehearse for the poses that constituted one's existence within "a universe of signs." Figure 15.6 gives a sample of the poses included in an article from *The Cosmopolitan*: the upraised arms of "entreaty," the collapse on the rug of "despair," and the heart-clutching gesture of "emotion" itself; also the "typical prayer pose" and "supplication." Which is more embarrassing—this early type of Shirley Temple posed by M. B. Parkinson (documenter of chorus girls in their tubs) who insinuates the seductiveness of the professional temptress (figure 15.7),[7] or the awfulness of Baby Lottie Morse posed to recite "Faith in the Red, White, and Blue" (figure 15.8), which is enough to make one contemplate doing to her what Homer Simpson did to Baby Adore in Nathanael West's *The Day of the Locust*? With examples like these continually set before the American female-child, how could she help but take the next step depicted in Gibson's drawing "Stage-Struck" (figure 15.9)?

If it is difficult for us to conceive of life as a series of emotional pictographs, we

15.2. George Du Maurier, "Repentance," from *Trilby* (1894).

15.3. Howard Chandler Christy, "Her husband and I turned on her together," from "The Lion's Mouth," *Scribner's Monthly Magazine*, December 1900.

must realize the seriousness once accorded to the scientific interpretation of expression and the pleasure derived from the arts of posing. The weight of studies such as Charles Darwin's *Expression of Emotions* of 1872 stands behind the attention given the subject by late-nineteenth-century women's magazines and etiquette books. Darwin had concluded that humankind shares a "community" of expressions. Since the language of body and mind were universal, it was possible for anyone at any time or place to identify the feelings of strangers in the crowd.[8] Upon such authority, S. L. Louis' *Decorum* could advise its readers in 1881 to study "the attitudes." Versed in these poses, they could at least display the outward behavior that suggested the qualities of the lady and the gentleman.[9] In 1899 *The Cosmopolitan* printed an essay on "How To Secure Expression in Photography." It maintained that photographs not only indicate the emotions being expressed (fear, surprise, authority, contemplation), they establish the sitter's sex. (Female: modesty, submission. Male: self-confidence.)[10] A brief piece in *Harper's Bazar* of 1905 noted too little variety of expression on the faces seen in the lobbies of large hotels and railroad stations,[11] but the writer's observation—that the modern face serves as a census report—supported the prevailing Darwiniam bent for schematic classifications and the popular interest in the relation of physiognomy, habit, and type.

The face was an important index of meaning. The body, viewed from head to toe, was perhaps even more an instrument of display. Seen in motion or arrested

15.4. Albert Beck Wenzell,
from "The Weaker Vessel,"
Good Housekeeping, June
1912.

on the verge of movement; rendered through the medium of photograph, silhouette, poster, or painting; supplied by a mechanical display figure, an actress on-stage, or the artist's model, the body allowed a wide margin of effects. It was freed from the necessity of detail as the face was not. It could accommodate the variables of distance, scale, and mobility while displaying the universality preached by teachers of "the attributes." As for the question of speech, champions of the pose claimed that it is the physical form that projects meaning, not the verbal notations that chance to accompany the body's signs.

Poetry or pieces of prose were frequently introduced by a member of the group who mounted the poses known as "living pictures." Sometimes it was the costumed performer who delivered literary fragments or a patriotic oration, but even then the focus remained on the gestures which complemented the recitation. *The New Peerless Speaker* of Henry M. Soper and *The Complete Speaker and Reciter* compiled by Frances P. Hoyle (both published in 1902) contain recitations, directions for tableau subjects, dialogues, pantomimes, and statue-posing. Words dominate these anthologies of verses, patriotic song lyrics, oratory, and comic recitations; but even there, care is taken to include photographs of the matching poses.[12] We see Baby Lottie getting her chance at a star turn, as well as toddlers in black-face or costumed as Uncle Sam. Books like these serve to remind us that the "attitude" derived from traditions that branched toward rhetoric and oratory on the one hand, and toward the eloquent silences of pantomime and tableaux on the other.[13]

15.5. J. Henry, " 'You nervy little devil, you!' " from Ferber, *Fanny Herself* (1917).

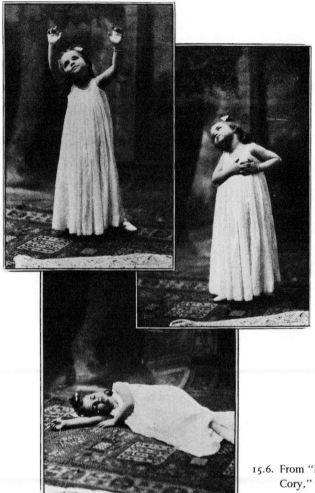

15.6. From "Photographs by
Cory," *The Cosmopolitan*,
January 1898.

Stage drama obviously draws upon the verbal arts; early movies and poster art just as obviously consort with gestures. But the fact remains that, just as an actress in the "talkies" can "do" an entire scene without words, silent movies and advertising art still make use of captions and other linguistic signs. The issue is not which emphasizes the art of pure gesture and which is dominated by the verbal. It is a matter of realizing how powerfully the pose—held within a frame of silence and stillness—*speaks* the reality of the moment.

True-blue Delsarteans—the school which inspired the American "science" of attitude and gesture throughout the 1880s and 1890s—always put the sign of the body first. The recitations included in *The Delsarte Recitation Book* range from silly comic dialect pieces to classroom standards like "The Charge of the Light Brigade." But the dominant theory rebukes the presence of the printed recitations. Don't say

15.7. M. B. Parkinson, New
York (1897).

LIBRARY OF CONGRESS

it, the book repeats over and over. Make "gestures" (which are the *verbs* of the visual sentence) and strike "attitudes" (which provide the *adverbs* that qualify the gestures).[14]

We today who delve into Delsartean manuals of gesture have every right to feel we have heard these same arguments from the lips of the deconstructionists. The theoretical position taken in *The Delsarte Recitation Book and Directory* by Elsie Wilbor reiterates the current skepticisms prompted by the indeterminancy of words. Literature is a fraud when it expects to be taken on its own authority. At least, physical gestures help "justify" and "prove" the interpretations brought to the statements they make. These days, of course, even the body is no privileged signifier. The profound faith once placed in physiognomy as the index of the individual soul, as the creature of physiological habit and psychological impulse, and as the locus of the essential truths of the fixed type does not go down easily with us; but even our behaviorists and semioticians have to admit an uneasy kinship with the Delsarteans, as well as with William James and Charles Sanders Peirce. And when

15.8. Baby Lottie Morse reciting "Faith in the Red, White, and Blue," from Hoyle, *The Complete Speaker and Reciter for Home, School, Church, and Platform* (1902).

15.9. Charles Dana Gibson, "Stage-Struck," *Collier's Weekly*, March 25, 1905.

Nicola Bradbury speaks of the power of the wordless gestures of Maggie Verver and Milly Theale in James' late novels;[15] when Jonathan Culler observes that pictures (vision) unify and that literature (speech) disrupts;[16] and when Myra Jehlen and George Steiner consider the discourse of denial by which women resist the yammer of male social systems, we are very close indeed to the concerns of the 1890s.[17]

Current critical discussions are a sophisticated and (sometimes) more elegantly worded version of the pronouncements made by the followers of Delsarte. Alike, they reiterate the relations between words, bodies, meaning, and private lives. Out of these commonly shared obsessions, women can still extract suggestions on how

15.10. Charles Dana Gibson, "Studies in Expression, An Imitation of the Lady of the House," *Life*, January 23, 1902.

to appropriate the right gestures to express whatever each believes to be her essential nature, even though women—now, as then—exist in a universe of signs which may very well be a community of cultural lies.

The arts of posing and gesticulation extended through all levels of American culture. Just as the simplified system perfected by the Eastman Company for loading photographic film and adjusting the focus made it possible for anyone to take snaps with the Kodak Brownie,[18] the codification of the Delsarte system encouraged the notion that no one need forgo "the attitudes" just because one was an amateur, not a professional. In a situation that emphasized true equality in the performance arts, schools, churches, social clubs, lodges, and municipal groups offered the occasions for public programs, while home theatricals became a popular supplement to family suppers and dances. Yes, but what could *a woman* gain from appearing before one sort of audience or another as a Type expressive of an Emotion? There were three possibilities: she could act out her dreams; she could order her inner life; she could demonstrate a deeply held principle or make a political statement.

Dressing up for masquerades and playing out imaginary roles formed an integral part of the American social life of the 1890s and 1900s. Chapter 5 has already suggested this fact. Feigning emotions and disguising old identities are problematic in the way they skewered certainties of class identification. They also admitted the possibility of subversion, as when inferiors aped their masters, here evidenced in Gibson's "An Imitation of the Lady of the House" (figure 15.10).[19] But small-town prudes and political conservatives might as well have saved their breath in the face of the general enthusiasm for dressing up and striking a pose which made the American social scene sometimes appear to be an unending sequence of costume parties.[20]

Fairy tales and folk figures supplied the popular female roles of Cinderella, Mother Goose, Red Riding Hood, and Columbine. Women from picturesque foreign places and historical periods were favorites. Grecian, Japanese, and sixteenth- and eighteenth-century costumes figured high on the list. Flower costumes held great appeal for both amateurs and professionals. But the primary figures cited by the costume-party manuals and the tableau handbooks were heroines of history, literature, and legend. Joan of Arc, Miss Liberty, Columbia, Juliet, Dolly Varden, Pocahontas, Molly Pitcher, Evangeline, and Priscilla turn up continually in their pages.

Changing places, acting out fantasies, being whatever you wished to be before midnight struck to pull you back into the old self: all this energy of transformation was abetted by Bartlett's *Evening of Statuary and Tableaux*, Butterick's *Character and Unique Fashions*, Willard's *Pictured Readings and Tableaux*, Fairfield's *Tableaux for Home and School*, and Irish and Young's *Pleasing Pantomimes and Tableaux*. But these were brief interludes whose intention was the genial entertainment of intimate social groups.[21] They were fun as far as they went, but that was not far enough for young women with notions of experimenting with the alteration of their public selves. The reenvisioned life is the insistent note one hears upon drawing near the fervent center of the Delsartean cult. The books put together by Delsarte's disciples have a clear message. Through text, drawings, photographs illustrative of the Delsarte method, women readers are guided toward ordered lives of "self-expression and health."[22]

The soul science of attitude and gesture was taken with great seriousness by François Delsarte, a Frenchman who lived between 1811 and 1871. When Delsarte delivered the address that defined his theories before the Philotechnic Society of Paris, he claimed weighty credentials.[23] His system was "Swedenborg geometrized." It combined elements of the cabala, scholasticism, and Neoplatonism, all dragged somewhat breathlessly into the nineteenth century. With spiritual antecedents such as these, it is not surprising to find Delsarte declaring that "the body is hideous," that the arts of "hideous realism" focus meanly upon the outer veils and masks of appearance, that naturalism is atheism, and that formalistic art is idolatry.[24] The soul is the only source of the pure art of the attitudes; only the outward poses of the attitudes enable the soul to arrive at "the eternal type" and the regeneration of its fallen nature.

"Delsarte Americanized" had less to say than had Delsarte himself about the vile distortions of bodily configurations and the need for the soul's redemption. The American version was far more interested in self-help, self-expression, and the emotional and physical well-being of its followers. Delsarteans adapted the essentials of the founder's system to American ideals and needs, but the high seriousness of the benefits it promised those who regularly performed its "gymnastics of expression" remained intact.[25]

Performers of the Delsarte method could depend upon its teachings because it was "scientific." It was scientific because the soul is bound to universal laws that can be studied, practiced until habit replaces conscious effort, and then "lived" as the basis for a permanent state of well-being. Delsartean purists, an exceedingly sober group, scorned association with brief, casual social entertainments. They believed that through what we would call behavior modification the body can be taught to express the soul, while the soul can be stimulated to express the highest aims of the individual will. "Freedom," "force," "grace," "superior," "expression," "control," "beauty," "sincerity," "signify," "elevated," and "vital": these are the central words of the gospel expounded throughout America by Delsarte's disciples.[26]

There are multifold connections between the principles of the Delsarte system and other prevalent tendencies in late-nineteenth-century culture and thought. Among these predilections are the classification of physical and spiritual types; interest in reciprocal relations between habit and will; unembarrassed borrowings from classical art and philosophy; preference for formulas that order personal and public lives; enthusiasm for scientific methods of self-advancement; insistence that every meaning has its clearly recognizable sign; beauty defined as outer repose and inward vitality; demands that artful expression be joined to spontaneous emotion; appeals to women to free themselves from society's self-demeaning control over their bodies and dress.

Unfortunately, the good intentions of the Delsarte system become trivialized once we look at the illustrations found in the canonical handbooks. For example, the drawings that accompany the text of Anna Morgan's *An Hour with Delsarte* are risible in the extreme. Morgan's book of 1889 is probably the most readable and sensible of the lot, but the earnestness of the lectures she gave before numerous women's groups would be undone if ever we allow a sense of humor to get in the way, as would the messianic effect of the Jane Fonda exercise tapes once we actually *look at* what is going on.

According to Anna Morgan, the Delsarte pupil begins her day's exercises by assuming "the natural pose"—body erect, arms at the side, face forward. Then the pupil (pictured in each of her carefully drilled moves) proceeds through a programmed series of attitudes. We are transported on the spot into the darkened movie theaters of the next generation where the Gish sisters, Marguerite Clark, and Mary Pickford positioned themselves in the same timeless stances of alarm and charm (figure 15.11). There is a great deal to be said, of course, in favor of the arts of silent film acting. It is also unfair to blame the Delsarte method out of hand for those wretched little child poseurs featured in figures 15.6, 15.7, and 15.8. Furthermore, as figure 15.12 suggests, classical and Shakespearean drama, as well as classical ballet and modern dance, continue to meditate upon the power of just such poses, as—once more with feeling—the performance arts continue to find expressive forms for unspeakable meanings.

All is ripe for satire, of course, whether blame is laid specifically upon the Delsarteans or placed indiscriminately against the period's rapturous pleasure over all manner of "dramaticals." Figure 15.13 from Anna Morgan's book is given rapid burial once we sight Fanny Brice's parody lament of the good girl betrayed (figure 15.14). Archie Gunn, always front row at the theater and as ready to tease as to applaud, knows how to twit the well-known actor William Faversham starring in one of the hits of the 1894 Broadway season, "The Masqueraders" (figure 15.15).

15.11. Rosa Mueller Sprague, "Now you stop!" from Morgan, *An Hour with Delsarte* (1889).

15.12. Rosa Mueller Sprague, "Alas, poor soul! What grief is thine?" from Morgan, *An Hour with Delsarte* (1889).

The wags of Harvard's Hasty Pudding Club are adept in the business of the lampoon, and the quickly readable gestures of the tableau tradition furnish them with excellent images for highly stylized mockery (figure 15.16). Still and all, however much the Delsarte method lent itself to ridicule, its repertoire of poses actively inspired the arts of graphic design. The Hasty Pudding sheet is an excellent example of theater poster art; only the words give away the joke.

The following two sets of illustrations demonstrate the ease with which the intense feelings conveyed by the attitudes could drop into formalistic patterns, just as they also demonstrate the reverse—patterns as the source of the signaled emotions. Figure 15.17 is a Gibson drawing of 1893. In a dramatic moment titled "That Evening Her Engagement Was Announced," the rejected suitor clutches the draperies of the passageway—funereal curtains about to fall shut around his heart.[27] Figure 15.18 appeared the previous year as a photographic illustration for Helen Ecob's *The Well-Dressed Woman*, a book-length manifesto of the need for women to express their true individuality through naturalness of costume and posture. This illustration is not intended as an emotional moment in a drama. Ecob simply wishes the model—by standing at the entry, set off by aesthetically pleasing draperies—to display the easy line of the "natural" clothing Ecob urges all women to adopt. Figure 15.19 is a cover drawing by Helen Dryden for *Vogue* of October 1914.

"Mine woes afflict this spirit sore."

15.13. Rosa Mueller Sprague, "Mine woes aflict this spirit sore," from Morgan, *An Hour with Delsarte* (1889).

Dryden's cover contains neither the drama of Gibson's drawing nor the motive for self-improvement that occasioned the Ecob illustration. The pose of the highly conventionalized female form is pure and impersonal design. The attitude of the body is the same as in the other examples (back to the viewer, swag of drapery held in the hand) and a personalized mood is vaguely detectable (there *is* that moon); but the need to provide signs indicative of an individual soul surprised in a moment of intense self-clarity lies outside the artist's intentions.

15.14. Fanny Brice as "Rose of Washington Square" (1920).

The second set of poses is somewhat related to the first in that young women—positioned sideways to the viewer—watch and wait at windows. In each instance a female figure is displayed in a setting where the aperture suggests a closing down or an opening out. Figure 15.20 is a photograph from F. P. Hoyle's *The Complete Speaker and Reciter* of 1902 which provides full instructions for staging the following amateur tableau.[28] " 'Watching at the Window.' The long-expected friend, lover or husband, is awaited with keen interest, or the approach of some danger brings the earnest looker to the window. A scene easily represented."

Figure 15.21 is an illustration of 1906 by Howard Chandler Christy titled "Awaiting His Coming." This is no religious allegory of the Bride as the Church who awaits Christ the Bridegroom. It is the American girl, newly engaged to be married. She stands at the open window with clasped hands and an overturned flowerpot, waiting with eagerness for the romantic moment when "she capitulates and gladly lays down her head upon his manly shoulder."[29]

The final pose of the group is a photograph taken on my mother's wedding day in 1914 (figure 15.22). The costume is a bona-fide bridal gown; its wearer is a real bride-to-be—as real as the ceremony following shortly after in the family parlor whose vows would be honored for nearly sixty-one years until my father's death

MR. FAVERSHAM
AS THE VILLAIN.
THE DOTTED LINES BY THE
ARM DENOTE HIS
FAVORITE
MODE OF EXPRESSING
CONTEMPT.

15.15. Archie Gunn, "Mr. Faversham as the Vil-
lain. . . ," *The Illus-
trated American,*
December 22, 1894.

at ninety-two. The pose is real but highly conventionalized, as in the case with most wedding photographs. The scene contains the standard signifiers for "wait-ing" and "expectation." It even adds further familiar visual flourishes (stained-glass window and folded hands) that suggest a worshipful maiden at prayer or Rossetti's Blessed Damozel waiting at heaven's bar. Pose and setting neatly sum up the moment just prior to the bridal sacrament that will transform the subject from one stage of young womanhood to the next.

According to the principles laid down by both François Delsarte and William James, physical acts initiate emotions and make them authentic. When your body assumes a pose in a particular setting, that pose becomes your sign. As you stand, so you feel and are. I cannot answer for the exact state of my mother's bottom-nature at the moment this photograph was taken. The facts of the case are the visual conventions lying behind the pose whose cultural mobility made them available to every female Tom, Dick, and Harry.

What is unusual about this particular rendition of the impending marriage cer-emony is the fact that the photographer was Merle Smith, the man who had been on hand to record my mother's progress from sixteen years of age to this June day in her twenty-second year. From the girl self-consciously posed on a bearskin rug as the jilted woman (see figure 5.52) and the kneeling angel-virgin (see Introduc-tion, figure 31) through the dozens of informally posed snaps taken in the larky company of her friends to the young woman on her marriage day, my mother had been the focus of Merle Smith's camera and a contributing partner to his command of "the attitudes."

Women appropriated the language of bodily attitudes for their own ends when they assumed poses for pleasing interludes of entertainment and for serious acts of disciplined self-enhancement. But did such poses have sufficient strength of refer-ence for the making of personal statements about social and political beliefs?

15.16. "The Dregs in the
Cup," Hasty Pudding
Club (1906).

ARCHIVES OF THE HASTY PUDDING CLUB, HARVARD

The material contained within the tableau handbooks is politically conservative. Nothing there to shock audiences at the school pageant, church sociable, or
party evenings at the big house on the hill. Scenes from American history place
women in the pose of "the beloved" of Hiawatha, Captain John Smith, or John
Alden. Wives and mothers of Presidents supply another category of favorite sub-

15.17. Charles Dana Gibson,
"That Evening Her En-
gagement Was An-
nounced," *Life*, May 25,
1893.

15.18. From Ecob, *The Well-
Dressed Woman* (1892).

15.19. Helen Dryden, *Vogue*,
October 1914.

jects. The lives of Martha Washington, Abigail Adams, Dolly Madison, and Nancy
Hanks are reduced to a matter of costumes and wigs. Biblical stories are combed
for examples of "the good women"—Ruth, Esther, and the repentant Magdalene.
The Fourth of July throws colored spots upon Columbias holding torches, cornu-
copias, spears, and flags, or upon Liberty figures who receive tributes from other

15.20(*left*). "Watching at the Window," from Hoyle, *The Complete Speaker and Reciter for Home, School, Church, and Platform* (1902).

15.21. Howard Chandler Christy, "Awaiting His Coming," from *The American Girl* (1906).

nations and extend the hand of generosity to grateful immigrants. As one might expect, the level of excitement picks up in 1898. Emphasis is given to female representations of the authoritative role newly taken up by the United States. Now the "America" figures have to express the nation's duty to unify the world.[30]

Powerful Columbias. Weak women. The instructions for a school recitation of "Though We Are Little Girls" sharply distinguished between boys who go out in the world to win fame through bravery in battle and girls who wait at home to hear the tales the boys will tell on their return.[31] Harriet Beecher Stowe and Clara Barton slip through the male mesh of "important" Americans to qualify for figuration in patriotic tableaux, as do Molly Pitcher and Barbara Fritchie, but the College Graduate, the New Woman, and the Club Woman are placed on display in order to be made fun of. Indeed, *American Heroines*, an instruction manual of 1900, proposes tableau poses that continually counter threatening female types with "the best types"—the Bride, the Mother, and Columbia.[32]

15.22. Irma Purman (June 1914).

Resolutely middle-class, small-town values pervade the tableau books from the mid-1880s well into the late 1920s (and beyond, gauging from my own memory of school pageants and inspirational programs sponsored by the local gas company). The entertainments of the wealthy also made clear the political position taken by the new plutocracy. Ward McAllister derived his fame from designing high-society costume balls and tableaux; when he compiled his memoirs at the end of his career, he emphasized his conviction that a powerful society must be exclusive and thoroughly organized.[33] The occasions McAllister planned and promoted (the Patriarch Balls, the Mother Goose Ball, the Hobby-Horse Quadrille) solidified that power and expressed his own social theory: fashion is a statement of progress because it manifests the beauty of women and the male genius for making money. In obedience to the principle of this theory the social entrepreneur designs occasions that display that beauty and that money. By these means, and through the avid encouragement of the popular press, the rest of the world *sees* what power signifies. McAllister made his great discovery about the need to organize visible social events at the time of the Centennial Exposition of 1876. From that moment on, he put his theories into practice throughout the 1880s and 1890s as carefully as though he were the head of the same business corporations which fed wealth to his clients. From Mrs. Astor's ballroom to Delmonico's to the Metropolitan Opera House, McAllister's chosen settings confirmed his basic political credo: display proves power.

There was no lack of satiric jibes against the pretentiousness of this rage for celebrity. Edith Wharton's *The House of Mirth* of 1905 and Charles Dana Gibson's drawing of the same year (figure 15.23) single out the meretriciousness that governed social and media events in the decades after the gross glory days of McAllister's reign. But even so, faith remained strong in the tableau as an effective mode for defining and confirming the authority of high society.

Social power was enhanced when the tableau form centered upon representations of national power. It was no accident that McAllister's first inspiration was the Banner Ball in 1876. It was also no accident that the major social event of the centennial year was the staging of a series of tableaux based on patriotic themes, as described by Mrs. E. M. W. Sherwood (the same woman who recorded the dinner table conversation about the New England Woman for *The Atlantic Monthly* in 1878). In 1893 Mrs. Sherwood wrote a little book detailing the social value of theatricals presented at big country houses and seaside villas. As the "apotheosis of entertainment," tableaux gave high society its best opportunity for expressing its belief in the heroic, the refined, and the historic.[34] But 1876 had been the brightest occasion to which "her people" had given their official stamp.[35] The entertainment centered upon a living picture based on Daniel Huntington's 1861 painting "Lady Washington's Court"—itself a statement about the aristocratic society lodged at the core of the new republic. The opulent affair was staged by descendants of the original members of the Washington family coterie. (The "Martha Washingtons" common to school pageants and women's clubs were not in the same class as these society women who appeared in the full regalia of brocades, velvets, and diamonds—Mrs. August Belmont, Mrs. John Jacob Astor, and Mrs. R. H. Hunt among them.)

Other tableaux preceded and followed the staging of the Huntington painting; scenes from the Puritan and Knickerbocker periods established the longevity of "true" American stock. The high point of the evening, however, came during the

15.23. Charles Dana Gibson, "Advertising à la Mode," *Life*, May 4, 1905.

"allegorical" section. Placed like the hostess at the head of the receiving line of a Newport ball, the figure of America—"beautiful, young, triumphant"—welcomed the richly costumed nations of the world. Among them were Miss Adelaide Townsend as England seated in a chariot, a Russia who leaned against a large stuffed polar bear, and Miss Stevens as Egypt (figure 15.24). But although these nations had their own moments of glory, once they approached America's side to form a "shield" of honor around her person, it was clear who commanded the occasion. American elite society and "America" were one and the same, the source of power over all.

The tableaux described by Ward McAllister and Mrs. Sherwood during the final years of the nineteenth century had no patience with radical statements. Nor were the charity tableaux sponsored by Mrs. Vanderbilt in 1907 or Mrs. Astor in 1914 (see figure 9.25) the right occasions for women to pictorialize their need to breathe in a freer political climate. In 1912 New York debutantes posed for the "Oriental Tableaux" staged by the society photographer James Breese of studio-orgies notoriety,[36] while the high-society circuit mounted elaborate versions of the same entertainments staged around the country by members of the middle class. Notwithstanding McAllister's theories of fashion as progress, these affairs were by and large politically conservative and socially static. There were also the masques performed by members of the artists' colonies clustered around Stockbridge, Massachusetts, and Cornish, New Hampshire (put on with merriment by friends of Daniel Chester French in 1900 and Augustus Saint-Gaudens in 1905),[37] as well as the "Friendship" masque photographed in great detail by Frances Benjamin Johnston in 1906 (see figures 9.9 and 9.22). Such costumed romps must have been fun to watch and participate in, but they had nothing to say about the progressive issues of the period.[38]

15.24. "Miss Stevens as Egypt," from "Some Society Tableaux," *The Cosmopolitan*, January 1898.

Nor was progressivism the primary point of the tableaux, pageants, and plays offered by the settlement houses. The amateur's enthusiasm brought to the performance of *Twelfth Night*, given by the residents of Denison House in Boston, was an end in itself. Whatever the activists of the Progressive Movement were out to achieve in 1906, the Chicago players in Hull House's *The Merry Wives of Windsor* were pleased to receive the "halo" of culture for their efforts.[39] An evening away from the workshops and factories gave young members of the cast a taste of middle-class pleasures and virtues. They learned lessons in cooperation and the "repression of egoism." They experienced the kind of "culture" upheld by the "better element" (those with "more ideals"). They benefited from the *esprit de corps* of rehearsals and the acclaim of the opening night audience.

The charge of bread and circuses placed against the Chicago Exposition could also be laid against settlement house theatricals. It is easy to assert that these entertainments disguised the presence of long-standing social evils and placated the poor without altering their economic condition. But the very fact that poses relied on established conventions could seem a gift for the recently displaced. Contemporary photographs taken of Greek and Italian immigrants participating in Nativity tableaux have the look of a people, torn loose from their pasts, who take heart from these simple exercises in tradition and continuity. Mary, Joseph, the Magi, and the Shepherds were recognizable signs, even in the Boston slums. The physical poses have a factuality that offered assurance that the religious values of the Old Country could withstand visual translation across the ocean. Best of all, the immigrants had no need to speak English to express those values. Body English sufficed.

But were the arts of posing ever applied to a woman's need to question and change her society? The members of the National American Woman Suffrage Association, for one, were adroit at incorporating the conventions of the tableau to their purposes. We have seen Inez Milholland in 1912 in the role of Cornelia, mother of the Gracchi and heroine of supreme will, and as a herald on horseback marching with the suffragists in 1913 through the streets of Washington, D.C., to the Treasury Building where tableaux were performed that featured women as Justice, Charity, Peace, Plenty, Columbia, and Liberty (see figures 1.16, 1.17, and 12.4). And Margaret Wycherly as "Woman" attempted in 1915 to associate her demands for the vote with the Liberty pose (see figure 12.14). For the sake of their cause, these feminists brought to bear costumes, props, and stage conventions which could have been drawn from the most reactionary of the tableau instruction books then in print. It was the nature of the occasion that determined whether pat formulas for amateur entertainments would ever be transformed into ideological declarations for the woman's movement.

No overt signs of political radicalism marked the charity-benefit performance of Sophocles' *Antigone* that the Saturday Morning Club presented in Bumstead Hall, Boston, in the spring of 1890.[40] Figures 15.25 and 15.26 show Mrs. Caroline C. Baker Burien in the lead role falling into two poses instantly familiar from inclusion in various Delsarte manuals. In these photographs the flow of dramatic action is stopped, framed as frozen instances. The tragic heroine expresses entreaty and despair as emotional absolutes. Her body becomes the *agon* Antigone must undergo in preparation for the moment of her grand defiance.

Antigone's story clearly invites a feminist reading. A young woman defies the authority of the king and the laws of male society. She imposes her will in order to uphold the sacred principles of the gods. Through her death, Creon the ruler experiences moral defeat, although the state he represents goes on as before. There is more to interest us, however, than any formulaic interpretation of the drama's text. There are the intentions the Saturday Morning Club brought to the production of *Antigone* and the varied reactions of their audience.

The Saturday Morning Club (founded in 1871 for the pleasure and stimulation of Maud Howe, daughter of Julia Ward Howe, herself a stalwart in the woman's rights movement) was alert to the position of women in contemporary society.[41] Befitting the members' social status, their approach was predictably middle class. But the Saturday Morning Club held to the principle that all women share a common sex and history. This earnest belief is reiterated throughout the "memories" set down in a handwritten account by Mary Gray Morrison as her record of the events leading up to the 1890 production of *Antigone*.

The original Greek *Antigone* had been performed by male actors before an all-male audience; 2,300 years later an all-female cast presented the drama before a Boston audience restricted to women.[42] But Morrison noted the resonances of the ancient story that carried forward into the present. The women in attendance in Bumstead Hall were affected precisely because the universality of Antigone's plight was underscored by the universalizing techniques of the production. Naturalistic details would have caused rents and divisions between ancient Greece and contemporary Boston, but the conventionalized gestures closed the cultural gap. As Morrison expressed it, "the ideal spirit" of women who were "less individual than typical" was given the power by which those women "appeal to us now as they will to all ages of human life." The story itself emphasized what happens when a woman pits "the eternal right" against the "human mandate" supported by male authority. *Antigone* is the universal in conflict with the expedient—the female principle in struggle against the masculine.

Once again we find the familiar equation, as ideologically important to dedicated feminists as to advocates of the True Woman. Females represent "the higher law" and "the eternal right." Male society functions at the lower level of the topical and the circumstantial. When staging, therefore, the "femaleness" of the absolute, the Saturday Morning Club had to give great care to "the simplest of the great emotions which never alter in humanity." At the same time, the group had to acknowledge the passage of time that continually "brings new feelings with new knowledge and new ways."[43]

Fifty club women dedicated themselves to a year of preparation which included coaching by a teacher from New York's American Academy of Dramatic Arts. Each detail of the performance presented "for the sisters alone" was meticulously worked out. The stylization given to the costumes, settings, and gestures received the greatest attention from the press. Through the expert use of convention, the young women achieved the effect noted by one newspaper report: the "great, broad band of human sympathy [that] knits together all ages and all civilizations." The same newspaper item affirmed that everything was done to insure that the "tears that fell for Antigone's fate," and "the perennial, human joy in her lofty devotion," were as powerful in Boston in 1890 as they had been in ancient Greece. It was also noted that the "Greekness" of the material was aided by the fact of "the sharp outline of feature and figure so characteristic of our New England women." Since the performers were themselves "severely and justly Greek in type," their pictorial impression supplemented "the most careful study of grouping and facial expression."

. . . the repose of figures during the exciting passages of the dialogue gave all the more opportunity for pose and expression to do their work upon the mind and heart. The attitudes of motionlessness well assumed by the chorus of maidens during the scene in which Antigone bewails the fate gave the eye the pleasure and to the heart the relief which comes from having some deep, common grief voiced by an artist.[44]

If the club's intention was to bring unanimity of response—an aim vouched for by the news account by Heloise Hersey cited above—the actual effect was somewhat different according to others in the audience.

Interesting divergences appear between reports in the Boston press about the *Antigone* and the goals addressed in Mary Gray Morrison's "Memories." The decision of these society women to exclude men from the audience naturally aroused

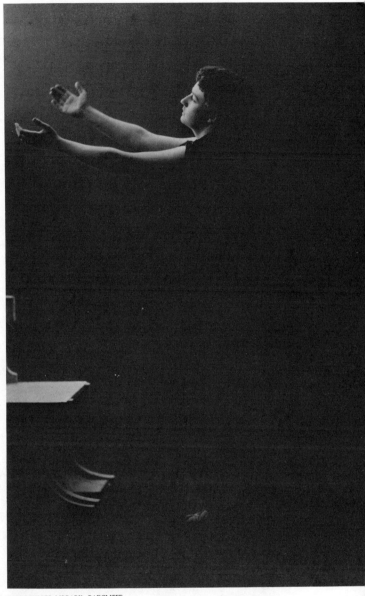

15.25. Mrs. Caroline C. Burien
as Antigone (1890).

the newspapers' curiosity. There was some criticism about the snobbish tone of the affair and the club's emphasis on "culture," but most of the stories were approving—unfortunately, for the wrong reasons. One paper headlined "Beauty Show. Only Ladies Were Admitted To See the Play Yesterday. The Affair Was an Artistic and Social Event." Another article announced "Antigone Acted by Girls. Maidens and Young Matrons of the Bluest Blood of Beacon Street Make Money for Charity by Their Portrayal of Creon's Cruelty and Antigone's Devotion."

15.26. Mrs. Caroline C. Burien as Antigone (1890).

The same newspaper led off the accompanying article with a little joke concerning feminine ignorance. A young woman excited by the upcoming social event asked her bookseller for a copy of Sophocles' play and was angered that he had not automatically set it aside since he knew she always wanted to read the "new stories . . . as fast as they come out."

Several accounts focused upon the costumes, describing the players' garb in detail as though they were models in a fashion show. One reporter gushed, "Nothing could be more beautiful than these maidens." Another remarked that the dress designers Worth and Redfern would lose their business if men could only see how lovely modern women look in Grecian garb. Still another praised "the grouping of the chorus, whose softly draped and prettily contrasting dresses gave tone and color to the scene, were picturesque and graceful, and added much to the charm of the performance."

Further misreadings appear in the papers' comments about the production and its organization. It was characterized largely in terms of the many "pretty feminine touches": tickets shaped like drachmas; programs of papyrus rolled on double rods; costumes that were "models of beauty and historical accuracy"; the "high grade of critical work and scholarly research"; the "modest absence of a flourish of trumpets"; and "a womanly reserve" concerning the club's sense of its achievements. This, then, was the public reception given the year of work devoted to bringing the story of Antigone's passion to a modern female audience. By and large, the newspaper coverage of the "charm" of the Saturday Morning Club's presentation in 1890 anticipated the way the "dainty" architecture of the Woman's Building at the 1893 Exposition would be judged according to similar gender diminishments. But the young women of Boston had had far more in mind than "pretty feminine touches" and "picturesque and graceful" dresses. They had hoped to bind their viewers through their use of stylized pose and gesture into an eternal sisterhood of "perennial sympathy and joy."[45]

The Saturday Morning Club had something else it wanted to say with its *Antigone*. Its members wished to suggest that the Greek idea of fate was the cause of the sense of impasse that characterized all history up to the 1890s. Under the philosophical mandate sanctioned by the Greeks, suffering was viewed as a permanent condition. In contrast, the young women of 1890 testified that their generation believed that "the old ideas of the gods had become too small" and that justice was the new spirit. As Mary Gray Morrison expressed it, women now existed in the intersection between the worlds of the past and the present where "the angels" of each world are seen "ascending and descending." The stage of Bumstead Hall provided, as it were, the threshold area where Antigone's "attitude" allowed ancient truths to flow into the hearts of modern women. Measured through a series of heart-stopping poses, Antigone's tragedy pictorialized the conjunction of two kinds of time and two different beliefs in the power of the individual will. The players offered images of "the eternal right" to the women who watched—images that would serve "the sisters" well in 1890. If the women in the audience but knew how, they could use those images as incentives to a future of resisting "Creon's law."

The Saturday Morning Club wanted to serve justice, but what of grace, the agent of mercy? Henry Adams, who found no hope for justice in the universe that figured in the theater of his mind, desired the presence of grace. Only that strange, whimsical power could offset the mad whirl of the supersensual chaos. In earlier times Western society had had the Virgin to intercede with the Father and the Son who presided over the enactments of stern justice, but now there was only the Dynamo, and who would wish to kneel in prayer to that impervious, impersonal force?

Grace was much talked about at the turn of the century. The fact that the word was usually associated with good taste and the aesthetics of bodily movement gives evidence of precisely the diminishment of meaning which exasperated Henry Adams about the secular age into which he had been lobbed at birth. Augustus Saint-Gaudens' sculptured figures exuded a grace of line because their source was Saint-Gaudens' unerring sense of taste, but Adams was unable to find in his friend's art the presence of that other, more profound grace which has the capacity to alter lives into something strange and new. The question for Adams' contemporaries was whether any of the available versions of grace were able to supply the power the old forms once had.

The Boston newspapers described the women who performed in *Antigone* as graceful, charming, tasteful models of beauty and fashion. It seemed that the "feminine" in them was all there was to look at. The sacred agency of femaleness that formerly had the power to apportion justice and mercy in earthly lives was either hidden in the Boston of 1890 or nonexistent. By the end of the nineteenth century only professional actresses appeared to have kept the way open for a return to what the old doctrines of grace once represented. It was the oddity of the culture of the time that the artifice of "the attitudes" and the somewhat disreputable traditions of the theater were the means by which the sense of the sacred might still infiltrate a society devoted to secular arts of display and an ignoble marketing of desires. It was a further paradox that the grace that mattered so much to the private self could come about only through the negation of the individual and by means of the elevation of the universal type.

One of the main sources for instruction in the principles of grace in late-nineteenth-century America was the Delsarte system of attitudes, but historians of the Western theater will name the particular moment in time for the reintroduction into Europe of the ancient system of stylized gestures that lay behind Delsarte. It was 1787, in Naples, at the villa of Sir William Hamilton. Johann Wolfgang von Goethe was among those attending a private performance presented by Emma Hart, an occasion Goethe never forgot.[46] He watched the future Lady Hamilton manipulate her shawl in a series of swift movements that allowed her to slip from one pose and persona to another, becoming Medea or Niobe in an instant. After that momentous day in 1787 it can be declared that the way was open for the Black Crook Girls, Loïe Fuller, Sarah Bernhardt, and the Saturday Morning Club.[47]

Three points must be extracted from the richness of details that threaten to smother any extended account of the links between Emma Hart's use of the attitudes and the monodrama, tableau, pantomime, opera, and ballet, as well as the various schools of dramatic expression. One is the rapidity by which Emma Hart could alter her look to express widely different emotions. Within a moment she transformed her nature from sibyl to bacchante to Mary Magdalene; the types she represented appeared upon the scene as quickly as, it is said, Grace descends to catch one unaware. Second is Goethe's observation that the everyday Emma Hart was a vulgar and rather boring woman, while the woman he watched in performance was the personification of grace.[48] Last, her arts can be traced through the next hundred years until we come to Delsarte and the definitions of gracefulness expounded by his disciples well into the 1890s.

The basic principles of Delsartean grace are these: the self is ordinarily a jumble of disjunctions and contradictions of the kind that act against a woman like Emma Hart "meaning" much of anything. But an Emma with her attitudes is a force of unity and significance. Form and content, signified and signifier, are joined. The body is free because the soul's inner will is in control. Artistry becomes habitual in its spontaneity. Skillful movements provide the effect of repose. No waste is apparent since the techniques by which the adept schools herself are so lavish. Through the Delsartean woman's adherence to conventions of type, the unique sincerity of her privileged form counters the pull of conformity to social norms.

In large part, Emma Hart's biography is the story of a woman's body passed around to a variety of male patrons of "good taste." But that body was sanctified when it leapt into motion as the expression of the essential self that lay deep within her nature. Emma possessed of the power of the attitudes was no longer restricted by her history as an artist's model and whore to the single role of the erotic Venus. Nor did she have to become that impossibility—the equivalent of the Christian Virgin—in order to be saved. While Emma performed, she became "the Venus Naturalis" of which Kenneth Clark has written—that exceptional form that transcends both the erotic and the spiritual natures and arrives at the fullest expression of the force of the female.[49]

This, then, is the theory and tradition which celebrated the merger of the graceful female form with the age-old values associated with Grace, whether glossed by the pagan imagination or by Christian doctrine: the values of unity, sincerity, economy, signficance. Once we encounter attempts in the late nineteenth century to express grace and the graceful, contradictions, of course, slip into view.

During the 1860s and 1870s Adah Isaac Menken became a sensation as the result of her performance in *Mazeppa*. Based on a long poem by Lord Byron, this stage piece relates the tale of a young cossack adventurer who is captured by his enemies and tied naked to the back of a wild horse set loose upon rocky crags and ravines.

Menken shrewdly pared away the original details of the story to focus upon Mazeppa's ride. A woman in a male role, she could have it both ways with her audience where she attired herself in a flesh-colored covering which gave her the look of nudity. Aided by dramatic lighting and production effects, Menken nightly rode across countless stages tied upside down, her "male" body arched in romantic agony. Theater posters that featured Menken as Mazeppa-in-bondage announced the coming attraction and packed the houses. A pose as visible and exciting as Mazeppa's was immediately appropriated by other image makers for their own purposes. A poster for the 1900 melodrama *Sporting Life* shows the heroine in the clutch of the villain as she lies in the same arching pose. Charles Schenk's model, posed for his 1902 volume *Draperies in Action*, did without stallion or body stocking (figure 15.27). In 1929 Daniel Chester French hired Ethel Cummings, a servant girl from nearby Stockbridge, to model for his "Andromeda" (figure 15.28), while Howard Chandler Christy painted pretty girls arched in the same pose for the pleasure of his friends.

When a standardized pose is offered within different contexts, the emotional signals it emits are hardly simple. Both Mazeppa, the young cossack hero, and Andromeda, the heroine of Greek myth, represent noble figures victimized by cruel captors.[50] The "attitude" staged for Menken's theater audience, the photographer's camera, and the sculptor's chisel consciously plays off these tales of suffering and threatened innocence. The pose stimulates responses as much sexual as spiritual. Ahead lies Fay Wray clutched in King Kong's grasp, numerous comic-book heroines, and the female object of pornographic movies—all frozen into the final stages of duress.

According to the sublime principles of Delsartean grace, the spiritual significance of the attitude elevated the universal ideals and repressed the earthy particularity of the body. But when theory of type (the means by which grace was defined in the Delsarte manuals) collided with lives of women (real and fictitious), a change took place. Grace available on the open market, and the material value of gracefulness in a society given to display and performance, were put to the world's tests.

Edith Wharton's Lily Bart, Stephen Crane's Maggie Johnson, Theodore Dreiser's Carrie Meeber, and Henry James' Miriam Rooth serve as literary points of reference, together with two actual stage personalities, Evelyn Nesbit and Alma Stanley. These examples demonstrate how young women moved with grace through lives pictorialized as a series of dream poses, in the end variously finding death, material success, notoriety, defeat, or the fullness of being.

Lily Bart and Maggie Johnson are women entrapped within dreams which dictate the poses they adopt. Joan Lidoff has described Lily as a repressed Sleeping Beauty, while Cynthia Griffin Wolff defines Lily's America as an aesthetic dreamscape that constricts the opportunities of those caught within its narrow spaces.[51] Early on, Lily becomes resigned to the fear she will never attain "the republic of the spirit" she once hoped to share with Lawrence Selden, but one evening she

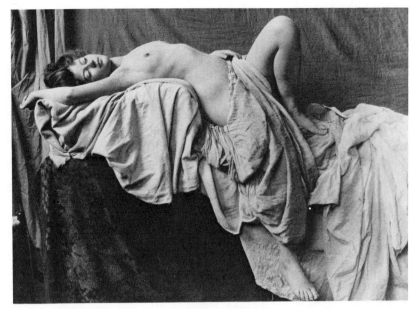

15.27. Charles Schenk, from
 Draperies in Motion
 (1902).

15.28. Daniel Chester French,
 "Andromeda" (1929–
 1931).

DANIEL CHESTER FRENCH PAPERS

experiences the thrill of revived hope. This is the evening at the Welly Brys' where she appears in a *tableau vivant* as Joshua Reynolds' "Mrs. Lloyd," the image she believes will reveal her true nature (figure 15.29). But Lily's previous history of poses (the means by which her casual public has come to a consensus of "what Lily is"—a "bad woman" out to marry money) overwhelm the charm and force of the "attitude" she assumes before the watching crowd. Reading Wharton's novel, we are reminded that the idle or malicious people who listen to what is *said about Lily* get her character wrong. But when we earnestly try to *look at her* correctly and to sort out her different dream poses, we too are defeated by the ambiguity of the evidence. The narrative determinism of *The House of Mirth* which has been often noted by the critics extends to us as much as to the novel's characters. Lily, her fellows in society, and we are, all together, fixed in our views by the effects of the dramatic scenes. The only distinctions permitted us are between good taste and bad taste, the graceful and the vulgar. As Selden kneels by the bed where Lily's body lies (an excellent "pose" for the lowering of the stage curtain, as anyone who has attended *Camille, La Traviata,* or *La Bohème* realizes), the contrary emotions stirred by the novel's conclusion make us doubt whether either justice or mercy has seeped into the final frame of the story.

Maggie Johnson's death calls forth fewer questions about the author's intent than Lily's does since Stephen Crane's irony actively directs what he would have us believe: for example, an inverse of what Maggie's mother thinks heaven thinks of herself. In just such an intensely pictorial and emotionally heightened scene, however—with Mrs. Johnson calling upon God to witness her goodness and proclaiming the just punishment of her wicked child—Crane meets Wharton on the common ground of the "dramatical." Crane's characters, like Wharton's, are presented through a series of socially determined poses, theatrical performances, and marketing displays; both authors picture tragic lives played out in a series of "hilarious halls" and houses of mirth.

Lily and Maggie are for sale; they are defined as *shapes* their potential buyers dream about. Male dreams exert pressures which leave the young women little room to pursue their own dreams or to develop their own characters.[52] Lily and Maggie fail by necessity because they possess too much gracefulness (their attractive bodies) and an insufficiency of Grace (that force capable of withstanding the blunt push of other people's desires).

In contrast to Lily Bart and Maggie Johnson, Evelyn Nesbit was clearly a success—a "personality" at sixteen and a national scenic treasure at twenty-two when she held the stage of the popular press during the Thaw murder trial of 1907. Nesbit was always ready to pose for other men's dreams.[53] She could fall into the attitudes of "Dawn," "Innocence," "Tired Butterfly"—anything (see figures 10.10, 10.13–10.15). When Harry Thaw bought her as his wife, she furnished his twisted imagination with yet another image: Ideal Beauty threatened by Stanford White, the Beast. Generous to a fault when it came to giving men what they asked for, Nesbit also provided White with the image of grace he said he needed to counter the

15.29. Joshua Reynolds, "Joanna Leigh, Mrs. R. B. Lloyd" (c.1776).

disorder he found on all sides. White's designs for the new "cathedrals" such as Madison Square Garden required a new kind of Virgin, and Nesbit with her flowerlike fragility (one which had miraculously escaped the smear of the "mire" of rape by "the Beast") was just the one to assume that role. Evelyn Nesbit won a place of honor in the modern city, as Maggie Johnson, rose blooming in the mud, could not.

In many ways, Evelyn Nesbit's was the perfect image to take command of the new century, an era one observer characterized as like either devil or angel. Saint-Gaudens called Nesbit angel and snake and detested her for causing the death of his friend Stanford White,[54] but it was this mix of innocence and guile which guaranteed her the wide constituency of appeal needed for success. According to Michael Mooney, the chronicler of the obsessions that surrounded Nesbit's person, her triumph lay in her ability to absorb everyone's dreams and to deny no one. Freudians know that is exactly what dreams must do—contain no margin for "no." Nesbit was the perfect model and actress, a quick study who learned her lines and assumed her poses with the naturalness that comes through the habitual exercise of artful attitudes, as any Delsartean would tell you.

The final years of Evelyn Nesbit's life were not particularly bright. There are stories of alcoholism and drugs, dwindling income, and unsatisfactory relations with inadequate men—all the shabby details which satisfy decent folk who prefer that people who live without "no" come to a properly obscure and unhappy end. In this respect, Nesbit's career is similar to that of another actress who also possessed a notable talent for contradictory poses. That woman's name was Alma Stanley.[55]

Between 1893 and 1896 James McNeill Whistler worked on a pastel of Alma Stanley as she appeared in the 1893 production, "The Sleep Walker," a contemporary farce (figure 15.30). In Whistler's rendition of "Stanley the Actress," the subject is dressed entirely in black and stands before a gray background. The only touch of color to set off her white face is the purple flower crouched upon her shoulder. In 1898 during a visit to Melbourne, Stanley posed as Niobe for a local photographer (figure 15.31). Through typification, Whistler reduced Stanley's figure to an elegant design of uncluttered signification that qualifies the "realism" of the play (which Stanley seems to have misremembered as being titled "The Street Walker"). In contrast, the classical type of Niobe, the Suffering Mother, was turned by the stare of the camera's lens into an exasperatingly naturalistic record of a very particular woman's face and bust mounted precariously on a fake marble pedestal. Alma Stanley was not done as great a service by Talma of Melbourne as by James McNeill Whistler of London, but the fact remains that the actress had the ability to image both contemporary woman and mythic mother.

Miriam Rooth, the actress-heroine of Henry James' novel of 1890 *The Tragic Muse*, represents the Delsarte theory directly put into practice. Miriam will never end her life like Alma Stanley or Evelyn Nesbit, drunken, wayward, and out of the good graces of her public. But has Miriam a "character" of her own? Just about

15.30. James Abbott McNeill
Whistler, "Alma Stanley
in 'The Street Walker'[?]"
(pastel on paper,
(c.1893–1896).

MUSEUM OF FINE ARTS, BOSTON

With all love to dear Minnie.
Alma
TALMA   Copyright.   119 Swanston St.
        Melbourne. 1898.   Melbourne

MUSEUM OF FINE ARTS, BOSTON

15.31. Carte de visite of Alma
Stanley as "Niobe"
(1898).

everyone in the novel asks this question when they watch, astounded, a woman who is always posing, always a "spectacle."[56]

Miriam's face is a mobile mask that fits what the "occasion" suggests. Her "identity," based upon "reflection," "mirrors" the people who surround her. Without need for intellect or virtue, she controls the social situation and the theater stage by means of whatever "character" she assumes for the moment. Her peculiar talents are change, growth, and creativity performed within "vacancy." Her acting method is the traditional "system" of the "attitudes" through whose sequence she slips with the rapidity of Emma Hamilton's shawls or Loïe Fuller's veils. Miriam Rooth exists to "represent beauty and harmony." She stirs the spectators and joins them together as an audience. "Spectacle," "occasion," "reflection," "vacancy," "harmony": these are important terms for the defining of Miriam's success, but the words James applies most often to her are "possession" and "authority." Hers is the power to fill the "empty space" of the stage. By means of the "vacancy" of her face and the "blank" of the spectators' minds, Miriam possesses and commands.

As James sees it, the lives of Miriam and her audience are flooded by the image of the Ideal which comes on great wings down to the earth for all to see. Descriptions such as these are traditionally used to delineate the presence of divine Grace, but James knew the aptness of this language for the arts of an actress in motion.

James' Miriam Rooth is not the American Girl. Half-Jewish, half-English, her "occasions" are those of the London stage. Dreiser's Carrie Meeber is the fictional figure of the period who best defines the possibility for grace in the American context of display, spectacle, and melodrama. At first viewing, Carrie and Miriam seem alike. Both begin as a "half-equipped little knight . . . dreaming wild dreams of some vague, far-off supremacy." Thousands of pretty girls who come to the city from country towns have that much to start with and no more,[57] and Carrie never conveys the obsessive strength of will that characterizes Miriam from the start. What, then, makes Carrie stand out at a time when every attractive American girl seemed to be part of a nationwide contest to see who would be named the prettiest, smartest, most talented?[58]

Part of the answer comes from observations made by Alan Dale, the theater reviewer. French and English show girls have looks but only that, Dale states in "Stage Beauty and Brains," an essay he wrote for *The Cosmopolitan* in 1911.[59] American girls possess brains and astutely developed professional skills. They progress past prettiness to "personality" by means of a distinctive "trademark" that comes from something they *do* very well. By adding animation and humor to their performances, American girls insure themselves a future in a shifting world of display where the fickle public quickly rejects old favorites for new faces and talents.

Carrie Meeber has lovely eyes, a nice figure, excellent posture, the fresh bloom of youth, and a sure taste in clothes. Her instincts are elastic. She responds at once to accidental moods of the audience and converts them into attention directed toward herself. Onstage, her liveliness of spirit prevents her from becoming a thickening Lillian Russell, dragged down by inertia. These native talents are enough to transform Carrie Meeber into Carrie Madenda. They assure her a place as a popular member of the troupe and the status of a celebrity living nicely on credit in expensive hotel suites. These talents do not explain, however, the success that comes to her as an idol of the theater public. That merit comes because she represents for her watchers an image of grace, power, and revelation.[60]

A great deal has been written about Carrie's passivity, her blankness and lack of individuality, but these are precisely the traits that contribute to her impact. Carrie shares with Miriam Rooth the ability to mirror the world, one of the primary qualities of the notable stage presence. She lacks, however, the eccentricity, articulateness, and Old World street knowledge that make Miriam seem far more willstrong than sweet little Carrie. But Carrie's great gift is that she longs. Her own deep feelings and insatiable desires radiate from her large eyes and sad mouth; her face is always on the verge of tears. Although Carrie is capable of taking a variety of roles (a necessity for successful display artists)—from Quaker Girl to Harem

Beauty—her central role is the first one she ever played, on the night of the Elks Club benefit. She is forever Laura, the thwarted, put-upon heroine, the young woman who releases that intensity of feeling which most experts in the genre recognize as the mark of melodrama and the source of its ageless appeal.[61]

At the sound of her stage name Carrie started. She began to feel the bitterness of the situation. The feelings of the outcast descended upon her. She hung at the wing's edge, wrapt in her own mounting thought. She hardly heard anything more, save her own rumbling blood.

Already she was moving forward with a steady grace, born of inspiration. She dawned upon the audience, handsome and proud, shifting, with the necessity of the situation, to a cold, white, helpless object, as the social pack moved away from her scornfully.

Hurstwood blinked his eyes and caught the infection. The radiating waves of feeling and sincerity were already breaking against the farthest walls of the chamber. *The magic of passion, which will yet dissolve the world, was here at work.* (My italics)

Peter Brooks' study of the melodramatic imagination points with unswerving accuracy to the tokens by which we experience the world as melodrama.[62] They include the attempt to express the unspeakable; gestures that point beyond themselves and act as vehicles for mysterious forces; the impulse to image the sacred in a voided world; testimony to a spectacular virtue that astonishes its viewers; the hope that the world might one day become equal to our expectations; tragic moments served up in popular, democratic forms; enjoyment taken in the formalistic patterns of theatrical poses; the assurance that life can be made legible and "meanings represented"; the participation, however brief, in "the magic of passion, which will yet dissolve the world."

But the melodramatic imagination is also the faith that the world is constituted of justice and that all parties will get what they deserve before the evening's entertainment is over. During the course of the stage action, there is no mercy for the innocent while they struggle in the grip of the villains and no mercy for the villains once the innocent seize control. In a strictly melodramatic interpretation of "the universe of signs," there is no display of grace and little concern for its necessity.

As narrative form *Sister Carrie* is firmly founded upon the principles of the melodramatic imagination. As a character, Carrie Meeber is thereby held to its rules. But Carrie's own desires counter those expectations throughout the novel. In doing so, her desires match those of Theodore Dreiser. Like his fictional creation, Dreiser longs for *something more than justice*—and for the extraordinary power granted to anyone with the special talent for public expressions of the nature of longing.

In the privacy of her room (before her mirror and in her rocking chair), Carrie vaguely dreams of "the Other." The Other is what theologians more precisely (since it is their business to be precise) call Grace. In public, Carrie brings onto the stage her consummate talent for grace—the aura which includes, but is much more than, her talent for taste, style, and natural movement. For Carrie's face and figure carry the look of someone who wants grace—has the dream of something more—despite the world's determination (and determinism) to deny that dream and to exact justice instead.

At the time Dreiser's novel was published in 1900, the literal minded were scandalized. Dreiser had not punished Carrie for her immorality, and novels are bad when bad women are not made to face their just deserts. But Carrie's world—a place of true melodrama—*is* based upon justice. She gets exactly what she *deserves* as reward for her skills as a stage personality. She wins celebrity, material ease, and a smooth ride into a marketable future. But Carrie does not get what she *desires*—the mercy beyond understanding that would take her beyond longing for "the Other" into the state of otherness itself. Therefore, the novel gives us Carrie Madenda as Lucky Carrie, but also Carrie Meeber as Poor Carrie.

Carrie Madenda's success is the result of a clear transaction between her presence and her adoring attendants. During her stage appearances her mobile face and pliable body express the unspeakable for which her audiences long. She is to them the *sign* of Grace—on display, night after night, purchasable for the price of a theater ticket.[63]

Epilogue: Looking Back

In 1905 John White Alexander was awarded the largest mural commission yet given to an American artist. He was assigned the decoration of the main entrance hall of the Carnegie Institute of Pittsburgh, which was still undergoing expansion since its inception in 1895. In May of 1907 the art critic Charles Caffin wrote a review for *Harper's Monthly* assessing Alexander's The Crowning of Labor" which was shortly to become, "as everything else in the institution, 'free to the people.' "[1]

The pleasure Caffin expressed over the art forms he saw lavished upon the walls of the great hall of the Carnegie Institute, and the interpretation he brought to the allegorical figures, provide us with a singularly revealing record of the hopes held by Americans of Caffin's class and aesthetic bent, as well as the visual means by which they believed their cultural expectations would be met. For it was Caffin's faith that, even when an American artist had undergone the shock of having "seen Pittsburgh,"[2] he was inspired to envision a society that was "better" and "other" than the circumstances allowed. It was also Caffin's belief that vision would enfold the crucial symbol of mediation between what is and what ought to be—winged female forms soaring midway between men and the gods.

Caffin's *Harper's Monthly* review reiterates the principles by which Americans are encouraged to define the pluralism of their culture according to the type linked with the modern—that is, the universal joined to the specific. John Alexander is praised for having had "the courage and discretion to get away from the traditional device of embodying the city as a woman, recognizing that the labor of Pittsburgh is man's labor and typifying it by a man." (Caffin notes that "the male types represent a conception of the rights and possibilities of labor that is a part of our present-day understanding," whereas "the girl types are drawn from such as we can see around us.") The review approves of the fact that "Mr. Alexander has given an import that is partly American in its ideal and partly local to Pittsburgh." But what matters the most to Caffin is that Alexander's murals depict an industrialized nation whose dreams are defined by allegorical types that rise above and look beyond the disturbing, dismaying realities down below.

Charles Caffin muses over the extraordinary response the offerings of the Carnegie Institute have prompted from the people of Pittsburgh. Attendance figures at the various cultural attractions and enrollments in the classes sponsored by the institute are cited to verify the popular enthusiasm, but Caffin realizes that the "mind fails to grasp the significance" of any statistics, however impressive they may seem. "One falls back on one's imagination, which sometimes brings one nearer to understanding than will any process of thinking. And to me the spirit of it all was revealed one dull November evening, as I stood on the rolling hills of Schenley Park, within which the Institute is situated."

Charles Caffin, art critic and American idealist, mounts the heights above Pittsburgh. As he looks about him, he sees the modern city in all its gloom and terror.

Immediately about one it is drear—the grass colorless and thin in the grip of winter; twilight laying a chill, damp hand upon one's face; intermittent lights pricking the gloom that closes round one, creeping up, as it seems, from a murky pit below the hills. Down there is the city, metropolis of mines and rolling mills, of factories and warehouses, the heart of a huge arterial system of commerce throbbing through the lives of countless men and women. And spread low above them is a pall. It is the breath of their nostrils, mingled with the murk and grime from the bowels of the earth and smoke from the fire of their furnaces. One shudders; it is appalling, the reek of foulness suffocating the souls of men; one's eyes turn from it involuntarily and seek the cleanliness of the sky. But lo! a marvel!

Suddenly the reek and smoke of the pits and the "reflection of the setting sun" enfold one another. Together they create a great column of vapor that rises "until it trembles softly with color, like the neck of some beautiful bird, far above one. Gradually the vapor expands into a volume of body, dappled with the plumage of little clouds, dyed as with molten colors, while higher still spread innumerable pinions, floating, sweeping, eddying in a slow surge of movement, changing as they move to violet, saffron, rose, and golden glory."

In an apotheosis of pollution, the sky above the modern city becomes suffused "with glory, tumultous, serene, superb, and tender."[3] The vision has been made possible by the union of the darkness of the mills and the radiance of the sun. A vision "to be seen in Pittsburgh often by any one with eyes in his soul," it was the same sight which prompted, "one may believe, Mr. Alexander's decoration." This was not the Pittsburgh known to the Wobblies; nor was Alexander's art—or any art—the source of inspiration to workers for whom both life and art were "impossible" in the words of Bill Haywood, one of the organizers of the Industrial Workers of the World.[4] But Caffin expressed the views of many that the "art idea" exemplified by Alexander's Pittsburgh murals presented a real and possible modern America.

The laborers engulfed in the glory-touched column of vapor are part of Alexander's grand design (figure 1). Not design limited by definition to the aesthetic and the decorative, but design as an emotional and conceptual plan that encloses all elements within the sweep of its purpose and meaning. At its center is Pittsburgh, represented by a male in black armor suspended in flames and smoke (figure 2). The modern industrial city emerges together with the figures of the steelers from "the bowels of the earth" and "the fire of their furnaces." How unlike the city and the laborers in point of origin and beauty of form are the females which drift down from "the cleanliness of the sky" (figure 3). These "creatures of the upper air" function for industrial America in the same way as the dream houri promised to warriors willing to die for the cause of Islam or as the Queen of the Joust who bequeaths her favors to the champion of the medieval tourney. They bring "gifts of cunning craftsmanship from the looms, the workshops, and the studios of the world. Like swallows homing at twilight, they skim the air, and poise, and wheel. The smoke-wreaths have taken shape in draperies that cling to their lovely forms and stream below their feet in buoyant volumes."

Herbert Duce, the poster man from Chicago, struggled to find images that could redeem the contradictions of the modern commercial city. John White Alexander also sought a happy resolution of desires potentially in conflict. As Caffin phrases it, "For while the application of mental and physical labor to material results is typified by a man, the reward of labor in wealth of resources and in the grace and heightening of life is symbolized by beautiful maiden forms."

Looking beyond has mastered the present. The future is assured. All the American "Pittsburghs" (male and materialistic to the core of their smoky depths) are saved through the vision of grace conveyed by the American Girls swirling down from the skies.

Looking beyond in 1900 usually meant looking up and above to the realm of "the ideal" and "the other." Whatever the merits of the aspiring imagination as impetus for material progress, the cultural pressure it placed upon women in turn-of-the-century America was often retrogressive in effect. The theories of perception and cognition proposed by Charles Sanders Peirce and Josiah Royce were intended to lead to social behavior grounded in freedom and reason, but other notions added to the mix were restrictive and unreasonable. All too frequently American women were enclosed within signs that raised them into the stiffling empyrean whence come all good American Girls.

Spiritual expectations also had devastating effect on the prose style, early and late, of those who anxiously wished to keep women up and above. Eugene Benson's essay of 1866 is a good example of the verbal fervor with which "The 'Woman Question' " was approached by a man in the mid-nineteenth century who wishes

1. John White Alexander, from "The Crowning of Labor," (1906–1907).

MUSEUM OF ART, CARNEGIE INSTITUTE

to answer it once and for all. As Benson assesses the problem, women must be kept from locating themselves on earth.[5]

The being to many of us apparently purposeless, is more benevolent than she seems. She carries with herself *grace and light,* her very presence is a charm, her glance an illumination. *She contents herself with being like the breeze that scatters, careless and diffusive,* from horizon to horizon, the perfumes and exhalations of life. So much the worse for us if we have not felt *the sweetness and the charm of that ungraspable influence penetrate us, giving to our being new powers and new joys.* (My italics)

Those who retain "an exalted conception of women's place in society" receive the "new powers and new joys" of grace. But the cost to the "exquisite creature" whose mission is to transmit this grace is that she remains "like the breeze," "careless and diffuse," without the dimmest sense of what is going on. As described by

2. John White Alexander, "The Apotheosis of Pittsburgh," detail from "The Crowning of Labor" (1906–1907).

Benson's earnest prose, the eternal feminine is restricted to the light and air radiating from the "exalted conception" of womankind nurtured by the idealizing masculine imagination.

By 1899 the prose style used to place women had calmed down somewhat. To the audience of a magazine like *The Cosmopolitan*, the "exquisite creature" is

3. John White Alexander, "The Apotheosis of Pittsburgh," detail from "The Crowning of Labor" (1906–1907).

now "the womanly woman." But the language of an essay by Professor Harry Thurston Peck still cannot break past what the *men* are looking at.[6]

And as woman is to-day and as she has been in the past, so man would have her in the future. *He does not wish for the evolution of a new type* of motherhood that substitutes the formulated resolutions of a "woman's congress" for the old-time instinct of self-devotion and tenderness and unfailing love. He does not yearn for a new type of wifehood; *for he does not wish the sort of wife who would be a species of domestic comet, a dissolving view,* or even one whom he could borrow money of; but he wishes one who, in the good old way, will have no interest apart from his, and who if she sets up a possible ideal will seek to find it in such an exercise of the gifts that God has given her as will insure the greatest service to society, to the state, and to humanity at large, by sending forth into the world those who have known and felt the purifying and ennobling influence of a perfect home. (My italics)

Where the male eye places the woman differs somewhat in these two essays of 1866 and 1899. In the earlier view, the woman is a presence, an eidolon vaguely located in that ideal world of light and breeze traditionally associated with the realms of Grace. In the later view, the woman is solidly the wife and mother. She is very much of this world, although kept outside the workaday places where men borrow money from one another. Although still the source of "purifying and ennobling influence," she is not in heaven but in the home-as-heaven. What matters most is that she herself has no ideal of her own. If she had an ideal, she would be displaced from the male ken; she would transform herself into "a species of domestic comet, a dissolving view." Professor Peck wants to be able *to see* his women, not to have them evolve out of sight into a world of their own envisioning.

The Ladies' Home Journal of January 1908 also presents "the womanly woman" as looked at by male eyes. This time it is Charles W. Eliot, the president of Harvard, who does the seeing. Eugene Benson's timeless "exquisite creature" and Harry Thurston Peck's nonevolving "womanly woman" are now neatly classified as "the Normal American Woman."[7] Appropriate to the period's rage for scientism and statistics, Professor Eliot's sentences crisply define his subject as "a woman of good parts who marries at twenty-four or thereabouts, and brings up a family of five or six children" (themselves catalogued as "dutiful, thoughtful and loving").

Popular sentiment was prone to more verbal gush than Harvard's president allowed himself. The lyrics of the "mother songs" favored during the 1910s lagged well behind in the 1860s with Eugene Benson. But Professor Eliot could hardly fail to agree with the view upheld by merchandisers and consumers of the emotions on the issue of "The Picture the World Loves Best" (figure 4). Versions of this predictable image appeared on the sheet-music covers written in 1916 by Beth Slaton Whitson and of two ballads from 1920 and 1921 (figures 5 and 6). The woman as Mother was made in heaven, but hers was a heaven relocated "down here" in the American home. Neither Herbert Duce's billboards nor John White Alexander's wall murals were as good a place as the home for men who wanted to look beyond, yet keep the image of their desire clearly in view.

4. "The Picture the World Loves Best" (1916).

But turn-of-the-century American women were, after all, human, and humans are volatile and possess energies that roll away from under the idealizing thumb like pellets of mercury. The conservative imagination was in trouble once women began to unfix themselves from the conceptual containers set by posters, murals, and the home-hearth.

The sensible solution to the agitation resulting from conflicting notions about the woman's place would be for both sexes to coexist within the same world of perception and the contingencies. Such coexistence naturally necessitated an adjustment of the dominant sight lines. Ideality would have to be brought to the level of a reality that encompassed the desires of men and the aspirations of women. Alas, when men did lower their gaze, too often they perceived women as having been dragged into a life that was "sordid and common . . . ignoble and obvious."[8] Having looked too high for too long, by the 1910s it seemed as though men were compensating by "pitching [their] note . . . low." The social consequences were as silly and destructive as when their perceptions took them to heaven's gates.

5. "I'm in Heaven
   When I'm in
   My Mother's
   Arms" (1920).

Eddie Cantor turned his enormous eyes upon "the Modern Maiden" in the same year that the United States, led by Columbia the Warrior, entered the war meant to save Europe from its own moral baseness. According to the lyrics of the song Cantor sang for the 1917 *Ziegfeld Follies*, the old assumptions had been overturned. The new American Girl was what angels and "the normal woman" were never meant to be. "High" she was, but not in terms of virtuous elevation above the squalor of material greed. She was "high" in being a costly product for sale to big spenders. She was, in fact, Paul Bourget's scheming American Beauty of 1895 set on public view before the spotlights of the Broadway stage in 1917.

6. "Angels, We Call Them
   Mothers Down Here" (1921).

LILLY LIBRARY

Imagine if you can what it means to angels
To listen to the wants of a modern maid,
To fill the bill would tax most any angel,
And footing the same would break one, I am afraid,
In Heaven they must feel the cost of living,
You've got to figure it out this way, you know,
When things are high down here
Upon the earth, it's clear
They must be higher *there* than here below:
CHORUS: Give me a lot of beaux
And lots of pretty clothes,
Give me a Pekinese
And seats for all the shows,
Give me a millionaire
To fall in love with me,
Take me to Rector's, pay the collectors,
One of those purely platonic protectors,

Give me a Limousine
And diamonds like a queen,
Give me most anything else you have to spare,
Give me the boy that I am after,
Let me retain my girlish laughter,
That's the Twentieth Century Maiden's Pray'r.[9]

Ahead lay 1931 and another ballad presented during the *Ziegfeld Follies'* annual attempt at "Glorifying the American Girl." (figure 7). The modern maiden of 1931 does not even expect an answer to her prayer (whose refrain, according to the directions, is sung "slow with earnestness"). No more was the nameless heroine of Bett Hooper's novel of the same year able to hope that prayers would save her from the fate of becoming Everyman's sexual hot-water bottle (see figure 5.23).

I am one of the hicks,
That came here from the sticks,
Trying to find the kind of fame, the name of Broadway stands for.
I am one of those fools that dreamed of riches and jewels,
But now I awake,
Find my mistake,
Can't get a break,
Broadway's a fake.
REFRAIN: I work in a "speak" that's dim and dingy
Where spenders are pretenders, cheap and stingy,
All I smell is rotten Scotch and gin, gee,
Cigarettes, Cigars!
Now I've learnt what smoking "coke" and "snow" means,
'Mong the bums who never learnt what "no" means,
Who ask me do I know what making dough means;
Cigarettes, Cigars!
To heaven I just sent up my lonely plea,
Is this where I must end up—
Oh, good Lord, answer me?
Ev'ry morning as the nighttime dies out,
I walk home to sleep and weep my eyes out;
Can't you hear a broken heart that cries out,
Cigarettes, Cigars![10]

This is the American Girl of 1931 set to words and music—another version of the working women John Sloan depicted back in 1909 in his painting "Three A.M." (figure 8). None were the American Girl men wanted to see when they lifted their eyes up to heaven, but they were the type of woman men found when they looked straight into the midst of the society of the new century.

George Parsons Lathrop and Will H. Low were practicing artists of the minor ranks during the final years of the nineteenth century. As your average artist chaps, they would not be expected to come forth with profound insights when they con-

7. Alberto Vargas, "Cigarettes, Cigars!" *Ziegfeld Follies* (1931).

tributed two of the "discussions on American art and artists" gathered in a book of that title in 1893. Their comments are not the full-grown trees of systematic argument, but they still offer some sturdy underbrush concerning the relations affecting an artist's desire, the images he forms, and the models and media he uses. Lathrop's comments confirm the continuing importance of the type, and Low's go further to suggest what happens to the nature of images based on type once the female subject chooses to *look back* at the male whose intention is to dream her into a settled place in his own scheme of things.

Lathrop's essay "My Favorite Model" skims through the opinions of several dozen

8. John Sloan, "Three A.M."
(1909).

PHILADELPHIA MUSEUM OF ART

of his artist friends. He makes no real attempt to specify the rules by which artists select their models or how they employ them in the studio as stimulation for the imagination. His airy dismissal of the layperson's natural interest in how artists carry out their work is exasperating at first glance.[11] Nothing of note occurs in the way of artists' seeing and thinking, he asserts. Be content to think that they pass their time "at hazard"—"taking a walk along the street or in the country, a stroll through 'society,' or, for that matter, *making an excursion into dreamland*" (my italics). He concludes, "Is not the world of art, in a fine and lofty way, something like a masquerade?"

There is, however, something useful kerneled inside Lathrop's remarks. Yes, young men growing up into their profession during the 1890s are apt to shrug off the old-

9. "Magdalen," from a painting by Murillo and photographs of Miss Teresa Vaughan and Miss Estella Clayton, from Low, "Contrasts of Life and Art" (1893).

From a photograph of Miss Teresa Vaughan.

From a painting by Murillo.

" MAGDALEN."

From a photograph of Miss Estelle Clayton.

fashioned demand for "truths." Yes, they prefer to believe that the images they create are essentially pleasing dreams and playful make-believe. Still, those images do not originate in mental chaos, nor result in idle marks upon the world's wall. Images follow discernible patterns. They inscribe their signature across the objects through which the artist makes his dreams visible. In Lathrop's words, "Who . . . has not been struck by the fact that in all of any one person's work *there is usually some prevailing type.*"

Will H. Low's essay "Contrasts of Life and Art" moves in a different direction from Lathrop's. Lathrop had lingered with the notion that models are simply the convenient means by which artists express the typical forms they favor most. By contrast, Low's interest lies in the question of *whose desire* (that of the artist or that of the model) is expressed by the different representational media of the painting and the photograph.

Low's little exercise in comparing models painted and models photographed goes this way. He reproduces a series of paintings of a female figure. Next to each painting he places photographs of models who assume the same pose (figure 9). Then Low examines the differences between the two sets of images in regard to the degree of "reality" and "beauty" found in each example—a particularly intriguing matter when, as here, fantasies of penitence are involved.

Low immediately grants the dissimilarities between paintings done strictly in the realistic mode and those that follow the traditions of ideal art.[12] But he is most intrigued by the fact that the impress of the model's presence in the studio alters when the medium is a photograph. He allows that the photographer's model is to some extent "merged in the character portrayed," but his final contention is that her "type" (to use Low's term) finally asserts itself and takes command of the resulting image. The woman is *there,* not *beyond* in some imaginative region governed by the artist's mind.

The conclusion Low reaches at the end of his little experiment in artistic forms is this: a photograph contains the model's look and her individuality; a painting represents the artist's desire and the dream he has converted into his reality.

Low elaborates, and usefully, on his insight. When photographed, the model remains herself, able to resist whatever "strong idea" the man with the camera may have in mind. It is *her* appearance, *her* personality, *her* type, which finally constitute the picture's subject. Low maintains it is quite different when it comes to paintings. In that artistic medium, "where action or strong emotion is to be expressed, the quality must, in almost any case, reside in the painter and be expressed by him on the canvas." That is, whenever the artist's aim is to represent his own emotions—the reality shaped around his desires—he turns to the canvas as the place to fix his model's image. Under those conditions, the personality of his hired help undergoes "a complete submission" to his will. Her nature is absorbed "into the exact sentiment of the figure represented." She no longer has the power to distract the artist from matching the image on the canvas with the idea in his mind.[13]

Will Low's observations have to be qualified, of course. They are somewhat narrow and a bit naïve. There has been sufficient evidence throughout this book to indicate the proclivity of photographers to create dreams every bit as much as painters do. On the other hand, we ought not to assume in haste that artists (whether wielding camera, brush, or sculptor's mallet) are Svengalis who impose their desires upon passive subjects; not when both parties to the exchange participate to some extent in the images taken and given from the existing supply of accepted poses and activated memories of past pictures. Nor should we seize upon Lathrop's and Low's generalizing remarks and convert them into absolute statements about the nature of gender relations in the studio, thereby splitting the product that results into opposed components: *male* (what artists do) and *female* (what is done to models).[14]

What we take away from the little essays by George Parsons Lathrop and Will H. Low is the reminder that a significant relationship links the one who does the looking and the one who is looked at. Notwithstanding the variables which shift and heave from instance to instance, the initiator of the interlocked process of perception, identification, interpretation, and conceptualization leads the action. *When* it is a man who perceives and a woman who is his subject, and when he sees her as an ideal or as the betrayer of ideality, and when he misreads the signs of her will-strong bottom-nature, then it is time to urge the women to do something to counter that look of command. But how can this resistance be possible if women have learned to acquiesce to male dreams?

By the 1910s American women tended to be freer in their behavior than during the previous decades, but they frequently followed what Elémire Zolla calls the necessity to conform voluntarily in spite of the absence of any official demand to do so.[15] Zolla's observation is prompted by his attempt to define the nature of images that remain committed to one set of dreams or another. He suggests that the study of national cultures indicates that members of large social units thrive on archetypes—images emanating from personal dream worlds of "entrancement," "magic," and "swoon" that possess the power to fix people in their grip. Groups "caught in the web of manifold, benumbing appearances" can undergo "a startling, fearsome reversal of their stiff, fragile, thoughtless, clumsy habits and persuasions," but this jolting reversal merely indicates that old archetypes have been replaced by new ones. Dreams, and the looks that nourish them, continually shift up and down, back and forth, leading nowhere.

In recent essay Nancy Miller argues that traditional literature failed, and continues to fail, to inscribe the true presence of women.[16] Taking the nineteenth-century novel as her particular case in point, Miller finds that this literary form supported accepted ideas about the representation of life by art. "Plausibility" (the truth test) was twisted to accommodate "propriety" (public opinion). (Neither, of course, would meet the criteria for the clear ideas—the Reality—advocated by Charles Sanders Peirce.) The determination of literary norms was the work of mid-nineteenth-century males who decided which type of woman stood for the sign of masculine dreams. As the consequence, women were not encouraged to do their own writing—their own "looking"—at dreams they possessed for themselves. They gained entrance into the official literature only as types, or as the purveyors of types, that conformed to whatever satisfied men.

Miller characterizes male dreams as consisting of ego, ambition, and eroticism. All are variations on the nature of power. Miller further contends that women still have to go silently into the night dreams of the masculine social imagination if they hope for inclusion within the literary canon. But Miller detects a female literature that then and now counters male dreams with its own desires, running like still waters beneath the surface of the acceptable. Men's dreams keep power in their hands and women in their places through the insistence that love is a woman's sole concern. But no, Miller states, women's dreams are—extravagantly so—about being "something else" than what men want them to be. Their dreams are about the usurpation of power, even if it entails their death, as in the case of "the drowning women" we saw floundering in chapter 8.

As we leave Miller's argument and its many examples drawn from the nineteenth-century imaging of women, the thought occurs how nice it would be if women could have more power and not so much death. Otherwise, the world war which came to *its* conclusion in 1918 was simply replaced by yet another power struggle that continues to this day.

The study of how women differ from men has become a major source for scholarly and polemical activities that refuse to abide by the old rules of setting up separate spheres or privileged canons. Its primary purpose is to refute the notion that men exist "down here" and women "up there." For as long as that conceptual division dominates, men can the more easily control the morally inferior world where historically superior things are taking place, while women are assigned the boring task of tending superior realms and leading inferior lives.

Not surprisingly, scholars are currently working with data that either emphasize the effects of traits that are biological and innate or that stem from habits that are cultural and acquired. Nor is it unexpected that some are interpreting the evidence in order to argue for a radical overthrow of the bad old situation that would push men into the lower depths of social and intellectual worth and put

10. Irma Purman and friends
(c.1912).

women on top as the sole controllers of the future. But the most absorbing of the recent analyses are contributed by anthropologists, biologists, and sociologists who have faith in, not scorn for, the differences which mark the sexes, while avoiding the dangers of the separate-but-equal line of argument.

Under scrutiny in the area of physiology and neurology are gender differentiations in mathematical skills, spatial perceptions, manual dexterity, memory retention, sensory sensitivity, and the relative strength of various parts of the body. For their part, psychologists are reexamining the old canards about male logic and female intuition. There is also an increased interest in finding out whether women possess distinctive patterns of verbalization and whether their sight is governed by factors different from those that control the way men see.

Exciting times lie ahead as the new women and new men of the current generation of scholars rearrange the scattered pieces of the epistemological process that might one day advance us all toward Peirce's final goal of a commonly perceived Reality. Let us trust that the ways by which women and men have been assigned different identities and apportioned different desires during particular periods in the nation's history will provide a useful basis for any rethinking of the nature of American culture, past and present. One question that should not be overlooked when conducting such appraisals is this: can women who have been *looked at* for too long ever master the art of *looking back?*

Sometimes the images created by the eye of the commercial illustrator or photographer are relatively neutral in meaning. The basic information the pictorializers distribute encourages viewers to speculate freely. Figure 10 is such an image. Eight young women, in their late teens and early twenties, line up for a photograph around 1912. Insofar as it is a bit unclear whether the women or their hats count the most, this is a picture the editors of fashion magazines like *The Delineator* could use for showing off the newest trends. On the other hand, it can be taken as a mood piece, evoking the pleasure of watching Girls in Their Summer Dresses. Or it might merit analysis by social historians studying the nuances of accepted female display in 1912: the exposure of ankles, the slender but uncorseted waistlines, the simple hairstyles. It is a photograph that feminist historians could cite as evidence of the important sisterly bonding young women experience during the interim before marriage. It might even occasion socioeconomic readings in light of what is *not* on view, since these are not factory workers, urban dwellers, newly arrived immigrants, activists in the cause of suffrage, or members of the deserving poor. From a very personal perspective, it allows a daughter to see what her mother (third from the right) looked like when only twenty but already in possession of a bottom-nature that would remain extraordinarily unaltered in the years (often very difficult, very sad) that lay ahead. But all in all, this photograph is essentially pictorialization of the dreamless sort. It is basically no more (although certainly not less) than an image of one group of New Women who were on the verge of deciding (and having decided for them) what all their newness would come to.

Figure 11 is one of the series of drawings Charles Dana Gibson prepared in 1901 for his picture narrative *A Widow and Her Friends*. The caption for this frame reads, "She is disturbed by a vision which appears to be herself." The widow has been kneeling in prayer, seeking counsel as to whether she ought to remarry. (The mats by the side of the beds of young American women in those days must have been worn threadbare from all the kneeling and praying we have seen depicted throughout this book.) Suddenly she is visited by a wretched wraith. Does this ghostly figure represent the bride she once was who covers her face in shame to think the widow would betray her vows of eternal fidelity to her first and only true love? Or does the vision weep for the future woe the widow will reap if she remarries? The first interpretation supports the male fantasy that requires self-sacrifice of widows unfortunate enough to outlive their husbands. The second suggests a female's fear and need for acts of self-preservation. Whichever omen the vision represents, Gibson's widow resolves her dilemma by becoming a nun—one of those "exquisite creatures" who attain elevation above earthly matters by pledging themselves as Brides of Christ. The widow will no longer be pressured to marry by the silly males who trail after her throughout the rest of Gibson's drawings for this *Life* story-in-sequence, but she wins only by disengaging herself from the conflict.[17] Her dream-vision has prompted her to remove herself from the world—our world—of male and female desires.

Coles Phillips designed the cover for the October 12, 1911, issue of *Life* (figure 12). "The Light Housekeeper" is ready with wedding ring, cookbook, spoon, bowl, milk bottle, apron, and a frown which can be taken in several ways but is not meant to be taken seriously in any case. This is neither Widow nor Nun but the Normal Woman who has yet to learn how "reasonable" Professor Charles W. Eliot

11. Charles Dana Gibson, "She is disturbed by a vision which appears to be herself," *Life*, June 27, 1901.

12. Coles Phillips, "The Light Housekeeper," *Life*, October 12, 1911.

13. McDougall, "Our Sweet Girl Graduates of 1895," *New York World*, June 23, 1895.

considers her position to be in a male society. Alas, she has nothing of her own mind's creation with which to counter abject normalcy. Although she looks back at her viewer, that look conveys no force. It is "light" indeed.

What, then, about images evidently meant to signal the New Woman? Will they have the right look? Figure 13 comes from the *New York World* of 1895, which finds it easy to satirize "Sweet Girl Graduates" educated for the express purpose of taking men's jobs away from them. Crisply drawn, sharply etched, these figures promote the slick bias by which the *World* can prophesy a future in which females are neither nuns nor housekeepers nor true women.

Inadvertently, the *World* pictures women of the type who will take command of their destinies like the heroine of Edna Ferber's 1917 novel *Fanny Herself* (figure

14). The caption (confirming the meaning of the Delsartean pose) reads, "Fanny's hands became fists, gripping the power she craved. 'Then I shall have arrived!' " This, we can say, is *a woman's dream* receiving its full expression at last, in picture and in text. The image has the look about it of a vision which sends the woman's gaze upward toward her own future.

Indeed, the career of Fanny Brandeis McChesney (to which Edna Ferber devoted four novels) moves her past a brief, unhappy first marriage, through struggles as a single mother and resentments over advances by ever-present mashers, to become first a smashingly successful drummer of women's underwear and finally the head of her company's sales and promotion department. But once Fanny slides into the arms of the perfect husband and lover, her woman's dreams of power are subverted by female dreams of romance. Fanny as conquering hero is reabsorbed into the official literature where (according to Nancy Miller's thesis) a woman's view of herself is forced to conform to the dictates of the male imagination.

Ruth Eastman prepared a cover for the May 1919 issue *Motor* (figure 15). It seems to depict a woman in possession of her own best dream which, as we all know, is to be capable of servicing her own automobile. But this is a girl who is very pretty in the accepted manner of the late 1910s, and one who is obviously posed according to the convention of "draperies in action." This image has little to do with the realities of dusty back-country roads. It certainly lacks the conviction of a woman with expertness at the jack and wrench. In place of the tools of command, a glance is cast upon the viewer that is more coy appeal than cool self-reliance. The Eastman image is merely a fashionable updating of the True Woman, as appropriate for a motoring magazine in which male fantasies of power juxtapose handsome automobiles with pretty women as, say, "September Morn" is for the wall of the mechanic's shop.[18]

Figure 16 is one of a group of photographs taken in 1909 of Cincinnati suffragists posed (to quote the caption) "to illustrate the woman police concept." A woman rigged out in costume is trying to imagine what it might be like to take over a traditional male role. But her hairdo (arranged in careful accommodation to the stiff policeman's hat) and the meticulous regimental detailing on the skirt pull her image toward the dream realm of women's fashion magazines or a Gilbert and Sullivan parody of Princess Ida as bobby. Figure 17 is a tableau that portrays the Delsartean attitude for "I have you!" as the make-believe policewoman apprehends the villainous culprit. If we could see the face of the second woman who is costumed here as a male criminal, we might not even think her skilled enough in her role to fit Cesare Lombroso's physiognomical category "the Female Offender." This photograph does better duty as an allegory of Law Victorious Over Crime than as a historical document about policewomen in the act of performing their duty. It remains, first to last, a conceptualization of "how woman policeman would look making an arrest." (A visual look, only; verbalization of the concept has not moved past the coinage "woman policeman.") These two photographs remind us of the consequences when, through lack of opportunity, women had to struggle even *to*

14. J. Henry, "Fanny's hands became fists, gripping the power she craved. 'Then I shall have arrived!' " from Ferber, *Fanny Herself* (1917).

15. Ruth Eastman, *Motor*, May 1919.

16. "The woman 'cop' (a dream)" (1909).

think how they might look if the day ever came when they too could assume the poses their society had allocated to men alone.

It is true that within nine years after the Cincinnati suffragists tried to discover the right images to represent their dreams of authentic power, women were enrolled in the ranks of the police reserves, one of the traditionally male occupations women were called to fill during World War I. News photographs show the uniformed reservists marching down Fifth Avenue on Armistice Day 1918. A dream has come partially true; a concept is transformed into a near approximation of the real thing. But only briefly. The men return from Europe. Women police reservists, subway guards, defense factory workers, and farm help are no longer needed or wanted in areas of male employment. Many of the New Women stop going forward with the currents set in motion by the war. They retreat once more into lives of going up or going down. Once again they are vulnerable to the looks of men whose dreams are in control.

17. "How woman policeman would look making an arrest" (1909).

LIBRARY OF CONGRESS

I conclude this book filled with hundreds of visual instances of female forms with six final examples. They are the doing of a representative group of male artists: Charles Dana Gibson, Coles Phillips, John Sloan, Thomas Eakins, Alfred Stieglitz, and Merle Smith of Montpelier, Indiana. What is arresting is that all but one of the young women are shown in the act of *looking back*. Even more arresting, only one of those looking back does it with effect.

In 1905 Gibson sketched the American Girl in an artist's studio (figure 18). Since her command to the sitter—"Keep still, please"—is the same one that women heard

18. Charles Dana Gibson, "Keep Still, Please," *Collier's Weekly*, April 29, 1905.

rather too often in those days, it is nice to see that the Girl is now on the artist's stool, holding her brush like a miniature rapier. But since the portrait she draws is decidedly not the Gibson Man, she is hardly creating a figure of her own desire, one capable of thwarting the hopes of all the foolish, ordinary-looking men in the world. She remains the figment of the male viewer's own fantasy that such a "looker" might conceivably pay *him* her attention. Once again, the Gibson Girl in her charm and compliancy stays well within the boundries set by the male perspective.

Coles Phillips' cover design of *Life* of 1909—"From the Mirror"—is a still weaker version of the Gibson motif (figure 19). The standardized prettiness of the Phillips Girl's face, the checked gingham of her milkmaid frock, the heart-shaped cutouts on the bench where she sits, and the narcissism of the endlessly regressing series of self-reflecting images lessen whatever counterforce this image of *a woman looking* might convey. Since she is looking at herself reflected mirrorlike in her viewer's eyes, she is mere pose and no substance.

19. Coles Phillips, "From the Mirror," *Life*, August 19, 1909.

John Sloan's 1915 watercolor "The Bachelor Girl" would seem to provide the image we seek, but not entirely (figure 20). Independent creator of her own dreams, this working woman is still not fully on her own or fully complete. First, Sloan's title repeats a convenient classification of the day. By 1915 the Bachelor Girl was as much a type as the Beautiful Charmer or the Outdoors Pal, although a type denoting one of the New Women entering the work force as a self-supporting individual. Second, the figure is viewed according to the pictorial conventions of perspective laid down in the Italian Renaissance by whose rules viewers master the scene by looking at it as through an open window or peephole. Third, the young woman is apparently a disciple of Madame Merle's theories of the power of

20. John Sloan, "The Bachelor
   Girl" (watercolor drawing)
   (1915).

21. Thomas Eakins, "Portrait of
   Margaret Eakins" (c.1880).

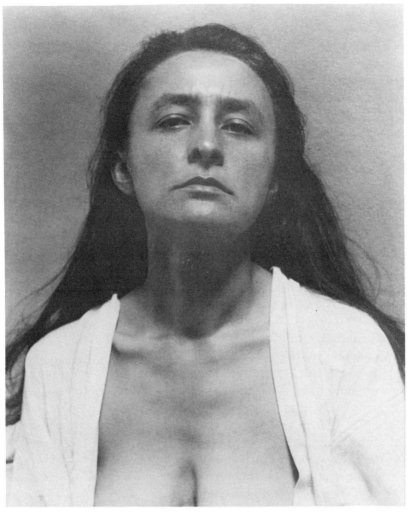

22. Alfred Stieglitz, "Georgia O'Keeffe" (1918).

social convention. She contemplates the dress which is part of her appearance be-fore the world, one of the mirroring signs by which she is known to others. Fourth, she is alone with herself, looking only at herself; we are given no evidence of how capable she is at dealing in power relations once someone else enters her line of vision. All this is well enough. This book has indicated that American women of will and self-possession could, indeed, not only survive but even thrive under such conditions. They could establish the reality of their presence in terms of prevailing conventions of type, or of pictorial perspective, or of dress and pose, and they often did it best during moments of private self-contemplation. But one element of im-portance is missing from Sloan's scene: the Bachelor Girl's necessary confrontation with society that requires from her a look to meet the looks imposed upon her.

Margaret Eakins stares sullenly back at the camera held by her brother Thomas, and Georgia O'Keeffe defiantly takes on the photographer's eye of Alfred Stieglitz (figures 21 and 22). Such looks dare male viewers either to elevate or to lower these women past the level of their own stubbornly self-protected natures. But these are photographs of women essentially on the defensive against the men in charge. They do not possess a weapon of their own for the social engagements into which they must advance in confidence if they are to be New Women for the new century.

There is no guarantee that the photograph taken by Merle Smith of my mother offers a better demonstration than the views by Gibson, Phillips, Eakins, or Stie-glitz of a look capable of countering the perceptions and conceptualizations that limited the women of her generation (figure 23). This 1916 photograph is a con-ventional "going on holiday" pose, complete with massively male golf clubs. The pose had been familiar in newspapers and magazines through Eastman Kodak ads of the Girl with the Brownie. Because of the details devoted to the suit-tailoring, the lace at the neck, and the intricately embellished hat, it might serve as a fash-ion-magazine illustration. But this photograph has something else that perhaps moves it beyond weak conventionality.

It was not in my mother's nature to express her very strong, very private char-acter in overtly pictorial terms or aggressively dramatic attitudes. During the world war that lay just ahead, she would have made a poor poster image for a Liberty with sword raised on high. But what is nice about this photograph is that—al-though it is only one of the scores of occasions she faced a camera once she had been classified as the Town Beauty by the age of sixteen—she at last, at the age of twenty-four, picks up her own camera and aims it directly at the man with the camera. She is about to push the button, to activate the trigger of the image-making weapon she holds. Reciprocal energy is released through this double image of perception and thought, action and counteraction. It is a small statement she makes here, and a quiet one, but her steady gaze says clearly enough, "Look, I can do it too!"

23. Irma Purman Banta (c.1916).

Notes

Introduction: Object, Image, Type, and the Conduct of Life

1. Consuelo Vanderbilt (1877–1964) was about ten years old when photographed. Married in 1895 to the ninth duke of Marlborough, she was separated from him in 1906. In 1921 she married Jacques Balsan.

2. Gertrude Lynch, "Racial and Ideal Types of Beauty." The quotations that follow are from pp. 223–224, 228, 231, 233.

3. Howard Chandler Christy, *The American Girl*, p. 12.

4. Henry James, *The Portrait of a Lady*, pp. 287–288.

5. The following analyses and sources provide the contexts for my discussion of Peirce and Royce, both in this chapter and chapters 9–10: Peirce, *Charles Sanders Peirce: Selected Writings*; Karl-Otto Apel, *Charles S. Peirce: From Pragmatism to Pragmaticism*; Frederick Copleston, *A History of Philosophy*; Walter Benn Michaels, "The Interpreter's Self: Peirce on the Cartesian 'Subject' "; Vincent G. Potter, *Charles S. Peirce: On Norms and Ideals*; Peter Fuss, *The Moral Philosophy of Josiah Royce*; Royce, *The Basic Writings of Josiah Royce*; Royce, *The Letters of Josiah Royce*; Royce, "Later Problems of Idealism and Its Present Position"; Ralph Barton Perry, *Present Philosophical Tendencies*.

It must be noted that there are several subtexts to the theoretical positions held by Peirce and Royce. One is provided by the feminist activities of Melusina Fay Peirce, who was married to Peirce between 1862 and 1875. See Dolores Hayden, *The Grand Domestic Revolution*, pp. 67–89. Another is an unsigned piece addressed to the Contributors' Club of *The Atlantic Monthly* (July 1906), 98:136–139, titled "Women and Woman." This entry takes the issue of the social impact of language usage directly into the feminist political arena by examining the advantages and disadvantages of the words "female" (a sex), "woman" (an abstraction), and "women" (an immediacy of reference).

6. Neil Harris, introduction to his *The Land of Contrasts*, pp. 14–15.

7. In "The Conception of God" in 1907 and the Gifford Lectures of 1900–1901 Royce argued that God alone is the perfect viewer and interpreter of "the picture." "Topics in Psy-

chology of Interest to Teachers" is contained in Royce's unpublished papers in the Harvard University archives and quoted by permission of Houghton Library. Pagination is taken from Peter Fuss, *The Moral Philosophy of Josiah Royce*, pp. 61–62, 74, 92. Royce's advice to teachers is adumbrated by the 1898 *Teacher's Manual* published by the Prang Educational Company of Boston, edited by John S. Clark and others, for the art training of elementary schoolchildren. Teachers were to instruct students in the drawing of "Type Forms," thereby awakening and directing the childrens' powers of idealization to definite ends or purposes. In 1896 Clark delivered a paper before the Pratt Institute titled "The Study of Type Forms and Their Value in Education," which Prang printed as a pamphlet in 1898.

8. The incident cited by Royce is analogous to what Henry James' heroines Isabel Archer and Daisy Miller in their ignorance initially get away with upon meeting the lions of life before they are attacked by those "signs" against which they have failed to develop protective "habits of conduct." Isabel and Daisy possess certain powers because they are not wise enough to be afraid, but also because their interpretants (particularly the males) misread the signs these young women manifest. By conceiving of Daisy and Isabel as "mere women," Winterborne—and Osmond (for a time)—are vulnerable to the force exerted by these American Girls. But the time comes when Daisy and Isabel, "named" by their social interpretants as dangerous types, are turned upon and quelled.

9. Frank Stockton's 1884 short story "The Lady or the Tiger?" achieved phenomenal popularity by posing this essential question.

10. Peter Fuss provides a highly useful review and analysis of the importance Royce placed upon the initial choice of images which thereafter help to shape all future social behavior. Chs. 3–5, *The Moral Philosophy of Josiah Royce*.

11. The bibliography (both primary and secondary) for the relation of women, home, and child-rearing is massive. The following partial list contains no consensus on the question whether nineteenth-century American mothers were providing necessary moral training; more often than not the essays and books express concern over the breakdown of the female model. Jane Addams, "Filial Relations"; "The American Ideal Woman," *Putnam's Monthly*; "As a Bachelor Sees Women," *The Ladies' Home Journal*; J. W. Bennett, "Your True Relation to Society"; Eugene Benson, "The 'Woman Question' "; Hjalmar Hjorth Boyesen, "German and American Women"; William H. Chafe, *Women and Equality: Changing Patterns in American Culture*; Mary Roberts Coolidge, *Why Women Are So*; Carl N. Degler, *At Odds: Women and the Family in America from the Revolution to the Present*; Margaret Deland, "The Change in the Feminine Ideal"; Frank A. DePuy, *The New Century Home Book: A Mentor for Home Life in All Its Phases*; Barbara Ehrenreich and Deirdre English, *For Her Own Good: 150 Years of the Experts' Advice to Women*; Charles W. Eliot, "The Normal American Woman"; Charlotte Perkins Gilman, *The Home: Its Work and Influence*; C. P. Gilman, *The Man-Made World, or Our Androcentric Culture*; C. P. Gilman, *Women and Economics*; Robert Grant, *The Art of Living*; Dolores Hayden, *The Grand Domestic Revolution*; Emma Churchman Hewitt, "The 'New Woman' in Her Relation to the 'New Man.' "

Prince Böjidar Karageorgevitch, "The Perversion of the Infant Mind in Matters of Taste"; David M. Katzman, *Seven Days a Week: Women and Domestic Service in Industrializing America*; Mary Holland Kinkaid, "The Feminine Charms of the Woman Militant"; Christopher Lasch, *Haven in a Heartless World*; Mary A. Livermore, *What Shall We Do with Our Daughters?*; Harry W. McVickar, *The Evolution of Woman*; Orison Swett Marden, *Woman and Home*; Maxine L. Margolis, *Mothers and Such: Views of American Women and Why They Changed*; Elaine Tyler May, *Great Expectations: Marriage and Divorce in Post-Victorian America*; Harry Thurston Peck, "For Maids and Mothers"; Stow Persons, *The Decline of American Gentility*; Carroll Smith-Rosenberg, *Disorderly Conduct*; Anna Garlin Spencer, *Women's Share in Social Culture*; Caroline Ticknor, "The Steel-Engraving Lady and the Gibson Girl"; "Topics of the Times—Home and Society," *Scribner's Monthly Magazine*; Virginia Tufte and Barbara Myerhoff, eds., *Changing Images of the Family*; Barbara Welter, *Dimity Convictions: The American Woman in the Nineteenth Century*; Margaret Gibbons Wilson, *The American Woman in Transition; The Woman's Book*.

12. This and the following quotation are from Royce's *The Basic Writings of Josiah Royce*, "The Religious Problem and the Theory of Being" (1899), pp. 475, 485.

13. The following are among the works which give information about and/or the flavor of the art training experienced by Americans during the final decades of the nineteenth century: Linda Ayres, "The American Figure: Genre Paintings and Sculpture," pp. 41–83; S. G. W. Benjamin, "Tendencies of Art in America—Part I"; *Book of American Figure Painters*; Richard J. Boyle, *American Impressionism*; David A. Brown, *Raphael and America*; William C. Brownell, "The Younger Painters of America—First Paper" and "Second Paper"; Kenyon Cox, *Artist and Public and Other Essays on Art Subjects*; K. Cox, *The Classic Point of View*; K. Cox, *Concerning Painting: Considerations Theoretical and Historical*; K. Cox, *Old Masters and New*; K. Cox, *Painters and Sculptors*; Margaret French Cresson, *Journey Into Fame: The Life of Daniel Chester French*; David H. Dickason, *The Daring Young Men: The Story of the American Pre-Raphaelites*; John H. Dryfhout, *The Work of Augustus Saint-Gaudens*; Charles C. Eldredge, *American Imagination and Symbolist Painting*; Lois M. Fink and Joshua C. Taylor, *Academy: The Academic Tradition in American Art*; Mrs. Daniel Chester (Mary) French, *Memories of a Sculptor's Wife; From Realism to Symbolism: Whistler and His World*, essays by Theodore Reff and Allen Staley; William H. Gerdts, *American Impressionism*; W. H. Gerdts, introduction, *The White, Marmorean Flock: Nineteenth-Century American Women Neoclassical Sculptors*; Kathryn Greenthal, *Augustus Saint–Gaudens. Master Sculptor*; Neil Harris, "The Gilded Age Reconsidered Once Again"; Gordon Hendricks, *The Life and Works of Thomas Eakins*; Patricia Hills, *Turn-of-the-Century America*; Donelson F. Hoopes, *American Narrative Painting*; Samuel Isham, *The History of American Painting*; Henry James, *William Wetmore Story and His Friends*; James J. Jarves, *The Art Idea: Sculptors, Painting, and Architecture in America*; Estelle Jussim, *Slave to Beauty: The Eccentric Life and Controversial Career of F. Holland Day*; Sylvester Rosa Koehler, *American Art*; S. R. Koehler, *American Etchings*; S. R. Koehler, "The Future of Art"; John La Farge, "The Field of Art: The American Academy at Rome"; Oliver W. Larkin, *Art and Life in America*; T. J. Jackson Lears, *No Place of Grace: Antimodernism and the Transformation of American Culture, 1880–1920*; Will H. Low, *A Chronicle of Friendship, 1873–1900*; W. H. Low, *A Painter's Progress*; E. V. Lucas, *Edwin Austin Abbey, Royal Academician*; Russell Lynes, *The Art-Makers of Nineteenth-Century America*; R. Lynes, *The Tastemakers*; Lillian B. Miller, *Patrons and Patriotism: The Encouragement of the Fine Arts in the United States, 1790–1860*; H. Wayne Morgan, *New Muses: Art in American Culture, 1865–1920*; Lewis Mumford, *The Brown Decades: A Study of the Arts in America, 1865–1895*; Eugen Neuhaus, *The History and Ideals of American Art*; Richard Ormond, *John Singer Sargent: Paintings, Drawings, Watercolors*.

William Ordway Partridge, *Art for America*; Bennard B. Perlman, *The Immortal Eight: American Painting from Eakins to the Armory Show, 1870–1913*; Mary Elizabeth Phillips, *Reminiscences of William Wetmore Story*; Patricia Jobe Pierce, *Edmund C. Tarbell and the Boston School of Painting, 1889–1980*; P. J. Pierce, *The Ten*; Ronald G. Pisano, *William Merritt Chase*; R. G. Pisano, *A Leading Spirit in American Art: William Merritt Chase*; Henry C. Pitz, "Charles Dana Gibson"; Michael Quick, *American Expatriate Painters of the Late Nineteenth Century*; M. Quick, *American Portraiture in the Grand Manner, 1720–1920*; Carter Ratcliff, *John Singer Sargent*; Sheldon Reich, *Alfred H. Maurer, 1868–1932*; Michael Richman, *Daniel Chester French: An American Sculptor*; Phyllis D. Rosenzweig, *The Thomas Eakins Collection of the Hirshhorn Museum and Sculpture Garden*; Homer Saint-Gaudens, *The American Artist and His Times*; George William Sheldon, *American Painters*; G. W. Sheldon, *Recent Ideals of American Art*; Regina Soria, *Perceptions and Evocations: The Art* of *Elihu Vedder;* Roger B. Stein, *John Ruskin and Aesthetic Thought in America, 1840–1900;* Russell Sturgis, *The Appreciation of Pictures;* R. Sturgis, *The Appreciation of Sculpture;* Joshua C. Taylor, *America as Art;* J. C. Taylor, *The Fine Arts in America;* Louise Hall Tharp, *Saint-Gaudens and the Gilded Age;* Margaret Farrand Thorp, *The Literary Sculptors;* Elihu Vedder, *The Digressions of V.;* H. Barbara Weinberg, "The Career of Francis Davis Millet"; H. B. Weinberg, introduction, *Illustrated Catalogue: The Masterpieces of the Centennial International Exhibition;* H. B. Weinberg, "Late-Nineteenth-Century American Painting"; H. B. Weinberg, "The Lure of Paris: Late-Nineteenth-Century American Painters and Their French Training"; Bruce Wilkinson, *Uncommon Clay, The Life and Works of Augustus Saint Gaudens.*

14. *U.S. Centennial Commission, International Exhibition, 1876: Reports and Awards.* The following quotation is from group 28, p. 280.

15. The role taken by the British government in instigating reforms in the nation's schools of design before and after the 1851 Exhibition is well told by Tobin Andrews Sparling, *The Great Exhibition: A Question of Taste.* Citing the advances made in the education of the public taste in England as a result of the 1851 London Exhibition, a writer for *Scribner's Monthly* voiced the hope that art schools would be established in the United States in the aftermath of the Centennial Exposition. See "Topics of the Times—American Art," *Scribner's Monthly Magazine.* The U.S. Centennial report was quick to cite the commercial advantages gained by Great Britain as a result of these reforms. See *U.S. Centennial Commission,* group 28, p. 282.

16. The report of the architects for group 26, the *U.S. Centennial Commission,* criticized the Exhibition's failure to solve "that important problem, viz, the amelioration of dwellings for the laboring and industrial classes" (pp. 10–11). It blamed the fact that geometrical drawings "have gradually been superseded by perspective views, while the latter too often have been, as on this occasion, supplanted by photographic views of the finished structures" (p. 8). Industrial arts (as well as the arts of the studio) were shifting from a solid grounding in the use of abstract geometry to "realistic" renderings (perspective sketches of projected houses which laymen were expected to "imagine" for future occupancy), or to even more "naturalistic" photographs of actual, completed structures which were intended as a "perception" of the house viewed by potential buyers. According to the report, this sequence moves from good to bad to worse in its effects upon the public's ability to comprehend dwelling places. Abstractions (understood by those educated in the science of geometric concepts) are closer to common comprehension than are "realistic" representations. In the tradition of the U.S. Centennial Commission report, the Pratt Institute of Brooklyn was founded in 1887 by Charles Pratt, a self-made manufacturer; both the commission and Pratt believed that technology and design based on geometric forms lent themselves to "the common task of helping man to help himself." See James R. Campbell, "The Pratt Institute"; *Pratt Institute, Circular of Information: Day Courses, 1920–1921.*

17. *U.S. Centennial Commission,* group 28, pp. 278–279.

18. The Prang Company not only sold materials to would-be artists, it furnished countless American homes with the artwork of others. Excellent sources of information concerning the part played by Prang in providing inexpensive art reproductions to the general public are Peter C. Marzio, "The Democratic Art of Chromolithography in America"; Clarence P. Hornung and Fridolf Johnson, *200 Years of American Graphic Art.*

19. Children taught by the Prang method were expected to sit up straight at their desks, hold pencils and paper in a prescribed way, and make marks according to specific instructions; at the same time, they were encouraged to "draw freely" and see in their tools "the means of reflecting themselves." Mary D. Hicks and John S. Clark, *The Use of Models: A Teacher's Assistant in the Use of the Prang Models,* pp. 9–10. In 1881 the need for small children to be taught "perception" and given "lessons in form" through the use of "simple

geometric solids,—the simplest objects which can be found"—was a stated fact. See introduction to Prang's *Preliminary Material for Teachers.*

20. Frank Lloyd Wright never forgot the impression made upon him as a child by the geometric building blocks sponsored by followers of Friedrich Froebel, German founder of the kindergarten movement in 1837, who—like the Prang instructors—believed in providing an early education in material forms. Wright's mother made a trip to the 1876 Philadelphia Centennial Exhibition in order to visit the Froebel display; she brought home to her seven-year-old son a set of building blocks. Wright always claimed that his childhood training in geometric forms affected his designs for the rest of his life. See *A Testament,* pp. 19–20.

21. Hugo B. Froehlich and Bonnie E. Snow, *Text Books of Art Education, Book V: Fifth Year,* p. 3. The following quotations are from pp. 3, 36, 52.

22. The Prang manual overlooks the fact that the use of wax or wooden "lay figures" as studio models was common practice. See chapter 3 for references to their employment by Daniel Chester French, Edwin Austin Abbey, and other professional artists. The following instruction books gave detailed instructions for their use: Eduoard Lanteri, *Modelling and Sculpture.* (Lanteri's volumes first appeared in 1902, 1904, and 1911); William Ordway Partridge, *Technique of Sculpture.* Figure 3.13 shows what a life-size lay figure looks like.

23. Kenyon Cox, *Painters and Sculptors,* pp. 8–9. The 1904 Prang manual, *Book 5* (p. 52), describes what students would draw if they set down on paper only what they *knew.* The results of these "concepts" would be as "subjective" as paintings we today would label as surreal ("your moonlight pictures would look like midday, your house would seem to be made of glass, and your railway tracks would stand up in the air like step-ladders") or paintings of the kind the Cubists were just then creating ("I can only see two sides of that house, but as there are really four I shall draw them all").

24. D. S. MacColl, *Nineteenth-Century Art.* The following references are from p. 2–3.

25. See Pete Daniel and Raymond Smock, *A Talent for Detail: The Photographs of Miss Frances Benjamin Johnston, 1889–1910.*

1. American Girls and the New Woman

1. The following two illustrations are drawn from the 1904 editions of *Text Books of Art Education, Books 2, 4,* prepared by Hugo B. Froehlich and Bonnie E. Snow. The authors' preface to the first edition (1887) of *The Use of Models* acknowledges that the theories behind this new educational concept were well established; it cites James Sully's *Outlines of Psychology with Special References to the Theory of Education,* and quotes from ch. 6, "On Perception": "It is now recognized that Form should be studied not only by the eye, but also by the hand; that touch furnishes 'the most direct mode of apprehending things,' and 'seems to bring us into the closest relation to external things.' " The Prang manual adds, "Ideas thus gained are real to the children, having been acquired through their own experience," then concludes by striking the note which William James and John Dewey as educators and Ernst Gombrich as art historian would later sound. "One of the most important means of developing ideas of form is 'making,' first, the type forms and afterwards objects based on them. 'Making' is also a form of *expression* of ideas of form, and still further affords an opportunity for the exercise of the creative ability of children—an ability which is too frequently ignored in education." For further information concerning the graded art instruction manuals prepared by the Prang Company, see John A. Nietz, *Old Textbooks,* pp. 337–339.

2. Froehlich and Snow, *Text Books of Art Education, Book 4,* pp. 34–35.

3. The most complete recent study which focuses entirely upon popular American views of female attractiveness between the 1870s and 1920 is Lois W. Banner, *American Beauty.* Also see Richard Corson, *Fashions in Makeup from Ancient to Modern Times;* Madge Gar-

land, *The Changing Face of Beauty;* Valerie Steele, *Fashion and Eroticism: Ideals of Feminine Beauty from the Victorian Era to the Jazz Age.* One of the best contemporary sources is Mary Eliza Haweis, *The Art of Beauty.*

4. Paul Bourget, visiting from France, was explicit on this issue of female sexual coldness. *Outre-Mer: Impressions of America,* pp. 77–78.

5. A useful summary and analysis of contemporary responses to "Daisy Miller" both in the United States and Great Britain is furnished by Elizabeth K. Helsinger, Robin Lauterbach Sheets, and William Veeder in *The Woman Question: Literary Issues, 1837–1883,* pp. 178–192.

6. William Dean Howells, *Heroines of Fiction,* 2:76.

7. *The American Code of Manners,* p. 144.

8. Thomas Beer, *The Mauve Decade: American Life at the End of the Nineteenth Century.* The following quotations are from pp. 35, 36, 52.

9. The increased intensity with which James characterized the type of the New England Woman is indicated by the difference between Gertrude Wentworth of *The Europeans* (1878) and Olive Chancellor of *The Bostonians* (1886). Gertrude is a problem to herself. Olive is a problem for others as well; her force as a woman of passionate principle is greater, far more ambiguous in nature, than anything Gertrude can express. What James dealt with lightly as a comedy of manners in the 1870s becomes a drama verging on the tragic by the late 1880s.

10. William Dean Howells, *Heroines of Fiction,* 2:180. Paul John Eakin's *The New England Girl: Cultural Ideals in Hawthorne, Stowe, Howells, and James* provides a book-length examination of the Howellsian thesis.

11. M. E. W. Sherwood, "New England Women."

12. Kate Stephens, "The New England Woman."

13. Contrast Kate Stephens' gloomy views as she looks back upon the plight of the New England spinster (the woman judged by her society as having had a valueless existence) with Louisa May Alcott's editorial written for the *New York Ledger* of April 11, 1868. Alcott's piece is the third of the series titled "Advice to Young Ladies" and concerns itself specifically with the group she calls "Happy Women." These come from the "class composed of superior women who, from various causes, remain single, and devote themselves to some earnest work . . . remaining as faithful to and as happy in their choice as married women with husbands and homes." Alcott presents a number of case histories, then concludes: "My sisters, don't be afraid of the words 'old maid,' for it is in your power to make this a term of honor, not reproach." Unmarried women must use the talents they possess "for the good of others," thereby finding happiness for themselves and making "of life no failure, but a beautiful success." Of course, what Stephens decries are the consequences for a woman who lives "for the good of others" without the ability to claim a place of her own in a society which holds that marriage furnishes women their sole chance at "placement."

As for statistics, not feelings, about the pros and cons of being unwed in Massachusetts, see Peter R. Uhlenberg's "A Study of Cohort Life Cycles: Cohorts of Native Born Massachusetts Women, 1830–1920," pp. 407–409. Uhlenberg gives figures for women who "are exposed to the risk of marriage, but do not succumb" and finds that their number increased from 1830 to 1890, then declined sharply by 1920. An important cause of this increase was the fact that there were more women with foreign-born parents, a group which tended to remain unmarried to a greater extent than women with native-born parents. (I wish to thank Kathryn Kish Sklar for directing me to Uhlenberg's article, and Geraldine Moyle for telling of the Alcott piece.)

14. Margaret Deland, "The Change in the Feminine Ideal," pp. 289–302.

15. The main source for material on the proliferation of American magazines is Frank Luther Mott, *A History of American Magazines,* vols. 3 and 4. Also see Clarence Hornung

and Fridolf Johnson, *200 Years of American Graphic Art*, and Edward W. Bok, *The Americanization of Edward Bok*, the autobiography of the influential editor of *The Ladies' Home Journal*.

16. Contemporary views (both favorable and derogatory) concerning the proliferation of illustrations and photographs used in the print media are expressed in the following: Alexander Black, "Photography in Fiction"; Sidney Fairfield, "The Tyranny of the Pictorial"; "Over-Illustration," *Harper's Weekly*; Frank Liston White, "Fifty Years of Book Illustrating in the United States." (I wish to thank Christoph K. Lohmann for calling several of these essays to my attention.) Also see Ralph F. Bogardus, *Pictures and Texts: Henry James, A. L. Coburn, and New Ways of Seeing in Literary Culture*; Theodore Bolton, *American Book Illustrators*; Charles Higgins, "Photographic Aperture: Coburn's Frontispiece to James's New York Edition"; Frank Weitenkampf, *The Illustrated Book*.

17. Mary Holland Kinkaid, "The Feminine Charms of the Woman Militant," pp. 146–155.

18. Inez Milholland Boissevain (1888–1916) graduated from Vassar in 1909 and received an L.L.B. from New York University in 1912. As a lawyer she specialized in criminal and divorce cases; she opposed capital punishment and worked for the causes of prison reform and legal aid. A Socialist, she was a member of the Women's Trade Union League, the NAACP, and the Fabian Society of England. In 1914 she addressed a meeting held at Cooper Union in support of Max Eastman and Art Young of *The Masses* who were being sued by the Associated Press for criminal libel. During 1915 she served as a war correspondent in Italy; she was expelled by the Italian government for her pacifist articles. In 1916 she took part in the garment workers' strike and died after collapsing during a speech in November that advocated women's suffrage. During the 1913 suffrage parade in Washington, D.C., she rode as one of the six mounted heralds (see figure 1.17). She testified about the hostility of the crowds lining the capital's streets to a Senate investigation committee called immediately after the event, as recorded in *Suffrage Parade*. This biographical data, gathered by Sharon M. Vardamis, is on file at the Schlesinger Library of Radcliffe College. An interesting aside to Kinkaid's use of Inez Milholland as the example of the feminist who *could* be a fine homemaker if she would is the piece "Feminists Design a New Type House" that appeared in the *New York Times* of April 15, 1914; comment is made how horrible it would be if Mrs. Boissevan (as she then was) ever became a household drudge.

19. Harriet Burton Laidlaw (1873–1949) graduated from Barnard College in 1902 and married a wealthy New York banker in 1905. She became active in the New York Woman Suffrage party organized by Carrie Chapman Catt in 1909. During 1911–13 she served as the second auditor of NAWSA; after 1917 she was one of the directors. This information appears in James, James, and Boyer, eds., *Notable American Women, 1607–1950*; the observation is made that Laidlaw was "known as a remarkably beautiful woman." Data is unavailable for Mrs. Thomas Jefferson Smith other than the notation on her photograph which states that she served as the recording secretary of NAWSA.

20. I am grateful to Steven Fink for calling attention to significant differences between Bridgman's painting and the photograph of Mrs. Smith, which alter the interpretation of the formalistic constants of elongated neck and rose included in each example. As Fink indicates, Mrs. Smith is erect, her eyes are cast demurely away from the viewer, and the rose is laid on her breast. The Bridgman figure reclines, gazing directly, somewhat provocatively, at the viewer, and the rose touches her lips, suggesting the kiss she is perhaps prepared to offer. The former pose is an image of chaste femininity; the latter is one of more open sensuality, hardly an appropriate model for James' Pansy Osmond. Fink's reading concurs with the fact that Bridgman's painting comes from his experiences in Algiers and Morocco prior to 1881; it is one of the odalisques common to mid-nineteenth-century art, albeit the fact that its exoticism (and eroticism) is tempered to American tastes. (For similar reasons, Raphael's Madonnas were preferred by contemporary American collectors over the

barely concealed sensuality of mannerist Madonnas painted by artists like Francesco Parmigianino. See David A. Brown, *Raphael and America*.)

21. *Our Girls: Poems in Praise of the American Girl, with Illustrations by Howard Chandler Christy*.

22. For further information concerning Annette Kellermann's career, see Lois Banner, *American Beauty*, pp. 207, 267, and Edward Wagenknecht, *American Profile, 1900–1909*, pp. 16, 265.

23. Mary Edwards Walker (1832–1919) received her medical degree from Syracuse Medical College in 1855. She married Albert Miller, but divorced him in 1869. She helped organize the Women's Relief Association during the Civil War. In 1863 she was appointed assistant surgeon; during her military service she wore a regular army uniform. In 1866 she was elected president of the National Dress Reform Association. She lectured for women's suffrage but became increasingly alienated from the suffragists and from the dress reform movement because of her pronounced eccentricities of behavior. (This information is from James, James, and Boyer, eds., *Notable American Women*.)

24. Romaine Brooks (1874–1970) was born in Rome of American parents. In 1896 she ran away from her mother's oppressive domination to pursue the life of a poor art student in Paris and Rome. After her mother's death in 1902, Brooks inherited a fortune. She exhibited at the Paris Salon of 1910, the London Academy of 1911, and thereafter at the Durand-Ruel Gallery in Paris. She was briefly married to John Ellingham Brooks, an English writer and pianist; she was said to have been in love with Alfred, Lord Douglas and perhaps with Gabriele D'Annunzio, but her primary emotional commitment was to lesbian unions. Called "thief of souls" by Robert de Montesquiou because of her skill as a portraitist, Brooks' work has received limited but intense interest. The National Collection of Fine Art (now the National Museum of American Art) held an exhibit of her paintings in 1970 which resulted in a catalog introduced by Joshua Taylor and a review by Hilton Kramer that appeared in the *New York Times* for April 25, 1971.

Further information is available in Meryle Secrest's biography *Between Me and Life* and an article by Edouard MacAvoy for *Le Figaro littéraire* (January 26, 1967). The National Museum of American Art owns several of Brooks' portraits and paintings, and her drawings, as well as an Ephemera File of autobiographical material. One of the most telling comments concerning Brooks as a woman who *saw* differently, thereby was ready to *look* different, is made by MacAvoy. Before he examined the bizarre drawings Brooks did between the ages of fifteen and seventeen, expressive of the terror her mother caused her, MacAvoy assumed that he would find the sketches of violets expected from well-bred young girls of the period. What he discovered shook him loose from his notions that "all charming young girls had to resemble each other in 1889."

25. Information concerning the rush of attention paid in print to the physical fitness of American women (in particular, their involvement in sports) is found in the following sources, among others: Lois W. Banner, *American Beauty*; Emily M. Bishop, *Self-Expression and Health: Americanized Delsarte Culture*; Foster R. Dulles, *America Learns To Play: A History of Popular Recreation, 1607–1940*; Helen Gilbert Ecob, *The Well-Dressed Woman*; Barbara Ehrenreich and Deirdre English, *For Her Own Good*; Alison Gernsheim, *Fashion and Reality*; Valerie Steele, *Fashion and Eroticism*. For contemporary comments from the popular tabloids, the following is a representative sampling: *Illustrated Police News and Town Life* (Boston), March 28, 1896 (p. 3), May 9, 1896 (p. 13); *New York Journal*, May 31, 1896 (p. 33); *New York World*, August 18, 1895 (pp. 27, 29, 30), August 25, 1895 (p. 31), June 16, 1895 (pp. 24, 31).

26. Fairfax Downey, *Portrait of an Era as Drawn by C. D. Gibson*, p. 252.

27. Paul Bourget, *Outre-Mer*, p. 86.

2. *Looking for the "Best" Type*

1. William Graham Sumner, *Folkways*, p. 12.

2. The following quotations from Paul Bourget's *Outre-Mer* are from pp. 86, 350. The same year that Bourget's book came out with its emphasis upon the pictorialization of the young American woman, Sydney Fairfield wrote on "The Tyranny of the Pictorial" for *Lippincott's Magazine*. The year 1895 was the time of the "craze for pictures," the "reign of the pictorial," and the "subordination of what is literary to what is pictorial" (pp. 861–862). Fairfield traces the public's general appetite for pictures to the "predominant curiosity regarding the female adorned and unadorned" (p. 862). He also sets up a strong cause-and-effect association between the use of the new color-printing processes and the increased inclusion of female images in advertisements for the sale of consumer products by artists "catering to this manufactured taste" (p. 862). But whether displayed in ads, periodicals, or gallery exhibits, the "astonishing financial success" of these images proves that "the glorification of feminine beauty is a pronounced tendency of the day" and that "woman is the one great subject for illustrations" (p. 863).

3. The following quotations are from pp. 24–25, 45–46, 48–49, of James Fullarton Muirhead's *The Land of Contrasts*. Muirhead collected his notes on American life during 1892–93 at the time of the Columbian Exposition while on assignment from Baedeker's to compile a new handbook on the United States.

4. The words of Charles Freer's complete statement could easily be taken from Henry James' *The Portrait of a Lady*: "It seems to have grown up like a young tree. The grey mysterious girl with round rosy cheeks and wondering eyes is about to step out of ivory darkness into an unknown world. She half hesitates, yet, shows no sign of fear. A marvelous creation, most beautifully suggestive. . . . The young woman stepping into an old world. Wonderful!! I am happy!" From Freer's letter to Roslind Birnie Philip of June 26, 1904, BP II 4/49 Birnie Philip Bequest, University of Glasgow. Quoted by Susan Hobbs in her essay "A Connoisseur's Vision: The American Collection of Charles Lang Freer."

5. The following quotations are from Bourget, *Outre-Mer*, p. 86. Also see *Charles Dana Gibson: A Study of the Man and Some Recent Examples of His Best Work* for comments concerning Gibson's adroit classification of "The Seven Types of the American Girl." These comments appeared in briefer form in "Charles Dana Gibson: The Man and His Art," *Collier's Weekly* (November 29, 1902), 30(9):8–9.

6. The following quotation is from Boyesen's essay "Types of American Women" (1890), p. 6.

7. Muirhead, *The Land of Contrasts*, p. 52.

8. Bourget, *Outre-Mer*, p. 81. In contrast to Bourget's sourness about the Girl as Doll, Boyesen and Muirhead were champions of the type (especially in her subclass "the pretty Western girl"). They liked "her candour, her frankness, her hail-fellow-well-met-edness, her apparent absence of consciousness of self or of sex, her spontaneity, her vivacity, her fearlessness." Boyesen, "Types of American Women," p. 7; Muirhead, *The Land of Contrasts*, p. 50.

9. Boyesen, "Types of American Women," p. 8.

10. The following quotations are from Boyesen's "Types of American Women," pp. 13–15, 17–20.

11. Johann Casper Lavater published *Physiognomische Fragmente* in Leipzig and Winterthur in 1775–78, with illustrations contributed by a number of various artists. This work was translated into English by Thomas Holcraft for its first London edition in 1789 as *Essays on Physiognomy*. The edition cited throughout my discussion is the second London edition of 1804. (The first American edition appeared in Boston sometime in the early 1790s). See

"Physiognomies in the Ancient World" by Elizabeth C. Evans concerning the interest in physical appearance (initiated by the Pseudo-Aristotle in the third century B.C.) leading to theories of "the type" by which classical writers of history, biography, and the panegyric developed iconistic emblems for human virtue. Graeme Tytler's *Physiognomy in the European Novel* examines (perhaps too uncritically) the influence of Lavater's notions throughout the nineteenth century on racial and literary responses to physical types.

12. As phrased in the book's subtitle, *For the Promotion of the Knowledge and Love of Mankind*, Lavater's hopes are clear. See vol. 2, pp. 7–13, for one of his statements concerning the relations he found between acts of classification and affection.

13. For the context of this illustration taken from Arnold Guyot's *Physical Geography* of 1866, and the next, from Adolph von Steinwehr and Daniel G. Brinton's *An Intermediate Geography* of 1878, see Ruth Miller Elson, *Guardians of Tradition: American Schoolbooks of the Nineteenth Century*. Elson and John Nietz in *Old Textbooks* examine the ways nineteenth-century American schoolchildren were instructed in the racial and civic hierarchies which placed "the Anglo-Saxon" at the top of the moral heap. Also see Frances Fitzgerald, *America Revised: History Schoolbooks in the Twentieth Century*; and Henry Vail, *A History of the McGuffey Readers*.

14. See Lois Banner, *American Beauty*; Madge Garland, *The Changing Face of Beauty*; and Valerie Steele, *Fashion and Eroticism*.

15. Essential studies of reactions of the American "nativists" to the influx of immigrants during the final decades of the nineteenth century and the first two decades of the twentieth century are Thomas Hartshorne, *The Distorted Image: Changing Conceptions of the American Character Since Turner*; John Higham, *Strangers in the Land: Patterns of American Nativism, 1860–1925*; Roy Lubove, *The Progressives and the Slums: Tenement House Reform in New York City, 1890–1917*. Also see Maxine Margolis, *Mothers and Such*, concerning fears about the contamination of pure-blooded American stock by the immigrants. Subsequent references will be made to contemporary texts that denounced the "hybrid" elements introduced by "the others" from alien lands.

16. Compare two contemporary responses ("romantic" and "scientific") to the classification of ethnic types that influenced artistic renditions offered to the American public. The strand of romanticism that recognized the specialness of national cultures and physical traits inspired the painter Francis Davis Millet to give meticulous attention to details of native costumes and facial expression. See H. Barbara Weinberg, "The Career of Francis Davis Millet." In contrast to Millet's enthusiasm for individualistic ethnic traits is the scientific approach taken by William Boyd and Henry J. Elliott to their creation of the gallery of "ethnological heads" (set along the pavilion windows of the first story) completed for the Library of Congress in 1896.

The Handbook of the New Library of Congress makes clear the importance the sculptors gave to the classification of national types. (The following quotations are from pp. 13–16.) "The series [of thirty-three heads] is unique in that it is the first instance of a comprehensive attempt to make ethnological science contribute to the architectural decoration of an important building. . . . The present idea was carried out with the assistance of Professor Otis T. Mason, the Curator of the Department of Ethnology in the National Museum for the last twelve years. . . . Any attempt at dramatic or picturesque, except what was natural to the type portrayed, was felt to be out of place. Each head was subjected to the strict test of measurement—such as the ratio of breadth to length to height, and the distance between the eyes and between the cheekbones—this being the most valuable criterion of racial differences." What prompted the extreme care taken by Mason, Boyd, and Elliott was truth to the type, not fidelity to the individual. "All portraiture was avoided, both as being somewhat invidious and unscientifically personal, and, more specially, because no one man can ever exemplify all the average physical characteristics of his race. On the other hand, the heads were never permitted to become merely ideal."

Francis Millet's responses to different races were direct and positive; as an artist he liked ethnic variety for its own sake; in contrast, the sculptor-anthropologists restricted themselves to precise measurement in denial of both portraiture and the ideal. Although Boyd and Elliott believed they were being true to principles of scientific objectivity, they gave away their personal feelings about what their calipers found when they set the heads of "savage and barbarous peoples" in opposition to the "educated" type of the "Blonde European" which furnished the Library of Congress with its "norm" for moral rightness. Also see Lois M. Fink, "Nineteenth Century Evolutionary Art," p. 108.

17. The sense of lost racial homogeneity is explicitly addressed by Henry James in passages from *The American Scene* that explore Central Park, the streets of the Lower East Side of New York, and the byways of Boston and Salem. James had returned to the United States in 1904–1905 after an absence of twenty years to find that the new faces and languages of the immigrants had put an end to familiarity as he understood the term. *The American Scene*, pp. 116–144, 177, 194–208, 265. On May 20, 1905, *Collier's Weekly* featured a picture by E. W. Kemble which underscores the belief held by many of the native-born that they were being rudely displaced from "their" land. Kemble's drawing depicts the Statue of Liberty with a sign dangling from her torch that reads "Standing Room Only." The caption asks, "Will It Come to This?"—then reports that on May 7 ten ships delivered 12,039 immigrants (mostly Italians) to New York's harbor, the greatest number to arrive in the United States in any single day. For an interesting comparison between the responses to the ethnic issue expressed by Henry James and his elder brother, see Larry C. Miller, "William James and Twentieth-Century Ethnic Thought."

18. Joseph Simms, *Physiognomy Illustrated; or, Nature's Revelations of Character*, p. 227. The first edition was published in 1874.

19. The well-known illustrator and jingoist Howard Chandler Christy elaborates upon the right occupation (farming) at the right moment (the colonial period) as the criteria for identifying "the true American." That American is the man who "must have made his living from the soil. Not to have done so proves an arrival from the Old World at a later than the colonial period of our history." *The American Girl*, p. 91. A cartoon by one William Walker (?) appeared in *Life* of January 30, 1902. Titled "Landing of Pilgrims as It Might Have Been," the grotesque figures in Pilgrim garb are stock Jews and Irish. What if *they* had come first? is a question Christy had not contemplated.

20. The next two quotations are from Robert Tomes, *The Bazar Book of Decorum*, pp. 25–26.

21. Daniel J. Boorstin, "Introduction: The Immigrant Vision," from Cynthia McCabe, *The Golden Door: Artist-Immigrants of America, 1876–1976*.

22. The following quotations are from Josiah Strong, *Our Country: Its Possible Future and Its Present Crisis*, pp. 56, 219–220.

23. Statistics were enthusiastically viewed as the means for procuring scientific validity for social and political opinions. There was a spate of publications filled with tables dedicated to revealing "the whole man," as exemplified by *Physiognomical Register for Recording the Indications of the Head, Face, Temperament, and Other Organic Conditions*, by J. A. Denkinger, M.D. Denkinger's prose style never lifts off the ground formed by his tables, but Strong's argument (delivered by a man whose express mission was to warn his countrymen against the alien hordes) constantly alternates statistics with jeremiads.

24. Joseph Simms, *Physiognomy Illustrated*, p. 20.

25. Mark Twain was in agreement with Simms' appraisal of the low worth of the Indian race. Chapter 19 of *Roughing It* (1872) is devoted to an attack upon the romanticization of

the Noble Savage which Twain here, and elsewhere, blames upon James Fenimore Cooper's "mellow moonshine of romance." Among the worst of "the prideless beggars" are the Goshutes who are descended, together with the Bushmen, "from the selfsame gorilla, or kangaroo, or Norway rat, whichever animal-Adam the Darwinians trace them to." Take into account that this is the Clemens/Mark Twain *persona* speaking (the erstwhile greenhorn from east of the Mississippi who is trying hard to "interpret" the West as it *really* is); also grant that much of the attempted humor of *Roughing It* is based upon the language and vision of hyperbole (after the manner of most late-nineteenth-century ethnic jokes). Even so, it is safe to say that Twain would concur with Simms' comparisons. Quotations are from *Roughing It*, pp. 144–146. A cigar label of 1885 shows a white hunter together with an Indian, with the legend "True Americans," but that sentiment was hardly the ruling one.

26. Sumner's *Folkways* of 1907 defined ethnocentrism as "this view of things in which one's own group is the center of everything, and all others are scaled and rated with reference to it. . . . Each group nourishes its own pride and vanity, boasts itself superior, exalts its own divinities, and looks with contempt on outsiders." *Folkways*, p. 13.

27. In 1891 Simms (himself pictured as heavily bearded) made much of the fact that men with full beards never know a day's illness, whereas shaving damages the nervous system. He backed this thesis by citing the example of the Reverend Henry Ward Beecher, who by submitting "to fashion through shaving" might be in danger of "damning souls instead of saving them." *Physiognomy Illustrated*, p. 525. By 1910 and Rocine's book, the clean-shaven American face was one of the signs of good racial stock and sound moral fiber.

28. The preface to *Heads, Faces, Types, Races* is typical of Rocine's style as one of the period's "success doctors." "Phrenology teaches us practical memory culture, how to develop self-confidence, improve digestion, develop the abdominal brain, increase personal magnetism, restore a failing sexuality" (p. 8).

29. See Rocine, *Heads, Faces, Types, Races*, pp. 298–299, for his detailed verbal attack on the Jewish race. The classic study of centuries of pictorial insults against the Jews is Eduard Fuchs' *Die Juden in der Karikatur*. Also note that Fuchs put together a similar study with his history of caricatures of women, *Die Frau in der Karikatur*. These two groups of social inferiors were creatures open to ridicule through the pictorialization of their physical grotesqueness. Anti-Semitism and misogyny merges in the 1913 drawings by J. Kuhn-Regnier; depictions of Susanna and the Elders, Samson and Delilah, and the Queen of Sheba and Solomon gave this caricaturist his chance to demean not only Jewish males but Jewesses, types who represented the height (or depth) of female repulsiveness.

30. Wenzell's "Long Branch Puzzle" first appeared in *Life* of August 9, 1894, a nasty version of the contemporary interest in drawings based on the general notion of "*Puzzle:* find the . . ." Gibson did a series of such illustrations for *Life* which had no racial implications but merely asked viewers to identify the odd man out in the pictured scene (e.g., the man who doesn't get the joke; the unmarried woman with charm but no money). Still, the joke in all versions is based on the type who does not fit into the group. The Wenzell drawing is also a variation on a *Life* cartoon of December 28, 1893, captioned "The Hebraization of the American Drama." A production of *The Merchant of Venice* is pictured in which all the roles are taken by Jews, with the exception of Shylock who is portrayed by a stock stage Irishman.

31. Mark Silk questions this comforting notion in his essay "Notes on the Judeo-Christian Tradition in America." The Kuhn-Regnier series from the Europe of 1913 (see note 29) dashes the thought that Christians automatically granted conceptual protection to the Jews of the Old Testament.

32. The following quotations are from George Barr McCutcheon's "What Is It To Be an American?"

33. Although McCutcheon does not take on the issue directly, he refers by implication to

a dilemma of the mid-1910s: where to place the Teutonic race in relation to the Anglo-Saxon forebears of "the true American" once that once-honored bloodline becomes associated with the hated Hun. See Rocine, *Heads, Faces, Types, Races*, p. 300; Higham, *Strangers in the Land*, pp. 195–202.

34. Simms, *Physiognomy Illustrated*, pp. 26–35), advances the argument that the science of physiognomy is the way to success in business. Bruce Barton took this notion all the way in 1925 with *The Man Nobody Knows: A Discovery of the Real Jesus*, for who can best the Best Man at the arts of business and advertising? Barton's belief that Jesus is the exemplary ad man is countered by V. G. Rocine's belief that the Ideal Type has no affinities to the type of the true American businessman. See figure 5.32.

35. Lila Gillian Farrell, *Human Nature Study*. This and the following quotations are from p. 3.

36. Henry Dwight Sedgwick, *The New American Type and Other Essays*, p. 16. The following quotations are from pp. 13–14, 16–17.

37. See Ruth Brandon, *A Capitalist Romance: Singer and the Sewing Machine*.

38. Sedgwick here contrasts the type that readers of Henry Adams will recognize. Compare Clover Hooper Adams, and Adams himself, with the nerveless, unimaginative "type of the McKinley era" which Adams shrewdly analyzed in the person of Senator Donald Cameron of Pennsylvania. Place Sedgwick's contrasting descriptions of the American female (mind and spirit) and the male (vigor and craft) in *The New American Type*, pp. 17, 20–24, next to Adams' description of Senator Cameron in *The Education of Henry Adams*, p. 333.

39. Samuel Murray's 1894 portrait of Susan Macdowell Eakins (twenty-four-inch shellacked and gessoed white plaster) is strikingly like John Singer Sargent's 1897 oil portrait of Catherine Vlasto in the inclusion of the fan and the cut of the evening dress. The Sargent portrait was executed when his sitter was twenty-two and in delicate health; she died two years later—"unmarried," according to notations perpetuated in the continuing series of provenience records attached to the painting's file until Abram Lerner (director of the Hirshhorn Museum) finally wrote in the margins an exasperated "Good heavens! She was only 24 years when she died. Do we have to remind people she died an old maid!"

40. George Miller Beard, *American Nervousness, Its Causes and Consequences*, pp. 26, 66–69.

41. Frank Norris, "Why Women Should Write the Best Novels; and Why They Don't," p. 20.

42. Generally speaking, the accepted physical type of the American Girl reflected the same normative appearance no matter the region of the United States, in the same way that the multifold ethnic, economic, and class variations at work throughout the nation were largely overlooked because of the imaginative commitment of the mainstream to a look based on so-called classical, northern European features. On occasion, physiognomical distinctions were made between young women called upon to represent the Southern type and the types of the East or the West. The *New York Herald* of March 15, 1896, ran a full page of photographs with the heading "Types of American Beauties." The women are posed almost identically and wear similar dresses, but there is a noticeable difference between the women from Cleveland and Buffalo and those from New Orleans. The former are stocky and square-jawed; the latter are delicate of feature and torso. The *Herald*'s selection reflects more than the obvious fact that several kinds of physical builds coexist in any period; they suggest that the sturdy and the fragile were both accepted as "Types of American Beauties." George Beard claimed that physical weakness is "all modern" and "pre-eminently American," while hoping for somewhat fatter women. *American Nervousness*, p. 339. The *Herald* sized up its female audience and found its members modern, American, frail, *and* fat.

43. Cesare Lombroso and William Ferrero's *The Female Offender* was originally published in Italy in 1893. Leonard D. Savitz, in his introduction to the edition of Gina Lombroso-

Ferrero's *Criminal Man* (based on Cesare Lombroso's classification) for the Reprint Series in Criminology, Law Enforcement, and Social Problems, details the enthusiastic reception given Lombroso's theories in the United States. Max Nordau's 1895 dedication of *Degeneration* to Lombroso indicates the nature of the European response to the problems of moral and aesthetic degeneracy, but (according to Savitz) Lombroso especially fit American tastes.

44. Lombroso's writings give another instance of a system of "scientific" classification offered with benign intentions, however frightening their actual implications. Lombroso insisted he did not sift out the "morally insane" in order that society might punish them. Such persons could not choose to be other than they were; they were victims of heredity. Having dropped back down the evolutionary ladder, they needed help from social institutions. Lombroso's categories were meant to have two beneficial results: social atavisms could be kept apart from decent people who would otherwise become their prey, and they could be made the recipients of reformatory therapies. Compare Lombroso's views with those of the American "success doctors," V. G. Rocine and Joseph Simms. Rocine and Simms worked to separate the population into (a) easy marks and (b) hard cases; both were subjects to be manipulated by super salesmen. Also compare Lombroso with American "protectionists" like Josiah Strong who wished to divide the world into (a) those who were welcome in the United States and (b) those who had to be kept out. In contrast, Lombroso hoped his classifications would prove to be both preventative and remedial, a concern with no appeal for Strong, Simms, or Rocine.

3. Artists, Models, and Real Things

1. Gordon Hendricks, *The Life and Works of Thomas Eakins*, p. 248.

2. An observation made by David Sellin in his essay "Eakins and the Macdowells and the Academy," p. 18.

3. Hendricks, *The Life and Works of Thomas Eakins*, p. 156. For Eakins' extensive use of photography in preparing his work, see *Thomas Eakins: His Photographic Works; Eakins at Avondale and Thomas Eakins*.

4. Chapter 12 deals extensively with the Columbian Exposition held in Chicago during the summer of 1893.

5. Henry James, notebook entry of February 22, 1891; from *The Notebooks of Henry James*, pp. 102–104.

6. This and the following quotations from "The Real Thing" are from the New York edition, pp. 314, 318, 326–327. See the excellent essay by Moshe Ron, "A Reading of 'The Real Thing.' " Ron asks epistemological questions which result in useful distinctions between "the real thing" and "character." He also argues that James' equation of "being" with "representation" goes against the basic traditions of Western Platonism.

7. Arthur Bartlett Maurice's "Representative American Story Tellers: I—Richard Harding Davis," p. 142, comments on the satisfaction given to "rural readers" when they read about details of high-society life. "They know they are getting 'the real thing.' "

8. Chapters 14–15 give further details concerning the increasing impact of the celebrity upon the popular imagination. Also consult Daniel J. Boorstin, *The Image: A Guide to Pseudo-Events in America*; William Aylott Orton, *America in Search of Culture*, p. 219; Warren I. Susman, " 'Personality' and the Making of Twentieth-Century Culture." Boorstin makes a particular point of the trademarks by means of which a person or thing usually gains instant recognition from the public.

9. For an example of Talcott Parsons' approach to "functionality," see "Definitions of Health and Illness in the Light of American Values and Social Structures," *Social Structures and Personality*," p. 262.

10. The following account and quotations are from pp. 139–140, 236–239, of Elihu Vedder's *The Digressions of V.*

11. Royal Cortissoz's remarks are from the foreword of the catalog prepared for the Yale University exhibition of the Abbey Collection, *Paintings, Drawings, and Pastels by Edwin Austin Abbey*, p. 3. The following observation by Henry James is from the same source.

12. The following quotations are from William H. Downes' essay "William Merritt Chase: A Typical American Artist," p. xxxix; an anonymous contributor writing on "The Chase Exhibition" in *The Outlook*; Perriton Maxwell in "William Merritt Chase—Artist, Wit, and Philosopher." Further information concerning Chase's life and career is available in Ronald G. Pisano's two books on Chase, *William Merritt Chase* and *A Leading Spirit in American Art*; the catalog for the *Chase Centennial Exhibition, November 1–December 11, 1949*; the National Museum of American Art, Chase Ephemera File.

13. William Merritt Chase, "How I Painted My Greatest Picture."

14. Copies of William Ordway Partridge's *Technique of Sculpture* were owned by Daniel Chester French and other leading sculptors.

15. Nathan Cabot Hale, introduction to Lanteri's *Modelling and Sculpture*, 1:vi.

16. Davida Johnson Clark bore a son to Saint-Gaudens in 1889. See John H. Dryfhout, *The Work of Augustus Saint-Gaudens*, Louise Hall Tharp, *Saint-Gaudens and the Gilded Age*, and Burke Wilkinson, *Uncommon Clay*, for the meager details available of this carefully concealed relationship.

17. Data concerning French's practices as a sculptor are drawn from the exhibit of 1981–82 arranged by Susan Frisch Lehrer and from "The Property Guidebook" compiled by Lehrer from the D. C. French Archives at Chesterwood (part of the National Trust for Historic Preservation). Further information comes from Margaret French Cresson *Journey Into Fame*; Mrs. Daniel Chester (Mary) French *Memories of a Sculptor's Wife*; Michael Richman *Daniel Chester French: An American Sculptor*; Margaret French Cresson, "Daniel French's Heaven—Reminiscences of Chesterwood"; and the National Museum of American Art, D. C. French Ephemera File. Also see the introduction to the biography by Caroline Ticknor, *May Alcott: A Memoir*, which D. C. French wrote in recognition of the aid that Alcott (*the* artist in Concord, Massachusetts, of the 1860s) gave him as a young and aspiring sculptor.

18. Mitchell Shapiro was interviewed by Paul Ivory, director of Chesterwood, on August 17, 1971, and Ethel Cummings was interviewed October 21, 1976. Shapiro photographed French's models around 1928 as aids to the sculptor's work. French requested natural lighting; he wished these studies to be treated as regular portrait sittings, not as dramatic scenes requiring artificial lighting. Cummings was born around 1909 and served as a domestic before she began to model for art student patients at the Austin Riggs Hospital in Stockbridge. French employed her at nearby Chesterwood from about 1926–27 to 1931, the time of his death. For his "Andromeda" (see figure 15.28) French posed Cummings arched over the mockup of a large rock with chains around her hands. Lehrer's exhibition listed a dozen other models by name and the many statues for which they posed. French's rigorous attention to direct observation is apparent in the preparation he undertook when sculpting wings for a memorial angel; a letter French wrote to William Brewster, professor of zoology at Harvard University, of October 5, 1890, details the close scrutiny he gave an owl's wings so he could make the feathers of the angelic wings lie just so. See Richman, *Daniel Chester French*, p. 72. (French's correspondence is part of the Brewster Papers, Museum of Comparative Zoology, Harvard University.)

19. See Mary French, *Memories of a Sculptor's Wife*, pp. 211, 216 for comments on models.

20. In *Woman and Demon: The Life of a Victorian Myth* Nina Auerbach offers an analysis of *Trilby* as part of her commentary upon female roles in nineteenth-century British fiction. Auerbach takes a different methodological approach from mine, and her emphasis is upon

British, not American, culture; but my reading is not at odds with hers since we both agree about the power Trilby exerts upon her viewers.

21. Edward Rosenberg, *From Shylock to Svengali: Jewish Stereotypes*, devotes a chapter to Du Maurier's anti-Semitic portrait. In 1895 Mary Kyle Dallas brought the stereotype even closer home to New York when she wrote a parody titled *Biltry*. Dallas heaps her anti-Semitic jokes upon the "Little Billee" character, however, not upon the Svengali figure. By reversing the gender roles as well, Dallas also manages to make a number of sexist jokes against the heroine (Little Beckie who paints candles) and her friends (bachelor girls who have set themselves up as would-be artists in a New York studio).

22. Du Maurier describes Trilby's "personality" photograph that was all the rage with her public as a likeness of the Venus de Milo. When Trilby sings, she is also likened by audiences to a "woman archangel" who flies on "white wings." Since Trilby has further been described as the type of Pre-Raphaelite beauty, she bears a heavy weight of art historical references; they fix her into the mold of several visual types. Add to all these the type of "the demon" of which Nina Auerbach writes. Which, then, is Trilby?

23. Arthur Bartlett Maurice, "Representative American Story Tellers," p. 142.

24. Visits to the studios of well-known artists were so much a part of the social scene by the 1880s that rules of behavior were laid down in the etiquette books. See S. L. Louis, *Decorum: A Practical Treatise on Etiquette and Dress of the Best American Society*. Visitors who did not abide by these rules are described by an irritated artist in "A Half-Hour with Studio Bores" by Charles De Kay.

25. In 1881 Oliver Wendell Holmes, Jr., published *The Common Law*. There he argued that absolutes are no longer applicable in any area of human conduct, including the law. Now that truth is to be taken as relative, law courts have to work out *ad hoc* definitions of correct social behavior. The society represented by Neville and his family still holds to the fixed standards Holmes had attempted to reexamine thirty years earlier.

26. Philip Fisher, "Acting, Reading, Fortune's Wheel: *Sister Carrie* and the Life History of Objects," pp. 264, 267.

27. See Else Honig Fine, *Women and Art*, pp. 113–114.

28. The anecdote concerning Susan Macdowell Eakins' dress is from Avis Berman, "Thomas Eakins: Master of Realistic Art," p. 28. See Frances Borzello, *The Artist's Model*, for a general study of the artist/model relationship.

4. The Aesthetics of Desire

1. The tale of Corinthea is reviewed by Pauline King, *American Mural Painting*; and by Rodolphe Louise Mégroz, *Profile Art Through the Ages*. Arthur S. Vernay repeats the same legend in *The Silhouette* but makes it a man who longs for his beloved.

2. Johann Casper Lavater, *Essays on Physiognomy*, 2:117–118. The tradition, techniques, and teaching of the silhouette are an important aspect of the history of the arts of Platonic forms which ground the black and white illustration, the photographic studio portrait, the poster, and the mural. In addition to the titles listed in note 1, see Katharine G. Buffum, *Silhouettes To Cut in School*; Augustin A. C. F. Edouart (the father of the modern silhouette), *A Treatise on Silhouette Likeness*; Emily Nevill Jackson, *The History of Silhouettes*; Norman Laliberté and Alex Mogelon, *Silhouettes, Shadows, and Cutouts*; Frederic Gordon Roe, *Women in Profile*. Ernst Gombrich continually refers to the silhouette tradition in his essays on the arts of representation; he gives it particular attention in "On Physiognomic Perception" and "Expression and Communication."

3. The quotations that follow are from Henry B. Brewster, *The Statuette and the Background*, pp. 4, 12–13, 15–16, 18–19, 28–29, 32–33, 51, 55, 74, 76, 81, 108, 124, 127.

4. Readers of Lila Gillian Farrell's *Human Nature Study* (discussed in chapter 2) will

immediately identify these three types: Rhoda is the Mental; Humphrey is the Thoracic; Walter is the Vital.

5. Frank Kermode, *The Sense of an Ending*, p. 64.

6. The first American edition—*The Tragedy of Pudd'nhead Wilson and The Comedy of Those Extraordinary Twins*—used a photograph of Mark Twain as its frontispiece; outline sketches decorating the text's margins distinguished Roxy as "white." The first London edition—*Pudd'nhead Wilson, a Tale by Mark Twain* (Chatto & Windus, 1894)—incorporated the Loeb illustrations from *The Century*.

7. Mark Sullivan, *Our Times*, vol. 1, *The Turn of the Century*, p. 196.

8. The following quotations are from Richard Bernheimer, *The Nature of Representation*, pp. 65–66, 172–175. Bernheimer's interest as a philosopher in the demoniac, the primary, and the denoted echoes the attention paid by the art historian Ernst Gombrich and the literary scholar Angus Fletcher, in *Symbolic Images: Studies in the Art of the Renaissance* and *Allegory: The Theory of a Symbolic Mode*, respectively.

9. See Murray Krieger, "Poetic Presence and Illusion: Renaissance Theory and the Duplicity of Metaphor."

10. Krieger's essay on the English Renaissance poets focuses upon their use of language to combat the loss of the infinite. He maintains that the plastic arts of the sixteenth century were incapable of representations of both the designated and the denoted. In contrast, painters and sculptors of the late-nineteenth-century American Renaissance strove to succeed where their contemporaries who were poets were failing.

11. Fletcher, *Allegory*, p. 323.

12. Marshall Brown, "The Logic of Realism." The following quotations are from pp. 224, 228–229, 233, 236.

13. Sylvester Rosa Koehler, "The Future of Art," p. 72. Howard Mumford Jones cites Herbert Spencer's declaration of 1883 that the United States had arrived at the pitch of activity and creation characteristic of the Italian Renaissance. See Jones, "The Renaissance and American Origins," p. 150. The notion had taken hold in art circles with Koehler's call in 1879 and two articles of the following year: William C. Brownell's two-part review, "The Younger Painters in America"; and an unsigned piece, "Art and Artists—the American Renaissance," in *The Californian*.

14. Jarves, *The Art Idea*, pp. 174–175, provides a typical passage listing what America lacks; and also what it has: the spirit of Benjamin Franklin.

15. The charges leveled against the Pre-Raphaelites by Jarves continued to be made through the end of the nineteenth century. Harry Quilter's "The New Renaissance" and William J. Stillman's "The Decay of Art" are rather more livid in expression than most, but Quilter and Stillman were joined by others with distaste for the morbid subjectivity and mechanistic camera focus they found in the British style. Edwin Austin Abbey often remarked that he alone remained under the influence of the Pre-Raphaelite art to which he was first introduced at the 1876 Philadelphia Centennial; he stayed loyal to this particular tradition of beauty, whereas his fellow artists preferred the French style. See Lucas, *Edwin Austin Abbey*, 1:14, 47. Roger B. Stein, *John Ruskin and Aesthetic Thought in America*, and David H. Dickason, *The Daring Young Men*, examine the feelings—hot and cold—incited by the Pre-Raphaelite approach. Chapter 10 discusses the example of Kenyon Cox's 1886 pictorial treatment of Dante Gabriel Rossetti's "The Blessed Damozel."

16. See Katharine Everett Gilbert and Helmut Kuhn, *A History of Esthetics*, pp. 526–527. The aestheticians involved include G. T. Fechner, Hermann Helmholtz, Adolf Hildenbrand, Heinrich Wolfflin, Alois Riegl, and Wilhem Dilthy in Germany, and Charles Darwin, Herbert Spencer, Grant Allen, and Bernard Bosanquet in Great Britain.

17. William Morris Hunt furnished the example which art critics continually held up as the sad case of what happens to a talented American bereft of an established artistic theory

to tutor his eye and hand. Hunt received sympathetic tongue-cluckings from those who deplored the age into which he was unlucky enough to be born since it left him vulnerable to the praise of viewers who equated good intentions with achievement. See Samuel Isham, *History of American Painting*, p. 30.

18. In 1886 Koehler sharply refuted the suggestion that the advancements taking place in American art were the result of the 1876 Centennial Exposition in Philadelphia. Quite the opposite. In Koehler's opinion, the Centennial Exposition had done harm through its focus on decorative arts. They held "art captive as the slave of private luxury," while encouraging a "sordid view" through the commercialization of products. *American Art*, p. 2.

19. Chapter 12 contains an extended discussion of varied responses to the Centennial Exposition of 1876 and the 1893 Columbian Exposition.

20. In 1886, the same year as Koehler's appraisal of American art, Mariana Van Rensselaer wrote the preface to *Book of American Figure Painters*. Van Rensselaer (one of the best art critics of her generation) opens by citing Ralph Waldo Emerson in regard to the view she and Emerson held in common: America is "a land of beginnings, of designs, of projects and expectations." She concludes with lines from Emerson's poem "Days" which urge one "to watch the uprise of successive mornings and to conspire with the new works of new days." Two other elements from this 1886 Lippincott volume are noteworthy beyond Van Rensselaer's continuing support of the Concord poets of Dawn with their vocabulary of hope. First, the physical facts behind the volume's printing processes; second, the nature of the volume's contents. Both indicate the directions "the new works of the new days" were to take after 1886.

The Lippincott editors state that they are making use of improved modes of reproduction and printing for the first time. The Forbes Company of Boston provided the photogravures; Ives of Philadelphia prepared the negatives from color works by means of the orthochromatic technique. In consequence of these innovations, every plate was of the very latest execution; nothing appearing in the volume had been designed before 1885. As for the contents: they were devoted to the art of the human figure and face. The very earliest American art, Van Rensselaer explains, had concentrated upon the portrait, but the first half of the nineteenth century had dismissed portrait studies in favor of the landscape. Changes taking place in the 1880s made possible a renewed emphasis upon the human form. See Estelle Jussim, *Visual Communication and the Graphic Arts*, for a detailed analysis of the ways "interpretation" was being altered by the new printing methods. Also see Neil Harris, "Iconography and Intellectual History," pp. 196–211.

21. The following quotations from Koehler's *American Art* are from pp. 1, 9, 12–13, 17–18.

22. The quotation here, included in Koehler's *American Art*, p. 9, is from a review Koehler wrote in 1880. He is selective in the type of "civilization" he hopes American artists will emulate, albeit in characteristically native ways. Like Jarves, he praises the Romantic movement in France and states his dislike of the pedantry of the German school and the morbidity of the English artists.

23. Neil Harris, among other recent historians, provides an excellent summation of the divisiveness rending American culture in the 1880s. See "The Gilded Age Reconsidered Once Again," p. 9.

24. See John Tomsich, *A Genteel Endeavor: American Culture and Politics in the Gilded Age*. Tomsich masses more than enough evidence to demonstrate the unhappy frame of mind possessed by "the Sunday Morning" pantheon of the lesser Olympians—Thomas Bailey Aldrich, William Osborn Stoddard, Charles Eliot Norton, Edmund Stedman, Bayard Taylor, and Richard Watson Gilder. Tomsich writes of "the genteel endeavor," "Its tool was culture, but its motivation was fear" (p. 365). It was fear steaming from the hopelessness these men felt that their desire for unity in sex, politics, and the arts could never be met. But just

as members of the middle class in no way made up the full constituency of the kingdom of yearning in the late nineteenth century, the aesthetics of desire practiced by the purveyors of genteel American cultural values is not the whole story.

25. New Yorkers tended to prefer paintings that were realistic, objective, and dealt with subjects from nature. Bostonians favored art that leaned toward idealism and self-expression. See Jarves, *The Art Idea*, p. 331. and Joshua Taylor, *Fine Arts in America*, p. 110.

26. Excellent sources concerning the development of an international style for American artists are Michael Quick's *American Expatriate Painters of the Late Nineteenth Century*, William H. Gerdts' *American Impressionism*, Richard J. Boyle's *American Impressionism*, and H. Barbara Weinberg's "The Lure of Paris: Late-Nineteenth-Century American Painters and Their French Training." The motives behind acceptance of the cosmopolitan style varied. It aided some to express their feelings about American life; others gained the satisfaction of becoming part of an extended art world and an escape from provincialism. But the note sounded here by Christian Brinton in his 1906 review of Samuel Isham's *The History of American Painting* remains a common one. Brinton rejects the notion that American artists abroad become "denationalised." They may take on cosmopolitan subjects, "but beneath mere subject lies that deeper, more significant psychological affinity which links each of them to the native race spirit. And it is just this alert, receptive race spirit transfusing canvases frankly imitative or frankly individual which constitutes American art" (p. 193).

27. See S. G. W. Benjamin, "Tendencies of Art in America," p. 105. The effects of the breaking away of young artists from the National Academy in order to form the American Art Association, later known as the Society of American Artists, are detailed by Koehler and Van Rensselaer in their essays of 1886 from *American Art* and *Book of American Figure Painters*; Lois M. Fink and Joshua C. Taylor, *Academy*; Patricia Jobe Pierce, *The Ten*.

28. S. G. W. Benjamin's 1880 essay "Tendencies of Art in America" explicitly states his belief that shifts in art follow the urgent lead of strong laws with a will of their own. His era's interest in determinism finds its way into aesthetic concerns as well as into areas of economics, politics, and the natural sciences. "The Absolute Necessity" prompted; the arts obeyed.

29. William Brownell, "The Younger Painters of America—First Paper," pp. 7–8. Brownell remained relatively calm in regard to his reservations concerning the new subjectivism. Others voiced more heated opposition to the display of highly personal feelings in art: William J. Stillman, "The Decay of Art" (1886), William Ordway Partridge, *Art for America* (1894), and Kenyon Cox in almost everything he wrote.

30. The stirrings in the art world summed up by Brownell in his essay of 1880 would soon, as Wayne Morgan has noted, "add to the momentum toward abstraction that triumphed after 1900." *New Muses*, p. 146. Janet Malcolm's review of the French art scene of the 1880s and 1890s concurs that the conditions were present for a shift from naturalism to "pictures 'formed by the mind' rather than by the eye—to an art of imitable and universal forms rather than of transitory and specific moments." "Photography: Maximilian's Sombrero," p. 93.

31. Whistler's art was itself part of that development in the direction of design and abstraction that emerged from the Pre-Raphaelites' intensity of response to closely observed natural details. For a useful review of the processes by which Whistler's art evolved, see the essays by Theodore Reff and Allen Staley collected in *From Realism to Symbolism*.

32. Inevitably, attempts are made to jam several genre tendencies under one label. Abbott Thayer is defined (with both desperation and acumen) as "the American Romantic-Realist." See "Abbott Thayer Celebrated in Washington," *Art News*, p. 57. Edwin Austin Abbey is (rightly) detected as working in between the "naïve heroics" of the mid-nineteenth century and the "ash-can-and-tenement realism" of the early twentieth century. See Kathleen A. Foster's essay "The Paintings."

33. Richard V. West, *Occasional Papers 1: The Walker Art Building Murals*, p. 30.

34. The following quotations are from John La Farge, *Considerations on Paintings*, pp. 70, 97–98, 101, 105, 118, 123, 204–205.

35. La Farge's comment could have been taken directly from William James' *The Principles of Psychology* of 1890, which continually underscores the pluralism of perceptions.

36. La Farge in his lectures of 1893 was not speaking against "authority" and "selection." He emphasized the strong relationship set up between the artist's brain, where memories are stored, and his hand, which repeats those memories through habit—a notion that is clearly Jamesian, Peircean, and Roycean in nature. La Farge also called for art's touchstones—"the influence of the best"— which provide the "relief" of placing order and meaning (via structure and form) upon a world of nature that remains chaotic if unaided by the piercing, selecting eye. Like James, Peirce, and Royce, La Farge noted that we try to *locate* ourselves in nature, thereby *composing* ourselves. "Composure" is the name of "beauty"— that which we love because we have *chosen* it. Also see La Farge, "The Field of Art: The American Academy at Rome" (1900), p. 253.

37. Royal Cortissoz, "Some Imaginative Types in American Art," pp. 178–179.

38. The following quotations are from Vernon Lee's "Imagination in Modern Art: Random Notes on Whistler, Sargent, and Besnard," pp. 515, 517.

39. Lee concludes that human thought (defined as "the lazy activity of day-dreaming, of mingled fancy and belief") reduces nature and instinct to order and makes good out of mischief. To the ancients, evil and good are merged, and Astarte is the reverse of Neith; to the moderns, as expressed by Vernon Lee at least, the "good half" appears to become the entire story.

40. Observation made by David Huntington in the catalog prepared in 1983 by the Detroit Institute of Arts for the exhibition "The Quest for Unity: American Art Between World's Fairs, 1876–1893," quoted in *Archives of American Art Journal*.

41. Jay Hambridge, *Dynamic Symmetry in Composition*, p. xvi. The following quotations are from p. 82.

42. Quoted from a letter by Howard Giles, instructor of the life class at the New York School of Fine and Applied Art; from Hambridge, *Dynamic Symmetry in Composition*, p. 48. Giles was joined in his enthusiasm by Denman W. Ross of Harvard who arranged for Hambridge to lecture on his theories at the university, and also by several artists of the period in addition to Henri and Bellows—Christine Herter and Leon Kroll among them. Also see Hambridge, *The Elements of Dynamic Symmetry*; Christine Herter, *Dynamic Symmetry: A Primer*.

43. Kenyon Cox, "Whistler and Absolute Painting," p. 637; Hambridge, *Dynamic Symmetry in Composition*, p. 83.

44. Charles H. Caffin, "The Art of Thomas W. Dewing," p. 721. What Caffin emphasized as the primary concern of the "new painting" had already been set forth in appraisals of the "new literature" by William Dean Howells in 1882 ("Henry James, Jr.") and by Henry James in 1884 and 1905 ("The Art of Fiction" and "The Lesson of Balzac"). The following quotations are from Caffin's essay, p. 724.

45. Caffin's description of the "modern" vision that deals with the confusions of pluralities and vastness by means of the focused eye has obvious affinities with "the camera vision" outlined by D. S. MacColl in 1902. See Introduction and chapter 8.

46. When Russell Sturgis spoke of "pure" form in his two works of 1904 and 1905, *The Appreciation of Pictures* and *The Appreciation of Sculpture*, he was not as laudatory as Caffin. Sturgis was no less firm in his conviction that form is what matters—not sentiment, anecdote, archaeological detail, or moral principles; but not necessarily *pure* form. If Whistler pursued color, Hambridge doted on rectangles, and Dewing concentrated on mood symbols, Sturgis liked the old-fashioned "flesh and blood side of art." But Sturgis' meat—derived

from good drawing that emphasized decorative patterns of force, dignity, and seriousness—also placed him in opposition to the young mavericks of "the Eight" who would see him, together with the likes of Caffin and Kenyon Cox, as too sophisticated and refined—*too official*—ever to act as their spokesman. Ashcans may be painted for the purpose of drawing attention to the dynamic symmetry of geometrical shapes; they can be part of Whistlerian arrangements in black and white (although the "music" those cans are analogous to are ragtime and the back-fence squallings of cats, not nocturnes). But the Eight painted scenes that were too anecdotal and sociological to suit the other "new realists" of their generation. Color, geometry, and *idea* were the aims of Whistler, Hambridge, and Dewing, and—in his own way—Sturgis. They were not enough for the Eight, who wanted to bring art and society together. So the internecine warfare continued within the varied ranks of the New Realists. Some stayed with flesh and blood; others went on to celebrate machines as icons for modern times; still others kept to the abstractions of form that spoke of the inner life.

47. Patricia Hills, "Turn-of-the-Century America," p. 97. Another, more extensive examination of the issue is given by Rebecca Zurier in *Art for the Masses (1911–1917)*, p. 126.

48. Richard Bernheimer, *The Nature of Representation*, p. 173.

49. *Our Girls* was published by Moffat, Yard of New York in 1907. Like many commercial illustrators of his generation, Christy produced lavishly decorated "gift books." In 1898 Christy's *Pastel Portraits from the Romantic Drama* was published by Scribner's. *Types of the American Girl* appeared in 1900 as a limited edition of portfolios of colored reproductions. In 1902 Christy switched from Scribner's to Bobbs-Merrill and prepared *The Courtship of Miles Standish* in 1903 and *Evangeline* in 1905. *The Christy Girl* followed in 1906, and the two Moffat, Yard gift books of 1906 and 1907—*Our Girls* and *The American Girl*. *Liberty Belles: Eight Epochs in the Making of the American Girl* was published by Bobbs-Merrill in 1908. Each of his projects celebrated a romanticized version of the American past summed up by images of pretty young women, whether as a gift book per se or a pictorialization of the historical romances of Thomas Nelson Page *(The Old Gentleman of the Black Stock)* and George Washington Cable *(The Cavalier)* in 1901 and 1902.

50. Paul Bourget, *Outre-Mer*, p. 50. The following quotations are from the same page.

51. Christy arrived on the New York art scene in 1892, a young man from Ohio on the make, a latter-day William Dean Howells. (Christy, like Howells, would do well at portraying American heroines, although from quite different motives and perspectives.) Christy first studied with William Merritt Chase, one of the best-known art teachers of the 1890s. He admired the paintings of Sargent, as well as the illustrations of Gustave Doré, Abbey, and Howard Pyle. When the boom in magazine illustrations (made possible by technical improvements that provided cheap, skillfully executed reproductions) made it clear that illustrators would have more success than painters, Christy decided the direction he would take, and in 1895 he gave himself full time to the trade. The early days were difficult since it was not easy to break into the circle of the top publishers and magazines where the steady contract money was, but by 1898 Christy had established himself, and the way was smooth from then on. These and more details concerning Christy's career and the publishing context which created and sustained his great success are available from the following sources: Susan E. Meyer, *America's Great Illustrators* and "Howard Chandler Christy"; Norris F. Schneider, *Howard Chandler Christy*. Also see the National Museum of American Art, Christy Ephemera File; *Howard Chandler Christy: Artist/Illustrator of Style*; Howard Chandler Christy, "Model-Lives."

52. Illustrations that featured dream-vision images indicative of loss and regret were hardly new in 1898 when Christy did his first sketch. A Melander and Brothers stereopticon view of 1880, "Memories of the Past," shows an elderly man musing over books and letters while the dim image of a woman in a bridal gown prompts his thoughts. Gibson picked up the motif as early as 1893 (e.g., "A Bachelor's Supper") and would continue to use it into the

early 1900s (e.g., "When a Man's in Love" and "The Weaker Sex—X," to list only a few of his many titles). So would Albert Beck Wenzell and the newcomer James Montgomery Flagg.

53. At the conclusion of World War I Christy was determined to stop drawing pretty girls for public pay and to dignify his career by turning full time to portrait-painting. (Christy continued to keep his hand in for the pleasure of his inner circle of artist friends, as his murals still visible at the Café des Artistes in New York make clear.) The art world received no surprises when Christy made his shift. His slick portrait treatment of persons of fashion and celebrity confirms the ease with which he could always paint to please, not to question, the values of Society and society, and how he could stay on top even when he changed the nature of his artistic media. His portraits include those of Mrs. Calvin Coolidge, Mrs. William Randolph Hearst, President Harding, Mussolini, Will Rogers, Mary Baker Eddy, Norman Vincent Peale, Eddie Rickenbacker, and the Prince of Wales; they all suggest the equation he made between appearance and public importance (that is, power). He finished his professional career with two patriotic murals. "We the People" was an allegory produced for the 1937 sesquicentennial of the Constitution, containing Miss Liberty wreathed by a halo. "The Signing of the Constitution," completed in 1940, was commissioned for the Capitol in Washington, D.C. (It caused some uproar over its excessive cost.) Before his death in 1945, Christy also did a spurt of war posters in which his energetically smiling girl stands, as always, to the fore.

54. Henry James, *The American Scene*, pp. 32–33. Also see Robert Grant, *The Art of Living* (1895), pp. 234–250.

55. Fairfax Downey, *Portrait of an Era*, p. 108. The following information about Gibson's formative years and his success as America's leading popular illustrator is largely drawn from Downey's book. Other useful sources include Susan E. Meyer, *America's Great Illustrators*; Henry C. Pitz, "Charles Dana Gibson"; and Robert Koch, "Gibson Girl Revisited." Also see the editor's remarks upon signing Gibson to an extended contract for *Collier's Weekly* (November 29, 1902), 30(9):8–9; Gary A. Best, "Charles Dana Gibson"; the National Museum of American Art, Gibson Ephemera File.

56. Downey describes how Gibson's visual imagination worked even as a child: "Storing away images of models in his mind, he would cut his silhouettes from memory and produce whole scenes from a single sheet." *Portrait of an Era*, p. 6.

57. An essay of 1899 claims that Gibson's drawing techniques altered after 1894 under the influence of his second trip to Paris in that year. "He gradually drew away from his fine-line drawings and told his story in a few bold strokes where he would formerly have used a hundred." From Charles Belmont Davis, "Mr. Charles Dana Gibson and His Art," p. 53. One recent critic reverses the nature of the influence by stating that it was Gibson's superior draughtsmanship that affected European pen-drawing by the late 1890s. See Henry C. Pitz, "Charles Dana Gibson," p. 54. From whichever direction it came, the technique became one of extreme economy of means. What remained constant was "the idea of a beautiful woman," however altered the methods for her representation. In Davis' words, "She is still called the Gibson Girl, but how much she is changed and how different she is if we but study her carefully" (p. 52).

Prior to 1890, Gibson's work for *Life* focused on politics and the cultural scene; during the 1890s through 1910, when his popularity reached its peak, Gibson gave a great deal of time to drawing scenes which did not feature his Girl, but his reputation rested largely on her. His ability to change his art techniques to match his idea of the Girl, and the capacity of his idea to develop, worked together perfectly for about twenty years. Then both images and idea reached their limit; neither could keep up with or continue to influence the public imagination. It is somewhat sad to note the ineffectuality of Gibson's attempts to bring his Girl into the decade of World War I. Prior to 1910 the image he provided was indeed "a portrait of an era." Unable to stay outside time, or to keep pace with time, that image vanished as a historical type and a cultural value, though it remains as a masterly formal design of black strokes upon white paper.

58. Susan Meyer lists prominent society figures who came to Gibson's studio, full of an amateur's enthusiasm and attended by chaperons, to model for his Girl. *America's Great Illustrators*, p. 217. The sequence of cause and effect is suspect if taken too narrowly. The clamor of would-be models in the mid-1890s came about as the result of the fame Gibson had already received. Gibson's marriage to one of the day's most celebrated beauties caused wide attention. See the *New York Times* of November 8, 1895, p. 8, and the *New York World* of August 16, 1895. The *World* placed the caption "The Face of Romance and the Face of Reality" next to illustrations representing Gibson, Irene Langhorne, and the Gibson Girl; the point was to compare the Girl that Gibson dreamed up with the young woman he was to marry. But if Gibson's ideal was made flesh by Irene Langhorne, the idea had come first. Downey quotes Gibson as having denied that there had ever been an Ur type which preceded the idea. The meeting with, and marrying of, Irene Langhorne had only one result: the Girl "was an ideal, rather than a portrait, until one night at Delmonico's Gibson discovered the girl who for him would be both." *Portrait of an Era*, p. 211.

59. Quoted in *Time*, January 1945. National Museum of American Art, Gibson Ephemera File.

60. *Charles Dana Gibson* (New York: Collier, 1905), n.p.

61. Undated reference, from *This Fabulous Century: Sixty Years of American Life*, p. 183.

62. One of Gibson's contemporaries remarked that Gibson drew "the girl of the period as his own young eyes saw her—that is to say, as she was, but clothed with a glamour that made her . . . shirt-waist and pompadour crow's nest topped by a hard stiff hat, accessories of grace." Downey, *Portrait of an Era*, p. 198.

63. C. Belmont Davis, "Mr. Charles Dana Gibson and His Art," p. 50.

64. In an undated cartoon, James Montgomery Flagg tried to clarify the lineage from the Gibson Girl to her imitators. He pictured the Girl surrounded by Gibson (arms folded), Christy, and Flagg (the latter two with drawing pads). The caption reads: "Charles Dana Gibson is the Papa of the 'Gibson Girl'—Howard Chandler Christy and James Montgomery Flagg *were not that good!* Let this end *that* stupidity! Next!" Susan E. Meyer, *America's Great Illustrators*, p. 32. In 1896 Frank Norris wrote an assessment of the American Girl depicted by Gibson and Albert Beck Wenzell. He notes that Wenzell's women are "entirely given over to society" and devoted to externals; they are depicted "in places, in conditions." In contrast, Norris remarks, Gibson's women are approached psychologically and inwardly; they are shown "in states of mind" and "in circumstances." From "A Question of Ideals: The American Girl of 1896 as Seen by Wenzel [*sic*] and by Gibson," pp. 166–168. Whatever similarities of pose, costume, and setting Gibson's imitators brought to their drawings, the inner life of their young women did not match that of Gibson's best images.

65. Davis, "Mr. Charles Dana Gibson and His Art," p. 52.

66. See *This Fabulous Century*, p. 183; Downey, *Portrait of an Era*, pp. 200–204; Robert Koch, "Gibson Girl Revisited," p. 73; Henry C. Pitz, "Charles Dana Gibson," p. 52, for an inventory of the many items licensed to bear the Gibson Girl imprint.

67. "Having copied to conquer, having obligingly lived up to what men thought [the women] ought to be," they "proceeded to oblige men to live up to them." Downey, *Portrait of an Era*, p. 192.

68. *Ibid.*, p. 186.

5. *Masking, Camouflage, Inversions, and Play*

1. The 1877 advertisement composed by Eakins also mentioned that "applicants should be of respectability and may on all occasions be accompanied by their mothers or other

female relatives." In 1885 a commentator noted the paradox of concealed face, exposed body. See David Sellin's essay "Eakins and the Macdowells and the Academy." Eakins' painting of William Rush and his nude model, accompanied by a chaperon, was criticized by the *New York Times* in 1878 as shocking because of the presence of her discarded clothes heaped on a chair. See Weinberg, "Late-Nineteenth-Century American Painting," p. 25.

2. See Kathleen Abbott, *Masks and Ikons; Alter Ego, Masks: Their Art and Use;* Wladyslaw Theodore Benda, *Masks;* Ellen Russell Emerson, *Masks, Heads, and Faces; Image and Identity: The Role of the Mask in Various Cultures.*

3. Michael Schau, *"All-American Girl"—the Art of Coles Phillips*, p. 21.

4. Ross Anderson, *Abbott Handerson Thayer*, pp. 12–13, 112–126; Susan Hobbs, "Nature Into Art: The Landscapes of Abbott Handerson Thayer"; Nelson C. White, *Abbott H. Thayer, Painter and Naturalist*, p. 14. Thayer's growing concern with nature's methods of coloration led to the book he wrote in collaboration with his son Gerald in 1909, *Concealing-Coloration in the Animal Kingdom, an Exposition of the Laws of Disguise Through Color and Pattern: Being a Summary of Abbott H. Thayer's Discoveries;* but he had begun to set down his ideas in journals such as *The Auk* by 1896.

5. "Thayer's law" was first presented to the public in the Smithsonian Report of 1897. Essentially, Thayer wished to stress a law of gradation in coloring which allows for mimicry. He believed that animals are darkest when most brilliantly lighted; the two effects (light and shadow) cancel one another, and animals melt into the background. It is not that the creatures are invisible, but that the viewer looks *through* them. For further comments upon Thayer's notions, see the exhibition catalog *Abbott H. Thayer*, Carnegie Institute; Homer Saint-Gaudens, "Abbott H. Thayer"; Ross Anderson, *Abbott Handerson Thayer*, pp. 113–126; Nelson C. White, *Abbott H. Thayer: Painter and Naturalist*, pp. 122–134.

6. Benson's unsigned article "Dress of American Women" appeared in *The Round Table*, January 2, 1864. "The Riot of the Women" (unsigned) ran in September 30, 1865, in denunciation of "the reign of scarlet"; yet another anonymous piece in the October 14, 1865, issue of *The Round Table* attacked the "Purple Women" whose extravagant dress was out of keeping during the austerities of the Civil War. It is interesting to note that, whatever praise Benson gave to the "generally soft, delicate, clearly cut type of American beauty" attired in muted colors, several of his own oil paintings depict women gathering flowers while wearing clothes as vivid as the natural colors around them. See Ella M. Forshay's exhibition catalog *Reflections of Nature: Flowers in American Art.* The experiences of World War II acted against the belief of Benson and his fellow essayist voiced in *The Round Table* that women in wartime should be as quiet as doves. Fashion magazines of the 1940s encouraged and expressed the public mood by featuring images of women wearing scarlet lipstick and bright attire as a boost to the general morale. (The attribution of the Benson essay was made by Robert J. Scholnick.)

7. Edith Wharton, *The Custom of the Country*, p. 22. The following quotations are from pp. 22, 28, 49, 65, 594.

8. Theodore Dreiser, *Sister Carrie*, p. 42. The following quotations are from pp. 42–43, 46–47. The Pennsylvania edition is based upon Dreiser's original manuscript, not the heavily cut version first published by Doubleday (New York) in 1900.

9. *Character and Unique Fashions: Suggestions for Fancy-Dress Costumes.*

10. William Wasserstrom, *The Heiress of All the Ages*, p. 129.

11. Beverly and her women friends have occasions when they dress in men's clothing, but they take no pleasure in what are for them embarrassing moments. See McCutcheon, *Beverly of Graustark*, p. 325. Stills from the 1926 movie starring Marion Davies indicate that gender inversions took a far more prominent role in the Hollywood version, but McCutcheon's Beverly is of the same mind as Cora C. Klein who admonished in *Practical Etiquette*, "It is very bad taste, even for a frolic, for a young girl to assume boy's clothes,

or get herself up in any way that will tend to make herself look masculine" (p. 129). There were many other young women, however, of Beverly's generation who enjoyed just such a "frolic."

12. But even before the hero learns the sex of Mercedes, his American "princess," he concludes that the Boy was "that Other Half which everyman is always unconsciously looking for." C. N. and A. M. Williamson, *The Princess Passes*, p. 368.

13. V. G. Rocine, *Heads, Faces, Types, Races*, p. 184. The description of the Reverend Mr. Caine that follows is from p. 39.

14. George Santayana's "The Genteel Tradition in American Philosophy" was delivered before the Philosophical Union of the University of California, Berkeley, in 1911; it was published by Scribner's in *Winds of Doctrine: Studies in Contemporary Opinion*, 1913.

15. Simms, *Physiognomy Illustrated*, pp. 435–437, anxiously ponders the plight of the woman who takes after her father and assumes male standards of behavior, but he is more concerned about the social dislocations caused by masculine energy and independence contained within a female body. Simms also stresses the dire consequences of prenatal influences that occur when a pregnant woman gazes too long upon male images, thereby warping the nature of her unborn girl-child. The illustration Simms uses here to represent the "incorrect" female is of Rosa Bonheur. It should be compared with the oil portrait painted in 1898 by Anna Elizabeth Klumpke, a lifelong admirer of the famous French artist.

16. See Helen Goodrich Buttrick, *Principles of Clothing Selection*; Jessica Daves, *Ready-Made Miracle: The American Story of Fashions for the Millions*; Steven Fraser, "Combined and Uneven Development in the Men's Clothing Industry"; Claudia B. Kidwell, *Cutting a Fashionable Fit: Dressmakers' Drafting Systems in the United States*; C. B. Kidwell and Margaret C. Christman, *Suiting Everyone: The Democratization of Clothing in America*; Daniel E. Ryan, *Human Proportions in Growth: Being the Complete Measurement of the Human Body*; Leon Stein, *The Triangle Fire*.

17. Elocution manuals often referred to the notion of masculine freedom in play. One example, meant to be presented by small girls, is titled "Why I'd Rather Be a Boy." It reads in its entirety, "Boys have good times. They can swim and skate and coast, ride horseback, climb trees, play hop-toad, make cartwheels of themselves, and slide down the banisters; and most girls can't." Frances B. Hoyle, *The Complete Speaker and Reciter*, "Little Folks' Speaker," p. 288.

18. These and most of the group photographs and snapshots to come (as well as those taken singly of my mother from the age of sixteen, included in the Introduction, chapter 1, and elsewhere) were taken by Merle Smith, a young professional photographer who married one of the women of my mother's group in Montpelier, Indiana. Smith was usually on the spot at informal gatherings, ready to take pictures to commemorate the event; he and the women worked together to stage special tableaux; he frequently used my mother as his favorite model to enact through more formalized "studio" studies the images he had in mind. Smith's presence at these visual events contributes a unique element: he was a professional but also one of "the crowd." It is impossible to tell exactly where his inspirations for shots ended and those of his friends began, since both photographer and subjects responded to a repertoire of images common to them all.

Useful works which analyze the specific problems and benefits of interpreting family photographs include James W. Davidson and Mark H. Lyttle, *After the Fact: The Art of Historical Detection*; Judi Hirsch, *Family Photographs: Content, Meaning, and Effect*; Michael Lesy, *Time Frames: The Meaning of Family Pictures*; Thomas J. Schlereth, *Artifacts and the American Past*, "Mirrors of the Past," pp. 11–47; George Talbot, *At Home: Domestic Life in the Post-Centennial Era, 1876–1920*. On p. xv of *Time Frames*, Lesy states best the circumstances which I know pertained to Merle Smith's renderings of the Montpelier scene: "The people who appear in the photographs in this book often strike (or have been directed to strike) theatrical poses, and make (or have been directed to make) symbolic gestures whose meanings are to be deciphered by their intimates and descendents. At times, they make gestures of their own free will; at other times, their actions are directed." The presence of the camera "transforms the people it beholds into actors, standing in sets, posing with symbolic props, the whole scene a private allegory of love, defined by the edge of an imaginary proscenium stage. . . . Sometimes the people pictured have been well rehearsed, know their parts, and enjoy them. Other times they 'forget' or improvise them, or even evade them."

As for the even larger matter of the interpretation of photographic images in relation to the culture, refer to this selected list of books and articles: Roland Barthes, *Camera Lucida: Reflections on Photography*; Brian Coe and Paul Gates, *The Snapshot Photograph: The Rise of Popular Photography, 1888–1939*; John Collier, Jr., *Visual Anthropology: Photography as a Research Method*; Michael Lesy, *Wisconsin Death-Trap*; Gisèle Freund, *Photography and Society*; Wright Morris, "Photographs, Images, and Words"; Joel Snyder, "Picturing Vision"; Joel Snyder and Neil Walsh Allen, "Photography, Vision, and Representation"; Susan Sontag, *On Photography*; John Szarkowski, *The Photographer's Eye*; Kendall L. Walton, "Transparent Pictures: On the Nature of Photographic Realism."

19. Material on J. C. Leyendecker is available from the National Museum of American Art, Leyendecker Ephemera File; Susan E. Meyer, *America's Great Illustrators*; Michael Schau, *J. C. Leyendecker*. The information concerning Leyendecker's art training, the progress of his commercial success, and his working technique places him solidly within the contemporary tradition of image-as-idea which he shared with artists ranging from Abbott Thayer to the compilers of dress-pattern book illustrations. Leyendecker's homosexuality influenced his choice of the male models who provided him "the look" he preferred; but when Leyendecker did artwork representing college athletes, he turned toward the conventions of the "manly" type personified at the turn of the century by Richard Harding Davis. See Fairfax Downey, *Richard Harding Davis: His Day*.

20. William James, *The Principles of Psychology*, 1:294.

21. See the perceptive reading of Cooley's book, and of *Mind, Self, and Society* (1934) by George H. Mead, written by Gregory Stone. Titled "Appearance and the Self," Stone's essay has much to say about Cooley's and Mead's contributions to the theory of "fantastic socialization," especially the section on "Play, Costume, and Dressing Out," pp. 236–241.

22. John Luther Long's short story "Madame Butterfly" appeared in *The Century*, January 1898). David Belasco presented his stage version in 1900. The first performance in the United States of Giacomo Puccini's opera was in 1906. By the time the photograph shown in figure 5.59 was taken (around 1910–11), the sad story of Cio-Cio-San had taken its place in the culture, together with other elements of imagery that had been filtering down since elite circles in Paris and London took up the *japonaise* look in the 1860s.

23. Taylor's biographer records the pleasure Taylor derived from dressing up for the roles of women he took in various dramatic groups and then going into local shops to see if he could fool the proprietors with his disguise. Frank Barkley Copley, *Frederic W. Taylor, Father of Scientific Management*, 1:88–89.

24. Scott Fitzgerald did not actually appear in the Triangle Club production; his low grades made him ineligible. The story of Fitzgerald's activities as the Club's lyricist is given in Donald Marsden, *The Long Kickline: A History of the Princeton Triangle Club*, pp. 90–101; Matthew J. Bruccoli, *Some Sort of Epic Grandeur*, pp. 62–63. Records indicate that "The Evil Eye" (not "Fie-Fie, Fi-Fi!" as mentioned in the *Times* caption) was the occasion of the Fitzgerald publicity photograph. For a review of the activities of the men at Harvard, see *An Illustrated History of the Hasty Pudding Club Theatricals*.

25. Robert C. Toll, *On with the Show: The First Centuries of Show Business in America*,

pp. 239–263. Toll's detailed account of the popularity of impersonators demonstrates that such acts made up an important segment of respectable "family" entertainment through the 1910s.

26. The frontispiece for the *Julian Eltinge Magazine and Beauty Hints* shows Eltinge as a male; the caption reads "The Man You All Know." One of the brief pieces of advice Eltinge writes, headed "The Woman Who Poses," admonishes women "be yourselves," then offers to send them six photographic poses of himself as a woman with the purchase of a jar of his cold cream. Epistemological complications increase with every page. *Photos:* "Julian Eltinge Made Beautiful as the Society Woman by Using the Julian Eltinge Cold Cream, Liquid Whiting, and Powder"; "See What the Julian Eltinge Cold Cream Does for a Man. It Will Do More for a Woman"; "The Handsomest Woman on the Stage Is a Man." *Random remarks:* "Woman's Brain Superior to Man's"; the observation that Eltinge never uses an understudy for his stage appearance since he is unique and has to "stand alone." *Conclusion:* photograph of Eltinge telling his mother about his beauty products. The Eltinge material is from the Theater Collection, Princeton University Library.

27. Consider, however, the argument advanced by Mary Vida Clarke in an essay of 1918 titled "Sauce for the Gander and Sawdust for the Goose." Clarke objects to the lack of sexually enticing males on the popular stage. Men in the audiences have their fantasies nourished by the parade of female beauties, but women are denied the pleasure of viewing interesting males. Major female stars are usually accompanied by weak and unattractive male ingenues or by other women dressed as young boys. Clarke concludes, "The equal rights that women demand should include the equality of opportunity for emotional satisfaction in the musical comedy of the future."

28. See "Actresses in Men's Roles," an item from the *New York Sun*; Robert C. Toll, *On with the Show*, p. 240.

29. The information concerning Vesta Tilley's career is drawn from *The Green Room Book or Who's Who on the Stage*, pp. 432–433; Toll, *On with the Show*, p. 259; and the autobiography written by Lady de Frece (née Matilda Alice Powles), *Recollections of Vesta Tilley*. Lady de Frece's account of her life (1864–1952) is resolutely sunny and very meager concerning the hard facts after the manner of many stage memoirs of that period. Intriguing details manage to seep through, however. From the first, Tilley believed she expressed herself best when dressed as a boy since "female costume was rather a drag" (p. 25). It took an hour for her to get dressed before her performances because she had to bind down her body to eliminate all feminine curves (p. 187). She received many ardently worded letters, visits, and floral tributes from her female admirers, and was given access to a diary which recorded the obsessive fascination felt toward her person by one young woman who followed her from performance to performance (pp. 233–235).

30. Recall that Leap Year is an "official," albeit infrequent, social occasion which gives women the license to speak their feelings and take a lead in their affairs. The Leap Year motif was a common one throughout the 1890s and into the 1910s and often received satiric and comic treatment. Charles Dana Gibson prepared several series for *Life* in which he pictured women in newly usurped male functions: the church, the military, the diplomatic corps, the law, athletics. In 1903 Gibson developed the series for *Collier's Weekly* called "The Weaker Sex" in which women, appearing in traditional dress and demeanor, enact variations on the age-old notion that women control men through their ability to overthrow male intellect (see figure 12.8). The following quotations are from George Barr McCutcheon's story "When Girl Meets Girl."

6. Literary Portraits and Types: Crises

1. James, *The Notebooks of Henry James*, p. 15.

2. Henry James, Preface, *The Portrait of a Lady*, 3:xi–xii. The following quotations from the preface and the novel are from pp. xi–xv, xvii, xxi, 24, 69, 144–145.

3. I am not willing to argue that the launching of an extended critique of "the type" was a fully conscious intention on James' part when writing the *Portrait*. I only say, Look at what is there in the novel, what is implied once we analyze the function of Isabel's portrait, and what her type as the American Girl does to shape the narrative's meaning.

4. Henry James, "The Art of Fiction," p. 406.

5. Christy, *The American Girl*, p. 65. James Montgomery Flagg's drawing of 1908 titled "The Assassins" depicts an irate mob of young women and men in pursuit of the fleeing figure of Father Time upon whom they wish to vent their anger. That the aftermath of marriage received serious treatment by some American writers is shown in Allen F. Stein, *After the Vows Were Spoken: Marriage in American Literary Realism*.

6. Mark Twain, preface, *The Comedy of Those Extraordinary Twins*, pp. 313–315. Once this supposedly comic tale proved to have elements that were both farcical and tragic, Mark Twain wrenched it apart (not very cleanly, as readers of *Pudd'nhead Wilson* realize) and published *The Tragedy of Pudd'nhead Wilson* and *The Comedy of Those Extraordinary Twins* as separate stories contained within the same volume.

7. See Peter Galassi, *Before Photography*, p. 27. Also see Viola Hopkins Winner, *Henry James and the Visual Arts*, p. 10; Rudolf Arnheim, "A Plea for Visual Thinking," p. 493; R. Arnheim, "Visual Thinking," pp. 1–15.

8. See John W. Crowley and Charles L. Crow, "Psychic and Psychological Themes in Howells' 'A Sleep and a Forgetting.' "

9. The following words in praise of the "Normal Woman" from Ecob's *The Well-Dressed Woman* (whose subtitle is "The Good, the True, the Beautiful") are from pp. 208, 216, 224. On pp. 227–228 Ecob quotes from William James' *The Principles of Psychology* in regard to the body as the innermost part of the material (outer) self.

10. Robert Langbaum, "The Exteriority of Self in Yeats's Poetry and Thought," p. 582. The following quotations are from pp. 582, 587.

11. Johann Casper Lavater, *Essays on Physiognomy*, 1:18. The following quotations (2:74–76; 1:18) incorporate remarks extracted by Lavater from Johann Georg Sulzer's "General Theory of the Fine Arts" (1771–74).

12. Paul K. Alkon, "Visual Rhetoric in *The Autobiography of Alice B. Toklas*." The following quotation is from p. 874.

13. See Graeme Tytler, *Physiognomy in the European Novel*, pp. 318–319.

14. Gertrude Stein, "What are Master-pieces and Why are there so few of them," p. 149.

15. The following quotations from Arthur C. Danto, *The Transfiguration of the Commonplace*, are from pp. 205, 207–208. Reasons *not* to take Danto's book seriously are outlined in a generally dismissive review by Flint Schier for *TLS* (February 4, 1893), p. 111. Schier focuses in particular upon Danto's somewhat shaky argument concerning the "transparency" of an artist's style, but I suggest that Danto leads his readers through stimulating conceptual terrain that is necessarily bumpy.

16. Whistler's remark is reported in "Whistler Unattached" by Andrew McLaren Young, an essay prepared for the catalog of the University of Glasgow exhibition mounted in 1971 at the Nottingham University Art Gallery. See the National Museum of American Art, Whistler Ephemera File.

17. On May 17, 1896, the *New York World* ran a story about "The Dancer," a statue executed by the Parisian sculptor Jean Alexandre Falguière. The notorious Clio de Mérode posed for the statue's head. The question raised by the newspaper account was whether the

rest of the nude figure duplicated the exact shape of de Mérode's body. Prurient interest was great. The public wanted to "know" the whole woman completely by extending her "style" from the head all the way down along the sinuously naked body.

18. Ellen Russell Emerson is cited in Frances Willard and Mary Livermore's volume *A Woman of the Century* (1893); an entry in *The Dictionary of American Biography* further elaborates upon her achievements. Ellen Russell was born in 1837, educated at Mt. Vernon Seminary in Boston, and married in 1862 to Edwin R. Emerson. She began her career as an ethnologist with work on the American Indian, which led to her first book, a comparative study of Indian myths published in 1884. After taking up Egyptology in Paris between 1886 and 1889, she wrote *Masks, Heads, and Faces* following further years of study. The following quotations are from pp. 1–2.

19. The following quotations from Arthur Bartlett Maurice's essay "Representative American Story Tellers" are from pp. 140, 142, 143.

20. Vacation cards stress the fact of geographical distances; they are mailed for the purpose of saying, "This is *where* I am," and also, "*I* am the one who is here." They remind those who receive them that the senders are old friends in new situations (persons who for that reason are somewhat different from what they are "back home"). The photographic formula reestablishes the status of the sender's usual identity, yet declares a deviation from the general state of affairs. The senders are indeed "on holiday" from the daily "average" of their identity.

21. The following quotations from Henry Dwight Sedgwick, *The New American Type and Other Essays*, are from pp. 30–31, 38, 40–43, 48.

22. The next three quotations are taken from *When Knighthood Was in Flower* of 1908 by Charles Major (250,000 volumes sold); *Dorothy Vernon of Haddon Hall* (1902), also by Major (illustrated by H. C. Christy who gives the sixteenth-century English heroine an American Girl pompadour); and Hallie Erminie Rives' novel of 1902, *Hearts Courageous*. The following are useful references to popular fiction of the turn of the century and the commercialization of what Laurence Burnham in "The Modern Heroine in Illustration" called "The 'Heroine Trust' ": David L. Cohn, *The Good Old Days: A History of American Morals and Manners as Seen Through the Sears, Roebuck Catalogs, 1905 to the Present;* Alice Payne Hackett, *Fifty Years of Best Sellers, 1895–1945;* James D. Hart, *The Popular Book: A History of America's Literary Taste;* Frank Luther Mott, *Golden Multitudes: The Story of Best Sellers in the United States.* These works bear out what Sedgwick had in mind (*The New American Type*, pp. 30–31) when distinguishing between "the proletarian reading mob" ("which reads dime novels"), "the lower bourgeois reading mob" ("which reads the novels of Albert Ross, E. P. Roe, and the like"), and "the upper bourgeois reading mob" ("which reads Winston Churchill, Charles Major, Thomas Dixon, Jr., Mary Hartwell Carterwood, Hallie Erminie Rives, and others . . . [and] which buys its books over the book-counter of department stores, on the train, at the news-stand, from the book-agent at the front door, or borrows them from circulating libraries").

It is instructive to compare the passages that follow in the main text with this description of a group of young Boston women whose "faces stand out clear and bright and not to be forgotten, as a very part of this charming scene." "Now a little brunette flashes her bright eyes from under a coquettish bonnet, that only makes the wearer more deliciously piquant than ever . . . ; near by is a blonde, tall and graceful, with merry blue eyes and pale hair with a glint of gold running through it that defies bands, combs, and pins, waving, crimping and curling just as it pleases, whether the wearer wills it or not; looking out from under a jaunty velvet hat is a sweet, shy face, with delicate color in the cheeks that comes and goes . . . the blue eyes grow more serious and intent, and the tender mouth graver and quieter. . . . Science softens under the sparks of their eyes, and philosophy becomes poetry in their pretty, pouting mouths." These young women are not drawn from a novel by Charles Major or George Barr McCutcheon, or from a gift book written and illustrated by Howard Chandler Christy. These are real "upper bourgeois types" in the class sense—the original members of the Saturday Morning Club of Boston, founded by Julia Ward Howe for the pleasure and instruction of her daughter in 1871.

The description is taken from a piece prepared in 1873 for the *Boston Post* and is included in *The Story of the Saturday Morning Club of Boston*, printed in 1932 on the occasion of the club's sixtieth anniversary. In chapter 15 I discuss at length the earnest production of *Antigone* put on by the Saturday Morning Club in 1890; there I address the problems the members had in conveying the seriousness of their ideas about the Sisterhood in the face of the trivialization made of their efforts by newspaper accounts which spoke mainly of their charm, beauty, and fashion. But as long as descriptions such as the one just quoted from p. 13 of the official club biography received their sanction, the club members would continue to be "seen" as they, it seems, chose to see themselves.

23. Paul Bourget, *Outre-Mer*, p. 83. William Dean Howells commented (in *Heroines of Fiction*, 1:90) that young women as they appeared in the pages of the contemporary novel were Nice Girls, not Real Girls; he did not go as far as Bourget in characterizing the latter type as depraved in any sense.

24. The following quotations from Jeanne Howell, *A Common Mistake*, are from pp. 24–25, 136–137. An advertising blurb placed at the back of *Biltry*, Mary Kyle Dallas' 1895 parody of *Trilby*, describes Howell's heroine as a representative of the "undisciplined, brilliant, nervous young womanhood of America," a person who misuses her own will in ways that Paul Bourget would appreciate.

25. Sylvia Gilchrist both attracts and repels the heart of the darkly handsome, sardonic lawyer Ballantine, who is very like the lawyer hero of Wharton's novel. Sylvia is surrounded by other skeptics, as is Wharton's Lily Bart; both groups bring in society's judgments of probable guilt against the young women based on what they "see" and what "people say." *A Common Mistake* concludes, as does *The House of Mirth*, with the hero kneeling in remorse at the bedside of the heroine who is dead through overdoses of soothing chloral and unbearable suspicion.

26. The following two passages are from pp. 8, 133, of George Barr McCutcheon's *Beverly of Graustark*, which ranked sixth on that year's best-seller list. Beverly Calhoun is a true "upper bourgeois heroine" who tells her friends that, for all her adventures, she is not the type of "the dime-store heroine" or "the yellow-book girl" (p. 14).

27. Henry James, *The Tragic Muse*, p. 56.

28. Edith Wharton, *The Custom of the Country*, pp. 195–196. Popple's purpose ("a pure question of color, of pattern") is contrasted with Van Degen's purpose (to take pleasure in the realistic likeness of a beautiful woman). The painter's desire initially makes the portrait-image take command: it has "the air of having been invited to 'receive' for Mr. Popple." But then Undine, who has been seated behind the easel, steps forward and becomes the thing looked at. It is significant that Wharton's description of Undine at this point emphasizes that the living woman appears "dead white," "shadowless," and "starred with the hard glitter of diamonds." What could be a more realistic likeness of the kind appreciated by Van Degen than Undine herself, yet in actual appearance she forms the image "of color, of pattern," aspired to by Popple's art; in particular that art which traces itself back to the ancient traditions of silhouette outline and grisaille. See J. Patrice Marandel, foreword, *Gray Is the Color: An Exhibition of Grisaille Painting*. The above quotations from *The Custom of the Country* are from pp. 188–189, 195.

29. The painting Bourget saw was Sargent's portrait of Isabella Stewart Gardner. It received a public showing upon its completion in 1888 at the St. Botolph Club in Boston, at which time the identity of the woman in the picture remained unknown. The following

quotations from Bourget's account of "The American Idol" are from pp. 107–108 of *Outre-Mer*.

30. Bourget's observations published in 1895 coincide with what Henry Adams stated as early as 1876 in his "Primitive Rights of Women" and with what was to be elaborated upon in Thorstein Veblen's *The Theory of the Leisure Class* (1899), Henry James' *The American Scene* (1907), and F. Scott Fitzgerald's *The Great Gatsby* (1925) and *Tender Is the Night* (1934). Bourget's equation of the jeweled idol worshiped by the men of Wall Street also echoes William James' famous evocation of the Bitch Goddess *Success*. More will be said in chapter 15 concerning the money value of females whom the male capitalistic society labored to possess as reward for its labors. At that point, further quotations drawn from Bourget's interpretation of the Sargent portrait serve to take this image beyond the relatively simple issue of women who are idolized at the cost of being converted into a male's collector's item.

31. Stephen Crane, *Maggie: A Girl of the Streets*, p. 24. The following quotations are from pp. 11–12, 27, 33, 52, 62, 67–68, 74.

32. Crane's observations are borne out by Jacob A. Riis' documentary account of life in the slums of New York's Lower East Side, first published in 1890: *How the Other Half Lives: Studies Among the Tenements of New York*.

33. Maggie Johnson also "looks" and "misreads," as when she "observed Pete" and found him a shining knight. The cumulative effect in *Maggie* of such acts of looking and misperceiving is confirmed by Crane's career-long emphasis on the consequences visited upon individuals and societies whose behavior is impaired by what Jeanne Howell identifies as "a common mistake." Whether it is Crane's Swede, Scratchy Wilson, Henry Fleming, members of military regiments, or small-town neighborhoods, characters in Crane's fictional world are severely flawed by their divergence from the central Peircean mandate. Rather than moving—as Peirce would have them do—from perception to conception on toward useful social conduct, the majority of Crane's characters lurch unproductively through this sequence of the would-be evolution of the consciousness, with the consequence that they and those at whom they look are harmed by the behavior that results.

34. *The Awakening* was not one of the novels which the general public at the time of its publication in 1899 reacted to with enthusiastic "waves of contagion." It is only recently that Chopin's novel has become "a mob book" for our own times.

35. In 1890 Jacob Riis alluded to the kind of death by water experienced by Crane's Maggie Johnson and other girls "of the street." *How the Other Half Lives*, p. 117.

7. Literary Portraits and Types: Possibilities

1. Henry James, *The Portrait of a Lady*, 4:436. The following quotations are from 3:xx, 16, 18, 21, 61, 67–68, 139–140, 143–145, 185; 4:3, 13–14, 19, 21–22, 105, 142–144, 179, 415.

2. In "Photography: A New Way of Looking," Rosalind Krauss cites Cartier-Bresson's desire to capture "the whole essence, in the confines of one single photograph." His is the belief in the camera's power to achieve "pictorial status" by means of a "single, formally satisfying and visually eloquent whole." But Krauss emphasizes the countermove made by photographers who place a series of images within "a single field." This mode, which accepts the impossibility of obtaining single images and makes a virtue of sequence, is also discussed by Leroy Searle in an essay written for the catalog to a Seattle Art Museum exhibition of photography, "Photographs in Sequence or Series" (1979), quoted by Krauss. Krauss refers to Thomas Eakins and Richard Avedon as imagists who "thought in sequence" —thereby not focusing on single images but rather on "the strip of postures, the array of moments in time." Charles Dana Gibson used the same technique. In his picture stories

"The Weaker Sex," "The Education of Mr. Pip," and "A Widow and Her Friends," Gibson makes the serial form tell his tale—just as did that other near-contemporary and experimenter with time, Gertrude Stein. See Mary Anderberg, "Silent Movies of the Page: The Serial Drawings of Charles Dana Gibson"; Richard Bridgman, *Gertrude Stein in Pieces*, p. 140.

3. There is a reprise of the same image of Isabel in the final chapter of the novel when Isabel sinks down upon the same bench just before Goodwood's appearance. In the earlier scene Isabel has just read a letter from Goodwood and will shortly after be confronted by Lord Warburton's proposal. The two scenes are not, however, copies; they image the differences in Isabel's external circumstances and in her inner consciousness.

4. Berenson's connoisseurship followed the lead of Morelli (1816–1891), who attempted to make a science of attribution from his conviction that artists have a fixed style that can be detected in the minute details of their works. To make out, say, similarities in several paintings of an earlobe gives the expert viewer a firm grasp on an artist's entire oeuvre.

5. *The Portrait of a Lady* furnishes many further examples of James' extensive and varied use of types—among them, his examination of national types (English, Italian, American) and of types of the suitor. Also note the literary strategy of James' placement of Madame Merle next to Isabel Archer. The former is presented as a relatively fixed portrait, not as a woman formed before the reader's eyes out of a series of developing types, as is the portrait of Isabel.

6. At the time of Houghton, Mifflin's publication of *The Evasion*, reviewers praised this 1906 novel. *The Boston Advertiser* found the story "peopled by real humans." *The Living Church* of Milwaukee compared it with Edith Wharton's *The House of Mirth* of the previous year and concluded that Frothingham's novel was "vastly superior"; in *The Evasion* "the people are truer to life, in fact are alive, very much alive."

7. As I indicated in chapter 4, the same observation was made in the 1870s by American art critics concerning the "adolescent" enthusiasms of the country's artists which robbed them of the strength they needed to match European "professionals." Artists without either "theory" or an "art idea" were unable to tell the difference between a Mrs. Monarch and a Miss Churm; they were still sophomoric when it came to distinguishing "real things."

8. This and the following quotations from the 1888 version of "The Art of Fiction" are from pp. 376–379, 390, 398 of *Partial Portraits*. For a detailed analysis of the differences between James' 1884 and 1888 essays, and between James' stand and that of Walter Besant, the man who initiated the argument, consult Mark Spilka, "Henry James and Walter Besant: 'The Art of Fiction' Controversy."

9. Henry James, "Guy de Maupassant," p. 269.

10. Henry James, "The Future of the Novel," p. 33.

11. R. P. Blackmur does something similar in the introduction to his collection of James' prefaces, *The Art of the Novel*. Blackmur represents James crouched over his memories of himself as an artist crouched over his writing desk; through this method, Blackmur furnishes a visual history of the origins of the images James the artist converted into the highly finished portraits of Isabel Archer, Christina Light, and Miriam Rooth. The following quotations are from James, "The Lesson of Balzac," pp. 79–80, 83, 86, 116.

12. James here makes the expected distinction between what the lyric poet does (reflects his or her own mind and feelings) and what the novelist achieves (represents the feelings of the narrative's characters). This division between novelists and poets breaks down, however, before James' main argument: that Balzac's art of the novel is the art of the author's own mind. William Dean Howells agreed on this point in the essay he wrote in 1882, "Henry James, Jr.," p. 25. James' manner of "character-painting" (so new, Howells observes, that many cannot understand it) is based upon "what a writer has to say rather than what he has to tell . . . what the novelist thinks about persons and situations."

13. James in a letter of H. G. Wells of July 10, 1915; from Edel and Ray, eds., *Henry James and H. G. Wells: A Record of Their Friendship*, p. 267.

14. This paraphrase of the view on types held by Georg Lukács *(Studies in European Realism)* is from James Clifford, " 'Hanging Up Looking Glasses at Odd Corners,' " p. 52.

15. Sergio Perosa cites the passage from James' *A Small Boy and Others* (1913) in which James recalls that from childhood on "the picture, the representative design, directly and strongly appealed to me, and was to appeal all my days." From *Henry James: Autobiography*, p. 149. But, Perosa notes, James' pictorial method faltered in the 1890s prior to its strong reappearance in the novels of the first decade of the twentieth century—the habit of pictorialization which was thereafter supplemented by the use of the scenic form he had polished during the 1890s. *Henry James and the Experimental Novel*, p. 43. I agree that the early portrait of Isabel Archer finds its later match in Kate Croy, Milly Theale, Charlotte Stant, and Marie de Vionnet, after the hiatus which led to representations of a kind we do not fully "see," exampled by the governess at Bly, Maisie Farrange, May Bartram, and Alice Staverton (all creations of James' fiction of the 1890s). True, this fiction also yields the highly visual images of Maisie's mother and the monkey countess; however, they fall into the special category of the grotesque, a type James always represented pictorially.

16. Since the "types" of art are not the same as "actual" persons found in life, types are set free from obedience to many of life's contingencies. Thus scrubbed clean of life's messiness, they stand ready to serve the artist's needs of identification and interpretation. See Mary Doyle Springer, *A Rhetoric of Literary Character: Some Women of Henry James*. A comparison of the two descriptions James gave to Lord Deepmere —in *The American* of 1877 and in the revised versions of 1907—indicates James' increased emphasis upon verbal patternings; the later version calls even more attention to eccentricity of type and thereby sets up an even more useful contrast between Deepmere and the central figures of the narrative.

17. Gertrude Stein, *The Autobiography of Alice B. Toklas*, p. 54.

18. Rocine, *Heads, Faces, Types, Races*, pp. 197–198, 299.

19. Gertrude Stein, "Melanctha," pp. 85–86.

20. Gertrude Stein, "Henry James," p. 292.

21. During the writing of "Melanctha" Stein "meditated and made sentences" that incorporated into Melanctha's story "the poignant incidents" Stein observed as she took long walks with her dog up the hill from the rue Ravignan. *The Autobiography of Alice B. Toklas*, p. 49. How like Melanctha's inner self is that of another young woman who wanders the city's streets in search of the same impossible balance of security and excitement: Lily Bart of Edith Wharton's 1905 novel *The House of Mirth*. There is also a marked similarity between the tormenting relationship Stein portrays as existing between Melanctha Herbert and Jeff Campbell and that which Wharton creates between Lily Bart and Lawrence Selden. Both narratives meet on much the same ground: both are "about" what love and life *feel* like; both are dramas of the state of never knowing and never trusting; both examine the consequences of doubt and lack of faith—the inability to forgive another for destroying the image a person needs to cherish of his or her own nature.

22. This and the following words and phrases are from Stein, *The Autobiography of Alice B. Toklas*, pp. 64, 91, 238.

23. Gertrude Stein, "The Gradual Making of *The Making of Americans*," pp. 85–88.

24. This and the following two quotations are from Stein, *The Autobiography of Alice B. Toklas*, pp. 119, 156, 211.

25. Melanctha may well have represented for Stein the repressed sexuality about which she felt compunction to write, yet needed to disguise through projecting aspects of her own bottom-nature upon the figure of the young black woman from Baltimore. The urgency Melanctha has to reveal her type to others was the opposite of Stein's impulse, however.

Stein encouraged outsiders to see her socially, superficially; she buried her own "type" within the portraits she wrote, while electing not to "live" too publicly.

26. The following quotations from Stein's "Portraits and Repetitions" are from pp. 102, 117.

27. William James, *The Principles of Psychology*, "The Stream of Thought," 1:224–290.

28. Stein, "Henry James," pp. 303, 305.

29. Stein, "Portraits and Repetitions," p. 103.

30. The following phrases and passages from Stein's "Henry James" are from pp. 299, 300, 303, 308, 311, 330.

31. See Stein's "Composition As Explanation," p. 230.

32. See Stein, *The Autobiography of Alice B. Toklas*, pp. 189–190.

33. Wendy Steiner, *Exact Resemblance to Exact Resemblance: The Literary Portraiture of Gertrude Stein*.

34. See Ralph Bogardus, *Pictures and Texts*; Charles Higgins, "Photographic Aperture: Coburn's Frontispieces to James's New York Edition."

8. Studio Studies and Still Lifes

1. Quoted from William Innes Homer, ed., *A Pictorial Heritage: The Photographs of Gertrude Käsebier*, p. 17.

2. Svetlana Alpers, for one, made clear her position that painters do not create "biographies" at the conference on "Theories of Reference and Representation" held during October 1983 on the campus of Indiana University. See the update by Svetlana and Paul Alpers on traditional objections laid against finding too close a sisterhood between "the sister arts" of literature and painting which offers a useful cautionary tale of the kind that never fully keeps the foolhardy from daring all: *"Ut Pictura Noesis?* Criticism in Literary Studies and Art History."

3. See Estelle Jussim, *Slave to Beauty*, for the context for F. Holland Day's photographs of blacks, pp. 107, 171; Deborah Jane Marshall, "The Indian Portraits," p. 31; Pete Daniel and Raymond Smock, *A Talent for Detail: The Photographs of Miss Frances Benjamin Johnston*. Marshall's essay speaks of Käsebier's desire to represent "a courageous and noble race"; however, Käsebier's granddaughter remarked of one of the male portraits that it "shows so well the character of the Indian, the secretness of the wrapped blanket, the cunning of the eyes, the cruelty of the mouth, the strength of bony structure, and the love of ornament." Käsebier's portrait of the Sioux Zit-Kala-Za perhaps avoided the kind of interpretation which perceives Indians as ignoble savages through its being that of a young woman given the dress, the pose, and the props of a painting by Thomas Dewing. Zit-Kala-Za was also photographed by Joseph T. Keiley; see Weston J. Naef, *The Collection of Alfred Stieglitz*.

4. Many women were artists. There was considerable contemporary discussion concerning their "special" talents and whether they were best suited for the "feminine" decorative arts or had the "force" to create in the area of the fine arts. Among the sources (both of the period and those resulting from recent scholarship), the following items are of particular note: Asher Benjamin, "Editorial—Women in the Arts"; Clara Erskine Clement, *Women in the Fine Arts from the Seventh Century B.C. to the Twentieth Century A.D.*; Elsa Honig Fine, *Women and Art*; Rena Tucker Kohlman, "America's Women Sculptors;" Lida Rose McCabe, "Some Painters Who Happen To Be Women"; Anna Lea Merritt, "A Letter to Artists: Especially Women Artists"; Karen Petersen and J. J. Wilson, *Women Artists*; Anne E. Peterson, "American Women in Photography"; Charlotte Streiper Rubinstein, *American Women Artists from Early Indian Times to the Present*; Lorado Taft, "Women Sculptors of America"; Frank Linstow White, "Our Women in Art"; Josephine Withers, *Women Artists*

in *Washington Collections; Women Artists of America, 1707–1964;* Helen Zimmerman, "The Work of Miss Bessie Potter."

In addition, there are the previously cited works regarding "the white, marmorean flock" and the photographic careers of Frances Benjamin Johnston and Gertrude Käsebier. Other sources which contain revealing details concerning the varied ways women artists entered the art world: Cecilia Beaux's autobiography, *Background with Figures;* Alastair Duncan, *Tiffany Windows;* Theodore C. Knauff, *An Experiment in Training for the Useful and the Beautiful;* Weston J. Naef, *The Collection of Alfred Stieglitz; Some Examples of the Work of American Designers: Dill and Collins, Co., Papermakers; The Woman's Book.*

5. Even a cursory study of the American art scene between 1880 and 1920 raises questions such as these: Is American portraiture best characterized as an instrument of the Realists, or are the sharp details and succinct outlines found in these paintings a lingering legacy from the Academicians? What differentiates the portraits of the Beaux Arts tradition from the blurred forms of the Tonalists and the idealized heads of the Symbolists? How does the somewhat wearisome debate between the champions of objective and of subjective art, respectively, hold up when one turns from a portrait by Thomas Eakins to a study by Thomas Dewing? Did the Ten use radically different techniques in rendering female heads from those employed by the maverick Eight, or were the differences discernible between the two groups mainly a matter of opposing epistemological opinions concerning portrait representation? If the latter, did the Eight and the Ten "see" as they did because of personal vision or because they were being pulled as a group by their theoretical short hairs? Did the portrait studies at the exhibitions of the Society of American Artists come closest to what the general public liked, or were the Art Students League exhibitions best for doing this? And who were the patrons buying these portraits; what amount of cash was involved; where was the younger generation of students coming from, and why were many deciding by the 1890s not to bother with training at the Parisian ateliers?

6. Henry James, *The Ambassadors,* 21:270–271. The following quotations are from 22:5–7, 9–10, 256.

7. In his essay "Some Imaginative Types in American Art," Royal Cortissoz observes that a figure is never as still as a landscape. Painted figures introduce the note of an "episode"; they remind the viewer that movement is about to start up (p. 172).

8. Patricia Hills, *Turn-of-the-Century America,* p. 74. The following quotations are from the same page.

9. Patricia Jobe Pierce, *The Ten,* p. 78; Patricia Hills, *Turn-of-the-Century America,* p. 74. The almost obligatory reference to Thorstein Veblen's theory concerning women of conspicuous consumption follows directly after in Hills' remarks. Also see Sarah Lea Burns, *The Poetic Mode in American Painting: George Fuller and Thomas Dewing,* p. 229, for her description of "the attenuated, pale, Pre-Raphaelite type . . . aloof and pensive in chambers hermetically sealed from the outside world."

10. The photograph of Helen Keller accompanied the article she wrote, "An Apology for Going to College."

11. Susan Hobbs, "Thomas Wilmer Dewing: The Early Years, 1851–1885," pp. 5–6. Ezra Tharp, in "T. W. Dewing," p. 156, made much of the elegant bone structure and skeletal perfection of Dewing's women. Good bones, and fine brains as well. Dewing told friends that he always exacted the latter of his models. See Nelson C. White, comments for "A Loan Exhibition: Thomas W. Dewing," held in 1963 at the Durlacher Galleries, New York. In many ways, the ideal Dewing woman fits the image of breeding, bones, and brains projected by the young Katharine Hepburn.

12. Two of the dots on the line between paintings of flowers and mountains and still lifes of women are provided by Maria Richards Oakey, the flower portraitist (who became the

wife of Thomas Dewing, painter of females whose psychic environment is silence), and by Abbott Thayer, noted for the hushed, almost sacerdotal silences with which he surrounds his female sitters. Lying well behind Oakey's flower paintings is the Dutch tradition of symbolic floral arrangements; coming just before Oakey in point of time are the flower paintings of the American artist Martin J. Heade. Ingvar Bergström writes with insight about the Netherlandish legacy in *Dutch Still-Life Painting in the Seventeenth Century.* Theodore Stebbins, Jr., points to the masked sensuality and the concealed forms characteristic of Heade's blossoms in *The Life and Works of Martin Johnson Heade.* Noting the pronounced languor of the "reclining" and "horizontal" forms of Heade's magnolia studies, Stebbins reads them as somewhat ominous signs that threatened the repressive sexual codes of mid-nineteenth-century America. Ella Forshay's 1984 exhibition at the Whitney Museum, "Reflections of Nature: Flowers in American Art," also adds weight to the recognition of the connections between flower studies and expressive human forms. Also see Jennifer Martin Beinenstock, "Portraits of Flowers: The Out-of-Door Still-Life Paintings of Marie Oakey Dewing"; John Wilmerding, "The American Object: Still-Life Paintings," pp. 84–111. For the relation between Thayer's studies of mountain forms and his art of the ideal, see Susan Hobbs, "Nature Into Art: The Landscapes of Abbott Handerson Thayer"; and Ross Anderson, *Abbott Handerson Thayer,* "The Meaning of Monadnock: The Landscapes of Abbott Thayer," pp. 85–111.

13. See John White, *The Birth and Rebirth of Pictorial Space,* pp. 189–192.

14. The following quotations and phrases from MacColl's *Nineteenth-Century Art* are from pp. 3, 13. What MacColl noticed in 1902 about the behavior of "the modern eye" was corroborated by his contemporaries and has been confirmed by later studies. Richard Boyle's book *American Impressionism* supplies the key phrase when summing up the same phenomenon: "the general lack of integration of the figure with . . . the setting" (p. 230).

15. Lewis Mumford, *The Brown Decades,* p. 103.

16. "Disguised symbolism" is the phrase used by Ingvar Bergström, *Dutch Still-Life Painting in the Seventeenth Century,* p. 291, to describe the "spiritual quality" whose residue pervades "early Netherlandish naturalistic art." The girl of Benson's painting is characterized as one who "appears like a model, modeling," whose function is "to represent an ideal of womanhood." (From folder notes on file at the Museum of Fine Arts, Boston). Her native "naturalism" is thereby disguised by the filter of idealism.

17. Two notable recent studies of late-nineteenth-century American malaise are T. J. Jackson Lears, *No Place of Grace: Antimodernism and the Transformation of American Culture, 1880–1920,* and Charles C. Eldredge *American Imagination and Symbolist Painting;* also see Peter Conn, "The Triumph of Reaction: Henry James," from *The Divided Mind.* Like Lears, Alan Trachtenberg is strongly critical of the arts of leisure of the late nineteenth century which excluded the conflicts tearing at the society. See *The Incorporation of America,* p. 183.

18. The essays contained within *Art as Experience,* first published in 1934, are based upon Dewey's 1931 Harvard lectures. Dewey addresses the psychological consequences of that sensed loss of stability which is arguably even more the mark of the age of Jamesian novels and Dewing portraiture than of the particular historical moment when Dewey proposed answers to that condition. The following quotations from *Art as Experience* are from pp. 15, 178, 253–257, 260, 268, 272–273, 275, 280, 322.

19. Gertrude Stein, "Portraits and Repetitions," p. 113.

20. This is how D. C. French described his statue. Although Michael Fried's remarks are directed to the artistic considerations of nineteenth-century France, Fried's essay "Painting Memories: On the Containment of the Past in Baudelaire and Manet" is pertinent to the American need for an art of memory and to the advantages that American artists gained once they learned to apply conventional forms with new vigor to the present day.

21. M. H. Spielmann, "Curiosities of Art: Coincidences and Resemblances in Works of Art." In the April 1905 issue of *Camera Work*, Roland Rood launched a vigorous defense of the arts of borrowing. Rood's essay "On Plagiarism" is largely directed to arguing the fact that arts which work with the general type and the universal inevitably draw upon forms and repetitions from the past; they lead, happily, to "a communism in art-thought" entirely different from notions of originality and "genius." Rood's conclusion is that an art limited to special cases intended for special groups must be fended off by a healthy appreciation of the arts of the general type appreciated by all the people. This democratic note was sounded over and over in regard to murals, posters, and public monuments, as chapters 12 and 13 will demonstrate. Also see Raymond Federman, "Imagination as Plagiarism."

22. The Barbizon tradition is carried forward, in its way, by a photograph from out of the Pacific Northwest, one of a series taken to promote Superior Drill Machinery (see "Help-meet," Introduction, figure 36). It is titled "Meditation" and features as its counterpart of Pearce's French peasant woman a bonneted, buxom American farm girl resting upon an example of the best of current New World technology.

23. There has been a tendency to make faulty equations between the chairs in which Dewing's women sit and their economic status. The bentwood chairs and rockers with which Dewing furnished the rooms of his paintings have been considered a giveaway to the position of affluence and privilege held by his women; they are among the "things" held against Dewing's women. This argument (which links "expensive" furniture to "elitist"—e.g., parasitic, unhappy—life) does not hold water. *Thonet: Thonet Bentwood and Other Furniture* and Christopher Wilk's *Thonet: 150 Years of Furniture* furnish enough data to call into question the notion of the expensiveness of mass-produced bentwood furniture (including pieces manufactured by small companies in Michigan, Illinois, Massachusetts, Indiana, and Wisconsin, as well as models imported by Thonet and other European design firms). "A sampling of American furniture catalogues from the turn of the century reveals that bentwood furniture of one kind or another was sold by most furniture dealers or manufacturers." Wilk, *Thonet: 150 Years of Furniture*, p. 138, n. 76. It was upholstered furniture that was costly. Even the highest grade of the Thonet rockers and chairs in 1904 ranged from $23.00 to $7.50. These were not prices the very poor could afford to pay, but they are hardly out of reach of the lower middle class. The 1885 catalog of the Heywood Brothers factories features oak chairs with cane backs and seats; the price list (most likely per dozen) shows armchairs and rockers at $33.00 and an armless style at $22.50.

The *Report to the President on Bent-Wood Furniture* continues the story into the 1920s. Domestic production at $2.58 per chair was having to fight against increased imports from Poland and Czechoslovakia. None of this "proves" that the appearance of a bentwood chair in a painting by Dewing or any other painter assures the depiction of a life of democratic virtue. On the other hand, the presence of those spare, unupholstered styles does not "prove" self-indulgence. After mass production was begun by the late 1870s, bentwood furniture began to appear in innumerable American banks, restaurants, hotels, and offices. It very likely provided part of the furniture for Silas Lapham's office. Clay Lancaster's essay "Taste at the Philadelphia Centennial" suggests that many visitors to the fair did not fully accept the Austrian bentwood furniture they saw there. It did not take long, however, for a thriving American market to appear.

24. Sargent's painting of 1911 was modeled in Paris by his niece, Rose Marie Ormond. The statement contained within the painting's file at the National Gallery of Art notes, "Portraiture is not intended here, only a presentation of languid, luxuriant femininity"; but a glance at the biography of Sargent's niece, who was the wife of Robert André Michel, introduces a sobering note of reality. Three years after Mme. Michel posed for her uncle's study of "languid, luxuriant femininity," her husband was killed in battle, fighting with the French army. In 1918, while attending a Good Friday service, she was killed when a shell hit the

church. Perhaps it could be seen as a happy fact, not a questionable one, that this young woman had had occasions to represent "repose" (or *Nonchaloir*, as the painting was originally titled).

25. Howells' utopian critique of American society in 1894, *A Traveler from Altruria*, cites Mrs. Makely as the dire example of such wasted women and inept lives. David M. Katzman reviews the treatment of "the servant problem" in the periodicals of the time in *Seven Days a Week: Women and Domestic Service in Industrializing America*, p. 223.

26. This comment, made of Edmund Tarbell and Frank Benson alike, is from Homer Saint-Gaudens' *The American Artist and His Times*, p. 182.

27. Eldredge locates the dream art of his American painters within the Symbolist tradition, and cites Edmund Wilson's *Axel's Castle* as his authority for the distinctions between the Symbolist and the Romantic that led the former into detachment from, and indifference to, society: "He will not assert his individual will . . . he will end by shifting the field of literature or art altogether . . . from an objective to a subjective world, from an experience shared with society to an experience savored in silence." *American Imagination and Symbolist Painting*, p. 37; from Wilson, *Axel's Castle*, p. 266. The notion that dwellers in "the real world" do well to avoid those who might entice them into the unrealities of subjectively wrought "other worlds" is an old one, with females perennially given the role of La Belle Dame Sans Merci, Undine, or one of the Lorelei. One version of the theme was the song sung by Anna Held in the 1890s which warned men to beware "the maiden with the dreamy eyes." Homer Saint-Gaudens, *The American Artist and His Times*, p. 142. But as Neil Harris has sensibly suggested in his essay "The Gilded Age Reconsidered Once Again," while remarking upon Eldredge's book, the art of the visionaries "was only one of many eddies" in the culture (p. 17).

28. The comic verse which accompanies this scene reads, "Little daubs of powder, / little daubs of paint / Make a very pretty thing / Of a thing that ain't." My thanks to Steven Fink for noticing that we see this woman from the back; only the frontal mirror view upsets the viewers' expectations that this may indeed be a pretty woman's face.

29. Henry James, *The Wings of the Dove*, 19:5–6; Edith Wharton, *The House of Mirth*, p. 43; Theodore Dreiser, *Sister Carrie*, p. 89.

30. Lavater, *Essays on Physiognomy*, 2:83.

31. Maurice Merleau-Ponty, "The Child's Relation with Others," pp. 125–141. The relationship between Merleau-Ponty's and other mirror theories is strong, including the variation provided by Josiah Royce's emphasis upon the importance of one's "first love" toward the creation of a consciousness. Judith Williamson's discussion of Jacques Lacan's "mirror phase" is apropos of Merleau-Ponty, Royce, and (her immediate concern) the nature of desire stimulated by the self that finds itself reflected in commercial advertisements. See Williamson, *Decoding Advertisements: Ideology and Meaning in Advertisements*, pp. 60–64. Virginia C. Fowler directly applies Lacan's theories to the American Girl in *Henry James's American Girl*, pp. 31–32.

9. *Images of the Ideal*

1. See the discussion of mid-nineteenth-century American sculptors of the neoclassical persuasion in the following: William J. Clark, Jr., *Great American Sculptures*; Russell Lynes, *The Art-Makers of Nineteenth-Century America*; Margaret Farrand Thorp, *The Literary Sculptors*; William H. Gerdts, Jr., *The White, Marmorean Flock*. Crawford's "Peri at the Gates of Heaven," Rogers' "The Lost Pleiad," and Powers' assorted damsels join with William Rush's "Allegory of the Waterworks" to suggest the range of allegorical female forms that extend from 1825 (for the Rush) to 1882 (for the Rogers).

2. The highly visible achievements of American women sculptors working within the

neoclassical tradition are detailed in the following sources: Linda Ayres, "The American Figure: Genre Paintings and Sculpture"; Karen Petersen and J. J. Wilson, *Women Artists*; Margaret Farrand Thorp, *The Literary Sculptors*; W. H. Gerdts, *The White, Marmorean Flock*.

3. See Henry-Russell Hitchcock and William Seale, *Temples of Democracy: The State Capitols of the U.S.A.* for an excellent examination of the rising enthusiasm for public architecture and design that found expression in the construction of state capitol buildings at the turn of the century. Alastair Duncan discusses the "business" of church construction (some 4,000 begun in the 1870s) in *Tiffany Windows*. Blashfield's career contains an encapsulation of the fortunes of such projects; he designed and executed murals and paintings for churches and capitols alike, as well as for universities, law courts, and private residences. See chapter 13 for more about Blashfield's contributions to the public arts of the ideal.

4. See Susan Hobbs, "Thomas Wilmer Dewing: The Early Years, 1851–1885."

5. See Ross Anderson, *Abbott Handerson Thayer*, p. 71; Thomas B. Brumbaugh, "Womanhood Idealized: The Late Works of Abbott H. Thayer."

6. As described in "Madame de Mauves," 13:217–218, 245. Euphemia de Mauves is "at once alert and indifferent, contemplative and restless"; she "never drooped nor sighed nor looked unutterable things."

7. Longmore can look at "bad" women as often as he pleases, but he is denied any direct enjoyment of the vision of bliss afforded by Claudine, the mistress of an artist he encounters during a country outing. Longmore is also kept apart from "the ideal woman" when Euphemia's image (which comes to him in a dream) remains no more than the gleam of a dress glimpsed on the opposite bank of the river which separates him from her longed-for presence.

8. According to *A Bibliography of Henry James*, eds. Leon Edel and Dan H. Lawrence, the original text of "The Quest of the Holy Grail" was printed for the Galleries 9 exhibition held in London during January 1895. The first revised text was printed by R. H. Russell of New York in June 1895. The second revised text was prepared for the 1901 Guildhall Art Gallery exhibition in London. The following quotation is taken from a book edition housed at the Boston Public Library; it was printed for the New York exhibition held at the American Art Galleries (sponsored by the American Art Association) in 1901. An undated letter of the autumn of 1895 from James refers to the slightness of the aid he gave to Mrs. Abbey in her preparation of the January 1895 catalog, but Abbey's biographer, E. V. Lucas, attributes the entire description of panel 5 to James.

9. Two small watercolors by La Farge are on view at the Isabella Stewart Gardner Museum in Boston—"The Study of the Water Lily" (c.1861–63) and "The Recording Angel" (1890). La Farge is best known, however, for the idealized figures he designed for stained-glass windows commissioned for churches and private homes. "Spring" (1901–1902), now part of the collection of the Philadelphia Museum, is a fine example of the Ideal as decorative design.

10. The hot-and-cold professional relationship between Edgar Degas and Mary Cassatt included expressions of the French artist's admiration for Cassatt's worth as a painter. There were, as well, his contemptuous remarks that she too often went in for painting poses of Jesus with his English nanny. See Ellen Wilson, *An American Painter in Paris: A Life of Mary Cassatt*, p. 169.

11. Charles C. Eldredge's *American Imagination and Symbolic Painting* includes bacchantes by Charles W. Stetson (1890) and Charles C. Curran (1892), but the weary hopelessness expressed by the American Symbolists provides "alienated texts" that lie outside the cultural mainstream. In contrast, bacchantes elicited public disapproval whenever they were too lively. Charles McKim donated a "Dancing Bacchante" by Frederick MacMonnies to the Boston Public Library, but protests drove it out of the library's inner courtyard and into the halls of the Metropolitan Museum. See William H. Jordy, *American Buildings and*

Their Architects, p. 372; Walter Muir Whitehall, "The Vicissitudes of Bacchante in Boston." The bacchantes shown in this chapter, however, are images that may be called "approved texts" because of their easy acceptance at the popular level. The relation of the bacchante to the Diana/Amazon figure and, in turn, the relation of these merged images to the figures of the New Woman that appear during World War I are examined in chapter 13.

12. Charles Le Brun, called by some the father of the French School of painting, formulated a detailed system of physiognomy in the late seventeenth century for the use of fellow artists. One of the scores of designs included in Le Brun's 1698 compilation of the human passions is the face whose eyes turn upward. This is the sign, Le Brun states, for the virtuous who respond to the light in heaven; in contrast, the wicked turn their faces downward toward darkness. See *A Series of Lithographic Drawings Illustrative of the Relation Between the Human Physiognomy and That of the Brute Creation*. Almost 200 years later, skeptics like Clover Hooper Adams would scoff at the studio full of sibyls she found at William Wetmore Story's place in Rome. *The Letters of Mrs. Henry Adams, 1865–1883*, letter of April 20, 1873, p. 95. But the convention of the upward glance (either to express a mortal's desire to receive divine truth, or the godlike ability to understand all) was as vigorous as ever. An analysis of how to perfect this "attitude" is provided by Webster Edgerly (pseudonym Edmund Shaftesbury) in *Lessons in the Art of Acting*, printed in 1889. Another example is assigned an explicit social meaning by its inclusion in an etiquette book of 1880, *The American Code of Manners*: "More than half the world wishes to be told *what to do*, and the attitude of *looking up* is said by sculptors to be the most graceful one which the human form can adopt" (pp. 9–10). By the late nineteenth century sibyls were often the writers of manuals of etiquette and suppliants were those who sought social, not sacred, guidance.

13. Oertel was born in Furth, Bavaria, in 1823; he emigrated to the United States in 1848. During the 1850s he made steel engravings for bank notes, painted some portraits, and tinted photographs. In 1857 Oertel was hired by Captain Montgomery Meigs, in charge of the national Capitol, to design decorations for the ceiling of the House of Representatives, but he was edged out of the job by Constantino Brumidi. By 1871 he had become an ordained priest of the Protestant Episcopal Church. Religious paintings and ecclesiastical wood carving were his main means of support: he also gave instruction in the arts—as during 1889–1891 when he taught at Washington University in St. Louis. His most ambitious project was the painting of four pictures for his "Redemption" series between 1895 and 1902, together with the paintings and woodwork he designed for the cathedral at Quincy, Illinois. Before he died in 1909, Oertel completed 1,183 separate "major" works. Information concerning Oertel's career as "a painter of ideas" comes from the biography by his son J. F. Oertel, *A Vision Realized: A Life Story of Rev. J. A. Oertel*; Charles E. Fairman, *Art and Artists of the Capitol*. The words for the hymn "Rock of Ages" predate the image by a century. They were written, perhaps in 1762, by Augustus Montague Toplady; they received first publication in 1775.

14. See Thomas H. Pauly, "In Search of 'The Spirit of '76.' "

15. Lyman Frank Baum, *The Art of Decorating Dry Goods Windows and Interiors*, p. 182.

16. According to Oertel's son, he died demented after years of frustration during which he attempted to advance his theories about the representation of Christian doctrine through emblematic art. The public which seized upon the figure of the young woman clinging to the cross seemed indifferent to what its creator had *to say about* the meaning of that or other images of his faith.

17. See George Mills Harper, introduction to *Thomas Taylor the Platonist: Selected Writings*; John H. Muirhead, *The Platonist Tradition in Anglo-Saxon Philosophy*; Luther A. Weigle, *American Idealism*. In *The End of American Innocence: A Study of the First Years of Our Own Time, 1912–1917* Henry F. May discusses the lingering hold retained by idealism in the public areas of politics and social reform. Joshua Taylor's chapter "The Persistence

of Traditional Ideals" in *Fine Arts in America*, Louise Tharp's *Saint-Gaudens and the Gilded Age*, and Lois Fink and Joshua Taylor's *Academy* offer other useful accounts of the place of idealism in the art world.

18. "The Rotary System" is the term Henry James used to describe the calculated plans for obsolescence that rapidly raze material forms in order that new ones may be erected. See *The American Scene*, pp. 253–254.

19. See Jonathan Culler, *The Pursuit of Signs: Semiotics, Literature, and Deconstruction*, p. 102; Edward Said, *Beginnings: Intention and Method*, pp. 372, 380.

20. The following résumé of George Richardson's views is taken from *Iconology; or, A Collection of Emblematical Figures, Moral and Instructive*.

21. Richardson's insistence in 1779 on the need for a new iconology for the times is matched by his concern (similar to that proposed by Lavater's *Essays on Physiognomy* of 1775–78) to advance art and to increase man's knowledge about human nature and society through the study of physiognomical types. Charles Le Brun's 1698 volume of drawings arranged according to a careful system of signs had also declared the same intention.

22. Henriette E. s'Jacob treats these difficult methodological questions in a book whose approach to the examination of the centuries-old tradition of angelic forms used in tomb decoration often approximates the manner and purposes of *Imaging American Women*. See *Idealism and Realism: A Study of Sepulchral Symbolism*.

23. Leon Battista Alberti (1404–1472) altered ancient notions of the nature of knowledge by introducing a copy theory of reality by which visual images result from sensible instances of mathematical ideas. When he added matter to mind, the European art world of the Renaissance exploded with creativity. But Alberti's discovery was, after all, an inspired *convention* for seeing and perceiving; it led to the creation of further conventions for the representation of new visual forms. See Joan Gadol, *Leon Battista Alberti*. Ronald Paulson argues that Joshua Reynolds was a master in the painting of closed forms based on conventional iconologies—static, whole, ideal. Reynolds' practice contrasted with that of Thomas Gainsborough who evolved an open system of painting capable of expressing the artist's deepest feelings. Paulson interprets the Reynolds/Gainsborough split as one between art as conventional, public, and "neoclassical," and art as personal, expressive, and "romantic" and "modern." Ronald Paulson, *Emblem and Expression: Meaning in English Art of the Eighteenth Century*. This divergence tore the American art world in half by the late nineteenth century, but the artists tied the differences they found to the ways they chose to handle artistic forms. Such differences were not primarily viewed as rents in the fabric of their world.

24. Ellen Russell Emerson, *Masks, Heads, and Faces*, p. 115. The following quotations are from p. 115.

25. Ellen Russell Emerson's 1892 observations concerning the tug of accurate details set over against statements of the universal apply to the procedures Daniel Chester French and Augustus Saint-Gaudens were currently carrying through in their sculpture. In 1887 Kenyon Cox noted that Saint-Gaudens was less interested in capturing the perfection of the type than in projecting individual qualities in his sculptured forms. Cox also insisted that Saint-Gaudens' statue of Deacon Chapin is not presented to us as a particular man but as "The Puritan." The bronze figure stands for the person; but it even more actively delineates the Puritan ideals defined by many late-nineteenth-century Americans. See Cox, "Augustus Saint-Gaudens."

26. William J. Stillman, "The Decay of Art," pp. 22–23. An even more explicit attack against the feminization of culture appears in Francis Marion Crawford, "False Taste in Art." An anonymous essay in *Lippincott's Magazine* of June 1882, "Art and Art-Life in New York," also clearly describes the city's art as feminine, although in generally approving tones. One association made by the essay is particularly ironic. The statement that "oil-

colors are certainly masculine and water-colors feminine" (p. 601) is made in face of the fact that the men who organized the American Water-Color Society in 1867 hoped to counter the reputation of that medium as weak, amateurish, and "feminine."

27. Ella E. Clark and Margot Edmonds study the growth of the legend surrounding the Indian woman who accompanied Lewis and Clark on their travels to the West, and append a list of the statues and paintings commissioned in honor of Sacagawea (six between 1904 and 1906 alone). See Clark and Edmonds, *Sacagawea of the Lewis and Clark Expedition.*

28. As one case in point, Russell Sturgis, *The Appreciation of Sculpture*, p. 264.

29. "Of Verities and Illusions," written by Charles H. Caffin in 1905 for *Camera Work*, suggests new standards drawn from a previously alien culture for the inspiration of lovers of the ideal. Japanese tranquillity, abstractions, and universals are compared with Western habits of aggressiveness and egotism; the Asian way wins completely. Henry Adams and George Cabot Lodge were but two of the disaffected writers of the period who turned to the Far East for solace once European history was seen to mock ideals of reason, harmony, and permanence.

30. Letters of September 23, 1880 and December 5, 1881 to George B. Coale, from Royce, *The Letters of Josiah Royce*, pp. 92, 105.

31. Letter of May 6, 1896 to Frank Thilly, *ibid.*, p. 346.

32. The following material (quoted and paraphrased) is drawn from vol. 1, Royce, *The Basic Writings of Josiah Royce*; in particular from "The Internal and External Meaning of Ideas" (1899)—Royce's version of Henry James' "The Real Thing"; "The Fourth Conception of God" (1899); "Immortality" (1906).

33. The summations of Peirce's position that follow are based on material from Peirce, *Charles S. Peirce: Selected Writings* and Vincent G. Potter's *Charles S. Peirce: On Norms and Ideals.*

34. Two useful evaluations of Santayana's position on the ideal are provided by Richard Colton Lyon's introduction to *Santayana on America*; and the introduction by Douglas L. Wilson for *The Genteel Tradition: Nine Essays by George Santayana.*

35. As we have seen (chapter 3, note 18), Daniel Chester French consulted a Harvard professor of zoology in his own examination of bird feathers. French's attentiveness to naturalistic detail was matched by Abbott Thayer who equipped his angels with magnificently rendered feathers. See Thomas B. Brumbaugh, "A Seated Angel by Abbott H. Thayer."

36. R. G. Collingwood's address of 1919 concerning Ruskin's art theories emphasizes the nearness of the art of perfection to the state of death; Gerardus van der Leeuw states that art which fulfills itself ceases to be art because "the holy" is "the wholly other" that resists images and words. See Collingwood, *Essays in the Philosophy of Art*, pp. 37–38; van der Leeuw, *Sacred and Profane Beauty: The Holy in Art*, pp. 4–7.

37. See Paul de Man, "Pascal's Allegory of Persuasion," pp. 1–25, concerning the necessary zero effect of allegory.

38. See Angus Fletcher, pp. 198, 323.

39. See Lillian S. Robinson and Lise Vogel, "Modernism and History," pp. 278–307. The argument here is not just against *thematic* imprisonment; it attacks the politically reactionary nature of literary and artistic formalism per se; that is, "modernism" defined as sexist, totalitarian, fascist.

40. In *American Art* (1886) Koehler comments upon the decay of the churchly sentiments and the "coldly reflecting and calculating nature" of official religious art (p. 19). For more on the status of religion in the United States and reactions to the sense of spiritual crisis, see Jackson Lears, *No Place of Grace*: James Ward Smith and A. Leland Jamison, eds., *The Shaping of American Religion*; Gerald Burney Smith, ed., *Religious Thought in the Last Quarter-Century*; Sidney Warren, *American Freethought, 1860–1914.*

41. Harry A. Bliss, *Memorial Art: Ancient and Modern Illustrations of the World's Most*

Notable Examples of Cemetery Memorials, p. 163. One monument company identifies the customers it satisfies the most as the dead! See *About Memorials: A Classification of the Usual Forms of Monumental Tributes*.

42. In addition to *Memorial Art* and *About Memorials*, the following suggest the activity of the grave-marker business at the turn of the century: *A Collection of 152 Original Monumental Designs, Compiled by Messrs. Cardoni and Morton*; A. Critchfield, *The Reporter's Illustrated Monumental Draughtsman*; Huger Elliott, *Memorial Art*; Hoffmann and Procházka, *Public and Private Monuments and Memorials*; and *Palliser's Memorials and Headstones*. A strange mix of hard-sell practicality and "scholarship" is present in many of these promotional pieces; they often devoted themselves equally to granite-based facts and figures and to theories concerning the arts of memory. One work which stays clear of theory is George A. Douglas, *The Experience of a Veteran Salesman of Memorial Monuments*. This delightful memoir is a monument salesman's version of Franklin's *Autobiography*; it tells how a "runaway apprentice" from Muncietown (Indiana) set out in 1851 to make his fortune. Through thrift, avoiding dishonest practices, learning how not to be a "med" (mediocre), a bit of pushing a wheelbarrow with marble stones through the streets, and overcoming the bad reputation of "tombstone gents," Douglas proves his motto: "Success' was my 'pass word' and I never lost sight of it." To celebrate his rise, he offers this "bright, sunny little volume, void of fiction and overflowing with good counsel," full of information for "the average man" who wants to know "the 'signs of the times.' "

43. In 1869 Sir Charles Eastlake concluded that "of all expressions in the head of a beautiful woman that of innocent, confiding, and devoted love is what will best tell in a picture." *Materials for a History of Oil Painting*, pp. 394–395. The truth of the matter, of course, kept coming out and had something to "tell" of its own. "Nym Crinkle's Feuilleton," a drama review appearing in the *New York Dramatic Mirror* of March 3, 1888, indicates how male pleasure in the ideal female kept encountering the will of actual women. The reviewer reports on "The Woman Hater" by D. D. Lloyd, a farce about a man who marries his dream of perfection. Once the wife achieves the married state she begins to act like herself, bewildering her husband as she no longer looks and behaves as she did while he was courting her. She laughs at him for thinking she will continue to "dress like a sylphide when I'm washing the windows." At this point the husband becomes a hater of women and marriage, betrayers of his ideals. The reviewer comments, "The masculine animal always keeps a pedestal somewhere to put a woman on. Sometimes he calls it an ivory throne. His misery is that he can't find a woman who will stay there. The angel insists on jumping off with his jasmine in her fist and breaking her divine neck." Male dreamers used aesthetic methods, as well as social and political ones, to keep female images on the pedestal, but by the end of the century the natural gap between the women on the ground and images on pedestals had widened even more. If some now object that a woman's jump down to earth that results only in the washing of windows was not much of a gain, consider that it was at least a *woman's* work, not a sylphide's; it was at least the start toward life in the world that requires no wings.

44. See the section concerning "Social Science, Secularization, and the Emergence of Weightlessness" from Jackson Lears' *No Place of Grace*, pp. 32–47. There Lears examines the causes that led to the sense "that modern character, as well as modern culture, had become weightless." The observation that religion lacked "lyrical lift" (p. 194) was made in 1892 by the Unitarian minister the Reverend Francis Tiffany.

45. In *A Chronicle of Friendship, 1873–1900* Will H. Low describes the collaborative efforts exerted in the 1870s in the design of St. Thomas Church of New York City by Augustus Saint-Gaudens, and John La Farge. Further information concerning the outpouring of their work separately or together is available in the following: untitled, unsigned note in *The American Architect and Building News*; Louise Hall Tharp, *Saint-Gaudens and the Gilded*

Age; Charles H. Caffin, "Mural Painting in America"; Pauline King, *American Mural Painting;* Henry Van Brunt, "The New Dispensation of Monumental Art: The Decoration of Trinity Church in Boston, and of the New Assembly Chamber at Albany"; Frederic P. Vinton, "William Morris Hunt: II. The Memorial Exhibition—the Paintings at Albany." Bruce Wilkinson, *Uncommon Clay.* The preeminence of mural art in America will be detailed in chapter 13.

46. White, "Intimate Letters of Stanford White: Correspondence with His Friend and Coworker, Augustus Saint-Gaudens," pp. 114–115.

47. Samuel Isham's remarks, taken from *The History of American Painting,* pp. 559–560, describe the generation of Dallas Archer which is portrayed in exactly these terms by Edith Wharton in her novel *The Age of Innocence.*

48. Sylvester Rosa Koehler, *American Art,* p. 40. The next three quotations from Koehler (p. 17) are, respectively, his paraphrase of an observation by William Morris Hunt, a quotation from Carl Hoff, and Koehler's own conclusion about the need for "occasion." The quotations that follow are from pp. 19–20, 22, 39, 46.

49. For example, *The Prang Elementary Course for the Seventh Year,* printed in 1898, included winged figures by Herbert Adams, Abbott Thayer, and Edwin H. Blashfield. The 1922 title of the Caproni order book—*Catalogue of Plaster Reproductions: From Antique, Medieval, and Modern Sculpture Suitable for Educational Institutions and Homes*— suggests that yet another generation of American schoolchildren had passed through the halls of elementary and high schools lined with plaster models of Greek and Neopolitan figures with wings, as well as the winged Victories newly created in celebration of America's participation in World War I. The many bacchantes made available to schools by the ever-eclectic Caproni were matched by the virtuousness of various winged females.

50. During the 1890s the firm of Palliser, Palliser and Company of 42d Street, New York City, put out a particularly stylish and erudite catalog. *Palliser's Memorials and Headstones, Also Mottos for Monuments, Epitaphs for Study or Application* is an encyclopedia of information (i.e., dozens of pages of sketches that gloss memorial motifs from many historical periods and countries). It includes a précis of a Royal Academy lecture on "The Proportion of the Human Figure" and a brief anthology of elegiac verse and lyrics on the subject of immortality. *Palliser's* is practical and up-to-date, offering suggestions on how to obtain estimates from contractors in "a business-like manner" and reporting on the usefulness of a Kodak for recording the variety of designs Palliser's makes available to its customers. In 1921 Harry A. Bliss, self-styled as a "Monument Photographer," prepared a less diffuse discussion of the topic. Bliss' *Memorial Art* was intended as a "text-book . . . for monument dealers and architects"; its illustrations were meant to be "of general interest." But both the Palliser catalog of 1891 and Bliss' book of 1921 assume that monument art is a concern of the public at large—one of the necessary facts in their lives.

51. Quoted from an article by A. A. Hopkins, contained in the National Museum of American Art, Blashfield Ephemera File. It is Hopkins who names and quotes J. A. Symonds as the likely source for Blashfield's notion of the angelic: Symonds, *Sketches and Studies in Southern Europe,* 1:279.

52. Taken from the unsigned, undated caption for a reproduction of "The Christmas Bells" included in the National Museum of American Art, Blashfield Ephemera File.

53. Oertel's remarks were prompted by his desire to explain the meaning of his painting "Father Time and His Family." See J. F. Oertel, *A Vision Realized,* pp. 50–51.

54. The following quotations from Huger Elliott, *Memorial Art,* pp. 164, 318–319. Elliott's remarks are part of his extended discussion of the problems which arise when the selection of civic monuments is left to committees comprised of ignorant citizens without guidance by minds trained in aesthetic matters; in turn, Elliott's discussion is part of his larger argu-

ment in favor of the City Beautiful movement which would install public objects of a high level of artistic achievement.

55. James Jackson Jarves, *The Art Idea*, p. 326.

56. On June 8, 1864, Robert Browning wrote to the American sculptor William Wetmore Story concerning the commission he had given Story to render a memorial portrait bust of Elizabeth Barrett Browning, who had died in 1861. "To strangers an idealisation might do very well. In the Tomb now constructing the central circle will contain no attempt at a portrait, much as I should desire it, but a simple 'Poetry,' with no pretence at anything but a symbol." Henry James, *William Wetmore Story and His Friends*, 2:146. The poetic approach did not always assure success, however. August Rodin, for one, botched the memorial he designed for James McNeill Whistler. He first planned a winged Victory, then changed his concept to a Venus de Milo climbing the Mountains of Fame. See the *New York Times Book Review* (July 8, 1923), p. 16.

57. Joshua C. Taylor asserts that post–Civil War art completely lost the capacity to locate symbolic and mimetic figures within a single pictorial space. *America as Art*, pp. 27–29. In chapters 11–12 I shall demonstrate that the attempt to do just this continued throughout the end of the nineteenth century and through the time of World War I in the making of visual patriotic statements.

58. Henriette s'Jacob discusses at length in *Idealism and Realism: A Study of Sepulchral Symbolism* the nature of *orants*, *imago clipeata*, and other traditional emblems for the guardians of dead souls. The former refers to images of souls in prayer; the latter, to images of the soul borne aloft.

10. Angels at the Threshold

1. See Charles Rosen and Henri Zerner, *Romanticism and Realism: The Mythology of Nineteenth-Century Art*, pp. 146–147.

2. Quoted in J. F. Oertel. *A Vision Realized*, p. 55.

3. Quoted by Nelson C. White in his foreword to the exhibition catalog *Abbott H. Thayer, 1849–1921*, prepared in 1961 for the Lyman Allyn Museum of New London, Connecticut.

4. For this and the following quotation, see Mrs. Arthur Bell (Nancy D'Anvers), "An American Painter: Abbott H. Thayer," pp. 250–251.

5. Samuel Isham, *The History of American Painting*, p. 472. Isham immediately contrasts Thayer as one who "spiritualizes" the Girl "until she becomes almost as a sacred thing" with the type of the young woman who appears in the paintings of Frank Benson, Edmund Tarbell, and Robert Reid: "others abating no whit of her charm and grace, still make her human,—a creature capable of playing tennis, pouring tea, or even sitting in a hammock; a creature that is real, and whom we have met." Like most who approach the somewhat hushed presence of the Thayer female, Isham finds he must equivocate about her "threshold" status.

6. During the years when Thayer was preoccupied with his theory of protective coloration, the art collector John Gellatly sent the painter actual Renaissance frames in the hope that they would inspire Thayer to return to the studio and prepare paintings to fill them. See Ross Anderson, *Abbott Handerson Thayer*, p. 26; Thomas B. Brumbaugh, "A Seated Angel by Abbott H. Thayer," p. 57. The following information concerning Thayer's practices in the studio (his use of photographs and/or models) is also taken from Anderson's introductory chapter and from Brumbaugh's article.

7. See Ross Anderson's chapter "Transcendental Domesticity: Images of Women in the Art of Abbott Thayer" in *Abbott Handerson Thayer*, pp. 43–83.

8. Edwin Howland Blashfield, *Commemorative Tribute to Abbott Handerson Thayer*, p.

2. In an undated letter to Emma Beach (whom he married in 1891 after the death of his wife Kate, who had been hospitalized as a mental patient since 1888), Thayer described the method he used in the studio to paint his daughter Mary complete with wings. "The wings are arranged on a board and perfectly firm against wind and jarring. They are nailed (the board is) to a timber in the bright light up there so that when Mary poses she fits into them and completes the picture." Quoted by Nelson White, *Abbott H. Thayer: Painter and Naturalist*, p. 51.

9. Brumbaugh, "A Seated Angel," p. 53.

10. *Ibid.*, p. 54. Brumbaugh takes exception to the notion that Thayer's paintings are "sentimental idealizations." Rather, he notes how many are "harshly realistic," while others are "monumental." See Brumbaugh, "The Monumental Art of Abbott H. Thayer," p. 1134.

11. Kenyon Cox, "Augustus Saint-Gaudens," *The Fine Arts*, vol. 10 of *Vocations, in Ten Volumes* (Boston: Hall & Locke, 1911), p. 339.

12. This and the next two quotations are from Kenyon Cox's essay "Augustus Saint-Gaudens," pp. 30, 34, 35.

13. From a letter of 1918 written by Thayer to John Gellatly cited in Brumbaugh, "A Seated Angel," p. 52: quoted by permission of the John Gellatly Papers, Archives of American Art.

14. Anderson, *Abbott Henderson Thayer*, pp. 37, 72.

15. Christy, *The American Girl*, pp. 61–62.

16. Henry Adams, "Primitive Rights of Women."

17. Richard Guy Wilson, "The Great Civilization—Cultural Conditions," p. 30.

18. This and the following quotations are from Homer Saint-Gaudens' essay "Abbott H. Thayer," pp. 84, 87.

19. Paul K. Alkon, in "Visual Rhetoric in *The Autobiography of Alice B. Toklas*," p. 872, refers to the Picasso mural of angels which hung over what Alkon describes as Stein's "sterile bed" The consequences to Stein's personal life of her lesbianism aside, Stein's literary use of types and her emphasis upon a present entity that has no more "past" than angels do have also been judged (too hastily) as sterile and inhuman.

20. See Lavater's *Essays on Physiognomy*, 3:33. Lavater is pleased to report on Winkelmann's insistence that only the physiognomist is capable of detecting the "internal sensation" by which truths are identified. The next quotation and figure 10.2 are from pp. 268–269.

21. See Lee R. Edwards, *Psyche as Hero: Female Heroism and Fictional Form*, pp. 7–8; Victor W. Turner, *The Ritual Process: Structure and Anti-Structure*, p. 81. Edwards proposes that the conditions she describes are characteristic of the general human condition rather than of a particular gender crisis. Contemporary accounts at the turn of the century tend to support both views: the specific plight of the woman in a male society and the ordeals endured by anyone of "the feminine type" pressed to the wall by "masculine" demands.

22. Henry Adams, *Mont-Saint-Michel and Chartres*, p. 250.

23. Joseph F. Byrnes, *The Virgin of Chartres: An Intellectual and Psychological History of the Work of Henry Adams*, chs. 3–6.

24. Henry James, *The American Scene*, pp. 345–350.

25. See the essay that accompanies this and other photographs concerning the problems of "modern" art photography which deals with classical motifs: Marguerite Tracy, "Shadows of Artists' Ideals."

26. Artists also face criticism if they use modern dress when viewers expect female forms representative of the eternal verities. A striking example of the hostility expressed toward this betrayal of audience expectations comes in the responses to Mary Cassatt's mural for the Columbian Exposition of 1893, where her "Modern Woman" was adversely compared

with Mary MacMonnies' "Primitive Woman." One of Cassatt's harshest critics, Frances Willard, remarked that the mural consisted of "modishly attired women" whose figures were "not drawn according to the canons of art accepted in America"; it seemed "too trivial and below the dignity of a great occasion." For this and other judgments concerning the "meaningless," "cynical," and "frankly realistic" nature of Cassatt's design (one which *failed to explain itself*), see Jeanne Madeline Weimann, *The Fair Woman*, pp. 313–319.

27. Henry Adams, *The Education of Henry Adams*, p. 442.

28. Kathleen A. Foster, "The Paintings," p. 3, emphasizes Abbey's command of "the newest bravura style" that resulted in "up-dated and enthusiastic creations from a school [Pre-Raphaelitism] that has lost almost all conviction."

29. See Thomas Hastings, *Commemorative Tributes to La Farge, Abbey, and Millet, 1912*, p. 6.

30. Gerardus van der Leeuw, *Sacred and Profane Beauty*, pp. 155–176.

31. See Joseph F. Byrnes, *The Virgin of Chartres*, p. 374; Jackson Lears, *No Place of Grace*, p. 283; Henry F. May, *The End of American Innocence*, p. 85; John Tomsich, *A Genteel Endeavor*, p. 477; Michael Quick, *American Expatriate Painters of the Late Nineteenth Century*, p. 119.

32. Royal Cortissoz, *Commemorative Tribute to Daniel Chester French*, p. 63.

33. Henry James, *William Wetmore Story*, 1:21.

34. Van Wyck Brooks, *America's Coming of Age*, p. 7. Art's harmony comes from having a "national culture" (p. 120), but this was impossible in a country divided between Highbrow (feminine) and Lowbrow (masculine)—between those who read and those who make money (pp. 17–18).

35. See Dewey, *Art as Experience*, pp. 41, 194, 290.

36. James' eulogy to Abbey, quoted by E. V. Lucas, *Edwin Austin Abbey*, 2:491. According to James' view, Abbey's career—carried out in imaginative worlds that shared the facts of ashcans and phototechnology with the romances of Shakespeare, Boccaccio, and Herrick—worked because of the concentration he brought to the processes of perception and conceptualization.

37. Whistler's comment is reported in Kenyon Cox's *Artist and Public*, p. 18.

38. The following quotations from Davis' *The Princess Aline* are from pp. 3, 6, 106–107, 128, 140, 145, 149.

39. Edith Morris is May Bartram to Carlton's John Marcher, as those familiar with Henry James' "The Beast in the Jungle" of 1898 will recognize. Edith playfully mocks the obsession that drives Carlton, and since Davis is writing a popular romance that will satisfy office boys (see chapter 3, note 7), the narrative ends happily. Davis' hero learns in time *whom* he loves and, in the process, learns *how* to love (at least in Davis' terms), thereby freeing himself from the dread consequences of his impossible quest.

40. Henry James, *Hawthorne*, pp. 42–43.

41. This story would be repeated many times whenever the male imagination found itself intimidated by the queenly force of a Lady Ashley, Nicole Warren, Caddy Compson, or Thea Fanchel. But rather this kind of majestic creature safe from the effects of time and familiarity than actually to possess a woman like the Princess Aline who would, according to Arthur Bartlett Maurice, have lost most of her charm had Carlton married her, becoming "fat and pudgy and altogether commonplace." Maurice, "Representative American Story Tellers," p. 140.

42. The distinctions Hugh Honour makes between classicism and romanticism are pertinent to the distinctions I make between love and desire. Honour notes that elements of a statue may follow neoclassical principles: its "noble composure," "rational treatment of hair and drapery," and "obvious indebtedness to Antique prototypes." At the same time that statue may reveal complexity of form and texture, individuality of characterization,

and "*a meditative, almost apprehensive, mood of yearning which is deeply unclassical*" (my italics). The classical tradition, as it were, holds to the belief that one "has it" and need not long for it. The romantic tradition expresses doubt; "having it" seems out of the question. Some works of literature and art are pure examples of their genre; attained love or thwarted desire (one or the other) are represented therein. But as Honour's examples suggest, a single piece of sculpture or painting can contain both the form of classicism ("love") and the mood of romanticism ("desire"). See Hugh Honour, *Romanticism*, pp. 128–129.

43. Henry Adams, *Mont-Saint-Michel and Chartres*, p. 198.

44. Richard Le Gallienne, "A Vindication of Eve," pp. 55–58.

45. See Anne d'Harnoncourt and Kynaston McShine, eds., *Marcel Duchamp*, pp. 260–263.

46. Letter of Saint-Gaudens of July 6, 1906; from White, "Intimate Letters of Stanford White," p. 406.

47. The fairy world was well represented throughout this period. See Charles C. Eldredge, *American Imagination and Symbolist Painting*, pp. 62–67, for his discussion of the prevailing taste in mermaids. Also see an unsigned essay in *American Artists and Their Work* concerning the popularity enjoyed by Frederick S. Church for his art of fairies and mermaids. In addition, the essayist credits Church with two important firsts: "the creation of an ideal of American womanly beauty" and the creation of "a national art" (p. 236). Note too that Evelyn Nesbit began her career modeling as nymphs and other fairy folk for Church. See Mooney, *Evelyn Nesbit and Stanford White*, pp. 27–30. *The* American female ideal and *the* national art linked with mermaids and fairies, and with Maude Adams and Evelyn Nesbit as almost perversely "innocent" ingenues, provide a different equation between female form and national values from that created by Thayer, Saint-Gaudens, and Cox.

48. The following quotations are from Kenyon Cox's essay "Sculptors of the Early Italian Renaissance." The essay is an early statement of the position Cox was to uphold as teacher, critic, and practicing artist for the next thirty years. He never lost his belief in the vitality of the Renaissance tradition which he considered influenced "the best art of our own day."

49. Cox classifies the three main sculptural traditions that attempt a "solution to this problem" of the shock of the Ideal: (a) the Greeks who "sought relief from the hard facts of nature in nobly ideal forms, abstracted from all accident and all individuality"; (b) Michelangelo who practiced an ideal art that was "rugged, Titanic, imperfect"—expressed in "rough-hewn, unfinished block"; (c) the Early Renaissance sculptors who used "lowness of relief" to gain emotional escape from too stark a rendition of truth. The third mode is the solution Cox prefers; it is the one also employed by Saint-Gaudens (and, to a lesser extent, by Daniel Chester French).

50. The Louvre bust Cox features has its twin in the marble bust in the Bargello of Florence, sculpted by (happy name!) Desiderio da Settignano.

51. Henry James, *The American Scene*, p. 53.

52. The book cover of *The Blessed Damozel* by Dante Gabriel Rossetti with Drawings by Kenyon Cox is decorated by two classical figures holding a palette and scroll and the initials DGR and KC; the sister arts of *Ars Poetica* and *Ars Plastica* are united. The book is dedicated to Cox's friend and fellow artist Will H. Low. The copy of the edition in the Princeton University Rare Book Collection is inscribed in Cox's handwriting: "A mon Cher Maitre J. L. Gérôme, Son Éleve Reconaissant." The text for the poem is based on the revised, more "mature" version of 1881. Rossetti's poem and Cox's illustrations are followed by an appendix by Mrs. Schuyler (Mariana) Van Rensselaer. She expresses somewhat predictable "American" responses toward Rossetti's style of painting and poetry and the Pre-Raphaelite movement in general: an art based on themes so literary, intellectual, and subtle they frequently require verbal explanations; themes limited to inward matters of "morbid" force that reveal little interest in "*the aspect of things*"; themes so personal they deal "not at all

with the vexed questions of the day." Van Rensselaer states that, by contrast, Cox shows both the soul and the remembered body and passions. She also praises Cox's use of the nude: his art "is not etherealized out of all likeness to the veritably living body, not refined away into something that is falsely deemed more pure because less vital than reality. . . . His figures are bodies, and not would-be spirits; but they are *nude* bodies, and not simply undraped; ideal, and not simply literal, transcripts from reality."

53. As long as the Damozel is fixed in a state of desire, her eyes are shown as closed. When it seems that she is reunited with her beloved, her lids are open. Like Kate Chopin's heroine Edna Pontellier, the Damozel has awakened from the false dream of reality shaped by her thwarted desire; or so she believes until the moment when she is again swept by the despair of her desiring.

54. Van Rensselaer identifies "the winged blesser of the bridal" as "a celestial Eros or Hymen," a figure "in keeping with the half-spiritual, half-terrestrial atmosphere of the poem." "The type is drawn, of course, from classic, not from Christian art. But it has a perennial underlying significance, deeper than any marks of time or race; and its value is increased by its familiarity to every mind. Mr. Cox has preserved this significance and value, and has infused the type with a new Christian feeling."

55. My interpretation of the signs of Daniel Chester French's statue directly contradicts the reading given it by a contemporary reviewer. In *The Washington Star* of January 1, 1925, Leila Mechlin praises the emotions expressed by the male figure: "the man, one step ahead, is leading, or lifting, the woman upward. In both instances the man is the protector and is imbued with gentleness as well as strength. There is tenderness, reverence in his touch, as well as passion." Margaret French Cresson describes another winged figure designed by her father for the Court of Honor at the San Francisco Fair of 1914: "a colossal figure, sexless, neither man nor woman, naked to the waist, with veiled head, seated aloft on a rugged mass of rock with great spreading wings and the arms extended in a compelling gesture of command." *Journey Into Fame*, p. 229. Whatever this enigmatic figure represented, the managers of the fair decided to relocate it to the Court of Mines; neither honor nor love was its apparent meaning.

11. Making the Right Occasions

1. The first reference is taken from Robert de la Sizeranne's "Is Photography Among the Fine Arts?" p. 102. The second concerning Ruskin's distinctions between false and genuine art is from his *Modern Painters*, p. 24.

2. Angus Fletcher, *Allegory*, pp. 8, 22, 229–233, 347.

3. See Lewis Perry, *Intellectual Life in America*, p. 314. As for one of the best ironists of the second half of the nineteenth century, William Dean Howells received early training in doubting allegorical statues. In his mid-teens Howells appraised the Columbus, Ohio, Courthouse and commented of "the image of Justice, having the scales in her hands," that the figure "would be a great deal more appropriate in grocery." From an entry of March 7, 1852, in Howells' diary. See Thomas Wortham, " 'The Real Diary of a Boy': Howells in Ohio, 1852–1853," p. 16. As for the difficulties acruing to a sustained belief in allegorical figures erected in public places at the start of the twentieth century, see the account of the hostile press given in 1909 to a large statue of "Purity" placed in Times Square: Michele H. Bogart, "The Importance of Believing in 'Purity.' "

4. The following quotations drawn from Koehler's "The Future of Art" are from pp. 73–74.

5. This and the next quotation are from James' *The American Scene*, pp. 162–163.

6. See Hugh Honour, *The New Golden Land: European Images of America from the Discoveries to the Present Time;* Howard Mumford Jones, *O Strange New World: American*

Culture, the Formative Years; Samuel Eliot Morison, *The European Discovery of America: The Northern Voyages, 500–1600.*

7. The following remarks form the gist of the argument advanced by William Aylott Orton, *America in Search of Culture,* pp. 30–33.

8. Edward Said asserts that Vico's sense of history is one of the modes that allow us to create a world beyond that in which we are daily conscious of transgressing God's laws, the Platonic forms, or Descartes' Ideas. *Beginnings,* p. 353.

9. Thomas A. Bailey, "The Mythmakers of American History."

10. See Richard David Mosier, *Making the American Mind: Social and Moral Ideas in the McGuffey Readers.* For a direct account of the influence the McGuffey Readers had upon one satisfied pupil, see Henry Vail, *A History of the McGuffey Readers.*

11. Gilbert's hymn of praise in honor of public art, "The Greatest Element of Monumental Architecture," is from *The American Architect* (August 5, 1929).

12. W. Rankin, "Art in America: Current Notes," p. 185.

13. Henry Adams, "American Ideals."

14. The following quotations from Henry James, *The American Scene,* are from pp. 146, 173–74, 191, 254, 291–292, 339–341, 344, 349, 358, 362–364, 393–394.

15. James, *Henry James: Autobiography, Notes of a Son and Brother,* p. 491.

16. Plans for Grant's Tomb abounded when a competition was announced in 1885. For a sampling of the edifices that did not get past the design stage (all of which make one wonder what James would have made of *them*), see Alison Sky and Michele Stone, *Unbuilt America: Forgotten Architects in the United States from Thomas Jefferson to the Space Age,* pp. 110–112.

17. Kenyon Cox took quite another view of the Saint-Gaudens "Sherman." In "The Sherman Statue," written for *The Nation* (June 18, 1903), Cox observed of the unveiling of the group, "No event has ever taken place in this country of equal artistic importance" (p. 491). Even the *idea* of "the Victory-led rider" was wholly new, an idea which has struck two artists at the same time (Saint-Gaudens and Reinhold Begas who designed a similar group in Berlin in honor of the Emperor Wilhelm). The next quotation, which validates the presence of the Victory, is also from p. 491 of Cox's essay. Cox returned to the Sherman group on other occasions. In *Artist and Public* (1914) he stated that without the inclusion of the figure of Victory, the stride of Sherman's mount would have no significance (p. 224). Theodore Roosevelt's approach was less aesthetic; he conflated the notion of "Victory" with the Sherman figure (which represented the nation's highest hopes) without singling out the female figure, then gave the entire grouping his unqualified praise. See Glenn Brown, "Roosevelt and the Fine Arts," p. 719. A later commentator passed on the matter of the group's coherence entirely on formalistic grounds; questions of emotional or conceptual principles did not enter into his evaluation. See Robert G. Berkelman, "America in Bronze: Augustus Saint-Gaudens." It would seem that James was one of the few who worried, as Richard Sennett still does, that the signs for democracy ought to be both (to use Sennett's words) "visible and legible." See Sennett, *Authority,* pp. 168–175.

18. Critics continue to discuss the possibility of providing both force and intelligibility of information. Men as diverse as Arnold Hauser and William Mills Ivins, Jr., have agreed on the need for open, evolving visual forms that meet the practical demands of a changing society without giving in to the dangerous desire for unity (the factor lying behind the craving for force). Ivins believes we can create special conventions for communication to fit periods of transition, while Hauser champions the joining (not the blending) of means (art) and ends (life). See Ivins, *Prints and Visual Communication;* Hauser, "The l'art pour l'art Problem."

19. Quoted by Henry F. May, *The End of American Innocence,* p. 101.

20. Margaret French Cresson, *Journey Into Fame,* pp. 231–233.

21. *Harper's Weekly* of 1860 yields three cartoons that represent the usual divisions then made between male and female aspects of political power. (a) A schoolmarm urges the need to support the Constitution through her instruction in the classroom; (b) a female figure stands for the Union which must be defended by her citizens; (c) "Young America"— he who wages aggressive attacks against the foes of Constitution and Union—is shown as the infant Hercules strangling the serpent Disunion. Females lecture about the moral good or represent it allegorically; males do the deeds that protect the good.

22. Figure 11.13 appeared as a promotion poster for the three-part series in *Godey's Magazine* (1896) that featured the woman who allegedly served as military adviser to President Lincoln. Lucinda B. Chandler's piece "Anna Ella Carroll: The Great Unrecognized Military Genius of the War of Rebellion" ran in September; Mary C. Francis followed in October with "More About Anna Ella Carroll"; a group of letters headed "The Case of Anna Ella Carroll" completed the discussion in the November issue. It is significant that the frontispiece used for the September article was taken from a "feminine" portrait of Carroll; it is in marked contrast to the "masculine" representation used on the advertising poster. Information on Carroll (1815–1893) is available in James, James, and Boyer, eds., *Notable American Women*.

23. The Liberty figure popularized by Edward Savage in the first years of the new republic represented an American goddess of youth and progress, one whose iconic significance continued to evolve once the colonies won their independence and consciously assumed the function as the world's model for a free, vigorous, developing nation. Joshua Taylor's *America as Art* provides a detailed review, not only of the various early versions of the female with Liberty cap and eagle, but also of the fact that this image *acquired* meaning as it grew together with the republic. Taylor ends his study with the 1860s, the decade he argues was the last in which the American allegorical cast of mind was capable of placing early images (such as Washington or Lincoln) within a fully visualized realm of ideas. I pick up several of Taylor's threads in order to move them on through the 1910s. I also argue that Americans continued to create a "new language of forms" well beyond the 1860s, through which they compressed a diversity of bodily images and abstract ideas into one visual format—a single field of meaning—which attempted to give an account of the nation's significance, contradictions and all.

24. See Hugh Honour, *The New Golden Land*, pp. 87–91.

25. *Ibid.*, p. 251.

26. In 1903 Edwin Howland Blashfield completed the mural titled "The Uses of Wealth" as a lunette for the Citizens Bank of Cleveland, Ohio. It depicts members of the laboring and professional classes attended by allegorical figures (male and female) whose attributes number cornucopia, key, sword, shield, globe, and torch. The central figure rushes forward in a swirl of airborne drapery bearing the legend "Benignitas Quae Constat Ex Opera et Industria Honestior Est, et Latius Patet, et Prodesse Potest Pluribus."

27. The description given of the "America" group in Weinberg, ed., *Illustrated Catalogue: Masterpieces of the Centennial International Exhibition*, 1:79–80, points up the diverse elements involved. "America" with an eagle feather headdress rides the bison; she is "the aboriginal earth-goddess, depending upon kindlier forces to illumine her path and guide her steps." The figure of "the United States" is "the serious virgin" who directs "America" by wielding the scepter that points to the "empire which 'westward takes its way.'" Also visible in this illustration are "Canada" (female) and "Mexico" (male); not shown is "South America," represented by a male conquistador. This inventory suggests that the raw energy of the American continent is channeled toward its proper moral purposes (fulfillment of its manifest destiny) by the political governance of the United States, which is also assigned the leadership of the futures of Mexico, Canada, and the countries of South America.

28. In "Captain John Smith" (1867), later collected in *Historical Essays* (1891), Henry

Adams reviews a number of early seventeenth-century accounts that would have invalidated any romantic image of Pocahontas had not John Smith's formulation of the supposed events in his *Generall Historie* of 1624 already swept away the historical facts, replacing them with an invention that was of great use to the late-nineteenth-century mind. The chorus for the popular song "My Pocahontas" (1907) indicates the ease with which the original American Girl entered the popular lore of the twentieth century (here, as the bride of John Smith): "The moon is beaming, My Pocahontas, Of you I'm dreaming; Now don't you know, I love you so, I'd give my life for you! My Pocahontas, Your eyes are gleaming, My Pocahontas, My heart is teeming; in my canoe, There's room for two; for two in my birch canoe." The Princeton Triangle Club produced "Po-ca-hon-tas" during the season of 1890–91, and revived it in 1897–98.

29. Christy's *Liberty Belles* presents the eight stages in the evolution of the American Girl and the adoring males who figure in seven of the sequences. Prior to the Western Girl, men are placed in romantic rapport with the young women; they are *there* at the woman's side, even if pictured in emotional subjugation to her charms. The Western Girl, in contrast, rides well ahead of the pack who urge their horses forward in vain pursuit (see Introduction, figure 10). As for the Queen, the final stage, she sits upon her throne, elevated and alone, in full command of the scene (see Introduction, figure 9).

30. Sacagawea was another figure from the myth of the Indian heroine who miraculously appears just in time to save male Americans bent on an Aeneas-like quest to found a new and nobler empire. Chapter 9, note 27, indicates Sacagawea's canonization between 1904 and 1906 by means of Eva Emery Dye's popular novel *The Conquest: The True Story of Lewis and Clark* (1902), periodical essays, purported histories, and the erection of statues and paintings in public places. The word is out that revisionists will shortly undermine this sanctified image of the "good" Indian who served the cause of white expansionism; but as Henry Adams knew, when he tried to correct the myth of Pocahontas, useful myths die hard.

31. For detailed discussions of the part played by the Western Girl in turn-of-the-century fiction, see Kevin Starr, *Americans and the California Dream, 1850–1915*; William Wasserstrom, *The Heiress of All the Ages*, pp. 39–51.

32. Angus Fletcher, *Allegory*, pp. 100–108.

33. See Ray Ginger, *Age of Excess*; R. Ginger, ed., *The Nationalizing of American Life, 1877–1900*; Fred Albert Shannon, *The Centennial Years*. Also see Neil Harris' essay "The Gilded Age Reconsidered Once Again."

34. We have James B. Campbell to thank for the period flavor of the praise given to Columbus for his "pluck and perseverance." *Campbell's Illustrated History of the World's Columbian Exposition*, 2:419. Also see R. Reid Badger, *The Great American Fair*, pp. 43–44.

35. James J. Jarves, *The Art Idea*, pp. 146–147, observed in 1864 that Protestantism has no Catholic saints to emulate; as a result it "deifies its military and civic heroes"—those who are progressive, rational, conquering, materialistic. Throughout this book Jarves wonders whether American democracy can create an art idea that will replace the dead European tradition, while providing something more than the vigor of its vulgarity and need for mastery.

12. Scaling Up to War (1876–1898)

1. See Lois M. Fink and Joshua C. Taylor, *Academy*, pp. 12–14; Gyorgy Kepes, *Language of Vision*, pp. 71, 86–97, for a sense of the methods by which the "natural external design" of an object is disclosed through studies in perspective and spatial relations.

2. John Flaxman, *Lectures on Sculpture, as Delivered Before the President and Members of the Royal Academy*. In 1878 a new edition of Flaxman's *Outlines* was brought out by a

Boston publisher; the reviewer for *The American Architect and Building News* (November 30, 1878) observed that the Flaxman designs had been "somewhat out of fashion of late, not because anything so good has taken their places, but as one of the results of the rebound from classicism to naturalism." Still, enough interest remained to prompt the book's publication. By the end of the century the sculpture of French and Saint-Gaudens and the mural art of Blashfield brought new life (and new responses) to the older tradition of outline, silhouette, and type for which Flaxman had stood almost a century before.

3. The 1838 London edition of Flaxman's lectures contains drawings of the Phidian Jupiter (forty feet high, with the winged Victory held on its outstretched palm) and of the Minerva which stood thirty-nine feet in height.

4. An inventory of items modeled by Story includes further titles under the category of "Colossal Statue." See the appendix to Mary Elizabeth Phillips, *Reminiscences of William Wetmore Story*, pp. 295–298. Henry James also remarks on Story's predilection for outsized designs in his biography of Story, 2:299–300, 302.

5. William Ordway Partridge, *Technique of Sculpture*, pp. 60–61, 67, 70.

6. A plate from the 1763 edition of the Paris *Encyclopédie* presents the de Medici figure and her proportions; see Fink and Taylor, *Academy*, p. 16.

7. "Diana" caused Saint-Gaudens and White no end of trouble and expense because they had not correctly calculated the scale of the original figure in relation to the size and elevation of its architectural setting. The first model had to be taken down because it was too large at eighteen feet; the replacement at thirteen feet had the needed proportions. "Diana" also appeared in other sizes and forms. The example at the Metropolitan Museum is six feet and lacks the drapery of the original. See John H. Dryfhout, *The Works of Augustus Saint-Gaudens*, pp. 154–155, 205–210; "Accessions and Notes. The Diana of Saint-Gaudens," p. 205.

8. Adams, *The Education of Henry Adams*, pp. 383–385. Also see *The American Scene*, p. 253, for Henry James' conjectures concerning the Aphrodite displayed in the Museum of Fine Arts, Boston; he decided that she was an alien image in the New England context.

9. See Adams' letter of January 24, 1908, to Homer Saint-Gaudens, from *Henry Adams and His Friends: A Collection of His Unpublished Letters*, Harold D. Cater, ed., p. 610.

10. The circumstances surrounding Sargent's decision to paint Mrs. Stokes in sports attire indicate how quickly the artist seized the chance "look" that pleased his imagination. See Doren Bolger Burke's notes for the painting contained in *American Paintings in the Metropolitan Museum of Art*, pp. 247–248. Unsatisfied with Edith Stokes in a blue satin evening dress, seated, and with a fan, Sargent responded at once when his sitter arrived one day at the studio "full of energy and her cheeks aglow from the brisk walk." Sargent scraped the original image off the canvas and began again with Edith Stokes dressed in her walking togs. (Mr. Stokes was a last-minute replacement for the Great Dane intended to fill out the painting.)

11. Cited by R. W. B. Lewis, *Edith Wharton*, p. 188.

12. From a syndicated newspaper interview of James Montgomery Flagg that appeared in 1955, five years before his death. National Museum of American Art, Flagg Ephemera File.

13. See Fairfax Downey, *Portrait of an Era*, p. 194. The following statistics for the heights of men and women for 1889 and 1910–18 are drawn from Milicent L. Hathaway and Elsie D. Foard, *Heights and Weights of Adults in the United States*, table 1. This information was given me by Mr. Abraham, National Center for Health Statistics, Rockville, Maryland; he also directed me to *Medico-Actuarial Mortality Investigation* (1912). The latter study concludes that the average height of males in the United States and Canada (based on 221,819 cases) was 5 feet 8.5; women (based on 136,504 cases) averaged 5 feet 4.75. Notwithstanding the relative shortness of most American women, artists often sought out tall women as inspiration for their studio work. Among the statuesque women were Maggie Keenan and

Mary Anderson who modeled for Abbey, Mary Lawton (6 feet) who posed for French's "Alma Mater," and Augusta Homer, exceptionally tall, slender, and straight of posture, who married Augustus Saint-Gaudens. Also see Lois Banner, *American Beauty*, Helen Ecob, *The Well-Dressed Woman*, Alison Gernsheim, *Fashion and Beauty*, and Valerie Steele, *Fashion and Eroticism*, for notations concerning the growing taste for statuesque women during the 1890s. Care must be taken, however, to distinguish between the mature, full-figured "older woman" preferred by the English and some Americans and the willowy figure of the younger women which captured the imagination of most American artists.

14. An unsigned essay appeared in *Camera Work* (April 1905) under the title "On the Elongation of Form." Its extended discussion brings into focus a number of diverse components: natural form modified by artificially adjusted bodily measurements; the current consensus concerning the American type; belief in universal standards of female beauty; cultural inclinations toward figures that were long and lithe. The essay opens by relating that—supplied with "exact anthropometrical measurements from Professor Sargent of the Harvard College Gymnasium taken from American-born students entering the college"—the Boston sculptor H. H. Kitson modeled the ideal types of young American males and females. "Professor Sargent's composite female figure is tall and slender, her build is firm and rounded, mature around the hips, with undeveloped bust, natural waist, and *an increased length* (the twenty-two inches that Beardsley considered essential for the beauty of the upper leg) from hip to knee as striking peculiarity" (my italics; p. 27).

The essayist says that this American type reminds one of "the languid damozels of the Pre-Raphaelites, of the 'stag-like' Dianas of the Fontainebleau school and, above all, of the graceful visions of female beauty as depicted by the early Florentines" (p. 28). This resemblance is not a mere coincidence; "all anthropometrical researches from Polycletus to our time show that there exists really only one type of ideal beauty for women" (p. 28). Actual women match the paintings and sculptures from the waist up only. They disguise their relatively short legs by wearing long skirts so they may appear as elongated as works of art. Women wear long skirts not out of modesty but from the desire to look like the "one sisterhood" of Greek statues, Rossetti's paintings, Shopas' Diana, Botticelli's angels, Saint-Gaudens' caryatids, and Dewing's women (p. 28). "Through elongation the intricacies of the human form became simpler, less plastic, more vague and subtle." By "losing her roundness of form the woman becomes androgynous, half-boy, half-girl. . . . The body becomes a vague embodiment of immortality" (p. 33). At this point emphasis diverges from the monumental females of the period ("statuesque," "painterly," and Michelangelesque in the classical sense of the "grand"); it looks toward the "linear" style of Greek geometrics pursued by Thomas Dewing. Dewing's paintings are praised as "pictures of women who might stand for the ideal American type": "those languid descendents of the Puritans" who blend "the Hellenic spirit and Florentine temper" with "the melancholia of modern times" (p. 34).

The essayist refers to "the gladiator-like proportions of the Milesian Venus, the robust beauties of Rubens and the stately dames of a Titian or Tintoretto," but suggests that once we "understand what form really is—that it is not merely for the senses, but that it may become expressive to the spirit—the better we will like this peculiar elongation of form" (p. 34). Elongation joined with slenderness resulted in the ideal American type of *the spirit*. In addition, as this chapter demonstrates, there was a growing interest in the ideal American type of *the will*, physically characterized by elongation combined, not with matronly embonpoint, but with statuesque attributes of the young female athlete. There was both the Dewing ideal and the Gibson ideal; the look of Isabel Archer and the look of Kate Croy.

15. See Marvin Trachtenberg, *The Statue of Liberty*, chs. 4–5.

16. See Downey, *Portrait of an Era*, pp. 206–210.

17. During the course of his 1893 lectures at the Metropolitan Museum concerning the cultural relativism of signs, John La Farge observed that Japanese reactions to the statue's torch were not altogether favorable. See *Considerations on Painting*, p. 257. Yet Emma Lazarus had consciously written her famous poem in honor of "The New Colossus." The opening lines of the verses inscribed on the pedestal dedicated October 28, 1886, read: "Not like the brazen giant of Greek fame, / With conquering limbs astride from land to land." The American colossus is described differently—as "a mighty woman"; "her name / Mother of Exiles," her eyes "mild"; her "silent lips" cry out, " 'Keep, ancient lands, your storied pomp!' " From *The Poems of Emma Lazarus*. Lazarus' poetic strategy is to remind Americans what their best symbols do *not* represent: the bad, old lives from which they have fled, as exemplified by the Russian pogroms of 1879–1883 which inspired her to write this poem.

18. John J. Garnett, *The Statue of Liberty: Its Conception, Its Construction, Its Inauguration*, p. 25.

19. "Notes and Clippings: The Statue of Liberty," *The American Architect and Building News*.

20. *Bartholdi Souvenir: A Sketch of the Colossal Statue Presented by France to the United States*.

21. Observations made in 1878 concerning Thomas Crawford's "Liberty" that crowns the dome of the U.S. Capitol suggest a distinction that was not always heeded: Crawford's sculptured form works as architectural embellishment, but not as allegory. The figure is limited to accepted conventions. Its public significance would be enhanced if it *meant* more, thereby satisfying the popular imagination that requires that its images go beyond mere decoration. See William J. Clark, *Great American Sculptures*, p. 69.

22. *Living and Symbolic Design Photographs, Composed of Officers and Men in the U.S. Army and Navy Service* was presented in a bound album by Mole and Thomas, photographers of Chicago, to Josephus Daniels, Secretary of the Navy in 1918. The photographs, taken from a tower seventy-five feet tall, were "passed" by the Committee on Public Information. The "information" they conveyed involved using scale to correct the distortions caused when such immense figures are looked at "normally" from the ground level. Thousands of yards of white tape were laid to create the "formations." "This presents a most grotesque figure on the ground, for the outlines conform to the laws of *true perspective*, and are just as distorted, only on the opposite side, as a photograph of the same design would be, if it were laid out on the ground in true and proportionate outline." Once one climbs the tower, the image makes sense; the scale and perspective serve to adjust the distortion. Naturalistic details are replaced by an idealizing overview. Among the designs photographed were the U.S. flag, the eagle, the U.S. shield, the Liberty Bell, and Woodrow Wilson—all inspirational symbols for the nation at war. The Statue of Liberty figure consisted of 18,000 men standing over an area about a quarter of a mile long. The grand design could have meant nothing to each of the men standing within the boundaries of those white tapes; it did, however, to the photographers and, supposedly, to the Secretary of the Navy.

23. A cartoon for the *New York Graphic* in 1874 depicts Columbia throwing a good-luck shoe at Nellie Grant's White House wedding. In scale and gesture, this Columbia is just another guest; at most, she is a fairy godmother with an edge on the other celebrants who have gathered to wish President Grant's daughter future good fortune.

24. Charlotte Perkins Gilman was outspoken in her attacks against a "man-made world" which preferred women who manifested "civilized 'feminine delicacy.' " In her crusade to revitalize the home and the institution of "perfect motherhood," Gilman declared that serious damage was done to race preservation and progress when women were kept "small, weak, soft, ill-proportioned." *Women and Economics*, pp. 46–182. (Gilman's book first appeared in 1899.)

25. Harriet Beecher Stowe, *Uncle Tom's Cabin*, 1:120.

26. Statistics for the height of U.S. senators in 1886 are taken from Hathaway and Foard, *Heights and Weights*, table 1.

27. "Daniel Chester French's Four Symbolic Groups for the New York Custom House," unsigned essay for *The Craftsman* (April 1906). The following quotation is from p. 83.

28. Christy, *The American Girl*, p. 12; the following quotations are from pp. 9, 20, 29, 69–70.

29. The quotation from the *New York Times* and the one which follows from Strong's *Our Country* are contained in Roy Lubove, *The Progressives and the Slums*, pp. 45, 54.

30. Franz Boas, *Changes in Bodily Form of Descendants of Immigrants*. Boas marshaled these figures in order to prove that environment is the major factor in size, not racial inheritance. He noted the changes in growth between first and second generation immigrants to the United States, the latter of whom were benefiting from improved sanitation, nutrition, and living conditions.

31. See John Higham, *Strangers in the Land*, concerning the rage of interest in eugenics stimulated by fears of the effects of foreign genetic contamination.

32. Andersen's text proposes that his city (dedicated to "Industry, Science, Fine Arts, Religion, Commerce—Peace") be centered by a Tower of Progress 300 meters tall. The city itself—the "imperial 'eternal' city"— would encompass six residential sections with a population of 100,000 to 120,000 persons each. See *Creation of a World Centre of Communication*.

33. In his text Andersen attributes certain gender qualities to "Evening" and "Night" (the female figures which would adorn the lower terraces of his proposed Fountain of Life alongside the male figures of "Morning" and "Day"). The female represents "the power of thought liberated in dreams" and is "the symbol of everlasting protection." The female also expresses the mysterious shadows of eternal love. But Andersen continues to argue that his bronze statuary groups are visually, as well as spiritually, almost identical. The male and female are shown "advancing in harmony and supporting each other without conscious effort. *Strong, supple limbs are given to both, with only a touch of added grace to the female figure, which is kept harmoniously in line with that of the male, and is almost equally developed.* The heads are carefully studied in the endeavor to make a type, in which love, simplicity and intellect should be united" (my italics).

34. Leon Edel, *The Life of Henry James*, discusses at length the relationship between James and his younger friend, Hendrik Christian Andersen; he suggests that James may have gone beyond heightened emotional attachment into physical expression of his homoerotic feelings. Letter from James to Andersen, 5:472–473.

35. See Alan Trachtenberg, *The Incorporation of America*. As the titles of three other books suggest, the movement toward centralization had been underway prior to the Columbian Exposition: Ray Ginger, ed., *The Nationalizing of American Life, 1877–1900*; John Higham, *From Boundlessness to Consolidation: The Transformation of American Culture, 1848–1860*; Robert H. Wiebe, *The Search for Order, 1877–1920*. But Trachtenberg's book emphasizes that incorporation was one of the central facts of American life by 1893.

36. Immense scale was hardly new to the American imagination urged on by public celebrations and national anniversaries. Erastus Salisbury Field worked on the 13-by-9-foot canvas of "Historical Monument of the American Republic" in the years around 1876. See Frederick B. Robinson, "Erastus Salisbury Field." The Philadelphia Centennial of 1876 and the Sesquicentennial International Exposition also prompted plans to erect a 1,000-foot Tower and to restore King Solomon's Temple in Philadelphia. See Sky and Stone, *Unbuilt America*, pp. 270, 128–131. But the designs for the Columbian Exposition left the visionaries' sketchpad to receive materialization as a great, if temporary city. See David F. Burg, "The Aesthetics of Bigness in Late Nineteenth Century American Architecture"; D. F. Burg, *Chica-*

go's *White City of 1893*; William H. Jordy, "American Architecture Between World's Fairs: Richardson, Sullivan, and McKim."

37. Will H. Low, "The Art of the White City," p. 511.

38. Statistics are available for Wellesley women in 1893, though not for women attending Smith College. See Hathaway and Foard, *Heights and Weights*, table 1.

39. *United States Centennial Commission*, group 28, p. 3.

40. William Dean Howells, "A Sennight of the Centennial," p. 96. The following quotations are from the same page. The artwork most frequently signaled out for praise was "The Dreaming Iolanthe," "an ideal subject" carved from butter. Viewers of the piece were amazed that so difficult a material was handled with such a "a high degree of talent, a fine ideal feeling, as well as exceeding delicacy and brilliancy of manipulation." *Frank Leslie's Illustrated Historical Register of the Centennial Exposition, 1876*, p. 156. Another favorite was the many fountains: the Statue of Religious Liberty erected by B'nai B'rith with several figures (female in armor holding the Constitution; youth holding an urn with sacred flame; eagle grasping the snake of slavery); Columbus; Elias Howe, inventor of the sewing machine; a soda-water fountain. James D. McCabe, *The Illustrated History of the Centennial Exhibition*, pp. 327, 329. Under "Topics of the Times—American Art," *Scribner's Monthly Magazine* of November 1876 observed the remarkable interest shown toward the art displays even though "respectable mediocrity is the rule" (p. 126). Clay Lancaster analyzes the effects upon viewers who had no sure way of reconciling the industrial displays with the art displays, especially when confronted with that hybrid "industrial art." Clay Lancaster, "Taste at the Philadelphia Centennial," pp. 296–297. Homer Saint-Gaudens believed that the Centennial hurt the art it meant to foster, while helping the cause of manufacturing and industry. *The American Artist and His Times*, p. 116. Mariana Van Rensselaer said the exhibits proved to the public that there was more to life than "Yankee steam and steel," and that American smugness had to be replaced by a heightened awareness of art. *Book of American Figure Painters*, n.p. The arts that benefited were those which relied upon the new technology, such as advertising, graphics, reproductions of the fine arts. Hornung and Johnson, *200 Years of American Graphic Art*, p. 73.

41. Richard Kenin's introduction to *Frank Leslie's Illustrated Historical Register* points out the masculine impact of the Centennial displays. In the Machinery Hall the Corliss engine stood together with the Krupp cannon. The Main Building was decorated with a huge bronze Pegasus and galvanized iron eagles. The 150-foot dome of the Art Building was topped by a colossal Columbus. The Educational Department stressed social engineering by which heredity taints could be controlled by "rational" genetics. Years later a Boston etiquette book referring to the disquieting effects of modern life upon manners—the "woman's sphere"—commented, "We have become so highly and uncomfortably civilized, our surroundings are so artificial, that there is some danger of our all turning into so many machines, each one being a part of the great central Corliss engine of our civilization." Florence Howe Hall, *Social Customs*, p. 22. In 1876 Howells observed that the best talents of American women were not to be found in displays of pincushions; instead, female skills were most clearly in evidence in the Machinery Hall where women were "everywhere seen in the operation and superintendence of the most complicated mechanisms." "A Sennight of the Centennial," p. 101. The dilemma remained: should women separate themselves from "the great central Corliss engine of our civilization," or learn to run it? Also see Samuel J. Burr, *Memorial of the International Exhibition*; Walter Smith, *Industrial Art*, vol. 2 of Weinberg, *Illustrated Catalogue: The Masterpieces of the Centennial International Exhibition*.

42. This observation was made by Ray Ginger, *Age of Excess*, pp. 155, 157. In her analysis of the developments in the technology of half-tone between 1876 and 1893, Estelle Jussim continually stresses the increase in accuracy and "information transfer" made possible by

the new techniques in photoengraving. *Visual Communication and the Graphic Arts*, pp. 4–5, 234.

43. See Peirce's Lowell Lectures of 1892–93 on the history of science, and his notes on nineteenth-century music: *Selected Writings*, pp. 263, 269–270.

44. See Walter Benn Michaels, "The Interpreter's Self: Peirce on the Cartesian 'Subject,' " pp. 383–402.

45. Remarked by Fred Albert Shannon, *The Centennial Years*, pp. 1–2.

46. See Helen Lefkowitz Horowitz, *Culture and the City: Cultural Philanthropy in Chicago from the 1880s to 1917*.

47. Alan Trachtenberg, *The Incorporation of America*, ch. 7, and Justus D. Doenecke, "Myths, Machines, and Markets: The Columbian Exposition of 1893." Trachtenberg and Doenecke emphasize the social disparities between class and race, as well as the suspect nature of the newly formed economic alliances between business and the arts. A more generous view of the intentions and achievements of the man in charge of planning, Daniel Burnham (e.g., his relations with the laborers who built the exhibition buildings and grounds), is offered by Thomas S. Hines, *Burnham of Chicago*, chs. 4–5.

48. Quoted by Jeanne Weimann, *The Fair Women*, p. 261. The next statement is from Henry Van Brunt's "Architecture at the World's Columbian Exposition," part 4, p. 729; quoted on pp. 261–262 of *The Fair Women*.

49. Weimann is eloquent on the subject of the advantages that came to the women who organized the Woman's Building. Notwithstanding the sometimes petty bickerings and the more significant internecine battles carried on among various factions of the women's groups in charge, the Columbian Exposition provided them a "splendid experience," one which "was never repeated; nor could it be, in all the international expositions with all the women's boards and women's buildings which have appeared since that time." *The Fair Women*, p. 597.

50. Henry Van Brunt, "Architecture at the World's Columbian Exposition," part 1, p. 96. Hubert Howe Bancroft's *Book of the Fair* furnishes one example of the mixed meanings conveyed to the visitors. "Halos of fresh thought descend and possess us. Questions and ambitions arise, instinct with new powers and new purposes . . . the aroma of culture fills the air, and knowledge is drawn in at every breath" (1:2). Although "everywhere the marvellous is made subservient to the useful and reasonable," the exhibits are "a triumph of the aesthetical no less than of the material" (1:4). Women are credited with having originated the industrial arts in ancient times, but the winged groups on top of the Woman's Building are "typical of feminine characteristics and virtues"—spirituality, love, sacrifice, literature, beneficence, home (1:260). Bancroft decides that the fair as a whole demonstrates the "heroic age of industrial development" that presents the world, "as in a mirror, the highest achievements of which mankind is capable" (2:973). When he alludes to Cassatt's mural in the Woman's Building which depicts women in modern dress pursuing the image of Fame that disappears from their grasp, is he suggesting that only men can win the one race that counts? The full title of Bancroft's two-volume work indicates the significance of what he found at Chicago: *The Book of the Fair: An Historical and Descriptive Presentation of the World's Science, Art, and Industry, as Viewed Through the Columbian Exposition at Chicago in 1893, Designed to Set Forth the Display Made by the Congress of Nations, of Human Achievement in Material Form, so as the More Effectually to Illustrate the Progress of Mankind in All the Departments of Civilized Life*.

51. See William H. Jordy, "American Architecture Between World's Fairs."

52. Among numerous contemporary accounts of the magical moment when the switch was thrown that lighted the Exposition grounds, Bancroft's description best conveys the awe and delight of the occasion. *Book of the Fair*, 1:402.

53. John Flaxman's earliest piece of "practical sculpture" was designed when he was nine

years old: a female figure in classical mode to be used as a lamp holder. Sidney Colvin, *The Drawings of Flaxman in the Gallery of University College, London*, p. 11. See Robert Jope-Slade, "Art and Electricity"; he asks that lamp designers discard worn-out design motifs and incorporate a wider range of conventions. Figure 14.36 depicts Loïe Fuller in motion in metal, the famous stage personality serving as a lighting fixture.

54. See Thomas H. Pauly, "In Search of 'The Spirit of '76,' " p. 461.

55. Bancroft describes the fifteen-foot Franklin statue and the Edison Tower ("the very apotheosis of electricity") in *Book of the Fair*, 1:403, 424. Certainly stress was placed on the men involved in the practical business considerations concerning electrical power. See Edward C. Kirkland, *Industry Comes of Age*, pp. 168–170; Ginger, *Age of Excess*, p. 225; Trachtenberg, *The Incorporation of America*, p. 68. But if men were in charge of the development of electricity, the symbol for that power was female. A design by D. C. French in 1882 had been one of the forerunners of the Beckwith designs. See Cresson, *Journey Into Fame*, p. 26. As early as 1860 *Harper's Weekly* included "The First Telegraphic Message from California," a drawing of a winged figure with stars on her skirt who walks along telegraph wires carrying a scroll inscribed "May the Union Be Perpetual." Werner Sollors' essay "Dr. Benjamin Franklin's Celestial Telegraph, or Indian Blessings to Gas-Lit American Drawing Rooms" is an intriguing examination of images which merged Franklin's experiments, the spiritualist movement, and the marginal place held by American Indians and women.

The notion that communication holds the diverse elements of the United States together is central to a painting shown at a 1915 exhibition of the Chesapeake and Potomac Telephone Company: a telephone switchboard operator (whose function is allegorical, though her dress is contemporary) grasps wires of telephone poles that flow out to city, farm, and factory. Together with "The Telephone," Carroll Beckwith also provided the 1893 fair with female companion figures: "The Arc Light," "The Morse Telegraph," "The Dynamo," and "The Spirit of Electricity." F. D. Millet gives a detailed description of the Beckwith group in his essay "The Decoration at the Exposition," pp. 1–42.

56. The murals prepared for the Woman's Building depicting contemporary women at work at various arts and crafts were picturesque in form and in theme. Allegorical murals of Ceres and Diana were displayed at the Agricultural Building, and in the Mechanical Arts Building the figure of Columbia was placed near the newest model of the Corliss engine to add a pleasant touch and homey feel. These allegorical figures may have been sublime through the fact of their figuration, but they were no less picturesque in detail and effect than the murals in the Woman's Building. All served to convey the readable message (much applauded by most who commented on the Exposition) that the spectators were in the presence of ethical principles, useful skills, and "the power and progress of a nation where all are free to strive for the highest rewards that energy and talent can win." Quotation from Bancroft, *Book of the Fair*, 1:673. F. Hopkinson Smith commented upon the combination of the picturesque with colossal size in his observations concerning the overall scale of the White City: "The Picturesque Side," p. 109. See Maud Howe Elliott, "The Building and Its Decoration"; Pauline King, *American Mural Painting*; and Will H. Low, *A Painter's Progress*, for other contemporary accounts, as well as the wealth of material gathered in Weimann's *The Fair Women* on the decorations that mixed the domestic with the grandiose.

57. This and the following quotation are from Bourget, *Outre-Mer*, pp. 108–109.

58. Bourget, "A Farewell to the White City," pp. 136–137. Bourget speaks of the national consciousness as one which "feels its work to be the creation of a personal ideal" of culture.

59. The phrase "the American Paradise of 1893" appears in the "Explanatory Introduction" to James B. Campbell's two-volume work *Campbell's Illustrated History of the World's Columbian Exposition*.

60. As described in Campbell, *Campbell's Illustrated History*, 2:364, visitors to the Fine

Arts Department were fascinated by paintings depicting the bloody events of the French Revolution and the custom of self-flagellation practiced in medieval Europe, but this was the kind of history they believed *their* nation had done away with.

61. F. Hopkinson Smith, "The Picturesque Side," p. 123, wrote of the apex attained by American artists—"the fixing forever of that position in the art of the world." Michael Quick observes that the popular success achieved by the art displayed at the Columbian Exposition prompted some expatriate artists to return home. *American Expatriate Artists*, p. 40.

62. J. A. Mitchell, "Types and People at the Fair," p. 54. Mitchell characterizes the American visitors to the Exposition as uniformly "practical people" who care most for exhibits that display "ingenuity and manual skills"; however, they also take pleasure in paintings, as long as they are of "comfortable subjects," preferring as they do "a taste of sugar" in the arts (pp. 48, 50). James B. Campbell also insisted that there was a consensus of response to both paintings and sculpture by the visitors; he noted that "giant and intricate machinery and other handiwork of man was oftimes passed with very little notice, while some little souvenir card with artistic decorations or stamping upon its surface would call forth expressions of delight." *Campbell's Illustrated History*, 2:591. However frequently men and women found mutual interest in the items on display, gender distinctions prevailed in the nature of the images themselves. W. Lewis Fraser's essay "Decorative Painting at the World's Fair: The Works of Gari Melchers and Walter MacEwen" details the contrasting work assigned to these artists: MacEwen did feminine themes with women and children; Melchers did masculine themes of heroism.

63. Henry Van Brunt, "Architecture at the World's Columbian Exposition," part 1, p. 89. Van Brunt declares his hope that the fair will serve as an object lesson to national legislators who keep "a costly architectural factory in Washington" so that "the unsubstantial pageant of Jackson Park will not have been in vain" (part 5, p. 907).

64. See Alan Trachtenberg, *The Incorporation of America*; Justus D. Doenecke, "Myths, Machines, and Markets: The Columbian Exposition."

65. F. D. Millet considered the buildings at the Exposition "simply as great sketches of possible permanent structures." "The Decoration of the Exposition," p. 9. In his history of the 1893 fair, R. Reid Badger speaks of the buildings as "snapshots." *The Great American Fair*, p. 7. Both Millet and Badger single out that particular quality of the unfinished by which many characterize "modernity."

66. Alan Trachtenberg attacks the corporate mentality that attempted to impose a rigidly elitist culture upon the masses. Thomas Hines agrees that Burnham erred in trying to perpetuate an unsuitable architectural style upon the future of American building. At the time, however, the men in charge of the Exposition (and the women who planned their own exhibits) were convinced that the occasion was the result of a typically American miracle of the processes shaping organized activity in the United States. It seemed to them to prove what Americans do best: (a) work with informal, personalized plans without the hindrance of government controls or the interference of large official groups; (b) construct and decorate a diverse number of buildings that are subsumed under a larger plan; that is, to organize projects in ways that are similar to states working independently of the federal government. Trachtenberg points out the artificiality and the regimentation of the conditions under which the workers were housed (pp. 210–211). At the time, however, the artists and architects in charge of the projects (who themselves lived for months in barracklike structures on the fair's site) expressed enthusiasm for the camaraderie and cooperation they experienced. See R. Reid Badger, *The Great American Fair*, pp. 19, 28; Henry C. Bunner, "The Making of the White City," p. 417; Thomas S. Hines, *Burnham of Chicago*, ch. 5.

67. Montgomery Schuyler, "Last Words About the World's Fair," 2:574.

68. Henry Van Brunt, "Architecture at the World's Columbian Exposition," part 1, p. 89. He incorporates the words of the plea made by Frederic Harrison.

69. Howells, *Letters of an Altrurian Traveller (1893–1894)*. Howells' series of twenty-three articles appeared in *The Cosmopolitan* between November 1892 and September 1894.

70. See William Ordway Partridge, *Art for America*, p. 57, for his fatuous declaration in 1894 that all citizens of the United States were free and most were prosperous.

71. Will H. Low, "The Art of the White City," pp. 504, 506. He specifically said that he regretted an actual high white wall had not been built to protect the beauties of the inner Exposition areas from the Midway and all that lay beyond.

72. Gilder, "The White City" and "The Vanishing City." Gilder's first poem concerns the transience of ancient cultures, while insisting that the soul of Greece lives again in Chicago at the Exposition. Art defeats Time and "Beauty walks forth to light the world forever." But Gilder's second poem emphasizes the brevity of the White City and man's inability to counter Time's ravages. "Then vanish, City of Dream, and be no more; / Soon shall this fair Earth's self be lost on the unknown shore." An essay by James Mayo on the Liberty Memorial, Kansas City, Missouri, suggests that emblematic structures which outlive their "occasion" serve as disturbing reminders of the nation's failure to live up to their image ("Resymbolization of a Symbol"). It is as well that the White City vanished when it did.

73. The Townsend Walsh Collection of the New York Public Library, Lincoln Center, contains souvenir programs for several Imre Kiralfy stage productions, each a treasure of the florid promotional style. *Imre Kiralfy's Gorgeous Spectacle America as Produced at the Chicago Auditorium 281 Times and Witnessed by 1,200,000 People* featured the production of "America" which ran between April 19 and November 11, 1893. Kiralfy's "Excelsior!" followed immediately on November 24 at Niblo's Garden in New York; it featured "novel electric effects by the Edison Electric Light Company" and "Apotheosis: The Crowning Tableaux: The Triumph of Light Over Darkness." Kiralfy had led up to the Exposition year with "Columbus and the Discovery of America," produced in 1892 in conjunction with the Barnum and Bailey Greatest Show on Earth. For more details of the Kiralfy style, see Elena Millie and Andrea Wyatt, "Tomorrow Night, East Lynne! American Drama as Reflected in the Theatre Poster Collection at the Library of Congress."

74. George R. Collins, introduction to Sky and Stone, *Unbuilt America*, pp. 1–13.

75. The following sources indicate the way models are used in the planning of new industrial, scientific, and social designs: Mary Hesse, *Models and Analogies in Science*; M. Hesse, "Models Versus Paradigms in the Natural Sciences"; Ralph R. Knoblaugh, *Modelmaking for Industrial Design*; Rom Harré, "The Constructive Role of Models"; Cesare Segre, "Culture and Modelling Systems"; Martin K. Starr, *Product Design and Decision Theory*.

76. This and the following quotation are from Adams, *The Education of Henry Adams*, pp. 342–343.

77. Henry James, *The American Scene*, p. 89.

78. Lewis Mumford's indictment of what he termed "the imperial age" of building comes in his chapters on "The Imperial Facade" and "The Age of the Machine" in *Sticks and Stones*.

79. Royal Cortissoz, "A National Monument of Art: The Congressional Library at Washington." The planning for the Library of Congress was actually an embattled affair, as Helen-Anne Hilker makes clear in "Monument to Civilization: Diary of a Building." In general, however, public praise was warm for the new building. Even Henry James was moved to observe that it suggested learning and grace, not merely the expenditure of money. *The American Scene*, p. 354.

80. Daniel H. Burnham, "White City and Capital City." In 1864 James Jarves called for

the careful planning of American cities (*The Art Idea*, pp. 324–325), just as the original designers of the nation's capital had desired to make something good out of the swampy wasteland of the District of Columbia. For further remarks on the need for municipal planning for arts and architecture, see Sylvester Baxter, "The Beautifying of Village and Town"; Edwin Howland Blashfield, "A Word for Municipal Art"; Frederic C. Howe, *The Modern City and Its Problems;* George Kriehn, "The City Beautiful"; Charles Mulford Robinson, *Modern Civic Art, or The City Made Beautiful;* "The Forty-Second Annual Convention of the American Institute of Architects." From the onset, nationalists wanted Washington, D.C., to be an "empirical demonstration" of the success of the American system and the maker of visible myths about a people who "convert forests into cities" and conquer space in order to liberate and elevate. See Margaret F. Thorp, *The Literary Sculptors*, p. 133, and Lillian B. Miller, *Patrons and Patriotism*, p. 11. For contemporary criticism of the City Beautiful movement, see Michele Bogart's "The Importance of Believing in 'Purity.' "

81. Antagonism between architects and the government agencies overseeing the building designs had a long history. An untitled, unsigned appraisal of the situation appeared in *The American Architect and Building News* (April 6, 1878). Also see P. B. Wight, "On the Present Condition of Architectural Art in the Western States."

82. Hitchcock and Seale's *Temples of Democracy* cites guidebooks from the turn of the century that detailed the pleasures visitors could expect while wandering through the corridors of the new state capitol buildings. The Library of Congress had its own handbook prepared by Herbert Small in 1901.

83. Hugo B. Froehlich and Bonnie E. Snow suggested drawing exercises that included depictions of marching children, the national flag, and scenes from George Washington's boyhood. *A Course of Study in Art*, p. 8. The 1898 *Teacher's Manual* for the fourth and fifth years focused upon the "beauty" of the U.S. flag and the national shield.

84. In 1897 the Prang Company put out an *Illustrated Catalogue of Pictures Adapted for Schoolroom Decoration*. It includes testimonials supporting the use of visual aids in the training of youthful minds (W. O. Partridge: "It is just as important to hang reproductions of great paintings and frescoes upon the walls as it is to place books under their eyes"). Among the available items are photographs ranging from the colossi of Memnon and the Colosseum to the National Capitol and the Court of Honor at the Columbian Exposition, and portrait-lithographs of Lincoln, Webster, "Our Poets" (Bryant, Emerson, Holmes, Lowell, Longfellow, Whittier), and the Pilgrim Ancestors (Alden, Standish, Elder Brewster), as well as Eastman Johnson's "Boyhood of Lincoln," a scene representing "Farragut Lashed to the Shrouds, Passing the Forts in Mobile Bay," pictures of Civil War battles, and landscapes of Yellowstone and New England. In 1900 the Art Study Company of Chicago published the first of a series of semimonthly *History Study Pictures: History, Geography, Literature*. Each volume contained ten reproductions from paintings and photographs that ranged from Flaxman's "Trojan Heroes" and illustrations by Gustave Doré and G. F. Watts inspired by Tennyson's *Idylls of the King* to select categories devoted to Columbus, Indians of History, Colonial Pictures, New England History, Lincoln, Washington, and Birthplaces of Liberty. The charge was fifteen cents for a single portfolio of ten pictures with text or one dollar for a series of ten portfolios.

85. In 1876 *The Galaxy* printed a rebuke against the ugliness of currency that was too natural and unheraldic in design; the need was for inspiring designs placed before the public during every exchange of money. See Cornelius Clarkson Vermeule, *Numismatic Art in America*, for the details. The model for the Liberty head coins was Mary Cunningham, though some criticized Saint-Gaudens at the time for using an Irish servant, not a "pure American." In Homer Saint-Gaudens' edition of *The Reminiscences of Augustus Saint-Gaudens*, pp. 329–333, the retort is made that it would have been even better to have used Irish features on a Swedish body with a drop of Negro blood since only Indians are "pure Amer-

icans." The 1916 dime designed by A. A. Weinman was supposedly modeled by Elsie Rachel Stevens, wife of Wallace Stevens.

86. Theodore Roosevelt's involvement in the design of U.S. coins and other public works of art should be noted. In 1912 Roosevelt formed the National Arts Commission with Daniel Chester French, Cass Gilbert, Edwin H. Blashfield, and Frederick Law Olmstead among its members. Roosevelt was especially pleased with the results of Saint-Gaudens' coinage designs. See Glenn Brown, "Roosevelt and the Fine Arts."

87. The year 1895 was the foundation date for the National Society of Mural Painters. For the fullest account see Pauline King, *American Mural Painting.* Besides the items listed in chapter 9, note 45, see the following:: Frank J. Mather, Jr., Charles R. Morey, and William J. Henderson, *The American Spirit in Art;* William A. Coffin, "The Decorations in the New Congressional Library"; Royal Cortissoz, introduction, *The Works of Edwin Howland Blashfield;* "Decorations of the Education Palace, Albany, N.Y."; John La Farge, "Puvis de Chavannes"; William Walton, "The Field of Art—Mural Painting in This Country Since 1898"; Richard V. West, *Occasional Papers 1—the Walker Art Building Murals.*

88. Constantino Brumidi's allegorical paintings for the interiors of the U.S. Capitol coincided with the incorporation of ideal sculpture, but the early murals of the 1860s were relatively isolated instances; they were viewed as too heavily in debt to the Italian tradition to be correct "American" forms of expression. See Charles E. Fairman, *Art and Artists of the Capitol;* Lillian B. Miller, *Patrons and Patriotism.*

89. Patricia Hills, "Turn-of-the-Century America," p. 68.

90. Homer Saint-Gaudens, *The American Artist and His Times,* p. 150; Samuel Isham, *The History of American Painting,* p. 556. Isham records the decline of seriousness in murals after 1900. Lacking insight into spiritual matters, they served best as decorations for ballrooms (p. 560). King also describes the growing use of mural designs in hotels, private houses, clubs, and banks. The allegorical mural was revived during the Depression by the WPA projects; decoration and social statements once again attempted connections on the walls of post offices across the country. See Karal Ann Marling, *Wall-to-Wall America: A Cultural History of Post-Office Murals in the Great Depression.* Also see the review of Marling's book which shows that problems of interpretation continue to plague the reading of more recent public statements, as they do murals dating from the turn of the century: Richard P. Horwitz, "Making Sense of Mural America."

91. Pauline King lists the artists involved in preparing the mural decorations for the Columbian Exposition, *American Mural Painting,* pp. 65–66, 88–89. Also see Jeanne Weimann, *The Fair Women,* for the contribution of women muralists.

92. King, *American Mural Painting,* p. 63. The next two quotations are from pp. 206–207, 234.

93. Charles Fairman tells of the eloquent plea offered, to no avail, before members of the House of Representatives in 1858 by Owen Lovejoy, congressman from Illinois. Referring to a mural depicting General Rufus Putnam and the Roman general Cincinnatus who left their plows to go off to defend their countrymen, Lovejoy said he could detect in it no "revolutionary reminiscence." "Overhead we have pictures of Bacchus, Ceres, and so on surrounded with cupids, cherubs &c to the end of heathen mythology. All this we have, but not a single specimen of the valuable breeds of cattle, horses, sheep, etc., which are now found in the country." Fairman, *Art and Artists of the Capitol,* p. 178.

94. Joshua Taylor, *America as Art,* p. 139.

95. Kenyon Cox, *Artist and Public and Other Essays on Art Subjects,* p. 14.

96. This and the following observations concerning the efficacy for modern American life of the public mural are drawn from Blashfield's often impassioned statements published as *Mural Painting in America. The Scammon Lectures Delivered Before the Art Institute of Chicago, March 1912, and Since Greatly Enlarged.*

97. The Ephemera File on Blashfield (1848–1936) in the library collection at the National Museum of American Art and Royal Cortissoz's introduction to Blashfield's *Works* make clear the position Blashfield held, next to John La Farge, as "our recognized *chef d'école*"— a "rank he won through the force of ideas beautifully expressed." (This comment is from the *New York Times* obituary.) Blashfield originally planned to be an engineer and studied in Germany and at MIT, but by 1876 he was in Paris training under Gérôme and Bonnat. In 1881 he returned to the United States—"uncontaminated by French influence." He took up mural painting during the 1880s when many other American artists were learning the basic techniques of that medium; like them, he finally received public recognition for his work at the Columbian Exposition.

Blashfield's murals blended the idealistic with the realistic; many were designed in honor of the patriot and the workingman; all were in "tribute to the young goddess of the nation"—"a fair and grave goddess, ineffably young and with a stern innocence of feature." These remarks and the next are from an essay by Elizabeth Luther Cary for the November 1916 issue of *The American Magazine of Art*, 7(1):4, 6. "In general, Mr. Blashfield respects the rather solemn temper of the American public toward art. . . . he meets the moral lessons involved with the seriousness of a dedicated teacher. He argues vigorously in his writings for the importance of significant story telling." Blashfield's murals celebrate "law and order, the making of nations, the heroes of progress and civilization. His types are those of deeply enlisted men and women intent upon duty." Blashfield himself argued in the Scammon Lectures that he created images for Americans which expressed feelings common to all: "We have suffered and fought in the cause of progress and civilization; remind us of it upon our walls. We have bred heroes; celebrate them."

98. Blashfield's representations of different nations and cultures at various stages of "the evolution of civilization" alternate male with female figures. The figure for America—the apex of civilized life—is male. This usage is in contrast to the many representations of this type during the period which were largely female, ranging from George Maynard's "Civilization" to Howard Chandler Christy's ultimate image of the "Liberty Belle" (see Introduction, figure 9).

99. "Mural Painting—an Art for the People and a Record of the Nation's Development," *The Craftsman*. The quotations are from pp. 59, 66. *The Craftsman* was edited by Gustav Stickley. See *No Place of Grace* for Jackson Lears' opinions concerning Stickley's disquiet over the direction taken by American culture in the new century, pp. 66–96.

100. The botched handling of Iowa's rural landscape in 1906 is a repetition of the mistakes viewed by Congressman Lovejoy in 1858 in the mural honoring General Putnam. See note 93. The need to mix realistic, contemporary details with allegorical, universal types continued to concern a number of observers of public art. See Russell Sturgis, *The Appreciation of Sculpture*, p. 157, and Jules Guerin, "The Mural Decorations," p. 258. (The essay by Guerin concerns the murals for the Lincoln Memorial.)

101. For a detailed listing of the murals painted by Abbey, and the meticulous procedures he followed in preparing his designs for placement in the interior spaces of the Pennsylvania State Capitol, see E. V. Lucas, *Edwin Austin Abbey*, vol. 2, chs. 37–38, 40. Two other Abbey murals at Harrisburg are less effective both as decoration and message than "The Spirit of Light." In one, workers toiling to uncover treasures in the earth appear unaware of the hovering triad of Science (helmeted, with drawn sword), Fortune (blindfolded and propelled by a whirling wheel), and Abundance (whose cornucopia filled with agrarian bounties is at odds with the industrial scene). In another mural, the sailing ships of the early explorers are led by Religion, Faith, and Hope—figures representing the motives that sent the first settlers to the North American continent. The images are drained of emotional power since the historical period (the 1600s) and the specified values (entirely spiritual,

alone) have even less to do with the state of Pennsylvania in 1909 than the airy figures adrift on the tide of gas and oil which Abbey depicted in "The Spirit of Light."

102. See Fairman, *Art and Artists of the Capitol*, pp. 384–388.

103. Clarke's letter of protest, printed in *Kate Field's Washington* on October 3, 1894, is cited on pp. 255–256 of Helen-Anne Hilker's article "Monument to Civilization: Diary of a Building." Clarke also noted that most of the "readable books" in the Library of Congress were written by women and that surely Harriet Beecher Stowe ought to be honored by having her likeness included as one of the portico busts or as one of the portrait statues in the main reading room.

104. Garry Wills provides an examination of the problems encountered by Horace Greenough and Jean Antoine Houdon in sculpting an appropriate "republican" image of George Washington. See "Washington's Citizen Virtue: Greenough and Houdon."

105. Religious paintings for public places did not go down well in the United States at the turn of the century and never had. See Donelson F. Hoopes, *American Narrative Paintings*, p. 14. John La Farge's Christs and Louis Tiffany's Saviors were restricted to the dim narthexes and side aisles of American churches, in the same way that V. G. Rocine's Reverend Mr. Caine was placed to the side where the meek and virtuous keep silence in the midst of the din of a burgeoning commercialized society. The sturdy presences of Washington, Penn, or Edison were etherealized through adding the figure of Columbia or the American Girl; females become the conveyers of the transcendent powers with which they reward the good male American. Elevate the male figure itself too high and the sense of the ridiculous or the sacrilegious rushes in. Estelle Jussim tells of the public anger over F. Holland Day's attempt to represent Christ's Passion photographically by having himself hoisted upon a cross on the grounds of his Norwalk, Connecticut, estate. Day's experience was a cautionary tale for anyone at the turn of the century who pushed the mimetic arts too close toward images of the sacred and for those who need to be reminded of the particular susceptibility of the camera for replacing painterly suggestion with mechanical naturalism. See Jussim, *Slave to Beauty*, ch. 9.

106. For his mural of Minnesota, Blashfield used the device of the triangular arrangement of figures borrowed from John Flaxman's neoclassical renditions of the classical Greek pediments. Blashfield came naturally to this technique since he had begun his boyhood training by copying out Flaxman's designs.

107. See Alan Wallach, "Thomas Cole and the Aristocracy."

13. Poster Lives (1898–1918)

1. Henry F. May, *The End of Innocence*, pp. 9–19.

2. As portrayed in the poster scene designed for Imre Kiralfy's 1893 spectacle "America," the pictured force is that of civilization and technology, not the force of armies. The impulse to transfer moral dominance into political influences is not, however, far behind; or into sheer entertainment, as with Arthur Voegtlin's "America" mounted at the Hippodrome in 1913. According to the reviewer for *The Theater* (October 1913), 18(152):xiv, the audience's attention is whisked rapidly from place to place, interlude to interlude—Columbus' landing, New York Central Railroad Station, New England farm, New Orleans levee, the Alamo, New York slum fire, Panama and huge steamships—with a final Grand Tableau "where patriotic feeling is stirred by the singing of America." The reviewer for the *New York Dramatic Mirror* (September 3, 1913), 70(1811):7, was more jaded in his response to the dull music, the lack of jokes, the ridiculous villain, but allowed that the spectacle was most effective. Patriotic feelings are certainly central to the spectacle's effect, but whereas Kiralfy made moral comments an important part of the evening's entertainment, Voegtlin

seems out for sheer fun. Both presentations are alike structurally, however; both present a welter of scenes lacking coherent connections. In either version of "America," if locales and people were not instantly recognizable as types, the audiences would be unable to identify, and enjoy, what they were seeing.

3. See Arthur Fish, "Triumphal Arches." For the checkered history of the arch designed to commemorate Admiral Dewey's victory in Manila Bay, see Marjorie P. Balge, "The Dewey Arch: Sculpture or Architecture?"; Mark Sullivan, *Our Times*, vol. 1, *The Turn of the Century*, p. 337. In 1900 L. Frank Baum detailed the ways merchants could erect their own "victory arches" to attract customers to street fairs. *The Art of Decorating Dry Goods Windows and Interiors*, p. 163.

4. Marjorie Balge's article "The Dewey Arch" describes the central role taken by Ward (president of the National Sculpture Society) in modeling the "Victory" perched on top of the arch.

5. Royalties from sales of both "The American Girl Battleship March" and "The American Girl Battleship Waltz" were donated to the fund. As one enthusiast wrote to Maude Mears, "We girls are wild to show our patriotism as well as the boys."

6. By 1889 John Philip Sousa's "Star-Spangled Banner" and "Hail Columbia" were routinely played at official functions, but a taste for the American Girl associated with men headed for war was encouraged in the decades just before the United States entered the First World War. Among the popular songs that used the motif of the Girl in cover art and lyrics: "Uncle Sam's Girls" (1904), "The Stars and Stripes and You" (1906), "I Want a Girl from Yankee Doodle Town" (1909), "Three Things I Love—Mother, sweetheart, and my country's flag" (1912), "Our American Girl" (1913). For Sousa's own assessment of the status of patriotic music in 1890, see John Philip Sousa, *National Patriotic and Typical Airs of All Lands*. The music presented at the Columbian Exposition also had its historian who wished to commemorate the use of "appropriate music of a superior order inspired by the patriotism and grandeur of the occasion": Hitchcock's *Musical, Pictorial and Descriptive Souvenir of the World's Columbian Exposition in Celebration of the Discovery of America*.

7. R. G. Collingwood, *The Principles of Art*, "Art as Magic," pp. 66–73.

8. These phrases are from the preface to *Cartoons of the War of 1898 with Spain from Leading Foreign and American Papers*. This collection (source of figures 13.8 and 13.18) set out to prove its proud claim that the war had been caused by the nation's newspapers; pictures, not words, had done the trick. Mark Twain and William and Henry James were among those who actively opposed the imperialistic aspirations of the United States.

9. Angus Fletcher, *Allegory*, p. 2.

10. Frances P. Hoyle, editor of *The Complete Speaker and Reciter for Home, School, Church, and Platform* (1902), included the fiery expansionist speech delivered by Senator Albert Beveridge of Indiana and the counterargument offered by Senator Hoare (see pp. 116–118).

11. Among the popular songs addressed directly to immigrant audiences were "They're All Good American Names" (1911), "We'll Build a Little Home in the U.S.A." (1915), and "Don't Bite the Hand That's Feeding You" (1915). The lyrics assume that the newcomers wish to be transformed into "real Americans" in order not to stand self-condemned as ingrates. John Higham reports on a public ceremony at Henry Ford's compulsory English School by which a visual metamorphosis took place on stage. Workers representing a variety of ethnic types climbed into a large caldron, then emerged homogenized as "Americans" waving the stars and stripes. See *Strangers in the Land*, pp. 247–248.

12. See Cynthia Jaffe McCabe, *The Golden Door: Artist-Immigrants of America, 1876–1976*; Fink and Taylor, *Academy*, pp. 66–67.

13. The following quotations from Henry, "Among the Immigrants," are from pp. 301, 309, 311.

14. See Neil Harris' discussion of Keppler's cartoon in "The Gilded Age Reconsidered Once Again," p. 9.

15. Figure 13.21 is the work of Maud Humphrey, whose popularity was based on her drawings of cherubic children mimicking adult activities. (Her reputation now rests on the fact that she was the mother of Humphrey Bogart who reputedly served his mother as a child model). See *American Artists and Their Work* for an evaluation of Humphrey's position in the American art scene when she was twenty-one and already well versed in studies of children and idealistic images of women.

16. Figure 13.22 is one of a series of silk-embroidered tapestries executed (after designs by her husband) by one Madame de Rudder of Belgium during the 1890s. See J. E. Whitby, "The Art Movement: An Unusual Form of Decorative Art."

17. Figure 13.23 is a sketch contributed by Edwin Howland Blashfield to *The Book of the Homeless*, compiled in 1916 by Edith Wharton. In *King Albert's Book: A Tribute to the Belgian King and People from Representative Men and Women Throughout the World*, p. 6, Hall Caine speaks of the "sublime duty" imposed by destiny upon Belgium. Traditionally identified as a heroine of freedom and spirit, the nation is now being destroyed by Germany, the Evil Eve. Columbia now carries on Belgium's former role; she comes to save Belgium and to make her once more mistress of her own home. Caine's use of language is revealing; the war is symbolically apportioned between three females—the wicked witch, the victim, the protectress and savior. I am indebted to R. Alan Price for bringing these two publications to my attention.

18. During World War I one of the most effective versions of "The Greatest Mother" trope was the Angel of Mons which was "seen" by hundreds along the battle lines. See Mark Girouard, *The Return to Camelot: Chivalry and the English Gentleman*, pp. 284–285.

19. The women photographed running the public transport, operating elevators, working in arms factories, and in other ways replacing men drafted into the armed services wear the practical work clothes required by their jobs. These uniforms also do duty as public symbols. The women are recognized as national heroines, not as feminists mannishly dressed in order to disrupt established social institutions. Among the photographs in the Prints and Photographs Division of the Library of Congress there is one, however, which is difficult to assess in these flattering terms. A uniformed black woman poses with a feather duster in her hand before the subway train she is hired to clean. Has the fact that she too is in uniform enhanced her social position in times of war; or is it only white women in uniform who are seen symbolically?

20. The "demonstrations" to which these determined women lent themselves were not for the purpose of getting the vote. Many photographs represent cooking demonstrations that instructed women how to stretch scarce foodstuffs. Others feature women rolling bandages or preparing other nurturing supplies. There is, however, a group of photographs taken of "Miss Hewitt's Campers" at Midvale, New Jersey, in 1916. These views of smartly uniformed, impeccably well-bred young women with brooms and rifles are an odd mix of the housewife and the soldier. They are reminiscent of the Mathew Brady photographs of army men posed in homey scenes outside the tents that were their haven from the battle lines. Since it is not yet wartime for the United States, there is the sense that Miss Hewitt's campers are participating in a costume party, notwithstanding the earnestness of their expressions. Michele J. Shover's excellent essay on women in World War I poster art mentions both images of the monumentally militant and of the domestic, while placing her emphasis upon the latter, politically conservative, forms. I am pointing up the importance of the monumental figures. They are no less politically conservative but are certainly emotionally more forceful than women with brooms. See Michele J. Shover, "Roles and Images of Women in World War I Propaganda." Sandra M. Gilbert views the effects of World War

I upon the women of Great Britain as liberating. The men in the trenches fell into depression and emotional and physical impotence; the women joyfully asserted their newfound sense of power. Actual American women seemed not to have gone to the extremes detailed by Gilbert; some of the poster art did, however, and beyond. See Gilbert's "Soldier's Heart: Literary Men, Literary Women, and the Great War," *Signs*, pp. 422–450.

21. See Joseph Darracott, ed., *The First World War in Posters*; Martin Hardie and Arthur K. Sabin, *War Posters Issued by Belligerent and Neutral Nations, 1914–1919*; Rickards, *Posters of the First World War*, for comparisons between American and European war posters.

22. See William Almon Wolff, "Leading Advertising Experts Commend Success of Marines' Publicity Campaign," pp. 5, 6, 70.

23. Flagg, who was appointed state military artist for New York and whose "I Want You" poster was printed in four million copies, stated that men go to war for adventure, not for ideals. See Susan E. Meyer, *James Montgomery Flagg*, p. 37. He, for one, did not need to "see" World War I through an image of the female which offered the veil of values other artists superimposed between the event and the viewer. Joseph Pennell's responses to the poster events offered by the war is fiercely "official." See *Joseph Pennell's Liberty-Loan Poster: A Text-Book for Artists and Amateurs, Governments and Teachers and Printers*.

24. For details of Gibson's active involvement in the poster work of World War I, and the organization of the nation's morale effort by George Creel, see Susan E. Meyer, *America's Great Illustrators*, p. 229; and Mark Sullivan, *Our Times*, vol. 5, *Over Here, 1914–1918*, pp. 426–440. Gibson was more in his element with illustrations for propaganda projects such as Wharton's *Book of the Homeless* to which he contributed a sweet-faced young woman, "The Girl He Left Behind Him," who writes her soldier an encouraging letter of love.

25. Charles Matlack Price and Horace Brown, *How To Put It—Patriotic Posters—the Stuff That Makes People Stop—Look—Act!*

26. The year before the war began Price wrote in praise of German poster art: "Arts and Decorations—the Essentials of the Poster."

27. William Dean Howells, "Editha," pp. 214–224. Howells never names the war to which Editha sends George Gearson; like Stephen Crane in *The Red Badge of Courage*, Howells elects to universalize the war fever that perpetually brings heightened dreams of glory to the romantic imagination.

28. Frederick Orin Bartlett, "DeLancey—Himself," pp. 40–47.

29. "The Red, White, and Blue"—a "Novelty March Song" of 1914 with words by George Arthur—is sung by a man whose sweetheart awakens patriotic feelings whenever he gazes into her face. The first verse links the nation's flag to the love he feels for her. "For my dear old country's banner, You unfurl, little girl, to my gaze." The song's chorus elaborates upon the flaglike qualities of her red lips, star-white teeth, and sky-blue eyes.

30. In "Leading Advertising Experts Commend Success of Marines.' Publicity Campaign," William A. Wolff details the advertising methods used to promote the Marine Corps. Wolff's remarks, and the comments he compiles from other advertising men, stress conscious parallels between consumer advertising and government propaganda. At the war's start the corps was like "a good automobile that isn't advertised," but through the efforts of men confident in "the product they had to advertise," the public was taught "to recognize the globe, anchor and eagle. . . . So every Marine you saw became a living, walking advertisement for his corps." Wolff cites the success of Flagg's poster "Tell That to the Marines!" which was "diabolically clever. It didn't overlook a single selling point." William C. (Pop) Freeman (who writes "snappy advertising talks" for newspaper syndicates) asks rhetorically, "Wouldn't it be a good idea for every trade-mark to have the backing of the label of the U.S.A.?" (If trademarks sell the corps, the U.S. government should push trademarks.) The ad men point to the "Truth in Advertising" advantage gained as the result of the marines' actual performance in combat; one admits that he was "sold" by the ad campaign to

the extent of sending his son to the corps. Werner S. Allison of the National Biscuit Company sums up the ties formed between product and sales techniques: "The war has brought advertising into its own and shown some of the infinite possibilities. It has demonstrated beyond the preadventure of a doubt that it has a deep-hold on the hearts and minds of the people, and when employed in an intelligent, commonsense manner, *brings a great popular response whether it is used to sell a commodity, a service, faith in the Government, morale, or a trademark*" (my italics). Quotations are from pp. 5, 6, 68, 70.

31. See Edward L.Bernays' *Crystallizing Public Opinion* for a description of his promotional techniques, and *Biography of an Idea: Memoirs of Public Relations Counsel Edward L. Bernays* for his "history" of his new profession.

32. The attribution of superlative beauty to Princess Eleanore is belied by Christy's illustrations. Christy always did best with pert young things. Here he has to convey the seriousness of a mature woman who is the sovereign of a beleaguered nation at war. His only solution is to make her dowdy and matronly. In compensation (and this is a true insight on Christy's part, however unwitting), DeLancey is the one imaged as "the beautiful woman." In terms of the narrative as well, DeLancey is the story's heroine, the one who follows the "male" command of his leader in combat, the princess.

33. In the same issue of *The Marines' Bulletin* as "DeLancey—Himself" (incorporated in the article by William A. Wolff on the advertising techniques used to promote the Marine Corps) there is a painting by Neysa McMein. It depicts a marine who offers a doll-like Santa Claus to the little blonde peasant girl he holds on his lap. The marine is the "mother" and the child is one of the "babies" he has come to save. From the following description of "Those Girl Marines" (included in the same issue, Christmas number 1918, 1[2]:61, together with photograph) women members of the corps were incapable of "saving"; only males were up to being protective mothers. "Since that fateful day last August when for the first time a lily white hand was raised as the Devil Dog Recruiting Station while a feminine voice sang out in dulcent tones 'I do,' question after question has been knocking at our door while the inquisitive eye of the public has been peeping through the keyhole. . . . So at last we have come across. Here are three of the fair Marines, as fair a trio as ever wore the winterfield, or snapped their heels as they hand their officers a 'slam.' "

34. Angus Fletcher, *Allegory*, p. 28. The following references to the relation between the sublime and the picturesque are from pp. 267, 275.

35. See T. J. Clark's characterization of Greenberg's position, "Clement Greenberg's Theory of Art." Clark is mainly referring to Greenberg's *Partisan Review* essays of 1939–1940, "Avant-Garde and Kitsch" and "Towards a Newer Laocoön."

36. T. J. Clark asks whether modernism does not simply reinstate aristocratic values abandoned by the bourgeoisie. Certainly posters do.

37. Edward Said, *Beginnings*, p. 20.

38. Words are usually necessary to poster art, as Michele J. Shover points out concerning those instances when "an image alone may not be dependable enough to convey the critical messages." Shover, "Roles and Images of Women in World War I Propaganda," p. 471. Rebecca Zurier examines the debate between the merits of unsupported images and images given explanatory captions that was carried on by the editors and artists of *The Masses*. See *Art for the Masses (1911–1917)*, pp. 103–108.

14. Poses on Display

1. See Alastair Duncan, *Tiffany Windows*, for the details of the success of Tiffany's "Ecclesiastical Department." Business was excellent throughout the 1890s; it reached its peak between 1900 and 1910.

2. The Devil's agent who loiters in the wake of young belles was a visual commonplace

in *Life* during the late 1880s and throughout the 1890s. Wenzell and Gibson were among the many illustrators who supplied drawings that twit secular revels before and after the Lenten season, and in so doing mock the season itself.

3. On the same day in 1896 as the *New York Journal* ran its celebratory drawings, up in Boston the cover of the *Illustrated Police News*, designed by Archie Gunn, featured Easter lilies from whose stems dangled smiling chorus girls.

4. L. Frank Baum, *The Art of Decorating Dry Goods Windows and Interiors*, p. 181. The following quotation is from p. 179. Another window-design manual of the period also featured the expected mix of the sacred and the secular. Easter is defined by George J. Cowan as the purchase of a new hat, but his *Window Backgrounds* takes care to display "the other side." Cowan describes the making of the "Ecclesiastical Window" which displays shoes, hats, and lingerie against a backdrop of stained glass, lilies, pipe organ, and the figure of a nun with a rosary.

5. Immediately after the end of the Civil War there had been a period of national prosperity. It was followed by a series of depressions beginning in the early 1870s. The bad times were 1873–78, 1882–85, 1893–97; the periods of revived prosperity were 1878–1882 and—to a lesser extent—1886–1892. By 1900 many considered the United States to be in sound economic health. In the study prepared by Willford I. King in 1915 the facts confirmed, however, that the rich were getting very rich and the poor even poorer. The poor made up 65% of the population (as calculated by King's methods and tables); the lower middle class was 15%; the upper middle class was 18%; the rich formed 2% of the total. For these figures and others, see Edward C. Kirkland, *Industry Comes of Age: Business, Labor, and Public Policy, 1860–1897*, pp. 2–10; Willford Isbell King, *The Wealth and Income of the People of the United States*; Rebecca Zurier, *Art for the Masses*, "Radicals, Revolutionaries, Rebels, and Reformers: What the Issues Were," pp. 67–68.

6. Neil Harris, "The Gilded Age Revisited: Boston and the Museum Movement," links the department store with the art museum as theatrical palaces of display and desire. For the impact upon the consumers' imagination of the Montgomery Ward Dream Book and the Sears-Roebuck Farmer's Friend, see Boris Emmet and John E. Jeuck, *Catalogues and Counters: A History of Sears, Roebuck and Co.*; Thomas J. Schlereth, *Artifacts and the American Past*, "Mail-Order Catalogs as Resources in Material Culture Studies." On September 9, 1909, *Life* ran a drawing by Orson Lowell titled "The Call of the World." It shows a young nun tempted by the clothes on display in Bernard Silver's store window. For those who associated the decay of American (i.e., Christian) morals with the influx of "alien tribes," it must have been impossible not to connect this weakening with the presence of Jewish merchants. L. Frank Baum and George J. Cowan could not be accused of being Jews for all their advocacy of almost pagan Easter windows, but those of an anti-Semitic cast of mind felt they had not far to go to trace the source of the corruption.

7. Charles Schenk, *Draperies in Action*. Schenk also offered a winged Victory, an angel with a book, a dancer in the style of Isadora Duncan, a maiden gazing into a hand mirror, and a haloed Virgin.

8. Herbert Cecil Duce, *Poster Advertising*, p. 96. The following quotations are from pp. 96–97, 99, 121–124.

9. See Campbell, *Campbell's Illustrated History*, 2:447. It can be argued that this very "California" icon was much more appropriate as a nationalistic display piece than "The Dreaming Iolanthe" carved of butter which had engaged the attention of visitors to the Philadelphia Centennial.

10. Daniel J. Boorstin in *The Image* follows through on observations made of the public's susceptibility to image-making by Edward L. Bernays, *Crystallizing Public Opinion*, and Walter Lippmann, *Public Opinion*. More recent appraisals of particular note are T. J. Jackson Lears, "From Salvation to Self-Realization: Advertising and the Therapeutic Roots of the

Consumer Culture, 1880–1930"; Judith Williamson, *Decoding Advertisements: Ideology and Meaning in Advertising*. For a rich sampling of advertisements, see Edgar R. Jones, *Those Were the Good Old Days—a Happy Look at American Advertising, 1880–1930*.

11. Richard D. Altick, *The Shows of London*; Martin Meisel, *Realizations: Narrative, Pictorial, and Theatrical Arts in Nineteenth-Century England*; Anne, Margaret, and Patrice Higonnet, "Facades: Walter Benjamin's Paris." Altick in particular emphasizes the public's desire to merge educational values with entertainment (p. 509).

12. It has not been necessary to wait for Daniel Boorstin or the Higonnets to expose the visual fraudulence of theater or marketplace. The irate piece titled "Over-Illustration" that appeared in *Harper's Weekly* on July 29, 1911, is typical of the disgust felt by some at that time over the public's taste for images. The anonymous *Harper's* critic observes that growing minds rely on inspiration for spiritual and mental development but that they are currently being corrupted by the "pictorial squalor" rife in the popular press. People cannot see *ideas* for the *pictures* that have replaced them.

13. One example of the previous taste for the didactic that elevates the mind and reforms the soul is a pamphlet of 1874 whose title insists upon the sober purposes of tableaux entertainments: Francis H. Jefferson, *A Series of Tableaux, Suitable for Dramatic Representation; Also Adapted to the Illustration of Temperance and Other Moral Games*.

14. The gap between consumer and producer might close to some extent depending upon the amount of imaginative activity required of the audiences. John Dewey has made the distinction between "esthetic" (limited to "experience as appreciating, perceiving, and enjoying"—as "undergoing") and "artistic" (experience expanded to "the active or 'doing' phase of art"). The former "denotes the consumer's rather than the producer's standpoint," while the latter tends to the "production of something visible, audible, or tangible." *Art as Experience*, p. 47. "Esthetic" response to the "artistic" spectacles presented onstage could remain passive or enter upon its own "active or 'doing' phase." A test case (one which might be judged either way) is provided by the public festival. See the following for contemporary discussions of the merits of such participatory pageants: William C. Langdon, *The Celebration of the Fourth of July by Means of Pageantry*; Charles M. Robinson, *Modern Civic Art, or The City Made Beautiful*, pp. 355–373.

15. John Dewey, *Art as Experience*, p. 47.

16. Dewey observes that bliss is not a stencil that is transferable; we must experience bliss individually, as well as hear about it through general reports made by the saints. *Art as Experience*, p. 92. Yes, but an awareness of the "type" of the saints' experience prepares one in advance for the particularized moment of personal bliss.

17. J. C. Leyendecker wrote a letter describing the steps in the process he followed: first, facing the problem of identification posed by the object he was assigned to represent (and sell); next, finding a mental image which provided the solution to the problem; thereafter, the making of a series of design sketches, the use of a live studio model to check out details of the imaged face and figure, and the final rendition of the design on paper which transcribed the image Leyendecker had pursued from the start. Michael Schau, *J. C. Leyendecker*, p. 35. An article on Leyendecker in *The International Studio* of January 1912 from the National Museum of American Art, Leyendecker Ephemera File, remarks on the extreme readability of the results, "one which conveys the intended meaning to the *greatest number* of people."

18. A. H. Harrison, *The History of Silhouettes and How To Make Them*, p. 7.

19. Quoted by William Welling, *Photography in America: The Formative Years, 1839–1900*, p. 389.

20. The following items suggest some of the sources that serve as histories and/or propose theories for the analysis of cultural evidence concerning the marketing of needs and desires. Advertisements: Robert Atwan, Donald McQuade, and John W. Wright, *Edsels, Luckies, and*

Frigidaires: Changing Images of Everyday Life Through a Century of Advertising; Ralph M. Hower, *The History of an Advertising Agency: N. W. Ayer and Son at Work, 1869–1939;* Frank S. Presbry, *The History and Development of Advertising;* Mark Sullivan, *Our Time,* vol. 2, *America Finding Herself;* Samuel Jay Keyser, "There Is Method in Their Adness: The Formal Structure of Advertisements"; T. J. Jackson Lears, "Some Versions of Fantasy: Toward a Cultural History of American Advertising, 1880–1930"; Judith Williamson, *Decoding Advertisements.*

Department stores: John William Ferry, *A History of the Department Store;* William Nelson Taft, *Department-Store Advertising;* Robert W. Twyman, *History of Marshall Field and Co., 1852–1906.*

Posters: *An Exhibition of Original Designs for Posters by Louis J. Rhead;* Charles Knowles Bolton, *The Reign of the Poster;* Edgar Breitenbach and Margaret Cogswell, *The American Poster;* Henry Cuyler Bunner, "American Posters Past and Present"; Ernest Elmo Calkins, "The Art of the Poster"; *Catalogue of an Exhibition of Illustrated Bill-Posters at the Rooms of the Grolier Club;* Patricia Frantz Kery, *Great Magazine Covers of the World;* Victor Margolin, *American Poster Renaissance;* Victor Margolin, Ira Brichta, and Vivian Brichta, *The Promise and the Product: 200 Years of Advertising Posters;* Brander Mathews, "The Pictorial Poster"; Ervine Metzl, *The Poster: Its History and Its Art;* F. L. Neuschaefer, "Psychology of Posters"; C. Matlack Price, *Poster Design: A Critical Study of the Development of the Poster in Continental Europe, England, and America;* Helen F. Sloan, *American Art Nouveau: Poster Period of John Sloan;* Roberta Wong, *American Posters of the Nineties.*

Also see Mary Douglas and Baron Isherwood, *World of Goods: Towards an Anthropology of Consumption;* Stuart Ewen and Elizabeth Ewen, *Channels of Desire: Mass Images and the Shaping of American Consciousness;* A. D. Faber, *Cigar Label Art;* Ian M. G. Quimby, *Material Culture and the Study of American Life.*

21. Estelle Jussim's *Visual Communication* makes the point that by 1900 printing technology had split into two areas of "visual communication": "craft" which transmitted information; "art" which expressed feelings. As Jackson Lears' essay "Some Versions of Fantasy" bears out, marketing goals and methods of advertisements tried to mediate, unsuccessfully, between realism and surrealism and between information and emotion.

22. "The Great Good Place," Henry James' story of 1900, is far less like Edward Bellamy's department store haven than like an elegant spa for persons fatigued by the pace of modern society. In the department store, expenditure is encouraged; at the spa, overt commerce between consumers and producers seems hushed, even though we are aware that turn-of-the-century watering places, whether in Europe or at Saratoga Springs, were flourishing business enterprises. In *Memorial Art* Huger Elliott compares department stores unfavorably to cemeteries since the former lack all pretense of tranquillity (though he admits that too many modern burial sites also seek the same "publicity" the big stores do). In *The American Scene* James observes that only the Presbyterian Hospital with its rows of white beds offers the rare calm amid the boom of the modern city which the narrator of "The Great Good Place" seeks. Hospitals and cemeteries, it would seem, not the marketplace, offer that refuge for the dying and the dead. To want something is to work harder. See Margolin, Brichta, and Brichta, *The Promise and the Product,* p. 73. The end of striving comes only when one no longer desires; the place without images for desiring is "good."

23. James, *Henry James: Autobiography, A Small Boy and Others* (1913), p. 101.

24. Hetta Lord Hayes Ward, "Fine Arts—the Art of Shop Windows."

25. See Ernest Elmo Calkins, 'The Art of the Poster"; Robert Grier Cooke, "Shop Window Display—'The People's Picture Galleries.' " There were dissenters, of course, who denounced the hideous posters defacing the public byways. See George Kriehn, "The City Beautiful," whose strong objections provide a perfect example of "educated taste" set in opposition to "popular taste." James Montgomery Flagg, known for his sarcasm, may have been parody-

ing the case for billboards, but his remarks (from his book *Boulevards All the Way—Maybe*) express a response to the American scene that prefers it "made" rather than "natural": "Unless you have seen it you cannot imagine what a sordid, dull thing landscape is minus billboards. Just plain sky and trees, brooks, valleys and hills. Nature is all very well in her way. As a setting for Rustless Soup and Malted Corsets and Delicious Gasoline it is perfect—but leave out those beautiful billboards and it is rather shocking—rather nude and insipid." Any child in those days facing a long automobile trip without the comfort of Burma Shave signs or Mail Pouch Tobacco barn roofs would have agreed with Flagg, not with Kriehn.

26. Robert Grier Cooke, "Shop Window Display—'The People's Picture Galleries,'" p. 117.

27. Edna Ferber, *Fanny Herself*, pp. 18–19.

28. Sylvester Baxter, Foreword, *Massachusetts Charitable Mechanic Association, 1795–1895: Exhibition of Posters, October 2 to November 30, 1895*.

29. Brander Mathews, "The Pictorial Poster," p. 748.

30. Grant's remark of 1893 is quoted in George McMichael's *Journey to Obscurity: The Life of Octave Thanet*, p. 133. Octave Thanet, by the way, as portrayed in McMichael's book is an exemplary case of a successful woman writer caught between conflicting tastes (high and popular) and political responses (advanced and reactionary) to her times.

31. Julian Ralph, *People We Pass: Stories of Life Among the Masses of New York City*, p. 63.

32. When a new celebrity replaces an older one in the ability to capture the public's attention, jealousy results—of the kind joshed by a cartoon that appeared in the *New York World* on June 16, 1895. An irate Statue of Liberty knocks over a man who has had the affrontery to ask her what she thinks of Trilby.

33. Eugene Benson, "The Pagan Element in Art." Also see Robert Scholnick, "Between Realism and Romanticism: The Curious Career of Eugene Benson." See the following for various contemporary responses to the indomitable will to be morally frivolous: Margaret Armour, "Aubrey Beardsley and the Decadents"; Dee Garrison, "Immoral Fiction in the Late Victorian Library"; *The Lark*, nos. 1–24, May 1895–April 1897.

34. Michael M. Mooney, *Evelyn Nesbit and Stanford White*, pp. 194–199. For surveys of the growth of burlesque, see Edward B. Marks, *They All Had Glamor: From the Swedish Nightingale to the Naked Lady*; Robert Toll, *On with the Show*.

35. Paul Bourget, *Outre-Mer*, pp. 77–79.

36. Frank Norris' sexually anguished character Vandover delivers an angry diatribe against the good girls of his set whose feigned ignorance of the world's vices helps send men toward their doom in the diseased arms of prostitutes. *Vandover and the Brute*, pp. 84–87.

37. See Martha Kingsbury, "The Femme Fatale and Her Sisters," pp. 183–205; also see Kingsbury's remarks concerning John Singer Sargent's rendition of the goddess Neith in "Sargent's Murals in the Boston Public Library," p. 157.

38. The reviewer of Crane's novel was in error, of course, when he described Maggie Johnson as one who performs in Bowery music halls. Maggie attends several such places in the company of Pete but never performs there herself.

39. See Lois Banner's *American Beauty*, ch. 7, for a full discussion of the period taste for voluptuous female figures which was on the wane by the mid-1890s. The celebrity Russell lost on the New York stage was later regained in another sense by her inclusion in the Gertrude Stein/Virgil Thomson opera "The Mother of Us All" (honoring Susan B. Anthony) as the type of the Showgirl.

40. Charles Sanders Peirce provides the theory that lies behind the potency of Fuller's potentiality. In "How To Make Our Ideas Clear," first published in *Popular Science Monthly*, 1878, Peirce defined an object's reality in terms of what it has in it to do, taking as his example a diamond. Diamonds are "known" by the fact that they cut glass. A diamond stored away in cotton does not cut glass, but the potential for that act (the fulfillment of

its reality) exists even while it is under wraps. Loïe Fuller swathed in yards of veilings is on the verge of proving her identity. Fuller setting those veils in motion is Fuller "cutting glass."

15. The Purchase of Grace

1. See Martin Meisel, *Realizations*; Peter Brooks, *The Melodramatic Imagination: Balzac, Henry James, Melodrama, and the Mode of Excess*; Kirsten Gram Holmstrom, *Monodrama, Attitudes, Tableaux Vivants: Studies on Some Trends of Theatrical Fashion, 1770–1815*.

2. See Edward Wagenknecht, *American Profile*, pp. 240–276; Neil Harris, *The Land of Contrasts*, pp. 159–190; Elena Millie and Andrea Wyatt, "Tomorrow Night, East Lynne!" pp. 114–151; Oral S. Coad and Edwin Mims, Jr., *The American Stage*.

3. Peter Brooks, *The Melodramatic Imagination*, p. 53.

4. Meisel, *Realizations*, p. 13.

5. Edith Wharton's novel of 1920 *The Age of Innocence* did not bother with illustrations. Wharton verbally created scene after scene grounded in the tradition of the "dramatical" gesture. Ellen Olenska is supposedly "the natural woman" set in contrast to a social milieu whose every artificial move is dictated by convention: the relation between Ellen and Newland Archer is supposedly realistic in its presentation, set in contrast to literary formulas based on the notion that True Love conquers all. Indeed, Ellen may be relatively free of obedience to such social conventions and narrative formulas, but not from those drawn from the world of the theater. For instance, the whole of chapter 9, in which Archer come to Ellen's little house. Everything in it, including its mistress, comes straight out of a stage director's handbook of pose, setting, costume, and lighting effects. Wharton's novel struggles to decide whether it is melodrama veering toward tragedy and/or a comedy of manners or whether it is an antidrama of everyday life. Wharton's concentrated use of dramatic conventions, carefully staged scenes, and the highly conscious posing of her heroine act to qualify the realism associated with the later mode.

6. Du Maurier's drawing follows the form of Harriet Hosmer's "Beatrice Cenci" (figure 1.36). It also recalls the poses of the Italian Magdalenes discussed and illustrated in terms of the painterly plagiarism of recognizable forms by M. H. Spielmann, "Curiosities and Resemblances in Works of Art."

7. Parkinson used the same model in series of equally obnoxious photographs. In one, the child apes the bathing beauty, hoisting high her skirt in front of a painted backdrop of sand and ocean; in another, she poses as a little mother merrily standing before washtub and scrubbing board.

8. Charles Darwin, *The Expression of the Emotions in Man and Animals*, pp. 12, 17.

9. Louis admits that there are few true gentlemen but that there is no crime "in counterfeiting [their] excellences." *Decorum*, p. 15.

10. C. Francis Jenkins, "How To Secure Expression in Photography." The page facing the start of Jenkins' article is the conclusion of a piece about lepers; it shows a photograph of a Filipino without a nose. The placement of this image across from photographs of attractive models running through a scale of facial expressions introduces an unexpected note of poignancy. Jenkins' theories are not meant to include the grotesque and the abnormal—only the ordinary, readily readable signs of which people with noses are capable.

11. Anne O'Hagan, "The Art of Facial Expression."

12. The full titles of Soper's and Hoyle's books demonstrate the range of their "complete" appeal: *The New Peerless Speaker and Complete Program Containing the Best Orations, Humorous, Dramatic, and Patriotic Readings and Recitations* and *The Complete Speaker and Reciter for Home, School, Church, and Platform*, respectively.

13. See Gilbert Austin, *Chironomia, or A Treatise on Rhetorical Delivery*; Holmstrom, *Monodrama, Attitudes, Tableaux Vivants*.

14. Elsie M. Wilbor, ed., *The Delsarte Recitation Book and Directory*, pp. 33, 69, 93, 99.

15. Nicola Bradbury, *Henry James: The Later Novels*, pp. 13–35.

16. Jonathan Culler, *The Pursuit of Signs*, p. 116.

17. Myra Jehlen, "Archimedes and the Paradox of Feminist Criticism," pp. 189–215; George Steiner, "The Distribution of Discourse."

18. See Brian Coe and Paul Gates, *The Snapshot Photograph*; Reese V. Jenkins, *Images and Enterprise: Technology and the American Photographic Industry, 1839 to 1925*. The usual notion is that snapshots guarantee spontaneity and informality when compared with the studied poses common to studio photography. This notion is refuted by Coe and Gates who report the many instances when humorous tableau scenes were carefully set up for the Kodak, as well as by the many photographs shown in chapter 5 of my mother and her friends. It has been commented that in a pictorial age and a photo culture everyone is ready to have his or her picture taken, in and out of the studio. See the following histories of photography which detail the care taken by studio photographers (such as Kurtz, Sarony, and Mora) to supply props and backgrounds, and the use of retouching and other tricks of lighting, all of which enhance the expressive effect of the photograph: Jennifer Harper, *City Work at Country Prices: The Portrait Photographs of Duncan Donovan*; Beaumont Newhall, *The History of Photography from 1839 to the Present Day*; Robert Taft, *Photography and the American Scene*. Also see Edward W. Earle, ed., *Points of View: The Stereograph in America*; Gisèle Freund, *Photography and Society*. Earle discusses the influence of the stereopticon views and Freund reports on the interclass use of the *cartes de visite*.

19. Charles Dana Gibson did a series of drawings for *Life* in 1892 under the general title "The Salons of New York." Almost every segment of society is lightly satirized for the pretentiousness of the poses it practices. Persons without a firm hold on their cultural identities strive to imitate those they perceive as "the best." Jews, bluestockings, blacks, and WASPS all come in for their share of deflation as they put on awkward shows of gentility (in ways quite unlike the maid in figure 15.10 who is doing her own mocking). Of all the groups Gibson pictures there, only the blacks gathered "At Mrs. Pinkney Johnson's" are *not* shown as physically ugly.

20. Karen Halttunen's *Confidence Men and Painted Women* reviews the turn to the counterfeit practiced by some members of the middle class by the mid-nineteenth century—a practice which paradoxically arose in defense against the social and moral threats posed by the infiltration into "real society" of persons of fraudulent identity. The burst of interest in masquerades and costume balls has been discussed in chapter 5. Further instances are given in Ward McAllister, *Society as I Have Found It*; in the description of the Orion ball held at Madison Square Garden featured in the *New York Journal* of February 16, 1896; in the description, with photographs, of the 1916 costume ball sponsored by the Society of Illustrators attended by James Montgomery Flagg, Howard Chandler Christy, and Charles Dana Gibson detailed in Susan Meyer, *America's Great Illustrators*, p. 32; in the suggested costumes proposed by Miss Oakey (Maria Richards Oakey Dewing), *Beauty in Dress*, ch. 17.

21. George B. Bartlett, *An Evening of Statuary and Tableaux; Character and Unique Fashions*; Ellen M. Willard, *Pictured Readings and Tableaux*; Frances Fairfield, *Tableaux for Home and School*; Marie Irish, O. E. Young, and others, *Pleasing Pantomimes and Tableaux*. Also see J. W. Bray, *Dramaticized Themes with Tableaux*; Joseph A. Hill, *Hill's Book of Tableaux or Living Symbolic Illustrations of the Principles, Moral and Benevolent Teachings, and Practices of the Prominent Secret Societies*; Francis H. Jefferson, *A Series of Tableaux, Suitable for Dramatic Representation*; Marie Irish, *Patriotic Celebrations*; Pollard's Artistic Tableaux*; J. V. Prichard, *Tableaux Vivants for Amateur Representations*; Nora A. Smith, *Plays, Pantomimes, and Tableaux for Children*; Sarah L. Stocking, *Shadow Pictures*; Martha Coles Weld, *Illustrated Tableaux for Amateurs*.

22. See Emily M. Bishop, *Self-Expression and Health*.

23. Genevieve Stebbins, *Delsarte System of Expression*, pp. 114, 384, 385, 392. Stebbins

includes the full text of Delsarte's address taken from an unpublished manuscript delivered at an unspecified date. Stebbins also enfolds Comte, Mill, Herbert Spencer, and Ruskin within the Delsartean tradition. The circle of influence widens even further with the addition of the teachings of Lavater. See Anna Morgan, *An Hour with Delsarte: A Study of Expression*. Delsarte's disciples included Robert Browning, Sarah Bernhardt, Walter Crane, Lord Leighton, and Steele MacKaye. See Frederick Sanburn, *A Delsartean Scrap-Book*.

24. This and the following notations are from Stebbins, *Delsarte System of Expression*, pp. 29, 63, 451, 65, 398.

25. In addition to Bishop, Morgan, Sanburn, and Stebbins cited in notes 21–23, see E. M. Booth, *Outlines of the Delsarte System of Expression*; Edward B. Warman, *Gestures and Attitudes*. The Delsarte phenomena received frequent mention in other ways: in etiquette books—Florence Howe Hall's *Social Customs*; in books of elocution—Frances Hoyle's *The Complete Speaker and Reciter*; in books on acting method—Webster Edgerly's *Lessons in the Art of Acting*. It was also found worthy of a full-scale parody: George M. Baker, *The Seldarte Craze*.

26. The influence of Delsartean principles lingered well into the twentieth century. Maureen Howard tells of a teacher of elocution she knew as a child who taught her pupils how "to harness . . . awkward moments into ideal gestures" because she believed that through adherence to the correct "attitudes" one could "know," thereby control, all aspects of existence. See *Facts of Life*, pp. 23–24.

27. Gibson's drawing appeared in the May 25, 1893, issue of *Life* without a caption. It accompanied a story titled "The American Comedy" in which the young woman is pledged to marry an English peer after her mother undermines the suit of young Trail, an American railroad man. The caption "That Evening Her Engagement Was Announced" was added by Scribner's to their 1906 edition of *The Gibson Book*, a two-volume collection of the best of Gibson's work to that date.

28. This photograph shows the actress Henrietta Crosman in the lead role of David Belasco's "Sweet Kitty Bellairs," a drama set in eighteenth-century Georgian England. The dramatic situation is different from the one Hoyle proposes. Kitty Bellairs is not waiting for her lover to appear; she watches at the window of an inn as the hero marches away with his regiment. This is yet another indication that a set pose cannot be finally fixed in its meaning but requires interpretation within specific contexts. It also bears out the importance of the view, supported by Belasco, that the director "must *think in pictures.*" From an article by Belasco, "How I Stage My Plays," for *Theatre Magazine* (December 1901), p. 32. The information concerning Belasco and "Sweet Kitty Bellairs" is from Lise-Lone Marker, *David Belasco: Naturalism in the American Theatre*.

29. Christy, *The American Girl*, p. 138.

30. A collection of tableaux published in 1899 includes an entertainment titled "The Modern Hesperides." Uncle Sam reviews the different kinds of government known throughout history; he decides the best is the republican form that exists in the United States, where it is in the hands of "the Anglo-Saxon." This type "is destined to rule the world because his genius for organization is based on general principles and not on mere personal influence"; he "leads the world in mechanical inventions, skilled labor, commercial power and capacity for government." J. W. Bray, *Dramatized Themes with Tableaux*, p. 46.

31. The opening stanza of this "Exercise for Four Little Girls" reads: "Though we are only little girls / We love to hear the story / Of how the soldiers dressed in blue / Marched forth to fame and glory." The recitation closes with: "Though we are only little girls / And have not much to say, / We love to honor the soldiers / Upon Memorial Day." From Marie Irish, *Patriotic Celebrations*, pp. 109–110.

32. All these types and historical figures, and many more, are included in Mrs. G. R. (Ellen L.) Sikes' *American Heroines: An Entertainment for Churches and Church Societies*,

Secular Societies, and Lodges. Sikes significantly shows her approval of the healthy, vigorous Golf Girl and the new Spinster who rides off on her bicycle and no longer lingers at home by her spinning wheel.

33. Ward McAllister, *Society as I Have Found It*, pp. 216–217. McAllister's title is misleading since he continually calls attention to the claim of having "created" society through his own powers of organization rather than having merely "found" it already formed.

34. M. E. W. Sherwood, *The Art of Entertaining*.

35. M. E. W. Sherwood, "Some Society Tableaux." Ward McAllister also reports on the social elegance of the same affair Mrs. Sherwood describes. *Society as I Have Found It*, pp. 324–326.

36. James L. Breese, "Oriental Tableaux: A Series of Beautiful Pictures from Oriental Literature, Posed by Society Débutantes of New York."

37. Descriptions of the elaborate masques put on by the D. C. French and Augustus Saint-Gaudens coteries are available in the archival materials housed at Chesterwood, the home of D. C. French; Sarah H. Begley, *Chesterwood Tableaux Vivants*; Kenyon Cox, "An Out-Door Masque in New England"; Bruce Wilkinson, *Uncommon Clay*; the National Museum of American Art, the Ephemera Files for both French and Saint-Gaudens. Bacchantes and Dianas proliferated in both settings since the artists' fetes were decidedly Grecian in motif. After Thayer's daughter Mary portrayed the Madonna in a tableau in 1890, Thayer painted her in the same pose. White, *Abbot H. Thayer, Painter and Naturalist*, p. 55. John White Alexander was another artist absorbed by the expressive possibilities of the tableau form. Aided by his wife, Alexander designed costuming, lighting, and color scenes for various theatrical events: he staged *Jeanne d'Arc* at the Harvard Stadium, worked with Maude Adams, and arranged many charity tableaux. Edwin H. Blashfield commented of his friend's interest, "It was an easy progression for him from his canvases to the moving-pictures of a pageant or a play." See Blashfield, *Commemorative Tribute to John White Alexander*. Consider that Saint-Gaudens coached Isadora Duncan, and that one of Duncan's lovers was Edward Gordon Craig who introduced many new ideas in stage design, and that Steele MacKaye, a fervent disciple of the Delsarte method, announced he wished to create a revolution in the American theater world based on Delsartean principles (see Stebbins, *Delsarte System of Expression*, p. 77), and one realizes the diverse but converging currents that helped to influence the look of early-twentieth-century stage productions.

38. Important exceptions to the rule of the political conservatism of most society tableaux (especially these under the direction of Hazel MacKaye, activist daughter of Steele MacKaye) were examined by Karen Blair in a paper presented at the UCLA conference on "The Dark Madonna: Community Rituals of Multi-Ethnic Women," November 8, 1985, titled "American Women and the Uses of Pageantry: Women's Clubs, 1900–1930." As for the use of "attitudes" and "types" in making feminist statements in the motion picture media, then and now, see Janet Bergstrom, "Yvonne Rainier: An Introduction"; Kay Sloan, "Sexual Warfare in the Silent Cinema: Comedies and Melodramas of Woman Suffragism."

39. See Madge C. Jenison, "A Hull House Play."

40. The proceeds from the Saturday Morning Club's production went to Boston's West End Nursery and the Society for the Prevention of Cruelty to Children. The following data concerning the *Antigone* is from the Schlesinger Library, Radcliffe College, including "Memories" by Mary Gray Morrison, dated October 1890, in the Saturday Morning Club papers.

41. The history of the founding of the group is given in *The Story of the Saturday Morning Club of Boston*.

42. Margaret Anglin appeared as Antigone in a performance given in 1910 at Berkeley, California—the first, she states (erroneously), ever performed in English. There is a photograph of Anglin in costume and appropriate "attitude" included in her essay for *Good*

Housekeeping of January 1912. (According to *The Story of the Saturday Morning Club*, p. 7, Sargent painted one of the members of the 1890 cast.)

43. Bearing out the theory T. S. Eliot expounded in "Tradition and the Individual Talent," the women attending the Saturday Morning Club's production were supposedly persuaded that they witnessed the enfolding of "the simplicity of the earlier life" within "the fulness of the later ages." The very Greekness of the play served "to bring out the Christian virtues," while the classic calm pointed up modern "nervousness." In "Difficult Daughter," a review of George Steiner's *Antigones* which Oliver Taplin wrote for *The New York Review of Books* (December 6, 1984), pp. 13–16. Taplin voices surprise that *Antigone* could ever be discussed today "without serious reference to the 'women's movement.' " He then proceeds to detail the strong connections that abide between the classical play and the current concerns of feminist scholarship.

44. Even the audience for *Antigone* offered studies in "the differing types of the Boston feminine head" once their hats and bonnets were removed (as Lorado Taft would agree!).

45. Although the 1932 history of the club has little to say about the *Antigone* production, note is made of the "tremendous welding power" prompted by participation in the program. "It unified the Club, strengthened club feeling and gave it an impulse along lines not foreseen." *The Story of the Saturday Morning Club*, p. 27.

46. Goethe, *Goethe's Travels in Italy*, p. 199.

47. For details of the earlier origins of "attitudes" and later developments of the tradition after Emma Hart's time, see Kirsten Gram Holmstrom, *Monodrama, Attitudes, Tableaux Vivants*, and Martin Meisel, *Realizations*. One of the areas whose fertility demands future study is the potent relationship between high and low culture and between the expressive means used mutually by the genius and by the hack. Since such studies frequently reveal that the flow often goes from popular to serious art (see Lois Banner on fashions, Rosen and Zerner on paintings, and Meisel on theater arts), our understanding of the nature of "culture" will be benefited when even more attention is given to formulaic poses and the "trickle up" principle by which these poses permeate every level and jurisdiction of society.

48. Holmstrom, *Monodrama*, p. 111.

49. Kenneth Clark, *The Nude: A Study in Ideal Form*. Chapter 4 concerns "Venus II" or the Venus Naturalis.

50. Andromeda as the type of Pure Womanhood Victimized figures significantly in Edith Wharton's *The Custom of the Country* (1913). In the play by Henry Arthur Jones "The Masqueraders" (1894), Andromeda emblemizes ideal truth. One of the reviewers wrote that in "a world of shapes and shadows and masqueraders" only "in Andromeda everything is real." See C. F. Nirdlinger, "Plays and Players."

51. Joan Lidoff, "Another Sleeping Beauty: Narcissism in *The House of Mirth*"; Cynthia Griffin Wolff, *A Feast of Words: The Triumph of Edith Wharton*, pp. 112–133. Wolff's reading of Wharton's novel makes fine use of references to the contemporary art scene, comprised of murals, neoclassical buildings, Art Nouveau style, and the tableau vivant, to suggest the forms that shaped the public image of Lily Bart. The semiotic structures of such dream lives, expressive of cultural formulas of behavior, were analyzed in an excellent seminar paper by one of my UCLA graduate students, Robert Fletcher, "Stylizations *and* Inventions: A Semiotic Analysis of Wharton's *The House of Mirth* and *The Custom of the Country*."

52. Both Maggie Johnson and Lily Bart fit the notion of the modern heroine adhered to by the commercial artists of the period: "make her pretty—which is virtually saying 'Make her without any particular character.' " Noted by Laurence Burnham in "The Modern Heroine in Illustration," p. 199. Of course, this allowed each artist to impose his own view of what "being pretty" is like. Lily Bart as Wharton describes her is slender and dark-haired.

There is a photograph of Wenzell in his studio preparing the illustrations for *The House of Mirth* using a slender, dark-haired model, yet the Lily Wenzell presents is buxom and blonde.

53. See Michael Mooney's biography of Nesbit for a résumé of her career which began when she modeled for a number of painters in Philadelphia and New York. *Evelyn Nesbit and Stanford White*, pp. 27–30. The following phrases concerning Nesbit's progress from model to showgirl to mistress to wife to national celebrity are taken from pp. 220, 308.

54. Chapter 12 mentioned the various types of the Venus which American imaginations tried to ignore, and spoke of Henry Adams' fear that the greatest of these—the Venus Genetrix—would never find her place in this country. Adams' Venus Genetrix (comparable to Kenneth Clark's Venus Naturalis) is the archetypal life force that flows from the generative core of the universe. Michael Mooney makes much of the fact that Evelyn Nesbit was likened at the time of Stanford White's murder to Venus. *Evelyn Nesbit and Stanford White*, p. 233. In this instance the association points to the legendary female force that kills, not to the energy that creates. According to Mooney, White's body lay in state in his Gramercy Park home near the statue of Venus Genetrix, found in the Tiber, which White had purchased for his collection. The *New York World* picked up on this arresting fact and commented that White had placed a Diana on top of Madison Square Garden, but that now he lay in the shadow of the Venus of death. As chapter 12 has suggested, perhaps the electric light bulb was the best (and the safest) form that Venus could take in America.

55. My thanks to Guy Szuberla for bringing to my attention the discrepancies between the title of the 1893 play by C. H. Abbott in which Stanley (1853–1931) starred and the title given the Whistler pastel.

56. Miriam Rooth's infinite variety is detailed in *The Tragic Muse*, 7:131, 142–143, 160–161, 189. See 7:210–213; 8:117–118, for specific references to the nature of her "identity" and to her personal and professional "character."

57. This description of Carrie Meeber (also applicable to Miriam Rooth) appears on p. 4 of Dreiser's *Sister Carrie*. *The Delineator*, of which Dreiser was editor between 1906 and 1910, ran an article by Ruth Batchelder, "The Country Girl Who Is Coming to the City." If Carrie had followed Batchelder's advice, she would never have left home. On the other hand, there is the heroine of James Montgomery Flagg's story in words and pictures, *Adventures of Kitty Cobb*. The early events of Kitty's life in the big city are very like Carrie's in their general pattern, but Kitty remains "good," marries the right young man, survives a minor lovers' quarrel, and gains lifelong happiness and the material niceties. If young women followed Flagg's version of "The Country Girl," they would hasten to the city as quickly as possible.

58. During the 1890s *Life* ran contests which spurred its readers to select their favorite Gibson Girl. The Sunday supplements of the period were filled with catchy competitions such as the one headlined in the *New York Journal* of June 14, 1896. See Lois Banner, *American Beauty*, ch. 12, for the evolution of institutionalized beauty contests during the 1920s. The first contest, held in 1921, was judged by one man alone—Howard Chandler Christy.

59. Alan Dale, "Stage Beauty and Brains," pp. 517–522. Compare what Vanderbank says about London's demand for female beauty in Henry James' *The Awkward Age* (1899). London wants "staring, glaring obvious knock-down beauty, as plain as a poster on a wall, an advertisement of soap or whiskey, something that speaks to the crowd and crosses the footlights, fetches such a price in the market that the absence of it . . . inspires endless terrors. . . . London doesn't love the latent or the lurking, has neither time, nor taste, nor sense for anything less discernible than the red flag in front of the steam-roller. It wants cash over the counter and letters ten feet high" (9:25.). Dale would be the last to claim that "staring glaring obvious knock-down beauty" didn't command its price on the American stage; he wants to suggest, however, that "something else" besides physical looks sells in the market-

place. Jackson Lears' essay "Some Versions of Fantasy" is especially telling on the connections advertising makes between intensity, entertainment, fantasy, and desire.

60. Chapter 19 of Dreiser's *Sister Carrie*, which describes Carrie's triumph at the Elks Club theatricals, introduces the notion of the special force she will increasingly exert upon susceptible male audiences, one which results from her "appealing grace"—"a power which to them was a revelation."

61. Peter Brooks, *The Melodramatic Imagination*, p. 8. William Ordway Partridge expressed his distaste for melodrama in *Art for America*, pp. 130–131. More on the mark are Brooks and Jacques Barzun who bear witness to the "reality" founded on the melodramatic imagination's talent for adding intensity to everyday events. Once when asked whether he'd like to meet Santayana, Henry James replied, "raising his hands to Heaven, 'Come! I would walk across London with bare feet on the snow to meet George Santayana. At what time! One thirty! I will come. At one thirty I shall inevitably, inexorably make my appearance!' " See Barzun, "James the Melodramatist," p. 518. Ida M. Tarbell was not pleased to observe that women had to exaggerate themselves in order to be paid attention to. See *The Business of Being a Woman*, p. 22. However, the kind of intensity which James practiced in the anecdote about Santayana was the kind the Tarbell woman could use to good effect. Intensity need not express itself in so exclamatory a manner, nor through physical exaggeration, as James well knew when writing his own tales. Grace can come quietly, wordlessly, on the wings of the dove, but that grace still partakes of an intensity that exaggerates the outlines of one's bottom-nature and converts it into creative energy.

62. Brooks, *The Melodramatic Imagination*, p. 8.

63. Ames, the Delsartean Svengali in Carrie's life, urges her to concentrate upon her talent for expressive longing. He admonishes her to leave behind frivolous musical comedy roles and to take on serious dramatic parts. It is as though Ames were encouraging Carrie to cease being like Bessie Clayton, Edna May, and Marie Doro (see figures 14.25, 14.29, 14.30) in order to pattern her career after Maude Adams, Margaret Anglin, and perhaps even Olga Nethersole (see figures 5.68, 14.24, 14.26).

Epilogue: Looking Back

1. This and the following quotations are from Charles H. Caffin, "The New Mural Decorations of John W. Alexander," pp. 845–856.

2. Theodore Drieser, in a letter of 1894 to Sara White, wrote of the discrepancy between the fine dreams inspired by the pastoral landscape and the depression caused by the starkness of the industrialized areas of the nation: "The very soil smacked of American idealism and faith, a fixedness in sentimental and purely imaginative American tradition, in which, I, alas! could not share. . . . I could not believe that it was more than a frail flower of romance. I had seen Pittsburgh." John J. McAleer, *Theodore Dreiser*, pp. 29–30.

3. In 1912 *Life* ran a sketch by G. W. Harting with the caption "Speaking of Pittsburgh." It depicts the cosmic atmosphere polluted by smoke that steams up from the earth, pouring from a source designated as Pittsburgh.

4. Rebecca Zurier tells of the time in 1913 when Bill Haywood, Max Eastman, and others met at Mabel Dodge's apartment. The conversation turned to the nature of proletarian art. Haywood referred to the Pittsburgh steelworker by saying, "Not only is art impossible to such a man, but life is impossible. He does not live." Eastman later included Haywood's remarks in his 1927 novel *Venture*. See Zurier, *Art for the Masses*, p. 134. The idealists could not be dissuaded, however. Edwin Austin Abbey designed murals for the Pennsylvania State Capitol at Harrisburg that continued to romanticize labor and to celebrate the worker. "Men at an Anvil" was done for the rotunda, as well as "The Spirit of Vulcan: Genius of the Workers in Iron and Steel."

5. Eugene Benson, "The 'Woman Question,' " pp. 751–756. Benson here incorporates a quotation from an unnamed source.

6. Harry Thurston Peck, "For Maids and Mothers," p. 162. In the headnote to Peck's essay, the editor mentions that the next issue will contain a response by Charlotte Perkins Gilman.

7. Charles W. Eliot, "The Normal American Woman," p. 15.

8. Eugene Benson, "The 'Woman Question,' " p. 756.

9. "The Modern Maiden's Prayer," with words by Ballard MacDonald and music by James F. Hanley.

10. "Cigarettes, Cigars!" with words by Mack Gordon and music by Harry Revel.

11. George Parsons Lathrop, "My Favorite Model," from *Discussions on American Art and Artists*, p. 170; the next quotation is from p. 169.

12. In "Photographic Appendix—Contrasts of Life and Art," from *Discussions on American Art and Artists*, p. 345, Will H. Low notes that in realistic paintings "the similarity between the model and the picture may be very great." In contrast, the artist who is "possessed of a certain idea and [who] works as it were from within outwards" may be as indebted to the model as is the realist, "but the result is less obviously portrait-like." The following quotations are from pp. 255–256.

13. In the same collection for *Discussions on American Art and Artists*, Hillary Bell contributes "The Studio and the Stage" (pp. 262–264). Bell's essay contributes a complicating factor to the general question of the differences between paintings (idealism) and photographs (realism): the introduction of the practiced mind and body of a professional actress who poses as model for the camera. In general, Bell believes, photographs represent the whole and particular woman; paintings are a composite of several women used to represent a type. But once the trained actress enters the game, that particularity and that wholeness of being (i.e., realism) is accentuated, and "the distinction between life and art [is] very strongly marked." Taking Bell's lead, we could conclude that in a contest of wills against Miriam Rooth as the photographer's model, the idealist painter hasn't a chance. It can still be argued that Miriam seen onstage, or in a painting by Nick Dormer, allows the type to reign, albeit the type of a whole and particular woman: the Tragic Muse.

14. Note that Lathrop, Low, and Bell refer generically to "artists" and "models," but in actuality their examples are all of female models, while most of the artists referred to are males.

15. Elémire Zolla, "Archetypes," p. 191. The following quotations are from the same page.

16. Nancy K. Miller, "Emphasis Added: Plots and Plausibilities in Women's Fiction."

17. My special thanks to Steven Fink for his shrewd suggestions regarding the interpretation of Gibson's "Widow" and also of figures 15, 18, and 19.

18. Howard Chandler Christy contributed two covers to *Motor* in 1923; together they suggest the range of possibilities available to that artist's imagination and that magazine's car/woman aesthetic. The May cover shows a classically gowned nymph with a lyre deep in a forest glade; in the foreground, a young man and woman sit in a sporty roadster. The October cover depicts a young woman in knickers changing a tire. The sexless, timeless nymph and the androgynous "advanced" woman bracket the boy/girl pair who are placed within that particular contemporary "environment"—the motorcar—considered most conducive to modern romance.

Bibliography

Abbott, Kathleen. *Masks and Ikons*. London: Enitharmon Press, 1973.

"Abbott Thayer Celebrated in Washington." *Art News* (September 1949), vol. 48, no. 6.

Abbott H. Thayer. Carnegie Institute. *Exhibition of Paintings by Abbott H. Thayer Held at Carnegie Institute, 1919*. Pittsburgh: 1919.

About Memorials: A Classification of the Usual Forms of Monumental Tributes with Illustrative Examples and Practical Suggestions as to Size, Material, and Cost. New York: 1892.

"Accessions and Notes: The Diana of Saint-Gaudens." [Preston Remington]. *Bulletin of the Metropolitan Museum of Art* (August 1928), 23, no. 8, 205.

Ackerman, James S. "On Judging Art Without Absolutes." *Critical Inquiry* (Spring 1979), 5(3):441–470.

"Actresses in Men's Roles" [*New York Sun*]. *Current Literature* (May 1901), 30:5, 620.

Adams, Henry. "American Ideals." *History of the United States of America During the Administrations of Thomas Jefferson and James Madison*. Vol. 1. New York: 1889.

Adams, Henry. "Captain John Smith," and "Primitive Rights of Women." *Historical Essays*. New York: 1891.

Adams, Henry. *The Education of Henry Adams*. Boston: Houghton Mifflin, 1918.

Adams, Henry. *Henry Adams and His Friends: A Collection of His Unpublished Letters*. Harold Cater, ed. Boston: Houghton Mifflin, 1947.

Adams, Henry. *Mont-Saint-Michel and Chartres*. Boston: Houghton Mifflin, 1913; 1st ed., 1904.

Adams, Marian Hooper. *The Letters of Mrs. Henry Adams, 1865–1883*. Ward Thoron, ed. Boston: Little, Brown, 1936.

Addams, Jane. "Filial Relations." *Democracy and Social Ethics*. New York: Macmillan, 1902.

Alcott, Louisa May. "Advice to Young Ladies: Being a Series of Twelve Articles, by Twelve Distinguished Women. No. III—Happy Women." *New York Ledger*, April 11, 1868, p. 1.

Alkon, Paul K. "Visual Rhetoric in *The Autobiography of Alice B. Toklas*." *Critical Inquiry* (June 1975), 1(4):849–881.

Allen, Elizabeth. *A Woman's Place in the Novels of Henry James.* London: Macmillan, 1984.

Alpers, Svetlana and Paul Alpers. "*Ut Pictura Noesis?* Criticism in Literary Studies and Art History." *New Literary History* (Spring 1972), 3(3):437–458.

Alter Ego, Masks: Their Art and Use. The Cooper Union Museum for the Arts of Decoration. New York: Cooper Union, 1951.

Altick, Richard D. *The Shows of London.* Cambridge, Mass.: Belknap Press of Harvard University Press, 1978.

"America," by Arthur Voegtlin. Review, *New York Dramatic Mirror* (September 3, 1913), 70(1811):7.

"America," by Arthur Voegtlin. Review, *The Theatre* (October 1913), 18(152):xiv.

American Architect and Building News, The. Unsigned, untitled (April 6, 1878), 3(119):117–118. (government-sponsored architecture).

American Architect and Building News, The. Unsigned, untitled (November 30, 1878), 4(153):177 (murals).

American Artists and Their Work. Vol. 2. New York: University Press, [1889].

American Code of Manners, The: A Study of the Usages, Laws, and Observances Which Govern Intercourse in the Best Social Circles, and of the Principles Which Underlie Them. Reprinted from "*Andrews' American Queen.*" New York: 1880.

"American Ideal Woman, The." *Putnam's Monthly* (November 1853), 2(11):527–531.

American Perspective, An: Nineteenth-Century Art from the Collection of Jo Ann and Julian Ganz, Jr. Washington, D.C.: National Gallery of Art, 1981.

Anderberg, Mary. "Silent Movies of the Page: The Serial Drawings of Charles Dana Gibson." *Thalia: Studies in Literary Humor* (Winter 1979–80), 2(3):34–53.

Andersen, Hendrik Christian. *Creation of a World Centre of Communication.* Ernest M. Hébrand, Architect. Paris: 1903.

Anderson, Ross. *Abbott Handerson Thayer.* Syracuse, N.Y.: Everson Museum, 1982.

Anglin, Margaret. "Domesticity and the Stage: How Play-Acting and Housekeeping Work Together for Good." *Good Housekeeping* (January 1912), 54:41–48.

Antigone of Sophocles, The, as Presented by the Saturday Morning Club, Bumstead Hall, Boston, in the Spring of 1890, "Memories" by Mary Gray Morrison. Schlesinger Library, Radcliffe College.

Apel, Karl-Otto. *Charles S. Peirce: From Pragmatism to Pragmaticism.* John Michael Krois, tr. Amherst: University of Massachusetts Press, 1981.

Argan, Guilio Carlo. "Ideology and Iconology." *Critical Inquiry* (Winter 1975), 2(2):297–305.

Armour, Margaret. "Aubrey Beardsley and the Decadents." *The Magazine of Art* (London) (December 1896), 20(1):9–12.

Arnheim, Rudolf. "A Plea for Visual Thinking." *Critical Inquiry* (Spring 1980), 6(3):489–498.

Arnheim, Rudolf. "Visual Thinking." In Gyorgy Kepes, ed., *The Education of Vision.* New York: Braziller, 1965.

"Art and Artists: The American Renaissance." *The Californian, Western Monthly Magazine* (June 1880), 1(6):571–572.

"Art and Art-Life in New York." *Lippincott's Monthly Magazine* (June 1882), 29(174):597–605.

"As a Bachelor Sees Women: In Which He Frankly Explains Why He Has Never Married." *The Ladies' Home Journal* (January 1908), 25:12.

Atwan, Robert, Donald McQuade, and John W. Wright. *Edsels, Luckies, and Frigidaires: Changing Images of Everyday Life Through a Century of Advertising.* New York: Delta Special, 1979.

Auerbach, Nina. *Woman and the Demon: The Life of a Victorian Myth.* Cambridge, Mass.: Harvard University Press, 1982.

Austin, Gilbert. *Chironomia, or a Treatise on Rhetorical Delivery.* Mary Margaret Robb and Lester Thonssen, eds. Carbondale and Edwardsville: Southern Illinois University Press, 1966.

Ayres, Linda. "The American Figure: Genre Paintings and Sculpture." In *An American Perspective.*

Badger, R. Reid. *The Great American Fair: The World's Columbian Exposition and American Culture.* Chicago: Hall, 1979.

Bailey, Thomas A. "The Mythmakers of American History." *The Journal of American History* (June 1968), 55(1):5–21.

Baker, George M. *The Seldarte Craze.* Boston: 1887.

Balge, Marjorie P. "The Dewey Arch: Sculpture or Architecture?" *Archives of American Art Journal* (1983), 23(4):2–6.

Balkin, Harry H. *Human Dictionary.* Boston: Balkin, 1923.

Bancroft, Hubert Howe. *The Book of the Fair: An Historical and Descriptive Presentation of the World's Science, Art, and Industry, as Viewed through the Columbian Exposition at Chicago in 1893, Designed to Set Forth the Display Made by the Congress of Nations, of Human Achievement in Material Form, so as the More Effectually to Illustrate the Progress of Mankind in All the Departments of Civilized Life.* 2 vols. Chicago: 1895.

Banner, Lois W. *American Beauty.* New York: Knopf, 1983.

Barthes, Roland. *Camera Lucida: Reflections on Photography.* New York: Hill and Wang, 1981.

Bartholdi Souvenir: A Sketch of the Colossal Statue Presented by France to the United States. New York: 1886.

Bartlett, Frederick Orin. "DeLancey—Himself." *The Marines' Bulletin* (Christmas number 1918), 1(2):40–47.

Bartlett, George B. *An Evening of Statuary and Tableaux: A Summer Evening's Entertainment.* Boston: 1888.

Barton, Bruce. *The Man Nobody Knows: A Discovery of the Real Jesus.* New York: Grosset & Dunlap, 1925.

Barzun, Jacques. "James the Melodramatist." *The Kenyon Review* (Autumn 1943), 5(4):508–521.

Batchelder, Ruth. "The Country Girl Who Is Coming to the City." *The Delineator* (November 1908), 72(5):836–837.

Baum, Lyman Frank. *The Art of Decorating Dry Goods Windows and Interiors.* Chicago: Show Window Publishing, 1900.

Baxter, Sylvester. "The Beautifying of Village and Town." *The Century* (April 1902), 63(6):844–851.

Baxter, Sylvester. Foreword, *Massachusetts Charitable Mechanic Association, 1795–1895: Exhibition of Posters, October 2 to November 30, 1895.*

Beard, George Miller. *American Nervousness, Its Causes and Consequences: A Supplement to Nervous Exhaustion (Neurasthenia).* New York: Arno Press, 1972; 1st ed., 1881.

Beaux, Cecilia. *Background with Figures.* Boston: Houghton Mifflin, 1930.

Beer, Thomas. *The Mauve Decade: American Life at the End of the Nineteenth Century.* New York: Knopf, 1926.

Begley, Sarah H. *Chesterwood Tableaux Vivants.* Stockbridge, Mass: 1982.

Bell, Mrs. Arthur [Nancy D'Anvers]. "An American Painter: Abbott H. Thayer." *The International Studio* (1899), 6:247–254.

Bell, Hillary. "The Studio and the Stage." In F. Hopkinson Smith et al., eds., *Discussions on American Art and Artists.*

Benda, Wladyslaw Theodore. *Masks.* New York: Watson-Guptill, 1944.

Benjamin, Asher. "Editorial—Women in the Arts." *Architecture* (October 1914), 30(4):211–214.

Benjamin, S. G. W. "Tendencies of Art in America—Part 1." *The American Art Review* (January 1880), 1(3):105–110.

Bennett, J. W. "Your True Relation to Society." *The Cosmopolitan* (August 1899), 27(4):369–374.

[Benson, Eugene.] "Dress of American Women." *The Round Table: A Saturday Review of Politics, Finance, Literature, Society, and Art* (January 2, 1864), 1(3):39–40.

Benson, Eugene. "The Pagan Element in Art." *The Galaxy* (June 1, 1866), 1:203–209.

Benson, Eugene. "The 'Woman Question.' " *The Galaxy* (December 15, 1866), 2:751–756.

Bergstrom, Janet. "Yvonne Rainier: An Introduction." *Camera Obscura* (1976), 1:55–73.

Bergström, Ingvar. *Dutch Still-Life Paintings in the Seventeenth Century*. Christina Hedström and Gerald Taylor, trs. New York: Yoseloff, 1956.

Berkelman, Robert G. "America in Bronze: Augustus Saint-Gaudens." *Sewanee Review* (October-December 1940), 48(4):494–509.

Berman, Avis. "Thomas Eakins: Master of Realist Art." *The Saturday Review of Literature* (June 1982), pp. 24–28.

Bernays, Edward L. *Biography of an Idea: Memoirs of Public Relations Counsel Edward L. Bernays*. New York: Simon & Schuster, 1965.

Bernays, Edward L. *Crystallizing Public Opinion*. New York: Boni & Liveright, 1923.

Bernheimer, Richard. *The Nature of Representation: A Phenomenological Inquiry*. H. W. Janson, ed. New York: New York University Press, 1961.

Berthoff, Warner. *The Ferment of Realism. American Literature 1884–1919*. Cambridge: Cambridge University Press, 1981.

Best, Gary A. "Charles Dana Gibson." *Bulletin of Bibliography* (March 1984), 41(1):12–18.

Bienenstock, Jennifer Martin. "Portraits of Flowers: The Out-of-Door Still-Life Paintings of Maria Oakey Dewing." *American Art Review* (December 1977), 4(13):48–55, 114–118.

Bishop, Emily M. *Self-Expression and Health: Americanized Delsarte Culture*. 5th ed., rev. Chautauqua, N.Y.: 1895.

Black, Alexander, *Miss America: Pen and Camera Sketches of the American Girl*. New York: 1898.

Black, Alexander. "Photography in Fiction: 'Miss Jerry,' the First Picture Play." *Scribner's Magazine* (September 1895), 18:348–360.

Blashfield, Edwin Howland. *Commemorative Tribute to Abbott Handerson Thayer. The American Academy of Arts and Letters, 1921*. New York: 1922.

Blashfield, Edwin Howland. *Commemorative Tribute to John White Alexander. Read in the 1917 Lecture Series of the American Academy of Arts and Letters*. New York: Academy of Arts and Letters, no. 17, n.d.

Blashfield, Edwin Howland. *Mural Painting in America. The Scammon Lectures Delivered Before the Art Institute of Chicago, March 1912, and Since Greatly Enlarged*. New York: Scribner's, 1913.

Blashfield, Edwin Howland. "A Word for Municipal Art." *Municipal Affairs* (December 1899), 3(4):582–593.

Blessed Damozel, The, by Dante Gabriel Rossetti, with Drawings by Kenyon Cox. New York: 1886.

Bliss, Harry A. *Memorial Art: Ancient and Modern Illustrations of the World's Most Notable Examples of Cemetery Memorials*. Buffalo: 1921.

Boas, Franz. *Changes in Bodily Form of Descendants of Immigrants*. Final Report, Reports of the United States Immigration Commission. Senate Documents no. 208, vol. 64 (61st Congress, 2d Session, 1909–1910). Washington, D.C.: GPO, 1911.

Bogardus, Ralph F. *Pictures and Texts: Henry James, A. L. Coburn, and New Ways of Seeing in Literary Culture*. Ann Arbor: UMI Research Press, 1984.

Bogart, Michele H. "The Importance of Believing in 'Purity,' " *Archives of American Art Journal* (1984), 24(4):2–8.

Bok, Edward William. *The Americanization of a Dutch Boy Fifty Years After*. New York: Scribner's, 1920.

Bolton, Charles Knowles. *The Reign of the Poster*. Boston: 1895.

Bolton, Theodore. *American Book Illustrators. Bibliographic Check Lists of 123 Artists*. New York: Bowker, 1938.

"Book Notices." *The American Architect and Building News* (November 30, 1878), 4(158):183. (Flaxman's *Outlines*).

Book of American Figure Painters. Philadelphia: 1886.

Boorstin, Daniel J. *The Image: A Guide to Pseudo-Events in America*. New York: Atheneum, 1980.

Boorstin, Daniel J. "Introduction: The Immigrant Vision." In Cynthia McCabe, *The Golden Door: Artist-Immigrants of America, 1876–1976*.

Booth, E. M. *Outlines of the Delsarte System of Expression, Arranged for Use of Classes*. Iowa City: Republican Co., 1884.

Borzello, Frances. *The Artist's Model*. London: Junction Books, 1982.

Bourget, Paul. "A Farewell to the White City." *The Cosmopolitan* (December 1893), 16(2):133–140.

Bourget, Paul. *Outre-Mer: Impressions of America*. New York: 1895.

Boyesen, Hjalmar Hjorth. "Types of American Women." *Literary and Social Silhouettes*. New York: 1894.

Boyle, Richard J. *American Impressionism*. Boston: New York Graphic Society, 1974.

Bradbury, Nicola. *Henry James: The Later Novels*. Oxford: Clarendon Press, 1979.

Brandon, Ruth. *A Capitalist Romance: Singer and the Sewing Machine*. Philadelphia: Lippincott, 1977.

Bray, Jeremiah, W. *Dramatized Themes with Tableaux*. Chicago: 1899.

Breese, James L. "Oriental Tableaux: A Series of Beautiful Pictures from Oriental Literature, Posed by Society Débutantes of New York." *Good Housekeeping* (June 1912), 54:776–783.

Breitenbach, Edgar and Margaret Cogswell. *The American Poster*. New York: American Federation of Arts, 1968.

Brewster, Henry B. *The Statuette and the Background*. London: Williams and Norgate, 1896.

Bridgman, Richard. *Gertrude Stein in Pieces*. New York: Oxford University Press, 1970.

Brinker, Menachem. "On Realism's Relativism: A Reply to Nelson Goodman." *New Literary History* (Winter 1983), 14(2):273–276.

Brinker, Menachem. "Verisimilitude, Conventions, and Beliefs." *New Literary History* (Winter 1983), 14(2):253–267.

Brinton, Christian. Review of *The History of American Painting* by Samuel Isham. *The Bookman* (April 1906), 23(2):192–194.

Brooks, Peter. *The Melodramatic Imagination: Balzac, Henry James, Melodrama, and the Mode of Excess*. New Haven: Yale University Press, 1976.

Brooks, Van Wyck. *America's Coming of Age*. New York: Huebsch, 1915.

Brown, David Alan. *Raphael and America*. Washington, D.C.: National Gallery of Art, 1983.

Brown, Glenn. "Roosevelt and the Fine Arts." *The American Architect* (December 10, 1919), 116(2294):711–719.

Brown, Marshall. "The Logic of Realism: A Hegelian Approach." *PMLA* (March 1981), 98(2):224–241.

Brownell, William C. "The Younger Painters of America—First Paper." *Scribner's Monthly Magazine* (May 1880), 20(1):1–15; 'Second Paper" (July 1880), 20(3):321–335.

Bruccoli, Matthew J. *Some Sort of Epic Grandeur*. New York: Harcourt Brace Jovanovich, 1981.

Brumbaugh, Thomas B. "The Monumental Art of Abbott H. Thayer." *Antiques* (June 1973), 103(6):1134–1140.

Brumbaugh, Thomas B. "A Seated Angel by Abbott H. Thayer." *Wadsworth Atheneum Bulletin*, 6th series (Spring and Fall 1971), 7(3):52–65.

Brumbaugh, Thomas B. "Womanhood Idealized: The Late Works of Abbott H. Thayer." *Art and Antiques* (September-October 1980), pp. 95–101.

Bruns, Gerald L. "Loose Talk About Religion from William James." *Critical Inquiry* (December 1984), 11(2):299–316.

Buffum, Katharine G. *Silhouettes To Cut in School*. Springfield, Mass.: Bradley, 1914.

Bunner, Henry Cuyler. "American Posters Past and Present." *The Modern Poster*. New York: 1895.

Bunner, Henry Cuyler. "The Making of the White City." *Scribner's Monthly Magazine* (October 1892), 12(4):399–418.

Burg, David F. "The Aesthetics of Bigness in Late Nineteenth Century American Architecture." In Marshall Fishwick and J. Meredith Neil, eds., *Popular Architecture*, pp. 484/106–492/114. Bowling Green, Ohio: Bowling Green Popular Press, 1978.

Burg, David F. *Chicago's White City of 1893*. Lexington: University Press of Kentucky, 1976.

Burke, Doreen Bolger. *American Paintings in the Metropolitan Museum of Art*. Vol. 3 of *A Catalogue of Works by Artists Born Between 1846 and 1864*. Kathleen Luhrs, ed. New York: Metropolitan Museum of Art, 1980.

Burnham, Daniel H. "White City and Capital City." *The Century* (February 1902), 58(4):619–620.

Burnham, Laurence. "The Modern Heroine in Illustration." *The Bookman* (April 1907), 25(2):191–199.

Burns, Sarah Lea. *The Poetic Mode in American Painting: George Fuller and Thomas Dewing*. Ph.D., dissertation, University of Illinois, 1979.

Burr, Samuel J. *Memorial of the International Exhibition*. Hartford, Conn.: 1877.

Buttrick, Helen Goodrich, *Principles of Clothing Selection*. New York: Macmillan, 1923.

Byrnes, Joseph F. *The Virgin of Chartres: An Intellectual and Psychological History of the Works of Henry Adams*. East Brunswick, N.J.: Associated University Press, 1981.

Caffin, Charles H. "The Art of Thomas W. Dewing." *Harper's Monthly Magazine* (April 1908), 116:714–724.

Caffin, Charles H. "Mural Painting in America." In Kenyon Cox, ed., *The Fine Arts*. Vol. 5 of *Vocations, in Ten Volumes*. William De Witt Hyde, ed. Young Folks Library. Boston: Hall & Locke, 1911.

Caffin, Charles H. "The New Mural Decorations of John W. Alexander." *Harper's Monthly Magazine* (May 1907), 114:845–858.

Caffin, Charles H. "Of Verities and Illusions." *Camera Work* (October 1905), 12:25–29.

Calkins, Ernest Elmo. "The Art of the Poster." *The International Studio* (December 1922), 76(307):215–220.

Campbell, James B. *Campbell's Illustrated History of the World's Columbian Exposition*. 2 vols. Chicago: 1894.

Campbell, James R. "The Pratt Institute." *The Century* (October 1893), 46(6):870–883.

Cartoons of the War of 1898 with Spain from Leading Foreign and American Papers. Chicago: 1898.

Catalogue of an Exhibition of Illustrated Bill-Posters at the Rooms of the Grolier Club. New York: November 1890.

Catalogue of Plaster Reproductions, from Antique, Medieval, and Modern Sculpture, Suitable for Educational Institutions and Homes. Boston: Caproni, 1922.

Chafe, William H. *Women and Equality: Changing Patterns in American Culture*. Oxford: Oxford University Press, 1977.

Chambers, Robert W. *The Common Law*. New York: Appleton, 1911.

Character and Unique Fashions: Suggestions for Fancy-Dress Costumes. New York: Butterick, 1897.

Charles Dana Gibson: A Study of the Man and Some Recent Examples of His Best Work.
New York: Collier, 1905.

Chase Centennial Exhibition, November 1–December 11, 1949. Indianapolis: John Herron
Art Museum, 1949.

"Chase Exhibition, The." *The Outlook* (January 29, 1910), p. 230.

Chase, William M. "How I Painted My Greatest Picture." *The Delineator* (December 1908),
72(6):967–969.

Chopin, Kate. *The Awakening.* New York: Norton, 1976; 1st ed., 1899.

Christy, Howard Chandler. *The American Girl as Seen and Portrayed by Howard Chandler
Christy.* New York: Moffat, Yard, 1906.

Christy, Howard Chandler. *Liberty Belles: Eight Epochs in the Making of the American
Girl.* Indianapolis: Bobbs-Merrill, 1912.

Christy, Howard Chandler. "Model-Lives." *Hearst's International Cosmopolitan* (July 1933),
95(1):32–35, 160–162; (October 1933), 95(4):44–45, 128–130.

Clark, Ella E. and Margot Edmonds. *Sacagawea of the Lewis and Clark Expedition.* Berkeley
and Los Angeles: University of California Press, 1979.

Clark, John S. *The Study of Type Forms and Their Value in Education.* Boston: Prang, 1898.

Clark, John S., Mary Dana Hicks, and Walter S. Perry. *Teacher's Manual: Elementary Course
in Art Instruction.* Boston: Prang, 1898.

Clark, Kenneth. *The Nude: A Study in Ideal Form.* Mellon Lectures in Fine Arts, 1953.
Bollinger Series 35–2. Princeton: Princeton University Press, 1956.

Clark, T. J. "Clement Greenberg's Theory of Art." *Critical Inquiry* (September 1982), 9(1):139–
156.

Clark, William J., Jr. *Great American Sculptures.* Philadelphia: 1878.

Clarke, Mary Vida. "Sauce for the Gander and Sawdust for the Goose." *The Dial* (December
14, 1918), 65:541–543.

Clement, Clara Erskine. *Women in the Fine Arts from the Seventh Century B.C. to the
Twentieth Century A.D.* Boston: Houghton, Mifflin, 1904.

Clifford, James. " 'Hanging Up Looking Glasses at Odd Corners': Ethnobiographical Prospects." In Daniel Aaron, ed., *Studies in Biography.* Harvard English Studies 8. Cambridge,
Mass: Harvard University Press, 1978.

Coad, Oral Sumner and Edwin Mims, Jr. *The American Stage.* Vol. 14 of *The Pageant of
America.*

Coe, Brian and Paul Gates. *The Snapshot Photograph: The Rise of Popular Photography,
1888–1939.* London: Ash & Grant, 1977.

Coffin, William A. "The Decorations in the New Congressional Library." *The Century* (March
1897), 53(5):694–711.

Cohn, David L. *The Good Old Days: A History of American Morals and Manners as Seen
Through the Sears, Roebuck Catalogs, 1905 to the Present.* New York: Simon & Schuster,
1940.

*Collection of 152 Original Monumental Designs, A, Compiled by Messrs. Cardoni and Mor-
ton.* Detroit: 1883.

Collier, John, Jr. *Visual Anthology: Photography as a Research Method.* New York: Holt,
Rinehart & Winston, 1967.

Collingwood, R. G. *Essays in the Philosophy of Art.* Alan Donagan, ed. Bloomington: Indiana University Press, 1964.

Collingwood, R. G. *The Principles of Art.* Cambridge: Clarendon Press, 1938.

Collins, Lyndhurst, ed. *The Use of Models in the Social Sciences.* London: Tavistock, 1976.

Colvin, Sidney. *The Drawings of Flaxman in the Gallery of University College, London.*
London: 1876.

Conn, Peter. *The Divided Mind: Ideology and Imagination in America, 1898–1917.* Cambridge: Cambridge University Press, 1983.

"Contributors' Club, The: Women and Woman." *The Atlantic Monthly* (July 1906), 98:136–139.

Cooke, Robert Grier. "Shop Window Displays—'The People's Picture Galleries.' " *The American Magazine of Art* (April 1921), 12(4):115–117.

Cooley, Charles Horton. *Human Nature and the Social Order.* New York: Scribner's, 1902.

Coolidge, Mary Roberts. *Why Women Are So.* New York: Holt, 1912.

Copleston, Frederick. *A History of Philosophy.* Vol. 8, *Modern Philosophy: Bentham to Russell.* Part 2, "Idealism in America: The Pragmatist Movement, the Revolt Against Idealism." Garden City, N.Y.: Image Books, 1966.

Copley, Frank Barkley. *Frederich W. Taylor, Father of Scientific Management.* Vol. 1. New York: Kelley, 1969; 1st ed., 1923.

Corson, Richard. *Fashions in Makeup from Ancient to Modern Times.* New York: Universe Books, 1972.

Cortissoz, Royal. *Commemorative Tribute to Daniel Chester French.* American Academy of Arts and Letters (November 10, 1932), no. 79, pp. 59–65.

Cortissoz, Royal. Foreword, *Paintings, Drawings, and Pastels by Edwin Austin Abbey, Gallery of Fine Arts, Yale University.* New Haven: 1939.

Cortissoz, Royal. Introduction, *The Works of Edwin Howland Blashfield.* New York: Scribner's 1937.

Cortissoz, Royal. "A National Monument of Art: The Congressional Library at Washington." *Harper's Weekly* (December 28, 1895), 39(2036):1240–1241.

Cortissoz, Royal. "Some Imaginative Types in American Art." *Harper's New Monthly Magazine* (July 1895), 91:164–179.

Cowan, George J. *Window Backgrounds: A Collection of Drawings and Descriptions of Store Window Backgrounds.* Chicago: Dry Goods Reporter, 1912.

Cox, Kenyon. *Artist and Public and Other Essays on Art Subjects.* New York: Scribner's, 1914.

Cox, Kenyon. "Augustus Saint-Gaudens." *The Century* (November 1887), 35(1):28–37.

Cox, Kenyon. *The Classic Point of View: Six Lectures on Painting.* New York: Scribner's, 1911.

Cox, Kenyon. *Concerning Painting: Considerations Theoretical and Historical.* New York: Scribner's, 1917.

Cox, Kenyon. *Old Masters and New.* New York: Fox, Duffield, 1905.

[Cox, Kenyon.] "An Out-Door Masque in New England." *The Nation* (June 29, 1905), 80(2087):519–520.

Cox, Kenyon. *Painters and Sculptors: A Second Series of Old Masters and New.* New York: Duffield, 1907.

Cox, Kenyon. "Sculptors of the Early Italian Renaissance." *The Century* (November 1884), 29(1):62–66.

Cox, Kenyon. "The Sherman Statue." *The Nation* (June 18, 1903), 76(1981):491–492.

Cox, Kenyon. "Whistler and Absolute Painting." *Scribner's Monthly Magazine* (April 1904), 35:637–638.

Crane, Stephen. *Maggie: A Girl of the Streets.* Vol. 1 of *The University of Virginia Edition of the Works of Stephen Crane.* Charlottesville: University Press of Virginia, 1969.

Crawford, Francis Marion. "False Taste in Art." *The North American Review* (July 1882), no. 308, pp. 89–98.

Cresson, Margaret French. "Daniel French's Heaven—Reminiscences of Chesterwood." *Historic Preservation* (April-June 1973), 25, no. 2, 18–27.

Cresson, Margaret French. *Journey Into Fame: The Life of Daniel Chester French.* Cambridge, Mass.: Harvard University Press, 1947.

Critchfield, A. *The Reporter's Illustrated Monumental Draughtsman. The only work ever* published devoted exclusively to monumental designing. A complete treatise on object, profile, elevation, plan, and perspective drawing in its application to monumental work. Chicago: 1895.

Crowley, John W. and Charles L. Crow. "Psychic and Psychological Themes in Howells' 'A Sleep and a Forgetting.' " *Emerson Society Quarterly* (First quarter 1977), 23(1):41–51.

Culler, Jonathan. *The Pursuit of Signs: Semiotics, Literature, and Deconstruction.* Ithaca: Cornell University Press, 1981.

Dale, Alan. "Stage Beauty and Brains." *The Cosmopolitan* (March 1911), 50(4):517–522.

Dallas, Mary Kyle. *Biltry.* New York: 1895.

"Daniel Chester French's Four Symbolic Groups for the New York Custom House." *The Craftsman* (April 1906), 10(1):75–83.

Daniel, Pete and Raymond Smock. *A Talent for Detail: The Photographs of Miss Frances Benjamin Johnston, 1889–1910.* New York: Harmony Books, 1974.

Danto, Arthur C. *The Transfiguration of the Commonplace: A Philosophy of Art.* Cambridge, Mass.: Harvard University Press, 1981.

Darracott, Joseph, ed. *The First World War in Posters.* New York: Dover, 1974.

Darwin, Charles. *The Expression of the Emotions in Man and Animals.* Authorized Edition. New York: Appleton, 1896.

Daves, Jessica. *Ready-Made Miracle: The American Story of Fashion for the Millions.* New York: Putnam's, 1967.

Davidson, James West and Mark Hamilton Lyttle. *After the Fact: The Art of Historical Detection.* New York: Knopf, 1982.

Davis, Charles Belmont. "Mr. Charles Dana Gibson and His Art." *The Critic* (January 1899), 34(859):48–55.

Davis, Richard Harding. *The Princess Aline.* New York: Harper, 1895.

"Decorations of the Education Palace, Albany, N.Y.—Town and Country Embellishment." *The Art World, a Monthly for the Public Devoted to the Higher Ideals, Combining The Craftsman* (March 1918), 4(6):495–499.

Degler, Carl N. *At Odds: Women and the Family in America from the Revolution to the Present.* New York: Oxford University Press, 1980.

de Kay, Charles. "A Half-Hour with Studio Bores." In F. Hopkinson Smith et al., eds., *Discussions on American Art and Artists,* pp. 153–159.

Deland, Margaret. "The Change in the Feminine Ideal." *The Atlantic Monthly* (March 1910), 105:289–302.

de Man, Paul. "Pascal's Allegory of Persuasion." In Stephen J. Greenblatt, ed., *Allegory and Representation: Selected Papers from the English Institute, 1979–1980,* n.s. 5. Baltimore: Johns Hopkins University Press, 1981.

Denkinger, J. A. *Physiognomical Register for Recording the Indications of the Head, Face, Temperament, and Other Organic Conditions.* Boston: 1895.

De Puy, Frank A. *The New Century Home Book: A Mentor for Home Life in All Its Phases; a Chronicle of the Progress of America and the World; a Compendium of the Nation's Greatest City; and a Guide for the Great Army of Home-Builders.* New York: Eaton & Mains, 1900.

Dewey, John. *Art as Experience.* New York: Putnam's Perigee Book, 1980; 1st ed., 1934.

D'Harnoncourt, Anne and Kynaston McShine. *Marcel Duchamp.* New York: Museum of Modern Art, 1973.

Dickason, David Howard. *The Daring Young Men: The Story of the American Pre-Raphaelites.* Bloomington: Indiana University Press, 1953.

Doenecke, Justus D. "Myths, Machines, and Markets: The Columbian Exposition of 1893." *Journal of Popular Culture* (Spring 1973), 6(3):535–549.

Douglas, George A. *The Experience of a Veteran Salesman of Memorial Monuments*. Cincinnati: Ebel, 1908.

Douglas, Mary and Baron Isherwood. *World of Goods: Towards an Anthropology of Consumption*. New York: Norton, 1982.

Downes, William H. "William Merritt Chase: A Typical American Artist." *The International Studio* (December 1909), 39:xxix–xxxvi.

Downey, Fairfax. *Portrait of an Era as Drawn by C. D. Gibson: A Biography*. New York: Scribner's 1936.

Downey, Fairfax. *Richard Harding Davis: His Day*. New York: Scribner's 1933.

Dreiser, Theodore. *Sister Carrie*. Philadelphia: University of Pennsylvania, 1981.

Dryfhout, John H. *The Work of Augustus Saint-Gaudens*. Hanover: University Press of New England, 1982.

Duce, Herbert Cecil. *Poster Advertising*. Chicago: Blakely, 1912.

Dulles, Foster Rhea. *America Learns to Play: A History of Popular Recreation, 1607–1940*. New York: Appleton-Century, 1940.

Du Maurier, George. *Trilby*. New York: 1894.

Duncan, Alastair. *Tiffany Windows*. New York: Simon & Schuster, 1980.

Dye, Eva Emery. *The Conquest: The True Story of Lewis and Clark*. New York: McClurg, 1902.

Eakin, Paul John. *The New England Girl: Cultural Ideals in Hawthorne, Stowe, Howells, and James*. Athens: University of Georgia Press, 1976.

Eakins at Avondale and Thomas Eakins: A Personal Collection. Chadds Ford, Pa.: Brandywine Conservancy, 1980.

Earle, Edward W., ed. *Points of View: The Stereograph in America—a Cultural History*. Foreword by Nathan Lyons. Rochester, N.Y.: Visual Studies Workshop Press, 1979.

Eastlake, Sir Charles. *Materials for a History of Oil Painting*. Vol. 2. London: 1847–1869.

Ecob, Helen Gilbert. *The Well-Dressed Woman: A Study in the Practical Application to Dress of the Laws of Health, Art, and Morals*. New York: 1892.

Edel, Leon. *The Life of Henry James*. Vol. 5, *The Master (1901–1916)*. Philadelphia: Lippincott, 1972.

Edel, Leon and Dan. H. Lawrence. *A Bibliography of Henry James*. London: Hart-Davis, 1957.

Edel, Leon and Gordon Ray, eds. *Henry James and H. G. Wells: A Record of Their Friendship*. Urbana: University of Illinois Press, 1958.

Edgerly, Webster [Edmund Shaftesbury, pseud.]. *Lessons in the Art of Acting. . . .* Washington, D.C.: 1889.

Edouart, Augustin Arnant Constance Fidèle. *A Treatise on Silhouette Likenesses*. London: Longmans, Green, 1835.

Edwards, Lee R. *Psyche as Hero: Female Heroism and Fictional Form*. Middleton, Conn.: Wesleyan University Press, 1984.

Ehrenreich, Barbara and Deirdre English. *For Her Own Good: 150 Years of the Experts' Advice to Women*. Garden City, N.Y.: Anchor Press/Doubleday, 1978.

Eldredge, Charles C. *American Imagination and Symbolist Painting*. New York: Grey Art Gallery and Study Center, 1979.

Eliot, Charles W. "The Normal American Woman." *The Ladies' Home Journal* (Journal 1908), 25:15.

Elliott, Huger. *Memorial Art*. Cambridge, Mass.: Granite Marble and Bronze, 1923.

Elliott, Maud Howe. "The Building and Its Decoration." *Art and Handicraft in the Woman's Building of the World's Columbian Exposition, Chicago, 1893*. Paris and New York: 1893.

Elson, Ruth Miller. *Guardians of Tradition: American Schoolbooks of the Nineteenth Century*. Lincoln: University of Nebraska Press, 1964.

Emerson, Ellen Russell. *Masks, Heads, and Faces, with Some Considerations Respecting the Rise and Development of Art.* London: 1892.

Emmet, Boris and John E. Jeuck. *Catalogues and Counters: A History of Sears, Roebuck and Co.* Chicago: University of Chicago Press, 1950.

Ephemera Files: see National Museum of American Art.

Evans, Elizabeth C. "Physiognomies in the Ancient World." *Transactions of the American Philosophical Society* (1969), n.s. 59, part 5, pp. 5–101.

Ewen, Stuart and Elizabeth Ewen. *Channels of Desire: Mass Images and the Shaping of American Consciousness.* New York: McGraw-Hill, 1982.

Exhibition of Original Designs for Posters by Louis J. Rhead, An. New York: 1895.

Faber, A. D. *Cigar Label Art.* Watkins Glen, N.Y.: Century House, 1919.

Fairfield, Frances. *Tableaux for Home and School.* Chicago: Denison, 1922.

Fairfield, Sidney. "The Tyranny of the Pictorial." *Lippincott's Monthly Magazine* (1895), 55:861–864.

Fairman, Charles E. *Art and Artists of the Capitol of the United States of America.* Washington, D.C.: GPO, 1927.

Farrell, Lila Gillian. *Human Nature Study.* Grand Rapids, Mich.: Human Nature Study Bureau, 1924.

Federman, Raymond, "Imagination as Plagiarism." *New Literary History* (Spring 1976), 7(3):563–578.

Ferber, Edna. *Fanny Herself.* New York: Stokes, 1917.

Ferry, John William. *A History of the Department Store.* New York: Macmillan, 1960.

Fine, Elsa Honig. *Woman and Art: A History of Women Painters and Sculptors from the Renaissance to the Twentieth Century.* Montclair, N.J.: Allanheld & Schram/Prior, 1978.

Fink, Lois Marie. "Nineteenth Century Evolutionary Art." *American Art Review* (January 1978), 4(4):74–81, 105–109.

Fink, Lois Marie and Joshua C. Taylor. *Academy: The Academic Tradition in American Art. An Exhibition Organized on the Occasion of the One Hundred and Fiftieth Anniversary of the National Academy of Design, 1825–1975.* National Collection of Fine Arts. Washington, D.C.: Smithsonian Institution Press, 1975.

Fish, Arthur. "Triumphal Arches." *The Magazine of Art* (August 1900), 23:445–449.

Fisher, Philip. "Acting, Reading, Fortune's Wheel: *Sister Carrie* and the Life History of Objects." In Eric J. Sundquist, ed., *American Realism: New Essays.* Baltimore: Johns Hopkins University Press, 1982.

Fitzgerald, Frances. *America Revised: History Schoolbooks in the Twentieth Century.* Boston: Little, Brown, 1979.

Flagg, James Montgomery. *Adventures of Kitty Cobb. Pictures and Text.* New York: Doran, 1912.

Flagg, James Montgomery. *Boulevards All the Way—Maybe.* New York: Doran, 1925.

Flaxman, John. *Lectures on Sculpture, as Delivered Before the President and Members of the Royal Academy.* 2d ed. London: 1838.

Fletcher, Angus. *Allegory: The Theory of a Symbolic Mode.* Ithaca: Cornell University Press, 1964.

Fletcher, Robert. "Stylizations and Inventions: A Semiotic Analysis of Wharton's *The House of Mirth* and *The Custom of the Country.*" U.C.L.A. graduate seminar paper submitted March 19, 1984.

Forshay, Ella M. *Reflections of Nature: Flowers in American Art.* New York: Whitney Museum of American Art, 1984.

Forster, Kurt W. "Critical History of Art, or Transfiguration of Values?" *New Literary History* (Spring 1972), 3(3):459–470.

"Forty-Second Annual Convention of the American Institute of Architects, Washington,

D.C., December 15, 16, and 17, 1908, "1908—Resume." *The Brickbuilder* (January 1909), 18(1):14–16.

Foster, Kathleen A. "The Paintings." *Edwin Austin Abbey (1852–1911). An Exhibition Organized by the Yale University Art Gallery*. New Haven: Yale University Press, 1973.

Fowler, Virginia C. *Henry James's American Girl*. Madison: University of Wisconsin Press, 1984.

Frank Leslie's Illustrated Historical Register of the Centennial Exposition, 1876. Facsimile, with a new introduction by Richard Kenin. New York: Paddington Press, 1974.

Fraser, Steven. "Combined and Uneven Development in the Men's Clothing Industry." *Business History Review* (Winter 1983), 57(4):522–547.

Fraser, W. Lewis. "Decorative Painting at the World's Fair: The Works of Gari Melchers and Walter MacEwen." *The Century* (May 1893), 46(1):14–21.

French, Mrs. Daniel Chester [Mary]. *Memories of a Sculptor's Wife*. Boston: Houghton, Mifflin, 1928.

Freund, Gisèle. *Photography and Society*. Boston: Godine, 1980.

Fried, Michael. "Painting Memories: On the Containment of the Past in Baudelaire and Manet." *Critical Inquiry* (March 1984), 10(3):510–542.

Froehlich, Hugo B. and Bonnie E. Snow. *A Course of Study in Art for the First Six Years in School. To Be Used with Text Books of Art Education*. New York: Prang, 1904.

Froehlich, Hugo B. and Bonnie E. Snow. Text Books of Art Education. Book 1: First Year; Book 2: Second Year; Book 4: Fourth Year; Book 5: Fifth Year. New York, Boston: Prang, 1904.

From Realism to Symbolism: Whistler and His World. An Exhibition Organized by the Department of Art History and Archaeology of Columbia University in the City of New York in Cooperation with the Philadelphia Museum of Art. New York: Columbia University Press, 1971.

Frothingham, Eugenia Brooks. *The Evasion*. Boston: Houghton, Mifflin, 1906.

Fuchs, Eduard. *Die Frau in der Karikatur*. Munich: Langen, 1906.

Fuchs, Eduard. *Die Juden in der Karikatur: Ein Beitrag zur Kulturgeschichte*. Munich: Langen, 1921.

Fuss, Peter. *The Moral Philosophy of Josiah Royce*. Cambridge, Mass.: Harvard University Press, 1965.

Gadol, Joan. *Leon Battista Alberti: Universal Man of the Early Renaissance*. Chicago: University of Chicago Press, 1969.

Galassi, Peter. *Before Photography: Painting and the Invention of Photography*. Museum of Modern Art. Boston: New York Graphic Society, 1981.

Garland, Madge. *The Changing Face of Beauty: Four Thousand Years of Beautiful Women*. New York: Barrows, 1957.

Garnett, John J. *The Statue of Liberty: Its Conception, Its Construction, Its Inauguration. The Official Programme*. New York: Dinsmore, 1886.

Garrison, Dee. "Immoral Fiction in the Late Victorian Library." *American Quarterly* (Spring 1976), 28(1):71–89.

Geertz, Clifford. *The Interpretation of Cultures: Selected Essays*. London: Hutchinson, 1975.

Gerdts, William H., Jr. *American Impressionism*. New York: Abbeville, 1984.

Gerdts, William H., Jr. Introduction, *The White, Marmorean Flock: Nineteenth-Century American Women Neoclassical Sculptors*. Catalog by Nicolai Cikovsky, Jr., Marie H. Morrison, and Carol Ockman. Poughkeepsie, N.Y.: Vassar College Art Gallery, 1972.

Gernsheim, Alison. *Fashion and Reality*. London: Faber & Faber, 1963.

Gibson Book, The. 2 vols. New York: Scribner's, 1906.

Gibson, Charles Dana. *Other People*. New York: Scribner's, 1911.

Gibson, Charles Dana. *The Social Ladder*. New York: Russell, 1902.

Gilbert, Cass. "The Greatest Element of Monumental Architecture." *The American Architect* (August 5, 1929), 136(2574):141–144.

Gilbert, Katherine Everett and Helmut Kuhn. *A History of Esthetics*. New York: Dover, 1972.

Gilbert, Margaret. "Notes on the Concept of a Social Convention." *New Literary History* (Winter 1983), 14(2):225–251.

Gilbert, Sandra M. "Soldier's Heart: Literary Men, Literary Women and the Great War," *Signs: Journal of Women in Culture and Society* (1983), 8(3):422–450.

Gilder, R. W. "The Vanishing City." *The Century* (October 1893), 46(6):868–869.

Gilder, R. W. "The White City." *The Century* (May 1893), 46(1):22.

Gilman, Charlotte Perkins. *The Home: Its Work and Influences*. New York: Source Book Press, 1970; 1st ed., 1903.

Gilman, Charlotte Perkins. *The Man-Made World, or Our Androcentric Culture*. New York: Source Book Press, 1970; 1st ed., 1911.

Gilman, Charlotte Perkins. *Women and Economics: A Study of the Economic Relation Between Men and Women as a Factor in Social Evolution*. New York: 1899.

Ginger, Ray. *Age of Excess: The United States from 1877–1914*. New York: Macmillan, 1965.

Ginger, Ray, ed. *The Nationalizing of American Life, 1877–1900*. New York: Free Press, 1965.

Girouard, Mark. *The Return to Camelot: Chivalry and the English Gentleman*. New Haven: Yale University Press, 1981.

Goethe, Johann Wolfgang von. *Goethe's Travels in Italy*. Translated from the German. London: 1885.

Gombrich, Ernst H. *Art and Illusion: A Study in the Psychology of Pictorial Representation*. London: Phaidon, 1960.

Gombrich, Ernst H. "On Physiognomic Perception" (pp. 45–55), "Expression and Communication" (pp. 56–69). *Meditations on a Hobby Horse and Other Essays on the Theory of Art*. London: Phaidon, 1963.

Gombrich Ernst H. *Symbolic Images: Studies in the Art of the Renaissance*. London: Phaidon, 1972.

Goodman, Nelson, "Realism, Relativism, and Reality." *New Literary History* (Winter 1983), 14(2):269–272.

Grant, Robert. *The Art of Living*. New York: 1895.

Grant, Robert. *The High Priestess*. New York: Scribner's, 1915.

Green Room Book or Who's Who on the Stage, The. John Parker, ed. New York: Kennerley, 1908.

Greenthal, Kathryn. *Augustus Saint-Gaudens. Master Sculptor*. The Metropolitan Museum of Art, New York. Boston: J. K. Hall, 1985.

Guerin, Jules. "The Mural Decorations." *Art and Archaeology* (June 1922), vol. 13, no. 6.

Guyot, Arnold Henry. *Physical Geography*. New York: 1866..

Habegger, Alfred. *Gender, Fantasy, and Realism in American Literature*. New York: Columbia University Press, 1982.

Hackett, Alice Payne. *Fifty Years of Best Sellers, 1895–1945*. New York: Bowker, 1945.

Hall, Florence Howe. *Social Customs*. Boston: Estes, 1911.

Halttunen, Karen. *Confidence Men and Painted Women: A Study of Middle-Culture in America, 1830–1870*. New Haven: Yale University Press, 1983.

Hambridge, Jay. *Dynamic Symmetry in Composition, as Used by the Artists*. Cambridge, Mass.: Hambridge, 1923.

Hambridge, Jay. *The Elements of Dynamic Symmetry*. New York: Dover, 1967; first published in *The Diagonal* (1919–1920).

Handbook of the New Library of Congress. Herbert Small, comp. Boston: Curtis & Cameron, 1901.

Hardie, Martin and Arthur K. Sabin. *War Posters Issued by Belligerent and Neutral Nations, 1914–1919.* London: Black, 1920.

Harper, George M. "Thomas Taylor in America." In Kathleen Raine and George M. Harper, eds., *Thomas Taylor the Platonist: Selected Writings.* Bollingen Series 88. Princeton: Princeton University Press, 1969.

Harper, Jennifer. *City Work at Country Prices: The Portrait Photographs of Duncan Donovan.* Toronto: Oxford University Press, 1977.

Harré, Rom. "The Constructive Role of Models." In Lyndhurst Collins, ed.,*The Use of Models in the Social Sciences.*

Harris, Neil. "The Gilded Age Reconsidered Once Again." *Archives of American Art Journal* (1983), 23(4):8–18.

Harris, Neil. "The Gilded Age Revisited: Boston and the Museum Monument." *American Quarterly* (Winter 1962), 14(4):545–566.

Harris, Neil. "Iconography and Intellectual History: The Half-Tone Effect." In Higham and Conkin, eds., *New Directions in American Intellectual History.*

Harris, Neil. Introduction, *The Land of Contrasts, 1880–1970.* New York: Braziller, 1970.

Harrison, A. H. *The History of Silhouettes and How To Make Them.* St. Louis: Freelance Publicity and Syndication Bureau, 1916.

Hart, James David. *The Popular Book: A History of America's Literary Taste.* New York: Oxford University Press, 1950.

Hartshorne, Thomas L. *The Distorted Image: Changing Conceptions of the American Character Since Turner.* Westport, Conn.: Greenwood Press, 1980.

Hastings, Thomas. *Commemorative Tributes to La Farge, Abbey, and Millet, 1912.* No. 15. New York: American Academy of Arts and Letters, 1922.

Hathaway, Milicent L. and Elsie D. Foard. *Heights and Weights of Adults in the United States.* Home Economics Research Report no. 10. Human Nutrition Research Division, Agricultural Research Service, U.S. Department of Agriculture. Washington, D.C.: August 1960.

Hauser, Arnold. "The *l'art pour l'art* Problem." *Critical Inquiry* (Spring 1979), 5(3):425–440.

Haweis, Mary Eliza. *The Art of Beauty.* London: 1878.

Hawkins, Anthony Hope. *The Prisoner of Zenda; Being the History of Three Months in the Life of an English Gentleman.* New York: 1894.

Hayden, Dolores. *The Grand Domestic Revolution: A History of Feminist Designs for American Homes, Neighborhoods, and Cities.* Cambridge, Mass.: MIT Press, 1981.

Helsinger, Elizabeth K., Robin Lauterbach Sheets, and William Veeder. *The Woman Question: Literary Issues, 1837–1883.* Vol. 3 of *The Woman Question: Society and Literature in Britain and America, 1837–1883.* New York: Garland, 1983.

Hendricks, Gordon. *The Life and Works of Thomas Eakins.* New York: Grossman, 1974.

Henry, Arthur. "Among the Immigrants." *Scribner's Monthly Magazine* (March 1901), 29(3):301–311.

Herter, Christine. *Dynamic Symmetry: A Primer.* New York: Norton, 1966.

Hesse, Mary B. *Models and Analogies in Science.* Notre Dame, Ind.: University of Notre Dame, 1966.

Hesse, Mary B. "Models Versus Paradigms in the Natural Sciences." In Lyndhurst Collins, ed., *The Use of Models in the Social Sciences.*

Hewitt, Emma Churchman. "The 'New Woman' in Her Relation to the 'New Man.' " *The Westminster Review* (March 1897), 147(3):335–337.

Hicks, Mary D. and John S. Clark. *The Use of Models: A Teacher's Assistant in the Use of the Prang Models. Form Study and Drawing in Primary Schools.* Boston: Prang, 1887.

Higgins, Charles. "Photographic Aperture: Coburn's Frontispieces to James's New York Edition." *American Literature* (January 1892), 53(4):661–675.

Higginson, Thomas Wentworth. *Women and the Alphabet.* Vol. 4 of *The Writings of Thomas Wentworth Higginson.* Boston: Houghton Mifflin, 1881, 1900.

Higham, John. *From Boundlessness to Consolidation: The Transformation of American Culture, 1848–1860.* Ann Arbor: Clements Library, 1969.

Higham, John. Introduction, Higham and Conkin, eds., *New Directions in American Intellectual History.*

Higham, John. *Strangers in the Land: Patterns of American Nativism, 1860–1925.* New York: Atheneum, 1981.

Higham, John, and Paul K. Conkin, eds. *New Directions in American Intellectual History. Wingspread Conference on New Directions, Racine, Wisconsin, 1977.* Baltimore: Johns Hopkins University Press, 1979.

Higonnet, Anne, Margaret, and Patrice. "Facades: Walter Benjamin's Paris." *Critical Inquiry* (March 1984), 10(3):391–419.

Hilker, Helen-Anne. "Monument to Civilization: Diary of a Building." *The Quarterly Journal of the Library of Congress* (October 1972), 29(4):234–266.

Hill, Joseph A. *Hill's Book of Tableaux or Living Symbolic Illustrations of the Principles, Moral and Benevolent Teachings, and Practices of the Prominent Secret Societies, Such as Masonic, Odd Fellows, K. of P., I.O.R.M., A.O.V.W., K. of H., G.A.R., A.O.H., R.A., D. of R., P.S., Grange, Etc. Also a Series Presenting in an Attractive Form the Great Truths of Religion, as Drawn from the Bible; Together with Curious Marriage Ceremonials of Nations, Arranged as Tableaux. Also a Series Expressly Prepared for our National Holidays in Addition to Which is a Large Collection Historical, Classical, and Miscellaneous.* Indianapolis: Fraternity Publishing, 1884.

Hills, Patricia. "Turn-of-the-Century America." *American Art Review* (January 1978), 4(4):66–73, 94–97.

Hills, Patricia. *Turn-of-the-Century America: Paintings, Graphics, Photographs, 1890–1910.* New York: Whitney Museum of American Art, 1977.

Hines, Thomas S. *Burnham of Chicago: Architect and Planner.* New York: Oxford University Press, 1974.

Hirsch, E. D., Jr. "Beyond Convention?" *New Literary History* (Winter 1983), 14(2):389–397.

Hirsch, Judi. *Family Photographs: Content, Meanings, and Effect.* New York: Oxford University Press, 1981.

History Study Pictures: History, Geography, Literature. Chicago: Art Study, 1900.

Hitchcock, Henry-Russell and William Seale. *Temples of Democracy: The State Capitols of the U.S.A.* New York: Harcourt Brace Jovanovich, 1976.

Hitchcock's Musical, Pictorial, and Descriptive Souvenir of the World's Columbian Exposition in Celebration of the Discovery of America. New York: 1893.

Hobbs, Susan. "A Connoisseur's Vision: The American Collection of Charles Lang Freer." *American Art Review* (August 1977), 4(2):76–101.

Hobbs, Susan. "Nature Into Art: The Landscapes of Abbott Handerson Thayer." *The American Art Journal* (Summer 1982), 14(3):4–55.

Hobbs, Susan. "Thomas Wilmer Dewing: The Early Years, 1851–1885." *The American Art Journal* (Spring 1981), 13(2):4–35.

Hoffmann and Procházka. *Public and Private Monuments and Memorials.* New York: 1896.

Holmes, Oliver Wendell, Jr. *The Common Law*. Boston: 1881.

Holmstrom, Kristin Gram. *Monodrama, Attitudes, Tableaux Vivants: Studies on Some Trends of Theatrical Fashion, 1770–1815*. Stockholm: Almquist & Wiksell, 1967.

Homer, William I., ed. *A Pictorial History: The Photographs of Gertrude Käsebier*. Wilmington: Delaware Art Museum, 1979.

Honour, Hugh. *The New Golden Land: European Images of America from the Discoveries to the Present Time*. New York: Pantheon, 1975.

Honour, Hugh. *Romanticism*. New York: Harper & Row, Icon Editions, 1979.

Hooper, Bett. *Virgins in Cellophane: From Maker to Consumer Untouched by Human Hand*. New York: Long & Smith, 1932.

Hoopes, Donelson F. *American Narrative Painting*. Los Angeles: Los Angeles County Museum of Art and Praeger Publishing, 1974.

Hornung, Clarence P. and Fridolf Johnson. *200 Years of American Graphic Art: A Retrospective Survey of the Printing Arts and Advertising Since the Colonial Period*. New York: Braziller, 1976.

Horowitz, Helen Lefkowitz. *Culture and the City: Cultural Philanthropy in Chicago from the 1880s to 1917*. Lexington: University Press of Kentucky, 1976.

Horwitz, Richard P. "Making Sense of Mural America." *American Quarterly* (Spring 1984), 36(1):139–144.

Howard Chandler Christy: Artist/Illustrator of Style. Allentown, Pa.: Allentown Art Museum, 1977.

Howard, Maureen. *Facts of Life*. Boston: Little, Brown, 1978.

Howe, Frederic Clemson. *The Modern City and Its Problems*. New York: Scribner's, 1915.

Howell, Jeanne. *A Common Mistake*. New York: Merriam, 1892.

Howells, William Dean. "Editha." *Harper's Monthly Magazine* (January 1905), 110:214–224.

Howells, William Dean. "Henry James, Jr." *The Century* (November 1882), 25:24–25.

Howells, William Dean. *Heroines of Fiction*. 2 vols. New York: Harper, 1901.

Howells, William Dean. *Letters of an Altrurian Traveller (1893–1894)*. Clara M. Kirk and Rudolph Kirk, eds. Gainesville, Fla.: Scholar's Facsimiles & Reprints, 1961.

Howells, William Dean. "A Sennight of the Centennial." *The Atlantic Monthly* (July 1876), 38:92–107.

Hower, Ralph M. *The History of an Advertising Agency: N.W. Ayer and Son at Work, 1869–1939*. Cambridge, Mass.: Harvard University Press, 1939.

Hoyle, Frances P. *The Complete Speaker and Reciter for Home, School, Church, and Platform*. Scull, 1902.

Illustrated Catalogue of Pictures Adapted for Schoolroom Decoration. Boston: 1897.

Illustrated History of the Hasty Pudding Club Theatricals, An. 3d. Cambridge, Mass.: Hasty Pudding Club, 1933.

Image and Identity: The Role of the Mask in Various Cultures. An Exhibition Organized by the UCLA Museum of Cultural History. Los Angeles: UCLA, Museum of Cultural History Galleries, 1972.

Irish, Marie. *Patriotic Celebrations: Monologues, Recitations, Motion Songs, Song Pantomimes, Exercises, Drills, and Dialogues for All Patriotic Occasions*. Chicago: Denison, 1910.

Irish, Marie, O. E. Young, and others. *Pleasing Pantomimes and Tableaux*. 1929.

Isham, Samuel. *The History of American Painting*. New York: Macmillan, 1905.

Ivins, William Mills, Jr. *Prints and Visual Communication*. Cambridge, Mass.: Harvard University Press, 1953.

Jackson, E[mily] Nevill. *The History of Silhouettes*. London: Connoisseur, 1911.

James, Edward T., Janet Wilson James, and Paul S. Boyer, eds. *Notable American Women,*

1607–1950: A Biographical Dictionary. Cambridge, Mass.: Belknap Press of Harvard University Press, 1971.

James, Henry, *The Ambassadors*. Vols. 21–22 of *Novels and Tales*.

James, Henry. *The American Scene*. New York: Harper, 1907.

James, Henry. "The Art of Fiction." *Partial Portraits*. New York: 1888.

James, Henry. *The Awkward Age*. Vol. 9 of *Novels and Tales*.

James, Henry. "The Future of the Novel." *The Future of the Novel*. Leon Edel, ed. New York: Vintage, 1956.

James, Henry. "Guy de Maupassant." *Partial Portraits*. New York: 1888.

James, Henry. *Hawthorne*. London: 1879.

James, Henry. *Henry James: Autobiography*. Frederick W. Dupee, ed. Princeton: Princeton University Press, 1983.

James, Henry. "The Lesson of Balzac." In *The Question of Our Speech*. Boston: Houghton, Mifflin, 1905.

James, Henry. "Madame de Mauves." Vol. 13 of *Novels and Tales*.

James, Henry. *The Notebooks of Henry James*. F. O. Matthiessen and Kenneth B. Murdoch, eds. New York: Braziller, 1955.

James, Henry. *The Novels and Tales*. New York edition, 26 vols. New York: Scribner's, 1908–1917.

James, Henry. *The Portrait of a Lady*. Vols. 3–4 of *Novels and Tales*.

James, Henry. "The Quest and Achievement of the Holy Grail: Wall Paintings in the Boston Public Library Installed in 1895 by Edwin Austin Abbey, R.A. An Outline of This Version of the Legend by Henry James." New York: American Art Association, 1901.

James, Henry. "The Real Thing." Vol. 18 of *Novels and Tales*.

James, Henry. *The Tragic Muse*. Vols. 7–8 of *Novels and Tales*.

James, Henry. *William Wetmore Story and His Friends from Letters, Diaries, and Recollections*. 2 vols. Boston: Houghton, Mifflin, 1903.

James, Henry. *The Wings of the Dove*. Vols. 19–20 of *Novels and Tales*.

James, William. *Principles of Psychology*. 2 vols. New York: 1890.

Jarves, James Jackson. *The Art Idea: Sculpture, Painting, and Architecture in America*. 5th ed. Boston: 1864.

Jefferson, Francis H. *A Series of Tableaux, Suitable for Dramatic Representation; Also Adapted to the Illustration of Temperance and Other Moral Games*. Central Falls and Lincoln, R.I.: 1874.

Jehlen, Myra. "Archimedes and the Paradox of Feminist Criticism." In *Feminist Theory: A Critique of Ideology*. Chicago: University of Chicago Press, 1982.

Jenison, Madge C. "A Hull House Play." *The Atlantic Monthly* (July 1906), 98:83–92.

Jenkins, C. Francis. "How To Secure Expression in Photography." *The Cosmopolitan* (June 1899), 27(2):131–136.

Jenkins, Reese V. *Images and Enterprise: Technology and the American Photographic Industry, 1839 to 1925*. Baltimore: Johns Hopkins University Press, 1975.

Jones, Edgar R. *Those Were the Good Old Days—a Happy Look at American Advertising, 1880–1930*. New York: Simon & Schuster, 1959.

Jones, Howard Mumford. *O Strange New World: American Culture, the Formative Years*. New York: Viking, 1964.

Jones, Howard Mumford. "The Renaissance and American Origins." *Ideas in America*. Cambridge, Mass.: Harvard University Press, 1944.

Jope-Slade, Robert. "Art and Electricity." *The Magazine of Art* (December 1896), 20(1):13–18.

Jordy, William H. "American Architecture Between World's Fairs: Richardson, Sullivan, McKim." *Archives of American Art Journal* (1983), 23(4):27–33.

Jordy, William H. *American Buildings and Their Architects.* Vol. 3. *Progressive and Academic Ideals at the Turn of the Twentieth Century.* Garden City, N.Y.: Doubleday, 1972.

Joseph Pennell's Liberty-Loan Poster: A Text-Book for Artists and Amateurs, Governments and Teachers and Printers, with Notes, an Introduction, and Essay on the Poster by the Artist, Associate Chairman of the Committee on Public Information, Division of Pictorial Publicity. Philadelphia: Lippincott, 1918.

Julian Eltinge Magazine and Beauty Hints: The Fascinating Widow. Central News and Press Exchange, 1904.

Jussim, Estelle. *Slave to Beauty: The Eccentric Life and Controversial Career of F. Holland Day, Photographer, Publisher, Aesthete.* Boston: Godine, 1981.

Jussim, Estelle. *Visual Communication and the Graphic Arts: Photographic Technologies in the Nineteenth Century.* New York: Bowker, Xerox Education, 1974.

Karageorgevitch, Prince Böjidar. "The Perversion of the Infant Mind in Matters of Taste." *The Magazine of Art* (January 1899), 22:119–120.

Katzman, David M. *Seven Days a Week: Women and Domestic Service in Industrializing America.* New York: Oxford University Press, 1978.

Keay, Carolyn. *American Posters of the Turn of the Century.* New York: St. Martin's Press, 1975.

Keller, Evelyn Fox and Christine R. Grontkowski. "The Mind's Eye." In Sandra Harding and Merrill B. Hintekka, eds., *Discovering Reality*, pp. 207–224. Boston: Reidel, 1983.

Keller, Helen. "An Apology for Going to College." *McClure's Magazine* (June 1905), 25(2): 190–196.

Kepes, Gyorgy. *Language of Vision.* Chicago: Theobald, 1944.

Kermode, Frank. *The Sense of an Ending: Studies in the Theory of Fiction.* New York: Oxford University Press, 1967.

Kery, Patricia Frantz. *Great Magazine Covers of the World.* New York: Abbeville, 1982.

Keyser, Samuel Jay. "There Is Method in Their Adness: The Formal Structure of Advertisement." *New Literary History* (Winter 1983), 14(3):305–334.

Kidwell, Claudia B. *Cutting a Fashionable Fit: Dressmakers' Drafting Systems in the United States.* Washington, D.C.: Smithsonian Institution Press, 1979.

Kidwell, Claudia B. and Margaret C. Christman. *Suiting Everyone: The Democratization of Clothing in America.* National Museum of History and Technology. Washington, D.C.: Smithsonian Institution Press, 1974.

King Albert's Book: A Tribute to the Belgian King and People from Representative Men and Women Throughout the World. New York: Hearst's International Library, 1914.

King, Pauline. *American Mural Painting: A Study of the Important Decorations by Distinguished Artists in the United States.* Boston: Noyes, Platt, 1902.

King, Willford Isbell. *The Wealth and Income of the People of the United States.* New York: Macmillan, 1915.

Kingsbury, Martha. "The Femme Fatale and Her Sisters." In Thomas B. Hess and Linda Nochlin, eds., *Woman as Sex Object: Studies in Erotic Art, 1730–1970.* New York: Newsweek, 1972.

Kingsbury, Martha. "Sargent's Murals in the Boston Public Library." *Winterthur Portfolio*, no. 11 (xi). Charlottesville: University of Virginia Press, 1976.

Kinkaid, Mary Holland. "The Feminine Charms of the Woman Militant: The Personal Attractiveness and Housewifely Attainments of the Leaders of the Equal Suffrage Movement." *Good Housekeeping* (February 1912), 54:146–155.

Kirkland, Edward C. *Industry Comes of Age: Business, Labor, and Public Policy, 1860–1897.* Vol. 6 of *The Economic History of the United States.* New York: Holt, Rinehart & Winston, 1961.

Klein, Cora C. *Practical Etiquette.* Chicago: Flannagan, 1899.

Knauff, Theodore C. *An Experiment in Training for the Useful and the Beautiful: A History.* Philadelphia: Philadelphia School of Design for Women, 1922.

Knoblaugh, Ralph R. *Modelmaking for Industrial Design.* New York: McGraw-Hill, 1958.

Koch, Robert. "Gibson Girl Revisited." *Art in America* (1965), 1:70–73.

Koehler, Sylvester Rosa. *American Art.* New York: 1886.

Koehler, Sylvester Rosa. *American Etchings.* Boston: 1886.

Koehler, Sylvester Rosa. "The Future of Art." *The American Art Review* (December 1879), 1(2):72–74.

Krauss, Rosalind. "Photography: A New Way of Looking, a Century of Surprises." *Vogue* (August 1982), pp. 62, 64.

Krieger, Murray. "Poetic Presence and Illusion: Renaissance Theory and the Duplicity of Metaphor." *Critical Inquiry* (Summer 1979), 5(4):597–620.

Kriehn, George. "The City Beautiful." *Municipal Affairs* (December 1899), 5(4):597–620.

Lady de Frece [Matilda Alice Powles]. *Recollections of Vesta Tilley.* London: Hutchinson, 1934.

La Farge, John. *Considerations on Painting. Lectures Given in the Year 1893 at the Metropolitan Museum of New York.* New York: 1895.

La Farge, John. "The Field of Art: The American Academy at Rome." *Scribner's Magazine* (August 1900), 28(2):253–256.

La Farge, John. "Puvis de Chavannes." *Scribner's Magazine* (December 1900), 28(6):672–684.

Laliberté, Norman and Alex Mogelon. *Silhouettes, Shadows, and Cutouts: History and Modern Use.* New York: Art Horizons, 1968.

Lancaster, Clay. "Taste at the Philadelphia Centennial." *Magazine of Art* (December 1950), 43(8):293–297.

Langbaum, Robert. "The Exteriority of Self in Yeats' Poetry and Thought." *New Literary History* (Spring 1976), 7(3):579–598.

Langdon, William Chauncy. *The Celebration of the Fourth of July by Means of Pageantry.* New York: Russell Sage Foundation, 1912.

Lanteri, Edouard. *Modelling and Sculpture: A Guide for Artists and Students.* 3 vols. New York: Dover, 1965.

Lark, The. Nos. 1–24, May 1895–April 1897. Includes "The Epi-Lark," no. 25 (May 1, 1897). San Francisco.

Larkin, Oliver W. *Art and Life in America.* Rev. ed. New York: Holt, Rinehart & Winston, 1960.

Lasch, Christopher. *Haven in a Heartless World: The Family Besieged.* New York: Basic Books, 1977.

Lathrop, George Parsons. "My Favorite Model." In F. Hopkinson Smith et al., eds., *Discussions on American Art and Artists.*

Lavater, Johann Casper. *Essays on Physiognomy, for the Promotion of the Knowledge and the Love of Mankind.* Vols. 1, 2, 3¹, 3². Thomas Holcroft, tr. 2d ed. London: 1804.

Lazarus, Emma. "The New Colossus." *The Poems of Emma Lazarus.* Vol. 2. Boston: 1889.

Lears, T. J. Jackson. "From Salvation to Self-Realization: Advertising and the Therapeutic Roots of the Consumer Culture, 1880–1930." In Richard Wightman Fox and T. J. Jackson Lears, eds., *The Culture of Consumption: Critical Essays in American History, 1880–1980,* pp. 1–38. New York: Pantheon, 1983.

Lears, T. J. Jackson. *No Place of Grace: Antimodernism and the Transformation of American Culture, 1880–1920.* New York: Pantheon, 1981.

Lears, T. J. Jackson. "Some Versions of Fantasy: Toward a Cultural History of American Advertising, 1880–1930." In Jack Salzman, ed., *Prospects 9* Cambridge: Cambridge University Press, 1984.

Lee, Vernon. "Imagination in Modern Art: Random Notes on Whistler, Sargent, and Besnard." *The Fortnightly Review* (October 1897), n.s. 62, pp. 513–521.

Leeuw, Gerardus van der. *Sacred and Profane Beauty: The Holy in Art*. David E. Green, tr. New York: Holt, Rinehart and Winston, 1963.

Le Gallienne, Richard. "A Vindication of Eve." *The Cosmopolitan* (May 1899), 27(1):55–58.

Lesy, Michael. *Time Frames: The Meaning of Family Pictures*. New York: Pantheon, 1980.

Lesy, Michael. *Wisconsin Death-Trap*. Preface by Warren Susman. New York: Pantheon, 1973.

Lewis, R. W. B. *Edith Wharton: A Biography*. New York: Harper and Row, 1974.

Lidoff, Joan, "Another Sleeping Beauty: Narcissism in *The House of Mirth*." *American Quarterly* (Winter 1980), 35(5):519–539.

Lieberson, Jonathan. "Interpreting the Interpreter." Review of *Local-Knowledge: Further Essays in Interpretive Anthropology* by Clifford Geertz. *The New York Review of Books* (March 15, 1984), pp. 39–46.

Lippmann, Walter. *Public Opinion*. New York: Harcourt, 1922.

Livermore, Mary A. *What Shall We Do with Our Daughters?* Boston: Lee & Shepard, 1883.

Living and Symbolic Design Photographs, Composed of Officers and Men in the U.S. Army and Navy Service. Mole and Thomas Photographers. 1918.

Lombroso, Cesare and William Ferrero. *The Female Offender*. London: 1895.

Lombroso-Ferrero, Gina. *Criminal Man, According to the Classification of Cesare Lombroso, with an Introduction by C. Lombroso*. Reprint, with a new introduction by Leonard D. Savitz. Montclair, N.J.: Patterson Smith, 1972.

Long, John Luther. "Madame Butterfly." *The Century* (January 1898), 55:374–392.

Louis, S. L. *Decorum: A Practical Treatise on Etiquette and Dress of the Best American Society*. Chicago: 1881.

Low, Will H. "The Art of the White City." *Scribner's Monthly Magazine* (October 1893), 14(4):504–512.

Low, Will H. *A Chronicle of Friendship, 1873–1900*. New York: Scribner's, 1908.

Low, Will H. *A Painter's Progress*. New York: Scribner's, 1910.

Low, Will H. "Photographic Appendix—Contrasts of Life and Art." In F. Hopkinson Smith et al., eds., *Discussions on American Art and Artists*.

Lubove, Roy. *The Progressives and the Slums: Tenement House Reform in New York City, 1890–1917*. Pittsburgh: University of Pittsburgh Press, 1962.

Lucas, E. V. *Edwin Austin Abbey, Royal Academician: The Record of His Life and Work*. 2 vols. New York: Scribner's, 1921.

Lynch, Gertrude. "Racial and Ideal Types of Beauty." *The Cosmopolitan* (December 1904), 38(2):223–233.

Lynes, Russell. *The Art-Makers of Nineteenth-Century America*. New York: Atheneum, 1970.

Lynes, Russell. *The Tastemakers*. New York: Harper, 1949.

Lyon, Richard Colton. Introduction, *Santayana on America*. New York: Harcourt, Brace & World, Harbinger Book, 1968.

McAleer, John J. *Theodore Dreiser: An Introduction and Interpretation*. New York: Holt, Rinehart, and Winston, 1968.

McAllister, [Samuel] Ward. *Society as I Have Found It*. New York: Arno Press, 1975; 1st ed., 1890.

McCabe, Cynthia Jaffe. *The Golden Door: Artist-Immigrants of America, 1876–1976*. Washington, D.C.: Smithsonian Institution, 1976.

McCabe, James D. *The Illustrated History of the Centennial Exhibition*. Philadelphia: National Publishing, 1876.

McCabe, Lida Rose. "Some Painters Who Happen To Be Women." *The Art World* (March 1918), 4(6):491–493.

MacColl, D. S. *Nineteenth-Century Art.* Maclehose, 1902.

McCutcheon, George Barr. *Beverly of Graustark.* New York: Dodd, Mead, 1904.

McCutcheon, George Barr. "What Is It To Be an American?" *The Field, the Country Gentleman's Newsletter* (August 31, 1918), 132(3427):193.

McCutcheon, George Barr. "When Girl Meets Girl." *Good Housekeeping* (June 1912), 54:750–760.

McMichael, George. *Journey to Obscurity: The Life of Octave Thanet.* Lincoln: University of Nebraska Press, 1965.

McVickar, Harry W. *The Evolution of Woman.* New York: Harper, 1896.

Malcolm, Janet. "Photography: Maximilian's Sombrero." *The New Yorker* (July 6, 1981), pp. 91–94.

Marandel, J. Patrice. Foreword, *Gray Is the Color: An Exhibition of Grisaille Painting.* Houston: Rice Museum, 1973–74.

Marden, Orison Swett. *Woman and Home.* New York: Crowell, 1915.

Margolin, Victor. *American Poster Renaissance.* New York: Watson-Guptill, 1975.

Margolin, Victor, Ira Brichta, and Vivian Brichta. *The Promise and the Product: 200 Years of Advertising Posters.* New York: Macmillan, 1979.

Margolis, Maxine L. *Mothers and Such: Views of American Women and Why They Changed.* Berkeley and Los Angeles: University of California Press, 1984.

Marker, Lise-Lone. *David Belasco: Naturalism in the American Theatre.* Princeton: Princeton University Press, 1974.

Marks, Edward B. *They All Had Glamour: From the Swedish Nightingale to the Naked Lady.* New York: Messner, 1944.

Marling, Karal Ann. *Wall-to-Wall America: A Cultural History of Post-Office Murals in the Great Depression.* Minneapolis: University of Minnesota Press, 1982.

Marsden, Donald. *The Long Kickline: A History of the Princeton Triangle Club.* Princeton: Princeton Triangle Club, 1968.

Marshall, Deborah Jane. "The Indian Portraits." In William I. Homer, ed., *A Pictorial Heritage: The Photographs of Gertrude Käsebier.*

Marzio, Peter C. "The Democratic Art of Chromolithography in America: An Overview." *Art and Commerce: American Prints of the Nineteenth Century.* Proceedings of a conference held in Boston, May 8–10, 1975. Museum of Fine Arts, Boston. Charlottesville: University of Virginia, 1978.

Mather, Frank J., Jr., Charles R. Morey, and William J. Henderson. *The American Spirit in Art.* Vol. 12 of *The Pageant of America.*

Matthews, Brander. "The Pictorial Poster." *The Century* (September 1892), 44(5):748–756.

Maurice, Arthur Bartlett. "Representative American Story Tellers: I—Richard Harding Davis." *The Bookman* (April 1906), 23(2):136–145.

Maxwell, Perriton. "William Merritt Chase—Artist, Wit, and Philosopher." *The Saturday Evening Post* (November 4, 1899), p. 347.

May, Elaine Tyler. *Great Expectations: Marriage and Divorce in Post-Victorian America.* Chicago: University of Chicago Press, 1980.

May, Henry F. *The End of American Innocence: A Study of the First Years of Our Own Time, 1912–1917.* Oxford: Oxford University Press, 1979.

Mayo, James. "Resymbolization of a Symbol." *Dimensions* (1981), 2(2):14–17.

Mead, George Herbert. *Mind, Self, and Society.* Charles W. Morrison, ed. Chicago: University of Chicago Press, 1934.

Medico-Actuarial Mortality Investigation. Vol. 1, *Introduction, Statistics of Height and Weight of Insured Persons*. . . . New York: Association of Life Insurance Medical Directors and the Actuarial Society of America, 1912.

Mégroz, Rodolphe Louis. *Profile Art Through the Ages: A Study of the Use and Significance of Profile and Silhouette from the Stone Age to Puppet Films*. New York: Philosophical Library, 1949.

Meisel, Martin. *Realizations: Narrative, Pictorial, and Theatrical Arts in Nineteenth-Century England*. Princeton: Princeton University Press, 1983.

Merleau-Ponty, Maurice. "The Child's Relations with Others." *The Primacy of Perception*. William Cobb, tr.; J. M. Edie, ed. Evanston: Northwestern University Press, 1964.

Merritt, Anna Lea. "A Letter to Artists: Especially Women Artists." *Lippincott's Monthly Magazine* (March 1900), 65(387):463–469.

Metzl, Ervine. *The Poster: Its History and Its Art*. New York: Watson-Guptill, 1963.

Meyer, Susan E. *America's Great Illustrators*. New York: Abrams, 1978.

Meyer, Susan E. "Howard Chandler Christy." *American Artist* (May 1978), 42:42–47, 98–101.

Meyer, Susan E. *James Montgomery Flagg*. New York: Watson-Guptill, 1974.

Michaels, Walter Benn. "The Interpreter's Self: Peirce on the Cartesian 'Subject.' " *Georgia Review* (Summer 1977), 31:383–402.

Miller, Larry C. "William James and Twentieth-Century Ethnic Thought." *American Quarterly* (Fall 1979), 31(4):533–555.

Miller, Lillian B. *Patrons and Patriotism: The Encouragement of the Fine Arts in the United States, 1790–1860*. Chicago: University of Chicago Press, 1966.

Miller, Nancy K. "Emphasis Added: Plots and Plausibilities in Women's Fiction." *PMLA* (January 1981), 96(1):36–48.

Millet, Francis D. "The Decoration at the Exposition." *Some Artists at the Fair*.

Millie, Elena and Andrea Wyatt. "Tomorrow Night, *East Lynne!* American Drama as Reflected in the Theatre Poster Collection at the Library of Congress." *The Quarterly Journal of the Library of Congress* (Winter 1980), 37(1):114–151.

Mitchell, J. A. "Types and People at the Fair." *Some Artists at the Fair*.

Mooney, Michael M. *Evelyn Nesbit and Stanford White: Love and Death in the Gilded Age*. New York: Morrow, 1976.

Morgan, Anna. *An Hour with Delsarte: A Study of Expression*. Boston: 1889.

Morgan, H. Wayne. *New Muses: Art in American Culture, 1865–1920*. Norman: University of Oklahoma, 1978.

Morison, Samuel Eliot. *The European Discovery of America: The Northern Voyages, 500–1600*. New York: Oxford University Press, 1971.

Morris, Wright, "Photographs, Images, and Words." *The American Scholar* (Autumn 1979), 48:457–469.

Mosier, Richard David. *Making the American Mind: Social and Moral Ideas in the McGuffey Readers*. New York: King's Crown Press, 1947.

Mott, Frank Luther. *Golden Multitudes: The Story of Best Sellers in the United States*. New York: Macmillan, 1947.

Mott, Frank Luther. *A History of American Magazines*. Vol. 3, *1865–1885*; vol. 4, *1885–1905*. Cambridge, Mass.: Belknap Press of Harvard University Press, 1938, 1957.

Muirhead, James Fullarton. *The Land of Contrasts: A Briton's View of His American Kin*. Boston: 1898.

Muirhead, John H. *The Platonic Tradition in Anglo-Saxon Philosophy: Studies in the History of Idealism in England and America*. London: Allen & Unwin, 1931.

Mumford, Lewis. *The Brown Decades: A Study of the Arts in America, 1865–1895*. New York: Harcourt, Brace, 1931.

Mumford, Lewis. *Sticks and Stones*. New York: Boni & Liveright, 1924.

"Mural Painting—an Art for the People and a Record of the Nation's Development." *The Craftsman* (April 1906), 10(1):54–66.

Naef, Weston J. *The Collection of Alfred Stieglitz: Fifty Pioneers of Modern Photography.* New York: Metropolitan Museum of Art, Viking Press, 1978.

National Museum of American Art. Ephemera Files:

Edwin Austin Abbey	James Montgomery Flagg
Edwin Howland Blashfield	Daniel Chester French
Mary Cassatt	Charles Dana Gibson
William Merritt Chase	J. C. Leyendecker
Howard Chandler Christy	Augustus Saint-Gaudens
Kenyon Cox	Abbott Handerson Thayer
Thomas Wilmer Dewing	James Abbott McNeill Whistler

Neuhaus, Eugen. *The History and Ideals of American Art.* Stanford: Stanford University Press, 1931.

Neuschaefer, F. L. "Psychology of Posters." *The American Art Student* (February 16–March 30, 1922), 4(6):5–6.

"New Woman, The." *New York World* (August 18, 1895), p. 25.

Newhall, Beaumont. *The History of Photography from 1839 to the Present Day.* Rev. and enl. ed. Museum of Modern Art, in collaboration with the George Eastman House. Garden City, N.Y.: Doubleday, 1964.

Nietz, John A. *Old Textbooks.* Pittsburgh: University of Pittsburgh Press, 1961.

Nirdlinger, C. F. "Plays and Players." Review of "The Masqueraders," by Henry Arthur Jones. *The Illustrated American* (December 22, 1894), pp. 9–13.

Norris, Frank. *The Literary Criticism of Frank Norris.* Donald Pizer, ed. Austin: University of Texas Press, 1964.

Norris, Frank. "A Question of Ideals: The American Girl of 1896 as Seen by Wenzel [sic] and by Gibson." *Wave* (December 26, 1896), p. 7. *The Literary Criticism of Frank Norris.*

Norris, Frank. *Vandover and the Brute.* Vol. 5 of *Complete Works of Frank Norris.* Port Washington, N.Y.: Kennikat Press, 1967; 1st ed., 1914.

Norris, Frank. "Why Women Should Write the Best Novels; and Why They Don't." *Boston Evening Transcript* (November 13, 1901), p. 20. *The Literary Criticism of Frank Norris.*

"Notes and Clippings: 'The Statue of Liberty.' " *The American Architect and Building News* (March 30, 1878), 3 (118):116.

"Nym Crinkle's Feuilleton." Review of "The Woman Hater," by D. D. Lloyd. *New York Dramatic Mirror* (March 3, 1888), 19 (479):1.

Oakey, Miss. [Maria Richards]. *Beauty in Dress.* New York: 1881.

Oertel, J. F. *A Vision Realized: A Life Story of Rev. J. A. Oertel, D. D., Artist, Priest, Missionary.* Boston: Christopher Publishing, 1928.

O'Hagan, Anne. "The Art of Facial Expression." *Harper's Bazar* (June 1906), 40(6):502–510.

"On the Elongation of Form." *Camera Work* (April 1905), 10:27–35.

Ormond, Richard. *John Singer Sargent: Paintings, Drawings, Water-colors.* London: Phaidon, 1970.

Orton, William Aylott. *America in Search of Culture.* Boston: Little, Brown, 1933.

Our Girls: Poems in Praise of the American Girl, with Illustrations by Howard Chandler Christy. New York: Moffat, Yard, 1907.

"Over-Illustration." *Harper's Weekly* (July 29, 1911), 55:6.

Pageant of America, The: A Pictorial History of the United States. 15 vols. Ralph Henry Gabriel, ed. New Haven: Yale University Press, 1925–29.

Palliser's Memorials and Headstones, Also Mottos for Monuments, Epitaphs for Study or Application. New York: 1891.

Palmenberg, J. R. *Display Forms.* New York: 1883.

Parsons, Talcott. "Definitions of Health and Illness in the Light of American Values and Social Structures." *Social Structures and Personality.* New York: Free Press, 1964.

Partridge, William Ordway. *The Angel of Clay.* New York: Putnam's, 1900.

Partridge, William Ordway. *Art for America.* Boston: 1894.

Partridge, William Ordway. *Technique of Sculpture.* Boston: 1895.

Paulson, Ronald. *Emblem and Expression: Meaning in English Art of the Eighteenth Century.* Cambridge, Mass.: Harvard University Press, 1975.

Pauly, Thomas H. "In Search of 'The Spirit of '76.'" *American Quarterly* (Fall 1976), 28(4):444–464.

Peck, Harry Thurston. "For Maids and Mothers." *The Cosmopolitan* (June 1899), 27(2):149–162.

Peirce, Charles Sanders. *Charles S. Peirce: Selected Writings (Values in a Universe of Chance).* Philip P. Wiener, ed. New York: Dover, 1966.

Perlman, Bennard B. *The Immortal Eight: American Painting from Eakins to the Armory Show (1870–1913).* New York: Exposition Press, 1962.

Perosa, Sergio. *Henry James and the Experimental Novel.* Charlottesville: University Press of Virginia, 1978.

Perry, Lewis. *Intellectual Life in America: A History.* New York: Franklin Watts, 1984.

Perry, Ralph Barton. *Present Philosophical Tendencies: A Critical Survey of Naturalism, Idealism, Pragmatism, and Realism Together with a Synopsis of the Philosophy of William James.* New York: Longmans, Green, 1912.

Persons, Stow. *The Decline of American Gentility.* New York: Columbia University Press, 1973.

Petersen, Karen and J. J. Wilson. *Women Artists: Recognition and Reappraisal from the Early Middle Ages to the Twentieth Century.* New York: Harper & Row, Colophon Books, 1976.

Peterson, Anne E. "American Women in Photography: A Historical Overview, 1850–1945." *Women Look at Women.* Library of Congress Traveling Exhibition.

Phillips, Mary Elizabeth. *Reminiscences of William Wetmore Story.* Chicago: 1897.

Pierce, Patricia Jobe. *Edmund C. Tarbell and the Boston School of Painting, 1889–1980.* John Douglas Ingraham, ed. Hingham, Mass.: Pierce Galleries, 1980.

Pierce, Patricia Jobe. *The Ten.* North Abington, Mass.: Pierce Galleries, 1976.

Pisano, Ronald G. *A Leading Spirit in American Art: William Merritt Chase.* Seattle: Henry Art Gallery, 1983.

Pisano, Ronald G. *William Merritt Chase.* New York: Watson-Guptill, 1979.

Pitz, Henry C. "Charles Dana Gibson." *The American Artist* (December 1956), 20 (10):50–55.

Pollard's Artistic Tableaux. New York: 1887.

Porter, Carolyn. *Seeing and Being: The Plight of the Participant Observer in Emerson, James, Adams, and Faulkner.* Middletown, Conn.: Wesleyan University Press, 1981.

Potter, David Morris. *History and American Society: Essays of David M. Potter.* Don E. Fehrenbacher, ed. New York: Oxford University Press, 1973.

Potter, Vincent G. *Charles S. Peirce: On Norms and Ideals.* Worcester: University of Massachusetts Press, 1967.

Pratt Institute, Brooklyn, New York, School of Fine and Applied Arts. Circular of Information: Day Courses, 1920–1921.

Preliminary Material for Teachers Using the Primary Course of Instruction in Drawing of the American Text-Books of Art Education. Boston: Prang, 1881.

Presbry, Frank S. *The History and Development of Advertising.* Garden City, N.Y.: Doubleday, Doran, 1929.

Price, C. Matlack. "Arts and Decorations—the Essentials of the Poster: The Appeal of an Informal Art." *Arts and Decoration* (September 1913), 3(11):374–376.

Price, C. Matlack. *Poster Design: A Critical Study of the Development of the Poster in Continental Europe, England, and America.* Enl. ed. New York: Bricka, 1922.

Price, C. Matlack and Horace Brown. *How To Put It—Patriotic Posters—the Stuff That Makes People Stop—Look—Act!* Washington, D.C.: National Committee of Patriotic Societies, 1918.

Prichard, J. V. *Tableaux Vivants for Amateur Representation.* New York: French, n.d.

"Quest for Unity, The: American Art Between World's Fairs, 1876–1893. Papers from a Symposium." *Archives of American Art Journal* (1983), 23(4):7.

Quick, Michael. *American Expatriate Painters of the Late Nineteenth Century.* Dayton: Dayton Art Institute, 1976.

Quick, Michael. *American Portraiture in the Grand Manner, 1720–1920.* Los Angeles: Los Angeles County Museum of Art, 1981.

Quilter, Harry. "The New Renaissance; or, The Gospel of Intensity." *Appleton's Journal* (November 1880), n.s. 53, pp. 453–460.

Quimby, Ian. *Material Culture and the Study of American Life.* H. F. Du Pont Museum, Winterthur, Del. New York: Norton, 1978.

Ralph, Julian. *People We Pass: Stories of Life Among the Masses of New York City.* New York: Harper, 1896.

Rankin, W. "Art in America: Current Notes." *The Burlington Magazine for Connoisseurs* (June 1908), 13(63):185–186.

Ratcliff, Carter, *John Singer Sargent.* New York: Abbeville 1982.

Reff, Theodore. "Le Papillon et le Vieux Boeuf." In *From Realism to Symbolism: Whistler and His World,* pp. 23–29.

Reich, Sheldon. *Alfred H. Maurer, 1868–1932.* Washington, D.C.: Smithsonian Institution Press, 1973.

Reitano, Joanne. "Working Girls Unite." *American Quarterly* (Spring 1984), 36(1):112–134.

Report to the President on Bent-Wood Furniture. United States Tariff Commission. Report no. 28, 2d series, 1930.

Richardson, George. *Iconology; or, A Collection of Emblematical Figures, Moral and Instructive.* 2 vols. London: 1779.

Richman, Michael. *Daniel Chester French: An American Sculptor.* Postscript by Paul W. Ivory. New York: Metropolitan Museum of Art for the National Trust for Historic Preservation, 1976.

Rickards, Maurice. *Posters of the First World War.* London: Evelyn, Adams & Macay, 1968.

Riis, Jacob A. *How the Other Half Lives: Studies Among the Tenements of New York.* Sam Bass Warner, Jr., ed. Cambridge, Mass.: John Harvard Library, Belknap Press of Harvard University Press, 1970.

Rio, Michel. "Images and Words." *New Literary History* (Spring 1976), 7(3):505–512.

Robinson, Charles Mulford. *Modern Civic Art, or The City Made Beautiful.* New York: Putnam's, 1904.

Robinson, Frederick B. "Erastus Salisbury Field." *Art in America* (October 1942), 30:244–253.

Robinson, Lillian S. and Lise Vogel. "Modernism and History." In Susan Koppelman Cornillon, ed., *Images of Women in Fiction: Feminist Perspective.* Bowling Green: Bowling Green Popular Press, 1973.

Rocine, V. G. *Heads, Faces, Types, Races.* Chicago: Vaught-Rocine, 1910.

Roe, Frederic Gordon. *Women in Profile: A Study in Silhouette.* London: Baker, 1970.

Ron, Moshe. "A Reading of 'The Real Thing.' " *Yale French Studies* (1979), 58:190–212.

Rood, Roland. "On Plagiarism." *Camera Work* (April 1905), 10:17–24.

Rosen, Charles and Henri Zerner. *Romanticism and Realism: The Mythology of Nineteenth-Century Art.* New York: Viking, 1984.

Rosenberg, Edgar. *From Shylock to Svengali: Jewish Stereotypes in English Fiction.* Stanford: Stanford University Press, 1960.

Rosenzweig, Phyllis D. *The Thomas Eakins Collection of the Hirshhorn Museum and Sculpture Garden.* Washington, D.C.: Smithsonian Institution Press, 1977.

Royce, Josiah. *The Basic Writings of Josiah Royce.* 2 vols. John J. McDermott, ed. Chicago: University of Chicago Press, 1969.

Royce, Josiah. "Later Problems of Idealism and Its Present Position." *Lectures on Modern Idealism.* New Haven: Yale University Press, 1919.

Royce, Josiah. *The Letters of Josiah Royce.* John Clendenning, ed. Chicago: University of Chicago Press, 1970.

Rubinstein, Charlotte Streifer. *American Women Artists from Early Indian Times to the Present.* Boston and New York: G. K. Hall and Avon Books, 1982.

Ruskin, John. *Modern Painters.* Vol. 1. New York: 1872.

Ryan, Daniel Edward. *Human Proportions in Growth: Being the Complete Measurement of the Human Body for Every Age and Size During the Years of Juvenile Growth, with Full Instructions for Use in Proportioning Garments.* New York: 1880.

Said, Edward W. *Beginnings: Intention and Method.* Baltimore: Johns Hopkins University Press, 1975.

Saint-Gaudens, Augustus. *The Reminiscences of Augustus Saint-Gaudens.* Homer Saint-Gaudens, ed. New York: Century, 1913.

Saint-Gaudens, Homer. "Abbott H. Thayer." *The International Studio* (January 1908), 33(131):81–87.

Saint-Gaudens, Homer. *The American Artist and His Times.* New York: Dodd, Mead, 1941.

Sanburn, Frederick. *A Delsartean Scrap-Book.* New York: 1890.

Santayana, George. "The Genteel Tradition in American Philosophy." *The Genteel Tradition: Nine Essays by George Santayana.* Douglas L. Wilson, ed. Cambridge, Mass.: Harvard University Press, 1967.

Schau, Michael. *"All-American Girl"—the Art of Coles Phillips.* New York: Watson-Guptill, 1975.

Schau, Michael. *J. C. Leyendecker.* New York: Watson-Guptill, 1974.

Schenk, Charles. *Draperies in Action, a Monthly Publication. Complete in Six Parts, Each Part Containing Six Plates.* New York: Schenk, 1902.

Schlereth, Thomas J. *Artifacts and the American Past.* Nashville: American Association for State and Local History, 1980.

Schneider, Norris F. *Howard Chandler Christy.* Zanesville, Ohio: 1975.

Scholnick, Robert. "Between Realism and Romanticism: The Curious Career of Eugene Benson." *American Literary Realism* (Autumn 1981), 14(2):242–253.

Schuyler, Montgomery. "Last Words About the World's Fair." In William H. Jordy and Ralph Coe, eds., *American Architecture and Other Writings,* vol. 2. Cambridge, Mass.: Belknap Press of Harvard University Press, 1961.

Secrest, Meryle. *Between Me and Life: A Biography of Romaine Brooks.* Garden City, N.Y.: Doubleday, 1974.

Sedgwick, Henry Dwight. *The New American Type and Other Essays.* Boston: Houghton, Mifflin, 1908.

Segre, Cesare. "Culture and Modeling Systems." *Critical Inquiry* (Spring 1978), 4(3):525–538.

Sellin, David. "Eakins and the Macdowells and the Academy." *Thomas Eakins, Susan Macdowell Eakins, Elizabeth Macdowell Kenton: An Exhibition of Paintings, Photographs, and Artifacts.* Roanoke, Va.: Progress Press, 1977.

Sennett, Richard. *Authority.* New York: Knopf, 1980.

Series of Lithographic Drawings Illustrative of the Relation Between the Human Physiognomy and That of the Brute Creation, A. From Designs by Charles Le Brun, with Remarks on the System. J. P. Blanquet, ed. London: 1827.

Shannon, Fred Albert. *The Centennial Years: A Political and Economic History of America from the Late 1870s to the Early 1890s.* Robert H. Jones, ed. Garden City, N.Y.: Doubleday, 1967.

Sheldon, George William. *American Painters.* New York: 1881.

Sheldon, George William. *Recent Ideals of American Art.* New York: 1888, 1889, 1890.

Sherwood, M. E. W. *The Art of Entertaining.* New York: Dodd, Mead, 1893.

Sherwood, M. E. W. "New England Women." *The Atlantic Monthly* (August 1878), 42(250):230–237.

Sherwood, M. E. W. "Some Society Tableaux." *The Cosmopolitan* (January 1898), 24(3):235–246.

Shover, Michele J. "Roles and Images of Women in World War I Propaganda." *Politics and Society* (1975), 5(4):469–486.

Sikes, Mrs. G. R. [Ellen L.]. *American Heroines: An Entertainment for Churches and Church Societies, Secular Societies, and Lodges.* Dayton: Lorenz, 1900.

Silk, Mark. "Notes on the Judeo-Christian Tradition in America." *American Quarterly* (Spring 1984), 36(1):65–85.

Simms, Joseph. *Physiognomy Illustrated; or, Nature's Revelations of Character: A Description of the Mental, Moral, and Volitive Dispositions of Mankind, as Manifested in the Human Form and Countenance.* 6th ed. New York: Murray Hill, 1891.

Sizeranne, Robert de la. "Is Photography Among the Fine Arts? A Symposium—1." *The Magazine of Art* (January 1899), 22:102–105.

s'Jacob, Henriette E. *Idealism and Realism: A Study of Sepulchral Symbolism.* Leiden: Brill, 1954.

Sky, Alison and Michelle Stone. *Unbuilt America: Forgotten Architects in the United States from Thomas Jefferson to the Space Age.* New York: McGraw-Hill, 1976.

Sloan, Helen F. *American Art Nouveau: Poster Period of John Sloan.* Lock Haven, Pa.: Hammermill Printing, 1967.

Sloan, Kay. "Sexual Warfare in the Silent Cinema: Comedies and Melodramas of Woman Suffragism." *American Quarterly* (Fall 1981), 33(4):412–436.

Smith, F. Hopkinson. "The Picturesque Side." In *Some Artists at the Fair.*

Smith, F. Hopkinson et al., eds. *Discussions on American Art and Artists.* Boston, New York, Chicago, San Francisco: American Art League, [1893].

Smith, Gerald Birney, ed. *Religious Thought in the Last Quarter-Century.* Chicago: University of Chicago Press, 1927.

Smith, James Ward and A. Leland Jamison, eds. *The Shaping of American Religion.* Vol. 1 of *Religion in American Life.* Princeton: Princeton University Press, 1961.

Smith, Nora Archibald. *Plays, Pantomimes, and Tableaux for Children.* New York: Moffat, Yard, 1918.

Smith-Rosenberg, Carroll. *Disorderly Conduct. Visions of Gender in Victorian America.* New York: Knopf, 1985.

Snyder, Joel. "Picturing Vision." *Critical Inquiry* (Spring 1980), 6(3):499–526.

Snyder, Joel and Neil Walsh Allen. "Photography, Vision, and Representation." *Critical Inquiry* (Autumn 1975), 2(1):143–169.

Sollors, Werner. "Dr. Benjamin Franklin's Celestial Telegraph, or Indian Blessing to Gas-Lit American Drawing Rooms." *American Quarterly* (Winter 1983), 35(5):459–480.

Some Artists at the Fair. New York: Scribner's, 1893.

Some Examples of the Work of American Designers: Dill and Collins, Co., Papermakers. Philadelphia, New York, Boston: 1918.

Sontag, Susan. *On Photography.* New York: Farrar, Straus & Giroux, 1977.

Soper, Henry M. *The New Peerless Speaker and Complete Program Containing the Best Orations, Humorous, Dramatic, and Patriotic Readings and Recitations.* Chicago: 1902.

Soria, Regina. *Perceptions and Evocations: The Art of Elihu Vedder.* Washington, D.C.: National Collection of Fine Arts,, 1979.

Sousa, John Philip. *National Patriotic and Typical Airs of All Lands.* Philadelphia: 1890.

Sparling, Tobin Andrews. *The Great Exhibition: A Question of Taste.* New Haven: Yale Center for British Art, 1982.

Spencer, Anna Garlin. *Women's Share in Social Culture.* New York: Kennerley, 1912.

Spielmann, M. H. "Curiosities of Art: Coincidences and Resemblances in Works of Art." Parts 1 and 2. *The Magazine of Art.* (November and December 1922), 22:16–23, 70–78.

Spilka, Mark. "Henry James and Walter Besant: 'The Art of Fiction' Controversy." *Novel* (Winter 1973), 6(2):101–119.

Springer, Mary Doyle. *A Rhetoric of Literary Character: Some Women of Henry James.* Chicago: University of Chicago Press, 1978.

Staley, Allen. "Whistler and His World." In *From Realism to Symbolism: Whistler and His World.*

Starr, Kevin. *Americans and the California Dream, 1850–1915.* New York: Oxford University Press, 1973.

Starr, Martin Kenneth. *Product Design and Decision Theory.* Englewood Cliffs, N.J.: Prentice-Hall, 1963.

Stebbins, Genevieve. *Delsarte System of Expression.* 6th ed. New York: Werner, 1902.

Stebbins, Theodore E., Jr. *The Life and Works of Martin Johnson Heade.* New Haven: Yale University Press, 1975.

Steele, Valerie. *Fashion and Eroticism: Ideals of Feminine Beauty from the Victorian Era to the Jazz Age.* New York: Oxford University Press, 1985.

Stein, Allen F. *After the Vows Were Spoken: Marriage in American Literary Realism.* Columbus: Ohio State University Press, 1984.

Stein, Gertrude. *The Autobiography of Alice B. Toklas.* New York: Random House, 1933.

Stein, Gertrude. "Composition as Explanation," "The Gradual Making of *The Making of Americans*," "Henry James," "Portraits and Repetitions," "What Are Master-pieces and Why Are There So Few of Them." *Look at Me Now and Here I Am: Writings and Lectures, 1909–1945.* Patricia Meyerowitz, ed. Baltimore: Penguin, 1971.

Stein, Gertrude. "Melanctha." *Three Lives.* New York: Modern Library, 1933; 1st ed., 1909.

Stein, Leon. *The Triangle Fire.* Philadelphia: Lippincott, 1962.

Stein, Roger B. *John Ruskin and Aesthetic Thought in America, 1840–1900.* Cambridge, Mass.: Harvard University Press, 1967.

Steiner, George. "The Distribution of Discourse." *On Difficulty and Other Essays.* New York: Oxford University Press, 1978.

Steiner, Wendy. *Exact Resemblance to Exact Resemblance: The Literary Portraiture of Gertrude Stein.* New Haven: Yale University Press, 1978.

Stephens, Kate. "The New England Woman." *The Atlantic Monthly* (July 1901), 88:60–66.

Stillman, William J. "The Decay of Art." *The New Princeton Review* (July 1886), 2(1):20–36.

Stocking, Sarah L. *Shadow Pictures.* 1884.

Stone, Gregory P. "Appearance and the Self." In Mary Ellen Roach and Joanne Bubolz Eicher, eds., *Dress, Adornment, and the Social Order.* New York: Wiley, 1965.

Story of the Saturday Morning Club of Boston, The. Organized by Mrs. Julia Ward Howe and Mrs. Robert E. Apthorp, November Second, Eighteen Hundred and Seventy-One, on the Occasion of Its Sixtieth Birthday. Boston: Wall, 1932.

Stowe, Harriet Beecher. *Uncle Tom's Cabin; or, Life Among the Lowly.* 2 vols. Boston: 1852.

Strong, Josiah. *Our Country: Its Possible Future and Its Present Crisis.* Rev. ed., based on the census of 1890. New York: 1885, 1891.

Sturgis, Russell. *The Appreciation of Pictures: A Handbook.* New York: Baker and Taylor, 1905.

Sturgis, Russell. *The Appreciation of Sculpture.* New York: Baker & Taylor, 1904.

Suffrage Parade. Hearings Before a Subcommittee of the Committee on the District of Columbia, United States Senate. Part 1 (March 6–17, 1913). Washington, D.C.: GPO, 1913.

Sullivan, Mark. *Our Times: The United States, 1900–1925.* 5 vols. New York: Scribner's, 1927–1933.

Sully, James. *Outlines of Psychology with Special Reference to the Theory of Education.* London: 1884.

Sumner, William Graham. *Folkways: A Study of the Sociological Importance of Usages, Manners, Customs, Mores, and Morals.* Boston: Ginn, 1907.

Susman, Warren I. " 'Personality' and the Making of Twentieth-Century Culture." In Higham and Conkin, eds., *New Directions in American Intellectual History.*

Symonds, J. A. *Sketches and Studies in Southern Europe.* New York: 1880.

Szarkowski, John. *The Photographer's Eye.* Museum of Modern Art. Garden City, N.Y.: Doubleday, 1966.

Taft, Lorado. "Women Sculptors of America." *The Mentor* (February 1, 1919), vol. 6, no. 24.

Taft, Robert. *Photography and the American Scene: A Social History, 1839–1889.* New York: Macmillan, 1938.

Taft, William Nelson. *Department-Store Advertising.* Scranton: International Textbook, 1929.

Talbot, George. *At Home: Domestic Life in the Post-Centennial Era, 1876–1920. An Exhibition, Spring 1976–Fall 1977.* Milwaukee: State Historical Society of Wisconsin, 1976.

Taplin, Oliver. "Difficult Daughter." Review of *Antigones*, by George Steiner. *The New York Review of Books* (December 6, 1984) 31(9):13–16.

Tarbell, Ida M. *The Business of Being a Woman.* New York: Macmillan, 1912.

Taylor, Joshua C. *America as Art.* National Collection of Fine Arts. Washington, D.C.: Smithsonian Institution Press, 1976.

Taylor, Joshua C. *The Fine Arts in America.* Chicago: University of Chicago Press, 1979.

Tharp, Ezra. "T. W. Dewing." *Art and Progress* (March 1914), 5(5):155–161.

Tharp, Louise Hall. *Saint-Gaudens and the Gilded Age.* Boston: Little, Brown, 1969.

Thayer, Gerald H. *Concealing-Coloration in the Animal Kingdom, an Exposition of the Laws of Disguise Through Color and Pattern: Being a Summary of Abbott H. Thayer's Discoveries.* New York: Macmillan, 1909.

This Fabulous Century: Sixty Years of American Life. Vol. 1, *1900–1910.* New York: Time-Life Books, 1969.

Thomas Eakins: His Photographic Works. Philadelphia: Pennsylvania Academy of the Fine Arts, 1969.

Thonet: Thonet Bentwood and Other Furniture. The 1904 Illustrated Catalogue. Introduction by Christopher Wilk. New York: Dover, 1980.

Thorp, Margaret Ferrand. *The Literary Sculptors.* Durham, N.C.: Duke University Press, 1965.

Ticknor, Caroline. *May Alcott: A Memoir.* Boston: Little, Brown, 1928.

Ticknor, Caroline. "The Steel-Engraving Lady and the Gibson Girl." *The Atlantic Monthly* (July 1901), 88:105–108.

Toll, Robert C. *On with the Show: The First Century of Show Business in America.* New York: Oxford University Press, 1976.

Tomes, Robert. *The Bazar Book of Decorum: The Care of the Person, Manners, Etiquette, and Ceremonials.* New York: 1870.

Tomsich, John. *A Genteel Endeavor: American Culture and Politics in the Gilded Age.* Stanford; Stanford University Press, 1971.

"Topics of the Times—American Art." *Scribner's Monthly Magazine* (November 1876), 13(1):126–127.

"Topics of the Times—Home and Society." *Scribner's Monthly Magazine* (April 1877), 13(6):870–871.

Trachtenberg, Alan. *The Incorporation of America: Culture and Society in the Gilded Age.* New York: Hill & Wang, 1982.

Trachtenberg, Alan. Introduction, *Democratic Vistas, 1860–1880.* New York: Braziller, 1970.

Trachtenberg, Marvin. *The Statue of Liberty.* New York: Viking, 1976.

Tracy, Marguerite. "Shadows of the Artist's Ideal." In F. Hopkinson Smith et al., eds., *Discussions on American Art and Artists*, pp. 257–261.

Tufte, Virginia and Barbara Myerhoff, eds. *Changing Images of the Family.* New Haven: Yale University Press, 1979.

Turner, Victor W. *The Ritual Process: Structure and Anti-Structure.* Harmondsworth, Eng: Penguin/Pelican, 1974.

Twain, Mark. *The Diaries of Adam and Eve.* New York: American Heritage Press, 1971.

Twain, Mark. *Roughing It.* Vol. 2 of *The Works of Mark Twain.* Berkeley and Los Angeles: University of California Press, 1972.

Twain, Mark. *The Tragedy of Pudd'nhead Wilson and The Comedy of Those Extraordinary Twins.* Hartford, Conn.: American Publishing, 1894.

Twyman, Robert W. *History of Marshall Field and Co., 1852–1906.* Philadelphia: University of Pennsylvania Press, 1954.

Tytler, Graeme. *Physiognomy in the European Novel: Faces and Fortunes.* Princeton: Princeton University Press, 1982.

Uhlenberg, Peter R. "A Study of Cohort Life Cycles: Cohorts of Native Born Massachusetts Women, 1830–1920." *Population Studies, a Journal of Demography* (November 1969), 23(3):407–420.

United States Centennial Commission, International Exhibition, 1876: Reports and Awards. Group 26 (Architecture and Engineering) and Group 28 (Education and Science). Francis A. Walker, ed. Philadelphia: 1877–78.

Vail, Henry. *A History of the McGuffey Readers. The Bookish Books.* Vol. 4. Cleveland: privately printed, 1910.

Van Brunt, Henry. *Architecture and Society: Selected Essays of Henry Van Brunt.* William A. Coles, ed. Cambridge, Mass.: Belknap Press of Harvard University Press, 1969.

Van Brunt, Henry. "Architecture at the World's Columbian Exposition." *The Century.* Part 1 (May 1892), 44(1):81–99; part 4 (September 1892), 44(5):720–731; part 5 (October 1892), 44(6):897–907.

Van Brunt, Henry. "The New Dispensation of Monumental Art: The Decoration of Trinity Church in Boston, and of the New Assembly Chamber at Albany." *The Atlantic Monthly* (May 1879), 43(259):633–641.

Van Rensselaer, Mrs. John King. "The Basis of New York Society." *The Cosmopolitan* (August 1899), 27(4):350–368.

Van Rensselaer, Mariana. Appendix. In *The Blessed Damozel by Dante Gabriel Rossetti with Drawings by Kenyon Cox.*

Van Rensselaer, Mariana. Preface. In *Book of American Figure Painters.*

Veblen, Thorstein. *The Theory of the Leisure Class: An Economic Study of Institutions.* New York: 1899.

Vedder, Elihu. *The Digressions of V.* New York: Johnson Reprint, 1970; 1st ed., 1910.

Vermeule, Cornelius C. *Numismatic Art in America: Aesthetics of the United States Coinage.* Cambridge, Mass.: Belknap Press of Harvard University Press, 1971.

Vernay, Arthur S. *The Silhouette [The Collector, vol. 1, no. 2]*. New York: 1911.

Vinton, Frederic P. "William Morris Hunt: II: The Memorial Exhibition—the Paintings at Albany." *The American Art Review* (January 1880), 1(3):93–103.

Von Steinwehr, Arnold and D. G. Brinton. *An Intermediate Geography*. New York: 1878.

Wagnenknecht, Edward. *American Profile, 1900–1909*. Amherst: University of Massachusetts Press, 1982.

Wallach, Alan. "Thomas Cole and the Aristocracy." *Arts Magazine* (November 1981), 56:94–106.

Walton, Kendall L. "Transparent Pictures: On the Nature of Photographic Realism." *Critical Inquiry* (December 1984), 11(2):246–277.

Walton, William. "The Field of Art—Mural Painting in This Country Since 1898." *Scribner's Monthly Magazine* (November 1906), 40(5):637–640.

Ward, Hetta Lord Hayes. "Fine Arts—the Art of the Shop Windows." *The Independent* (December 29, 1892), 44(2300):7(1859)–8(1860).

Warman, Edward B. *Gestures and Attitudes: An Exposition of the Delsarte Philosophy of Expression, Practical and Theoretical*. Boston: 1892.

Warren, Sidney. *American Freethought, 1860–1914*. New York: Gordian Press, 1966.

Wasserstrom, William. *The Heiress of All the Ages: Sex and Sentiment in the Genteel Tradition*. Minneapolis: University of Minnesota Press, 1959.

Webster, Jean. *Daddy-Long-Legs*. Illustrations by the author. New York: Century, 1912.

Weigle, Luther A. *American Idealism*. Vol. 10 of *The Pageant of America*.

Weimann, Jeanne Madeline. *The Fair Women*. Introduction by Anita Miller. Chicago: Academy Chicago, 1981.

Weinberg, H. Barbara. "The Career of Francis Davis Millet." *Archives of American Art Journal* (1977), 17(1):2–18.

Weinberg, H. Barbara. "Late-Nineteenth-Century American Painting: Cosmopolitan Concerns and Critical Controversies." *Archives of American Art Journal* (1983), 23(4):19–26.

Weinberg, H. Barbara. "The Lure of Paris: Late-Nineteenth-Century American Painters and Their French Training." In Theodore F. Stebbins, Jr., Carol Troyen, and Trevor J. Fairbrother, eds., *A New World: Masterpieces of American Painting, 1760–1910*. Boston: Museum of Fine Arts, 1983.

Weinberg, H. Barbara, ed. Introduction, *Illustrated Catalogue: The Masterpieces of the Centennial International Exhibition, 1876*. 3 vols. Vol. 1, Edward Strahan, *The Art Gallery* (Philadelphia 1876); vol. 2, Walter Smith, *Industrial Art* (Philadelphia 1877). From A Garland Series: The Art Experience in Late Nineteenth-Century America. New York: Garland, 1977.

Weitenkampf, Frank. *The Illustrated Book*. Cambridge, Mass.: Harvard University Press, 1938.

Weld, Martha Coles. *Illustrated Tableaux for Amateurs*. Vol. 1. New York: 1886.

Welling, William. *Photography in America: The Formative Years, 1839–1900*. New York: Crowell, 1978.

Welter, Barbara. *Dimity Convictions: The American Woman in the Nineteenth Century*. Athens: Ohio University Press, 1976.

West, Richard V. *Occasional Papers 1—the Walker Art Building Murals*. Brunswick, Maine: Bowdoin College, Museum of Art, 1972.

Wharton, Edith. *The Age of Innocence*. New York: Appleton, 1920.

Wharton, Edith. *The Book of the Homeless*. New York: Scribner's, 1916.

Wharton, Edith. *The Custom of the Country*. New York: Scribner's, 1913.

Wharton, Edith. *The House of Mirth*. New York: Scribner's, 1905.

"Which Is the American Princess? Gertrude Vanderbilt . . . or Bertha Krieg, the Bowery Girl?" *New York Journal* (January 12, 1896), p. 27.

Whitby, J. E. "The Art Movement: An Unusual Form of Decorative Art." *The Magazine of Art* (December 1898), 22:83–87.

White, Frank Liston. "Fifty Years of Book Illustrating in the United States." part 2. *The Independent* (January 28, 1892), 44(2252):119.

White, Frank Liston. "Our Women in Art." *The Independent* (August 1892), 44(2282):1187.

White, John. *The Birth and Rebirth of Pictorial Space*. London: Faber & Faber, 1957.

White, Nelson C. *Abbott H. Thayer: Painter and Naturalist*. Hartford: Connecticut Printers, 1951.

White, Nelson C. Foreword, *Abbott H. Thayer, 1849–1921*. New London, Conn.: Lyman Allyn Museum, 1961.

White, Stanford. "Intimate Letters of Stanford White: Correspondence with His Friend and Co-worker, Augustus Saint-Gaudens." Homer Saint-Gaudens, ed. In *The Architectural Record* (August 1911), 30(2):106–116; (September 1911), 30(3):283–298; (October 1911), 30(4):399–406.

Whitehall, Walter Muir. "The Vicissitudes of Bacchante in Boston." *The New England Quarterly* (December 1954), 27:435–454.

Wiebe, Robert H. *The Search for Order, 1877–1920*. New York: Hill & Wang, 1967.

Wight, P. B. "On the Present Condition of Architectural Art in the Western States." *The American Art Review* (February 1880), 1(4):137–143.

Wilbor, Elsie M., ed. *Delsarte Recitation Book and Directory*. New York: 1890.

Wilhelm, C. "Flowers and Fancies: From the Garden to the Stage." *The Magazine of Art*. (November 1898), 22;1–8.

Wilk, Christopher. *Thonet: 150 Years of Furniture*. Woodbury, N.Y.: Barron's, 1980.

Wilkinson, Burke. *Uncommon Clay: The Life and Work of Augustus Saint-Gaudens*. New York: Harcourt Brace Jovanovich, 1985.

Willard, Ellen M. *Pictured Readings and Tableaux*. Chicago: Denison, 1915.

Williamson, C. N. and A. M. *The Princess Passes: A Romance of a Motor-Car*. New York: Holt, 1905.

Williamson, Judith. *Decoding Advertisements: Ideology and Meaning in Advertising*. London: Boyars, 1978.

Wills, Garry. "Washington's Citizen Virtue: Greenough and Houden." *Critical Inquiry* (March 1984), 10(3):420–441.

Wilmerding, John. "The American Object: Still-Life Paintings." In *An American Perspective*.

Wilson, Douglas L. Introduction, Santayana, *The Genteel Tradition: Nine Essays by George Santayana*.

Wilson, Edmund. *Axel's Castle*. New York: Scribner's, 1931.

Wilson, Ellen. *An American Painter in Paris: A Life of Mary Cassatt*. New York: Farrar, Straus and Giroux, 1971.

Wilson, Margaret Gibbons. *The American Woman in Transition: The Urban Influence, 1870–1920*. Westport, Conn.: Greenwood Press, 1979.

Wilson, Richard Guy. "The Great Civilization—Cultural Conditions." *The American Renaissance, 1876–1917*. New York: Brooklyn Museum, 1979.

Winner, Viola Hopkins. *Henry James and the Visual Arts*. Charlottesville: University Press of Virginia, 1970.

Withers, Josephine. *Women Artists in Washington Collections: Her Feminine Colleagues. Photographs and Letters Collected by Frances Benjamin Johnston in 1900*, by Toby Quitslund. College Park: Maryland Art Gallery and Women's Caucus for Art, 1979.

Wolff, Cynthia Griffin. *A Feast of Words. The Triumph of Edith Wharton*. New York: Oxford University Press, 1977.

Wolff, William Almon. "Leading Advertising Experts Commend Success of Marines' Publicity Campaign." *The Marines' Bulletin* (Christmas number, 1918), 1(2):4–6, 68–71. New York: U.S. Marine Corps Recruiting Publicity Bureau, 1918.

Woman Artists of America, 1707–1964. Newark, N.J.: Newark Museum Association, 1965.

Woman's Book, The. 2 vols. New York: Scribner's 1894.

Wong, Roberta. Introduction, *American Posters of the Nineties.* Boston: Boston Public Library, 1974.

Wortham, Thomas. " 'The Real Diary of a Boy': Howells in Ohio, 1852–1853." *The Old Northwest* (Spring 1984), 10(1):3–40.

Wright, Frank Lloyd. *A Testament.* New York: Horizon, 1957.

Zimmerman, Helen. "The Work of Miss Bessie Potter." *The Magazine of Art* (September 1900), 23:522–524.

Zolla, Elémire. "Archetypes." *The American Scholar* (Spring 1979), 48:191–207.

Zurier, Rebecca. *Art for the Masses (1911–1917): A Radical Magazine and Its Graphics.* New Haven: Yale University Art Gallery, 1985.

Picture Credits

Preface

1. Bancroft Library, University of California, Berkeley.
2. Courtesy of the Willner Family.
3, 4, and 6. Library of Congress, Prints and Photographs Division.
5. New York Public Library, Art and Architecture Division.
7. Butler Institute of Art, Youngstown, Ohio.

Introduction

2, 21. The U.S. Food Administration, National Archives, Washington, D.C.
4. Indiana University, Lilly Library, Starr Sheet Music Collection.
5, 6, 8, 22–24, 27, 33, 35, 36. Library of Congress, Prints and Photographs Division.
7. Isabella Stewart Gardner Museum, Boston.
16. Metropolitan Museum of Art, New York. Alfred Steiglitz Collection, 1933. (33.43.389)
20. Chesterwood Museum Archives, Stockbridge, Mass., property of the National Trust for Historic Preservation.
25. National Archives, War Department, General, Washington, D.C.
26. Smithsonian Institution, Washington, D.C. Archives Center, National Museum of American History, Warshaw Collection. (S.175a, p. 17)
38. Smithsonian Institution, Washington, D.C. Archives Center, National Museum of History, Division of Photography History. (73.15.23)
39. Smithsonian Institution, Washington, D.C. National Portrait Gallery. Gift of Visiting Nurse Service of New York.

1. American Girls and the New Woman

1.6. Smithsonian Institution, Washington, D.C. National Museum of American Art. Gift of William T. Evans.

1.8, 1.18, 1.22, 1.23, 1.26, 1.27, 1.29–1.35, 1.37, 1.39, 1.46, 1.47. Library of Congress, Prints and Photographs Division.

1.9. Brooklyn Museum. Gift of Mr. Sam A. Lewisohn.

1.10. Phillips Collection, Washington, D.C.

1.11, 1.51. Columbia University, Solton and Julia Engel Collection, Rare Books and Manuscript Library.

1.13. Pennsylvania Academy of the Fine Arts, Temple Fund Purchase.

1.17. Radcliffe College, Schlesinger Library.

1.19. Smithsonian Institution, Washington, D.C. National Portrait Gallery. Gift of Mrs. Austin D. Barney, Philip C. Barney, and Mrs. Halleck Lefferts.

1.20. Smithsonian Institution, Washington, D.C. National Portrait Gallery. Gift of the Girl Scouts of the United States.

1.21. Smithsonian Institution, Washington, D.C. National Museum of American History, Division of Political History.

1.38. Smithsonian Institution, Washington, D.C. National Museum of American Art. Gift of Romaine Brooks.

1.41. Courtesy of Mr. and Mrs. Peter Becker.

1.43. National Archives, Office of War Information, Washington, D.C.

2. Looking for the "Best" Type

2.1. Courtesy of Earl Davis.

2.2. Smithsonian Institution, National Museum of American History, Division of Photographic History. (4135.B6.3)

2.3. Smithsonian Institution, Washington, D.C. Freer Gallery of Art.

2.11. Courtesy of Walter and Naomi Rosenblum.

2.13, 2.22, 2.25. Library of Congress, Prints and Photographs Division.

2.15. Courtesy of Henry C. White.

2.23, 2.24. Yale University, Collection of American Literature, Beinecke Rare Book and Manuscript Library.

2.27. Smithsonian Institution, Washington, D.C. National Portrait Gallery.

2.28. Colorado Springs Fine Arts Center, Taylor Museum.

2.29. Philadelphia Museum of Art. Given by Friends of the Philadelphia Museum of Art. Centennial Gift. (1976-156-1)

2.30. Smithsonian Institution, Washington, D.C. Joseph H. Hirshhorn Museum and Sculpture Garden.

3. Artists, Models, and Real Things

3.1. Detroit Institute of Arts. Founders Society Purchase, Merrill Fund. (57.235)

3.2. Private collection of the Harold O. Love family, photograph courtesy of Smithsonian Institution, Washington, D.C., National Museum of American Art.

3.3. Pennsylvania Academy of the Fine Arts, Temple Fund Purchase.

3.4. Dartmouth College Library, Saint-Gaudens Collection, photograph courtesy of Saint-Gaudens National Historical Site.

3.5, 3.7. Saint-Gaudens National Historic Site, Cornish, N.H.

3.6. Saint-Gaudens National Historical Site, photograph courtesy of Fogg Art Museum, Harvard University.

3.8. Los Angeles County Museum of Art. Mr. and Mrs. Herbert M. Gelfand Collection.

3.9. Brooklyn Museum. Robert B. Woodward Memorial Fund.

3.10. Chesterwood Museum Archives, Stockbridge, Mass., property of the National Trust for Historic Preservation.

3.13. Yale University Art Gallery. Gift of Vincent Price.

3.16. Pennsylvania Academy of the Fine Arts. Commissioned by the School.

3.17. Smithsonian Institution, Washington, D.C. National Portrait Gallery.

3.18, 3.19. Smithsonian Institution, Washington, D.C. Joseph H. Hirshhorn Museum and Sculpture Garden.

4. The Aesthetics of Desire

4.3. Museum of Fine Arts, Boston. (91.130)

4.4. Philadelphia Museum of Art. Given by Mrs. Thomas Eakins and Miss Mary Adeline Williams. (29-184-10)

4.5. Princeton University Library, Department of Rare Books and Special Collections.

4.6. Courtesy of the Trustees of the Boston Public Library.

4.7, 4.10, 4.11. Library of Congress, Prints and Photographs Division.

4.8. Corcoran Gallery of Art, Museum Purchase, 1911.

5. Masking, Camouflage, Inversions, and Play

5.1. Philadelphia Museum of Art. Given by Mrs. Thomas Eakins and Miss Mary Adeline Williams. (29-184-49)

5.2. Harvard University, Houghton Library.

5.4. Metropolitan Museum of Art, New York. Rogers Fund. (11.31)

5.5 Los Angeles County Museum of Art. Mr. and Mrs. William Preston Harrison Collection.

5.6, 5.62. Delaware Art Museum. John Sloan Collection.

5.7. Rijksmuseum Kröller-Müller, Otterlo, Netherlands.

5.8, 5.9, 5.12. Smithsonian Institution, Washington, D.C. National Museum of American Art. Gift of the Heirs of Abbott H. Thayer.

5.11. Philadelphia Museum of Art. George W. Elkins Collection. (E24-4-14)

5.13. Philadelphia Museum of Art. W. P. Wilstach Collection. (W'03-1-7)

5.15. Collection of Jo Ann and Julian Gantz, Jr. Courtesy of Los Angeles County Museum of Art.

5.33, 5.36, 5.39, 5.40, 5.45. Library of Congress, Prints and Photographs Division.

5.35, 5.65, 5.70–5.74. Indiana University, Lilly Library, Starr Sheet Music Collection.

5.61, 5.64. Princeton University, Triangle Club Archives.

5.66, 5.67. Princeton University, Princeton University Theater Collection.

6. Literary Portraits and Types: Crises

6.1. University of California, Los Angeles. University Research Library, Department of Special Collections.

6.2. Pennsylvania Academy of the Fine Arts. Gift of Mr. and Mrs. Henry R. Hallowell, 1964.

6.3. Library of Congress, Prints and Photographs Division.

6.4. Isabella Stewart Gardner Museum, Boston.

7. Literary Portraits and Types: Possibilities

7.1. Museum of Modern Art, New York. Philip Johnson Fund (by exchange and gift of Mr. and Mrs. Bagley Wright).

7.2. Metropolitan Museum of Art, New York. Gift of William Merritt Chase, 1891. (91.11)

7.3. Museum of Fine Arts, Boston. Anonymous Loan. (1.1975)

8. *Studio Studies and Still Lifes*

9. *Images of the Ideal*

10. Angels at the Threshold

10.1. Smithsonian Institution, Washington, D.C. National Museum of American Art. Gift of John Gellatly.

10.9. Saint-Gaudens National Historic Site, Cornish, N.H.

10.10, 10.13–10.15. Smithsonian Institution, Washington, D.C. National Museum of American History, Division of Photographic History. (4135.B5.6, 7, 8, 37)

10.12, 10.20. Library of Congress, Prints and Photographs Division.

10.17–10.19. Princeton University Library, Department of Rare Books and Special Collections.

10.23. Corcoran Gallery of Art, Washington, D.C. Museum Purchase.

11. Making the Right Occasions

11.1. Columbus Museum of Art. Gift of Ferdinand Howald.

11.2, 11.13, 11.15, 11.16, 11.20, 11.22. Library of Congress, Prints and Photographs Division.

11.3. © Art Institute of Chicago. Wirt D. Walker Collection. All rights reserved.

11.4. Isabella Stewart Gardner Museum, Boston.

11.6. Blenheim Palace Collection. Courtesy of His Grace the Duke of Marlborough.

11.8. Photograph courtesy of Saint-Gaudens Historical Site, Cornish, N.H.

11.14. Bibliotèque Nationale, Paris.

11.18. Corcoran Gallery of Art, Washington, D.C. Gift of William Wilson Corcoran.

11.21. Princeton University Library. Department of Rare Books and Special Editions.

11.23. Oakland Museum of Art, Kahn Collection.

12. Scaling Up to War (1876–1898)

12.1. Smithsonian Institution, Washington, D.C. Freer Gallery of Art.

12.2. Chesterwood Museum Archives, Stockbridge, Mass., property of the National Trust for Historic Preservation.

12.3, 12.5, 12.29. Saint-Gaudens National Historical Site, Cornish, N.H.

12.4, 12.14–12.16, 12.33, 12.34, 12.36. Library of Congress, Prints and Photographs Division.

12.6. Metropolitan Museum of Art, New York. Bequest of Edith Minturn Phelps Stokes, 1938. (38.104)

12.12, 12.37. New-York Historical Society.

12.13. Bibliotèque Nationale, Paris.

12.17. The Daniel Chester French Papers, National Trust for Historic Preservation.

12.21, 12.22. Library of Congress, Rare Books and Special Collections.

12.28. Columbia University, Avery Architectural and Fine Arts Library.

13. Poster Lives (1898–1918)

13.1. New York Public Library at Lincoln Center, Astor, Lenox, and Tilden Foundations, Billy Rose Theatre Collection.

13.2. San Francisco Public Library Collection.

13.3–13.5, 13.29, 13.31. Indiana University, Lilly Library, Starr Sheet Music Collection.

13.11, 13.13–13.15, 13.17, 13.19–13.21, 13.24, 13.27, 13.28, 13.33–13.35, 13.38. Library of Congress, Prints and Photographs Division.

13.12. New York State Historical Association, Cooperstown.

13.25, 13.37, 13.40. National Archives, Washington, D.C. U.S. Food Administration.

13.26. Liberty Memorial Museum, Kansas City, Mo.

13.32. National Archives, Washington, D.C. Office of Naval Records and Library.

13.36. Courtesy of Joan Weekes Smith and Verna Rudd Kenvin.

14. Poses on Display

14.1. Indiana University, Lilly Library, Starr Sheet Music Collection.

14.2, 14.4, 14.6, 14.15–14.17, 14.30, 14.31, 14.37, 14.38. Library of Congress, Prints and Photographs Division.

14.13, 14.18. Smithsonian Institution, Washington, D.C. Archives Center, National Museum of American History, Warshaw Collection. (S.132, S.175a, p. 72)

14.27. Princeton University, Triangle Club Archives.

14.32. Metropolitan Museum of Art, New York. Robert Lehman Collection, 1975 (M5).

14.36. Courtesy of Lillian Nassau.

15. The Purchase of Grace

15.1. Smithsonian Institution, Washington, D.C. Joseph H. Hirshhorn Museum and Sculpture Garden.

15.7. Library of Congress, Prints and Photographs Division.

15.14. Indiana University, Lilly Library. Starr Sheet Music Collection.

15.16. Harvard University, Archives of the Hasty Pudding Club.

15.25, 15.26. Radcliffe College, Schlesinger Library.

15.28. The Daniel Chester French Papers, National Trust for Historic Preservation.

15.29. Private Collection in England.

15.30. Museum of Fine Arts, Boston. Charles Henry Hayden Fund. (31.505)

15.31. Melbourne Photo Studio—Talma. Copy photo, Courtesy of Museum of Fine Arts, Boston.

Epilogue

1, 2, 3. Museum of Fine Art, Carnegie Institute, Pittsburgh.

4, 5, 6, 7. Indiana University, Lilly Library, Starr Sheet Music Collection.

8. Philadelphia Museum of Art. Given by Mrs. Cyrus McCormick. (46-10-1)

16. 17. Library of Congress, Prints and Photographs Division.

20. © Art Institute of Chicago. Olivia Shaler Swan Memorial Collection. All rights reserved.

21. Daniel Wolf, Inc., New York.

22. Metropolitan Museum of Art, New York. On loan from Georgia O'Keeffe. (L49.56.42)

Name Index

Abbey, Edwin Austin, 149, 151, 154, 193-94, 395, 420, 436, 439, 543, 545-46, 707n22, 717n11, 719n15, 721n32, 723n51, 741n8, 749n28, 756n13, 776n101, 782n4; art, 547
Ackerman, James, xxix
Adam, 213, 448, 451
Adams, Abigail, *see* Subject Index: Heroines
Adams, Bristow, art, 257
Adams, E. D., 414
Adams, Henry, xxix, 130, 170, 348, 414, 431, 433-36, 438-39, 448, 456, 474, 476, 484, 493, 502, 504, 523, 527, 538, 562, 586, 623, 660, 715n38, 733n30, 744n29, 753-54n28, 754n30, 781n54
Adams, Herbert, 746n49
Adams, J. H., art, 423
Adams, Lottie, *see* Subject Index: Artists' models
Adams, Marian (Clover) Hooper (Mrs. Henry), 504, 715n38, 742n12
Adams, Maude, 269, 451, 750n47, 779n37, 782n63; art, 274, 451
Addams, Jane, 62, 345
Alberti, Leon Battista, 349, 614, 743n23
Alcott, Abbie May, 717n17
Alcott, Louisa May, 514, 534, 708n13
Alden, John, 540, 648, 764n84
Aldrich, Thomas Bailey, 720n24
Alexander the Great, 622
Alexander, John White, 543, 545-46, 672-74, 779n37; art, 675-77

Alkon, Paul, 296-97
Allen, Elizabeth, xxxv
Allen, Grant, 719n16
Allen, Judge Florence Ellenwood, 69-71; art, 69
Allison, Werner S., 771n30
Alpers, Svetlana, 736n2
Altick, Richard, 608
Andersen, Hendrik Christian, 519-21, 758n32, 758n33, 758n34; art, 521-22
Anderson, C. H., 407, 416; art, 365, 410
Anderson, Mary, *see* Subject Index: Artists' models
Angelico, Fra, 389, 631
Anglin, Margaret, 618-19, 779n42, 782n63; art, 621
Anthony, Susan B., 65, 71, 345, 546-47, 624, 775n39; art, 72, 84, 548
Apelles, 327
Apollo, 121, 128, 198, 200
Appleseed, Johnny, 496
Archangel Michael, 456-57
Argan, Guilio, xxix
Aristotle, 111, 171, 336, 622, 626
Arnold, Matthew, 295
Astor, Mrs. John Jacob, 97, 109, 421, 652-53; art, 98
Attucks, Crispus, 475
Auerbach, Nina, 717-18n22
Aurelius, Marcus, 18
Aurora, 165
Avedon, Richard, 733n2

Bacchus, 765n93
Balkin, Harry, 253, 257, 294-95, 475; art, 253
Balsan, Jacques, 703n1
Balzac, Honoré de, 325, 327-29, 734n12
Bancroft, Hubert H., 760n50, 760n52, 761n55
Banner, Lois, xxxiv, 707n3, 775n39, 780n47, 781n58
Barber, Alice, *see* Alice Barber Stevens
Barth, John, 493
Bartholdi, Frederic, xxviii, 481, 488, 508, 511-13, 530, 532
Bartlett, Frederick Orin, 579, 585-88, 590
Bartlett, George B., 642
Barton, Bruce, 715n34
Barton, Clara, *see* Subject Index: Heroines
Barye, Antoine Louis, 160
Barzun, Jacques, 782n61
Batchelder, Ruth, 781n57
Baudelaire, Charles Pierre, 738n20
Baum, L. Frank, 407, 597, 614, 699, 768n3, 772n6
Bayes, Nora, 257
Beard, George Miller, 134-35, 715n42
Beardsley, Aubrey, 406, 597, 756n14, 775n33
Beatrice (Portinari), 611
Beaux, Cecilia, xxxvii, 62, 355, 437, 737n4; art, xl, 63
Becker, Maurice, xxxv, xxxvii; art, xxxvi
Beckwith, J. Carroll, 532, 535, 761n55; art, 531
Beecher, Henry Ward, 714n27
Beer, Thomas, 51
Begas, Reinhold, 752n17
Belasco, David, 268, 728n22, 778n28
Bell, John, art, 494
Bell, Mrs. Arthur (N. D'Anvers), 429
Bellamy, Edward, 774n22
Bellow, Saul, 749n41
Bellows, George, 201, 349; art, 351
Belmont, Mrs. August, 652
Bembo, Peter, 236
Benjamin, Walter, xxix, 608, 773n11
Benson, Eugene, 230, 670, 674-76, 678, 726n6, 775n33
Benson, Frank W., 187, 318, 349, 355, 543, 738n16, 740n26, 747n5; art, 353
Bentley, Miss, art, 451; *see also* Subject Index: Artists' models
Benton, Thomas Hart, 500
Bercovitch, Sacvan, 52
Berenson, Bernard, 322, 614, 734n4
Bergström, Ingvar, 349
Berkeley, Bishop George, 497
Bernays, Edward L., 585, 771n31, 772n10
Bernhardt, Sarah, 618, 661, 778n23
Bernheimer, Richard, 185-88, 206, 290
Berthoff, Warner, xxxv
Besant, Walter, 325, 734n8
Besnard, Paul Albert, 722n38
Beveridge, Senator Albert, 768n10

Bierstadt, Albert, 171
Black, Alexander, xxxvii
Blackmur, R. P., 734n11
Blair, Karen, 779n38
Blake, William, 18, 355
Blashfield, Edwin Howland, 1, 382, 422-23, 540, 543-46, 549-50, 589, 741n3, 746n49, 753n2, 755n2, 764n80, 765n86, 765n96, 767n106, 769n17, 779n37; art, 3, 383-84, 425, 544, 546-47, 549-50, 573
Blashfield, Evangeline Wilbour, 382; art, 383
Bliss, Harry A., 418
Bloomer, Amelia J., 65
Boas, Franz, 519, 758n30
Boccaccio, Giovanni, 749n36
Bogart, Humphrey, 769n15
Bok, Edward, 600
Boldini, Giovanni, 342
Bonheur, Rosa, 727n15
Bonnat, Leon J. F., 766n97
Boone, Daniel, 475, 496
Boorstin, Daniel, 117, 585, 608, 610, 716n8, 773n12
Booth, Evangeline, 565; art, 566
Bosanquet, Bernard, 719n16
Botticelli, Sandro, 194, 756n14
Bourget, Paul, 93-94, 97-98, 100-1, 208, 295, 299, 304, 308, 394, 446-47, 487, 534-35, 595, 620-21, 680, 708n4, 732n24, 732n29, 733n30
Boyd, William, 712n16
Boyesen, Hjalmar Hjorth, 93, 99-104, 119-20, 123-24, 299
Boyle, John J., 360-61, 491; art, 363
Boyle, Richard, 738n14
Bradbury, Nicola, 640
Bradley, Will, xv, 30
Brady, Matthew, 769n20
Brainerd, Sibyl, 493; art, 495
Brandegee, Robert Bolling; art, 69
Breese, James, 72, 620, 653; art, 75
Brett, John, 223
Brewster, Elder, 764n84
Brewster, Henry Bennet, 180-88, 192-93, 197-98, 200
Brewster, William, 717n18
Brice, Fanny, 643; art, 646
Bridgman, Frederick A., 71, 374, 709n20; art, 74
Brinker, Menachem, xxix
Brinton, Christian, 721n26
Brinton, Daniel G., 712n13; art, 107
Brooks, Peter, 633-34, 670, 782n61
Brooks, Romaine, 78, 82, 281, 710n24; art, 80
Brooks, Van Wyck, 438
Brown, Horace, 577, 588
Brown, Marshall, 188
Brownell, William, 192, 721n29, 721n30
Browning, Elizabeth Barrett, 747n56
Browning, Robert, 747n56, 778n23
Brumbaugh, Thomas, 747n6, 748n9, 748n10

Brumidi, Constantino, 560, 742n13, 765n88
Brunelleschi, Filippo, 349
Bruns, Gerald L., xxx
Brush, George de Forest, 130, 135; art, 133
Bryant, William Cullen, 500, 540, 764n84
Buffon, George Louis Leclerc, comte de, 111, 335
Bunker, Dennis Miller, 155, 194; art, 157, 194
Bunyan, Paul, 496
Burien, Mrs. Caroline C. Baker, 655; art, 657-58
Burke, Doren Bolger, 775n10
Burnham, Daniel, 530, 539, 760n47, 762n66, 763n80
Buttrick, Helen, 642; art, 256
Byron, Lord, George, 661

Cable, George Washington, 723n49
Cabot, Polly, art, 133
Caffin, Charles H., 202-5, 371, 672-74, 722n45, 723n46
Caine, Hall, 769n17
Caine, the Reverend Mr., 254, 767n105
Cameron, Senator Donald, 715n38
Cameron, Elizabeth (Mrs. Donald), 433, 456
Campbell, James B., xxviii, 761n59, 762n62
Canova, Antonio, xxxviii
Cantor, Eddie, 680
Carqueville, Will, 30
Carroll, Anna Ella, 753n22; art, 489
Cartherwood, Mary Hartwell, 731n22
Cartier-Bresson, Henri, 733n2
Cary, Elizabeth Luther, 766n97
Cassatt, Mary, 355, 369, 370-71, 399, 535, 542, 741n10, 748n20, 760n50; art, 371, 402
Catt, Carrie Chapman, 65, 709n19
Cellini, Benvenuto, xxxvii
Cenci, Beatrice, 78, 776n6; art, 79
Ceres, 765n93
Chambers, Robert, 32, 34, 145, 148, 164, 168, 170-73, 175, 230, 232, 235, 295, 306-7, 437
Chase, William Merritt, 151-52, 154, 168, 193, 319-21, 355, 369, 717n12, 723n51; art, 153, 320
Chastellux, Marquis de, 96
Chatterton, Thomas, 270
Chavannes, Puvis de, 23, 543, 765n87
Cheret, Jules, 625
Chief Joseph, 467
Chopin, Kate, 232, 311-15, 751n53
Christy, Howard Chandler, 7, 27, 73, 125, 130, 136, 168, 206-13, 216, 218, 277, 280, 291, 367, 401-2, 431, 469, 492-93, 496, 507, 516-19, 560, 572-73, 576, 585, 634, 646, 662, 713n19, 723n49, 723n51, 723n52, 725n64, 731n22, 732n22, 754n29, 766n98, 771n32, 777n20, 781n58, 783n18; art, 8-9, 64, 76, 128, 209, 211, 279, 404, 495, 576-77, 583, 635, 650
Church, Frederick S., 750n47
Churchill, Winston, 731n22
Cincinnatus, 765n93

Clark, John S., 704n7
Clark, Davida Johnson, art, 155; *see also* Subject Index: Artists' models
Clark, Kenneth, 661, 781n54
Clark, Marguerite, 643
Clark, Mary Vida, 729n27
Clark, Mrs., *see* Subject Index: Artists' models
Clarke, Sarah Freeman, 546
Clayton, Bessie, 622, 782n63; art, 624
Clayton, Estella, art, 685
Clemens, Samuel Langhorn, 51, 118, 182, 292, 325, 448, 451, 713n25, 730n6, 768n8; art, 119, 183-84
Coburn, Alvin Langdon, 338
Colacurcio, Michael, 52
Cole, Thomas, 552; art, 551
Collingwood, R. G., 255, 744n36
Colonna, Vittoria, 188, 411
Columbine, *see* Subject Index: Heroines
Columbus, Christopher, 144, 414, 496, 540, 754n34, 759n40-n41, 764n84, 767n2
Commons, John, 483
Comte, Auguste, 778n23
Conkling, Senator Roscoe, 567
Conn, Peter, xxx, xxxiv
Conrad, Joseph, 180
Cooley, Charles Horton, xxxvii, 266, 274, 282, 728n21
Coolidge, Mrs. Calvin, 724n53
Cooper, James Fenimore, 93, 714n25
Corelli, Marie, 597
Corinthea, 179-80, 191, 205, 212, 336, 718n1
Cornelia, *see* Subject Index: Heroines
Cortissoz, Royal, 149, 198, 205, 538, 737n7, 766n97
Courbet, Gustave, 193
Cowan, George J., 772n4, 772n6
Cox, Charles, art, 87
Cox, Kenyon, 25, 193-94, 205, 437, 452, 454-57, 459, 482-83, 519, 543, 545, 568, 719n15, 721n29, 723n46, 743n25, 749n37, 750n47, 751n54, 752n17, 779n37; art, 196, 455, 458-59, 520, 571
Craig, Edward Gordon, 779n37
Crane, Stephen, 5, 213, 232, 237-38, 310-11, 313, 315, 628, 662, 664, 666, 733n33, 770n27, 775n38, 780n52
Crane, Walter, 778n23
Crawford, Thomas, 380, 740n1, 757n21
Creel, George, 770n24
Cresson, Margaret French, 751n55
Crèvecoeur, Hector St. John de, 93, 96, 112, 125, 191
Crockett, Davy, 496
Crossman, Henrietta, 778n28
Culler, Jonathan, 640
Cummings, Ethel, *see* Subject Index: Artists' models
Cunningham, Mary, *see* Subject Index: Artists' models

Cupid, 217, 446, 457, 597, 765n93
Cushing, Otho, art, 461

Dale, Alan, 625, 628, 669, 781n59
Dallas, Mary Kyle, 718n21, 732n24
Daly, Robert, 52
Daniels, Josephus, 757n22
D'Annunzio, Gabriele, 710n24
Dante Alighieri, 201, 217, 611
Danto, Arthur C., 298-99, 301, 435
Dare, Virginia, *see* Subject Index: Heroines
Darwin, Charles, 57, 230, 232, 310, 635, 719n16
Daumier, Honoré, xxxv
Davey, Florence, 349; art, 351
Davies, Arthur B., 632; art, 633
Davies, Marion, 726n11
Davis, Charles Belmont, 214, 724n57
Davis, Richard Harding, 164, 208, 258, 301-2, 440-47, 449, 460, 496, 716n7, 728n19, 749n39; art, 259
Davis, Stuart, 94; art, 95
Day, F. Holland, 340, 412, 767n105, 736n3; art, 340
Degas, Edgar, 367, 388, 741n10
Delacroix, Eugene, 574
Deland, Margaret, 59-62, 65, 67, 103
Delsarte, Francois, 32, 610, 638-45, 647, 655, 660-62, 666, 692, 777-78n23, 778n26, 779n37, 782n63
deMan, Paul, 471
Demuth, Charles, 465-66; art, 466
Derain, Alice, 329
Derrida, Jacques, 471
Dewey, Admiral George, 553, 555, 768n3
Dewey, John, 5, 20, 89, 349-55, 358, 366, 401, 438-39, 611, 707n1, 738n18, 773n14, 773n16
Dewing, Thomas W., 135, 188, 202-5, 291, 316, 325, 345, 347, 352, 355, 369, 371, 373, 374, 382, 398, 431, 436, 469, 501, 722n46, 736n3, 737n11, 738n12, 738n18, 739n23, 756n14; art, 205, 346, 350, 373, 385, 471
Dickens, Charles, 95, 288
Dickinson, Emily, 439
Dilthy, Wilhem, 719n16
Dixon, Thomas Jr., 731n22
Dodge, Mabel, 782n4
Dodge, William, 543
Donatello, 482
Doré, Gustave, 723n51, 764n84
Doro, Marie, 85, 622, 782n63; art, 86, 625
Douglas, Alfred, Lord, 710n24
Douglas, George A., 745n42
Dreiser, Theodore, 5, 87, 145, 152, 174-75, 237, 246, 325, 370, 572, 610, 634, 662, 669-71, 781n57, 782n2
Drexel, Mrs. Joseph W., 143, 176
Dryden, Helen, 644-45; art, 649
Duce, Herbert, 602, 606-7, 634, 674, 678
Duchamp, Marcel, 449
Du Feure, Georges, 625

Dumas, Alexandre, 161, 171
Du Maurier, George, 145, 148, 160-62, 164, 171, 174, 232, 250, 268, 306-7, 509-10, 634; art, 163, 510, 635
Duncan, Isadora, 772n7, 779n37
Duse, Eleonora, 618
Dyce, William, 223
Dye, Eva Emery, 754n30

Eakin, Paul John, 708n10
Eakins, Margaret, 698, 700
Eakins, Susan Macdowell, 131, 176-78, 715n39, 718n28; art, 133, 177
Eakins, Thomas, xxxiii, 13, 57-58, 131, 135, 143-44, 151, 176-78, 192-94, 221, 240, 291, 316, 325, 328, 382-83, 412, 436, 439, 695, 700, 716n2, 725n1, 733n2, 737n5; art, 56, 177, 195, 222, 698
Eastlake, Sir Charles, 745n43
Eastman, Max, 782n4
Eastman, Ruth, 692; art, 693
Ecob, Helen Gilbert, 294-95, 301, 644-45, 730n9; art, 649
Eddy, Mary Baker, 51, 724n53
Eddy, Sarah J., art, 72
Edel, Leon, 758n34
Edgerly, Webster (Edmund Shaftsbury), 742n12, 778n25
Edison, Thomas A., 530, 532, 614-15, 761n55, 767n105
Edouart, Augustin A. C. F., 718n2
Edson, Mrs. Charles Farwell, 66
Edward, Prince of Wales, 724n53
Edwards, Lee R., 433
Eickemeyer, Rudolph, Jr., 97; art, 98, 450, 453-54
Eldredge, Charles C., 366, 738n17, 740n27
Eliot, Charles W., 678, 689-90
Eliot, T. S., 780n43
Elliott, Emory, 52
Elliott, Henry J., 712n16
Elliott, Maud Howe, 761n56
Eltinge, Julian, 268-69, 729n26; art, 272-73
Emerson, Ellen Russell, 193, 301, 389, 412-13, 731n18
Emerson, Ralph Waldo, 439, 720n20, 764n84
Emperor Wilhelm, 752n17
Eros, Lord of Love, 435, 446, 457, 751n54
Escott, T. H. S., 96
Esther, *see* Subject Index: Heroines
Eustis, Mrs. James B., 400; art, 402
Evangeline, *see* Subject Index: Heroines
Ewen, Stuart and Elizabeth, xxxiv

Fairfield, Frances, 642
Falguière, Jean Alexandre, 730n17
Falk, Benjamin, 401-2, 631-32; art, 405, 566, 630
Farragut, Admiral David G., 764n84
Farrell, Lila Gillian, 126, 718n4

Faulkner, William, 749n41
Faversham, William, 643
Fechner, G. T., 719n16
Federman, Raymond, 739n21
Ferber, Edna, 616-17, 634, 691-93; art, 637, 693
Fernande (Olivier), 329
Fichte, Johann G., 415
Field, Erastus Salisbury, 758n36
Fink, Denman, 560-62; art, 563
Fink, Mike, 496
Fink, Steven, 709n20, 740n28, 783n17
Fisher, Harrison, 46, 73, 174, 251; art, 48, 75, 251
Fisher, Philip, 174
Fitzgerald, F. Scott, 62, 268, 517, 728n24, 733n30, 749n41; art, 271
Flagg, James Montgomery, 27, 240, 246-49, 369, 433, 508, 560, 562, 576, 724n52, 725n64, 730n5, 755n12, 770n23, 770n30, 774n25, 777n20, 781n57; art, 241, 246-49, 370, 434
Flaxman, John, 499, 540, 754n2, 760n53, 764n84, 767n106
Fletcher, Angus, 188, 465, 495, 497, 558, 588, 719n8
Fletcher, Robert, 780n51
Foley, Margaret, 381
Fonda, Jane, 643
Ford, Henry, 768n11
Foringer, A. E., art, 568
Forshay, Ella M., 726n6, 738n12
Forster, Kurt, xxix
Foucault, Michel, 589-90
Fowler, Virginia, xxxv, 740n31
Fox, Della, 270-71; art, 275
Francesca, Piero della, 565, 597
Franklin, Benjamin, 530, 532, 719n14, 745n42, 761n55
Frazee, Hazel, art, 574
Freeman, Florence, 381
Freeman, William C. (Pop), 770n30
Freer, Charles, 97, 420, 711n4
French, Daniel Chester, xxviii, 19, 154-56, 158, 160, 355, 420, 437, 458, 481, 483, 515, 522, 525, 529, 533, 564-65, 653, 662, 707n22, 717n14, 738n20, 743n25, 744n35, 750n49, 751n55, 755n2, 756n12, 761n55, 765n86, 779n37; art, 20, 159, 355, 420, 461, 502, 517, 663
French, Mary (Mrs. Daniel C.), 160
Freud, Sigmund, 589-90, 666
Frick, Henry C., 187
Fried, Michael, 738n20
Frieseke, Frederick, 363; art, 365
Fritchie, Barbara, *see* Subject Index: Heroines
Froebel, Friedrich, 707n20
Froehlich, Hugo and Bonnie Snow, art, 46
Frohman, Charles, 85, 622
Frothingham, Eugenia Brooks, 324-25
Fuchs, Edward, 714n29

Fuller, Loïe, 618, 624-25, 628, 631-32, 661, 668, 761n53, 776n40; art, 629-30, 633
Fullerton, Morton, 507-8, 552

Gainsborough, Thomas, 54, 743n23
Galle, Philipp, 486, 488, 493, 496, 520; art, 490
Gardner, Isabella Stewart, 394, 534, 732n29; art, 309
Gautier, Marguerite (Camille), 161-62, 171-72
Geertz, Clifford, xxx
Gellatly, John, 747n6, 748n13
Gérôme, Jean Leon, 143, 161, 750n52, 766n97
Gerson, Alice, 152
Gibson, Charles Dana, xxxiv, 18, 27, 30, 32, 82, 88, 97, 112, 136, 138-39, 152, 168, 172, 211-18, 250, 258, 260-61, 280, 302, 317, 367, 369, 435, 440, 446-47, 458, 460, 508-9, 516, 519, 555, 557-58, 560, 576-77, 597, 611, 614, 617-18, 622, 634, 641, 644-45, 652, 689, 695-96, 700, 711n5, 714n30, 723n52, 724n55, 724n56, 724n57, 725n58, 725n62, 725n64, 725n66, 729n30, 733n2, 756n14, 770n24, 772n2, 777n19, 777n30, 778n27; art, 19, 34, 47, 82, 86, 89-90, 99, 105, 116, 139, 169, 215-17, 259, 264, 436, 441-43, 445, 460, 509, 511, 520, 557, 561, 583, 598, 616, 619-20, 627, 640-41, 649, 653, 690, 696
Gibson, Irene Langhorne, 81, 213, 725n58; art, 81, 89
Gilbert, Cass, 475, 477, 483, 606, 765n86
Gilbert, C. Allan, art, 59
Gilbert, Mrs. H. Bramhall, 469; art, 472
Gilbert, Margaret, xxix
Gilbert, Sandra M., 769-70n20
Gilbert, William and Sir Arthur Sullivan, 212, 692
Gilbert, Yvette, 618
Gilder, Richard Watson, 537, 720n24, 763n72
Giles, Howard, 722n42
Gilman, Charlotte Perkins, 361, 515, 757n24
Gish, Lillian and Dorothy, 643
Glintenkamp, Henry J., 575; art, 581
Goethe, Johann Wolfgang von, 401, 660
Golding, Elaine, 76-77; art, 76-77
Gombrich, Ernst, xxix, 185, 707n1, 718n2, 719n8
Goodman, Nelson, xxix
Gould, J. J., Jr., xxxvii; art, xxxix
Grable, Betty, 562
Grady, Mr., 418-19, 435, 439; art, 419
Grant, Nellie, 757n23
Grant, Robert, xxxix-xl, 618, 724n54
Grant, Ulysses S., 144, 467, 477-78, 757n23
Gray, Dolly, 553, 555
Greenberg, Clement, 497, 589, 771n35
Greenough, Horace, 767n104
Greer, Germaine, 461
Grontkowski, Christine R., xxix
Guerin, Fritz W., 567; art, 401, 570
Guerin, Jules, 766n100; art, 554

Gunn, Archie, 618, 625, 643, 772n3; art, 494, 619, 622, 624, 647
Guy, Seymour Joseph, art, 234
Guyot, Arnold, 105, 107, 712n13

Habegger, Albert, xxxvii
Halsey, Forrest, art, 622
Hambridge, Jay, 201, 204, 212, 722n42, 722n46
Hamerton, Philip, 96
Hamilton, Sir William, 660
Hanks, Nancy, *see* Subject Index: Heroines
Harding, Warren G., 724n53
Hardy, Thomas, 52
Harley, Katherine, 77, 85; art, 77
Harris, Neil, xxx, xxxiv, 16, 720n20, 720n23, 740n27, 769n14, 772n6
Harrison, Frederic, 763n68
Hart, Emma (Lady Hamilton), 660-61, 668, 780n41
Hauser, Arnold, 461, 752n18
Haweis, Mary Eliza, 708n3
Hawkins, Anthony Hope, 250
Hawthorne, Nathaniel, 93, 151, 165, 208, 240, 371, 514
Hayden, Sophie, 527-28
Haywood, Bill, 673, 782n4
Hayworth, Rita, 562
Heade, Martin J., 738n12
Healy, George P. A., 377, 380, 382; art, 379
Hearst, Mrs. William Randolph, 724n53
Hearst, William Randolph, 105, 109, 595, 625
Hegel, Georg W. F., 188, 193, 415, 525
Held, Anna, 740n27
Held, John, 123
Helmholtz, Hermann, 719n16
Hemingway, Ernest, 70, 441, 749n41
Henri, Robert, 201, 205
Henry, Arthur, 560-61
Henry, J., 634; art, 637, 693
Hepburn, Katharine, 737n11
Hephaestus, 529
Heraclitus, 333
Hercules, xxxix, 753n21
Herrick, Robert, 149, 749n36
Hersey, Heloise, 656
Herter, Albert, 400
Herter, Christine, 722n42
Hiawatha, 648
Higginson, Thomas Wentworth, xxxv
Higham, John, xxx, 768n11
Hildenbrand, Adolf, 719n16
Hills, Patricia, 204, 345
Hine, Lewis, 67, 109, 121, 560; art, 110
Hines, Thomas, 762n66
Hirsch, E. D., xxix
Hirschfeld, Al, 618
Hoare, Senator George Frisbie, 558-59, 768n10

Hobbs, Susan, 347, 711n4
Hoff, Carl, 746n48
Hollins, Marion, 76, 85; art, 76
Holmes, Oliver Wendell Jr., 718n25, 764n84
Homer, Winslow, 429
Honour, Hugh, 472, 485, 487, 749n42
Hooper, Bett, 244-50, 682
Hosmer, Harriet, 78, 386, 500, 776n6; art, 79
Houdon, Jean Antoine, 767n104
Howard, Maureen, 778n26
Howe, Elias, 757n40
Howe, Julia Ward, 546, 655, 732n22
Howe, Maud, 655, 732n22
Howell, Jeanne, 304-5, 319, 732n24, 733n33
Howells, William Dean, 51-52, 85, 89, 292, 328, 361, 449, 452, 454, 524-25, 536-37, 579, 581, 584-85, 588, 590, 708n10, 722n44, 723n51, 730n8, 732n23, 734n12, 739n23, 740n25, 751n3, 763n69, 770n27
Hoxie, Vinnie Ream, 381
Hoyle, Frances P., 636, 640, 646; art, 640, 650
Hughes, Edward, art, 70
Humphrey, Maude, 769n15; art, 572
Hunt, Mrs. R. H., 652
Hunt, William Morris, 418, 542, 719n17, 746n45, 746n48
Huntington, David, 652, 722n40

Inches, Mrs. Charles E., 320; art, 321
Irish, Marie, 642
Isham, Samuel, 419, 426, 429, 439, 765n90
Ivanowski, Sigismond de, 620, 670; art, 616, 623
Ivins, William M. Jr., 752n18
Ivory, Paul, 717n18

Jackson, Andrew, 187, 475, 539
Jackson, Jane, 149-50; art, 150
Jackson, General Stonewall, 496
James, Alice, 439
James, Henry, xxix, xxxiv-xxxv, 5, 13, 32, 51, 63, 89, 93, 130, 149, 151, 175, 188, 192, 198, 215, 290, 292, 296-97, 301, 324-26, 329, 333, 335, 338, 374, 381, 395, 435, 438-39, 446, 456, 469, 477-84, 519-20, 523, 526-27, 539, 586, 614-15, 713n17, 738n18, 743n18, 749n36, 752n16, 758n34, 768n8, 782n61; WORKS: *The Ambassadors*, 54, 148, 328, 342-45, 394, 735n15; *The American*, 189, 354, 735n16; *The American Scene*, 211, 435, 468-69, 476-79, 538, 713n17, 755n8; "The Art of Fiction," 325-26, 722n44, 734n8; *The Awkward Age*, 781n59; "The Beast in the Jungle," 735n15, 749n39; *The Bostonians*, 52, 85, 134, 708n9; "Daisy Miller," 1, 49, 52, 62, 100, 288-89, 391, 394, 562, 704n8, 708n5; *The Europeans*, 52-53, 708n9; "The Future of the Novel," 326; *The Golden Bowl*, 85, 217, 395, 640, 735n15; "The Great Good Place," 613-14, 744n22; "Guy de Maupassant," 326; "The Jolly Corner," 735n15; "The Lesson of Balzac,"

325-28, 722*n*44, 734*n*12; "Madame de Mauves," 48, 390-95, 741*n*6; "Partial Portraits," 325; *The Portrait of a Lady*, 10, 12-13, 45-46, 52, 72, 78, 85, 97, 185, 218, 287-91, 295-96, 301, 313, 315-25, 328, 331, 333-35, 345, 357, 391, 394, 697, 704*n*8, 709*n*20, 711*n*4, 730*n*3, 734*n*3, 734*n*91, 756*n*14; *The Princess Casamassima*, 734*n*11; "The Real Thing," 145-48, 155, 158, 160-62, 171, 176, 221, 230, 233, 294-95, 298, 301, 734*n*7, 744*n*32; *A Small Boy and Others*, 614; *The Tragic Muse*, 307-8, 662, 666, 668-69, 734*n*11, 783*n*13; "The Turn of the Screw," 198, 394, 407, 735*n*15; "William Wetmore Story," 437, 755*n*4; *The Wings of the Dove*, 48, 85, 291, 328, 370, 394, 640, 735*n*15, 756*n*14; art, 3

James, William, xxx, xxxiv, xlv, 5, 13, 20, 32, 88-89, 188, 194, 263, 265, 275, 293, 333, 348, 414-16, 438-39, 487, 525, 639, 647, 707*n*1, 713*n*17, 722*n*35, 722*n*36, 730*n*9, 733*n*30, 768*n*8

Jameson, Fredric, 174

Janet, Pierre, 293

Jarves, James Jackson, 189, 204, 206, 425, 720*n*22, 763*n*80

Jehlen, Myra, 640

Jesus Christ, 126, 165, 254, 456-57, 469-70, 595, 597, 646, 715*n*34, 741*n*10, 767*n*105; art, 255

Johnson, Adelaide, 546

Johnson, Andrew, 477

Johnson, Eastman, 764*n*84

Johnston, Frances Benjamin, 27-28, 30, 383, 399, 653, 736*n*3, 737*n*4, 780*n*50; art, 29, 386, 400, 516

Jones, Henry Arthur, 780*n*50

Jones, Howard Mumford, 472, 719*n*13

Julius II, pope, 187

Jussim, Estelle, 720*n*20, 767*n*105

Kant, Immanuel, 62, 288, 415, 611

Käsebier, Gertrude, 35, 339-40, 396, 435, 736*n*3, 737*n*4; art, 39, 341, 397

Keats, John, 213, 411

Keenan, Maggie, *see* Subject Index: Artists' models

Keiley, Joseph T., 736*n*3

Keller, Evelyn, xxix

Keller, Helen, 346, 737*n*10; art, 347

Kellermann, Annette, 78, 710*n*22; art, 79

Kemble, Edward W., 182, 713*n*17; art, 184

Kendall, William Sergeant, art, 259

Kent, Rockwell, 229

Keppler, Joseph, 567, 769*n*14

Kermode, Frank, 182

Key, Francis Scott, 500

Keyser, Samuel Jay, xxxvii

Khayyam, Omar, 62, 452

King, Hetty, 270; art, 275

King, Pauline, 543

King, Willford I., 722*n*5

King Arthur, 411

Kinkaid, Mary Holland, 64-67, 70, 619

Kiralfy, Imre, 537, 763*n*73, 767*n*2; art, 554

Kirchner, Raphael, art, 3

Kissinger, Henry, 466; art, 467

Kitchener, Horatio, Lord, 576

Kitson, H. H., 756*n*14

Klayman, Leon, 466-67

Klein, Cora C., 726*n*11

Klumpke, Anna Elizabeth, 727*n*15

Koehler, Sylvester Rosa, 21-22, 189-93, 197, 204, 206, 419-20, 426, 437, 467-68, 471, 720*n*22

Krieg, Bertha, 105-6, 108-9

Krieger, Murray, 719*n*10

Kroll, Leon, 722*n*42

Kuhn-Regnier, J., 714*n*29

Lacan, Jacques, 740*n*31

La Farge, John, 193-97, 205, 396-97, 418, 420, 436, 542-43, 611, 722*n*36, 741*n*9, 745*n*45, 757*n*17, 766*n*97, 767*n*105; art, 398

Laidlaw, Harriet Burton (Mrs. James Lees), 66, 71, 81, 709*n*19; art, 73

Lamartine, Alphonse de, 112

Lander, Louisa, 381

Langbaum, Robert, 295

Lange, Dorothea, 360

Lanteri, Édouard, 154, 158, 707*n*22

Larche, Raoul, 631; art, 629

Lathrop, George Parsons, 682-86

Lavater, Johann Casper, 104, 111, 121, 128, 165, 179, 296-97, 304, 373, 432-33, 610, 711*n*11, 743*n*21, 748*n*20, 778*n*23; art, 106, 434

Lawton, Mary, *see* Subject Index: Artists' models

Lazarus, Emma, 757*n*17

Lears, Jackson, 418, 738*n*17, 782*n*59

Le Brun, Charles, 396, 742*n*12, 743*n*21

Lee, Light Horse Harry, 496

Lee, Robert E., 478

Lee, Vernon, 198, 200

Leeuw, Geraldus, van der, 436, 744*n*36

Le Gallienne, Richard, 448

Léger, Fernand, art, 228

Lehrer, Susan Frisch, 156, 717*n*17

Leigh, Joanna (Mrs. Lloyd), 610, 664; art, 665

Leighton, Frederick, Lord, 778*n*23

Lerner, Abram, 715*n*39

Lessing, Gotthold, 129

Leutze, Emanuel, 491, 560; art, 493

Lewis, Edmonia, 380-81

Lewis, Meriwether and William Clark, 100, 744*n*27

Leyendecker, J. C., 200-1, 258-59, 280, 575, 589, 611-12, 728*n*19, 773*n*17; art, 202, 260

Lichenstein, Roy, 316; art, 316

Lidoff, Joan, 662

Lieberson, Jonathan, xxx

Lincoln, Abraham, 28, 144, 477, 501, 514, 540, 753n22, 753n23, 764n84
Lincoln, Mary Todd, 514
Linnaeus, Carl von, 111, 335
Lippmann, Walter, 772n10
Lloyd, D. D., 745n43
Lodge, George Cabot, 744n29
Loeb, Louis, 182; art, 183
Lohmann, Christoph K., 709n16
Lombroso, Cesare, 136-39, 210, 692, 715n43, 716n44; art, 137
Long, John Luther, 728n22
Longfellow, Henry Wadsworth, 454, 493, 540, 764n84
Louis, S. L., 635
Lovejoy, Owen, 765n93, 766n100
Low, Juliette Gordon, 70-71; art, 70
Low, Will H., 523, 537, 682-83, 685-86, 745n45, 750n52, 761n56, 763n71, 783n12; art, 524, 685
Lowell, James Russell, 469-71, 540, 764n84
Lowell, Orson, 17, 722n6; art, 61
Lukács, Georg, 328, 735n14
Lynch, Gertrude, 4-5

McAllister, Ward, 651-53, 777n20, 779n33, 779n35
MacAvoy, Edouard, 710n24
McCan, Mrs. Martha Nelson, 66
MacColl, D. S., 25-26, 348-49, 722n45
McCutcheon, George Barr, 46, 125-26, 250-51, 275-80, 301, 305-6, 466, 496, 732n22; art, 48, 251
MacDonald, Georgia, 562
McEwen, Walter, 543, 762n62
MacKay, Mrs. Clarence, 65-66, 81; art, 66
MacKaye, Hazel, 779n38
MacKaye, Steele, 770n38 778n23, 779n37
McKim, Charles, 741n11
McKinley, William, 601, 715n38
McMein, Neysa, 771n33
MacMonnies, Frederick, 522-23, 525, 529, 533, 535, 542, 741n11
MacMonnies, Mary, 749n26
MacMorris, Daniel, art, 575
MacNeil, Hermon A., 541
McVickar, Harry, 1, 32, 35; art, 3, 9, 35, 50
Madison, Dolly, *see* Subject Index: Heroines
Maillol, Aristide, 437
Major, Charles, 303, 731n22
Makart, Hans, 487, 493
Manet, Edouard, 363, 738n20
Marianne, 574
Marling, Karal Ann, 765n90
Marlowe, Julia, 269-70; art, 274
Martiny, Philip, 522
Mason, Otis T., 712n16
Matisse, Henri, 328-29, 335-36, 355, 437
Matthews, Brander, 618
Matthiessen, F. O., 187

Maurer, Alfred, 174, 237; art, 176, 239
Maurice, Arthur Bartlett, 301-2, 749n41
May, Edna, 620, 782n63; art, 622
May, Edward Harrison, art, 131
May, Henry, 553
May, Phil, 617
Mayer, Hy, 597; art, 599
Maynard, George, 543, 766n98
Mead, George H., 728n21
Mears, Maude, 554, 768n5; art, 556
Mechlin, Leila, 751n55
Medici, de, Lorenzo I, 187
Meigs, Captain Montgomery, 742n13
Meisel, Martin, 608, 633, 780n47
Melchers, Gari, 543, 762n62
Melville, Herman, 151, 294, 452, 454-55, 662
Menken, Adah Isaac, 661-62
Mephistopheles, 595, 597, 771n2
Mercury, 532
Merleau-Ponty, Maurice, 374, 740n31
Mérode, Clio de, 730n17
Metcalf, Willard, 543
Michel, Rose Marie Ormond, 739n24
Michelangelo Buonarroti, 160, 164-65, 188, 411, 750n49, 756n14
Milholland, Inez (Mrs. Eugen Boissevain), 66, 81, 612, 655, 709n18; art, 68
Mill, John Stuart, 778n23
Miller, Nancy, 687, 692
Millet, Francis D., 536, 712n16, 713n16, 761n55, 762n65
Mills, Harriet May, 66
Milton, John, 185, 274, 405
Monroe, Harriet, 527
Montesquiou, Robert de, 710n24
Mooney, Michael, 666, 781n54
Morelli, Giovanni, 322, 734n4
Morgan, Anna, 643-45; art, 644-45
Morgan, J. P., 187
Morgan, Wayne, 721n30
Morison, Samuel Eliot, 472
Morrison, Mary Gray, 632, 655-56, 659, 779n40
Morse, Baby Lotte, 634, 636; art, 640
Morse, Samuel F. B., 378, 380, 382; art, 379
Morse, Susan Walker, 378-80; art, 379
Morton, Levi P., 567
Moser, Koloman, art, 224
Mother Goose, *see* Subject Index: Heroines
Mott, Lucretia, 546
Mowbray, H. Siddons, 543
Moyle, Geraldine, 708n13
Mozier, Joseph, 240; art, 242
Muirhead, James Fullarton, 93-97, 100, 295, 299, 711n3
Mumford, Lewis, 538, 763n78
Murillo, Bartolome, 166, 685

Murray, Samuel, 131; art, 133
Mussolini, Benito, 724n53

Nadelman, Elie, 383-84, 386; art, 387-89
Nankivell, Frank, 595; art, 596
Nation, Carrie, 51, 396
Nesbit, Evelyn, 62, 172, 450, 452, 456, 662, 664, 666, 750n47, 781n53, 781n54; art, 450, 453-54
Nethersole, Olga, 620, 782n63; art, 622
Nietzsche, Friedrich W., 487
Nordau, Max, 716n43
Norris, Frank, 134, 213, 294, 725n64, 775n36
Norton, Charles Eliot, 720n24

Oakey, Maria Richards (Mrs. T. W. Dewing), 737n12, 777n20
Oertel, Johannes A., 407, 423, 428-29, 742n13; art, 408
O'Ferrall, Trilby, 160-62, 164, 171, 232, 250, 509-10, 634, 718n20, 718n22, 775n32
O'Keeffe, Georgia, 700; art, 699
Olmstead, Frederick Law, 765n86
O'Neill, Rose, 35; art, 39
Opper, F. O., 601; art, 604
Ormond, Rose Marie (Mme. Robert Michel), 739n24
Orzai, Emmanuel-Joseph-Raphael, 625

Page, Anne, *see* Subject Index: Artists' models
Page, Thomas Nelson, 723n49
Palmenberg, J. R., 624, 628; art, 615
Palmer, Bessie Potter, 525
Palmer, Elsie, 130; art, 132
Parkinson, M. B., 366-67, 369, 396, 634; art, 368, 397, 639
Parmigiano, Francesco, 71, 710n20
Parsons, Talcott, 148, 716n9
Partridge, William Ordway, 145, 148, 152, 154, 158, 162, 164-65, 167-68, 174, 198, 235, 306-7, 417, 500, 707n22, 717n14, 721n29, 763n70, 764n84, 782n61; art, 167
Pascal, Blaise, 744n37
Paulson, Ronald, 743n23
Paus, Herbert, 575
Paxton, William McGregor, 358; art, 359
Pearce, Charles Sprague, 359, 543, 737n22; art, 362
Pease, Mrs. Walter, art, 75
Peck, Harry Thurston, 678
Peirce, Charles Sanders, xxxi, 5, 13-16, 20, 32, 45-46, 82, 88-89, 93, 99, 103, 182, 188, 193, 196, 200, 211, 213, 275, 317, 337, 412, 414-17, 457, 525-26, 538, 558, 587, 589-90, 608, 612, 639, 674, 687-88, 722n36, 733n33, 744n33, 760n43, 775n40
Peirce, Melusina Fay, 703n5
Penfield, Edward, 27, 250, 575, 589; art, 252, 580, 582

Penfield, Mrs. Jean Nelson, 65
Penn, William, 767n105
Pennell, Joseph, 770n23
Perosa, Sergio, 735n15
Peter Pan, 451
Petty, George, 562
Phaedre, 289
Phidias, 187, 429, 755n3
Phillips, Coles, 223, 231, 240, 358, 532, 599, 689, 695-96, 700; art, 224, 231, 360, 533, 600, 628, 690, 697
Phillips, H. S., art, 489
Picabia, Francis, art, 298
Picasso, Pablo, 225, 297-98, 328-29, 331-32, 336, 355, 373-74, 437, 748n19
Pickford, Mary, 643
Pierce, Patricia Jobe, 345
Pitcher, Molly, *see* Subject Index: Heroines
Plotinus, 414
Pocahontas, art, 495; *see also* Subject Index: Heroines
Poe, Edgar Allan, 185, 306, 308
Poland, Luke P., 567
Polycletus, 756n14
Pope, Alexander, 328
Pope Julius II, 187
Porter, Sarah, 69-71
Potter, David, xxxv
Poussin, Nicolas, 23, 412, 414
Powers, Hiram, 13, 171, 380, 484, 740n1
Price, Bessie, *see* Subject Index: Artists' models
Price, C. Matlack, 577, 588, 770n26
Price, R. Alan, 769n17
Prince, George, art, 572
Priscilla, *see* Subject Index: Heroines
Puccini, Giacomo, 268, 728n22
Pulitzer, Joseph, 105, 109
Pumpelly, Elsie, *see* Subject Index: Artists' models
Purman, Irma (Mrs. John Banta), 7, 32, 35, 45-46, 87-88, 91, 258-59, 261-63, 265-68, 280-81, 402, 404-5, 646-47, 688-89, 700, 727n18; art, 10-11, 33, 35, 38-39, 47, 87, 91, 258, 261, 265-68, 281, 406, 599, 627, 651, 688, 701
Purman, Russell, art, 474
Putnam, General Rufus, 765n93, 766n100
Pyle, Howard, 723n51

Ralph, Julian, 618
Raphael, 187, 348, 411-12, 414, 709n20
Rau, William, 367, 369, 622, 659; art, 368-69
Reed, Ethel, 30
Redfern, Charles Poynter, 659
Red Riding Hood, *see* Subject Index: Artists' models
Rehan, Ada, 612
Reid, Robert, 369, 543, 747n5

Reitano, Joanne, xxxiv
Rembrandt van Rijn, 195
Reynolds, Joshua, 328, 349, 610, 664, 743n23; art, 665
Rhead, Louis, 30, 398, 595; art, 594
Ribot, Theodore, 293
Richardson, George, 412, 743n20, 743n21
Richardson, Henry Hobson, 530
Richardson, Samuel, 242, 277
Rickenbacker, Eddie, 724n53
Riegl, Alois, 719n16
Riga, Cesare, 396, 412
Riis, Jacob A., 67, 469, 471, 519-20, 560, 733n32
Rimmer, William, 458
Rio, Michel, xxix
Rives, Hallie Erminie, 303, 731n22
Roberts, Edith, art, 79
Rocine, V. G., 118-19, 121, 123, 125-26, 130, 134, 206, 210, 253-54, 297, 317, 330, 349, 446, 560, 606, 714n28, 715n34, 716n44, 767n105; art, 121, 136, 254-55
Rockwell, Norman, 115
Rodin, Auguste, 437, 747n56
Rogers, Robert, 386, 740n1
Rogers, Will, 724n53
Rolfe, John, 28
Ron, Moshe, 716n6
Rood, Roland, 739n21
Roosevelt, Theodore, 121, 124, 135, 226, 254, 488, 501, 558, 606, 752n17, 765n86; art, 121
Ross, Betsy, *see* Subject Index: Heroines
Ross, Denman W., 722n42
Rossetti, Dante Gabriel, 457-58, 595, 647, 719n15, 750n52, 756n14; art, 196, 458-59
Rostand, Edmond, 269
Rousseau, Henri, 329
Rousseau, Jean-Jacques, 174
Royce, Josiah, xxxi, xlv, 5, 14, 17-21, 45-46, 88-89, 182, 193, 196, 200, 213, 275, 317, 415-17, 438-39, 457, 538, 587, 674, 704n7, 704n10, 722n36, 740n31, 744n32
Rubens, Jean Paul, 756n14
Rudder, Madame de, 769n16; art, 573
Rudi, François, 574
Rush, William, 144, 726n1, 740n1
Ruskin, John, 22, 452, 454, 465, 744n36, 751n1, 778n23
Russell, Bertrand, 246
Russell, Lillian, 618, 625, 628-29, 632, 669, 775n39; art, 630
Ruth, *see* Subject Index: Heroines

Sacagawea, *see* Subject Index: Heroines
Said, Edward, 498, 589, 752n8
Saint-Gaudens, Augusta, 756n13
Saint-Gaudens, Augustus, 154-58, 174, 188, 212, 418-19, 428, 430-31, 449-51, 476, 481-84, 488, 501-4,
519, 540-41, 608, 653, 660, 666, 717n16, 743n25, 745n45, 746n46, 750n47, 755n2, 755n7, 756n13, 756n14, 764n85, 765n86, 779n37; art, 156-58, 175, 450, 482, 503, 505, 541
Saint-Gaudens, Homer, 726n5, 740n26, 759n40, 764n85, 765n90
Santayana, George, xxxiv, 254, 416, 438, 586, 744n34, 782n61
Sappho, 165
Sargent, John Singer, 130, 135, 149, 198, 200, 223-25, 308, 320-21, 325, 340, 361, 363, 383, 394, 458, 469, 507, 534, 543, 715n39, 722n38, 732n29, 733n30, 739n24, 755n10, 775n37, 780n42; art, 132, 199, 225, 309, 321, 364, 470, 473, 506
Savage, Edward, 753n23
Savitz, Lernard D., 715n43
Savonarola, Girolamo, 168
Schenk, Charles, 598, 662; art, 600, 663
Schevill, William, 35; art, 39
Schier, Flint, 730n15
Scholnick, Robert J., 726n6
Schopenhauer, Arthur, 415
Schuyler, Montgomery, 536
Scott, Sir Walter, 288, 489
Scudder, H. E., 452
Searle, Leroy, 733n2
Sedgwick, Henry Dwight, 129-31, 135, 302-5, 310-11, 731
Sennett, Mack, 78
Sennett, Richard, 752n17
Seton, Mrs. Ernest Thompson, 65-66
Settignana, Desidero da, 750n50
Shakespeare, William, 149, 194, 250, 269, 643, 654, 714n30, 749n36
Shapiro, Mitchell, 158, 717n18
Sheldon, George, 358
Sherman, General William Tecumsah, 481, 484, 503, 519, 541, 752n17; art, 482
Sherwood, Mrs. M. E. W., 52-55, 57-58, 60, 652-53
Shirlaw, Walter, 543
Shopas, 756n14
Shover, Michele J., 769n20, 771n38
Silk, Mark, 714n31
Simmons, Edward, 543
Simms, Joseph, 118, 121, 123, 125-26, 130, 134, 180, 210, 255, 297, 714n26, 716n44, 727n15; art, 114, 119-20
Singer, Isaac Merrit, 130, 135; art, 131
Sir Galahad, 395, 510
s'Jacob, Henrietta C., 743n22, 747n58
Sklar, Kathryn Kish, 708n13
Sloan, John, xxxvii, 225, 268, 682, 695, 697, 700; art, xxxviii, 227, 270, 684, 698
Small, Herbert, 764n82
Smedby, William, 617
Smith, Bessie (Mrs. Stanford White), 450; art, 450
Smith, Captain John, 28, 218, 496, 648, 753n28

Smith, F. Hopkinson, 761n56
Smith, Franklin W., art, 540
Smith, Merle, 647, 695, 700, 727n18
Smith, Mrs. Thomas Jefferson, 71, 81, 709n19, 709n20; art, 74
Socrates, 149, 174, 179, 406, 414, 611
Soper, Henry M., 636
Sophocles, 171, 655-57, 659-60
Sousa, John Philip, 768n6
Southworth, E.D.E.N., 514
Speilmann, M. H., 356, 776n6
Spencer, Herbert, 117, 171, 719n13, 719n16, 778n23
Spilka, Mark, 734n8
Sprague, Rosa Mueller, art, 644-45
Springer, Mary Doyle, 328, 735n16
St. Méry, Moreau de, 96
Standish, Miles, 764n84
Stanlaws, Penrhyn, art, 259
Stanley, Alma, 662, 666, 668, 781n55; art, 667-68
Stanton, Elizabeth Cady, 65, 547; art, 84, 548
Stebbins, Emma, 381
Stedman, Edmund, 720n24
Stein, Gertrude, xlv, 5, 13, 24, 26, 32, 70, 123, 225, 293, 296-98, 317, 325, 329, 333-39, 355-56, 374, 432, 734n2, 748n19; WORKS: *The Autobiography of Alice B. Toklas*, 176, 296, 298, 300-1, 329-30, 336, 735n21, "Composition As Explanation," 736n31; "The Gradual Making of *The Making of Americans*," 331-32, 735n23; "Henry James," xlv, 333-34, 336, 413; *The Making of Americans*, 176, 493; "The Mother of Us All," 775n39; "Portraits and Repetitions," 332, 355, 736n26; *Tender Buttons*, 332; *Three Lives*, 175, 298, 328-32, 735n21; art, 125, 127, 298, 337-38
Steiner, George, 640
Steiner, Wendy, 337
Stephens, Kate, 54-58, 60, 62, 101-2, 654, 708n13
Sterner, Albert, 576
Stevens, Alice Barber, 168, 170, 288; art, 169
Stevens, Elsie Rachel, 765n85
Stevens, Wallace, 608
Stevenson, Robert Louis, 288
Stickley, Gustav, 545, 766n99
Stieglitz, Alfred, 12-13, 695, 700, 737n4; art, 699
Stillman, Bessie, 386-87, 396; art, 390
Stillman, William J., 413-14, 721n29
Stockton, Frank, 704n9
Stoddard, William Osborn, 720n24
Stokes, Edith [Mrs. I.N.P.], 507, 755n10; art, 506
Stokes, Isaac Newton Phelps, 755n10; art, 506
Story, William Wetmore, 400, 402, 437, 500, 742n12, 747n56, 755n4; art, 403
Stowe, Harriet Beecher, 515, 546, 567, 650, 767n103
Strong, Josiah, 117-18, 123, 125, 130, 180, 210, 518, 716n44
Sturgis, Russell, 206, 722n46, 744n28, 766n100
Sully, James, 707n1

Sulzer, Johann Georg, 730n11
Summerall, Major General Charles P., 483
Sumner, William Graham, 93
Sunshine, 274; art, 278
Sutton, Vida, 65
Svengali, 160-61, 171, 250, 686, 782n63
Swedenborg, Emanuel, 642
Swinton, Mrs. George, 469; art, 470
Symonds, John A., 409, 422, 746n51

Taft, Lorado, 612, 736n4, 780n44
Taplin, Oliver, 780n43
Tarbell, Edmund, 187, 318, 361, 740n26, 747n5; art, 364
Tarbell, Ida M., xxviii, xxxv, 782n61
Taylor, Bayard, 720n24
Taylor, Frederick Winslow, 268, 728n23; art, 271
Taylor, Joshua, 543, 753n23
Tempest, Florenze, 271, 273-75; art, 277-78
Temple, Shirley, 634
Tennyson, Alfred, Lord, 454, 540, 764n84
Terry, Ellen, 618
Thanet, Octave, 775n30
Thaw, Harry, 450, 620, 664
Thayer, Abbott Handerson, 32, 57-58, 112, 192, 225-29, 232-33, 240, 386-90, 398-99, 417, 420, 428-32, 435-37, 439, 451, 543, 722n32, 726n4, 726n5, 728n19, 738n12, 744n35, 746n49, 747n5, 747n6, 748n8, 748n10, 750n47, 779n37; art, 56, 115, 229, 238, 390-93, 399, 430
Thayer, Emma Beach, 229, 748n8
Thayer, Gerald, 229, 387, 429, 726n4
Thayer, Gladys, 389, 429; art, 392
Thayer, Mary, 429-30, 748n8, 779n37; art, 430
Thompson, Cephas Giovanni, 380, 382; art, 381
Thompson, D'Arcy, 201
Thompson, Miss, *see* Subject Index: Artists' models
Thomson, Rodney, art, 17
Thomson, Virgil, 775n39
Thoreau, Henry David, 151, 398, 558
Thucydides, 558
Ticknor, Caroline, 717n17
Tiffany, Louis, 595, 741n3, 767n105, 771n1
Tilley, Vesta, 271-73, 729n29; art, 276
Tintoretto, Il, 756n14
Titian, 756n14
Tocqueville, Alexis de, 93, 96
Tojetti, Domenico, 497, 560; art, 497
Toklas, Alice B., 298, 329
Toll, Robert C., 269
Tomes, Robert, 116, 130
Tomsich, John, 720n24
Toplady, Augustus Montague, 742n13
Toulouse-Lautrec, Henri, 625
Trachtenberg, Alan, xii, 738n17, 758n35, 762n66
Treidler, Adolph, 27, 576; art, 28
Turner, Frederick Jackson, 551

Turner, Joseph Mallord, 224
Turner, Victor W., 433
Tweed, William M., 467

Uhlenberg, Peter R., 708n13
Uncle Sam, 27, 565, 567-68, 576, 636, 778n30

Van Buren, Amelia C., 57; art, 56
Vanderbilt, Cornelius II, 420, 431
Vanderbilt, Mrs. Cornelius II, 510, 532, 653; art, 511
Vanderbilt, Gertrude, 105-6, 108-9; art, 108
Vanderbilt, Consuelo (Duchess of Marlborough), 1, 109, 469, 703n1; art, 4, 473
Van Rensselaer, Mrs. John King, 472
Van Rensselaer, Euphemia White (Mrs. John Church Cruger), 377-80
Van Rensselaer, Mariana (Mrs. Schuyler), 193, 720n20, 750n52, 751n54, 759n40
Van Winkle, Mrs. A., 80
Vardamis, Sharon M., 709n18
Vargas, Alberto, 562; art, 683
Vaughan, Teresa, art, 685
Veblen, Thorstein, 229-30, 240, 615-16, 733n30, 737n9
Vedder, Elihu, xxxv, 148-49, 151, 154, 223, 397, 402, 452, 532, 543, 717n10; art, 150, 226, 531
Verrocchio, Andrea, 482
Vico, Giovanni Battista, 752n8
Virgin Mary, 71, 165, 186, 310, 399, 433, 435, 448, 484, 534, 547, 631, 660-61, 666, 772n7
Vlasto, Catherine, 715n39
Voegtlin, Arthur, 769n2
Volk, Douglas, art, 580
Von Steinwehr, Adolph, 712n13; art, 107
Vonnoh, Bessie Potter, 358; art, 361

Wald, Lillian, 35, 78; art, 39
Waldo, Deliverance Mapes (Mrs. Samuel L.), 377, 380; art, 378
Waldo, Samuel L., 377, 382; art, 378
Walker, Dr. Mary Edwards, 78, 281, 710n23; art, 80
Walker, Henry Oliver, 543
Wallace, J. Laurie, 144
Walton, Kendall, xxx
Ward, J. Q. A., 553, 768n4
Warhol, Andy, 608
Washington, George, 28, 158, 475, 491, 501, 547, 601, 652, 753n23, 764n83, 764n84, 767n104, 767n105; art, 548
Wasserstrom, William, 249
Watts, George Frederick, 764n84
Weber (Joseph) and (Lew) Fields, 622, 624
Webster, Daniel, 28, 764n84
Webster, Jean, 242-44, 247-49; art, 243-45
Weir, J. Alden, 46, 187; art, 49

Weir, John Ferguson, 165, 369, 371; art, 166, 172
Wenzell, Albert Beck, 123, 420-21, 507, 560, 595, 634, 714n30, 724n52, 725n64, 772n2, 781n52; art, 122, 167, 424, 507, 596, 636
West, Benjamin, 300-1; art, 301
West, Nathanael, 634
Wharton, Edith, 5, 89, 192, 292, 324, 374, 439; works: *The Age of Innocence*, 48, 172, 232, 448-49, 593, 746n47, 776n5; *The Book of the Homeless*, 573, 769n17, 770n24; *The Custom of the Country*, 233-37, 240, 307-8, 310, 447, 732n28, 780n50; *The House of Mirth*, 172, 232, 304-5, 370, 507, 610, 622, 652, 662, 664, 732n25, 734n6, 735n21, 780n52; art, 234, 507, 573
Whately, Bishop Richard, 61-62
Whistler, James Abbott McNeill, 1, 97, 193, 201, 204, 293-300, 318, 340, 369, 393, 439-40, 586, 666, 721n31, 722n38, 722n46, 747n56; art, 4, 98, 667
White, Clarence, 10, 12-13; art, 12
White, Stanford, 154, 419, 450, 501, 664, 666, 746n46, 755n7, 781n54
Whitman, Walt, 60, 62, 191, 513-14
Whitney, Anne, 381
Whitson, Beth Slaton, 678
Whittier, John Greenleaf, 540, 764n84
Wilbor, Elsie, 639
Wildhack, Robert, 46; art, 49
Willard, Archibald, 532
Willard, Frances, 345, 546, 642, 749n26; art, 84
Williams, Anna W., 540
Williams, Esther, 77
Williams, Mary Adeline, art, 195
Williamson, Judith, 740n31
Williamson, C. N. and A. M., 250, 252, 275, 446
Wilson, Edmund, 740n27
Wilson, Woodrow, 519, 757n22
Winklemann, Johann J., 432-33, 748n20
Winter, Charles, xxxv, xxxvii; art, xxxvi, 81
Wise, Gene, xxx
Wolff, Cynthia Griffin, 662, 780n51
Wolff, William A., 770n30, 771n33, 780n51
Wolfflin, Heinrich, 719n16
Wollerman, Alma, 57, 387, 390; art, 391
Worth, Charles Frederick, 659
Wright, Frank Lloyd, 23, 707n20
Wright, H., art, 33
Wycherly, Margaret, 510-11, 513, 655; art, 512

Yankee Pedlar, 496
Yeats, William Butler, 295-96, 458
Young, Andrew McLaren, 730n16

Zenobia, *see* Subject Index: Heroines
Zit-Kala-Za, 340, 736n3; art, 341
Zolla, Elémire, 686
Zorn, Anders, 174, 342; art, 175
Zurier, Rebecca, 723n47, 771n38, 782n4

Subject Index

Actresses, 619, 636

Advertising, 2, 205-6, 223, 259, 533, 575, 578-79, 585, 608, 612-13, 715n34, 740n31, 770n30, 771n33, 772-73n10, 773n20, 774n221, 781n59; **billboard posters,** 291, 603, 605-6, 611, 613, 616-17, 678, 775n25; **cigar labels,** 571-72, 714n25; **trademarks,** 147, 574, 589, 716n8, 770n30

Altrurian Traveler, 536

American Akademe, 408

Androgeny, 32, 258, 519, 521, 756n14, 783n18

Apollo Belvedere, 28, 105

Apologue character, 328

Arcadia, 412, 536

Armory Show, 437

Art Associations, 204, 456, 499, 612, 721n27, 737n5, 741n8, 744n26, 746n50, 754n2, 765n86, 777n20

Art galleries, *see* Art museums, galleries

Art genres: **allegory,** xxxiv, xxxix, 13, 91, 143, 149, 156, 164, 171, 200, 225, 235, 260, 347, 349, 378, 380, 382-83, 386, 390, 394-396, 405, 409, 411, 414, 417-19, 432, 440, 448, 456, 465, 469, 474, 483, 495, 500, 510, 532, 545, 547, 567, 578, 588, 673, 692, 728n18, 740n1, 744n37, 751n3, 753n23, 757n21, 761n55, 761n56, 765n88, 765n90, 766n100, 783n12; **architecture,** xxxvii, 22, 475-76, 478, 529-30, 542-43, 552, 554, 618, 706n16, 757n21, 762n63, 764n81; **calendar art,** 206, 291, 406, 426, 532, 692; **caryatid,** 96-97, 431, 756n14; **cemetery, memorial art,** xxxii, 154, 158, 396, 407, 409, 421, 505, 564, 746n50,

747n58, 774n41; **civic art,** xxxii, xxxvii, xxxix, 410, 414, 427, 467, 475, 499, 529, 538-39, 542, 544-45, 552, 598, 608, 739n21, 741n3, 746n54, 752n11, 754n30, 765n86, 765n96; **coinage,** 538, 540-42, 764n85, 765n86; **colossi,** xxxix, 113, 145, 260, 468, 480-81, 499-500, 505, 508, 512-13, 515, 522-23, 528-29, 545, 764n84, 755n4, 757n17, 761n56; **commercial art,** 5, 21, 91, 200, 205, 212, 223, 357, 414, 543, 588-89, 595, 688, 728n19, 740n31, 780n52; **decorative arts,** 32, 720n18, 736n4, 769n16; **design, pattern,** 200-1, 203, 205, 212, 222-23, 346, 371, 397, 511, 542-45, 551, 576, 578, 588-89, 595, 612, 622, 644-45, 674, 706n16, 725n57, 732n28, 741n9, 754n1; **grisaille,** 723n28; **history painting,** 546-48, 618; **industrial art,** 21-22, 759n40, 760n50; **landscape,** 342, 344-45, 348, 720n20, 737n7, 764n84; **magazine and newspaper illustrations,** xxxiii, 145, 357, 406, 420, 543, 611, 617, 620, 709n16, 718n2, 723n51; **monument,** 32, 407, 418-20, 425-27, 431; **mural,** 32, 168, 171, 198, 347, 383, 395, 411, 418, 420, 458, 465, 475, 496, 530, 532, 535, 538, 542-47, 552, 598, 673-74, 678-79, 718n2, 724n53, 739n21, 741n3, 746n45, 748n19, 748n26, 753n26, 755n2, 760n50, 761n56, 765n87, 765n88, 765n90, 765n91, 765n96, 775n37, 776n101, 780n51; **nude,** 726n1, 731n17, 751n52; **patriotic art,** 30, 465, 471, 481, 495, 498, 547, 636, 724n53; **photography,** xxx, 7, 10, 12-13, 24, 32, 67, 76, 123, 158, 213, 296, 302, 339, 341, 396, 402, 435, 443, 573-75, 636, 685-86,

Art genres (*Continued*)

706*n*16, 709*n*16, 718*n*2, 727*n*18, 728*n*18, 731*n*20, 733*n*2, 748*n*25, 762*n*65, 776*n*10, 777*n*18, 783*n*13; **political cartoon,** 768*n*8; **portrait head,** 305, 310, 635, 720*n*20, 732*n*15; **post card,** 302, 731*n*20; **poster,** xxxvii, 2, 27, 30, 32, 205, 223, 259, 311, 357, 465, 483, 485, 492-93, 520, 549, 555, 560, 562, 564-65, 572, 574-79, 584, 586-90, 595, 606, 616-17, 625, 632, 634, 636, 638, 644, 662, 679, 700, 718*n*2, 724*n*53, 739*n*21, 753*n*22, 770*n*20, 771*n*36, 774*n*25, 781*n*59; **print reproduction,** 89, 396, 546, 617, 720*n*20; **propaganda art,** 483, 530, 555, 567-79, 612, 769*n*19, 770*n*30, 771*n*38; **religious art,** 144, 382, 420-21, 427, 436-37, 542, 741*n*3, 742*n*16, 744*n*40, 751*n*54, 759*n*40, 767*n*105, 771*n*1; **sculpture,** xxxvii, 152, 154-56, 158-59, 164, 212, 381, 414, 455, 475-76, 478, 499-500, 542, 552, 598, 618, 686, 740*n*1, 750*n*49, 757*n*21; **sheet music cover,** 357, 396, 402, 407, 420-21, 553, 564, 593, 678; **silhouette,** 7, 25, 146, 179, 205, 212-13, 232, 243, 336, 575, 578, 612, 614, 622, 636, 718*n*2, 732*n*28, 755*n*2; **"sister arts,"** 339, 341, 736*n*2, 750*n*52; **stained glass,** 416, 418, 426-27, 741*n*9, 772*n*4; **statuary** (bronze, marble, stone), xxxix, 32, 165, 198, 240, 380-81, 414, 416, 418, 427-28, 448, 465, 476, 481, 496, 542, 546, 608, 758*n*33, 759*n*41; **stereoptican,** 617, 723*n*52, 777*n*18; **still life,** 342, 344-45, 348, 738*n*12; **victory arch,** 465, 553, 768*n*3, **visionary art,** 366, 758*n*36; **window display,** 396, 407, 597, 611, 613-16, 620, 624, 628, 632, 772*n*4

Artistic and historic sites: **Altamira caves,** 187; **Athens** (Acropolis), 96, 437, 442-43, 508; **Boston** (Public Library), 198, 383, 395, 420, 543, 741*n*8, 742*n*11, 775*n*37, (Shaw Memorial), 155, (Trinity Church), 542, 746*n*45; **Bowdoin College, Me.** (Walker Art Building), 543, 765*n*87; **Cleveland** (Citizen's Bank), 753*n*26; **Kansas City, Mo.** (Liberty Memorial), 763*n*72; **New York City** (Brooklyn Bridge), 188, (Criminal Courts Building), 543, (Custom House), 158, 516, (Grand Army Plaza), 481, (Grant's Tomb), 477-78, 752*n*16, (Madison Square Garden), 154, 188, 501, 666, 777*n*20, (Parish House, Church of the Ascension), 382, (Presbyterian Hospital), 774*n*22, (Saint Thomas Church), 745*n*45; **Philadelphia** (Fairmount Park), 190, 523, (Independence Hall), 476, 478; **Pittsburgh** (Museum of Art, Carnegie Institute), 672-73; **Richmond** (Robert E. Lee Memorial), 478; **Rome** (Vatican), 96; **Washington, D.C.** (Library of Congress), 366, 496, 543, 545-46, 713*n*16, 763*n*79, 764*n*82, 765*n*87, 767*n*103, (Lincoln Memorial) 766*n*100 (National Capitol), 479-80, 546, 560, 724*n*53, 742*n*13, 757*n*21, 764*n*84, 765*n*88; **Wilkes-Barre, Pa.** (Courthouse), 543

Artists' models, 12-13, 21, 112, 115, 123-24, 144,

146-49, 152, 154-56, 158-60, 162, 164-65, 170-74, 176-77, 221, 232, 240, 306-7, 390, 407, 429-30, 442, 450-51, 503, 622, 636, 661-62, 666, 683, 685-86, 717*n*16, 717*n*18, 725*n*58, 726*n*1, 738*n*16, 747*n*6, 755*n*13, 764*n*85, 765*n*85, 773*n*17, 781*n*53, 783*n*14

Artists' studios, 152, 158, 160, 168, 412, 414, 430-31, 717*n*17, 718*n*24, 779*n*37

Art movements, periods, styles: **abstractionism,** 13, 193, 335, 349, 383, 721*n*30, 723*n*46, 744*n*29; **academicism,** 21-22, 152, 205, 500, 737*n*5; **aestheticism,** 193; **American Renaissance,** 187-89, 192-93; **Art Nouveau,** xxxiii, 223, 383, 595, 625, 780*n*51; **Asian art,** 13, 222, 415, 617, 641, 728*n*22, 744*n*29, 757*n*17; **Barbizon School,** 359, 739*n*22; **Beaux Arts,** 529, 737*n*5; **Belle Epoque,** xxxiii, 597; **Boston School,** 187, 318; **Byzantine art,** 308, 421; **City Beautiful,** 497, 536, 538-39, 747*n*54, 764*n*80, 775*n*25; **classicism,** 30, 115-16, 144, 198, 200-1, 301, 335, 367, 382-83, 388-89, 392, 396-98, 411, 413-14, 433, 435, 437, 442, 452, 456, 483, 500, 522, 540, 545, 553, 574, 628, 641, 643, 659, 685, 746*n*49, 748*n*25, 749*n*42, 750*n*49, 751*n*54, 755*n*2, 756*n*14, 757*n*17, 763*n*72, 767*n*106, 780*n*43; **Cubism,** 24, 26, 225, 707*n*23; **Dutch art,** 738*n*12, 738*n*16; **early Italian Renaissance,** 452, 750*n*49, 756*n*14; **the Eight,** 204, 723*n*46, 737*n*5; **Fontainbleau,** 756*n*14; **Impressionism,** 25, 222, 224, 414; **Italian Renaissance,** 26, 149, 187, 308, 348, 356, 386, 411, 429, 431, 435-36, 456, 497, 522, 529, 556, 614, 697, 719*n*13, 743*n*23, 450*n*48; **Jugenstil,** 421; **modernism,** 24-26, 201, 348, 356, 384, 409, 413, 431, 435, 437, 589, 744*n*39, 756*n*14, 762*n*65, 771*n*36, 780*n*43; **naturalism,** 25, 148, 349, 363, 383, 396, 413, 425-26, 452, 611-12, 706*n*16, 721*n*30, 738*n*16, 755*n*2, 767*n*105, 778*n*28; **neoclassicism,** 13, 24, 194, 240, 335, 380-81, 383, 414, 436, 499, 532, 740*n*1, 741*n*2, 743*n*23, 749*n*42, 767*n*106, 780*n*51; **plein air,** 21, 193, 339; **Pointillists,** 224; **postimpressionism,** 193; **Pre-Raphaelite,** 13, 189, 222-23, 231, 295, 388, 398, 414, 718*n*22, 719*n*15, 721*n*31, 737*n*9, 749*n*28, 750*n*52, 756*n*14; **realism,** 143-44, 147, 149, 151-52, 154, 156, 178, 188, 193, 197, 205, 383, 436, 483, 589, 685, 706*n*16, 721*n*25, 721*n*32, 723*n*46, 732*n*28, 737*n*5, 748*n*10, 749*n*26,, 766*n*100, 774*n*21, 776*n*5, 783*n*12, 783*n*13; **romanticism,** 144, 147, 149, 151, 154, 156, 178, 193, 436, 452, 712*n*16, 720*n*22, 721*n*32, 740*n*27, 743*n*23, 749*n*42; **surrealism,** 707*n*23, 774*n*21; **Symbolists,** 193, 409, 737*n*5, 740*n*27, 742*n*11; **The Ten,** 204, 737*n*5; **Tonalists,** 737*n*5

Art museums, galleries, 543, 613-14, 772*n*6

Art periods, *see* Art movements, periods styles

Art schools, xxxiii, 21, 143, 151, 189, 221, 440, 560, 704*n*7, 705*n*13, 706*n*16, 707*n*1, 722*n*42, 737*n*5

Art styles, *see* Art movements, periods, styles

Athletics, sports, 69, 76-77, 85, 88, 91, 135, 710*n*25, 755*n*10, 779*n*32

"Attributes," 45, 378, 753n26

Autobiography, biography, 300-1, 318, 326, 338-39, 661

Beauty contests, 78, 781n58
Belgium, 569, 589, 769n17
Black Crook Girls, 624, 661
Black Friday, 467
Body, 305, 632, 635, 639, 642, 655, 662, 730n9, 731n17
Bottom-natures, 13, 265, 293-97, 306, 312, 331-32, 335-37, 343, 370, 374, 647, 686, 689, 782n61
Bourse, 529
Brand names, products, xxxvii, 24, 30, 32, 35, 73, 112, 130, 158, 223, 238, 258-59, 291, 367, 420, 546, 567, 579, 589, 595, 599-601, 606, 609, 611-12, 618, 624, 641, 700, 739n22, 746n50, 763n73, 771n30, 777n18

Camera vision, 25-26, 348-49, 444, 722n45, 738n14
Capitalism, 347, 733n30
Celebrity, personality, 147, 149, 172, 231, 443, 611, 618, 622, 624, 632, 664, 669, 671, 716n8, 718n22, 724n53, 775n32, 781n53
Centralization, *see* Standardization, centralization
Child models, 401, 634, 776n7
Christmas, *see* Easter, Christmas
Classicism (literary), 406, 656, 712n11
Classicism (philosophical), 350
Cliche, stereotype, 8, 206, 351, 355
Clubs, *see* Organizations, clubs
Colleges, universities, educational institutions, 18-19, 28-30, 66, 90, 123, 158, 168, 170, 242, 268, 294, 332, 336, 338, 383, 414, 477, 523, 525, 527, 529, 533, 617, 620, 644, 678, 717n18, 722n42, 738n18, 744n35, 756n14, 759n38, 766n97, 779n37
Commercial artists, 17, 87, 89, 95, 113, 263, 460, 490, 548, 558, 570, 578-79, 594, 625, 634, 691, 693
Commercialization, 260, 396, 413, 551, 559, 598, 615, 674, 706n15, 720n18, 767n105
Common law, 170, 172-73, 230
Communication, xxxvii, 761n55
Concord Transcendentalists, 228, 408, 730n26
Conduct, 14-15, 19, 69, 82, 230, 258, 292, 317, 411, 590, 606, 704n10, 718n25, 780n51
Constitution (U.S.), 473-75, 478-49, 724n53, 753n21, 759n40
Consumerism, xxxiv, 32, 88, 347, 578, 600, 608, 610, 613, 671, 678, 711n2, 739n23, 775n25, 770n30, 773n14
Contemplation, meditation, 342-43, 345, 348-49, 351-55, 358, 369, 373, 396, 401, 700, 739n22
Conventions, xxx, xxxv, 7, 9, 13, 22-23, 25-26, 32, 74, 78, 186, 195-96, 241, 261, 267, 282, 290, 301, 325, 349, 355, 359, 361, 365-66, 369, 386, 397, 405-8, 412-13, 425-6, 428, 431-32, 443, 497, 609, 645,

647, 654, 656, 661, 692, 700, 738n20, 743n23, 752n18, 757n21
Corliss engine, 188, 525-26, 529-30, 532, 759n41, 761n56
Cosmopolitanism, 721n26
Costumes, xxxii, 238-39, 266, 275, 280-81, 301, 586-87, 642, 644, 659, 728n21
Crédit Mobilier, 467, 567

Declaration of Independence, 191, 477
Deconstruction, 639
Degeneracy, decadence, 129, 137-38, 203, 413, 437, 606, 624, 712n15, 716n43, 772n6, 775n33
Delmonico's, 213, 652, 725n58
Denoted and designated subjects, 185-87, 192, 201, 203, 206, 210, 213-14, 290, 292, 294, 308, 316, 404-5
Department stores, 2, 504, 597-98, 613, 620, 772n6, 774n20, 774n22
Determinism, 721n28
Disguise, *see* "Protective coloration," invisibility, disguise
Display, 609-10, 625, 652, 660, 662, 669
Dreams, 90, 366, 401, 536-37, 589, 641, 662, 664, 666, 683-87, 689, 692, 694, 772n39, 723n52, 740n27, 741n7
Dream theory, *see* Play and dream theory
Dress patterns, 728n19
Durand-Ruel Gallery, 710n24

Easter, Christmas (selling seasons), 396, 407, 421, 423, 593, 595, 597, 616, 772n4
Education, public schools, 21-25, 27, 30, 45, 105, 414, 427, 523, 538, 540, 542, 638, 641, 704n7, 707n19, 707n20, 707n23, 712n13, 746n49, 764n83, 773n11
Electricity, 188, 476, 510, 530, 532-33, 536, 623-24, 628, 631, 760n52, 761n53, 761n55, 763n73, 781n54
Ellis Island, 109, 559, 561-62
Elocution, *see* Recitation, elocution
Elongation, 500, 503, 513, 756n14
English Renaissance poets, 188
Ethnic types, *see* Racial, ethnic types
Euclidian perspective, 348, 499
Eugenics, *see* Genetics, eugenics
Evolution, 21, 104, 109, 121, 124, 134, 136, 138, 206, 211, 333, 383, 411-12, 516, 545, 560, 678, 716n44, 733n33, 754n29
Exclusion, inclusion, 197-98, 200-1, 203-4, 261-63, 281, 326
Expatriate artists, xxxv, 721n26, 762n61
Expositions, 613; **Atlanta** (1895), 32; **Chicago Columbian** (1893), xxviii, 91, 144-45, 190, 200, 208, 422, 446, 462, 468, 481, 496-97, 515, 519, 522-23, 525-30, 532-39, 542, 549, 551-52, 601, 607-8, 614, 654, 711n3, 716n4, 720n19, 748n26, 758n36, 760n47,

Expositions (*Continued*)
  760n49, 762n61, 763n71, 763n72, 764n84, 765n91,
  766n97, 768n6, (Woman's Building), 525, 527-28,
  535, 542, 659, 760n49, 760n50, 761n56; **London,**
  (1851), 706n15; **Philadelphia Centennial** (1876),
  xxvii-xxviii, 1, 21-22, 144, 190, 200, 382, 414,
  462, 481, 489, 492, 496, 523-27, 529, 532, 549, 562,
  567, 569, 652, 706n16, 707n20, 719n15, 720n18,
  739n23, 758n36, 772n9, (U.S. Centennial Commission Report), 21-23, 523-25, 706n15, 706n16,
  724n53, 758n36; **San Francisco** (1915), 613, 751n55

"Fantastic Socialization," xxxvii, 266, 275, 282,
  728n21
Fantasy, 209, 258, 302, 353-54, 357, 366, 451, 469,
  508, 574, 614, 620, 642, 685, 729n27, 774n21, 782n59
Fashion, 652, 659, 689, 700, 726n6, 727n16, 780n47
Female and male impersonators, 268-75, 729n25
Female types: **Amazon, Warrior Queen,** 399-400,
  484-85, 487-89, 491-96, 498, 501-2, 520, 543, 550,
  552, 562, 564, 571-73, 575, 577, 585, 588, 590, 680,
  742n11; **America, Columbia, Republic,** xxviii,
  xxxiii, 1, 27, 91, 100, 112, 394, 412, 465, 480, 584-
  86, 489, 492-93, 497, 500, 509, 515, 518, 520, 522-
  23, 529-30, 532-33, 535, 549, 553, 555, 557-58, 562,
  564-65, 567-69, 571-72, 587, 589, 601, 642, 649-50,
  653, 655, 680, 753n26, 757n23, 761n56, 766n98,
  767n105, 769n17; **American Girl,** xxxi, xxxiii, 1-
  2, 7, 9, 21, 46, 48, 51-53, 57-58, 69, 76, 78, 85, 88-
  90, 94-101, 103-5, 109, 112-14, 123-24, 128-29, 131-
  336, 139, 144, 152, 170, 206, 208, 210-11, 213, 250,
  289-92, 295-96, 299, 316, 322, 324, 340, 391-92,
  417, 433, 440-41, 443-47, 460, 469, 481, 483, 493,
  495-96, 500, 505, 509-10, 516-23, 540-43, 549, 552-
  54, 559-60, 562, 574, 577, 589-90, 593, 595, 597-
  98, 608, 620, 646, 669, 674, 680, 682, 695-96, 715n42,
  725n64, 730n3, 740n31, 747n5, 754n28, 754n29,
  767n105, 768n6; **American Idol,** 308, 394, 447, 521,
  532, 534-35, 551, 447, 662-63, 717n18, 733n29,
  780n50; **Angel,** 156, 158, 267, 305, 382, 389-90,
  417, 428-31, 448, 450, 462, 484-85, 498, 545, 562,
  564, 571, 585, 590, 595, 743n22, 745n43, 756n14,
  769n18, 772n7; **Aspiring Woman,** 101-2; **Bacchante,** 399-400, 501, 661, 742n11, 746n49, 779n37;
  Beautiful Charmer, xxvii, 7, 46-51, 57-58, 62, 67-
  68, 70-71, 74, 81, 88, 94, 97, 101-2, 289, 378, 380,
  483, 485, 495-96, 502, 543, 562, 595, 680, 697;
  Blessed Damozel, 408, 459, 462, 647, 751n53; **Bluestocking,** 103, 357, 777n19; **Diana,** 154, 398-400,
  448, 501, 503, 629, 742n11, 755n7, 756n14, 761n56,
  779n37, 781n54; **Dollarprinzessin, Bitch Goddess,**
  487-88, 493, 733n30; **Drowning Woman,** 311, 313-
  17, 370, 687; **Dynamo,** 58, 433, 484, 534, 631, 660;
  Eve, xxviii, 57, 60, 448, 529, 769n17; **Fairy, nymph,
  mermaid,** 530, 750n47, 783n18; **Fatal Woman,** 622,
  626, 718n22, 740n27, 775n37; **Heiress,** 1, 91, 97,
  108, 251, 378, 487, 517; **La Femme Inconnu,** 452,
  456, 458; **Liberty,** 27, 394, 412, 465, 485, 500, 522,
  540, 542, 549, 562, 601, 642, 649, 655, 700, 724n53,
  753n23, 764n85; **Madonna,** 71, 166, 186, 308, 399,
  457, 565, 571, 606, 710n20, 779n37; **Magdalene,**
  356, 597, 649, 661; **Mother,** 57, 109, 136, 292, 414,
  484-85, 492, 495-96, 552, 565, 571-72, 575, 588,
  599, 650, 678, 769n18; **New England Woman,** 46,
  48, 51-58, 62, 67, 101, 134, 652, 656, 708n9, 708n13;
  New Woman, xxvii, xxxi, xxxiii, xxxix, 1, 48,
  57-59, 61-62, 67-68, 71, 74, 81, 83-87, 103, 119,
  138-39, 170, 172-73, 230, 255, 259, 276, 280, 312,
  380, 399, 400, 428, 484, 496, 502, 557, 560, 650,
  680, 689, 691, 694, 697, 700, 742n11, 783n18; **Normal Woman,** 103, 678, 680, 689, 730n9; **Outdoors
  Pal,** xxvii, 7, 46, 48, 88, 135, 251, 259, 280, 282,
  380, 444, 446-47, 483, 496, 557-58, 697; **Princess,**
  7, 104, 108, 251; **Psyche,** 435, 457, 550; **Queen,**
  443-44, 446-47, 469, 493, 516, 518, 754n29; **Red
  Cross Nurse,** 484-85, 542, 562, 575, 589; **Sibyl,** 149,
  400-1, 404, 661, 742n12; **Spinster,** 55, 57, 715n39,
  779n39, 779n32; **Suffragist,** 7, 62, 65, 67, 71, 81,
  138-39; **Titaness,** 51, 139, 271, 280, 311, 607, 656,
  692; **Venus,** 303, 420, 500, 502-3, 534, 661, 718n22,
  747n56, 755n6, 756n14, 780n49, 781n54; **Victory,**
  88, 442, 482-84, 522, 540, 746n49, 747n56, 752n17,
  775n3, 768n4, 772n7; **Virgin,** 58, 267, 429, 449,
  753n27; **Western Girl,** 7, 493, 711n8, 754n31;
  Winged Female, xxxii, 388, 391, 408, 411, 415,
  417-22, 425-29, 431-32, 437, 445-47, 459-61, 483,
  516, 535, 541, 545-46, 549-50, 599, 672, 718n22,
  746n49, 748n8, 761n55; **miscellaneous types,** xxviii,
  xxxv, 7, 50-51, 62, 71, 73, 81, 97, 100-4, 119, 123,
  162, 170, 173, 194, 198, 200, 207, 210, 236, 292,
  310, 316, 345, 357, 400, 437, 446, 449, 529, 550,
  562, 571, 573, 623, 650, 655, 661, 666, 689, 691,
  697, 711n8, 722n39, 732n23, 751n3, 755n3, 761n56,
  764n80, 773n16, 775n39, 779n32
Feminine traits, *see* Masculine, feminine traits
Feminism, xxx, 15, 32, 61, 64-65, 67, 69, 71, 74, 78,
  82, 85, 88, 102, 330, 502, 513, 547, 549, 573, 610,
  612, 619, 624, 655-56, 659, 689, 692, 694, 703n5,
  709n18, 709n19, 710n23, 732n22, 779n38, 780n45
"Feminization of American Culture," 413, 440,
  743n26
Formalism, 148, 193, 200, 330, 346-47, 349, 361, 476,
  482, 519, 642, 644, 744n39, 752n17
Frankfurt School, 174

Garment industry, 255
Gender distinctions, 109, 111, 118, 206, 240, 242,
  247, 250, 253, 255, 257-59, 261, 263, 269, 275, 280,
  302, 310, 635, 686, 688, 715n38, 726n11, 727n17,
  728n19, 733n30, 758n33, 762n62
Genetics, eugenics, 136, 758n31, 759n41
Genres, 341

Genteel tradition, xxxiv-xxxv, 51, 249, 254, 416, 418, 552, 617, 720-21n24, 727n14
Geometrics, 22-24, 45, 201, 203-4, 409, 706n16, 707n19, 707n20, 723n46, 756n14
Gilded Age, 190, 487, 523, 769n14
Gnostics, 611
Grace: grace, 660, 662, 664, 669, 671; Grace, 643, 661, 670, 678, 782n61

Hamiltonianism, 475
Heroes, 324, 414, 546, 585, 587, 589, 754n35, 766n97
Heroines, 28, 67, 162, 165, 218, 236, 239, 414-15, 492-94, 496, 574, 641-42, 649-50, 652, 655, 662, 723n51, 731n22, 744n27, 754n28, 754n30, 769n19, 778n32, 780n52
High and low cultures, xxxiv, 192, 310-11, 780n47
Historic sites, *see* Artistic and historic sites
History (living in), 5, 7, 32, 103, 138, 204, 230, 301, 326, 346, 388, 413, 429, 474-75, 525, 545, 607
Home, marriage, motherhood, xxxii, 19, 55-57, 63, 65, 67, 69, 88, 102, 138, 261, 291-92, 360, 417, 432, 448, 484, 528, 552, 579, 588-89, 678-79, 704n11, 757n24
Homogeneity, *see* Unity, homogeneity
Homosexuality, *see* Lesbianism, homosexuality

Idealism, *see* Platonism, neoplatonism, idealism,
Immensity, xxviii, 500, 513-14, 758n36
Immigrants, xxxiii, 27, 105-6, 108-9, 112-13, 117, 203, 476, 508, 518, 559-60, 562, 618, 650, 654, 689, 712n15, 713n17, 757n17, 768n11
Imperialism, xxxii-xxxiii, 206, 208, 268, 446, 462, 469, 480, 495, 497, 500, 515-16, 520, 529, 551-53, 606, 768n8
Inclusion, *see* Exclusion, inclusion
"Indiana Normal," 258
Industrialization, xxxiii, 347, 551, 615, 674, 782n2
International style, 192
Invisibility, *see* "Protective coloration," invisibility, disguise
Irony, 236-37

King Albert's Book, 576, 769n17
Knickerbocker period, 652

Laocoön, 28, 538-39
Lay figure, mannequins, 149, 151, 154, 158, 165, 707n22
Leap year, 276, 280, 729n30
Lesbianism, homosexuality, 78, 82, 281, 330, 710n24, 728n19, 748n19, 758n34
Literary genres: **etiquette book,** 49, 116, 130, 635, 718n24, 726n11, 742n12, 759n41; **gift book,** 291, 420-21, 535, 723n49, 732n22; **guidebooks** (Baedeker), 94, 96, 711n3, 764n82; **"inversion narratives,"** 276, 281; **muckraking exposes,** xxviii, 67; **popular fiction, best-sellers, "mob books,"** xxxvii,

59, 105, 145, 148, 164, 241, 244, 250, 280, 302-5, 310-11, 313, 334, 402, 440, 445, 617, 634, 731n22, 732n26, 733n34; **song lyrics,** 465, 553, 613, 636, 678
London Academy (1911), 710n24
LOPH Club, 262, 266, 281

McGuffey Readers, 45, 475, 752n10
Magazines: *The American Architect,* 527, *The Atlantic Monthly,* 52-54, 58, 61, 63, 524, 652; *The Auk,* 726n4; *The Bookman,* 162, 164, 301; *The Century,* xxxv, xxxvii 182-83, 208, 398, 452, 455-56, 728n22; *The Chap Book,* 200, 202; *Collier's,* xxxiii, 47, 49, 260, 509, 617, 619, 640, 696, 713n17, 724n55, 729n30; *The Cosmopolitan,* 4-5, 72, 75, 448, 469, 472, 567, 569, 617, 634-35, 638, 654, 669, 676; *The Craftsman,* 545; *The Delineator,* 152, 615-16, 623, 689, 781n57; *The Galaxy,* 764n85; *Godey's,* xxxiii, 489, 514, 753n22; *Good Housekeeping,* 63, 66-68, 70, 277, 279, 618-19, 621, 636, 779-80n42; *Granite Marble & Bronze,* 423, 425-26; *Harper's Bazar,* 64, 635; *Harper's Monthly,* xxxv, 202, 208, 672; *Harper's Weekly,* 753n21, 761n55, 773n12; *Illustrated Police News,* 625, 772n3; *The International Studio,* 429; *Julian Eltinge Magazine and Beauty Hints,* 269, 272, 729n26; *Kate Field's Washington,* 767n103; *Ladies' Home Journal,* 600, 602, 678; *Leslie's Illustrated Historical Register,* 2, 565, 759n40; *Leslie's Monthly Magazine,* 567; *Life,* 16-17, 19, 61, 86-87, 90, 95, 99, 212-13, 215-17, 231, 264, 358, 360, 370, 436, 458, 460-61, 516, 518, 557, 598, 616, 620, 628, 641, 649, 653, 689-90, 696-97, 714n30, 724n57, 729n30, 772n6, 777n19, 778n27, 781n58, 782n3; *Lippincott's,* xxxix; *The Living Church,* 734n6; *McClure's,* 347, 617; *Mlle. New York,* 406; *The Marine's Bulletin,* 579, 585; *The Masses,* xxxvi-xxxvii, 81, 94-95, 465, 575, 581, 709n18, 771n38; *Motor,* 692-93, 783n18; *The Nation,* 752n17; *The Platonist,* 408; *Popular Science Monthly,* 775n40; *Puck,* 62, 484-86, 488, 491, 601, 604; *Punch,* 62; *Round Table,* 231, 726n6; *Scribner's,* 59, 89, 208, 212, 259, 520, 524, 531, 560-61, 563, 601, 635, 706n15, 759n40; *The Theater,* 767n2; *Truth,* 597, 599; *Vogue,* 644, 649; *The Yellow Book,* xxxiii, 406
Male impersonators, *see* Female and male impersonators
Mannequins, *see* Lay figure, mannequins
Margin, the, 433, 436, 456, 478
Marine Corps, 585, 587, 770n30, 771n33
Marketing, the marketplace, xxxii-xxxiii, xxxvii, 88, 146-47, 160, 294, 396, 461, 508, 522, 559-60, 578, 598, 602, 609, 613, 628, 632, 660, 662, 664, 671, 739n23, 773n12, 773n20, 774n21, 781n59
Marriage, *see* Home, marriage, motherhood

Marxism, 611

Masculine, feminine traits, 253-55, 263, 281-82, 366, 411, 413-14, 418, 431, 433, 435, 438-39, 478, 481, 523, 525-27, 529-30, 532, 534, 542, 549, 606, 631, 656, 659-60, 664, 686-87, 692, 736n4, 743-44n26, 745n43, 748n21, 749n34, 753n21, 753n22, 759n41, 762n62, 766n98, 767n105, 778n31; male, female genders, 120, 125, 127-28, 138, 181, 189, 210, 214-15

Masks, 221, 266, 349, 412

Meditation, see Contemplation, meditation

Melting pot theory, 112

Memory, 223, 293, 355, 357, 738n20, 745n42

Middle Ages, 448, 502, 544, 603, 606, 622, 762n60

Mirrors, 30, 327, 341, 355, 366-67, 369-74, 382, 668-69, 696, 700, 740n28, 740n31, 772n7

Miss Hewitt's campers, 769n20

Modern doubt, 415, 419, 450n42

Modernism (literary), 333, 336

Monroe Doctrine, 555

Morphology, 201, 213

Motherhood, see Home, marriage, motherhood

Motion, 624, 631, 669

Nationalism, 9, 28, 211, 213, 465-66, 475, 481, 499, 500-1, 505, 508, 510, 513, 520, 522, 525, 534, 539, 549, 559-60, 587, 652, 713n16, 721n26, 764n80, 772n9; see also Patriotism

Nativists, 111, 114, 116-18, 123, 203, 712n15

Naturalism (literary), 329, 350

Neoplatonism, see Platonism, neoplatonism, idealism

Neurasthenia, 67, 129-30, 134-35, 484

Newport, R. I., 97, 435, 620, 653

Newspapers: Sunday supplements, 30, 73, 78, 168, 172, 233, 576, 781n58; TITLES: The Boston Advertiser, 734n6, Boston Evening Transcript, 134, Boston Herald, 564, Cleveland World, 594-95, New York Daily Graphic, xxxi, 15-16, 113, 484, 487, 757n23, New York Dramatic Mirror, 745n43, 767n2, New York Herald, 33, 553, 715n42, New York Journal, 8, 90, 105-8, 595, 597, 618-19, 625, 628-29, 772n3, 781n58, New York Ledger, 708n13, New York Sun, 508, 618, 729n28, New York Times, 268, 271, 518, 725n58, 728n24, 730n15, 758n29, 766n97, New York World, xxxi, 83-84, 103, 138, 214, 596, 691, 725n58, 730n17, 775n32, 781n54, Philadelphia Press, 227, St. Louis Globe-Democrat, 558-59, 568, 570, Washington Star, 751n55, Washington Times, 75, 79, 405, 579, 583

Oratory, see Rhetoric, oratory

Oregon Trail, 551

Organizations, clubs (local, national, international), 70-71, 115, 126-29, 239, 268, 483, 519,

551, 567, 575-77, 617, 642, 644, 656, 673-74, 710n23, 727n14, 728n24, 732n29, 754n28, 757n22, 765n90

Paris Salon (1910), 422, 710n24

Patriotism, xxxii, 206-7, 210, 212, 216, 475, 477, 513, 525, 544, 549, 553, 567, 598, 634, 652, 767n2, 768n5, 770n29; see also Nationalism

Performance arts, 641, 643

Permanence, timelessness, 104, 168, 306, 336, 411-12, 417, 475, 574, 606, 609, 642, 656, 744n29

Personality, see Celebrity, personality

Philosophy (nineteenth century), 5, 13-14, 21, 189

Photo and print technology, 212, 561, 711n2, 720n20, 749n36, 760n42

Photojournalism, 67

"Physiognomical awareness," 297, 299, 304, 312, 334

Physiognomy, xxxii, 7, 32, 104-5, 109, 111-13, 115-18, 121, 124, 128-29, 134, 179, 213, 233, 237, 253, 255, 275, 280, 296-97, 299, 301, 317-18, 357, 432, 516, 528, 545, 559, 574, 606, 622, 635, 639, 692, 712n11, 715n34, 715n42, 742n12, 743n21, 748n20

Picturesque, see Sublime and picturesque

"Pittsburgh," 673-74, 782n3

Plagiarism, 356, 739n21, 776n6

Platonism, Neoplatonism, idealism, xxvii, xxxi, xxxiii 5, 13-14, 45, 55, 103, 116, 138, 144, 148, 151, 152, 154, 164-65, 167-68, 174, 179, 194, 235, 344, 367, 394-96, 405, 407, 409-15, 432, 437-38, 452, 455, 499, 521, 544, 585, 611, 642, 662, 674, 716n6, 718n2, 721n25, 742n17, 752n8

Play and dream theory, 354, 685, 728n21

Popular culture, xxxiii, 91, 206, 212, 214, 269, 423, 426, 593, 610, 617, 634, 641, 670, 678, 706n18, 707n3, 728n22, 739n21, 746n54, 754n28, 757n21, 768n2, 771n30, 773n12

Pornography, 367, 451, 662

Poses, 32, 46, 262, 280, 301, 316, 357, 396, 609-10, 612, 614, 617, 622, 632, 634-35, 638, 641, 643, 647, 654, 660, 662, 664, 670, 685-86, 692, 696, 728n18, 776n5, 777n18, 780n47; "attitudes," 261, 267, 610, 636, 638-39, 642-44, 647, 659-62, 664, 668, 692, 742n12, 778n26, 779n38, 779n42, 780n47; "dramatical," xxxii, 609, 618, 632, 634, 643, 664, 776n5

Pragmatism, 349, 354, 438

Presences, 185, 193, 204, 328, 405, 477, 504

Print media, 30, 88, 97, 233, 235-37, 540, 542, 584, 586, 613, 617, 620, 623, 652, 656-57, 660, 664, 695, 700, 708n15, 709n16, 710n25, 732n22, 768n8

Print technology, see Photo and print technology

Products, see Brand names, products

Progressive movement, 67, 654

Promotion, publicity, 236, 399, 585, 587, 598, 609, 613, 617, 632, 772-73n10, 774n22

"Protective coloration," invisibility, disguise, xxxii

117, 222-23, 225-27, 229-32, 234, 236-37, 239-40, 251, 310-11, 560, 726n4, 726n5

Public schools, *see* Education, public schools

Publishers, 2; Art Study Company of Chicago, 764n84; Bobbs-Merrill, 493, 723n49; Dodd, Mead, 456; Harper and Bros., 182, 440; Houghton Mifflin, 734n6; Moffat, Yard, 723n49; Prang Educational Company, 23-25, 45, 212-13, 257, 420, 540, 704n7, 706n18, 707n20, 746n49, 764n84; Scribner's, xxxvii, 723n49

Puritans, Puritanism, 52-54, 200, 345, 437, 475, 540, 652, 743n25, 756n14

Racial, ethnic types, 4-5, 7, 28, 52, 54, 57, 61, 91-94, 97, 99, 103-6, 108-9, 112-14, 116-21, 123, 125-26, 129-30, 134-35, 138, 161, 165, 181-82, 197, 200, 203, 210, 255, 307, 331-32, 336, 340-41, 433, 472-73, 480, 489, 497, 515-16, 518, 540, 545, 559-61, 569, 574, 586, 589, 624, 669, 712n16, 713n25, 714n30, 715n33, 731n18, 734n5, 736n3, 744n27, 754n30, 756n14, 761n55, 764n85, 769n19, 768n11, 772n6, 777n19, 778n30

Racism, xxxii, 175, 180, 203, 206, 213, 330-31, 565, 610, 653, 713n23, 714n25, 715n33, 718n21, 772n6

Reading, 358, 369

"Real things," xxxii, 5, 144, 156, 158, 170, 172, 201, 205, 236, 293-95, 330, 415, 716n6, 734n7

Realism (literary), 161, 296, 329

Realism (philosophical), 174-75, 350

Recitation, elocution, 636, 638, 650, 727n17

Regularity, symmetry, 46, 91, 114-16, 132

Religion, religious groups, 112, 117, 564-65, 593, 595, 654, 661, 714n31, 744n40, 745n44, 754n35

Repetition, 356

Repose, relaxation, 201, 354-55, 357-58, 361, 363, 661

Reverie, 293, 355, 358-59, 366, 380, 401, 740n24

Rhetoric, oratory, 636

"Rock of Ages," 407, 416, 423, 742n13

Romanticism, 151, 175

Roses at the breast, 69, 71-74, 85

Rotary system, 411, 743n18

Sales catalogs, 598, 613, 772n6

Saturday Morning Club, The, 610, 655-56, 659-61, 732n22, 779n40

Scale, 260, 499-500, 511-13, 515, 518-21, 528, 533, 544, 551, 755n7, 761n56

Selves, 32; averages, means, 226, 293-94, 297, 299, 312, 328, 332, 336-37, 366, 374; originals, 233, 297, 299, 313, 328, 332; social selves, 265-66, 269, 294, 306, 310, 312, 333, 367

Semiotics, 406-7, 448, 639, 780n51

"Servant Problem, The," 112, 361, 740n25

Settlement houses, 617, 654

Sexism, 175, 180, 206, 610, 714n29, 718n21, 744n39

Sexuality, 161-62, 164, 207, 210, 212, 257-58, 275, 304, 308, 310-311, 441, 451, 483, 502-3, 595, 597, 620-24, 708n4, 709n20, 714n28, 729n27, 735n25, 738n12, 775n36

Shakespearean negative capability, 147, 298

Shapes, 664

Social classes, xxxiv-xxxv, xxxvii, 7, 52, 66, 105-6, 108-9, 112, 116, 147, 192, 250, 302-3, 345, 358-61, 363, 371, 380, 532, 539, 589, 610, 617, 619, 622, 651-55, 682, 689, 706n16, 721n24, 766n97, 776n101, 771n36, 772n5, 777n20, 782n4

Social sciences, 109, 118

Somatic psychology, 293

Sports, *see* Athletics

"Spirit of '76, The" 407, 532

Standardization, centralization, xxxiii, 255, 758n35

State capitols, xxxix, 382, 538-39, 764n82; **Albany, N.Y.,** 542, 746n45; **Des Moines, Iowa,** 496, 539, 545, 766n100; **Harrisburg, Pa.,** 539, 546, 766n101, 782n4; **Madison, Wis.,** 539; **Providence, R.I.,** 539; **St. Paul, Minn.,** 475, 496, 539, 545, 549, 767n106

Statistics, 109, 508, 515, 519, 523, 678, 708n13, 713n23, 758n26, 759n38, 772n5

Statue of Liberty, xxviii, 27, 113, 260, 465, 481, 508, 510-13, 530, 532, 600, 713n17, 757n22, 775n32

Stereotype, 8, 206, 351, 355

Stillness, silence, 296, 306, 342-43, 345, 347, 350, 357, 459, 638, 738n12, 740n27

Studio photographers, 73, 75, 78-79, 86, 399, 401-2, 405, 451, 511, 513-14, 526, 625-26, 629-30, 638, 666, 757n22, 777n18

Subjectivism, 721n29

Sublime and picturesque, 498-99, 510-11, 513, 574, 588-89, 761n56, 769n17, 771n34

Symmetry, *see* Regularity, symmetry

Taste, 425, 527, 660-61, 664, 766n15, 759n40, 775n25, 775n30

Technology, xxxiii, xxxvii, 2, 22, 32, 437, 522, 535-36, 538, 545, 549, 589, 613, 706n16, 723n46, 739n22, 759n40, 759n42, 767n2

Theater, xxxiii, 260, 269-775, 280, 367, 585, 587, 590, 598, 610, 613-14, 616-18, 624-25, 632-33, 644, 660, 669-70, 680, 773n12, 779n37, 780n47

Theater and opera productions: *Algy,* 271-73; *America* (Kiralfy), 763n73, 767-68n2; *America* (Voegtlin), 767-68n2; *Antigone,* 610, 655-57, 659-60, 665, 732n22, 780n44; *Camille,* 664; *Columbus and the Discovery of America,* 763n73, *Excelsior!,* 763n73; *The Girl from Up There,* 620; *L'Aiglon,* 269; *La Bohème,* 664; *La Traviata,* 664; *Madame Butterfly,* 268; *The Masqueraders,* 643, 780n50; *Mazeppa,* 661-62; *The Mikado,* 212; *Sappho,* 620; *Sporting Life,* 662; *Sweet Kitty Belairs,* 778n28; *Twilbee,* 268; *The Woman Hater,* 745n43

Theater genres: **burlesque, vaudeville,** 492, 572, 613, 617-18, 620, 775*n*34; **classical drama,** 643; **masque, costume balls,** xxxii, 238-40, 383, 641, 651-53, 684, 777*n*20, 779*n*37; **melodrama,** 609, 618, 632-34, 669-70, 782*n*61; **motion picture,** 613-14, 634, 638, 643, 734*n*2, 779*n*38; **musical comedy,** 613, 618, 622, 729*n*27; **Noh drama,** 296; **pageant,** 67, 611, 648, 651, 654, 773*n*14; **pantomime,** 614, 618, 633, 636, 661; **spectacle,** xxxii, 32, 609-11, 614, 617-18, 668-69, 767*n*2; **tableau,** xxxii, 32, 266, 296, 380, 399, 442, 537, 609-10, 614, 617, 633, 636, 644, 646, 648, 650-55, 661, 727*n*18, 767*n*2, 773*n*13, 777*n*21, 778*n*30, 780*n*51

Theoretical models, 147, 537, 539, 763*n*75

Threshold lives, 52, 433, 435, 438, 447, 449, 478-79, 535, 562, 747*n*5

Timelessness, *see* Permanence, timelessness

Type, the, xxxii, 156, 162, 164, 168, 377-78, 380, 382-83, 386, 388, 391, 393-96, 400, 404, 406, 408, 411, 415, 417, 426, 432, 440, 449, 451-52, 456, 460, 500, 543, 641, 656, 659-60, 704*n*7

Unity, homogeneity, xxx-xxxi, xxxiii, 6, 93, 126, 130, 411, 417, 527, 535, 537, 540, 616-17, 640, 661, 713*n*17, 720*n*24, 744*n*29, 749*n*34, 752*n*18, 768*n*11

Universities, *see* Colleges, universities, educational institutions

Urbanization, 32

Wars: **Civil War,** 55, 93, 144, 187, 191, 380, 414, 426, 478, 513, 584, 710*n*23, 726*n*6, 747*n*57, 764*n*84, 772*n*5; **Spanish-American War,** xxviii, 208, 230, 377, 381, 426, 478, 481, 483, 549, 551, 554-55, 557-558, 567-58, 579, 589-90, 601, 768*n*8; **World War I,** xxvii-xxviii, xxxvii, 1, 27, 30, 125-26, 210, 212, 222, 225, 229, 271, 380, 382, 414, 482-83, 485, 493, 516, 520, 529, 532, 549-50, 562, 564-65, 567, 569, 571-79, 581, 584-88, 590, 687, 694, 700, 724*n*53, 724*n*57, 739*n*24, 746*n*49, 747*n*57, 757*n*22, 768*n*6, 769*n*18, 769-70*n*20, 770*n*23, 770*n*29, 771*n*38; **World War II,** 562, 726*n*6

Washington, D.C., 478-81, 538-39

Whigs, 475

Wilfred Owen Brigade, 466

Will, 48, 100-1, 394, 447, 487, 489, 525-26, 528-29, 534, 551, 590, 620, 643, 659, 661, 669, 686, 700, 756*n*14

Winged males, 456, 458, 599, 751*n*55

Women artists, xxxvii, 21, 30, 32, 340-41, 461, 736*n*4, 737*n*4, 750*n*2

Women's clubs, 60, 610, 780*n*45

Women's magazines, 279, 635

Women's sphere, 59, 101, 135, 210, 308, 431, 435, 439, 462, 478-79, 513, 532, 567, 573, 675, 687, 759*n*41

Wordworthian ego, Shakespearean negative capability, 147, 298

Ziegfeld Follies, 1, 257, 273, 280, 572, 680, 682